## STANDARD 7: CONCEPTS OF WHOLE NUMBER OPERATIONS

In grades K–4, the mathematics curriculum should include concepts of addition, subtraction, multiplication, and division of whole numbers so that students can—

- develop meaning for the operations by modeling and discussing a rich variety of problem situations;
- relate the mathematical language and symbolism of operations to problem situations and informal language;
- recognize that a wide variety of problem structures can be represented by a single operation;
- develop operation sense.

## STANDARD 8: WHOLE NUMBER COMPUTATION

In grades K–4, the mathematics curriculum should develop whole number computation so that students can—

- model, explain, and develop reasonable proficiency with basic facts and algorithms;
- use a variety of mental computation and estimation techniques;
- use calculators in appropriate computational situations;
- select and use computation techniques appropriate to specific problems and determine whether the results are reasonable.

## STANDARD 9: GEOMETRY AND SPATIAL SENSE

In grades K–4, the mathematics curriculum should include two- and three-dimensional geometry so that students can—

- describe, model, draw, and classify shapes;
- investigate and predict the results of combining, subdividing, and changing shapes;
- develop spatial sense;
- relate geometric ideas to number and measurement ideas;
- recognize and appreciate geometry in their world.

## STANDARD 10: MEASUREMENT

In grades K–4, the mathematics curriculum should include measurement so that students can—

- understand the attributes of length, capacity, weight, area, volume, time, temperature, and angle;
- develop the process of measuring and concepts related to units of measurement;
- make and use estimates of measurement;
- make and use measurements in problem and everyday situations.

## STANDARD 11: STATISTICS AND PROBABILITY

In grades K–4, the mathematics curriculum should include experiences with data analysis and probability so that students can—

- collect, organize, and describe data;
- construct, read, and interpret displays of data;
- formulate and solve problems that involve collecting and analyzing data;
- explore concepts of chance.

## STANDARD 12: FRACTIONS AND DECIMALS

In grades K–4, the mathematics curriculum should include fractions and decimals so that students can—

- develop concepts of fractions, mixed numbers, and decimals;
- develop number sense for fractions and decimals;
- use models to relate fractions to decimals and to find equivalent fractions;
- use models to explore operations on fractions and decimals;
- apply fractions and decimals to problem situations.

## STANDARD 13: PATTERNS AND RELATIONSHIPS

In grades K–4, the mathematics curriculum should include the study of patterns and relationships so that students can—

- recognize, describe, extend, and create a wide variety of patterns;
- represent and describe mathematical relationships;
- explore the use of variables and open sentences to express relationships.

Please refer to the inside back cover for the Curriculum Standards for Grades 5–8.

# MATHEMATICS
## *for Elementary Teachers*

AN INTERACTIVE
APPROACH

# MATHEMATICS
## *for Elementary Teachers*

AN INTERACTIVE
APPROACH

Thomas Sonnabend
*Montgomery College*

Saunders College Publishing
**Harcourt Brace College Publishers**
Fort Worth   Philadelphia   San Diego
New York   Orlando   Austin   San Antonio
Toronto   Montreal   London   Sydney   Tokyo

Requests for permission to make copies of any part of the work should be mailed to Permissions Department, Harcourt Brace Jovanovich, Publishers, 8th Floor, Orlando, Florida 32887.

Text Typeface: Palatino
Compositor: Better Graphics
Acquisitions Editor: Robert Stern
Developmental Editor: Nicholas Murray
Managing Editor: Carol Field
Project Editors: Martha Brown; Rebecca Gruliow
Copy Editor: Martha Colgan
Manager of Art and Design: Carol Bleistine
Art Director: Anne Muldrow
Art Assistant: Caroline McGowan
Text Designer: Alan Wendt
Cover Designer: Lawrence R. Didona
Text Artwork: Grafacon, Inc.; Rolin Graphics
Director of EDP: Tim Frelick
Production Manager: Bob Butler
Marketing Manager: Monica Wilson

---

**About the Cover**

The shape on the cover is a Mobius strip. To find out more about this amazing shape, see the Special Exercise on page 450.

---

Printed in the United States of America
MATHEMATICS FOR ELEMENTARY TEACHERS: AN INTERACTIVE APPROACH

0-03-020709-6

Library of Congress Catalog Card Number: 92-050826

2345 016 987654321

# Preface

The NCTM Standards state that "prospective teachers must be taught in a manner similar to how they are to teach—by exploring, conjecturing, communicating, reasoning, and so forth." This necessitates devoting more class time to discussing and discovering ideas and less time to lecturing.

Can a mathematics book actively involve students in developing and explaining mathematical concepts? Yes, by using a carefully organized, interactive lesson format that promotes student involvement and gradually leads the student to a deeper understanding of mathematical ideas. The interactive format also allows for more class discussion and small group work.

To implement the NCTM Standards, one needs a textbook that provides numerous opportunities for investigation and discourse. Rather than having a few special puzzle and investigation problems, this textbook presents a substantial collection of exercises in every lesson and homework set that involve reasoning, investigating, or communicating.

Most people do not enjoy reading mathematics textbooks. Can a mathematics textbook be interesting to read and study? Yes, if the mathematical presentation is straightforward and clear, and the lesson content is enriched with investigations, appropriate uses of technology, humor, history, and interesting applications. A text for this course should also make it clear how the topics in each chapter relate to both the NCTM Standards and the current school mathematics curriculum.

You are looking at the result of my effort to address all these concerns while covering new topics and examining underlying concepts and connections in elementary-school mathematics. This textbook is the culmination of 13 years of work with university, college, and community college students.

Teaching elementary school is one of the most important and challenging professions in our society. It is my hope that this textbook provides material for a more interesting course that produces more competent teachers with a better sense of what elementary-school mathematics is all about.

## Distinctive Features

This textbook places *greater emphasis* on

- discovery, discussion, and explanation of concepts that involve students and deepen their understanding
- investigations and activities that require higher-level thinking
- applications of mathematics that connect mathematical concepts to everyday life
- explaining a concept or solving a problem in more than one way so that future teachers can see a variety of approaches
- how material relates to the current elementary-school curriculum
- difficult concepts in the elementary-school mathematics curriculum that future teachers have trouble explaining
- connecting lessons, homework exercises, and chapter review exercises
- multiple representations of concepts so that students develop a broader understanding
- inductive and deductive reasoning, showing how these two processes are used throughout mathematics
- models for arithmetic operations that establish the connection between an operation and its everyday applications
- common student error patterns in arithmetic and measurement that prepare future teachers for diagnosing student difficulties
- spatial perception and perspective drawing so that students become more adept at three-dimensional geometry
- algebra as a mathematical language and a generalization of arithmetic
- important statistical applications including statistical deceptions, surveys, and standardized tests

In order to make time for these topics, this textbook places less emphasis upon (1) topics most students have studied or will study in other mathematics or education courses and (2) topics that are relatively more remote from the current elementary-school curriculum. Such topics include arithmetic and algebra skills, formal logic, geometry terminology, congruent triangle proofs, and isometries.

### Other Features

- Students use relevant NCTM Standards to review each chapter and increase their awareness of specific standards.

- Charts at the end of each chapter show grade-level coverage of related elementary-school topics.

- Computer exercises throughout the textbook employ BASIC to study number theory, algebra, statistics, and probability; Logo and automatic drawers to study geometry and measurement; and MINI-TAB to study statistics.

- Extensive coverage of geometry and measurement topics strengthens students' spatial and analytical abilities.

- Extensive coverage of statistics and probability incorporates many realistic applications.

- Mental computation and estimation with whole numbers, fractions, decimals, and percents make use of properties of operations and complement the use of calculators.

- Humor and historical vignettes humanize the mathematics.

## Teaching and Learning Aids

The following features make it easier for students and professors to make more effective use of this book.

- Chapter introductions set the stage for each new chapter.

- Subsection headings help students understand how each lesson is organized.

- Exercises within each lesson actively involve students in developing and reinforcing concepts.

- Lessons gradually lead students to a deeper understanding of difficult concepts in the elementary-school curriculum.

- Selected lesson exercises are marked **D** as especially suitable for discussion.

- Answers to most lesson exercises provide students with the opportunity to check their work as they develop new ideas.

- Important definitions, theorems, and properties are boxed with boldfaced headings.

- All mathematical terms are set boldface.

- Color is used to highlight mathematical ideas and add clarity to figures.

- Sample textbook pages show newer topics in elementary-school mathematics, thus increasing student awareness of recent changes.

- A "friendly" writing style and cartoons, drawings, and photographs stimulate student interest.

- Homework exercises are categorized as basic, extension, computer, and special so that instructors can select the appropriate level and type of homework exercises.

- Answers to most odd-numbered homework exercises and all chapter review exercises provide students with adequate feedback.

- Calculator and computer exercises are marked.

- Chapter study guides list important concepts and terms by section to help students recall major ideas.

- Chapter review exercises help students prepare for exams.

- Suggested reading lists for each chapter direct students to interesting resource material.

## Chapter Organization and Features

Chapter 1 introduces mathematical reasoning processes and problem solving techniques that are used throughout the course. Its broader view of mathematical reasoning includes inductive and deductive reasoning as well as patterns and problem solving.

Chapter 2 covers set concepts that are used later in the course to clarify other concepts. Venn diagrams are used to solve problems in Chapters 1 and 2.

Chapters 3–7 cover the number systems from whole numbers to real numbers. Categories for each whole number operation (e.g., compare and take away) are studied in depth in Chapter 3 and used with other number systems in Chapters 5–7. Mental computation and estimation are also used with each number system. In number theory (Chapter 4), students do proofs and learn two different methods for solving certain problem types. In Chapters 5–7, students learn how to explain difficult procedures in integer, fraction, and decimal arithmetic using models and realistic applications. Students also compare different representations of real numbers.

Chapters 8–10 cover geometry and measurement. In Chapter 8, the van Hiele model is used to develop categories and definitions of quadrilaterals. Sections on space figures and spatial perception strengthen students' spatial abilities. In Chapter 9, students connect transformation geometry to congruence, symmetry, and similarity, and students analyze a series of constructions using congruence properties. In Chapter 10, students perform a series of activities to learn about the metric system and to develop area formulas in a logical sequence.

Chapter 11, Algebra and Coordinate Geometry, follows and extends arithmetic from Chapters 3–7 and geometry and measurement from Chapters 8–10. Students learn different ways to represent a function or relation.

Multiple representations (words, tables, graphs, and formulas) are used in solving realistic application problems. Algebra is studied as a mathematical language.

Chapter 12 is the ideal place for BASIC programming. This optional chapter connects introductory BASIC with algebraic formulas from Chapter 11. The hands-on approach leads beginners through the essential ideas of BASIC. Students then use the computer as another approach to solving algebra, number theory, and measurement problems.

For those who complete Chapter 12, BASIC branches and loops can then be used with statistics and probability in Chapters 13 and 14. Chapter 13 emphasizes choosing the most appropriate graph or statistic to summarize results. Choices include the relatively new stem-and-leaf plots and boxplots. The extensive applications of statistics include statistical deceptions, surveys, and standardized tests.

In Chapter 14, students learn the connection between theoretical and experimental probabilities and use simulations to generate experimental probabilities. Students see the importance of probability in insurance, drug testing, and gambling games.

## Course Outlines

This textbook provides for some flexibility in organizing the course. The textbook contains more than enough material for two four–semester-hour mathematics courses for preservice elementary teachers. The material in Chapters 1–7 should be studied in sequence; however, a number of sections and parts of sections can be omitted.

In Chapters 1–7 you should cover the following material.

1. Chapter 1

2. In Section 2.1, review set notation and define whole numbers. In Section 2.2, cover "intersection and union."

3. In Section 3.1, cover "models for place value" and "rounding." Cover Sections 3.2 and 3.3. In Section 3.4, cover the properties. Cover Section 3.5.

4. In Section 4.1, cover "factors." In Section 4.2, cover "multiples," "divisibility tests for 2, 5, and 10," and "divisibility tests for 3 and 9." Cover Sections 4.3 and 4.4.

5. Cover Section 5.1 and "inverses" in Section 5.3.

6. Cover Chapter 6.

7. Cover Sections 7.1, 7.3, and 7.4.

After studying the basic material in Chapters 1–7, the major ideas of Chapters 8–14 can be studied independently of one another with the following exceptions.

| Material | Prerequisite |
| --- | --- |
| Logo in Chapters 9 and 10 | Sections 8.6, 8.7 |
| Chapter 10 | Chapter 8 |
| Section 10.6 | Section 9.4 |
| Section 11.5 | Chapters 8–10 |
| Sections 12.2–12.4 | Sections 7.3, 10.4, 11.3, 11.4 |
| Section 14.4 | Section 13.3 |
| BASIC in Chapters 13 and 14 | Chapter 12 |

### One-Semester Course

Design a one-semester course that suits your needs, with the following conditions.

1. Cover the required sections and parts of sections in Chapters 1–7 as already outlined.
2. You can skip optional Sections 3.6 and 7.5, investigations, extension exercises, and special exercises.
3. Round out the course with additional material from Chapters 1–7, or select sections from Chapters 8–14. Depending upon the length of your course, the ability of your students, and the amount of time you spend on extension exercises, you might be able to cover about 5 to 15 more sections. Suggestions for additional material would include Sections 8.1–8.5, 9.1, 10.1–10.3, 13.1–13.3, 14.1 and 14.2.

### Two-Semester Course

In two four-semester one-hour courses, one can cover most of the sections in the book, depending upon the number of homework exercises covered. One could skip some of Sections 3.6, 7.5, 9.2, 10.6, 11.5, Chapter 12, and Section 14.4 or 14.5, or optional subsections that are listed in the *Instructor's Manual*.

## Supplement for Students

The *Student Resource Manual* provides additional hands-on activities for each chapter. These activities utilize material cards that come with the manual. Also included are activities that focus on calculators, critical thinking, connections, and the NCTM standards.

# Supplements for Teachers

The *Instructor's Manual* contains teaching suggestions, overhead transparency masters, and exercise answers that are not given in the textbook. The *Test Bank* contains sample test questions for each chapter. The *Computerized Test Bank*, available in IBM and Macintosh formats, contains the questions from the *Test Bank*.

## Manipulatives Kit

This kit will consist of Cuisenaire mathematics manipulatives. The kit includes geometric solids, connecting cubes, and the following materials for the overhead projector: a geoboard, fraction tiles, base-ten blocks, and a tangram puzzle. This kit will be provided free to professors upon adoption of the text.

## Sample Elementary Textbook Kit

This kit consists of Instructor's Editions of the Harcourt Brace Jovanovich 1992 publications *Mathematics Plus*, Grades 3 and 6. This kit will be provided free to professors upon adoption of this book.

# Acknowledgments

First, I would like to thank my wife Celia for her support, encouragement, and tolerance during the past 5 years, not to mention her many suggestions based upon her own extensive experience as an elementary-school teacher. I am also grateful for the encouragement and advice provided by my mother, my sister, my stepfather, my friends, Judge Robert Mark, and author Dan Benice.

Next, I would like to thank the editors at Saunders College Publishing, Acquisitions Editor Bob Stern, Production Editors Becca Gruliow and Martha Brown, Developmental Editor Nick Murray, the copyeditor, Martha Colgan, and the proofreader, Viqi Wagner, who saw the potential in my work and helped to develop and polish the manuscript. Thanks also to editorial assistants Liz Barnett, Maria Cozzolino, Alicia Jackson, Karyn Valerius, and Beth Oryl, who helped in taking care of thousands of details. The attractive design of the book is due to the direction and creativity of Anne Muldrow and the many graphic artists who rendered the figures, with special thanks to the cartoonists at Rolin Graphics. Thanks also to Bob Butler and the production staff, who kept the book moving through production and smoothed out some bumps along the way.

Next, I would like to thank my professors from graduate school, who provided many inspiring ideas that led to the development of this textbook. They included Neil Davidson, Jim Fey, Zal Usiskin, Stephen Willoughby, Jim Henkelman, and Mildred Cole—six outstanding mathematics educators.

Finally, I would like to thank my colleagues, my students, and the many reviewers whose helpful suggestions significantly improved this book. The names and affiliations of principal reviewers are as follows.

## Principal Reviewers

Judy Bergman, *University of Houston*
Peter Braunfeld, *University of Illinois (Urbana)*
Gail Cashman, *former Montgomery College student*
Gregory Davis, *University of Wisconsin (Green Bay)*
Donald Dessart, *University of Tennessee*
Iris B. Fetta, *Clemson University*
Alan Hoffer, *Boston University*
William A. Miller, *Central Michigan University*
Pamela Pospisil, *Montgomery College*
Alice I. Robold, *Ball State University*
Sharon Ross, *California State University (Chico)*
Elizabeth Shearn, *University of Maryland*
Jane F. Sheilack, *Texas A & M University*
Keith Shuert, *Oakland Community College*
Jim Trudnowski, *Carroll College*
C. Ralph Verno, *West Chester University*
Stephen S. Willoughby, *University of Arizona*

I would also like to thank reviewers Christine A. Browning (Western Michigan University), Terry Crites (Northern Arizona University), Jerilyn Grignon (University of Wisconsin-Madison), and William Nibbelink (University of Iowa), who evaluated special features of the book.

# Contents Overview

# Contents

# Introduction ———

## Why Learn Mathematics?

As a teacher, you will introduce the next generation of students to mathematics, teaching them arithmetic, geometry, and statistics. Your students will solve problems, think logically, find patterns, and apply their knowledge to practical situations.

But why does anyone teach children mathematics as part of their education? Mathematics offers a unique way of looking at the world. Mathematics gives simple, abstract descriptions that illuminate general relationships among quantities or shapes while simplifying or ignoring qualities. Mathematics can show that, ounce for ounce, Brand A is a better buy than Brand B, focusing upon the amount and the price while ignoring other differences in the products and the companies that produce them. Such mathematical information can help one decide which brand to buy.

Furthermore, the logical, objective approach of mathematics is applied to many situations. Mathematics has had an impact on nearly every area of life, from philosophy to economics to art. Philosophers apply the logic of mathematics to ultimate questions. Economists employ quantitative methods to describe financial trends. Artists use geometry when they represent our three-dimensional world on canvas.

Finally, mathematics is the language of technological societies. Businesses use mathematics in record-keeping and analysis. As a consumer and citizen, each of us needs mathematics to make financial decisions and to interpret statistics in political and economic news.

What have your mathematical experiences been like? Is it one of your favorite subjects? Or have you felt like Peppermint Patty?

1

Reprinted by permission of UFS, Inc.

Use the questionnaire that follows to examine your mathematical attitudes and background and to introduce yourself to your instructor. Respond to the questionnaire on a separate sheet of paper and pass it in to your instructor.

**Questions About Your Mathematical Background and Experiences**

Name _____

Circle the courses that you have taken.

GENERAL MATH          ALGEBRA 1          GEOMETRY          ALGEBRA 2
PRECALCULUS          CALCULUS          STATISTICS          COMPUTERS

Most Recent Math Course: _____   _____   _____
                                         Title      Term or year    School

Write a few paragraphs answering some of the following questions.

- What do you like about mathematics or mathematics classes?
- What do you dislike about mathematics or mathematics classes?
- How have you felt about your mathematics teachers?
- How do you feel about taking this course?

# 1

# Mathematical Reasoning

How do we determine what is true in mathematics classes and in everyday life? You have been doing mathematics for many years, yet you may know little about the approaches you use over and over again in solving problems.

The two central processes of mathematics are inductive and deductive reasoning. Becoming aware of these reasoning processes will give you a better understanding of how you and your students learn mathematics. After studying these processes, you will use them throughout this course to make and prove conjectures.

Mathematics is sometimes called the study of patterns. Induction and deduction are used to generalize mathematical patterns, to extend them, and to prove generalizations about them.

In recent years, a greater emphasis has been placed on helping all students develop problem-solving abilities in a more structured way. Elementary-school books now teach some version of Polya's four-step problem-solving procedure: Read, plan, solve, and check.

When it comes to the second step, making a plan, the elementary-school curriculum now includes specific processes and strategies for problem solving. The most useful ones are induction, deduction, choosing the operation, making a table, and drawing a picture. More specialized strategies include guessing and checking and working backwards. These processes and strategies are introduced in Chapters 1 and 3.

# 1.1 Inductive Reasoning

How do we form our beliefs? For example, do you believe that your friend Alan is trustworthy?

Alan

Perhaps you would answer "yes" if your previous encounters with Alan suggest that he is trustworthy.

Similarly, many mathematical ideas arise from observing a pattern in a series of examples. The following "number magic" will allow your entire class to form a generalization based upon a pattern in your individual results.

## Lesson Exercise 1.1

(a) Follow these instructions.

Pick a number.

Multiply it by 2.

Add 10.

Divide by 2.

Subtract your original number.

(b) What number do you end up with?

(c) So why all the fanfare? Well, pick a different number and follow the instructions in part (a) again (or find out what everyone else in the class got). What number do you end up with this time? Are you mystified?

(d) Make a generalization based upon your results in part (a) and part (c).

You may wonder how the "magic" in Lesson Exercise 1.1 works. When we return to it later in the chapter, you'll be able to show why it works for any starting number.

The four introductory drawings and Lesson Exercise 1.1 illustrate inductive reasoning. Inductive reasoning works like this. You might be adding pairs of odd numbers and see a pattern in the results: $1 + 3 = 4$, $3 + 7 = 10$, and $35 + 31 = 66$. Then, you make a generalization: The sum of any two odd numbers is an even number. This process of making a generalization is called **inductive reasoning**.

> **Definition: Inductive Reasoning**
>
> **Inductive reasoning** involves making a generalization based upon a number of specific results or examples.

Inductive reasoning is the basis of experimental science and a fundamental part of mathematics. A scientist uses inductive reasoning to formulate a hypothesis based upon a pattern in experimental results. A mathematician uses inductive reasoning to form a reasonable generalization from a pattern in the series of examples.

In addition, many of our beliefs, prejudices, and theories are based upon this process. This lesson will help you make intelligent use of inductive reasoning in mathematics and in everyday life. Use inductive reasoning with care, since your generalizations may turn out to be wrong. For example, your friend Alan may eventually turn out to be untrustworthy.

## Making Generalizations

The essence of inductive reasoning is making generalizations (also called "conjectures") that appear to be true. The following example and exercises will help you become familiar with the process of making generalizations.

### Example 1.1

Does every number squared equal itself? Make a generalization based upon the following two examples: $0^2 = 0$ and $1^2 = 1$.

**Solution**

The answer to the question is "yes" for both these examples. Then, by inductive reasoning, I generalize that every number squared equals itself. However, this turns out to be a false generalization. This statement is false for all other decimal numbers. It would have been wiser to use more than two examples, including some numbers other than 0 and 1 (since 0 and 1 have special properties for multiplication). ■

In each of the following exercises, use inductive reasoning to make a generalization based upon the examples given. Write each generalization as a complete sentence.

### Lesson Exercise 1.2

What is the product of two odd numbers?

*Examples:* $5 \cdot 9 = 45$     $3 \cdot 7 = 21$
*Generalization:* _____

### Lesson Exercise 1.3

*Examples:* The last two times I went on a picnic, it rained.
*Generalization:* _____
_____
_____

Figure 1-1 shows how the second-grade textbook *Mathematics Plus* (Harcourt Brace Jovanovich, 1992) asks the child to make a generalization after a series of subtraction problems.

Of course, we would prefer that our generalizations are always true. In everyday life, we settle for generalizations that are true *most* of the time. When we wake up each morning, we assume that the refrigerator will be working and that we will have hot water. Such generalizations are reasonable and usually true. They give our lives order and enable us to plan ahead. However, such generalizations would not meet mathematical standards. In mathematics, we seek generalizations that are *always* true.

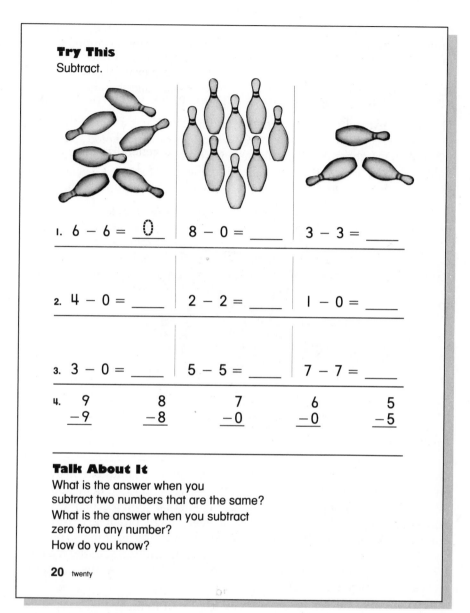

**Try This**
Subtract.

1. 6 − 6 = _0_       8 − 0 = ____       3 − 3 = ____

2. 4 − 0 = ____       2 − 2 = ____       1 − 0 = ____

3. 3 − 0 = ____       5 − 5 = ____       7 − 7 = ____

4.   9          8          7          6          5
    −9         −8         −0         −0         −5
   ____       ____       ____       ____       ____

**Talk About It**
What is the answer when you
subtract two numbers that are the same?
What is the answer when you subtract
zero from any number?
How do you know?

**20** twenty

From *Mathematics Plus*, Grade 2 (San Diego: Harcourt Brace Jovanovich, 1992), p. 20.

**Figure 1-1**

Unfortunately, inductive reasoning does not always lead to true generalizations. While the mathematical generalization you made in Lesson Exercise 1.2 turns out to be true, the mathematical generalization in Example 1.1 is false. Often a false generalization results when one selects a small or nonrepresentative set of examples. By observing a larger number of individual events, one can make more reasonable generalizations that are more likely to be true.

## Using Counterexamples to Disprove False Generalizations

How can one recognize false generalizations? Often it is a matter of finding just one exception. For over 1900 years, people accepted Aristotle's (384–322 B.C.) generalization that heavier objects fall at a faster rate than lighter objects. To test this generalization, Galileo (1564–1643) is alleged to have dropped two metal objects, one much heavier than the other, from

the Leaning Tower of Pisa. The objects hit the ground simultaneously! This one **counterexample** disproved Aristotle's longstanding generalization.

One usually cannot be sure whether a generalization reached by induction is true, because one cannot examine every single possibility. Although one cannot *prove* a generalization is true by picking examples, one can show a generalization is false by finding just *one* counterexample! Example 1.2 illustrates how one counterexample is used to show that a mathematical generalization is false.

### Example 1.2

Are all triangles isosceles (that is, having two or more congruent sides)? If not, find a counterexample.

**Solution**

No, all triangles are not isosceles, because the shape in Figure 1-2 is a triangle and it is not isosceles. ■

Figure 1-2

In Lesson Exercises 1.4 and 1.5, decide whether the generalization is reasonable or false. If possible, try a few other specific examples. If the generalization is false, disprove it by giving a counterexample. (The **D** in front of an exercise (such as Lesson Exercise 1.5) indicates that this is a good exercise to discuss as a class or in groups. Communicating your ideas orally or in writing helps to clarify them.)

## Lesson Exercise 1.4

I take a number and add it to itself. Then I take the same number and multiply it by itself. I obtain the same answer either way in two examples. $0 + 0 = 0 \cdot 0$ and $2 + 2 = 2 \cdot 2$. So I generalize that this will always work.

## **D** Lesson Exercise 1.5

I add the first two, three, and four odd numbers.

$$1 + 3 = 2^2 \qquad 1 + 3 + 5 = 3^2 \qquad 1 + 3 + 5 + 7 = 4^2$$

From this, I generalize that the sum of the first $N$ odd numbers is $N^2$ where $N = 2, 3, 4, \ldots$ (*Hint:* Write the next two examples that follow the pattern and see if they are true.)

How can you make more *reasonable* generalizations and detect faulty ones? By checking more examples and a greater variety of them.

## Applications of Inductive Reasoning

At its best, inductive reasoning leads to reasonable generalizations. In mathematics, these generalizations would then be proved true (if possible) using deductive reasoning. (Deductive reasoning will be discussed in the next section.) In everyday life, however, a reasonable generalization based upon a large number of examples is often the best we can do. It is often impossible to prove such a generalization is true.

Because nonmathematical generalizations are often impossible to prove, one should be careful about making them. Unfortunately, people are not always careful about making nonmathematical generalizations. Consider prejudice. A prejudice is a generalization about a whole group of people. Some people learn prejudices from their family or community, but prejudices can also be developed using inductive reasoning.

After I meet a few people from a certain group and observe a particular common characteristic, I may assume that all people from that group share that same characteristic. No matter what generalization I make about a group of people, there are bound to be some exceptions.

In Lesson Exercise 1.6, consider how some superstitions arise from inductive reasoning. (Note the use of the instruction *Explain* in the exercise. In this book, *Explain* means you should write an explanation that you would give to an elementary-school student. The explanation can be brief, but should proceed step-by-step from start to finish.)

## D Lesson Exercise 1.6

*Explain* how someone could use inductive reasoning to develop a superstition.

## D Lesson Exercise 1.7

Give an example of how you have used inductive reasoning to form a general idea.

## An Investigation: Sums of Consecutive Whole Numbers

An important part of mathematics is exploring new situations and making conjectures about them. The following investigation can be done in class (alone or in groups) or as homework.

## Lesson Exercise 1.8

Use inductive reasoning to answer the following questions.
(a) Is the sum of any three consecutive whole numbers divisible by 3?
(b) Is the sum of any four consecutive whole numbers divisible by 4?
(c) Is the sum of any five consecutive whole numbers divisible by 5?
(d) Investigate further examples and complete the following generalization:
   The sum of $N$ consecutive whole numbers is divisible by $N$ when
   $N =$ _____ .

## Answers to Selected Lesson Exercises

1.2 The product of two odd numbers is an odd number.

1.3 Every time I go on a picnic it rains.

1.4 False. $3 + 3 \neq 3 \cdot 3$

1.5 reasonable

1.6 A person may associate events that have oc-curred in succession a few times, such as a black cat crossing one's path and something bad happening soon after. After such experiences, the person generalizes that every time a black cat crosses one's path, bad luck will soon follow.

## 1.1 Homework Exercises _____ *LL8l*

### Basic Exercises

**1.** Consider the following number trick.

Pick any number at all.

Add 8.

Multiply by 2.

Subtract 10.

Subtract your original number.

(a) Try the trick with two or three different numbers.

(b) What is the general pattern in your results?

**2.** $3 \cdot 5 = 5 \cdot 3$    $6 \cdot 2 = 2 \cdot 6$    $1 \cdot 9 = 9 \cdot 1$
Write a generalization based upon these results.

**3.** A Martian met three people from Boston, and they all wore high heels. Now, the Martian thinks everyone from Boston wears high heels. Clearly, this generalization is false. Did the Martian use inductive reasoning correctly?

**4.** Why is it usually impossible to show that a statement is true by checking examples?

**5.** How can a proposed generalization be disproved?

In Exercises 6–10(a), decide whether the generalization made is reasonable or false. If it's false, give a counterexample.

**6.** *Examples:*

*Generalization:* All four-sided figures have four right angles.

**7.** *Examples:* José likes to drink beer and watch football on TV.
Brad likes to drink beer and watch football on TV.
*Generalization:* All men like to drink beer and watch football on TV.

**8.** *Examples:* $1 + 2 = \dfrac{2(3)}{2}$

$$1 + 2 + 3 = \dfrac{3(4)}{2}$$

$$1 + 2 + 3 + 4 = \dfrac{4(5)}{2}$$

*Generalization:* The sum of the first $N$ counting numbers is $N(N + 1)/2$ for $N = 2, 3, 4, \ldots$.

**9.** *Examples:*

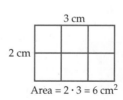 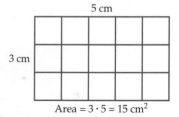

*Generalization:* The area of a rectangle in square units equals its length times its width.

**10.** (a) A farmer uses fertilizer for 3 years in a row, and his corn crop yield improves each year. Based upon these results, he generalizes that fertilizer improves corn crop yield.

(b) If the generalization in part (a) is true, what other factors should the farmer consider in deciding whether or not to use this fertilizer to grow corn?

**11.** Ready for some math magic?

$$112 \times 124 = 13,888$$

No, of course that's not the whole bit! Read on.

(a) Reverse the digits in each factor and multiply.

$$211 \times 421 = \underline{\hspace{1cm}}$$

(b) What is interesting about the result in part (a)?

(c) $312 \times 221 = \underline{\hspace{1cm}}$
$213 \times 122 = \underline{\hspace{1cm}}$

(d) Make a generalization based upon the results to parts (a) and (c).

(e) Try some other examples and decide whether your generalization is reasonable or false.

**12.** (a) $12,345,679 \times 36 = \underline{\hspace{2cm}}$
(b) $12,345,679 \times 45 = \underline{\hspace{2cm}}$
(c) Try to extend this pattern.
(d) *Explain* how this pattern works.
(Hint: What is $12,345,679 \times 9$?)

 **13.** Galileo used inductive reasoning to develop hypotheses about the length of a pendulum and the period of a full swing.

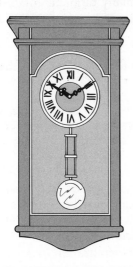

Use the following data to develop your own hypothesis.

| L (length of pendulum) | P (period of a full swing) |
|---|---|
| 1 unit | 1 second |
| 2 units | 1.41 seconds |
| 3 units | 1.73 seconds |
| 4 units | 2 seconds |
| 9 units | 3 seconds |

(a) If the pattern continues, what is the *length* of a pendulum that has a *period* of 4 seconds?

(b) What is the general relationship between the length and the period?

(c) Write a formula relating $L$ to $P$.

(d) Use your formula from part (c) to estimate the period of a pendulum 5 units long.

**14.** How would one use inductive reasoning to form a prejudice?

**15.** Give an example showing how each of the following groups might use inductive reasoning.
(a) students     (b) mathematicians

**16.** Give an example showing how each of the following groups might use inductive reasoning.
(a) teachers
(b) college admissions officers

**17.** (a) *Explain* how each of the following generalizations can be formed using inductive reasoning and (b) whether or not you agree with the generalization.
(1) There will always be wars.
(2) Boys are better than girls at mathematics.
(3) A movie sequel is never as good as the original movie.

*Extension Exercises*

**18.**

| E (weight on Earth) | 100 lb | 200 lb | 300 lb |
|---|---|---|---|
| M (weight on Mars) | 38 lb | 76 lb | 114 lb |

(a) An astronaut in a space suit might weigh about 400 lb on Earth. If the pattern continues, what would be her weight on Mars?

(b) If someone's weight doubles on Earth, what do you think would happen to the person's weight on Mars?

(c) Make a conjecture about the general relationship between weight on Earth and weight on Mars based upon these data. (Compare each $E$ value to the corresponding $M$ value.)

(d) Write an equation relating $E$ to $M$ based upon your conjecture.

19. Try some examples and decide whether each of the following statements is probably true or definitely false.

(a) The product of any three consecutive whole numbers is divisible by 3.

(b) The product of any four consecutive whole numbers is divisible by 4.

(c) The product of any five consecutive whole numbers is divisible by 5.

(d) Investigate further examples and state a generalization of your results.

20. (a) Is every number that is divisible by 4 also divisible by 3?

(b) Is any number that is divisible by 5 also divisible by 3?

(c) Is any number that is divisible by 6 also divisible by 3?

(d) Investigate further examples and state a generalization of your results.

21. When people clasp their hands, do they all prefer to put their right thumb on top?

*Special Exercise*
22.

Western Europe          United States

Mapmakers often draw adjacent states or countries in different colors. One of the most famous problems in mathematics is the map-coloring problem. It asks: How many different colors are needed to color any map drawn on a flat surface or sphere so that adjacent regions are different colors?

In 1878, Arthur Cayley posed this problem to the London Mathematical Society. Ninety-eight years later, Wolfgang Haken and Kenneth Appel of the University of Illinois found and proved the answer using over 1000 hours of computer time.

(a) How many different colors are needed to color the map of Western Europe so that no two adjacent regions are the same color?

(b) How many colors are needed for the U.S. map? (You don't have to color in every state.)

(c) Based upon your results to parts (a) and (b), make a conjecture about the answer to the map-coloring question.

## 1.2  Deductive Reasoning

It's the first day of class. A middle-aged woman walks in the door and heads directly to the front of the room. Next, she lays her things on the teacher's desk. What would you conclude about this person?

Or how about this? I'm thinking of a one-digit odd number that is greater than 5 and divisible by 3. Can you deduce what number it is?

In drawing conclusions from information given in the preceding examples, one can use a second important reasoning process: deductive reasoning. One of the most famous deductive thinkers is Sherlock Holmes. Notice how he uses deductive reasoning in the following scene.

## A Famous Application of Deductive Reasoning

The following scene is adapted from "The Adventures of the Dancing Men" by Sir Arthur Conan Doyle. Places! Action! Let the show begin.

HOLMES: (*cooly*) So Watson, you were just discussing gold investments.
WATSON: (*astonished*) How on earth did you know that?!
HOLMES: In a few moments, you'll say it's so absurdly simple.
WATSON: (*in a huff*) I certainly will not.
HOLMES: After seeing chalk between your index finger and thumb, I feel sure that you were discussing gold investments.
WATSON: (*still confused*) What is the connection?
HOLMES: Let me explain and diagram my argument using step-by-step deductive reasoning.

1. You have chalk between your index finger and thumb.

2. Therefore, you must have played billiards.

3. You must have played billiards with Thurston since you always play with him.

4. Thurston had an option to invest in gold no later than today and wanted you to invest with him, so you must have discussed it.

$$\text{chalk on} \rightarrow \text{played} \rightarrow \text{was with} \rightarrow \text{discussed gold}$$
$$\text{fingers} \quad \text{billiards} \quad \text{Thurston} \quad \text{investment}$$

WATSON: How absurdly simple! You've done a proof like I used to do in high school geometry class.

Curtain (and applause)

In reaching his conclusion, Sherlock Holmes used deductive reasoning. Each statement in his explanation necessarily leads to the next statement when combined with certain assumptions. For example, Holmes combined the fact that Watson had chalk between his index finger and thumb with the assumption that if Watson had chalk on his fingers then he must have been playing billiards. The necessary conclusion is that Watson was playing billiards.

---

**Definition: Deductive Reasoning**

**Deductive reasoning** is the process of reaching a necessary conclusion from given facts or hypotheses.

Deductive reasoning is used by detectives solving crimes, mathematicians drawing conclusions, and philosophers thinking logically. When the assumptions are true, deductive reasoning produces certain results. Now, it's your turn to solve a mystery using deductive reasoning.

## Lesson Exercise 1.9

The painting "By Numbers" was stolen from Jane Dough's Illinois home last night. Can you find the thief?

The only suspects are Jane Dough (the owner of the house), Jeeves (the butler), Sharky (the pool man), and Fluffy (the pet Doberman pinscher). The police have gathered the following evidence:

1. The painting was stolen between 8:00 and 9:00 P.M. last night.
2. Fluffy can't carry a painting.
3. Jeeves has been visiting Mumsy in Liverpool all week.
4. Sharky and Jane's fingerprints were on the canvas.
5. Jane was at the movie "Return of the Stepson of Darth Vader's Cousin" from 7:30 to 10:00 P.M. last night with three friends.

## Drawing Conclusions

The essence of deductive reasoning is drawing a necessary conclusion (from given hypotheses). The following lesson exercise illustrates how applying a geometry theorem to a particular figure requires deductive reasoning.

## Lesson Exercise 1.10

Fill in a conclusion that follows from the given hypotheses.

*Hypotheses: ABCD* is a parallelogram.

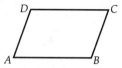

*Theorem:* The opposite sides of a parallelogram are congruent.

*Conclusion:* _____

In the preceding exercise, you applied the theorem that the opposite sides of a parallelogram are congruent to a particular parallelogram *ABCD*. Mathematicians also use deductive reasoning in applying a definition to a particular case, as is done in the following lesson exercise. The following exercise also introduces a second common format used in deductive reasoning: the "if-then" format.

## Lesson Exercise 1.11

Fill in a conclusion that follows from the given hypotheses.

If all numbers that are divisible by 2 are even, and 264 is divisible by 2, then _____ .

In the preceding exercise, the definition of an even number was applied to the number 264. In the "if-then" statement, the hypotheses come after the word "if," and the conclusion is stated after the word "then." In Lesson Exercise 1.11, the hypotheses are (1) "all numbers that are divisible by 2 are even numbers," and (2) "264 is divisible by 2." The conclusion is "264 is an even number."

## Lesson Exercise 1.12

Consider the following statement: If $x = 4$ and $y = x + 3$, then $y = 7$.
(a) What are the hypotheses?
(b) What is the conclusion?

The mathematician, like the detective, uses deductive reasoning in a process of elimination. This is illustrated in the following exercise.

## Lesson Exercise 1.13

(a) Fill in the blank and (b) identify the hypotheses and conclusion.

Two distinct lines in a plane are either parallel or intersecting. Distinct lines $a$ and $b$ in a plane are not parallel. Therefore, _____ .

Aristotle (384–322 B.C.), the father of deductive reasoning, was the first to study logic systematically. He stated the most famous example of deductive reasoning. It consists of two hypotheses and a necessary conclusion.

Example 1.3 models Aristotle's famous example of deductive reasoning with a Venn diagram (set picture). Aristotle didn't have the luxury of using a Venn diagram. John Venn (1834–1923) invented these diagrams used for illustrating set relationships over 2000 years after Aristotle's death.

### Example 1.3

Deduce the conclusion and represent it with a Venn diagram.

*Hypotheses:* All people are mortal.
Socrates is a person.

*Conclusion:* _____

**Figure 1-3**

#### Solution

Since Socrates is a person and all people are mortal, we can conclude that Socrates must be mortal. The same conclusion can be confirmed using Venn diagrams, as shown in Figure 1-3. The first hypothesis, "All people are mortal," is shown by drawing a circle representing the set of "all people" inside a circle representing the set of "all mortals." This Venn diagram shows that the set of "all mortals" contains the set of "all people." The second hypothesis, "Socrates is a person," is shown by drawing a point representing Socrates inside the circle representing the set of "all people," since the set of "all people" contains Socrates. (A point is used to represent a single element.)

And now look! The point representing Socrates is also inside the circle representing mortals. So the set of "mortals" contains Socrates. We have our conclusion: Socrates is mortal. ■

### Lesson Exercise 1.14

Deduce the conclusion to the following and represent both hypotheses in a Venn diagram.

*Hypotheses:* All doctors are college graduates.
All college graduates finish high school.

*Conclusion:* _____

Figure 1-4 shows how the first-grade textbook of *Mathematics Plus* asks children to draw a conclusion from a set of pictures.

## Does Deductive Reasoning Always Work?

Are the conclusions that result from deductive reasoning always true? What if one of the hypotheses is false? Try the following lesson exercise.

Name _____ **Thinking Mathematically**

Write the child's name on the correct bag.

Tanya          Dave          Kristin

two hundred eighty-nine **289**

From *Mathematics Plus*, Grade 1 (San Diego: Harcourt Brace Jovanovich, 1992), p. 289.

**Figure 1-4**

## Lesson Exercise 1.15

(a) Fill in the blank and (b) identify the hypotheses and conclusion. If Boston is a city, and all cities are states, then

_____.

Lesson Exercise 1.15 illustrates that valid (correct) deductive reasoning can sometimes lead to a false conclusion.

valid

FALSE     reasoning     FALSE
HYPOTHESIS     ⟶     CONCLUSION

Lesson Exercise 1.16 contains another example of this type.

## Lesson Exercise 1.16

Deduce the conclusion to the following.

*Hypotheses:* A square is also a rectangle.
             All rectangles have 6 sides.
*Conclusion:* _____

When deductive reasoning is done correctly, it is called valid deductive reasoning, and the conclusion is called a "valid conclusion." In **valid** deductive reasoning, the conclusion automatically follows from the hypotheses. Deductive reasoning is said to be **invalid** (done incorrectly) when the conclusion does not automatically follow from the hypotheses. The use of the words "valid" and "invalid" does *not* indicate whether any hypothesis or conclusion is true or false.

Lesson Exercises 1.15 and 1.16 are examples of how valid deductive reasoning can lead to a false conclusion. Both Lesson Exercises 1.15 and 1.16 have a false conclusion that results from having a false hypothesis. In order to guarantee that the conclusion reached by deductive reasoning is true, all the hypotheses must be true.

---

**True Conclusions from Deductive Reasoning**

If the hypotheses are true and the deductive reasoning is valid, then the conclusion must be true.

---

In analyzing a deductive sequence, check to see whether the hypotheses and conclusion are true or false, and check whether reasoning from the hypotheses to the conclusion is valid (done correctly) or invalid.

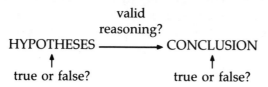

## Venn Diagrams and Deductive Reasoning

Sometimes people use deductive reasoning even though it does not apply to a situation. Examples 1.4 and 1.5 illustrate *invalid* deductive reasoning. Venn diagrams, which were used earlier to illustrate valid conclusions, are also helpful in detecting invalid deductive reasoning. If deductive reasoning is valid, it is impossible to draw a Venn diagram that satisfies the hypotheses but not the conclusion. If deductive reasoning is invalid, it *is* possible to draw a Venn diagram that satisfies all the hypotheses but not the conclusion.

### Example 1.4

Is the following conclusion valid? If so, draw a Venn diagram that illustrates it. If not, draw a Venn diagram showing that the conclusion does not follow from the two hypotheses.

*Hypotheses:* All dogs are animals.
          All cats are animals.
*Conclusion:* All dogs are cats.

### Solution

The conclusion does not seem to follow from the two hypotheses. If the conclusion is invalid, there should be a Venn diagram that satisfies the hypotheses but not the conclusion (see Figure 1-5). Such a diagram would be a counterexample to the conclusion. The first hypothesis, "All dogs are animals," is shown by drawing a circle representing the set of all dogs inside a circle representing the set of "all animals."

Similarly, the hypothesis "All cats are animals" is represented by drawing a circle representing "all cats" inside the circle representing "all animals."

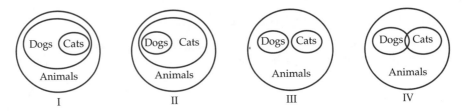

**Figure 1-5**

It is possible to draw a diagram (I, III, or IV) that satisfies the hypotheses but contradicts the conclusion. The "dog" circle does not have to be inside the "cat" circle as the conclusion suggests, so the conclusion does not necessarily follow from the hypotheses. ■

The result of Example 1.4 can be illustrated as follows.

invalid
reasoning

HYPOTHESIS ⎯⎯⎯→ CONCLUSION
(true)                          (false)

The error in Example 1.4 is obvious. However, advertisers sometimes use the same form of faulty reasoning, and many people do not notice it. Example 1.5 illustrates this technique.

### Example 1.5

Does the conclusion follow from the two hypotheses? If so, draw a Venn diagram that illustrates it. If not, draw a Venn diagram showing that the conclusion does not follow from the two hypotheses.

*Hypotheses:* All beautiful women use Coverall lipstick.
          Sally uses Coverall lipstick.
*Conclusion:* Sally is a beautiful woman.

### Solution

The Venn diagram in Figure 1-6 satisfies the hypotheses but not the conclusion. Therefore, the deductive reasoning must be invalid. The point representing Sally does not have to be inside the "beautiful woman" circle. In fact, Sally may be a child!  ■

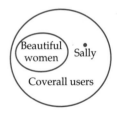

**Figure 1-6**

Note that Figure 1-6 and diagram III in Figure 1-5 have the same structure. This diagram results from one common form of invalid deductive reasoning. As shown in Figure 1-7, if $A$ is in $C$ and $B$ is in $C$, then the deduction that $B$ is in $A$ is invalid.

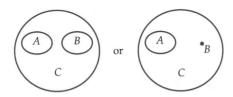

**Figure 1-7**

In Lesson Exercises 1.17 and 1.18, *assume the first two statements (hypotheses) are true*, and decide whether the third statement (conclusion) can be deduced from the first two. If the conclusion is valid, draw a Venn diagram that illustrates this. If the conclusion is invalid, draw a Venn diagram that disproves it.

**D** Lesson Exercise 1.17
___

A rectangle is a polygon. A triangle is a polygon. Therefore, a rectangle is a triangle.

**D** Lesson Exercise 1.18
___

Harold uses Some laundry detergent. People who use Some have clean clothes. Therefore, Harold has clean clothes.

## A Game: Pica-Centro

Pica-Centro is a game of deductive reasoning for two players that Douglas Aichele describes in his May 1972 article in the *Arithmetic Teacher*. The object of the game is to determine the three-digit number your opponent secretly selects by using deductive reasoning (and a little luck).

To begin the game, Player A secretly chooses a three-digit number with three different digits. Player B then keeps guessing three-digit numbers until Player B can determine Player A's number. For example, suppose Player A secretly picks the number 807. Player B records guesses as follows.

| Guesses Player (B) | Responses Player (A) | |
| --- | --- | --- |
| Digits | Pica Correct Digit Wrong Position | Centro Correct Digit Correct Position |
| 7  4  2 | 1 | 0 |
| 4  2  5 | 0 | 0 |
| 3  8  7 | 1 | 1 |
| 8  0  7 | 0 | 3 |

For each of Player B's guesses, Player A tells how many digits are correct and whether they are in the correct position, as shown in the table, above. This process continues until Player B finds Player A's number. Then the players switch roles.

**D** Lesson Exercise 1.19
___

Find a partner and play a game of Pica-Centro.

## Answers to Selected Lesson Exercises

**1.9** Sharky

**1.10** $\overline{AB} \cong \overline{CD}$ and $\overline{AD} \cong \overline{BC}$

**1.11** 264 is an even number.

**1.12** (a) $x = 4$ and $y = x + 3$  (b) $y = 7$

**1.13** (a) $a$ and $b$ are intersecting.

(b) The first two statements about the lines are the hypotheses, and the answer to part (a) is the conclusion.

**1.14** All doctors finish high school.

**1.15** (a) Boston is a state.

**1.16** All squares have six sides.

**1.17** no

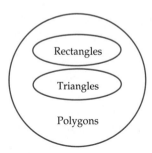

**1.18** yes

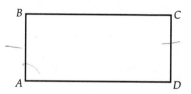

## 1.2  Homework Exercises

### Basic Exercises

1. Use deductive reasoning to fill in a conclusion that follows from the given statements and draw a Venn diagram (set picture).
   All rectangles are parallelograms. All parallelograms are quadrilaterals.
   *Conclusion:* _____

2. Use deductive reasoning to fill in the conclusion.
   Watson was playing billiards today. Watson only plays billiards with Thurston.
   *Conclusion:* _____

3. (a) Fill in the blank and (b) identify the hypotheses and conclusion.

   If *ABCD* is a rectangle, and the opposite sides of a rectangle are parallel, then

   _____.

4. What will guarantee that the conclusion reached by valid deductive reasoning is true?

5. The first person to study deductive reasoning systematically was
   (a) Sherlock Holmes
   (b) my mathematics teacher
   (c) Sylvester Stallone
   (d) Newton
   (e) Aristotle

In Exercises 6–9, decide whether or not the conclusion can be deduced from the first two hypotheses. If so, draw a Venn diagram that supports your answer. If not, draw a Venn diagram that satisfies the hypotheses but not the conclusion.

6. *Hypotheses:* All cockroaches are young.
   All young things are beautiful.
   *Conclusion:* All cockroaches are beautiful.

7. *Hypotheses:* All elephants have trunks.
   All trees have trunks.
   *Conclusion:* All elephants are trees.

8. *Hypotheses:* Two is a whole number.
   All whole numbers can be written as fractions.
   *Conclusion:* Two can be written as a fraction.

9. *Hypotheses:* Models drink diet cola.
   I drink diet cola.
   *Conclusion:* I am a model.

In Exercises 10 and 11, decide whether or not the third statement can be deduced from the two hypotheses.

10. *Hypotheses:* Martina is taller than Gabriela.
    Gabriela is taller than Steffi.
    *Conclusion:* Martina is taller than Steffi.

11. *Hypotheses:* Martina beat Gabriela at tennis.
    Gabriela beat Steffi at tennis.
    *Conclusion:* Martina will beat Steffi at tennis.

12. Consider the following Pica-Centro game.

| Guesses | Responses | |
|---|---|---|
| | Pica | Centro |
| | Correct Digit | Correct Digit |
| Digits | Wrong Position | Correct Position |
| 5  3  2 | 2 | 0 |
| 4  2  3 | 1 | 0 |

Which digit is definitely part of the secret number? Justify your answer.

13. Consider the following Pica-Centro game.

| Guesses | Responses | |
|---|---|---|
| | Pica | Centro |
| | Correct Digit | Correct Digit |
| Digits | Wrong Position | Correct Position |
| 5  2  3 | 2 | 0 |
| 0  1  2 | 0 | 0 |
| 6  7  8 | 0 | 1 |
| 9  7  6 | 0 | 0 |

(a) Which digits can be eliminated?
(b) Which digit is in the correct position in the third guess? Explain why.
(c) Which two digits are correct in the first guess?
(d) What is the correct position of the two correct digits in the first guess? Explain why.
(e) What is the secret number?

14. Consider the following Pica-Centro game.

| Guesses | Responses | |
|---|---|---|
| | Pica | Centro |
| | Correct Digit | Correct Digit |
| Digits | Wrong Position | Correct Position |
| 3  0  7 | 0 | 0 |
| 2  6  4 | 1 | 1 |
| 6  8  4 | 0 | 1 |
| 1  5  3 | 1 | 0 |

Find the secret number.

In Exercises 15 and 16, use deductive reasoning to fill in a conclusion that follows from all the given statements.

15. If you have your teeth cleaned twice a year, you will have less tooth decay. If you have less tooth decay, you will lose fewer teeth.

    *Conclusion:* _____

16. If my students don't like me, they will complain to the dean. If the dean hears complaints about me, then I won't get a raise in salary. If I give low grades, then my students won't like me.

    *Conclusion:* _____

In Exercises 17 and 18, use deductive reasoning to fill in a conclusion that follows from all the given statements.

17. *Hypotheses:* Some adults watch television. People who watch television don't have time to read.
    *Conclusion:* _____

18. *Hypotheses:* Some people throw litter on the street. People who throw litter do not care about their surroundings.
    *Conclusion:* _____

19. Fill in the blank with a deduction suggested by the advertiser and state whether or not it is true.

    If I use Listermint mouthwash then

    _____.

20. Complete the following to create an example of valid deductive reasoning.

    *Assumptions:* All elephants are good dancers.
    _____

    *Conclusion:* _____

21. What conclusions can be drawn about Sandy based upon the diagram (at the top of the next column)?

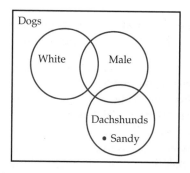

22. Joe and Sue are the same age. Joe is younger than Paul. Paul is older than Jane. Is Joe older than Jane, younger than Jane, or can't you tell from the given information?

## Extension Exercises

Photo courtesy of Library of Congress.

**23.** Assume the following statements are true.

All people are created equal.
People have the right to life, liberty, and the pursuit of happiness.
A government should be supported only so long as it protects these rights.

(a) These statements are taken from a famous document, although the word *men* has been changed to *people*. What is the name of this document?

(b) Based upon the above three statements, which of the following statements MUST be true or MUST be false?
  (1) Men and women are created equal.
  (2) Everyone has a right to a good job.
  (3) People should support a government even if it doesn't protect their liberty.

**24.** Everyone in the Smith family has dressed up for Halloween. Match each family member out of costume to the same family member in costume. Write a deductive explanation of your answer.

Ma     Pa     Igor     Lurch     Migraine     Nancy

25. Raymond Smullyan, a contemporary mathematician, devised the following puzzle:

*The Politician Puzzle*

100 politicians attended a convention. Each politician was either crooked or honest. Also
1. At least one of the politicans was honest.
2. Given any two politicians, at least one of the two was crooked.
How many politicians were honest and how many were crooked?

26. Lewis Carroll (real name: Charles Dodgson), author of *Alice's Adventures in Wonderland*, was also a mathematics professor who devised logic puzzles. The following are from his book *Symbolic Logic*. In each part, draw a valid conclusion that follows from all the given statements.
   (a) Everyone who is sane can do logic.
       No lunatics are fit to sit on a jury.
       None of your sons can do logic.
   (b) No ducks waltz.
       No officers decline to waltz.
       All my poultry are ducks.
   (c) No birds, except ostriches, are 9 feet high.
       There are no birds in this aviary that belong to anyone but me.
       No ostrich lives on mince pies.
       I have no birds less than 9 feet high.

27. (a) Draw a Venn diagram that represents the following statements.
       All dolphins are swimmers.
       All swimmers wear bathing suits.
       No tigers wear bathing suits.

   (b) Which of the following statements are confirmed by your diagram?
       (1) All dophins wear bathing suits.
       (2) If you are not a tiger, then you wear a bathing suit.
       (3) All dolphins are tigers.
       (4) If you are not a swimmer, then you are not a dolphin.

28. The Three Stooges are a real pain. When you ask one of them a question, they all answer. Furthermore, one of them always lies, and the other two answer truthfully. I asked them who is the smartest. They replied:

   CURLY: I am not the smartest.

   MOE: Larry is the smartest.

   LARRY: Curly is the smartest.

   Who is really the smartest and who is the liar?
   Explain how you found the solution.

29. While on a trip, you approach a fork in the road and don't know whether to bear right or left. You meet a native there who either always tells the truth or always lies (but you don't know which). What single question could you ask to find the correct route?

30. You want to determine whether the following statement is true for the cards shown: "If a 1 is printed on one side then a 2 is printed on the other side." Which of these cards *must* you turn over?

   $\boxed{1}$  $\boxed{2}$  $\boxed{3}$

**31.** Three boxes contain yellow and white tennis balls. One box has all yellow tennis balls; one has all white tennis balls; and one has some yellow and some white balls.

Unfortunately, all three boxes are labeled incorrectly! How can you determine the correct labeling after selecting just one ball?

| Y | | W | | W and Y |
|---|---|---|---|---|

**32.** Mr. Barber is a barber who shaves every man in town who does not shave himself. Who shaves Mr. Barber?

*Special Exercises*

**33.** (a) Fill the numbers in the puzzle. Each number should be used once.

| 3 Digits | 4 Digits | 5 Digits |
|----------|----------|----------|
| 632 | 1562 | 12683 |
| 683 | 1793 | 14623 |
| 904 | 3081 | 98729 |
| 913 | 8421 | |
| 981 | | |

(b) Give an example showing how you used deductive reasoning to fill in the numbers in this puzzle.

**34.** The following puzzle is adapted from the magazine "Murder Ink."

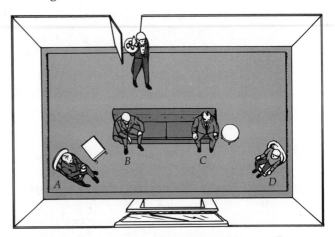

Boggs has been found dead. Four men, seated on the sofa and two chairs in front of the fireplace as shown above, are discussing the murder. Their names are Howell, Scott, Jennings, and Wilton. They are, not necessarily respectively, a general, a schoolmaster, an admiral, and a doctor.

1. The waiter brings a whiskey for Jennings and a beer for Scott.
2. In the mirror over the fireplace, the general sees the door close as the waiter departs. The general then speaks to Wilton, next to him.
3. Neither Howell nor Scott has any sisters.
4. The schoolmaster does not drink alcohol.
5. Howell is the admiral's brother-in-law. Howell is sitting in a chair, and the schoolmaster is next to him on his left.
6. The murderer suddenly moves to drop something in Jennings' whiskey. No one has moved from their seats.

(a) Tell the position of each man, give his profession, and name the murderer.
(b) Give an example showing how you used deductive reasoning to solve this puzzle.

**35.** Make up your own mystery like the one in the preceding exercise.

# 1.3  Inductive and Deductive Reasoning

Mathematicians use inductive and deductive reasoning to create new mathematics. First, they propose generalizations (using induction) and then, they try to prove the logical validity of their generalizations (using deduction).

In this lesson, you'll first learn to tell the difference between induction and deduction. Then, you'll see how mathematicians use these two processes in succession to create new mathematics.

## Inductive vs. Deductive Reasoning

By permission of Johnny Hart and Creators Syndicate, Inc.

**Figure 1-8**

## Lesson Exercise 1.20

Are the men in the cartoon in Figure 1-8 discussing deductive or inductive reasoning?

How can one avoid mixing up inductive reasoning and deductive reasoning? Remember, inductive reasoning leads to a possible generalization from specific examples; deductive reasoning draws a necessary conclusion from given assumptions. Induction involves an "inductive leap" from specific examples to a general idea. Deduction leads to a conclusion that *follows automatically* from the given assumptions.

Can you tell the difference? Find out in the following exercises.

In Lesson Exercises 1.21 through 1.23, identify whether inductive or deductive reasoning is being used.

## Lesson Exercise 1.21

The fingerprints on the wall match yours. I know that everyone has a unique set of fingerprints. I conclude that you touched the wall.

## Lesson Exercise 1.22

I meet two people from France who wear berets. I conclude that all people from France wear berets.

## Lesson Exercise 1.23

Given: $m = n + 6$ and $n = -8$. I conclude that $m = -2$.

## Inductive and Deductive Reasoning

Many mathematical ideas are developed using a two-step process. First, inductive reasoning is used to make a generalization about an observed pattern in a variety of examples. Then, deductive reasoning demonstrates that the general statement *must* be true if certain assumptions are made.

Remember the mystifying number trick from Section 1.1? You observed that no matter what number you started with, you always ended up with 5. Unfortunately, no matter how many examples you tried, you could not be sure you would *always* end up with 5.

Inductive reasoning carries the risk of an incorrect generalization, so the conclusion it produces lacks the certitude required in mathematics. A mathematician would use deductive reasoning to prove that the number trick always produces a 5.

### Example 1.6

Prove that the following number trick always results in 5.

Pick a number.
Multiply by 2.
Add 10.
Divide by 2.
Subtract your original number.

### Solution

Mathematicians use algebra and deductive reasoning to prove general results about numbers. In the case of the number puzzle, instead of starting with a number such as 3 or $-2$, start with a variable $N$ that could represent any number. Then go through all the steps in the puzzle and deduce what happens to the variable along the way.

1. Pick a number.        $N$
2. Multiply by 2.        _____ (deduction?)

What goes in the blank? If you take $N$ and multiply by 2, you obtain $2N$.

Next, how do we deduce the result of step 3 from step 2?

2. Multiply by 2.          $2N$
3. Add 10.                       _____ (deduction?)

Take $2N$ and add 10 and you obtain $2N + 10$. Continuing this series of steps and deductions yields the following proof.

1. Pick a number.                    $N$
2. Multiply by 2.                    $2N$
3. Add 10.                      $2N + 10$
4. Divide by 2.                  $N + 5$
5. Subtract your original number.      5

Deductive reasoning shows that no matter what $N$ you start with, you will end up with 5.  ■

## Lesson Exercise 1.24

Consider the following number trick.

Pick any number at all.

Subtract 3.

Multiply by 2.

Subtract your original number.

Add 6.

(a) Try two or three different numbers and use inductive reasoning to make a conjecture about what will happen with any number.
(b) Use deductive reasoning to prove your generalization from part (a).

Mathematics is our unique attempt to construct a system of ideas based upon precise deductive reasoning. A mathematical system begins with a few simple assumptions and then, through step-by-step logical arguments, arrives at new conclusions. The conclusions of deductive reasoning are irrefutable if the assumptions are correct.

Ancient Greek philosophers required that all their mathematical theorems be based upon deductive reasoning, and it has remained that way for over 2000 years! Mathematicians will not accept any statement as a theorem of mathematics unless it has been proved deductively.

## The Converse of a Statement

"If your fingerprints are on the murder weapon, then you must have touched it." This statement is generally true, although Sherlock Holmes once had to disprove it to solve a case. Would the following also be generally true? "If you touched the murder weapon, then your fingerprints must be on it." This last statement is the converse of the first.

The **converse** is the new "if-then" statement formed by interchanging the hypothesis and the conclusion. When you have shown an "if-then" statement is true, you may also want to examine the related "if-then" statement called the converse.

The following is another example of a statement and its converse.

*Statement:* If a number is divisible by 10, then the number is even.
*Converse:* If a number is even, then the number is divisible by 10.

### Lesson Exercise 1.25

The statement just given is true. Is the converse also true? Try some examples and see whether the converse is probably true or definitely false.

### Lesson Exercise 1.26

If $x + 3 = 5$ then $x = 2$.
(a) Is this statement true?
(b) Write its converse.
(c) Is the converse true or false?

Lesson Exercises 1.25 and 1.26 suggest the following.

---

**Statements and Their Converses**

The converse of a true "if-then" statement may be either true or false.

---

The extension (homework) exercises address two other statements that are related to an "if-then" statement, the contrapositive and the inverse.

## "If and Only If"

It would be convenient if all conditional statements were in an "if-$A$-then-$B$" format, but they are not. Two other common forms are the following.

$$X = 2 \text{ if } X + 3 = 5$$

You have mononucleosis *only if* you have a fever and sore throat.

How are the "*A*-if-*B*" and "*A*-only-if-*B*" formats related to the "if-*A*-then-*B*" format? The two preceding statements can be rewritten using the "if-then" format.

$$X = 2 \text{ if } X + 3 = 5$$

is the same as

$$\text{If } X + 3 = 5 \text{ then } X = 2$$

## Lesson Exercise 1.27

Which of the following are equivalent to the statement, "You have mononucleosis only if you have a fever and sore throat"?
(a) People who have mononucleosis must have a fever and sore throat.
(b) If you have a fever and a sore throat, then you must have mononucleosis.
(c) If you have mononucleosis, then you have a fever and sore throat.

The preceding example and exercise are special cases of the following.

---

**"If" Statements and "Only-If" Statements**

"*A* if *B*" means "If *B*, then *A*."
"*A* only if *B*" means "If *A*, then *B*."

---

This shows the relationship between the three common formats.

## Lesson Exercise 1.28

Write the following statements in an "if-then" format.
(a) You may teach only if you have a college degree.
(b) *N* is an even number if *N* is divisible by 2.

A commonly used, more powerful format combines the "if" and "only-if" formats. Consider a compound statement that contains both "if" and "only if"!

$$x = 2 \text{ if and only if } x + 3 = 5$$

An "if-and-only-if" statement is actually two statements in one. The statement "$x = 2$ if and only if $x + 3 = 5$" means

**1.** $x = 2$ if $x + 3 = 5$ and
**2.** $x = 2$ only if $x + 3 = 5$

These two statements can be rewritten in the "if-then" format as

**1.** If $x + 3 = 5$, then $x = 2$ and
**2.** If $x = 2$, then $x + 3 = 5$

So an "if-and-only-if" statement describes a very strong connection between two conditions. It gives you two statements in one: a statement *and* its converse. It means that the two conditions (separated by "if and only if") are equivalent. For example, to say, "$x + 3 = 5$" is equivalent to saying, "$x = 2$." Whenever one is true, the other must be true; whenever one is false, the other must be false.

---

**If-and-Only-If Statements**

"*A* if and only if *B*" means

1. If *A*, then *B*, *and*
2. If *B*, then *A*.

---

In other words, "*A* if and only if *B*" means that *A* implies *B* and *B* implies *A*. This relationship is often written symbolically as $A \longleftrightarrow B$. "If and only if" is a standard phrase used in many mathematical definitions and theorems. Look for it later on in this book. Remember: "If and only if" indicates a theorem or definition that satisfies *two* "if-then" statements.

## Lesson Exercise 1.29

Write the following statement as two "if-then" statements.

Whole number $A$ is a factor of whole number $B$ if and only if $A \cdot C = B$, where $C$ is a whole number.

## Answers to Lesson Exercises

1.20 inductive reasoning

1.21 deduction

1.22 induction

1.23 deduction

**1.24** (a) You end up with the original number.

(b) Assume that $N$ = your original number. Then the following deductions must be true.

(1) Subtract 3 and you get $N - 3$.

(2) Multiply by 2 and you get $2N - 6$.

(3) Subtract your original number $N$ and you get $N - 6$.

(4) Add 6 and you end up with $N$.

No matter what number $N$ you start out with, you will end up with the same $N$.

**1.25** No. The number 4 would be a counter-example.

**1.26** (a) yes

(b) If $x = 2$, then $x + 3 = 5$.

(c) true

**1.27** (a) and (c)

**1.28** (a) If you teach, then you have a college degree.

(b) If $N$ is divisible by 2, then $N$ is even.

**1.29** If whole number $A$ is a factor of whole number $B$, then $A \cdot C = B$, where $C$ is a whole number. If $A \cdot C = B$, where $A$, $B$, and $C$ are whole numbers, then $A$ is a factor of $B$.

## 1.3 Homework Exercises

*Basic Exercises*

1. What kind of reasoning involves a leap from given statements to a conclusion?

2. Which type of reasoning leads to a true conclusion whenever the given statements are true?

3. Make up an example of valid deductive reasoning that leads to a false conclusion.

In Exercises 4–8, identify whether induction or deduction is being used.

4. My mother and grandmother were homemakers. I conclude that all women are homemakers.

5. My teacher gives a quiz five Thursdays in a row. I conclude that she will give a quiz every Thursday.

6. Given that $AB = CD$ and $AB = 6$ cm, I conclude that $CD = 6$ cm.

7. The last two Friday the 13th's, I had bad luck. I conclude that Friday the 13th is an unlucky day for me.

8. Since $4 \times 6 = 24$ and $2 \times 8 = 16$, I conclude that the product of two even numbers is an even number.

9. Our courts accept fingerprints as evidence because, after millions of comparisons, no two sets of identical sets of fingerprints have been found. This is an example of _____ reasoning.

10. How do mathematicians use inductive and deductive reasoning in sequence to develop a new idea?

11. Consider the following number trick.

Pick a number.

Multiply by 3.

Subtract your original number.

Add 8.

Divide by 2.

(a) Try two or three different numbers and use inductive reasoning to make a conjecture about what will happen with any number.

(b) Why don't your results to part (a) *prove* that the number trick adds 4 to any number?

(c) Use deductive reasoning to prove your generalization from part (a).

(d) *Explain* how you used deductive reasoning to derive the result of the fourth step using the result of the third step.

12. Consider the following number trick.

Pick a number.

Subtract 8.

Add your original number.

Divide by 2.

Add 5.

(a) Try two or three different numbers and use inductive reasoning to make a conjecture about what will happen with any number.

(b) Use deductive reasoning to prove your generalization from part (a).

(c) *Explain* how you used deductive reasoning to derive the result of the third step using the result of the second step.

13. How do you write the converse of an "if-then" statement?

14. Consider the following statement: If a figure is a square, then the figure has exactly four sides.

(a) Is the statement true?

(b) Write the converse of the statement.

(c) Is the converse true?

15. Consider the following statement: If you have a fever, then you are sick.

(a) Is the statement true?

(b) Write the converse of the statement.

(c) Is the converse true?

16. Write the following statements in an "if-then" format.

(a) You can graduate only if you have taken a writing course.

(b) The number 5 is odd if 4 is even.

17. Write the following statements in an "if-then" format.

(a) You may be successful if you are smart.

(b) A triangle is equilateral only if it is isosceles.

18. Write the following statement as two "if-then" statements: A triangle is a right triangle if and only if it has a right angle.

19. Write the following statement as two "if-then" statements: A triangle has two congruent sides if and only if it has two congruent angles.

20. Write the following two statements as one "if-and-only-if" statement.

If you are my parent, then I am your child.

If I am your child, then you are my parent.

21. Write the following two statements as one "if-and-only-if" statement.

If $2x = 4$, then $x = 2$.

If $x = 2$, then $2x = 4$.

22. Four friends are trying to decide whether to jump into a cold swimming pool. Greg will jump in only if everyone else does. Suzanne will go in if at least one other person does. Mike will go in only if Suzanne has decided to go in. Gina will jump in regardless of what the others do.

How many will jump in the pool?

### Extension Exercises

23. Make up a number puzzle in which a person will always end up with the number 2. (Make it complicated enough so that someone else could not easily see how it works.)

24. Make up a number puzzle in which a person will always end up with a number that is 6 more than the person's original number.

25. (a) Try some examples and answer the following question. What is the sum of two even numbers?

(b) Fill in the blanks in the following deductive proof.

(1) Assume your two even numbers are $2M$ and $2N$, where $M$ and $N$ are whole numbers.

(2) The sum of the two even numbers is

_____ .

(3) $2M + 2N = 2 ($_____$)$.

(4) $2(M + N)$ is an even number because

_____ .

(5) So the sum of two even numbers is an even number.

26. In this lesson, you studied the converse of a statement. Another related statement of this

type is the inverse. To make the **inverse** of a statement, negate the hypothesis and the conclusion of the statement.

*Statement:* If it is raining, then I shall wear a raincoat.
*Inverse:* If it is not raining, then I shall not wear a raincoat.

(a) Write the inverse of the following statement: If $x + 3 = 5$, then $x = 2$.
(b) Write the inverse of the following statement: If I confess, then I am guilty.
(c) If possible, write a true "if-then" statement that has a false inverse.

27. Write the inverse of the following statements.
(a) If I drive a truck, then I need a driver's license.
(b) If a girl uses nose powder, then her nose looks beautiful.

28. The **contrapositive** of a statement combines the converse and the inverse. To make the contrapositive, interchange the hypothesis and conclusion *and* negate them both.

*Statement:* If a number is divisible by 100, then the number is even.
*Contrapositive:* If a number is not even, then the number is not divisible by 100.

(a) Write the contrapositive of the following statement: If $x + 3 = 5$, then $x = 2$.
(b) Write the contrapositive of the following statement: If I confess, then I am guilty.
(c) If possible, write a true "if-then" statement that has a false contrapositive.

29. Consider the following statement: If you are a U.S. Marine, then you are a real man.
(a) Write the converse.
(b) Write the contrapositive.
(c) Write the inverse.

30. Suppose the following statement is true: If it was raining, then I drove to work.
(a) Write the converse.
(b) Write the contrapositive.
(c) Write the inverse.

(d) Which of the three statements in parts (a), (b), and (c) is (are) true?

31. Suppose the following statement is true: If a four-sided figure is a square, then it is a rectangle.

Which of the following must also be true?
(a) If a four-sided figure is a rectangle, then it is a square.
(b) If a four-sided figure is not a square, then it is not a rectangle.
(c) If a four-sided figure is not a rectangle, then it is not a square.

32. Suppose the following statement is true: If it rains today, then I will scream.

Which of the following must also be true?
(a) If I do not scream today, then it is not raining.
(b) If I do scream today, then it is raining.
(c) If it does not rain today, then I will not scream.

33. (a) Based upon the preceding exercises, whenever an "if-then" statement is false, its contrapositive
(1) is true     (2) is false
(3) could be true or false
(b) Based upon the preceding exercises, whenever an "if-then" statement is true, its contrapositive
(1) is true     (2) is false
(3) could be true or false

34. Suppose the following advertising claim is true: "If you rent a car from Mary, then you will be able to travel around with ease." Is it then true that "if you do not rent a car from Mary, you will not be able to travel around with ease"?

35. Which of the following are the same as "if $A$, then $B$" and which are the same as "if $B$, then $A$"?
(a) $A$ implies $B$.
(b) $A$ follows from $B$.
(c) $A$ is a sufficient condition for $B$.
(d) $A$ is a necessary condition for $B$.
(e) If $A$ is false, then $B$ is false.

*Special Exercise*

**36.** Fill in the correct numbers using the following clues.

1. Each number from 1 to 16 is used once.
2. Each row and each column adds up to 34.
3. *K* is twice as large as *G* and three times *E*.
4. *J* and *N* add up to *F*.
5. *H* is 5 times *C*.
6. *B* and *D* are two-digit numbers.

| A | B | C | D |
|---|---|---|---|
| E | F | G | H |
| I | J | K | L |
| M | N | O | P 8 |

## 1.4  Patterns

Look out the window. At first glance, the world appears complex and confusing, but in reality it is full of patterns. Patterns give order to the world. In mathematics, we find patterns in shapes and quantities.

Human beings are better than other animals at finding mathematical patterns. The ability to find patterns is supposed to be a sign of intelligence.

Experimenters at Tulane University wanted to teach a rat the concept of "two." The rat had to choose among three doors: One door had one mark, one had two marks, and one had three marks. In each trial, the food was behind the door with two marks. How long would it take you to discover such a pattern? It took the rat 1500 trials.

Reprinted by permission of NEA, Inc. © 1975 by NEA, Inc.

**Figure 1-9**

People are better at finding mathematical patterns than rats. (Sometimes, we find patterns even where they don't exist, as the cartoon in Figure 1-9 shows.)

**D** Lesson Exercise 1.30

Describe any patterns you see in your classroom.

The ability to see patterns is important in mathematical problem solving. Working with patterns also develops number sense. In this lesson, you will study three common types of mathematical pattern problems: sequences, finding a rule, and patterns in sums.

Discovering and extending patterns requires inductive and deductive reasoning. First, conjecturing a general pattern based on examples is inductive reasoning. Then, proving the generalization or writing new examples of a pattern using a general rule requires deductive reasoning.

## Sequences

The first set of numbers children study is the **counting** (or **natural**) **numbers** {1, 2, 3, . . . }. A 3-year-old child who is 94 cm tall may grow about 6 cm per year until age 9, setting up the following pattern: 94 cm, 100 cm, 106 cm, 112 cm, 118 cm, 124 cm, 130 cm. These are two examples of number sequences. A **sequence** is an ordered arrangement of numbers, figures, or letters.

Lesson Exercise 1.31

Find the next term in the following sequence.

$$2, 5, 11, 23, \underline{\qquad}$$

Many number sequences follow a pattern based upon addition, subtraction, multiplication, division, or a combination of these operations. In each example, *induction* is used to find a general rule. Then the general rule is used to *deduce* the next term.

**Example 1.7**

Find the next term in each of the following sequences.
(a) A 64-g mass of a radioactive substance decays as shown every 5 years (its half-life).

   64 g, 32 g, 16 g, 8 g, \underline{\qquad}

(b) 5, 18, 70, 278, \underline{\qquad}

**Solution**
(a) It appears that each new term is obtained by dividing the preceding term by 2. (*induction*) If so, the next term would be 4 g. (*deduction*)
(b) It appears that each new term is obtained by multiplying the preceding term by 4 and subtracting 2. (*induction*) If so, the next term is 1110. (*deduction*)  ■

Try to complete the sequences in Lesson Exercises 1.32 and 1.33.

## Lesson Exercise 1.32

The number of petals in many varieties of flowers is found in the following sequence (called the **Fibonacci sequence**).

$$1, 1, 2, 3, 5, \underline{\phantom{x}}, \underline{\phantom{x}}, \underline{\phantom{x}}, \underline{\phantom{x}}, \underline{\phantom{x}}, \underline{\phantom{x}}$$

## Lesson Exercise 1.33

1, 2, 5, 14, _____

(a) The next term is _____.
(b) In guessing the general rule for the sequence, you used _____ reasoning.
(c) In applying the general rule to find the next term, you used _____ reasoning.

Figure 1-10 shows a sequence problem one would find in the first-grade textbook *Mathematics Plus*.

Some number sequences involve squares, cubes, or squares or cubes combined with addition or subtraction.

### Example 1.8

Find the next term in the following sequence: 2, 5, 10, 17, _____ .

**Solution**
It appears that each term is 1 more than a square number (1, 4, 9, 16). (*induction*) If so, the next term is $25 + 1 = 26$. (*deduction*)  ■

## Lesson Exercise 1.34

Find the next term in the following sequence: 2, 7, 14, 23, _____ .

Finding a rule for a sequence often involves the following steps.

**1.** See if the sequence is a simpler one involving only one of the following: addition, subtraction, multiplication, division, squares, or cubes.

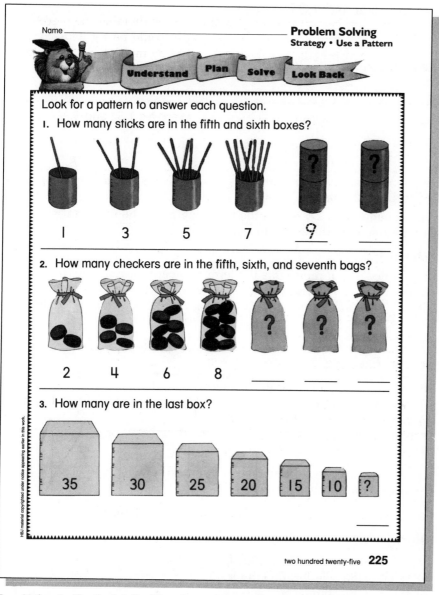

Name _____

**Problem Solving**
Strategy • Use a Pattern

Understand  Plan  Solve  Look Back

Look for a pattern to answer each question.

1. How many sticks are in the fifth and sixth boxes?

  1      3      5      7      9      _____

2. How many checkers are in the fifth, sixth, and seventh bags?

  2      4      6      8      _____  _____  _____

3. How many are in the last box?

  35     30     25     20     15     10     ?

  _____

two hundred twenty-five **225**

From *Mathematics Plus*, Grade 1 (San Diego: Harcourt Brace Jovanovich, 1992), p. 225.

**Figure 1-10**

2. If Step 1 does not uncover the rule, a more complicated sequence
   may involve multiplication, division, squares, or cubes *combined with*
   addition or subtraction. Look for this type of rule.

Now try two sequence problems, which fit into one of these categories.

## Lesson Exercise 1.35

2, 10, 42, 170, ——

## Lesson Exercise 1.36

1, 8, 27, 64, ——

The rule for some sequences can be stated algebraically.

### Example 1.9

The sequence 3, 9, 27, 81 has the following rule. The $n$th term $= 3^n$. Use the rule to deduce the 7th term.

#### Solution

In the rule "$3^n$," $n$ represents the term number. For example, the 1st term is $3^1$, or 3. The 2nd term is $3^2$, or 9. To find the 7th term, substitute 7 for $n$ in the rule. The 7th term is $3^7 = 2187$. (*deduction*) ■

## Lesson Exercise 1.37

The rule for a sequence is, the $n$th term $= 2n + 1$.
(a) What is the 1st term?
(b) What are the next three terms?

The reverse process, finding the formula for the $n$th term of a given sequence, is more challenging.

### Example 1.10

Consider the sequence 2, 6, 10, 14, . . .
(a) What is the rule for the $n$th term?
(b) What is the 50th term?

#### Solution

(a) The rule for the $n$th term relates each term to its *position* rather than to the preceding term.

| Position | 1 | 2 | 3 | 4 |
|---|---|---|---|---|
| Number | 2 | 6 | 10 | 14 |

What one rule relates 1 to 2, 2 to 6, 3 to 10, and 4 to 14? It does not involve a single arithmetic operation or squaring or cubing. Next, try multiplication with addition or subtraction. The pattern is close to multiplication by 3 or 4. Multiply each position by 4 and you obtain the sequence 4, 8, 12, 16, . . . , in which each term is 2 more than the corresponding term in the sequence in question. So the sequence rule is "4 times the position minus 2," or "The nth term = 4n − 2." (*induction*)

(b) The 50th term is 4 · 50 − 2 = 198. (*deduction*) ■

## Lesson Exercise 1.38

Consider the sequence 4, 7, 10, 13, . . .
(a) What is the next term?
(b) What is the rule for the nth term?
(c) What is the 60th term?
(d) Does part (b) require inductive or deductive reasoning?
(e) Does part (c) require inductive or deductive reasoning?
(f) Look at Lesson Exercises 1.37 and 1.38 and Example 1.10 and complete the following generalization.
 If the difference between each successive pair of terms in a sequence is the same number $k$, then the nth term = _____.

## Lesson Exercise 1.39

Consider the sequence 0, 3, 8, 15, . . .
(a) What is the next term?
(b) What is the rule for the nth term?
(c) What is the 100th term?

The following chart summarizes the use of induction and deduction with sequences.

| *induction* | | *deduction* | |
|---|---|---|---|
| numerical ⟶ | general | general rule and ⟶ | apply rule to |
| examples | rule | given sequence | extend sequence |

## Finding a Rule

In many everyday situations, a rule relates two sets of numbers. For example, when tickets are sold, the total amount of money collected is directly related to the number of tickets sold. One can often express such a rule with a formula.

## Lesson Exercise 1.40

Suppose you light a 10-inch candle when the lights go out, and you re-cord the following data.

| H (candle height in inches) | 10 | 8 | 6 | |
|---|---|---|---|---|
| T (elapsed time in hours) | 0 | 1 | 2 | 3 |

(a) Fill in the last value for H.
(b) What is H when T = 5?
(c) Describe the relationship between H and T.
(d) Write a formula: H = _____
(e) Graph each pair of values for T and H.

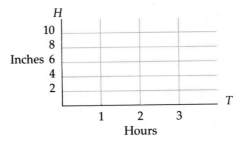

(f) What pattern do you see in the graph? _____

In "find-a-rule" patterns, the objects come in pairs. The same pattern or rule always relates the first object to the second object. The rules often involve arithmetic, as they did with sequences. There may be more than one possible rule. The object is to find a rule that works for all given pairs of numbers or objects.

## Lesson Exercise 1.41

Fill in the blanks by finding a rule that works for each number pair.

| Hours of Labor | | Charge |
|---|---|---|
| 1 | ⟶ | $30 |
| 2 | ⟶ | $40 |
| 3 | ⟶ | $50 |
| 4 | ⟶ | 60 |
| N | ⟶ | 10 |

(*Hint:* The charge includes a set fee for travel and an hourly wage.)

In Lesson Exercise 1.42, look for a pattern that relates each number in one group to its corresponding "partner" in the other group, rather than looking for patterns within one group of numbers.

## Lesson Exercise 1.42

| X | 1 | 2 | 3 | 4 | 5 |
|---|---|---|---|---|---|
| Y | 2 | 5 | 10 | 17 | |

(a) Fill in the last value for Y.
(b) Write a formula relating Y to X: Y = _____
(c) What is Y when X is 8?
(d) Answering part (c) by assuming your formula in part (b) is an example of _____ reasoning.
(e) Complete a *number sequence* statement that is comparable to part (a). Find the 5th term of _____ .
(f) Write a rule for the nth term of your sequence in part (e).

## Patterns in Sums

Pythagoras and his followers were the first to study numbers for their own sake. The Pythagoreans thought of quantities geometrically. They represented numbers with dots.

## Lesson Exercise 1.43

What is the common name for the following set of numbers?

1      4      9

Thinking of numbers geometrically reveals patterns in sums and establishes a connection between arithmetic and geometry.

## Lesson Exercise 1.44

$$1 \quad\quad = (\ )^2$$
$$1 + 3 \quad = (\ )^2$$
$$1 + 3 + 5 = (\ )^2$$

(a) Fill in the missing numbers.
(b) Draw geometric dot pictures of the three sums that show the pattern. (*Hint:* Use squares.)
(c) What would the next equation be if the pattern continues? Is this equation true?
(d) The sum of the first three odd numbers is _____ squared.
(e) The sum of the first four odd numbers is _____ squared.
(f) Write a generalization for any counting number $N$ based upon parts (d) and (e).
(g) Part (f) involves _____ reasoning.
(h) Use your generalization to compute $1 + 3 + 5 + 7 + \cdots + 79$.

Square number patterns are part of a branch of mathematics called number theory, a subject you will study further in Chapter 4. Number theory also includes such familiar topics as factors, multiples, and prime numbers.

Other patterns in sums may be too complicated to show geometrically, but your experience with number sequences will be helpful.

## Lesson Exercise 1.45

$$2^2 - 1^2 = 3$$
$$3^2 - 2^2 = 5$$
$$4^2 - 3^2 = 7$$

(a) If the pattern continues, what is the next equation? Is the next equation true?
(b) Complete the following generalization.
For any counting number $C$, $C^2 -$ _____ = _____ .
(c) Show that your equation in part (b) is true.
(d) Part (b) involves _____ reasoning and part (c) involves _____ reasoning.

Your calculator may have special keys such as $\boxed{x^2}$ (the squaring key) and $\boxed{y^x}$ (the $y$-to-the-$x$-power key) for working with exponents. (On some calculators, the power key is $\boxed{x^y}$ .)

You could compute $4^2$ in the preceding exercise with the squaring key by pressing $\boxed{4}\,\boxed{x^2}$. The $\boxed{y^x}$ key is used to compute "$y$ to the power $x$." For example, to compute $5^3$, one could press $\boxed{5}\,\boxed{y^x}\,\boxed{3}\,\boxed{=}$. You may want to use the exponent keys to do some of the homework exercises.

## Answers to Selected Lesson Exercises

**1.31** 47

**1.32** 8, 13, 21, 34, 55, 89

**1.33** (a) 41      (b) inductive      (c) deductive

**1.34** 34

**1.35** 682

**1.36** 125

**1.37** (a) 3      (b) 5, 7, 9

**1.38** (a) 16      (b) $3n + 1$      (c) 181
    (d) inductive      (e) deductive
    (f) $k \cdot n$ plus a constant

**1.39** (a) 24      (b) $n^2 - 1$      (c) 9999

**1.40** (a) 4      (b) 0
    (c) $H$ starts at 10 and $T$ at 0. When $T$
    increases by 1, $H$ decreases by 2.
    (d) $H = 10 - 2T$
    (f) The points all lie on a straight line.

**1.41** $60; $20 + 10N$

**1.42** (a) 26      (b) $Y = X^2 + 1$
    (c) 65      (d) deductive
    (e) 2, 5, 10, 17, . . .      (f) $n^2 + 1$

**1.43** square numbers

**1.44** (a) 1, 2, 3
    (b)

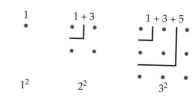

    (c) $1 + 3 + 5 + 7 = 4^2$; yes
    (d) 3      (e) 4
    (f) The sum of the first $N$ odd numbers is
    $N$ squared.
    (g) inductive      (h) $(40)^2 = 1600$

**1.45** (a) $5^2 - 4^2 = 9$; yes
    (b) $c^2 - (c - 1)^2 = (c + c - 1)$
    (c)     $c^2 - (c - 1)^2 \overset{?}{=} (c + c - 1)$
      $c^2 - (c^2 - 2c + 1) \overset{?}{=} 2c - 1$
      $c^2 - c^2 + 2c - 1 \overset{?}{=} 2c - 1$
             $2c - 1 = 2c - 1$
    (d) inductive; deductive

## 1.4  Homework Exercises

*Basic Exercises*

In Exercises 1–6, find the next term in each sequence.

  **1.** (a) 1, 16, 81, 256, \_\_\_\_
    (b) Explain how you used both induction and deduction in solving Exercise 1(a).

  **2.** 3, 7, 15, 31, \_\_\_\_

  **3.** 10, \_\_\_\_, 8, 14, 6, 16

  **4.** −1, 2, 7, 14, \_\_\_\_

  **5.** 4, 12, 14, 42, 44, \_\_\_\_

  **6.** man, 2; lion, 4; cockroach, 6; spider, \_\_\_\_; cat, \_\_\_\_ (The last answer is not ten!)

  **7.** (a) Find two different reasonable answers for the next term in the sequence 1, 2, 4, \_\_ .
    (b) What rule did you use to obtain each of your answers?

  **8.** In 1772, an astronomer named Bode found a pattern in the distance of the six known planets from the sun (where the distance from the earth to the sun is 10 units).

| Planet | Actual Distance | Bode's Pattern |
|--------|-----------------|----------------|
| Mercury | 4 | 4 |
| Venus | 7 | $4 + 3 \quad = \quad 7$ |
| Earth | 10 | $4 + (3 \times 2) \quad = \quad 10$ |
| Mars | 15 | $4 + (3 \times 2^2) \quad = \quad 16$ |
| ?????? |  | $4 + (3 \times 2^3) \quad = \quad 28$ |
| Jupiter | 52 | $4 + (3 \times 2^4) \quad = \quad 52$ |
| Saturn | 96 | $4 + (3 \times 2^5) \quad = \quad 100$ |

(a) What might be an explanation for the extra equation between Mars and Jupiter?

(b) What would the equation after Saturn's be?

(c) In 1781, the next planet, Uranus, was discovered. It is 192 units from the sun. Is this close to Bode's prediction?

(d) In 1801, the asteroid Ceres was discovered 28 units from the sun. How does this relate to Bode's model?

(e) Neptune, the planet after Uranus, is 301 units from the sun. How close is this to Bode's prediction?

9. The Fibonacci sequence, named after a twelfth-century Italian mathematician, begins with two 1's. Each term after that is obtained by adding the preceding two terms:

$$1, 1, 2, 3, 5, 8, \ldots$$

(a) Write the first ten terms of the sequence.

(b) Compare the sum of the first 3 terms to the 5th term and the sum of the first 4 terms to the 6th term. What pattern do you see?

(c) Does the relationship in part (b) appear to work for other sums of initial terms?

(d) Write a generalization of your results.

10. Describe a situation in which someone would count 10, 20, 30, 40, 50, 60.

11. All living things contain carbon. Radioactive carbon-14 can be used to figure out the age of fossils. Carbon-14 has a half-life of 5600 years, meaning that *half its mass decays every 5600 years.*

(a) Complete the following table.

| Time (years) | 0 | 5600 | | | |
|--------------|---|------|---|---|---|
| Fraction of C-14 Left | 1 | 1/2 | 1/4 | | |

(b) Prehistoric charcoal paintings from Lascaux, France, were found to have about 1/7 of the original C-14. Estimate their age.

12. Strontium-90 is a common waste product of the production of nuclear weapons and nuclear energy. It has a half-life of 28 years. Some scientists estimate that it will be safe when about $\frac{1}{100}$ of it is left. About how long will this take?

13. Counting only blood relatives, state the total number of

(a) parents a person has.

(b) grandparents a person has.

(c) greatgrandparents a person has.

(d) Assuming there are 4 generations per century, how many ancestors would a person have had 300 years prior to his or her birth?

14. The rule for a sequence is, the $n$th term = $n + 4$. Write the first four terms of the sequence.

15. The rule for a sequence is, the $n$th term = $10 - n$. Write the first five terms of the sequence.

16. What is the 9th term in a sequence with the following characteristics?

1. Starting with the 3rd term, each odd-numbered term is the sum of the two terms that precede it.

2. The 1st term is 1.
3. The 4th term is 6.
4. The 5th term is 10.
5. Starting with the 4th term, each even-numbered term is double the term two places to its left.

17. (a) Write the even numbers as a number sequence.
    (b) Write a rule for the $n$th term of the sequence.
    (c) What rule do you see relating each term to the next one?

18. (a) Write the odd numbers as a number sequence.
    (b) Write a rule for the $n$th term of the sequence.
    (c) What rule do you see relating each term to the next one?

19. Examine the following design.

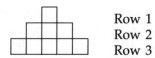

    Row 1
    Row 2
    Row 3

    (a) If the design were to continue downward, how many squares would there be in the 50th row?
    (b) What would be the total number of small squares in the first 50 rows?

20. Examine the following designs.

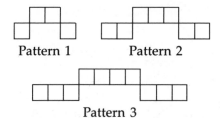

    Pattern 1        Pattern 2

    Pattern 3

    (a) How many squares would be in Pattern 5?
    (b) How many squares are in Pattern $N$, where $N = 1, 2, 3, \ldots$ ?

21. Consider the following sequence.

    11, 13, 15, 17, . . .

    (a) What is the next term?
    (b) What is the rule for the $n$th term?
    (c) What is the 40th term?
    (d) Does part (c) require induction or deduction?

22. Consider the following sequence.

    2, 6, 12, 20, . . .

    (a) What is the next term?
    (b) What is the rule for the $n$th term?
    (c) What is the 20th term?

23. Consider the following sequence.

    3, 6, 11, 18, 27, . . .

    (a) What is the next term?
    (b) What is the rule for the $n$th term?
    (c) What is the 30th term?

24. Consider the following sequence.

    50, 49, 48, 47, . . .

    (a) What is the rule for the $n$th term?
    (b) What is the 25th term?

25. Consider the following sequence.

    2, 9, 16, 23, . . .

    (a) What is the rule for the $n$th term?
    (b) What is the 100th term?

26. Determine how many numbers are in the following sequence.

    3, 9, 15, 21, 27, . . . , 159

27. Determine how many numbers in the following sequence are less than 10,000.

    3, 9, 27, 81, . . .

28. Read the following table.

| N (number sold) | 1 | 2 | 3 | 4 | 5 |
|---|---|---|---|---|---|
| P (profit) | 1 | 3 | 5 | 7 | |

(a) Write a formula that relates each $N$ value to its corresponding $P$ value.

(b) Use your rule to fill in the last value of $P$.

(c) You found a rule in part (a) using _____ reasoning.

(d) Graph each pair of values for $N$ and $P$ on a graph.

(e) What pattern do you see in your graph?

(f) Write a rule for the $n$th term of

$$1, 3, 5, 7, \ldots$$

**29.** Read the following table.

| L (length) | 1 | 2 | 3 | 4 | 5 |
|---|---|---|---|---|---|
| V (volume) | 1 | 8 | 27 | 64 | |

(a) Find a rule that relates $L$ to $V$:
$V = $ _____.

(b) Use your rule to fill in the last value of $V$.

(c) Write a rule for the $n$th term of

$$1, 8, 27, 64, \ldots$$

**30.** Read the following table.

| X | 1 | 2 | 3 | 4 | 5 |
|---|---|---|---|---|---|
| Y | 5 | 12 | 31 | 68 | |

(a) Find a rule that relates $X$ to $Y$:
$Y = $ _____. (*Hint:* See the preceding exercise.)

(b) Use your rule to fill in the last value of $Y$.

**31.** Study the pattern of squares and rectangles.

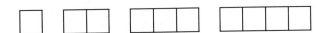

(a) Complete the following chart.

| S (number of squares) | 1 | 2 | 3 | 4 | N |
|---|---|---|---|---|---|
| P (perimeter) | | 4 | | | |

(b) Graph each pair of values for $S$ and $P$.

(c) What pattern do you see in your graph?

**32.** (a) How many two-person matches will be played in a single elimination tournament with 16 contestants? (After a single loss, a player is eliminated.)

(b) How many matches will be played in a single elimination tournament with $2^N$ contestants, where $N = 0, 1, 2, 3, \ldots$?

**33.** Find a rule that works for all of the following number pairs and use that rule to fill in the blanks.

| Expenses | | Reserves |
|---|---|---|
| 0 | → | 8 |
| 1 | → | 7 |
| 2 | → | 6 |
| 3 | → | _____ |
| N | → | _____ |

**34.** A physicist drops an object from the top of a tall building. The following chart shows how long the object takes to fall different distances. Fill in the blanks continuing the pattern.

| Time (sec) | | Distance (ft) |
|---|---|---|
| 0 | → | 0 |
| 1 | → | 16 |
| 2 | → | 64 |
| 3 | → | 144 |
| 4 | → | _____ |
| N | → | _____ |

**35.**

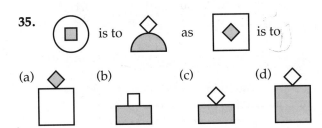

**36.** The Pythagoreans called certain numbers "triangular." The first three are shown below.

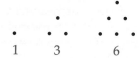

1     3     6

(a) What is the next triangular number?
(b) Each triangular number can be written as the sum of consecutive numbers. Show how this works with a dot drawing.
(c) Make dot drawings that show how 4, 9, and 16 are the sum of two triangular numbers.
(d) What generalization does part (c) suggest?

**37.** Examine the following pattern.

$$3^2 + 4^2 \qquad = (\ )^2$$
$$3^3 + 4^3 + 5^3 = (\ )^3$$

(a) Fill in the missing number.
(b) What would be the next line if the pattern continues? Is it a correct equation?

**38.** Examine the following pattern.

$$2^2 - 0^2 = 4$$
$$3^2 - 1^2 = 8$$
$$4^2 - 2^2 = 12$$

(a) What would be the next line if the pattern continues? Is it a correct equation?
(b) Complete the following generalization. For any counting number $C$,
$$C^2 - \underline{\quad} = \underline{\qquad}.$$
(c) Prove that your equation in part (b) is correct by showing that both sides are equal.

**39.** Examine the following pattern.

$$1^2 + 2^2 + 2^2 = (\ )^2$$
$$2^2 + 3^2 + 6^2 = (\ )^2$$
$$3^2 + 4^2 + 12^2 = (\ )^2$$

(a) Fill in the missing numbers.
(b) What would the next equation be if the pattern continues? Is this equation true?
(c) Complete the following generalization of the pattern. For any counting number $N$,
$$N^2 + \underline{\quad} + \underline{\quad} = (\ )^2.$$
(d) Show that the two sides of your equation in part (c) are equal.

*Extension Exercises*

**40.** Examine these multiplication facts.

$$2 \times 9 = 18$$
$$3 \times 9 = 27$$
$$4 \times 9 = 36$$
$$5 \times 9 = 45$$
$$6 \times 9 = 54$$

(a) Name two patterns you see in these multiplication facts of 9.
(b) Do the patterns you mentioned in part (a) also work for $7 \times 9$, $8 \times 9$, and $9 \times 9$?

**41.**

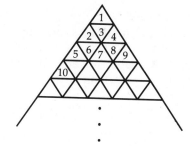

(a) If the pattern continues, where would 125 be located?
(b) Is 125 on a triangle that points up or down?
(c) Where would 457 be located?
(d) Is 457 on a triangle that points up or down?

**42.** (a) Look at the table below and find an approximate formula for obtaining the flash number $N$ from the ASA film speeds.

| ASA Film Speed ($S$) | 100 | 200 | 400 | 800 |
|---|---|---|---|---|
| Flash Number ($N$) | 120 | 170 | 240 | 340 |

(b) Use your formula to find the flash number for an ASA film speed of 64.

**43.** While a finite sum has a definite answer, infinite sums can be tricky.

(a) The sum of

$$(1 - 1) + (1 - 1) + (1 - 1) + \cdots$$

appears to be ____.

(b) The sum of

$$1 - (1 - 1) - (1 - 1) - (1 - 1) \cdots$$

appears to be ____.

(c) Write

$$(1 - 1) + (1 - 1) + (1 - 1) + \cdots$$

without parentheses.

(d) Write $1 - (1 - 1) - (1 - 1) - \cdots$ without parentheses.

(e) Is $(1 - 1) + (1 - 1) + (1 - 1) + \cdots$ the same as

$$1 - (1 - 1) - (1 - 1) - \cdots ?$$

**44.** A cubical set of ten blocks has edges of 1 cm, 2 cm, 3 cm, . . . , 10 cm. Is it possible to build two five-cube "towers" that have the same height by stacking cubes one on top of the other?

In Exercises 45–48, find the next term in the sequence.

**45.** 2, 9, 39, 161, ____

**46.** 4, 10, 5, 17, 7, 31, ____

**47.** 7, 9, 40, 74, 1526, ____

**48.** $x, 2x - 4, 4x - 12, 8x - 28,$ ____

**49.** Make up two of your own challenging number sequence exercises.

**50.** (a) Investigate the rule for the $n$th term of sequences with a constant difference between successive terms (called **arithmetic**) like 5, 7, 9, 11, . . . . Look for examples in the lesson and in previous homework exercises.

(b) Generalize your results from part (a) by completing the following. If the difference between successive terms is $d$ and the first term is $f$, the rule for the $n$th term is ____.

**51.** (a) Two different color stripes are painted (equally spaced) on a stick, as shown. How many different distinguishable sticks can be made by changing the position of the colors?

(b) Three different color stripes are painted (equally spaced) on a stick. How many different distinguishable sticks can be made by changing the position of the colors?

(c) Four different color stripes are painted (equally spaced) on a stick. How many different distinguishable sticks can be made?

**52.** (a) Three different color stripes are painted (equally spaced) on a ring, as shown. How many different distinguishable rings can be made by changing the position of the colors?

(b) Four different color stripes are painted (equally spaced) on a ring. How many different distinguishable rings can be made?

53. In a **geometric sequence**, each term is multiplied by the same number to obtain the next term. For example, in the sequence 3, 6, 12, 24, . . . , each term is multiplied by 2 to obtain the next term.

Find the next term of each geometric sequence.
(a) 2, 8, 32, \_\_\_\_
(b) 8, 4, \_\_\_\_

54. (a) Make up the first five terms of a geometric sequence of your choice.
(b) Compute the difference between each pair of successive terms.
(c) Would these differences form a geometric sequence?
(d) Repeat parts (a), (b), and (c) for two other geometric sequences and write a conclusion.

55. If a fixed number is added to each term of a geometric sequence, is the resulting sequence geometric? Try some examples and decide.

56. If each term of a geometric sequence is multiplied by a fixed number, is the resulting sequence geometric? Try some examples and decide.

57. Bounce a ball of your choice and describe mathematically how it bounces.

58. Select a current elementary-school mathematics textbook. What kind of pattern problems does it have?

*Special Exercises*

59. Carl Frederich Gauss (1777–1855) was one of the greatest mathematicians who ever lived (Figure 1-11). According to one story, when

Photo courtesy of Library of Congress.

**Figure 1-11**

Gauss was 10, his teacher, desiring to keep the children occupied, asked them to add a sum like $1 + 2 + 3 + \cdots + 98 + 99 + 100$. Expecting the students to be busy for a half hour or so, the teacher was astonished when Gauss came up with the answer in less than a minute. How did Gauss do it?

(a) Gauss paired off the numbers.

$$1 + 2 + 3 + \cdots + 98 + 99 + 100$$

What do you notice about the pairs?
(b) How many of these pairs are there?
(c) What is the sum?

**60.** Use the method of the preceding exercise to find the sum of the following.

$$5 + 10 + 15 + \cdots + 290 + 295 + 300$$

**61.**

| $x$ | 1 | 2 | 3 | 4 | 5 | 6 | $N$ |
|---|---|---|---|---|---|---|---|
| $y$ | 1 | 3 | 6 | 10 | 15 | | |

(a) When $x = 6$, $y =$ _____.
(b) When $x = N$, $y =$ _____.

**62.** The following diagram shows that

$$1 + 2 = \frac{1}{2}(2 \times 3).$$

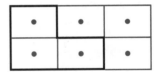

(a) Make a similar diagram showing that

$$1 + 2 + 3 = \frac{1}{2}(3 \times 4).$$

(b) Suggest a shortcut for computing

$$1 + 2 + 3 + \cdots + 98 + 99 + 100$$

using the same approach and see if you obtain the correct sum.

**63.** A 15-row auditorium seats 15 people in the first row, 16 in the second, 17 in the third, and so on. Use shortcuts to find the total number of seats in the auditorium.

## 1.5  Problem Solving

For too long, school mathematics has emphasized learning isolated facts and skills while devoting little time to mathematical reasoning. The most important part of school mathematics is not learning specific facts and skills; rather, it is learning how these facts and skills are used by citizens analyzing data, consumers deciding what to buy, and workers dealing with technology or finance.

Admittedly, it is easier to teach children to perform routine computations and to memorize facts and formulas, but as teachers we must tackle a more significant task: developing children's problem-solving ability. The National Council of Teachers of Mathematics (NCTM) says, "Problem solving must be the focus of school mathematics." You have already studied two of the most important components of mathematical reasoning: induction and deduction. The next two sections will further develop your problem-solving ability.

What is problem solving? In order to understand what problem solving is, it would be helpful to know what a "problem" is. A **problem** has two characteristics: (1) it requires a solution, and (2) the solution is not immediately obvious. The best classroom problems offer a situation of interest to the learner in which the need for mathematics arises naturally.

## Types of Problems

What kinds of problems are studied in elementary school? Read and solve the following three examples of elementary-school problems.

### Lesson Exercise  1.46

Pièrre has 21 oranges. He gives Jane 12. How many oranges does Pièrre have left?

### Lesson Exercise  1.47

The members of the Environment Club want to raise $50 by selling apples at $.25 each. So far, they have sold 120 apples. How many more apples must they sell?

### Lesson Exercise  1.48

Farmer Laura had 36 cows. If she sold all but 10, how many cows does she have left?

Like the preceding three problems, many elementary-school problems fit into one of three categories: (1) one-step translation problems, (2) multi-step translation problems, and (3) puzzle problems.

A **one-step translation** problem can be solved with a single arithmetic operation. Lesson Exercise 1.46 is an example of a one-step translation problem, the most common type in elementary school. One-step translation problems illustrate common applications of arithmetic and help reinforce arithmetic skills. Some mathematics educators would rather not call these "problems," since they become familiar and routine for most students who practice doing them.

A **multi-step translation** problem can be solved with two or more arithmetic steps. Lesson Exercise 1.47 is an example of a multi-step translation problem. Multi-step translation problems also illustrate common applications of arithmetic and reinforce arithmetic skills, but they require higher-level thinking than one-step problems. Elementary textbooks now contain more multi-step problems.

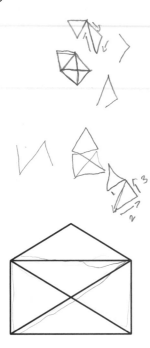

A **puzzle** problem is often solved by some unusual approach or insight. Lesson Exercise 1.48 is an example of a puzzle problem. Puzzle problems are nonroutine problems that develop flexible thinking.

These classifications are not precise; they depend upon a student's background. Lesson Exercise 1.46 might be a routine one-step subtraction problem for a second-grader but nonroutine for a first-grader who might solve it by counting back.

Read Lesson Exercises 1.49–1.51 and tell whether each would usually be classified as a one-step translation problem, a multi-step translation problem, or a puzzle problem.

### Lesson Exercise 1.49

A classroom has five rows of desks. There are six desks in each row. If all but two desks are occupied, how many children are in the class?

### Lesson Exercise 1.50

Draw the figure shown in Figure 1-12 without lifting your pencil off the paper or retracing any line segments.

**Figure 1-12**

### Lesson Exercise 1.51

Sidney has eight incredibly good chocolate brownies. Four of us are waiting to eat them. If we all eat the same number of brownies, how many will we each eat?

Photo courtesy of G. L. Alexanderson, Santa Clara University.

**Figure 1-13**

## Problem Solving

*Solving problems is the specific achievement of intelligence and intelligence is the specific gift of mankind: solving problems can be regarded as the most characteristically human activity . . . you can learn it only by imitation and practice.* (George Polya, *Mathematical Discovery*, p. ix, J. Wiley, 1962.)

George Polya (1887–1985, Figure 1-13), a brilliant teacher and mathematician, advocated problem-solving activities in mathematics beginning with his famous book, *How to Solve It* (1945). More recently, organizations such as NCTM have promoted this idea, and it has become a standard topic in the elementary-school mathematics curriculum. Until recently, school mathematics focused upon computational skills; now, problem solving is considered to be of central importance in mathematics, and computational skills play a supporting role.

Thanks to George Polya, we can learn specific methods for solving problems that increase our chances of being successful. First of all, George Polya described four steps that can be used in analyzing many mathematical and nonmathematical problems. The four steps are as follows.

---

**Four Steps in Problem Solving**

  1. Understand the problem.
  2. Devise a plan.
  3. Carry out the plan.
  4. Look back.

---

A mathematician could use these steps to solve a mathematics problem. A doctor could use them to treat an illness. A mechanic could use them to repair a car. Elementary-school mathematics textbooks utilize three-, four-, five-, or six-step variations of this approach.

People frequently solve problems without thinking about each step in Polya's plan. However, if one is having difficulty with a problem, the four-step plan is a useful guide. First, see if you understand the terms and conditions of the problem. What do you know, and what do you want to figure out? Second, in devising a plan, consider how the unknown is connected to the data given in the problem. Also, how does the problem relate to concepts you know or other problems you have solved? Third, in carrying out the steps of your plan, refer back to your overall plan if you lose track of it. Check each step of your work. Finally, look back, reviewing and checking your results. Have you answered the original question using appropriate units? Is there a way to check your answer or see if it is reasonable? Look back over the problem to improve your understanding of it. You can use this knowledge to solve related problems in the future.

Most elementary textbook series introduce the problem-solving steps early on. Figure 1-14 shows how the second-grade textbook of *Mathematics Plus* introduces Polya's steps.

Simply put, the four steps are: understand, plan, solve, and check. How are these four steps used in solving problems? Try them out as you work on Lesson Exercises 1.52 and 1.53.

Name _____

**Problem Solving**
Strategy • Make a Model

Understand   Plan   Solve   Look Back

Here are the steps to help you solve problems.

1. **Understand**   Read the problem.  Underline the question.
Ring the facts that are given.

José won 6 prizes.

Then he won 2 more.

How many prizes did he win?

2. **Plan**   Ring what you should do.

join      take away

3. **Solve**   Use counters to model the problem.  Then write the number sentence.

___ ◯ ___ = ___

4. **Look Back**   Read the problem again. Answer the question.

José won _____ prizes at the fair.
Is your answer correct?  Ring **Yes** or **No**.          Yes    No

**Talk About It**
How do you know that your answer is correct?

thirteen **13**

From *Mathematics Plus*, Grade 2 (San Diego: Harcourt Brace Jovanovich, 1992), p. 13.

**Figure 1-14**

## Lesson Exercise 1.52

Eleven years ago, Jamaal's daughter was 1/4 his age, and his dog Yapper was 2. Eleven years from now, Jamaal's daughter will be 1/2 his age. How old are Jamaal and his daughter now?

***Understanding the Problem***
(a) What are you supposed to figure out?
(b) Do you have enough information to do it?
(c) Is there any information that is not needed?

***Devising a Plan***
(d) You can solve this problem using a guess-and-revise (trial-and-error) approach or using algebraic equations. Which will you try? (Guess-and-revise is easier for most people.)
(e) Which of the following will you use in solving the problem: a calculator, paper and pencil, or mental computation?

***Carrying Out the Plan***
(f) Carry out your plan and obtain an answer.

***Looking Back***
(g) Check your answer.
(h) Make up a similar problem that can be solved in the same way.

## **D** Lesson Exercise 1.53

Consider the following problem.

Wanda Cash spent one-fourth of her money at a grocery store. Then she sat on a bench for 10 minutes. After that, she spent half of what was left at a record store. Now she has $6. How much money did Wanda start out with?

***Understanding the Problem***
(a) What are you supposed to figure out?
(b) What information do you have?

***Devising a Plan***
A good strategy for this problem is called **working backward**. Start at the end and work backward step by step until you reach the beginning.

***Carrying Out the Plan***
(c) Try the working backward strategy on this problem.

***Looking Back***
(d) Check your answer.
(e) Make up another problem like this one.

### An Investigation: Counting Squares

**D** Lesson Exercise 1.54

(a) Solve the following problem using Polya's four steps. Make up one appropriate activity or question and answer it for each of the four steps. See Lesson Exercises 1.52 and 1.53 for ideas.

How many different squares (of all sizes) are in the following picture?

(b) How many different squares are in the following picture?

(c) How many different squares are in the following picture?

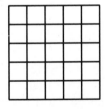

(d) Describe a general method for finding the total number of squares in a figure such as those in parts (a), (b), and (c).

(e) Solve a famous problem. How many different squares are there on an 8-by-8 checkerboard?

The four-step approach does not guarantee that you will be able to solve a problem, but it does provide some guidance. Previous experience solving problems is also a great help in solving new problems.

## Answers to Selected Lesson Exercises

| | |
|---|---|
| **1.46** 9 | **1.49** multi-step |
| **1.47** 80 | **1.50** puzzle problem |
| **1.48** 10 | **1.51** one-step translation |

1.52 (a) The current ages of Jamaal and his daughter.
   (b) yes     (c) Yapper's age
   (f) 55; 22 years

1.53 (a) How much money Wanda started out with.
   (c) She has $6 now. So before she went to the record store, she had $12. And before she went to the grocery store, she had $16.
   (d) Start with $16. Spend 1/4 of it at the grocery store. That leaves $12. Spend 1/2 of that at the record store. That leaves $6.

1.54 (a) *Understanding the Problem*  What are you supposed to find? (the total number of squares of all sizes in the picture)

   *Devising a Plan*  How will you do this? (Group the squares by size. Count all the 1-by-1 squares. Then count all the 2-by-2 squares and, finally, count all the 3-by-3 squares.)

*Carrying Out the Plan*  Carry out your plan and obtain an answer.

| Size | Number of Squares |
|------|-------------------|
| 1 by 1 | 9 |
| 2 by 2 | 4 |
| 3 by 3 | 1 |
| Total | 14 |

*Looking Back*  Make up another problem like this one. How many different squares are in the following picture?

After solving this problem and the previous one, develop a general solution for solving the same kind of problem with any size square.

## 1.5   Homework Exercises

*Basic Exercises*

Tell whether Exercises 1–3 would usually be classified as one-step translation, multi-step translation, or puzzle problems.

1. There are 10 boys and 12 girls going on a field trip. Each car will hold 5 children and 1 parent. How many cars are needed?

2. A classroom has four rows with five desks in each row. How many desks are there in all?

3. About how many marbles would fit inside a basketball?

4. Describe each of Polya's four steps for solving a problem with one word.

5. Explain how a doctor treating an illness could use Polya's four steps.

6. Consider the following problem: "The area of a square field is 49 m². What is the length of a fence that goes around the outside of the field?" Describe a plan for solving this problem.

7. Seth Borgas buys two shirts for $12.98 each and a hat for $8.98. The sales clerk says the total cost is $48.94. Without computing the exact answer, tell whether the clerk's total seems reasonable. Why or why not?

8. Make up a word problem about the Country Kitchen's menu that involves multiplication and addition.

The Country Kitchen
Roadside squirrel     $1.50
Twice-baked kelp     $1.05
Scalloped corn       $ .60
Pond water           $ .10

9. A family is taking a 500-mile car trip. Make up a word problem about the trip that uses multiplication and subtraction.

10. Solve the following problem using Polya's four steps. Make up an appropriate question or activity and answer it for each of Polya's four steps. The problem is as follows. "You have 10 black socks, 10 white socks, and 4 red socks in a drawer. How many would you have to pull out on a dark morning to be sure of obtaining a matching pair?"

11. Solve the following problem using Polya's four steps. Make up an appropriate question or activity and answer it for each of Polya's four steps. The problem is as follows. "How many cuts does it take to divide a log into five cross-sectional (cylindrical) pieces?"

12. (a) A 2-by-2-by-2 cube is built from eight 1-by-1-by-1 cubes. How many cubes of all sizes would there be?
    (b) A cube 4-by-4-by-4 is built from sixty-four 1-by-1-by-1 cubes. How many cubes of all sizes would there be?

13. How many cuts does it take to divide a log into
    (a) six equal cross-sectional pieces?
    (b) seven equal cross-sectional pieces?
    (c) N equal cross-sectional pieces?

14. (a) The Bathula family has 2 sons. Each son has 3 sisters. How many children are there?
    (b) The Dulfano family has T sons. Each son has N sisters. How many children are there?

15. A pizza restaurant has 10 different toppings for their cheese and tomato pizza: mushrooms, peppers, pepperoni, sausage, onion, anchovies, tuna, pickles, shredded wheat, and celery. How many different kinds of pizza can they serve by varying the combination of the toppings? (*Hint:* Try the same kind of problem with 1 topping, then 2 toppings, and so on, and look for a pattern.)

16. Fill in the missing numbers.

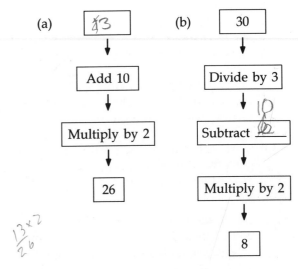

17. Consider the following problem. Chick N. Little bought 3 dozen eggs, but 2 eggs were broken. How many good eggs were there?
    (a) Write a problem about 12-year-old Bea Young and her father that involves computing $3 \times 12 - 2$ to find his age.
    (b) Write a problem about the total number of people in rows of chairs that uses the same $3 \times 12 - 2$ computation.

18. A 10-minute call from Maryland to Akron costs $2.82. A 14-minute call costs $3.94. What is the cost for the first minute and for each additional minute?

19. Find three numbers whose sum is 10 and whose product is as large as possible.

20. Remove two toothpicks so that you have 2 squares of different sizes.

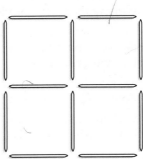

**21.** Move only three dots to make the following design:

```
  •   •   •   •
    •   •   •
      •   •
        •
```

look like this:

```
        •
      •   •
    •   •   •
  •   •   •   •
```

*Extension Exercises*

**22.** Connect the nine dots by drawing four lines without lifting your pencil off the paper or retracing any lines.

```
  •   •   •
  •   •   •
  •   •   •
```

**23.** You have 16 coins and a balance. Fifteen of the coins are regular, and one is a lighter counterfeit coin. Explain how you could locate the counterfeit coin with only three weighings.

**24.** You have 24 coins and a balance. Twenty-three of the coins are regular, and one is a lighter, counterfeit coin. Explain how you could locate the counterfeit coin with only three weighings.

**25.** Consider the entire set of problems that are like the preceding two exercises. What is the largest number of coins you could start with and be sure to locate the counterfeit coin in (a) three weighings? (b) two weighings?

**26.** The goal in each part of this exercise is to switch the position of the coins. A coin may move forward one space or may jump over a single coin.
(a) A penny (*P*) and nickel (*N*) are placed as shown.

| *P* | | *N* |
|---|---|---|

How many moves are needed to switch the pennies and nickels?

(b)

How many moves are needed to switch the pennies and nickels?

**27.** In word boxes, you can go from box to box as long as you move one step down or to the right. For example, for the word "BE," the word box allows you to complete the chart as follows.

```
        ¹ B
    ² B   E
```

| Number of Letters | Number of Paths Starting at | | Total Number of Paths |
|---|---|---|---|
| | Box 1 | Box 2 | |
| 2 | 1 | 1 | 2 |

(a) Complete the chart for "ZIP."

```
            ¹ Z
        ² Z   I
    ³ Z   I   P
```

| Number of Letters | Number of Paths Starting at | | | Total Number of Paths |
|---|---|---|---|---|
| | Box 1 | Box 2 | Box 3 | |
| 3 | | | | |

(b) Complete a similar chart for MATH.
(c) Based upon the results for two-, three-, and four-letter words, guess how many paths there would be for a word that has *N* letters.

**28.** (a) A number is divisible by 8. It has three digits that add up to 13. Guess the number.
(b) Find three other possible answers.

*Special Exercise*

29. A woman lines up five red checkers and five black checkers.

R   R   R   R   R   B   B   B   B   B
1   2   3   4   5   6   7   8   9   10

She asks: Can you switch the positions of only four checkers so that the black and red checkers alternate?

(a) How would you do it?

(b) If you start with only 1 pair of checkers, how many checkers would you have to move to solve the same problem?

(c) If you start with 3 pairs of checkers, how many checkers would you have to move to solve the same problem?

(d) What is the general pattern in the number of checkers that must be moved in parts (a), (b), and (c)?

(e) Does this pattern work for 2 pairs of checkers?

(f) Does it work for 4 pairs of checkers?

(g) Can you think of a different rule that would work for parts (e) and (f)?

(h) Make a conjecture about how many checkers must be moved in the same problem involving 25 pairs of checkers.

(i) Make a conjecture about how many checkers must be moved in the same problem involving 50 pairs of checkers.

## 1.6  Problem-Solving Strategies

Do you ever have difficulty solving mathematics problems? Devising a plan, the second step of Polya's procedure, is often the most difficult step. Elementary-school children now learn specific strategies that they can use to solve a variety of problems. Learning these strategies can make any student a better problem solver.

Children now do sets of problems that focus upon specific processes or strategies. The following problem-solving strategies are discussed in this book.

---

**Problem-Solving Processes and Strategies**

1. Using inductive reasoning
2. Using deductive reasoning or logic
3. Guessing and checking
4. Making a table or list
5. Drawing a picture
6. Choosing an operation
7. Working backward
8. Using a graph
9. Using an equation
10. Resting and trying again

---

These problem-solving strategies are now included in most elementary-school textbooks. You have already studied induction and deduction. Choosing an operation and working backward will be introduced in Chapter 3. Chapter 11 discusses using graphs and equations to solve problems.

In this section, you will study three useful problem-solving strategies: guessing and checking, making a table, and drawing a picture. Examples of each strategy follow.

The best way for you or your students to learn a problem-solving strategy is to practice using it first by itself. After each of the three individual strategies becomes familiar, you can try to solve problems in which you must decide which of the three strategies to use.

## Guessing and Checking

Sometimes you have to be bold in mathematics! The guessing-and-checking strategy requires you to start by making a guess and then checking how close your answer is. Next, based upon this result, you revise your guess and try again. Figure 1-15 (see page 66) shows how the fifth-grade textbook of *Mathematics Plus* presents guessing and checking.

Try guessing and checking in the following exercise.

## Lesson Exercise 1.55

Sandy mailed 18 postcards and letters, which cost $4.62 in postage. If mailing a postcard costs $.19 and mailing a letter costs $.29, how many of each did she mail? (*Guess and check.*)

Consider guessing and checking when you have a question with a limited number of possible answers, and you can check how close a guess is to the correct answer.

## Making a Table or List

Organizing information often makes it easier to solve a problem. Example 1.11 illustrates how making a table can help in solving a problem.

### Example 1.11

A cashier wants to make change for $1 using nickels, dimes, and quarters. Furthermore, he will use at least 2 quarters and no more than 8 coins all together. How many ways are there to do this? (*Make a table.*)

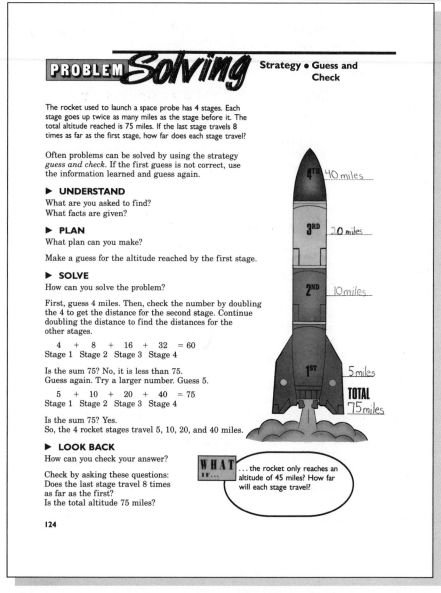

**PROBLEM Solving**                          Strategy • Guess and
                                                         Check

The rocket used to launch a space probe has 4 stages. Each
stage goes up twice as many miles as the stage before it. The
total altitude reached is 75 miles. If the last stage travels 8
times as far as the first stage, how far does each stage travel?

Often problems can be solved by using the strategy
*guess and check*. If the first guess is not correct, use
the information learned and guess again.

▶ **UNDERSTAND**
What are you asked to find?
What facts are given?

▶ **PLAN**
What plan can you make?

Make a guess for the altitude reached by the first stage.

▶ **SOLVE**
How can you solve the problem?

First, guess 4 miles. Then, check the number by doubling
the 4 to get the distance for the second stage. Continue
doubling the distance to find the distances for the
other stages.

    4   +   8   +   16   +   32   = 60
Stage 1  Stage 2  Stage 3  Stage 4

Is the sum 75? No, it is less than 75.
Guess again. Try a larger number. Guess 5.

    5   +   10   +   20   +   40   = 75
Stage 1  Stage 2  Stage 3  Stage 4

Is the sum 75? Yes.
So, the 4 rocket stages travel 5, 10, 20, and 40 miles.

▶ **LOOK BACK**
How can you check your answer?

Check by asking these questions:
Does the last stage travel 8 times
as far as the first?
Is the total altitude 75 miles?

**WHAT IF...** . . . the rocket only reaches an
altitude of 45 miles? How far
will each stage travel?

124

From *Mathematics Plus*, Grade 5 (San Diego: Harcourt Brace Jovanovich, 1992), p. 124.

**Figure 1-15**

Solution

*Understanding the Problem*   The cashier must use 2, 3, or 4 quarters and no more than a total of 8 coins to make $1.

*Devising a Plan*   All the solutions can be organized into a table.

*Carrying Out the Plan*   Fill out the table in an *organized* way.

| Quarters | Dimes | Nickels |
|----------|-------|---------|
| 4 | 0 | 0 |
| 3 | 2 | 1 |
| 3 | 1 | 3 |
| 3 | 0 | 5 |
| 2 | 5 | 0 |

There are 5 different ways.

*Looking Back*   Check the table to see that all combinations are included. They are.   ■

Tables enable one to organize information in a simple, clear way.

## Lesson Exercise 1.56

It will take 11 quarts of paint to paint your new apartment. Quarts cost $3.50 and gallons cost $8.50. (*Note:* 1 gallon = 4 quarts.)
(a) What are the different ways you can purchase the paint for the job? (*Make a table or list.*)
(b) Which is the least expensive?

Consider making a table or list when you have a limited number of options that can be listed in an organized way, and you want to examine all these options.

## Drawing a Picture

Sometimes, a drawing or a diagram makes it clearer how to solve a problem. For example, Venn diagrams can be helpful in examining deductive reasoning. Solve Lesson Exercise 1.57 by *drawing a picture.*

**D** Lesson Exercise 1.57

A well is 30 ft deep. An athletic snail at the bottom climbs up 3 ft each day and slips back 2 ft each night. On what day will the snail reach the top of the well? (*Hint:* Draw a picture. The answer is *not* the 30th day!)

Consider drawing a picture for any problem involving measurements or geometric shapes. Besides using problem-solving strategies, successful problem solvers tend to: (1) approach new problems with more confidence, (2) analyze and explore the conditions of the problem, and (3) obtain a lot of experience solving problems.

## An Investigation: Problem Analysis

The following lesson exercises are all related to the preceding puzzle problem. By doing this series of problems, you will develop a deeper understanding of this kind of puzzle problem.

Lesson Exercise 1.58

A well is 30 ft deep. A muscle-bound worm at the bottom climbs up 4 ft each day and slips back 1 ft each night. On what day will it reach the top of the well? (*Draw a picture.*)

Lesson Exercise 1.59

A well is 50 ft deep. A muscle-bound worm at the bottom climbs up 4 ft each day and slips back 2 ft each night. On what day will it reach the top of the well? (*Draw a picture.*)

Lesson Exercise 1.60

A well is 80 ft deep. Complete a worm/snail problem so that the slimy animal reaches the top on the
(a) 20th day.     (b) 19th day.     (c) 18th day.

## Answers to Selected Lesson Exercises

**1.55** 6 postcards and 12 letters

**1.56** (a)

| Number of Gallons | Number of Quarts | Total Cost |
|:---:|:---:|:---:|
| 0 | 11 | $38.50 |
| 1 | 7 | $33.00 |
| 2 | 3 | $27.50 |
| 3 | 0 | $25.50 |

(b) Three gallons would be the least expensive.

**1.57** 28th day

**1.58** 10th day

**1.59** 24th day

## 1.6   Homework Exercises

*Basic Exercises*

1. Which step of Polya's four-step scheme involves the consideration of various problem-solving strategies?

2. Find two consecutive even numbers whose product is 50,624. (*Guess and check.*)

3. A baseball league has 6 teams: the Bats, the Diamonds, the Flies, the Goose Eggs, the Hot Dogs, and the Relish. If every team plays every other team 4 times, how many games must be scheduled? (*Make a table.*)

4. A bank sells the following packets of traveler's checks: five $20 bills, three $50 bills, three $100 bills, and five $100 bills. How many different ways are there to buy $500 in traveler's checks? (*Make a table.*)

5. During 6 weeks in the summer, each of 4 workers will take 3 weeks off. No more than 2 workers may be off at one time, and everyone wants at least two consecutive weeks off. Complete the following schedule.

|       | Week 1 | Week 2 | Week 3 | Week 4 | Week 5 | Week 6 |
|-------|--------|--------|--------|--------|--------|--------|
| Molly | X      |        |        | X      | X      |        |
| Paul  | X      |        | X      | X      |        |        |
| Wong  |        |        |        |        |        |        |
| Clio  |        |        |        |        |        |        |

6. (a) A square has an area of 81 square units. What is its perimeter? Recall that the perimeter is the distance around the outside. (*Draw a picture and use the correct units.*)

   (b) Computing the perimeter of a square when you know the length of each side involves what type of reasoning, inductive or deductive?

7. Craig Chandler is 5 years older than Linda. The product of their ages is 1184. How old are they? (*Guess and check.*)

8. A well is 100 ft deep. A muscle-bound worm at the bottom climbs up 5 ft each day and slips back 2 ft each night. On what day will it reach the top of the well? (*Draw a picture.*)

9. A well is 60 ft deep. Complete a worm/snail problem so that the slimy animal reaches the top on the
   (a) 20th day.   (b) 19th day.   (c) 18th day.

10. A telephone company offers two plans for local calls. Plan A charges $.09 per call. Plan B charges $4 for the first 50 calls and $.06 for each call after that. Determine under what conditions each plan is cheaper. (*Make a table and guess and check.*) The table headings are shown below.

| Number of Calls | Cost of Plan A | Cost of Plan B |
|-----------------|----------------|----------------|
|                 |                |                |
|                 |                |                |
|                 |                |                |

11. An office staff includes a manager, an assistant manager, two secretaries, and two sales agents. Construct a 7-week vacation schedule for them, taking into consideration the following constraints. (See top of p. 70.)
    (1) The manager gets 3 weeks off. Everyone else gets 2 weeks off.
    (2) The manager is taking weeks 5, 6, and 7 off. Everyone else gets 2 consecutive weeks off.
    (3) No more than two people can be on vacation at one time.
    (4) At least one secretary and one sales agent must be present in the office each week.
    (5) When the manager is away, the assistant manager and both sales agents must be at work.

|                    | Week 1 | Week 2 | Week 3 | Week 4 | Week 5 | Week 6 | Week 7 |
|--------------------|--------|--------|--------|--------|--------|--------|--------|
| Manager            |        |        |        |        | X      | X      | X      |
| Assistant manager  |        |        |        |        |        |        |        |
| Secretary I        |        |        |        |        |        |        |        |
| Secretary II       |        |        |        |        |        |        |        |
| Sales agent I      |        |        |        |        |        |        |        |
| Sales agent II     |        |        |        |        |        |        |        |

**12.** Find $\sqrt{1444}$ without using a calculator $\boxed{\sqrt{\phantom{x}}}$ key. (*Guess and check.*)

**13.** Find the solution of $x^3 - 5x^2 + 28 = 0$. (*Guess and check.*)

**14.** Make up word problems that can be solved with each of the following strategies.
(a) guess and check
(b) draw a picture     (c) make a table

**15.** An apartment has two adjacent rectangular rooms, each 9 ft by 12 ft. They share a 9-ft-long wall. What is the perimeter of the apartment? (*Use one of the three strategies.*)

**16.** A 10-pound bag of mixed nuts contains 20% peanuts. How many pounds of peanuts should be added to change the mixture to 80% peanuts? (*Use one of the three strategies.*)

**17.** After throwing 25 darts at the following target, what is the *highest* score below 100 that it is *impossible* to score? (*Use one of the three strategies.*)

*Extension Exercises*

**18.** (a) A woman has 40 yards of fencing for her yard. What is the maximum rectangular area she can enclose? (*Draw a picture, make a table, and guess and check.*)
(b) A woman has $F$ yards of fencing for her yard. What is the maximum rectangular

area she can enclose? (*Draw a picture, make a table, and guess and check.*)

**19.** (a) A woman wants to enclose 100 yd² of field with a rectangular fence. What is the minimum perimeter of fencing she can use?
(b) A woman wants to enclose $N$ yd² of field with a rectangular fence. What is the minimum perimeter of fence she can use?

**20.** A travel agency is planning a one-week trip to Italy that has an initial cost of $2000 plus $1140 per person. At a price of $1600, 15 people will sign up. Past experience suggests that for each $20 decrease in the price, an additional person will sign up. Also, for each $20 increase in the price, one less person will sign up. Approximately what price will maximize the profit? (*Make a table and guess and check.*)

**21.** A farmer wants to transport a fox, a goose, and a bag of corn across a river in a boat. He

can take only one of the three across on each trip. He cannot leave the fox and the goose alone, since the fox will eat the goose. He cannot leave the goose and the corn alone, since the goose will eat the corn. How will he get the fox, the goose, and the corn across the river? (*Draw a picture and guess and check.*)

22. A man and two small children want to cross the river in a small boat. The boat is only big enough to hold either the man or the two children, both of whom can row. How can all three get across the river in the boat?

23. There are 20 children in a class, including exactly 10 girls and 12 eight-year-olds. How many eight-year-old girls could there be? Give *all* possible answers. (*Draw a picture and guess and check.*)

24. There are 26 children in a class, including exactly 12 girls and 20 eight-year-olds. How many eight-year-old girls could there be?

25. There are C children in a class, including exactly G girls and E eight-year-olds. Assume $G < E < C$. How many eight-year-old girls could there be?

26. (a) I'm inviting 20 people to a party, and I want to seat them all at one long table. I'm going to put together a series of card tables that seat one person on each side. They will form one long table. If I arrange them in one long row, how many card tables will I need?
    (b) Give a general solution for seating 2N people (N is a whole number greater than 3). How many tables would be needed?

27. Another option for the party in the previous exercise is to use rectangular tables as shown.

What is a formula relating the number of chairs (C) to the number of tables (T)?

28. In the preceding exercise, one student gives the answer $C = 2 + 4T$, and another gives the answer $C = 6 + 4(T - 1)$. Are both answers correct? Explain why or why not.

29. Another way to set up rectangular tables (see the previous exercise) gives more room for serving platters on the table.

What is the formula relating the number of chairs to the number of tables?

30. At a party of people who have never met, everyone wants to shake hands with everyone else. How many handshakes will occur if there are
    (a) 2 people at the party?
    (b) 3 people at the party?
    (c) 4 people at the party?
    (d) 8 people at the party? Use the pattern from parts (a), (b), and (c).

31. A group of girls are running in a race. How many orders of finish are possible if there are
    (a) 2 runners?    (b) 3 runners?
    (c) 4 runners?    (d) N runners?
    (e) Making a generalization in part (d) involves _____ reasoning.

32. (a) A farmer was asked by a passing stranger how many rabbits and chickens she has. The clever farmer replied, "Between the rabbits and the chickens, there are 76 eyes and 126 feet." How many rabbits and chickens does she have?
    (b) Repeat part (a) for E eyes and F feet.

33. Look at a current textbook series for Grades 1–6. What do they teach about problem-solving strategies in each grade?

## Summary

What methods of reasoning do mathematicians use? Can you use these methods to analyze problems in your daily life? Or will trying them only give you a headache?

Two methods commonly used to discover new ideas in mathematics and everyday life are inductive and deductive reasoning. Induction involves making a reasonable generalization from specific examples. Scientists and mathematicians use induction to develop general hypotheses or theorems. People may also develop prejudices and superstitions using induction.

To verify conjectures, one uses deductive reasoning, the process of drawing a necessary conclusion from given assumptions. Detectives use deduction in drawing conclusions, and mathematicians use deduction to prove theorems. Mathematicians often develop new ideas using induction to make a generalization or state a theorem followed by deduction to prove that the generalization or theorem must be true.

Both types of reasoning can lead to false conclusions. Induction is not totally reliable because what happens a few times may not always happen. Superstitions and prejudices are examples of erroneous generalizations. Deductions are sometimes false because valid deductive reasoning based upon false assumptions can lead to a false conclusion.

A superior ability to find patterns distinguishes human beings from other animals and machines. Mathematicians develop new ideas by recognizing and generalizing patterns. Finding a pattern makes use of induction, and extending the pattern based upon a general rule requires deduction. Finding and extending patterns enables people to make predictions about the future and to develop classifications. Pattern problems are sometimes used on intelligence tests.

Problem solving is now a focus of school mathematics. Children study three kinds of problems: one-step translation problems, multi-step translation problems, and puzzle problems. In solving most of these problems, four steps can be followed: (1) understand the problem, (2) devise a plan, (3) carry out the plan, and (4) check and assess your results.

Devising a plan or strategy is often the hardest step. Three strategies commonly used to solve mathematics problems are guessing and checking, making a table, and drawing a picture. Arithmetic, algebra, and geometry problems can sometimes be solved more easily with these strategies.

## Study Guide

To review Chapter 1, see what you know about each of the ideas or terms listed below that you have studied. You could also use this list to generate your own questions about Chapter 1.

# The NCTM Curriculum Standards and Mathematical Reasoning

The National Council of Teachers of Mathematics (NCTM) *Curriculum and Evaluation Standards for School Mathematics* (1989) is the most important document about the current elementary-school mathematics curriculum. Some states and communities have told textbook publishers they will only use books that follow "The Standards."

At the end of each chapter, you can learn about "The Standards" and review the chapter by considering how "The Standards" relate to the material you have just studied. If you have access to elementary-school textbooks, you can also investigate how these materials incorporate "The Standards."

---

**Selected NCTM Curriculum Standards**

There are about 50 objectives for students in Grades K–4 and 70 objectives for students in Grades 5–8. The following standards come from these two lists of objectives.

- Recognize and apply inductive and deductive reasoning.
- Use mathematics in their daily lives.
- Recognize, describe, extend, and create a wide variety of patterns.
- Describe and represent relationships with tables, graphs, and rules.
- Develop and apply strategies to solve a wide variety of problems.
- Reflect on and clarify their thinking about mathematical ideas and situations.

---

1. Describe how each standard listed relates to the material you studied in Chapter 1.
2. Select any current elementary-school mathematics textbook series and describe a sample lesson or exercise that illustrates each standard listed.

## Review Exercises

1. What is deductive reasoning?

In Exercises 2–4, identify whether induction or deduction is being used.

2. People have died in the past. I assume everyone will die in the future.

3. I know Alicia is in the bedroom, the kitchen, or the bathroom. I do not find her in the bedroom or the kitchen. I conclude that she is in the bathroom.

4. I know that $x > y$ and $y > z$. I conclude that $x > z$.

5. Explain how an auto mechanic repairing an engine could use Polya's four steps.

6. Does the conclusion given follow from the two hypotheses? If so, draw a Venn diagram that illustrates it. If the conclusion is invalid, draw a Venn diagram that shows this.

   *Hypotheses:* All squares have four sides. All rhombuses have four sides.
   *Conclusion:* Therefore, all rhombuses are squares.

7. *Explain* how a student might use inductive reasoning.

8. Is the sum of any three consecutive counting numbers divisible by 3?

9. (a) Write the converse of the following statement: If it is raining, then the ground gets wet.
   (b) Is the converse true?

**10.** Consider the following number trick.

Pick a number.

Add 5.

Multiply by 3.

Subtract 9.

Subtract your original number.

Divide by 2.

Prove that you will always end up with three more than you started.

**11.** (a) Write a formula for the $n$th term in the following sequence.

$$20, 19, 18, 17, \ldots$$

(b) What is the 40th term?

(c) Make up a chart of $x$ and $y$ values that is analogous to the sequence in part (a).

(d) Does part (a) involve inductive or deductive reasoning?

**12.** (a) Fill in the missing numbers.

$$1 = (\ )^3$$
$$3 + 5 = (\ )^3$$
$$7 + 9 + 11 = (\ )^3$$

(b) What would the next equation be if the pattern continues? Is the equation true?

**13.** Examine the following pattern.

$$4^2 - 1^2 = 3 \cdot 5$$
$$5^2 - 2^2 = 3 \cdot 7$$
$$6^2 - 3^2 = 3 \cdot 9$$

(a) Write the next example that follows the pattern.

(b) Complete the following generalization. For any counting number $N$ greater than two, $N^2 - \underline{\hspace{1cm}} = \underline{\hspace{1cm}}$.

(c) Prove that your equation in part (b) is true.

**14.** Make up an example of a multi-step translation problem.

**15.** How many rectangles are there in the figure?

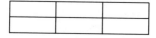

**16.** Consider the following problem: You took 11 orders for either a tuna salad sandwich ($1.90) or a buckwheat Newburg ($1.50) but forgot how many of each. If the bill comes to $17.70, how many of each were ordered?

(a) What would be a good strategy for solving this problem?

(b) Solve the problem using your strategy.

**17.** An employer wishes to select 2 people for a job from Alice, José, Mary, and Reggie. How many ways are there to do this?

**18.** Examine the following figure.

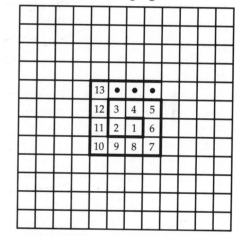

(a) If the pattern in the square continues, what number will appear in the upper right-hand corner?

(b) Where will the number 120 appear?

**19.** A well is 40 ft deep. A snail climbs up 9 feet each day and slips back 5 feet at night. How long will the snail take to reach the top of the well?

**20.** A well is 40 ft deep. Make up a snail problem in which the snail reaches the top on the
(a) 18th day.     (b) 19th day.

**21.** (a) Mack, Ahmad, Mona, and Rosie each own a pet. The pets are an ant, a crocodile, a gorilla, and a sea turtle. Determine who owns each pet by using the following facts.

1. Mack is allergic to crocodiles and gorillas.

2. Mona and the owner of the gorilla live in the same apartment building.
3. Ahmad is not allowed to have a pet larger than a goldfish in his building.

(b) Does this problem involve induction or deduction?

 **22.**

$$142857 \times 1 = 142857$$
$$142857 \times 2 = 285714$$
$$142857 \times 3 = 428571$$

(a) Write the next example continuing the pattern.

(b) Make a generalization about the digits in the result.

(c) How long does the pattern continue? Try 5, 6, and 7 as factors.

## Computer Exercises

**1.** (a) RUN the following BASIC program on a computer. What is the output?

```
10 FOR N = 1 TO 7 STEP 2
20 PRINT N
30 NEXT N
```

In parts (b) through (d), type in a new line 10 to create a program that prints the sequence in the given order.

(b) 2, 4, 6, 8
(c) 7, 11, 15, 19, 23
(d) 11, 8, 5, 2, −1 (*Hint:* Use a negative number after STEP.)

**2.** (a) RUN the following BASIC program on a computer. What is the output?

```
10 FOR N = 1 TO 5
20 PRINT 3*N
30 NEXT N
```

(b) What does * mean in BASIC?

In parts (c) through (e), type in a new line 20 to create a program that prints the sequence in the given order.

(c) 1, 4, 9, 16, 25
(d) 6, 10, 14, 18, 22
(e) 10, 8, 6, 4, 2

## Mathematical Reasoning in Elementary School

The following chart shows at what grade levels selected mathematical reasoning topics typically appear in elementary-school mathematics textbooks. Underlined numbers indicate grades in which the most time is spent on the given topic.

| Topic | Typical Grade Level in Current Textbooks |
|---|---|
| Using deductive reasoning | 2, 3, <u>4</u>, <u>5</u>, 6 |
| Number sequences | 1, 2, <u>3</u>, <u>4</u>, <u>5</u>, 6 |
| Finding patterns | 1, 2, 3, 4, 5, 6 |
| Problem-solving steps (Polya) | 2, <u>3</u>, <u>4</u>, <u>5</u>, <u>6</u> |
| Problem-solving strategies | 1, 2, <u>3</u>, <u>4</u>, <u>5</u>, <u>6</u> |

## Suggested Readings

Brown, S. and M. Walter. *The Art of Problem Posing*. Palo Alto, CA: Dale Seymour, 1983.

Burns, M. *The Book of Think*. Boston, MA: Little, 1976.

Charles, R. and F. Lester. *Teaching Problem Solving: What, Why, and How*. Palo Alto, CA: Dale Seymour, 1982.

Equals. *Get It Together*. Berkeley, CA: Equals, 1989.

Gardner, Martin. *Aha! Insight*. NY: Freeman, 1978.

Jacobs, Harold. *Mathematics: A Human Endeavor*. 2nd ed. NY: Freeman, 1982.

National Council of Teachers of Mathematics. *Curriculum and Evaluation Standards for School Mathematics*. Reston, VA: NCTM, 1989.

National Council of Teachers of Mathematics. 1980 Yearbook. *Problem Solving in School Mathematics*. Reston, VA: NCTM, 1980.

National Council of Teachers of Mathematics. 1983 Yearbook. *The Agenda in Action*. Reston, VA: NCTM, 1983.

National Council of Teachers of Mathematics. 1989 Yearbook. *New Directions for Elementary School Mathematics*. Reston, VA: NCTM, 1989.

National Council of Teachers of Mathematics. *Professional Standards for Teaching Mathematics*. Reston, VA: NCTM, 1990.

Polya, G. *How to Solve It*. 2nd ed. Princeton, NJ: Princeton U. Press, 1973.

(*Note:* Recent issues of the *Arithmetic Teacher* would be another good source for most of the topics covered in this book.)

# 2

# Sets

$E$very area of mathematics utilizes sets in some way. For example, Chapters 3, 4, 5, and 7 each concern a particular set of numbers (e.g., whole numbers). You will also study different sets of shapes (e.g., rectangles, parallelograms) and the relationships among them. Graphing involves sets of ordered pairs. In statistics, one studies data sets, and in probability one examines sets of possible outcomes. You have already used set pictures (Venn diagrams) to illustrate logical relationships.

This chapter introduces the basic ideas of sets, but this book as a whole does not place great emphasis on set theory. Neither does the current elementary-school mathematics curriculum.

## 2.1　Sets

GEORGE BOOLE

Photo courtesy of Library of Congress.

**Figure 2-1**

George Boole (1815–1864, Figure 2-1) developed set theory. Born to a lower-class family, Boole taught himself six foreign languages and a good deal of mathematics. He believed that the essence of mathematics lies in its deductive organization.

Georg Cantor (1845–1918, Figure 2-2), a German mathematician, extended set theory to include infinite sets, a topic that was so controversial that it caused one of his former teachers to turn against him. Partly as a result of being ridiculed by this teacher, Cantor suffered a nervous breakdown and died in a mental hospital.

Today, Boole and Cantor's work with finite and infinite sets is an accepted part of mathematics. In this text, sets will be used to define whole number addition and multiplication and will serve as a model for each of the four whole number operations in Chapter 3.

In the 1960s and early 1970s, some elementary-school teachers used sets to explain counting and arithmetic. Some of you may remember studying sets as children. Others may claim to be too young to remember 1970. Still others like myself can't believe it still isn't 1970.

Teaching that was heavily based upon set theory was not well received in elementary schools, and today sets are generally not studied as a separate topic in elementary school. However, we still talk about sets of numbers or shapes, about subsets, and about the set of objects two sets have in common. Venn diagrams are introduced in some middle-school programs as an aid to problem solving.

## Sets

What education courses must you pass to receive state teacher certification? Who in your class likes to eat pizza? The answers to these questions would be sets.

A **set** is a collection of objects. These objects are called **members** or **elements** of a set. The expression "$x \in A$" means that $x$ is a member of set $A$. The expression "$x \notin A$" means that $x$ is *not* a member of set $A$.

To define a set, one can list the members and enclose them in braces. For example, the set of primary colors is {red, yellow, blue}.

### Lesson Exercise 2.1

Fill in each blank with $\in$ or $\notin$.
(a) 4 _____ {2, 4, 6}
(b) orange juice _____ the set of all junk foods

*Georg Cantor*

Photo courtesy of Library of Congress.

**Figure 2-2**

A set with no members is called an **empty** or **null set.** For example, the set of all pink elephants in your math class is an empty set. An empty set is denoted by the symbol { } or ø.

### Lesson Exercise 2.2

Make up another example of an empty set.

People invented numbers so they could count objects. At first, people used only the first few counting numbers. The infinite set of counting or natural numbers is the result of thousands of years of work in expanding this initial set of numbers and developing more efficient notation.

We take the symbol 0 for granted, but at first people thought a symbol for "nothing" was unnecessary. Once 0 was included as a symbol for "nothing" and as a placeholder, numerations systems made significant advances (see Chapter 3).

By putting together 0 and the set of counting numbers, one obtains the set of whole numbers.

---

**Definition: Whole Numbers**

The set of **whole numbers** $W = \{0, 1, 2, 3, \ldots\}$.

---

## Finite and Infinite Sets

If the number of elements in a set is a whole number, the set is a **finite set.** The set of days of the week is a finite set containing seven elements. The set of whole numbers is an **infinite set** because it does not contain a finite number of elements. A more formal definition of an infinite set appears in the homework exercises.

### Lesson Exercise 2.3

Decide whether each of the following sets is a finite set or an infinite set.
(a) the set of whole numbers less than 6
(b) the set of all the pancakes in Arizona right now
(c) the set of whole numbers greater than 6

One might compare two sets to see if they are identical or if they contain exactly the same number of elements. Two sets are **equal** if and only if they contain exactly the same elements. For example, if $A = \{2, 3\}$ and $B = \{3, 2\}$, then $A = B$. Two sets are **equivalent** if, and only if, they contain the same *number* of elements. One can show that two sets are equivalent by placing their elements in a **one-to-one correspondence,** in which one pairs the elements of the two sets so that, for each element of one set, there is exactly one element of the other. For example, the sets $\{1, 2\}$ and $\{Bill, Sue\}$ are equivalent sets since they both contain two elements. This can be verified by establishing a one-to-one correspondence, as in Figure 2-3.

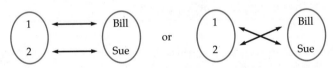

Figure 2-3

The following exercise addresses the differences between equal and equivalent sets.

### Lesson Exercise 2.4

$A = \{1, 2, 3\}$　　　　　$B = \{1, 3, 5\}$　　　　　$C = \{1, 2, 3, 4\}$
$D = \{Sara, John, Will\}$　　$E = \{bat, ball, glove, cap\}$　　$F = \{1, 3, 2\}$
(a) Which sets are equivalent?
(b) Which sets are equal?
(c) If two sets are equivalent, are they equal?
(d) If two sets are equal, are they equivalent?

## Subsets

If you wanted to decide which days to exercise, you would choose from the 7 days of the week. Let

$$U = \{\text{Sunday, Monday, Tuesday, Wednesday,}$$
$$\text{Thursday, Friday, Saturday}\}$$

and asssume you decide upon a 3-day schedule, either $A$ or $B$, or a very light exercise schedule, $C$.

$$A = \{\text{Monday, Wednesday, Friday}\}$$
$$B = \{\text{Tuesday, Thursday, Saturday}\}$$
$$C = \{\ \}$$

Set $A$ is an example of a subset of $U$, since each element of $A$ is contained in $U$ (see Figure 2-4). For the same reason, $B$ and $C$ are also subsets of $U$.

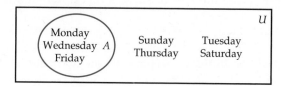

**Figure 2-4**

The definition of a subset is as follows.

---

**Definition: A Subset**

Set $A$ is a **subset** of $B$, written "$A \subseteq B$," if and only if every element of $A$ is also an element of $B$.

---

When $A$ is not a subset of $B$, written "$A \not\subseteq B$," this means that $A$ contains an element that is *not* in $B$.

## Lesson Exercise 2.5

Which of the following sets is a subset of $\{4, 6, 8\}$?
(a) $\{4, 8\}$     (b) $\{3\}$     (c) $\{\ \}$

In the preceding exercise, you may have wondered why $\{\ \}$ is a subset of $\{4, 6, 8\}$. In order to be a subset, every element in $\{\ \}$ must also be in $\{4, 6, 8\}$. Since there are no elements in $\{\ \}$, it is true that every element in $\{\ \}$ is also in $\{4, 6, 8\}$!

You may be familiar with $\subset$, the notation for a **proper subset.** The expression "$A \subset B$" means that every element of $A$ is also an element of $B$, *and* that *B* contains at least one element that is *not* in *A*. So, {1, 2} is a proper subset of {1, 2, 3} but {1, 2, 3} is not a proper subset of {1, 2, 3}. The symbols ⊆ and ⊂ are analogous to ≤ and < for relationships between numbers.

How does one distinguish between ⊆ and ∈? The symbol ⊆ shows a relationship between *sets* as in "{8} ⊆ {8, 10}." The symbol ∈ shows that one object is a member of a set, as in "8 ∈ {8, 10}" or "{8} ∈ {{8}, {10}}."

**D** Lesson Exercise 2.6
___

Fill in each blank with ∈ or ⊆.
(a) 12 _____ {10, 11, . . . , 19}      (b) {2, 4} _____ {2, 4, 6}

## An Investigation: Subsets

Is there a pattern in the number of subsets that different sets have?

## Lesson Exercise 2.7
___

(a) *Understanding the Problem*   What are you supposed to do in this investigation?
(b) *Devising a Plan and Carrying Out the Plan*   Complete the following table. (Remember that the empty set is a subset of every set.)

| Set | List of Subsets | Number of Subsets |
|---|---|---|
| {1} | { }   {1} | 2 |
| {1, 2} | | |
| {1, 2, 3} | | |
| {1, 2, 3, 4} | | |

(c) *Explain* why {1, 2, 3, 4} has twice as many subsets as {1, 2, 3}.
(d) Based upon your response to part (a), a set with *N* elements appears to have _____ subsets.
(e) *Looking Back*   In part (d), you used _____ reasoning.

## Answers to Selected Lesson Exercises

2.1 (a) ∈     (b) ∉

2.2 the set of all positive numbers less than 0

2.3 (a) finite     (b) finite     (c) infinite

2.4 (a) *A*, *B*, *D*, and *F* are equivalent and *C* and *E* are equivalent.
     (b) *A* = *F*     (c) no     (d) yes
2.5 (a), (c)
2.6 (a) ∈     (b) ⊆

## 2.1 Homework Exercises

### Basic Exercises

1. Name five English words that refer to a set (for example, a coin "collection" or a "herd" of cattle).

2. List the members of the set of whole numbers less than 20 that are perfect squares.

3. Name two sets of which you are a member.

4. Let $A$ be the set of odd numbers. Are the following true or false?
   (a) $11 \in A$   (b) $10 \in A$
   (c) $6 \notin A$   (d) $\{3\} \in A$

5. Which of the following would be an empty set?
   (a) the set of purple crows
   (b) the set of odd numbers that are divisible by 2

6. Decide whether each set is a finite set or an infinite set.
   (a) the set of whole numbers greater than 6
   (b) the set of all the grains of sand on Earth
   (c) the set of all perfect square numbers

7. Which of the following represent equal sets?
   $D = \{$orange, apple$\}$   $F = \{$apple, orange$\}$
   $A = \{1, 2\}$   $G = \{1, 2, 3\}$
   $E = \{\ \}$   $N = \emptyset$   $H = \{5, 6\}$

8. Which of the following represent equivalent sets?
   $D = \{$orange, apple$\}$   $F = \{$apple, orange$\}$
   $A = \{1, 2\}$   $G = \{1, 2, 3\}$
   $E = \{\ \}$   $N = \emptyset$   $H = \{5, 6\}$

9. Historical evidence reveals that some hunting tribes counted using equivalent sets. The tribal mathematician would place a rock in a pile for each hunter who left on an expedition. What do you think the mathematician did when the hunters returned?

10. (a) True or false? If two sets are not equal, then they are not equivalent.
    (b) If part (a) is true, give an example that supports it. If part (a) is false, give a counterexample.

11. How can a first-grader use the idea of one-to-one correspondence to determine which of two sets of blocks has more elements?

12. Which of the following sets are subsets of $\{1, 3, 5, 7\}$?
    (a) $\{1, 3, 5, 7\}$   (b) $\{9, 11, 13, \ldots\}$
    (c) $\{\ \}$   (d) $\{5\}$

13. Rewrite the following expressions using symbols.
    (a) $A$ is a subset of $B$.
    (b) The number 2 is not a member of set $T$.

14. If $A \subseteq \emptyset$, then $A = $ _____.

15. Fill in each blank with $\in$ or $\subseteq$.
    (a) $\{\ \}$ _____ $\{1, 3\}$
    (b) Jean _____ $\{$Tom, Jean$\}$

16. A committee $C = \{$Bobbie, Rupert, Sly, Jenny, Melissa$\}$ requires a majority vote to pass any new rules. Complete the following list of winning coalitions using just the first letter of each person's name. (Make an organized list.)
    $\{B, R, S\}$   $\{B, R, S, J\}$

17. The United Nations Security Council has 15 members, of which 5 are permanent and 10 are elected for 2-year terms. No measure can pass unless all 5 permanent members (the United States, the Russian Federation, the United Kingdom, France, and China) vote for it. Overall, nine votes are needed to pass a proposal.
    (a) How many votes are needed from temporary members?
    (b) You may refer to the 10 temporary members as $T_1, T_2, T_3, \ldots, T_{10}$. List five different winning coalitions containing exactly nine members.

### Extension Exercises

18. Decide which symbol, $\in$, $\notin$, $\subseteq$, or $\nsubseteq$, is equivalent to the underlined word in each sentence.
    (a) German shepherds <u>are</u> dogs.

(b) Juanita <u>is</u> Spanish.

(c) Jane <u>is not</u> a skydiver.

19. How many one-to-one correspondences are possible between each of the following?
    (a) two sets each having 2 members
    (b) two sets each having 3 members
    (c) two sets each having 4 members
    (d) two sets each having $N$ members

20. How can you create a one-to-one correspondence between the points of the triangle and the points of the circle?

21. (a) A box contains 2 kinds of fruit. How many pieces must you pick to be sure of getting at least 2 of one kind?
    (b) A box contains 2 kinds of fruit. How many pieces must you pick to be sure of getting at least 3 of one kind?
    (c) A box contains 2 kinds of fruit. How many pieces must you pick to be sure of getting at least 4 of one kind?
    (d) A box contains 2 kinds of fruit. How many pieces must you pick to be sure of getting at least $N$ of one kind?

22. (a) A box contains 3 kinds of fruit. How many pieces must you pick to be sure of getting at least 2 of one kind?
    (b) A box contains 3 kinds of fruit. How many pieces must you pick to be sure of getting at least 3 of one kind?
    (c) A box contains 3 kinds of fruit. How many pieces must you pick to be sure of getting at least 4 of one kind?
    (d) A box contains 3 kinds of fruit. How many pieces must you pick to be sure of getting at least $N$ of one kind?

23. A box contains $K$ kinds of fruit. How many pieces must you pick to be sure of getting at least $N$ pieces of one kind?

24. Set $A$ is **infinite** if and only if it can be put into a one-to-one correspondence with a proper subset of itself. For example, {0, 1, 2, 3, . . . } is infinite because it can be put into a one-to-one correspondence with its proper subset {10, 11, 12, 13, . . . }.

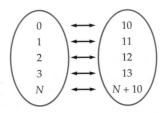

Show that the following sets are infinite.
    (a) {0, 2, 4, 6, 8, . . . }
    (b) {20, 21, 22, . . . }

25. Georg Cantor was the first to apply set theory to infinite sets. This led to some strange and surprising results.
    (a) Make a conjecture about which set has more elements, $W = \{0, 1, 2, 3, . . . \}$ or $E = \{0, 2, 4, 6, . . . \}$.
    (b) Cantor reasoned that two equivalent infinite sets (like finite sets) are those that can be put into a one-to-one correspondence. How did he match the members of $W$ and $E$ in a one-to-one correspondence to show that they are equivalent sets?

26. (a) Make up a nonempty set and list all possible subsets.
    (b) How does the number of subsets with an even number of elements compare to the number of subsets with an odd number of elements? (*Note:* 0 is an even number.)
    (c) Repeat parts (a) and (b) for a different nonempty set.
    (d) Propose a generalization of your results.

27. Write a description in words of each set.
    (a) {4, 8, 12, 16, . . . }
    (b) {3, 13, 23, 33, . . . }

## 2.2   Set Operations

A set operation is something you do to two sets that results in another set, just as the operation of addition on two numbers, such as 2 + 3, results in another number, 5. This section covers three set operations: intersection, union, and Cartesian products.

### Intersection and Union

Should Pam and Kurt get married? Pam likes skydiving, bronco busting, and chess. Kurt likes Sumo wrestling, mountain climbing, and chess. What interests do they have in common?

If $A$ is the set of Pam's interests and $B$ is the set of Kurt's interests, the answer to the question is the intersection of sets $A$ and $B$ (members of $A$ *and* $B$), written $A \cap B$. The only member of $A \cap B$ is "chess." "And" is a key word suggesting intersection. In everyday language and in mathematics, "and" indicates that both conditions must be true.

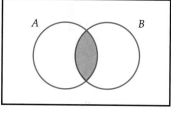

$A \cap B$

**Figure 2-5**

---

**Definition: Intersection**

The **intersection** of sets $A$ and $B$, written $A \cap B$, is the set containing the elements that are in both $A$ and $B$.

---

The shaded part of the set picture in Figure 2-5 is $A \cap B$. If $A$ and $B$ have no elements in common, then $A \cap B = \{\ \}$ or ø.

### Lesson Exercise 2.8

The math club membership $M = \{$Joe, Sam, Li, Clara$\}$ and the science club membership $S = \{$Juan, Li, Martha$\}$
(a) What is $M \cap S$?
(b) What characteristic do members of $M \cap S$ have?
(c) Does $S \cap M = M \cap S$?

### Lesson Exercise 2.9

$A \cap A =$ _____.

### D Lesson Exercise 2.10

If $B \cap C = C$, what is the relationship between $B$ and $C$?

---

When two or more sets are joined together, the new set formed is called the union of those sets. Getting back to Pam and Kurt, Pam has a sports car and an airplane, and she has a bicycle that they received as an engagement gift. Set $C$ = {car, plane, bicycle}. Kurt has a motorcycle, a skateboard, and that same bicycle. Set $D$ = {motorcycle, skateboard, bicycle}. If they marry, they will combine these vehicles to form the union of such items belonging to either Pam *or* Kurt *or both*, denoted $C \cup D$. $C \cup D$ = {car, plane, bicycle, motorcycle, skateboard}.

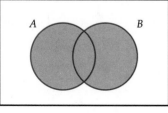

$A \cup B$

**Figure 2-6**

---

**Definition: Union**

The **union** of sets $A$ and $B$, written $A \cup B$, is the set containing all elements that are either in $A$ or in $B$ or in both $A$ and $B$.

---

"Or" is a key word suggesting union. "Or" has a slightly different meaning in mathematics than it sometimes does in everyday speech. In everyday speech, "or" often means "one or the other (but not both)." In mathematics, "$A$ or $B$" means "$A$ or $B$ *or both*." The shaded area in the set picture in Figure 2-6 is $A \cup B$.

Union and intersection are called **set operations** because they replace two sets by a third set just as arithmetic operations replace two numbers by a third number. Two properties of set operations are discussed in the homework exercises.

Lesson Exercises 2.11 and 2.12 refer back to Lesson Exercise 2.8.

## Lesson Exercise 2.11

(a) In Lesson Exercise 2.8, what is $M \cup S$?
(b) Does $M \cup S = S \cup M$?

## Lesson Exercise 2.12

The math club ($M$) and science club ($S$) have a joint activity. The people attending would represent which set?
(a) $M \cup S$     (b) $M \cap S$     (c) neither (a) nor (b)

## **D** Lesson Exercise 2.13

If $B \cup C = C$, then how are sets $B$ and $C$ related?

## **D** Lesson Exercise 2.14

Fill in each blank with $\in$, $\cup$, $\cap$, or $\subseteq$.
(a) {3, 5} _____ {6} = {3, 5, 6}
(b) 3 _____ {1, 2, 3}
(c) {3} _____ {1, 2, 3}

## Two-Set Venn Diagrams

*All* teachers are college graduates. *No* dirty clothes smell nice. These statements can all be illustrated using two-set Venn diagrams, as shown in Figure 2-7.

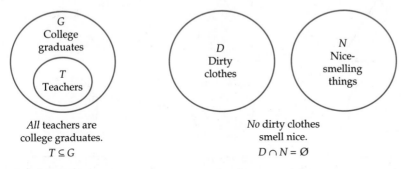

*All* teachers are
college graduates.
$T \subseteq G$

*No* dirty clothes
smell nice.
$D \cap N = \emptyset$

**Figure 2-7**

## Lesson Exercise 2.15

Draw two-set Venn diagrams illustrating the following statements, and write the relationship between the two sets using symbols.
(a) All fish are good swimmers.
(b) No U.S. senators are teenagers.

## Lesson Exercise 2.16

(a) Write a sentence describing the set relationship shown in Figure 2-8.

(b) Use symbols to represent the relationship between sets $A$ and $P$.

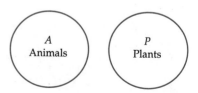

**Figure 2-8**

## Lesson Exercise 2.17

Let $U$ = {all students at your college}, $M$ = {students taking a math course}, and $S$ = {students taking a science course}.

Which region (I, II, III, or IV) of the Venn diagram in Figure 2-9 contains students
(a) taking mathematics but not science?
(b) taking mathematics and science?
(c) taking neither mathematics nor science?

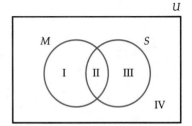

**Figure 2-9**

## Attribute Blocks

As a teacher, you will sometimes use objects or models to introduce ideas to your students. Attribute blocks are manipulatives (objects) used in

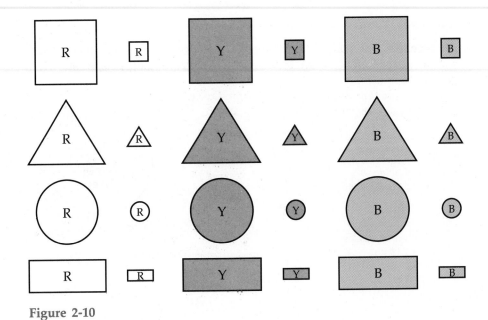

Figure 2-10

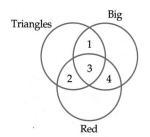

Figure 2-11

elementary school to study shapes, sets, and classification. Attribute blocks are so named because they have a variety of attributes: shape, color, size, and (sometimes) thickness. A typical set of attribute blocks is shown in Figure 2-10. You can buy a set or make one of your own.

## Lesson Exercise 2.18

What attribute blocks in Figure 2-11 belong in the overlapping part?

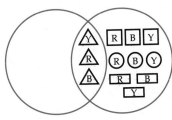

Figure 2-12

## Lesson Exercise 2.19

What attribute blocks in Figure 2-12 belong in the left section?

## Lesson Exercise 2.20

What attribute blocks in Figure 2-13 belong in Sections 1, 2, 3, and 4?

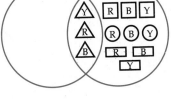

Figure 2-13

## Cartesian Products

Suppose you have 3 different shirts and 2 different pairs of pants. If everything matches, how many different outfits could you create? The answer involves the Cartesian product, another set operation. The **Cartesian product** of two sets is the set that shows all the ways one can pair a member of one set with a member of the other set.

## Lesson Exercise 2.21

(a) Suppose you have 3 shirts, $S = \{$purple, yellow, green$\}$, and 2 pairs of pants, $P = \{$red, blue$\}$. How many possible shirt-pant outfits could you create?

(b) Complete the following. The Cartesian product
$S \times P = \{$(purple, red), (purple, blue), (     ,     ),
(    ,     ), (    ,     ), (    ,     ) $\}$.

The Cartesian product $S \times P$ is a set of *ordered* pairs. The shirt color is written first and the pants color second. The ordered pair "(purple, red)" would mean "purple shirt and red pants," and it is in $S \times P$, but "(red, purple)," meaning "red shirt and purple pants," is not in $S \times P$.

In the preceding exercise, you saw that if $S$ has 3 elements and $P$ has 2 elements, then $S \times P$ has 6 elements. What happens in other cases?

## Lesson Exercise 2.22

(a) If $A$ has 3 elements and $B$ has 1 element, then $A \times B$ has _____ elements.

(b) If $A$ has 3 elements and $B$ has 3 elements, then $A \times B$ has _____ elements.

(c) If $A$ has $m$ elements and $B$ has $n$ elements, then $A \times B$ has _____ elements.

As the preceding exercise suggests, if $A$ has $m$ elements and $B$ has $n$ elements, then $A \times B$ has $mn$ elements. Use this principle to do the next two exercises.

## Lesson Exercise 2.23

Marissa has 10 shirts and 7 skirts. How many different shirt-skirt outfits can she create?

## Lesson Exercise 2.24

Barry has 6 shirts, 5 pairs of pants, and 3 pairs of shoes. How many different shirt-pant-shoe outfits can he create?

## Answers to Selected Lesson Exercises

2.8 (a) $\{$Li$\}$
(b) They are members of both the math and science clubs.
(c) yes

2.9 $A$

2.10 $C \subseteq B$

2.11 (a) $\{$Joe, Sam, Li, Clara, Juan, Martha$\}$
(b) yes

2.12 (a)

2.13 $B \subseteq C$

2.14 (a) $\cup$     (b) $\in$     (c) $\subseteq$

2.15 (a)

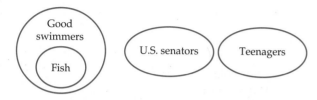

2.16 (a) No animals are plants.
    (b) $A \cap P = \varnothing$

2.17 (a) I     (b) II     (c) IV

2.18 the small and large blue squares

2.19 the large red, blue, and yellow triangles

2.20 1 = {big blue and yellow triangles},
    2 = {small red triangles},
    3 = {big red triangles},
    4 = {big red squares, circles, and rec-
        tangles}

2.21 (a) 6

2.22 (a) 3

2.23 70

2.24 90

## 2.2   Homework Exercises

### Basic Exercises

1. $A = \{1, 3, 5, 7, 9, 11\}$ and
   $B = \{3, 6, 9, 12, 15, 18\}$.
   (a) $A \cap B =$ _____
   (b) $A \cup B =$ _____
   (c) Does $A \cap B = B \cap A$?
   (d) Is $A \subseteq B$?

2. The operation $\cap$ is **commutative** because
   $A \cap B = B \cap A$ for all sets $A$ and $B$. Is the
   operation $\cup$ commutative?

3. (a) The operation $\cap$ is **associative** because
       $(A \cap B) \cap C = A \cap (B \cap C)$ for all sets $A$
       and $B$. Is the operation $\cup$ associative?
   (b) Support your answer to part (a) by shad-
       ing two Venn diagrams and comparing
       them.

4. $U$ is the set of all months of the year, $T$ is
   the set of all 30-day months, and $S$ is the set
   of school vacation months (June, July, and
   August). What is
   (a) $T \cap S$?     (b) $T \cup S$?
   (c) In parts (a) and (b) you used sets $T$ and
       $S$, set definitions, and _____
       reasoning.

5. $A$ has 3 members and $B$ has 2 members.
   (a) What is the largest number of members
       $A \cup B$ could have?
   (b) What is the smallest number of members
       $A \cup B$ could have?

6. $A$ has $a$ members and $B$ has $b$ members.
   (a) What is the largest number of members
       $A \cup B$ could have?
   (b) What is the smallest number of members
       $A \cup B$ could have?

7. In an apartment complex of 30 apartments,
   20 apartments receive the *New York Times*
   and 14 apartments receive the *Sporting News*.
   (a) What is the largest number of apartments
       that could receive *both* publications?
   (b) What is the smallest number of apart-
       ments that could receive *both*
       publications?

8. Use symbols to represent the following statements.
   (a) $E$ is the intersection of $F$ and $G$.
   (b) The union of $A$ and $E$ is $E$.

9. A logician says, "Tomorrow will be rainy or
   cold." What is the logician possibly predict-
   ing for tomorrow?

10. Assume $2 \in (A \cup B)$. Which of the following statements could be true?
    (a) 2 is in $A$ but not in $B$.
    (b) 2 is in $B$ but not in $A$.
    (c) 2 is in both $A$ and $B$.
    (d) 2 is in neither $A$ nor $B$.

11. Fill in each blank with $\in$, $\cup$, $\cap$, or $\subseteq$.
    (a) $1 \underline{\quad \in \quad} \{1, 2\}$
    (b) $\{1, 3, 5\} \underline{\quad \cap \quad} \{5\} = \{5\}$
    (c) $\{6, 7\} \underline{\quad\quad} \{5, 6, 7\}$

12. If possible, make up two sets such that the number of elements in $A$ plus the number of elements in $B$ is
    (a) less than the number of elements in $A \cup B$.
    (b) equal to the number of elements in $A \cup B$.
    (c) greater than the number of elements in $A \cup B$.

13. Make up two sets $A$ and $B$ such that the number of elements in $A$ equals the number of elements in $A \cap B$.

14. Draw two-set Venn diagrams illustrating the following statements and use symbols to represent the relationship between the two sets.
    (a) All musicians are creative people.
    (b) No square is a triangle.

15. Draw two-set Venn diagrams illustrating the following statements and use symbols to represent the relationship between the two sets.
    (a) All parallelograms are quadrilaterals.
    (b) No man is an island.

16. (a) Write a sentence describing the set relationship shown in the figure.

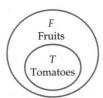

    (b) Use symbols to represent the relationship between sets $F$ and $T$.

17. Let $U = \{$all adults$\}$, $T = \{$adults who watch television$\}$, and $R = \{$adults who read books$\}$.

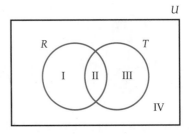

    Which region (I, II, III, or IV) of the Venn diagram contains adults
    (a) who watch television and read?
    (b) who watch television but do not read?
    (c) who do not watch television and do not read?

18. Suppose $P = \{$people who like prunes$\}$, $G = \{$people who like grapes$\}$, and $R = \{$people who like raspberries$\}$. The regions of a Venn diagram of sets $P$, $G$, and $R$ are labeled 1–8.

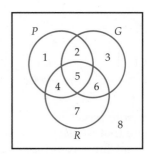

    Which region or regions would contain
    (a) your name?
    (b) people who like raspberries and grapes?
    (c) people who like raspberries and grapes but not prunes?
    (d) people who like raspberries?
    (e) people who like raspberries but not grapes?

19. Consider a set of attribute blocks. $T = \{$triangles$\}$ and $R = \{$red$\}$.
    (a) What is $T \cup R$?
    (b) What is $T \cap R$?

20. Using the set of attribute blocks described in the lesson, tell which ones would belong in the right-hand section?

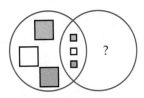

21. Which attribute blocks belong in Sections I, II, III, and IV?

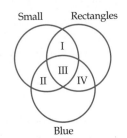

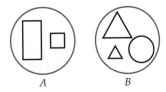

All the attribute pieces in set A have a certain attribute that the shapes in set B do not have. What attribute could this be?

23. The universal set contains all the attribute blocks. Define sets for each Venn diagram so that at least one piece goes in each section.

(a) 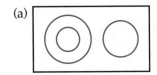          (b)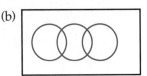

24. Teachers sometimes have children sort keys. Name two different attributes of keys that could be used to sort them.

25.

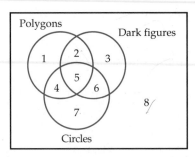

Which region would each figure go in?

(a)  (b)       (c)       (d)

26. You could classify U.S. paper money by the number on the bill or by the person on the bill. What other attributes are used to classify money or coins? Consider other countries and board games, too!

27. True or false?
    (a) If $A \subseteq B$, then $B \subseteq A$.
    (b) $A \cup \emptyset = \emptyset$
    (c) $A \cap \emptyset = \emptyset$
    (d) $0 \in \emptyset$

28. $A = \{1, 2\}$ and $B = \{0, 2, 4, 6\}$
    (a) $A \times B =$ _____
    (b) How many ordered pairs are in $A \times B$?

29. Find sets A and B so that $A \times B$ has 6 members.

30. Lois has 2 different skirts and 6 different shirts. How many possible shirt-skirt outfits can she create?

31. Chef Robert is making a dinner with an appetizer, entree, and vegetable. He will choose his menu from 3 appetizers, 6 entrees, and 5 vegetables. How many different menus can he create?

32. The Cartesian product, $A \times B$, is {(Joe, Mary), (Joe, Elisa), (Marco, Mary), (Marco, Elisa)}. What are the elements of sets A and B?

*Extension Exercises*

**33.**

Reprinted with special permission of NAS, Inc. © Field Enterprises, Inc., 1976.

   (a) What do the percentages add up to?

   (b) Why could the percentages add up to more than 100% and the data still be correct?

**34.** $W$ is the set of overweight people, $S$ the set of cigarette smokers, and $E$ the set of people who exercise regularly. Describe the following sets in words.

   (a) $W \cap S$       (b) $W \cup S$

   (c) $W \cap S \cap E$

**35.** $U$ is the set of all college students, $M$ the set of male college students, $F$ the set of female college students, $E$ the set of education majors, and $Y$ the set of college students under 22 years of age.

   (a) Describe $E \cap F$ in words.

   (b) $M \cup F =$ _____

   (c) $M \cap F =$ _____

**36.** Results of a survey asking people about their preferred alcoholic beverage are shown below.

| Age | Don't Drink (N) | Drink Beer or Wine (B) | Drink Hard Liquor (H) |
|---|---|---|---|
| 18–30 (Y) | 40 | 42 | 18 |
| 31–55 (M) | 26 | 46 | 28 |
| over 55 (E) | 21 | 43 | 36 |

Using the letters in parentheses from the table to represent each set, tell how many people are in each of the following sets.

   (a) $Y$      (b) $E \cap B$    (c) $M \cap N$

   (d) $Y \cup M$   (e) $N$      (f) $Y \cup M \cup E$

**37.** Blood-types can be illustrated by a Venn diagram. There are three antigens, A, B, and Rh, that may or may not be present in any human's blood. If you have the A antigen or B antigen in your blood, that letter appears in your blood-type. If you have the Rh antigen in your blood, a plus sign (+) appears in your blood-type.

But if you have neither the A nor the B antigen in your blood, the letter O appears in your blood type, and if you don't have Rh, a minus sign (−) appears in your blood-type. You probably wonder how anyone ever made up this system to type blood. I wonder too.

   (a) The blood-types can be shown nicely in a Venn diagram. I started it for you. Fill in the types in the other regions.

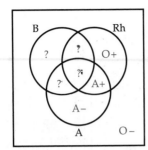

(b) The approximate percentages of each blood-type in the world are as follows.

|   | A | O | B | AB |
|---|---|---|---|---|
| + | 37% | 32% | 11% | 5% |
| − | 6% | 6.5% | 2% | 0.5% |

Fill these percentages in the appropriate regions of the Venn diagram.

(c) The following chart can be used for transfusions.

| Blood-type | Can Receive |
|---|---|
| O | A, B, AB, O |
| A | A, AB |
| B | B, AB |
| AB | AB |

Which blood-type is the "universal donor"?

**38.** (a) At a college, 90% of all first-year students take English and 80% take mathematics. What is the minimum percentage of students who take both subjects?

(b) At the same college, 75% of the first-year students take social science. What is the minimum percentage of students who take all three subjects?

**39.** The shaded area represents

(a) $B \cap C$

(b) $(A \cap B) \cup (B \cap C)$

(c) $(B \cup A) \cap C$

(d) $(B \cap C) \cap B$

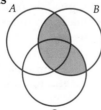

**40.** $C$ is the interior of the circle, $S$ is the interior of the square, and $H$ is the interior of the hexagon. Shade $(C \cap S) \cup (C \cap H)$.

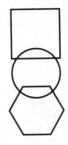

**41.** How can you create a one-to-one correspondence between the points of $\overline{AC}$ and the points of $\overline{AB} \cup \overline{BC}$?

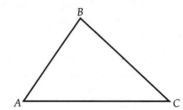

**42.** Assume that the following information is true.

$A \subseteq B$     $B \subseteq C$     $a \in A$
$b \in B$     $c \in C$     $d \notin B$

Which of the following must be true?

(a) $a \in C$     (b) $b \in A$     (c) $c \notin A$
(d) $A \subseteq C$     (e) $d \notin A$

**43.** The counting numbers 1, 2, 3, 4, 5, 6, and 7 can be placed in the 7 regions of a three-set Venn diagram so that the 4 numbers in each circle have the same sum. See if you can complete the diagram.

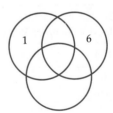

# Summary

Sets are an organizing concept in mathematics. In elementary-school arithmetic, one examines the operations and properties of sets of numbers. Geometric shapes can also be grouped into sets according to various characteristics such as the number of sides. In statistics, data are collected in sets. In probability, one studies sets of possible outcomes.

Sets can be represented by a list of elements, a verbal description, or symbols. In studying two sets, one may want to compare their elements. If one set is contained in the other, then it is a subset of the other set.

One can operate on two sets to create a third set that is related to the other two. The intersection of two sets contains all objects that are in both sets. The union of two sets contains all objects that are in one set or the other set or both. The Cartesian product of two sets creates ordered pairs using the elements of the two sets.

"Children's geometric ideas can be developed by having them sort and classify models of plane and solid figures" (*Curriculum and Evaluation Standards*, NCTM, p. 49) such as attribute blocks. Attribute blocks can also be used within Venn diagrams to give a visual representation of relationships among sets.

# Study Guide

To review Chapter 2, see what you know about each of the following ideas or terms that you have studied. You can also use this list to generate your own questions about Chapter 2.

# The NCTM Curriculum Standards and Sets

**Selected NCTM Curriculum Standards**

The following standards come from the NCTM document.

- Relate physical materials, pictures, and diagrams to mathematical ideas.
- Relate everyday language to mathematical language and symbols.
- Recognize and apply deductive and inductive reasoning.
- Develop common understandings of mathematical ideas, including the role of definitions.

1. Describe how each standard listed relates to the material you studied in Chapter 2.
2. Select any current elementary-school mathematics textbook series and describe a sample lesson or exercise that illustrates each standard listed.

## Review Exercises

1. Draw a Venn diagram illustrating the following statement, and use symbols to represent the relationship between the two sets: "All elementary-school teachers are college graduates."

2. What attribute blocks belong in Section I?

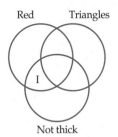

3. Let $R = \{31, 32, 33, 34, 35\}$ and let $W$ be the set of whole numbers. Determine whether the following are true or false.
   (a) $R \subseteq W$   (b) $10 \notin R$   (c) $R \cup W = W$

4. Fill in each blank with $\in$, $\cup$, $\cap$, or $\subseteq$.
   (a) $\{7, 9\}$ _____ $\{7, 9, 10\} = \{7, 9\}$
   (b) $8$ _____ $\{3, 5, 8\}$

5. How many subsets does $\{3, 5, 7\}$ have?

6. This semester, 1000 students registered for classes at a college; 300 of them signed up for math.
   (a) What is the smallest number of students who could have registered for a course other than math?
   (b) What is the largest number of students who could have registered for a course other than math?

7. In which region does each of the following belong?

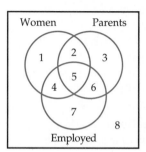

   (a) a 7-year-old boy who plays when he's not in school
   (b) a man with two children who works
   (c) you

8. Use the following information to determine how many households in a community have dogs.
   (1) Seven households only have cats.
   (2) Six households have no pet.
   (3) Two households only have dogs.
   (4) There are no other pets in the community other than cats and dogs.
   (5) There are 18 households.

9. A partition of a set divides it into nonempty proper subsets. Two partitions of the set {1, 2, 3} are shown.

(a) How many different partitions are there of {1, 2, 3}?
(b) How many different partitions are there of {1, 2, 3, 4}?

## Computer Exercise

1. (a) RUN the following BASIC program a few times, inputting different numbers each time.

   ```
   10 PRINT "TYPE A WHOLE NUMBER
   AND PRESS RETURN/ENTER."

   20 INPUT N
   30 IF N > 9 AND N < 100 THEN PRINT
   N
   ```

   (b) What numbers will this program print?
   (c) Change AND to OR in line 30 to create a new program. Predict which numbers it will print. Then RUN the program a few times to check your hypothesis.

## Sets in Elementary School

While set language is used in all areas of mathematics, set theory is not currently studied in most elementary schools as it was in the 1960s and early 1970s. The following chart shows at what grade level set topics typically appear in elementary-school mathematics textbooks.

| Topic | Typical Grade Level in Current Textbooks |
|---|---|
| One-to-one correspondence | 1 |
| Venn diagrams | 4, 5, 6 (enrichment topic) |

## Suggested Readings

Eves, Howard. *Great Moments in Mathematics After 1650*. Washington, DC: Mathematical Association of America, 1983.

Goodnow, J. *Moving on with Attribute Blocks*. Oak Lawn, IL: Creative Publications, 1989.

National Council of Teachers of Mathematics. 1964 Yearbook. *Topics in Mathematics for Elementary School Teachers*. Reston, VA: NCTM, 1964.

Vilenkin, N. *Stories about Sets*. New York, NY: Academic Press, 1969.

# 3

# Whole Numbers

Many of us take whole numbers for granted not fully appreciating that whole numbers have many significant applications, and that they provide the basis for working with fractions, decimals, and integers. Whole numbers help us locate streets and houses. They help us keep track of how many bananas we have. And in a country with about 250 million people, they help us keep track of the federal budget and the rate of unemployment.

## 3.1 Numeration Systems

Today most countries use the simple, efficient base-ten place-value system. Simple as it appears, it took thousands of years to develop. Using place value and a base, one can express amounts in the hundreds or thousands with only a few digits! Big deal, you say? Try writing a number such as 70 using tally marks (see Figure 3-1 on facing page).

### The History of Numeration Systems

People first used numbers to count objects. Before people understood the abstract idea of a number such as "four," they associated the number 4 with sets of objects such as four cows or four stars. A major breakthrough occurred when people began to think of "four" as an abstract quantity that could measure the size of a variety of concrete sets.

No one knows for sure, but the first numeration system was probably a tally system. The first nine numbers would have been written as follows.

A system such as this, having only one symbol, is very simple, but large numbers are difficult to read and write. Computation with large numbers is also slow.

98

Five thousand years ago, even before your professors were born, the ancient Egyptians improved the tally system by inventing additional symbols for 10, 100, 1000, and so on. Symbols for numbers are called **numerals.** Most of our knowledge about Egyptian numerals comes from the Moscow Papyrus (1850? B.C.) and the Rhind Papyrus (1650 B.C.).

Egyptian numerals are rather pretty symbols called hieroglyphics (see Figure 3-2). Using symbols for groups as well as for single objects was a major advance that made it possible to represent large quantities much more easily. The ancient Egyptian numeration system uses ten as a **base,** since the symbols represent the powers of ten: $10^0$, $10^1$, $10^2$, $10^3$, and so on. The Egyptian system is **additive,** since the value of a number is the sum of the values of the numerals. 99||| represents 100 + 100 + 1 + 1 + 1, or 203.

| Egyptian Numerals | | Value |
|---|---|---|
| / | (staff) | 1 |
| ∩ | (heel bone) | 10 |
| 9 | (scroll or coil of rope) | 100 |
| ⚱ | (lotus flower) | 1,000 |
| ⌐ | (pointing finger) | 10,000 |
| ⌒ | (tadpole or fish) | 100,000 |
| ☩ | (astonished man) | 1,000,000 |

**Figure 3-2**

**Figure 3-1**

**D** Lesson Exercise 3.1

(a) Speculate as to why the Egyptians chose some of the symbols shown in Figure 3-2.
(b) Write 635 using Egyptian numerals.

You can see from Lesson Exercise 3.1 (b) that the early Egyptian system requires more symbols than our base-ten system. The Egyptians later shortened their notation by creating single symbols for each number from 1 to 9 and for each multiple of 10 from 10 to 90, as shown in Figure 3-3.

Thus, 7 changed from ||||||| to Z. This change necessitated memorizing more symbols, but it significantly shortened the notation (Figure 3-4).

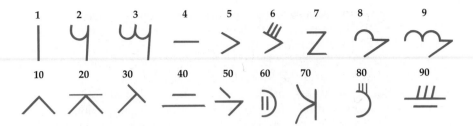

Figure 3-3

The Babylonians made another significant improvement by developing a system based on **place value,** in which the value of a numeral changed according to its position. A place-value system reduces the number of different symbols needed.

$$\text{⟨⟨⟨⟨⟨⟨⟨⟨}_{672} \qquad \text{⟨⟨⟨⟨⟨⟨⟨⟨⟨}_{4372}$$

Figure 3-4

In the improved Egyptian system, 672 required eight symbols and 4372 required nine. The Babylonians shortened these numerals by using place value for numbers greater than 59, base 60, and two symbols: $<$ for 10 and $\Upsilon$ for 1.

Since $<\Upsilon$ represents 11 and $<\Upsilon\Upsilon$ represents 12, $<\Upsilon<\Upsilon\Upsilon$ could represent eleven 60's plus twelve 1's, or $11 \cdot 60 + 12 \cdot 1 = 672$. $\Upsilon<\Upsilon<\Upsilon\Upsilon$ could represent $1 \cdot 60^2 + 11 \cdot 60 + 12 = 4372$. These examples of Babylonian numerals require fewer symbols than the corresponding Egyptian numerals.

The 3800-year-old tablet in Figure 3-5 shows Babylonian numerals.

## Lesson Exercise 3.2

What base-ten numeral could represent the same number as $\Upsilon\Upsilon<<\Upsilon\Upsilon\Upsilon<<<<$ ?

The Babylonians lacked a symbol for zero until 300 B.C. Before that time, it was impossible to distinguish between certain numerals. For example, 83 and 3623 are $1 \cdot 60 + 23$ and $1 \cdot 60^2 + 23$, both written as $\Upsilon<<\Upsilon\Upsilon\Upsilon$. While the Babylonians sometimes put a space between groupings to indicate an empty place, this was not always done.

The University Museum, University of Pennsylvania (neg. #69434).

**Figure 3-5**

Around 300 B.C., the Babylonians invented ⚈ as a separation symbol. The expression $1 \cdot 60^2 + 23$ was then written as 𝒀⚈ ≪ 𝒀𝒀𝒀. Even then, they did not use ⚈ on the right, so 1 and 60 were both written as 𝒀.

## Lesson Exercise 3.3

Which system requires memorizing the smallest number of different symbols?
(a) the tally system      (d) the Babylonian system
(b) the early Egyptian system      (e) our base-ten system
(c) the late Egyptian system

Between them, the Egyptians and Babylonians developed the foundations of our numeration system: a set base (10), unique symbols for one through nine, place value, and a symbol for zero.

## Our Base-Ten Place-Value System

Between A.D. 200 and 1000, the Hindus and Arabs developed the base-ten numeration system we use today, which is appropriately known as the **Hindu-Arabic** numeration system. The Hindus, around A.D. 600, were the first to treat 0 not only as a place holder but also as a separate numeral.

## Lesson Exercise 3.4

Which numeration system generally uses the smallest total number of symbols to represent large numbers?

(a) the tally system
(b) the early Egyptian system
(c) the late Egyptian system
(d) the Babylonian system
(e) our Hindu-Arabic system

We use a base-ten place-value (Hindu-Arabic) system to represent any member of the set of whole numbers, $W = \{0, 1, 2, 3, \ldots\}$. The Hindu-Arabic system has three important features: (1) a symbol for zero, (2) a way to represent any whole number using some combination of ten basic symbols (called **digits**), and (3) **base-ten place value,** in which each digit in a numeral, according to its position, is multiplied by a specific power of ten. Each place has ten times the value of the place immediately to its right.

The following diagram shows the first four place values for whole numbers, starting with the "ones" place on the far right.

| T | H | T | O |
|---|---|---|---|
| h | u | e | n |
| o | n | n | e |
| u | d | s | s |
| s | r | | |
| a | e | | |
| n | d | | |
| d | s | | |
| s | | | |
| $(10^3)$ | $(10^2)$ | $(10^1)$ | $(1)$ |
| 3 | 4 | 2 | 6 |

So 3426 is 3 thousands, 4 hundreds, 2 tens, and 6 ones. This **expanded notation** shows the value of each place. The numeral 3426 can also be written in expanded notation as

$$3 \times 1000 + 4 \times 100 + 2 \times 10 + 6$$

or

$$3 \times 10^3 + 4 \times 10^2 + 2 \times 10^1 + 6$$

## Lesson Exercise 3.5

A number has digits $\underline{A}\ \underline{B}\ \underline{C}$. Write this numeral in expanded notation.

## Lesson Exercise 3.6

What is the difference between a place-value numeration system such as the Hindu-Arabic system and a system such as the Egyptian system that does not have place value?

You may be so accustomed to using place value that you don't give it a second thought. The early Babylonians and Romans made some use of place value in their systems. Our own place-value system was first developed by the Hindus and was significantly improved by the Arabs.

Until the twelfth century, the abacus was the most convenient tool for doing computations. At that time, paper became more readily available, offering a new material for doing arithmetic. A battle ensued from 1100 to 1500 between the *abacists,* who wanted to use Roman numerals, and an abacus, and the *algorists,* who wanted to use the Hindu-Arabic numerals and to work on paper. By 1500, the algorists had prevailed.

## Models for Place Value

To understand and communicate mathematical concepts, one must be able to relate concrete and pictorial models to abstract ideas. For example, children learn about base ten using a variety of concrete materials such as Dienes blocks. Dienes blocks for base ten come in the shapes shown in Figure 3-6.

| Block | Name | Value |
|-------|------|-------|
|  | Unit | 1 |
|  | Long | 10 |
|  | Flat | 100 |
|  | Block | 1000 |

**Figure 3-6**

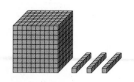

**Figure 3-7**

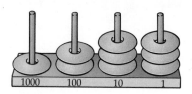

**Figure 3-8**

## Lesson Exercise 3.7

What number is represented in Figure 3-7?

Another widely used place-value model is the abacus. A simplified abacus like the one shown in Figure 3-8 may be used in elementary school after children have had experience with more concrete models, such as base-ten blocks. The abacus in Figure 3-8 shows 1233.

## Lesson Exercise 3.8

What makes the abacus more abstract than base-ten blocks?

The abacus was developed over 2400 years ago as a calculating device. Today, many people still use an abacus for computation.

### Rounding

### 24,000 Attend U-2 Concert

If you recently read about attendance at a concert or looked up the population of the world, you probably read an approximate, or rounded, figure. A number is always rounded to a specific place (for example, to the nearest thousand). The following exercise concerns rounding of whole numbers between 24,000 and 25,000.

## Lesson Exercise 3.9

(a) If a whole number between 24,000 and 25,000 is closer to 24,000, what digits could be in the hundreds place?
(b) If a whole number between 24,000 and 25,000 is closer to 25,000, what digits could be in the hundreds place?

As you saw in the preceding exercise, numbers between 24,000 and 24,500 are closer to 24,000 than to 25,000, and they have 0, 1, 2, 3, or 4 in the hundreds place. In rounding to the nearest thousand, these numbers would be rounded *down* to 24,000. However, numbers that are between 24,500 and 25,000, such as 24,589, would be rounded *up* to 25,000 because they are closer to 25,000 than to 24,000. All of these numbers have 5, 6, 7, 8, or 9 in the hundreds place.

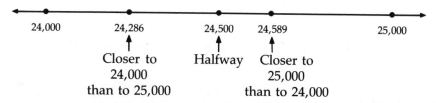

The number 24,500 is exactly halfway between 24,000 and 25,000, so it could be rounded either way. The rule used in our schools is to round up all such numbers that are exactly in the middle.

---

**Rounding Whole Numbers**

Rules for rounding a whole number to a specific place:

1. Locate the place and then check the digit one place to its right.

2. Round *up* if the digit to the right is 5 or more, and round *down* if it is 4 or less.

---

## Lesson Exercise 3.10

Exactly 386,212 people attended a rock concert given by the Earaches.
(a) Round this number to the nearest thousand.
(b) Use a number line to show that your answer makes sense.

## Lesson Exercise 3.11

A newspaper headline says "83,000 SEE KITTENS DEFEAT THE DUST BUNNIES." If this is a rounded figure the actual attendance could have been between what two numbers?

---

Whole-number rounding will be used in estimation later in this chapter.

## Answers to Lesson Exercises

3.1 (a) A staff would have been something the Egyptians would have used in traveling. The scroll relates to their development of papyrus. The lotus flower, tadpoles, and fish would have been found in a culture that developed around the Nile River. The astonished man is amazed by the amount of 1,000,000.

(b) 𝟗𝟗𝟗𝟗𝟗𝟗∩∩‖‖‖

3.2 8620

3.3 (a)

3.4  (e)

3.5  $100 \times A + 10 \times B + C$

3.6  In a place-value system, the value of a numeral changes depending upon its location. In a system that does not have place value, the value of a numeral is always the same.

3.7  1030

3.8  The abacus distinguishes place value using position but not size. Base-ten blocks do use size.

3.9  (a) 0, 1, 2, 3, or 4       (b) 5, 6, 7, 8, or 9

3.10 (a) 386,000

(b)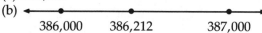

386,000      386,212          387,000

3.11 82,500 and 83,499 (inclusive) if attendance is rounded to the nearest thousand

## 3.1   Homework Exercises

### Basic Exercises

1. Tell whether each word in quotes is used like a numeral (that is, as a symbol) or like a number (an idea).
   (a) "Cat" is a three-letter word.
   (b) A "cat" is a warm, furry animal.

2. Write the following Egyptian numerals as Hindu-Arabic numerals.

   (a) 𓏺𓏺𓃾𓃾𓃾𓃾   (b) 𓏤𓏼𓏦

3. Write 328 as an early Egyptian numeral.

4. What are three important characteristics of our base-ten numeration system?

5. (a) Do both of the following Egyptian numerals represent the same number?

   𓃾𓏦 𓏦𓃾

   (b) What difference between Egyptian and Hindu-Arabic numerals is suggested by part (a)?

6. Recall that the basic Roman numerals have base-ten values as follows.

| Roman numeral | I | V | X | L | C | D | M |
|---|---|---|---|---|---|---|---|
| Hindu-Arabic numeral | 1 | 5 | 10 | 50 | 100 | 500 | 1000 |

In using Roman numerals, one adds the value of a symbol written to the right of a symbol of equal or greater value. When I, X, or C occurs to the left of a symbol of greater value, one subtracts the value of the I, X, or C. For example, XI is 11 and IX is 9.
(a) Give the Hindu-Arabic numeral for MDCCCCLIX.
(b) Give the Hindu-Arabic numeral for CXL.
(c) Write 472 (base ten) as a Roman numeral.

7. How many symbols would be needed to write 642 using each of the following?
(a) tallies
(b) late Egyptian numerals
(c) Roman numerals

8. Write the following base-ten numbers using expanded notation.
(a) 407      (b) 3125

9. A base-ten numeral has the digits $\underline{A}\ \underline{B}\ \underline{C}\ \underline{D}$. Write this numeral using expanded notation.

10. A base-ten numeral has the digits $\underline{A}\ \underline{A}\ \underline{A}$. The value of the $A$ at the far left is _____ times the value of the $A$ at the far right.

11. Rewrite each of the following as a base-ten numeral.
(a) $(8 \times 10^3) + (6 \times 10) + 2$
(b) $(2 \times 10^4) + (3 \times 10^3) + (4 \times 10^2) + 5$

12. What number is represented in each part?

(a)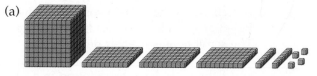

(b) 2 flats and 7 units

13. What number is represented?

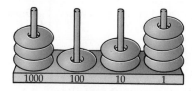

14. How would you represent 380 using base-ten blocks?

15. Chip trading is another common place-value model. Chip trading uses colored chips and a mat. In base ten, the columns on the mat represent powers of ten. For example, 4523 is represented by 4 red, 5 green, 2 blue, and 3 yellow chips.

| Red | Green | Blue | Yellow |
|-----|-------|------|--------|
| 4   | 5     | 2    | 3      |

(a) How would you represent 372?
(b) Ten blue chips can be traded in for one _____ chip.
(c) Which is more abstract, chip trading or base-ten blocks? Explain why.

16. If you counted using hands and fingers, you could represent 8 by "1 hand and 3 fingers." How would you represent 12 (base ten) in the hand-finger system?

17. Round the following numbers to the nearest hundred.
(a) $625, the price of lunch for two at La Vielle Chaussure
(b) $36,412, the one-game salary of a superstar athlete

18. Give the place to which each number has been rounded.

| | Original Number | Rounded Number |
|-----|------|---------|
| (a) | 418  | 420     |
| (b) | 418  | 400     |
| (c) | 368,272 | 370,000 |

19. The 1980 population of Cleveland was 1,898,825. Round this number to the nearest million.

20. About 8000 people attended a baseball game. If this figure has been rounded to the nearest thousand, the actual attendance was between what two numbers?

21. If the quarterback is right, what is the largest number of people that could be there watching?

© 1991, Carchria Biological Supply Company

22. Match the amount in each part with one of the following estimates.

4    40    400    4,000
4,000,000    400,000,000

(a) the number of students in a typical elementary school
(b) the population of Chicago
(c) the number of miles an adult can walk in an hour
(d) the distance, in miles, from Boston to San Diego
(e) the population of North America

**23.** What is the largest number you can enter into your calculator?

*Extension Exercises*

**24.** Using 10 of the largest Dienes block shape you have, you can form a new larger shape.
  (a) Describe how you would form a 10,000 piece.
  (b) Is a 10,000 piece a cube, a long, or a flat?
  (c) Describe how you would form a 100,000 piece.
  (d) Is a 100,000 piece a cube, a long, or a flat?

**25.** Write a ten-digit numeral in which the first digit tells the number of zeroes in the numeral, the second digit tells the number of 1's, the third digit tells the number of 2's, and so on. (*Hint:* There are no 8's or 9's in the numeral.)

**26.** Consider the following problem: "A number is called a palindrome if it reads the same forwards and backwards; for example, 33 and 686. How many palindromes are there between 1 and 1000 (inclusive)?"
  (a) Devise a plan and solve the problem.
  (b) Make up a similar problem and solve it.

**27.** Computers use base two, not base ten. Counting is done in groups of two, and only two different digits, 0 and 1, are used. Computers are composed of electronic "switches," which are represented by either a 1 (meaning "on") or a 0 ("off"). For example,

| Base-Two Place Value | | | |
|---|---|---|---|
| Eights $2^3$ | Fours $2^2$ | Twos $2^1$ | Ones 1 |
| | 1 | 0 | 1 |

So $101_{\text{base two}} = 5$ (base ten).
  (a) Write $1101_{\text{two}}$ as a base-ten numeral.
  (b) Write 17 (base ten) as a base-two numeral.
  (c) $1011_{\text{two}} + 111_{\text{two}} = $ _____ (base two).

**28.** In base seven, one counts in groups of seven.
  (a) What digits would base seven use?
  (b) Complete the place values for base seven.

| | | Sevens | Ones |
|---|---|---|---|
| | | $7^1$ | 1 |

  (c) Write $346_{\text{seven}}$ as a base-ten numeral.
  (d) Write 251 (base ten) as a base-seven numeral.

**29.** Writing a time using hours, minutes, and seconds is comparable to using what base?

**30.** Some of Jasper Johns' paintings are composed of numerals. Find examples of his work with numerals and write a few sentences describing each example.

---

## 3.2  Addition and Subtraction of Whole Numbers

Addition and subtraction involve more than computing $3 + 6$ or $63 - 27$. Computational skills are not useful unless you know when to use them in solving problems. Children should learn how to recognize situations that call for addition or subtraction.

## Addition Definition and Closure

In elementary school, teachers explain what addition is by giving examples. Later on, one can formally define important ideas such as addition. The idea of combining sets (that is, union) is used to define addition. An example would be if you combined 2 fresh bananas with 3 older bananas to obtain a total of 5 bananas.

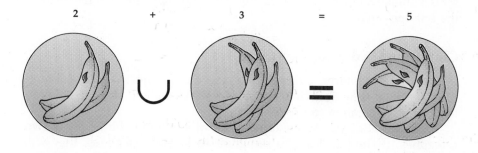

> **Definition: Whole-Number Addition**
>
> If set $A$ contains $a$ elements, set $B$ contains $b$ elements, and $A \cap B = \emptyset$, then $a + b$ is the number of elements in $A \cup B$.

In the addition equation $a + b = c$, $a$ and $b$ are called **addends**, and $c$ is called the **sum**. The + ("plus") sign first appeared in print in 1489 as a symbol for an excess amount. The Dutch mathematician Vander Hoecke used the + sign for addition (and the − sign for subtraction) in 1574.

## Lesson Exercise 3.12

(a) If one adds any two whole numbers, is the result always a whole number?

(b) Would a whole-number addition problem ever have more than one answer?

Your responses to the preceding exercise should confirm that the sum of two whole numbers is a unique whole number. For example, $3 + 5$ equals 8, a unique whole number. This is called the closure property of addition for whole numbers.

> **The Closure Property of Addition of Whole Numbers**
>
> If $a$ and $b$ are whole numbers, then $a + b$ is a unique whole number.

**Closure** requires that the result of an operation on two members of a set is a unique member of the same set, "unique" meaning that the result is the only possibility.

## Classifying Addition Applications

Research with children indicates that the most difficult aspect of word problems in arithmetic is choosing the correct operation. How do children learn which operation to use?

Consider addition. Many applications of addition fall into one of two categories. If children learn to recognize these two categories, they will recognize most real-world problems that call for addition. The following exercise will introduce you to the classification of addition applications.

**D** Lesson Exercise 3.13

Make up two word problems that can be solved by adding 3 and 5.

Do your word problems fit into one of the following categories? Many addition applications do.

1. **Combine Sets**   Combine two nonintersecting sets and find out how many objects are in the new set.

   *Example:*   Tina has 3 cute beagle puppies and Maddy has 5. How many puppies do they have altogether (Figure 3-9)?

   Figure 3-9

2. **Combine Measures**   Combine two measures of the same type and find the total measure.

   *Example:* Laura is going to Paris for 3 days and to London for 5 days. How long is the whole trip (Figure 3-10)?

**Figure 3-10**

The difference between categories 1 and 2 is the difference between "sets" and "measures." Set problems involve objects that *can be counted* with whole numbers, objects such as apples, dogs, and people. Measure problems involve measures such as distance, weight, and time, which are not limited to having whole number values. Most arithmetic applications can be classified as either set problems or measure problems.

Not all addition applications fit into the "combine sets" or "combine measures" categories, but these categories identify specific characteristics of addition applications. Children learn to recognize these two addition categories in elementary school. Although your future students may not learn the terms combine sets and combine measures, these categories will help you (the teacher) to identify more specifically what your students do or do not understand. For example, a child may know what 2 + 4 equals but may not be able to recognize combining sets as an addition situation.

## Lesson Exercise 3.14

Classify the addition situation in the cartoon in Figure 3-11.

By permission of Johnny Hart and Creators Syndicate, Inc.

**Figure 3-11**

## Lesson Exercise 3.15

Classify the following addition application: "Hy Climber climbs to an altitude of 3600 ft. If he climbs 400 more feet, what is his new altitude?"

Teachers first model the concepts of combining sets and combining measures for children using manipulatives (objects) and pictures. Manipulatives and pictures establish connections between addition and everyday applications of it.

### Example 3.1

Explain the solution to Lesson Exercise 3.14 using a set of identical blocks and relate it to addition.

**Solution**

Take 2 blocks. Then take 3 more. How many altogether? 5. This illustrates $2 + 3 = 5$. ■

## Lesson Exercise 3.16

Show how to solve Lesson Exercise 3.15 using a number line and relate the result to addition.

As Example 3.1 and Lesson Exercise 3.16 suggest, problems involving combining sets can be represented with a set of identical objects, and problems involving combining length measures can be represented with a number line.

A major intellectual breakthrough occurred when people realized that addition applies to all kinds of objects. The equation $3 + 4 = 7$ describes a relationship that applies to sets of people, apples, and rocks. The power of mathematics lies in the way we can apply basic ideas like addition to such a wide variety of situations.

Using addition with many different kinds of sets also has its drawbacks. Numbers emphasize similarities between different situations. People must then make allowances for differences in the *qualities* of the living things or objects being analyzed. While 3 peaches plus 4 peaches is the same mathematically as 3 bombs plus 4 bombs, peaches and bombs are rather different.

## Lesson Exercise 3.17

Angela has 2 apples and buys 3 more. Now she has 5 apples. What information about the apples is ignored in this description?

## Subtraction Definition

In school, children learn how subtraction is related to addition.

## Lesson Exercise 3.18

Name an addition equation that is equivalent to $6 - 2 = 4$.

In answering Lesson Exercise 3.18, you used the following definition to convert a subtraction equation into an equivalent addition equation.

---

**Definition: Whole-Number Subtraction**

For any whole numbers $a$ and $b$, $a - b = c$ if and only if $a = b + c$ for a unique whole number $c$.

---

In the subtraction equation $a - b = c$, $c$ is called the **difference**. You can illustrate the relationship between addition and subtraction with a diagram.

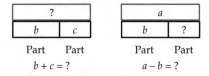

| ? |
|---|
| $b$ | $c$ |

Part    Part

$b + c = ?$

| $a$ |
|---|
| $b$ | ? |

Part    Part

$a - b = ?$

Because of this relationship, subtraction is called the inverse operation of addition. Although subtraction is defined by using addition, most children first understand subtraction as the process of removing objects from a set.

## Classifying Subtraction Applications

Children can learn to recognize applications that call for subtraction by recognizing the common categories of these applications.

**D** Lesson Exercise 3.19

---

Make up two word problems that can be solved by subtracting 2 from 6. Try to create two different types of problems.

---

Do your problems fit into any of the following categories?

1. **Take Away Sets**   Take away some objects from a set of objects.

   *Example:* Dan had 6 pet fish. Two of them died. How many are left (Figure 3-12)?

**Figure 3-12**

2. **Take Away Measures**   Take away a certain measure from a given measure.

   *Example:* A lumberjack has 10 ft of rope. He uses 6 ft of rope to tie some logs. How much rope is left (Figure 3-13)?

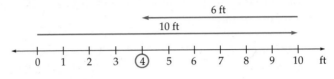

   Figure 3-13

Figure 3-14

| 56 in. | |
|---|---|
| 51 in. | ? |

Figure 3-15

3. **Compare Sets**   Find how many more objects one set has than another.

   *Example:* Maria has 6 cuddly kittens and Pete has 2. How many more kittens does Maria have than Pete (Figure 3-14)?

4. **Compare Measures**   Find how much larger one measure is than another.

   *Example:* Sue is 56 inches tall. Twelve months ago, she was 51 inches tall. How much has Sue grown in the last year (Figure 3-15)?

Once they learn to recognize these four types of subtraction situations, children will usually know when to use subtraction in solving problems.

   In Lesson Exercises 3.20 and 3.21, classify each subtraction application.

## Lesson Exercise 3.20

Hy Climber climbs to an altitude of 3600 ft. The summit is at 4000 ft. How much further does he have to climb?

## Lesson Exercise 3.21

The following is a true story. I used to have 3 umbrellas. I no longer have 2 of them. I lost 1 on the subway and the other to an early internal breakdown. How many umbrellas do I have now?

   The take-away and compare models of subtraction are usually introduced with manipulatives and pictures in elementary school.

## Lesson Exercise 3.22

*Explain* how to solve Lesson Exercise 3.20 using a number line and tell what arithmetic equation it illustrates.

## An Investigation: Number Chains

### Lesson Exercise 3.23

A **number chain** is created by adding and subtracting. The number in each square in Figure 3-16 is the sum of the numbers on either side of it.

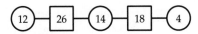

**Figure 3-16**

What is the relationship between the far-left-hand and far-right-hand numbers on the number chain in Figure 3-17?

**Figure 3-17**

(a) *Understanding the Problem*  If you put 10 in the far-left-hand circle, what number results in the far-right-hand circle?

(b) *Devising and Carrying Out a Plan*  Try some other numbers in the far-left-hand circle and fill in the remaining circles. Look for a pattern.

(c) Make a generalization of your results from part (b).

(d) *Looking Back*  Did you use inductive or deductive reasoning in part (c)?

(e) Start with $X$ in the far-left-hand circle and fill in all the other circles to prove your conjecture in part (c).

### Lesson Exercise 3.24

Consider the number chain in Figure 3-18.
(a) Fill in the circles with numbers that work.
(b) If possible, find a second solution.
(c) Start with $X$ in the upper-left-hand circle and fill in all the circles.
(d) What does your answer in part (c) tell you about the relationship between the numbers in opposite corners?

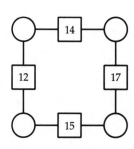

**Figure 3-18**

## Answers to Selected Lesson Exercises

3.12 (a) yes     (b) no

3.13 See the examples that follow Lesson Exercise 3.13.

3.14 combine sets

3.15 combine measures

3.16 Go to 3600 ft. Go up 400 ft more. You end up at 4000 ft. This illustrates that 3600 ft + 400 ft = 4000 ft.

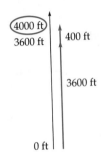

3.17 Are they fresh? What kind of apples are they? How much did she pay? What will she do with them? Were they sprayed with pesticides?

3.18 2 + 4 = 6

3.19 See the examples that follow Lesson Exercise 3.19.

3.20 compare measures

3.21 take away sets

3.22 Hy is at 3600 ft and he wants to reach 4000 ft. How much higher is 4000 ft than 3600 ft? 400 ft. So 4000 − 3600 = 400 ft.

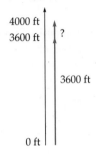

3.23 (a) 23     (d) inductive

## 3.2  Homework Exercises

### Basic Exercises

1. Which of the following sets are closed under addition?
   (a) {2, 4, 6, 8, . . . }
   (b) {1, 3, 5, 7, . . . }
   (c) {0, 1}

2. Which category of addition, combine sets or combine measures, is illustrated in the following problem? "Mary sold 61 apples yesterday and 48 apples today. How many apples did she sell in the last two days?"

3. The Samuels built a house and lived in it for 8 years. They sold it to the Wangs, who have now lived there for 11 years. How old is the house?
   (a) Which category of addition is illustrated?

   (b) Name some other significant information that is not included in the problem.

4. (a) What addition fact is illustrated in the diagram?

   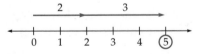

   (b) How would you use a number line to explain to a child why 4 + 2 = 6?

5. (a) What addition fact is illustrated by placing the rods together as shown?

   (b) Which category of addition is illustrated?

6. Use the definition of subtraction to rewrite each of the following subtraction equations as an addition equation.
   (a) $7 - 2 = ?$
   (b) $N - 72 = 37$
   (c) $586 - N = 23$

In Exercises 7 and 8, classify each application as one of the following: take away sets, take away measures, compare sets, or compare measures.

7. Mary is 4 feet, 8 inches tall and Sidney is 4 feet, 3 inches tall. How much taller is Mary?

8. Kong had 14 bananas. Kong ate 3. How many are left?

9. Explain how to solve the preceding exercise using blocks and tell what arithmetic equation it illustrates.

10. (a) What subtraction fact is shown?

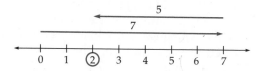

   (b) How would you use a number line to explain $5 - 2 = 3$ to a child?

11. (a) What subtraction fact is illustrated?

   (b) Which category of subtraction is illustrated?

12. (a) What subtraction fact is illustrated?

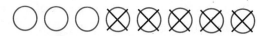

   (b) What category of subtraction is illustrated?

13. Make a drawing showing $8 - 2 = 6$ using
   (a) take away sets.
   (b) compare sets.
   (c) compare measures.

14. If $a - b = c$, then $a - (b + 1) =$ _____.

15. The following two third-grade problems require subtracting 12 from 30. How do they differ in tone?
   (a) Jody Winer has 30 records. She gave 12 to her brother. How many records does she have left?
   (b) Jody Winer has 30 records. Her brother has 12. How many more records does she have than her brother?

16. Is whole-number subtraction closed? (*Hint:* Check the two parts of the closure property.)

17. Explain why you cannot use addition to solve the following problem. "Assume I get 10 units of enjoyment from eating 1 dish of ice cream. How much enjoyment will I get from eating 2 dishes of ice cream?"

18. Explain why you cannot use addition to solve the following problem. "How much is 1 cup of water plus 1 cup of sugar?"

19. What operation and classification are illustrated by the following problem? "A clerk takes 24 cartons of orange juice out of the storeroom. Now 10 cartons are left in the storeroom. How many were there to start with?"

20. What operation and classification are illustrated by the following problem? "A rectangular field is 20 ft by 26 ft. What is its perimeter (distance around the outside)?"

21. Make up a realistic problem illustrating the combine-measures category of addition.

22. Make up a realistic problem illustrating the compare-sets category of subtraction.

23. Write a word problem that requires computing $10 - (3 + 5)$.

24. Solve the following using addition and subtraction: "Margarita starts off with $\$A$. She buys food for $\$F$ and clothes for $\$C$, and then she receives a paycheck for $\$P$. Write an expression representing the total amount of money she has now."

**25.** The political party in power sometimes tries to redraw the boundaries of a voting district in a way that gives it control of a greater number of districts. Find two possible ways to form 4 voting districts containing between 135,000 and 160,000 voters in the region shown. Each precinct must remain intact, and a district cannot contain a region that does not share a common border with at least one other region in that district. The numbers in the diagram represent the population in thousands in each precinct.

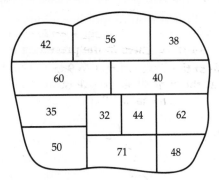

**26.** You are familiar with the "greater than" ($>$) symbol. Did you know that "greater than" can be defined using addition? For whole numbers $a$ and $b$, $a > b$ when $a = b + k$ for some counting number $k$.
(a) Use the definition to show why $8 > 6$.
(b) Write a definition for "less than" ($<$) using subtraction.

**27.** "Less than" and "greater than" can be defined in terms of a number line.

0  1  2  3  4  5  6

(a) For whole numbers $a$ and $b$, $a > b$ means that $a$ is located to the _____
(left, right)
of $b$ on the number line.
(b) Write a similar definition of $a < b$.

*Extension Exercises*

**28.** (a) If possible, write each of the following numbers as the sum of two or more con-

secutive counting numbers. For example, $13 = 6 + 7$ and $14 = 2 + 3 + 4 + 5$.

1 =                6 =
2 =                7 =
3 =                8 =
4 =                9 =
5 =               10 =

(b) Propose a hypothesis regarding what kinds of counting numbers can be written as the sum of two or more consecutive counting numbers.

**29.** Last night, three women checked in at the Quantity Inn and were charged $30 for their room. Later, the desk clerk realized he had charged them a total of $5 too much. He gave the bellperson five $1 bills to bring to the women. The bellperson wanted to save them the trouble of splitting $5 three ways, so she kept $2 and gave them $3.

     Each woman had originally paid $10 and received $1 back. So it cost them $9 apiece. This means they spent $27 plus the $2 "tip." What happened to the other dollar?

**30.** Consider the following problem: "How could you measure 1 oz of syrup using only a 4-oz container and a 7-oz container?"
(a) Devise a plan and solve the problem.
(b) Make up a similar problem.

**31.** Consider the following problem: "Under what conditions for whole numbers $a$, $b$, and $c$ would $(a - b) - c$ be a whole number?"
(a) Devise a plan and solve the problem.
(b) Make up a similar problem.

**32.** It took 600 digits to label the pages of a book starting with page 1. How many pages does the book have?

**33.** Make up a set containing one element that is closed under addition.

**34.** Consider the following problem: "Last year, your salary was $A$ and your expenses were $B$. This year, you received a salary increase of $X$, but your expenses increased by $Y$.

Write an expression showing how much of your salary will be left this year after you have paid all your expenses."

(a) Devise a plan and solve the problem.

(b) Make up a similar problem.

35. All the pairs of whole numbers that add up to 6 comprise a **fact family**.

$$0 + 6, 1 + 5, 2 + 4, 3 + 3, 4 + 2, 5 + 1, 6 + 0$$

(a) Plot the points (0, 6), (1, 5), (2, 4), (3, 3), (4, 2), (5, 1), and (6, 0).

(b) What geometric pattern do you see in the points?

(c) On a separate graph, plot the points for the fact family of 7.

(d) What geometric pattern do you see in the points in part (c)?

(e) Make a generalization based upon your results to parts (b) and (d).

(f) Is part (e) an example of induction or deduction?

36. (a) Find six pairs of solutions to $x - y = 3$ for whole numbers $x$ and $y$.

(b) Graph $x - y = 3$ for whole numbers $x$ and $y$.

(c) Repeat parts (a) and (b) with $x - y = 4$.

(d) Propose a generalization about $x - y = k$, in which $x$, $y$, and $k$ are whole numbers.

37. (a) Draw lines across the clock face that divide it into 3 regions such that the sum of the numbers in each region is the same.

(b) Draw lines across the clock face that divide it into 6 regions such that the sum of the numbers in each region is the same.

38. Consider the following problem: "Place the digits 1 to 9 in the squares so that all horizontal, vertical, and diagonal sums of three numbers equal 15."

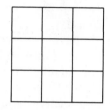

(a) Devise a plan and solve the problem.

(b) Make up a similar problem.

39. Explain why the number 9 could *not* be in one of the corners in the preceding exercise.

40. Fill in the digits from 1 to 9 in the circles so that the sum on each side of the triangle is the same *and* as small as possible.

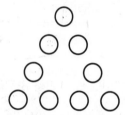

41. Each letter represents a digit. Find a possible solution.

$$
\begin{array}{r}
A \\
A \\
A \\
+ \ B \\
\hline
BA
\end{array}
$$

*Special Exercise*

42. By quantifying characteristics and adding them together, you can estimate your risk of cardiac arrest. Not a cheery topic, but useful to know.

(a) Fill in the following questionnaire adapted from one by The Executive Health Group.

**Risk of Heart Disease**

1. Cigarette smoking
   (0) never          (1) none in past year
   (2) smoked in past year or under 10 a day
   (3) 20 a day      (5) 40 or more a day
2. Family history (parents, grandparents)
   (0) no heart disease before age 75
   (1) one relative with heart disease between age 60 and 75
   (2) two relatives with heart disease between age 60 and 75
   (3) one relative with heart disease under age 60
   (4) two relatives with heart disease under age 60
3. Diabetes (parents, grandparents, siblings)
   (0) none          (1) one relative
   (2) two relatives
   (4) you have diabetes between the age of 20 and 60
4. Exercise
   (subtract 1) regular aerobic exercise
   (0) intense exercise during and after work
   (1) moderate exercise during and after work
   (2) sedentary work and intense recreation
   (3) sedentary work and moderate recreation
   (4) sedentary work and light exercise
   (5) no exercise

5. Disposition
   (0) always easy-going
   (1) usually easy-going
   (2) frequently impatient
   (3) generally aggressive
   (4) constantly ambitious
   (5) hard-driving, angry
6. Age/gender
   (0) under 45, F
   (1) under 40, M
   (2) 45–55, F, or 40–50, M
   (3) over 55, F
   (4) 50–60, M
   (5) over 60, M
7. Blood pressure
   (0) low      (3) medium      (6) high
8. HDL cholesterol (if known)
   (0) under 3      (3) 6 to 7.9
   (1) 3 to 4.5     (4) 8 to 9.9
   (2) 4.6 to 5.9   (5) 10 or over
9. Weight
   (0) not much overweight
   (1) about 10 lb overweight
   (2) about 23 lb overweight
   (3) about 38 lb overweight
   (4) about 53 lb overweight

To obtain your score, add up the numbers of all your choices. The results are as follows: 0–17 (low risk to acceptable), 18–22 (average), 23–32 (above average; try to lower some risk factors), 33 and up (high; consult with a physician).

(b) Which factors in the questionnaire are most under your personal control?

## 3.3  Multiplication and Division of Whole Numbers

Well, what were you expecting to study after addition and subtraction, scuba diving? To understand multiplication and division better, you will classify the kinds of situations that call for multiplication or division. Sound familiar?

## Multiplication Definition

Historically, people developed multiplication as a shortcut for certain addition problems such as 4 + 4 + 4.

### Lesson Exercise 3.25

Write 4 + 4 + 4 as a multiplication problem.

This repeated-addition model of multiplication can be used to define multiplication of whole numbers.

---

**Definition: Whole-Number Multiplication**

For any whole numbers $a$ and $b$ where $a \neq 0$, $a \times b = \underbrace{b + b + \cdots + b}_{a \text{ terms}}$.

If $a = 0$ then $0 \times b = 0$.

---

According to the definition, $3 \times 4 = 4 + 4 + 4$. However, because multiplication is commutative (see Section 3.4), $4 \times 3 = 4 + 4 + 4$ is also an acceptable equation in elementary school. In $a \times b = c$, $a$ and $b$ are called **factors** and $c$ is called the **product.**

An English minister, William Oughtred (1574–1660), created over 150 mathematical symbols, only 3 of which are still in use, the most important being the symbol $\times$ for multiplication. Some seventeenth-century mathematicians objected that the symbol $\times$ for multiplication would be confused with the letter $x$.

### Lesson Exercise 3.26

(a) If you multiply any two whole numbers, is the result always a whole number?
(b) Would a whole-number multiplication problem ever have more than one answer?

Your responses to the preceding exercise should suggest that whole-number multiplication is closed.

---

**The Closure Property of Multiplication of Whole Numbers**

If $a$ and $b$ are whole numbers, then $a \cdot b$ is a unique whole number.

---

### Classifying Multiplication Applications

Multiplication is used in a variety of applications, which usually fall into five categories.

**D** Lesson Exercise 3.27

Make up two word problems that can be solved by computing 3 × 4. Try to create two different types of problems.

Do your problems fit into any of the following categories?

1. **Repeated Sets**  Find the total number of objects given a certain number of equivalent sets, in which each set has the same number of objects.

   *Example:* I bought 3 packages of tomatoes. Each package contained 4 tomatoes. How many tomatoes did I buy (Figure 3-19)?

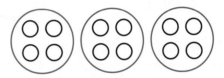

Figure 3-19

2. **Repeated Measures**  Find the total measure that results from repeating a given measure a certain number of times.

   *Example:* On a long car trip, I average 50 miles per hour. How far will I travel in 6 hours (Figure 3-20)?

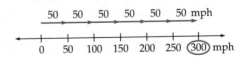

Figure 3-20

3. **Row-by-Column Sets**  Find the total number of objects needed to occupy a given number of rows and columns.

   *Example:* A class has 4 rows of desks with 3 desks in each row. How many desks are there (Figure 3-21)?

Figure 3-21

4. **Row-by-Column Measures** Find the total measure in square units given the number of rows (width) and columns (length) of squares. (This category establishes an important connection between multiplication and area.)

*Example:* A rug is 4 feet by 3 feet. What is its area in square feet (Figure 3-22)?

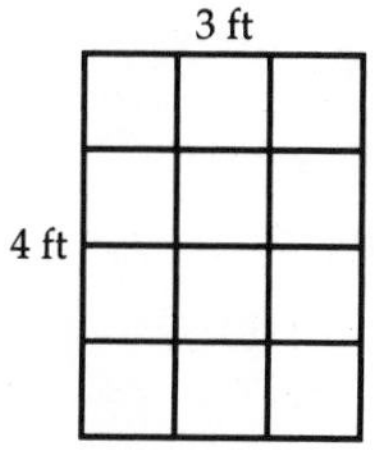

5. **Combinations** Find the total number of different pairs formed by matching any object from one set with any object from a second set.

*Example:* I have 3 shirts and 4 pairs of pants. If all the items match, how many different shirt-pant outfits can I create (Figure 3-23)?

**Figure 3-22**

$$
\begin{array}{cccc}
S_1P_1 & S_1P_2 & S_1P_3 & S_1P_4 \\
S_2P_1 & S_2P_2 & S_2P_3 & S_2P_4 \\
S_3P_1 & S_3P_2 & S_3P_3 & S_3P_4
\end{array}
$$

Organized List

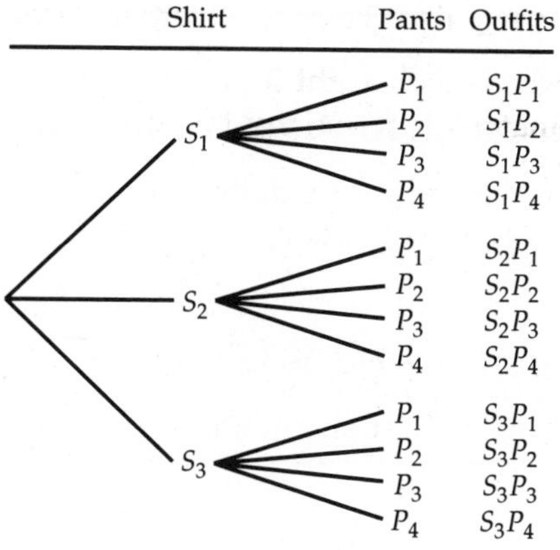

Tree Diagram

**Figure 3-23**

Anyone who can recognize these situations will usually know when to multiply to solve a problem. Lesson Exercises 3.28 and 3.29 will give you practice in recognizing different types of multiplication situations.

## Lesson Exercise 3.28

Classify the following multiplication application: "A juice pack contains 3 cartons of juice. How many cartons are in 4 juice packs?"

## Lesson Exercise 3.29

Classify the following multiplication application: "A rectangular tabletop is 5 feet long and 4 feet wide. What is its area?"

In elementary school, repeated sets, repeated measures, row-by-column sets, and row-by-column measures are usually introduced with manipulatives and pictures.

## Lesson Exercise 3.30

Explain how to solve Lesson Exercise 3.28 using a set of identical blocks and tell what arithmetic equation it illustrates.

## Lesson Exercise 3.31

Explain how to solve Lesson Exercise 3.29 using paper squares and tell what arithmetic equation it illustrates.

## Division Definition

Just as subtraction is defined in terms of addition, division is defined in terms of multiplication.

## Lesson Exercise 3.32

What multiplication equation corresponds to $12 \div 3 = 4$?

In answering Lesson Exercise 3.32, you used the following relationship between multiplication and division.

---

**Definition: Whole-Number Division**

If $x$, $y$, and $q$ are whole numbers, and $y \neq 0$, then $x \div y = q$ if and only if $x = y \cdot q$.

---

In $x \div y = q$, $x$ is called the **dividend,** $y$ is called the **divisor,** and $q$ is called the **quotient.** The division ($\div$) symbol first appeared in print in 1659 in a work by the Swiss mathematician Johann Rahn. The definition of division establishes that division is the inverse operation of multiplication. The connections among whole-number operations are summarized in the following diagram.

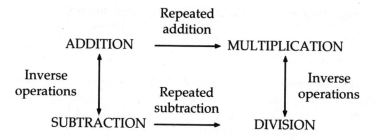

All of these connections have already been discussed, except for division as repeated subtraction. Imagine that a child (who does not know division) has 8 cookies to distribute. She serves 2 cookies per person, and she wants to figure out how many people she can serve. She could use repeated subtraction to determine the answer.

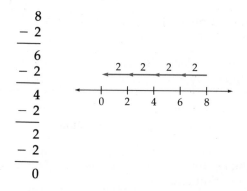

Whole-number division problems such as $8 \div 2$ can be thought of as asking how many times 2 can be subtracted from 8 until nothing remains. The answer is 4.

The preceding definition of division applies to examples with whole-number quotients and no remainder. For other whole-number division problems with nonzero divisors, one can always find a whole-number quotient and a whole-number remainder. For example, $13 \div 4 = 3\ R\ 1$.

## Lesson Exercise 3.33

Write an equation using multiplication and addition that is equivalent to $13 \div 4 = 3\ R\ 1$.

The preceding exercise illustrates the division algorithm.

---

**The Division Algorithm**

If $a$ and $b$ are whole numbers with $b \neq 0$, then there exist unique whole numbers $q$ and $r$ such that $a = bq + r$, in which $0 \leq r < b$.

---

The division algorithm equation $a = bq + r$ means:

$$\text{dividend} = \text{divisor} \cdot \text{quotient} + \text{remainder}$$

## Classifying Division Applications

Have you ever needed to divide 12 by 3? What types of situations require computing $12 \div 3$?

**D** Lesson Exercise 3.34

Make up two word problems that can be solved by dividing 12 by 3. Try to create two different types of problems.

---

Do your problems fit into any of the following categories?

1. **Repeated Sets**   Find how many sets of a certain size can be made from a group of objects.

   *Example:* I have a dozen eggs. How many 3-egg omelets can I make (Figure 3-24)?

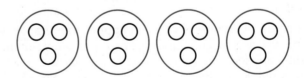

Figure 3-24

2. **Repeated Measures**   Find how many measurements of a certain size equal a given measurement.

   *Example:* A walk is 12 miles long. How long will it take if a walker averages 3 miles per hour (Figure 3-25)?

**Figure 3-25**

3. **Partition Sets**   Find how many are in each group when you divide a set of objects equally into a given number of groups.

*Example:* We have 12 yummy strawberries for the 3 of us. How many will each person get if we are fair about it (Figure 3-26)?

**Figure 3-26**

4. **Partition Measures**   Find the measure of each part when you divide a given measurement into a given number of equal parts.

*Example:* Let's divide this delicious 12-inch submarine sandwich equally among the three of us. How long a piece will we each receive (Figure 3-27)?

| 12 | | |
|---|---|---|
| ? | ? | ? |

**Figure 3-27**

5. **Row-by-Column Sets**   Find the number of rows (or columns) given an array of objects and the number of columns (or rows).

*Example:* Twelve people are seated in 3 rows. How many people are there in each row (Figure 3-28)?

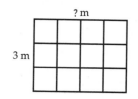

**Figure 3-28**

6. **Row-by-Column Measures**   Find the number of rows (or columns) of squares given a rectangular arrangement of square units and the number of columns (or rows) of squares. For example, one could find the width of a rectangle given its area and length.

*Example:* A rug has an area of 12 m² and a length of 3 m. What is its width (Figure 3-29)?

**Figure 3-29**

Students who recognize these types of situations will usually know when to divide to solve a problem. The hardest distinction for people to make is between the "repeated" categories (1 and 2) and the "partition" categories (3 and 4). For 12 ÷ 3, a "partitioning" problem would say, "Divide 12 into 3 equal parts," and a "repeating" problem would say "How many 3's make 12?" Note that the partitioning categories (3 and 4) include equal-sharing problems.

In Lesson Exercises 3.35, 3.36, and 3.37, classify the division applications.

## Lesson Exercise 3.35

Willie Loman sold 20 pairs of fireproof shoes last week. If he worked 5 days, how many pairs did he sell each day on the average?

## Lesson Exercise 3.36

The Arcurris drove 2000 km last week. About how far did they drive each day on the average?

## Lesson Exercise 3.37

My National Motors Gerbil gets 80 miles per gallon. How many gallons would I use on a 400-mile trip?

Repeated sets and measures, partition sets and measures, and row-by-column sets and measures are usually introduced with manipulatives and pictures in elementary school.

## Lesson Exercise 3.38

How would you solve Lesson Exercise 3.35 using a set of identical blocks?

## Lesson Exercise 3.39

How would you *explain* Lesson Exercise 3.37 to a child using a number line?

The following chart summarizes the most common classifications of arithmetic applications.

---

Classifying Arithmetic Applications

**Addition**
1. Combine sets
2. Combine measures

**Subtraction**
1. Take away sets
2. Take away measures
3. Compare sets
4. Compare measures

**Multiplication**
1. Repeated sets
2. Repeated measures
3. Row-by-column sets
4. Row-by-column measures
5. Combinations

**Division**
1. Repeated sets
2. Repeated measures
3. Partition sets
4. Partition measures
5. Row-by-column sets
6. Row-by-column measures

---

## Division by Zero

The most intriguing division problems are those involving zero. What is $4 \div 0$? $0 \div 0$? $0 \div 4$? According to the definition of division, $4 \div 0$ and $0 \div 0$ are undefined because you cannot have 0 as a divisor. However, $0 \div 4$ is defined. Elementary-school children often ask why the first two problems are undefined while the third is defined.

**D** Lesson Exercise 3.40

Why do we make problems like $4 \div 0$ undefined?

---

Expressions involving division by zero are most easily examined by converting the expression into a related multiplication equation. They can also be analyzed using any of the six division categories. The repeated-sets model is usually the easiest to use.

**Example 3.2**

*Explain* the result of $4 \div 0$ using multiplication or the division category of your choice.

**Solution**

***Method 1***  Using the inverse of multiplication model, $4 \div 0 = ?$ would mean $0 \times ? = 4$. There is no solution to $0 \times ? = 4$, so we make $4 \div 0$ undefined.

***Method 2***  Using repeated sets, $4 \div 0$ would mean, "How many sets of 0 will make 4?" No number of sets of 0 will make 4. So we make $4 \div 0$ undefined.  ■

**D** Lesson Exercise 3.41

*Explain* the result of $0 \div 4 = ?$ using multiplication or the division category of your choice.

**D** Lesson Exercise 3.42

*Explain* the result of $0 \div 0 = ?$ using multiplication or the division category of your choice.

## Working Backward

In Chapter 1, you studied problem-solving strategies such as induction, guess and check, and drawing a picture. In the previous two sections, you have seen how children can learn to choose the correct operation to solve a problem. Now, you can add another strategy, **working backward,** to your repertoire. Working-backward problems involve the four operations of arithmetic you have just studied. The following example illustrates this strategy.

### Example 3.3

Hy Roller got his weekly paycheck. He spent half of it on a gift for his mother. Then he spent $8 on a pizza. Now he has $19. How much was his paycheck?

**Solution**

***Understanding the Problem***  You know that he ended up with $19, and you know how he spent his money. How much did he start with?

***Devising a Plan***  Draw a diagram and then work backward.

*Carrying Out the Plan*   The diagram shows the sequence from the beginning to the end of the problem.

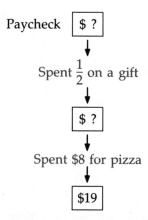

Now work backward and fill in the question marks. He ended up with $19. What did he have before he spent $8 on the pizza? $27.

So Hy had $27 just after he spent $\frac{1}{2}$ on a gift. How much did he start with? 2 × $27, or $54.

*Looking Back*   After you obtain an answer, start with $54 and work forward to check the answer. Start with $54. Spend $\frac{1}{2}$ on a gift. That leaves $27. Spend $8 on a pizza. That leaves $19. It checks!   ■

One could solve the preceding example using inverse operations.

| Original Problem | Same Problem Working Backward |
|:---:|:---:|
| □ | □ |
| ↓ ÷2 | ↑ ×2 |
| □ | □ |
| ↓ −8 | ↑ +8 |
| $19 | $19 |

Now you try one.

### Lesson Exercise 3.43

(a) Hy Roller received a raise in his weekly pay. After he received his first new paycheck, he spent $6 on tacos. He spent $\frac{1}{2}$ of what was left on a gift for his father. Now he has $25. How much is his weekly pay? (Draw a diagram and work backward.)

(b) Does working backward involve inductive reasoning or deductive reasoning?

## An Investigation: Operating on 3's

### Lesson Exercise 3.44

Using four 3's and any of the four operations, try to write equations equal to all the numbers from 1 to 10. Here, 0 is done as an example.
$$0 = 3 - 3 + 3 - 3$$

## Answers to Selected Lesson Exercises

**3.25** $3 \times 4$

**3.26** (a) yes     (b) no

**3.27** See the examples that follow Lesson Exercise 3.27.

**3.28** repeated sets

**3.29** row-by-column measures

**3.30** Make 4 sets of 3 blocks each. How many blocks in all? 12. So $3 \times 4 = 12$.

**3.31** Arrange 5 rows of squares with 4 in each row to create a rectangle with length 5 and width 4. How many squares in all? 20. The area is 20 square feet. This illustrates $5 \times 4 = 20$.

**3.32** $3 \times 4 = 12$

**3.33** $3 \times 4 + 1 = 13$

**3.34** See the examples that follow Lesson Exercise 3.34.

**3.35** partition sets

**3.36** partition measures

**3.37** repeated measures

**3.38** Take 20 blocks. Divide them into 5 equal-sized groups. How many in each group? 4. So $20 \div 5 = 4$.

**3.39** How many jumps of 80 will it take to reach 400? 5. So $400 \div 80 = 5$.

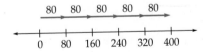

**3.41** $0 \div 4 = ?$ is the same as $4 \times ? = 0$. So $? = 0$. Therefore, $0 \div 4 = 0$.

**3.42** $0 \div 0 = ?$ is the same as $0 \times ? = 0$. So $?$ could stand for any number! Since each division problem must have one definite answer, we say $0 \div 0$ is undefined.

**3.43** (a) $56     (b) deductive

## 3.3 Homework Exercises

*Basic Exercises*

1. Rewrite $7 + 7 + 7$ as a multiplication problem.

In Exercises 2–5, classify each application as one of the following: repeated sets, repeated measures, row-by-column sets, row-by-column measures, or combinations.

2. In an election, 5 people are running for president and 3 people are running for vice president. How many different pairs of candidates can be elected to the two offices?

3. Each person in the United States creates about 6 pounds of solid garbage per day. How much solid garbage does a person dispose of in a year?

4. An index card is 3 in. by 5 in. What is its area?

5. Tacos come 10 to a box. How many tacos are in 3 boxes?

6. How would you explain to a child why the area of the rectangle shown is 6 ft²?

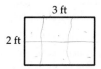

3 ft

2 ft

7. The following two word problems require multiplying 8 by 3. Which problem illustrates a more realistic use of mathematics?
   (a) Bill has 8 pencils. Courtney has 3 times as many. How many pencils does Courtney have?
   (b) Concert tickets cost $8 each. How much would 3 tickets cost?

8. (a) What multiplication problem is shown in the diagram?

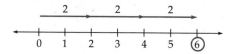

2      2      2

0  1  2  3  4  5  ⑥

(b) How would you use a number line to explain to a child that $3 \times 4 = 12$?

9. Make a drawing showing $2 \times 5 = 10$ using
   (a) repeated sets.
   (b) repeated measures.
   (c) row-by-column sets.

10. What is the next number in each sequence?
    (a) 7, 15, 31, _____
    (b) 20, 37, 71, 139, _____

11. Fill in the blanks in each part by following the same rule used in the completed examples.
    (a) $4 \rightarrow 26$     (b) $3 \rightarrow 10$
         $5 \rightarrow 35$         $4 \rightarrow 14$
         $6 \rightarrow 46$         $5 \rightarrow 18$
         $8 \rightarrow$ _____     $10 \rightarrow$ _____
         $X \rightarrow$ _____      $X \rightarrow$ _____
    (c) The process of making a conjecture about the general formula in the last blank in parts (a) and (b) is an example of _____ reasoning.

12. (a) $11^2 =$ _____     (b) $111^2 =$ _____
    (c) Without a calculator, guess the value of $1111^2$ and $11,111^2$.
    (d) Use a calculator to check your answers to part (c).

13. (a) Write the number of small squares using an exponent other than 1.

(b) Write the number of small cubes using an exponent other than 1.

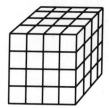

**14.** Use the definition of division to rewrite each division equation as a multiplication equation.
(a) $40 \div 8 = ?$    (b) $32 \div N = 6$
(c) $0 \div N = C$

In Exercises 15–18, classify each application as one of the following: repeated sets, repeated measures, partition sets, partition measures, row-by-column sets, or row-by-column measures.

**15.** A car travels 180 miles in 4 hours. What is its average speed?

**16.** If I deal out a deck of 52 cards to 4 people, how many cards will each person receive?

**17.** A car travels 180 miles, averaging 45 miles per hour. How long does this trip take?

**18.** A teacher wants to seat 30 students evenly in 5 rows. How many children sit in each row?

**19.** (a) What division fact is illustrated in the diagram?

(b) How would you use a number line to explain to a child that $10 \div 5 = 2$?

**20.** (a) What division fact is illustrated in the diagram?

(b) Use a set-partition picture to show that $6 \div 3 = 2$.

**21.** Make a drawing illustrating $10 \div 5 = 2$ using
(a) row-by-column sets.
(b) partition measures.
(c) repeated sets.

**22.** How many possible remainders, including 0, are there when a whole number is divided by each of the following?
(a) 5    (b) 6    (c) a counting number $N$

**23.** Helmer Junghans has 37 photographs to put in a photo album. Write a question whose answer is
(a) 10.    (b) 1.    (c) 9.

**24.** You are sewing buttons on a blouse whose front is 22 in. long. The first button is 2 in. from the top, and the buttons are 3 in. apart. How many buttons do you need?

**25.** The Hersheys buy a 6-slice pizza for the 4 members of their family. They each eat an equal number of slices and give any leftover slices to their pet goat Dainty.
(a) How many slices do they each eat?
(b) How many slices does Dainty get?
(c) Is the answer to part (a) a quotient, a remainder, or neither?
(d) Is the answer to part (b) a quotient, a remainder, or neither?

**26.** (a) Ninety-seven children want to go on a field trip in school buses. Each bus holds 40 children. How many buses are needed?
(b) Is the answer a quotient, a remainder, or neither?

**27.** Explain the result to $7 \div 0$ using multiplication or the division category of your choice.

**28.** Explain the result to $0 \div 0$ using multiplication or the division category of your choice.

**29.** Try $4 \div 0$ on a calculator. What is the result? Why did this occur?

**30.** (a) Fill in the missing numbers.

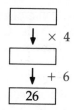

(b) What kind of reasoning, inductive or deductive, do you use to fill in the blanks?

**31.** Sharon takes a number, adds 2 to it, and then multiplies the result by 3. She ends up with $N$. What was the original number in terms of $N$?

32. Carroll Matthews went to a gambling casino. He did not look in his wallet beforehand, but he remembers how he spent his money. He paid $5 for parking. Then he spent $3 on an imitation orange juice drink. Then he lost half of his remaining money gambling. Now he has $14. How much did Carroll start with?

33. Frank picked some daisies. He gave half of them to his wife. Then he divided what was left evenly among his brother, his daughter, and his horse. They each got 6 daisies. How many daisies did he pick?

34. Make up a realistic problem illustrating the repeated-measures model of multiplication.

35. Make up a realistic problem illustrating the partition-sets model of division.

36. Is whole-number division closed? (*Hint:* Check the two parts of the closure property.)

37. What is the next number in the sequence 8, 23, 68, 203, . . . ?

38. Complete the following number pairs in each part using the same rule from the two completed examples.
   (a) $20 \rightarrow 0$
   $30 \rightarrow 1$
   $40 \rightarrow 2$
   $50 \rightarrow \underline{\quad}$
   $N \rightarrow \underline{\quad}$
   (b) $12 \rightarrow 7$
   $14 \rightarrow 8$
   $30 \rightarrow \underline{\quad}$
   $N \rightarrow \underline{\quad}$

39. A $5 \times 5$ square grid has 16 squares on the border.

How many squares would an $n \times n$ grid have on the border? (Simplify your answer.)

40. At a restaurant, you can order a chicken, turkey, cheese, or roast beef sandwich on rye, wheat, or white bread. How many different kinds of sandwiches can you order?

41. What two operations and categories are used in each of the following problems?
   (a) At a carnival, Puneet tried to knock down 4 rows of 3 pins. On his first throw, he hit 7 pins. How many were left?
   (b) Wally ate 2 pears. Juanita ate twice as many. How many pears did the two of them eat all together?

42. What two operations and categories are illustrated in each of the following applications?
   (a) How many miles must you travel each day to complete a 3260-mile car trip in 2 weeks?
   (b) A National Motors Capon travels 276 miles on 12 gallons of gas. How far will it travel on a full 20-gallon tank of gas?

43. What two operations and categories are illustrated in each of the following applications?
   (a) You have 10 carnival tickets. Then you go on a ride costing 2 tickets and use 3 tickets to buy corn-on-the-cob. How many tickets do you have left?
   (b) An auditorium has 20 rows with 28 seats in each row. If 16 seats are empty at a concert, how many people are seated there?

44. Write a realistic word problem that requires computing $(4 \times 8) - 5$.

45. Write a realistic word problem that requires computing $(3 + 6) \times 7$.

46. Gwen Cyrkiel buys $A$ shirts for $\$B$ each and $C$ skirts for $\$D$ each. What is the total cost of all her purchases?

47. For whole numbers $a$, $b$, and $c$ with $a$ an even number and $b \neq 0$, if $a \div b = c$, then $a \div 2b = \underline{\quad\quad}$.

48. For whole numbers $a$, $b$, and $c$, if $ab = c$, then $(2a)(3b) = \underline{\quad\quad}$.

49. (a) $5^{100}$ has 70 digits. What is the last digit? (*Hint:* Use inductive reasoning.)
   (b) $T$ is a one-digit whole number. If the last digit of $T^{100}$ is $T$, what are the possible values of $T$?

**50.** $3 + 6 = 9$ is to $2^3 \cdot 2^6 = 2^9$ as $5 - 2 = 3$ is to _____ .

**51.** You need to measure 7 oz of medicine, and all you have are two transparent 2-oz measuring cups and a glass. How could you do it?

**52.** The square of a number is 9 less than 10 times the number. What is the number? (Guess and check.)

**53.** Suppose the sum of two numbers is even and their product is odd. What can you deduce about the two numbers?

*Extension Exercises*

**54.** $25 \times 25 = 625$
   $26 \times 24 = 624$
   $27 \times 23 = 621$

   (a) Predict the answer to the next multiplication problem that extends the pattern.
   (b) Check your guess in part (a).
   (c) Repeat parts (a) and (b).
   (d) Start with $40 \times 40 = 1600$ and repeat parts (a) and (b) three times.
   (e) Make a generalization about your results.
   (f) Show algebraically why your generalization is true.

**55.** All books now have an ISBN (International Standard Book Number) such as 0-86576-009-8 (*Precalculus Mathematics in a Nutshell*). The first digit indicates the language of the country in which the book is published (for example, 0 for English). The digits 86576 represent the publisher (William Kaufmann, Inc.). The digits 009 identify the book to the publisher. Finally, the last digit is the **check digit** used to check that the rest of the number is recorded correctly. To obtain an ISBN check digit:

*Step 1.* Multiply the first nine digits by 10, 9, 8, 7, 6, 5, 4, 3, and 2, respectively. For 0-86576-009-8, $(0 \times 10) + (8 \times 9) + (6 \times 8) + (5 \times 7) + (7 \times 6) + (6 \times 5) + (0 \times 4) + (0 \times 3) + (9 \times 2) = 245$.

*Step 2.* Divide the sum by 11 and find the remainder.

$$245 \div 11 = 22 \text{ R } 3$$

*Step 3.* Subtract the remainder from 11 to match the check digit.

$$11 - 3 = 8 \quad \text{Yes, it checks!}$$

The check digit is used to check ISBN numbers that are copied onto order forms. Check the following ISBN numbers to see if they seem to be correct.
(a) ISBN   0-03-008367-2
(b) ISBN   0-7617-1326-8

**56.** (a) Graph $x \div y = 2$ for whole numbers $x$ and $y$.
   (b) Graph $x \div y = 3$ for whole numbers $x$ and $y$.
   (c) Write a generalization about the graph of $x \div y = k$, in which $k$ is a counting number.

**57.** In a two-person game of Last Out, the players take turns removing either one or two chips. The person who removes the last chip loses the game. If you go first, and the game starts with 11 chips, describe a winning strategy. (Work backward).

**58.** A true-false test has 5 questions. How many different ways can the test be answered if each question is answered true or false?

**59.** Complete the last column of the following chart.

| | Given | Find | Operation/Category |
|---|---|---|---|
| (a) | How many in each group (assume the same number in each group) How many groups there are | How many there are in all | |
| (b) | How many there are in all How many groups there are | How many in each group (assume the same number in each group) | |

60. Whole-number multiplication can also be defined using the Cartesian product (Chapter 2). For whole numbers $a$ and $b$, if set $A$ contains $a$ elements and set $B$ contains $b$ elements, then $a \cdot b$ is the number of elements in $A \times B$.
   (a) Use this definition with $A = \{1, 2\}$ and $B = \{1, 2, 3\}$ to explain why $2 \cdot 3 = 6$.
   (b) This definition is closely related to one of the five categories of multiplication. Which one?

61. Consider the following problem: "A mystery number divided by 6 is 28 more than that very same mystery number divided by 10. What is the mystery number?" Devise a plan and solve the problem.

62. Consider the following problem: "Find a two-digit number that is twice the product of its digits."
   (a) Devise a plan and solve the problem.
   (b) Make up a similar problem.

63. At a Chinese restaurant, $A$ people divide the check evenly. They ordered dishes costing $\$B$, $\$C$, $\$D$, $\$E$, and $\$F$. They add 20% for tax and tip. How much will each person pay?

*Special Exercise*

64. Write a report on alternative algorithms for multiplication of whole numbers.

## 3.4   Whole Numbers: Properties, Algorithms, and Error Patterns

Properties of whole-number operations make it easier to memorize basic facts and do certain computations. If you learn $7 \times 9 = 63$, then you know what $9 \times 7$ equals. The sum $(24 + 2) + 8$ is more easily computed as $24 + (2 + 8)$. These properties are also the basis for the efficient procedures we use to add and multiply larger numbers. The properties have names such as "commutative," "associative," "identity," and "distributive." Do you feel your memory being jarred?

### The Commutative and Associative Properties

Is a "night light" the same as a "light night"? Is $7 \times 9$ the same as $9 \times 7$? These questions involve the commutative property. In mathematics, the commutative property says that you can change the *order* of two numbers in certain arithmetic operations and still obtain the same answer. Which of the four whole-number operations are commutative? Investigate this question in Lesson Exercises 3.45 and 3.46.

## Lesson Exercise 3.45

Answer the following questions to help determine whether whole-number addition is commutative.
(a) Does $6 + 8 = 8 + 6$?
(b) For any two whole numbers $x$ and $y$, do you think $x + y = y + x$?
(c) Your answer to part (b) is based upon _____ reasoning.

## Lesson Exercise 3.46

Try some examples and see whether you think the following whole-number operations are commutative. Give a counterexample for any operation that is not commutative.
(a) subtraction      (b) multiplication      (c) division

By now you should be convinced that whole-number addition and multiplication are commutative.

---

**The Commutative Property of Addition for Whole Numbers**

For any whole numbers $x$ and $y$, $x + y = y + x$.

---

**The Commutative Property of Multiplication for Whole Numbers**

For any whole numbers $x$ and $y$, $xy = yx$.

---

The commutative properties can be stated in words as follows: When you add two whole numbers, you can add them in either order, and when you multiply two whole numbers, you can multiply them in either order. Figure 3-30 illustrates these properties using measures.

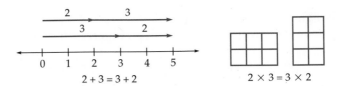

Figure 3-30

Note that the commutative property applies to expressions involving *one* operation: either addition or multiplication. But how do human beings use this property? It makes learning the addition and multiplication tables a lot easier.

## Lesson Exercise 3.47

How does the commutative property reduce the number of one-digit addition facts (for example, $3 + 5 = 8$) that must be memorized?

What about the associative (grouping) property? This property says that the grouping of numbers for an arithmetic operation will not change the answer. So which whole-number operations are associative? The following exercises will help you decide.

## Lesson Exercise 3.48

Answer the following questions and see whether you think whole-number addition is associative.
(a) Does $(6 + 3) + 5 = 6 + (3 + 5)$?
(b) Does $(24 + 2) + 18 = 24 + (2 + 18)$?
(c) Do you think $(x + y) + z = x + (y + z)$ for all whole numbers?

## Lesson Exercise 3.49

Try some examples and see whether you think the following whole-number operations are associative. Give a counterexample for any operation that is not associative.
(a) subtraction      (b) multiplication      (c) division

Are you now entirely convinced that whole-number addition and multiplication are commutative and associative? They are.

---

**The Associative Property of Addition for Whole Numbers**

For any whole numbers $x$, $y$, and $z$, $(x + y) + z = x + (y + z)$.

---

**The Associative Property of Multiplication for Whole Numbers**

For any whole numbers $x$, $y$, and $z$, $(xy)z = x(yz)$.

The associative properties can be stated in words as follows: When you add a series of whole numbers, parentheses have no effect on the results, and when you multiply a series of whole numbers, parentheses also have no effect on the results. In these kinds of problems, you can move parentheses around or remove them altogether.

Figure 3-31 illustrates these properties using sets.

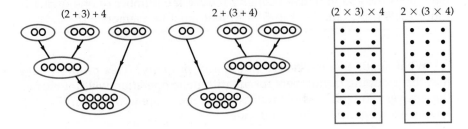

**Figure 3-31**

Like the commutative property, the associative property applies to expressions involving *one* operation: either addition or multiplication. We use the associative property in algebra to simplify an expression such as $8 \cdot (3x)$.

## Lesson Exercise 3.50

(a) Simplify $8 \cdot (3 \cdot x)$. You have learned how to do this in algebra class, but you may not understand how it relates to multiplication properties.

(b) What property says that, for a whole number $x$,
$8 \cdot (3 \cdot x) = (8 \cdot 3) \cdot x$?

(c) Explain why $8 \cdot (3 \cdot x) = 24x$.

Together, the commutative and associative properties allow us to reorder and regroup numbers in an addition problem in any way we want! For example, we can change $46 + (28 + 4) + 2$ to $(46 + 4) + (28 + 2)$ using the commutative and associative properties. The same reordering and regrouping may be done to any multiplication problem.

## Lesson Exercise 3.51

(a) Rewrite $8 \cdot (4 \cdot 7) \cdot 25$ to make it easier to compute mentally.

(b) What properties justify your answer to part (a)?

## The Identity Property

Some whole-number operations have a unique number called an identity element. The following exercises will guide you through an investigation of identity elements.

## Lesson Exercise 3.52

What whole number, if any, can go in both blanks in the following statement?

For all whole numbers $w$, $w +$ _____ $=$ _____ $+ w = w$.

## Lesson Exercise 3.53

What whole number, if any, can go in both blanks in the following statement?

For all whole numbers $w$, $w \cdot$ _____ $=$ _____ $\cdot w = w$.

## Lesson Exercise 3.54

What whole number, if any, can go in both blanks in the following statement?

For all whole numbers $w$, $w -$ _____ $=$ _____ $- w = w$.

## Lesson Exercise 3.55

What whole number, if any, can go in both blanks in the following statement?

For all whole numbers $w$, $w \div$ _____ $=$ _____ $\div w = w$.

Based upon Lesson Exercises 3.52 through 3.55, you can see that only addition and multiplication had a unique whole number that would go in both blanks and work for all whole numbers. These special numbers are called **identity elements.**

---

**Identity Elements for Whole-Number Addition and Multiplication**

0 is the unique additive identity such that, for all whole numbers $w$, $w + 0 = 0 + w = w$.

1 is the unique multiplicative identity such that, for all whole numbers $w$, $w \cdot 1 = 1 \cdot w = w$.

---

There is no identity element for whole-number subtraction or division. Don't let this upset you too much. Let's return to addition and multiplication and enjoy the fact that these operations do have identities.

## Lesson Exercise 3.56

(a) What one-digit addition facts use the identity property?
(b) What one-digit multiplication facts use the identity property?

Together, the commutative and identity properties of addition significantly reduce the number of separate addition facts that need to be memorized. In multiplication, the commutative and identity properties, along with the fact that $0 \times a = 0$ for all whole numbers $a$, greatly reduce the number of separate multiplication facts that children must memorize. You will learn additional strategies children can use to memorize addition and multiplication facts if you take a mathematics methods course in a school of education.

## The Distributive Property

The distributive property plays an important part in the procedure for multiplying numbers such as $34 \times 2$. The distributive property is the only property in this lesson that involves two different operations at the same time. The distributive property of multiplication over addition is

$$F \cdot (G + H) = (F \cdot G) + (F \cdot H)$$

## Lesson Exercise 3.57

(a) Try some examples and see whether you think the distributive property of multiplication over addition holds for all whole numbers.
(b) The conclusion is based upon _____ reasoning.

Lesson Exercise 3.57 suggests that the whole numbers possess the distributive property of multiplication over addition.

> **The Distributive Property of Whole-Number Multiplication over Addition**
>
> For any whole numbers $x$, $y$, and $z$, $x \cdot (y + z) = (xy) + (xz)$.

Figure 3-32 illustrates the distributive property using a set diagram.

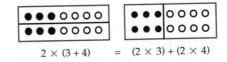

$$2 \times (3 + 4) \quad = \quad (2 \times 3) + (2 \times 4)$$

**Figure 3-32**

People use the distributive property in algebra to combine like terms. Consider the following exercise.

## Lesson Exercise 3.58

If $x$ is a whole number, the distributive property of multiplication over addition would say $7 \cdot x + 3 \cdot x =$ _____ .

Do any other distributive properties work for whole-number operations?

## D Lesson Exercise 3.59

(a) $F + (G \times H) = (F + G) \times (F + H)$ would be called the distributive property of _____ over _____ .
(b) Try some whole-number examples and see whether you think the property in part (a) is true.

## D Lesson Exercise 3.60

(a) $F \times (G - H) = (F \times G) - (F \times H)$ would be called the

_____ .

(b) Try some whole-number examples and see whether you think the property in part (a) is true.
(c) The conclusion in part (b) is based upon _____ reasoning.

As Lesson Exercise 3.60 suggests, another distributive property holds for whole numbers.

---

**The Distributive Property of Whole-Number Multiplication over Subtraction**

For any whole numbers $x$, $y$, and $z$, $x \cdot (y - z) = (xy - xz)$.

---

## Lesson Exercise 3.61

A storekeeper buys 24 televisions for $99 each. A method for mentally multiplying $24 \times 99$ is to compute $(24 \times 100) - (24 \times 1)$. Use the distributive property to explain why these two expressions are equal.

The following chart summarizes all the properties of whole-number operations presented in this section.

> **Properties of Whole-Number Operations**
>
> Whole-number addition is commutative and associative.
>
> Whole-number multiplication is commutative and associative.
>
> The additive identity for whole numbers is 0.
>
> The multiplicative identity for whole numbers is 1.
>
> Multiplication is distributive over addition and subtraction for whole numbers.

## The Addition Algorithm

People have developed procedures to perform paper-and-pencil computations involving larger numbers more easily. In spite of having such procedures, people in the Middle Ages considered whole-number arithmetic a college-level subject! Today, children in elementary school study some of the best of these computational procedures, called **algorithms.** We typically use algorithms to perform computations with two- and three-digit numbers.

"Algorithm" is a term you can use to impress friends at parties when they ask, "What *are* you studying in that math class, anyway?" Tell them, "We're analyzing a few algorithms."

In the most common addition algorithm, children line up digits according to place value and proceed from right to left, adding the digits in each column. This method is sufficient to compute the answer to a problem such as 32 + 42, in which the sum of the digits in each column is less than 10 (see Figure 3-33).

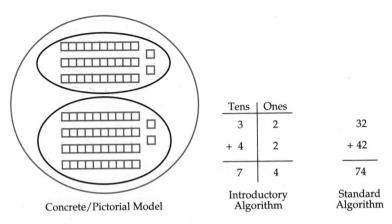

Concrete/Pictorial Model

| Tens | Ones |
|------|------|
| 3 | 2 |
| + 4 | 2 |
| 7 | 4 |

Introductory Algorithm

```
  32
+ 42
----
  74
```

Standard Algorithm

**Figure 3-33**

If the digits in any column add up to 10 or more, regrouping is needed. Dienes (base-ten) blocks help children understand the addition algorithm. They are especially useful for showing how regrouping works.

## Lesson Exercise 3.62

Suppose you want to compute $\begin{array}{r} 38 \\ +54 \end{array}$.

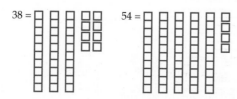

**Figure 3-34**

Describe how you would get the answer 92 by adding the blocks shown in Figure 3-34 and trading in. Follow the same sequence of steps that one uses in computing $\begin{array}{r} 38 \\ +54 \end{array}$ with paper and pencil.

One can use the properties of whole-number operations to show how the addition algorithm works. For example, in computing $\begin{array}{r} 56 \\ +32 \end{array}$ why are we allowed to add 2 + 6 and then add 50 + 30 to that result?

## D Lesson Exercise 3.63

Fill in the properties that justify the last three steps.

| | |
|---|---|
| 56 + 32 = (50 + 6) + (30 + 2) | Expanded notation |
| = 50 + (6 + 30) + 2 | + is associative |
| = 50 + (30 + 6) + 2 | _____ |
| = (50 + 30) + (6 + 2) | _____ |
| = (6 + 2) + (50 + 30) | _____ |

As Lesson Exercise 3.63 demonstrates, the commutative and associative properties are the basis for the addition algorithm.

## The Subtraction Algorithm

In studying the subtraction algorithm, children first solve problems that do not require regrouping. Children line up digits according to place value and proceed from right to left, subtracting each digit from the one above it. This process is sufficient to compute the answer to a problem such as 74 − 32 (see Figure 3-35).

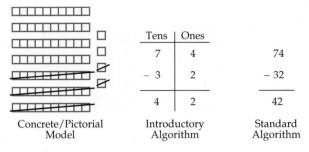

| | Tens | Ones | | |
|---|---|---|---|---|
| | 7 | 4 | | 74 |
| | − 3 | 2 | | − 32 |
| | 4 | 2 | | 42 |

Concrete/Pictorial          Introductory          Standard
Model                Algorithm            Algorithm

**Figure 3-35**

If the top digit in any column is less than the bottom digit, the child must use regrouping. Base-ten blocks help demonstrate regrouping in a problem such as 54 − 38.

## Lesson Exercise 3.64

Suppose you want to compute $\begin{array}{r} 54 \\ -38 \end{array}$ . Using words and pictures, describe how you would get the answer (16) by subtracting and trading in blocks. Follow the same sequence of steps that you would use in computing $\begin{array}{r} 54 \\ -38 \end{array}$ with paper and pencil.

The **equal-additions algorithm** is another subtraction algorithm that has been used in some U.S. schools in the last 60 years. The equal-additions algorithm is based upon the concept that there are an infinite number of equivalent subtraction problems having a given difference. Many European schools used this algorithm in the fifteenth and sixteenth centuries. See how you think it compares to the standard algorithm.

## Lesson Exercise 3.65

Suppose you add the same amount to both numbers in a subtraction problem. What will happen to the answer? Try the following.
(a) What is 86 − 29?
(b) Add 1 to both numbers in part (a) and subtract. Do you obtain the same answer?
(c) Add 11 to both numbers in part (a) and subtract. Do you obtain the same answer?

## Lesson Exercise 3.66

As the preceding exercise suggests, you can add the same amount to both numbers in a subtraction problem without the changing the result. For example, this could be used to change 53 − 27 into 56 − 30, an easier problem.
(a) Rewrite 44 − 18 as an equivalent but easier subtraction problem.
(b) Rewrite 322 − 96 as an equivalent but easier subtraction problem.

## Lesson Exercise 3.67

The property developed in the preceding two exercises is the basis for the equal-additions algorithm. For example, in computing 563 − 249, one needs to add 10 to the 3. To compensate, one adds 10 to 249. Then, the subtraction can be done without regrouping.

$$
\begin{array}{ccc}
5\ 6\ 3 & 5\ 6^13 & 5\ 6^13 \\
-2\ 4\ 9 & -2^54\ 9 & -2^54\ 9 \\
& & \overline{3\ 1\ 4}
\end{array}
$$

(a) Compute 86 − 29 using the equal-additions algorithm.
(b) How do you think this algorithm compares to the standard algorithm?

---

Research shows that children can learn to do subtraction quickly and accurately with either the standard algorithm or the equal-additions algorithm. However, the standard algorithm is easier for children to understand since it is based upon place-value trades that can be easily illustrated with manipulatives such as base-ten blocks.

## The Multiplication Algorithm

In the standard multiplication algorithm, each digit in one factor is multiplied by each digit in the other factor (Figure 3-36).

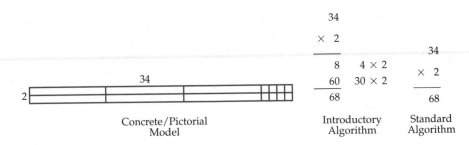

Figure 3-36

Why are we allowed to multiply 2 × 4 and 2 × 30 and add the results together?

**D** Lesson Exercise 3.68

Fill in the properties that justify the last two steps.

34 × 2 = (30 + 4) × 2          Expanded notation
       = (30 × 2) + (4 × 2)    _____
       = (4 × 2) + (30 × 2)    _____

The preceding exercise illustrates how the distributive property is used in the multiplication algorithm. Multiplying larger numbers is merely an extension of this process (Figure 3-37).

Lesson Exercise 3.69

Draw a base-ten-blocks picture (an array) showing 34 × 52 = 1768.

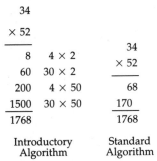

Figure 3-37

## The Division Algorithm

The standard long-division algorithm for whole numbers is more complicated and somewhat unlike the algorithms for the other three operations. Instead of lining up the digits of the numbers as in the other operations, one writes the divisor to the left of the dividend. Unlike the other three operations, one finds the quotient from *left to right*. And while one simply computes one-digit basic facts to perform the other algorithms, the division algorithm may require rounding the divisor (if it is more than one digit) and the dividend and then using estimation to obtain digits in the quotient.

Because the standard algorithm is quite difficult, a second algorithm, the **subtractive (or scaffold) algorithm** has been taught in a few U.S. schools in recent times. Today, most schools present a sequence of subtractive examples that lead up to standard long division.

**Example 3.4**

Compute 4972 ÷ 21 using repeated subtraction and the subtractive algorithm.

**Solution**

You must determine how many times the divisor 21 can be *subtracted* from 4972 to obtain 0 or a remainder less than the divisor 21. One could start by subtracting groups of 100 21's and continue as shown until the remainder is less than 21. The right-hand column is a record of how many 21's have been subtracted. (*Note:* In each step, the groupings of 21's you subtract may be of any size, but it helps to do this efficiently.)

```
21 | 4972
       2100      100  (×21)
       2872
       2100      100  (×21)
        772
        630       30  (×21)
        142
        126        6  (×21)
         16       236
```

So, 4972 ÷ 21 = 236 R 16.  ■

Compare Example 3.4 to the standard algorithm.

```
          236 R 16
    21 | 4972
         42
         77
         63
         142
         126
          16
```

standard algorithm

## Lesson Exercise 3.70

(a) Compute 8421 ÷ 22 using the subtractive algorithm.
(b) Compute 8421 ÷ 22 using the standard algorithm.
(c) What are the advantages and disadvantages of each algorithm?

As you have seen, the subtractive algorithm is longer and easier to understand than the standard long-division algorithm.

## Common Error Patterns in Algorithms

The bad news is that not all students learn the algorithms just the way you teach them. Confused students may initially develop their own erroneous procedures. The goods news is that you get to play detective in trying to uncover students' error patterns.

Children's written work is the first evidence of many learning difficulties. Try your luck at finding the error patterns in the following exercises.

In Lesson Exercises 3.71 through 3.74, (a) complete the last example, repeating the error pattern in the completed examples and (b) describe the error pattern.

### Lesson Exercise 3.71

| 49 | 67 | 92 |
|---|---|---|
| +37 | +43 | +39 |
| 76 | 100 | |

### Lesson Exercise 3.72

| 92 | 408 | 921 |
|---|---|---|
| −39 | −322 | −376 |
| 67 | 126 | |

### Lesson Exercise 3.73

| 36 | 42 | 72 |
|---|---|---|
| × 8 | × 6 | × 9 |
| 568 | 302 | |

### Lesson Exercise 3.74

| 121 | 184 | |
|---|---|---|
| 4 ⟌ 623 | 8 ⟌ 912 | 3 ⟌ 782 |

## Alternate Low-Stress Algorithms

In the 1976 NCTM yearbook, Barton Hutchins describes alternate algorithms that are easier for some children. Today, his subtraction algorithm and a modified version of his addition algorithm are sometimes used with older students who have been unable to master the corresponding standard algorithm.

The modified form of Hutchins' low-stress addition algorithm is called **scratch addition**.

**Example 3.5**

Compute 57 + 86 + 39 using scratch addition.

Solution

Scratch addition only requires addition of single digits. Write the example vertically.

57       Add the numbers in the units place, starting at the top.
8$\not{6}_3$       If the sum is 10 or more, "scratch" a line through the last digit
+39       added and write the number of units just below it.

57       Continue adding units.
8$\not{6}_3$
+3$\not{9}$
  2

1 2
5 7       Count the number of scratches in the column and write it at
$\not{8}_5\not{6}_3$       the top of the next column. Repeat the procedure for each
+ 3 $\not{9}$       successive column. ∎
1 8 2

## Lesson Exercise 3.75

(a) Compute 38 + 97 + 246 using scratch addition.
(b) What is easier about scratch addition?

Hutchins' **low-stress subtraction** algorithm for regrouping differs from the standard procedure in two ways. First, the renamed minuend (top number) is written between the minuend and the subtrahend. Second, all regrouping is done before any subtraction.

**Example 3.6**

Compute 324 − 168 using low-stress subtraction.

Solution

Write the problem vertically and draw a box between the minuend and the subtrahend where the renamed minuend will go.

3 2 4
[        ]
− 1 6 8

First, do all needed regrouping in the minuend. Start with the ones. 8 is bigger than 4, so regroup from the tens to the ones.

3 2 4

$\boxed{1^14}$

− 1 6 8

Next, check the tens. 6 is bigger than 1, so regroup from the hundreds to the tens.

| 3 2 4 | Now subtract. | 3 2 4 |
|---|---|---|
| $\boxed{2^11^14}$ | ⟶ | $\boxed{2^11^14}$ |
| − 1 6 8 | | − 1 6 8 |
| | | 1 5 6 ■ |

## Lesson Exercise 3.76

(a) Compute 827 − 469 using low-stress subtraction.
(b) What is easier about low-stress subtraction?

The homework exercises contain examples of older algorithms that are not as efficient or easy to understand as those we teach.

## Answers to Selected Lesson Exercises

**3.45** (a) yes      (c) inductive

**3.47** After memorizing any fact with two different addends (e.g., 3 + 5 = 8), you will also know a companion fact with the addends reversed (e.g., 5 + 3 = 8). This reduces the number of basic facts that need to be learned from 100 to 55.

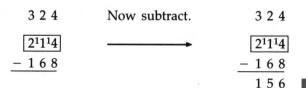

**3.48** (a) yes      (b) yes

**3.50** (a) $24x$
  (b) associative property of $x$
  (c) By the associative property, $8 \cdot (3 \cdot x) = (8 \cdot 3) \cdot x$, which equals $24x$.

**3.51** (a) $4 \cdot 25 \cdot 8 \cdot 7$
  (b) commutative and associative properties

**3.52** 0

**3.53** 1

**3.54** none

**3.55** none

**3.56** (a) 0 + any number or any number + 0
  (b) 1 × any number or any number × 1

**3.57** (b) inductive

**3.58** $(7 + 3) \cdot x$

**3.59** (a) addition over multiplication

**3.60** (a) multiplication over subtraction
(c) inductive

**3.61** $24 \times 99 = 24 \times (100 - 1) = (24 \times 100) - (24 \times 1)$

**3.62** Start with 3 tens and 8 ones, and 5 tens and 4 ones. Next, combine 8 ones and 4 ones to obtain 12 ones. Trade 10 ones in for 1 ten, leaving 2 ones. Combine 1 ten, 3 tens, and 5 tens to obtain 9 tens. The sum is 9 tens, 2 ones = 92.

**3.63** + is commutative; + is associative; + is commutative

**3.64** Start with 5 tens and 4 ones. You cannot take away 8 ones from 4 ones. Regroup 5 tens, 4 ones as 4 tens, 14 ones. Now take 8

ones away from 14 ones, leaving 6 ones. Take away 3 tens from 4 tens, leaving 1 ten. The difference is 1 ten, 6 ones = 16.

**3.65** (a) 57    (b) yes    (c) yes

**3.66** (a) $46 - 20$    (b) $326 - 100$

**3.68** distributive; + is commutative

**3.71** (a) 121

**3.72** (a) 655

**3.73** (a) 728

**3.74** (a) 221

**3.76** (b) It requires less switching back and forth between different procedures (regrouping and subtracting).

## 3.4  Homework Exercises

*Basic Exercises*

1. Explain all the different ways to compute $3 \cdot 2 \cdot 4$ by multiplying.

2. $X$ and $Y$ are whole numbers. $X + (Y + 3) = (X + Y) + 3$ illustrates the _____ property of _____ .

3. Four sets of 3 is the same as 3 sets of 4 because of the _____ property of _____ .

4. (a) What whole-number operations are commutative?
   (b) What whole-number operations are associative?

5. Draw a set picture illustrating that $(2 \times 4) \times 5 = 2 \times (4 \times 5)$.

6. Some people confuse $8 \div 2$ and $2 \div 8$.
   (a) $8 \div 2 \neq 2 \div 8$ is a counterexample disproving what property?
   (b) Explain the difference between $8 \div 2$ and $2 \div 8$.

7. Give a counterexample showing that whole-number subtraction is not associative.

8. You buy a simulated astroturf carpet for $38, a talking waste basket for $57, and a half-

pound chocolate moose for $2. What is the easiest way to compute your total bill?

9. A carpet that is 6 ft by 9 ft costs $5 per square foot. Explain an easy way to compute mentally the total cost of the carpet.

10. Three items cost $246, $38, and $4. Explain an easy way to compute mentally the total cost.

11. How does the commutative property reduce the number of one-digit multiplication facts that must be memorized?

12. Is the operation of putting on your shoes and socks commutative?

13. In English, the meaning of phrases may change depending upon which words are associated. "Slow-motion picture" and "slow motion picture" have different meanings. Therefore, the phrase "slow-motion picture" is not associative. Which of the following phrases is associative?
   (a) man eating shark
   (b) smart handsome stranger
   (c) hot dog salesperson
   (d) high-school student

14. In English, the meaning of a phrase may

change depending upon the order of the words. Does changing the order change the meaning of the following phrases?
(a) hall light     (b) love lost

15. Do the problems in the first column with a calculator. Then find a pattern you can use to do the problems in the second column without a calculator.
(a) $37 \times 3 =$ _____    $37 \times 12 =$ _____
     $37 \times 6 =$ _____    $37 \times 18 =$ _____
     $37 \times 9 =$ _____    $37 \times$ _____ $= 888$
(b) $3367 \times 3 =$ _____    $3367 \times 15 =$ _____
     $3367 \times 6 =$ _____    $3367 \times 21 =$ _____
     $3367 \times 9 =$ _____    $3367 \times$ _____ $= 40{,}404$

16. Without computing their exact values, tell which is larger, $3^{14}$ or $9^{10}$.

17. $6 + 0 = 0 + 6 = 6.\ 8 + 0 = 0 + 8 = 8.$ These examples illustrate that _____ is the _____ for _____ .

18. What one-digit multiplication facts use the identity property?

19. Show how to fill in the blank without computing $12 \times 34$.
$(12 \times 34) - 48 = 12 \times$ _____ .

20. Use the distributive property to show why $8x + 6x = 14x$.

21. Show two methods of computing the total area that illustrate the distributive property.

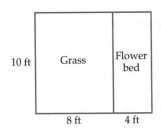

22. You drove your car on two different days for business purposes, going 120 miles and 62 miles. The company will reimburse you at a rate of 20 cents per mile. Show two ways of computing the total cost that illustrate the distributive property.

23. If $W$ is a whole number, name the property that justifies why
$$(8 + 2W) + 5W = 8 + (2W + 5W)$$

24. If $x$ is a whole number, justify each of the following steps.
$$
\begin{aligned}
(x + 3)(x + 6) &= x(x + 6) + 3(x + 6) &&\text{_____} \\
&= x^2 + 6x + 3x + 18 &&\text{_____} \\
&= x^2 + (6 + 3)x + 18 &&\text{_____} \\
&= x^2 + 9x + 18 &&\text{Basic addition fact}
\end{aligned}
$$

25. Describe how to compute $182 + 336$ using base-ten blocks. Follow the sequence of steps that one uses in computing $182 + 336$ with paper and pencil.

26. Fill in the blank with the property that justifies the step.
$$
\begin{aligned}
36 + 8 &= (30 + 6) + 8 &&\text{Expanded notation} \\
&= 30 + (6 + 8) &&\text{_____}
\end{aligned}
$$

27. When you add $39 + 48$ using the standard algorithm, you add $9 + 8 + 30 + 40$ and regroup. The following shows why this method is correct. Fill in the blanks with properties you studied in this lesson.
$$
\begin{aligned}
39 + 48 &= (30 + 9) + (40 + 8) &&\text{Expanded notation} \\
&= 30 + (9 + 40) + 8 &&\text{_____} \\
&= 30 + (40 + 9) + 8 &&\text{_____} \\
&= (30 + 40) + (9 + 8) &&\text{_____} \\
&= (9 + 8) + (30 + 40) &&\text{_____} \\
&= \phantom{.}17\phantom{.} + (30 + 40) &&\text{Addition fact} \\
&= 7 + 10 + (30 + 40) &&\text{Expanded notation} \\
&= 7 + (10 + 30 + 40) &&\text{_____}
\end{aligned}
$$

28. In subtracting 87 from 325, 325 must be regrouped as _____ hundreds, _____ tens, and _____ ones.

29. Show how to compute $336 - 182$ using base-ten blocks. Follow the sequence of steps that one uses in computing $336 - 182$ with paper and pencil.

**30.** Compute the following using the equal-additions algorithm.

(a)  72      (b)    821
    −47          −376

**31.** In multiplying $62 \times 3$, we use the fact that $(60 + 2) \times 3 = (60 \times 3) + (2 \times 3)$. What property does this equation illustrate?

**32.** Before learning the standard multiplication algorithm, children might learn to multiply 74 by 23, as shown in the following.

$$
\begin{array}{r}
74 \\
\times 23 \\
\hline
222 \leftarrow 3 \times 74 \\
1480 \leftarrow 20 \times 74 \\
\hline
1702
\end{array}
$$

Multiply 86 by 42 using this introductory algorithm.

**33.** Draw a base-ten-block picture showing $26 \times 32 = 832$.

**34.** Compute the following using the subtractive algorithm.

(a) $437 \div 7$      (b) $8921 \div 37$

**35.** The beginning of the division algorithm for $197 \div 3$ is shown here. Explain the meaning of the $6 \times 3 = 18$ and the 17.

$$
\begin{array}{r}
6\phantom{00} \\
3\overline{\smash{)}197} \\
18\phantom{0} \\
\hline
17
\end{array}
$$

**36.** Name three consecutive counting numbers whose sum is

(a) 84.      (b) 411.

(c) $N$, a counting number divisible by 3.

In Exercises 37–44, (a) complete the last example, repeating the error pattern in the completed examples and (b) describe the error pattern.

**37.**
$$
\begin{array}{rrr}
\overset{1}{76} & \overset{1}{98} & 87 \\
+\ 6 & +\ 7 & +\ 8 \\
\hline
142 & 175 &
\end{array}
$$

**38.**
$$
\begin{array}{rrr}
\overset{1}{62} & \overset{1}{52} & 57 \\
+\ 57 & +84 & +76 \\
\hline
110 & 37 &
\end{array}
$$

**39.**
$$
\begin{array}{rrr}
\overset{1}{86} & \overset{1}{72} & 93 \\
-48 & -37 & -28 \\
\hline
48 & 45 &
\end{array}
$$

**40.**
$$
\begin{array}{rrr}
40 & 306 & 809 \\
-27 & -215 & -763 \\
\hline
20 & 101 &
\end{array}
$$

**41.**
$$
\begin{array}{rrr}
36 & 42 & 72 \\
\times\ 8 & \times\ 6 & \times\ 9 \\
\hline
248 & 242 &
\end{array}
$$

**42.**
$$
\begin{array}{rrr}
82 & 41 & 27 \\
\times\ 37 & \times\ 79 & \times 32 \\
\hline
574 & 369 & \\
246 & 287 & \\
\hline
820 & 656 &
\end{array}
$$

**43.**
$$
\begin{array}{ccc}
36 & 57 & \\
6\overline{\smash{)}378} & 5\overline{\smash{)}375} & 8\overline{\smash{)}512} \\
36 & 35 & \\
\hline
18 & 25 & \\
18 & 25 &
\end{array}
$$

**44.**
$$
\begin{array}{ccc}
26 & 15 & \\
4\overline{\smash{)}824} & 5\overline{\smash{)}525} & 6\overline{\smash{)}1254}
\end{array}
$$

**45.** Describe two errors children might make in computing $27 \times 30$.

**46.** Compute the following using scratch addition.

(a)  386      (b)   4679
     97            345
     58          + 276
   + 87

**47.** Compute the following using low-stress subtraction.

(a)  68      (b)   324
    −39          −157

**48.** **Lattice multiplication** was passed along from the early Hindus and Chinese to the Arabs to medieval Europe. It appeared in the earliest known arithmetic book, which was published in Italy in 1478. Today, it is sometimes taught as an enrichment topic in the upper elementary grades. The algorithm for $27 \times 34$ is shown here.

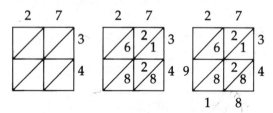

**Step 1:**
Write the numbers.

**Step 2:**
Multiply.

**Step 3:**
Sum the numbers on each diagonal.

So $27 \times 34 = 918$.

(a) Compute $38 \times 74$ using lattice multiplication.
(b) Compute $123 \times 35$ using lattice multiplication.
(c) How do you think this algorithm compares to the standard one?

**49.** The **Russian peasant multiplication algorithm** was used thousands of years ago by the Egyptians and until recently by Russian peasants. The Russian peasant algorithm for multiplying employs halving and doubling. Remainders are ignored when halving. The algorithm for $33 \times 47$ is shown here.

| Halving | Doubling | |
|---|---|---|
| Smaller → 33 | (47) | ← Larger |
| factor    16 | 94 | factor |
| 8 | 188 | |
| 4 | 376 | |
| 2 | 752 | |
| 1 | (1504) | |

Circle and add all the numbers in the doubling column that are paired with *odd* numbers in the halving column. $47 + 1504 = 1551$, so $33 \times 47 = 1551$.

(a) Compute $28 \times 52$ using this algorithm.
(b) Compute $18 \times 127$ using this algorithm.
(c) How does it compare to the standard algorithm?

**50.** A cashier may count off your change using the **cashier's subtraction algorithm.** If you give the cashier $40 for a $27 purchase, a cashier using this algorithm would say $28, $29, $30, $40 while giving you change. Explain how the algorithm works in this example.

*Extension Exercises*

**51.** Describe how to compute $26 \times 7$ using base-ten blocks to model the algorithm. Follow the same sequence of steps that one uses in computing $\begin{array}{r} 26 \\ \times\ 7 \\ \hline \end{array}$ with paper and pencil.

**52.** Describe how you would compute $246 \div 2$ using the partition model with base-ten blocks. Start with the hundreds.

**53.** Find the quotient and *remainder* of $8569 \div 23$ using a calculator.

**54.** $A$, $B$, and $C$ are whole numbers, and $A \neq 0$ and $B \neq 0$. For each equation, find one set of numbers that makes the equation true and one set of numbers that makes the equation false.

(a) $A \div B = B \div A$
(b) $C \div (A \div B) = (C \div A) \div B$
(c) $A - (B - C) = (A - B) - C$
(d) $A - B$ is a whole number.
(e) $A \div B$ is a whole number.
(f) $A \times (C \div B) = (A \times C) \div (A \times B)$
(g) $A - (C \div B) = (A - C) \div (A - B)$

**55.** (a) When you double both addends, what happens to the sum?
(b) Use the distributive property to prove your answer to part (a).
(c) What kind of reasoning did you use in part (a)?
(d) What kind of reasoning did you use in part (b)?

**56.** (a) When you double both numbers in a subtraction problem, what happens to the difference?
(b) Use the distributive property to prove your answer to part (a).

**57.** When you multiply $39 \times 48$ using the standard algorithm, you multiply and add partial products $(9 \times 8) + (30 \times 8) + (9 \times 40) + (30 \times 40)$. The following shows why this is correct. Fill in the blanks with properties you studied in this lesson.

$$
\begin{aligned}
39 \times 48 &= (30 + 9) \times (40 + 8) \\
&= [(30 + 9) \times 40] + [(30 + 9) \times 8] \\
&= [(30 \times 40) + (9 \times 40)] + [(30 \times 8) + (9 \times 8)] \\
&= [(30 \times 8) + (9 \times 8)] + [(30 \times 40) + (9 \times 40)] \\
&= [(9 \times 8) + (30 \times 8)] + [(9 \times 40) + (30 \times 40)]
\end{aligned}
$$

expanded notation

_____

_____

_____

_____

**58.** (a) Explain why someone might incorrectly compute $2 \cdot (3 \cdot 4)$ as $2 \cdot 3 \cdot 2 \cdot 4$.
(b) How would you explain the correct answer to this person?

**59.** (a) Select a three-digit number whose first and third digits are different.
(b) Reverse the digits of your number and subtract the smaller of the two numbers from the larger.
(c) Select another three-digit number and do the same thing.
(d) Select another three-digit number and do the same thing.
(e) What pattern do you see in your answer?
(f) Finding the general pattern from examples involves _____ reasoning.

**60.** Fill in each box using each digit from 1 to 9 once.

$$
\begin{array}{c}
\square\square\square \\
-\ \square\square\square \\
\hline
\square\square\square
\end{array}
$$

**61.** Fill in the missing digits.

$$
\begin{array}{r}
2?? \\
6 \overline{\smash{)}\,?2??} \\
\underline{??} \\
3 \\
? \\
\underline{??} \\
?? \\
\hline
0
\end{array}
$$

**62.** (a) Each letter represents a digit. Can you break the code?

$$
\begin{array}{r}
B\ A \\
\times\ \underline{C\ A} \\
F\ A\ B \\
\underline{D\ B\ E} \\
C\ F\ D\ B
\end{array}
$$

(b) What properties of the operations or the numbers did you use?

*Special Exercises*

**63.** Consider the set of numbers $A = \{5, 6, 7, 8\}$ with a made-up operation called $*$. The rules for $*$ are shown in the table.

| * | 5 | 6 | 7 | 8 |
|---|---|---|---|---|
| 5 | 8 | 7 | 6 | 5 |
| 6 | 7 | 6 | 5 | 8 |
| 7 | 6 | 5 | 8 | 7 |
| 8 | 5 | 8 | 7 | 6 |

(a) Is $*$ commutative for set $A$?
(b) Is there a number $I$ (an identity element) in $A$ such that $I * a = a * I = a$ for all numbers $a$ in $A$?
(c) Does $(5 * 6) * 8 = 5 * (6 * 8)$?
(d) Is $*$ associative for set $A$?

**64.** Consider the set of whole numbers and the operation $\nabla$, which takes the largest of any two numbers as the result. For example, $3 \nabla 6 = 6$ and $8 \nabla 2 = 8$.
(a) Is $\nabla$ commutative for whole numbers?
(b) Is there an identity number for $\nabla$ in $W$?
(c) Is $\nabla$ associative for whole numbers?

## 3.5   Whole Numbers: Mental Computation and Estimation

Believe it or not, your ancestors used to do all their arithmetic without electronic calculators! In order to cope with this hardship, they developed a repertoire of computational shortcuts. Today, most adults solve more complicated arithmetic problems with a calculator. But what happens if you don't have a calculator with you? Will you be limited to doing one-digit arithmetic?

### Left-to-Right Addition and Multiplication

Do you enjoy doing something differently than the way it's "normally" done? Sometimes it's a good idea! Addition and multiplication can sometimes be done mentally by working from left to right instead of from right to left.

### Example 3.7

A woman buys a dress for $46 and a coat for $79. How could she mentally compute the total cost?

**Solution**

Two break-apart methods can be used, breaking apart one *or* both addends using the place value of the number.

*Method 1*   Add the entire first number to the tens place of the second number. Then add the ones digit from the second number. Think $46 + $70 = $116 and $116 + $9 = $125.

*Method 2*  Add the tens, add the ones, and then add the answers together. Think $40 + 70 = 110$ and $6 + 9 = 15$. The answer is $\$110 + \$15 = \$125$.  ■

Do Lesson Exercise 3.77 mentally using one of the methods from Example 3.7.

## Lesson Exercise 3.77

(a) A man buys a coat for $56 and a cassette player for $78. How could he mentally compute the total cost?
(b) What property makes $50 + 6 + 70 + 8 = 50 + 70 + 6 + 8$?

Multiplication can also be done from left to right.

### Example 3.8

A restaurant uses 68 gallons of water per day. Explain how to compute mentally how much the restaurant would use in a week.

**Solution**

Multiply from left to right. Think $7 \times 60 = 420$ and $7 \times 8 = 56$. Add $420 + 56 = 476$ gallons.  ■

## Lesson Exercise 3.78

A car trip in the mountains takes 9 hours of driving at an average of 35 miles per hour. How could you mentally compute the total distance traveled?

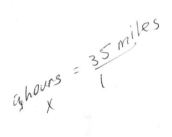

## Estimation

In order to estimate, one converts a problem to a similar but easier problem that can be computed mentally. Estimation shows another side of mathematics, in which one seeks a reasonable result rather than an exact one. Adults use estimation either to obtain an approximate answer without having to use a calculator or to check work done with a calculator or by another person.

**D** Lesson Exercise 3.79

Name a situation in which you have used estimation.

The three most useful strategies for whole-number estimation are rounding, the compatible-numbers strategy, and the front-end strategy.

## Rounding Strategy

How many calories should you eat each day? If you are a young adult, like I used to be, you could multiply your weight in pounds by 19 to get a rough calorie estimate.

**D** Lesson Exercise 3.80

May Wong is a 14-year-old weighing 93 pounds. How would you estimate how many calories she should consume to maintain her weight if the recommended number of calories is 18 times the number of pounds she weighs?

Did you use rounding to estimate the answer to the preceding exercise? You could have estimated $93 \times 18$ by rounding the factors to 90 and 20, multiplying 9 by 2 mentally, and adding two zeroes. So the answer is about 1800 calories. In symbols, this is written: $93 \times 18 \approx 1800$, in which the symbol $\approx$ means "is approximately equal to."

The rounding strategy involves two steps.

---

**Rounding Strategy**

1. Round the numbers to obtain a problem you can compute mentally.

2. Add, subtract, or multiply the rounded numbers to obtain an estimate.

---

Use the rounding strategy to estimate the answer to Lesson Exercises 3.81 and 3.82.

Lesson Exercise 3.81

A stadium seats 58,921 people. If only 3,426 tickets are left for next Sunday's match between the Poodles and the Goulash, *explain* how you would estimate the number of tickets that have been sold.

**D** Lesson Exercise 3.82

In estimating $A - C$, in which $A > C$, you round $A$ up and $C$ down. Your estimate will be
(a) too high     (b) too low     (c) Could be too high or too low

## The Compatible Numbers Strategy

In division, rounding does not always yield a simpler problem.

**D** Lesson Exercise 3.83

A group of milking cows produces 712 oz of milk one fine day. How would you estimate the number of quarts produced? (One quart contains 32 oz.)

In the preceding exercise, you needed to estimate $712 \div 32$. You could have rounded it to $700 \div 30$ or $710 \div 30$, but a better choice would be $750 \div 30$ or $700 \div 35$. For example, $712 \div 32 \approx 750 \div 30 = 25$. The average per cow is a little less than 25 quarts.

The computation $750 \div 30$ is an example of **compatible numbers,** a set of numbers whose sum, difference, product, or quotient is easy to compute mentally.

The compatible numbers strategy involves two steps.

---

**The Compatible-Numbers Strategy**

1. Round the two numbers to nearby compatible numbers.
2. Perform the computation with the compatible numbers and use the answer as an estimate.

---

Use the compatible-numbers strategy to estimate in the following exercises.

Lesson Exercise 3.84

You want to pay for an $8462 National Motors Ulcer in 24 easy interest-free monthly payments. How could you estimate the cost of a monthly payment?

**D** Lesson Exercise 3.85

$A$ and $C$ are whole numbers. In estimating $A \div C$, you round $A$ up and $C$ down. If you assume that $C \neq 0$, your estimate will be
(a) too high      (b) too low   (c) could be too high or too low

You can also use compatible numbers to estimate when adding three or more numbers by adding groups of numbers that total approximately 100 or 1000 (or some other round number).

Example 3.9

A movie theater had six shows of "Return of the Dodecahedron" on a Saturday. The number of tickets sold at the six shows were 64, 27, 59, 32, 41, and 77. How could you estimate the total number of tickets sold using the compatible-numbers strategy?

**Solution**

Add compatible numbers.

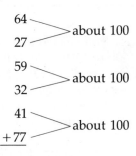

The sum is about 300 tickets.   ■

## Lesson Exercise 3.86

(a) The next day the movie theater of the preceding example had six more shows. The total number of tickets sold at the six shows were 36, 52, 51, 98, 71, and 96. Explain how to estimate the total number of tickets sold using the compatible-numbers strategy.
(b) What properties allow you to reorder and regroup the numbers?

## The Front-End Strategy

Front-end estimation is especially useful in addition. It is based upon adding a column of numbers from left to right. The estimate is made by adding the digits in the left-hand column and is then adjusted by considering the digits in the next column over to the right.

Figure 3-38 shows an example of the front-end strategy from *Mathematics Unlimited*, Grade 4.

Estimation is a relatively new topic in school. If you are not familiar with the front-end strategy, study the example in Figure 3-38 before solving the next exercise.

## Lesson Exercise 3.87

A salesperson sells three used cars for $3793, $4091, and $2807. *Explain* how you would use front-end estimation to estimate the salesperson's total sales.

## Estimating Sums

**A.** At the Lenawee County Fair, there were 478 students from Stark School, 216 students from Central School, and 193 students from Kaye School. About how many students from the three schools came to the fair?

To find about how many, you estimate.
Estimate 478 + 216 + 193.

| Add the front digits. | Write zeros for the other digits. |
|---|---|
| 478 | 478 |
| 216 | 216 |
| + 193 | + 193 |
| 7 | about **700** |

Rough estimate: 700
About 700 students from the three schools came to the fair.

**B.** You can adjust your estimate by looking at the other digits. Look for number pairs that add together to about 100.

478   +   216                    +    193

These add together to          This is about 100.
about 100.

100 + 100 = 200

Adjusted estimate: 700 + 200 = 900
About 900 students from the three schools came to the fair.

From *Mathematics Unlimited*, Grade 4 (San Diego, CA: Harcourt Brace Jovanovich, 1992), p. 41.

**Figure 3-38**

## Answers to Selected Lesson Exercises

**3.77** (a) Compute 50 + 70 = 120 and 8 + 6 = 14. Then 120 + 14 = 134.
(b) commutative property of addition

**3.78** Think $9 \times 30 = 270$ and $9 \times 5 = 45$. Add 270 + 45 = 315 miles.

**3.81** Round the problem to 59,000 − 3000 = 56,000 tickets.

**3.82** (a)

**3.84** $8462 \div 24 \approx 8000 \div 20 = \$400$

**3.85** (a)

**3.86** (a) 36 + 71, 52 + 51, 98 and 96 are each about 100. The sum is about 400.
(b) commutative and associative

**3.87** Add 3 + 4 + 2 thousand = $9000. Add another $700 + $800 to obtain $10,500.

## 3.5   Homework Exercises

*Basic Exercises*

1. The distance from Washington, D.C., north to Baltimore is 39 miles; the distance from Baltimore north to Philadelphia is 97 miles.
   (a) Explain how to compute mentally the total distance from Washington, D.C., to Philadelphia.
   (b) What property justifies the expression $30 + 9 + 90 + 7 = 30 + 90 + 9 + 7$?

2. A watermelon costs 39¢ per pound.
   (a) Explain how to compute mentally the cost of a 6-pound watermelon.
   (b) What property justifies the expression $39 \times 6 = (30 \times 6) + (9 \times 6)$?

Explain how to compute Exercises 3–5 mentally.

3. $(500)^3 =$ _____

4. The distance form Memphis to Albuquerque is 1000 miles. How long would it take to drive averaging 50 miles per hour?

5. A restaurant serves 4000 people per week. How many will it serve in 300 weeks?

6. (a) How many digits could the product of two three-digit whole numbers have?
   (b) A four-digit whole number is divided by a two-digit whole number. How many digits could the quotient have?

7. *Explain* how you would use rounding to estimate mentally $5692 + 8091 + 3721$.

8. An auditorium has 56 rows, each seating 23 people.
   (a) Explain how you would use rounding to estimate mentally the total number of seats by rounding.
   (b) Which category of multiplication is illustrated?

9. The distance from Boston to Buffalo is about 437 miles.
   (a) Explain how you would mentally estimate the time the drive would take if you averaged 55 mph.
   (b) Which category of division is illustrated?

10. A college has 4832 students and 324 teachers.
    (a) Explain how you would mentally estimate the number of students per teacher (called the "student-teacher ratio").
    (b) Which category of division is illustrated?

11. Use mental computation to write a realistic multiplication word problem that has an answer of 72,000.

12. *Explain* how you would mentally compute the following using the compatible-numbers strategy.

$$\begin{array}{r} 59 \\ 32 \\ 42 \\ + 97 \end{array}$$

13. $A$ and $C$ are two-digit whole numbers. In estimating $A \div C$, you round $A$ up and $C$ down. Would your estimate be too high, too low, or is it impossible to tell?

14. Without computing the products, tell which pairs of factors have the same product?
    (a) $36 \times 22$ and $18 \times 11$
    (b) $14 \times 22$ and $7 \times 44$
    (c) $35 \times 66$ and $105 \times 22$

15. You can mentally divide by 25 if you think of four 25's making 100 (or four quarters making a dollar, if you prefer). In other words, each 100 has four 25's. Try the following.
    (a) $200 \div 25$ (Think of four 25's per 100.)
    (b) $700 \div 25$
    (c) How many quarters in $9?
    (d) $650 \div 25$
    (e) How many quarters in $4.25?

16. Three towns with populations of 3692, 1527, and 4278 make up a voting district. *Explain* how to estimate the total population of the voting district using front-end estimation.

17. The Department of Education spent the following amounts on three projects: $3,462,871; $830,212; and $21,172,806. Explain how to estimate the total expense to

the nearest *million* dollars using the front-end or rounding strategy.

18. About how long would it take you to read a 300-page novel?

19. **Clustering** is a method of estimating a sum when the numbers are all close to one value. For example, $3648 + 4281 + 3791 \approx 3 \cdot (4000) = 12,000$. Show how to estimate the following using the clustering strategy.
    (a) $897 + 706 + 823 + 902 + 851 \approx$
    _____
    (b) $36,421 + 41,362 + 40,987 + 42,621 \approx$
    _____

20. In each situation, tell whether it makes more sense to compute mentally or to use a calculator. Assume the calculator is stored somewhere nearby.
    (a) You want to estimate the total revenue at a baseball game with 38,542 people who paid an average of about $5 per ticket.
    (b) You just purchased 264 scientific calculators for your school at $18 each and you want to check the total bill.

21. How could you use a calculator *and* mental computation to figure the cost of buying 20 carpets that are 18 ft by 24 ft, if each square foot costs $5?

22. In each exercise, estimate the second factor so that the product falls in the range given. Check your guess on a calculator and revise it as needed.
    (a) $300 \times$ _____ = (between 6000 and 6500)
    (b) $46 \times$ _____ = (between 700 and 750)
    (c) $67 \times$ _____ = (between 2500 and 2600)

23. In each exercise, estimate the divisor so that the quotient falls in the range given. Check your guess on a calculator and revise it as needed.
    (a) $463 \div$ _____ = (between 80 and 90)
    (b) $3246 \div$ _____ = (between 200 and 300)
    (c) $4684 \div$ _____ = (between 65 and 70)

24. (a) Place the digits 4, 5, 6, 8, and 9 in the blanks to obtain an answer that is as

close as possible to 50,000.
$$\text{\_\_ \_\_ \_\_ \_\_} \times \text{\_\_} \approx 50,000$$
(b) Use a calculator to see how close you came.
(c) Make a second guess and try to get closer to 50,000.
(d) Check your second guess on a calculator.

25. (a) Calculate $15^2$, $25^2$, and $35^2$.
    (b) Devise a shortcut for mentally squaring a two-digit counting number that ends in 5.
    (c) Try your shortcut on $65^2$ and check your guess on a calculator.

26. Select 5 different digits. Use 2 digits to form one factor and 3 digits to form the other factor.
    (a) Obtain the largest possible product using your 5 digits.
    (b) Obtain the smallest possible product using your 5 digits.

27. Consider the following problem: "Use each of the digits from 1 to 6 once to obtain the largest possible product."

$$\begin{array}{r} ?\,?\,? \\ \times\ ?\,?\,? \\ \hline \end{array}$$

(a) Devise a plan and solve the problem.
(b) Make up a similar problem.

28. Select 6 different digits. Use each of the digits once and obtain the largest possible quotient.

29. Predict which of the following problems have the smallest and largest answers. Then compute the answers with a calculator.
    (a) $46 \times 72$     (b) $42 \times 76$
    (c) $24 \times 67$     (d) $74 \times 26$

30. What two numbers have a sum of 109 and a product of 1978?

31. Use estimation to tell whether the following

calculator answers are reasonable. Explain why or why not.

(a) $657 + 542 + 707 = \boxed{543364}$

(b) $26 \times 47 = \boxed{1222}$

(c) $3650 \div 25 = \boxed{1825}$

32. (a) Compute the following using a calculator.

$15{,}873 \times 7 =$ _____
$15{,}873 \times 14 =$ _____
$15{,}873 \times 21 =$ _____

(b) Based upon the pattern in part (a), guess the following products.

$15{,}873 \times 35 =$ _____
$15{,}873 \times 63 =$ _____

33. For each computation, tell which computation method you would use (mental computation, paper and pencil, or calculator) and why.

(a) $87{,}347 \times 144$   (b) $750 + 422 + 250$
(c) $782 - 246$

*Extension Exercises*

34. **Compensation** is another method of mental computation in which the changes made to each number in an arithmetic problem balance out. The result is that the overall problem is easier to do, and it still has the same answer! For example:

$$783 + 597 = 780 + 600 = 1380$$
$$352 - 238 = 354 - 240 = 114$$
$$288 \div 36 \ = 72 \div 9 \ \ = 8$$

In parts (a), (b), and (c), change the example to an easier problem and compute the result mentally.

(a) $896 + 364$   (b) $821 - 489$
(c) $3600 \div 72$
(d) Show algebraically why compensation to $x + y$ using an amount $c$ does not change the result.
(e) Show algebraically why compensation to $x - y$ using an amount $c$ does not change the result.

35. Show how to compute the following mentally using compensation.
(a) $389 + 895$    (b) $4990 + 3627$
(c) $762 - 89$

36. There is a shortcut for multiplying a whole number by 99. For example, consider $15 \times 99$.
(a) Why does $15 \times 99 = (15 \times 100) - (15 \times 1)$?
(b) Compute $15 \times 99$ mentally using the formula in part (a).
(c) Compute $95 \times 99$ mentally using the same method.

37. (a) Develop a shortcut for multiplying $8 \times 999$ mentally. (*Hint:* See the previous exercise.)
(b) Compute $6 \times 999$ mentally using the same shortcut.
(c) Show how this shortcut is based upon the distributive property.

38. (a) Develop a shortcut for multiplying by 25 mentally in a computation such as $24 \times 25$.
(b) Compute $44 \times 25$ using the same shortcut.

39. (a) Develop a shortcut for multiplying by 15 mentally in a computation such as $24 \times 15$.
(b) Compute $42 \times 15$ using the same shortcut.

40. $33 \times 37 = 1221$
$46 \times 44 = 2024$
$58 \times 52 = 3016$

(a) Make up another example of this type.
(b) How can these examples be computed mentally?
(c) Prove that the shortcut always works. (*Hint:* Represent the two digits of the two numbers by $a\ b$ and $a\ 10 - b$ and write them in expanded notation.)

41. Michigan has about 10 million people, each using 70 gallons of water per day. Explain how to compute mentally how much water these people use in a 30-day month.

**42.** Consider the following problem: "Find four consecutive whole numbers whose product is 303,600." Devise a plan and solve the problem.

**43.** Estimate the total number of restaurants in the United States.

**44.** About how many pounds of food do you eat each day?

**45.** Look at a current series of mathematics textbooks for Grades 1–6. What do they teach about estimation and mental computation in each grade?

## 3.6 Place Value and Algorithms in Other Bases

You are well acquainted with base-ten place value and arithmetic. This familiarity will make it harder for you to understand the difficulties your students will encounter in learning about place value and arithmetic for the first time.

Studying place value and the algorithms in less familiar number systems will enable you to re-experience learning these concepts. Working in other bases will also deepen your understanding of place value and the algorithms.

### Other Numeration Systems

Today, most countries use base-ten numeration systems. The basis for this is people's tendency to count on their fingers.

In fact, any counting number greater than 1 could be used as a base. The Babylonians used base 60, the Mayans used base 20, and some ancient tribes used base 2. Today, computers work with base 2, 8, and 16, and some goods such as eggs and pencils are grouped in dozens and grosses (groups of 12 and $12^2$).

In representing 19 items, one could group them in different ways, as shown in Figure 3-39.

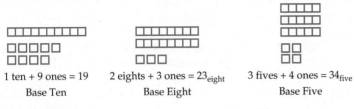

1 ten + 9 ones = 19          2 eights + 3 ones = $23_{eight}$          3 fives + 4 ones = $34_{five}$

Base Ten                          Base Eight                          Base Five

**Figure 3-39**

Consider base eight, the **octal** system, which is used in computers. Just as base ten has ten digits (0, 1, 2, 3, 4, 5, 6, 7, 8, 9), base eight has eight digits (0, 1, 2, 3, 4, 5, 6, 7).

## Lesson Exercise 3.88

What digits would base five have?

Counting with the eight digits of base eight goes like this: 0, 1, 2, 3, 4, 5, 6, 7, 10, 11, 12, . . . . In order to indicate a numeral in a base other than ten, one writes the base as a subscript, as in $12_{eight}$.

Figure 3-40 illustrates the meaning of some base-eight numerals and their representations using base-eight blocks.

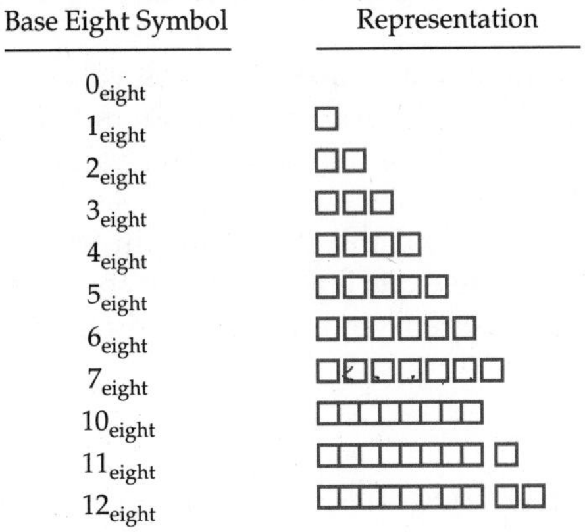

| Base Eight Symbol | Representation |
|---|---|
| $0_{eight}$ | |
| $1_{eight}$ | ▢ |
| $2_{eight}$ | ▢▢ |
| $3_{eight}$ | ▢▢▢ |
| $4_{eight}$ | ▢▢▢▢ |
| $5_{eight}$ | ▢▢▢▢▢ |
| $6_{eight}$ | ▢▢▢▢▢▢ |
| $7_{eight}$ | ▢▢▢▢▢▢▢ |
| $10_{eight}$ | ▭▭▭▭▭▭▭▭ |
| $11_{eight}$ | ▭▭▭▭▭▭▭▭ ▢ |
| $12_{eight}$ | ▭▭▭▭▭▭▭▭ ▢▢ |

**Figure 3-40**

## Lesson Exercise 3.89

What base-ten numeral is the same as $32_{eight}$?

Base-eight place value works like base-ten place value. In base ten, each place value is ten times larger than the place value to its right. In base eight, each place value is eight times larger than the place to its right, with the right-hand place for whole numbers being the ones place.

| 100 | 10 | 1 | ← **Place values expressed** → | 64 | 8 | 1 |
|---|---|---|---|---|---|---|
| 3 | 1 | 4 | **using base-ten numerals** | 3 | 1 | 4 |

$$314 = 3(100) + 1(10) + 4(1)$$

$$314_{eight} = 3(64) + 1(8) + 4(1)$$
$$= 204$$

Thus, $314_{eight}$ is the same as 204.

## Lesson Exercise 3.90

Convert $326_{eight}$ to base ten.

## Lesson Exercise 3.91

Convert $2134_{five}$ to base ten. (*Hint:* First, write place value columns for base five.)

One can also convert base-ten numerals to any other base.

### Example 3.10

Convert 150 to base eight.

**Solution**

Base-eight numbers use groups of 1, 8, 64, 512, and so on. Start with the largest grouping that is less than or equal to 150, namely, 64. How many 64's are there in 150? 2.

$$\begin{array}{r} 2 \\ 64 \overline{\smash{\big)}\ 150} \\ \underline{128} \\ 22 \end{array}$$

This leaves 22. Proceed to the next lowest grouping, 8's. How many 8's in 22? 2.

$$\begin{array}{r} 2\ R\ 6 \\ 8 \overline{\smash{\big)}\ 22} \end{array}$$

This leaves 6 ones. So $150 = (2 \times 64) + (2 \times 8) + 6$, or $226_{eight}$. ■

## Lesson Exercise 3.92

(a) Convert 302 to base eight.
(b) Convert 302 to base five.

## Algorithms in Base Five

The base-ten arithmetic algorithms also work in other bases. Studying algorithms in other bases will increase your understanding of them. How does one compute $34_{five} + 22_{five}$? How is it similar to base-ten addition?

**Example 3.11**

Compute     $\begin{array}{r} 34_{\text{five}} \\ +22_{\text{five}} \end{array}$

**Solution**

Follow the same steps as in the base-ten algorithm, but remember that the base-five digits are 0, 1, 2, 3, and 4 and regrouping (carrying) involves groups of 5 rather than groups of 10.

*Step 1*

$$\begin{array}{r} 1 \\ 34_{\text{five}} \\ +22_{\text{five}} \\ \hline 1_{\text{five}} \end{array}$$

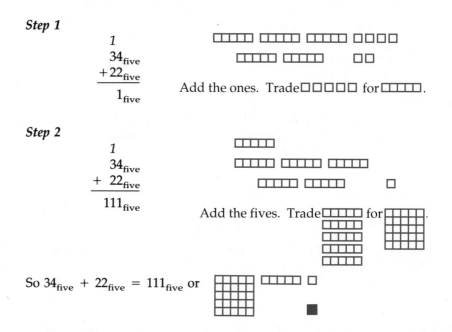

Add the ones. Trade ☐☐☐☐☐ for ▭▭▭.

*Step 2*

$$\begin{array}{r} 1 \\ 34_{\text{five}} \\ +\ 22_{\text{five}} \\ \hline 111_{\text{five}} \end{array}$$

Add the fives. Trade ▭▭ for ⊞.

So $34_{\text{five}} + 22_{\text{five}} = 111_{\text{five}}$ or

## Lesson Exercise  3.93

Compute $24_{\text{five}} + 14_{\text{five}}$.

## Lesson Exercise  3.94

Compute $32_{\text{five}} - 14_{\text{five}}$. Remember: Regrouping (borrowing) involves 5's, not 10's.

Next, consider the multiplication algorithm. A base-five multiplication table will be helpful.

## Lesson Exercise 3.95

Complete the base-five multiplication table.

| × | 0 | 1 | 2 | 3 | 4 |
|---|---|---|---|---|---|
| 0 | 0 | 0 | 0 | 0 | 0 |
| 1 | 0 | 1 | 2 | 3 | 4 |
| 2 | 0 | 2 | 4 | 11 | 13 |
| 3 |   |   |   |   |   |
| 4 |   |   |   |   |   |

Example 3.12 utilizes this table to compute $23_{five} \times 14_{five}$.

### Example 3.12

Compute    $23_{five}$

$\times 14_{five}$

**Solution**

Follow the same steps as in the base-ten algorithm. Refer to the base-five multiplication table to obtain the basic facts. First, multiply $4_{five} \times 3_{five}$, which the table says is $22_{five}$. Put down the 2 and carry the 2.

$$
\begin{array}{r}
2 \\
23_{five} \\
\times 14_{five} \\
\hline
2_{five}
\end{array}
$$

Then $4_{five} \times 2_{five} = 13_{five} + 2_{five} = 20_{five}$.

$$
\begin{array}{r}
2 \\
23_{five} \\
\times\ 14_{five} \\
\hline
202_{five}
\end{array}
$$

Next, compute $10_{five} \times 23_{five}$ and add the partial products.

$$
\begin{array}{r}
23_{five} \\
\times\ 14_{five} \\
\hline
202_{five} \\
230_{five} \\
\hline
432_{five}
\end{array}
$$

■

## Lesson Exercise 3.96

Compute $44_{\text{five}} \times 22_{\text{five}}$.

Long division in base five can be done using a long-division algorithm analogous to the base-ten algorithm.

### Example 3.13

Compute $1442_{\text{five}} \div 4_{\text{five}}$.

**Solution**

Using long division, follow the same steps as in base ten. First, how many times can $4_{\text{five}}$ go into $14_{\text{five}}$? 2. (You can refer to the base-five multiplication table.) $2_{\text{five}} \times 14_{\text{five}} = 13_{\text{five}}$. Subtract this from $14_{\text{five}}$ and bring down the next digit in the next dividend.

$$
\begin{array}{r}
2 \phantom{000} \\
4_{\text{five}} \overline{\left) 1442_{\text{five}} \right.} \\
\underline{13 \phantom{00}} \\
14 \phantom{00}
\end{array}
$$

Next, divide $4_{\text{five}}$ into $14_{\text{five}}$. It goes in 2 times, as it did before. Continuing the algorithm in this manner yields the following results.

$$
\begin{array}{r}
221 \text{ R } 3 \\
4_{\text{five}} \overline{\left) 1442_{\text{five}} \right.} \\
\underline{13 \phantom{00}} \\
14 \phantom{0} \\
\underline{13 \phantom{0}} \\
12 \\
\underline{4} \\
3 \quad \blacksquare
\end{array}
$$

## Lesson Exercise 3.97

Compute $1343_{\text{five}} \div 3_{\text{five}}$.

The homework exercises include problems involving alternate algorithms in other bases.

## Answers to Selected Lesson Exercises

3.88  0, 1, 2, 3, 4

3.89  26

3.90  214

3.91  294

3.92  (a) $456_{\text{eight}}$
      (b) $2202_{\text{five}}$

3.93  $43_{\text{five}}$

3.94  $13_{\text{five}}$

**3.95** Base-five multiplication table

| × | 0 | 1 | 2 | 3 | 4 |
|---|---|---|---|---|---|
| 0 | 0 | 0 | 0 | 0 | 0 |
| 1 | 0 | 1 | 2 | 3 | 4 |
| 2 | 0 | 2 | 4 | 11 | 13 |
| 3 | 0 | 3 | 11 | 14 | 22 |
| 4 | 0 | 4 | 13 | 22 | 31 |

**3.96** $2123_{five}$

**3.97** $244_{five}$ R 1

## 3.6 Homework Exercises

### Basic Exercises

1. How would you group

   X X X X X X X X X X X X X

   in each of the following bases?
   (a) base eight    (b) base five

2. How many different digits are needed for base 12?

3. Write the first 12 counting numbers in base three.

4. What base-eight numeral follows $377_{eight}$?

5. Convert each of the following to base ten.
   (a) $75_{eight}$    (b) $423_{five}$    (c) $213_{eight}$

6. Convert each of the following base-ten numerals to numerals in the indicated base.
   (a) 46 to base eight
   (b) 26 to base five
   (c) 324 to base five

7. (a) Using quarters, nickels, and pennies, what is the minimum number of coins needed to make 86¢?
   (b) Write a mathematics problem involving bases that is equivalent to the problem in part (a).

8. How can one distinguish even whole numbers from odd ones in the following systems?
   (a) base eight    (b) base five

9. Consider the following problem: "How can one recognize a base-five numeral that is divisible by 5?" Devise a plan and solve the problem.

10. Change $36_{eight}$ to base five.

11. Which is larger, $1011_{five}$ or $72_{eight}$?

12. Write a numeral for the following set using the base indicated by the grouping.

13. Write a base-five numeral represented by the base-five blocks shown. (Make all possible trades first.)

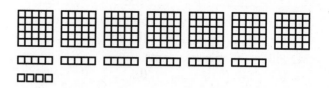

14. Perform the following computations.
    (a) $23_{five}$          (b) $324_{five}$          (c) $432_{five}$
        $+34_{five}$             $+132_{five}$             $+233_{five}$

15. Perform the following computations.
    (a) $41_{five}$          (b) $312_{five}$          (c) $432_{five}$
        $-23_{five}$             $-133_{five}$             $-143_{five}$

16. *Explain* how to compute $31_{five} + 22_{five}$ using base-five blocks. Follow the same sequence of steps used in the addition algorithm.

17. *Explain* how to compute $43_{\text{five}} - 24_{\text{five}}$ using base-five blocks. Follow the same sequence of steps used in the subtraction algorithm.

18. Perform the following computations.
(a) $\begin{array}{r} 34_{\text{five}} \\ \times\,23_{\text{five}} \\ \hline \end{array}$   (b) $\begin{array}{r} 412_{\text{five}} \\ \times\,321_{\text{five}} \\ \hline \end{array}$

19. Perform the following computations.
(a) $213_{\text{five}} \div 4_{\text{five}}$   (b) $4123_{\text{five}} \div 3_{\text{five}}$

20. Compute $324_{\text{five}} \div 4_{\text{five}}$ using the following algorithms.
(a) subtractive algorithm
(b) standard algorithm
(c) Which algorithm do you prefer? Why?

21. Complete the following base-eight addition and multiplication tables.

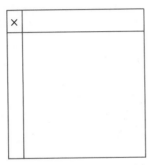

| + | 0 1 2 3 4 5 6 7 |
|---|---|
| 0 | |
| 1 | |
| 2 | |
| 3 | |
| 4 | |
| 5 | |
| 6 | |
| 7 | |

| × | |
|---|---|
| | |

22. Perform the following computations.
(a) $\begin{array}{r} 32_{\text{eight}} \\ +\,66_{\text{eight}} \\ \hline \end{array}$   (b) $\begin{array}{r} 132_{\text{eight}} \\ -\,\phantom{1}66_{\text{eight}} \\ \hline \end{array}$   (c) $\begin{array}{r} 24_{\text{eight}} \\ \times\,35_{\text{eight}} \\ \hline \end{array}$

23. Perform the following computations.
(a) $124_{\text{eight}} \div 4_{\text{eight}}$   (b) $756_{\text{eight}} \div 3_{\text{eight}}$

24. Fill in the missing digits.
(a) $\begin{array}{r} 1\ \ 3\ \ \underline{\phantom{0}}_{\text{eight}} \\ +\,2\ \underline{\phantom{0}}\ 4_{\text{eight}} \\ \hline \underline{\phantom{0}}\ \ 2\ \ 1_{\text{eight}} \end{array}$   (b) $\begin{array}{r} 2\ \ 0\ \ \underline{\phantom{0}}\ \underline{\phantom{0}}_{\text{five}} \\ -\,1\ \ 0\ \ 2\ \ 2_{\text{five}} \\ \hline \underline{\phantom{0}}\ \underline{\phantom{0}}\ \ 1\ \ 3_{\text{five}} \end{array}$

*Extension Exercises*

25. Consider the following problem: "An inspector wants to check the accuracy of a scale in weighing any whole-number amount from 1 to 15 pounds. What is the smallest number of weights the inspector needs, and what would they be?"

(a) What amounts must the inspector be able to weigh?
(b) Devise a plan and solve the problem.
(c) Make up a similar problem.

26. Computers use base 2 since it contains two digits, 0 and 1, that correspond to electronic switches being "off" or "on" in the computer. Computers sometimes take numbers in base 8 or 16 rather than base 10 because they are easier to convert to base 2. Can you figure out why?
(a) Convert $555_{\text{eight}}$ to base two.
(b) Describe an easier way for you or a computer to do part (a). (*Hint:* Work with each digit separately.)
(c) Use the shortcut from part (b) to convert $642_{\text{eight}}$ to base two.

27. In base 16 (**hexadecimal**), the digits are 0 through 9 and *A, B, C, D, E,* and *F* for 10 through 15.
(a) Convert $B6_{\text{sixteen}}$ to base ten.
(b) Convert $B6_{\text{sixteen}}$ to base two.
(c) How can a computer convert $B6_{\text{sixteen}}$ into base two without first converting it to base ten?

28. (a) Convert $11101_{\text{two}}$ to base eight.
(b) Convert $101101_{\text{two}}$ to base sixteen.

29. A magician asks a volunteer to think of a number from 1 to 15. The magician then shows the following four cards and asks the volunteer which cards contain the volunteer's number.

| 1 3 | 2 3 | 4 5 | 8 9 |
|---|---|---|---|
| 5 7 | 6 7 | 6 7 | 10 11 |
| 9 11 | 10 11 | 12 13 | 12 13 |
| 13 15 | 14 15 | 14 15 | 14 15 |

By adding the numbers in the upper left corner of the selected cards, the magician finds the secret number.
(a) Pick a number from 1 to 15 and show that the trick works.
(b) Explain how the trick works using base-two place value.

30. In base 12, the **duodecimal** system, one uses 12 digits: 0, 1, 2, 3, 4, 5, 6, 7, 8, 9, $T$, and $E$ ($T$ and $E$ represent ten and eleven).
    (a) Convert $E6_{twelve}$ to base ten.
    (b) Convert 80 to base twelve.

31. Pencils are often packed by the dozen or by the gross (144).
    (a) Inventory shows that a college bookstore has 3 gross, 2 dozen, and 8 pencils. How many pencils do they have?
    (b) Write a mathematics problem involving bases that is equivalent to the problem in part (a).

32. Perform the following computations.
    (a) $\begin{array}{r} 321_{four} \\ +233_{four} \\ \hline \end{array}$
    (b) $\begin{array}{r} 1001_{two} \\ -110_{two} \\ \hline \end{array}$

33. Perform the following computations.
    (a) $\begin{array}{r} 35_{six} \\ \times 42_{six} \\ \hline \end{array}$
    (b) $\begin{array}{r} 312_{four} \\ \times 132_{four} \\ \hline \end{array}$

34. Perform the following computations.
    (a) $123_{six} \div 3_{six}$     (b) $123_{seven} \div 3_{seven}$

35. Compute $\begin{array}{r} 243_{five} \\ +231_{five} \\ \hline \end{array}$ using scratch addition.

36. Compute $\begin{array}{r} 321_{seven} \\ -255_{seven} \\ \hline \end{array}$ using low-stress subtraction.

37. Compute $(452_{six}) \cdot (35_{six})$ using lattice multiplication.

38. For what base $b$ would $56_b + 44_b = 111_b$?

39. Consider the following problem: "$37_{eight} = 133_b$. What base is $b$?"
    (a) Devise a plan and solve the problem.
    (b) Make up a similar problem.

40. For what bases $a$ and $b$ would $12_a = 22_b$?

41. For what bases $b$ would $32_b + 25_b = 57_b$?

42. For what values of $a$ and $b$ does $a_b = b_a$?

## Summary

Our Hindu-Arabic numeration system took a long time to develop. By contrasting the Hindu-Arabic system with older systems such as ancient Egyptian and Babylonian numeration, one gains a greater appreciation of the time it took to develop a base-ten place-value system that has a symbol for zero. Children today study place value with concrete materials such as the base-ten blocks and the abacus.

"One essential component of what it means to understand an operation is recognizing conditions in real-world situations that indicate that the operation would be useful in those situations. Other components include building an awareness of models and the properties of an operation, seeing relationships among operations, and acquiring insights into effects of an operation on a pair of numbers" (NCTM, *Curriculum and Evaluation Standards*, p. 41).

In order to know when to add, subtract, multiply, or divide in everyday life, one must recognize common application categories for each operation. Although educators do not agree on the exact number or names of the categories, it is clear that each operation has anywhere from two to seven different classifications. These categories can be illustrated with pictures or objects.

Whole-number operations possess properties that simplify certain computations as well as memorization of the addition and multiplication tables. Addition and multiplication are commutative and associative, and the distributive property holds for multiplication over addition and multiplication over subtraction. The whole numbers also possess identity elements—0 for addition and 1 for multiplication.

Algorithms are faster and more efficient methods for paper-and-pencil computation involving larger numbers. Elementary-school children study simpler, introductory algorithms before learning more efficient procedures for all four operations. Manipulatives such as base-ten blocks clarify the steps in the algorithms. The addition and multiplication algorithms are based upon the commutative, associative, and distributive properties.

Adults frequently use mental computation and estimation. Our school curriculum has not reflected this usage. The elementary-school curriculum is beginning to devote more time to teaching children about whole-number computations that are especially easy to compute mentally. Children are also learning more about estimating using rounding, compatible numbers, and front-end strategies.

One can develop a deeper understanding of place value and algorithms for the four operations by studying other bases. Computers are well suited to base two, with its two digits that correspond to "on" and "off."

## Study Guide

To review Chapter 3, see what you know about each of the following ideas or terms that you have studied. You can also use this list to generate your own questions about Chapter 3.

## The NCTM Curriculum Standards and Whole Numbers

**Selected NCTM Curriculum Standards**

The following standards come from the NCTM document.

- Relate physical materials, pictures, and diagrams to mathematical ideas.
- Recognize that a wide variety of situations can be represented by a single operation.
- Relate the mathematical language and symbolism of operations to problem situations and informal language.
- Understand how the basic arithmetic operations are related to one another.
- Develop, analyze, and explain procedures for computation and techniques for estimation.
- Relate various representations of concepts or procedures to one another.

1. Describe how each standard listed relates to the material you studied in Chapter 3.
2. Select any current elementary-school mathematics textbook series and describe a sample lesson or exercise that illustrates each standard listed.

## Review Exercises

1. (a) Make a set picture illustrating why $3 \times 5 = 5 \times 3$.
   (b) What property is illustrated?

2. Show how to compute $362 - 187$ using the equal-additions algorithm.

3. Find one set of whole numbers $A$, $B$, and $C$, in which $B \neq 0$ and $C \neq 0$, that make the following equation true; then find one set that makes the equation false.

$$(A \div B) + (A \div C) = A \div (B + C)$$

4. (a) What is an easy way to compute $(8 \times 24) + (8 \times 16)$?
   (b) What property justifies your answer to part (a)?

5. Suppose the number 36,472 is rounded to 36,500. Give the place to which 36,472 is being rounded.

6. Describe the difference between a numeration system that has place value and one that does not.

7. *Explain* the meaning of $3 \div 0 = $ _____ using multiplication or the division category of your choice.

8. What is the total number of symbols needed to write 37 using each of the following?
   (a) tallies
   (b) late Egyptian numerals
   (c) Roman numerals

**9.** Make a drawing showing $7 - 3 = 4$ using compare measures.

**10.** You are planning a 2270-mile trip. Your car gets 37 miles per gallon.
  (a) Explain how you would mentally estimate how much gas you will need.
  (b) Which category of division is illustrated?

**11.** (a) Is whole-number division associative?
  (b) If so, give an example. If not, give a counterexample.

**12.** "A box holds 10 diskettes. How many boxes does Diane Lorenz need to hold 40 diskettes?" What operation and category are illustrated in this problem?

**13.** "My math class has 36 students and your class has 27 students. How many more students are there in my class?" What operation and category are illustrated in this problem?

**14.** "Ira Reed bought 6 cans of tennis balls. Each can contained 3 tennis balls. Since then, he has lost 2 balls. How many tennis balls does he have left?" What two operations and categories are illustrated in this problem?

**15.** "A truck can carry up to 1600 lb. If the driver weighs 200 lb, how many crates each weighing 40 lb can the truck carry?" What two operations and categories are illustrated in this problem?

**16.** In each part, complete the last example, repeating the same error pattern that occurs in the two completed examples.

(a)
```
  82      46      89
+ 79    + 37    + 74
─────   ─────   ─────
 1511    713
```

(b)
```
  37      426      371
- 10    - 302    - 130
─────   ─────   ─────
  20      104
```

(c)
```
   5        2
  37       27       48
× 48     × 93     × 57
─────   ─────    ─────
 296       81
 178      203
─────   ─────
2076     2111
```

**17.** *Explain* how to compute $326 + 293$ using Dienes (base-ten) blocks. Follow the same sequence of steps as the standard algorithm.

**18.** (a) Each letter in the following expression represents a digit. Find a possible solution.

$$\begin{array}{r} AA \\ + BBB \\ \hline ACD \end{array}$$

  (b) *Explain* how you solved the problem in part (a).

**19.** A man earns $D$ dollars per hour. If he works $H$ hours and then spends $S$ dollars for taxes and expenses, how much money does he have left?

**20.** Joy spent $30 on groceries. Then she spent half of her remaining money on a book. She now has $8. How much money did she start out with?

**21.** Convert 100 to base six.

**22.** Compute $1324_{\text{seven}} \div 6_{\text{seven}}$.

**23.** Find bases $a$ and $b$ such that $11_a = 22_b$.

# Computer Exercise

**1.** Ask your teacher for instructions about how to make output stop or pause and resume with your school's computers. (A program is often stopped by pressing CTRL and BREAK. CTRL and Num Lck may cause it to pause. Press any key to resume.)
  (a) RUN the following BASIC program. What is the output?

```
10 LET N = 0
20 LET N = N + 3
30 PRINT N
40 GOTO 20
```

(b) Change lines 10 and 20 so the program starts with the number 10 and counts by 5's.

(c) Guess the output of the following program and RUN it to check your prediction.

```
10 LET N = 1
20 LET N = N * 3
30 PRINT N
40 GOTO 20
```

## Whole Numbers in Elementary School

The following chart shows at what grade level selected whole-number topics typically appear in elementary-school mathematics textbooks. Underlined numbers indicate grades in which the most time is spent on the given topic.

| Topic | Typical Grade Level in Current Textbooks |
|---|---|
| Place value | 1, 2, 3, 4, 5 |
| Addition concepts | 1, 2 |
| Addition algorithm | 1, 2, 3 |
| Subtraction concepts | 1, 2 |
| Subtraction algorithm | 1, 2, 3 |
| Multiplication concepts | 2, 3, 4 |
| Multiplication algorithm | 3, 4, 5 |
| Division concepts | 3, 4 |
| Division algorithm | 3, 4, 5, 6 |
| Working backward | 4, 5, 6 |
| Estimation | 2, 3, 4, 5, 6 |

## Suggested Readings

*Arithmetic Teacher*. February 1989 Focus Issue on Number Sense. Reston, VA: NCTM, 1989.

Ashlock, R. *Error Patterns in Computation*. 3rd ed. Columbus, OH: Merrill, 1982.

Eves, H. *Introduction to the History of Mathematics*. 5th ed. Philadelphia, PA: Saunders College Publishing, 1983.

National Council of Teachers of Mathematics. *Historical Topics for the Mathematics Classroom*. Reston, VA: NCTM, 1989.

National Council of Teachers of Mathematics. 1978 Yearbook. *Developing Computational Skills*. Reston, VA: NCTM, 1978.

National Council of Teachers of Mathematics. 1986 Yearbook. *Estimation and Mental Computation*. Reston, VA: NCTM, 1986.

National Council of Teachers of Mathematics. 1989 Yearbook. *New Directions for Elementary School Mathematics*. Reston, VA: NCTM, 1989.

# 4

# Number Theory

Written records indicate that until the Pythagoreans came along around 500 B.C., people used numbers primarily in practical applications. The Pythagoreans believed that numbers revealed the underlying structure of the universe, so they studied patterns of counting numbers. This was probably the first significant work in the field of mathematics that we now call number theory.

Number theory is useful in certain computations with fractions and in algebra, but it has fewer applications outside mathematics than other topics in this course. So why do people study it? Because they appreciate the beauty of mathematics and find excitement in discovering number patterns, and they enjoy successfully using their minds to prove whether or not these patterns apply to all whole or counting numbers.

## 4.1 Factors

Pythagoras was the charismatic leader of a group of 300 called the Pythagoreans who lived about 2500 years ago. One of the female Pythagoreans was Theano, a student of Pythagoras, who later married him. After Pythagoras died, Theano continued his work. The Pythagoreans observed some rather strange rules: (1) never to eat meat or beans except after a religious sacrifice, (2) never to walk on a highway, and (3) never to let swallows sit on their roofs.

They were also mathematicians. Believing that numbers were the basis of all things, they associated numbers with ideas, just as some people today believe that 7 is lucky or 13 is unlucky. The Pythagoreans associated the number 1 with reason (a consistent whole), 2 with opinion (two sides), 4 with justice (balanced square and product of equals), and 5 with marriage (unity of their first odd or masculine and even or feminine numbers).

Their interest in numbers also led them to investigate factors. The Pythagoreans labeled a few special numbers "perfect" or "amicable" depending upon what factors they possessed.

181

## Definition of a Factor

Before finding out which numbers are perfect or amicable, you'll need to review factors. As you learned in Chapter 3, the term "factor" is used in describing the parts of any multiplication problem such as $2 \times 5 = 10$.

$$2 \times 5 = \phantom{xx} 10$$
$$\uparrow \phantom{x} \uparrow \phantom{xxxxx} \uparrow$$
$$\text{Factors} \phantom{xx} \text{Product}$$

## Lesson Exercise 4.1

Write the two division equations that are equivalent to $2 \times 5 = 10$.

In the equation $10 \div 5 = 2$, 5 is the divisor, and in the equation $10 \div 2 = 5$, 2 is the divisor. So one refers to 2 and 5 as either the "divisors" or the "factors" of 10. Although the word "factor" generally refers to multiplication and "divisor" to division, factors and divisors are the same in number theory.

---

**Definition: Factor or Divisor**

If $A$ and $B$ are whole numbers, with $A \neq 0$, then $A$ is a **factor** or **divisor** of $B$ if and only if there is a whole number $C$ such that $A \cdot C = B$.

---

To say that $A$ is a factor of $B$ means that $A$ divides $B$ evenly, say $C$ times, with $C$ being a whole number.

$$A \overline{\smash{)}B}^{\,C} \quad or \quad A \cdot C = B$$

If asked to explain why 6 is a factor of 30, you might say that it is because 6 divides 30 evenly ($30 \div 6 = 5$). Using the *definition* of a factor to explain why 6 is a factor of 30 requires using a *multiplication* equation. By the definition, 6 is a factor of 30 because there is a whole number 5 such that $6 \cdot 5 = 30$.

One advantage of defining "factor" using multiplication instead of division is that a multiplication equation is easier to work with in proofs involving factors.

## Lesson Exercise 4.2

(a)  Use the definition of a factor to explain why 2 is a factor of 40.
(b)  If 2 is a *factor* of R, then there must be a whole number N such that
_____. (Write a multiplication equation.)
(c)  Applying the definition to 2 and R in part (b) to fill in the blank involves _____ reasoning.

The notation 2 | 12 means "2 is a factor of 12" or "2 divides 12." In a | b,
the first number, a, represents the divisor or factor. To symbolize that 5 is
not a factor of 12, one writes 5 ∤ 12.

## Lesson Exercise 4.3

(a)  Name all the factors of 12.
(b)  Show the factor pairs of 12 using rectangles. The rectangles for 2
and 6 are done for you in Figure 4-1.
(c)  The number 12 is divisible by _____ (list all possibilities).
(d)  Use the definition of a factor to explain why 8 ∤ 12.

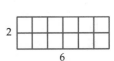

**Figure 4-1**

## An Investigation: Factors

## Lesson Exercise 4.4

(a)  Find three examples of counting numbers that have exactly 3 different factors.
(b)  Propose a generalization about counting numbers that have exactly 3
different factors.

## Perfect and Amicable Numbers

What makes a counting number perfect? According to the Pythagoreans, a
**perfect number** equals the sum of all its factors that are less than itself. The
factors of 6 are 1, 2, 3, and 6. All the factors of 6 that are less than 6 add up
to 6: 1 + 2 + 3 = 6. How perfect!

## Lesson Exercise 4.5

Test each number to determine if it is a perfect number.

(a) 20    (b) 28    (c) 38

Before 1950, only 12 perfect numbers were known. Since then, people have used computers to find about 15 more perfect numbers.

The Pythagoreans also studied amicable numbers. According to the Pythagoreans, two numbers are **amicable** (or **friendly**) if and only if each is the sum of the factors of the other (excluding the numbers themselves as factors). They found only one pair of amicable numbers, 284 and 220. The sum of the factors of 220 that are less than 220 (1 + 2 + 4 + 5 + 10 + 11 + 20 + 22 + 44 + 55 + 110) is 284. The sum of the factors of 284 that are less than 284 (1 + 2 + 4 + 71 + 142) is 220.

If two Pythagoreans were good friends, they would wear medallions with amicable numbers written on them.

It was over 2000 years later that Fermat (1636) found another pair of amicable numbers (17,296 and 18,416).

## Theorems about Factors

Patterns they noted in the factors of particular numbers led the Pythagoreans and other Greek mathematicians to investigate more general questions about factors. For example, if $A$ is a divisor of $B$, then $A$ must also be a divisor of what other numbers?

In Lesson Exercises 4.6–4.8, use inductive reasoning to make an educated guess regarding whether each statement is true or false. Remember that in mathematics, a "true" statement must *always* be true. If a mathematical statement is false in even one instance, it is "false." Give an example if you think a statement is true, and give a counterexample if you discover a statement that is false.

## Lesson Exercise 4.6

True or false? If $A$ is a factor of an even number, then $A$ is even.

## Lesson Exercise 4.7

True or false? If $A \mid 1200$, then $A \mid 2400$.

## Lesson Exercise 4.8

In Lesson Exercise 4.7, why isn't $A = 7$ a counterexample?

When you see the phrase "there exists," you need to find only one instance of it being true, as in the following exercise.

## Lesson Exercise 4.9

True or false? There exist counting numbers $A$, $B$, and $C$ such that $A \mid (B + C)$ and $A \mid BC$.

You may have guessed that the general statement in Lesson Exercise 4.7 is true. But how can you be sure? In this same situation, the classical Greeks, whenever possible, proved their conjectures using deductive reasoning or found a counterexample to disprove their conjectures. Euclid organized and published many of the Greeks' proofs in the *Elements*.

Deductive proofs about factors usually employ the definition of a factor. The following exercises will help prepare you for these proofs.

## Lesson Exercise 4.10

Suppose $A$, $B$, and $C$ are counting numbers and $A \cdot B = C$. What can you deduce about factor relationships among $A$, $B$, and $C$?

## Lesson Exercise 4.11

Suppose $A \mid B$. Using the definition of a factor, one can deduce that

_____.

### Example 4.1

Prove that if $A \mid 1200$, then $A \mid 2400$.

**Solution**

In Lesson Exercise 4.7, you saw that any example you selected works. For example, when $A = 2$, $2 \mid 1200$ and $2 \mid 2400$.

To show that the statement is true for any counting number $A$ when $A \mid 1200$, use the definition of a factor on the hypothesis $A \mid 1200$.

**1.** $A \mid 1200$

**2.** $A \mid 1200$ means that there is a whole number $W$ such that $A \cdot W = 1200$.

**3.** ?

**4.** ?

The last (fifth) step of the proof is:

**5.** $A \mid 2400$

Now, try to work backwards from the last step. If Step 5 says $A \mid 2400$, how would we show that in Step 4? By finding a whole number ? such that $A \cdot ? = 2400$.

**1.** $A \mid 1200$

**2.** $A \cdot W = 1200$, in which $W$ is a whole number

**3.** ?

**4.** $A \cdot \underline{\hspace{1em}} = 2400$, in which $\underline{\hspace{1em}}$ is a whole number

**5.** $A \mid 2400$

Now, how do you get from Step 2 to Step 4? To make $A \cdot W = 1200$ look like $A \cdot ? = 2400$, multiply both sides by 2. This is Step 3. Since we know that $2W$ is a whole number, this shows that $A \mid 2400$, since $A \cdot 2W = 2400$.

**1.** $A \mid 1200$

**2.** $A \cdot W = 1200$, in which $W$ is a whole number

**3.** $A \cdot 2W = 2400$

**4.** $A(2W) = 2400$, in which $2W$ is a whole number

**5.** $A \mid 2400$ ■

Try to prove the statement in the following exercise. The proof should go step by step from the hypothesis to the conclusion.

## Lesson Exercise 4.12

Prove that if $3 \mid A$, then $3 \mid 5A$, in which $A$ is a whole number.

The statements in Lesson Exercises 4.13–4.16 are possible theorems about divisors. Use inductive reasoning to determine which of these statements might be true. Give a counterexample for any statement that is false. If you believe that a statement is true, use deductive reasoning to show that it is true. In all statements, $A$, $B$, and $C$ are whole numbers, with $A \neq 0$.

**D** Lesson Exercise 4.13

True or false? If $A \mid B$, then $B \mid A$.

**D** Lesson Exercise 4.14

True or false? If $A \mid B$ and $A \mid C$, then $A \mid (B + C)$.

**D** Lesson Exercise 4.15

True or false? If $A \mid B$, then $A \mid BC$.

**D** Lesson Exercise 4.16

True or false? If $A \mid BC$, then $A \mid B$ and $A \mid C$.

Were you able to prove the statements in Lesson Exercises 4.14 and 4.15? Lesson Exercise 4.14 is a new theorem called the Divisibility-of-a-Sum Theorem. Lesson Exercise 4.15 is called the Divisibility-of-a-Product Theorem. Both these theorems have the word "divisibility" in them. For counting numbers $A$ and $B$, $A$ is **divisible** by $B$ if and only if $B$ is a factor of $A$. The Divisibility-of-a-Sum-Theorem is illustrated in Figure 4-2 and stated as follows.

---

**The Divisibility-of-a-Sum Theorem**

For any whole numbers $A$, $B$, and $C$, with $A \neq 0$, if $A \mid B$ and $A \mid C$, then $A \mid (B + C)$.

---

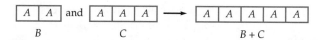

Figure 4-2

This theorem is useful in explaining why the divisibility tests in the next lesson work. See if you can apply the theorem in the following exercise.

Lesson Exercise 4.17

According to the Divisibility-of-a-Sum Theorem, if $5 \mid 4000$ and $5 \mid 200$ then _____.

> **The Divisibility-of-a-Product Theorem**
>
> $A$, $B$, and $C$ are whole numbers with $A \neq 0$. If $A \mid B$, then $A \mid BC$.

See whether you can apply the Divisibility-of-a-Product Theorem in the following exercises.

### Lesson Exercise 4.18

According to the Divisibility-of-a-Product Theorem, if $A$ and $C$ are whole numbers, with $A \neq 0$, in which $A \mid 3$, then _____.

### Lesson Exercise 4.19

Explain how you could use the Divisibility-of-a-Product Theorem to recognize that $6 \mid (12 \cdot 37)$.

## Answers to Selected Lesson Exercises

**4.1**  $10 \div 5 = 2; 10 \div 2 = 5$

**4.2**  (a) 2 is a factor of 40 because $2 \cdot 20 = 40$.
(b) $2N = R$     (c) deductive

**4.3**  (a) 1, 2, 3, 4, 6, 12
(b)

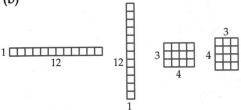

(c) 1, 2, 3, 4, 6, 12
(d) 8 is not a factor of 12 because there is no whole number $C$ such that $8C = 12$.

**4.4**  (a) 4, 9, 25

**4.5**  (a) no     (b) yes     (c) no

**4.6**  false

**4.7**  true

**4.8**  Because $7 \nmid 1200$.

**4.9**  true

**4.10**  $A$ and $B$ are factors of $C$.

**4.11**  $A$ times some whole number equals $B$.

**4.12**  1. $3 \mid A$
2. $3C = A$, in which $C$ is a whole number
3. $3(5C) = 5A$, in which $5C$ is a whole number
4. $3 \mid 5A$

**4.13**  false

**4.14**  true
1. $A \mid B$ and $A \mid C$
2. $A \cdot D = B$ and $A \cdot E = C$, in which $D$ and $E$ are whole numbers
3. $A \cdot D + A \cdot E = B + C$
4. $A \cdot (D + E) = B + C$, in which $D + E$ is a whole number
5. $A \mid (B + C)$

**4.15**  true
1. $A \mid B$
2. $AD = B$, in which $D$ is a whole number
3. $A(DC) = BC$, in which $DC$ is a whole number
4. $A \mid BC$

4.16 false

4.17 5 | 4200

4.18 A | 3C

4.19 6 | 12, so 6 is a factor of 12 times any whole number such as 12 · 37.

## 4.1  Homework Exercises

### Basic Exercises

1. (a) Name all the factors of 28.
   (b) Use the definition of a factor to explain why 6 is not a factor of 28.

2. Use the definition of a factor to explain why 11 | 0.

3. True or false? 8 ∤ 2.

4. Test each of the following numbers to see if it is a perfect number.
   (a) 120      (b) 315      (c) 496

5. In 1866, a 16-year-old Italian student named Niccolo Paganini found the second-lowest pair of amicable numbers. One is 1184. What is the other?

Decide whether the statements in Exercises 6–11 are true or false. Assume that $A$, $B$, $C$, and $K$ are whole numbers, with $A \neq 0$. If a statement is true, explain why or give an example. If it is false, explain why or give a counterexample.

6. True or false? If 2 ∤ $B$, then 4 ∤ $B$.

7. True or false? If $A \mid B$, then $A \mid KB$.

8. True or false? If $A \mid B$, then $B \mid A$.

9. True or false? If $A \mid B$ and $A \mid C$, then $A \mid (B + C)$.

10. True or false? There exist $A$, $B$, and $C$ such that if $A \mid B$, then $AC \mid B$.

11. True or false? There exist $A$, $B$, and $C$ such that if $A \mid BC$, then $A \mid B$ and $A \mid C$.

12. If 2 | $B$, then there exists a whole number $C$ _____.

13. If $3 \cdot A = B$, then ____ is a factor of ____ and ____ is a factor of ____.

14. The statement "If 5 | 20 and 5 | 40, then 5 | 60" is an instance of what theorem?

15. The statement "If 5 | 20, then 5 | 200" is an instance of what theorem?

16. According to the Divisibility-of-a-Sum Theorem, if 10 | 1000 and 10 | 20, then _____.

17. According to the Divisibility-of-a-Sum Theorem, if $C$ is a whole number such that 8 | $C$ and 8 | 16, then _____.

18. If 3 | $A$, then 3 | 2$A$. This is an instance of what theorem?

19. According to the Divisibility-of-a-Product Theorem, if $A$ and $C$ are whole numbers, with $A \neq 0$, and $A \mid 8$, then _____.

20. (a) You want to arrange 20 blocks into a rectangular shape. What are all the ways this can be done?
    (b) What mathematical concept does part (a) illustrate?

### Extension Exercises

In Exercises 21–29, assume that $A$, $B$, and $C$ are whole numbers, with $A \neq 0$. Decide whether each statement is true or false. If it is true, prove it. If it is false, give a counterexample.

21. True or false? If 5 | $B$, then 10 | $B$.

22. True or false? 1 | $B$ for all $B$.

23. True or false? If $A \mid B$, then $A \mid B^2$.

24. True or false? If $A \mid B$, then $A \mid (B + 1)$.

25. True or false? If $B$ and $C$ are divisible by 2, then $BC$ is divisible by 2.

26. True or false? If $B > C$ and $B$ and $C$ are divisible by $A$, then $B - C$ is divisible by $A$.

27. True or false? If $B \neq 0$ and $A \mid B$ and $B \mid C$, then $A \mid C$.

28. True or false? The product of two even numbers is even. (*Hint:* $C$ is **even** if and only if $C = 2W$ for some whole number $W$.)

29. True or false? The product of two odd numbers is odd. (*Hint:* $C$ is **odd** if and only if $C = 2W + 1$ for some whole number $W$.)

30. Use the Divisibility-of-a-Product Theorem to show why, for whole numbers $x$ and $y$ with $x \neq 0$, $x \mid x^2y^2$.

31. Prove that for any whole number $N \geq 2$, $3 \mid (N^3 - N)$. (*Hint:* Factor $N^3 - N$.)

32. Consider the following problem. "Investigate the result of adding 1 to the product of 4 consecutive whole numbers."

*Understanding the Problem*

(a) Give an example of adding 1 to the product of 4 consecutive whole numbers.

*Devising a Plan and Carrying Out the Plan*

(b) Repeat part (a) for 4 different consecutive whole numbers.

(c) Propose a generalization.

*Looking Back*

(d) Prove your generalization using $N$ as the first whole number.

## 4.2  Divisibility

Three drugstore owners pool their resources to buy 3456 bottles of aspirin. Can they divide the bottles evenly among themselves?

What is a shortcut for determining if a number such as 3456 is divisible by 3? The shortcut can be discovered by looking at the multiples of 3.

### Multiples

Do different numbers that are divisible by 3 have anything in common? Consider 0, 3, 6, 9, 12, 15, 18, 21, 24, 27, . . . .

In order to study divisibility by 3, you would look at the multiples of 3, {0, 3, 6, 9, 12, 15, 18, 21, 24, 27, . . . }. Multiples are generated when you count by a number starting at 0. The multiples of 3 could be written as $3 \cdot 0$, $3 \cdot 1, 3 \cdot 2, 3 \cdot 3, 3 \cdot 4$, or 3 times any whole number.

The definition of a multiple is based upon the definition of a factor. A number $B$ is a **multiple** of $A$ if and only if $A$ is a factor of $B$. For example, 20 is a multiple of 5 because 5 is a factor of 20.

### Lesson Exercise 4.20

List the multiples of 8.

## Lesson Exercise 4.21

According to the definition, 50 is a multiple of 10 because there is a whole number _____ such that _____ · _____ = _____ .

Students sometimes confuse factors and multiples because they are closely related ideas. Try the following.

## Lesson Exercise 4.22

Fill in each blank with "factor(s)" or "multiple(s)."

(a) 7 is a _____ of 14.

(b) 30 is a _____ of 10.

(c) $8x$ is a _____ of $x$ when $x$ is a whole number.

(d) Every counting number has an infinite set of _____ .

## Divisibility Tests for 2, 5, and 10

Is 77,846,379,820 divisible by 2, 5, or 10? No one who knows their numbers would actually try dividing such a large number by 2, 5, or 10. There is a shorter way.

The divisibility tests for 2, 5, and 10 are all based upon checking the last digit of the number. Do you see the patterns in the last digits of each of the following sets of numbers?

Numbers divisible by 2: {0, 2, 4, 6, 8, 10, 12, 14, 16, 18, . . . }

Numbers divisible by 5: {0, 5, 10, 15, 20, 25, . . . }

Numbers divisible by 10: {0, 10, 20, 30, 40, 50, . . . }

See whether you can describe the divisibility tests in the following exercise.

## Lesson Exercise 4.23

Fill in the blanks.

(a) A whole number is divisible by 2 if and only if _____ .

(b) A whole number is divisible by 5 if and only if _____ .

(c) A whole number is divisible by 10 if and only if _____ .

The divisibility tests for 2, 5, and 10 are as follows.

---

**Divisibility Tests for 2, 5, and 10**

- A whole number is divisible by 2 if and only if its ones digit is divisible by 2.
- A whole number is divisible by 5 if and only if its ones digit is 0 or 5.
- A whole number is divisible by 10 if and only if its ones digit is 0.

---

These divisibility tests are grouped together because they all require checking the last digit of the whole number.

## Lesson Exercise 4.24

Without dividing, determine whether each number in parts (a)–(c) is divisible by 2, 5, and/or 10.

(a) 8,479,238    (b) 1,046,890    (c) 317,425
(d) Applying the divisibility rules to answer parts (a), (b), and (c) is an example of _____ reasoning.

## D Lesson Exercise 4.25

Complete the number so that it is divisible by 2 but not by 5 or 10. Place one digit in each blank.

$$8 \ 6 \ 3, \ 1 \ \_\_ \ \_\_$$

---

Divisibility tests are useful in studying number theory and fractions. Later in this chapter, divisibility tests will be used to factor a number and to test whether a number is prime. In Chapter 6, divisibility tests will be used to simplify fractions and to find common denominators.

## Divisibility Tests for 3 and 9

Do you know how to tell if a number if divisible by 3 or 9? Both divisibility tests require adding up the digits of the number.

Numbers divisible by 3: {0, 3, 6, 9, 12, 15, 18, . . . }
Numbers divisible by 9: {0, 9, 18, 27, 36, 45, . . . }

## Lesson Exercise 4.26

(a) State the divisibility tests for 3 and 9, if you recall them. Use the sets just listed to check your guesses.
(b) What is the relationship between divisibility by 3 and divisibility by 9?

The rules are as follows.

---

**Divisibility Tests for 3 and 9**

- A whole number is divisible by 3 if and only if the sum of all its digits is divisible by 3.
- A whole number is divisible by 9 if and only if the sum of all its digits is divisible by 9.

---

These divisibility tests are grouped together because they both require computing the sum of the digits.

## Lesson Exercise 4.27

Without dividing, determine whether each number is divisible by 3 or 9.

(a) 468,172      (b) 32,094

## Lesson Exercise 4.28

Complete the number so that it is divisible by 3 and 9. Place one digit in each blank.

$$1\ 0,\ 8\ 2\ 1,\ 7\ \underline{\phantom{x}}\ \underline{\phantom{x}}$$

## Lesson Exercise 4.29

Without dividing, complete the following chart.

| Number | Divisible by | | | | |
| | 2 | 3 | 5 | 9 | 10 |
|---|---|---|---|---|---|
| 8172 | X | X | | X | |
| 403,155 | | | | | |
| 800,002 | | | | | |
| 68,710 | | | | | |

In Lesson Exercises 4.30–4.32: (a) Try some examples and decide whether the statements are true or false. (b) If a statement is true, give an example that supports it. If a statement is false, give a counterexample. (c) Draw a Venn diagram showing the relationship between the sets of numbers in each statement.

**D** Lesson Exercise 4.30

True or false? If a number is divisible by 6, then it is divisible by 3.

**D** Lesson Exercise 4.31

True or false? If a number is divisible by 2 and 4, then it is divisible by 8.

**D** Lesson Exercise 4.32

True or false? If a number is not divisible by 2, then it is not divisible by 4.

## What Makes the Divisibility Tests Work?

The divisibility tests are based upon two concepts: expanded notation and the Divisibility-of-a-Sum Theorem. Recall that a number such as 364 in expanded notation is $(3 \cdot 100) + (6 \cdot 10) + 4$.

Now, you may be wondering how expanded notation and the Divisibility-of-a-Sum Theorem relate to the divisibility tests.

**Example 4.2**

Prove that if $\underline{A}\ \underline{B}\ \underline{C}\ \underline{0}$ is a four-digit number, then $\underline{A}\ \underline{B}\ \underline{C}\ \underline{0}$ is divisible by 10. (A, B, and C represent the first three digits of the number.) In other words, a four-digit number that ends in 0 is divisible by 10.

**Solution**

**Understanding the Problem**   Assume that a number has the form $\underline{A}\ \underline{B}\ \underline{C}\ \underline{0}$ and show that it must be divisible by 10.

**Devising a Plan**   Write $\underline{A}\ \underline{B}\ \underline{C}\ \underline{0}$ as a sum using expanded notation and show that each term in the sum is divisible by 10.

**Carrying Out the Plan**   $\underline{A}\ \underline{B}\ \underline{C}\ \underline{0} = (A \cdot 1000) + (B \cdot 100) + (C \cdot 10)$. We know that $A \times 1000$, $B \times 100$, and $C \times 10$ are all divisible by 10. So, by the Divisibility-of-a-Sum Theorem, $(A \cdot 1000) + (B \cdot 100) + (C \cdot 10)$, which equals $\underline{A}\ \underline{B}\ \underline{C}\ \underline{0}$, is also divisible by 10.

*Looking Back*   There are no ones, and all the other place values are divisible by 10 no matter what digit is in the place. Then the sum of the place values will also be divisible by 10.  ■

Now it's your turn.

## Lesson Exercise 4.33

Prove that if a three-digit number ends in 5 or 0 (denoted $\underline{A}\ \underline{B}\ \underline{0}$ or $\underline{A}\ \underline{B}\ \underline{5}$), then the number is divisible by 5.

## Lesson Exercise 4.34

Parts (a)–(c) will prepare you to prove part (d).
In this problem, assume that in a four-digit number $\underline{A}\ \underline{B}\ \underline{C}\ \underline{D}$, the sum $A + B + C + D$ is divisible by 3. Then try to show that $\underline{A}\ \underline{B}\ \underline{C}\ \underline{D}$ is divisible by 3.
(a)  Write $\underline{A}\ \underline{B}\ \underline{C}\ \underline{D}$ in expanded notation.
(b)  Now regroup the expanded notation. Fill in the blank so that the entire expression equals your answer to part (a).

$(999 \times A) + (99 \times B) + (99 \times C) +$ _____

(c)  So $\underline{A}\ \underline{B}\ \underline{C}\ \underline{D} = (999 \times A) + (99 \times B) + (9 \times C) + A + B + C + D$. What do we know about $A + B + C + D$?
(d)  Prove that if $\underline{A}\ \underline{B}\ \underline{C}\ \underline{D}$ is a four-digit number and $A + B + C + D$ is divisible by 3, then $\underline{A}\ \underline{B}\ \underline{C}\ \underline{D}$ is divisible by 3.

## Answers to Selected Lesson Exercises

4.20 {0, 8, 16, 24, 32, . . . }

4.21 5, 10 · 5 = 50

4.22 (a) factor
      (b) multiple
      (c) multiple
      (d) multiples

4.23 See the box that follows the exercise.

4.24 (a) 2
      (b) 2, 5, 10
      (c) 5
      (d) deductive

4.25 The last digit is 2, 4, 6, or 8.

4.26 (b) Any whole number that is divisible by 9 is also divisible by 3.

4.27 (a) neither
      (b) 3, 9

4.28 two digits with a sum of 8

4.29

| Number | Divisible by | | | | |
|---|---|---|---|---|---|
|  | 2 | 3 | 5 | 9 | 10 |
| 8172 | X | X |  | X |  |
| 403,155 |  | X | X | X |  |
| 800,002 | X |  |  |  |  |
| 68,710 | X |  | X |  | X |

**4.30** true; 6 is an example

**4.31** false for 4

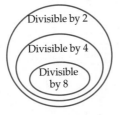

**4.32** true; 7 is an example

**4.33** $\underline{A}\ \underline{B}\ \underline{5} = (A \cdot 100) + (B \cdot 10) + 5$ and
$\underline{A}\ \underline{B}\ \underline{0} = (A \cdot 100) + (B \cdot 10)$
$(A \cdot 100)$, $(B \cdot 10)$, and 5 are all divisible by
5. Therefore, $(A \cdot 100) + (B \cdot 10) + 5$ and
$(A \cdot 100) + (B \cdot 10)$ are divisible by 5.

**4.34** (a) $(A \cdot 1000) + (B \cdot 100) + (C \cdot 10) + D$
(b) $A + B + C + D$
(c) It is divisible by 3.
(d) $\underline{A}\ \underline{B}\ \underline{C}\ \underline{D} = 999 \cdot A + 99 \cdot B + 9 \cdot C + (A + B + C + D)$
$999 \cdot A$, $99 \cdot B$, $9 \cdot C$, and $(A + B + C + D)$ are all divisible by 3.
Therefore, $(999 \cdot A) + (99 \cdot B) + (9 \cdot C) + (A + B + C + D) = \underline{A}\ \underline{B}\ \underline{C}\ \underline{D}$ is divisible by 3.

## 4.2·  Homework Exercises

*Basic Exercises*

1. What are the multiples of 7?

2. *X* is a whole number. What are the multiples of *X*?

3. Explain why 3 is not a multiple of 6.

4. Name a number that is a factor and a multiple of 15.

5. Fill in each blank with "multiple" or "factor."
   (a) 1 is a _____ of every counting number.
   (b) 3 is a _____ of 12.
   (c) 25 is a _____ of 5.
   (d) $2X$ is a _____ of $8X^3$ when $X$ is a whole number not equal to 0.

6. Without dividing, complete the following chart.

| Number | Divisible by | | | | |
|---|---|---|---|---|---|
| | 2 | 3 | 5 | 9 | 10 |
| 5260 | | | | | |
| 8197 | | | | | |
| 345,678 | | | | | |

7. There will be 219 children in next year's third grade. If the school has 9 teachers, can the school assign each teacher the same number of students?

8. Three sisters earn a reward of $37,500 for solving a mathematics problem. Can they divide the money equally?

9. Complete each number so that it is divisible by the indicated number or numbers. Determine all possible answers.
   (a) 4 1, __ 7 2 (by 3)
   (b) 8 2 6, 3 __ __ (by 2 and 5)
   (c) 4 1 7, 2 __ __ (by 2, 3, and 10)

10. Consider the numbers 0, 1, 4, 8, and 64.
    (a) Tell which number does not belong with the others and why.
    (b) Give a reason why each of the other numbers could be given as the answer to part (a).

11. (a) Suppose you want to mail a package requiring $1.96 in postage using $.25 stamps and $.15 stamps. Is it possible to find stamps totaling the exact amount needed?
    (b) Explain the result to part (a) using divisibility.

12. How would you use a calculator to determine if a whole number $A$ is divisible by $B$?

In Exercises 13–16, (a) Tell whether the statement is true or false. (b) If the statement is true, tell why or give an example that supports it; if the statement is false, give a counterexample. (c) Draw a Venn diagram showing the correct relationship among the sets of numbers in each statement.

13. True or false? If a number is divisible by 5, then it is divisible by 10.

14. True or false? If a number is not divisible by 5, then it is not divisible by 10.

15. True or false? If a number is divisible by 6 and 8, then it is also divisible by 48.

16. True or false? If a number is divisible by 8 and 10, then it is also divisible by 40. (Use inductive reasoning.)

17. If $15 \mid N$, then what other counting numbers must be factors of $N$?

18. If $M$ is a multiple of 20, then $M$ must also be a multiple of what other whole numbers?

*Extension Exercises*

19. Prove that if a three-digit number is even ($\underline{A}\ \underline{B}\ \underline{0}$, $\underline{A}\ \underline{B}\ \underline{2}$, $\underline{A}\ \underline{B}\ \underline{4}$, $\underline{A}\ \underline{B}\ \underline{6}$, $\underline{A}\ \underline{B}\ \underline{8}$), then the number is divisible by 2.

20. Prove that if the sum of the digits of a four-digit number $\underline{A}\ \underline{B}\ \underline{C}\ \underline{D}$ is divisible by 9, then the number itself is divisible by 9.

21. (a) What is the divisibility test for 100?
    (b) A leap year must be divisible by 4. Furthermore, if a leap year is divisible by 100, then it must also be divisible by 400. Which of the following are leap years?
    (1) 1776     (2) 1994     (3) 1996
    (4) 2000     (5) 2010

22. Devise a divisibility test for 4. (*Hint:* Look at the last two digits of any number that is divisible by 4.)

23. Devise a divisibility test for 25.

24. Devise a divisibility test for 6.

25. (a) Devise a divisibility test for 4 in base eight.
    (b) Devise divisibility tests for 2 and 7 in base eight.

26. Consider the following problem: "The ages of a woman and her granddaughter have a surprising property. First of all, they were born on the same day of the year. And for the last 6 years in a row, the grandmother's age has been divisible by her granddaughter's age! How old are they today?"
    (a) Devise a plan and solve the problem.
    (b) Check your answer.

27. Find a nine-digit number such that the first two digits form a numeral divisible by 2, the first three digits form a numeral divisible by 3, and so on up to the nine-digit numeral, which is divisible by 9.

In Exercises 28–32, if the statement is true, prove it. If the statement is false, give a counterexample. Assume that $A$ and $B$ are whole numbers with $B \neq 0$.

28. True or false? If $A$ is divisible by 2, then $4 + A$ is divisible by 2.

29. True or false? If a whole number is divisible by $A + B$, then it is divisible by $A$.

30. True or false? The sum of any five consecutive whole numbers is divisible by 5.

31. True or false? If $A$ is a multiple of $B$, then $2A$ is a multiple of $B$.

32. True or false? If the sum of all the digits of a number is divisible by 6, then the number is divisible by 6.

33. $A$, $B$, $C$, and $D$ are whole numbers. The number $A \cdot B \cdot (C + D)$ is even whenever _____ is even. (Any or all may be correct.)
    (a) $A$      (b) $B$      (c) $C$      (d) $D$

34. 8! is shorthand for $8 \cdot 7 \cdot 6 \cdot 5 \cdot 4 \cdot 3 \cdot 2 \cdot 1$. Similarly, $10! = 10 \cdot 9 \cdot 8 \cdot 7 \cdot 6 \cdot 5 \cdot 4 \cdot 3 \cdot 2 \cdot 1$.
    (a) Guess how many terminal zeroes the number equal to 8! has. (For example, 100 has two terminal zeroes.) Check your answer on a calculator.
    (b) Repeat part (a) for 10!
    (c) How can you tell how many terminal zeroes you will get?
    (d) Without computing, tell how many terminal zeroes 6! and 15! will have.

35. (a) Choose a two-digit number and reverse the digits. Subtract the smaller number from the larger. Is the difference divisible by 9?

(b) Repeat part (a) with a different number.
(c) Prove that the difference will always be divisible by 9.

36. $10^2 - 8^2$ is divisible by 18.
    $20^2 - 3^2$ is divisible by 23.
    (a) Write another statement that fits this pattern and see if it is true.
    (b) Use algebra to explain why this pattern works for $a^2 - b^2$ in which $a$ and $b$ are counting numbers and $a > b$.

37. Form an eight-digit number by writing a four-digit number twice in succession (for example, 12,341,234).
    (a) Is your number divisible by 73?
    (b) Repeat part (a) with another number of this type.
    (c) Propose a generalization.
    (d) Prove your generalization.

38. Find the remainder when $3^{888,888}$ is divided by
    (a) 4.      (b) 5.

*Special Exercise*

39. (a) Think of any three-digit number.
    (b) Write it down twice to form a six-digit number (e.g., 382,382).
    (c) Is your number divisible by 7?
    (d) Is your number divisible by 11?
    (e) Is your number divisible by 13?
    (f) Repeat parts (a)–(e) with a new number.
    (g) What is $7 \times 11 \times 13$?
    (h) What is $382 \times 1001$?
    (i) Can you explain why your six-digit numbers were divisible by 7, 11, and 13?

## 4.3   Prime and Composite Numbers

The Greeks were the first to study numbers systematically. They discovered a subset of the whole numbers that contains the building blocks of all whole numbers greater than 1.

## Prime Numbers and Composite Numbers

The **prime numbers** are the essential components of whole numbers greater than 1.

**D** Lesson Exercise 4.35

Try to write a definition of a prime number. (*Hint:* Say something about factors.)

Compare your definition to the first part of the following.

> **Definitions: Prime and Composite Numbers**
>
> A whole number greater than 1 is **prime** if it has exactly two different factors (divisors): 1 and itself. A whole number greater than 1 is **composite** if it has more than two different factors (divisors).

The number 11 is prime since it has exactly two factors: 1 and 11. The number 10 is composite (and not prime) since it has four factors: 1, 2, 5, and 10.

Lesson Exercise 4.36

How many factors does 1 have?

Since 1 has only one factor, it is neither prime nor composite. The Pythagoreans who studied prime numbers 2500 years ago called 1 the unity that generates all prime and composite numbers.

In geometric terms, you can represent a prime number with exactly two rectangles with counting-number dimensions. You can represent a composite number with more than two such rectangles (see Figure 4-3). (Note that 1, which is neither prime nor composite, also has exactly one rectangle with counting-number dimensions.)

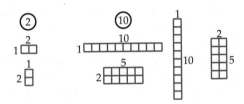

Figure 4-3

Lesson Exercise 4.37

Classify the following numbers as prime or composite and draw all possible rectangles with counting-number dimensions for each number.
(a) 8     (b) 7

Lesson Exercise 4.38

Name all prime numbers that are less than 20.

Children use prime numbers to find common denominators and to simplify fractions.

## The Prime Number Test

It's fairly easy to see that 2, 3, 5, 7, and 11 are primes. But how can you tell if a larger number is prime?

**D** Lesson Exercise 4.39

How would you check to see if 367 is prime?

In the preceding exercise, one would know that 367 is prime if it were not divisible by 2, 3, 4, 5, . . . , 365, 366. However, it is not necessary to try all these numbers as divisors. This procedure can be shortened. Consider the following questions.

Lesson Exercise 4.40

(a) If 2 is not a divisor of a number (such as 367), then what other numbers could not possibly be divisors of the number?
(b) If 3 is not a divisor of a number (such as 367), then what other numbers could not possibly be divisors of the number?

The approach of Lesson Exercise 4.40 would go as follows for 367.

$2 \nmid 367$. Therefore, 4, 6, 8, 10, . . . , 366 are not divisors of 367. (The Divisibility-of-a-Product Theorem says 4, 6, 8, . . . cannot be divisors unless 2 is a divisor.)

$3 \nmid 367$. Therefore, 6, 9, 12, . . . , 366 are not divisors of 367. The divisor 4 is already eliminated.

$5 \nmid 367$. Therefore, 10, 15, 20, 25, . . . , 365 are not divisors of 367. The divisor 6 is already eliminated.

7 ∤ 367. Therefore, 14, 21, 28, 35, . . . , 364 are not divisors of 367. The divisors 8, 9, and 10 are already eliminated.

What numbers do we have to check as divisors? Only primes. If *they* are not divisors, other whole numbers greater than 1 (which are all multiples of primes) could not be divisors either.

Do we need to check all primes less than 367? No. There's an additional shortcut! It results from the fact that every composite number $X$ has a prime factor less than or equal to $\sqrt{X}$.

To see why this is true, consider 360. Any larger factor of 360, such as 180, has a smaller companion factor (in this case, 2).

$$
\begin{aligned}
360 &= 180 \cdot 2 \\
&= 120 \cdot 3 \\
&= 90 \cdot 4 \\
&= 72 \cdot 5 \\
&= 60 \cdot 6 \\
&= 40 \cdot 9 \\
&= 36 \cdot 10 \\
&= 30 \cdot 12 \\
&= 24 \cdot 15 \\
&= 20 \cdot 18
\end{aligned}
$$

In fact, any factor larger than $\sqrt{360} \approx 19$ has a companion factor smaller than $\sqrt{360} \approx 19$. So if a number does not have a factor less than or equal to its square root, then it is prime. Putting the two ideas together, one needs only to check prime numbers less than or equal to the square root of the number.

---

**The Prime Number Test**

To determine if a number $N$ is prime, find out if any prime number less than or equal to the $\sqrt{N}$ is a divisor of $N$.

---

 **Example 4.3**

You want to determine if 367 is prime.

(a)  What is the minimum set of numbers you must try as divisors?

(b)  Use the prime number test to determine if 367 is prime.

**Solution**

(a)  A calculator shows that $\sqrt{367} \approx 19.2$. So we need to test all prime numbers less than 19.2 as divisors. This would include 2, 3, 5, 7, 11, 13, 17, and 19.

(b) By divisibility tests, $2 \nmid 367$, $3 \nmid 367$, and $5 \nmid 367$.

$$367 \div \phantom{0}7 = 54 \text{ R } 6, \text{ so } 7 \nmid 367$$
$$367 \div 11 = 34 \text{ R } 9, \text{ so } 11 \nmid 367$$
$$367 \div 13 = 29 \text{ R } 6, \text{ so } 13 \nmid 367$$
$$367 \div 17 = 22 \text{ R } 9, \text{ so } 17 \nmid 367$$
$$367 \div 19 = 20 \text{ R } 3, \text{ so } 19 \nmid 367$$

(You could also check the divisors 11, 13, 17, and 19 with a calculator.)

367 is not divisible by any prime number $\leq \sqrt{367}$. This means that 367 cannot have any prime factors less than 367. Therefore, 367 is a prime number. ■

D Lesson Exercise 4.41

Use the prime number test to determine if the following numbers are prime.

(a) 347      (b) 253

## Prime Factorization of Composite Numbers

Is it possible to factor any composite number using only prime numbers {2, 3, 5, 7, 11, 13, 17, 19, 23, . . . }? For example, $8 = 2 \cdot 2 \cdot 2$ and $264 = 2 \cdot 2 \cdot 2 \cdot 3 \cdot 11$. In other words, is it possible to write any composite number as a product of prime numbers?

D Lesson Exercise 4.42

(a) Select a composite number. Can you write it as a product of primes?
(b) Can you find a different set of prime factors for this same number?
(c) Repeat parts (a) and (b) for a different composite number.
(d) What generalization can you make from parts (a)–(c)?
(e) Part (d) is an example of _____ reasoning.

After studying many examples, Greek mathematicians conjectured that every composite number could be written as a product of a unique set of prime numbers. Euclid, a mathematics professor at the University of Alexandria, proved this in Book 9 of his *Elements*.

The prime numbers are the building blocks for all whole numbers greater than 1. Every whole number greater than 1 is prime or can be expressed using prime factors. The prime factorization is like a signature for each composite number. For example, $12 = 2 \cdot 2 \cdot 3 = 2^2 \cdot 3$ and $26 = 2 \cdot 13$.

It is customary to write the prime factors in increasing order and to use exponents as a shorthand for repeated factors. The possibility of writing any composite number as a unique product of prime numbers is so important that it is called the Fundamental Theorem of Arithmetic.

---

**The Fundamental Theorem of Arithmetic**

Every composite number has exactly one prime factorization.

---

Two methods are commonly used to find prime factorizations. Most middle-school textbooks teach the **factor-tree** method. The other method I will call the "prime-divisor" method.

**Example 4.4**

Find the prime factorization of 84 using both the factor-tree and prime-divisor methods.

Solution

*The Factor-Tree Method*   Start with 84 and find any two factors (for example, 2 and 42).

Then continue finding prime factors of these factors until all the factors are prime.

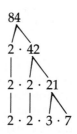

The result, $2 \cdot 2 \cdot 3 \cdot 7$, is the prime factorization of 84. Repeated factors are usually written with exponents.

$$84 = 2^2 \cdot 3 \cdot 7$$

*The Prime-Divisor Method*   In this method, try all prime numbers in increasing order as divisors, beginning with 2. Use each prime number as a divisor as many times as possible.

| | |
|---|---|
| Try 2. | ⟶ 2 ⎵ 84 |
| It works twice. | ⟶ 2 ⎵ 42 |
| Next, try 3. | ⟶ 3 ⎵ 21 |
| 7 is prime. | 7 |

The divisors and final quotient give the prime factorization of 84.

$$84 = 2 \cdot 2 \cdot 3 \cdot 7 \quad \blacksquare$$

Try the following exercise using both methods from Example 4.4.

## Lesson Exercise 4.43

Find the prime factorization of 120 using both methods.

## Famous Unsolved Problems

Some mathematics problems have remained unsolved for centuries. Since number theory deals only with numbers, its unsolved problems are the simplest to describe and the most well known. Do you want to be famous? Just solve one of these problems!

One famous unsolved problem concerns twin primes. **Twin primes** are any two consecutive odd numbers, such as 3 and 5, that are prime.

## Lesson Exercise 4.44

(a) Find all twin primes less than 100.
(b) Look at the number between each pair of twin primes greater than 3. What property do all these numbers have?
(c) Do you think there are an infinite number of twin primes?

Euclid proved that there are an infinite number of primes. Number theorists believe that there are also an infinite number of twin primes, but no one has been able to prove it!

Another famous unsolved problem is Goldbach's conjecture. Goldbach (1690–1764) said that every even number greater than 2 is the sum of two primes. No one knows for sure whether this is true or false.

## Lesson Exercise 4.45

Show that Goldbach's conjecture is true for the following numbers.

(a) 8     (b) 22     (c) 120

## Lesson Exercise 4.46

Goldbach's conjecture has been checked for all even numbers up to 100 million (using a computer), and it works! Why isn't this a sufficient proof?

## Answers to Selected Lesson Exercises

**4.36** one

**4.37** (a) composite    (b) prime

**4.38** 2, 3, 5, 7, 11, 13, 17, 19

**4.40** (a) multiples of 2    (b) multiples of 3

**4.41** (a) yes    (b) no

**4.42** (a) yes    (b) no    (e) inductive

**4.43** $120 = 2^3 \cdot 3 \cdot 5$

**4.44** (a) 3 and 5, 11 and 13, 17 and 19, 29 and 31, 41 and 43, 59 and 61, 71 and 73
(b) They are all divisible by 6.

**4.45** (a) $8 = 3 + 5$    (b) $22 = 11 + 11$
(c) $120 = 47 + 73$ or $7 + 113$ or $11 + 109$ or $13 + 107$ or $19 + 101$; and so on

**4.46** This is inductive reasoning. Some even number greater than 100 million may turn out to be a counterexample.

## 4.3   Homework Exercises

*Basic Exercises*

1. Classify the following numbers as prime or composite and draw all possible rectangles with counting-number dimensions for each number.
   (a) 47    (b) 51

2. In 1978, Hugh Williams discovered the following prime number with 317 ones. 11,111,111, . . . ,111. Explain why this number is not divisible by 2, 3, or 5.

3. One can often obtain a prime number by performing the following steps. Try them with the numbers 1 through 10 and see how many prime numbers you end up with.

   Step 1. Choose a counting number.
   Step 2. Multiply it by the next highest counting number.
   Step 3. Add 17 to your result.

4. The formula $2^n - 1$ often produces prime numbers when $n$ is a counting number.
   (a) Compute $2^n - 1$ for n = 2, 3, 4, 5, and 6.
   (b) Which of your resulting numbers are prime?

 5. Many mathematicians have tried to find formulas that produce only prime numbers. Fermat conjectured that $2^{2^n} + 1$ would be prime for n = 0, 1, 2, 3, . . . . The resulting numbers, called **Fermat numbers,** are $2^{2^0} + 1 = 3$, $2^{2^1} + 1 = 5$, $2^{2^2} + 1 = 17$, and so on.
   (a) The first five Fermat numbers are prime. Find the fourth Fermat number.
   (b) The sixth Fermat number is a composite number divisible by 641. Find this number and show that it is divisible by 641.

6. Is 1 prime or composite?

7. In order to determine if 431 is prime, what is the minimum set of numbers you must *try* as divisors?

8. In order to determine if 817 is prime, what is the minimum set of numbers you must *try* as divisors?

9. Use the Prime Number Test to classify the following numbers as prime or composite.
   (a) 71    (b) 697

10. Use the Prime Number Test to classify the following numbers as prime or composite.
    (a) 91    (b) 579

11. According to the Fundamental Theorem of Arithmetic, every composite number has _____.

12. Consider a property similar to the Fundamental Theorem of Arithmetic. Show that every composite number greater than 1 can-

not be *uniquely* expressed as a sum of prime numbers.

13. Find the prime factorization of each number using both methods.
    (a) 76     (b) 320

14. Write the prime factorizations of the following numbers.
    (a) 90     (b) 3155

15. Find all twin primes between 101 and 150.

16. **Triplet primes** are any three consecutive odd numbers that are prime.
    (a) Find a set of triplet primes.
    (b) Why can't there be any other sets of triplet primes?

17. Show that Goldbach's conjecture is true for the following numbers.
    (a) 12     (b) 30     (c) 108

18. In how many ways can 28 be expressed as the sum of two prime numbers?

19. The number 5 can be written as $1 + 2^2$. Find three other prime numbers that have the form $1 + W^2$ for some whole number $W$.

### Extension Exercises

20. Complete the following table for counting numbers from 1 to 50. The numbers 1 through 6 have already been placed in the appropriate columns.

| Total Number of Divisors | | | | | | | | | |
|---|---|---|---|---|---|---|---|---|---|
| 1 | 2 | 3 | 4 | 5 | 6 | 7 | 8 | 9 | 10 |
| 1 | 2 | 4 | 6 | | | | | | |
| | 3 | | | | | | | | |
| | 5 | | | | | | | | |

Describe any patterns you see in the numbers in any particular column.

21. (a) Choose any prime number greater than 3. Square it. Add 17. Find the remainder that results when you divide by 12.

(b) Repeat part (a) for two other prime numbers greater than 3.

(c) Make a table of numbers from 1 to 102 with six numbers in each row. Circle all prime numbers. Where are all prime numbers other than 3 located?

(d) All prime numbers greater than 3 have the form $6n + 1$ or $6n - 1$, in which $n$ is a counting number. Show why the procedure in part (a) always results in a remainder of 6.

22. Here is a way to find five consecutive composite numbers. First, compute $2 \times 3 \times 4 \times 5 \times 6 = 720$. Then, using the Divisibility-of-a-Sum Theorem, fill in the blanks.
    (a) $2 \mid 720$ and $2 \mid 2$, so _____ .
    (b) $3 \mid 720$ and $3 \mid 3$, so _____ .
    (c) $4 \mid 720$ and _____ .
    (d) Complete the pattern of parts (a), (b), and (c).

23. Use the method of the preceding exercise to find 10 consecutive composite numbers.

24. Euclid proved that if $p$ is prime and $2^p - 1$ is prime, then $(2^p - 1)2^{p-1}$ is perfect. This formula has been used to discover the 27 known perfect numbers. Use the formula to determine if the following values of $p$ result in perfect numbers.
    (a) 2     (b) 3     (c) 5     (d) 6

25.
$$2 \qquad\quad + 1 = 3$$
$$2 \times 3 \quad\; + 1 = 7$$
$$2 \times 3 \times 5 + 1 = 31$$

(a) Write the next two equations that continue the pattern.

(b) The numbers 3, 7, and 31 are prime. Are the numbers on the right side of your equations in part (a) prime?

(c) Show that the next equation continuing the pattern results in a composite number divisible by a prime number between 50 and 60.

26. (a) Is $3^2 \cdot 2^4$ a factor of $3^4 \cdot 2^7$?
    (b) Is $3^2 \cdot 2^5$ a factor of $3 \cdot 2^7$?

27. Suppose that $x$ and $y$ are whole numbers.
    (a) Is $x^3 y^5$ a factor of $x^2 y^8$?
    (b) Is $x^2 y^2$ a factor of $x^3 y^5$?

28. (a) Find all factors of $2^3$.
    (b) Find all factors of $3^4$.
    (c) How many factors does $2^3 \cdot 3^4$ have?
    (d) Find all factors of $3^2$.
    (e) Find all factors of $5^2$.
    (f) How many factors does $3^2 \cdot 5^2$ have?
    (g) Based upon your results in parts (a)–(f), if $p$ and $q$ are prime, how many factors does $p^m \cdot q^n$ have?

29. Without computing the results, explain why each of the following problems will result in a composite number.
    (a) $3 \times 5 \times 7 \times 11 \times 13$
    (b) $(3 \times 4 \times 5 \times 6 \times 7 \times 8) + 2$
    (c) $(3 \times 4 \times 5 \times 6 \times 7 \times 8) + 5$

30. Sophie Germain (1776–1831) studied divisibility problems like the following. Suppose we want $x^3 \div p$ to have a remainder of 2 for accounting number $x$ and an odd prime $p$. For example, $2^3 \div 3$ has a remainder of 2. If possible, in parts (a)–(c), find an $x$ such that:
    (a) $x^3 \div 5$ has a remainder of 2.
    (b) $x^3 \div 7$ has a remainder of 2.
    (c) $x^3 \div 11$ has a remainder of 2.
    (d) What pattern do you see in the values of $x$?

*Special Exercises*

31. The Sieve of Eratosthenes was developed by Eratosthenes, a Greek mathematician, about 2200 years ago as a method for finding all prime numbers less than a given number. Follow the directions to find all prime numbers less than or equal to 50.

| 1  | 2  | 3  | 4  | 5  | 6  | 7  | 8  | 9  | 10 |
|----|----|----|----|----|----|----|----|----|----|
| 11 | 12 | 13 | 14 | 15 | 16 | 17 | 18 | 19 | 20 |
| 21 | 22 | 23 | 24 | 25 | 26 | 27 | 28 | 29 | 30 |
| 31 | 32 | 33 | 34 | 35 | 36 | 37 | 38 | 39 | 40 |
| 41 | 42 | 43 | 44 | 45 | 46 | 47 | 48 | 49 | 50 |

(a) Copy the list of numbers.
(b) Cross out 1 because 1 is not prime.
(c) Circle 2. Count by 2's from there and cross out 4, 6, 8, . . . , 50 because all these numbers are divisible by 2 and therefore are not prime.
(d) Circle 3. Count by 3's from there and cross out all numbers not already crossed out because these numbers are divisible by 3.
(e) Circle the smallest number not yet crossed out. Count by that number and cross out all numbers that are not already crossed out.
(f) Repeat part (e) until there are no more numbers to do. The circled numbers are all the prime numbers.
(g) List all the primes between 1 and 50.

32. At Hexagon High, the students play mathematical pranks. There are exactly 400 lockers numbered 1 to 400. One day, the 400 students filed into school one by one. The first student opened every locker. The second student closed every even-numbered locker. The third student changed (opened or closed) every third locker (3, 6, 9, . . . ). The fourth student changed every fourth locker and so on. After all the students were finished, which lockers were open?

## 4.4   Common Factors and Multiples

After studying factors and multiples of individual whole numbers, it is natural to examine the factors and multiples that two whole numbers have in common. With the exception of 0, any two whole numbers have a largest common factor and a smallest nonzero common multiple.

### The Greatest Common Factor (GCF)

You can use greatest common factors to simplify both numerical and algebraic fractions. The **greatest common factor (GCF)** of two counting numbers is the largest number that is a factor of both numbers. For example, 20 and 16 have common factors of 1, 2, and 4. So the greatest common factor of 20 and 16, or GCF(20, 16) = 4.

Lesson Exercise 4.47

(a) What are the common factors of 20 and 30?
(b) What is the greatest common factor of 20 and 30?

Note that the definition of greatest common factors excludes 0. The following exercise concerns what would happen if 0 were included in the definition.

## Lesson Exercise 4.48

Suppose 0 were included in the definition of the greatest common factor. What would the greatest common factor of 0 and any other whole number be?

What follows are two methods for finding the greatest common factor: the factor-list method and the prime-factorization method. (A third method, the Euclidean algorithm, is presented in the extension exercises.)

**The Factor-List Method**

**1.** List all factors.

60: 1, 2, 3, 4, 5, 6, 10, 12, 15, 20, 30, 60

140: 1, 2, 4, 5, 7, 10, 14, 20, 28, 35, 70, 140

**2.** List all common factors.

1, 2, 4, 5, 10, 20

**3.** So GCF (60, 140) = 20.

**The Prime-Factorization Method**

**1.** Write the prime factorizations.

$60 = 2 \cdot 2 \cdot 3 \cdot 5$

$140 = 2 \cdot 2 \cdot 5 \cdot 7$

(*Note:* Since 2, 2, and 5 are on both lists, 2 is a common factor, $2 \cdot 2$ is a common factor, and $2 \cdot 5$ is a common factor, but we want the greatest common factor.)

**2.** Multiply all common prime factors.

$2 \cdot 2 \cdot 5$

**3.** So GCF = 20.

The factor-list method is less abstract, so children can more easily understand why it works. For this reason it is the first method children study in school. Although both methods work well for small numbers, the prime-factorization method is usually superior for larger numbers that have many factors.

 ## Lesson Exercise 4.49

Compute the GCF of 546 and 650 using whatever method you think is easier.

When two counting numbers have no common factors other than 1, they are said to be **relatively prime.** If the numerator and denominator of a fraction are relatively prime, the fraction is in simplest form. For example,

$\frac{7}{10}$ is in simplest form because 7 and 10 are relatively prime. In general, $A$ and $B$ are **relatively prime** if and only if GCF $(A, B) = 1$. For example, 7 and 10 are relatively prime because GCF $(10, 7) = 1$. Note that $A$ and $B$ need not be prime numbers to be relatively prime.

## Lesson Exercise 4.50

Which of the following pairs of numbers are relatively prime?

(a) 8 and 6      (b) 8 and 25      (c) 13 and 21

## Lesson Exercise 4.51

(a) If $A$ and $B$ are prime numbers, are $A$ and $B$ relatively prime? Try some examples and make an educated guess.
(b) Your guess in part (a) is based upon ——————— reasoning.

## The Least Common Multiple (LCM)

Least common multiples of denominators are the least common denominators used to add and subtract fractions. The **least common multiple (LCM)** of two counting numbers is the smallest counting number that is a multiple of both numbers. For example, the nonzero multiples of 10 are 10, 20, 30, 40, 50, . . . , and the nonzero multiples of 8 are 8, 16, 24, 32, 40, 48, . . . . So the least common multiple (LCM) of 10 and 8 is 40, or LCM $(10, 8) = 40$. This can be illustrated with a repeated-measures diagram, as shown in Figure 4-4.

Note that 40, 80, 120, 160, . . . are all common nonzero multiples of 10 and 8. Any two counting numbers have an infinite set of common multiples.

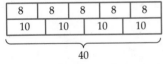

Repeated measures diagram

**Figure 4-4**

## Lesson Exercise 4.52

(a) Name three common multiples of 10 and 15.
(b) What is the least common multiple of 10 and 15?
(c) Draw a repeated-measures diagram that supports your answer.

## Lesson Exercise 4.53

(a) Is 18 a common multiple of 3 and 6?
(b) Is 40 a common multiple of 5 and 8?
(c) Based upon parts (a) and (b), what number would you expect to be a common multiple of counting numbers $M$ and $N$?
(d) What kind of reasoning did you use in part (c)?
(e) Use the definition of a multiple to prove that your answer to part (c) is true.

Lesson Exercise 4.53 verifies the following theorem.

---

**Products as Common Multiples**

$MN$ is a common multiple of $M$ and $N$ for all counting numbers $M$ and $N$.

---

Computing the product of two counting numbers is an easy way to find a common multiple. However, the result may not be the *least* common multiple. Two methods for finding the least common multiple are the multiple-lists method and the prime-factorization method. Both methods are used here to find the LCM of 10 and 8.

**The Multiple-Lists Method**

1. List the multiples of each number.

   10: 10, 20, 30, 40, 50, . . .

   8: 8, 16, 24, 32, 40, 48, . . .

2. Find the first common multiple.

   10, 20, 30, 40, 50, . . .

   8, 16, 32, 40, 48, . . .

3. So the LCM = 40.

**The Prime-Factorization Method**

1. Write the prime factorizations.

   $$10 = 2 \cdot 5$$
   $$8 = 2 \cdot 2 \cdot 2$$

2. Multiply all prime numbers that appear in either factorization. Use each prime number the largest number of times it appears in either factorization. The least common multiple of 10 and 8 must contain $2 \cdot 5$ (which is 10) and $2 \cdot 2 \cdot 2$ (which is 8). So it is $2 \cdot 5 \cdot$ _____ . In order for the LCM to contain 8, we need two more 2's as factors. $2 \cdot 5 \cdot \underline{2 \cdot 2} = 40$.

3. So the LCM = 40. (*Note:* $2 \cdot 2 \cdot 2 \cdot 5$ contains $2 \cdot 2 \cdot 2$, or 8, and $2 \cdot 5$, or 10, so it is a multiple of both 8 and 10.

The multiple-list method is less abstract, so children can more easily understand why it works. For this reason, it is the first method taught in school. While both methods work well for smaller numbers, the prime-factorization method is usually superior for larger LCM's.

**D** Lesson Exercise 4.54

Compute the LCM of 120 and 72 using both methods.

## Lesson Exercise 4.55

Compute the LCM of 62 and 80 using either method.

## An Investigation: Least Common Multiples

## Lesson Exercise 4.56

Consider the following problem: "When is *MN* the least common multiple of counting numbers *M* and *N*?"
(a) Restate the question in your own words.
(b) Devise a plan and solve the problem.

## Answers to Selected Lesson Exercises

**4.47** (a) 1, 2, 5, 10     (b) 10

**4.48** the other whole number

**4.49** 26

**4.50** (b), (c)

**4.51** (a) yes   (b) inductive

**4.52** (a) 30, 60, 90     (b) 30
(c)
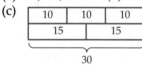

**4.53** (a) yes     (b) yes     (c) *MN*
(d) inductive
(e) *MN* is a whole number times *M*, so it is a multiple of *M*.
*MN* is a whole number times *N*, so it is a multiple of *N*.

**4.54** 360

**4.55** 2480

## 4.4   Homework Exercises

### Basic Exercises

1.  (a) Complete the Venn diagram.

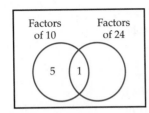

(b) Use the diagram to find the common factors of 10 and 24.
(c) Use the diagram to find the GCF of 10 and 24.

2.  (a) Compute the GCF of 42 and 120 using factor lists.
(b) Compute the GCF of 42 and 120 using prime factorizations.

3.  Compute the GCF of 126 and 270 using prime factorizations.

4.  Compute the GCF of 20, 48, and 172.

5.  (a) Find the GCF of 4 with each of the following: 5, 6, 7, 8, 9, 10, 11, and 12.
(b) Write a generalization of your results in part (a).

6.  $a = 3^2 \cdot 5 \cdot 11^4$ and $b = 3 \cdot 5^4 \cdot 7 \cdot 11$. Why isn't 11 the GCF?

7. $a = 2^2 \cdot 3^4 \cdot 5^7$ and $b = 2^3 \cdot 3 \cdot 5^6$. What is GCF $(a, b)$? (You may write your answer as a prime factorization.)

8. $a = 5 \cdot 7 \cdot 11^3$ and $b = 2^3 \cdot 5^2 \cdot 7 \cdot 11$. What is GCF $(a, b)$?

9. Which of the following pairs of numbers are relatively prime?
   (a) 11 and 12      (b) 34 and 51
   (c) 157 and 46

10. Which of the following pairs of numbers are relatively prime?
    (a) 28 and 33      (b) 14 and 15
    (c) 186 and 97

11. (a) Name three common multiples of 10 and 12.
    (b) How many common multiples do 10 and 12 have?
    (c) What is the LCM of 10 and 12?

12. Suppose 0 were included as a possible multiple in the definition of common multiples. What would be the LCM of any two whole numbers?

13. Place the numbers 2, 6, 10, 16, 24, 40, and 48 in the correct regions of the Venn diagram.

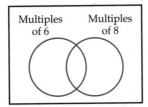

Multiples of 6 and 8

14. (a) Find the LCM of 20 and 32 using multiple lists.
    (b) Find the LCM of 20 and 32 using prime factorizations.
    (c) Draw a repeated-measures diagram that supports your answer.

15. Compute the LCM of 108, 32, and 20.

16. Two buses leave the terminal at 8 AM. Bus 36 takes 60 minutes to complete its route; bus 87 takes 75 minutes.

(a) When is the next time the two buses will arrive together at the terminal (if they are on time)?
(b) Draw a repeated-measures diagram that supports your answer.

17. Ben exercises every 3 days and Isabel every 2 days. Ben and Isabel both exercised today. How many days in the next 30 days will one of them be exercising when the other is not?

18. You have a balance and an unlimited supply of 3-oz and 5-oz weights. It is possible to weigh any whole-number amount of ounces using these weights on one or both balances!
    (a) How would you weigh the following amounts of a substance with the 3- and 5-oz weights?
       (1) 13 oz      (2) 2 oz      (3) 1 oz
    (b) Find another set of weights (measured in ounces) of two different denominations that you could use to weigh any whole-number amount of ounces.

19. $a = 2 \cdot 3^2 \cdot 5^7 \cdot 7 \cdot 11$ and $b = 2^3 \cdot 3^4 \cdot 5 \cdot 11$.
    (a) What is LCM$(a, b)$?
    (b) What is GCF$(a, b)$?

20. $a = 2^5 \cdot 7 \cdot 11^3$ and $b = 2^3 \cdot 3 \cdot 7^2 \cdot 11$.
    (a) What is LCM$(a, b)$?
    (b) What is GCF$(a, b)$?

21. $a = 2^3 \cdot 5^2 \cdot 7^3$
    GCF$(a, b) = 2 \cdot 5^2 \cdot 7$ and
    LCM$(a, b) = 2^3 \cdot 3^2 \cdot 5^4 \cdot 7^3$.
    Find $b$.

22. $a = 2 \cdot 3^2 \cdot 7^3$ and GCF$(a, b) = 2 \cdot 3^2 \cdot 7$. Give two possible values for $b$.

23. For what counting numbers $a$ and $b$ would $7^a = 5^b$?

24. The lowest common denominator for two fractions is the same as the _____ of the denominators.
    (a) LCM      (b) GCF      (c) neither

25. In simplifying $\frac{30}{45}$, divide the numerator and denominator by the _____ of 30 and 45.
    (a) LCM     (b) GCF     (c) neither

26. If A is a counting number, then GCF($A$, $A^2$) = _____ .

27. Without multiplying out the bases, tell which number in each pair is larger.
    (a) $2^{10}$ or $4^4$     (b) $3^{12}$ or $10^6$

In Exercises 28–30, A and B are counting numbers. If you think a statement is true, give an example. If a statement is false, give a counterexample.

28. True or false? If A and B are relatively prime, then A is prime and B is prime.

29. True or false? If $A$ is a factor of $B$, then $A$ is a factor of every multiple of $B$.

30. True or false? The LCM of two prime numbers is their product.

31. Find the greatest common factor of $3x^2y$ and $6y^2$, in which $x$ and $y$ are counting numbers.

32. Find three common multiples of $x^2$ and $xy$, in which $x$ and $y$ are counting numbers.

*Extension Exercises*

33. You want to pack new "Fiber 'n Wood Chips" cereal boxes standing up in a carton. The cereal boxes and all possible cartons are 10 in. high. The cereal boxes are 8 in. long and 3 in. wide. Which of the following cartons could be used to pack them without any wasted space between boxes?

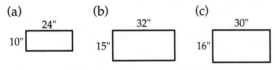

(a)          (b)          (c)
    24"          32"          30"
10"[  ]    15"[    ]    16"[    ]

(Top view: All boxes are 10" high.)

34. Suppose that, in the preceding exercise, you want to use a box with a square base (since it would use less material). What would be the smallest possible dimensions of the base?

35. Consider the following problem. "John has a cloth that is 30 in. by 48 in. He wants to cut out the largest possible squares of the same size and use all the material. How big could the squares be?"
    (a) Select a problem-solving strategy.
    (b) Solve the problem.

36. A and B are counting numbers. If LCM($A$, $B$) = $B$, then GCF($A$, $B$) = ___ .

37. How are GCF($a$, $b$) and LCM($a$, $b$) related?
    (a) Select three different pairs of counting numbers greater than 2 and fill in the table.

| $a$ | $b$ | GCF($a$, $b$) | LCM($a$, $b$) | GCF($a$, $b$)·LCM($a$, $b$) |
|---|---|---|---|---|
|  |  |  |  |  |
|  |  |  |  |  |

    (b) Make a generalization based upon your results in part (a).

38. What is the largest counting number that is a factor of every number in the set $1 \cdot 3 \cdot 5$, $3 \cdot 5 \cdot 7$, $5 \cdot 7 \cdot 9$, $7 \cdot 9 \cdot 11$, . . . ?

39. The **Euclidean algorithm,** a procedure for finding the GCF of counting numbers $a$ and $b$, appears in Book 7 of Euclid's *Elements*. The method uses a series of divisions according to the following flowchart.

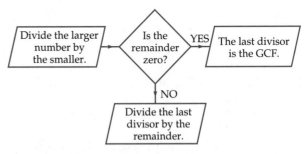

For example, here is how to find GCF(15, 40) using the Euclidean algorithm.

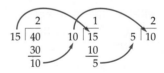

The last divisor, 5, is the GCF.

(a) Use this method to find GCF(40, 104).
(b) The Euclidean algorithm is based upon the fact that if $a = bq + r$, then GCF($a$, $b$) = GCF($b$, $r$). For GCF(15, 40),

$40 = 15 \cdot 2 + 10$. This leads to GCF(15, 40) = GCF(10, 15) = GCF(5, 10) = GCF(0, 5) = 5. Write the corresponding series of equal GCFs for part (a) and verify that they are all equal.

## Summary

"Number theory offers many rich opportunities for explorations that are interesting, enjoyable, and useful. These explorations have payoffs in problem solving, in understanding and developing other mathematical concepts, in illustrating the beauty of mathematics, and in understanding the human aspects of the historical development of number" (NCTM, *Curriculum and Evaluation Standards*, p. 91).

The classical Greeks were the first to study patterns in the set of counting numbers in detail, breaking down the counting numbers greater than 1 into their basic components. This analysis led to the study of factors (divisors) and multiples (by reversing factor-number relationships). The Divisibility-of-a-Sum Theorem and the Divisibility-of-a-Product Theorem describe the relationships between factors of different numbers. These theorems can be used with expanded notation to show how divisibility tests work. Elementary-school children learn divisibility tests for 2, 3, 5, 9, and 10.

The crowning achievement of ancient number theory was the discovery of the basic building blocks of counting numbers greater than 1: prime numbers. All composite numbers can be uniquely factored using prime numbers. This result is called the Fundamental Theorem of Arithmetic.

The Greeks also studied the relationship between the factors and multiples of counting numbers. Any two counting numbers have a greatest common factor and a least common (nonzero) multiple. In simplifying fractions, one divides the numerator and denominator by their greatest common factor. In order to find the lowest common denominator for adding or subtracting two fractions, one can compute the least common multiple of the denominators.

Number theory continues to fascinate mathematicians because it contains seemingly simple conjectures that have remained unanswered for hundreds of years. People have tested these conjectures for many examples, but no one has been able to prove these statements.

## Study Guide

To review Chapter 4, see what you know about each of the following ideas or terms listed that you have studied. You can also use this list to generate your own questions about Chapter 4.

# The NCTM Curriculum Standards and Number Theory

**Selected NCTM Curriculum Standards**

   The following standards come from the NCTM document.

- Develop common understandings of mathematical ideas including the role of definitions.
- Discuss mathematical ideas and make conjectures and convincing arguments.
- Recognize and apply deductive and inductive reasoning.
- Develop and apply number theory concepts (e.g., primes, factors, and multiples) in real world and mathematical problem situations.

1. Describe how each standard listed relates to the material you studied in Chapter 4.
2. Select any current elementary-school mathematics textbook series and describe a sample lesson or exercise that illustrates each standard listed.

## Review Exercises

1. Find a three-digit number $N$ for which $N - 8$ is divisible by 8, $N - 7$ is divisible by 7, $N - 6$ is divisible by 6, and $N - 5$ is divisible by 5.

2. By the definition of a multiple, $N$ is a multiple of 8 if and only if _____.

3. Write the prime factorization of 312.

4. The numbers $A$ and 10 are relatively prime. Give two possible values of $A$.

5. To simplify $\frac{28}{40}$, you divide the numerator and denominator by _____ , which is the _____ of 28 and 40.

6. Use the Divisibility-of-a-Product Theorem to explain why, for any whole number $x > 2$, $(x - 2) \mid (x - 2)(x + 3)$.

In Exercises 7–9, assume that $A$, $B$, and $C$ are counting numbers. If a statement is true, give an example that illustrates it. If a statement is false, give a counterexample.

7. True or false? If $A \mid B$ and $A \nmid C$ then $A \nmid (B + C)$.

8. True or false? The GCF of any two prime numbers is 1.

9. True or false? If $A \mid B$, then $A \mid B^2$.

In Exercises 10 and 11, if the statement is true, prove it. If the statement is false, give a counterexample.

10. $X$, $Y$, and $Z$ are whole numbers, with $X \neq 0$ and $Y \neq 0$. True or false? If $XY \mid Z$, then $XY \mid (XY + Z)$.

11. True or false? The LCM of any prime number and any composite number is their product.

12. Complete the number so that it is divisible by 3, 5, and 10. 3 2, 0 0 5, _ 2 _. Determine all possible answers.

13. $a = 2 \cdot 5^2 \cdot 11^3$ and $b = 2^3 \cdot 3 \cdot 5^4 \cdot 11^2$.
    (a) What is GCF $(a, b)$?
    (b) What is LCM $(a, b)$?

14. Suppose that you want to determine if 577 is prime. Using the Prime Number Test, what is the minimum set of numbers you must try as divisors?

15. Use expanded notation and the Divisibility-of-a-Sum Theorem to prove that if a three-digit numeral ends in 0 or 5 ($\underline{A}\,\underline{B}\,\underline{0}$ or $\underline{A}\,\underline{B}\,\underline{5}$), then the number is divisible by 5.

## Computer Exercise

1. (a) RUN the following BASIC program using the number 47 as input.

   10 PRINT "PICK A WHOLE NUMBER GREATER THAN 1."
   20 INPUT N
   30 FOR I = 2 TO N
   40 PRINT I, N/I

   50 IF I > SQR(N) THEN GOTO 70
   60 NEXT I
   70 END

   (b) How can you tell that 47 is prime?

   In parts (c) and (d), use the program to see if the given number is prime.

   (c) 353     (d) 527

## Number Theory in Elementary School

The following chart shows at what grade levels selected topics in number theory typically appear in elementary-school mathematics textbooks. Underlined numbers indicate grades in which the most time is spent on the given topic.

| Topic | Typical Grade Level in Current Textbooks |
|---|---|
| Divisibility tests | 5, <u>6</u> |
| Factors | 4, <u>5</u>, 6 |
| Prime and composite numbers | 5, <u>6</u> |
| Multiples | 4, <u>5</u>, <u>6</u> |
| GCF and LCM | <u>5</u>, <u>6</u> |

## Suggested Readings

Brown, S. *Some Prime Comparisons*. Reston, VA: NCTM, 1978.

Burton, D. *The History of Mathematics*. Boston, MA: Allyn & Bacon, 1985.

National Council of Teachers of Mathematics. *Historical Topics for the Mathematics Classroom*. Reston, VA: NCTM, 1989.

National Council of Teachers of Mathematics. 1989 Yearbook. *New Directions for Elementary School Mathematics*. Reston, VA: NCTM, 1989.

# 5

## Integers

As far back as 200 B.C., Chinese accountants used negative numbers. But 1700 years passed before Giralumo Cardano (1501–1576) gave the first detailed description of negative numbers and their properties.

Cardano was a doctor who did mathematics and astrology in his spare time. After publishing a horoscope of the life of Jesus Christ, Cardano was imprisoned for heresy. In spite of this scandal, he was later appointed as an astrologer to the papal court! Some sources claim that Cardano killed himself in 1576 so that his prediction of the date of his death would be correct.

Not everyone accepted Cardano's negative numbers. René Descartes called them "false" numbers. However, by the eighteenth century, negative numbers were widely used.

Today, negative numbers retain their importance in accounting. If you have $80 and spend $100, you have a net worth of −$20. People also use negative numbers to measure temperatures, golf scores, and changes in stock prices.

In mathematics, the set of integers results from enlarging the set of whole numbers to create solutions for every whole-number subtraction problem (for example, $6 - 10$). The set of integers retains many properties and patterns of whole-number operations.

## 5.1 Addition and Subtraction of Integers

Using numbers greater than or equal to 0 is sufficient for measurements such as weight, area, and the number of raisins in a bowl of cereal. Such measurements have a lower limit of 0.

In some measurement scales such as temperature, the scale extends above *and* below 0.

Figure 5-1 illustrates common uses of negative numbers. An investor does not like negative numbers, but golfers love them!

**Figure 5-1**

## Lesson Exercise 5.1

What is the meaning of the − sign in
(a) a temperature of −5°C?     (b) a golf score of −4?
(c) a federal budget balance of −$140 million (called a deficit)?

## The Set of Integers

When you add or multiply any two whole numbers, the result is a whole number. However, some whole-number subtraction problems, such as

$2 - 5$, do not have whole-number answers. These subtraction problems provided the mathematical motivation for creating negative integers.

How are negative numbers defined mathematically? For each positive number to the right of 0 on a number line, there is a corresponding negative number the same distance to the left of 0. For example, 3 is 3 units to the right of 0, and "negative 3," written $-3$, is 3 units to the left of 0. The set $\{-1, -2, -3, \ldots\}$ is called the set of **negative integers.**

By combining the set of whole numbers with the set of negative integers, one obtains . . . (drum roll) . . . the set of integers!

---

**Definition: Integers**

The union of the set of whole numbers and the set of negative integers is called the **integers.**

---

The set of integers is $I = \{\ldots -3, -2, -1, 0, 1, 2, \ldots\}$. The integers can be ordered on a number line.

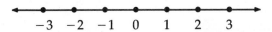

The integers are an extension of the whole numbers. With whole numbers, we can only count forward from 0, or move to the right from 0 on a number line. With integers, we can count forward or backward from 0, and move to the right *or* left from 0 on a number line. A larger number is always to the right of a smaller number on the standard integer number line. For integers $m$ and $n$, $m > n$ if and only if $m$ is located to the right of $n$ on the number line.

## Lesson Exercise 5.2

What number is 2 units to the left of $-130$ on the standard number line?

---

The number $-5$ is called "negative 5" or "the opposite of 5." A number and its opposite (for example, 5 and $-5$) are the same distance from 0 but on opposite sides.

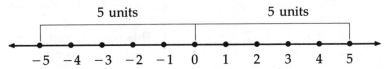

The opposite of $-5$, written $-(-5)$, is 5. If $x$ is an integer, $x$ can be positive, negative, or zero, and consequently, $-x$ can be negative, positive, or zero. Thus, calling $-x$ "the opposite of $x$" instead of "negative $x$" may be less confusing.

The distance between 0 and an integer is called the **absolute value.** The absolute value of both 5 and $-5$ is 5. In symbols,

$$|5| = 5 \quad \text{and} \quad |-5| = 5$$

### Lesson Exercise 5.3

If possible, find integers $m$ and $n$ such that
(a) $|m + n| < |m| + |n|$.     (b) $|m + n| = |m| + |n|$.
(c) $|m + n| > |m| + |n|$.

Integer arithmetic is more abstract than whole-number arithmetic. People are sometimes surprised by the answers to integer arithmetic problems. The remainder of this lesson shows how to explain the results of integer addition and subtraction.

### Integer Addition

You reach an intersection and are unsure about whether to turn right or left. So you turn right and drive for 2 miles. Uh oh. This can't be the right way, so you turn around and head 3 miles in the opposite direction. Where are you now in relation to the intersection? This trip is an application of integer addition.

You can use a number-line model to answer this question. Recall from Chapter 3 that adding a positive integer (counting number) represents a move to the right on the number line. Adding a negative integer would represent a move to the left. In the case of your drive in the country, the question is the same as computing 2 (2 to the right) + $-3$ (3 to the left). Example 5.1 shows how to compute $2 + -3$ using a number line (combine measures category).

#### Example 5.1

Explain how to compute $2 + -3$ using a number line.

**Solution**

Go to 2. Add the second number, $-3$, by moving 3 to the left from 2 (see Figure 5-2).

You end up at $-1$. So $2 + -3 = -1$. This process corresponds to going 2 miles to the right and 3 miles to the left. You end up 1 mile to the left of where you started. ■

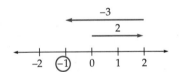

**Figure 5-2**

Try a similar example and then try to make a generalization.

**D** Lesson Exercise 5.4

(a) Explain how to compute $1 + -4$ using a number line.
(b) If $a$ and $b$ are whole numbers (such as 1 and 4) and $b > a$, then a formula relating integer addition $a + -b$ to *whole-number* addition or subtraction is $a + -b =$
   (1) $b - a$    (2) $-(b - a)$    (3) $a + b$    (4) $-(a + b)$

Another type of addition involving a positive plus a negative is a problem such as $5 + -3$, which has the form $a + -b$, with $a > b$. The following exercise concerns this type of problem.

**D** Lesson Exercise 5.5

(a) Explain how to compute $5 + -3$ using a number line.
(b) If $a$ and $b$ are whole numbers (such as 5 and 3), with $a > b$, then a formula relating integer addition $a + -b$ to *whole-number* addition or subtraction is $a + -b =$
   (1) $-(a - b)$    (2) $a + b$    (3) $a - b$    (4) $-(a + b)$

The formulas in Lesson Exercises 5.4(b) and 5.5(b) for adding integers with unlike signs ($a + -b$) can be combined into a single rule. Consider the distance each integer ($a$ and $b$) is from 0. Subtract the shorter distance from the longer distance (either $b - a$ or $a - b$). Then use the sign of the number further from 0 in your answer: $-(b - a)$ or $a - b$.

The other possibility in adding a positive and negative integer of the form $a + -b$ is that $a = b$.

Lesson Exercise 5.6

(a) Explain how to compute $3 + -3$ using a number line.
(b) In general, for whole number $a$, $a + -a =$ _____.

Finally, consider the sum of two negative integers.

Lesson Exercise 5.7

(a) Explain how to compute $-3 + -2$ using a number line.
(b) Part (a) suggests that for whole numbers $a$ and $b$, $-a + -b =$
   (1) $-(a + b)$    (2) $b - a$    (3) $a + b$    (4) $a - b$

Lesson Exercises 5.4–5.7 suggest the general rules for addition involving negative integers. Each rule relates integer addition to whole-number addition or subtraction. These rules comprise the *definition* of integer addition.

---

**Definition: Addition Involving Negative Integers**

If $a$ and $b$ are whole numbers, then

1. $a + -b = a - b$      if $a > b$.
2. $a + -b = -(b - a)$    if $b > a$.
3. $a + -a = 0$.
4. $-a + -b = -(a + b)$.

---

Consider the following applications of integer addition.

## Lesson Exercise 5.8

(a) In today's mail, you will receive a check for $282 and a bill for $405. Write an integer addition equation that gives your overall gain or loss.
(b) What type of addition application is this?

---

Although most applications fall into set or measure categories, money does not fit clearly into either category. Money is taught as a meaurement in school, since money measures the value of goods and services. Yet money also comes in countable units (sets) such as dollars or cents. In this text, applications concerning money will be classified as "measures/sets," indicating that money has characteristics of both measures and sets.

Can you write a realistic application of a given integer addition problem? You might use temperature, money, or a journey. Try the following.

## Lesson Exercise 5.9

Write a realistic word problem that models $-60 + -87$.

---

## Integer Subtraction

In elementary school, a child who is learning whole-number subtraction may ask: "What is $3 - 5$?" The child is asking a question that motivates the creation of negative numbers.

## Lesson Exercise 5.10

Try to determine the result of 3 − 5 by
(a) using a temperature or money application.
(b) extending a pattern in whole-number subtraction.
(c) using a number line.
(d) solving an equivalent addition problem (using the fact that subtraction is the inverse operation of addition).

This section covers all the approaches in the preceding exercise. First, let's define integer subtraction. Mathematicians set up integer subtraction to be consistent with whole-number arithmetic and integer addition. Integer subtraction is defined as the inverse operation of integer addition. Just as a whole-number problem such as 8 − 2 is equivalent to 8 = 2 + ?, an integer problem such as 3 − (−2) is equivalent to 3 = −2 + ?.

---

**Definition: Integer Subtraction**

For two integers $x$ and $y$, $x − y = n$ if and only if $x = y + n$.

---

This definition enables someone who knows integer addition to solve integer subtraction problems. Use this definition in the following exercise.

## Lesson Exercise 5.11

Rewrite each example as an addition example and find the answer.
(a) −2 − 1 = n     (b) 3 − (−2)     (c) −2 − (−3)

Students sometimes confuse the opposite or negative sign with the minus or subtraction sign in problems such as −2 − 1. The expression −2 − 1 is "negative 2 minus 1." Many middle-school books initially write negative numbers with a raised negative sign, like ⁻2, to distinguish it from the minus sign in subtraction. This practice is usually discontinued by the time students reach algebra class.

Another way to explain the answer to 3 − 5 is to find an application of it. When in everyday life would such a problem occur? Integer subtraction most commonly occurs in situations involving money or temperatures. Using take-away, 3 − 5 could represent an application such as "I had $3 and I spent $5. What is my net worth now?"or "The temperature was 3°C and it went down 5°. What is the temperature now?" In both cases, the answer is −2 with the appropriate units (−$2 or −2°C).

## Lesson Exercise 5.12

Make up a temperature or money problem for each of the following and give the result.
(a) $-2 - 1$     (b) $3 - (-2)$   (*Hint:* Use a temperature comparison.)
(c) $-2 - (-3)$

Integer subtraction results are an extension of whole-number subtraction results. One can explain the result of $3 - 5$ in relation to subtraction problems that have whole-number results. The difficulty is that 5 is greater than 3. Begin with related problems in which a whole number less than 3 is being subtracted. Use a few familiar examples to establish the pattern.

$$
\begin{aligned}
3 - 1 &= \phantom{-}2 \\
3 - 2 &= \phantom{-}1 \\
3 - 3 &= \phantom{-}0 \\
3 - 4 &= -1 \\
3 - 5 &= -2
\end{aligned}
$$

Use at least three whole-number examples to establish a pattern.

Use the same approach in the following exercise to explain the results of $3 - (-2)$, $-2 - 1$, and $-2 - (-3)$.

## Lesson Exercise 5.13

(a) To find the result of $3 - (-2)$, fill in the blanks, continuing the same pattern.

$$
\begin{aligned}
3 - \phantom{(-}2\phantom{)} &= 1 \\
3 - \phantom{(-}1\phantom{)} &= 2 \\
3 - \phantom{(-}0\phantom{)} &= 3 \\
3 - (-1) &= \underline{\phantom{xx}} \\
3 - (-2) &= \underline{\phantom{xx}}
\end{aligned}
$$

(b) Find the result of $-2 - 1$ by extending a pattern in whole-number subtraction. (*Hint:* The difficulty is the $-2$.)
(c) Find the result of $-2 - (-3)$ by starting with the result of $-2 - 1$ from part (b) and extending the pattern.

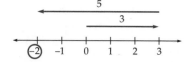

**Figure 5-3**

Like integer addition, integer subtraction can be illustrated using a number line. To show $3 - 5$, first go to 3. Then move 5 to the left. You end up at $-2$. So $3 - 5 = -2$ (see Figure 5-3).

The following exercise involves showing addition and subtraction on an integer number line.

## Lesson Exercise 5.14

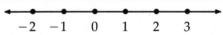

$-2$   $-1$   $0$   $1$   $2$   $3$

(a) On the standard number line, adding a positive integer is shown as a move to the _____.

(b) On the standard number line, adding a negative integer is shown as a move to the _____.

(c) On the standard number line, subtracting a positive integer is shown as a move to the _____.

(d) Based upon parts (a)–(c), it would make sense for subtraction of a negative integer to be shown as a move to the _____.

Apply the ideas of the preceding exercise to the same numerical examples.

## Lesson Exercise 5.15

*Explain* how to compute each of the following using a number line.
(a) $-2 - 1$     (b) $3 - (-2)$     (c) $-2 - (-3)$

Using the definition, applications, patterns, or a number line, one finds that $3 - 5 = -2$, $-2 - 1 = -3$, $3 - (-2) = 5$, and $-2 - (-3) = 1$. But there is a shorter way: the integer subtraction rule. The rule tells how to rewrite an integer subtraction problem as an equivalent integer addition problem. You probably remember this rule, but do you know why it works?

The rule can be explained using a number line.

## Lesson Exercise 5.16

(a) Why is subtracting a positive number (such as 3) the same as adding its opposite $(-3)$? (*Hint:* Use a number line.)

(b) Why is subtracting a negative number (such as $-5$) the same as adding its opposite (5)?

(c) Make a generalization based upon parts (a) and (b).

The preceding exercise suggests the rule for subtracting integers.

---

**The Integer Subtraction Rule**

Subtracting an integer is the same as adding its opposite. If $x$ and $y$ are integers, $x - y = x + -y$.

---

For example, $-2 - (+1) = -2 + -1 = -3$. So any subtraction problem can be rewritten as an addition problem. In order to compensate for changing the subtraction sign to an addition sign, the sign of the number being subtracted must also be changed.

How would you compute $-2 - (+1)$ on a calculator? Most calculators have a $\boxed{+/-}$ change-of-sign key that takes the opposite of the number on the display. To enter $-2$, you would press $\boxed{2}\ \boxed{+/-}$. (The $\boxed{-}$ key is used for subtraction, not negative signs.) To compute $-2 - (+1)$, press

$$\boxed{2}\ \boxed{+/-}\ \boxed{-}\ \boxed{1}\ \boxed{=}$$

 Lesson Exercise 5.17

---

Use the integer subtraction rule to compute the following. Then check your results with a calculator.
(a) $420 - (-506)$      (b) $-208 - 80$

Lesson Exercise 5.18

---

At 2 PM the temperature was 14°C. Since then it has dropped 38°.
(a) Write an integer subtraction equation for this situation.
(b) What is the temperature now?
(c) What subtraction category is illustrated?

---

It is more difficult to find applications in which a larger negative number is subtracted from a smaller negative number. One application would be a money problem in which subtracting a negative amount represents taking away (that is, paying) part of a debt or bill.

Lesson Exercise 5.19

---

Make up a money problem for $-6 - (-3)$ and give the result.

## Answers to Selected Lesson Exercises

5.1  (a) 5 degrees below 0       (b) 4 under par
(c) a debt of $140 million

5.2   −132

5.3   (c) is impossible

5.4   (a) Go to 1. Then move 4 to the left.

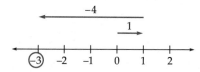

You end up at −3. So 1 + −4 = −3.
(b) (2)

5.5  (b) (3)

5.6  (b) 0

5.7   (a) Go to −3. Then move 2 to the left.

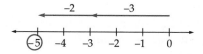

You end up at −5. So −3 + −2 = −5.
(b) (1)

5.8  (a) $282 + −$405 = −$123
(b) See the discussion that follows the exercise.

5.11 (a) 1 + $n$ = −2; $n$ = −3
(b) −2 + $n$ = 3; $n$ = 5
(c) −3 + $n$ = −2; $n$ = 1

5.12 (a) The temperature is −2°C and it goes down 1°. What is the temperature now?
−3°C. So −2 − 1 = −3.

(b) How much higher is 3°C than −2°C? 5°. So 3 − (−2) = 5.
(c) How much higher is −2°C than −3°C? 1°. So −2 − (−3) = 1.

5.13 (a) 4, 5
(b) 3 − 1 = 2, 2 − 1 = 1, 1 − 1 = 0, 0 − 1 = −1, −1 − 1 = −2, −2 − 1 = −3
(c) −2 − 1 = −3, −2 − 0 = −2, −2 − (−1) = −1, −2 − (−2) = 0, −2 − (−3) = 1

5.14 (a) right     (b) left     (c) left     (d) right

5.15 (a) Go to −2. Move 1 to the left. You end up at −3. So −2 − 1 = −3.
(b) Go to 3. Move 2 to the right. You end up at 5. So 3 − (−2) = 5.
(c) Go to −2. Move 3 to the right. You end up at 1. So −2 − (−3) = 1.

5.16 (a) In subtracting a positive integer $a$, you move $a$ units to the left, and in adding −$a$, you would move $a$ units to the left.
(b) In subtracting a negative integer −$a$, you move $a$ units to the right, and in adding $a$, you would move $a$ units to the right.

5.17 (a) 926     (b) −288

5.18 (a) 14 − 38 = −24
(b) −24°C
(c) take away measures

5.19 Milly has $6 in bills to pay. A bill for $3 is paid (taken away). Now, how do things stand? She has $3 in bills. So −6 − (−3) = −3.

## 5.1  Homework Exercises

### Basic Exercises

−1. Explain the meaning of the − sign in
(a) making −2 yards on a football play.
(b) a U.S. trade balance of −$4 billion.
(c) an altitude of −50 ft.

0. Find an example of a place where negative numbers appear in the newspaper.

1. Which of the following are integers?
(a) −4     (b) 0     (c) $\frac{2}{3}$     (d) $\frac{-8}{4}$

2. What number is 3 to the right of −100 on the standard number line?

3. What is the largest negative integer?

4. $a < 0$. Then $-a$ is
 (a)  positive      (b)  zero      (c)  negative

5. (a)  For what integers $x$ is $|x| < x$?
 (b)  For what integers $x$ is $|x| = x$?
 (c)  For what integers $x$ is $|x| > x$?

6. If possible, find integers $a$, $b$, and $c$ such
 that
 (a) $|a + b + c| < |a| + |b| + |c|$.
 (b) $|a + b + c| = |a| + |b| + |c|$.
 (c) $|a + b + c| > |a| + |b| + |c|$.

7. (a) $|-3| = $ _____      (b) $|-7| = $ _____
 (c) If $x < 0$, then $|x| = $ _____.

8. 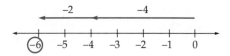       $A$ and $B$ are 9 units
    $A$    $0$  $B$        apart. $A$ is twice as far
                 from 0 as $B$. What are $A$
                 and $B$? (Guess and
                 check.)

9. What integer *addition* problem is shown on
 the number line?

 $$-2 \qquad\qquad -4$$

 $$\overset{\ominus}{-6} \quad -5 \quad -4 \quad -3 \quad -2 \quad -1 \quad 0$$

10. (a)  *Explain* $6 + -2$ using a number line.
 (b)  Describe an application that corresponds
  to your addition equation.

11. (a)  *Explain* $-5 + 3$ using a number line.
 (b)  What addition category is illustrated?

12. If $a$ and $b$ are whole numbers, and $a > b$,
 then a formula relating $-a + b$ to whole-
 number subtraction is $-a + b = $
 (a) $a - b$         (b) $a + b$
 (c) $-(a - b)$      (d) $-(a + b)$

13. In today's mail you will receive a check for
 $86, a bill for $30, and a bill for $20.
 (a)  Write an integer addition equation that
  gives the overall gain or loss.
 (b)  What application category is this?

14. An ion contains 42 protons, each with a single positive charge, and 44 electrons, each
 with a single negative charge.
 (a)  What is the overall positive or negative
  charge of the ion?
 (b)  Write an addition equation for this situation.
 (c)  What addition category is illustrated?

15. Fill in the blanks, continuing the same pattern.

 $$2 + 2 = 4$$
 $$2 + 1 = 3$$
 $$2 + 0 = 2$$
 $$\overline{\qquad\qquad}$$
 $$\overline{\qquad\qquad}$$

16. $-1 + 0 + 1 + 2 = 2$. What is the sum of
 $-99 + (-98) + \cdots + 98 + 99$?

17. Use the definition of subtraction to rewrite
 each subtraction equation as an addition
 equation.
 (a) $7 - 10 = ?$      (b) $-3 - (-2) = ?$

18. Which of the following are correct ways to
 say $-3 - (-2)$?
 (a)  "minus 3 minus negative 2"
 (b)  "negative 3 minus negative 2"
 (c)  "minus 3 minus minus 2"
 (d)  "the difference between minus 3 and
  minus 2"
 (e)  "the difference between negative 3 and
  negative 2"

19. Which of the following is a correct way to
 say $-(-6)$?
 (a)  "minus minus 6"
 (b)  "the opposite of negative 6"
 (c)  "minus negative 6"

20. Make up a temperature or money problem
 for $4 - 8$ and give the result.

**21.** Make up a temperature or money problem for $-6 - 4$ and give the result.

**22.** Show how $4 - 7$ can be solved by extending a pattern in *whole-number subtraction*. (*Hint:* Start with $9 - 7$ or $4 - 2$.)

**23.** Show how $5 - (-2)$ can be solved by extending a pattern in *whole-number subtraction*.

**24.** On a standard number line
   (a) subtracting 3 is the same as moving _____ units to the _____.
   (b) adding $-3$ is the same as moving _____ units to the _____.
   (c) What conclusion is suggested by parts (a) and (b)?
   (d) Make a broader generalization based upon part (c).

**25.** *Explain* how to compute $5 - (-2)$ on a number line.

**26.** *Explain* how to compute $-6 - (-3)$ on a number line.

**27.** Compute the following without a calculator. Then check your result with a calculator.
   (a) $-51 - 22$    (b) $-32 - (-70)$

**28.** A football team runs four plays with results of $+6$ yd, $+10$ yd, $+3$ yd, and $-5$ yd.
   (a) What is the net yardage?
   (b) How could you use this example to explain why $14 - (-5) = 19$?

**29.** Suppose that $a$ and $b$ are whole numbers, and $a < b$. Then $-a - b =$
   (a) $a + b$         (b) $-a + b$
   (c) $-a + -b$       (d) $a + -b$

**30.** Suppose that $x$ and $y$ are negative integers, and $x > y$. Then $x - y$ is
   (a) positive    (b) zero    (c) negative

**31.** True or false? All whole numbers are integers.

**32.** $I = \{ \ldots, -3, -2, -1, 0, 1, 2, \ldots \}$;
   $P = \{1, 2, 3, \ldots \}$;
   $N = \{-1, -2, -3, \ldots \}$; and
   $W = \{0, 1, 2, 3, \ldots \}$.
   (a) $N \cup W =$ _____
   (b) $N \cap P =$ _____

**33.** An elevator is at an altitude of $-10$ ft. The elevator goes down 30 ft.
   (a) Write an integer equation for this situation.
   (b) What is the new altitude?
   (c) What subtraction category is illustrated?

**34.** Euclid was born around 360 B.C.
   (a) If he lived for 50 years, when did he die?
   (b) Write an integer equation for this situation.
   (c) What operation and category are illustrated?

**35.** Consider the following problem. "A football team gains 5 yards on their first play and loses 12 on the second play."
   (a) What is their net gain or loss?
   (b) What operation and category are illustrated? (Give two possible answers.)

**36.**

|  | Continent | |
|---|---|---|
|  | North America | Europe |
| **Highest Point** | Mt. McKinley | Mt. Elbrus |
| Altitude | 6194 m | 5642 m |
| **Lowest Point** | Death Valley | Caspian Sea |
| Altitude | $-86$ m | $-28$ m |

   (a) What is the difference between the highest and lowest elevations in North America?
   (b) What is the difference between the highest and lowest elevations in Europe?
   (c) What operation and category are illustrated in parts (a) and (b)?

**37.** Fill in the chart.

| Stock | Monday Price | Tuesday Price | Change |
|---|---|---|---|
| Maytag | $32 | $31 | −1 |
| Wang | $65 | $62 | |
| Texas Oil & Gas | $87 | | −4 |
| K-Mart | | $53 | −2 |

**38.**

| Wind Chill Temperature in °F | | | | | | |
|---|---|---|---|---|---|---|
| **Wind Speed** | **Actual Temperature in °F** | | | | | |
| | 50° | 40° | 30° | 20° | 10° | 0° |
| 10 mph | 40 | 28 | 16 | 4 | −8 | |
| 20 mph | 32 | 18 | 4 | −10 | −24 | |
| 30 mph | 28 | 13 | −2 | −17 | −32 | |
| 40 mph | 26 | 10 | −6 | −22 | −38 | |

(a) The temperature is 40°F, and there is a 30-mph wind. What is the wind chill temperature?

(b) The weather report said the temperature is 10°F, and it feels like −25°F. What is the wind speed?

(c) Use the pattern in each row to fill in the last column of the chart.

(d) The temperature is 50°F, and the wind speed is 15 mph. Estimate the wind chill temperature.

*Extension Exercises*

**39.** Another model for integer addition is the charged particle model. A positive (+) sign represents positive 1, and a negative (−) sign represents −1. The picture illustrates that −4 + 2 = −2, since positive and negative charges cancel out.

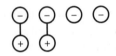

Draw a similar diagram showing why −3 + 6 = 3.

**40.** The charged particle model can also be used to show take-away subtraction. To compute 4 − (−2), start with 4 positive charges and take away 2 negative charges. In order to make this possible, show 4 as 6 positive charges and 2 negative charges.

⊕ ⊕ ⊕ ⊕ ⊕ ⊕        ⊕ ⊕ ⊕ ⊕ ⊕ ⊕
⊖ ⊖
    4              Take away −2    =    6

(a) Draw a similar diagram showing why 3 − (−4) = 7.

(b) Use the particle model to show why −2 − 4 = −6.

**41.** Which integers can be written as a sum of each of the following?
(a) two consecutive integers
(b) three consecutive integers

**42.** Consider the following subtraction algorithm for 52 − 27.

$$\begin{array}{r} 5\,2 \\ -2\,7 \\ \hline -5 \\ 3\,0 \\ \hline 2\,5 \end{array} \quad \begin{array}{l} (2-7) \\ (50-20) \end{array}$$

Will this algorithm work for all whole-number subtraction problems?

**43.** The sum of two integers is 4. The difference of the two integers is 10. What are they? (Guess and check.)

**44.** Consider the following problem: "For what integers x, y, and z does (x − y) − z = x − (y − z)?"
(a) Devise a plan and solve the problem.
(b) Make up a similar problem.

**45.** Decide whether each statement is true or false for all integers x and y. If a statement is true, give an example that supports it. If it is false, give a counterexample.
(a) True or false? $|x - y| = |y - x|$.
(b) True or false? $|x - y| = |x| - |y|$.

**46.** Fill in each of the numbers $-8$, $-6$, $-4$, $-2$, 0, 2, 4, 6, 8 in one square so that every row, column, and diagonal has the same sum.

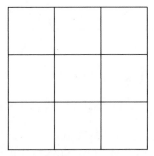

**47.** Fill in each of the numbers $-15$, $-12$, $-9$, $-6$, $-3$, 0, 3, 6, 9 in one square so that

every row, column, and diagonal has the same sum.

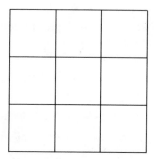

**48.** Are there more integers than whole numbers? Show that the sets are equivalent by establishing a one-to-one correspondence between the whole numbers and the integers.

*Special Exercise*

**49.** How can you increase your chances of living a longer life? The following predictor of life expectancy is adapted from Wallechinsky and Wallace's *People's Almanac #2*.

(a) Start with 72 and add the integers for all applicable descriptors.

- Male          $-3$                              Female          $+4$
- Urban residence over 2,000,000          $-2$          Rural residence under 10,000          $+2$
- Job with regular heavy labor          $+3$          Exercise five times per week          $+2$
- Alone for each 10 years since 25          $-1$          Live with spouse/friend          $+5$
- Easily angered, very aggressive          $-3$          Easygoing, a follower          $+3$
- Happy          $+1$                              Unhappy          $-2$
- College graduate          $+1$                    Graduate degree          $+2$
- One grandparent lived to 85          $+2$
- Parent died of stroke, heart attack before 50          $-4$
- Immediate family under 50 has cancer, heart disease, diabetes          $-4$          Grandparents lived to 80          $+6$
- Smoke > two packs/day          $-8$          Smoke 1 to 2 packs          $-6$
  Smoke one-half to one pack          $-3$
- Drink at least one-quarter bottle liquor/day          $-1$
- 50 or more pounds overweight          $-8$          30 to 49 pounds overweight          $-4$
  10 to 29 pounds overweight          $-2$
- 30 to 39 years old          $+2$          40 to 49          $+3$          50 to 69          $+4$

The number you obtain is your life expectancy.
(b) According to this scoring system, besides
your current age, what are the three
most important factors affecting life expectancy?

## 5.2   Multiplication and Division of Integers

Integer multiplication and division are similar to whole-number multiplication and division. In multiplying and dividing integers, the one new issue
is whether the result is positive or negative. This lesson shows how to
explain the sign of an integer product or quotient using patterns, applications, and definitions.

### Integer Multiplication

Why would someone want to multiply $-4 \times 3$ in everyday life? Suppose
the temperature drops 4° per hour for 3 hours. How much does it change
all together? $-12°$. This problem suggests that $-4 \times 3 = -12$. Temperature and money applications are useful models of integer multiplication.

### Lesson Exercise 5.20

(a) Write a temperature or money application for $-5 \times 2$ and give the
result. (In your question, ask for the "change" over time so the person answering must include the negative sign or a word such as
"decreases.")
(b) What category is illustrated by your application?

Another way to determine the sign of an answer to a multiplication
problem is to extend patterns in whole-number multiplication. Extending
whole-number multiplication patterns can establish the result of multiplying a positive integer by a negative integer and a negative integer by a
positive integer.

## Lesson Exercise 5.21

Fill in the blanks, continuing the same pattern. (*Note:* One begins with enough whole-number examples—at least three—to establish a pattern.)

(a)  $2 \cdot 3 = 6$
    $1 \cdot 3 = 3$
    $0 \cdot 3 = 0$
    $-1 \cdot 3 =$ _____
    $-2 \cdot 3 =$ _____

(b) Extend a pattern in whole-number multiplication to determine $2 \cdot -2$.

(c) Based upon parts (a) and (b), it appears that a negative integer times a positive integer or a positive integer times a negative integer results in a _____.

(d) Proposing a general rule based upon a pattern in examples requires _____ reasoning.

---

One can use the knowledge that a negative integer times a positive equals a negative to establish the result of a negative integer times a negative. Lesson Exercise 5.22 shows how to do this by extending a pattern.

## Lesson Exercise 5.22

Fill in the blanks, continuing the same pattern.

(a)  $-2 \cdot 3 \ \ = -6$
    $-2 \cdot 2 \ \ = -4$
    $-2 \cdot 1 \ \ = -2$
    $-2 \cdot 0 \ \ = \ \ 0$
    $-2 \cdot -1 =$ _____
    $-2 \cdot -2 =$ _____
    $-2 \cdot -3 =$ _____

(b) Based upon part (a), a negative integer times a negative integer results in a _____.

---

In Lesson Exercise 5.20 you created an application to model the multiplication of a positive integer by a negative. Next, consider the most difficult integer multiplication situation to model, a negative integer times a negative.

The following example explains how to set up an application of $-3 \times -2$.

### Example 5.2

Describe an application that suggests why $-3 \times -2 = 6$.

### Solution

Temperature, money, and mailing problems are particularly suitable. Whichever one you use, you must say that the amount is *now* 0. Then, when you ask the question at the end of the problem, go back in time.

|  | Temperature | Money | Mailing |
|---|---|---|---|
| Now 0 | It is now 0°C. | I have $0. | I have no cards left. |
| −2 | The temperature has been dropping 2° per hour. | I have been spending/losing $2 per hour. | I mailed 2 greeting cards each day. |
| −3 (Back 3 in time) | What was the temperature 3 hours ago? | How much did I have 3 hours ago? | How many cards did I have 3 days ago? |
| Answer | 6°C | $6 | 6 |
|  | So $-3 \times -2 = 6$. | So $-3 \times -2 = 6$. | So $-3 \times -2 = 6$. ■ |

Now you try one.

### Lesson Exercise 5.23

Describe an application problem that suggests why $-5 \times -6 = 30$.

The results of Lesson Exercises 5.20–5.23 support the rules for multiplication involving negative integers. Each rule relates integer multiplication to whole-number multiplication. These rules comprise the definition of integer multiplication (when combined with the rules for whole-number multiplication).

---

**Definition: Multiplication Involving Negative Integers**

If $a$ and $b$ are whole numbers, then

$$a \cdot -b = -(a \cdot b)$$
$$-a \cdot b = -(a \cdot b)$$
$$-a \cdot -b = a \cdot b$$

For *nonzero* $a$ and $b$, this means that a

"positive · negative = negative"
"negative · positive = negative"
"negative · negative = positive"

---

## Lesson Exercise 5.24

Use the rules just presented to compute $-3 \times 4$.

## Integer Division

When in everyday life would someone do division involving negative numbers? Suppose that a town's population drops by 400 in 5 years. What is the average population change per year? $-80$ people. This problem suggests that $-400 \div 5 = -80$. Population, money, and temperature problems offer useful models of integer division.

## Lesson Exercise 5.25

Write a temperature or money problem for $-12 \div 3$ and give the result.

Just as whole-number division is defined as the inverse of whole-number multiplication, integer division is defined as the inverse of integer multiplication.

---

**Definition: Integer Division**

If $x$, $y$, and $q$ are integers and $y \neq 0$ then $x \div y = q$ if and only if $x = y \cdot q$.

---

This definition enables someone who knows integer multiplication to solve integer division problems. Using this definition, one can convert any integer division problem with a nonzero divisor into an equivalent multiplication problem and solve it. For example, $-42 \div 6 = n$ is equivalent to $6 \times n = -42$. Thus, $n = -7$. So $-42 \div 6 = -7$. Use this approach to determine the rules for integer division in the following exercises.

## Lesson Exercise 5.26

(a) Rewrite $-8 \div 2 = n$ as a multiplication question and solve it.
(b) The result of part (a) suggests that a negative integer divided by a positive integer results in a _____.

## Lesson Exercise 5.27

(a) Rewrite $10 \div -5 = n$ as an equivalent multiplication problem and solve it.
(b) The result of part (a) suggests that a positive integer divided by a negative integer results in a _____.

## Lesson Exercise 5.28

(a) Rewrite $-12 \div -3 = n$ as an equivalent multiplication problem and solve it.
(b) The result of part (a) suggests that a negative integer divided by a negative integer results in a _____.

The following chart summarizes the rules for division involving negative integers.

| Division Involving Negative Integers | |
|---|---|
| If $a$ and $b$ are whole numbers, with $b \neq 0$, then | For *nonzero a* and *b*, this means that a |
| $-a \div b = -(a \div b)$ <br> $a \div -b = -(a \div b)$ <br> $-a \div -b = a \div b$ | "negative $\div$ positive $=$ negative" <br> "positive $\div$ negative $=$ negative" <br> "negative $\div$ negative $=$ positive" |

## Lesson Exercise 5.29

Use the rules just presented to compute $-24 \div -8$.

The introductory applications of division modeled a negative integer divided by a positive. It is more difficult to describe applications of a positive integer divided by a negative and a negative integer divided by a negative.

## Lesson Exercise 5.30

The temperature was 8° higher 2 hours ago.
(a)  What was the average temperature change per hour?
(b)  Write an integer division equation for this application.
(c)  What division category is illustrated?
(d)  This problem could be reworded as: "The temperature dropped 8° in the last 2 hours. What was the average temperature change per hour?" Write an integer division equation for this application.

The homework exercises include an application modeling a negative integer divided by a negative.

## Common Error Patterns

As a teacher, you will encounter certain common errors in your students' integer arithmetic. The following problems will give you practice in detecting them.

In Lesson Exercises 5.31–5.33, (a) complete the last two examples, repeating the error pattern in the completed examples, and (b) describe the error pattern.

## Lesson Exercise 5.31

$4 - 6 = \underline{2}$        $8 - 11 = \underline{3}$      $2 - 7 = \underline{5}$
$6 - 10 = \underline{\quad}$        $10 - 12 = \underline{\quad}$

## Lesson Exercise 5.32

$-6 \times -5 = \underline{-30}$      $-4 \times 2 = \underline{-8}$      $-3 \times -2 = \underline{-6}$
$-5 \times -4 = \underline{\quad}$      $-3 \times -6 = \underline{\quad}$

## Lesson Exercise 5.33

$-8 + 5 = \underline{-13}$      $-4 + -4 = \underline{-8}$      $-2 + 6 = \underline{-8}$
$3 + -6 = \underline{\quad}$      $-2 + 8 = \underline{\quad}$

## Answers to Selected Lesson Exercises

5.20 (a) Min has been spending $5 an hour for 2 hours. What is her overall change in finances? $-\$10$. So $-5 \times 2 = -10$. (*Note:* If you say "How much did she *lose*?" the person will answer $10 and may think the answer is *positive* 10.)
   (b) repeated sets/measures

5.21 (a) $-3, -6$
   (b) $2 \times 2 = 4, 2 \times 1 = 2, 2 \times 0 = 0,$ $2 \times -1 = -2, 2 \times -2 = -4$
   (c) negative      (d) inductive

5.22 (a) 2, 4, 6      (b) positive

5.24 $-12$

5.25 $-4$

5.26 (a) $2 \times n = -8$, so $n = -4$.
   (b) negative

5.27 (a) $-5 \times n = 10$, so $n = -2$.
   (b) negative

5.28 (a) $1n \times -3 = -12$, so $n = 4$.
   (b) positive

5.29 3

5.30 (a) $-4°$ per hour
   (b) $8 \div -2 = -4$
   (c) partition measures
   (d) $-8 \div 2 = -4$

5.31 (a) 4, 2

5.32 (a) $-20, -18$

5.33 (a) $-9, -10$

## 5.2   Homework Exercises

### Basic Exercises

1. Fill in the blanks, continuing the same pattern.

$$-5 \cdot 2 = -10$$
$$-5 \cdot 1 = \phantom{0}-5$$
$$-5 \cdot 0 = \phantom{00}0$$
$$\underline{\phantom{-5 \cdot 0 = 0}}$$
$$\underline{\phantom{-5 \cdot 0 = 0}}$$

2. Show how $-2 \times 4$ can be solved by extending a pattern in whole-number multiplication.

3. Mike lost 6 pounds each week for 4 weeks.
   (a) What was the total change in his weight?
   (b) Write an integer equation for this situation.
   (c) What application category is illustrated?

4. A school population has been dropping 15 students per year.
   (a) How many more students were there at the school 2 years ago?
   (b) Write an integer equation for this situation.
   (c) What application category is illustrated?

5. Make up a dieting, money, population change, or temperature problem for $4 \times -5$.

6. Make up an application that suggests why $-3 \times -5 = 15$.

7. Make up an application that suggests why $-4 \times -6 = 24$.

8. Write a temperature or money problem for $-20 \div 5$ and give the result.

9. If $a$ and $b$ are integers, what conditions would make each of the following true?
   (a) $a \times b = 0$      (b) $a \times b < 0$

10. Consider $(-2)^N$, in which $N$ is a whole number. For what values of $N$ is the result negative?

11. If $x$ is a negative integer, which is larger, $(x + x + x + x)$ or $(x \cdot x \cdot x \cdot x)$?

12. Rewrite each problem as an equivalent multiplication problem and give the solution.
   (a) $-54 \div -6 = \underline{\phantom{xxx}}$
   (b) $32 \div -4 = \underline{\phantom{xxx}}$

13. Rewrite each problem as an equivalent multiplication problem and give the solution.
   (a) $0 \div -3 = \underline{\phantom{xxx}}$      (b) $-3 \div 0 = \underline{\phantom{xxx}}$

**14.** Fill in the blanks, continuing the same pattern.

$$8 \div 2 = 4$$
$$4 \div 2 = 2$$
$$0 \div 2 = 0$$
$$\underline{\hspace{3cm}}$$
$$\underline{\hspace{3cm}}$$

**15.** A store lost \$480,000 last year.
  (a) What was the average net change per month?
  (b) Write an integer equation for this situation.
  (c) What application category is illustrated?

**16.** The temperature was 8° lower 2 hours ago.
  (a) What was the average temperature change per hour?
  (b) Write an integer equation for this situation.
  (c) What application category is illustrated?

**17.** Make up a dieting, money, or temperature problem for $-40 \div -5$ and give the result.

**18.** Make up a dieting, money, or temperature problem for $-35 \div 7$ and give the result.

**19.** Which of the following is not the product of 9 and an integer?
  (a) 180,018      (b) $-39,999$
  (c) $-4554$      (d) 9,000,063

**20.** If $x$ is a member of $\{-3, -2, -1, 0, 1, 2\}$ and $y$ is a member of $\{-6, -4, -2, 0, 2, 4\}$, find the largest and smallest possible values of each of the following.

  (a) $|x + y|$   (b) $x - y$   (c) $xy$   (d) $\frac{x}{y}$

In Exercises 21 and 22, (a) complete the last two examples, repeating the error pattern in the completed examples, and (b) describe the error pattern.

**21.** $-3 + -4 = \underline{\phantom{7}}7$      $-8 + -2 \ = \underline{\phantom{10}}10$
   $-2 + -3 = \underline{\hspace{1cm}}$      $-6 + -1 \ = \underline{\hspace{1cm}}$

**22.** $3 - (-6) = \underline{\phantom{-3}}-3$      $4 - (-5) = \underline{\phantom{-1}}-1$
   $6 - (-2) = \underline{\hspace{1cm}}$      $-3 - (-2) = \underline{\hspace{1cm}}$

**23.** Why might the error pattern in Exercise 21 occur?

**24.** Describe two errors a child might make in computing $-28 - 65$.

**25.** Tell what you could deduce about three consecutive integers if their product is
  (a) positive.      (b) zero.      (c) negative.

**26.** If $x$ is a positive integer, $(-x)^3$ is
  (a) positive      (b) zero      (c) negative

**27.** If $y$ is a negative integer, $(-y)^5$ is
  (a) positive      (b) zero      (c) negative

*Extension Exercises*

**28.** Fill in the following integers in the blanks in the box. You may use the same number more than once.

$$-4 \quad 2 \quad 1 \quad -8 \quad -2$$

**29.** The expression $3 \times -2$ can be written as $-2 + -2 + -2 = -6$ using repeated addition. Show how to compute the following using repeated addition.
  (a) $4 \times -8$      (b) $2 \times -5$

**30.** Consider the following problem. "If $x$ and $y$ are integers, and $x < y$, what values of $x$ and $y$ would make $x^2 < y^2$?" Devise a plan and solve the problem.

**31.** If $x$ and $y$ are integers, and $x < y$, what values of $x$ and $y$ would make $x^3 < y^3$?

**32.** If $x$ and $y$ are integers, and $x < y$, what values of $x$ and $y$ would make $-x < -y$?

**33.** Place a check in the appropriate column for each expression.

| Expression | Value of $X$ | Value of Expression | | |
| --- | --- | --- | --- | --- |
| | | Negative | 0 | Positive |
| $X^4$ | $X < 0$ | | | |
| $X^3 - 6$ | $X < 0$ | | | |
| $-3X$ | $X < 0$ | | | |

**34.** Place a check in the appropriate column for each expression.

| Expression | Values of $X$ and $Y$ | Value of Expression | | |
| --- | --- | --- | --- | --- |
| | | Negative | 0 | Positive |
| $-3X + 2Y$ | $X < 0, Y > 0$ | | | |
| $-3X + 2Y$ | $X > 0, Y < 0$ | | | |
| $2X^2 + Y^2$ | $X < 0, Y > 0$ | | | |

*Special Exercises*

**35.** How good an inflation fighter are you? This test is adapted from one published by the Center for Science in the Public Interest. Fill in the blanks and then add the numbers in the right-hand column to obtain a total score.

(a) Servings of chicken or turkey per week                $2 \times$ ____ = ____

(b) Potatoes or servings of rice or spaghetti per week                $2 \times$ ____ = ____

(c) Hot dogs, bacon, luncheon meat servings per week                $-2 \times$ ____ = ____

(d) Servings of steak, roast beef, or lamb per week      $-3 \times$ ____ = ____

(e) Servings of soda or fruit "drink" per day                $-2 \times$ ____ = ____

(f) Do you use butter rather than margarine? (Yes is $-4$.)                ____

(g) Alcoholic drinks per week                $-2 \times$ ____ = ____

(h) Do you make a shopping list? (Yes is $+3$.)                ____

(i) Do you regularly use unit pricing? (Yes is $+10$.)                ____

(j) Do you regularly buy store ($+10$) or national brands ($-10$)?                ____

(k) Do you try to buy things on special? (Yes is $+5$.)                ____

(l) How many times do you eat out per week?                $-6 \times$ ____ = ____

Total                _____

**Scoring:** $-20$ and below    You must have a lot of money to spend.

   $-19$ to 15    Okay, but you could improve.

   16 and up    You are saving $$ on food!

**36.** *Four Negative Two's:* Using only four negative two's and any combination of arithmetic symbols, write expressions equal to 1, 2, 3, . . . 9. The first one is done for you.

$$-2 \div -2 + (-2) - (-2) = 1$$

**37.** Look at two current elementary-school textbooks and report how they explain that the product of two negative numbers is a positive number.

## 5.3  Integer Properties and Algorithms

Does $-3 \cdot (4 \cdot 5) = -3 \cdot 4 \cdot 5$, or does $-3 \cdot (4 \cdot 5) = -3 \cdot 4 \cdot -3 \cdot 5$? Why does $-5x + 2x = -3x$? You can answer these questions if you understand integer properties.

First, let your mind relax. Now, let those whole-number properties you studied in Chapter 3 re-enter your consciousness. Do you recall that whole-number addition is commutative and associative, and that it has the identity number 0? Furthermore, do you recall that whole-number multiplication is commutative and associative, and that it has the identity number 1? And that whole numbers have the distributive properties of multiplication over addition and multiplication over subtraction?

Why recall these properties at this particular point in time? Well, wouldn't it be wonderful if integer arithmetic had these properties, too? It does!

### Whole-Number Properties Retained!

Integer operations retain the same commutative, associative, identity, and distributive properties as whole-number operations. The following list summarizes these properties.

---

**Properties of Integer Operations**

1. Integer addition and multiplication are closed. For any integers $x$ and $y$, $x + y$ is a unique integer and $xy$ is a unique integer.

2. Integer addition and multiplication are commutative. For any integers $x$ and $y$, $x + y = y + x$, and $xy = yx$.

3. Integer addition and multiplication are associative. For any integers $x$, $y$, and $z$, $(x + y) + z = x + (y + z)$ and $(xy)z = x(yz)$.

4. The unique additive identity for integers is 0, and the unique multiplicative identity for integers is 1. For any integer $x$, $x + 0 = 0 + x = x$ and $x \cdot 1 = 1 \cdot x = x$.

5. Integer multiplication is distributive over addition, and integer multiplication is distributive over subtraction. For any integers $x$, $y$, and $z$, $x(y + z) = xy + xz$ and $x(y - z) = xy - xz$.

---

The following exercises utilize these properties.

### Lesson Exercise 5.34

---

(a)  What is the easiest way to add $(3 + -5) + 5$?

(b)  What property does part (a) illustrate?

---

## Lesson Exercise 5.35

What property guarantees that for any integer $y$, $-2 \cdot (3y) = -2 \cdot 3 \, (y)$?

## Lesson Exercise 5.36

$I$ is an integer. According to the distributive property of multiplication over addition, $-5I + 2I = $ _____.

What about integer subtraction and division? Are they commutative or associative?

## Lesson Exercise 5.37

(a) Since 2 and 3 are integers, $2 - 3 \neq 3 - 2$ shows that integer subtraction is not _____.
(b) Explain why any commutative or associative property that does not hold for all whole numbers could not possibly hold for the set of integers.

### Inverses

So far, the integers have had all the same properties as the whole numbers. Big deal, you say? Well, it is nice to have some consistency. How would you like it if gravity stopped working?

Something different is also nice once in a while. The integers do have one additional property for addition that the whole numbers do not have. This additional property concerns the fact that mathematicians use integers to solve problems such as $3 + $ _____ $= 0$ and $4 + $ _____ $= 0$. The numbers that go in the blanks are the additive inverses of 3 and 4.

> **Definition: Additive Inverse**
>
> The integer $y$ is an **additive inverse** of the integer $x$ if and only if $x + y = y + x = 0$ (the additive identity).

Any integer added to its additive inverse should result in the additive identity, 0. Do all integers have unique additive inverses that are also integers? The results of Lesson Exercises 5.38 and 5.39 will help you decide.

## Lesson Exercise 5.38

Fill in each blank with all possible answers.

(a)  3 + _____ = 0 and _____ + 3 = 0. Therefore, _____ is an additive inverse of 3.

(b)  $-8$ + _____ = 0 and _____ + $-8$ = 0. Therefore, _____ is an additive inverse of $-8$.

(c)  Did each part have a unique (exactly one) answer?

## Lesson Exercise 5.39

What is the additive inverse of each of the following?

(a) 7     (b) $-2$     (c) 0

Lesson Exercises 5.38 and 5.39 should convince you that every integer has a unique additive inverse that is an integer.

---

**Additive Inverses for Integers**

For each integer $x$, there is a unique integer $-x$ such that
$x + -x = -x + x = 0.$

---

## Closure

One reason for creating integers is to provide answers to problems such as $2 - 3$. Does this result in integer subtraction being closed?

## Lesson Exercise 5.40

If $x$ and $y$ are integers, do you think $x - y$ is always a unique integer?

Lesson Exercise 5.40 may have led you to the following conclusion.

---

**The Closure Property for Integer Subtraction**

Integer subtraction is closed. For any two integers $x$ and $y$, $x - y$ is a unique integer.

---

## Algorithms

All integer arithmetic problems can be converted to whole-number arithmetic problems with positive or negative signs in front of them. For example, $34 - 52 = -(52 - 34)$, and $-86 \times 7 = -(86 \times 7)$. Thus the whole-number algorithms can also be used in integer problems with larger numbers.

### Lesson Exercise 5.41

$-456 + 78 = ?$
(a) $456 + 78$    (b) $456 - 78$    (c) $-(456 - 78)$    (d) $-(456 + 78)$

### Lesson Exercise 5.42

$876 \div -23 = ?$
(a) $876 \div 23$    (b) $-(876 \div 23)$    (c) $876 - 23$    (d) $-(876 - 23)$

## An Investigation: Order in Subtraction

Integer subtraction is not commutative, but $x - y$ is related to $y - x$ for all integers $x$ and $y$.

### Lesson Exercise 5.43

If $x - y = 2$, then $y - x =$ _____. (*Hint:* Try some numbers for $x$ and $y$.)

### Lesson Exercise 5.44

For integers $a$ and $b$, how does $a - b$ compare to $b - a$?
(a) Devise a plan.
(b) Carry out the plan.
(c) Make a generalization based upon your results.
(d) What kind of reasoning is used to make a generalization from examples in part (c)?

### Lesson Exercise 5.45

For what integer values of $m$ and $n$ does $m - n = n - m$?

## Answers to Selected Lesson Exercises

5.34 (a) Add $-5 + 5$ and then add 3.
     (b) associative property of $+$

5.35 associative property of $x$

5.36 $(-5 + 2)I$

5.37 (a) commutative
(b) If a rule does not apply to *all* whole numbers, then it cannot apply to *all* integers, since every whole number is also an integer. Whatever was a counterexample for whole numbers would also be a counterexample for the integers.

5.38 (a) $-3, -3, -3$   (b) 8, 8, 8   (c) yes
5.39 (a) $-7$   (b) 2   (c) 0
5.40 yes
5.41 (c)
5.42 (b)
5.43 $-2$

## 5.3   Homework Exercises

*Basic Exercises*

1. (a) What integer operations are commutative?
   (b) What integer operations are associative?

2. During 3 consecutive years, a man gains 14 pounds, loses 37 pounds, and then loses 14 pounds.
   (a) Write an integer *addition* expression that represents his overall change.
   (b) What is an easy way to add the numbers?

3. What is an easy way to multiply $-5 \times (7 \times -8)$?

4. What property guarantees that for an integer $m$, $4 \cdot (-3m) = (4 \cdot -3)m$?

5. What properties guarantee that for an integer $n$, $2n + 8 + n + -6 = (2n + n) + (8 + -6)$?

6. In adding a series of integers, it is often easier to add all the negative numbers and positive numbers separately and then add the results together.
   (a) Compute $(-6 + 4) + (4 + -3) + (-7 + 5)$ mentally using this method.
   (b) Compute $-5 + -2 + 6 + -3 + 8 + 7$ mentally using this method.
   (c) What two properties enable you to add integers in a different order and still obtain the same answer?

7. How can you compute $-27 \times 6$ using a distributive property?

8. The equation $-5 \times -3 = -3 \times -5$ illus-

trates the _____ property of _____.

9. For an integer $n$, the distributive property of multiplication over subtraction states that $2n - 5n = $ _____.

10. For an integer $n$, the distributive property of multiplication over addition states that $-6n + -3n = $ _____.

11. (a) $-12 \times 99 = -12 \times (100 - 1) = $ _____ $-$ _____ $= $ _____
    (b) Part (a) uses what integer property?
    (c) Use the same procedure from part (a) to compute $-34 \times 99$. Do as much of it mentally as you can.

12. Give a counterexample that shows that integer subtraction is not commutative.

13. After studying whole-number operations, explain why you would know that integer division is not associative.

14. What is the integer identity element for addition?

15. The examples $-3 \times 1 = -3$ and $-5 \times 1 = -5$ illustrate that _____ is the _____ for _____.

16. Any number added to its additive inverse equals ____.

17. What property guarantees that $6 - 12$ has a unique integer answer?

18. $82 - (-47) = $ ?
    (a) $82 + 47$   (b) $-(82 + 47)$
    (c) $82 - 47$   (d) $-(82 - 47)$

**19.** $-63 + 78 = ?$
  (a) $-(78 - 63)$     (b) $78 - 63$
  (c) $78 + 63$

*Extension Exercises*

**20.** Fill in the blanks, following the same rule in the completed examples.

$$-2 \rightarrow 3$$
$$-4 \rightarrow 5$$
$$6 \rightarrow -5$$
$$-5 \rightarrow \underline{\quad}$$
$$8 \rightarrow \underline{\quad}$$
$$N \rightarrow \underline{\quad}$$
$$\underline{\quad} \rightarrow -17$$

**21.** If $a \div b = 10$, then $b \div a = \underline{\qquad}$.

**22.** Consider the following problem. "For non-zero integers $a$ and $b$, how does $a \div b$ compare to $b \div a$?"
  (a) Devise a plan and solve the problem.

(b) For what integer values of $a$ and $b$ does $a \div b = b \div a$?

**23.** Suppose that you did not know that $-2 \cdot 4 = -8$. You could prove that $-2 \cdot 4 = -8$ using the additive inverse property and whole-number multiplication.
  (a) Since $2 \cdot 4$ is the additive inverse of $-2 \cdot 4$, write an addition equation that shows their relationship.
  (b) How does this show that $-2 \cdot 4 = -8$?

**24.** Suppose you did not know that $-2 \cdot -4 = 8$. You could use the result of the preceding exercise to prove it. How would this be done?

**25.** An **even** integer is any integer that can be written in the form $2m$, in which $m$ is an integer. Show that the product of two even integers is even.

**26.** Show that the sum of two even integers is even.

## Summary

"As students reach grade 5, they begin to recognize—in both arithmetic and geometric settings—the need for numbers beyond whole numbers . . . . The integer $-1$ becomes necessary so that the whole number problem $2 - 3$ has a solution, such as when a player loses three points in a game when he or she only has two points. As students expand their mathematical horizons . . . they need to understand both the common ideas underlying these number systems and the differences among them" (NCTM, *Curriculum and Evaluation Standards*, pp. 91–2).

People use negative integers to measure stock prices, golf scores, and altitudes. Integers were also developed as solutions to whole-number subtraction problems such as $2 - 3$ that have no whole-number solution.

With integers, as with whole numbers, addition and multiplication are defined, and then subtraction is defined as the inverse of addition, and division is defined as the inverse of multiplication. The results of integer arithmetic can be illustrated by using definitions, by extending whole number patterns, by using applications such as temperature and money, or by using a number line.

The set of integers retain the commutative, associative, and distributive properties of whole-number operations. Both sets have the same identity elements for addition (0) and multiplication (1). The set of integers has two important additional properties that whole numbers do not have: additive inverses and closure for subtraction.

## Study Guide

To review Chapter 5, see what you know about each of the following ideas or terms listed that you have studied. You can also use this list to generate your own questions about Chapter 5.

## The NCTM Curriculum Standards and Integers

**Selected NCTM Curriculum Standards**

The following standards come from the NCTM document.

- Understand and appreciate the need for numbers beyond the whole numbers.
- Formulate problems from mathematical situations.
- Extend their understanding of whole-number operations to integers.
- Understand how basic arithmetic operations are related to one another.
- Develop, analyze, and explain techniques for computation.

1. Describe a topic you studied or an exercise you completed in this chapter that illustrates each standard listed.
2. Select any current elementary-school mathematics textbook series and describe a sample lesson or exercise that illustrates each standard listed.

# Review Exercises

1. Give an example showing that integer subtraction is not associative.

2. What integer operations are commutative?

3. Make up a temperature or money problem for $-3 - 6$.

4. Write a realistic application that is solved by computing $-3 \times -5$.

5. Show how $4 - (-2)$ can be solved by extending a pattern in whole-number subtraction.

6. Explain how to compute $-4 - (-2)$ using a number line.

7. (a) An army that loses 300 soldiers is how much better off than an army that loses 800 soldiers?
   (b) Write an integer equation for this situation.
   (c) What subtraction category is illustrated?

8. Sandy lost 18 pounds in 9 months. What was the average monthly change in her weight?
   (a) Write an integer equation and solution for this situation.

(b) What operation and category are illustrated?

9. An elevator is at an altitude of $-30$ ft. If it goes up 20 ft, what is its new altitude?
   (a) Write an integer equation and solution for this situation.
   (b) What operation and category are illustrated?

10. For what integer value of $a$ and $b$ does $a \div b = b \div a$?

11. $-86 - 47 = $ ?
    (a) $86 + 47$
    (b) $86 - 47$
    (c) $-(86 + 47)$
    (d) $-(86 - 47)$

12. If $a$, $b$, and $c$ are whole numbers, then $a + -b + c = $ ? (Select all correct answers.)
    (a) $a + b - c$      (b) $(a + c) - b$
    (c) $b - (a + c)$    (d) $-(b - a + c)$
    (e) $-(b - a) + c$

13. Name a *property* that the integers have that whole numbers do not.

# Computer Exercise

1. (a) For integers $x$ and $y$, in which $y < 0$, when is $x \div y < x$? Use the following BASIC program to investigate.

   10 PRINT "TYPE IN AN INTEGER AND
      A NEGATIVE INTEGER SEPARATED
      BY A COMMA."
   20 INPUT X, Y

   30 LET Z = X/Y
   40 PRINT X, Y
   50 IF Z < X THEN PRINT "TRUE,
      X ÷ Y < X."

   (b) Write a general conclusion to your investigation.

# Integers in Elementary School

The following chart shows at what grade level selected integer topics typically appear in elementary-school mathematics textbooks.

| Topic | Typical Grade Level in Current Textbooks |
|---|---|
| Integer concepts | 6 |
| Adding and subtracting integers | 6 |
| Multiplying and dividing integers | 6 (enrichment) |

## Suggested Readings

Ashlock, R. *Error Patterns in Computation.* 3rd ed. Columbus, OH: Merrill, 1982.

National Council of Teachers of Mathematics. 1986 Yearbook. *Estimation and Mental Computation.* Reston, VA: NCTM, 1986.

# 6

# Rational Numbers as Fractions

The ancient Egyptians were using fractions long before the invention of negative integers. The Rhind Papyrus (1600 B.C.) gives a systematic treatment of unit fractions $\left(\dfrac{1}{\text{counting number}}\right)$. Teachers follow this historical order when they teach fractions before integers in elementary school.

Practical applications that led to the development of fractions include sharing problems (for example, 4 loaves of bread for 10 people) and measuring problems $\left(\text{for example, } 2\dfrac{1}{2} \text{ ft}\right)$. Today, we also talk about $\dfrac{3}{4}$ of a tank of gas or a $\dfrac{2}{3}$ majority to override a veto in Congress.

This chapter examines a subset of the set of fractions called the rational numbers, that is, fractions that have an integer numerator and a nonzero integer denominator. In a mathematical development of number systems, one expands the whole numbers to the integers in order to have answers to all subtraction problems. Still lacking answers to many whole-number and integer division problems (such as $2 \div 3$), one can expand the integers to form the rational number system, which provides answers to all integer division problems with nonzero divisors.

## 6.1  Rational Numbers

The Babylonians and Egyptians used fractions in agriculture and business over 3500 years ago. Today, the increased use of computers has reduced the importance of fractions relative to decimals. However, fractional notation is still useful for certain sharing and measuring applications. In this section, you'll examine the different uses of fractions and different methods for comparing the size of two fractions.

Lesson Exercise 6.1

Why do you think a fraction was used in the speed limit sign in Figure 6-1 (see page 253)?

Copyright: *The Fresno Bee.*

**Figure 6-1**

## Rational Numbers and Elementary Fractions

When you hear the word "fractions," how do you react?

Reprinted by permission of UFS, Inc. © 1966, United Feature Syndicate, Inc.

The fractions that children study in elementary school will be referred to as elementary fractions. **Elementary fractions** are numbers $\frac{a}{b}$ in which $a$ and $b$ are whole numbers and $b \neq 0$. Elementary fractions include $\frac{2}{3}$, $\frac{1}{2}$, and $\frac{11}{4}$ $\left(\text{or } 2\frac{3}{4}\right)$, whereas $\frac{-2}{3}$ and $\frac{\sqrt{2}}{3}$ are not elementary fractions. In a fraction $\frac{a}{b}$, $a$ is called the **numerator** and $b$ is called the **denominator.**

Why do we use the terms "numerator" and "denominator"? Well, suppose I cut an apple pie into 8 equal pieces. Any serving would be in eighths (the denomination). The number of pieces that someone eats determines the numerator. If you eat 3 (number) pieces of eighths (de-nomination), then you have eaten $\frac{3}{8}$ of the pie. You also must have been rather hungry.

An elementary fraction can be classified according to the relative size of its numerator and denominator. If $a < b$, then $\frac{a}{b}$ is a **proper fraction.** If $a > b$, then $\frac{a}{b}$ is an **improper fraction.**

Children in elementary school study elementary fractions. In second-ary-school mathematics, students learn the union of the set of elementary fractions with the set of negatives of elementary fractions: the rational numbers. Some time is also devoted to other types of fractions, such as fractions that contain square roots.

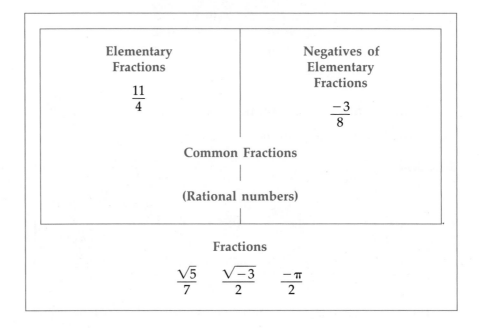

This chapter will focus on rational numbers.

Definition: Rational Numbers

**Rational numbers** are all numbers that *can be written* as a quotient (ratio) of two integers $\frac{p}{q}$ , in which $q \neq 0$.

The set of rational numbers includes all integers, since any integer can be written in rational form. For example, $-4 = \frac{-4}{1}$. Many decimals such as 0.3 are rational numbers since $0.3 = \frac{3}{10}$. Percents such as 42% are rational, since $42\% = \frac{42}{100}$. Decimals and percents will be discussed further in Chapter 7.

What numbers are *not* rational? It is impossible to write $\sqrt{2}$ and $\sqrt{3}$ as an integer over a nonzero integer! This will be proved for $\sqrt{2}$ in Chapter 7.

## Lesson Exercise 6.2

Which of the following are rational numbers?

(a) $\frac{-3}{4}$    (b) 5    (c) $\sqrt{2}$    (d) 0    (e) 0.37

Both elementary fractions and common fractions (rational numbers written as fractions) are subsets of the set of fractions. A **fraction** is a number $\frac{a}{b}$ in which $a$ is any kind of number and $b$ is any nonzero number (not necessarily integers). Examples of fractions include $\frac{11}{4}$, $\frac{-3}{8}$, $\frac{\sqrt{5}}{7}$, $\frac{\sqrt{-3}}{2}$, and $-\frac{\pi}{2}$.

All properties in this chapter will be stated for elementary fractions or rational numbers, although these properties and rules usually apply to all fractions.

## Four Meanings of an Elementary Fraction

Do you realize that elementary fractions have four meanings that children typically learn in elementary school?

**D** Lesson Exercise 6.3

What are different things the fraction $\frac{2}{3}$ can represent?

Did you come up with the following uses of $\frac{2}{3}$?

**Four Meanings of Elementary Fractions**

1. **Fraction of a whole:** $\frac{2}{3}$ means "Divide a whole into 3 equal parts and count 2 of them."

2. **Location on a number line:** $\frac{2}{3}$ is a number between 0 and 1. Divide the interval from 0 to 1 into 3 equal parts and count 2 parts over from 0 to 1.

$$0 \qquad \frac{1}{3} \qquad \frac{2}{3} \qquad 1$$

3. **Division:** $\frac{2}{3}$ means $2 \div 3$, the numerator divided by the denominator.

4. **Fraction of a set or measure:** $\frac{2}{3}$ means "Divide a measure into 3 equal parts and count 2 of them."

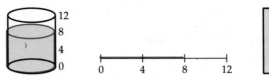

*or* "Divide a set into 3 equal groups and shade 2 out of every 3."

Note that $\frac{2}{3}$ can also represent a ratio. This meaning of $\frac{2}{3}$ will be addressed in Chapter 7.

## Lesson Exercise 6.4

*Explain* four common meanings of $\frac{3}{4}$.

Everyday applications of elementary fractions match up with these four meanings.

## Lesson Exercise 6.5

Match each application with a fraction meaning.

(a)  2 desserts split equally among 4 people
(b)  a scarf $3\frac{1}{2}$ ft long
(c)  2 slices of an 8-slice pizza
(d)  $\frac{3}{5}$ of a group of 20 prefer juice over soda.

(1)  fraction of a whole
(2)  location on a number line
(3)  division
(4)  fraction of a set

Which of the four meanings apply to rational numbers less than 0? Try the following.

## Lesson Exercise 6.6

Which of the four meanings are easily applied to $\frac{-3}{4}$?

As you may have discovered in the preceding exercise, two of the four meanings work well with negative rational numbers: location on a number line and division.

$$-1 \qquad \frac{-3}{4} \qquad\qquad 0 \qquad \frac{-3}{4} = -3 \div 4$$

As you know, improper fractions can be rewritten as mixed numerals $C\frac{A}{B}$ in which $C\frac{A}{B} = C + \frac{A}{B}$. This process can be explained using the fraction models.

**D** Lesson Exercise 6.7

Show why $\frac{9}{4} = 2\frac{1}{4}$ using

(a) division.        (b) the fraction-of-a-whole meaning.

## Equivalent Fractions for Rational Numbers

A friend of mine went on a diet. Instead of cutting a cake into 9 equal pieces and eating 6, he cut it into 6 equal pieces and only ate 4. Fractions such as $\frac{4}{6}$ and $\frac{6}{9}$ that look different may represent the same rational number. **Equivalent fractions** are two fractions that represent the same number.

Equivalent elementary fractions represent the same part of a whole. What is the pattern in the numerators and denominators of equivalent elementary fractions?

Lesson Exercise 6.8

By splitting thirds into equal parts, one can create equivalent fractions.

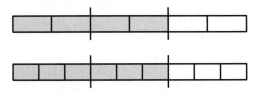

The diagrams show that $\frac{2}{3} = $ _____ $ = $ _____ .

The pattern could be extended without end: $\frac{2}{3} = \frac{4}{6} = \frac{6}{9} = \frac{8}{12} = \frac{10}{15}$, and so on, indefinitely. In general, you can rename a fraction by multiplying or dividing its numerator and denominator by the same positive whole number.

What about multiplying the numerator and denominator by the same negative integer? Does $\frac{2 \times {}^-2}{3 \times {}^-2} = \frac{{}^-4}{{}^-6}$ ?

## Lesson Exercise 6.9

Use division rules for integers and equivalent elementary fractions to show why $\dfrac{-4}{-6} = \dfrac{2}{3}$.

---

A number-line model can be used to show that the same pattern applies to negative rational numbers.

$$-\frac{2}{3} = -\frac{4}{6} = -\frac{6}{9} = -\frac{8}{12} = -\frac{10}{15} = \cdots$$

and so on.

The Fundamental Law of Fractions describes the general relationship between fractions.

---

**The Fundamental Law of Fractions**

For any rational number $\dfrac{a}{b}$ and any integer $c \neq 0$, $\dfrac{a}{b} = \dfrac{ac}{bc}$.

---

The Fundamental Law of Fractions states that you can multiply the numerator and denominator of a rational number $\dfrac{a}{b}$ by the same nonzero integer $c$ to convert it from $\dfrac{a}{b}$ to $\dfrac{ac}{bc}$ without changing the value of the fraction. You can also divide the numerator and denominator by the same nonzero integer $c$ to convert it from $\dfrac{ac}{bc}$ to $\dfrac{a}{b}$ without changing its value.

## Lesson Exercise 6.10

Use the Fundamental Law of Fractions to show why $\dfrac{3}{4} = \dfrac{6}{8}$.

---

## Lesson Exercise 6.11

Can you *add* the same counting number to the numerator and denominator of an elementary fraction $\frac{a}{b}$ without changing its value? That is, does $\frac{a}{b} = \frac{a+c}{b+c}$ for counting numbers $a$, $b$, and $c$?

## Simplifying Elementary Fractions

In simplifying an elementary fraction such as $\frac{12}{20}$, one divides the numerator and denominator by the same counting number. The following exercise illustrates this process.

## Lesson Exercise 6.12

(a) To write $\frac{12}{20}$ in simplest form in one step, divide the numerator and denominator by _____.

(b) To write $\frac{28}{42}$ in simplest form in one step, divide the numerator and denominator by _____.

(c) In parts (a) and (b), how is the answer related to the numbers in the original numerator and denominator?

(d) Give a general procedure for simplifying an elementary fraction based upon your response to part (c).

When the numerator and denominator of an elementary fraction have a greatest common factor (GCF) greater than 1, you can divide the numerator and denominator by the GCF, and the resulting fraction will be in simplest form! Try this method in the following exercise.

**D** Lesson Exercise 6.13

Find the GCF of 148 and 260 and use it to simplify $\frac{148}{260}$.

In simplifying fractions that have larger numerators and denominators, such as $\frac{148}{260}$, the GCF may make the work easier. Most fractions children encounter in elementary school $\left(\text{for example, } \frac{8}{16}\right)$ can be simplified just as easily without finding the GCF. But when children end up doing $\frac{8}{16} = \frac{4}{8} = \frac{2}{4} = \frac{1}{2}$ and ask why it took so many steps, you can tell them about the GCF. It always gets the simplification done in *one* step!

## Verifying the Equivalence of Fractions

In one group, 18 out of 30 $\left(\frac{18}{30}\right)$ people prefer butter to guns, and in a second group, 24 out of 40 people $\left(\frac{24}{40}\right)$ prefer butter to guns. How do the group preferences compare?

Since $\frac{18}{30} = \frac{3}{5}$ and $\frac{24}{40} = \frac{3}{5}$, the same fraction of each group prefers butter. This process illustrates how putting two given fractions into simplest form shows whether or not they are equivalent. This is one of three common ways to show that two fractions are equivalent.

---

**Three Methods for Verifying the Equivalence of Fractions**

1. **Simplest form:** Write both fractions in simplest form and see if they are equal.

2. **Least common denominator:** Write both fractions with the least common denominator (LCM of the denominators) and see if the numerators are equal.

3. **Compare cross products:** $\frac{a}{b} = \frac{c}{d}$ if and only if $ad = bc$.

---

It is easy to understand how the first two methods work. Try them in the following exercise.

## Lesson Exercise 6.14

Show that $\frac{8}{20} = \frac{6}{15}$ by

(a) putting both fractions in simplest form.
(b) writing both fractions with the least common denominator.

---

The third method, comparing cross products, is more difficult to understand. You can use Method 2 (least common denominator) and algebra to show why the equations $\frac{a}{b} = \frac{c}{d}$ and $ad = bc$ are equivalent in Method 3.

### Lesson Exercise 6.15

(a) What is a common denominator for $\frac{a}{b}$ and $\frac{c}{d}$ ?

(b) Rewrite the fractions in $\frac{a}{b} = \frac{c}{d}$ with a common denominator.

(c) Explain why $\frac{a}{b} = \frac{c}{d}$ is equivalent to $ad = bc$.

### Lesson Exercise 6.16

Show that $\frac{8}{20} = \frac{6}{15}$ by comparing cross products.

To solve for a missing numerator or denominator in one of two equivalent fractions, one can use either the Fundamental Law of Fractions or cross products.

### Lesson Exercise 6.17

$$\frac{3}{2} = \frac{15}{N}$$

(a) Solve for $N$ by using the Fundamental Law of Fractions. $\Big($Hint: What number was multiplied by the numerator and denominator of $\frac{3}{2}$ ?$\Big)$

(b) Solve for $N$ by using equal cross products.

### Lesson Exercise 6.18

Two companies conduct surveys asking people whether they want stricter handgun control. The first company asks 500 people and the second asks 1000. Describe results from the two surveys that would be considered equivalent.

## Unequal Elementary Fractions

Someone who has a basic understanding of elementary fractions will have little difficulty determining which of two elementary fractions with the same denominator is larger $\Big($for example, $\frac{5}{6} > \frac{2}{6}\Big)$. In general, for whole numbers $a$, $b$, and $c$ with $c \neq 0$, if $a > b$, then $\frac{a}{c} > \frac{b}{c}$.

When denominators are unequal, it may be more difficult to determine which of two elementary fractions is larger. For example, how do $\frac{7}{12}$ and $\frac{5}{9}$

compare in size? One way to find out is to rename both fractions with a common denominator and then see which one has a larger numerator.

$$\frac{7}{12} = \frac{7 \cdot 3}{12 \cdot 3} = \frac{21}{36} \quad \text{and} \quad \frac{5}{9} = \frac{5 \cdot 4}{9 \cdot 4} = \frac{20}{36}$$

Since $\frac{21}{36} > \frac{20}{36}$, we know that $\frac{7}{12} > \frac{5}{9}$.

Comparing cross products can also be used to compare the size of fractions. The following exercise develops the rule for comparing cross products of unequal elementary fractions.

**D** Lesson Exercise 6.19

Suppose $\frac{a}{b}$ and $\frac{c}{d}$ are elementary fractions, and $\frac{a}{b} > \frac{c}{d}$. Find a common denominator and derive an equivalent inequality.

Exercise 6.19 shows that $\frac{a}{b} > \frac{c}{d}$ and $ad > bc$ are equivalent for whole numbers $a$ and $c$ and counting numbers $b$ and $d$.

---

**Comparing Cross Products of Unequal Elementary Fractions**

If $a$ and $c$ are whole numbers and $b$ and $d$ are counting numbers, then $\frac{a}{b} > \frac{c}{d}$ if and only if $ad > bc$.

---

**Example 6.1**

How do $\frac{3}{7}$ and $\frac{5}{11}$ compare in size?

**Solution**

**The LCD Method**  Write both fractions with the lowest common denominator and compare them. The lowest common denominator is 77.

$$\frac{3}{7} = \frac{3 \cdot 11}{7 \cdot 11} = \frac{33}{77} \quad \text{and} \quad \frac{5}{11} = \frac{5 \cdot 7}{11 \cdot 7} = \frac{35}{77}$$

So $\frac{5}{11} > \frac{3}{7}$.

**The Compare-Products Method**  Compare the cross products:

$3 \cdot 11 < 5 \cdot 7$. So $\frac{3}{7} < \frac{5}{11}$.

Note that the product with the numerator of a fraction matches up with that fraction in the comparison.  ■

## Lesson Exercise 6.20

In one class, 6 out of 20 students prefer swimming over soccer. In another class, 10 out of 32 students prefer swimming over soccer. Compare the preferences of the two classes using the LCD method and compare-products method.

## Answers to Selected Lesson Exercises

**6.1**  to catch people's attention

**6.2**  (a), (b), (d), (e)

**6.4**  $\frac{3}{4}$ represents:

fraction of a whole
(shade 3 of 4 equal
parts)

fraction of a set
(shade 3 out of
every 4)

$3 \div 4$

(divide the
numerator by
the denominator)

(divide the interval
from 0 to 1 into 4
equal parts and count
over 3)

**6.5**  (a)—(3)     (b)—(2)     (c)—(1)     (d)—(4)

**6.6**  number-line location and division

**6.7**  (a) $\frac{9}{4} = 9 \div 4 = 2\frac{1}{4}$

(b) $\frac{9}{4}$ means 9 quarters.

This makes $2\frac{1}{4}$.

**6.8**  $\frac{4}{6} = \frac{6}{9}$

**6.9**  $\frac{-4}{-6} = -4 \div -6 = 4 \div 6 = \frac{4}{6} = \frac{2}{3}$

**6.10**  $\frac{3}{4} = \frac{3 \cdot 2}{4 \cdot 2} = \frac{6}{8}$

**6.11**  no

**6.12**  (a) 4     (b) 14
(c) 4 = GCF(12, 20)     14 = GCF(28, 42)
(d) The answer follows the exercise.

**6.13**  GCF = 4, $\frac{148}{260} = \frac{148 \div 4}{260 \div 4} = \frac{37}{65}$

**6.14**  (a) $\frac{2}{5} = \frac{2}{5}$
(b) LCM(20, 15) = 60
$\frac{8}{20} = \frac{24}{60}$ and $\frac{6}{15} = \frac{24}{60}$

**6.15**  (a) $bd$
(b) $\frac{ad}{bd} = \frac{bc}{bd}$
(c) $\frac{a}{b} \overset{?}{=} \frac{c}{d}$ is the same as $\frac{ad}{bd} \overset{?}{=} \frac{bc}{bd}$. To com-

pare $\frac{ad}{bd}$ and $\frac{bc}{bd}$, one only needs to check $ad \overset{?}{=} bc$.

**6.16** $8 \cdot 15 \overset{?}{=} 20 \cdot 6$     Yes, $120 = 120$.

**6.17** (a) $2 \cdot 5 = 10 = N$
(b) $3N = 2 \cdot 15$. So $3N = 30$, or $N = 10$.

**6.19** $ad > bc$

**6.20** $LCD: \frac{6}{20} ? \frac{10}{32} \rightarrow LCD = 160 \rightarrow \frac{6}{20} = \frac{48}{160}$

and $\frac{10}{32} = \frac{50}{160}$. So $\frac{6}{20} < \frac{10}{32}$.

*Compare products:* $\frac{6}{20} < \frac{10}{32}$ since $6 \cdot 32 < 10 \cdot 20$.

## 6.1   Homework Exercises

*Basic Exercises*

**1.** If $\frac{c}{d}$ is a proper fraction, then $c$ ___?___ $d$.

   (a) >     (b) =     (c) <

**2.** Show that each number is rational by writing it as a quotient of two integers.

   (a) 3     (b) $-3$     (c) $4\frac{1}{2}$
   (d) $-5.6$     (e) $25\%$

**3.** Which of the following are rational numbers?

   (a) $-7$     (b) $\frac{2}{3}$     (c) $\sqrt{3}$     (d) $0.2$

**4.** $W$ is the set of whole numbers, $I$ is the set of integers, and $Q$ is the set of rational numbers.
   (a) Is $I \subseteq Q$?
   (b) $W \cap Q =$ _____

**5.** Complete each diagram so that it shows $\frac{3}{5}$.

(a) 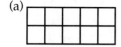     (b)
0                               1

**6.** A child shows $\frac{4}{5}$ as . What is

   wrong with the diagram?

**7.** *Explain* four common meanings of $\frac{1}{3}$.
   (Use some drawings).

**8.** *Explain* four common meanings of $\frac{5}{8}$.
   (Use some drawings.)

**9.** Match each application with a fraction model.

| Application | Fraction Model |
|---|---|
| (a)  your height in inches | (1)  fraction of a whole |
| (b)  fraction of those surveyed who jog | (2)  location on a number line |
| (c)  the fraction of the day you are asleep | (3)  division |
| (d)  evenly sharing 3 pizzas among 5 people | (4)  fraction of a set |

**10.** (a) What fractions can you find in a daily newspaper?
   (b) What denominators appear most often?

**11.** Show why $\frac{13}{3} = 4\frac{1}{3}$ using
   (a) division.     (b) the fraction-of-a-whole meaning.

**12.** *Explain* why $\frac{1}{3} > \frac{1}{4}$ using the fraction-of-a-whole meaning.

**13.** *Explain* why $\frac{0}{5} = 0$.

**14.** *Explain* why $\frac{0}{0}$ is undefined.

**15.** Make two different designs by shading half of each figure.

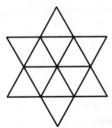 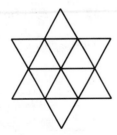

**16.** Use division rules for integers to show why $\dfrac{-4}{7} = \dfrac{4}{-7}$.

**17.** Which of the following are equal to $\dfrac{-3}{5}$?

(a) $-\dfrac{3}{5}$    (b) $\dfrac{-3}{-5}$    (c) $\dfrac{3}{-5}$    (d) $\dfrac{3}{5}$

**18.** Show why $\dfrac{1}{2} = \dfrac{2}{4}$ using the

(a) fraction-of-a-whole meaning.
(b) Fundamental Law of Fractions.

**19.** Use fractions to explain the error made by the man in this cartoon.

" CUT MY PIZZA INTO FOUR PIECES...
NO WAY I COULD EAT EIGHT."

© 1991 Carolina Biological Supply Company.

**20.** The relationships between the numerators and denominators of equivalent fractions can be studied using points on a graph.

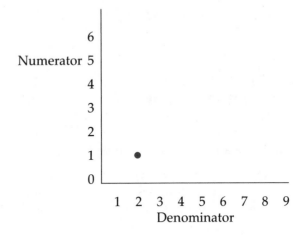

The graph shows the point representing $\dfrac{1}{2}$.

(a) Plot points for $\dfrac{2}{4}$, $\dfrac{3}{6}$, and $\dfrac{4}{8}$.

(b) Connect all four points. What patterns do you see?

(c) Plot points for $\dfrac{2}{3}$, $\dfrac{4}{6}$, and $\dfrac{6}{9}$.

(d) Connect the points from part (c). What patterns do you see?

(e) Write a generalization of the results to parts (b) and (d).

(f) Making a generalization based upon the examples of parts (b) and (d) is an example of _____ reasoning.

**21.** If $x$ and $y$ are counting numbers, use the Fundamental Law of Fractions to show why $\dfrac{x}{y} = \dfrac{2x^2}{2xy}$.

**22.** Name a situation in fraction arithmetic in which one would change

(a) $\dfrac{12}{15}$ to $\dfrac{4}{5}$.    (b) $\dfrac{4}{5}$ to $\dfrac{12}{15}$.

23. Describe an everyday situation in which one would use $\frac{15}{100}$ instead of $\frac{3}{20}$.

24. Make up a numerical counterexample which shows that the algebra is incorrect.

$$\frac{x}{y + x} = \frac{\overset{1}{\cancel{x}}}{y + \underset{1}{\cancel{x}}} = \frac{1}{y + 1}$$

25. Write each fraction in simplest form. (Assume that $x$, $y$, and $z$ are counting numbers.)
    (a) $\frac{168}{464}$   (b) $\frac{xy^2}{xy^3z}$   (c) $\frac{48}{264}$   (d) $\frac{2^8 - 2^7}{2^7 - 2^6}$

26. (a) Write an elementary fraction that is in simplest form.
    (b) What is the GCF of its numerator and denominator?
    (c) Repeat parts (a) and (b) for a different fraction.
    (d) Write a generalization based upon your results.
    (e) In part (d), you used _____ reasoning.

27. Suppose that you rewrite $\frac{4}{6}$ as $\frac{2}{3}$. Explain why it is misleading to call this "reducing."

28. By what do you multiply both sides of $\frac{a}{b} = \frac{c}{d}$ to obtain $ad = bc$, assuming $b \neq 0$ and $d \neq 0$?

29. Use all three methods to show that $\frac{4}{6} = \frac{6}{9}$.

30. Use all three methods to show that $\frac{9}{12} = \frac{15}{20}$.

31. Solve for $N$.
    (a) $\frac{N}{2} = \frac{5}{4}$   (b) $\frac{4}{N} = \frac{N}{9}$   (c) $\frac{5}{N} = \frac{6}{M}$

32. Solve for $N$.
    (a) $\frac{55}{90} = \frac{N}{18}$   (b) $\frac{5}{15} = \frac{7}{N}$   (c) $\frac{3}{4} = \frac{N}{M}$

33. Two companies conduct surveys asking people if they favor stronger controls on air pollution. The first company asks 1500 people and the second asks 2000. In the first group, 1200 say yes. Make up results for the second group that would be considered equivalent.

34. The third grade is voting on whether to go to a movie or a play. In Ms. Chan's class, 12 out of 20 students prefer going to the movie. In Ms. Brussat's class, 15 out of 25 students prefer going to the movie. Explain in what sense both classes equally prefer the movie over the play.

35. Use the LCD method and the compare-products method to show how $\frac{4}{7}$ and $\frac{8}{15}$ compare in size.

36. In one class, 14 out of 23 students would rather go to an aquarium than a circus. In another class, 17 out of 30 students would rather go to an aquarium than a circus. Use the LCD or compare-products method to compare their preferences.

37. In one fifth-grade class, there are 35 students, 16 of whom are boys. In the other class, there are 32 students, 14 of whom are boys. Write two multi-step mathematical questions that could be asked about one or both of these classes.

38. Teachers can use familiar objects to illustrate fractions. Name a common object that is naturally divided into each of the following.
    (a) halves   (b) fourths   (c) twelfths

39. If you select a card at random from a regular deck of 52 cards, what fraction of the time would you expect to pick each of the following?
    (a) an ace
    (b) a picture card (jack, queen, or king)

*Extension Exercises*

**40.** Cuisenaire rods are from 1 to 10 cm long in the colors indicated (actual widths are 1 cm).

**41.** If 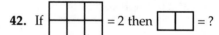 = 4 then ☐ = ?

**42.** If ☐ = 2 then ☐☐ = ?

☐  white

☐  red

☐  green

☐  purple

☐  yellow

☐  dark green

☐  black

☐  brown

☐  blue

☐  orange

Any Cuisenaire rod can be used as the unit rod.

(a) If the red rod is a unit, what fraction does the white rod represent?

(b) If the orange rod is a whole, what fraction does the green rod represent?

(c) If the white rod represents $\frac{1}{4}$, what does the red rod represent?

(d) If the purple rod is $\frac{2}{3}$, what color represents a whole?

**43.** $\dfrac{1+1}{4+3}$ is between $\dfrac{1}{4}$ and $\dfrac{1}{3}$.

(a) Is $\dfrac{2+5}{3+6}$ between $\dfrac{2}{3}$ and $\dfrac{5}{6}$ ?

(b) If $\dfrac{a}{b}$ and $\dfrac{c}{d}$ are positive and $\dfrac{a}{b} < \dfrac{c}{d}$, is $\dfrac{a+c}{b+d}$

between $\dfrac{a}{b}$ and $\dfrac{c}{d}$ ? Try more examples and decide whether this is reasonable, or find a counterexample to show that it is false.

**44.** Using only the digits 1, 3, 7, and 8, replace each question mark by a digit to make a true statement. (Guess and check.)

$$?\dfrac{?}{?} = \dfrac{?\,?}{?}$$

**45.** Prove: If $a$ and $b$ are counting numbers and $a > b$, then $\dfrac{1}{a} < \dfrac{1}{b}$.

*Special Exercise*

**46.** Copy the picture and cut out all nine squares. Fit the nine pieces together into one large square so that all the edges that touch have equivalent fractions.

| $\phantom{000}$ 1 $\phantom{000}$ | $1\dfrac{1}{3}$ | $\dfrac{1}{2}$ |
|---|---|---|
| 0 $\qquad \dfrac{1}{4}$ | $\dfrac{7}{7}$ | $\dfrac{2}{5}$ |
| $\dfrac{2}{16} \qquad \dfrac{4}{3}$ $\qquad \dfrac{3}{4}$ | $\dfrac{2}{6} \quad \dfrac{1}{3} \quad \dfrac{2}{8}$ | $\dfrac{6}{8} \quad \dfrac{1}{3} \quad \dfrac{3}{6}$ $\qquad \dfrac{10}{12}$ |
| $\dfrac{1}{3} \qquad \dfrac{4}{10}$ | $\dfrac{2}{4} \quad \dfrac{5}{6} \quad \dfrac{0}{3}$ | $\dfrac{1}{8} \quad \dfrac{1}{2}$ |

---

6.2

## Addition and Subtraction of Rational Numbers

You plan to spend $\dfrac{3}{4}$ hour doing mathematics homework and $\dfrac{1}{2}$ hour doing English. What is the total amount of time you will need? You have $\dfrac{1}{4}$ yd of fabric and you need a total of $\dfrac{1}{2}$ yd. How much more do you need to purchase?

To solve the first problem, you would add $\dfrac{1}{4}$ and $\dfrac{1}{2}$. To solve the second, you would subtract $\dfrac{1}{2}$ minus $\dfrac{1}{4}$. Adding and subtracting rational numbers are the subjects of this lesson.

## Adding and Subtracting Fractions That Have Like Denominators

Children first add and subtract fractions that have the same denominators. They can solve problems like the following: "Pamela walks $\frac{1}{5}$ of a mile to school and then $\frac{3}{5}$ of a mile from school to Kurt's house. How far did she walk altogether? How much further was the second walk than the first?"

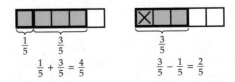

$$\frac{1}{5} + \frac{3}{5} = \frac{4}{5} \qquad\qquad \frac{3}{5} - \frac{1}{5} = \frac{2}{5}$$

**Figure 6-2**

Pictures and manipulatives help clarify why one should not add or subtract the denominators (see Figure 6-2). The general addition and subtraction rules for like denominators can be given algebraically . . . by you! Complete the following.

## Lesson Exercise 6.21

(a) For rational numbers, $\dfrac{a}{c} + \dfrac{b}{c} = $ _____ .

(b) For rational numbers, $\dfrac{d}{f} - \dfrac{e}{f} = $ _____ .

The rules for adding and subtracting rational numbers that have the same denominator are as follows.

---

**Addition of Rational Numbers That Have Like Denominators**

$$\frac{a}{c} + \frac{b}{c} = \frac{a + b}{c}$$

---

**Subtraction of Rational Numbers That Have Like Denominators**

$$\frac{d}{f} - \frac{e}{f} = \frac{d - e}{f}$$

---

Use the rules for adding and subtracting rational numbers that have like denominators to compute the following.

## Lesson Exercise 6.22

Assume that the following fractions represent rational numbers.

$$\frac{4x}{x+2} - \frac{3x}{x+2} = \underline{\hspace{2cm}}$$

## Adding Elementary Fractions That Have Unlike Denominators

Does $\frac{1}{2} + \frac{1}{3} = \frac{2}{5}$? According to the National Assessment of Educational Progress (NAEP), about 30% of the seventh graders in the United States think so (40% think the answer is $\frac{5}{6}$, and 30% get some other answer).

How would you convince someone who thinks $\frac{1}{2} + \frac{1}{3} = \frac{2}{5}$ that $\frac{2}{5}$ is the wrong answer? Fraction pictures are helpful in showing why $\frac{1}{2} + \frac{1}{3} \neq \frac{2}{5}$. Pictures of $\frac{1}{2}, \frac{1}{3}$, and $\frac{2}{5}$ are shown in Figure 6-3.

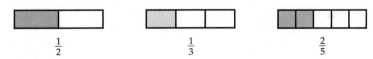

$$\frac{1}{2} \qquad\qquad \frac{1}{3} \qquad\qquad \frac{2}{5}$$

**Figure 6-3**

Clearly, $\frac{1}{2} + \frac{1}{3} \neq \frac{2}{5}$ because $\frac{1}{2}$ by itself is more than $\frac{2}{5}$! Once a child realizes that $\frac{2}{5}$ is the wrong answer, the child will want to know how to get the correct answer.

## D Lesson Exercise 6.23

How would you explain why you must have a common denominator to compute $\frac{1}{2} + \frac{1}{3}$?

$\frac{1}{2} + \frac{1}{3} =$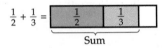

$\underbrace{\phantom{xxxxxxxxxxx}}_{\text{Sum}}$

**Figure 6-4**

To show that a common denominator is needed, try determining the sum of $\frac{1}{2}$ and $\frac{1}{3}$ without a common denominator.

What part of the whole is shaded to show the sum in Figure 6-4? There is no way to tell, because $\frac{1}{2}$ and $\frac{1}{3}$ are in different units (denominations). The answer cannot be determined without a *common denominator*.

When both fractions are written in terms of the same units (denominations), it is possible to compute the sum. We cannot add halves and thirds any more than we can add feet and inches (without converting to common units). After rewriting both fractions with a common denominator (sixths), one can use a combine-measures pictures to show the sum (see Figure 6-5).

$\frac{1}{2} + \frac{1}{3} = \frac{3}{6} + \frac{2}{6} =$  $= \frac{5}{6}$

**Figure 6-5**

Aren't common denominators wonderful? Without them, we could not name sums or differences of fractions that have unlike denominators.

## Lesson Exercise 6.24

Use fraction pictures to

(a) *explain* why you need a common denominator to compute $\frac{1}{2} + \frac{1}{4}$.

(b) show how you compute the sum.

## Subtracting Elementary Fractions That Have Unlike Denominators

Marilyn read the first $\frac{1}{4}$ of a book yesterday. Today she is about $\frac{1}{3}$ of the way through. What fraction of the book has she read today? This example requires subtracting fractions that have unlike denominators.

Fraction pictures clarify subtraction rules for unlike denominators. The following example explains why one needs a common denominator to compute $\frac{1}{3} - \frac{1}{4}$.

**Example 6.2**

Use fraction pictures to *explain* why you need a common denominator to subtract $\frac{1}{3} - \frac{1}{4}$, and show how you compute the answer.

**Solution**

Use the take-away-measures meaning of subtraction. How much is $\frac{1}{3}$ "take away" $\frac{1}{4}$?

Show $\frac{1}{3}$.

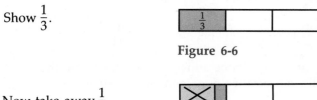

**Figure 6-6**

Now take away $\frac{1}{4}$.

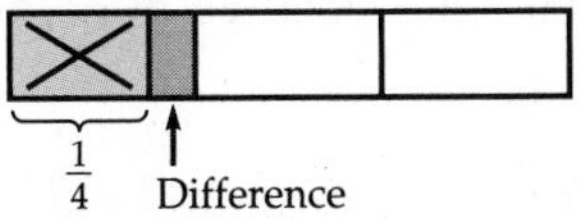

**Figure 6-7**

We cannot name the difference unless we use a common denominator (twelfths).

After changing $\frac{1}{3}$ to $\frac{4}{12}$ and $\frac{1}{4}$ to $\frac{3}{12}$, one can see the result of taking $\frac{3}{12}$ away from $\frac{4}{12}$. $\frac{1}{3} - \frac{1}{4} = \frac{4}{12} - \frac{3}{12} = $ ⊠⊠⊠▯▯▯▯▯▯▯▯▯ $= \frac{1}{12}$ ■

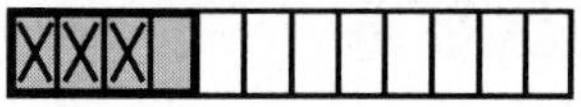

Note that one can also use compare-measures subtraction with two separate fraction bars and see how much longer $\frac{4}{12}$ is than $\frac{3}{12}$.

**Lesson Exercise 6.25**

Use fraction pictures to

(a) *explain* why a common denominator is needed to compute $\frac{1}{2} - \frac{1}{3}$.

(b) show how to compute the difference.

## Rational Numbers That Have Unlike Denominators

Before you can add or subtract rational numbers that have unlike denominators, you must rewrite them with a common denominator. As you saw in Section 6.1, you can find the least common denominator (LCD) using the least common multiple (LCM) of all the denominators. For example, the LCD for $\frac{1}{6}$ and $\frac{7}{8}$ is the LCM of 6 and 8, which is 24.

$$\frac{1}{6} + \frac{7}{8}$$

$$\text{LCM} = 24$$

$$\frac{1 \cdot 4}{6 \cdot 4} + \frac{7 \cdot 3}{8 \cdot 3} = \frac{4}{24} + \frac{21}{24} = \frac{25}{24} = 1\frac{1}{24}$$

Negative rational numbers can be added and subtracted in the same way. In order to retain the positive denominator, we shall always write $\frac{-3}{5}$ rather than $\frac{3}{-5}$.

The general rules for adding and subtracting rational numbers that have unlike denominators are as follows.

---

**Addition of Rational Numbers That Have Unlike Denominators**

To add rational numbers $\frac{a}{b} + \frac{c}{d}$ in which $b > 0$, $d > 0$, and $b \neq d$:

1. Rename each fraction with the least common denominator, that is, LCM($b$, $d$).
2. Add the fractions using the addition rule for like denominators.

---

**Subtraction of Rational Numbers That Have Unlike Denominators**

To subtract rational numbers $\frac{a}{b} - \frac{c}{d}$ in which $b > 0$, $d > 0$, and $b \neq d$:

1. Rename each fraction with the least common denominator, that is, LCM($b$, $d$).
2. Subtract the fractions using the subtraction rule for like denominators.

Use these rules in Lesson Exercise 6.26.

## Lesson Exercise 6.26

Compute $\dfrac{3}{40} - \dfrac{1}{32}$.

Are you aware that fractions can be added with any common denominator? However, if you do not use the *least* common denominator, additional simplification will be required at the end.

$$\frac{3}{4} + \frac{1}{6} = \frac{9}{12} + \frac{2}{12} = \frac{11}{12} \quad \text{or} \quad \frac{3}{4} + \frac{1}{6} = \frac{18}{24} + \frac{4}{24} = \frac{22}{24} = \frac{11}{12}$$

$$\text{(LCD)} \qquad\qquad\qquad\qquad \left(\begin{array}{c}\text{other common}\\\text{denominator}\end{array}\right)\text{(extra step)}$$

Until the seventeenth century, most people used the *product* of all the denominators as the common denominator. For the last 300 years, most people have used the least common denominator instead. Today, children usually find the least common denominator in textbook examples, and they rarely need prime factorizations to do it.

Children learn addition and subtraction involving negative rational numbers in junior high school. Since they have already studied elementary fraction and integer arithmetic, they can relate any rational number addition or subtraction problem to elementary fraction and integer arithmetic.

## Lesson Exercise 6.27

$$-2\frac{7}{30} + 4\frac{5}{18} = ?$$

(a) $4\dfrac{5}{18} - 2\dfrac{7}{30}$     (b) $2\dfrac{7}{30} + 4\dfrac{5}{18}$     (c) $-\left(4\dfrac{5}{18} - 2\dfrac{7}{30}\right)$

Do you recall how to change a mixed number such as $1\dfrac{3}{4}$ into an improper fraction? You can verify the results using addition of fractions.

Lesson Exercise 6.28

(a) What is a shortcut for converting $6\frac{2}{3}$ to an improper fraction?

(b) $6\frac{2}{3} = \frac{6}{1} + \frac{2}{3}$. Add $\frac{6}{1} + \frac{2}{3}$. Is your answer the same as your answer to part (a)?

The classifications for whole-number operations apply to some addition and subtraction applications involving rational numbers.

Lesson Exercise 6.29

What operation and category are illustrated in the following problem? "Last week, you worked $37\frac{1}{2}$ hours, and this week you worked 45 hours. How many more hours did you work this week?"

## Answers to Selected Lesson Exercises

6.21  (a) $\dfrac{a + b}{c}$     (b) $\dfrac{d - e}{f}$

6.22  $\dfrac{x}{x + 2}$

6.24  (a) $\frac{1}{2} + \frac{1}{4}$ would equal the shaded region shown,

| | | |
|---|---|---|
| $\frac{1}{2}$ | $\frac{1}{4}$ | |

but we cannot name the sum unless we use a common denomination (fourths).

(b) $\frac{1}{2} + \frac{1}{4} = \frac{2}{4} + \frac{1}{4} =$ 

| | | | |
|---|---|---|---|

$= \frac{3}{4}$

6.25  (a) Show $\frac{1}{2}$.

| | |
|---|---|
| $\frac{1}{2}$ | |

Now take away $\frac{1}{3}$.

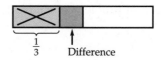

$\frac{1}{3}$     Difference

We cannot name the difference unless we use a common denomination (sixths).

(b) $\frac{1}{2} - \frac{1}{3} = \frac{3}{6} - \frac{2}{6} =$ 

| | | | | | |
|---|---|---|---|---|---|

$= \frac{1}{6}$

6.26  $\dfrac{7}{160}$

6.27  (a)

6.28  (a) $\dfrac{20}{3}$     (b) $\dfrac{20}{3}$, yes

6.29  subtraction, compare measures

## 6.2  Homework Exercises

*Basic Exercises*

1. Assume that the following fractions are rational.

   (a) $\dfrac{x}{n} + \dfrac{2x}{n} =$ _____

   (b) $\dfrac{4x}{x+1} - \dfrac{2x}{x+1} =$ _____

2. Use fraction pictures to
   (a) *explain* why a common denominator is needed to compute $\dfrac{1}{2} + \dfrac{2}{5}$.
   (b) show how to compute the sum.

3. Use fraction pictures to
   (a) *explain* why a common denominator is needed to compute $\dfrac{1}{3} + \dfrac{1}{4}$.
   (b) show how to compute the sum.

4. Use fraction pictures to
   (a) *explain* why a common denominator is needed to compute $\dfrac{1}{3} - \dfrac{1}{5}$.
   (b) show how to compute the difference.

5. Use fraction pictures to
   (a) *explain* why a common denominator is needed to compute $\dfrac{1}{4} - \dfrac{1}{6}$.
   (b) show how to compute the difference.

6. (a) Find the lowest common denominator of $\dfrac{5}{44}$ and $\dfrac{3}{28}$.
   (b) Give two other common denominators.
   (c) Compute $\dfrac{5}{44} - \dfrac{3}{28}$.

7. $\dfrac{2}{51} + \dfrac{1}{21} =$ _____

8. Assume that the following fractions represent rational numbers.

   (a) $\dfrac{1}{a} + \dfrac{2}{b} =$ _____    (b) $\dfrac{3}{2c} - \dfrac{2}{5c} =$ _____

9. $\dfrac{1}{2^3 \cdot 3} - \dfrac{1}{3^2 \cdot 5^2} =$ _____

10. $-43\dfrac{1}{2} + 32\dfrac{1}{2} = ?$

    (a) $-\left(43\dfrac{1}{2} + 32\dfrac{1}{2}\right)$
    (b) $\left(43\dfrac{1}{2} - 32\dfrac{1}{2}\right)$    (c) $-\left(43\dfrac{1}{2} - 32\dfrac{1}{2}\right)$

11. Write $4\dfrac{1}{5}$ as a sum; show that it equals $\dfrac{21}{5}$.

12. What operation and category are illustrated in the following problem? "You buy $\dfrac{3}{4}$ lb of Swiss cheese and $\dfrac{1}{2}$ lb of provolone. How many pounds of cheese have you purchased?"

13. You are working on a project that will take about $4\dfrac{1}{2}$ hours.

    (a) If you have been working on it for $1\dfrac{3}{4}$ hours, how much more time will it take?
    (b) What operation and classification are illustrated here?

14. In an apartment complex, $\dfrac{7}{8}$ of the people speak English as their native language, and $\dfrac{1}{16}$ speak Spanish as their native language.

    (a) What fraction speak a language other than English or Spanish as their native language?
    (b) What operations and classifications are illustrated here?

**15.** Make up a realistic problem for $5\frac{1}{4} - 2\frac{1}{2}$ and give the answer.

**16.** What fraction of the figure is shaded?

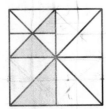

$$\frac{7}{32}$$

**17.** The sum of two fractions is $\frac{7}{12}$. Their difference is $\frac{1}{4}$. What are the two fractions? (Guess and check.)

### Extension Exercises

**18.** (a) What would the next equation be if the pattern continues? Is the equation true?

$$\frac{1}{2} = \frac{1}{3} + \frac{1}{6}$$
$$\frac{1}{3} = \frac{1}{4} + \frac{1}{12}$$

(b) Complete the general equation showing the pattern in part (a).

$$\frac{1}{N} = \underline{\hspace{2cm}}$$

(c) Show that it is true.

**19.** The ancient Egyptians represented all elementary fractions other than 0 and $\frac{2}{3}$ as the sum of unequal **unit fractions,** fractions that have a numerator of 1. For example, $\frac{2}{7} = \frac{1}{4} + \frac{1}{28}$. They did this to avoid certain computational difficulties. Write each of the following as the sum of unequal unit fractions.

(a) $\frac{3}{4}$　　(b) $\frac{3}{26}$　　(c) $\frac{5}{8}$　　(d) $\frac{7}{9}$

**20.** In the December 1991 *Mathematics Teacher,* Arthur Howard describes situations in which the standard algorithm for adding fractions does not yield the correct answer. For example, suppose two third-grade classes go on a field trip. One class has 10 girls out of a class of 25 and the other has 12 girls out of a class of 24. What fraction of the whole group will be girls?

$$\frac{10}{25} \oplus \frac{12}{24} = \frac{10 + 12}{25 + 24} = \frac{22}{49}$$

This example illustrates nonstandard fraction addition, denoted $\oplus$, in which the "reference unit" (denominator) of the sum is the *sum* of the reference units of the addends. In other words, one adds the denominators of the addends!

(a) Make up a problem about fruit that is solved using $\oplus$.

(b) Make up a problem that is solved using an analogous $\ominus$ operation.

**21.** *Within each part,* the question mark represents the same counting number. Find the missing numbers. All fractions are in simplest terms. (Guess and check.)

(a) $\frac{2}{?} + \frac{1}{2} = \frac{9}{?}$　　(b) $\frac{?}{5} - \frac{4}{15} = \frac{1}{?}$

**22.** Some calculators can handle fractions. If $\boxed{F}$ is the fraction key, $\frac{3}{8}$ would be entered as $\boxed{3}\,\boxed{F}\,\boxed{8}$. It would appear as $\boxed{3 \underline{\quad} 8}$. What would the display show after the following keystrokes are completed?

$$\boxed{3}\,\boxed{F}\,\boxed{8}\,\boxed{+}\,\boxed{1}\,\boxed{F}\,\boxed{4}\,\boxed{=}$$

**23.** Prove, for rational numbers, if $\frac{a}{b} = \frac{c}{d}$, then

$$\frac{a + b}{b} = \frac{c + d}{d}.$$

**24.** A **Farey sequence of order $n$** lists all rational numbers in simplest fraction form in increasing order from 0 through 1 with denominators that do not exceed $n$. The

Farey sequence of order 3 is

$$\frac{0}{1}, \frac{1}{3}, \frac{1}{2}, \frac{2}{3}, \frac{1}{1}.$$

(a) Write the Farey sequence of order 4.
(b) Write the Farey sequence of order 5.

(c) If $\frac{a}{b}$ and $\frac{c}{d}$ are consecutive fractions in a Farey sequence, what is the relationship between $ad$ and $bc$?

---

## 6.3  Multiplication and Division of Rational Numbers

You are planning a chicken dinner. Each person will eat about $\frac{1}{4}$ of a chicken. How many chickens will you need for 6 people? Next, you want to dye some shirts. Suppose it takes $\frac{3}{4}$ cup of dye to dye a shirt. How many shirts can you dye with 10 cups?

To solve the first problem, you would multiply $\frac{1}{4}$ by 6. To solve the second, you would divide 10 by $\frac{3}{4}$. Multiplying and dividing rational numbers are the subjects of this lesson.

### Multiplying Rational Numbers

Before studying multiplication of fractions, most children know how to find $\frac{1}{2}$ of 8 or $\frac{2}{3}$ of 6. These computations are really multiplication problems. Why? Just as $2 \times 8$ is the same as two sets of 8, $\frac{1}{2} \times 8$ is the same as $\frac{1}{2}$ of a set of 8 or, more simply, $\frac{1}{2}$ of 8. Similarly, $\frac{2}{3} \times 6$ is the same as $\frac{2}{3}$ of 6.

The product of a proper fraction and a whole number can be completed using this relationship.

$$\frac{1}{2} \times 8 = \frac{1}{2} \text{ of } 8 \quad \boxed{\because}\,|\,\because = 4 \qquad \frac{2}{3} \times 6 = \frac{2}{3} \text{ of } 6 \quad \boxed{\text{0}}|\boxed{\text{0}}|\,: = 4$$

This relationship can also be used in fraction word problems.

Lesson Exercise 6.30

$\frac{4}{5}$ of a group of 20 people watch television. Write a fraction arithmetic
equation that shows how to find the size of this group.

After studying how to multiply a whole number by a fraction, children
study the product of two proper fractions, such as $\frac{1}{2} \times \frac{3}{4}$. Example 6.3
shows how to find the result of $\frac{1}{2} \times \frac{3}{4}$ using a diagram.

**Example 6.3**

*Explain* how to compute $\frac{1}{2} \times \frac{3}{4}$ using a diagram.

**Solution**

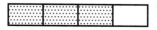

**Figure 6-8**

$\frac{1}{2} \times \frac{3}{4}$ is the same as $\frac{1}{2}$ of $\frac{3}{4}$. Show $\frac{3}{4}$ and then take $\frac{1}{2}$ of it. Place dots in $\frac{3}{4}$
of a rectangular diagram to show $\frac{3}{4}$ , as shown in Figure 6-8.

**Figure 6-9**

To show $\frac{1}{2}$ of $\frac{3}{4}$ , darken $\frac{1}{2}$ of the *dotted* part, as in Figure 6-9.

What part of the whole figure is darkened? $\frac{3}{8}$.
So, $\frac{1}{2}$ of $\frac{3}{4} = \frac{1}{2} \times \frac{3}{4} = \frac{3}{8}$.  ■

**D** Lesson Exercise 6.31

*Explain* how to compute $\frac{1}{2} \times \frac{3}{5}$ using the diagram method of
Example 6.3.

The results of Example 6.3 and Lesson Exercise 6.31 suggest the multiplication rule for fractions.

## Lesson Exercise 6.32

(a) Complete the chart, showing results from Example 6.3 and Lesson Exercise 6.31.

| Factors (as proper or improper fractions) | Product (as a proper or improper fraction) |
|---|---|
| $\frac{1}{2} \times \frac{3}{4}$ | |
| $\frac{1}{2} \times \frac{3}{5}$ | |

(b) The results from part (a) suggest that the general rule for multiplying rational numbers is: $\frac{a}{b} \times \frac{c}{d} = $ _____ .

---

Lesson Exercise 6.32 suggests the rule for multiplying rational numbers. This rule is the definition of multiplication of rational numbers.

---

**Definition: Multiplication of Rational Numbers**

$$\frac{a}{b} \times \frac{c}{d} = \frac{ac}{bd}$$

---

Because the definition is written for proper and improper fractions, we must rewrite mixed numbers as improper fractions before applying this rule.

Another interesting process in multiplying fractions is simplifying the resulting fraction before completing the multiplication. This is no longer referred to as "canceling" in textbooks; it is now called a "shortcut" or "simplifying by dividing by a common factor."

**D** Lesson Exercise 6.33

---

In multiplying $\frac{3}{7} \times \frac{10}{21}$, why is one allowed to simplify as follows?

$$\frac{\overset{1}{\cancel{3}}}{7} \times \frac{10}{\underset{7}{\cancel{21}}}$$

---

In school, most children learn to "cancel" a factor from the numerator of one fraction with the denominator of *another fraction*.

$$\frac{3}{7} \times \frac{10}{21} = \frac{\overset{1}{3}}{7} \times \frac{10}{\underset{7}{21}} = \frac{10}{49}$$

This is a shortcut for the following procedure.

$$\frac{3}{7} \times \frac{10}{21} = \frac{3 \times 10}{7 \times 21} = \frac{\overset{1}{3} \times 10}{7 \times \underset{7}{21}} = \frac{10}{49}$$

$$\longrightarrow$$

| | Definition of multiplication | | Simplifying a *single* fraction |

After writing the product of the two fractions as one fraction, $\dfrac{(3 \times 10)}{(7 \times 21)}$, the Fundamental Law of Fractions allows us to simplify the fraction to

$$\frac{\overset{1}{3} \times 10}{7 \times \underset{7}{21}}$$

Then, we can multiply to obtain the answer $\dfrac{10}{49}$ in simplest form.

When children use the shortcut in school, they "cancel" before combining the two fractions into one, which makes the process faster but more mysterious. It is not clear to them why the top of one fraction and the bottom of a *different* fraction can be divided by the same nonzero number.

## Lesson Exercise 6.34

Multiply as shown in the preceding example. (Do not use the "shortcut.")

(a) $\dfrac{4}{9} \times \dfrac{3}{8}$     (b) $1\dfrac{1}{6} \times 2\dfrac{2}{5}$

## Dividing Rational Numbers

"Joe buys 4 lb of Swiss cheese. He and his wife eat a total of $\dfrac{1}{2}$ lb of Swiss cheese each day. For how many days will the cheese last?" Before learning the division rule, children solve problems such as this that model a whole number divided by an elementary fraction. This kind of problem can be solved using pictures and the repeated-measures model of division.

**Example 6.4**

*Explain* how to compute $4 \div \frac{1}{2}$ using a measurement picture.

**Solution**

The expression $4 \div \frac{1}{2}$ means "How many $\frac{1}{2}$'s does it take to make 4?"

It takes two $\frac{1}{2}$'s to make each whole.

| $\frac{1}{2}$ | $\frac{1}{2}$ | $\frac{1}{2}$ | $\frac{1}{2}$ | $\frac{1}{2}$ | $\frac{1}{2}$ | $\frac{1}{2}$ | $\frac{1}{2}$ |
|---|---|---|---|---|---|---|---|

0    1    2    3    4

Therefore, it takes eight $\frac{1}{2}$'s to make 4. So $4 \div \frac{1}{2} = 8$. ■

## Lesson Exercise 6.35

*Explain* how to compute $3 \div \frac{1}{4}$ using a measurement picture.

Like division of whole numbers and integers, division of rational numbers is defined in terms of multiplication.

## Lesson Exercise 6.36

If division of rational numbers is defined like whole-number and integer division, then $\frac{a}{b} \div \frac{c}{d} = \frac{e}{f}$ means _____ × _____ = _____ as long as $\frac{c}{d} \neq 0$.

Lesson Exercise 6.36 suggests the following definition of rational-number division.

---

**Definition: Division of Rational Numbers**

If $\frac{a}{b}$ and $\frac{c}{d}$ are rational numbers and $\frac{c}{d} \neq 0$, then $\frac{a}{b} \div \frac{c}{d} = \frac{e}{f}$ if and only if $\frac{a}{b} = \frac{c}{d} \times \frac{e}{f}$.

---

## Lesson Exercise 6.37

Use the definition of division to write $\frac{8}{25} \div \frac{2}{5} = N$ as a multiplication equation and then find the answer by inspection.

The results from Example 6.4 and Lesson Exercises 6.35 and 6.37 suggest the shortcut procedure for dividing fractions.

## Lesson Exercise 6.38

Refer back to Example 6.4 and Lesson Exercises 6.35 and 6.37 to obtain the answers in the first column. Multiply to find the answers in the second column.

(a) $\frac{4}{1} \div \frac{1}{2} = $ _____　　$\frac{4}{1} \times \frac{2}{1} = $ _____

(b) $\frac{3}{1} \div \frac{1}{4} = $ _____　　$\frac{3}{1} \times \frac{4}{1} = $ _____

(c) $\frac{8}{25} \div \frac{2}{5} = $ _____　　$\frac{8}{25} \times \frac{5}{2} = $ _____

(d) Parts (a)–(c) suggest that for rational numbers $\frac{a}{b}$ and $\frac{c}{d}$ with $\frac{c}{d} \neq 0$,

$\frac{a}{b} \div \frac{c}{d} = $ _____.

Lesson Exercise 6.38 suggests the general invert-and-multiply rule.

---

**Division of Rational Numbers**

$$\frac{a}{b} \div \frac{c}{d} = \frac{a}{b} \times \frac{d}{c} = \frac{ad}{bc} \qquad (c \neq 0)$$

---

## Lesson Exercise 6.39

Compute $\frac{5}{6} \div \frac{3}{4}$ using the invert-and-multiply rule. Put the answer in simplest form.

The invert-and-multiply rule is a shortcut for division that uses the reciprocal of a rational number. The **reciprocal** of a rational number $\frac{a}{b}$, in which $a \neq 0$, is $\frac{b}{a}$.

## Lesson Exercise 6.40

Any nonzero rational number multiplied by its reciprocal equals _____.

You are familiar with the invert-and-multiply rule for dividing rational numbers and have seen how it can be developed from examples. One can show how the invert-and-multiply rule works in any rational number division problem. For example, consider $\frac{2}{5} \div \frac{7}{9}$.

$$\frac{2}{5} \div \frac{7}{9} \;=\; \frac{\frac{2}{5}}{\frac{7}{9}} \;=\; \frac{\frac{2}{5} \times \frac{9}{7}}{\boxed{\frac{7}{9} \times \frac{9}{7}}} \;=\; \frac{\frac{2}{5} \times \frac{9}{7}}{1} \;=\; \frac{2}{5} \times \frac{9}{7}$$

Division re-written as a fraction

↑
Omitted when shortcut is used

Fundamental Law of Fractions

So, $\frac{2}{5} \div \frac{7}{9} = \frac{2}{5} \times \frac{9}{7}$. It's the invert-and-multiply rule! The invert-and-multiply rule is simply a shortcut for the longer procedure just shown.

## D  Lesson Exercise 6.41

Use the division model of fractions and the Fundamental Law to show that $\frac{3}{5} \div \frac{2}{7}$ is the same as $\frac{3}{5} \times \frac{7}{2}$.

The categories of whole-number operations also apply to some situations involving multiplication and division of rational numbers. In Lesson Exercises 6.42 and 6.43, tell what operation and classification are illustrated.

## Lesson Exercise 6.42

A computer printer produces a page in $\frac{1}{2}$ minute. How many pages would it print in 30 minutes?

## Lesson Exercise 6.43

Last year, 20 people signed up for a course called "Mathematics is Awesome." The word got around, and this year $3\frac{1}{2}$ times as many people signed up. How many people signed up this year?

## An Investigation: Multiplying Elementary Fractions

### Lesson Exercise 6.44

Consider the following problem: "In multiplying an elementary fraction $\frac{a}{b}$ by an elementary fraction $\frac{c}{d}$ , tell what conditions would make the product (1) greater than $\frac{a}{b}$ , (2) equal to $\frac{a}{b}$ , and (3) less than $\frac{a}{b}$."

(a) Devise a plan and solve the problem.

(b) Use the results of this problem to analyze $\frac{a}{b} \div \frac{c}{d}$ (with $c \neq 0$) in a similar way.

Instead of computing the answers, apply your generalizations from the preceding exercise to answer the following.

### Lesson Exercise 6.45

$\frac{3}{16} \times \frac{4}{5}$ is     (a) greater than $\frac{3}{16}$     (b) equal to $\frac{3}{16}$     (c) less than $\frac{3}{16}$

### Lesson Exercise 6.46

$9\frac{1}{2} \div \frac{3}{4}$ is     (a) greater than $9\frac{1}{2}$     (b) equal to $9\frac{1}{2}$     (c) less than $9\frac{1}{2}$

## Answers to Selected Lesson Exercises

6.30  $\frac{4}{5} \times 20 = 16$

6.31  $\frac{1}{2} \times \frac{3}{5}$ is $\frac{1}{2}$ of $\frac{3}{5}$.

Show $\frac{3}{5}$.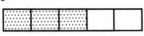

Darken $\frac{1}{2}$ of $\frac{3}{5}$.

$\frac{3}{10}$ of the figure is darkened. So $\frac{1}{2} \times \frac{3}{5} = \frac{3}{10}$.

6.32  (a) $\frac{3}{8}$ , $\frac{3}{10}$     (b) $\frac{ac}{bd}$

6.34  (a) $\frac{4}{9} \times \frac{3}{8} = \frac{\overset{1}{4} \times \overset{1}{3}}{\underset{3}{9} \times \underset{2}{8}} = \frac{1}{6}$

(b) $1\frac{1}{6} \times 2\frac{2}{5} = \frac{7}{6} \times \frac{12}{5} = \frac{7 \times \overset{2}{12}}{\underset{1}{6} \times 5} = \frac{14}{5} = 2\frac{4}{5}$

6.35  $3 \div \frac{1}{4}$ means how many $\frac{1}{4}$'s does it take to make 3? It takes 4 quarters to make 1.

| $\frac{1}{4}$ | $\frac{1}{4}$ | $\frac{1}{4}$ | $\frac{1}{4}$ |   | $\frac{1}{4}$ | $\frac{1}{4}$ | $\frac{1}{4}$ | $\frac{1}{4}$ |   | $\frac{1}{4}$ | $\frac{1}{4}$ | $\frac{1}{4}$ | $\frac{1}{4}$ |

So, it takes 12 quarters to make 3.

So $3 \div \frac{1}{4} = 12$.

(*Note:* The diagram can also be drawn on a number line as it was in Example 6.4.)

**6.36** $\dfrac{c}{d} \times \dfrac{e}{f} = \dfrac{a}{b}$

**6.37** $\dfrac{4}{5}$

**6.38** (a) 8, 8   (b) 12, 12   (c) $\dfrac{4}{5}, \dfrac{4}{5}$   (d) $\dfrac{ad}{bc}$

**6.39** $1\dfrac{1}{9}$

**6.40** 1

**6.41** $\dfrac{3}{5} \div \dfrac{2}{7} = \dfrac{\frac{3}{5}}{\frac{2}{7}} = \dfrac{\frac{3}{5} \times \frac{7}{2}}{\frac{2}{7} \times \frac{7}{2}} = \dfrac{\frac{3}{5} \times \frac{7}{2}}{1} = \dfrac{3}{5} \times \dfrac{7}{2}$

*Note:* The second step in Exercise 6.41 can also be justified as multiplication by 1 in the following form:

$$\dfrac{\frac{7}{2}}{\frac{7}{2}}$$

**6.42** division, repeated measures

**6.43** multiplication, repeated sets

**6.45** (c)

**6.46** (a)

## 6.3   Homework Exercises

### Basic Exercises

1. You want to budget $\dfrac{3}{4}$ of your $1500 monthly paycheck for expenses. Write a fraction arithmetic equation that gives the amount you want to budget.

2. Using repeated addition, $3 \times \dfrac{2}{7}$ is the same as $\dfrac{2}{7} + \dfrac{2}{7} + \dfrac{2}{7} = \dfrac{6}{7}$. Similarly, $4 \times \dfrac{3}{7}$ is the same as _____ .

3. Write $3\dfrac{1}{2} + 3\dfrac{1}{2} + 3\dfrac{1}{2}$ as a multiplication problem.

4. *Explain* how to compute $\dfrac{1}{4} \times \dfrac{2}{3}$ using a diagram.

5. *Explain* how to compute $\dfrac{1}{5} \times \dfrac{1}{3}$ using a diagram.

6. *Explain* how to compute $\dfrac{2}{3} \times \dfrac{5}{6}$ using a diagram.

7. *Explain* how to compute $\dfrac{3}{4} \times \dfrac{4}{5}$ using a diagram.

8. What fraction product is illustrated by the grid?

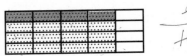

9. Multiply as shown in the lesson. Do not use the shortcut.
   (a) $\dfrac{5}{9} \times \dfrac{7}{10}$   (b) $2\dfrac{1}{3} \times 1\dfrac{1}{5}$

10. Multiply as shown in the lesson.
    (a) $4\dfrac{1}{2} \times 2\dfrac{2}{3}$   (b) $\dfrac{3}{5} \times \dfrac{-2}{9}$

11. *Explain* how to compute $2 \div \dfrac{1}{4}$ using a measurement picture.

12. *Explain* how to compute $3 \div \dfrac{1}{2}$ using a measurement picture.

13. Make up a money problem that is modeled by $5 \div \dfrac{1}{10}$.

14. Use the definition of division to rewrite $\dfrac{10}{21} \div \dfrac{2}{3} = \dfrac{n}{m}$ as a multiplication equation and find the answer by inspection.

15. $A \times B = 1$. $A$ is 9 times $B$. What are $A$ and $B$? (Guess and check.)

16. Use the division model of fractions and the Fundamental Law to show that $\frac{3}{5} \div \frac{1}{4}$ is the same as $\frac{3}{5} \times \frac{4}{1}$.

17. Use the division model of fractions and the Fundamental Law to show that $\frac{1}{2} \div \frac{3}{4}$ is the same as $\frac{1}{2} \times \frac{4}{3}$.

18. Use the division model of fractions and the Fundamental Law to show that $\frac{9}{10} \div \frac{2}{3}$ is the same as $\frac{9}{10} \times \frac{3}{2}$.

19. Compute the following for nonzero integers $x$ and $y$.
    (a) $\frac{x}{5} \div \frac{x}{7}$    (b) $\frac{x^2}{y} \div \frac{x}{3}$

20. (a) $1 + \frac{1}{5} =$ \_\_\_\_\_

    (b) $1 + \dfrac{1}{1 + \frac{1}{5}} =$ \_\_\_\_\_

    (c) $1 + \dfrac{1}{1 + \dfrac{1}{1 + \frac{1}{5}}} =$ \_\_\_\_\_

    (d) What pattern do you see in the results to parts (a)–(c)?
    (e) Without computing, guess the answer to the following.
    $$1 + \cfrac{1}{1 + \cfrac{1}{1 + \cfrac{1}{1 + \frac{1}{5}}}}$$

21. If $A \times \frac{2}{3} = B$, then what number multiplied by $B$ equals $A$?

22. Suppose $\frac{9}{10}$ of all elementary teachers are women and $\frac{1}{10}$ of these women like mathe-matics better than any other subject. What fraction of elementary teachers are women whose favorite subject is math?

23. A recipe for 4 people calls for $\frac{1}{3}$ cup of corn oil. If you make the same dish for 2 people, how much corn oil should you use?

24. To override a presidential veto, at least $\frac{2}{3}$ of the Senate must vote to override. How many votes are needed to ensure passage?

25. A recipe calls for $\frac{1}{4}$ cup of flour per person.
    (a) If you are cooking for 6 people, how much flour should you use?
    (b) What operation and category are illustrated in part (a)?

26. Last year, a farm produced 1360 oranges. This year, they produced $2\frac{1}{2}$ times as many oranges.
    (a) How many oranges did they produce?
    (b) What operation and category are illustrated in part (a)?

27. A wall is $82\frac{1}{2}$ inches high. It is covered with $5\frac{1}{2}$-inch square tiles.
    (a) How many tiles go from the floor to the ceiling?
    (b) What operation and category are illustrated in part (a)?

28. Norma and Irving want to split a delicious $10\frac{1}{2}$-inch submarine sandwich equally. What division category is illustrated?

29. An adult pays $231 for plane tickets for himself and a child. If the child goes for half-price, how much is the adult fare?

30. A baker takes $\frac{1}{2}$ hour to decorate a cake.
    (a) How many cakes can she decorate in $H$ hours?
    (b) What operation and category are illustrated in part (a)?

**31.** Carol Ramos spent $\frac{1}{2}$ her money at the movies. Then she spent $\frac{1}{3}$ of what was left at the store. Now she has $4 left. How much did she start with?

**32.** Sid spent $6 at the movies. Then he spent $\frac{1}{3}$ of what remained for a magazine. Now he has $D$ dollars. What did he start out with?

**33.** Make up a realistic application problem for $\frac{3}{4} \times 22$.

**34.** Make up a realistic application problem for $20 \div \frac{3}{4}$.

*Extension Exercises*

**35.** Crazy King Loopy has just died. Loopy's will instructs his attorney, Ward E. Claus, to divide up his prize collection of 17 hogs as follows: $\frac{4}{9}$ of the hogs go to his eldest daughter Wacky, $\frac{1}{3}$ go to his son Harpo, and $\frac{1}{6}$ go to young Loopy II. Ward has no idea how he is going to carry out the will.

Fortunately, the court sage, Wiggy, tells Ward to borrow another hog, and then he will be able to carry out the will. Ward tries it, and it works! Ward returns the extra hog when he is done.
(a) How many hogs does each child receive?
(b) Why does Wiggy's approach seem to work?
(c) In the end, were the conditions of the will fulfilled, or did everyone receive more hog than they were supposed to?

**36.** Suppose that each time a rubber ball is dropped, it rebounds to half the height from which it fell. The ball is dropped from a height of 20 feet.
(a) How high does it bounce on the first bounce?
(b) How high does it bounce on the second bounce?

(c) How high does it bounce on the $N$th bounce?

**37.** Consider the situation described in the preceding exercise. How far has the ball traveled when it hits the ground for the
(a) first time?
(b) second time?
(c) third time?
(d) fourth time?
(e) Estimate the total distance the ball will travel before it stops bouncing.

**38.** Suppose a pollution control bill is supported by $\frac{3}{5}$ of all voters who are Democrats, $\frac{2}{5}$ of all Republicans, and $\frac{1}{2}$ of all Independents. If $\frac{2}{5}$ of the population is Democratic, $\frac{3}{10}$ is Republican, and $\frac{3}{10}$ is Independent, what fraction of all voters support the bill?

**39.** Consider the following problem: "A particular ball bounces to $\frac{1}{4}$ of the height it reached on the preceding bounce. After being dropped and bouncing up and down, it hits the ground for the third time, having traveled $37\frac{1}{2}$ feet. What was its original height?" Devise a plan and solve the problem.

**40.** Consider the following problem: "Ross had a bag of oranges. He gave $\frac{1}{4}$ of them to his mother. Then he gave $\frac{1}{3}$ of what was left to his friend Rita. Next, he gave $\frac{1}{2}$ of what was left to his mathematics professor. Ross has 3 oranges left. How many did he start with?" Devise a plan and solve the problem.

**41.** Consider the following problem. "A survey shows that $\frac{2}{3}$ of a group prefer Johnson and $\frac{1}{3}$ prefer Perkins. You must persuade 5 or more people to switch to Perkins in order for Perkins to gain a majority. How many people are in the group?" Devise a plan and solve the problem.

**42.** A student finishes $\frac{2}{5}$ of a paper in one evening. About how many evenings will it take to do the whole paper working at the same rate?

**43.** An item is on sale for $\frac{1}{10}$ off the regular price. The regular price is what fraction more than the sale price?

**44.** Five painters are painting a house. They all work at about the same rate, and they need 7 days to finish the job. However, at the end of 3 days, 2 painters quit. How long will it take the remaining 3 painters working at their normal rate to finish the job?

**45.** Find the smallest positive rational number that is divisible (a whole number of times) by $\frac{3}{4}$ and $\frac{2}{5}$.

**46.** Units of measurement can be treated like fractions. For example, if a man travels 10 miles per hour for 6 hours, how far does he travel?

$$10 \, \frac{\text{miles}}{\text{hour}} \times 6 \text{ hours} = 10 \times 6 \, \frac{\text{miles}}{\text{hour}} \times \text{hours}$$
$$= 60 \text{ miles}$$

Carry the units along throughout each of the following exercises.

(a) Swiss cheese costs 4 dollars per pound. How much would $3\frac{1}{2}$ pounds cost?

(b) An ad claims that a car travels 495 miles on a full tank of gas. If the car gets 30 miles to the gallon, how many gallons does the gas tank hold?

**47.** Consider the following diagram.

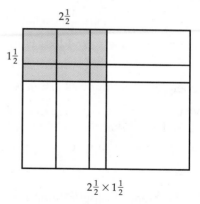

(a) Find $2\frac{1}{2} \times 1\frac{1}{2}$ from the diagram.

(b) Make a similar diagram for $3\frac{1}{2} \times 2\frac{1}{2}$ and give the answer.

(c) Repeat part (b) for $4\frac{1}{2} \times 3\frac{1}{2}$.

(d) Find a shortcut for computing $a\frac{1}{2} \times b\frac{1}{2}$, in which $a = b + 1$ for counting numbers $a$ and $b$.

(e) Use your shortcut to compute $18\frac{1}{2} \times 19\frac{1}{2}$.

**48.** Consider the following diagrams.

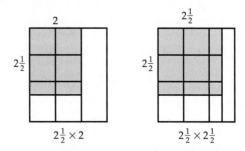

(a) Find $2\frac{1}{2} \times 2\frac{1}{2}$ from the diagram.

(b) Make a similar diagram for $3\frac{1}{2} \times 3\frac{1}{2}$ and give the result.

(c) Repeat part (b) for $4\frac{1}{2} \times 4\frac{1}{2}$.

(d) Find a shortcut for computing $a\frac{1}{2} \times a\frac{1}{2}$, for a counting number $a$.

(e) Use your shortcut to compute $29\frac{1}{2} \times 29\frac{1}{2}$.

49. If $x$ and $y$ are nonzero rational numbers, with $x > y$, under what conditions is each of the following true?

(a) $\frac{1}{x} > \frac{1}{y}$   (b) $\frac{1}{x} = \frac{1}{y}$   (c) $\frac{1}{x} < \frac{1}{y}$

50. (a) If $m$ and $n$ are counting numbers and $m > n$, then which is larger, $\left(\frac{1}{2}\right)^{n}$ or $\left(\frac{1}{2}\right)^{m}$?

(b) If $m$ and $n$ are counting numbers and $m > n$, for what positive rational numbers $a$ is $a^m < a^n$?

51. (a) Write half of $2^3$ as a power of 2.
(b) Write half of $2^4$ as a power of 2.
(c) Write half of $2^N$ as a power of 2.
(d) Make up an analogous problem involving $3^N$.

52. Sometimes, the difference of two fractions equals their product. For example,
$\frac{3}{7} - \frac{3}{10} = \frac{3}{7} \times \frac{3}{10}$ and $\frac{2}{3} - \frac{2}{5} = \frac{2}{3} \times \frac{2}{5}$.
(a) What is the relationship between the two fractions in each example?
(b) Make up two more examples that work.
(c) Show algebraically that the product and difference of two fractions of this type will always be equal. (*Hint:* It takes only two variables to write all the numerators and denominators.)

53. Until the seventeenth century, many people divided fractions *after* finding a common denominator.

(a) Show that this method works for $\frac{1}{3} \div \frac{3}{4}$.
(b) Do you think this method is easier than the standard rule?

54. Assume that $b$, $c$, and $d \neq 0$. The statement $\frac{a}{b} \div \frac{c}{d} = \frac{a \div c}{b \div d}$ is
(a) always true
(b) sometimes true
(c) never true

55. A typist completes $P$ pages per day. How many days would it take to type a paper that is $L$ pages long?

56. Within each part, the question mark represents the same counting number. Find the missing numbers. All fractions are in simplest form. (Guess and check.)

(a) $2\frac{?}{3} \times 4\frac{?}{5} = 11\frac{11}{15}$   (b) $\frac{??}{10} \div 3 = \frac{30}{??}$

*Special Exercises*

57. How thick is a page in this book?

58. Fill in the chart.

| Days | 1 | $\frac{1}{2}$ | $\frac{1}{4}$ | $\frac{3}{4}$ | $\frac{1}{8}$ | $\frac{3}{8}$ | $\frac{5}{8}$ | $\frac{7}{8}$ |
|---|---|---|---|---|---|---|---|---|
| Hours | 24 | | | | | | | |

(b) Compute the following arithmetic problems using hours and then using days. Check one answer against the other one.

| Days | $\frac{1}{4} + \frac{1}{8} = $ ___ | $\frac{7}{8} - \frac{1}{2} = $ ___ |
|---|---|---|
| Hours | $6 + $ ___ $ = $ ___ | ___ $-$ ___ $ = $ ___ |

## 6.4   Properties of Rational Numbers

The properties of whole-number and integer operations discussed in Chapters 3 and 5 hold for rational-number operations. However, the rational-number system possesses some additional properties.

### Integer Properties Retained!

Do rational-number operations retain the same commutative, associative, identity, inverse, closure, and distributive properties as integer operations? Yes! The following list summarizes these properties.

---

**Properties of Rational-Number Operations**

1. Addition, subtraction, and multiplication of rational numbers are closed.

2. Addition and multiplication of rational numbers are commutative.

3. Addition and multiplication of rational numbers are associative.

4. The unique additive identity for rationals is 0 and the unique multiplicative identity for rationals is 1.

5. All rational numbers have a unique additive inverse that is rational. For any rational number $\frac{a}{b}$ , there is a unique rational number $-\frac{a}{b}$ such that $\frac{a}{b} + -\frac{a}{b} = -\frac{a}{b} + \frac{a}{b} = 0$.

6. Multiplication is distributive over addition, and multiplication is distributive over subtraction in the rational number system.

---

The following exercises make use of these properties.

### Lesson Exercise 6.47

(a) What is an easy way to multiply $(9 \times 28) \times \frac{1}{4}$ ?

(b) What property or properties are illustrated?

### Lesson Exercise 6.48

What is the additive inverse of $\frac{3}{4}$ ?

The properties also justify some procedures used in algebra.

## Lesson Exercise 6.49

If $x$ is rational, what property guarantees that

$$\left(x + \frac{1}{2}\right) + 2 = x + \left(\frac{1}{2} + 2\right)?$$

## Lesson Exercise 6.50

According to the distributive property of multiplication over subtraction for rational numbers $n$, $\frac{7}{2}n - \frac{5}{2}n =$ _____ .

What about rational-number subtraction and division? Are they commutative or associative?

## Lesson Exercise 6.51

After studying whole numbers and integers, explain how you know that rational-number subtraction and division are neither commutative nor associative.

## Multiplicative Inverses

Add any rational number to its additive inverse, and the result is the additive identity (0). The same idea applies to a multiplicative inverse.

## Lesson Exercise 6.52

Any rational number multiplied by its multiplicative inverse should result in what number?

Do all rational numbers have multiplicative inverses that are rational numbers?

## Lesson Exercise 6.53

What is the multiplicative inverse of each of the following?

(a)  $-4$    (b) $\frac{2}{3}$

Lesson Exercise 6.54

(a) Do you think all rational numbers have multiplicative inverses that are rational numbers? Try some examples.
(b) Only one rational number does not have a multiplicative inverse. What is it?

Lesson Exercises 6.53 and 6.54 should convince you that all nonzero rational numbers have a unique rational multiplicative inverse.

---

**Multiplicative Inverses for Nonzero Rational Numbers**

All rational numbers except 0 have a unique multiplicative inverse that is rational. That is, for each nonzero rational number $\frac{a}{b}$ there is a unique rational number $\frac{b}{a}$ such that $\frac{a}{b} \times \frac{b}{a} = \frac{b}{a} \times \frac{a}{b} = 1$.

---

## Denseness

Another property that some sets of numbers have and others do not is denseness.

---

**Definition: Dense**

A set of numbers is **dense** if, between any two numbers in the set, there is another number in the set.

---

Are the whole numbers dense? Try the following exercise.

## Lesson Exercise 6.55

If you pick any two whole numbers, is there always a whole number between them?

As you saw in Lesson Exercise 6.55, whole numbers are not dense.

## **D** Lesson Exercise 6.56

Find a counterexample that shows that the set of integers is not dense.

If whole numbers and integers are not dense, why did I even bring the topic up? Because, perhaps, rational numbers are dense! Do you think that between any two rational numbers, there is another rational number? Example 6.5 shows two ways of finding a rational number between two given rational numbers.

## Example 6.5

Find a rational number between $\frac{1}{5}$ and $\frac{1}{6}$.

**Solution**

***The Decimal-Conversion Method*** Although decimals haven't been discussed yet in this book, you already know how to convert fractions to decimals using the division model.

Change both fractions to decimals using a calculator. Then find a decimal between them and change it into a fraction.

On my calculator, $\frac{1}{5} = \boxed{0.2}$ and $\frac{1}{6} = \boxed{0.1666667}$. The decimal 0.19 is between $\frac{1}{5}$ and $\frac{1}{6}$. The decimal $0.19 = \frac{19}{100}$. So $\frac{19}{100}$ is a rational fraction between $\frac{1}{5}$ and $\frac{1}{6}$.

***The Common-Denominator Method*** Write both fractions with a common denominator. $\frac{1}{5} = \frac{6}{30}$ and $\frac{1}{6} = \frac{5}{30}$. There is no whole number between the numerators 5 and 6, so use a larger common denominator:

$\frac{1}{5} = \frac{6}{30} = \frac{12}{60}$ and $\frac{1}{6} = \frac{5}{30} = \frac{10}{60}$. Now it is clear that $\frac{11}{60}$ is between $\frac{10}{60}$ and $\frac{12}{60}$, so it is between $\frac{1}{5}$ and $\frac{1}{6}$. ■

 Lesson Exercise 6.57

Find a rational number between $\frac{50}{51}$ and $\frac{51}{52}$.

Example 6.5 and Lesson Exercise 6.57 offer evidence that the rational numbers are dense.

---

**The Denseness Property of Rational Numbers**

Between any two rational numbers, there is another rational number.

---

There are an infinite number of rational numbers *between* any two rational numbers. It's amazing, isn't it? If you pick any two rational numbers, you can keep finding numbers between them . . . forever. For example, take the numbers used in Example 6.5.

According to Example 6.5,

$\frac{19}{100}$ is between $\frac{1}{6}$ and $\frac{1}{5}$.

And $\frac{18}{100}$ is between $\frac{1}{6}$ and $\frac{19}{100}$.

And $\frac{17}{100}$ is between $\frac{1}{6}$ and $\frac{18}{100}$.

And so on.

## Answers to Selected Lesson Exercises

**6.47** (a) $28 \times \frac{1}{4} \times 9$

    (b) associative, or commutative and associative for multiplication

**6.48** $\frac{-3}{4}$

**6.49** associative property of addition

**6.50** $\left(\dfrac{7}{2} - \dfrac{5}{2}\right)n$

**6.51** The counterexamples for whole-number and integer subtraction and division would also be counterexamples for rational numbers. If a rule does not apply to *all* whole numbers, then it cannot apply to *all* rational numbers, since every whole number is also a rational number.

**6.52** 1

**6.53** (a) $-\dfrac{1}{4}$   (b) $1\dfrac{1}{2}$

**6.54** (b) 0

**6.55** no

**6.56** There is no integer between 1 and 2.

**6.57** Decimals such as 0.9804 and 0.9805 are between $\dfrac{50}{51}$ and $\dfrac{51}{52}$.

## 6.4   Homework Exercises

*Basic Exercises*

1. (a) What rational-number operations are commutative?
   (b) What rational-number operations are associative?

2. For any rational number $x$, what property guarantees that
$$\dfrac{5}{2}x + (2x + 7) = \left(\dfrac{5}{2}x + 2x\right) + 7?$$

3. According to the associative property of multiplication for a rational number $x$,
$$\dfrac{1}{2} \cdot (4 \cdot x) = \underline{\hspace{2cm}} .$$

4. What is an easy way to multiply $\dfrac{1}{7} \times 33 \times 14$?

5. What is an easy way to multiply
$$\dfrac{1}{3} \times \left(\dfrac{1}{5} \times 18\right) \times 20?$$

6. $\dfrac{2}{3} + 0 = 0 + \dfrac{2}{3} = \dfrac{2}{3}$

   $-3\dfrac{5}{8} + 0 = 0 + -3\dfrac{5}{8} = -3\dfrac{5}{8}$

   These examples illustrate that \_\_\_\_\_ is the _____ for _____ .

7. What is the additive inverse of $-2\dfrac{1}{2}$ ?

8. One reason that we need rational numbers is to provide answers to whole-number and integer division problems.
   (a) Are the rational numbers closed under division? (That is, if $x$ and $y$ are rational numbers, is $x \div y$ a rational number?)
   (b) Would the set of rational numbers, excluding 0, be closed under division?

9. After studying whole numbers and integers, explain how you would know that rational-number subtraction is not commutative.

10. Give a counterexample that shows that rational-number division is not associative.

11. According to the distributive property of multiplication over addition for a rational number $n$, $-\dfrac{4}{3}n + \dfrac{2}{3}n = \underline{\hspace{2cm}}$

12. Use the distributive property to compute $4\dfrac{1}{2} \times 2\dfrac{3}{4}$ by rewriting it as $\left(4 + \dfrac{1}{2}\right)\left(2 + \dfrac{3}{4}\right)$.

13. What is the multiplicative inverse of $-2\dfrac{1}{2}$ ?

14. Any nonzero number multiplied by its multiplicative inverse equals \_\_\_\_\_ .

15. (a) What property do rational numbers have that whole numbers and integers do not have?
    (b) What property do all nonzero rational numbers have that whole numbers and integers do not have?

16. Find a rational number between $-\dfrac{1}{9}$ and $-\dfrac{1}{10}$.

17. True or false? Every rational number is an integer.

**18.** True or false? Some whole numbers are not rational numbers.

**19.** True or false? The next largest integer after 6 is 7.

**20.**
$$\left(1 + \frac{1}{2}\right)\left(1 + \frac{1}{1}\right) = \underline{\quad}$$

$$\left(1 + \frac{1}{3}\right)\left(1 + \frac{1}{2}\right)\left(1 + \frac{1}{1}\right) = \underline{\quad}$$

$$\left(1 + \frac{1}{4}\right)\left(1 + \frac{1}{3}\right)\left(1 + \frac{1}{2}\right)\left(1 + \frac{1}{1}\right) = \underline{\quad}$$

(a) Fill in the blanks.
(b) What would the next equation be if the pattern continues? Is the equation true?

**21.** True or false? If $a$, $b$, $c$, and $d$ are nonzero integers, and $a < b$ and $c = d$, then $\frac{a}{c} < \frac{b}{d}$.

*Extension Exercises*

**22.**
$$\frac{1}{3} + \frac{1}{2 \cdot 3} = \underline{\quad\quad}$$

$$\frac{1}{4} + \frac{1}{3 \cdot 4} = \underline{\quad\quad}$$

$$\frac{1}{5} + \frac{1}{4 \cdot 5} = \underline{\quad\quad}$$

(a) Fill in the blanks.
(b) If the pattern continues, what would the next equation be? Is the equation true?
(c) Write the general formula suggested by parts (a) and (b).
$$\underline{\quad} + \underline{\quad} = \underline{\quad}$$
(d) Writing a general formula based upon the examples in parts (a) and (b) requires _____ reasoning.
(e) Prove that your formula in part (c) is correct. (*Hint:* Find the common denominator on the left side of the equation and add the two fractions.)

**23.** Many students are not sure why one can find $\frac{1}{4}$ of 40 by computing $40 \div 4$. Show why $\frac{1}{4}$ of 40 is the same as $40 \div 4$ by changing $\frac{1}{4}$ of 40 first to a multiplication problem, and then from there into a division problem.

**24.** Consider the following problem. "You have a piece of construction paper that is 24 in. by 28 in. What is the maximum number of $8\frac{1}{2}$ in. by 11 in. pieces that you can cut out of it?" Devise a plan and solve the problem.

**25.** Draw a Venn diagram that includes the following sets: rational numbers, whole numbers, and integers.

**26.** Consider the sum
$$S = \frac{1}{2} + \frac{1}{2^2} + \frac{1}{2^3} + \frac{1}{2^4} + \cdots + \frac{1}{2^{20}}.$$
(a) Write $2S$ as a sum of fractions.
(b) Subtract the given expression for $S$ from your expression for $2S$ and simplify the result. What do you obtain?
(c) How could you write the sum
$$\frac{1}{2} + \frac{1}{2^2} + \frac{1}{2^3} + \frac{1}{2^4} + \cdots + \frac{1}{2^N}$$
in a simpler way?

**27.** (a) Following steps analogous to those in the last exercise, find a simpler way to write
$$S = \frac{1}{3} + \frac{1}{3^2} + \frac{1}{3^3} + \frac{1}{3^4} + \cdots + \frac{1}{3^{40}}.$$
(b) How could you write the sum
$$\frac{1}{3} + \frac{1}{3^2} + \frac{1}{3^3} + \frac{1}{3^4} + \cdots + \frac{1}{3^N}$$ in a simpler way?

**28.** Show that multiplication of rational numbers $\frac{x}{w}$ and $\frac{y}{z}$ is commutative.

**29.** Show that multiplication of rational numbers $\frac{u}{v}$, $\frac{w}{x}$, and $\frac{y}{z}$ is associative.

**30.** Tell whether each of the following is true or false. If the equation is true, prove it. If it is false, give a counterexample. Assume that $\frac{w}{z}$, $\frac{x}{z}$, and $\frac{y}{z}$ are rational numbers.

(a) $\left(\frac{w}{z} - \frac{x}{z}\right) + \frac{y}{z} = \frac{w}{z} - \left(\frac{x}{z} + \frac{y}{z}\right)$

(b) $\left(\frac{w}{z} + \frac{x}{z}\right) \div \frac{y}{z} = \left(\frac{w}{z} \div \frac{y}{z}\right) + \left(\frac{x}{z} \div \frac{y}{z}\right)$

if $y \neq 0$

## 6.5   Elementary Fractions: Estimation, Mental Computation, and Error Patterns

In the rare instance that you should make an error in arithmetic with elementary fractions, estimation might help you detect your error. For example, if you computed that $3\frac{1}{4} + 2\frac{2}{3} = \frac{11}{20}$ (the error pattern in Lesson Exercise 6.67) or $8\frac{1}{2} \div 2\frac{2}{3} = \frac{16}{51}$ (the error pattern in Lesson Exercise 6.65), estimating would tell you that the answer could not be right.

### The Rounding Strategy

The rounding strategy is often the best for estimating in addition, subtraction, and multiplication problems involving elementary fractions. Round the numbers to create a problem that you can compute mentally. In most cases, fractions are rounded to the nearest integer.

     Use rounding to estimate in the following exercise.

### Lesson Exercise 6.58

A factory assembles about $8\frac{1}{4}$ cars per day. How could you estimate the number of cars the factory will assemble in $3\frac{1}{2}$ days?

### The Compatible-Numbers Strategy

Are you a flexible person? If so, you'll like using the compatible-numbers strategy with elementary fractions. Rounding to the *nearest* whole number is not always the best approach in fraction multiplication or division.

     Rounding may not work in multiplication when at least one factor is close to or less than $\frac{1}{2}$. This factor can be rounded to the closest fraction that has a 1 in the numerator and a counting number in the denominator, such as $\frac{1}{2}$, $\frac{1}{3}$, or $\frac{1}{4}$. Then change the other factor to a compatible number.

### Example 6.6

A new electric eyeglass defogger regularly sells for $820, but Nutty Mike's is offering it for $\frac{2}{5}$ off the regular price. How could you estimate the amount of the discount?

**Solution**

We need to estimate $\frac{2}{5}$ of $820. We cannot round $\frac{2}{5}$ to the nearest whole number, 0. Doing so would make the estimate 0 no matter how large the dollar amount is! Instead, round $\frac{2}{5}$ to $\frac{1}{2}$ or $\frac{1}{3}$ , which will be easier to use than $\frac{2}{5}$ , and round $820 to a compatible number.

$$\frac{2}{5} \times \$820 \approx \frac{1}{2} \times \$800 = \$400$$

So $\frac{2}{5}$ of $820 is about $400. Or

$$\frac{2}{5} \times \$820 \approx \frac{1}{3} \times \$900 = \$300$$

So $\frac{2}{5}$ of $820 is about $300.  ■

## Lesson Exercise 6.59

Nutty Mike's is offering $\frac{3}{5}$ off the price of a $604 electric bookmark. How could you estimate the discount?

---

The following example illustrates the use of the compatible-numbers strategy for division.

### Example 6.7

How could you estimate $83\frac{3}{4} \div 26\frac{1}{4}$?

**Solution**

Use the compatible-numbers strategy. Rounding to the nearest whole numbers ($84 \div 26$) or to the nearest ten ($80 \div 30$) would not be the best choice. Rounding to compatible numbers such as $80 \div 20$, $90 \div 30$, or $75 \div 25$ would be preferable.

$$83\frac{3}{4} \div 26\frac{1}{4} \approx 80 \div 20 = 4 \qquad \text{or} \qquad 83\frac{3}{4} \div 26\frac{1}{4} \approx 90 \div 30 = 3$$

Both 3 and 4 are good estimates.  ■

## Lesson Exercise 6.60

You want to lay panels $17\frac{1}{4}$ in. wide across a wall that is $384\frac{1}{2}$ in. wide. How could you estimate how many panels you will need?

---

## Mentally Multiplying a Mixed Number by a Whole Number

Do you know a way to do the mental computation in the following exercise?

### Lesson Exercise 6.61

Celia bicycles $5\frac{1}{2}$ miles per hour for 8 hours. How could you use a short-cut to compute mentally the distance she travels?

Computations like the one in the preceding exercise can be done mentally using a shortcut. Rather than changing $8 \times 5\frac{1}{2}$ to $\frac{8}{1} \times \frac{11}{2}$, you can multiply $8 \times 5 = 40$ and add $8 \times \frac{1}{2} = 4$. So $8 \times 5\frac{1}{2} = 40 + 4 = 44$. This shortcut works because $8 \times 5\frac{1}{2} = 8 \times \left(5 + \frac{1}{2}\right) = (8 \times 5) + \left(8 \times \frac{1}{2}\right) = 40 + 4 = 44$.

### Lesson Exercise 6.62

What property guarantees that $8 \times \left(5 + \frac{1}{2}\right) = (8 \times 5) + \left(8 \times \frac{1}{2}\right)$?

### D Lesson Exercise 6.63

On a car trip, the Durst family drives 50 miles per hour for $6\frac{1}{2}$ hours. How could you mentally compute the total distance traveled?

## Mentally Dividing a Whole Number by $\frac{1}{N}$

Can you visualize a measurement picture of $7 \div \frac{1}{3}$ that makes it easy to compute the answer without the invert-and-multiply rule? You can picture measures of 1 to compute problems like $7 \div \frac{1}{3}$.

It takes 3 thirds to make 1, so it takes $7 \times 3$ thirds to make 7. Therefore, $7 \div \frac{1}{3} = 21$.

| $\frac{1}{3}$ $\frac{1}{3}$ $\frac{1}{3}$ | | | | | | |

## Lesson Exercise 6.64

A 30-inch rug is being made out of $\frac{1}{2}$-inch strips. How many strips are needed? *Explain* how to compute the answer mentally using measurement pictures.

## Common Error Patterns

Your future students will amaze you with their own ingenious procedures (which often do not work) for fraction arithmetic. Repetition of incorrect procedures results in error patterns in children's work.

In Lesson Exercises 6.65–6.68, (a) complete the last two examples, repeating the error pattern in the completed examples; (b) describe the error pattern; and (c) state how the error might be detected using estimation.

## Lesson Exercise 6.65

$$\frac{1}{3} + \frac{2}{5} = \frac{3}{8} \qquad \frac{2}{5} + \frac{1}{5} = \frac{3}{10} \qquad \frac{2}{3} + \frac{4}{7} = \frac{6}{10}$$

$$\frac{1}{4} + \frac{3}{4} = \underline{\quad} \qquad \frac{1}{2} + \frac{2}{3} = \underline{\quad}$$

## Lesson Exercise 6.66

$$\frac{2}{3} \div \frac{1}{4} = \frac{3}{8} \qquad 8 \div \frac{1}{2} = \frac{1}{16} \qquad 8\frac{1}{2} \div 2\frac{2}{3} = \frac{16}{51}$$

$$\frac{4}{7} \div \frac{2}{3} = \underline{\quad} \qquad \frac{7}{8} \div 2 = \underline{\quad}$$

## Lesson Exercise 6.67

$$\frac{8}{4} = \underline{\ 2\ } \qquad \frac{3}{6} = \underline{\ 2\ } \qquad \frac{3}{9} = \underline{\ 3\ }$$

$$\frac{12}{3} = \underline{\quad} \qquad \frac{1}{4} = \underline{\quad}$$

## Lesson Exercise 6.68

$$3\frac{1}{4} = \frac{3}{12} \qquad 5\frac{1}{4} \qquad 6\frac{1}{6}$$
$$+\ 2\frac{2}{3} = \frac{8}{12} \qquad +\ 2\frac{1}{2} \qquad +\ 4\frac{1}{4}$$
$$\overline{\qquad} \qquad \frac{11}{12}$$

## Answers to Selected Lesson Exercises

**6.58** $8\frac{1}{4} \times 3\frac{1}{2} \approx 8 \times 4 = 32$ cars

**6.59** $\frac{3}{5}$ of $604 \approx \frac{1}{2} \times \$600 = \$300$

**6.60** $384\frac{1}{2} \div 17\frac{1}{4} \approx 400 \div 20 = 20$ panels

**6.62** distributive property of multiplication over addition

**6.63** 325 miles

**6.64** 60 strips. How many halves make 30? Two halves make each whole. So it takes $30 \times 2$ halves $= 60$ to make 30 wholes.

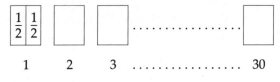

**6.65** (a) $\frac{4}{8}, \frac{3}{5}$

(b) The child is adding the denominators.

(c) The answers are each smaller than one of the addends.

**6.66** (a) $\frac{14}{12}, \frac{16}{7}$

(b) The child is inverting the first fraction and multiplying it by the second.

(c) Each divisor is larger than the dividend, so the quotient could not be more than 1.

**6.67** (a) 4, 4

(b) The child always divides the smaller number into the larger.

(c) Fractions with denominators that are larger than their numerators cannot be greater than 1.

**6.68** (a) $\frac{3}{4}, \frac{5}{12}$

(b) The child is adding only the fractional parts of the mixed numbers.

(c) Rounding to the nearest whole number and adding would show that both sums are much too small.

## 6.5 Homework Exercises

### Basic Exercises

**1.** (a) How could you estimate $\frac{5}{6} + \frac{10}{11}$?

(b) Is your estimate too high or too low?

**2.** The Westwood Dribblers have a trip of $836\frac{1}{10}$ miles to their away basketball game. So far, they have traveled $381\frac{7}{10}$ miles. How could u estimate the distance they have left to travel?

3. A recipe calls for $5\frac{3}{4}$ cups of sugar to make one pound of belly busters. How could you estimate how much sugar is needed to make $8\frac{1}{4}$ pounds of belly busters?

4. $26\frac{7}{3600} \times 32\frac{9}{60}$ is about
   (a) 7000   (b) 100   (c) 60   (d) 900

5. $A, B, C, D, E,$ and $F$ are counting numbers. You estimate $A\frac{B}{C} - D\frac{E}{F}$ by rounding $A\frac{B}{C}$ up and $D\frac{E}{F}$ down. Will your estimate be too high or too low, or is it impossible to tell?

6. A $327 stereo is selling for $\frac{2}{5}$ off during a sale. How could you estimate the sale price?

7. An author takes $14\frac{3}{4}$ hours to write a mathematics lesson. How could you estimate how many lessons she can write in a grueling $62\frac{1}{2}$-hour work week?

8. $286\frac{3}{1900} \div 6\frac{1}{4}$ is about
   (a) 280   (b) 1800   (c) 30   (d) 50

9. Fill in possible missing numbers.
   (a) $\frac{1}{?} \times 33 \approx 4$   (b) $\frac{1}{?} \times 70 \approx 23$

10. Order the following products from smallest to largest using estimation and number sense.
    (a) $\frac{4}{5} \times 17\frac{1}{8}$   (b) $\frac{4}{5} \times 23\frac{2}{5}$
    (c) $\frac{1}{2} \times 16\frac{11}{12}$   (d) $\frac{3}{4} \times 16\frac{11}{12}$

11. The product of A, B, and C is approximately
    (a) $\frac{1}{10}$   (b) $1\frac{1}{4}$   (c) 3   (d) 4   (e) 5

12. What property guarantees that
    $8 \times \left(3 + \frac{1}{4}\right) = (8 \times 3) + \left(8 \times \frac{1}{4}\right)$?

13. Fatco stock sells for $6\frac{1}{2}$ dollars per share. Mentally compute the cost of 50 shares. Show how you did it.

14. A job pays $40 per hour for $3\frac{3}{4}$ hours. Mentally compute the total pay. Show how you did it.

15. A clothing manufacturer needs $\frac{1}{2}$ yd of material to make a T-shirt. How many T-shirts can she make with 50 yd of material?
    (a) *Explain* how to compute the answer mentally.
    (b) What operation and category are illustrated?

16. A baker takes $\frac{1}{4}$ hour to create a flower decoration for a cake.
    (a) How many cakes can he decorate in 32 hours? *Explain* how to compute the answer mentally.
    (b) What operation and category are illustrated?

17. $872\frac{7}{16} \div \frac{3}{8}$ is approximately
    (a) $\frac{1}{1,000,000}$
    (b) 40   (c) 320   (d) 2200

**18.**
$$\frac{\square}{\square} \div \frac{\square}{\square}$$

Place the numbers 2, 3, 7, and 9 in the four boxes to make
(a) the largest possible quotient.
(b) the smallest possible quotient.

**19.** For each computation, tell which computation method (mental computation, paper and pencil, or calculator) you would use and why.

(a) $24 \times \frac{1}{8}$    (b) $\frac{2}{7} + \frac{4}{5}$    (c) $\frac{1}{8} \times 3752$

In Exercises 20–23, (a) complete the last two examples, repeating the error pattern in the completed examples and (b) describe the error pattern.

**20.** $\frac{13}{36} = \frac{1}{6}$    $\frac{16}{64} = \frac{1}{4}$    $\frac{15}{25} = \frac{1}{2}$

$\frac{21}{42} = \underline{\quad}$    $\frac{17}{27} = \underline{\quad}$

**21.**   $4\frac{1}{5} = 3\frac{11}{5}$      $3\frac{1}{3}$      $8\frac{2}{5}$

$\underline{- 2\frac{2}{5} = 2\frac{2}{5}}$    $\underline{- 1\frac{2}{3}}$    $\underline{- 3\frac{3}{5}}$

$1\frac{9}{5} = 2\frac{4}{5}$

**22.**   $14\frac{3}{5}$      $12\frac{4}{5}$      $8\frac{1}{12}$

$\underline{- 8\frac{1}{2}}$    $\underline{- 6\frac{1}{3}}$    $\underline{- 5\frac{1}{2}}$

$6\frac{2}{3}$

**23.** $\frac{1}{2} + \frac{3}{4} = \frac{2+3}{4+4} = \frac{5}{8}$    $\frac{2}{3} + \frac{1}{6} = \underline{\quad}$

$\frac{1}{5} + \frac{9}{10} = \underline{\quad}$

**24.** Why might the error pattern in Exercise 21 occur?

**25.** Why might the error pattern in Exercise 22 occur?

**26.** Describe two errors children might make in computing $\frac{3}{5} \times \frac{1}{6}$.

**27.** Fill in the next two fractions that will continue the same pattern.

(a) $\frac{1}{6}, \frac{1}{12}, \frac{1}{24}, \underline{\quad}, \underline{\quad}$

(b) Write a rule for the $N$th term.

**28.** Fill in the blanks, following the rule in the completed examples.

| (a) | | | (b) | | |
|---|---|---|---|---|---|
| 9 | → | 6 | 4 | → | 14 |
| 12 | → | 8 | 8 | → | 28 |
| 15 | → | ___ | 10 | → | ___ |
| 18 | → | ___ | 5 | → | ___ |
| ___ | → | 20 | ___ | → | 70 |
| $N$ | → | ___ | $N$ | → | ___ |

*Extension Exercises*

**29.** Using mental computation, one can see that $20\frac{1}{2} \times 2\frac{1}{2}$ is
(a) less than 44
(b) between 44 and 50
(c) more than 50

**30.** People mentally multiply whole numbers by 25 by changing a problem such as $25 \times 44$ into $100 \times \frac{44}{4}$ or $100 \times 11$.

(a) Show why $25 \times 44 = 100 \times \frac{44}{4}$.

(b) How could you use this same approach to compute $25 \times 84$?

**31.** One can avoid regrouping in some fraction subtraction problems by using equal addition.

For example, $3\frac{1}{5} - 1\frac{2}{5} = 3\frac{4}{5} - 2 = 1\frac{4}{5}$.

Show how to use this method to compute
(a) $8\frac{1}{3} - 3\frac{2}{3}$.    (b) $5\frac{1}{4} - 2\frac{3}{4}$.

**32.** Consider the following problem. "The Hershey family took a trip. They started out with a full tank of gas. When they were $\frac{2}{3}$ of the way, the gas tank was about $\frac{1}{4}$ full. Can they complete the trip without stopping for gas?"
(a) Select a problem-solving strategy to use.
(b) Solve the problem.

**33.** Does 1 = 4? Does 10 = 15? Find the incorrect step in each of the following.
(a) $1 = \dfrac{2}{1+1} = \dfrac{2}{1} + \dfrac{2}{1} = 4$. So 1 = 4.
(b) $10 = \dfrac{20}{2} = \dfrac{10+10}{2} = \dfrac{10}{2} + 10 = 15$.
    So 10 = 15.

**34.** A common error pattern in adding fractions is to add the numerators and denominators, as in $\dfrac{1}{2} + \dfrac{2}{3} = \dfrac{3}{5}$. In fact, if $A$, $B$, $C$, and $D$ are counting numbers, then
$$\frac{A}{B} + \frac{C}{D} \underset{(< \text{ or } >)}{\phantom{=}} \frac{(A+C)}{(B+D)}.$$

**35.** $\dfrac{1}{2} + \dfrac{1}{3} = \dfrac{5}{6}$   $\dfrac{1}{4} + \dfrac{1}{5} = \dfrac{9}{20}$
(a) What is a shortcut for adding the fractions shown?
(b) Make up two more examples that work the same way.
(c) Write an algebraic equation using two variables that describes the general pattern in each equation.
(d) Writing a general equation based upon examples requires _____ reasoning.
(e) Show algebraically that your equation in part (c) is true.

**36.** Two positive fractions have a sum of 2 and a product of $\dfrac{7}{16}$. What are they? (Guess and check.)

## Summary

"The fraction $\frac{2}{3}$ becomes necessary as the only solution to the problem $2 \div 3$ . . . the need to measure more precisely than to the nearest inch gives rise to numbers like $3\frac{5}{8}$ inches" (NCTM, *Curriculum and Evaluation Standards*, p. 92).

The set of integers is expanded to form the set of rational numbers so that nonzero integer division problems with nonzero divisors will have answers. In elementary school, children study the nonnegative subset of rational numbers that I have called elementary fractions.

Elementary fractions are quite versatile. They can represent a fraction of a whole, a division problem, a location on a number line, or a fraction of a set. You can represent any rational number as a division problem or a location on a number line.

"Area models are especially helpful in visualizing numerical ideas from a geometric point of view. For example, area models can be used to show that $\frac{8}{12}$ is equivalent to $\frac{2}{3}$ " (NCTM, *Curriculum and Evaluation Standards*, p. 88). Algebraically, one can verify the equivalence of fractions by writing them in simplest form, finding a least common denominator, or comparing cross products. One can find which of two unequal fractions is larger by the latter two of these three methods.

Arithmetic rules for rational numbers are consistent with these models. As with whole-number and integer arithmetic, with rational numbers addition and multiplication are defined, and then subtraction is defined as the inverse of addition and division as the inverse of multiplication. Fraction pictures help children understand the results of fraction arithmetic. The common categories of the four whole-number operations fit many word problems involving rational numbers. Estimation enables students to use their facility with whole numbers to develop their intuition about elementary fraction arithmetic.

Rational numbers include all the numbers most children study in elementary school. Whole numbers, elementary fractions, and integers are all rational numbers. Whole numbers, integers, and rational numbers all possess the commutative and associative properties for addition and multiplication and the distributive properties for multiplication over addition and for multiplication over subtraction. The integers and rational numbers also have unique additive inverses, and nonzero rational numbers have unique multiplicative inverses. The rational numbers are also dense.

Children now study estimation and mental computation with fractions in school. They learn how to recognize problems that are easy to compute and how to use the rounding and compatible-numbers strategies to estimate.

## Study Guide

To review Chapter 6, see what you know about each of the following ideas or terms listed that you have studied. You can also use this list to generate your own questions about Chapter 6.

# The NCTM Curriculum Standards and Rational Numbers

### Selected NCTM Curriculum Standards

The following standards come from the NCTM document.

- Understand and appreciate the need for numbers beyond the whole numbers.
- Develop concepts of fractions and mixed numbers.
- Develop and use order relations for fractions.
- Recognize relationships among different topics in mathematics.
- Use models to explore operations on fractions.
- Apply fractions to problem situations.
- Develop, analyze, and explain procedures for computation and techniques for estimation.

1. Describe how each standard listed relates to the material you studied in Chapter 6.
2. Select any current elementary-school mathematics textbook series and describe a sample lesson or exercise that illustrates each standard listed.

# Review Exercises

1. *Explain* how to compute $24 \times 2\frac{1}{2}$ mentally.

2. $A$ is an integer. If $\frac{A}{20} > \frac{20}{35}$, then $A$ _____ .

3. *Explain* four common meanings of $\frac{5}{6}$. (Use some drawings.)

4. Show why $\frac{7}{4} = 1\frac{3}{4}$ using the fraction-of-a-whole model.

5. Name a property that the nonzero rational numbers have that the integers do not have.

6. $-3\frac{1}{2} - \left(-2\frac{1}{4}\right) = ?$
   (a) $3\frac{1}{2} - 2\frac{1}{4}$
   (b) $-\left(3\frac{1}{2} - 2\frac{1}{4}\right)$
   (c) $3\frac{1}{2} + 2\frac{1}{4}$

7. $-5\frac{1}{2} + 26\frac{1}{4} =$ _____

8. *Explain* why $\frac{5}{0}$ is undefined.

9. (a) You have 5 ounces of peanuts. How many $\frac{3}{4}$-ounce servings can you make?
   (b) What operation and category does this problem illustrate?

10. Suppose you give $\frac{1}{10}$ of your earnings to charity and pay $\frac{1}{3}$ of your earnings in taxes.
    (a) What fraction of your earnings is left for other expenses?
    (b) What operations and classifications are illustrated here?

11. Patty bought $1\frac{3}{4}$ pounds of Swiss cheese for 5 lunches during the work week.
    (a) How much cheese will she have for each day?
    (b) What operation and category are illustrated?

12. (a) Use the least-common-denominator method to show how $\frac{4}{9}$ and $\frac{2}{5}$ compare in size.
    (b) Use the compare-products method to show how $\frac{4}{9}$ and $\frac{2}{5}$ compare in size.

13. Use fraction pictures to *explain* why you need a common denominator to add $\frac{2}{3} + \frac{1}{6}$ and show how you compute the answer.

14. $472\frac{1}{4} \div \frac{3}{16}$ is approximately
    (a) 2500   (b) 100   (c) 9   (d) $\frac{1}{10,000}$

15. Use the division model of fractions and the Fundamental Law to show that
    $\frac{2}{5} \div \frac{7}{9} = \frac{2}{5} \times \frac{9}{7}$.

16. (a) What is an easy way to multiply
    $\frac{1}{5} \times 8 \times \left(15 \times \frac{3}{4}\right)$?
    (b) What property or properties did you use?

17. Give an example illustrating the distributive property of multiplication over addition for rational numbers.

18. *Explain* how to compute $\frac{2}{3} \times \frac{3}{5}$ using a diagram.

**19.** (a) Complete the last problem, repeating the error pattern in the completed examples.

$$\frac{1}{4} + \frac{2}{3} = \frac{4}{7} + \frac{6}{7} = \frac{10}{7} = 1\frac{3}{7}$$

---

$$\frac{3}{5} + \frac{1}{9} = \frac{12}{14} + \frac{6}{14} = \frac{18}{14} = 1\frac{4}{14} = 1\frac{2}{7}$$

---

$$\frac{2}{5} + \frac{1}{4} =$$

---

(b) Describe the error pattern.

(c) Explain how the error pattern in the first example could be detected using estimation. (*Hint:* Why should the answer be less than 1?)

## Computer Exercise

**1.** (a) Run the following BASIC program using numbers of your choice.

```
10 PRINT "TYPE IN FRACTIONS A/B
   AND C/D BY TYPING A, B, C, D
   WITH B AND D ≠ 0."
20 INPUT A, B, C, D
30 PRINT A * C "/" B * D
```

(b) What is the purpose of the program?

(c) Revise line 30 so the program prints the result of $\frac{A}{B} \div \frac{C}{D}$.

## Elementary Fractions in Elementary School

The following chart shows at what grade levels selected elementary fraction topics typically appear in elementary-school mathematics textbooks.

| Topic | Typical Grade Level in Current Textbooks |
|---|---|
| Fraction concepts | 1, 2, 3, <u>4</u>, <u>5</u>, <u>6</u> |
| Fraction addition and subtraction | 4, <u>5</u>, 6 |
| Fraction multiplication | 5, <u>6</u> |
| Fraction division | 5, <u>6</u> |

## Suggested Readings

*The Arithmetic Teacher.* February, 1984 Focus Issue on Rational Numbers. Reston, VA: NCTM, 1984.

Ashlock, R. *Error Patterns in Computation.* 3rd ed. Columbus, OH: Merrill, 1982.

National Council of Teachers of Mathematics. 1975 Yearbook. *Mathematics Learning in Early Childhood.* Reston, VA: NCTM, 1975.

National Council of Teachers of Mathematics. 1978 Yearbook. *Developing Computational Skills.* Reston, VA: NCTM, 1978.

National Council of Teachers of Mathematics. 1986 Yearbook. *Estimation and Mental Computation.* Reston, VA: NCTM, 1986.

National Council of Teachers of Mathematics. 1989 Yearbook. *New Directions for Elementary School Mathematics.* Reston, VA: NCTM, 1989.

# 7

# Decimals, Percents, and Real Numbers

All rational numbers can be written as fractions or as decimals. Each notation has its advantages.

The ancient Egyptians developed fraction notation over 3500 years ago for measuring and accounting, but fraction notation is often awkward for comparing the size of two numbers or for doing computations. Decimal notation is one of the great labor-saving inventions of mathematics. Simon Stevin (1548–1620), a Flemish engineer, was the first to discuss decimal notation and decimal arithmetic in some detail.

Decimal notation uses an extension of our whole number place-value system to represent numbers. As a result, decimal arithmetic algorithms use whole-number/integer algorithms with additional rules for shifting and placing decimal points.

Decimals are also significant in mathematics because, as the Pythagoreans discovered over 2000 years ago, rational numbers alone are insufficient for measuring all lengths. The first irrational (that is, "not rational") decimal numbers that the Pythagoreans found were certain square roots.

Although the set of rational numbers is dense, it does not represent every point on the standard number line. The fact that decimal numbers include both rational and irrational numbers makes it possible to label every point on a number line and to measure any length. The union of the set of rational and irrational numbers is called the set of real numbers.

## 7.1 Decimals: Place Value and Arithmetic

**Sally's Car Clinic**
**Parts and Labor $362.25**

**GNP Is $3.4 Billion**

Whether it is a GNP of $3.4 billion, an atom of diameter 0.00000004 cm, or car repairs costing $362.25, people usually report statistics in decimal notation. In most everyday applications, decimal notation is easier to use than fractions, and decimal computations are easier to do than fractional computations. Furthermore, calculators and computers generally give output in decimal form, and the metric system employs decimal notation.

## Place Value

What amount does 3426.517 represent? Decimal place value is an extension of whole-number place value, and it has a symmetry that is shown in the following diagram. The place values match up around the center: tens, hundreds, thousands, . . . and tenths, hundredths, thousandths match up.

| 3 | 4 | 2 | 6 | . | 5 | 1 | 7 |
|---|---|---|---|---|---|---|---|
| t | h | t | o | . | t | h | t |
| h | u | e | n |   | e | u | h |
| o | n | n | e |   | n | n | o |
| u | d | s | s |   | t | d | u |
| s | r |   |   |   | h | r | s |
| a | e |   |   |   | s | e | a |
| n | d |   |   |   |   | d | n |
| d | s |   |   |   |   | t | d |
| s |   |   |   |   |   | h | t |
|   |   |   |   |   |   | s | h |
|   |   |   |   |   |   |   | s |

The decimal point is read "and." The number 3426.517 is read "three thousand, four hundred, twenty-six and five hundred seventeen thousandths."

## Lesson Exercise 7.1

(a) In our numeration system, each place you move to the left multiplies place value by _____.

(b) Each place you move to the right divides place value by _____, which is the same as multiplying by _____.

Like whole numbers, other decimal numbers can be written using expanded notation to show place value.

### Example 7.1

Write 46.28 using expanded notation.

**Solution**

$$46.28 = (4 \times 10) + 6 + \left(2 \times \frac{1}{10}\right) + \left(8 \times \frac{1}{100}\right) \blacksquare$$

## Lesson Exercise 7.2

(a) Write 0.317 in expanded notation.

(b) Does 0.317 equal 3 tenths, 1 hundredth, and 7 thousandths or does it equal 317 thousandths? Answer the question by showing that the sum in part (a) equals $\frac{317}{1000}$.

Pictorial models clarify the relative size of decimal numbers. Elementary-school textbooks use decimal squares to picture 1, $\frac{1}{10}$, and $\frac{1}{100}$. A decimal square represents 1. Divide the square into 10 equal rectangles, as shown in Figure 7-1, and each rectangle represents $\frac{1}{10}$. Divide the square into 100 equal squares, and each small square represents $\frac{1}{100}$.

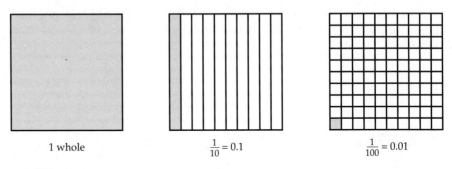

| 1 whole | $\frac{1}{10} = 0.1$ | $\frac{1}{100} = 0.01$ |

**Figure 7-1**

Many other decimal numbers can be represented in a similar fashion. For example, here 0.63 is shown in an excerpt from *Mathematics Unlimited, Grade 6* (Figure 7-2).

## Lesson Exercise 7.3

Use decimal square pictures to *explain* why 0.4 > 0.32.

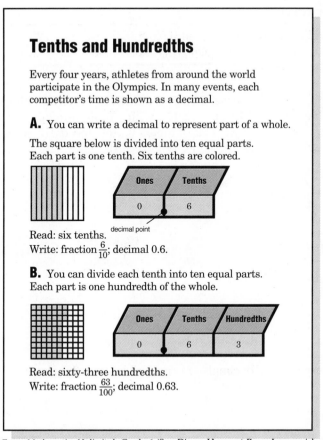

From *Mathematics Unlimited*, Grade 6 (San Diego: Harcourt Brace Jovanovich, 1992), p. 38.

**Figure 7-2**

Another pictorial model that shows the relative size of decimals is a number line. Each decimal represents a location on the number line. For example, 0.64 is between 0.6 and 0.7, as shown in Figure 7-3.

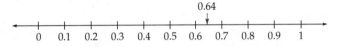

**Figure 7-3**

As with whole numbers and fractions, if a decimal number $u$ is located to the right of a decimal number $v$ on this number line, $u > v$.

## Lesson Exercise 7.4

(a) Why might a child think that 0.52 > 0.8?

(b) Use a number line to *explain* why 0.8 > 0.52.

The preceding exercise contains examples of terminating decimals. **Terminating decimals** can be written with a finite number of digits to the right of the decimal point. The numbers 8., 0.6 and 0.317 are terminating decimals, while 0.3444 . . . is not (Figure 7-4).

**Figure 7-4**

Nonterminating decimals are covered later in the chapter.

## Exponents

Exponents are often used in expressing large and small positive numbers in a briefer format. Decimal place values can be expressed using powers of 10.

What does $10^3$ mean? You are probably most comfortable with positive exponents. Zero and negative integer exponents are defined so that certain properties of positive exponents extend to all integer exponents.

## D Lesson Exercise 7.5

Suppose that a student knows how to compute $10^c$, when $c$ is a counting number.

(a) How could you suggest what $10^0$, $10^{-1}$, and $10^{-2}$ should equal by extending a pattern? (*Hint:* Start with $10^3 = 1000$.)

(b) Describe the pattern.

Lesson Exercise 7.5 suggests an appropriate definition of zero and negative-integer exponents.

---

**Zero and Negative-Integer Exponents**

For all $A > 0$ and integers $N$:

$$A^0 = 1$$

$$A^{-N} = \frac{1}{A^N}$$

---

The powers of 10 relate to decimal place value as follows.

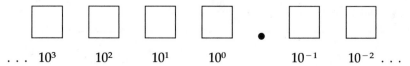

$$\ldots \; 10^3 \qquad 10^2 \qquad 10^1 \qquad 10^0 \qquad\qquad 10^{-1} \qquad 10^{-2} \; \ldots$$

These definitions are also consistent with exponent properties with which you are familiar.

**D** Lesson Exercise 7.6

(a)  $(2^3) \cdot (2^4) = (2 \cdot 2 \cdot 2) \cdot ($_____$) = 2^{\,?}$

(b)  What is the shortcut for multiplying $2^3 \cdot 2^4$?

(c)  Using the same rule (shortcut), $2^3 \cdot 2^0 =$ _____.

(d)  If $2^3 \cdot 2^0 = 2^3$, then $2^0$ must equal _____.

(e)  Using the same rule, $2^3 \cdot 2^{-1} =$ _____.

(f)  Use part (e) to find the value of $2^{-1}$ that makes the rule work.

## Adding and Subtracting Decimals

You buy two packages of cheese weighing 0.36 lb and 0.41 lb, and you want to compute the total weight. Or you find a record for $6.42 at one store and for $6.98 at another store, and you want to know the difference in price. These situations call for addition and subtraction of decimal numbers.

One can model simple decimal addition with decimal squares.

Lesson Exercise 7.7

Show how to compute $0.3 + 0.4$ in a single decimal square by shading in two different colors.

The decimal-square picture in Lesson Exercise 7.7 indicates how $0.3 + 0.4$ is related to $3 + 4$. The total number of shaded columns in the decimal square is $3 + 4 = 7$. Since each column represents 0.1 (1 tenth), the shaded area represents 0.7 (7 tenths).

The rules for adding and subtracting terminating decimals are similar to those for adding and subtracting whole numbers, since decimal place value is a consistent extension of whole-number place value. The rules for addition and subtraction can be determined by rewriting terminating decimals as fractions.

## Lesson Exercise 7.8

Show that $0.36 + 0.40 = \dfrac{(36 + 40)}{100}$.

The equation in Lesson Exercise 7.8 indicates that one can compute the whole-number sum $36 + 40$, and then place the decimal point. This means that $0.36 + 0.40$ can be computed in place-value columns as follows.

$$
\begin{array}{rcr}
36 \text{ hundredths} & & 0.36 \\
+40 \text{ hundredths} & \rightarrow & +0.40 \\
\hline
76 \text{ hundredths} & & 0.76
\end{array}
$$

The decimal point in the sum is lined up with the decimal points in the addends. This is the familiar addition algorithm.

---

**Adding Terminating Decimals Vertically**

Line up the decimal points, add the numbers (ignoring the decimal points), and insert the decimal point in the sum directly below those in the addends.

---

Decimal subtraction is defined in terms of addition. For decimal numbers $a$, $b$, and $c$, $c - b = a$ if and only if $a + b = c$. So a problem such as $0.76 - 0.40 = $ _____ becomes $0.40 + $ _____ $= 0.76$.

Using the definition, we know that if

$$
\begin{array}{cc}
+0.36 \text{ then} & 0.76 \\
+0.40 & -0.40 \\
\hline
0.76 & 0.36
\end{array}
$$

This relationship indicates why subtraction problems can also be done in columns after lining up corresponding places.

---

**Subtracting Terminating Decimals Vertically**

Line up the decimal points, subtract the numbers (ignoring the decimal points), and insert the decimal point in the difference directly below those in the other two numbers.

---

Simple decimal subtraction can be modeled with decimal squares.

## Lesson Exercise 7.9

The decimal-square picture shows 0.3.

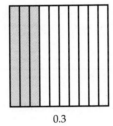

0.3

Draw a second decimal square that shows the result of 0.3 − 0.1 using a take-away approach.

---

The classifications of whole-number operations also apply to many decimal word problems. Consider one of the problems from the beginning of this section.

## Lesson Exercise 7.10

What subtraction category is illustrated in the following problem? "A record costs $6.42 at one store and $6.98 at another. What is the difference in price?"

## Multiplying Decimals

What is the cost of 0.6 lb of cole slaw that sells for $.89 per pound? About how much would 5 bananas weigh if one banana weighs 0.3 lb? These applications call for multiplication of decimals.

Simple decimal multiplication can be modeled with decimal squares.

Lesson Exercise 7.11

Explain how to compute $0.6 \times 0.4$ using decimal-square pictures.
First, dot 0.4 of a decimal square. Then in a new picture, darken 0.6
("6 tenths") of each column of the 0.4.

The explanation in Lesson Exercise 7.11 employs the same approach
you studied with multiplication of fractions in Section 6.3. Like addition
and subtraction, decimal multiplication is related to whole-number and
fraction multiplication.

**D** Lesson Exercise 7.12

In multiplying the decimals 0.6 and 0.89, we multiply 6 by 89 and
then place the decimal point. Rewrite 0.6 and 0.89 as fractions and use
rational-number multiplication and its properties to show that
$$(0.6)(0.89) = (6)(89)\left(\frac{1}{1000}\right).$$

The preceding exercise relies on rational-number multiplication and its
properties.

$$(0.6)(0.89) = \left(\frac{6}{10}\right)\left(\frac{89}{100}\right) = \frac{6 \cdot 89}{1000} = (6 \cdot 89) \cdot \frac{1}{1000}$$

|  | multiply whole numbers | indicates number of decimal places in the product |
|--|--|--|

This shows that $(0.6)(0.89)$ can be computed as $6 \cdot 89 = 534$ and then
$534 \cdot \frac{1}{1000} = 0.534$. The number of decimal places in the product (three
places: thousandths) comes from multiplying tenths (one place) times
hundredths (two places). The decimal places in the factors can be counted
and these numbers added to place the decimal point in the product. This
relationship is an example of the following rule.

---

**Multiplying Terminating Decimal Numbers**

Multiply the two numbers, ignoring the decimal points. The
number of decimal places in the product is the sum of the number
of decimal places in the two factors.

---

The categories for whole-number multiplication also apply to some decimal applications.

## Lesson Exercise 7.13

What operation and category are illustrated in the following problem? "About how much would 5 bananas weigh if one banana weighs 0.3 lb?"

---

## Dividing Decimals

Suppose 4 laps around a track is a distance of 0.8 miles and you want to know how long each lap is. Children begin decimal division by studying examples like this one that have whole-number divisors and terminating decimals as dividends and quotients.

Decimal squares can be used to compute $0.8 \div 4$.

## Lesson Exercise 7.14

In computing $0.8 \div 4$ with a decimal square, first show 8 tenths.

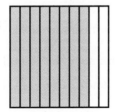

Then, how could you use this picture to compute $0.8 \div 4$ by partitioning?

---

In the preceding exercise, each of the 8 columns represents 1 tenth, so the 2-column result represents 2 tenths. This example illustrates how $0.8 \div 4$ is computed by dividing 8 by 4 and then placing the decimal point in the quotient above the decimal point in the dividend.

$$\frac{2 \text{ tenths}}{4 \overline{)8 \text{ tenths}}} \rightarrow \frac{0.2}{4 \overline{)0.8}}$$

This suggests the following procedure.

> **Dividing a Decimal Number by a Whole Number**
>
> Divide, ignoring the decimal point, and place the decimal point in the quotient directly over the decimal point in the dividend.

Now that you have studied problems involving whole-number divisors, what about problems with decimal divisors? These problems are converted to problems with *whole-number* divisors by moving the decimal points in the divisor and the dividend the same number of places to the right. But why does this method work?

$$0.4\,\overline{)\,0.08}\qquad\text{becomes}\qquad 4\,\overline{)\,0.8}$$

(unfamiliar, new)                    (Hey, we just
                                      studied these!)

What allows us to move the decimal point in the dividend and the divisor the same number of places? It had better not affect the answer to the division problem. If it does, we can't go around teaching children to do it!

## Lesson Exercise 7.15

Consider $8 \div 4$.

(a) Multiply both original numbers by 1000. Is the quotient still the same?

(b) Multiply both original numbers by 3. Is the quotient still the same?

(c) Multiply both original numbers by $\frac{1}{2}$. Is the quotient still the same?

(d) Multiply both original numbers by $\frac{1}{10}$. Is the quotient still the same?

(e) Multiply two decimal numbers $A$ and $B$ ($B \neq 0$) by any decimal number $C$ ($C \neq 0$). Why does $A \cdot C \div B \cdot C = A \div B$? (*Hint:* Consider fractions.)

Lesson Exercise 7.15 verifies the following conclusion.

> **Equivalent Division**
>
> If $A$, $B$, and $C$ are decimal numbers, with $B \neq 0$ and $C \neq 0$, then
> $$A \div B = A \cdot C \div B \cdot C.$$

This means that we can multiply both numbers in a division problem by the same nonzero number without affecting the quotient. The Equivalent-Division property is merely a different form of the Fundamental Law of Fractions! The expression $A \div B = A \cdot C \div B \cdot C$ is the same as $\dfrac{A}{B} = \dfrac{A \cdot C}{B \cdot C}$. This conclusion can also be justified using multiplication by 1. For nonzero $B$ and $C$,

$$A \div B = \frac{A}{B} = \frac{A}{B} \cdot \boxed{\frac{C}{C}} = \frac{AC}{BC} = AC \div BC.$$

## Lesson Exercise 7.16

(a) By what do you multiply both the divisor and dividend when you change $0.4\,\overline{)\,0.08}$ to $4\,\overline{)\,0.8}$?

(b) Write $0.08 \div 0.4$ as a fraction and show that it is the same as $0.8 \div 4$.

(c) Compute $0.08 \div 0.4$.

As Lesson Exercise 7.16 indicates, the Equivalent-Division property (i.e., Fundamental Law of Fractions) can be used to convert any decimal divisor problem into a whole-number divisor problem by moving the decimal points in the divisor and the dividend the same number of places to the right.

Decimal division is also used to convert fractions into decimals.

## Lesson Exercise 7.17

(a) $\dfrac{3}{11}$ means _____ ÷ _____.

(b) Complete the division in part (a) and tell why the decimal representation of $\dfrac{3}{11}$ is called a "repeating decimal."

Decimal division is also useful in certain applications. Can you correctly classify the following division application?

## Lesson Exercise 7.18

"A National Motors Finite SST travels 460.8 miles on 16.2 gallons of gas. How many miles does the Finite SST get per gallon?" What division category is illustrated?

## An Investigation: Multiplying and Dividing Decimals

### Lesson Exercise 7.19

Consider the following problem: "In multiplying positive decimals $x$ and $y$, determine what would make the product
(a) greater than $x$.    (b) equal to $x$.    (c) less than $x$."
Devise a plan and solve the problem.

### Lesson Exercise 7.20

In dividing positive decimal $x$ by positive decimal $y$, determine what would make the quotient $x \div y$
(a) greater than $x$.    (b) equal to $x$.    (c) less than $x$.

Instead of computing the answers, apply your generalizations from Lesson Exercises 7.19 and 7.20 to do Lesson Exercises 7.21 and 7.22.

### Lesson Exercise 7.21

Peaches cost $.69 per lb. You buy 0.8 lb. The price would be
(a) greater than $.69.    (b) $.69.    (c) less than $.69.

### Lesson Exercise 7.22

You need 12 kg of soil, and each bag holds 0.8 kg. How many bags do you need?
(a) more than 12    (b) 12    (c) fewer than 12

## Answers to Selected Lesson Exercises

7.1 (a) 10    (b) 10, $\frac{1}{10}$

7.2 (a) $\left(3 \times \frac{1}{10}\right) + \left(1 \times \frac{1}{100}\right) + \left(7 \times \frac{1}{1000}\right)$

(b) $\frac{3}{10} + \frac{1}{100} + \frac{7}{1000} = \frac{300}{1000} + \frac{10}{1000} + \frac{7}{1000} = \frac{317}{1000}$

7.3 0.4 and 0.32 are shown. To show 0.4, shade 4 out of every 10 squares. To show 0.32, shade 32 out of the 100 squares. The area shaded for 0.4 is larger, so 0.4 > 0.32.

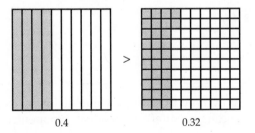

7.4 (a) It reminds the child of 52 > 8.
   (b) Locate them both on the number line and show that 0.8 is to the right of 0.52.

7.5 (a) $10^3 = 1000$, $10^2 = 100$, $10^1 = 10$, $10^0 = 1$, $10^{-1} = 0.1$, $10^{-2} = 0.01$
   (b) When the exponent decreases by 1, the result is divided by 10.

7.6 (a) $2^7$   (b) Add the exponents.   (c) $2^3$
   (d) 1   (e) $2^2$   (f) $\frac{1}{2}$

7.7

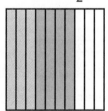

0.3 + 0.4 = 0.7

7.8 $0.36 + 0.40 = \dfrac{36}{100} + \dfrac{40}{100} = \dfrac{(36 + 40)}{100}$

7.9

0.3 − 0.1 = 0.2

7.10 compare sets/measures

7.11 $0.6 \times 0.4$ means 0.6 ("6 tenths") of 0.4. Dot 0.4 of a decimal square.

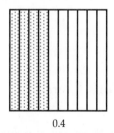

0.4

Now darken 6 tenths of the 0.4.

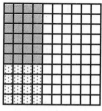

0.6 of 0.4

0.24 of the decimal square is darkened. So $0.6 \times 0.4 = 0.24$.

7.12 $(0.6)(0.89) = \left(\dfrac{6}{10}\right)\left(\dfrac{89}{100}\right) = (6)(89)\left(\dfrac{1}{1000}\right)$

7.13 multiplication, repeated measures

7.14

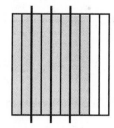

0.8 ÷ 4 = 0.2

7.15 (a) yes   (b) yes   (c) yes   (d) yes
   (e) $A \cdot C \div B \cdot C = \dfrac{AC}{BC} = \dfrac{A}{B} = A \div B.$

**7.16** (a) 10

(b) $0.08 \div 0.4 = \dfrac{0.08}{0.4} = \dfrac{0.08 \times 10}{0.4 \times 10} = \dfrac{0.8}{4}$

$= 0.8 \div 4$

(c) 0.2

**7.17** (a) $3 \div 11$      (b) $0.272727 \ldots$; the digits 2 and 7 repeat over and over.

**7.18** partition, measures

**7.21** (c)

**7.22** (a)

## 7.1   Homework Exercises

*Basic Exercises*

1. If you move the decimal point in a number two places to the left, the value of the number is divided by _____ or multiplied by _____.

2. Write the following decimal numbers using expanded notation.
   (a) 0.31      (b) 32.017

3. Write each of the following as a decimal number.
   (a) forty-one and sixteen hundredths
   (b) seven and five thousandths

4. (a) Write 0.296 using expanded notation.
   (b) The number 0.296 is read "two hundred ninety-six thousandths." Show that $\dfrac{296}{1000}$ equals the sum in part (a).

5. Use decimal square pictures to *explain* why $0.40 = 0.4$.

6. Use decimal square pictures to *explain* why $0.11 < 0.2$.

7. (a) Why might a student think that $-2.3 > -2.1$?
   (b) Use a number line to *explain* why $-2.1 > -2.3$.

8. (a) Why might a student think that $-0.4 > -0.17$?
   (b) Use a number line to *explain* why $-0.4 < -0.17$?

9. Show how to find the value of $10^0$ by extending a pattern in positive exponents.

10. Show how to find the value of $10^{-3}$ by extending a pattern in positive exponents.

11. (a) How can you write $10^{-N}$ ($N$ is a positive integer) with a positive exponent?
    (b) How can you write $X^{-N}$ ($X$ and $N$ are positive integers) with a positive exponent?

12. Which is larger, $3^{-4}$ or $4^{-3}$?

13. Do you recall the shortcut for dividing numbers with the same base, such as $\dfrac{2^6}{2^4}$?
    (a) $\dfrac{2^6}{2^4} = \dfrac{2 \cdot 2 \cdot 2 \cdot 2 \cdot 2 \cdot 2}{2 \cdot 2 \cdot 2 \cdot 2} = 2^?$
    (b) What is the shortcut for dividing $\dfrac{2^6}{2^4}$?

    Use the shortcut from part (b) in parts (c), (d), and (e). It works with all integer exponents. Assume that $X$ is a positive number.
    (c) $\dfrac{10^7}{10^4} =$ _____
    (d) $\dfrac{5^7}{5^{-3}} =$ _____
    (e) $\dfrac{X^6}{X^2} =$ _____

14. Show how to compute $0.2 + 0.3$ in a single decimal square by shading in two different colors.

15. Show that $0.321 + 0.127 = \dfrac{(321 + 127)}{1000}$.

**16.** Consider the following addition problem.

$$\begin{array}{r} 1 \\ 0.36 \\ + \; 0.27 \\ \hline 0.63 \end{array}$$

  (a) When you add 6 + 7 and separate the 13 into 3 and 10, this 10 represents 10 _____.

  (b) The 1 that is regrouped represents 1 _____.

  (c) Are the amounts in parts (a) and (b) equal?

**17.** Draw a sequence of two decimal-square pictures that show how to compute 0.4 − 0.3 using a take-away approach.

**18.** What operation and category are illustrated in the following problem?
"Joe bought a bag of gourmet plant food for $9.89. How much change will he receive back from a $100 bill?"

**19.** At a Chinese restaurant, Szechuan chicken costs $7.50, Hunan shrimp costs $9.25, and moo shi pork costs $6.95. Write two multi-step mathematics problems that could be answered using this information.

**20.** Explain how to compute 0.5 × 0.6 using decimal-square pictures.

**21.** What decimal multiplication problem is illustrated by the following decimal square picture?

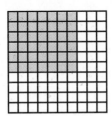
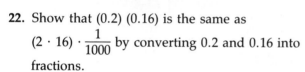

**22.** Show that (0.2) (0.16) is the same as

$(2 \cdot 16) \cdot \dfrac{1}{1000}$ by converting 0.2 and 0.16 into fractions.

**23.** Show that (2.64) (0.3) is the same as

$(264 \cdot 3) \cdot \dfrac{1}{1000}$ by converting 2.64 and 0.3 into fractions.

**24.** Compute the answer to 0.7 × 0.4 by converting both factors into fractions and multiplying.

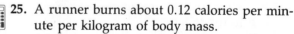

**25.** A runner burns about 0.12 calories per minute per kilogram of body mass.
  (a) How many calories does a 60-kg runner burn in a 10-minute run?
  (b) What category is illustrated?

**26.** Draw a decimal-square picture that shows that 0.6 ÷ 3 = 0.2.

**27.** What do you multiply both numbers by when you change 72 ÷ 3.6 to 720 ÷ 36?

**28.** Use fractions to show why $0.32\,\overline{\smash{)}6.4}$ is the same as $32\,\overline{\smash{)}640}$.

**29.** If you were asked to compute 5000 ÷ 12, you could solve a simpler equivalent problem such as 2500 ÷ 6 using the Equivalent-Division property. Change each problem to a simpler one.

  (a) 6000 ÷ 24     (b) $8 \div \dfrac{2}{3}$

**30.** (a) $\dfrac{2}{9}$ means _____ ÷ _____.

  (b) Complete the division and explain why the decimal representation of $\dfrac{2}{9}$ is called a repeating decimal.

**31.** What operation and category are illustrated in the following problem?
"A baker needs 2 kg of flour to make a loaf of bread. How many loaves can he bake from 5 kg of flour?"

**32.** During 1987 and 1988, the federal government gave Michael Dukakis $46 million.
  (a) What was his average spending per day?
  (b) What operation and category are illustrated?

**33.** What operations and categories are illustrated in the following?
"Molly bought 4 tires for $37.28 each, an air pump for $11.43, and 2 windshield wipers for $3.10 each. How much did these items cost altogether?" (Assume that tax is already included.)

**34.** What operations and categories are illustrated in the following?
"At the beginning of a 4-day car trip, an odometer read 58,427.7. At the end of the trip, it read 59,271.5. What was the average number of miles driven each day?"

**35.** If $A \times 0.3 = B$, then _____ $\times B = A$.

 **36.** Match each fraction with its location on the number line.

$$\frac{126}{66} \qquad \frac{436}{318} \qquad \frac{67}{38}$$

$$A \ \ B \ C \ D \ E$$

**37.** Write the next number in the sequence 0.8, 0.16, 0.032, 0.0064, . . .

 **38.** Multiply $0.15 \times 0.2$ on your calculator. Explain why the answer does not have three decimal places, as the multiplication rule would suggest.

**39.** If a computer does a computation in 0.0002 seconds, how many computations could it do in 1 minute?

**40.** (a) Fill in the blanks.

$$0.1089 \times 9 \ = \ _____$$
$$0.10989 \times 9 \ = \ _____$$
$$0.109989 \times 9 \ = \ _____$$

(b) What is the next equation if the pattern continues?
(c) Is your equation in part (b) true?

**41.** (a) Fill in the parentheses.

$$1 \times 2 + 0.25 = (\ )^2$$
$$2 \times 3 + 0.25 = (\ )^2$$

(b) What is the next equation if the pattern continues?
(c) Is your equation in part (b) true?

**42.** Consider the following information about the following aspirin products. All these products are essentially the same.

| Product | Number of Pills | Dosage | Price | Cost per Pill | Cost per 100 mg |
|---------|-----------------|--------|-------|---------------|-----------------|
| Bufferin‡ | 100 | 325 mg | $5.67 | | |
| Ex. St. Bufferin‡ | 100 | 500 | $7.77 | | |
| Bayer | 100 | 325 | $4.77 | | |
| Max. Bayer | 60 | 500 | $4.77 | | |
| Anacin† | 100 | 400 | $4.99 | | |
| Giant Buff. Asp.‡ | 100 | 325 | $1.59 | | |

† contains caffeine    ‡ contains buffers

(a) Using a calculator, fill in the last two columns of the chart.
(b) Which product is the best buy?

(c) Some companies sell higher-dosage aspirin. Instead of taking 2 Extra Strength Bufferin for 15 cents, you could take _____ Giant Buffered Aspirins at a cost of _____ cents and obtain a similar dosage.

43. In general, a car that has automatic transmission gets about 2 mpg (miles per gallon) less than the same type of car with manual transmission. Assume that a particular car gets 30 miles per gallon with automatic transmission.
   (a) If gas costs $1.10 per gallon and you drive 10,000 miles per year, an automatic transmission increases your gas costs about _____ per year.
   (b) Maintenance for an automatic transmission costs about $160 more per year than for a manual transmission. The extra cost of an automatic transmission for maintenance and gas each year for this car is about _____.

44. An air conditioner decreases a car's average annual mileage by about 2 mpg. If gas costs $1.10 per gallon and you drive 10,000 miles per year, an air conditioner increases gas costs about _____ per year. (Make up the car's mileage per gallon.)

45. An intermediate-sized car gets about 5 mpg less than a subcompact car. Driving 10,000 miles per year and paying $1.10 per gallon of gas would cost about _____ more for gas in the intermediate-sized car than in the subcompact.

*Extension Exercises*

46. A 22-year-old woman owns a 2-year-old car. Consider the following facts. She drives it about 8000 miles per year. Maintenance costs $.08 per mile. Gas costs an average of $1.30 per gallon. The car averages 26 miles per gallon. Insurance costs $480 per year.
   (a) About how much does maintenance cost for a year?
   (b) About how much does gas cost for a year?

(c) Excluding car loan payments, about how much does it cost to operate the car for a year?

47. (a) Graph $xy = 16$ for positive decimals $x$ and $y$.
   (b) Graph $xy = 12$ for positive decimals $x$ and $y$.
   (c) Write a generalization about the graph of $xy = k$, in which $k$ is a counting number.

48. Make up two different decimal multiplication problems that have an answer of 0.2. Do not use 1 as a factor.

49. Consider the following problem: "In charging a customer, a cashier interchanges dollars and cents in the price of an item and gives the customer an extra $11.88 in change for a $20 bill. What is the correct price of the item?"
   (a) Devise a plan and solve the problem.
   (b) Find all possible solutions.

50. Consider the following problem: "The sum of 2 two-digit decimal numerals is 0.42. Their product is 0.0297. What are the numbers?" Devise a plan and solve the problem.

51. If $x > 0$, for what values of $x$ is $x^{-3}$ a negative number?

52. Assume that $x^y = 1$, in which $x > 0$ and $y > 0$. Give all possible solutions.

53. (a) In base five, what would be the place value of the first two digits to the right of the decimal point?
   (b) Write $24.21_{\text{five}}$ in expanded notation.

54. Compute $3.12_{\text{five}} + 2.33_{\text{five}}$.

55. (a) Write $\frac{1}{3}$ as a decimal.
   (b) Write $\frac{1}{3}$ in base 3.
   (c) Write $\frac{1}{3}$ in base 6.
   (d) Name another base in which $\frac{1}{3}$ would be a terminating decimal and write it as a decimal in that base.

*Special Exercises*

**56.** The following chart gives the energy consumption of some common electric appliances.

| Appliance | Usage | KWH (kilowatt-hours) Used |
|---|---|---|
| Oven | 1 hour | 1.1 |
| TV (color) | 1 hour | 0.3 |
| Refrigerator | 1 month | 120 |
| Frost-free refrigerator | 1 month | 200 |
| Dishwasher | 1 cycle | 0.6 |
| Fan | 1 hour | 0.2 |
| Room air conditioner | 1 hour | 1.5 |
| Vacuum cleaner | 15 minutes | 0.2 |
| Clock | 1 month | 1.8 |
| Iron | 1 hour | 0.8 |
| Light bulb (100 W) | 1 hour | 0.1 |
| Baseboard heater | 1 hour | 2 |
| Clothes washer | 1 cycle | 0.2 |
| Clothes dryer | 1 cycle | 3 |
| Water heater | 1 month | 350 |

Use a rate of $.08 per kilowatt-hour and find the cost of the following.
(a)  watching color TV for 2 hours
(b)  doing one load of laundry in the washer and dryer
(c)  running a refrigerator for 1 month
(d)  running a water heater for 1 month
(e)  running a room air conditioner for 8 hours

**57.** Refer to the chart in the previous exercise and consider the following. A couple owns an oven, a refrigerator, two clocks, two room air conditioners, a vacuum cleaner, a color TV, a water heater, an iron, and eight 100-watt bulbs. Assume that they run the air conditioner for 100 hours.

Estimate how much they will use each appliance in a month and then estimate their total electric bill for the month at a rate of $.09 per kilowatt-hour.

## 7.2   Decimals: Estimation, Mental Computation, and Error Patterns

You have a basket full of groceries, and you want to estimate the total bill. You need 8 gallons of gas and want to estimate the cost. These problems require decimal estimation.

### The Rounding Strategy

Decimal estimation, not surprisingly, is very similar to fraction estimation. The rounding strategy is usually best for estimating in decimal addition, subtraction, and most multiplication problems. Decimals are usually rounded to the nearest whole number to create a problem that can be computed mentally.

Figure 7-5 shows how the fifth-grade textbook of *Mathematics Unlimited* introduces decimal estimation with rounding.

## Estimating Decimal Products

**A.** Wally burns coal in his fireplace for heat. He burns 1.75 kg of coal each hour. If he uses the fireplace for 4.5 hours, about how much coal does he use?

Estimate 4.5 × 1.75.

You can estimate decimal products the same way you estimate whole-number products.

**Round both factors to their greatest place.**

$$1.75 \rightarrow 2$$
$$\times\ 4.5 \rightarrow 5$$

**Multiply the factors.**

$$\begin{array}{r} 2 \\ \times\ 5 \\ \hline 10 \end{array}$$

Wally burns about 10 kg of coal in 4.5 hours.

From *Mathematics Unlimited*, Grade 5 (San Diego: Harcourt Brace Jovanovich, 1992), p. 106.

**Figure 7-5**

## Lesson Exercise 7.23

(a) You buy 8.6 m of material costing $7.79 per meter. How could you estimate the total cost by rounding each factor to the nearest whole number?

(b) Why would it also be reasonable to estimate the answer using 8 m × $8 per meter?

You can also use estimation in decimal multiplication to place the decimal point in the answer. Because it involves understanding rather than memorization, some people prefer this method to using the rule for counting decimal places in the factors.

### Example 7.2

How could you use *estimation* to place the decimal point in the following?

6 × 19.95 is      (a) 1197      (b) 119.7      (c) 11.97      (d) 1.197

**Solution**

6 × 19.95 ≈ 6 × 20 = 120. So the decimal point in the answer 1197 must go between the 9 and 7. The answer is choice (b), 119.7. ■

### Lesson Exercise 7.24

Consider the following problem: "The total cost of 12 shirts that are $7.95 each is
(a) $95.40.      (b) $954.      (c) $9.54.      (d) $.954."
How could you use estimation to select the correct choice?

## The Compatible-Numbers Strategy

You can use compatible-numbers estimation to place the decimal point when one or both of the numbers in a multiplication problem are close to or less than 0.5. This type of problem can be done by rounding to a nearby simple fraction with a 1 in the numerator. Then change the other factor into a compatible number.

Recall the following useful equivalences from your childhood days.

| Fraction | $\frac{1}{2}$ | $\frac{1}{3}$ | $\frac{1}{4}$ | $\frac{1}{5}$ | $\frac{1}{10}$ |
|---|---|---|---|---|---|
| Decimal Equivalent | 0.5 | 0.333 . . . | 0.25 | 0.2 | 0.1 |

Example 7.3 illustrates the use of the compatible-numbers strategy in multiplication.

### Example 7.3

Place the decimal point in the answer to 4.87 × 0.26 *by estimating*. (Do not count the decimal places in the factors.)

**Solution**

$$\begin{array}{r} 4.87 \\ \times 0.26 \\ \hline 2922 \\ 974\phantom{0} \\ \hline 12662 \end{array}$$

But where does the decimal point go?

$$4.87 \times 0.26 \approx 4 \times \frac{1}{4} = 1.$$

The answer is about 1, so the decimal point goes between the 1 and the 2. So $4.87 \times 0.26 = 1.2662.$  ■

## Lesson Exercise 7.25

The answer to $83.5 \times 0.412$ has the sequence of digits 34402. *Use estimation* to *explain* where the decimal point goes.

The compatible-numbers strategy works for estimating in decimal division just as it does for whole-number and fraction division. Rounding to the *nearest* whole number is not always the best approach.

## Lesson Exercise 7.26

Suppose that 6.8 lbs of crabmeat costs $58.20. How could you estimate the cost per pound?

One can use estimation to check results obtained with a calculator.

## Lesson Exercise 7.27

I did the following computations on my calculator. Estimate each answer. Then tell whether the given answer must be incorrect.
(a) $86 \div 0.7 = 12.286$      (b) $365 \times 0.05 = 18.25$

## Mentally Multiplying or Dividing by Powers of 10

The shortcut for multiplying by a counting-number power of 10 is suggested by the pattern in the following lesson exercise.

## D Lesson Exercise 7.28

Fill in the blanks.
(a) $9.52 \times 10$        or $9.52 \times 10^1$    = _____
(b) $9.52 \times 100$       or $9.52 \times 10^2$    = _____
(c) $9.52 \times 1000$      or _____     = _____
(d) Propose a general rule based upon your answers to parts (a)–(c).
(e) Explain how you used inductive reasoning to answer part (d).

Lesson Exercise 7.28 suggests the following rule.

---

**Multiplying a Decimal Number by a Power of 10**

Multiplying a decimal number by $10^N$ ($N = 1, 2, 3, \ldots$) is the same as moving the decimal point $N$ places to the right.

---

## Lesson Exercise 7.29

Explain how to compute $4.6 \times 10^3$ mentally.

In 1987, Van Gogh's painting *Irises* sold for a record $53.9 million. The amount 53.9 million means "53.9 times 1 million," or $53.9 \times 10^6$. So $53.9 million = $53,900,000$, which would buy a lot of real flowers. Figure 7-6 shows how 53.9 million is related to 53 million and 54 million.

**Figure 7-6**

##  Lesson Exercise 7.30

According to the National Safety Council, the cost of motor vehicle accidents in 1989 was $93.9 billion.
(a) Write this number in decimal notation (without the word "billion").
(b) If there are about 90 million drivers, what is the average cost per driver?

Now consider dividing a number by a counting-number power of 10. What is a shortcut for dividing by a power of 10 such as 100 or 1000?

##  Lesson Exercise 7.31

Complete the following.
(a) $9.52 \div \phantom{0}10$    or    $9.52 \div 10^1 = $ _____
(b) $9.52 \div \phantom{0}100$   or    $9.52 \div 10^2 = $ _____
(c) $9.52 \div 1000$  or    $9.52 \div 10^3 = $ _____
(d) Based upon parts (a)–(c), dividing a decimal number by $10^N$, *in which* $N = 1, 2, 3, \ldots$ appears to be the same as moving the decimal point _____ places to the _____.

The preceding exercise suggests the following rule.

---

**Dividing a Decimal by a Power of 10**

Dividing a decimal number by $10^N$ ($N = 1, 2, 3, \ldots$) is the same as moving the decimal point $N$ places to the left.

---

## Lesson Exercise 7.32

A store buys 1000 candy bars for $75. How much did it pay for each candy bar?
(a) *Explain* how to compute the answer mentally.
(b) What operation and category are illustrated?

---

The shortcut for multiplying or dividing by a power of 10 can be extended to exponents that are negative integers. Consider the following examples.

$$3.47 \times 10^2 \quad = 347$$
$$3.47 \times 10^1 \quad = 34.7$$
$$3.47 \times 10^0 \quad = 3.47$$
$$3.47 \times 10^{-1} = 0.347$$
$$3.47 \times 10^{-2} = 0.0347$$

## Lesson Exercise 7.33

Describe a shortcut you can use to multiply by negative-integer powers of 10.

---

The shortcut for multiplying a decimal number by an integer power of 10 is as follows.

---

**Multiplying a Decimal Number by an Integer Power of 10**

To multiply $A \times 10^c$, in which $c$ is an integer, the decimal point in $A$ is moved $c$ places to the right if $c \geq 0$ and $-c$ places to the left if $c < 0$.

---

## Lesson Exercise 7.34

Write $5.67 \times 10^{-6}$ using decimal notation.

## Scientific Notation

Archimedes (287–212 B.C.) was one of the first to use very large numbers. He supposedly computed the number of grains of sand needed to fill the entire universe ($10^{63}$). But why did he do this?

According to my wife, he was at the beach with some of his friends who taunted him. "If you're so smart Archi, how many grains of sand would fill the universe?" Submitting to peer pressure, Archimedes proceeded to find out.

It is easier to write large numbers such as $10^{63}$ in shorthand notation. How do calculators deal with such large numbers? Try the following and find out.

 Lesson Exercise 7.35

(a) Compute 400,000 × 360,000 by hand.
(b) Compute 400,000 × 360,000 on your calculator. Did you obtain something like $\boxed{1.44 \quad 11}$? If you got an error message or $E$, your calculator cannot deal with very small or very large numbers. Try this computation on a classmate's calculator that does show the correct answer.

The answer to Lesson Exercise 7.36 (b) is in scientific notation. It means $1.44 \times 10^{11}$. Some calculators, and all computers, use scientific notation to abbreviate very large positive numbers and positive numbers that are close to 0. A computer might write $1.44 \times 10^{11}$ as $\boxed{1.44 \quad E\ 11}$. Scientific notation shows a number as an integer power of 10 multiplied by a number between 1 and 10 (including 1 but not 10).

---

**Scientific Notation**

$N \times 10^{P}$, in which $1 \leq N < 10$ and $P$ is an integer.

---

Scientific notation is a useful shorthand for numbers that have many digits. Scientists, calculators, and computers each employ slightly different scientific notation.

People using scientific notation also need to know how to convert decimal notation into scientific notation.

**Example 7.4**

Write the 1992 world population—5,400,000,000—in
(a) scientific notation.    (b) billions.

**Solution**

(a) First, move the decimal point to obtain a number between 1 and 10.

$$5.400000000$$

How many places was the decimal point shifted? 9. The 9 gives the *magnitude* of the exponent of 10. Should the exponent be 9 or $-9$ ($5.4 \times 10^9$ or $5.4 \times 10^{-9}$)? Use estimation to decide. Which could equal 5,400,000,000?

$$5,400,000,000 = 5.4 \times 10^9$$

(b) Since 1 billion $= 10^9$, $5.4 \times 10^9$ is 5.4 billion. ■

## Lesson Exercise 7.36

A snail moves at a rate of about 0.00036 miles per hour. Write this rate in scientific notation.

## Common Error Patterns

Students regularly make certain errors in decimal arithmetic. The following exercises will help you recognize some common error patterns.

In Lesson Exercises 7.37–7.39, (a) complete the last two examples, repeating the error pattern in the completed examples, (b) describe the error pattern, and (c) if possible, explain how estimation could be used to detect errors.

## Lesson Exercise 7.37

| 0.6 | 0.8 | 0.7 | 0.9 | 0.5 |
|-----|-----|-----|-----|-----|
| + 0.3 | + 0.9 | + 0.6 | + 0.2 | + 0.8 |
| 0.9 | 0.17 | 0.13 | | |

## Lesson Exercise 7.38

| 0.6 | 0.3 | 0.7 | 0.8 | 0.6 |
|-----|-----|-----|-----|-----|
| × 0.9 | × 0.2 | × 0.3 | × 0.7 | × 0.4 |
| 5.4 | 0.6 | 2.1 | | |

## Lesson Exercise 7.39

$$0.3 \overline{\smash)3.21} \quad \overset{17}{\phantom{}} \qquad 5 \overline{\smash)15.25} \quad \overset{3.5}{\phantom{}} \qquad 8 \overline{\smash)5.672} \qquad 4 \overline{\smash)36.16}$$

## Answers to Selected Lesson Exercises

**7.23** (a) $72

(b) Rounding one factor up and the other down may yield a more accurate estimate.

**7.24** $12 \cdot 7.95 \approx 12 \cdot 8 = 96$. The answer is (a).

**7.25** $83.5 \times 0.412 \approx 80 \times \frac{1}{2} = 40$. The answer is 34.402.

**7.26** $58.2 \div 6.8 \approx 56 \div 7 = \$8/\text{lb}$

**7.27** (a) is wrong

**7.28** (a) 95.2    (b) 952    (c) 9520

(e) a generalization based upon a pattern in some examples

**7.29** 4600

**7.30** (a) $93,900,000,000    (b) $1043

**7.31** (a) 0.952    (b) 0.0952    (c) 0.00952

(d) $N$, left

**7.32** (a) Dividing by 1000 requires moving the decimal point in $75 three places to the left to obtain $.075.

(b) partition sets/measures

**7.34** 0.00000567    **7.35** (a) 144,000,000,000

**7.36** $3.6 \times 10^{-4}$

**7.37** (a) 0.11, 0.13

(b) The sum from the tenths column is all placed to the right of the decimal point in the answer.

(c) All the sums are less than either of the addends.

**7.38** (a) 5.6, 2.4

(b) The product is given the same number of decimal places as each of the factors.

**7.39** (a) 0.79, 9.4

(b) Zeroes are omitted from the quotient.

## 7.2   Homework Exercises

*Basic Exercises*

**1.** Mount Everest has an altitude of 8847.6 m and Mount Api has an altitude of 7132.1 m.

(a) How could you estimate how much higher Mount Everest is than Mount Api?

(b) What operation and category are illustrated?

**2.** A job pays $4.35 per hour. How could you estimate how much the job pays for a 32-hour work week?

**3.** A 3-line ad in a newspaper costs $1.79 per line per day. The cost to run such an ad for 4 days is about

(a) $5    (b) $8    (c) $12    (d) $22

(e) $54

**4.** The answer to $3.74 \times 42.8125$ has the digits 16011875. How could you use estimation to explain where the decimal point goes?

**5.** In everyday life, not all rounding of decimals is done to the nearest whole number. For example, if you mail a 1.1-oz letter, the post office charges you the 2-oz rate. Name another situation in which all fractional amounts are rounded up.

**6.** You can use the clustering strategy to estimate total costs. For example, in estimating the total costs of grocery items at $1.29, $.45, $2.45, and $1.09, you could group items that add up to about $1.00 or $2.00. The first two items cost about $2, plus $2 for the third, plus $1 for the fourth makes a total of about $5. Mentally estimate the total of each of the following groups of prices.

(a) $1.59, $.30, $3.10, $1.15, $.72, $2.00, $1.59, $.89, $2.29

(b) $3.71, $2.62, $.51, $.30, $26.95, $9.98, $4.25

7. A long-distance call from Cleveland to Pittsburgh costs $.2696 per minute. The cost of a 12.2-minute call is about
   (a) $28    (b) $4000    (c) $.40    (d) $3

8. Ray takes 18 strides to walk across a room. His stride is about 0.68 m long. How could you estimate the distance across the room?

9. A 46-oz can of apple juice costs $1.29. How could you estimate the cost per ounce?

10. Without computing the product, fill in each blank.
    (a) $4.6 \times 8 = 2.3 \times$ _____
    (b) $8.2 \div 0.3 = 16.4 \div$ _____.

11. To estimate the positive decimal problem $A \div B$, $A$ is rounded up and $B$ is rounded down. Will the estimate be too high or too low? Or is it impossible to tell?

12. The length of a table to the nearest tenth of a centimeter is 153.7 cm. The exact length of the table is between _____ cm and _____ cm.

13. *Explain* how to compute $24 \div 0.5$ mentally. (*Hint:* Change 0.5 to a fraction.)

14. *Explain* how to compute $30 \div 0.25$ mentally.

15. I did the computations below on my calculator. Tell by estimating which answers could not be correct.
    (a) $2.4 \times 0.6 = 14.4$
    (b) $2.13 - 0.625 = 1.505$
    (c) $374 \times 0.011 = 41.14$
    (d) $43.74 \div 2.2 = 19.88181818$

16. Estimate $0.3174 \times 345.92$. Then do the problem on your calculator. Decide whether your calculator answer is reasonable.

17. Rosa bought 100 board feet of walnut board at $3.29 per board foot. What was the total cost?
    (a) *Explain* how to compute the answer mentally.
    (b) What operation and category are illustrated?

18. Multiplying a decimal number by $10^N$, in which $N = 1, 2, 3, \ldots$, is the same as moving the decimal _____ places to the _____.

19. The 1991 U.S. federal budget included a debt of about $3.6 trillion. Write this number without the word "trillion."

20. Write each of the following population figures in millions (using the word "million").
    (a) United States: 275,580,000
    (b) Paris: 2,672,000
    (c) world: 5,400,000,000

21. The distance from Earth to Saturn is about 800 million miles. About how long would it take to reach Saturn traveling 35,000 mph?

22. Large numbers are difficult to grasp. How long is a million seconds? Would it be a week? A month? A year? 5 years?
    (a) Guess.
    (b) Figure out the answer.

23. How long is a billion seconds? Would it be a week? A month? A year? 5 years?
    (a) Guess.
    (b) Figure out the answer.

24. Write the following in decimal notation.
    (a) $3.62 \times 10^7$    (b) $4268 \div 10^6$

25. Which of the following are equal?
    (a) $8 \div 0.23$    (b) $800 \div 0.0023$
    (c) $80 \div 2.3$    (d) $0.8 \div 0.023$
    (e) $80 \div 0.023$

26. A store buys 1000 "Honk if you love quiet" bumper stickers for $43. How much did they pay for each bumper sticker?
    (a) *Explain* how to compute the answer mentally.
    (b) What operation and category are illustrated?

27. A television signal travels 1 mile in $5.4 \times 10^{-6}$ second. Write this number in decimal notation.

**28.** Which is larger, $3.2 \times 10^{-6}$ or $3.2 \times 10^{-5}$?

**29.** A computer display shows $\boxed{3.4 \quad E\ 12}$. Write this number in scientific notation.

**30.** (a) If your calculator has an $\boxed{x^y}$ key, use it to compute $5^{10}$ using the following keystrokes: $\boxed{5}\ \boxed{x^y}\ \boxed{10}\ \boxed{=}$.
(b) Compute $4^{20}$ using this approach.

**31.** Each day, the earth picks up approximately $1.2 \times 10^7$ kg of dust from outer space. Does it seem like most of it falls in your house or apartment?
(a) Write this number in standard decimal form.
(b) Name this number.

**32.** Many scientists believe that the earth is about $5 \times 10^9$ years old.
(a) Write this number in decimal form.
(b) Name this number.

**33.** Why is $48 \times 10^3$ not correct scientific notation?

**34.** The mass of an oxygen atom is 0.000 000 000 000 000 000 000 013 g. Write this number in scientific notation.

**35.** It would take 3,000,000,000,000,000,000,000,000 candles to give off as much light as the sun.
(a) Write this number in scientific notation.
(b) What advantages does scientific notation have over regular decimal notation in this case?
(c) Write this number as it would appear on a calculator display.

**36.** The U.S. government has a large debt. The *interest* on the debt in 1992 was about $206 billion.
(a) Write this number in decimal form.
(b) Write this number in scientific notation.

**37.** The chart at the top of the next column gives the distance in meters of each planet from the sun.

| Planet | Distance from Sun (meters) |
| --- | --- |
| Mercury | $5.8 \times 10^{10}$ |
| Venus | $1.1 \times 10^{11}$ |
| Earth | $1.5 \times 10^{11}$ |
| Mars | $2.3 \times 10^{11}$ |
| Jupiter | $7.8 \times 10^{11}$ |
| Saturn | $1.4 \times 10^{12}$ |
| Neptune | $2.9 \times 10^{12}$ |
| Uranus | $4.5 \times 10^{12}$ |
| Pluto | $5.9 \times 10^{12}$ |

(a) Which planet is about 10 times as far from the sun as the Earth?
(b) Pluto is about _____ times as far from the sun as the Earth is.
(c) Mercury is about _____ times as far from the sun as the Earth is.

**38.** The average person in the United States discards 6 pounds of trash each day. The population of the United States is about 280 million people. How much trash does the U.S. population discard in a year? Write your answer in scientific notation.

**39.** The 1980 estimated population of the United States was 225 million. An average of 1900 cigarettes per person were smoked that year.
(a) Compute the total number of cigarettes smoked in the United States (in 1980) in scientific notation.
(b) Write this number in decimal form.
(c) Name this number.

**40.** Numbers can be multiplied in scientific notation. Fill in the reason for each step.

$280 \times 260,000$

$= (2.8 \times 10^2) \times (2.6 \times 10^5)$ _____

$= (2.8 \times 2.6) \times (10^2 \times 10^5)$ _____

                        (two properties)

$= 7.28 \times 10^7$             rules of exponents and multiplication

**41.** A radar device bounces waves off a plane. The waves take $4 \times 10^{-6}$ seconds to travel back and forth. If waves travel $1.8 \times 10^5$ miles/sec, how far away is the plane?

In Exercises 42–44, (a) complete the last two examples, repeating the error pattern in the completed examples and (b) describe the error pattern.

**42.**

$$\begin{array}{cccc} 42 & 8.1 & 63 & 4.2 \\ -\ 3.71 & -\ 3.71 & -\ 5.29 & -\ 3.17 \\ \hline 39.71 & 4.41 \end{array}$$

**43.**

$$\begin{array}{cccc} 6.2 & 3.5 & & \\ 4\,\overline{)26} & 8\,\overline{)29} & 7\,\overline{)36} & 5\,\overline{)93} \end{array}$$

**44.**

$$\begin{array}{cccc} 16.2 & 14.1 & 12.3 & 8.2 \\ -\ 3.7 & -\ 2.5 & -\ 6.7 & -\ 4.8 \\ \hline 13.5 & 12.4 \end{array}$$

**45.** Describe two errors children might make in computing $0.7 \times 0.8$.

**46.** Fill in the blanks, following the rule in the completed examples.

$$0.6 \rightarrow 1.36$$
$$0.4 \rightarrow 1.16$$
$$0.2 \rightarrow \underline{\hspace{2em}}$$
$$N \rightarrow \underline{\hspace{2em}}$$

**47.** *Explain* how to compute $20 \times 4.25$ mentally. $\left(\textit{Hint:}\ \text{Think of } 4.25 \text{ as } 4\tfrac{1}{4}.\right)$

*Extension Exercises*

**48.** In some computer languages (e.g., Pascal and FORTRAN), the computer can be commanded to truncate a decimal numeral. **Truncating** (denoted TRUNC) means taking the integer part of a real number and discarding the decimal part.

$$\text{TRUNC}(6.8) = 6 \text{ and } \text{TRUNC}(-236.715) = -236.$$

Truncate the following.
(a) 46.81792    (b) $-278.987$    (c) 4.325
(d) When is the result of truncating different from rounding?

**49.** Use estimation and mental computation to order the following numbers from smallest to largest.

$$x = 0.00211 + 0.00321$$
$$y = 0.00211 - 0.00321$$
$$z = (0.00211)(0.00321)$$
$$w = 0.00211 \div 0.00321$$

**50.** A job pays \$4.75 an hour. *Explain* how to compute the pay for 40 hours mentally.

**51.** A job pays \$5.75 an hour. *Explain* how to compute the pay for 20 hours mentally.

**52.** (a) Without using a calculator, tell which of the following are less than 42 and which are greater.
(1) $42 \div 2.7$    (2) $42 \div 0.1$
(3) $42 \div 1.01$    (4) $42 \div 0.999$
(b) Check your answers with a calculator.

**53.** If $326 \div A$ is greater than 326, then $A$ is _____.

**54.** Does $(a^b)^c = a^{b^c}$ for all counting numbers $a$, $b$, and $c$?

*Special Exercise*

**55.** The following game requires two people and a calculator. Play a game of "100 POINT" with a partner. The rules of 100 POINT are as follows.
1. Player 1 keys any number into the calculator.
2. Then each player in turn multiplies the number on the calculator by another number, trying to obtain 100 or "100 point something" (e.g., 100.54). The first player to succeed wins the round.

## 7.3   Ratio and Proportion

In selecting a college, you might have been interested in comparing the number of students and the number of teachers or the number of men and the number of women.

### Ratios

Suppose Brain Strain College has 800 students and 50 teachers. We could say there are 750 more students than teachers, or 16 times as many students as teachers. Which would be a more useful comparison?

### Lesson Exercise 7.40

A second college, Tom Cruise College, has 775 students and 25 teachers.
(a) There are _____ more students than teachers.
(b) There are _____ times as many students as teachers.
(c) Which would be better for comparing this college to Brain Strain College, part (a) or part (b)?

---

Both colleges have 750 more students than teachers, but Brain Strain has significantly fewer students per teacher. The number of students per teacher (called the "student-teacher ratio") gives the more useful figure.

The student-teacher ratio at Brain Strain College is 16 to 1. At Tom Cruise College, it is 31 to 1. These ratios could also be written using colons (16:1 and 31:1) or as fractions $\left(\frac{16}{1} \text{ and } \frac{31}{1}\right)$. Ratios tell us that Tom Cruise College has about twice as many students per teacher as Brain Strain College.

In many cases, the most useful comparison between two sets or two measures is how many times larger one set or measure is than the other. This is what a ratio of two sets shows. Common applications include ratios of students to teachers, miles to gallons, men to women, pounds to cubic feet, and dollars to hours.

A ratio compares two numbers. A ratio is another name for a fraction or quotient.

---

**Definition: Ratio**

A **ratio** is a comparison of two numbers $a$ and $b$, with $b \neq 0$. It can be written $a$ to $b$, $a{:}b$, or $\frac{a}{b}$.

In order to have a correspondence between ratios and fractions, the second number in a ratio is not allowed to be 0, as in the ratio of men to women on the New York Yankees (25 to 0?), since $\frac{25}{0}$ is undefined. One can compare the same two groups in accordance with the definition by looking at the ratio of women to men on the New York Yankees $\left(0 \text{ to } 25, \text{ or } \frac{0}{25}\right)$.

People often use ratios to compare the relative size of two groups or measurements.

## Lesson Exercise 7.41

A car travels 650 miles on 20 gallons. What is the ratio of miles to gallons?

## Proportions

Suppose you're driving one of those cars with automatic cruise control. You set it at 50 mph and sit back and relax. ZZZZ. Wake up! You still have to steer the car.

The car travels 50 miles/hour. You will travel 100 miles in 2 hours, 150 miles in 3 hours, and so on. When you double the driving time, the miles traveled will also double. When you triple the driving time, the miles traveled will also triple.

The ratios of miles to hours, for example, 100 to 2 and 150 to 3, are equal because $\frac{100}{2} = \frac{150}{3}$. The equation $\frac{100}{2} = \frac{150}{3}$ is a proportion. A **proportion** states that two ratios are equal. In this application, one would say that the distance traveled "is proportional to" the driving time.

## Lesson Exercise 7.42

The weight of a pile of bricks is proportional to its volume. Suppose that 10 ft$^3$ of bricks weigh 30 lb.
(a) How much would 40 ft$^3$ of bricks weigh?
(b) Write a proportion that relates the two piles of bricks.

In Chapter 6, you learned that two rational numbers, $\frac{a}{b}$ and $\frac{c}{d}$, are equal if and only if their cross products are equal, that is, if $ad = bc$. This tells us that $\frac{a}{b} = \frac{c}{d}$ is a proportion if and only if $ad = bc$. The cross-product equation $ad = bc$ is often used to find a missing number in the proportion $\frac{a}{b} = \frac{c}{d}$.

Sometimes you can find the unknown number in a proportion by looking at the relationships between the numerators and denominators. Then you don't have to find cross products! Try this in Lesson Exercise 7.43(b).

## Lesson Exercise 7.43

The ratio of boys to girls in a class is 4:5.
(a)  What is the ratio of girls to boys?
(b)  There are 20 girls in the class. How many boys are there? (Write a proportion and see whether you can solve it *without* doing the cross multiplication.)

How are proportions used? Proportions with one unknown number occur in a wide variety of applications, including gas mileage, recipes, map scales, currency conversion, and time needed to complete a task.

 **Example 7.5**

Suppose that you want to know how far your car will go on a full 10-gallon tank of gas. Based upon your records, your car recently traveled 109 miles on 4 gallons of gas.
(a)  Estimate how far you can go on a full tank.
(b)  Compute the exact answer using a proportion.

**Solution**

The miles traveled are proportional to the number of gallons (Figure 7-7).

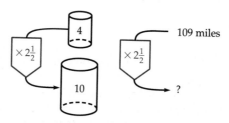

**Figure 7-7**

(a)  Since 10 is $2\frac{1}{2}$ times 4, you will go about $2\frac{1}{2}$ times as far.

$$2\frac{1}{2} \times 109 \text{ miles} \approx 250 \text{ miles}$$

(b)  Solve the problem as follows.

(1) Select a variable for the unknown. Let $D$ = the distance you can travel on a full tank.

(2) Write a proportion. Make sure your units match up when you write the proportion. (There is more than one correct way to write it.)

$$\frac{109 \text{ miles}}{4 \text{ gallons}} = \frac{D \text{ miles}}{10 \text{ gallons}}$$

Other correct proportions would include

$$\frac{109 \text{ miles}}{D \text{ miles}} = \frac{4 \text{ gallons}}{10 \text{ gallons}}$$

$$\frac{D \text{ miles}}{109 \text{ miles}} = \frac{10 \text{ miles}}{4 \text{ gallons}}$$

and $\quad \dfrac{4 \text{ gallons}}{109 \text{ miles}} = \dfrac{10 \text{ gallons}}{D \text{ miles}}$

(3) Solve the proportion using cross products.

$$\frac{109}{4} = \frac{D}{10}$$

So $4D = 1090$.

Dividing both sides by 4, we obtain $D = \dfrac{1090}{4} = 272.5$ miles.   ∎

## Lesson Exercise 7.44

You want to cook a new dish called "seaweed surprise" for 7 people. The recipe for 4 people calls for 18 ounces of seaweed.

(a) Estimate how much seaweed you would need.

(b) Find the answer using a proportion. (Make sure that your units match up.)

(c) Estimate how many friends would accept a subsequent dinner invitation.

When you solve a proportion using cross products, you multiply and then divide. You intuitive types will be interested in knowing that problems that are done with proportions can also be done without actually writing a proportion. You can solve such a problem by using some multiplication and/or division that is based upon your understanding of the proportional relationships.

 **Example 7.6**

Solve the problem in Example 7.5 without writing a proportion.

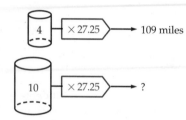

**Figure 7-8**

**Solution**

***The Unitary Method***   Figure out how many miles per *unit* (gallon) the car gets by dividing $\dfrac{109 \text{ miles}}{4 \text{ gallons}} = 27.25$ miles/gallon (Figure 7-8).

Then, to figure out the mileage for 10 gallons, compute $27.25 \times 10 = 272.5$ miles.

***The Multiplier Method***   This method was used to make the estimate in Example 7.5(a). Figure out *how many times* further you are going by dividing $\dfrac{10 \text{ gallons}}{4 \text{ gallons}} = 2.5$. The multiplier is 2.5 (Figure 7-9).

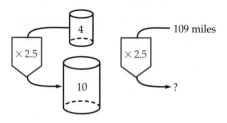

**Figure 7-9**

To figure out the mileage for 10 gallons, *multiply* $109 \times 2.5 = 272.5$ miles. ■

---

**D** Lesson Exercise 7.45

Solve Lesson Exercise 7.44 without writing a proportion.

---

**D** Lesson Exercise 7.46

 Luis takes $3\frac{1}{2}$ hours to type 16 pages. How long will it take him to type 44 pages?
(a) Estimate the answer.
(b) Solve the problem using a proportion.
(c) Solve the problem without writing a proportion.
(d) Which was easier for you, part (b) or part (c)?

---

## Answers to Selected Lesson Exercises

**7.40** (a) 750     (b) 31     (c) (b)

**7.41** 65:2 or 32.5:1

**7.42** (a) 120 lb     (b) $\dfrac{10}{30} = \dfrac{40}{120}$

**7.43** (a) 5:4     (b) 16

**7.44** (b) $31\frac{1}{2}$ oz

**7.45** Multiply $\dfrac{7}{4} \times 18$.

**7.46** (b) and (c) 9.625 hours

## 7.3   Homework Exercises

*Basic Exercises*

**1.** Is 4:3 the same as 8:6?

**2.** Is 7:4 the same as 6:3?

**3.** An all-female college has 600 students.
   (a) What is the ratio of men to women?
   (b) Why is the ratio of women to men un-defined?

**4.** Two sets have a ratio of 10 to 3. Determine whether the ratio of the two sets will change if the number of members in each set is
   (a) doubled.     (b) increased by 10.

**5.** The *pitch* of a roof is the ratio of its rise (height) to its span (width).

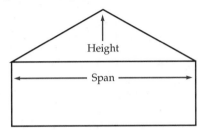

A roof has a rise of 8 ft and a span of 30 ft.
   (a) What is its pitch?
   (b) Write the pitch as a fraction in simplest form.
   (c) What does the pitch tell about the roof?

**6.** The following table shows the frequencies of notes in a musical scale. Simple ratios exist between some of the frequencies.

| Note | Middle C | D | E | F | G | A | B | High C |
|------|----------|-----|-----|-----|-----|-----|-----|--------|
| Frequency | 256 | 288 | 320 | 342 | 384 | 420 | 480 | 512 |

Giving answers in simplest fractional terms, find the ratio of frequencies of
   (a) middle C to E.
   (b) middle C to G.
   (c) middle C to high C.
   (d) E to G.

**7.** The following table lists the number of students and teachers in eight major public

school systems in the 1988 *Digest of Education Statistics.*

| Metro Area | Number of Students | Number of Teachers | Student-Teacher Ratio |
|------------|--------------------|--------------------|-----------------------|
| New York City | 936,153 | 54,031 | |
| Los Angeles | 592,881 | 24,678 | |
| Chicago | 394,587 | 21,693 | |
| Miami | 268,047 | 14,665 | |
| Philadelphia | 191,141 | 10,914 | |
| Baltimore | 189,572 | 10,716 | |
| Tampa | 119,022 | 6,892 | |
| San Diego | 117,168 | 4,737 | |

   (a) Complete the last column of the chart, showing the ratio of students to teachers.
   (b) Which city has the lowest student-teacher ratio?
   (c) Which city has the highest student-teacher ratio?
   (d) Would you rather go to a school with a higher or lower student-teacher ratio?

**8.** Molly is 50, and her grandson Robert is 5. As they get older, the *ratio* of Molly's age to Robert's age will
   (a) increase        (b) decrease
   (c) stay the same    (d) none of these

**9.** Estimate the answer and then solve for $Q$ in each proportion.
   (a) $\dfrac{Q}{5} = \dfrac{7}{3}$     (b) $\dfrac{Q}{12} = \dfrac{4}{Q}$

**10.** Which of the following proportions can be solved easily without computing cross products?
   (a) $\dfrac{3}{7} = \dfrac{T}{14}$     (b) $\dfrac{4}{5} = \dfrac{3}{N}$
   (c) $\dfrac{5}{10} = \dfrac{13}{J}$    (d) $\dfrac{9}{7} = \dfrac{10}{K}$

**11.** Solve for $R$ in each proportion just by looking at the relationship between each pair of fractions.
   (a) $\dfrac{5}{7} = \dfrac{R}{14}$     (b) $\dfrac{3}{R} = \dfrac{6}{10}$     (c) $\dfrac{R}{18} = \dfrac{5}{6}$

**12.** If a British pound is worth $1.63, how many pounds can I buy for $10?
   (a) Estimate the answer.
   (b) Solve the problem using a proportion. (Make sure that the units in the proportion match up.)
   (c) Solve the problem without writing a proportion.

**13.** Last year at the Laundromat Users convention, 3216 people ate 1011 chickens at the Saturday afternoon picnic. This year, 3800 people are expected to attend. How many chickens would you order?

**14.** If 15 pounds of fertilizer takes care of 2000 ft² of lawn, how much would be needed for a rectangular lawn that is 80 ft by 100 ft?

**15.** A couple drinks 3 quarts of orange juice and 2 quarts of skim milk each week. At this rate, how much orange juice and skim milk would they drink in four days?
   (a) Estimate the answer.
   (b) Solve the problem using a proportion.
   (c) Solve the problem without writing a proportion.

**16.** A school has 1200 students and a student-teacher ratio of 30 to 1. How many additional teachers must be hired to reduce the student-teacher ratio to 24 to 1?

**17.** In a large city, 2 million cars are used to commute to work. The average number of people per car is 1.2. If the average number of people per car were increased to 1.5, how many fewer cars would be used?

**18.** Frozen orange juice concentrate is usually mixed with water in a ratio of 3 parts water to 1 part concentrate. How much orange juice can be made from a 12-oz can of concentrate?

**19.** A college has a male-female ratio of 3 to 2. If there are 1100 students, how many men and women are there?

**20.** Suppose that a representative survey of adults in a large city shows that 663 support a sales tax increase and 837 are against it. If the adult population of the city is 4,200,000, predict how many adults support the sales tax increase.

**21.** A 20-ft-long pipe of uniform width and density is cut into two pieces. One piece is 12 ft long and weighs 140 pounds. How much does the other piece weigh?

**22.** Maria ate 5 times as many cookies as Debbie. They ate a total of 18 cookies. How many did each one eat?

**23.** Two triangles are **similar** if and only if the lengths of corresponding sides are proportional. The two triangles shown here are similar, and their corresponding sides are in corresponding positions.

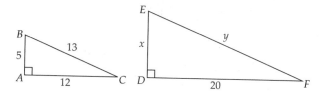

Find $x$ and $y$ by solving proportions.

**24.** A store sells 3 one-pound bags of pasta for $1.87. How much would 2 cost? (*Note:* Stores generally round up *all* fractions of a penny.)

**25.** If 10 oranges cost $1.89, how much will 12 oranges cost?

**26.** (a) An 18-ounce jar of peanut butter costs $1.98. What is the cost per ounce (called the **unit price**)?
   (b) A 32-ounce jar of peanut butter costs $3.88. What is the cost per ounce?
   (c) Which jar is a "better buy" (which has the lower unit price)?

**27.** Consider the following two sizes of corn flakes packages. Which is a better buy?

| Item Price | Unit Price | | Item Price | Unit Price |
|---|---|---|---|---|
| $1.25 | $1.67 per pound | | $1.59 | $1.41 per pound |
| Soggy's Corn Flakes 12-oz box | | | Soggy's Corn Flakes 18-oz box | |

**28.** A 14-oz package of organic mushrooms costs $2.40. A 20-oz package of organic mushrooms costs $3.26. Which package is a better buy?

**29.** Suppose that a 22-oz bag of Giant wheat bread costs $.69. A 22-oz bag of Wonder wheat bread costs $1.29, and 1 lb of Pepperidge Farm wheat bread costs $1.19.
(a) Which product would you buy?
(b) If all three brands had an equal unit price, which would you buy?
(c) What is the most you would pay for a 1-lb loaf of Pepperidge Farm bread if prices of the other loaves are as just listed?

**30.** Describe how someone might conduct a study to determine approximately how many students at your college are left-handed.

*Extension Exercises*

 **31.** A 24-oz jar of Lipton Iced Tea mix costs $3.29. It contains about $\frac{1}{2}$ oz of tea and $23\frac{1}{2}$ oz of sugar. How much would it cost you to mix your own tea and sugar the same way using Lipton Tea (8 oz for $3.79) and sugar (5 lb for $2.39)?

 **32.**

|                       | Town A  | Town B  |
|-----------------------|---------|---------|
| Population            | 346,812 | 182,312 |
| Number of Restaurants | 641     | 311     |

(a) If you had only this information, which town would appear to be a better place to open a restaurant?
(b) What other information should you obtain before deciding?

**33.** A car averages about 24 miles per gallon, a bus averages about 6 miles per gallon, and an electric train averages about 2 miles per gallon. Under what conditions would each vehicle be the most fuel-efficient?

 **34.** Proportions can be used to estimate populations. A ranger catches and tags 10 fish in Lake Leisure. Then she tosses them back in

the lake and lets all the fish mingle. Then the ranger catches 20 fish, finding that 6 of them are tagged. So she guesses that about $\frac{6}{20}$ of the fish in the lake are tagged. Estimate the number of fish in Lake Leisure.

 **35.** The ranger in the previous problem goes to a Lake Boggy. She catches and tags 20 fish. Then she releases them back into the lake. Now, she catches 50 fish and finds that 4 of them are tagged. Estimate the number of fish in Lake Boggy.

**36.** It takes 15 minutes to cut a log into 3 pieces. How long would it take to cut a similar log into 4 pieces? (The answer is not 20 minutes.)

**37.** Consider the following problem: "Three years ago, Francisco and Michael invested $3000 and $5500, respectively, in a business. Today the business is worth $10,000. What is Francisco's share of the business worth?" Devise a plan and solve the problem.

**38.** A family has what they estimate to be a 30-day supply of food. However, after 10 days, only an 18-day supply is left. If they continue to eat at the same rate, the food will last a total of how many days?

**39.** A college class has a male-female ratio of 5:3. Then 3 more women join the class, changing the ratio to 10:7. How many students are now in the class?

**40.** Two classes have the same number of students. Class *A* has a boy-girl ratio of 3 to 5, and class *B* has a boy-girl ratio of 1 to 1. What is the ratio of boys in class *A* to boys in class *B*?

**41.** A class has 18 students. Each of the following could be the ratio of girls to boys except for
(a) 1:1    (b) 2:1    (c) 3:1    (d) 5:1
(e) 8:1

**42.** A college has a male-female ratio of *M* to *F*. What fraction of all the students are female?

**43.** A car gets $M$ miles on $G$ gallons. What is the distance it can travel on $H$ gallons?

**44.** A painter finds that $G$ gallons of paint will cover $A$ square feet. How many gallons are needed to cover $B$ square feet?

**45.** A family drinks $Q$ quarts of milk in $D$ days. How many quarts will they drink in $C$ days?

*Special Exercises*

**46.** Write 16 different proportions using the following numbers. Do not write any fractions that equal 1.

$$1 \quad 2 \quad 4 \quad 6 \quad 8 \quad 12$$

**47.** Draw a floor plan of your home that is to scale.

## 7.4   Using Percents

Do you think it is fair that a salesperson who sells twice as much should earn twice the commission, or that someone who owes three times as much money should pay three times as much interest? In situations such as these, many people consider it fair to charge the same rate on amounts of all different sizes. Percents were devised for just such situations!

"Shirts are 20% off the regular price."

"The inflation rate for 1986 was 3%."

"The sales tax in Maryland is 5%."

"The salesperson's commission is 10%."

"The annual interest rate is 8%."

"The annual finance rate on credit card debts is 15%."

"All employees will receive a 5% raise this year."

These are all common applications of percents. People have used percents since the late fifteenth century in computing interest and taxes.

What does the word "percent" mean? "Cent" in "percent" means *100*, just as it does in the words "century" and "centipede." "Percent" means *per 100*. For example, "50 percent" means 50 per 100, or $\frac{50}{100}$, or $\frac{1}{2}$ (Figure 7-10.)

In general, $N\% = \dfrac{N}{100}$.

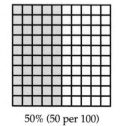

50% (50 per 100)

**Figure 7-10**

### Percents, Fractions, and Decimals

You cannot understand percents unless you understand fractions or decimals. The three concepts are connected. The definition of a **percent** (%), $N\% = \dfrac{N}{100}$, is used to convert it to a fraction or decimal. Consider the following examples.

$$4\% = \frac{4}{100} = 0.04 \quad \text{and} \quad 0.8\% = \frac{0.8}{100} = \frac{8}{1000} = 0.008.$$

## Lesson Exercise 7.47

Based upon the preceding examples, a shortcut for changing a percent to a decimal involves dropping the percent sign *and* moving the decimal point _____ places to the _____ to compensate.

The process is reversed in changing elementary fractions or decimals to percents. The decimal 0.37 and the fraction $\frac{1}{8}$ can be converted to percents as follows.

### Example 7.7

Give the percent equivalents of 0.37 and $\frac{1}{8}$.

**Solution**

After writing the number in decimal form, multiply it by 100% (which is 1).

$$0.37 = 0.37 \times 100\% = 37\%$$

$$\frac{1}{8} = 0.125 = 0.125 \times 100\% = 12.5\%$$

## Lesson Exercise 7.48

(a) Fill in the blanks, using the method shown in Example 7.7.

$$0.084 = \underline{\hspace{1cm}} \times \underline{\hspace{1cm}} = \underline{\hspace{1cm}}_{\text{Percent}}$$

$$\frac{3}{5} = \underline{\hspace{1cm}}_{\text{Decimal}} = \underline{\hspace{1cm}} = \underline{\hspace{1cm}}_{\text{Percent}}$$

(b) Part (a) and Example 7.7 suggest that a shortcut for changing a decimal into a percent involves moving the decimal point _____ places to the _____.

Why was the percent notation developed, when people already had fraction and decimal notation? A percent gives a fixed rate per hundred. This is especially suitable for financial applications such as tax rates, sales commissions, and interest rates. Percents are also used to describe statistical data in sports, education, and science.

## Basic Percent Problems

People who work with tax rates, sales commissions, and interest rates invariably end up solving basic percent problems. Example 7.8 presents two methods for solving the most common type of percent application: finding a percent of a number.

 Example 7.8

Abby buys a dress for $38. The sales tax is 6%. How much sales tax does she have to pay?

**Solution**

***The Multiplication Method***  As with fractions and decimals, 6% *of* 38 means 6% × 38. Since this problem involves money, using decimals makes more sense. 6% of 38 = 0.06 × 38 = $2.28.

***The Proportion Method***  A number line helps illustrate the proportional relationship. One can show 6% of $38 by making a percent scale and a corresponding dollar ($) scale on opposite sides of the same number line, as in Figure 7-11. The amount of $38 represents 100%, and you want to know what amount 6% would be.

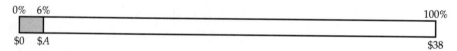

**Figure 7-11**

This picture suggests some proportions. Traditionally, one ratio is written for the percents and the other for the amounts (dollars in this case).

$$\frac{6\%}{100\%} \text{ or } \frac{6}{100} = \frac{\$A}{\$38} \text{ or } \frac{A}{38}$$

So $\frac{6}{100} = \frac{A}{38}$.

Computing cross products yields

$$6 \cdot 38 = 100 \cdot A$$
$$228 = 100 \cdot A$$
$$2.28 = A$$

She will pay $2.28 in sales tax.  ∎

## Lesson Exercise 7.49

I have a credit card debt of $200 for one year. How much interest will I be charged if the annual finance rate is 18%?
(a) Solve the problem using multiplication.
(b) Solve the problem using a proportion.

Another fairly common type of percent problem involves finding what percent one number is of another. What percent is represented by each of the following examples?

"16 out of 50 prefer mushrooms."

"a score of 23 out of 30"

"His $22,500 salary will be increased by $800."

"$1.20 sales tax on $19.99."

"$300 simple annual interest on a principle of $4000"

You can represent all of these examples with percents by writing the two numbers that are being compared as a fraction and then converting the fraction to a percent. The denominator is the total amount or the amount before a change, fee, or increase.

### Example 7.9

May scored 23 out of 30 on a mathematics test. What percent score is this?

**Solution**

***The Division Method***   23 out of 30 is $\frac{23}{30}$. To find out what percent this is, change $\frac{23}{30}$ to a percent.

$$\frac{23}{30} = 0.7667 = 0.7667 \times 100\% = 76.67\%$$

Test scores are usually rounded to the nearest percent, so the score would be 77%.

**Figure 7-12**

***The Proportion Method***   Draw a number-line picture (Figure 7-12). A score of 30 represents 100%, and you want to know what percentage 23 represents.

$$\frac{23}{30} = \frac{N\%}{100\%} \text{ or } \frac{N}{100}$$
$$23 \cdot 100 = 30 \cdot N$$
$$2300 = 30N$$
$$76.67 = N$$

Test scores are usually rounded to the nearest percent. Her score is 77%. ■

 Lesson Exercise 7.50

In a survey asking 35 sixth-grade students whether they would prefer listening to opera, eating squid, or defrosting a freezer, 16 students said that they would prefer defrosting a freezer. What percent does this represent?
(a) Solve the problem using division.
(b) Solve the problem using a proportion.

A less common application is to find a number when a percent of the number is known. The following exercise is just such a situation.

Lesson Exercise 7.51

Consider the following problem. "A group of 105 fifth-grade students attended a school play. They represented 84% of the entire fifth grade. How many students are in the fifth grade?"
(a) Use *N* to represent the unknown number. Write an equation using *N* and solve it.
(b) Draw a number-line diagram showing percent and number scales for this problem. Then write a related proportion and solve it.

## Percent Increases and Decreases

### Best Sellers at 35% Off

### Utility Costs Increase by 14%

Some percent problems involve finding a percent increase or decrease. These can be done as two-step problems. Consider the following example.

**Example 7.10**

A coat at the Outerwear House costs $140, but today it's 30% off! What is the sales price?

**Solution**

*Method 1: Multiply and Subtract* This can be done in two steps. First compute the 30% discount in dollars.

$$30\% \text{ of } \$140 = 30\% \times \$140 = 0.30 \times \$140 = \$42.$$

Second, subtract the discount from the regular price. $140 − $42 = $98. The sales price is $98.

*Method 2: Subtract and Multiply* Make a bar diagram, as in Figure 7-13. As the diagram shows, "30% off the regular price" means 70% of

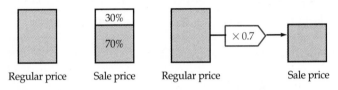

**Figure 7-13**

the regular price (100% − 30% = 70%). Find 70% of $140 = 0.70 × $140 = $98. The sales price is $98. ∎

## Lesson Exercise 7.52

I had $1000 in the bank for a year earning 12% simple interest. The year is over. How much money do I have in that account now?
(a) Solve this by multiplying and adding.
(b) Draw a bar diagram illustrating the relationship and solve by adding and multiplying.

 

There are two teachers, an experienced teacher who earns $43,870, and a fairly new teacher who earns $28,800. Both receive their annual raise. How could the two raises be compared? One way is to compare the percent increase (the change in the number of dollars *per each $100* earned) that each teacher received.

How is the percent change computed? The two-step method is as follows. First, compute the amount of the increase or decrease. Second, compute what percent this amount is of the *original* amount.

**Example 7.11**

This year, Maria Gomez's salary increased from $28,800 to $32,256. What percent increase is this?

**Solution**

***Method 1: Subtract and Divide***   Compute the amount of the increase: $32,256 − $28,800 = $3456. Second, compute what percent this increase is of the *original* amount: $3456 is what % of $28,800?

$$\frac{\$3456}{\$28,800} = 0.12 = 0.12 \times 100\% = 12\%.$$

Maria received a 12% increase.

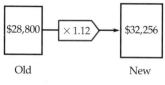

Old          New

**Figure 7-14**

***Method 2: Divide and Subtract***   Find the multiplier that produces 32,256 from 28,800 (Figure 7-14).

$\frac{32,256}{28,800} = 1.12$. Change 1.12 to a percent. $1.12 \times 100\% = 112\%$.

So 32,256 is 112% of 28,800. The increase is $112\% − 100\% = 12\%$.  ■

The following exercise is similar to Example 7.11.

**D** Lesson Exercise 7.53

 This year, Sally Martin's salary increased from $43,870 to $48,300. Find what percent increase this is to the nearest tenth of a percent by
(a) using the subtract-and-divide method.
(b) using the divide-and-subtract method.
(c) How does this increase compare to Maria Gomez's increase in Example 7.11?
(d) Describe another way of comparing their increases that would result in Sally's increase being larger than Maria's.
(e) Would you say Sally and Maria's raises are comparable, or did one come out better than the other?

You can also find the original amount if you are given the percentage increase or decrease and the final result.

 Lesson Exercise 7.54

Consider the following problem. "This year, a school's enrollment decreased exactly 6% to 423 students. What was the enrollment before this decrease?
(a) What percent is 423 of last year's enrollment?
(b) Write an equation and solve it.

## Compound Interest

**New Rates**

| Account | Yield | Rate |
|---|---|---|
| 6-month CD $100 minimum | 8.60% | 8.60% |
| 1-year CD $100 minimum | 8.87% | 8.50% |

Do you have some money in the bank? In this section, we'll focus on the kind of interest you are earning.

**Simple interest** pays interest only on the original money (the "principal") you deposited. With **compound interest,** you also earn interest on your interest. Most banks pay compound interest on your savings, usually more than once a year, either semiannually (twice a year), quarterly (four times a year), monthly, or daily (360 or 365 times a year).

Are you better off receiving compound interest than simple interest? Suppose that, in Lesson Exercise 7.52, I had received 12% interest compounded semiannually. Instead of receiving 12% interest at the end of the year, I receive 6% after 6 months and 6% more interest after 12 months. This is semiannual (twice a year) compounding.

### Example 7.12

Compute 12% interest on $1000 compounded semiannually.

**Solution**

$$\$1000 - \boxed{\times 1.06} \longrightarrow \_\_\_\_ - \boxed{\times 1.06} \longrightarrow \_\_\_\_$$

| time | 6 months | 12 months |
|---|---|---|
| amount | $1000 + 6%($1000)<br>$1000 + $60<br>$1060 | $1060 + 6%($1060)<br>$1060 + $63.60<br>$1123.60 |

So you end up with $1123.60. ∎

In Example 7.12, the interest is $123.60, and in Lesson Exercise 7.52, the interest is $120. You receive more money with the semiannual compounding in Example 7.12 because you receive 6% interest on the $60 interest (an extra $3.60) from the first 6 months.

### Example 7.13

The total annual interest in Example 7.12 is $123.60 on $1000. What percent interest is this? (This percent is known as the **effective annual yield.**)

Solution

$$\frac{\$123.60}{\$1000} = 0.1236 \quad \text{and} \quad 0.1236 \times 100\% = 12.36\%$$

So the effective annual yield on 12% interest compounded semiannually is 12.36%.  ■

Example 7.13 shows that when you receive 12% interest compounded semiannually for a year, you actually receive more than 12% of your investment in interest.

Bank ads often quote the effective annual yield.

---

**Definition: Effective Annual Yield**

The **effective annual yield** is the interest rate compounded annually, which is equivalent to the given compound interest rate.

---

**D** Lesson Exercise 7.55

A bank pays 12% interest compounded quarterly.
(a) What percent interest will the bank pay every 3 months?
(b) Compute the total interest for the year on $1000, assuming you leave all your money and the interest in the bank.
(c) What is the effective annual yield on 12% compounded quarterly?
(d) Is it higher than 12% compounded semiannually?

---

In computing 12% interest compounded quarterly, you first compute

$$1000\left(1 + \frac{0.12}{4}\right)$$

Then, in the next quarter, you multiply this amount $1000\left(1 + \frac{0.12}{4}\right)$ by $\left(1 + \frac{0.12}{4}\right)$ again. After four quarters, you would have multiplied

$$1000\left(1 + \frac{0.12}{4}\right)\left(1 + \frac{0.12}{4}\right)\left(1 + \frac{0.12}{4}\right)\left(1 + \frac{0.12}{4}\right)$$
$$= 1000\left(1 + \frac{0.12}{4}\right)^4.$$

So the resulting amount $A$ is $1000\left(1 + \dfrac{0.12}{4}\right)^4$.

In general, you accumulate the amount

$$A = P\left(1 + \frac{R}{N}\right)^{T \cdot N}$$

in which 1000 is the principal $P$, 0.12 is the annual rate $R$, 4 is the number of payments per year $N$, and $T$ the number of years in the bank.

---

**Formula for Compound Interest**

A formula for computing compound interest is $A = P\left(1 + \dfrac{R}{N}\right)^{TN}$

in which $P$ is the principal, $T$ is the time in years, $A$ is the amount after time $T$, $R$ is the rate of interest, and $N$ is the number of times interest is paid each year.

---

*Do not memorize this formula.* Look it up when you need it.

 **Example 7.14**

A bank pays 12% interest compounded semiannually. Use the compound-interest formula to find out how much you will have at the end of the year if you deposit $1000.

**Solution**

$$A = P\left(1 + \frac{R}{N}\right)^{TN}$$

$R = 0.12$, $P = 1000$, $N = 2$, $T = 1$, and $A = ?$. Substituting in the formula,

$$A = 1000\left(1 + \frac{0.12}{2}\right)^{2 \cdot 1} = 1000(1.06)^2 = \$1123.60$$

This is the same answer as in Example 7.12. ■

 Lesson Exercise 7.56

Do Lesson Exercise 7.55 (b) using the compound-interest formula.

Lesson Exercise 7.57

Many banks compound interest daily, paying interest 360 or 365 times per year. If Ben deposits $1000 for a year, earning 12% interest compounded daily (360 times per year), how much money will he have at the end of the year?

## Answers to Selected Lesson Exercises

**7.47** 2, left

**7.48** (a) $0.084 \times 100\% = 8.4\%$
$0.6 = 0.6 \times 100\% = 60\%$
(b) 2, right

**7.49** $36

**7.50** $45\frac{5}{7}\%$ or about 45.71%

**7.51** (a) $0.84N = 105$, so $N = 125$

(b) $\frac{84}{105} = \frac{100}{N}$. So $N = 125$.

**7.52** $1120

**7.53** (a) 10.1%    · (c) lower
(d) Compare the dollar amount of each increase.

**7.54** (a) 94%
(b) $0.94N = 423$, so $N = 450$.

**7.55** (a) 3%           (b) $1125.51
(c) 12.55%       (d) yes

**7.57** $1127.47

## 7.4   Homework Exercises

*Basic Exercises*

1. What does the word "percent" mean?

2. 14% means
   (a) _____ per 100
   (b) _____ per 50

3. Convert each percent to a fraction and a decimal.
   (a) 34%     (b) 180%     (c) 0.6%

4. Convert each decimal to a percent.
   (a) 0.79     (b) 5.24     (c) 0.00083

5. Convert each fraction to a percent.
   (a) $\frac{1}{25}$   (b) $\frac{3}{16}$

 6. A salesperson earns a 12% commission. If she sells a $2400 computer, what is her commission?
   (a) Solve the problem using multiplication.
   (b) Solve the problem with a proportion and draw a number-line model.
   (c) If she sells 3 times as many computers, her commission will be _____ times as much.

7. The sales tax on a $9.59 item is $7\frac{1}{2}\%$. How much is the tax?

8. A department store is considering running a 60-second TV ad. Assume that the average viewer who responds to the ad will bring the store an additional $10 of profit. The marketing department has gathered the following information.

**60-Second Television Ad**

| Time Slot | Cost | Estimated Number of Viewers | Estimated Viewer Response |
|---|---|---|---|
| 9:15 AM | $1400 | 13,000 | 1.0% |
| 1:15 PM | 900 | 10,000 | 1.2% |
| 7:15 PM | 1600 | 20,000 | 0.9% |

(a) Forecast which time slots are profitable.
(b) Which time slot should be the most profitable?

9. Each year in the United States, we produce about 110 million tons of air pollution from carbon monoxide. Motor vehicles produce about 82 million tons of this pollutant. What percent of the carbon monoxide do motor vehicles produce?
   (a) Solve the problem using division.

(b) Solve the problem with a proportion and draw a number-line model.

10. On our last trip to England, my wife and I needed to exchange dollars for pounds. One bank charged a 0.5% commission fee with a minimum charge of 2.50£ (British pounds). Another bank charged a 2% commission with a minimum charge of 2£. If the exchange rate at both banks was $1.76 for 1£ before fees, how many pounds would you receive at each bank for each of the following?
(a) $100    (b) $1000

11. You paid $1.20 in tax when purchasing an electric coffee stirrer for $19.99. What percent sales tax is this? (Use either method.)

12. Weigh a grape and a raisin (a dried grape) and estimate what percent of the grape is water.

13. A fruit juice has the following list of ingredients: grape juice, apple juice, and passion fruit juice. Ingredients are listed in order from most abundant to least abundant. At least what percent of the drink is grape juice?

14. Consider the following problem. "A salesperson earns a commission of 8% of total sales. This week she earned $798.40. What were her total sales for the week?"
(a) Write an equation (that is, not a proportion) and solve it.
(b) Write a proportion and solve it.

15. There are 184 comedy films at Fantasy Island Video. This represents about 18% of their collection. How many films do they have? Give all possible answers. (There are 57 of them!)

16. Your new credit card has an annual finance charge of 15% simple annual interest.
(a) Suppose you borrow $500 for a year. How much interest will you owe?
(b) Suppose you cannot afford to pay back the $500 for an additional 9 months. How much additional interest will you owe?

17. A credit card company charges 12% simple annual interest on debts.
(a) What percent interest does the company charge per month?
(b) What percent interest does the company charge per day?

18. You buy a $5000 savings certificate that pays 8% simple annual interest. How much interest will you earn in 6 months?

19. How much money must I put in an account earning 6% simple annual interest so that I will have $5000 at the end of 1 year?

20. The U.S. water use (in billions of gallons) in 1990 was approximately as follows.

| Irrigation | Utilities | Domestic | Industrial | Total |
|---|---|---|---|---|
| 145 | 195 | 42 | 43 | 425 |

What percent of the water is used for domestic purposes?
(a) Solve the problem using division.
(b) Solve the problem with a proportion.
(c) If domestic water use were cut in half, overall water use would decrease by _____%.

21. Sylvia scored 64 out of 70 on a quiz. Write her score as a percent.

22. If you want to increase a price by 6%, by what single number could you multiply the old price to obtain the new price?

23. A baseball glove sells for $15.98. How much will it cost at 20% off?
(a) Solve the problem by multiplying and subtracting.
(b) Solve the problem by subtracting and multiplying.
(c) If the sales tax is 4%, what is the total price of the glove?

24. In 1988, our annual car insurance for one car rose from $463 to $574. What percent increase is that?
(a) Solve the problem by dividing and subtracting. (Round to the nearest tenth of a percent.)

(b) Solve the problem by subtracting and dividing.

(c) Given that we had no accidents or traffic violations, is this a reasonable increase?

**25.** My car was worth $8300 when it was new. Now it is worth only $3500. By what percent has its value depreciated (decreased)?

**26.** Sam has $20 and Mike has $10. Sam has _____% more money than Mike, and Mike has _____% less money than Sam.

**27.** I deposit $2000 in a bank that pays 12% interest compounded monthly.

(a) How much money will I have in the account after 1 year?

(b) What is the effective annual yield?

**28.** I deposit $4000 in a bank that pays 10% interest compounded daily (300 times per year).

(a) How much money will I have in the account after 1 year?

(b) What is the effective annual yield?

**29.** Five-percent annual inflation is the same mathematically as 5% interest compounded annually. If a car cost $10,000 in 1993, what would it cost in 2003, assuming an annual inflation rate of 5%?

**30.** You are offered a 6-year job for a total of $240,000.

(a) Which of the following pay plans is probably worth the most? Why?

(1) $40,000 each year

(2) annual payments in order of $30,000; $34,000; $38,000; $42,000; $46,000; $50,000

(3) annual payments in order of $50,000; $46,000; $42,000; $38,000; $34,000; $30,000

(b) When given these three choices, people most often selected option 2, which is probably the worst pay plan. Why would someone prefer it?

**31.** The world population in 1992 was about 5.4 billion. It is expected to grow about 1.6% annually in the near future.

(a) Forecast the world population in 1993.

(b) Forecast the world population in 2000. (*Hint:* Use an exponent.)

(c) Forecast the world population in 2050.

**32.** The U.S. population in 1992 was about 260 million. It is expected to grow about 0.6% annually in the near future.

(a) Forecast the U.S. population in 1993.

(b) Forecast the U.S. population in 2000.

(c) Forecast the U.S. population in 2050.

**33.** Look in a newspaper to determine how interest rates for savings accounts compare to interest rates for car loans.

**34.** An airline ticket costs $218, including 8% tax. What was the base fare?

**35.** A store owner makes a 25% profit (on the wholesale price) by selling a dress for $80. How much is the profit in dollars?

**36.** Twenty years ago, Gil had an annual income of $6530. If inflation for the last 20 years has been about 200%, what annual income will he need this year to keep pace with inflation?

**37.** Driving 40 mph instead of 60 mph on the highway increases gas mileage by 20%. A car that gets 28 mpg at 60 mph will get _____ mpg at 40 mph.

**38.** Paolo works for a company that manufactures variables. This year, Paolo's salary increased from $8S$ to $10S$. What percent increase is this?

**39.** Write two multi-step mathematical questions that can be answered using the following data.

|  | Regular Price | Sale Price |
|---|---|---|
| Gazelle Joggers | $78.50 | $75.00 |
| Hippo Running Shoes | $29.95 | $19.95 |
| Fatiguers Running Shoes | $35.00 | $31.99 |
| Bolt Running Shoes | $50.00 | $40.00 |

**40.** (a) Complete the chart.

| Number | 0 | 10 | 20 | 30 | 40 |
|---|---|---|---|---|---|
| 38% of the Number | 0 | 3.8 | | | |

(b) Plot your points on graph paper using axes like those shown.

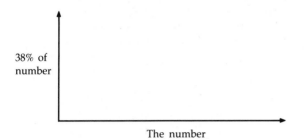

38% of number

The number

(c) Use your graph to estimate the following: 10 is 38% of _____ .

**41.** A store marks down an item 30% to a price of $225.60.

(a) Complete the chart.

| Original Price | $0 | $100 | $200 | | |
|---|---|---|---|---|---|
| 30% Off the Price | $0 | | | | |

(b) Plot your points on graph paper using axes like those shown.

30% off the price

Original price

(c) Use your graph to estimate the original price if the sale price is $225.60.

**42.** You are offered two real estate sales jobs. One pays 9% commission. The other job pays $50 per week and 6% commission. If sales tend to average about $2000 per week, which job would pay more?

**43.** Explain the following expressions.
(a) "We are with you 100%."
(b) "Let's split it 50-50."

**44.** As of 1992, the United States and Canada have different kinds of health-care systems. In Canada, all citizens are insured; in the United States, about 35 million people (14%) are uninsured. Canada uses a single insurer in each of its ten provinces; the United States has about 1500 different health insurers. Researchers at the Organization for Economic Cooperation and Development compared the two systems.

| | Population (1987) | Total Cost (1987) | Total Administrative Costs (1987) |
|---|---|---|---|
| U.S. | 251 million | $515 billion | $124 billion |
| Canada | 26 million | $39 billion | $4.3 billion |

(a) Compute the per capita (per person) costs in the United States and Canada.
(b) What percent of the total cost represents administrative costs in each country?
(c) If the United States reduced its administrative costs from 24% to 11%, how much would be saved?

| | Infant Mortality Deaths per 1000 Births (1986) | Persons per Physician (1986–7) | Life Expectancy (1985) |
|---|---|---|---|
| U.S. | 10.4 | 488 | 75.3 years |
| Canada | 7.9 | 463 | 77.1 years |

(d) What do the data suggest about the comparative performance of the two health-care systems?

*Extension Exercises*

 **45.** (a) The sign in the cartoon is making a prediction. What sort of prediction is it?

A&M Homewares Inc. Drawing by Joseph Farris; © 1974 The New Yorker Magazine, Inc.

(b) If *A* is 15% less than *B*, is *B* 15% greater than *A*? (*Hint:* Try substituting numbers for *A* and *B*.)

**46.** Hi-C Orange Drink costs $2.09 for 64 oz. It contains 10% orange juice, about 1.7 oz of sugar, plus water and artificial color. How much would it cost you to make 64 oz of orange drink yourself using canned orange juice ($2.19 for 46 oz), sugar ($2.39 for 5 lb), and water?

**47.** Consider the following problem. "A business manager must pay $35,000 per year in fixed expenses, and she pays 40% of her total sales to her workers. How much money must she make to earn a $40,000 profit after paying her expenses and her workers?" Devise a plan and solve the problem.

**48.** Taxes are commonly classified as progressive, intermediate, or regressive. A **progressive tax** requires people with higher income to pay a higher percent of their income as tax. An **intermediate tax** requires people at every income level to pay the same percent income tax, and a **regressive tax** requires people with lower incomes to pay a higher percent of their income as tax. Classify each of the following tax structures as progressive, intermediate, or regressive.

(a)

| Total Yearly Income | Percent Tax |
|---|---|
| $30,000 | 8% |
| $25,000 | 10% |
| $20,000 | 12% |

(b)

| Total Yearly Income | Tax |
|---|---|
| $30,000 | $2000 |
| $25,000 | $2000 |
| $20,000 | $2000 |

(c) Maryland has a sales tax rate of 5%. The average person with $30,000 in yearly income buys about $4000 worth of sales-taxed items, while the average person with $10,000 in yearly income buys about $2000 worth of sales-taxed items. Classify this sales tax as progressive, intermediate, or regressive.

**49.** Fill in tax amounts so that the tax is *regressive* and those with higher incomes pay more money in tax.

| Total Yearly Income | Tax Amount |
|---|---|
| $30,000 | _____ |
| $20,000 | _____ |
| $10,000 | _____ |

50. (a) Suppose that Congress is considering raising the highest tax bracket from 40% to 50%. Would this be a 10% increase or a 25% increase? Explain the reasoning behind each interpretation.
    (b) Suppose that Congress is considering raising another tax bracket from 30% to 40%. What is the fairest way to compare this increase to that in part (a)?

51. Your salary increases 8%, but prices increase 10%. What percent of your old purchasing power is your new purchasing power?

52. A store owner buys a compact stereo for $200. She wants to price it so she can offer a 10% discount off the posted price and make a profit of 40% of the price she paid. What will the posted price of the stereo be?

53. If inflation is 10% a year for 3 years in a row, the 3-year price increase is
    (a) less than 30%
    (b) 30%
    (c) greater than 30%

54. A $80 dress is marked down 10% one week. The next week, an additional 25% is taken off the sale price. Find a single percent discount equal to these two successive discounts.

55. A car is marked up 30% from its wholesale price. During a sale, the retail price is reduced by 20%. What percent higher is the sale price than the wholesale price?

56. After two annual raises of 20%, Margaret receives an annual salary of $69,840. What was her salary two years ago?

57. An investment earns 10% per year. How many years would it take for your investment to double if you leave your interest in the account? (*Hint:* The answer is not 10 years.)

58. How much should you put in a bank that offers 9% interest compounded annually if you want to have $5000 after 5 years? (Guess and check.)

59. If the pattern shown in the diagram continues, what percent of the interior would be shaded in the eighth triangle?

Triangle 1          Triangle 2          Triangle 3

60. A student answers *A* out of *B* questions correct on a test. If all the questions count the same, write the student's test score as a percent.

61. A car accelerates from a speed of *N* mph to *M* mph ($M > N$). What percent increase is this?

62. (a) Look through a newspaper or magazine for an article that uses percents.
    (b) Write a mathematical expression or equation to represent each use.
    (c) Comment on whether the percents used in each case convey useful information.

*Special Exercises*

The U.S. Dept. of Agriculture (USDA) has certain standards for names used to describe various meat products. Some of them are shown here.

---

**USDA Standards for Meat**

**hamburger:** no more than 30% fat

**hot dog** or **bologna:** no more than 30% fat and 10% added water

**smoked pork sausage:** no more than 50% trimmable fat

**egg rolls with poultry:** at least 12% poultry meat

**breaded poultry:** no more than 30% breading

**poultry chop suey:** at least 4% poultry meat

**poultry pies:** at least 14% poultry meat

**poultry with gravy:** at least 35% poultry meat

**poultry salad:** at least 25% poultry meat

**poultry soup** (condensed): at least 4% poultry meat

**poultry soup** (ready-to-eat): at least 2% poultry meat

---

63. Based upon USDA standards, give the government restrictions on each of the following products.
    (a) Chun King chicken egg rolls
    (b) Weaver chicken rondelets (breaded chicken patties)
    (c) Ball Park franks
    (d) Swift Premium turkey roast (boneless meat with gravy)
    (e) Campbell's chicken noodle soup (condensed)

64. Which is required by the USDA to have more meat: chicken salad, chicken pot pie, or chicken chop suey?

---

## 7.5   Percents: Mental Computation and Estimation

Calling all unconventional people. You can work out many percents more quickly by *not* using standard procedures.

### Computing 1%, 10%, 25%, 50% or 100% of a Number

An eight-concert subscription series to the West Dakota Symphony Orchestra sells at a 10% discount off the $160 single-seat price. How much is the savings? 10% of $160. Some people would compute 10% of 160 as follows.

$$
\begin{array}{r}
160 \\
\times\, 0.10 \\
\hline
0\ 00 \\
16\ 0 \\
\hline
16.00
\end{array}
$$

Sure, the answer is right, but it was a lot more trouble than it was worth. A quicker way to find 10% (or 1%) of a number is to move the decimal point of the number. Since 10% is $\frac{1}{10}$ , 10% of 160 can be found by moving the decimal point in 160 one place to the left to obtain the answer, 16.

You should be able to compute 1%, 10%, 25%, 50%, and 100% of most whole numbers without converting the percent into a decimal and multiplying. Generalize these shortcuts in Lesson Exercises 7.58 and 7.59.

## Lesson Exercise 7.58

(a)  How do you find 100% of a number?

(b)  Computing 50% of a number is the same as dividing the number by _____ .

(c)  Computing 25% of a number is the same as dividing the number by _____ .

## Lesson Exercise 7.59

(a)  Finding 10% of a number is the same as dividing by _____ , which means you could move the decimal point in the number _____ place(s) to the _____ .

(b)  Finding 1% of a number is the same a dividing by _____ , which means you could move the decimal point in the number _____ place(s) to the _____ .

As Lesson Exercises 7.58 and 7.59 suggest, you can use the following procedures.

**Computing 100%, 50%, 25%, 10%, and 1% of a Number**

100% of a number is that number.

50% of a number is half the number, so divide the number by 2.

25% of a number is one quarter of the number, so divide the number by 4.

10% of a number is $\frac{1}{10}$ of the number, so divide the number by 10, moving the decimal point one place to the left.

1% of a number is $\frac{1}{100}$ of the number, so divide the number by 100, moving the decimal point two places to the left.

Apply these shortcuts in Lesson Exercises 7.60 and 7.61.

## Lesson Exercise 7.60

Mentally compute    (a) 100% of 642.    (b) 50% of 286.
                               (c) 25% of 4000N.

## Lesson Exercise 7.61

A $25 shirt is selling at a 10% discount. Mentally compute the discount and the sale price.

## Computing Other Percents

Now for some more amazing feats of mental computation! Certain other percents of a number, such as 5%, 30%, 75%, and 200%, can sometimes be computed mentally using our understanding of 1%, 10%, 25%, and 100%, respectively.

**Example 7.15**

How could one mentally compute
(a) 200% of 14?    (b) 5% of 300?    (c) 30% of 620N?

**Solution**

(a) To find 200% of 14, compute 2 times 100% of 14.

$$2 \times 14 = 28$$

(b) To find 5% of 300, compute 5 times 1% of 300.

$$5 \times 3 = 15$$

Note that you could also compute

$$\frac{1}{2} \text{ of } 10\% \text{ of } 300 = \frac{1}{2} \text{ of } 30 = 15$$

(c)  To find 30% of 620N, compute 3 times 10% of 620N.

$$3 \times 62N = 186N \quad \blacksquare$$

## Lesson Exercise 7.62

The number of high-school girls playing basketball in 1992 was 300% of 160,000, the number who played in 1975. How could you mentally compute how many girls were playing high-school basketball in 1992?

## Lesson Exercise 7.63

How could you mentally compute      (a) 6% of 200?      (b) 40% of 12N?

## Estimating Percents

You can also estimate A% of B using mental computation. Round the problem and compute mentally or, if you prefer, use the compatible-numbers strategy. The compatible-numbers strategy requires rounding the percent to a nearby fraction. The following table lists some percents and their fraction equivalents.

| Percent | 5% | 10% | 20% | 25% | $33\frac{1}{3}\%$ | 50% | $66\frac{2}{3}\%$ | 75% | 100% |
|---|---|---|---|---|---|---|---|---|---|
| Unit Fractions | $\frac{1}{20}$ | $\frac{1}{10}$ | $\frac{1}{5}$ | $\frac{1}{4}$ | $\frac{1}{3}$ | $\frac{1}{2}$ | $\frac{2}{3}$ | $\frac{3}{4}$ | $\frac{1}{1}$ |

### Example 7.16

How could one estimate 32% of 527?

**Solution**

*Method 1: Rounding*   Round the problem to 30% of 500 and compute mentally. This is 3 times 10% of 500. Since $3 \times 50 = 150$, estimate that 32% of 527 ≈ 150.

*Method 2: Compatible Numbers*   Round 32% to a nearby unit fraction $\left(\frac{1}{3}\right)$, so that 32% of 527 is about $\frac{1}{3}$ of 540 = 180. So 32% of 527 ≈ 180.   ■

Lesson Exercise 7.64

A salesperson earns a 22% commission. Show how to estimate her commission for selling a $648 washing machine using both the rounding and compatible-numbers methods.

John got 34 right out of 48 questions on a test. Approximately what percent did he answer correctly? The following example shows how to answer this question.

### Example 7.17

John answered 34 questions correctly out of 48. Show how to estimate the percentage of questions he answered correctly.

**Solution**

34 out of 48 is $\frac{34}{48} \approx \frac{3}{4} = 75\%$. John answered about 75% of the questions correctly.  ■

Lesson Exercise 7.65

4 out of 17 children in a class like olive loaf. How could you estimate the percentage of children who like olive loaf?

## Estimating Tips

You've just finished a feast. Chef Skippy fixed his special baked zucchini with peanut sauce, buttered apples, and licorice balls. It came to $12.26 plus $.74 tax. What's a reasonable tip?

One common application of percent estimation is estimating the tip in a restaurant. People typically leave about 15% of the bill.

## Lesson Exercise 7.66

Describe every method you know for computing the tip on a bill of $12.26 plus $.74 tax.

The following example illustrates three methods for estimating a tip.

### Example 7.18

How could you mentally compute an appropriate tip for the following bill from Skippy's restaurant?

|        |        |
|--------|--------|
| Bill   | $12.26 |
| 6% tax | .74    |
| Total  | $13.00 |

**Solution**

*Method 1*   Estimate 10% and then add half of the estimate (5%) to obtain 15%.

If the bill is $12.26, 10% is about $1.22, and half of $1.22 is about $.60. A 15% tip is about $1.22 + $.60 ≈ $2.

*Method 2*   Find $\frac{1}{6}$ of the bill after rounding the total to a compatible number $\left(\frac{1}{6} \approx 16.7\%\right)$.

Estimate $\frac{1}{6}$ of $12.26. Round it to $\frac{1}{6}$ of $12, or $2. So the tip should be about $2.

*Method 3*   Multiply the tax by a whole number that will make it about 15%.

The tax is 6%. For an 18% tip, triple the tax ($2.22). Leave $2 or $2.25.  ■

## Lesson Exercise 7.67

Show how to use each of the three methods to estimate the tip on the following bill.

|       |        |
|-------|--------|
| Bill  | $8.79  |
| Tax   | $ .70  |
| Total | $9.49  |

## Answers to Selected Lesson Exercises

**7.58** (a) It is the number.     (b) 2     (c) 4

**7.59** (a) 10, 1, left     (b) 100, 2, left

**7.60** (a) 642     (b) 143     (c) 1000N

**7.61** The discount is $2.50, and the price is $22.50.

**7.62** 480,000

**7.63** (a) 1% of 200 = 2 and 2 × 6 = 12
(b) 10% of 12N = 1.2N and 1.2N × 4 = 4.8N

**7.64** 22% of 648 ≈ 20% of $650 = $130

**7.65** 4 out of 17 = $\frac{4}{17} \approx \frac{1}{4}$ = 25%

**7.67** 10% of 8.79 ≈ $.90; $.90 + $\frac{1}{2}$($.90) = $1.35

$\frac{1}{6}$ of $8.79 ≈ $\frac{1}{6}$ of $9 = $1.50; tax is 8% →
double it → ($.70) · 2 = $1.40

## 7.5   Homework Exercises

### Basic Exercises

1. How could you mentally compute each of the following?
   (a) 50% of 222     (b) 25% of 6
   (c) 10% of 470     (d) 1% of 37

2. A $400 television is selling at a 25% discount. Mentally compute its sales price.

3. A salesperson earns a 10% commission on $88 worth of sales. What is her commission?

4. How could you mentally compute each of the following?
   (a) 200% of 7     (b) 8% of 400
   (c) 75% of 12Y²

5. Many nutritionists recommend getting about 60% of your calories from carbohydrates. How could you mentally compute the number of calories in a 2000-calorie-per-day diet that should come from carbohydrates?

6. A $7000 Specific Motors Flounder Supersport is discounted by 6% from this list price. How could you mentally compute the dollar amount of the discount?

7. A quart of milk cost $.60 in 1988. By 1992, it had increased 20%. Explain how to compute mentally the 1992 price of a quart of milk.

8. Compute mentally and fill in each blank.
   (a) 50% of _____ is 22.
   (b) 25% of _____ is 80.
   (c) 20% of _____ is 110.

9. Compute mentally and fill in each blank.
   (a) 200% of _____ is 36.
   (b) 10% of _____ is 180.
   (c) 1% of _____ is 74.

10. A computer discounted 50% sells for $750. Mentally compute the original price.

11. (a) 50% of _____ is 4N.
    (b) 20% of _____ is N².
    (c) 80% of _____ is 20N.

12. (a) 38 is _____% of 100.
    (b) 11 is _____% of 50.
    (c) 21 is _____% of 25.
    (d) 50 is _____% of 40.

13. Estimate what percent of the square is shaded.

14. The best compatible-numbers estimate for 72% of 87 is
    (a) $\frac{1}{4}$ of 88     (b) $\frac{1}{2}$ of 90     (c) $\frac{3}{4}$ of 80

15.     $\frac{1}{3}$   $\frac{1}{5}$   $\frac{1}{7}$   $\frac{1}{10}$

    (a) Which of these fractions have a simple representation as a percent?

(b) Which of these fractions do not have a simple representation as a percent?

16. The Cereal Bowl seats 95,000. The stadium is 64% full for a clash between the Ballerinas and the Fieldmice. Explain how to estimate the attendance mentally.

17. The voting-age population in the United States is about 136 million, of which 56% vote in a presidential election. Explain how to estimate how many people vote.

18. If you take an extra summer job paying $4200, you will have 35% taken out of your paycheck in taxes. How could you estimate your take-home pay?

19. Use estimation to order the following expressions from smallest to largest.

| | |
|---|---|
| 80% of 28 | 52% of 807 |
| 37% of 420 | 19% of 400 |

20. Use estimation to tell whether the following calculator answers are reasonable. Explain why or why not.
    (a) 15% of 724 = $\boxed{10860}$
    (b) 22% of 58,000 = $\boxed{12760}$
    (c) 86% of 94 = $\boxed{109.3023256}$

21. For each computation, tell which computational method (mental computation, paper and pencil, or calculator) you would choose and why.
    (a) 42% of $736 (exact answer)
    (b) 42% of $736 (estimate)
    (c) 20% of $8000

22. Your luncheon at the Tastee Health Food Restaurant consisted of blanched tofu, holistic corn dogs, and milk-fed guacamole. The meal cost $9.50 plus tax. If the service was satisfactory, estimate how much you would leave for a tip.

Estimate the tip on the bills in Exercises 23–25.

23.
| | |
|---|---|
| Bill | $21.07 |
| 7% tax | $ 1.48 |
| Total | $22.55 |

24.
| | |
|---|---|
| Bill | $42.78 |
| Tax | 2.14 |
| Total | $44.92 |

25.
| | |
|---|---|
| Bill | $8.75 |
| Tax | .35 |
| Total | $9.10 |

*Extension Exercises*

26. When you borrow money with simple interest, the interest $I = PRT$, in which $P$ is the principal, $R$ is the rate of interest, and $T$ is the time in years. Show how to estimate the cost of borrowing $5400 at a rate of 12% for 2 years and 2 months.

27. Start with 100. Decrease it by 50%. Now increase your answer by 50%.
    (a) What number do you end up with?
    (b) Explain why you did not end up with 100.

28. Consider the following number trick.

    Pick a number.

    Multiply by 10.

    Add 50.

    Take 20% of the result.

    Subtract 10.

    Divide by 2.

    (a) Start with two or three different numbers and make a conjecture about what the trick does to any number.
    (b) Prove your generalization from part (a).

29. (a) Place the digits 4, 5, 6, 8, and 9 in the blanks to obtain an answer as close as possible to 300.

    __ __% of __ __ __ ≈ 300

    (b) Use a calculator to see how close you came.
    (c) Make a second guess and try to get closer to 300.
    (d) Check your second guess on a calculator.

**30.** Use estimation to fill in each blank with a number that will make the statement true. Check your guess with a calculator and revise it as needed.

(a) 42% of _____ is between 600 and 700.

(b) 64% of _____ is between 1000 and 1100.

(c) 7% of _____ is between 11 and 14.

**31.** Use estimation to order the following expressions from smallest to largest.

| | |
|---|---|
| 31% of 642 | 11% of 1000 |
| 48% of 117 | 86% of 90 |

**32.** If $A$ is 25% of $B$, then $B$ is _____% of $A$.

**33.** If $A$ is 25% more than $B$, then $B$ is _____% of $A$.

**34.** Consider the following problem. "The number of boys in a class is 25% the number of girls. What percent of the whole class is boys?"

(a) Devise a plan and solve the problem.

(b) Make up a similar problem and solve it.

## 7.6  Rational, Irrational, and Real Numbers

What is the relationship between rational numbers and decimals? Can all rational numbers be written as decimals? Do all decimals represent rational numbers?

### Rational Numbers as Decimals

The division model of fractions tells us that a rational number $\frac{p}{q}$ is the same as $p \div q$. Any rational fraction can be converted into a decimal by dividing the numerator by the denominator. What do rational fractions look like as decimals?

**D** Lesson Exercise 7.68

Change some rational fractions into decimals. Use long division rather than a calculator. What kind of decimals do you obtain?

Decimals come in three forms: terminating decimals, infinite repeating decimals, and infinite decimals that have no repeating block. Examples would be 0.3 (terminating), 0.313131 . . . (infinite repeating), and 0.31643847162 . . . (infinite with no repeating block). In the last decimal number, 0.31643847162 . . . , assume that there is no infinitely repeating block of digits.

## Lesson Exercise 7.69

Which of these three forms represent rational fractions?

As you may have surmised, all rational fractions can be represented by terminating or (infinite) repeating decimals. Why is this the case? In converting a rational fraction $\frac{p}{q}$ into a decimal, we divide $q$ into $p$. If at some point the division works out evenly, we have a **terminating decimal,** as is the case for $\frac{3}{8}$.

$$\frac{3}{8} = 8\overline{\smash{\big)}\,3.000}^{\,0.375}$$

If each step in the division has a remainder, the remainders will repeat at some point. For example, dividing 7 into 2 $\left(\text{or } \frac{2}{7}\right)$:

$$\frac{2}{7} = 7\overline{\smash{\big)}\,2.0^6 0^4 0^5 0^1 0^3 0^2 0^6 0^4 0\ldots}^{\,0.2\ 8\ 5\ 7\ 1\ 4\ 2\ 8\ 5\ldots}$$

↑<br>Remainders begin<br>to repeat.

Why must the remainders begin to repeat? In this case, with 7 as the divisor, there are only six possible remainders: 1, 2, 3, 4, 5, and 6, so the remainders must start to repeat after no more than six divisions.

A decimal such as 0.285714285714 . . . is a **repeating decimal,** with an infinite number of digits to the right of the decimal point and a repeating block of digits. A bar indicates that the block of digits beneath it repeats an infinite number of times.

$$0.\overline{285714} = 0.285714285714285714\ldots$$

If it is true that all terminating and repeating decimals are rational numbers, then it should be possible to convert any terminating or repeating decimal to a rational fraction. Do you know how to use place value to convert terminating decimals to fractions? Do so in Lesson Exercise 7.70.

## Lesson Exercise 7.70

Convert 0.072 into a fraction.

Infinite (repeating) decimals can be converted to fractions using patterns.

## Lesson Exercise 7.71

(a)  Convert $\frac{1}{9}$ and $\frac{2}{9}$ into decimals.

(b)  Based upon the pattern in part (a), write $\frac{7}{9}$ in decimal form.

(c)  Convert $\frac{1}{99}$ and $\frac{2}{99}$ to decimals.

(d)  Based upon the pattern in part (c), write $\frac{7}{99}$ in decimal form.

(e)  Based upon the pattern in part (c), write $\frac{13}{99}$ in decimal form. Use division to check your guess.

(f)  Based upon the patterns you have seen, conjecture how to write $\frac{278}{999}$ as a decimal.

The general formula suggested in the previous exercise is

$$0.\overline{a_1a_2a_3 \ldots a_n} = \frac{a_1a_2a_3 \ldots a_n}{10^n - 1}$$

in which $a_1 \ldots a_n$ are the digits. Note that the denominator has all 9's (i.e., 9, 99, 999, and so on), and the numerator contains the digits in the repeating block. Apply this formula in the following exercise.

## Lesson Exercise 7.72

Convert the following repeating decimals to fractions.
(a) $0.\overline{8}$     (b) $0.\overline{37}$     (c) $0.\overline{02714}$

The preceding examples and exercises suggest that any repeating or terminating decimal represents a rational number. Some other types of repeating decimals appear in the homework exercises.

## Irrational Numbers

All rational numbers can be written as terminating or repeating decimals.

## Lesson Exercise 7.73

What other kinds of decimals are there besides terminating and repeating decimals?

A **nonrepeating** (infinite) **decimal** has an infinite number of nonzero digits to the right of the decimal point, but it does not have an infinite repeating block of digits. Two famous examples begin as follows.

$$1.414213562419339\ldots$$
$$3.141592653589793\ldots$$

Nonrepeating decimals are called **irrational** (not rational) **numbers** because they cannot be written as rational fractions. The first irrational number ($\sqrt{2}$) was discovered over 2400 years ago, possibly by Pythagoras or one of his disciples. The discoverer probably found $\sqrt{2}$ as the length of the diagonal of a square with sides of length 1.

Using the Pythagorean Theorem (see Chapter 10)

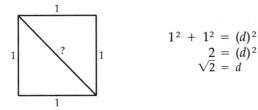

$$1^2 + 1^2 = (d)^2$$
$$2 = (d)^2$$
$$\sqrt{2} = d$$

People have used computers to determine $\sqrt{2}$ to millions of decimal places. And still it has no repeating block of numbers!

$\sqrt{2} = 1.41421\ \ 35624\ \ 19339\ \ 16628\ \ 19759\ \ 88713\ \ 07959\ldots$ and so on.

How did the ancient Greeks know they had discovered an irrational number? One of them wrote a deductive proof that the $\sqrt{2}$ is irrational. Aristotle describes the proof in one of his books. In order to prove that the $\sqrt{2}$ is irrational, we shall use the fact that the square of any counting number greater than 1 has an even number of factors in its prime factorization. For example, $36 = 2 \cdot 2 \cdot 3 \cdot 3$ and $400 = 2 \cdot 2 \cdot 2 \cdot 2 \cdot 5 \cdot 5$. (The prime factors come in pairs.)

## Lesson Exercise 7.74

Give another example of the square of a counting number and show that it has an even number of factors in its prime factorization.

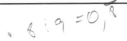

Now to show that $\sqrt{2}$ is irrational.

## Lesson Exercise 7.75

We'll assume that $\sqrt{2}$ is a *rational* number $\frac{p}{q}$ and show that this is impossible.

(a) Suppose $\sqrt{2} = \frac{p}{q}$ in which $p$ and $q$ are counting numbers. Square both sides and you obtain _____.

(b) Solve your equation from part (a) for $p^2$.

(c) So $2q^2 = p^2$. Imagine prime factoring $2q^2$ and $p^2$. Since $p^2$ is the square of a counting number, it has an _____ number

$$\text{(even, odd)}$$

of prime factors.

Since $2q^2$ is 2 times a perfect square, it has an _____

$$\text{(even, odd)}$$

number of prime factors.

In Lesson Exercise 7.75(c), you found that two equal numbers, $2q^2$ and $p^2$, appear to have different numbers of prime factors. This is impossible, according to the Fundamental Theorem of Arithmetic. Therefore, our assumption that $\sqrt{2} = \frac{p}{q}$ must be wrong, since all our deductive reasoning from that point on was valid. Thus, $\sqrt{2}$ is irrational!

## Lesson Exercise 7.76

(a) Name two more square roots that you think are irrational numbers.

(b) Name a square root that *is* a rational number.

Soon after the Greeks proved that $\sqrt{2}$ is irrational, they proved that the square roots of 3, 5, 6, 7, 8, 10, 11, 12, 13, 14, 15, and 17 are also irrational.

The most famous irrational number of all is $\pi$. For thousands of years, people wondered how the distance around a circle (the circumference) compared to the distance across the circle through the center (the diameter).

**D** Lesson Exercise 7.77

 To measure in this problem, you will need a string and a ruler. (A compass would also be useful.)

(a) Draw three circles of different sizes.
(b) Measure the circumference $C$ and diameter $d$ of each and complete the following chart.

*Handwritten:* $9\frac{1}{2} + 2\frac{3}{4}$

| C | d | C + d | C − d | C × d | C ÷ d |
|---|---|-------|-------|-------|-------|
| 14 | 4¼ | 18 ¼ | 9 3/4 | 59.5 | 3.29 |
| 3 | ¾ | 3 3/4 | 2 1/4 | 9/4 | |
| 9 1/2 | ¾ | 12 1/4 | $9\frac{1}{2} - 2\frac{3}{4}$ | | |

*Handwritten (right side):*
$14 \times 4\frac{1}{2} = 56\frac{1}{2}$

$14 : 4 = 7$

$3 \cdot \frac{3}{4} = \frac{9}{4}$

$14 \cdot$

$9\frac{1}{2} - 2\frac{3}{4}$

$9\frac{1}{2} \cdot$

$C : d = \pi$

$C = d \cdot \pi$

(c) Which of the last four columns have answers that are about the same?
(d) What generalization does part (c) suggest?

Did you find that $\dfrac{C}{d}$ is always a little more than 3? The exact quotient is represented by the symbol $\pi$. By definition, $\pi = \dfrac{C}{d}$, or $C = \pi d$.

At first, people assumed that $\pi$ would be a simple number such as 3 or 3.1. The Rhind Papyrus (1650? B.C.) shows that the Egyptians used a value of $\pi \approx 3.16$ to solve problems involving circles. Archimedes (240 B.C.) found the value of $\pi$ to two decimal places as 3.14. Archimedes drew inscribed and circumscribed polygons around a circle and computed their perimeter (Figure 7-15).

He knew that the perimeter of the circle was in between these two numbers. But it was not until 1761 that Johann Lambert *proved* that $\pi$ is irrational. In 1989, Gregory and David Chudnosky of Columbia University used two computers to calculate $\pi$ to 1,011,196,691 decimal places.

$$\pi = 3.14159 \ \ 26535 \ \ 89793 \ \ 23846 \ \ 26434 \ldots$$

**Figure 7-15**

**Lesson Exercise 7.78**

A wheel has a diameter of 30 in. Approximate its circumference.

## Real Numbers

**Real numbers** are all numbers that can be written as decimal numbers. The set of real numbers is the union of two sets: the rational numbers and the irrational numbers.

## Lesson Exercise 7.79

Give two examples of real numbers.

The following chart compares the two types of real numbers: rational and irrational.

**Real Numbers**

| Rational numbers | Repeating or terminating decimals |
| --- | --- |
| Irrational numbers | Infinite nonrepeating decimals |

All of the numbers in this book can be organized into an overall set picture.

**Real Numbers**

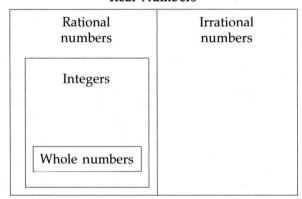

You may be wondering if there are any other kinds of numbers besides real numbers. In order to find solutions to $x^2 = a$, in which $a < 0$, we need imaginary numbers such as $\sqrt{-3}$, which are covered in some high-school and college mathematics courses.

### Example 7.19

Which of the following describe 2.6?
(a) a whole number          (d) an irrational number
(b) an integer              (e) a real number
(c) a rational number

**Solution**

2.6 is not a whole number or integer because of the .6. 2.6 is rational because it can be written as $\frac{26}{10}$. Since 2.6 is rational, it cannot be irrational. Since 2.6 is rational, it is also a real number.  ■

## Lesson Exercise 7.80

Complete the following chart by placing a $\checkmark$ in the appropriate columns.

|  | Whole Number | Integer | Rational Number | Irrational Number | Real Number |
|---|---|---|---|---|---|
| **2.6** |  |  | $\checkmark$ |  | $\checkmark$ |
| **3** |  |  |  |  |  |
| $\sqrt{2}$ |  |  |  |  |  |
| **−1** |  |  |  |  |  |
| $-2\frac{1}{2}$ |  |  |  |  |  |

## Multiple Representations of Real Numbers

Why do we need both fractions and decimals to represent quantities? Each notation has its advantages. Sometimes it is easier to represent a number as a fraction than as a decimal, and sometimes it isn't.

## Lesson Exercise 7.81

State whether each quantity is easier to represent *with a fraction* than with a decimal.

(a) $\frac{1}{10}$   (b) $\frac{1}{11}$   (c) $\frac{3}{7}$   (d) $-\frac{4}{5}$

It is usually easier to compare the size of numbers in decimal form than in fraction form.

### Lesson Exercise 7.82

If you have a calculator, what is an easy way to determine whether $\frac{3}{8}$ or $\frac{11}{29}$ is larger?

Some addition problems are easier to do with fractions; some are easier with decimals.

### Lesson Exercise 7.83

State whether you think each addition problem is easier to do with fractions or with decimals.

(a) $\frac{2}{7} + \frac{3}{7}$ or $0.\overline{285714} + 0.\overline{428571}$     (b) $\frac{1}{4} + \frac{7}{100}$ or $0.25 + 0.07$

(c) Describe more generally when it is easier to do addition with fractions and when it is easier to use decimals.

In some problems, the preferred choice of notation may depend upon whether you want an exact or an approximate answer.

### Lesson Exercise 7.84

Last year, your salary increased from $21,000 to $27,000, an increase of $28\frac{4}{7}\%$ or 28.6%.

(a) Classify each percent as exact or approximate.
(b) Describe an advantage of each answer.

### Lesson Exercise 7.85

The numbers $\frac{25}{100}$, $\frac{1}{4}$, 0.25, and 25% all represent the same amount. For each representation, describe a situation in which it would be the best choice. For example, $\frac{25}{100}$ would be the appropriate notation for writing a check.

Why do we use special irrational number symbols (such as $\sqrt{2}$ and $\pi$) and decimal representations for the same numbers?

Lesson Exercise 7.86

(a) Why is it easier to write $\sqrt{273}$ than its decimal representation?
(b) A farmer wants to buy some fencing. You determine that the amount of fence he needs is $\sqrt{273}$ ft. What would be a more useful way to give the farmer the information?

## Rational Number Properties Retained!

What properties do real numbers have? Real-number operations retain all the properties of rational numbers! The following list summarizes these properties.

---

**Properties of Real-Number Operations**

Addition, subtraction, and multiplication of real numbers are closed.

Addition and multiplication of real numbers are commutative.

Addition and multiplication of real numbers are associative.

The unique additive identity for real numbers is 0, and the unique multiplicative identity for real numbers is 1.

All real numbers have a unique additive inverse that is real, and all nonzero real numbers have a unique multiplicative inverse that is real.

Multiplication is distributive over addition, and multiplication is distributive over subtraction for the set of real numbers.

---

The following exercises make use of these properties.

## Lesson Exercise 7.87

Give an example showing that real-number (decimal) addition is commutative.

## Lesson Exercise 7.88

$3.6 + -3.6 = -3.6 + 3.6 = 0$ illustrates what property of real numbers?

## Lesson Exercise 7.89

Using the distributive property of multiplication over addition for real numbers, $2x + \sqrt{2}x =$ _____ for all real numbers $x$. What about real subtraction and division?

## Lesson Exercise 7.90

The real numbers include all the other sets of numbers in Chapters 3, 5, and 6. If a property such as the associative property for subtraction does not work for whole numbers, explain why it could not work for real numbers.

Some of the properties of all the number systems you have studied are summarized in the following chart.

| Property | Operation | Whole Numbers | Integers | Rational Numbers | Irrational Numbers | Real Numbers |
|----------|-----------|---------------|----------|------------------|--------------------|--------------|
| COMMUTATIVE | + | ✓ | ✓ | ✓ | ✓ | ✓ |
|  | × | ✓ | ✓ | ✓ | ✓ | ✓ |
| ASSOCIATIVE | + | ✓ | ✓ | ✓ | ✓ | ✓ |
|  | × | ✓ | ✓ | ✓ | ✓ | ✓ |
| IDENTITY | + | ✓ | ✓ | ✓ |  | ✓ |
|  | × | ✓ | ✓ | ✓ |  | ✓ |
| INVERSES | + |  | ✓ | ✓ |  | ✓ |
|  | × |  |  | ✓ |  | ✓ |

## Lesson Exercise 7.91

Tell why 0 cannot be the additive identity and 1 cannot be the multiplicative identity for irrational numbers.

## The Completeness Property

I'll bet you've worked with a lot of number lines in your time. What set of numbers would fill up the entire number line? The rational numbers are dense, but they don't fill up the whole number line. There are gaps between them. For example, between 1 and 2, we find $\sqrt{2}$ and $\sqrt{3}$, which are not rational. It takes both the rational and irrational numbers together—the real numbers—to fill up the number line completely.

The capacity of the real numbers to fill up the entire number line is called the **completeness property.**

---

**Completeness Property for Real Numbers**

Every point on the number line corresponds to a real number, and every real number corresponds to a point on the number line.

---

## Lesson Exercise 7.92

Explain why the set of integers does not complete the number line.

---

## Answers to Selected Lesson Exercises

**7.68** terminating and infinite repeating

**7.69** terminating and repeating

**7.70** $\dfrac{9}{125}$

**7.71** (a) $0.\overline{1}$ and $0.\overline{2}$     (b) $0.\overline{7}$
     (c) $0.\overline{01}$ and $0.\overline{02}$    (d) $0.\overline{07}$
     (e) $0.\overline{13}$            (f) $0.\overline{278}$

**7.72** (a) $\dfrac{8}{9}$   (b) $\dfrac{37}{99}$   (c) $\dfrac{2714}{99,999}$

**7.73** infinite nonrepeating

**7.74** $81 = 3 \cdot 3 \cdot 3 \cdot 3$

**7.75** (a) $2 = \dfrac{p^2}{q^2}$    (b) $p^2 = 2q^2$
     (c) even, odd

**7.76** (a) $\sqrt{3}$ and $\sqrt{34}$    (b) $\sqrt{4}$

**7.78** 94.2 in.

**7.79** 3, 8.765

**7.80** 3 is whole integer, rational, real; $\sqrt{2}$ is irrational and real; $-1$ is integer, rational, real; $-2\dfrac{1}{2}$ is rational and real

**7.81** (a) no    (b) yes    (c) yes    (d) no

**7.82** For each fraction, divide the numerator into the denominator and compare the decimal representations.

**7.83** (a) fractions    (b) decimals
     (c) Fractions are easier when you have a common denominator that has factors other than 2 and 5. Decimals are easier for fractions that are easily converted to decimals.

**7.84** (a) The fraction is exact; the decimal is approximate.
     (b) The fraction is more precise. The decimal is usually easier to work with.

**7.85** The fraction $\dfrac{1}{4}$ could be a probability, 0.25 an amount of money, and 25% a tax rate.

**7.86** (a) The decimal representation is an infinite nonrepeating decimal.
     (b) Give a decimal approximation of $\sqrt{273}$.

**7.90** All counterexamples for whole numbers are also counterexamples for real numbers.

**7.91** They are not part of the set of irrational numbers.

**7.92** There are numbers in between any two integers. For example, $\dfrac{1}{2}$ is on the number line between 0 and 1 and $\dfrac{1}{2}$ is not an integer.

## 7.6   Homework Exercises

*Basic Exercises*

1. Convert the following fractions to decimals.
   (a) $\frac{3}{5}$     (b) $2\frac{2}{9}$

2. Convert the following decimals to fractions.
   (a) 0.731     (b) −13.04

3. Which is larger, $0.\overline{34}$ or $0.3\overline{4}$?

4. Convert the following decimals to fractions.
   (a) $0.\overline{4}$     (b) $0.\overline{32}$     (c) $0.\overline{267}$

5. Convert the following decimals to fractions.
   (a) $52.\overline{35}$     (b) $0.\overline{3917}$     (c) $0.\overline{9}$

6. One can use the results from the lesson to convert other types of repeating decimals to fractions. For example,

$$0.43\overline{2} = \frac{43\frac{2}{9}}{100} = \frac{\frac{389}{9}}{100} = \frac{389}{900}$$

   Use this method to convert the following decimals to fractions.
   (a) $0.2\overline{1}$     (b) $0.3\overline{41}$

7. Make up a geometric problem whose answer is $\sqrt{5}$.

8. The origin of $\pi$ was in computing the ratio of the _____ to the _____ .

9. A wheel has a circumference of 76 in. What is its diameter?

10. Make up an algebraic equation (other than $x = \sqrt{3}$) with a solution of $x = \sqrt{3}$.

11. (a) Find the value of $\sqrt{5}$ on a calculator.
    (b) Why can't this number be the exact value of $\sqrt{5}$?

12. (a) Enter any positive number. Press the square root key repeatedly. What number do you reach eventually?

(b) Repeat part (a), starting with a different number.
(c) Generalize your results.

13. Classify the following numbers as rational or irrational.
    (a) $\sqrt{11}$     (b) $\frac{3}{7}$     (c) $\pi$     (d) $\sqrt{16}$

14. Classify the following as rational or irrational.
    (a) 0.333. . .
    (b) 0.817
    (c) 0.42638275643. . .
    (d) 0.121121112. . .

15. Police can estimate the speed $s$ (in miles per hour) of a car by the length $L$ (in feet) of its skid marks. On a dry highway, $s \approx \sqrt{24L}$. On a wet highway, $s \approx \sqrt{12L}$.
    (a) Estimate the speed of a car that leaves 54-ft skid marks on a wet highway.
    (b) Estimate the speed of a car that leaves 54-ft skid marks on a dry highway.
    (c) Classify your answers to parts (a) and (b) as rational or irrational.

16. On a clear day, the distance $D$ in kilometers you can see to the horizon from a height of $H$ meters is given by

$$D = \frac{\sqrt{H}}{3.57}$$

    (a) How far can you see from a height of 40 m?
    (b) Graph $D$ vs. $H$ for $0 \le H \le 100$.

17. A pendulum is constructed by tying a weight on a string. The time to make one complete

swing back and forth depends upon the length of the string.

| Length in cm | → | Take square root | → | Divide by 5 | → | Time in seconds |

(a) How long would a 40-cm pendulum take to complete one swing?

(b) A pendulum takes 4 seconds to complete a swing. How long is the pendulum?

(c) A formula relating time $T$ to length $L$ is $T =$ _____ .

(d) A formula relating length $L$ to time $T$ is $L =$ _____ .

**18.** Match each word in column $A$ to a word in column $B$.

| $A$ | $B$ |
| --- | --- |
| Terminating | Rational |
| Repeating | Irrational |
| Infinite nonrepeating | |

**19.** Your calculator display shows $\boxed{0.3333333}$ . Name two different exact values this might represent.

**20.** Your calculator display shows $\boxed{2.9999999}$ . Name two different exact values this might represent.

**21.** Complete the chart.

| | Whole | Integer | Rational | Irrational | Real |
| --- | --- | --- | --- | --- | --- |
| $\frac{1}{3}$ | | | ✓ | | ✓ |
| $\sqrt{13}$ | | | | | |
| $-6$ | | | | | |
| $\sqrt{9}$ | | | | | |
| $-0.317$ | | | | | |

**22.** Complete the chart.

| | Whole | Integer | Rational | Irrational | Real |
| --- | --- | --- | --- | --- | --- |
| $\sqrt{\frac{7}{2}}$ | | | | ✓ | ✓ |
| 4.21 | | | | | |
| $-\sqrt{16}$ | | | | | |
| $\pi$ | | | | | |
| 51 | | | | | |

**23.** True or false? All rational numbers are real numbers.

**24.** Draw a Venn diagram with the following sets: real numbers, rational numbers, whole numbers.

**25.** (a) How many whole numbers are there between 3 and $-3$? (This would not include 3 and $-3$.)

(b) How many integers are there between 3 and $-3$?

(c) How many real numbers are there between 3 and $-3$?

**26.** State whether each quantity is easier to represent *with a fraction* than a decimal.

(a) $\frac{1}{3}$   (b) $\frac{3.}{20}$   (c) $\frac{5}{2}$

**27.** State whether each quantity is easier to represent *with a fraction* than a decimal.

(a) $-\frac{14}{50}$   (b) $8\frac{1}{6}$   (c) $\frac{9}{10}$

28. If you have a calculator, what is an easy way to determine which fraction is larger, $\frac{5}{7}$ or $\frac{12}{17}$?

29. Make up an addition problem that is easier to do with fractions than with decimals.

30. Make up a subtraction problem that is easier to do with decimals than with fractions.

31. Name a fraction that is difficult to represent as a percent.

32. A telephone company plans to raise monthly rates by 3%, which amounts to $28 million. Which number would probably be more upsetting to consumers?

33. In school, 3.14 and $\frac{22}{7}$ are often used as approximations for $\pi = 3.141592654 \ldots$. Which school approximation is closer to the actual value of $\pi$?

34. Different mathematicians have used decimal and fraction approximations for $\pi$. Which of the following is closest to $\pi = 3.141592654 \ldots$?
    (a) Babylonians (around 1700 B.C.): $\frac{25}{8}$
    (b) Archimedes (around 200 B.C.): $\frac{223}{71}$
    (c) Tsu Ch'ung-chih (around A.D. 480): $\frac{355}{113}$
    (d) Bhaskara (around A.D. 1150): $\frac{3927}{1250}$

35. Why is it easier to use the symbol $\pi$ than its decimal representation?

36. The distance around a running track is $50\pi + 360$ yds.
    (a) What is a more useful way to express this distance?
    (b) Is your answer to part (a) exact or approximate?

37. People reporting measurements usually state a margin of error. For example, $16.0 \pm 0.2$ cm means the actual measure is somewhere between $16.0 - 0.2 = 15.8$ cm and $16.0 + 0.2 = 16.2$ cm. Give the highest and lowest value of each of the following.
    (a) an SAT score of $520 \pm 30$ points
    (b) A candidate is preferred by $64\% \pm 2\%$.
    (c) The length is $35 \pm 1$ ft.

38. Which real-number operations are associative?

39. $0.37 + 0.516 = 0.516 + 0.37$ illustrates the _____ property of _____ .

40. What properties guarantee that for any decimal $x$, $-4x + 3 + 5.5 + 6x = (-4x + 6x) + (3 + 5.5)$?

41. What is the additive inverse of $-0.41798$?

42. What is the multiplicative inverse of $0.1$?

43. Give a counterexample that shows that real-number subtraction is not commutative.

44. What is the easiest way to multiply $0.6 \times 4.2 \times 5$?

45. How would you mentally compute $6.5 \times 8$?

46. According to the distributive property of multiplication over subtraction, $6.4x - 2.1x =$ _____ .

47. Give an example showing that real-number addition is not distributive over multiplication.

48. Tell whether each equation is true for no real number, some real number or numbers, or all real numbers.
    (a) $x \cdot 1 = x$
    (b) $2x - 4 = 10$
    (c) $2 + x = x$

49. Tell whether each equation is true for no real numbers, some pairs of real numbers, or all pairs of real numbers.
    (a) $x + y = 3$
    (b) $xy = yx$
    (c) $x + y = x + y + 3$

50. What property do real numbers have that rational numbers do not have?

51. Explain why the set of rational numbers does not complete the number line.

**52.** Explain why the set of whole numbers is not complete.

*Extension Exercises*

**53.** (a) Which of the following fractions can be rewritten with a denominator of 10, 100, 1000, etc.?

(1) $\frac{4}{5}$    (2) $\frac{3}{25}$

(3) $\frac{7}{9}$    (4) $\frac{3}{200}$    (5) $\frac{1}{7}$

(b) Which fractions in part (a) can be represented by terminating decimals?
(c) Prime factor each denominator in part (a).
(d) Try to generalize your results by filling in the blanks. Fractions (in simplest form) that can be rewritten as terminating decimals have denominators that are divisible by no prime number other than _____ or _____ .

**54.** As the preceding exercise suggests, a rational number $\frac{a}{b}$ in simplest form is a terminating decimal if and only if $b$ is divisible by no prime numbers other than 2 or 5. Factor the denominator of each fraction and determine whether it is a terminating or repeating decimal.

(a) $\frac{8}{9}$    (b) $\frac{7}{500}$    (c) $\frac{11}{30}$    (d) $\frac{7}{20}$

**55.** If $\frac{x}{y}$ is a rational number in simplest fraction form, with $y > x > 0$ and $y = 2^a \cdot 5^b$ for whole numbers $a$ and $b$, how are $a$ and $b$ related to the number of digits in the terminating decimal representation of $\frac{x}{y}$?

**56.** According to Einstein's Theory of Relativity, something strange happens to the mass of an object that moves at a velocity close to the speed of light. The mass $m$ at velocity $v$ is

$$m = \frac{m_0}{\sqrt{1 - \dfrac{v^2}{c^2}}}$$

in which $m_0$ is the mass at rest and $c$ is the speed of light.
(a) If an object moves at a velocity of $0.8c$, what is its mass?
(b) What do you think happens to the mass as the velocity gets closer to $c$?
(c) Find the mass at a velocity of $0.99c$.

**57.** A common algebraic error is to assume that $\sqrt{M + N} = \sqrt{M} + \sqrt{N}$ for all real numbers $M$ and $N$. For what decimal values of $M$ and $N$ does $\sqrt{M + N} = \sqrt{M} + \sqrt{N}$? Make an educated guess after trying some examples.

**58.** Consider the following problem. "Name two irrational numbers whose product is 6."
(a) Devise a plan and solve the problem.
(b) Make up a similar problem.

**59.** Are the real numbers dense? That is, between any two real numbers, is there another real number? Try the following to find out.
(a) Find a real number between 1.41 and 1.42.
(b) Find a real number between 1.41 and $\sqrt{2}$ ($\sqrt{2} = 1.4142135\ldots$) if you can.
(c) Do you think that the real numbers are dense?

**60.** Is $\sqrt{5} - 2$ rational or irrational?

**61.** The sum of a rational number and an irrational number is
(a) rational    (b) irrational
(c) could be either

**62.** (a) $0.010110111\ldots + 0.101001000\ldots$

= _____

(b) Part (a) shows that the sum of two _____ numbers can be a _____ number.

**63.** True or false? If $x > 0$, then $x + \frac{1}{x} \geq 2$. If it is true, prove it. If it is false, find a counterexample.

**64.** Prove that $\sqrt{3}$ is not rational.

**65.** Prove that $\sqrt[3]{2}$ is not rational.

## Summary

The rules for decimal place value and arithmetic are extensions of the rules for whole-number place value and arithmetic. The primary question in decimal arithmetic is where to place the decimal point in the answer. The rules for placing decimal points can be explained using place value and rational-number properties. The models for whole-number operations apply to many decimal problems.

Decimal estimation relies primarily on the same strategies as fraction estimation, namely, rounding and the compatible-numbers strategy. One can mentally multiply or divide a decimal number by a power of 10 by moving the decimal point of the number. This same technique is used in converting a decimal number into scientific notation, an exponential shorthand used by scientists.

Many everyday applications of mathematics involve proportional relationships. A proportion states that two ratios are equal. Proportions with one missing quantity can be solved using cross products, or more intuitively, with a unitary or multiplier approach. Common ratios that occur in proportion problems include male-female ratios, student-teacher ratios, and miles per gallon. Proportions also occur in situations involving water bills, real estate taxes, map scales, surveys, and foreign currency rates.

Percents developed from the use of hundredths in fractions and decimals. People use percents to describe taxes, inflation, interest rates, finance charges, salary increases, discounts, and test scores. In all these cases, percents give the rate per 100. These applications of percents can usually be solved with algebra or proportions and modeled by number line pictures.

It is helpful to know the fraction equivalents of some basic percentages in order to compute some percentage problems mentally using shortcuts. Rounding can be used to estimate solutions to many other percentage problems.

The set of all decimal numbers is called the real numbers. Decimals are either terminating, infinite repeating, or infinite nonrepeating decimals. Terminating and repeating decimals represent rational numbers. With rational numbers, one has the option of using either decimal or fraction notation.

Nonrepeating decimals are called irrational numbers. Examples of irrational numbers include $\sqrt{2}$, $\sqrt{5}$, and $\pi$. The only way to write the exact value of an irrational square root or $\pi$ is to use a special symbol.

Real-number operations possess all the properties that whole-number, integer, and rational-number operations possess. The real numbers also satisfy the completeness property.

## Study Guide

To review Chapter 7, see what you know about each of the following ideas or terms listed that you have studied. You can also use this list to generate your own questions about Chapter 7.

# The NCTM Curriculum Standards and Decimals, Percents, and Real Numbers

**Selected NCTM Curriculum Standards**

The following standards come from the NCTM document.

- Extend their understanding of whole number operations to decimals.
- Apply decimals to problem situations.
- Develop, analyze, and explain procedures for computation and techniques for estimation.
- Develop number sense for decimals.
- Develop, analyze, and explain methods for solving proportions.
- Understand and apply ratios, proportions, and percents to a wide variety of situations.
- Investigate relationships among fractions, decimals, and percents.
- Understand, represent, and use numbers in a variety of equivalent forms (fraction, decimal, percent, and scientific notation) in real-world and mathematical problem situations.

1. Describe how each standard listed relates to the material you studied in Chapter 7.
2. Select any current elementary-school mathematics textbook series and describe a sample lesson or exercise that illustrates each standard listed.

## Review Exercises

1. (a) Write 0.0037 in expanded notation.
   (b) Write 0.0037 in scientific notation.

2. Use decimal square pictures to explain why $0.3 > 0.25$.

3. It took $G$ gallons of paint to paint 3 classrooms. How much paint would it take to paint $C$ similar classrooms?

4. While you are on a trip, you buy a $9.49 shirt. The cashier charges you $10.06. What percent is the sales tax?

5. If 100 balloons cost $.76, *explain* how you would mentally compute the charge per balloon.

 6. Consider the following problem. "The average 130-pound person needs 2000 calories per day. How many calories does the average 150-pound person need?
   (a) Solve the problem with a proportion.
   (b) Show how to solve the problem without writing a proportion.

7. If $\sqrt{m} > m$, what are the possible values of $m$?

 8. In a presidential election, 44 million people voted. This represented 52% of the registered voters. How many registered voters were there?

9. The price of a dress is marked down 30%. Then it is marked down an additional 20%. Find a single percent discount equal to these two successive discounts.

10. Complete the last example, repeating the same error pattern in the completed examples.

    $6 \div 0.3 = 0.2$     $0.8 \div 0.4 = 0.02$
    $1.2 \div 0.3 =$ _____

11. *Explain* how to compute 1% of $7250 mentally.

12. Use fractions to show why $42 \div 0.06$ is the same as $4200 \div 6$.

13. $42.764764 \div 0.48917563645639$ is about
    (a) 9    (b) 40    (c) 1    (d) 90    (e) 20

14. *Explain* how to compute 150% of 46 mentally.

15. What operation and category are illustrated in the following problem? "A man loses 8 lb in 10 days. What is his average weight loss per day?"

16. What operation and category are illustrated in the following problem? "Before driving to work, your odometer reads 26,872.6 miles. When you arrive at work, it reads 26,880.4. How long is the drive?"

17. $\sqrt{17}$ is
    (a) a whole number
    (b) an integer
    (c) a rational number
    (d) an irrational number
    (e) a real number

18. Name a property that real numbers have that the whole numbers do not.

19. Give an example of the distributive property of multiplication over subtraction for real numbers.

20. Write 23.7 million in scientific notation.

21. Explain how to compute $0.2 \times 0.3$ using decimal square pictures.

# Computer Exercise

1. Algebra students sometimes ask about the equation in line 30 of each BASIC program. Try different numbers with the computer and find out what real numbers make the equation true.

    (a) 10 PRINT "TYPE 3 REAL NUMBERS SEPARATED BY COMMAS."
    20 INPUT A, B, C
    30 IF A * (B * C) = A * B * A * C THEN PRINT "YES"
    40 IF A * (B * C) >< A * B * A * C THEN PRINT "NO"

    (b) 10 PRINT "TYPE 2 REAL NUMBERS SEPARATED BY COMMAS."
    20 INPUT A, B
    30 IF (A − B) * (A + B) = (A * A − B * B) THEN PRINT "YES"
    40 IF (A − B) * (A + B) >< (A * A − B * B) THEN PRINT "NO"

    (c) SQR is the square root function in BASIC.

    10 PRINT "TYPE 2 REAL NUMBERS SEPARATED BY COMMAS."
    20 INPUT A, B
    30 IF SQR(A + B) = SQR(A) + SQR(B) THEN PRINT "YES"
    40 IF SQR(A + B) >< SQR(A) + SQR(B) THEN PRINT "NO"

## Decimals and Percents in Elementary School

The following chart shows at what grade level selected decimal topics typically appear in elementary-school mathematics textbooks.

| Topic | Typical Grade Level in Current Textbooks |
|---|---|
| Decimal place value | 3, 4, <u>5</u>, <u>6</u> |
| Decimal addition and subtraction | 3, <u>4</u>, <u>5</u>, 6 |
| Decimal multiplication | 5, <u>6</u> |
| Decimal division | 5, <u>6</u> |
| Ratio | 5, 6 |
| Proportion | 6 |
| Percents | 5, <u>6</u>, |
| Decimal estimation | 4, 5, 6 |
| Scientific notation | 6 (enrichment topic) |

## Suggested Readings

*Arithmetic Teacher*. February, 1989 Focus Issue on Number Sense. Reston, VA: NCTM, 1989.

Davis, P. *The Lore of Large Numbers*. New York: Random House, 1961.

National Council of Teachers of Mathematics. *A Sourcebook of Applications of School Mathematics*. Washington, DC: MAA, 1980.

National Council of Teachers of Mathematics. 1969 Yearbook. *More Topics in Mathematics for Elementary School Teachers*. Reston, VA: NCTM, 1969.

National Council of Teachers of Mathematics. 1992 Yearbook. *Calculators in Mathematics Education*. Reston, VA: NCTM, 1992.

# 8

# Introductory Geometry

The oldest recorded examples of geometry are ancient cave drawings of circles, squares, and triangles. Ancient pottery and weaving include examples of geometric designs. The root meaning of the word "geometry" is "earth measure," which derives from the use of geometry by the Egyptians and Babylonians in land surveying over 4000 years ago. The Egyptians and Babylonians also used geometry in agriculture, architecture, and astronomy. The Great Pyramid of Gizeh in Egypt has a square base with sides that are all 756 ft long, with an error of less than 1 inch!

About 2500 years ago, the Greeks developed an important new approach to geometry, organizing geometric ideas into a logical sequence. They began with the most basic figures and terms and deduced all other concepts of plane geometry.

Today, school geometry follows this historical sequence. Children first study geometry in an informal, concrete manner. Then, in high school, many students study geometry using a more formal, deductive approach.

## 8.1 Beginning Geometry

We all begin geometry when we notice shapes in our surroundings. Children come to elementary school with an awareness of objects and shapes. School geometry builds upon this awareness by beginning with space figures and plane figures suggested by objects in the environment. Then, a more systematic study of geometry begins with the most basic figures—points, lines, and planes—and proceeds in a deductive sequence.

## Shapes in Our World

The informal study of geometry begins with objects in our environment.

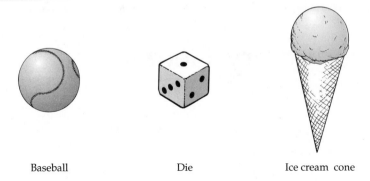

Baseball                    Die                    Ice cream  cone

The surfaces of objects also suggest geometric figures.

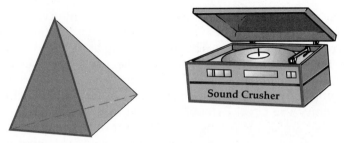

Sound Crusher

Geometric shapes are idealized versions of objects we see.

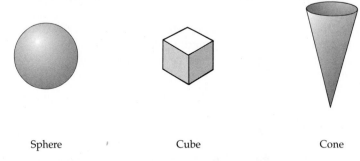

Sphere              Cube                  Cone

According to Plato, the perfect geometric shapes in our minds are part of the ultimate reality, whereas objects in the world are imperfect.

**D** Lesson Exercise 8.1

(a) Find three objects in your classroom that suggest common geometric figures.
(b) Find surfaces of three objects in your classroom that suggest common geometric figures.

## Points, Lines, and Planes

After an initial introduction to geometry through shapes suggested by objects, how should one begin a more systematic study of geometry? In his famous book, *The Elements*, Euclid (300 B.C.?) begins **Euclidean geometry** with a description of points, lines, and planes. "Point," "line," and "plane" are undefined terms that we can understand using everyday objects and our intuition. Points, lines, and planes are suggested by our surroundings, as shown in Figure 8-1.

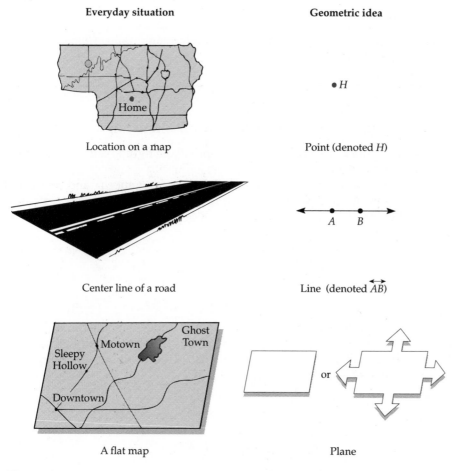

**Everyday situation**

Location on a map

Center line of a road

A flat map

**Geometric idea**

• *H*

Point (denoted *H*)

Line (denoted $\overleftrightarrow{AB}$)

Plane

**Figure 8-1**

A location on a map and a grain of sand suggest a point. A **point** represents an exact location. A taut wire and the center line on a road suggest a line. A **line** is straight; it extends indefinitely in two directions and has no thickness. The arrows on a line indicate that it extends without limit.

A map and a piece of paper suggest a plane. A **plane** is flat; it has no thickness, and it extends endlessly in all directions.

Mathematicians and philosophers have debated where geometric ideas such as a line come from. Why all the fuss, you ask? Because, in your whole life, you will never see a geometric line!

**D** Lesson Exercise 8.2

How does a geometric line differ from a drawing of a line?

**D** Lesson Exercise 8.3

(a) True or false? If $A$ and $B$ are points in a plane, then $\overleftrightarrow{AB}$ lies entirely in the plane.
(b) Draw a picture that supports your answer.

## Plane Figures, Space Figures, and Dimension

A **plane figure** is a set of points in a plane. Plane figures can be zero-, one-, or two-dimensional.

People use the term "dimension" in everyday speech and in art, but the concept of dimension is quite difficult to explain precisely. A point is **zero-dimensional;** it is just a location. A set of discrete points is also zero-dimensional.

• <br>
•   •   • <br>
•

Zero-dimensional figures

To generate a **one-dimensional figure,** move a point through a distance. A line, for example, is one-dimensional; it has length but no thickness. Informally, any shape that is constructed from an "infinitely thin" wire is also one-dimensional (Figure 8-2).

One-dimensional figures

**Figure 8-2**

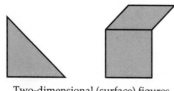

Two-dimensional (surface) figures

**Figure 8-3**

Move a line through a distance to generate a two-dimensional figure. Any plane figure that is not zero- or one-dimensional is **two-dimensional.** Informally, any shape that is constructed from an "infinitely thin" piece of paper is two-dimensional. Two-dimensional figures have area but no volume (Figure 8-3).

A **three-dimensional** or **space figure** does not lie in a single plane, and it has volume. Informally, any shape that is constructed from modeling clay is three-dimensional.

## Lesson Exercise 8.4

What is the dimension (0, 1, 2, or 3) of the geometric figure *suggested* by each of the following?
(a) a very thin string       (b) a gorilla       (c) a map

## Line Segments, Rays, and Angles

After introducing the terms "point" and "line," Euclid uses these terms to define line segments and rays. Line segments and rays are suggested by our surroundings, as shown in Figure 8-4.

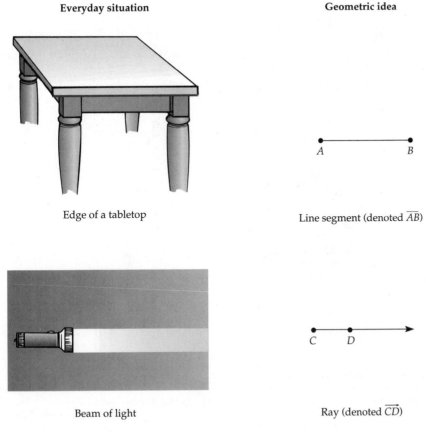

| Everyday situation | Geometric idea |
| --- | --- |
| Edge of a tabletop | Line segment (denoted $\overline{AB}$) |
| Beam of light | Ray (denoted $\overrightarrow{CD}$) |

**Figure 8-4**

## Lesson Exercise 8.5

Try to write definitions of "line segment" and "ray" using the terms "point" and "line."

Line segments and rays are subsets of a line. A **line segment** consists of two points on a line and all the points between them. The idea of making a line segment out of points is used in dot-matrix printers and stadium scoreboards, as shown in Figure 8-5.

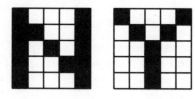

Figure 8-5

A **ray** (for example, $\overrightarrow{CD}$ in Figure 8-4) is a subset of a line that consists of a point (C) together with all points on the line ($\overleftrightarrow{CD}$) on one side of the point (C).

Next, consider the ways in which angles are also suggested by our surroundings (see Figure 8-6).

| Everyday situation | Geometric idea |
|---|---|

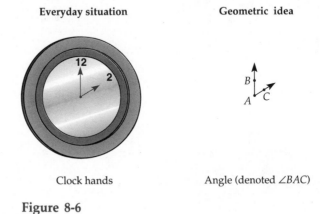

| Clock hands | Angle (denoted $\angle BAC$) |
|---|---|

Figure 8-6

## Lesson Exercise 8.6

Try to write a definition of "angle" using the term "ray."

An **angle** is the union of two rays that have a common endpoint. The two rays are called **sides,** and the common endpoint is called the **vertex.** The angle in Figure 8-3 has sides $\overrightarrow{AB}$ and $\overrightarrow{AC}$ and vertex $A$.

## Lesson Exercise 8.7

Give a simpler name for each of the following.

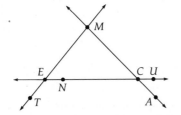

(a) $\overline{ME} \cup \overline{ET}$

(b) $\overline{NU} \cap \overrightarrow{CE}$

(c) $\overleftrightarrow{ME} \cap \overline{CN}$

## Measuring Angles

To give the position of a storm in relation to a town (see Figure 8-7), a meteorologist might use an angle measure.

Surveyors, navigators, and meteorologists all measure angles as a part of their work. Mathematicians use angle measures to classify angles. In Section 8.3, you will study a surprising pattern in the angle measures of polygons. The following background information will prepare you.

Measuring an angle is quite different from measuring a length. The measure of an angle tells the amount of rotation involved in moving from one ray to the other. Over 4000 years ago the Babylonians chose degrees as the unit for angle measure. You can measure angles in degrees using a protractor.

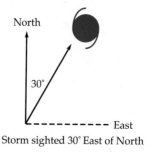

Storm sighted 30° East of North

**Figure 8-7**

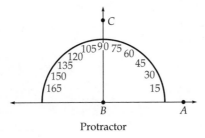

Protractor

**Figure 8-8**

As you can see, $\angle ABC$ measures 90° on the protractor pictured in Figure 8-8. This is written $m\angle ABC = 90°$.

**D** Lesson Exercise 8.8

A ship $S$ is sighted from point $U$ on the shoreline $\overleftrightarrow{UN}$.
(a) Estimate the measure of $\angle SUN$.
(b) Measure $\angle SUN$ with a protractor.

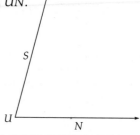

## Types of Angles

Mathematicians describe and categorize shapes. Then they look for common properties within a category.

Throughout this chapter, geometric figures will be placed into categories. The first example of classifying shapes in this chapter is the categorization of angles according to their measure. Angle categories are suggested by our surroundings.

Lesson Exercise 8.9

What type of angle is most common in the room you are in now?

The most common angles in a classroom are usually **right angles** (90°) and **straight angles** (180°). Right angles appear in everything from books to boxes to corners of rooms (Figure 8-9).

Right angle                          Straight angle

**Figure 8-9**

**D** Lesson Exercise 8.10

Two right angles with a common side, $\angle ABC$ and $\angle ABD$, form a
straight angle ($\angle CBD$). Give an example of an object that illustrates this
property and, if applicable, state the practical value of the property in
your example.

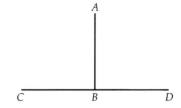

Other angle measures between 0° and 180° are not as common. These
angles are placed into two groups: **acute angles** (greater than 0° and less
than 90°) and **obtuse angles** (greater than 90° and less than 180°). Some
examples are shown in Figure 8-10.

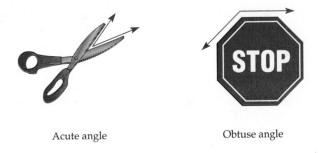

Acute angle                          Obtuse angle

**Figure 8-10**

Angles with measures greater than 180° or less than 0° are used in
trigonometry but will not be discussed in this textbook.

Lesson Exercise 8.11

Name an object in your classroom that suggests an acute angle.

We can compare two angles by measuring them. Two angles with the
same measure are called **congruent angles.** The term "congruent" applies
to any set of geometric figures that are the same size and shape.

Lesson Exercise 8.12

(a) True or false? All acute angles are congruent.
(b) Give an example that supports your answer.

## Parallel and Intersecting Lines

Our surroundings suggest the common relationships between two lines, as shown in Figure 8-11.

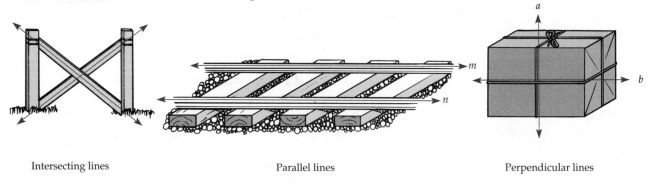

| Intersecting lines | Parallel lines | Perpendicular lines |

**Figure 8-11**

### Lesson Exercise 8.13

Try to write definitions of "intersecting lines," "parallel lines," and "perpendicular lines."

Compare your definitions to the following. Two **intersecting lines** have exactly one point in common. Two lines are **parallel** if and only if they lie in the same plane and do not intersect. In Figure 8-11, parallel lines $m$ and $n$ are denoted $m \parallel n$. Two lines that intersect at right angles are **perpendicular.** In Figure 8-11, perpendicular lines $a$ and $b$ are denoted $a \perp b$.

### D Lesson Exercise 8.14

(a) True or false? In a plane, two lines that are both perpendicular to a third line must be parallel to each other.
(b) In your classroom, identify a model of this situation that supports your answer.

## Answers to Selected Lesson Exercises

**8.2** A geometric line is perfectly straight, extends forever in two directions, and has no width; it has no arrowheads.

**8.3** (a) true    **8.4** (a) 1    (b) 3    (c) 2

**8.7** (a) $\overline{MT}$    (b) $\overline{NC}$    (c) { }

**8.10** doors of a cabinet; the property enables them to fit together and for the bottom of the two doors to be level

**8.12** (a) false    **8.14** (a) true

## 8.1  Homework Exercises

*Basic Exercises*

1. The word "geometry" can be split into "geo-" and "-metry." What do you think these two roots mean?

2. How does the dictionary define the word "point"?

3. The Northwood marching band wants to form a letter $N$ using 10 people. Design the $N$.

4. Tell what geometric figure each of the following suggests.
   (a)

Photo courtesy of the Department of the Army.

   (b) a special piece of glass that disperses light into its color components
   (c) the edge of a box

5. (a) True or false? If a line $\overleftrightarrow{AB}$ intersects a point in plane $c$, then $\overleftrightarrow{AB}$ lies in plane $c$.
   (b) Make a drawing that supports your answer.

6. Suppose a point $P$ lies in a plane. Are there any points in the plane that are exactly 100 miles from $P$? If so, how many?

7. How is a geometric point different from a dot?

8. Give three possible names for the line shown here.

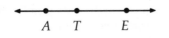

$$A \quad T \quad E$$

9. What is the dimension (0, 1, 2, or 3) of the geometric figure *suggested* by each of the following?
   (a) a pillow        (b) a piece of very thin wire
   (c) a sheet of paper

10. (a) Find three objects in your home that suggest common space figures.
    (b) Find three objects in your home that suggest common plane figures.

11. What shapes do you see in each of the structures pictured?
    (a) water tank

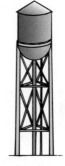

    (b) Eskimo igloo (*Hint:* It's half of something.)

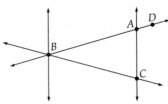

12. Euclid lived about _____ years ago.
    (a) 50        (b) 200        (c) 500
    (d) 2000      (e) 10,000

13. How is $\overrightarrow{AB}$ different from $\overrightarrow{BA}$?

14. What is the vertex of $\angle PAT$?

15. How is a line segment different from a line?

16. Give a simpler name for each of the following.
    (a) $\overrightarrow{AB} \cup \overrightarrow{AC}$
    (b) $\overrightarrow{AB} \cup \overrightarrow{AD}$
    (c) $\overleftrightarrow{BA} \cap \overleftrightarrow{AC}$

17. Show all the different patterns you can make by using these points as the endpoints of one to six line segments. It is not necessary to draw the same pattern in all different positions.

18. Estimate the measure of each marked angle. Then measure the angle with a protractor.

(a)          (b)

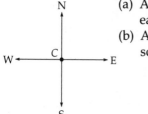

19. Why can't an angle be measured in inches?

20. Make an enlarged copy of the following drawing. Use a protractor to draw a ray with endpoint C in the given direction.

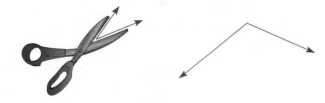

     (a) A storm is observed 30° east of south.
     (b) A ship is sighted 25° south of west.

21.

A ship reports a bearing of 50° north of east from station A and 30° west of north from station B. Locate the ship on the grid.

22. Pete and Charissa are on duty at observation towers A and B in a national forest. If there is a fire at F, how can Pete and Charissa measure angles and precisely locate the fire without leaving their towers? Assume that they can communicate by radio and that they each have a map of the park and a protractor.

F
•

•
A                           •
                                B

23. Name two capital letters that contain two or more acute angles and no obtuse or right angles.

24. True or false? All right angles are congruent.

25. Which of the following road intersection designs makes it easier to see cars coming from other directions?

90° | 90°                    135° 45°

26. If possible, draw two angles that intersect at exactly
(a) one point.      (b) two points.
(c) three points.

27. Draw four points A, B, C, and D so that $\overleftrightarrow{AB}$, $\overleftrightarrow{AC}$, $\overleftrightarrow{AD}$, $\overleftrightarrow{BC}$, $\overleftrightarrow{BD}$, and $\overleftrightarrow{CD}$ are
(a) the same line.
(b) six different lines.
(c) four different lines.

28. (a) True or false? In a plane, two lines that are perpendicular to a third line are parallel to each other.
(b) In your home, identify a model of this situation that supports your answer.
(c) How might the property in part (a) be useful to a carpenter?

29. Into how many sections is a plane separated by the removal of each of the following?
(a) one line      (b) two parallel lines
(c) two intersecting lines

**30.**

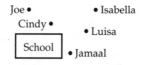

Assume that no one can see anyone else by looking through the school building.
(a) Who can see Joe?
(b) Who can see Cindy?
(c) Who can see Luisa and Jamaal?
(d) Shade the region of points from which Joe can be seen.

**31.**

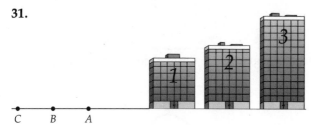

Which buildings can be seen from each of the following?
(a) A    (b) B    (c) C
(d) Shade the region of points from which only building 1 can be seen.

*Extension Exercises*

**32.** Give the angle formed at each of the following times of day by the minute and hour hands of a clock.
(a) 5:00    (b) 3:30    (c) 2:06

**33.** Name two morning times of day at which the minute and hour hands form a
(a) 150° angle.    (b) 105° angle.

**34.** Place eight dots so that there are exactly two dots on each circle and each line.

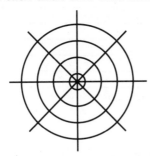

**35.** If possible, draw four lines in a plane that separate the plane into
(a) 10 sections.    (b) 11 sections.

**36.** When a billiard ball bounces off the side of a billiard table, it forms two congruent angles, as shown.

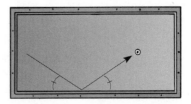

Use a protractor and trial and error to find how billiard ball *A* should be aimed so that it hits the bottom and right cushions (sides) and then strikes ball *B*.

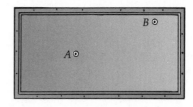

**37.** Where would you first bounce the ball off a wall so that it will end up in the hole?

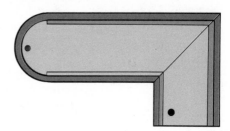

*Special Exercise*

**38.** Read *The Dot and the Line* by Norton Juster and describe how the author uses geometric shapes as symbols.

## 8.2  Plane Figures

After seeing how surfaces of objects suggest plane figures and studying basic terms such as "line segment," "angle," "parallel," and "perpendicular," one is prepared for a more detailed study of plane figures.

### Simple Closed Curves

In elementary school, children study plane figures that are simple closed curves. See whether you can write a definition of a simple closed curve in the following exercise.

### Lesson Exercise 8.15

Based upon the diagrams in Figure 8-12, write a definition of a simple closed curve.

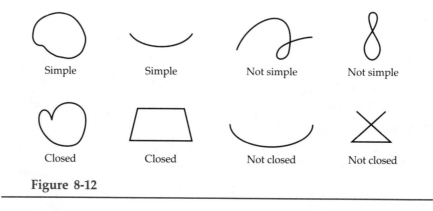

Figure 8-12

A **simple closed curve** does not cross itself and encloses a part of the plane. A simple closed curve divides the plane into three disjoint sets of points: the interior, the curve itself, and the exterior (Figure 8-13).

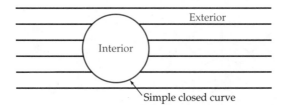

Figure 8-13

In elementary school, children study two main groups of simple closed plane figures: polygons and circles.

## Polygons

Many surfaces in our environment approximate polygons (see Figure 8-14).

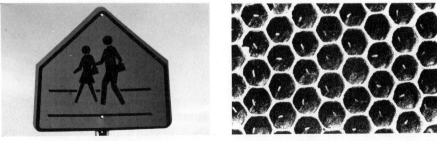

Beehive photo (neg. no. 286786) courtesy of Department of Library Services, American Museum of Natural History.
Photo of school crossing sign by Tom Sonnabend.

**Figure 8-14**

See whether you can write a definition of a polygon in the following exercise.

## Lesson Exercise 8.16

Based upon the diagrams in Figure 8-15, write a definition of a polygon.

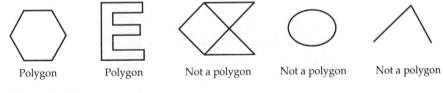

| Polygon | Polygon | Not a polygon | Not a polygon | Not a polygon |

**Figure 8-15**

What is a polygon? After a while, geometry teachers tire of the well-known response "a dead parrot." A **polygon** is a simple closed plane curve bounded by line segments.

## Lesson Exercise 8.17

Which of the following figures are polygons? If a figure is not a polygon, explain why not.

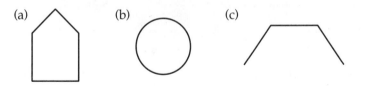

(a)      (b)      (c)

Polygons having from three to eight sides are shown in Figure 8-16. Elementary-school children usually study all of them except the heptagon.

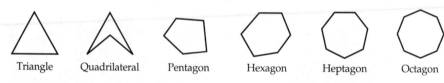

Triangle     Quadrilateral     Pentagon     Hexagon     Heptagon     Octagon

**Figure 8-16**

These polygons also have three to eight angles, respectively. Each vertex of an angle is called a **vertex** (plural: "vertices") of the polygon. A **diagonal** is a line segment other than a side that joins two vertices of a polygon (Figure 8-17).

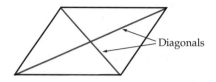

Diagonals

**Figure 8-17**

In buildings and bridges, engineers sometimes use diagonals to reinforce a structure, as shown in Figure 8-18.

Photo courtesy of Library of Congress.

**Figure 8-18**

Diagonals are used to define convex polygons, the kind children study in elementary school. No portion of any diagonal of a **convex** polygon lies in its exterior (see Figure 8-19). (All triangles are convex polygons, since they do not have diagonals.)

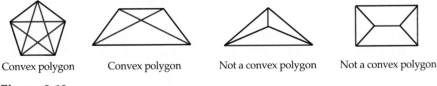

Convex polygon     Convex polygon     Not a convex polygon     Not a convex polygon

**Figure 8-19**

The term "convex" is also used with lenses (Figure 8-20).

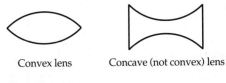

Convex lens     Concave (not convex) lens

**Figure 8-20**

## An Investigation: Diagonals of Polygons

The number of diagonals in polygons follows a pattern. A triangle has no diagonals. A quadrilateral (see Figure 8-21) has a total of two diagonals, with one diagonal from each vertex.

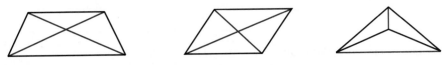

**Figure 8-21**

Put the results in a table.

| Polygons | | | | |
|---|---|---|---|---|
| **Number of Vertices** | 3 | 4 | 5 | 6 |
| **Number of Diagonals from Each Vertex** | 0 | 1 | | |
| **Number of Diagonals** | 0 | 2 | | |

## Lesson Exercise 8.18

(a) Complete the table just presented.
(b) Based upon the pattern in your completed table, predict how many
    diagonals there are in a heptagon (a seven-sided polygon).
(c) Draw a heptagon and its diagonals and check your prediction.

What is the general formula for the number of diagonals in a polygon
that has $N$ sides? The following exercise will help you answer this intriguing question.

## D Lesson Exercise 8.19

Now consider a polygon that has $N$ sides.

| Polygons | | | | | | |
|---|---|---|---|---|---|---|
| Number of Vertices | 3 | 4 | 5 | 6 | 7 | $N$ |
| Number of Diagonals from Each Vertex | 0 | 1 | 2 | 3 | 4 | |
| Number of Diagonals | 0 | 2 | 5 | 9 | 14 | |

(a) How many vertices does it have?
(b) How many diagonals can be drawn *from* a vertex?
(c) How is the total number of diagonals related to the number of vertices
    and the number of diagonals from each vertex?
(d) How many diagonals does the polygon have?

Were you able to complete Lesson Exercise 8.19? The result is the
following.

> **Diagonals of a Polygon**
>
> A polygon that has $N$ sides has $\dfrac{N(N-3)}{2}$ diagonals.

## Lesson Exercise 8.20

(a) Use the formula to find the number of diagonals that a 20-sided
    polygon has.
(b) The process of assuming that the formula is true and applying it in
    part (a) involves _____ reasoning.

The most common polygons are triangles and quadrilaterals. These two classes of polygons can be subdivided further.

## Triangles

Triangular shapes appear occasionally in nature; they also possess a rigid structure that strengthens supports in buildings and furniture (see Figure 8-22).

Photo of diatom courtesy of Dr. George W. Andrews.

Photo of bridge courtesy of Library of Congress.

**Figure 8-22**

One way in which mathematicians classify triangles is by the number of congruent sides. Consider how this could be done in the following exercise.

## Lesson Exercise 8.21

(a) How many congruent sides can a triangle have?
(b) If you remember, give the name for each group of triangles in part (a).

The previous exercise produces three categories of triangles: **scalene triangles,** which have no congruent sides; **isosceles triangles,** which have at least two congruent sides; and **equilateral triangles,** which have three congruent sides (see Figure 8-23).

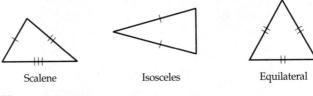

Scalene          Isosceles              Equilateral

**Figure 8-23**

You can use these definitions to classify any triangle.

## Lesson Exercise 8.22

Which of the following categories include a triangle with three congruent sides?
(a) scalene     (b) isosceles     (c) equilateral

## Quadrilaterals

How should children learn about geometric shapes? While teaching high-school mathematics in Holland, Dina van Hiele-Geldof and Pierre van Hiele developed a theory about stages of learning in geometry. According to the van Hieles, school geometry should begin with recognition, followed by analysis and then informal deduction.

The first level, **recognition,** concerns recognizing a shape as a whole without worrying about components (such as sides and angles) and properties. In **analysis,** students focus on the components and properties of shapes, such as how many sides they have and whether they have some congruent sides or angles. Students use the parts of a figure to describe and define the figure. In **informal deduction,** students become aware of relationships between different classes of figures (for example, they see that all squares are parallelograms). At this level, students also use deduction to find relationships among the properties of a figure, such as knowing whether a quadrilateral that has four congruent sides must also have four congruent angles.

How would a teacher present a unit on quadrilaterals using the van Hiele levels? At the first level, we *recognize* quadrilaterals in our environment (Figure 8-24).

Photos of door and street lamp by Tom Sonnabend.

Photo (neg. no. 2A12497) of halite crystals by A. Singer. Courtesy of Department of Library Services, American Museum of Natural History.

**Figure 8-24**

At the recognition level, the student would compare shapes that are quadrilaterals with shapes that are not. Figure 8-25 shows some examples.

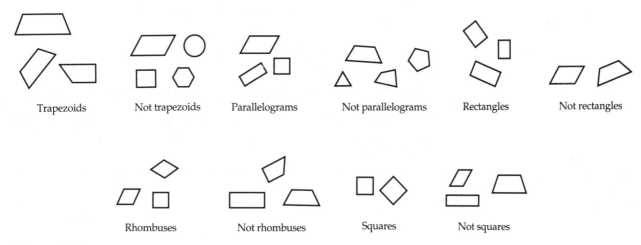

**Figure 8-25**

At the next level, analysis, the student analyzes properties of quadrilaterals, while still being unaware of any formal definition.

## Lesson Exercise 8.23

In which of the preceding five quadrilaterals are both pairs of opposite sides congruent?

The next phase of the analysis level is to compare and contrast properties of different quadrilaterals.

## Lesson Exercise 8.24

(a) Name two properties of sides that all squares and all rhombuses share.
(b) Name a property of sides or angles that all squares have that some rhombuses do not have.

## Lesson Exercise 8.25

(a) Name two properties that all parallelograms and all rectangles share.
(b) Name a property that all rectangles have that some parallelograms do not have.

At the third level, informal deduction, students use properties to define shapes and examine alternate definitions.

## Lesson Exercise 8.26

Based upon the preceding exercises and diagrams, write a definition of a trapezoid, a parallelogram, a rectangle, a rhombus, and a square.

One possible set of definitions for common quadrilaterals is as follows.

---

**Definitions: Common Quadrilaterals**

- A **trapezoid** is a quadrilateral that has exactly one pair of parallel sides.
- A **parallelogram** is a quadrilateral in which each pair of opposite (nonintersecting) sides is parallel.
- A **rectangle** is a quadrilateral that has four right angles.
- A **rhombus** is a quadrilateral that has four congruent sides.
- A **square** is a quadrilateral that has four congruent sides and four right angles.

---

Definitions such as these enable mathematicians to communicate using a shared understanding of terminology. A definition *may* give a minimum set of properties that define a shape; it may also list additional properties that clarify what the shape is like.

For example, the preceding definition of a rectangle does not give a *minimum* set of properties. The next exercise addresses this issue.

## Lesson Exercise 8.27

A rectangle can be defined as a quadrilateral that has right angles. What is the *minimum* number of right angles that makes a quadrilateral a rectangle? (*Hint:* Try to draw quadrilaterals with one, two, and three angles that are *not* rectangles.)

---

As Lesson Exercise 8.27 suggests, a rectangle *can* be defined as "a quadrilateral that has three right angles," but elementary and high-school texts usually add other properties that clarify what a rectangle is. Typical definitions are "a rectangle is a quadrilateral that has four right angles" or "a rectangle is a parallelogram that has four right angles."

The five classes of quadrilaterals overlap. At the level of informal deduction, definitions are used to find relationships among classes of figures. See whether you can answer the following questions by referring to the definitions.

## Lesson Exercise 8.28

(a) According to the preceding definitions, would every square be a type of rectangle?
(b) Is every trapezoid also a parallelogram?
(c) Is every square also a rhombus?

## D Lesson Exercise 8.29

Suppose $P$ = {parallelograms}, $Rh$ = {rhombuses}, $S$ = {squares}, $Re$ = {rectangles}, $T$ = {trapezoids}, and $Q$ = {quadrilaterals}.
(a) $Rh \cap Re$ = _____      (b) $T \cap P$ = _____

## D Lesson Exercise 8.30

With the help of your answers to Lesson Exercises 8.28 and 8.29, decide which of the following Venn diagrams is correct.

(a)

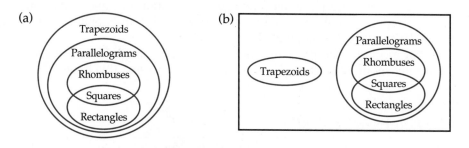

(b)

(c)

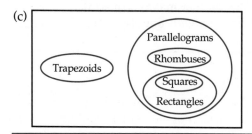

## Circles

Another shape sometimes appears in clocks and in nature. It is suggested by the top of a can and the outline of a wheel. You know this plane figure well: it is the circle (Figure 8-26).

Photo of clock courtesy of Library of Congress.

Photo of diatom courtesy of Dr. George Andrews.

**Figure 8-26**

## Lesson Exercise 8.31

(a) Suppose that a radio program can be received anywhere within 20 km of the radio station. If the land is flat and has few obstacles, what shape is the border of the region where the station can be received?

(b) Based upon part (a), complete the following definition of a circle. A circle is the set of points in a plane that are

_____.

The preceding exercise suggests the following definition of a circle.

> **Definitions: Circle, Radius, and Center**
>
> A **circle** is the set of points in a plane that are the same distance (the **radius**) from a given point (the **center**); see Figure 8-27.

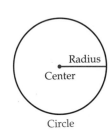

**Figure 8-27**

Note that the word "radius" is used to refer to both a *segment* joining the center to the circle and the *length* of that segment.

## Lesson Exercise 8.32

(a) What property of a circle makes it work as a wheel?

(b) How could you describe the size of a circular object such as a bicycle wheel?

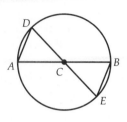

**Figure 8-28**

The diameter is a commonly used measurement of circular objects. (Two other common measures, area and circumference, will be examined in Chapter 10.)

## Lesson Exercise 8.33

In Figure 8-28, $\overline{AB}$ and $\overline{DE}$ are diameters of a circle with center $C$, and $\overline{AD}$ and $\overline{BC}$ are not diameters. Define "diameter."

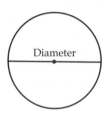

**Figure 8-29**

A **diameter** is a line segment that (1) has two points of the circle as endpoints and (2) passes through the center of the circle (Figure 8-29).

Just as with the radius, the term "diameter" can be used to describe the segment or its length. The intersecting diameters of some wheels suggest central angles. So do the hands of a clock (see Figure 8-30). A **central angle** is an angle whose vertex is the center of a circle.

Photo courtesy of Library of Congress.

**Figure 8-30**

## Lesson Exercise 8.34

Consider the following problem. "Name a time of day when the minute and hour hands of a clock form a 75° angle." Devise a plan and solve the problem.

## Answers to Selected Lesson Exercises

8.17 (a) is; (b) is not bounded by line segments, and (c) is not closed.

8.18 (a)

| Number of Vertices | 3 | 4 | 5 | 6 |
|---|---|---|---|---|
| Number of Diagonals from Each Vertex | 0 | 1 | 2 | 3 |
| Number of Diagonals | 0 | 2 | 5 | 9 |

    (b) 14

8.19 (a) $N$   (b) $N - 3$   (d) $\dfrac{N(N - 3)}{2}$

8.20 (a) 170   (b) deductive

8.21 (a) none, two, or three

8.22 (b), (c)

8.23 parallelogram, rectangle, rhombus, square

8.24 (a) Both pairs of opposite sides are parallel and equal.
    (b) four right angles

8.25 (a) Both pairs of opposite sides are parallel and equal.
    (b) four right angles

8.27 three

8.28 (a) yes    (b) no    (c) yes

8.29 (a) S    (b) { }

8.30 (b)

8.31 (a) circle

8.32 (a) It has uniform curvature.
    (b) You could measure the diameter, circumference, or area.

8.34 3:30

## 8.2 Homework Exercises

### Basic Exercises

1. Draw a curve that is simple but not closed.

2. Which of the following shapes are polygons? If a shape is not a polygon, explain why not.

(a)    (b)    (c)    (d)    (e)

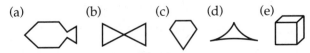

3. What polygon is suggested in each case?

(a)

(b)

Photo by Tom Sonnabend.

4. Sketch a pentagon that has exactly three right angles.

5. Sketch a hexagon that has exactly two acute angles.

6. Form the following shapes on a geoboard.
   (a) a pentagon that has one pair of parallel sides
   (b) a quadrilateral that has no parallel sides but two pairs of congruent, adjacent sides

7. Which of the following polygons are convex?

(a)    (b)    (c)    (d)

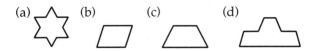

8. Find the maximum number of intersection points for
   (a) a triangle and a square.
   (b) a triangle and a convex pentagon.
   (c) a square and a convex pentagon.
   (d) a regular polygon that has $n$ sides and a regular polygon that has $m$ sides, $n < m$.

9. Draw all the diagonals of the hexagon.

10. A polygon that has $N$ sides has $\dfrac{N(N-3)}{2}$ diagonals. How many diagonals does an octagon have?

11. Some painters utilize the triangular form. Leonardo DaVinci used it in the *Mona Lisa*, and Hans Memling used it in his *Madonna and Child*. What mood or effect might the triangular form create?

12. True or false? No scalene triangle is isosceles.

13. Consider the following problem. "How many triangles are contained in the following shape?" Devise a plan and solve the problem.

14. How many squares are in the following design?

15. Complete a square that has the segment shown as one of its sides.

16. If possible, form each of the following shapes on a geoboard. Then make a drawing to record your results.
    (a) parallelogram　　　(b) rhombus
    (c) trapezoid

17. How could you use some of the segments shown to form each of the following?
    (a) a parallelogram
    (b) a trapezoid
    (c) a rhombus

| Group 1 | Group 2 | Group 3 |
|---------|---------|---------|
| _____  |         |         |
| _____  |         |         |
| _____  | _____  | _____ |
| _____  | _____  |         |

18.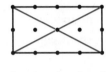

    (a) Refer to the drawing. Which of the following appear to be true?
      (1) The diagonals have the same length.
      (2) The diagonals are perpendicular.
      (3) The diagonals bisect each other.
    (b) What van Hiele level is represented in part (a)?

19.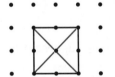

    Refer to the drawing. Which of the following appear to be true?
    (1) The diagonals have the same length.
    (2) The diagonals are perpendicular.
    (3) The diagonals bisect each other.

20. In which of the following shapes are both pairs of opposite sides parallel?
    (a) rhombus　　　(b) square
    (c) trapezoid　　(d) rectangle
    (e) parallelogram

21. Which of the following shapes have at least one right angle?
    (a) rhombus        (b) square
    (c) trapezoid      (d) rectangle
    (e) parallelogram

22. Take a sheet of paper. Use paper-folding to show that the opposite sides of a rectangle are congruent.

23. Cut a rectangular shape along its diagonal to form two congruent pieces. Sketch and name all the shapes you can form by putting the two pieces together in different ways.

24. A carpenter has made a rectangular door. How can he use a tape measure to be sure that the door has right angles?

25. (a) Guess the root meaning of the word "triangle."
    (b) Guess the root meaning of the word "rectangle."

26. A square is defined in the text as "a quadrilateral that has four congruent sides and four right angles," but this is not a *minimum* set of conditions. Make drawings to determine which of the following also define a square.
    (a) a quadrilateral that has four congruent sides and three right angles
    (b) a quadrilateral that has two congruent sides and four right angles
    (c) a quadrilateral that has three congruent sides and four right angles
    (d) a quadrilateral that has two *adjacent* congruent sides and four right angles

27. A square is also which of the following?
    (a) quadrilateral      (b) parallelogram
    (c) rhombus            (d) rectangle

28. Is every rhombus a parallelogram? If so, give an example. If not, give a counterexample.

29. The diagonals of a rectangle are congruent. Why does this statement imply that the diagonals of a square must also be congruent?

30. Which set picture best represents the relationship between rhombuses and rectangles? Label the correct circles appropriately.

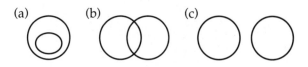

31. Suppose that $P$ = {parallelograms}, $S$ = {squares}, $T$ = {trapezoids}, and $Q$ = {quadrilaterals}.
    (a) $P \cap S$ = _____
    (b) Is $T \subseteq Q$?
    (c) $P \cup Q$ = _____

32. Suppose that $Re$ = {rectangles}, $Rh$ = {rhombuses}, $S$ = {squares}, and $P$ = {parallelograms}.
    (a) $Re \cap Rh$ = _____
    (b) Is $Rh \subseteq P$?
    (c) $S \cup P$ = _____

33. The **midpoint** of a side divides it into two equal lengths.
    (a) Draw a large quadrilateral on a sheet of paper.
    (b) Use a ruler to locate the midpoint of each side.
    (c) Connect the midpoints.
    (d) What shape appears to be the result?
    (e) Repeat steps (a)–(d) for a second quadrilateral.
    (f) Make a generalization based upon your answers to part (d).

34. (a) Draw a large rectangle on a sheet of paper.
    (b) Use a ruler to locate the midpoint of each side.
    (c) Connect the midpoints.
    (d) What shape appears to be the result?
    (e) Repeat steps (a)–(d) for a second rectangle.
    (f) Make a generalization based upon your answers to part (d).

**35.** Fill in the blanks to describe the circle that has center *N*.

Circle *N* is the set of _____ in a plane that are _____ from _____.

**36.** Why does dipping a finger in a pool of water create circular ripples?

**37.** The diameter of a circle divides its interior into two congruent regions. How can someone use this property in dividing a circular pizza or pie in half?

**38.** The diagram of a bicycle wheel has *C* as its center.

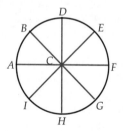

(a) Name a central angle and give its measure.
(b) What kind of triangle is △*CDE*?

*Extension Exercises*

**39.** In 1884, Ezra Gilliland designed a phone system that allowed 15 people to speak to one another. How many connections were

needed? (*Hint:* How many segments are needed to connect 15 points in pairs?)

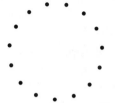

**40.** At a party, 15 friendly people all want to shake hands with each other. How many handshakes would this require?

**41.** Some mathematics books define a trapezoid as "a quadrilateral that has at least one pair of parallel sides." If this definition is used, which of the following Venn diagrams would be correct?

(a)

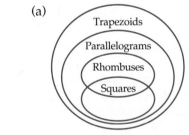

(b)

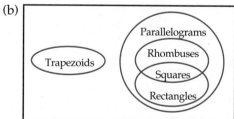

(c)

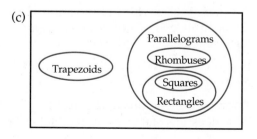

**42.** Draw a polygon on the grid that meets all of the following conditions.

```
•   •   •   •   •
•   •   •   •   •
•   •   •   •   •
•   •   •   •   •
•   •   •   •   •
```

(a) It is a hexagon.
(b) Not all of its sides are congruent.
(c) It has exactly two acute angles.
(d) It has exactly three dots in its interior.

**43.** If possible, sketch two parallelograms that intersect at exactly
(a) one point.      (b) two points.
(c) three points.   (d) four points.

**44.** If possible, sketch two parallelograms that intersect at exactly
(a) five points.    (b) six points.
(c) seven points.   (d) eight points.

**45.** If possible, draw a triangle and a circle that intersect at exactly
(a) one point.      (b) two points.
(c) three points.   (d) four points.

*Computer Exercises*

**46.** Computer software like the Geometric Supposer (Sunburst Communications), Geometer's Sketchpad (Key Curriculum), UCSMP Geometry Software (Scott Foresman), and Geometry Inventor (Wings for Learning) are all "automatic drawers" that allow students to draw and measure angles, segments, polygons, and circles. Students can use these drawings to investigate and discover properties of triangles, quadrilaterals, and circles. Some of the properties

in the following exercises are discussed later in this textbook.

If it is available at your school, use an automatic drawer to explore properties of
(a) the sides of a parallelogram.
(b) the angles of a parallelogram.
(c) the diagonals of a parallelogram.

**47.** Use an automatic drawer to explore properties of the angles of
(a) a triangle.
(b) an isosceles triangle.
(c) an equilateral triangle.

*Special Exercises*

**48.**

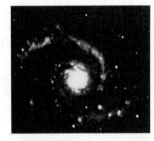

Photo courtesy of NASA.
Photo (neg. no. 2A12055) by A. Singer. Courtesy of Department of Library Services, American Museum of Natural History.

The equiangular spiral shape appears in the stars and in animals. You can graph one using a circular grid.

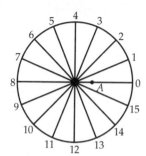

(a) Draw a segment from radius 1 that is perpendicular to radius 0 at point *A*. Label the intersection point with radius 1 as *B*.

(b) Draw a segment from radius 2 that is perpendicular to radius 1 at *B*. Label the intersection point with radius 2 as *C*.

(c) Continue this pattern for all 15 radii.

(d) Draw a smooth curve through points *A*, *B*, *C*, and so on that resembles an equiangular spiral.

49. A series of straight line segments can be used to define a curved figure. Strange, but true! Trace the circle (shown in the next column) on a piece of paper.

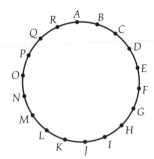

(a) Draw the following segments: $\overline{AI}$, $\overline{BJ}$, $\overline{CK}$, $\overline{DL}$, . . . , $\overline{RH}$.

(b) Using a different color, draw: $\overline{AH}$, $\overline{BI}$, $\overline{CJ}$, $\overline{DK}$, . . . , $\overline{RG}$.

(c) Using another color, draw the next set of segments that continues the pattern.

## 8.3   Angle Measures of Polygons

Although most floor tiles are square, many other designs can be used. Some quilts also utilize interlocking, repeating patterns. What shapes can be used for floor tiles or quilt patterns? Figure 8-31 shows some examples.

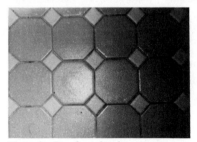

Photos by Tom Sonnabend.

**Figure 8-31**

We can answer this question by studying the angle measures of polygons, beginning with the simplest polygon, the triangle.

### The Angles of a Triangle

The sum, in degrees, of the angle measures of any triangle is the same. Do you know what the sum is? Try the following.

**D** Lesson Exercise 8.35

(a) Take a sheet of paper and draw three congruent triangles. Number the angles in each triangle as shown in Figure 8-32.

**Figure 8-32**

(b) Cut out the triangles.
(c) Now place the three triangles together in a tiling pattern, as shown in Figure 8-33.
(d) What does the sum of the three angle measures ($\angle 1$, $\angle 2$, and $\angle 3$) appear to be?

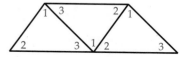

**Figure 8-33**

Lesson Exercise 8.35 (d) suggests the following property.

---

**Angle Measures of a Triangle**

The sum of the three angle measures of a triangle is 180°.

---

This property is helpful in finding angle measures of triangles.

Lesson Exercise 8.36

An equilateral triangle has three equal sides and three equal angles. What is the measure of each angle?

## The Angles of a Polygon

It is possible to find the sum of the angle measures of any polygon without measuring its angles! One can use the sum of the angle measures of a triangle to deduce the sum of the angle measures in any convex polygon. First, consider quadrilaterals.

Lesson Exercise 8.37

(a) What is the sum of the angle measures of any square or rectangle?
(b) Cut out four copies of a quadrilateral that has no parallel sides (Figure 8-34) and label the angles of each quadrilateral 1, 2, 3, and 4.
(c) Fit the four quadrilaterals together in a tiling pattern so that $\angle 1$, $\angle 2$, $\angle 3$, and $\angle 4$ share a common vertex. What is the sum of the angle measures of $\angle 1$, $\angle 2$, $\angle 3$, and $\angle 4$?

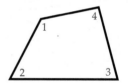

**Figure 8-34**

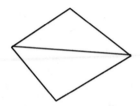

**Figure 8-35**

The angle measures of all convex quadrilaterals have the same sum! This fact can be proved by drawing a diagonal of any convex quadrilateral to form two triangles, as shown in Figure 8-35.

## Lesson Exercise 8.38

(a) What is the sum of the three angle measures of each triangle in the quadrilateral shown in Figure 8-35?
(b) What is the sum of the four angle measures of the quadrilateral?

Lesson Exercise 8.38 verifies the following property.

---

**Angle Measures of a Convex Quadrilateral**

The sum of the four angle measures of any convex quadrilateral is 360°.

---

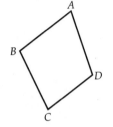

**Figure 8-36**

## Lesson Exercise 8.39

(a) Explain why the following is not correct. Consider quadrilateral *ABCD* (Figure 8-36). *ABCD* can be divided into four triangles, as shown in Figure 8-37. The interior angle measures of each triangle add up to 180°, so the interior angle measures of *ABCD* add up to 4 · 180° = 720°.
(b) How could you compute the sum of the interior angle measures of the quadrilateral using the four triangles?

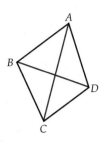

**Figure 8-37**

## Lesson Exercise 8.40

Consider the pentagon in Figure 8-38.
(a) What is the sum of its angle measures? Write the answer in the chart.

| Polygons (Convex) | | | | | | |
|---|---|---|---|---|---|---|
| **Number of Sides** | 3 | 4 | 5 | 6 | 7 | N |
| **Number of Triangles Formed** | 1 | 2 | | | | |
| **Sum of Interior Angle Measures** | 180° | 360° | | | | |

(b) Use inductive reasoning or more drawings to complete the chart.
(c) Write a generalization of your results.

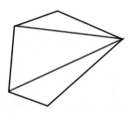

**Figure 8-38**

As the pattern in Lesson Exercise 8.40 suggests, you can divide any convex polygon that has *N* sides into *N* − 2 triangles by drawing all the possible diagonals from any single vertex. This result leads to the following conclusion.

---

**Angle Measures of a Convex Polygon**

The sum of the angle measures of any $N$-sided convex polygon is $(N - 2) \cdot 180°$.

---

This property of angle measures also applies to polygons that are *not* convex; however, such polygons have angle measures greater than 180° (which are not addressed in this textbook).

## Lesson Exercise 8.41

What is the sum of the angle measures of a convex octagon?

---

Many shapes in the world suggest regular polygons (see Figure 8-39).

Photo of honeycomb (neg. no. 286786) courtesy of Department of Library Services, American Museum of Natural History.

**Figure 8-39**

A **regular polygon** has sides that are all congruent and angles that are all congruent.

## Lesson Exercise 8.42

You want to construct a STOP sign in the shape of a regular octagon. How many degrees are there in each interior angle of a stop sign?

---

## Tessellations

To return to the opening question, what shapes can be used as tiles?

All of the patterns in Figure 8-40 (see page 430) are called tessellations. A plane **tessellation** is a complete covering of a plane by shapes in a repeating pattern, without gaps or overlapping.

Figure 8-40

Figure 8-41

Which *regular* polygons tessellate the plane? First, consider squares. If you've seen a few tile floors, you know that squares can be used. But why?

Pick a vertex of a square (Figure 8-41).

Can we cover the plane region around the chosen point with additional squares, with no gaps or overlaps?

Yes! Squares tessellate, as shown in Figure 8-42.

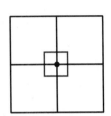

Figure 8-42

## Lesson Exercise 8.43

In Figure 8-42, the angle measures around the marked point add up to _____ degrees.

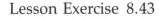

## D Lesson Exercise 8.44

Do equilateral triangles tessellate? Make a drawing or cut out at least six congruent equilateral triangles.

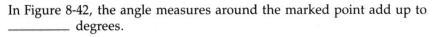

## D Lesson Exercise 8.45

Do regular pentagons tessellate?

## Lesson Exercise 8.46

(a) Complete the chart.

| Regular Polygons | Total Number of Degrees | Measure of Each Interior Angle |
|---|---|---|
| Triangle | | |
| Quadrilateral (square) | 360° | 90° |
| Pentagon | | |
| Hexagon | | |
| Heptagon | | |
| Octagon | | |
| Dodecagon (12 sides) | | |

(b) Without drawing the shapes or making cutouts, tell which figures in the chart will tessellate the plane.

## Answers to Selected Lesson Exercises

**8.36** 60°

**8.37** (a) 360°

**8.38** (a) 180°      (b) 360°

**8.39** (a) Together, the angles of the four triangles do not form the four angles of
the quadrilateral.
(b) $(4 \cdot 180°) - 360° = 360°$

**8.40** (b)

| Polygons (convex) | | | | | | |
|---|---|---|---|---|---|---|
| Number of Sides | 3 | 4 | 5 | 6 | 7 | $N$ |
| Number of Triangles Formed | 1 | 2 | 3 | 4 | 5 | $N - 2$ |
| Sum of Interior Angle Measures (in degrees) | 180° | 360° | 540° | 720° | 900° | $(N - 2)180°$ |

**8.41** 1080°

**8.42** 135°

**8.43** 360

**8.44** yes

**8.45** no

**8.46** (a)

| Regular Polygons | Total Number of Degrees | Measure of Each Interior Angle |
|---|---|---|
| Triangle | 180° | 60° |
| Quadrilateral | 360° | 90° |
| Pentagon | 540° | 108° |
| Hexagon | 720° | 120° |
| Heptagon | 900° | $128\frac{4}{7}°$ |
| Octagon | 1080° | 135° |
| Dodecagon (12 sides) | 1800° | 150° |

(b) Regular triangles, quadrilaterals, and
hexagons tessellate the plane.

## 8.3   Homework Exercises

*Basic Exercises*

1. (a) Draw a large triangle on a sheet of paper.
   (b) Measure each angle.
   (c) Do the three angle measures add up to
   180°? If not, why not?

2. Explain why a triangle cannot have an obtuse angle and a right angle.

3. Tell whether each of the following is a possible triangle or an impossible triangle.
   (a) an isoceles triangle that has an obtuse
   angle
   (b) a scalene triangle that has a right angle

4. $\triangle KAR$ is regular and $m\angle PKR = 108°$. Fill in
the missing angle measures.

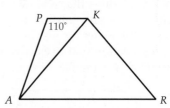

5. A quadrilateral has two right angles. What
can you deduce about the measures of the
other two angles?

6. Explain how you could divide a hexagon into

triangles to show that the sum of the interior angle measures of a convex hexagon is 720°.

7. Explain what is wrong with the following.

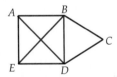

Pentagon *ABCDE* can be divided into five triangles, as shown. Therefore, the sum of the interior angles measures of the pentagon is 5 · 180° = 900°.

 8. What is the sum of the interior angle measures of a 40-sided convex polygon?

9. (a) Is a rhombus a regular polygon? Why or why not?
   (b) Is a rectangle a regular polygon? Why or why not?

10. A Canadian nickel has the shape of a regular dodecagon (12 sides). How many degrees are in each angle?

11. Beehive cells approximate regular hexagons.
    (a) When bees make the cells, what size interior angles would they make?
    (b) Use a protractor to draw a regular hexagon. Then divide it into three congruent rhombuses.

12. In this lesson, you saw that regular triangles, squares, and regular hexagons tessellate the plane. There are also eight possible semi-regular tessallations that use two or more different regular polygons to tessellate the plane. The following figure shows a semi-regular tessellation that uses two regular triangles and two regular hexagons.

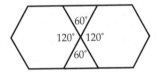

Using the chart at the end of the lesson, try to sketch the other seven possible semi-regular tessellations.

13. Draw or cut out four congruent copies of each type of figure and determine if they tessellate.
    (a) a parallelogram      (b) a trapezoid

14. Draw or cut out six congruent copies of each type of figure and determine if they tessellate.
    (a) an isosceles triangle
    (b) a scalene triangle

*Extension Exercises*

15. (a) How many rectangles are in the following diagram?

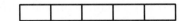

   (b) How many rectangles are in the following diagram?

   (c) How many rectangles are in the following diagram?

   (d) Describe a general rule relating the total number of rectangles to the number of sections in a diagram of this type.
   (e) Use your rule from part (d) to determine how many rectangles would be in the following diagram.

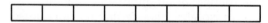

**16.** What is the measure of ∠A in the pentagram? (Assume that *FGHIJ* is regular.)

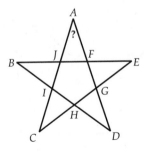

**17.** A certain regular polygon has *n* sides.
   (a) What is the measure of each interior angle in terms of *n*?
   (b) How do you know that the expression in part (a) is less than 180°?

**18.** Each angle of a certain regular polygon measures 174°. How many sides does it have?

**19.** Consider the following problem. "In a basketball tournament, each of eight teams plays every other team once. How many matches are there?" Devise a plan and solve the problem. (*Hint:* Draw a regular octagon.)

**20.** (a) How many equilateral triangles are shown?

   (b) How many equilateral triangles are shown?

(c) How many equilateral triangles are shown?

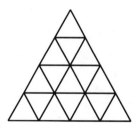

*Special Exercises*

**21.** (a) Trace the square and cut it along the lines into seven pieces.

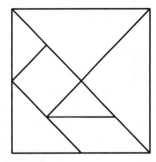

   Presto! You have made a Chinese tangram puzzle set. This type of geometric puzzle is at least 4000 years old! So how does it work? You rearrange the seven pieces into all different shapes. For example, after taking it apart, you can try to reconstruct the original square.
   (b) Try an introductory problem. Cover the following picture with two tangram pieces.

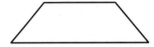

   (c) What fraction of the original square is covered by the parallelogram piece?

*(Exercise continues)*

(d) Cover the following figure with all seven pieces.

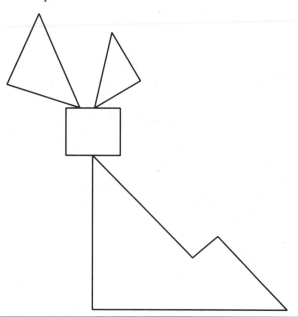

(e) Use all seven pieces to cover a whale.

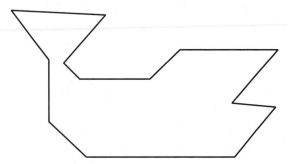

(f) Use all seven pieces to make a triangle.

22. If possible, form each of the following shapes using exactly four tangram pieces.
    (a) triangle          (b) square
    (c) parallelogram     (d) trapezoid

---

## 8.4  Three-Dimensional Geometry

Space figures are the first shapes children perceive in their environment. But children cannot systematically study and categorize three-dimensional shapes in school until they have studied one- and two-dimensional shapes.

In elementary school, children learn about the most basic classes of space figures: prisms, pyramids, cylinders, cones, and spheres. This lesson concerns the definitions of these space figures and the properties of their faces, vertices, and edges.

As a basis for studying space figures, first consider relationships among lines and planes in space. These relationships are helpful in analyzing and defining space figures.

### Lines in Space

What are possible relationships between two lines in space? As in two dimensions, two lines could be parallel or intersecting. But there is another possibility in three dimensions!

**D** Lesson Exercise 8.47

Using two pencils to represent lines in space, see whether you can find another possible relationship, in addition to their being parallel or intersecting.

In space, two lines can be parallel, intersecting, or skew. **Skew** lines are two lines that cannot be contained in a plane. Skew lines are not parallel and they do not intersect. Two drawings of skew lines are shown in Figure 8-43.

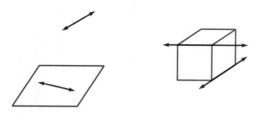

**Figure 8-43**

**D** Lesson Exercise 8.48

(a) True or false? A line that is parallel to one of two skew lines must intersect the other.
(b) Identify a model of this situation in your classroom that supports your answer.

## A Line and a Plane in Space

What are the possible relationships between a line and a plane in space? One possibility is that they are parallel. A line and a plane are **parallel** if and only if they do not intersect.

**D** Lesson Exercise 8.49

Use a piece of paper to represent a plane and a pencil or pen to represent a line. See whether you can find three possible relationships between a line and a plane.

Did you find the following possibilities in Lesson Exercise 8.49?

**A Line and a Plane in Space**

*Either*

**1.** The line is parallel to the plane.

*or*

**2.** The line intersects the plane at a single point.

*or*

**3.** The line lies in the plane.

From *SMP 11–16 Book* R3 (New York: Cambridge Univ. Press, 1987). © Cambridge University Press, 1987. Reprinted with the permission of Cambridge University Press.

**D** Lesson Exercise 8.50

(a) True or false? If a line lies in a plane, and a second line intersects the plane, then the two lines must intersect.

(b) In your classroom, identify a model of this situation that supports your answer.

**D** Lesson Exercise 8.51

(a) True or false? If a line is parallel to a plane, and a second line lies in the plane, then the two lines do not intersect.

(b) In your classroom, identify a model of this situation that supports your answer.

## Planes in Space

What are the possible relationships between two planes in three dimensions? One possibility is that the two planes are parallel. Two planes are **parallel** if and only if they do not intersect.

## Lesson Exercise 8.52

Using two pieces of paper to represent planes, find the possible relationships between two planes.

Did you find the following possibilities in Lesson Exercise 8.52?

---

**Two Planes in Space**

*Either*

**1.** The two planes intersect in a line.

*or*

**2.** The two planes are parallel.

---

## Lesson Exercise 8.53

(a) True or false? Two planes that are parallel to a third plane must be parallel to each other.
(b) In your classroom, identify a model that supports your answer.

## Lesson Exercise 8.54

True or false? Two planes may intersect at exactly one point.

Parallel planes are used in defining a prism, the most common type of polyhedron (plural: "polyhedra" or "polyhedrons") in school geometry.

## Polyhedra

Many everyday objects, such as boxes and crystals (Figure 8-44), resemble polyhedra.

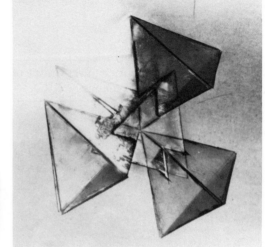

Photo (neg. no. 116114) by Julius Kirschner. Courtesy of Library Services, American Museum of Natural History.

**Figure 8-44**

To define a polyhedron, we will use the terms "simple closed surface" and "polygonal region." A simple closed surface in space is analogous to a simple closed curve in a plane. A **simple closed surface** separates space into three disjoint sets: points inside the surface, points on the surface, and points outside the surface. A **polygonal region** is a polygon together with its interior (Figure 8-45).

Polygonal region          Polygon

**Figure 8-45**

The shapes in Figure 8-46 are polyhedra.

Rectangular prism       Triangular pyramid

**Figure 8-46**

The shapes in Figure 8-47 are *not* polyhedra.

Sphere

Cone

**Figure 8-47**

## Lesson Exercise 8.55

Use the preceding information to write a definition of a polyhedron.

A **polyhedron** is a simple, closed space figure bounded by polygonal regions. All of the surfaces of a polyhedron are flat, not curved. The polygonal surfaces of polyhedra are called **faces.** The sides of each face (polygonal region) are called **edges,** and the vertices of the polygons are also **vertices** (corners) of the polyhedron.

For example, in the cube shown in Figure 8-48, square *ADHE* and its interior comprise a *face,* $\overline{AD}$ is an *edge,* and *A* is a *vertex.*

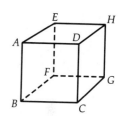

**Figure 8-48**

## Lesson Exercise 8.56

(a) How many faces does a cube have?
(b) How many vertices (corners) does a cube have?
(c) How many edges does a cube have? Count them in groups, beginning on the top of the cube.

## Prisms

Die          VCR

**Figure 8-49**

Cubes and rectangular solids are both a special type of polyhedron called a prism. A **prism** has congruent polygonal regions as its bases (usually the top and bottom), and the corresponding vertices are connected by parallel line segments (Figure 8-49). The faces that are not bases are called **lateral faces.**

A prism is named by the kind of base it has (Figure 8-50).

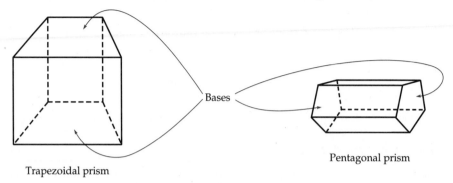

Bases

Trapezoidal prism

Pentagonal prism

**Figure 8-50**

In more formal terms, a **prism** is a polyhedron formed by two congruent polygonal bases in parallel planes connected by three or more parallelogram-shaped regions. A prism that has lateral faces that are rectangular regions is a **right prism** (Figure 8-51).

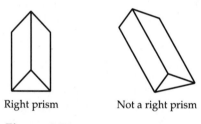

Right prism          Not a right prism

**Figure 8-51**

Note that any kind of prism can be split into congruent layers, as shown in Figure 8-52.

**Figure 8-52**

**D** Lesson Exercise 8.57

(a) Draw a triangular prism.
(b) How many faces does it have?
(c) How many vertices does it have?
(d) How many edges does it have?

Your results from Lesson Exercises 8.56 and 8.57 should have been as follows.

| Figure | Faces | Vertices | Edges |
|---|---|---|---|
| Cube | 6 | 8 | 12 |
| Triangular prism | 5 | 6 | 9 |

Figure 8-53 shows how the fourth-grade textbook of *Mathematics Unlimited* introduces the topic.

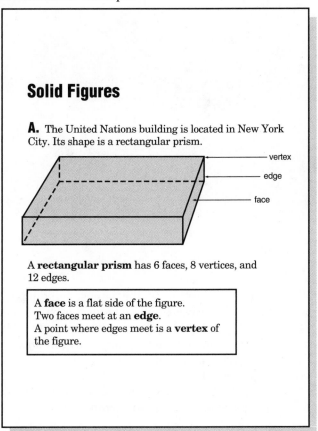

From *Mathematics Unlimited*, Grade 4 (San Diego, CA: Harcourt Brace Jovanovich, 1992), p. 328.

**Figure 8-53**

## D  Lesson Exercise 8.58

(a) Add two more rows to the table for a rectangular prism and a pentagonal prism and fill in the number of faces, vertices, and edges each has.

(b) What pattern do you see in each row of the table?

## Pyramids

Neg. no. 331002. Photo: Lowenfish. Courtesy of Department of Library Services, American Museum of Natural History.

**Figure 8-54**

**Figure 8-55**

The ancient Eyptians constructed some of the largest buildings in the world (Figure 8-54). Some contain over 2 million stones, each weighing at least a ton! These buildings suggest another important group of polyhedra: pyramids. A pyramid can be formed by taking any polygon and a point above the plane of the polygon and connecting all the vertices of the polygon to that point (Figure 8-55).

Pyramids are named by the kind of base they have (Figure 8-56). The Great Pyramid of Egypt approximates a square pyramid.

Square pyramid          Triangular pyramid

**Figure 8-56**

In more formal terms, a **pyramid** is a polyhedron that has a polygonal base. Its lateral faces are triangular regions with a common vertex. The following table summarizes the data we have collected so far about different polyhedra and the number of faces, vertices, and edges they have.

| Figure | Faces | Vertices | Edges |
|---|---|---|---|
| Cube | 6 | 8 | 12 |
| Triangular prism | 5 | 6 | 9 |
| Rectangular prism | 6 | 8 | 12 |
| Pentagonal prism | 7 | 10 | 15 |
| Triangular pyramid | | | |
| Square pyramid | | | |

## Lesson Exercise 8.59

(a) Fill in the last two rows of the chart.
(b) Use inductive reasoning to hypothesize how the number of edges of each polyhedron is related to the number of faces and vertices it has.

The pattern you observed in Lesson Exercises 8.58 and 8.59 holds for all polyhedra. Euler's formula describes this pattern algebraically.

---

**Euler's Formula**

For all polyhedra, $F + V - E = 2$, in which $F$ is the number of faces, $V$ the number of vertices, and $E$ the number of edges.

---

Euler (1707–1783) (pronounced "oiler") was the most prolific mathematician who ever lived (Figure 8-57). Even during the last 17 years of his life, when he was blind, Euler developed many new mathematical ideas.

## Regular Polyhedra and Euler's Formula

Although there are an infinite number of regular polygons, there are only five regular polyhedra! A **regular polyhedron** is a polyhedron that has faces that are congruent, regular polygonal regions, and the number of

Photo courtesy of Library of Congress.

**Figure 8-57**

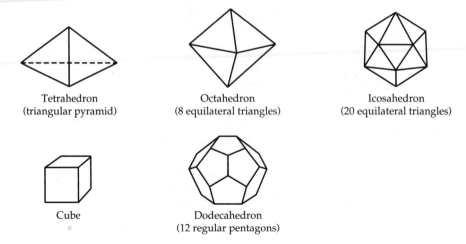

Tetrahedron
(triangular pyramid)

Octahedron
(8 equilateral triangles)

Icosahedron
(20 equilateral triangles)

Cube

Dodecahedron
(12 regular pentagons)

**Figure 8-58**

edges that meet at each vertex is the same. The ancient Greeks proved that the only regular polyhedra are the five shown in Figure 8-58.

Natural crystals occur in the shape of the tetrahedron (for example, chrome alum), the cube (salt), and the octahedron (sodium sulphantimoniate). In the following exercise, determine if Euler's formula works for regular polyhedra.

## Lesson Exercise 8.60

(a) Complete the table.

| Regular Polyhedron | Faces | Vertices | Edges |
|---|---|---|---|
| Tetrahedron | | | |
| Octahedron | 8 | | |
| Icosahedron | 20 | 12 | 30 |
| Cube | | | |
| Dodecahedron | 12 | | 30 |

(b) Does Euler's formula work for all regular polyhedra?

## Cylinders, Cones and Spheres

Some everyday objects suggest space figures that are not polyhedra: cylinders, cones, and spheres (Figure 8-59).

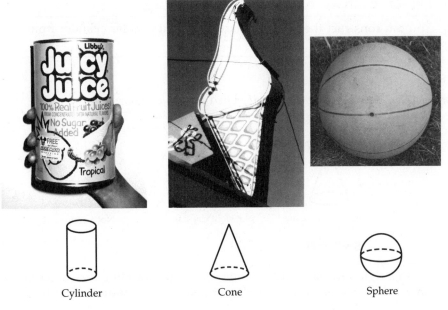

Cylinder                    Cone                    Sphere

Photos by Tom Sonnabend.

**Figure 8-59**

## Lesson Exercise 8.61

Why aren't cylinders, cones, and spheres polyhedra?

The most common types of cylinders are right circular cylinders.

Right circular cylinder    Not right circular cylinders    Not a cylinder

**Figure 8-60**

Circular cylinders have parallel bases that are circular regions. In a **right circular cylinder** (Figure 8-60), the segment connecting the center of the circular bases is perpendicular to the bases.

Lesson Exercise 8.62

You can construct the lateral surface of a right circular cylinder from a polygon. Which one?

The familiar type of cone is called a right circular cone.

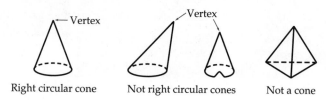

Right circular cone    Not right circular cones    Not a cone

**Figure 8-61**

In a **right circular cone,** the line segment connecting the center of the circular base to the vertex (see Figure 8-61) is perpendicular to the base.

Lesson Exercise 8.63

(a) Name a property that all cones and pyramids have in common.
(b) What van Hiele level is the question in part (a)?

## Answers to Selected Lesson Exercises

8.48 (a) false

8.50 (a) false

8.51 (a) true

8.53 (a) true

8.54 false

8.56 (a) 6     (b) 8     (c) 12

8.57 (b) 5     (c) 6     (d) 9

8.58 (a) rectangular prism: 6, 8, 12; pentagonal prism: 7, 10, 15

8.59 (a) 4, 4, 6 and 5, 5, 8

8.60 (a)

| Regular Polyhedron | Faces | Vertices | Edges |
| --- | --- | --- | --- |
| Tetrahedron | 4 | 4 | 6 |
| Octahedron | 8 | 6 | 12 |
| Icosahedron | 20 | 12 | 30 |
| Cube | 6 | 8 | 12 |
| Dodecahedron | 12 | 20 | 30 |

(b) yes

8.61 Their faces are not polygonal regions.

8.62 a rectangle

8.63 (a) They have exactly one base.
(b) analysis

## 8.4  Homework Exercises

*Basic Exercises*

1. (a) True or false? In space, two lines that are perpendicular to a third line are parallel to each other.
   (b) In your surroundings, identify a model of this situation that supports your answer.

2. What are skew lines?

3. In space, point A is not on a line b. How many lines pass through A that
   (a) intersect b?
   (b) are perpendicular to b?
   (c) are parallel to b?
   (d) are skew to b?

4. In space, point A is on line b. How many lines pass through A that
   (a) intersect b?
   (b) are perpendicular to b?
   (c) are parallel to b?
   (d) are skew to b?

5. What are the three possible relationships between a line and a plane in space?

6. (a) True or false? Two lines that are parallel to the same plane are parallel to each other.
   (b) In your surroundings, identify a model of this situation that supports your answer.

7. (a) True or false? A plane contains line m but not line n, and m ∥ n. Then the plane is parallel to n.
   (b) In your surroundings, identify a model of this situation that supports your answer.

8. Point A is not on line b. How many different planes contain point A and line b?

9. Is every line in a horizontal plane horizontal?

10. Is every line in a vertical plane vertical?

11. Draw a sketch of two perpendicular planes.

12. True or false? Two planes, a and b, intersect a third plane in parallel lines. Planes a and b are parallel.

13. True or false? Three planes may intersect at exactly one point.

14. Into how many sections can space be separated by the removal of two planes?

15. (a) The ceiling and floor of a room suggest _____ planes.
    (b) The ceiling and side wall of a room suggest _____ planes.

16. *ABCDEFGH* is a cube.

   (a) Name two skew lines in the drawing.
   (b) The plane that contains *ABEF* is parallel to the plane that contains _____.
   (c) The plane that contains *ABCD* is _____ to the plane that contains *BCGF*.
   (d) What is the intersection of the plane containing *E, F, G,* and *H* with the plane containing *B, C, F,* and *G*?

17. True or false? If a line contains two points of a triangle, then the line lies entirely in the plane of the triangle.

18. (a) True or false? Any set of four points is contained by one plane.
    (b) In your home, identify a model of this situation that supports your answer.

19. (a) True or false? If a line intersects one of two parallel lines, then it intersects the other also.
    (b) In your home, identify a model of this situation that supports your answer.

20. True or false? Through a given point not on plane P, there is exactly one line parallel to P.

21. True or false? Through a given point not on plane P, there is exactly one plane parallel to P.

**22.** True or false? Line *m* intersects plane *P* and is not perpendicular to it. Then there is no line in *P* perpendicular to *m*.

**23.** Which of the following are polyhedra?

(a)     (b)

(c) cylinder    (d) hexagonal prism

**24.** (a) Name two properties that prisms and pyramids have in common.
(b) At what van Hiele level is the question in part (a)?

**25.** (a) How many faces does a hexagonal prism have?
(b) How many edges?
(c) How many vertices?

**26.** The figure shown is a cube.

(a) What kind of quarilateral is *EGCA*?
(b) What kind of triangle is △*EGH*?

**27.** (a) What simple change in the definition of a circle would make it the definition of a sphere?
(b) What are the possible shapes of the intersection of a plane and a sphere?

**28.** Name the space figure that would be formed if each shape were folded on the broken lines.

(a)     (b)     (c)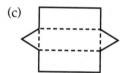

**29.** Which of the following pictures is the correct layout of the faces of the block?

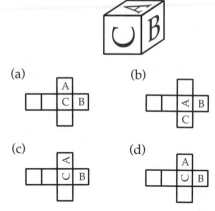

(a)    (b)

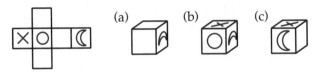

(c)    (d)

**30.** Which assembled cube on the right matches the disassembled cube on the left?

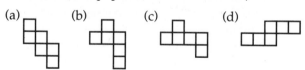

(a)    (b)    (c)

**31.** Which of the following patterns fold into a cube? (Use paper cutouts as needed.)

(a)    (b)    (c)    (d)

**32.** Shown here is a layout of the faces of a rectangular prism *ABCDEFGH*. Label the missing vertices.

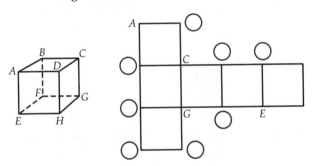

**33.** (a) Sketch a pyramid that has a hexagonal base.
   (b) How many faces does it have?
   (c) How many vertices?
   (d) How many edges?

**34.** A pyramid has a heptagonal base. How many faces, vertices, and edges does it have?

**35.** Determine if Euler's formula is true for the following figures.

(a)   (b) 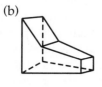  (c)

**36.** Draw a cone.

**37.** Draw a pentagonal prism.

**38.** Name each figure.

(a)     (b)

**39.** Name a space figure that approximates the shape of each of the following.
   (a) a new piece of chalk
   (b) your refrigerator at home

**40.** What property of (right) prisms and cylinders makes them more suitable than pyramids or cones for the shape of a garbage can?

**41.** What property of (right circular) cones and cylinders makes them more suitable than prisms or pyramids for the shape of an ice cream cone?

**42.** Write a description of the shape of a milk carton.

*Extension Exercises*

**43.** Decide whether each of the following describes a point, line, plane, segment, or ray.
   (a) all points that are equidistant from two parallel planes
   (b) in space, all points that are equidistant from both endpoints of a line segment
   (c) all points that are 3 inches below a line

**44.** A line and a plane are **perpendicular** if and only if they intersect, and the line is perpendicular to every line in the plane that passes through the intersection point.

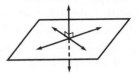

True or false? If two lines are perpendicular to the same plane, then they are parallel to each other.

**45.** True or false? If a line is perpendicular to one of two parallel planes, then it is perpendicular to the other.

**46.** Investigate whether chair legs are approximately perpendicular to the floor and summarize your results.

**47.** Two planes are **perpendicular** if and only if one plane contains a line that is perpendicular to the other plane.

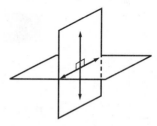

True or false? If two planes are perpendicular to a third plane, then they are parallel to each other.

**48.** Why are there no such things as skew planes?

49. A prism has a base with $n$ sides.
    (a) How many faces does it have?
    (b) How many vertices does it have?
    (c) How many edges does it have?
    (d) Does Euler's formula work for prisms?

50. A pyramid has a base with $n$ sides.
    (a) How many faces does it have?
    (b) How many vertices does it have?
    (c) How many edges does it have?
    (d) Does Euler's formula work for pyramids?

51. Take a regular polyhedron. Connect the centers of adjacent faces and you get . . . another polyhedron (called the **dual**)!
    What shape is obtained by connecting the centers of adjacent faces of

(a)
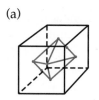
a cube?

(b)

a tetrahedron?

(c)

an octahedron?

    (d) A regular polyhedron has $x$ vertices, $y$ faces, and $z$ edges. Conjecture how many vertices, faces, and edges its dual has.

52. Construct or obtain models of a square pyramid and a triangular pyramid with congruent equilateral triangles for all their triangular faces. (You could use cardboard.) Place the two shapes together to form a polyhedron with the smallest number of faces. How many faces does it have?

*Special Exercise*

53. A plane surface suggested by a sheet of paper has two sides. In fact, a piece of paper always has two sides, right? Not always. The remarkable Möbius strip has only 1 side! The front cover of this book has a drawing of a Möbius strip. You can make one yourself using scissors, paper, and tape.
    (a) Cut out two strips of paper. Tape the ends of one strip to make a regular loop. Before taping together the ends of the second strip, give it a half-twist to create a Möbius strip.

    (b) Use a pencil to draw a line on one side of each paper loop. Continue each line until you reach your starting point.
    (c) What is the difference in your results in part (b) for each loop?

## 8.5  Spatial Perception

Figure 8-62

It's amazing that a figure sketched on a flat surface can appear to have a third dimension, as in Figure 8-62. Representing three-dimensional figures on a two-dimensional surface posed a serious problem for artists up until the Renaissance. Today, artists have no problem making flat drawings that create the illusion of three dimensions. This knowledge resulted from many years of experimentation.

### Visual Perception

Although the M. C. Escher drawing in Figure 8-63 is two-dimensional, it appears to be three-dimensional. Our brains tend to look for depth, the third dimension, even in a flat picture. Some optical illusions are based upon the tendency to perceive depth in a flat drawing.

**Figure 8-63**

In Lesson Exercises 8.64 and 8.65, use your eyes. NO MEASURING ALLOWED!

## Lesson Exercise 8.64

Which one of the following is true?
(a)  The circles in Figure 8-64 are the same size.
(b)  The top circle is larger.
(c)  The bottom circle is larger.

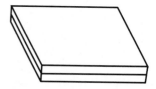

**Figure 8-64**

## Lesson Exercise 8.65

Will a dime fit inside the parallelogram in Figure 8-65?

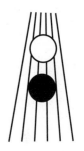

**Figure 8-65**

In Lesson Exercises 8.64 and 8.65 we perceive depth. In Lesson Exercise 8.64, the white ball appears further back. Our brains expect objects that are further away to look smaller. Since the white ball looks to be the same size as the "closer" black ball, we see the white ball as larger. In Lesson Exercise 8.65, we assume that the top of the parallelogram is further back than the bottom, making it seem larger.

While our eyes help us make sense of our surroundings, these examples illustrate that our visual perception is not always reliable for evaluating spatial relationships. However, once we understand visual perception, we can make sketches of solids on paper that are helpful in analyzing three-dimensional relationships.

## Drawing Solids

When solids are drawn on paper, some parallel and perpendicular relationships are retained, while others are not. First, consider a cube. What follows is an introductory method for drawing a cube. You will eventually develop your own shortcuts.

## Lesson Exercise 8.66

Get a pencil and paper and follow these steps.

**Step 1**   Draw a square (Figure 8-66).

Figure 8-66

**Step 2**   Draw a second identical square "behind" it (Figure 8-67).

Figure 8-67

**Step 3**   Connect the corresponding vertices (Figure 8-68).

Figure 8-68

**Step 4**   Erase the three edges that cannot be seen from the front, or draw them as broken lines (Figure 8-69).

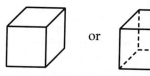

Figure 8-69

## Lesson Exercise 8.67

(a) Draw another cube for practice.
(b) Label the vertices of your cube as shown in Figure 8-70.
(c) Name two perpendicular lines in the cube that are drawn perpendicular.
(d) Name two perpendicular lines in the cube that are not drawn perpendicular to each other.
(e) Name two surfaces of the cube that are contained in parallel planes.

**Figure 8-70**

Next, draw a triangular prism.

## Lesson Exercise 8.68

**Step 1**   Draw a triangle (Figure 8-71).

**Figure 8-71**

**Step 2**   Draw a second identical triangle above it (Figure 8-72).

**Figure 8-72**

**Step 3**   Connect the corresponding vertices (Figure 8-73).

**Figure 8-73**

**Step 4**   Redraw as broken lines the part that cannot be seen from the front, as in Figure 8-74.

**Figure 8-74**

## Lesson Exercise 8.69

Draw another triangular prism for practice.

## Viewpoints of Space Figures

We never see a solid in its entirety; we see it from a viewpoint (Figure 8-75).

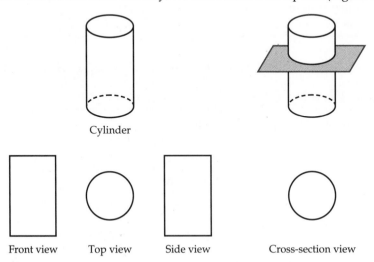

Cylinder

Front view        Top view        Side view        Cross-section view

**Figure 8-75**

Artists, architects, and photographers study how objects appear from different viewpoints. Such knowledge enriches our understanding and our experience in a world replete with geometric shapes and spatial relationships. Architects draw plans using views (called "elevations"). A view accurately shows the proportions, while a perspective drawing does not.

## Lesson Exercise 8.70

Name the space figure that has the front view, top view, and side view shown in Figure 8-76.

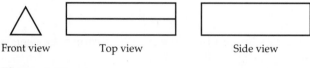

Front view        Top view        Side view

**Figure 8-76**

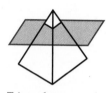

Triangular pyramid

**Figure 8-77**

## Lesson Exercise 8.71

Draw the cross-sectional view of the space figure in Figure 8-77.

## Perspective Drawing

In the Middle Ages in Europe, many artists painted scenes that had religious themes. In these symbolic works, the artists were not concerned about accurately representing people and objects. In the late thirteenth, fourteenth, and fifteenth centuries, however, European painters became more interested in accurately drawing their surroundings, but they were not sure exactly how to do it.

LAC 95586, 15th century, Bartholemew the Englishman, Book of Properties, Amiens, Bibliotheque. © Giraudon/ Art Resource, N.Y.

**Figure 8-78**

## Lesson Exercise 8.72

What is unrealistic about the fifteenth-century painting shown in Figure 8-78?

The painting in Figure 8-78 does not realistically depict how chairs and desks look.

Renaissance painters learned how to portray three dimensions realistically in paintings. These painters realized that they needed geometry to solve the problem of depicting three dimensions on a flat canvas. Piero della Francesca, the great fifteenth-century painter and mathematician,

66149. Piero della Francesca, Flagellatum, Urbino. © Alinari/Art Resource, N.Y.

**Figure 8-79**

used the idea of a vanishing point to create more realistic paintings, like the one in Figure 8-79.

If the lines running *from the front to the back* of the picture were extended, they would all intersect at one point (the vanishing point) just below the middle of the picture.

## Lesson Exercise 8.73

Find two parallel lines in the painting in Figure 8-79 that do not pass through the vanishing point. Explain why not.

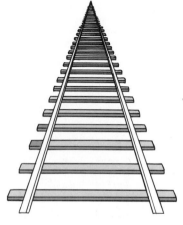

**Figure 8-80**

How is the illusion of depth created in a drawing? In a drawing of railroad tracks that go off into the horizon, like those in Figure 8-80, the parallel rails appear to meet at a point on the horizon called the **vanishing point.** Drawings based upon a vanishing point are called **one-point perspective drawings.**

A second method of drawing a cube utilizes one-point perspective. This method is more difficult than the method most people use, but the result is more realistic.

## Lesson Exercise 8.74

To draw a cube with one-point perspective, follow these steps.

**Step 1**   Draw the front of the cube and choose a vanishing point (Figure 8-81).

**Step 2**   Use a ruler to connect the vertices to the vanishing point (Figure 8-82).

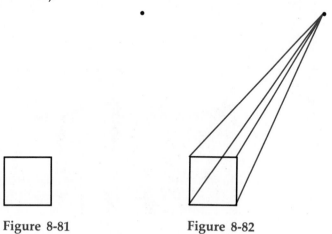

Figure 8-81                    Figure 8-82

**Step 3**   Draw the back of the cube (Figure 8-83).

**Step 4**   Darken the edges that would be seen from the front (Figure 8-84).

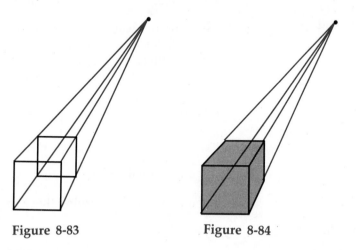

Figure 8-83                    Figure 8-84

## Lesson Exercise 8.75

Where is the vanishing point for the drawing in Figure 8-85?

Figure 8-85

## Answers to Selected Lesson Exercises

**8.64** (a)

**8.65** no

**8.67** (c) $\overline{AE}$ and $\overline{EH}$     (d) $\overline{AE}$ and $\overline{AB}$
(e) *ADHE* and *BCGF*

**8.70** triangular prism

**8.72** All of the furniture looks crooked.

**8.73** Lines going from left to right across the floor or ceiling are drawn parallel but do not pass through the vanishing point. Only parallel lines from the front to back meet at the vanishing point.

## 8.5   Homework Exercises

*Basic Exercises*

**1.**

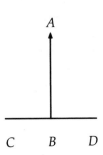

(a) Which appears to be longer, $\overline{AB}$ or $\overline{CD}$?
(b) Measure and find the correct answer.
(c) Why does our visual perception tend to elongate $\overline{AB}$?

**2.**

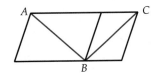

(a) Which one of the following statements appears to be true?
(1) $\overline{AB}$ and $\overline{BC}$ are the same length.
(2) $\overline{AB}$ is longer.
(3) $\overline{BC}$ is longer.
(b) Measure and find the correct answer.

**3.**

These two photos show the same person on opposite sides of the same room! Explain how this optical illusion is created.

**4.** Draw a cube.

**5.** Here is another way to sketch a cube.
Draw three line segments like these.     Draw every other edge parallel to one of these segments.

**6.** Draw a triangular prism.

**7.** Draw a cylinder by following these steps.

**Step 1**   Draw an oval.

**Step 2** Draw a second identical oval above it.

**Step 3** Connect the ovals with two line segments.

**Step 4** Redraw as a broken line the part of the bottom oval that cannot be seen from the front.

8. Draw a square pyramid by following these steps.

**Step 1** Draw a base.

**Step 2** Draw a point above it.

**Step 3** Connect the vertices of the base to the point.

**Step 4** Redraw the hidden edges as broken lines (or erase them).

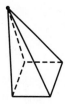

9. Draw a hexagonal prism.

10. Use a grid line like the one shown here to draw a cylinder that has diameter $d = 3$ units and height $h = 4$ units.

$d = 2 \quad h = 2$

11. Name the space figure that has the front view, top view, and side view shown.

Front view      Top view      Side view

**12.** In each case, identify the cross section cut by the plane.

(a)      (b)

**13.** A cone is cut by planes as shown. What is the resulting cross section?

(a)      (b)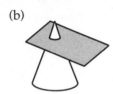

**14.** An engineering company designs the following piece. Draw a picture of the cross section.

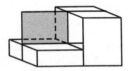

**15.** If a cube is intersected by a plane passing through the three points shown, what shape is the cross section?

**16.** Name two figures other than a cube that have a square cross section. Use drawings to support your answers.

**17.** Why do drinking glasses usually have circular cross sections?

**18.** Shown here is a picture of a set of cubes, along with two-dimensional front and bottom views.

      Front view      Bottom view

Draw the front and bottom view for each of the following stacks of cubes. (Assume that no cubes are hidden other than those that support visible cubes.)

(a)         (b)

**19.** The following diagram shows the rear view of a building. Draw the front view.

Rear view

**20.** Draw the front and top view of the buildings.

**21.** Sketch the front and top views of the building in which you live.

**22.** On its surfaces, a cube has the four shapes shown. Look at the four shapes and the two views of the cube.

Which of the following shows the cube correctly?

(a)    (b)    (c)    (d)

**23.** Below are three different views of a cube. Which letter must appear twice on the cube?

**24.** (a) Locate the vanishing point in Albrecht Dürer's *St. Jerome in His Study.*

192341. Dürer, *St. Jerome in His Study*, engraving. © Marburg/Art Resource, N.Y.

  (b) Find two parallel lines that do not pass through the vanishing point. Explain why not.

**25.** Find the vanishing point in the drawing.

**26.** You can draw block letters using a vanishing point, as shown. Draw your first or last name in block letters using a vanishing point.

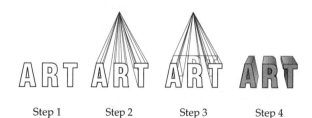

Step 1          Step 2          Step 3          Step 4

**27.** The figure shown is intersected by a plane. Match the figure to the correct picture of its intersection with the plane.

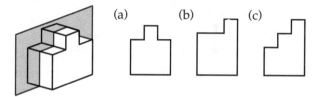

(a)          (b)          (c)

**28.** Draw a cube with one-point perspective.

**29.** In the game of pick-up sticks, a player picks up the sticks one stick at a time, always taking the stick on top. In what order should the sticks in the diagram be picked up?

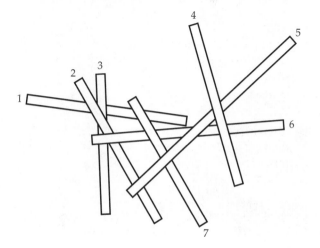

**30.** Explain why the man reading the book on perspective in the cartoon thinks it's hogwash.

By permission of Johnny Hart and Creators Syndicate, Inc.

**31.** The drawing by William Hogarth shown here is called *False Perspective*. Make a list of all the perspective errors you can find.

The Bettmann Archive.

**32.** What is odd about the perspective in the Escher drawing shown here?

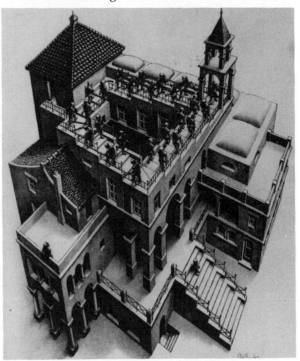

© 1990 M. C. Escher Heirs/Cordon Art—Baarn—Holland.

*Extension Exercises*

33. (a) Copy the figure.

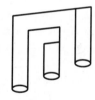

(b) What is odd about the figure?

34. Explain why it is impossible for $\overleftrightarrow{AB}$ to intersect the *congruent* boxes as shown.

35. Draw a table with one-point perspective.

36. Consider the following problem. "Color six small squares so that no two colored squares are in the same column, the same row, or the same diagonal." Devise a plan and solve the problem.

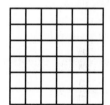

37. In drawing railroad tracks in perspective, how much space should there be between parallel tracks? Look at drawings 1 and 2 and answer the questions that follow.

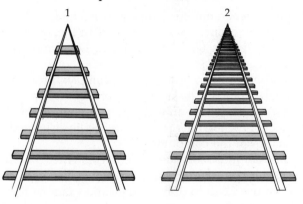

(a) Which picture of the railroad tracks, 1 or 2, looks more realistic?

(b) Measure the distance between the successive horizontal ties in each figure. Which figure has evenly spaced ties?

(c) The vanishing point is used to draw tracks correctly. Follow these steps and make your own drawing with a ruler and pencil.

*Step 1* Use a vanishing point to draw the rails. Then draw the front and back ties.

*Step 2* Label the front $\overline{AB}$ and the back $\overline{CD}$.

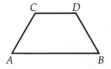

*Step 3* To locate the tie between $\overline{AB}$ and $\overline{CD}$, draw $\overline{AD}$ and $\overline{BC}$. Then draw a new tie parallel to $\overline{AB}$ through the point where $\overline{AD}$ and $\overline{BC}$ intersect.

*Step 4* Erase your guidelines.

38. How would you locate the first tie in the following drawing? (*Hint:* Use the midpoint of the second tie and see the previous exercise.)

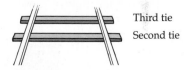

Third tie

Second tie

39. Make a perspective drawing with five railroad tracks.

40. The targets for a shooting match are set up on a field.

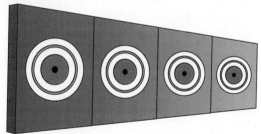

Copy the figure and add targets on the left and right as follows.

(a) Draw the left edge of the first target, and draw the vanishing point.

(b) Connect the top and bottom of the left edge to the vanishing point.

(c) Draw the right edge of the last target.

(d) Use the diagonals to locate the targets in between.

**41.** Create your own drawing using one-point perspective.

**42.** Mold a piece of clay into the shape of a cube. How could you slice it into three congruent square pyramids?

*Special Exercises*

**43.** Suppose that a wooden cube is painted blue on the outside and then cut into smaller cubes as shown.

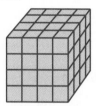

(a) How many small cubes would there be?

(b) How many cubes would have exactly one surface painted blue? (*Hint:* There is a pattern in the location of these cubes.)

(c) How many cubes would have exactly two surfaces painted blue?

(d) How many cubes would have exactly three surfaces painted blue?

(e) How many cubes would have exactly four surfaces painted blue?

(f) How many cubes would have no surfaces painted blue?

**44.** Someone builds a 5-by-5-by-5 model of cubes as shown and paints the outside of the model.

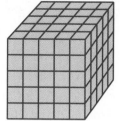

How many cubes will have each of the following?

(a) one face painted

(b) two faces painted

(c) three faces painted

(d) four faces painted

(e) zero faces painted

**45.** Repeat the preceding question for the following models.

(a) 6-by-6-by-6 model

(b) *n*-by-*n*-by-*n* model

## 8.6   Introducing Logo

Logo, an excellent computer programming language for children, was developed by Seymour Papert and his co-workers at MIT in the 1960s. In his book *Mindstorms*, Papert explains why he developed Logo and why you, the reader, should use it.

First, Logo enables children to learn how to solve complex problems and think logically. In Logo, complex tasks can be broken down into simpler components. Second, Logo offers an ideal learning environment. The child has more control over the learning process and receives immediate, individualized feedback from the computer.

Logo is easier to begin than most computer languages. After 5 or 10 minutes of instruction, a child can start making drawings in Logo. In elementary schools, children use Logo to draw shapes and examine their properties.

## Basic Commands

Once the computer is set up to do Logo, the following activities will introduce you to the language. Type the following:

CLEARSCREEN

and press the RETURN or ENTER key. Pressing this key lets the computer know that you are finished typing in a line of information. (*Note:* In MIT Logo, use DRAW instead of CLEARSCREEN.)

Do you now see a triangle in the center of your screen? Called a "turtle," it is really a triangle. Experiment with moving the turtle around by typing the following commands. Type:

FD 40

Be sure to leave a space between the D and the 4. Press RETURN or ENTER. FD stands for "forward." The number tells the turtle how far to move. Type:

CS

and press RETURN or ENTER. CS is short for CLEARSCREEN. (Again, use DRAW in MIT Logo.) Now try typing an FD command with a different number. Enter:

FD 8

How far did the turtle move this time? (Throughout this chapter, when you are instructed to "enter" a command, type the command and press the RETURN or ENTER key.)

## Lesson Exercise 8.76

Enter CS (clear screen) and then enter FD 100. What happens this time?

You can also move the turtle by typing BK (back), RT (right turn), or LT (left turn), followed by a blank space and a number. Enter:

BK 60

and press RETURN or ENTER. The RT and LT commands are slightly different. You have to watch the turtle more closely. Enter:

RT 90

What happened? (Did you remember to press RETURN or ENTER afterwards?)

Enter:

RT 180

Name ______________________________ **Technology Connection**
**Computer**

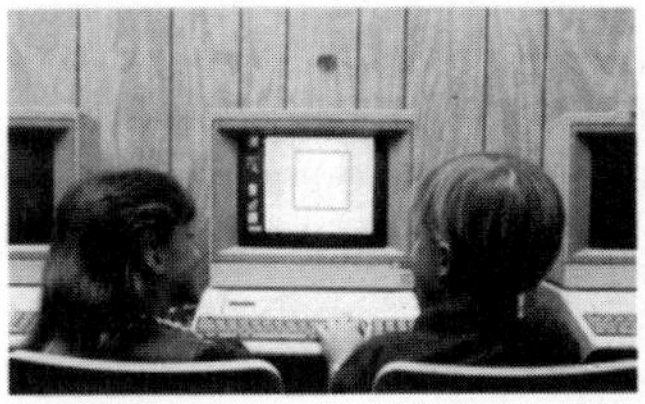

Use a computer.

Work with a friend.

Use the LOGO turtle to make a line, a square, and a rectangle.
In the box, draw what you made.

1. Make a line.
   Enter RT 90 FD 80

2. Make a square.
   Enter FD 70 RT 90 FD 70 RT 90 FD 70 RT 90 FD 70

3. Make a rectangle.
   Enter FD 50 LT 90 FD 80 LT 90 FD 50 LT 90 FD 80

4. Make a square or rectangle of your own. Write the commands you use. In the box, draw a shape like the one on the computer. **Answers will vary.**

Enter

FD ____ RT ____ FD ____ RT ____ FD ____ RT ____ FD ____

From *Mathematics Plus*, Grade 2 (San Diego, CA: Harcourt Brace Jovanovich, 1992), p. 276.

**Figure 8-86**

## Lesson Exercise 8.77

What does the 90 or 180 after RT stand for?

## Lesson Exercise 8.78

Enter CS (clear screen). Now try to draw a picture using a series of commands.

## Lesson Exercise 8.79

Draw a square using Logo.

Figure 8-86 shows how the second-grade textbook of *Mathematics Plus* introduces drawing squares and rectangles with Logo.

A square with sides of length 40 can be drawn by repeating the commands FD 40 and RT 90 four times. Logo has a REPEAT command that can save you from having to write the repeated command over and over. Enter:

CS
REPEAT 4 [FD 40 RT 90]

The last command repeats the moves inside the brackets four times.

## **D** Lesson Exercise 8.80

Consider the following series of commands.

FD 50
RT 120
FD 50
RT 120
FD 50
RT 120

(a) Without the aid of the computer, draw the result of these commands.
(b) Using REPEAT, write a single line that is equivalent to the six given lines.
(c) Clear the screen. Enter your REPEAT command and see what results.

## Drawing Polygons

So far, you've seen how to draw an equilateral triangle and a square. Were you surprised that the equilateral triangle is drawn with RT 120 instead of RT 60? (If not, *I'm* surprised.) Figure 8-87 shows why RT 120 was used.

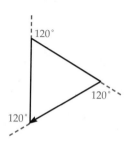

**Figure 8-87**

The angle measure of the turns is related to the *exterior* angle measure of the regular polygon. In a square, the exterior and interior angles happen to have the same measure (Figure 8-88).

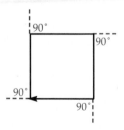

**Figure 8-88**

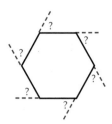

**Figure 8-89**

**D** Lesson Exercise 8.81

(a) Look at the regular pentagon drawn in Figure 8-89. Write a REPEAT command that will draw it with sides of length 30.
(b) Enter your answer to part (a) into the computer and see whether it works.

**Figure 8-90**

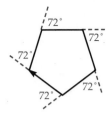

**Figure 8-91**

**D** Lesson Exercise 8.82

(a) What is the measure of each interior angle of a regular hexagon (see Figure 8-90)? (*Hint:* See Section 8.3.)
(b) What is the measure of each exterior angle in Figure 8-91?
(c) Write a Logo command that draws a regular hexagon.
(d) Enter your answer to part (c) into the computer and see if it works.

Is there a pattern in the angle turns used in drawing regular polygons? You be the judge. Examine the following chart.

| Drawing Regular Polygons | |
|---|---|
| **Sides** | **Angle of Logo turn** |
| 3 | 120° |
| 4 | 90° |
| 5 | 72° |
| 6 | 60° |
| N | ? |

**D** Lesson Exercise 8.83

What is the pattern in the chart on page 468? If you understand it, give the angle (in degrees) of Logo turns to draw an *N*-sided regular polygon.

When you draw a polygon that has a large number of sides, what shape does it resemble? Try drawing a 360-sided polygon!

Lesson Exercise 8.84

(a) Enter REPEAT 360 [FD 1 RT 1].
(b) What shape does the 360-sided polygon approximate?

## Glossary of Logo Commands

Here is a reference list of Logo commands. If you have some free time at the computer, try out some new commands.

| Command | Abbreviation | Function | Example |
|---|---|---|---|
| FORWARD | FD | moves turtle forward | FD 60 |
| BACK | BK | moves turtle back | BK 50 |
| RIGHT | RT | turns the turtle to *its* right | RT 120 |
| LEFT | LT | turns the turtle to *its* left | LT 90 |
| CLEARSCREEN (DRAW in MIT Logo) | CS | clears the screen | CS |
| PENUP | PU | turtle moves without leaving a trail | PU |
| PENDOWN | PD | turtle will leave a trail when it moves | PD |
| HOME | | returns turtle to center of screen | HOME |
| SHOWTURTLE | ST | shows turtle shape on screen | ST |
| HIDETURTLE | HT | conceals turtle shape | HT |

## Answers to Selected Lesson Exercises

8.77 the number of degrees in the turn

8.81 (a) *Hint:* Use RT 72.

8.82 (a) 120°    (b) 60°

8.83 angle of turn $= \dfrac{360°}{N}$

8.84 (b) circle

## 8.6   Homework Exercises

*Basic Exercises*

1. Sketch the figure that each of the following Logo programs would draw. Check your answer on a computer.

    (a) RT 45      (b) LT 60
        FD 50          FD 20
        RT 90          RT 120
        FD 50          FD 20
                       RT 120
                       FD 20
                       LT 30
                       FD 30
                       LT 30
                       FD 20
                       RT 120
                       FD 20
                       RT 120
                       FD 20

2. Sketch the figure that each of the following Logo programs would draw. Check your answer on a computer.

    (a) RT 135     (b) FD 40
        FD 60          LT 45
        LT 45          FD 30
        FD 40          RT 90
                       FD 30
                       RT 90
                       FD 30
                       LT 135
                       FD 30

3. What letter does the following Logo program draw?

    RT 90
    FD 20
    BK 40
    FD 20
    RT 90
    FD 50

4. What letter does the following Logo program draw?

    FD 40    RT 90    FD 20
    BK 20    RT 90    FD 20
    LT 90    FD 15

5. (a) What is the measure of each interior angle of a regular octagon?
   (b) What is the measure of each exterior angle?

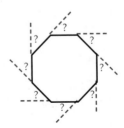

   (c) Write a Logo command that draws a regular octagon.
   (d) Enter your answer to part (c) into the computer and see whether it works.

6. Write a Logo command that draws a 10-sided polygon.

7. Write a Logo command that draws a figure that approximates a circle.

8. Write a Logo program that draws each picture shown.

    (a)              (b)

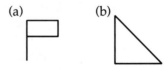

9. Write a Logo program that draws a letter *M*.

10. Write a Logo program that draws each picture shown.

    (a)

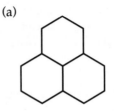

    (b)

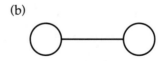

**11.** Write a single REPEAT command that draws the picture shown.

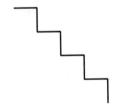

*Extension Exercises*

**12.** Experiment with the command
REPEAT ____ [FORWARD 1 RIGHT ____]
by filling in different numbers in the blanks.

**13.** Write a single REPEAT command that draws the star.

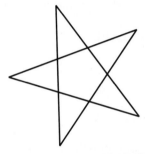

**14.** Write Logo steps to draw a cube.

**15.** Complete the proof that the sum of the exterior angle measures of a triangle is 360°.

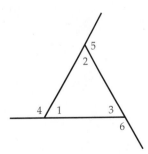

$m\angle 4 + m\angle 1 =$ _____ degrees,
$m\angle 5 + m\angle 2 =$ _____ degrees, and
$m\angle 6 + m\angle 3 =$ _____ degrees.

Combine these equations, to obtain
$m\angle 4 + m\angle 5 + m\angle 6 + m\angle 1 + m\angle 2 + m\angle 3 =$
_____ degrees. Since $m\angle 1 + m\angle 2 + m\angle 3 =$
_____ degrees, we know that
$m\angle 4 + m\angle 5 + m\angle 6 =$ _____ degrees.

**16.** Prove that the sum of the exterior angle measures of a quadrilateral is 360°. Use the preceding exercise as a model.

## 8.7  Logo Procedures

If you want to program the computer to do a more complex task, construct a "procedure" that performs a sequence of simpler tasks.

### Procedures

Suppose that you want the computer to draw a square. Instead of telling it to draw each part of the square separately, you can write a Logo program that gives all the commands needed to draw a square. Store this program, called a **procedure,** in the computer, and you can use it whenever you want the computer to draw a square.

The turtle knows the words FORWARD and BACK. Does it know the word SQUARE? Type:

SQUARE

and press the ENTER or RETURN key.

Logo does not understand this word . . . yet. You can give the word a meaning in Logo.

## Lesson Exercise 8.85

Write a command to draw a square.

To construct a Logo procedure to draw a square, begin with a title. Enter:

TO SQUARE

Note how the prompt from the computer has changed from ? to >. This means that you are *inside a program* and the computer is storing whatever you type into its memory.

Now enter a command to draw a square.

REPEAT 4 [FD 40 RT 90]

Finally, end the procedure.

END

(*Note:* If you are ever stuck in a program or want to redo it, the easiest way to exit from a program (and change from > back to ?) is to enter END.)

Now enter SQUARE again and see if the computer understands SQUARE now.

SQUARE

Aha!

---

**Defining a Logo Procedure**

1. Type TO followed by a name.
2. Type all the commands needed to perform the procedure.
3. Type END.

---

You have repeated commands. What happens when you repeat a procedure? Enter:

CS
REPEAT 6 [SQUARE RT 60]

**D** Lesson Exercise 8.86

Experiment by combining SQUARE with other commands to make designs.

If you are finished with this procedure, you can erase it from the computer by typing ERASE SQUARE. Enter:

ERASE SQUARE
SQUARE

The computer has lost its memory!

**D** Lesson Exercise 8.87

Write a procedure TRIANGLE that draws an equilateral triangle with sides of length 40.

## Variables

When you want to vary the dimensions of a figure, use variables in your Logo program. Create a new SQUARE procedure that allows you to input the length L of the sides of the square. Enter:

CS
TO SQUARE :L
REPEAT 4 [FD :L RT 90]
END

Now the computer has memorized the SQUARE program. The colon after SQUARE tells the computer that a number will be given to enter in memory location L. Enter:

SQUARE 20
SQUARE 40
SQUARE 60

To draw a rectangle, you need to input two numbers: a length and a width.

**D** Lesson Exercise 8.88

(a) Write a procedure RECTANGLE :L :W that will draw a rectangle using *any length and width* that are given as input when the procedure is called. It should begin:

TO RECTANGLE :L :W

(b) Once the procedure is written, run your procedure on the computer using a command such as:

RECTANGLE 40 30

## Combining Procedures

Often, a complicated task can be broken down into simpler tasks. You can draw the "house" in Figure 8-92 by drawing a square and a triangle.

Do you still have the TRIANGLE (Lesson Exercise 8.87) and SQUARE :L procedures in the computer's memory? If not, type them in. Then enter:

"A house"

**Figure 8-92**

TO HOUSE
SQUARE 40
FD 40 RT 30    *(moves from bottom left corner to top left corner of square)*
TRIANGLE
END
HOUSE

Did this work? Depending upon how your triangle program begins, you may have to make an adjustment. (Adjustments may also be needed with certain computers and monochrome monitors.)

## A Project: Creating a Design

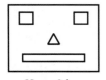

Happy? face

**D** Lesson Exercise 8.89

Write a longer procedure that makes a design using triangles, squares, and rectangles. The designs in Figure 8-93 are possibilities. Use them as an inspiration to create your own design.

Luxury cruiser

**Figure 8-93**

(*Hint:* To move the turtle invisibly from one place to another, use PENUP so that nothing is drawn on the screen. Then use PENDOWN when you want to resume drawing on the screen.)

## Answers to Selected Lesson Exercises

8.85 See the previous lesson.

8.87 *Hint:* An equilateral triangle is a regular

polygon. Find the measure of its exterior angles.

## 8.7   Homework Exercises

*Basic Exercises*

1. (a) Type in a procedure SQUARE that draws a square with sides that are 35 units long.
   (b) Try the following.

   REPEAT 6 [RT 60 SQUARE]

2. (a) Type in a procedure PENTA that draws a pentagon with sides that are 35 units long.
   (b) Try the following.

   RT 90
   REPEAT 6 [FD 10 RT 60 PENTA]

3. (a) Write a procedure HEXA :S that draws a regular hexagon with sides of any length S. The length will be given as input when the procedure is run.
   (b) Run your procedure on a computer.

4. (a) Write a procedure OCTA :S that draws a regular octagon with sides of any length S. The length will be given as input when the procedure is run.
   (b) Run your procedure on a computer.

5. Guess what each of the following will draw. Then run each one and see what happens.
   (a) REPEAT 5 [FD 50 RT 144]
   (b) REPEAT 13 [RT 60 REPEAT 3 [FD 30 RT 90]] (Do not press RETURN or ENTER until you finish typing the entire line.)

6. Write a Logo procedure that draws the six-pointed star.

7. Write a procedure that draws an 80° angle and its bisector.

*Extension Exercises*

8. (a) Write a procedure POLYGON :N that draws a regular polygon with N sides. N will be input when the procedure is run.
   (b) Run your procedure on a computer.

9. Write a Logo procedure to draw the following.

(a)                              (b)

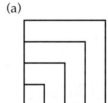                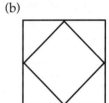

10. On graph paper, draw a cube like the one shown here. Use the coordinates to write a procedure in Logo that draws a cube.

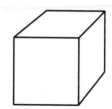

11. Write a Logo procedure to draw the following.

    (a)                           (b)

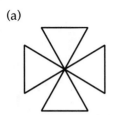
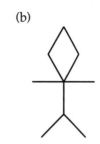

12. Write a program to draw the following.

13. Write a program to draw *one* of the following shapes.

    (a)                           (b)

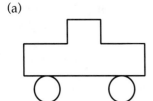

14. Write a procedure that makes a design using triangles, squares, and rectangles.

15. In this exercise, you will create a program that writes the word "Logo."
    (a) Write a procedure to draw an L.
    (b) Write a procedure to draw a letter o. Make it a little smaller than the L.
    (c) Write a procedure to draw a letter g. Make it about the same size as the o.
    (d) Write a master procedure that writes the word "Logo."

16. (a) Write a program
    PGRAM :SIDE1 :SIDE2 :ANGLE
    that draws a parallelogram with two given lengths and one angle measure.
    (b) Why is only one angle measure needed?

*Special Exercise*

17. (a) Without running it, tell what the following set of commands would draw.

    FD 20
    RT 15
    BK 25
    LT 35

    (b) Type the following program into a computer.

    ```
    TO SUN
    FD 20
    RT 15
    BK 25
    LT 35
    SUN
    END
    ```

    (c) Type SUN to perform your program. Type CTRL and G when you want the program to stop.
    (d) Explain the output of the program.

## Summary

Geometry began when people first observed three-dimensional shapes in their surroundings. The surfaces of three-dimensional objects suggested two-dimensional shapes. Young children today discover geometry in the same way. "In learning geometry, children [K–4] need to investigate, experiment, and explore with everyday objects and other physical materials" (NCTM, *Standards,* p. 48).

Ideal geometric shapes do not exist in the world. We abstract them from our surroundings. Geometric shapes then take on a life of their own. It was the work of the ancient Greeks, culminating with Euclid around 300 B.C., that gave us the logically organized Euclidean geometry. Euclidean geometry begins with the undefined terms "point," "line," "plane," and "space," and builds geometry from there. Formal geometry proceeds in a certain order because one cannot, for example, define a prism without first being familiar with points, line segments, and polygons.

In geometry, shapes are classified. Within each classification, mathematicians look for common properties. Once these properties are established, they can be applied to all kinds of objects in the world that approximate the shape being studied. This chapter contains classifications of angles, lines, polygons, and space figures.

In learning geometry, the van Hieles suggest working first on recognizing whole figures, then analyzing their properties, and then writing precise definitions and identifying relationships between different classes of figures. The van Hiele levels work especially well in the study of quadrilaterals.

Geometry offers interesting opportunities for investigations. For instance, the total number of diagonals of various polygons is related to the number of sides. The sums of the angle measures in convex polygons follow a pattern. Euler's formula describes another pattern in the numbers of faces, vertices, and edges in any polyhedron.

In studying space figures, we confront the difficulty of visualizing spatial relationships represented by diagrams and the issue of portraying three-dimensional shapes on two-dimensional surfaces. Renaissance mathematician-artists were the first to develop a system of perspective drawing based upon their understanding of the way we see the world. A teacher needs spatial ability in order to represent solids on the blackboard.

Geometry can be studied on the computer using Logo, probably the best computer language yet developed to teach young children. Children can quickly start using it, and it does not require a large vocabulary. After a short time, a student can grapple with some challenging geometry problems and create some beautiful designs. Logo also teaches the concepts of top-down programming and subroutines (procedures).

## Study Guide

To review Chapter 8, see what you know about each of the following ideas or terms listed that you have studied. You can also use this list to generate your own questions about Chapter 8.

# The NCTM Curriculum Standards and Geometry

**Selected NCTM Curriculum Standards**

The following standards come from the NCTM document.

- Identify, describe, compare, and classify geometric figures.
- Recognize and appreciate geometry in their world.
- Understand and apply geometric properties and relationships.
- Visualize and represent geometric figures with special attention to developing spatial sense.

1. Describe how each standard listed relates to the material you studied in Chapter 8.
2. Select any current elementary-school mathematics textbook and describe a sample lesson or exercise that illustrates each standard listed.

## Review Exercises

1. Why does the formal study of geometry begin with points and lines rather than with a study of three-dimensional figures?

2. Name two ways in which a sheet of paper differs from a plane.

3. Give a simpler name for each of the following.
    (a) $\overrightarrow{BA} \cup \overrightarrow{BC}$
    (b) $\overleftrightarrow{AD} \cap \overline{BE}$

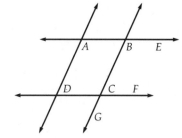

4. Point $A$ is on line $b$. How many different planes contain point $A$ and line $b$?

5. True or false? Through a point not on a given line, there is exactly one line that is skew to the given line.

6. (a) True or false? Two intersecting lines cannot both be parallel to a given plane.
    (b) In your home, identify a model of this situation that supports your answer.

7. Make an accurate drawing of a cube using one-point perspective.

8. Locate the next tie in correct perspective.

9. A parallelogram is also which of the following?
    (a) rectangle      (b) quadrilateral
    (c) trapezoid      (d) rhombus

10. Is every rhombus a type of square? If not, give a counterexample.

11. Which of the following shapes have four equal angle measures?
    (a) rhombus      (b) square
    (c) trapezoid      (d) rectangle
    (e) parallelogram

12. Sketch two parallelograms that intersect at exactly five points.

13. Use the angle sum property of a triangle to explain why the interior angle measures of a pentagon add up to 540°.

14. Draw a picture and explain why a regular hexagon does or does not tessellate the plane.

15. How many faces, vertices, and edges does a hexagonal pyramid have?

16. A certain prism has 21 edges. How many faces does it have?

17. What would the following sequence of Logo commands draw?

FD 50
LT 45
FD 50
RT 90
FD 50
RT 135
FD 30

18. Write a Logo command that draws a regular octagon.

19. What would the following sequence of Logo commands draw?

REPEAT 4 [FD 50 RT 60]
RT 90
FD 85

20. Make a sketch of a repeating tile pattern that uses squares and regular octagons.

## Geometry in Elementary School

The following chart shows at what grade level selected geometry topics typically appear in elementary-school mathematics textbooks.

| Topic | Typical Grade Level in Current Textbooks |
|---|---|
| Two- and three-dimensional figures | 1, 2, 3, 4, 5, 6 |
| Measuring angles | 5, 6 |
| Points, lines, and planes | 4, 5, 6 |
| Polygons (five or more sides) | 3, 4, 5, 6 |
| Radius, diameter, chord | 4, 5, 6 |
| Faces, edges, and vertices | 4, 5, 6 |
| Drawing space figures | 6 |

## Suggested Readings

*Arithmetic Teacher.* February, 1990 Focus Issue on Spatial Sense. Reston, VA: NCTM, 1990.

Bergamini, D. (ed.) *Mathematics.* New York: Time, 1963.

Chazan, D., and R. Houde. *How to Use Conjecturing and Microcomputers to Teach Geometry.* Reston, VA: NCTM, 1989.

Equals. *Get It Together.* Berkeley, CA: Equals, 1989.

Fuys, D., D. Geddes, and R. Tischler. *The Van Hiele Model of Thinking in Geometry Among Adolescents.* Reston, VA: NCTM, 1988.

Gardner, M. *Aha!* New York: W. H. Freeman, 1978.

Hill, J. (ed.) *Geometry for Grades K–6.* Reston, VA: NCTM, 1987.

Juster, Norton. *The Dot and the Line.* New York: Random House, 1963.

Lange, M. *Geometry in Modules.* Reading, MA: Addison-Wesley, 1975.

Minnesota Educational Computer Consortium (MECC). *Apple Logo in the Classroom.* St. Paul: MECC, 1983.

National Council of Teachers of Mathematics. 1973 Yearbook. *Geometry in the Mathematics Classroom.* Reston, VA: NCTM, 1973.

National Council of Teachers of Mathematics. 1984 Yearbook. *Computers in Mathematics Education.* Reston, VA: NCTM, 1984.

National Council of Teachers of Mathematics. 1987 Yearbook. *Learning and Teaching Geometry, K–12.* Reston, VA: NCTM, 1987.

O'Daffer, P., and S. Clemens. *Geometry: An Investigative Approach.* 2nd ed. Reading, MA: Addison-Wesley, 1992.

Papert, S. *Mindstorms: Children, Computers, and Powerful Ideas.* New York: Basic Books, 1980.

# 9

# Congruence, Symmetry, and Similarity

Many artistic and architectural designs often utilize patterns of congruent shapes. Sometimes, each individual shape is symmetric, that is, all of its parts match up to one another in a certain way.

People use similarity relationships in planning designs. In technical terms, similar figures are the same shape, although they may be of different sizes. For example, a scale model of a building is "similar" to the planned building.

Congruence, symmetry, and similarity are all related to motion geometry. By moving a geometric figure to different positions or changing its size, one can tell whether it is symmetric or if it is congruent or similar to another geometric figure.

Over 2500 years ago, the Greeks used straightedge-and-compass constructions to construct or copy geometric shapes. Many of these constructions can be analyzed using congruence properties.

## 9.1 Congruence and Rigid Motions

In Chapter 8, you learned about congruent line segments and angles. Congruence is one of the most important ideas of geometry. Photocopies and mass-produced items are examples of approximately congruent objects (Figure 9-1, page 483). The Dutch artist M. C. Escher drew some interesting, interlocking congruent shapes (Figure 9-2, page 483).

Photo courtesy of Library of Congress.

**Figure 9-1**

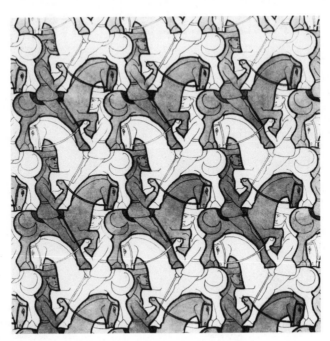

© 1990 M. C. Escher Heirs/Cordon Art—Baarn—Holland.

**Figure 9-2**

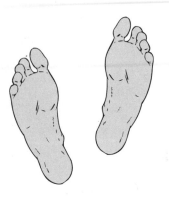

### Rigid Motions

Ask a child whether two flat shapes are the same (that is, congruent), and the child may place one shape on top of the other to be sure (Figure 9-3). In general, it is true that two plane figures are congruent if and only if one can fit exactly over the other.

The set of **rigid motions** (or **isometries**) describes the various ways to move a geometric figure around while preserving the distances between points in the figure. The three basic rigid motions are rotations (turns), translations (slides), and reflections (flips).

The page shown in Figure 9-4 from the sixth-grade textbook of *Mathematics Plus* gives an example of each motion.

How do these three basic motions work? In Lesson Exercise 9.1, begin with a turn (rotation) that moves the plane around a fixed point.

**Figure 9-3**

# TRANSLATIONS, ROTATIONS, AND REFLECTIONS

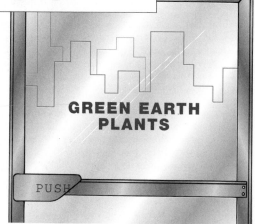

This is what a new sign on a window looked like from inside the store. Alex's boss, Mr. Weeks, was not happy. Do you know why?

Mr. Weeks was unhappy because people approaching the store could not read the sign.

You can move a geometric figure three ways.

You can slide the figure along straight lines. This is called a **translation**.

You can turn the figure around a point. This is called a **rotation**.

You can flip the figure over a line. This is called a **reflection**.

**Translation**

**Rotation**

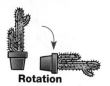

**Reflection**

From *Mathematics Plus*, Grade 6 (San Diego, CA: Harcourt Brace Jovanovich, 1992), p. 364.

**Figure 9-4**

## Lesson Exercise 9.1

(a) Place a piece of thin paper on this page and trace the shape $ABC$ and point $O$ from Figure 9-5.
(b) Now place your pencil point on $O$ and turn the tracing paper a little. You have just done a rotation around the point $O$!

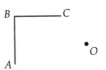

**Figure 9-5**

To describe any clockwise rotation, we specify a fixed center point, the measure of the angle through which we turn the plane around the center point, and the direction of the turn (clockwise).

## Lesson Exercise 9.2

Suppose that you turn ⌐ a full turn clockwise around point $C$ (Figure 9-6) so that it ends up back in the same place. How many degrees have you rotated the shape?

**Figure 9-6**

## Lesson Exercise 9.3

Suppose that you rotate the shape clockwise halfway around point $C$, as shown in Figure 9-7. How many degrees have you rotated the shape?

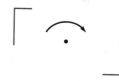

**Figure 9-7**

Lesson Exercises 9.2 and 9.3 illustrate two important rotations: the 360° full turn and the 180° half-turn. Now try doing a rotation yourself.

## Lesson Exercise 9.4

(a) Copy the grid and picture from Figure 9.8 on a piece of paper.
(b) Now, use tracing paper to trace $O$ and $\triangle ABC$ and then rotate $\triangle ABC$ 90° clockwise around point $O$.
(c) After completing the rotation, trace over the triangle in its new position (called the "image") so that it shows up on your original paper drawing. Then remove the tracing paper and draw the image in pencil or pen.

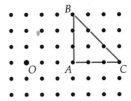

**Figure 9-8**

Next, try to find more general relationships between a point and its image under a rotation.

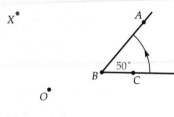

**Figure 9-9**

## Lesson Exercise 9.5

Consider ∠ABC and points X and O in Figure 9-9.

(a) Find the image X′ of point X under a counterclockwise rotation of m∠ABC around point O.

(b) Describe the relationships you observe among any of the following: XO, X′O, BA, BC, m∠XOX′, and m∠ABC.

Compare your response to Lesson Exercise 9.5(b) with the end of the following general statement. In the plane, a counterclockwise **rotation** of m∠ABC around point O maps a point X to X′ so that XO = X′O and m∠XOX′ = m∠ABC (see Figure 9-10).

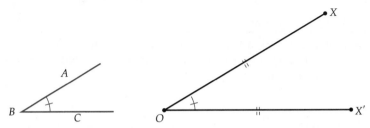

**Figure 9-10**

There's a new geometric dance called the translation. You stand on one foot and slide 2 inches to the right (see Figure 9-11). (It's easier on a recently waxed floor.)

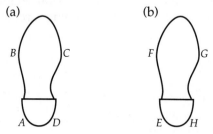

**Figure 9-11**

How do you do a translation (slide)? In a translation, each point of the plane moves the same distance in the same direction along a line. If footprint (a) in Figure 9-11 slides 4 centimeters to the right, it will coincide with footprint (b).

So footprint (b) is the image of footprint (a) under a translation of 4 centimeters to the right. In order to describe a translation, you need a distance and a direction.

## Lesson Exercise 9.6

(a) Copy the grid and picture from Figure 9-12 on a piece of paper.
(b) Now use tracing paper to trace $\triangle ABC$ and translate (slide) it 2 units down.
(c) Trace over the triangle in its new position so it shows up on your original paper. Then remove the tracing paper and draw the image in pencil or pen.

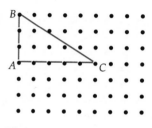

Figure 9-12

Next, try to find more general relationships between a point and its image under a translation.

## Lesson Exercise 9.7

(a) Using tracing paper with Figure 9-13, find the image $X'$ of point $X$ under a translation of length $AB$ in the direction of $A$ to $B$ $\left(\textbf{directed}\right.$ $\textbf{segment } \overrightarrow{AB}\left.\right)$. Copy the entire diagram on the tracing paper. Then, figure out where to slide point $A$.
(b) Describe any relationships you observe between $\overline{XX'}$ and $\overline{AB}$.

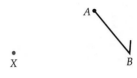

Figure 9-13

Compare your response to Lesson Exercise 9.7(b) with the end of the following general statement. In a plane, a **translation** of length $AB$ in the direction of $A$ to $B$ maps a point $X$ to $X'$ so that $XX' = AB$ and $\overrightarrow{XX'}$ and $\overrightarrow{AB}$ point in the same direction (Figure 9-14).

Finally, how do you do a reflection (a flip)? Wait a second. Don't start doing body flips over those desks. It's dangerous.

Let's use a triangle instead. A reflection is suggested by folding a shape across a line. If this page of the book were folded on line $m$ in Figure 9-15, $\triangle ABC$ would coincide with $\triangle DEF$. In a reflection through line $m$, $\triangle ABC$ and $\triangle DEF$ would be interchanged.

So $\triangle DEF$ is the image of $\triangle ABC$, and $\triangle ABC$ is the image of $\triangle DEF$ under a reflection through line $m$. In order to describe a reflection (a flip), you need a line of reflection.

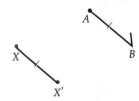

Figure 9-14

## Lesson Exercise 9.8

Look at $\triangle ABC$ and its image $\triangle DEF$ in Figure 9-15.

(a) Why is this motion called a reflection?
(b) If one is available, place a mirror to verify that $\triangle DEF$ is the reflected image of $\triangle ABC$.

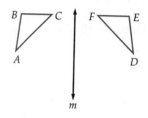

Figure 9-15

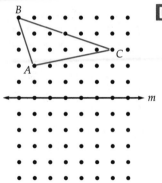

Figure 9-16

**D** Lesson Exercise 9.9

(a) Copy the grid and picture (from Figure 9-16) on a piece of paper.
(b) Now use tracing paper to trace $m$ and $\triangle ABC$.
(c) Flip the paper over, but make sure that line $m$ stays in the same position. (Do *not* interchange the position of the arrowheads of line $m$.)
(d) Trace over the triangle in its new position so that it shows up on your original paper. Then remove the tracing paper and draw the image in pencil or pen.

Next, try to find more general relationships between a point and its image under a reflection.

Figure 9-17

Lesson Exercise 9.10

Consider line $m$ and point $X$ in Figure 9-17.

(a) Find the image of $X$ under a reflection through line $m$.
(b) Describe any relationships you observe between $m$ and $\overline{XX'}$.

Compare your response to Lesson Exercise 9.10(b) with the following definition. In a **reflection** through line $m$, each point $X$ (not on $m$) in the plane is paired with $X'$ so that $m$ is the perpendicular bisector of $\overline{XX'}$. If $X$ is on $m$, then $X' = X$.

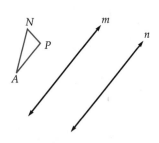

Figure 9-18

Lesson Exercise 9.11

In Figure 9-18, assume $m \parallel n$.

(a) Find the image of $\triangle NAP$ after a reflection through $m$. Label the image $\triangle N'A'P'$.
(b) Find the image of $\triangle N'A'P'$ after a reflection through $n$. Label the image $\triangle N''A''P''$.
(c) What single motion maps $\triangle NAP$ to $\triangle N''A''P''$?

## Rigid Motions and Congruence

How are rotations, translations, and reflections related to congruence? Why do they all appear together in this section of the text?

## Lesson Exercise 9.12

Look back at the images in Lesson Exercises 9.4, 9.5, 9.7, and 9.8. In which of these exercises is the image the same size and shape as the original figure?

## Lesson Exercise 9.13

If I translate a geometric figure and then reflect it, will it still be the same size and shape?

Your responses to Lesson Exercises 9.12 and 9.13 suggest the following test that relates rigid motions and congruence.

---

**A Test for Congruence**

Two plane drawings are congruent if one can be moved onto the other using a rotation, translation, or reflection, or some combination of these motions.

---

## Lesson Exercise 9.14

Trace one of each pair of geometric figures in Figure 9-19 and use a rotation, translation, or reflection to determine if the two shapes are congruent. If the shapes are congruent, state which motion you used to show this.

(a)    (b)    (c)

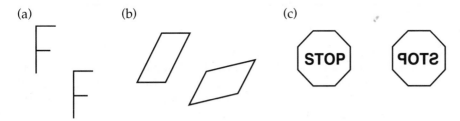

**Figure 9-19**

## Lesson Exercise 9.15

What *combination* of motions could be used to map one **F** onto the other in Figure 9-20?

·**Figure 9-20**

Motions indicate congruent pairs of angles or line segments. The symbol for congruence is ≅.

## Lesson Exercise 9.16

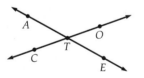

Figure 9-21

(a) Find a specific motion that maps ∠ATC in Figure 9-21 onto another angle.
(b) Based upon part (a), it appears that ∠ATC ≅ _____ .
(c) Using motion geometry, find another pair of angles in Figure 9-21 that might be congruent.

Angles such as ∠ATC and ∠ETO in Lesson Exercise 9.16 that are formed by two intersecting lines are called **vertical angles.** ∠ETC and ∠ATO are also vertical angles. Using rotations to prove that vertical angles are congruent requires a more rigorous study of rotations.

Next, consider two parallel lines and a line (called a **transversal**) that intersects them both.

## Lesson Exercise 9.17

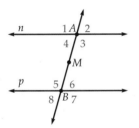

Figure 9-22

In Figure 9-22, $n \parallel p$ and $M$ is the midpoint of $\overline{AB}$.

(a) Find a specific motion that maps ∠1 to another angle in the diagram.
(b) Based upon part (a), it appears that ∠1 ≅ _____ .
(c) Repeat parts (a) and (b) until you have listed all possible sets of congruent angles.

Notice that each of the two parallel lines in Figure 9-22 forms four numbered angles with the transversal. Each angle (such as ∠1) in one group corresponds in position to an angle in the other group (such as ∠5). Thus, ∠1 and ∠5 are called **corresponding angles.** Other pairs of corresponding angles are ∠2 and ∠6, ∠3 and ∠7, and ∠4 and ∠8.

In Figure 9-22, ∠5 and ∠3 are nonadjacent angles on alternate sides of the transversal and are between ("inside") the parallel lines. Therefore, ∠5 and ∠3 are called **alternate interior angles.** The other pair of alternate interior angles are ∠4 and ∠6.

In Lesson Exercise 9.17, you probably made conjectures about some of the corresponding or alternate interior angles. Propose more general conjectures in the following exercise.

## Lesson Exercise 9.18

Look back at the diagram in Lesson Exercise 9.17 and make a conjecture about

(a) alternate interior angles.
(b) corresponding angles.

Lesson Exercises 9.17 and 9.18 should suggest the following theorem.

> **Parallel Lines and Corresponding and Alternate Interior Angles**
>
> If two parallel lines are cut by a transversal, then each pair of corresponding angles and each pair of alternate interior angles is congruent.

## Glide Reflections

It is not always possible to move one of two congruent figures onto the other using a *single* rotation, translation, or reflection (see Figure 9-23).

This observation led to the creation of a fourth rigid motion, the glide reflection, which combines a translation and a reflection.

The glide reflection of $\mathsf{P}$ on $\overrightarrow{AB}$ (direction of $A$ to $B$) in Figure 9-24 has two steps. First, reflect the flag through $\overleftrightarrow{AB}$, and then translate the result using $\overrightarrow{AB}$.

**Figure 9-23**

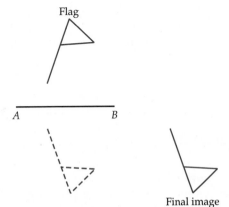

Flag

A                     B

Final image

**Figure 9-24**

So a **glide reflection** is a reflection followed by a translation along the line of reflection.

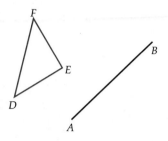

Figure 9-25

## Lesson Exercise 9.19

See Figure 9-25 and perform a glide reflection of $\triangle DEF$ on $\overrightarrow{AB}$ (direction of $A$ to $B$).

Using this fourth rigid motion, we can say that two plane figures are congruent if and only if one figure can be moved onto the other using a single rotation, translation, reflection, or glide reflection.

## Congruent Figures

Motions show that one whole figure is congruent to another. We can also show that two figures are congruent by matching up their parts.

Figure 9-26

## Lesson Exercise 9.20

What would you have to know about the sides and angles of two triangles (Figure 9-26) to know that the triangles are congruent?

The specific conditions that make two figures congruent vary according to the complexity of the figure. The **corresponding parts** of two congruent figures are the congruent parts that match up in the two figures.

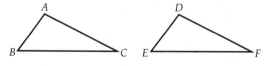

Figure 9-27

In naming congruent triangles such as $\triangle ABC \cong \triangle DEF$ in Figure 9-27, the order of the letters indicates the corresponding vertices. In this case, the corresponding vertices would be as follows:

$$A \longleftrightarrow D \quad\quad B \longleftrightarrow E \quad\quad C \longleftrightarrow F$$

These correspondences can be used to match up congruent angles and sides. For example, $\angle A \cong \angle D$ and $\overline{BC} \cong \overline{EF}$.

You may be wondering about the difference between the congruence sign ($\cong$) and the equal sign ($=$) in geometry. Congruent figures or parts of figures, such as $\overline{BC}$ and $\overline{EF}$, have the same shape and size, and this congruence is expressed as $\overline{BC} \cong \overline{EF}$. An equal sign most commonly is used to indicate that some *measure* of two geometric figures is the same. The expression "$BC = EF$" means that the length of $\overline{BC}$ equals the length of $\overline{EF}$. The expressions $BC$ and $EF$ represent *numbers* (lengths), whereas the terms $\overline{BC}$ and $\overline{EF}$ represent line segments.

The following chart shows the corresponding notations for equality and congruence of line segments and angles.

|  | Equality | Congruence |
|---|---|---|
| Line segments | $BC = EF$ | $\overline{BC} \cong \overline{EF}$ |
| Angles | $m\angle A = m\angle D$ | $\angle A \cong \angle D$ |

## Lesson Exercise 9.21

In Figure 9-28, $RANT \cong BCDA$. Complete the following expressions.

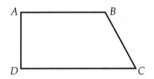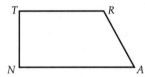

**Figure 9-28**

(a) $m\angle C =$ _____    (b) $\overline{NT} \cong$ _____

## Tessellations as Art

Artistic tessellations utilize congruent figures and motions as a basis for creating designs. Recall that all triangles, quadrilaterals, and regular hexagons tessellate the plane.

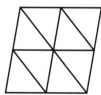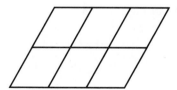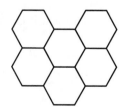

**Figure 9-29**

The Dutch artist M. C. Escher (1898–1972) used the shapes shown in Figure 9-29 as a basis for creating more ingenious tessellations. Escher was inspired by Moorish art he saw during his travels to Spain in the 1930s.

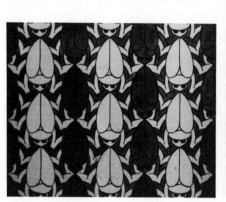
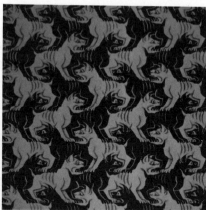

Photos © 1990 M. C. Escher Heirs/Cordon Art—Baarn—Holland.

**Figure 9-30**

## Lesson Exercise 9.22

If the design in Figure 9-30 covered an entire plane, name two different motions that would map the design onto itself.

**Figure 9-31**

**Figure 9-32**

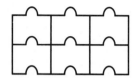

**Figure 9-33**

**Figure 9-34**

How did Escher create nonpolygonal tessellations? Watch closely. I'll start with a square. Each square must change in exactly the same way.

Suppose I add a bump on top of the square (Figure 9-31).

In order to make this new shape tessellate, I take away the same bump from the opposite side (Figure 9-32).

This procedure enables each square to be transformed in the same way, creating a new set of congruent figures that tessellate the plane. The result is shown in Figure 9-33.

Now, I'll continue by adding and subtracting a curve. Each change in the shape must not affect its ability to fit together in a tiling pattern (Figure 9-34).

The result is shown in Figure 9-35.

**Figure 9-35**

Now, how about adding a design inside (Figure 9-36)?

Figure 9-36

## Lesson Exercise 9.23

Complete the transformations in Figure 9-37 so that the new shape will tessellate.

(a)
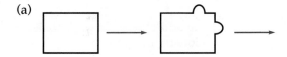

(b)
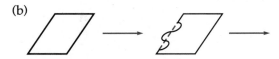

Figure 9-37

## Lesson Exercise 9.24

Make up your own tessellation and fill it in on one of the grids in Figure 9-38.

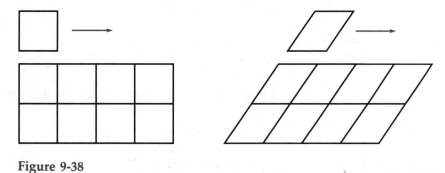

Figure 9-38

## Answers to Selected Lesson Exercises

9.2  360°

9.3  180°

9.8  (a) One triangle looks like a mirror reflection of the other when the line is used as the mirror.

**9.11** (c) a translation

**9.12** all of them

**9.13** yes

**9.14** Parts (a) and (c) contain congruent figures.

**9.15** rotation and reflection

**9.16** (a) 180° rotation     (b) $\angle ETO$
    (c) A half-turn around $T$ appears to map $\angle ATO$ onto $\angle ETC$.

**9.17** (c) $\angle 1 \cong \angle 3 \cong \angle 5 \cong \angle 7$ and $\angle 2 \cong \angle 4 \cong \angle 6 \cong \angle 8$

**9.20** Three sides of one triangle are congruent to three corresponding sides of the other triangle, and three angles of one triangle are congruent to the three corresponding angles of the other triangle.

**9.21** (a) $m\angle A$     (b) $\overline{DA}$

## 9.1   Homework Exercises

### Basic Exercises

**1.** Find the image of the flag after a 270° clockwise rotation around point $C$.

**2.** (a) Copy the grid and picture on a piece of paper.

   (b) Now use tracing paper to trace point $O$ and the ⌐.

   (c) Rotate the ⌐ 180° clockwise around point $O$.

   (d) Show the image of the ⌐ on your original grid.

**3.** If a point $P$ is rotated clockwise 32° around point $O$, then $m\angle POP' =$ _____ and $PO =$ _____ .

**4.** Some airport runways are numbered using a compass position in 10-degree units. For example, 36 would mean 360°. Use a protractor

to add a new runway labeled 11 to the following diagram.

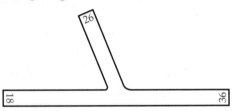

**5.** Using a ruler, find the image of the flag under a translation 4 cm to the left.

**6.** Show the image of the triangle after a translation 3 units to the right and 2 units down.

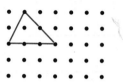

**7.** A point $P$ is translated using $\overrightarrow{AB}$. If $P$ is not on $\overleftrightarrow{AB}$, then $\overleftrightarrow{PP'} \parallel$ _____ and $\overleftrightarrow{PA} \parallel$ _____ .

8. Show the image of the ⌐ after a reflection through line *m*.

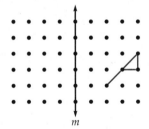

9. (a) Show the image of △*ABC* after a reflection through line *n*.

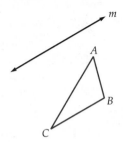

   (b) How many image points seem to be needed to draw the image of △*ABC*?

10. Show the image of *ABCD* after a reflection through line *t*.

11. If the line shown in the diagram is a mirror, draw the image of the shape on the other side of the mirror. Do not use tracing paper.

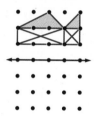

12. What set of points does a reflection map to itself?

13. Without tracing paper, draw the image of each figure after a 180° rotation around *C*.

   (a) 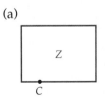     (b)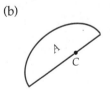

14. Find the center of rotation for each object and its image.

   (a) 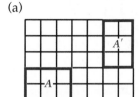     (b)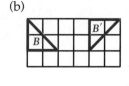

15. (a) Give the center point and degree of rotation that maps $\overline{AB}$ to $\overline{A'B'}$.

   (b) Give the line of reflection that maps $\overline{AB}$ to $\overline{A'B'}$.

16. Some ambulances have AMBULANCE written on the front. Why is it done this way?

17. A set of golf clubs can be made for right-handed or left-handed golfers. The two sets of clubs would be congruent but would have different **orientations**. Name two other kinds of objects that are sometimes made congruent but with different orientations.

18. A heavy container must be moved as shown. The easiest way is to move it to an adjacent

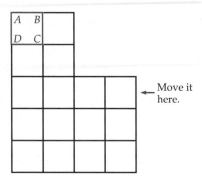

square by rotating the container around one of its corners.

(a) Fill in the boxes along the way and label the corners to show a way to move the container from start to finish.
(b) Describe the specific motion used in each step.

19. A dog is tied in front of a house. Draw the limits of the dog's range.

20. What rigid motion is suggested by each of the following?
    (a) a tree falling to the ground
    (b) a pair of shoes
    (c) a train traveling straight down a railroad track

21. Open some jars at home. Record how many degrees you rotate each top in order to remove it.

22. The cartoon at the top of the next column shows that two successive reflections through parallel lines would be the same as what single motion?

Barbershop mirrors. Drawing by Chas. Addams; © 1957, 1985. The New Yorker Magazine, Inc.

23. Find the image of the ⌐ after a translation 2 centimeters to the right followed by a reflection over line $t$.

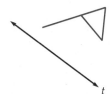

24. Assume that $m \perp n$.

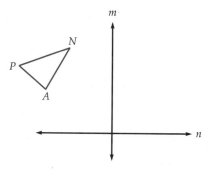

(a) Find the image of △NAP after a reflection through m. Label the image △N'A'P'.

(b) Find the image of △N'A'P' after a reflection through n. Label the image △N"A"P".

(c) What single motion maps △NAP to △N"A"P"?

**25.** (a) True or false? The image of a vertical line after a reflection is a vertical line.

(b) Give an example that supports your answer.

**26.** The image of a plane figure under a

_____ is congruent to the figure.

(a) rotation     (b) translation
(c) reflection   (d) all of these

**27.** (a) Do the segments in each picture appear to be congruent?

(1) $\overline{AB} \cong \overline{BC}$          (2) $\overline{EF} \cong \overline{GH}$

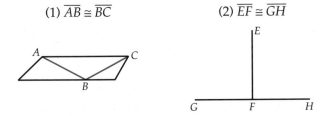

(b) Check their congruence with tracing paper.

**28.** Trace one of each pair of figures and use a rotation, translation, or reflection to determine if the two figures are congruent. If the figures are congruent, state which motion you used to show their congruence. Describe the motion as specifically as possible.

(a)          (b)          (c)

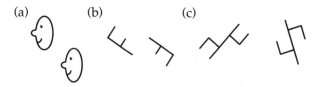

**29.** Draw two congruent figures such that one figure cannot be mapped onto the other using a *single* rotation, translation, or reflection.

**30.** The relationship between motions and congruence also applies to space figures. Which of the following pairs of figures are congruent?

(a)          (b)          (c)

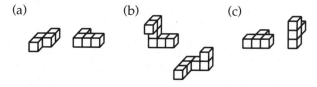

**31.** The motion of the man and the Z's do not correspond.

(a) In the cartoon, does the man's motion approximate a rotation, a translation, or a reflection?

By permission of Johnny Hart and Creators Syndicate, Inc.

(For Exercise 31)

(b) Which of the three motions is applied to the Z's?

32. Use tracing paper and find the line of reflection that flips one figure onto the other. (Guess and check.)

33. Use tracing paper and find the center of rotation used to turn △ABC onto △A'B'C'. (Guess and check.)

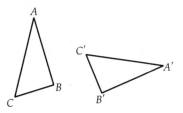

34. BART is a parallelogram.

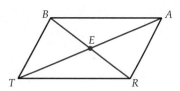

(a) What single motion maps $\overline{BA} \rightarrow \overline{RT}$ and $\overline{BT} \rightarrow \overline{RA}$?

(b) Based upon part (a), it appears that $\overline{BA}$ _____ $\overline{RT}$ and $\overline{BT}$ _____ $\overline{RA}$.

(c) Find a specific motion that maps ∠ABT to another angle in the diagram.

(d) Based upon part (c), it appears that ∠ABT ≅ _____ .

(e) Repeat parts (c) and (d) for ∠BTR.

35. Assume that △ACT is an isosceles triangle, with $\overline{AC} \cong \overline{AT}$ and M the midpoint of $\overline{CT}$.

(a) Name a specific motion that maps $\overline{AC} \rightarrow \overline{AT}$.

(b) Name a second specific motion that maps $\overline{AC} \rightarrow \overline{AT}$.

(c) Find a motion that suggests which two angles in the triangle are congruent and name them.

36. Rotate the sign (from *Unexpected Hanging* by Martin Gardner) 180°. What does it say?

> NOW   NO
> SWIMS
> ON   MON

37. (a) Place a mirror on the line. What is the reflection of the name MATT?

(b) Make up another name that matches its own vertical reflection.

38. Find the image of the flag after a glide reflection on $\overrightarrow{AB}$.

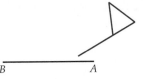

39. What would make each of the following congruent?
(a) two line segments     (b) two squares
(c) two rays

40. △MAY ≅ △HUT.
(a) Which angle of △HUT corresponds to ∠M?
(b) TH = _____

41. (a) Select one of the repeated figures in the drawing by Escher shown at the top of the next page. Find a center point and the number of degrees of a clockwise rotation that maps it onto another figure.

©1990 M. C. Escher Heirs/Cordon Art—Baarn—Holland.

(b) Select one of the repeated figures. Find a line of reflection that maps it onto another figure.

**42.**

Select one of the repeated figures. Describe a specific motion that maps it onto another figure.

**43.** (a) Begin with a square. Alter one side and translate the alteration to the opposite side. Does the resulting figure tessellate the plane?

(b) Repeat part (a) with a different tessellating polygon.

**44.** Complete the following transformations so that the new shape will tessellate.

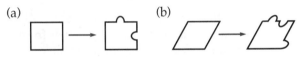

(a)          (b)

**45.** Make up your own tessellation.

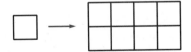

**46.** Make up your own tessellation.

*Extension Exercises*

**47.** How was this photograph taken?

Courtesy of the Eames Office and IBM. © The Eames Office 1989.

**48.** Susan King wants to use two mirrors to see the back of her head. She stands facing one mirror $1\frac{1}{2}$ ft away. She holds a second mirror facing the opposite way, 1 ft behind her head. Her head is about 6 in. thick. How far from her eyes will the back of her head appear to be in the mirror? (Draw a picture.)

**49.** Suppose that you want to be able to stand in front of a wall mirror and see yourself from head to toe. Find the minimum possible height of the mirror, and tell how it would be positioned.

In Exercises 50–52, fill in the blanks with any of the following words that make the statement true: "rotation," "translation," "reflection."

**50.** Under a _____ in a plane, one point is fixed and all other points move.

**51.** Under a _____ in a plane, no points remain fixed.

**52.** After a _____ in a plane, two lines that are parallel have images that are parallel to each other.

**53.** (a)  What are the coordinates of A, B, and C?

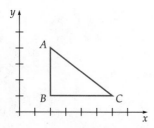

(b)  Suppose that a mapping changes the coordinates of each point as follows.

$$(x, y) \rightarrow (x - 4, y + 1)$$

Find image points A', B', and C' using this rule. (Use graph paper or an automatic drawer.)

(c)  Plot A', B', and C'.

(d)  What motion maps $\triangle ABC$ to $\triangle A'B'C'$?

**54.** (a)  What are the coordinates of A, B, and C?

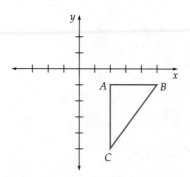

(b)  Suppose that a mapping changes the coordinates of each point as follows.

$$(x, y) \rightarrow (y, x)$$

Find image points A', B', and C' using this rule.

(c)  Plot A', B', and C'.

(d)  What motion maps $\triangle ABC$ to $\triangle A'B'C'$?

**55.** (a)  What are the coordinates of A, B, and C?

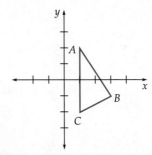

(b)  Suppose that a mapping changes the coordinates of each point as follows.

$$(x, y) \rightarrow (-x, y)$$

Find image points A', B', and C' using this rule.

(c)  Plot A', B', and C'.

(d)  What motion maps $\triangle ABC$ to $\triangle A'B'C'$?

**56.** Consider the following problem. "What is the effect of the mapping $(x, y) \rightarrow (x, 2y)$ on different figures on a coordinate grid? Check all four quadrants." Devise a plan and solve the problem.

**57.** A sheet of paper is folded in quarters, and a square is cut out of the center. What will the paper look like when it is unfolded?

For each design, the folded and cut paper is shown on the left. Guess what the unfolded design will look like. Then try it and see.

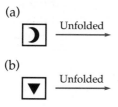

**58.** Draw two points $A$ and $A'$ that are 5 cm apart.
   (a) Find parallel lines $m$ and $n$ so that the translation from $A$ to $A'$ is the same as a reflection through line $m$ followed by a reflection through line $n$.
   (b) If your lines $m$ and $n$ are both between $A$ and $A'$, find another solution in which they are not. If they are not both between $A$ and $A'$, find another solution in which they are.

**59.** (a) How many trapezoids are in the star diagram?
   (b) How many rhombuses are in the star diagram?

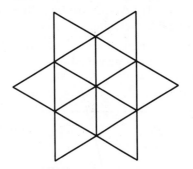

***Computer Exercises***

**60.** (a) What motion is illustrated by the following?

```
TO FLAG
FD 60
REPEAT 4 [RT 90 FD 20]
BK 60
END

FLAG
RT 110
FLAG
```

   (b) Write a procedure that draws a flag and its image after a 200° counterclockwise rotation.

**61.** Write a procedure that draws an equilateral triangle and its image after a 140° clockwise rotation around one of its vertices.

**62.** Use the FLAG procedure (see Exercise 60) in another procedure that draws a flag and then draws its image 30 units to the right. (*Hint:* Use PU in between drawing the flag and its image.)

**63.** Write a Logo procedure that uses another procedure SQUARE to draw a series of four squares that tessellate.

**64.** Write a Logo procedure that uses another procedure HEXAGON to draw three regular hexagons that tessellate.

**65.** Use an automatic drawer to draw two parallel lines and a transversal.

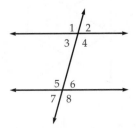

(a) Investigate the angle measures.
(b) Clear the screen and repeat part (a) after drawing a transversal at a different angle.
(c) Write generalizations of your results.

*Special Exercise*

**66.** Pentominos are made up of five connected squares. Each square must be connected to some other square on at least one *complete* side.

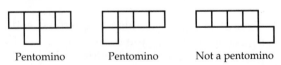

Pentomino　　　Pentomino　　　Not a pentomino

(a) Which two of the following pentominos are congruent? What motion maps one congruent pentomino onto the other?

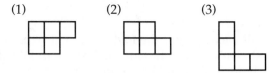

(1)　　　　　(2)　　　　　(3)

(b) Draw 12 different (noncongruent) pentomino shapes.
(c) Cut out the 12 different pentomino shapes. See whether you can put them together to form a single rectangle.

## 9.2　Constructions and Congruence

Ancient Greek mathematicians enjoyed the challenge of copying plane figures by drawing a series of line segments (using a straightedge) and circles (using a compass), since they considered lines and circles to be the basic units of geometry. Many plane figures can be copied or divided into two equal parts using only lines and circles.

The ancient Greeks succeeded in constructing nearly everything they attempted, but they were unable to trisect an angle or to construct a square equal in area to a given circle. We now know that these two constructions are impossible.

Today, we do constructions as historical rituals and as thought-provoking puzzles. As you do your constructions, think of the ancient Greeks who puzzled over the same problems, wondering what they could and could not construct with limited tools.

## Lesson Exercise 9.25

Before doing anything fancy, draw the basic figures—a circle and a line segment—with your compass and straightedge, respectively.

## Constructing Congruent Figures

What kind of congruent figures can be constructed with a compass and a straightedge? For starters, you should be able to draw a circle and a line segment congruent to those that you drew in Lesson Exercise 9.25.

## Lesson Exercise 9.26

### Copying a Circle

(a) Do two circles with radii of equal length have to be congruent?
(b) Part (a) is the basis for copying a circle. Place the point of your compass at the center of the circle (from Lesson Exercise 9.25) and the pencil point on any point of the circle (Figure 9-39).
(c) Hold this distance (the radius) and use it to draw a congruent circle elsewhere on the paper.

**Figure 9-39**

## Lesson Exercise 9.27

### Copying a Line Segment

(a) What makes two line segments congruent?
(b) Use your compass to span the length of the segment (from Lesson Exercise 9.25) by placing the compass point on one endpoint and the pencil point on the other (Figure 9-40).
(c) Hold this distance and move the compass elsewhere. Mark these two points on the paper and connect them with your straightedge.

**Figure 9-40**

The first two constructions of congruent figures are not all that impressive. Let's move on to some more interesting constructions. (*Note:* If you prefer to investigate with an automatic drawer the conditions that make two triangles congruent, see the last computer exercise in the homework exercises.)

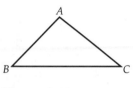

**Figure 9-41**

## Lesson Exercise 9.28

**Copying a Triangle (SSS method)**

(a) Can you figure out a way to construct a copy of △*ABC* (Figure 9-41) by copying each of its sides? If not, go on to part (b).

If your method did work, compare it to the method outlined in parts (b)–(e).

(b) Copy $\overline{BC}$ using the method of Lesson Exercise 9.27. Label the copy $\overline{EF}$ (Figure 9-42).

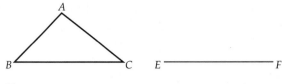

**Figure 9-42**

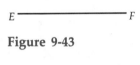

**Figure 9-43**

(c) Place the point of your compass on *B* and the pencil point on *A*. Now use the same span to draw an arc with center *E* and radius *BA* (Figure 9-43).

(d) Place the point of your compass on *C* and the pencil point on *A*. Now use the same span to draw an arc with center *F* and radius *CA* (Figure 9-44) that intersects the last arc you drew.

(e) Label the intersection point *D*. Draw $\overline{DE}$ and $\overline{DF}$. Voila! △*DEF* ≅ △*ABC* (Figure 9-45).

**Figure 9-44**

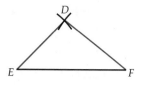

**Figure 9-45**

    The construction in Lesson Exercise 9.28 suggests that making *EF* = *BC*, *DE* = *AB*, and *DF* = *AC* will make △*DEF* ≅ △*ABC*. This is an example of a property called the SSS (three sides) property of triangle congruence.

---

**SSS Triangle Congruence**

If three sides of one triangle are congruent to the three corresponding sides of another triangle, then the two triangles are congruent.

## Lesson Exercise 9.29

Which pairs of triangles must be congruent by SSS?

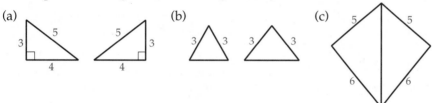

(a)               (b)                          (c)

You've copied circles, line segments, and triangles. Now try copying an angle.

Figure 9-46

## Lesson Exercise 9.30

**Copying an Angle** (Figure 9-46)

(a) Draw a ray with endpoint *D* (Figure 9-47).
(b) Draw an arc with center *A* and mark points *B* and *C* on the sides of ∠*A* (Figure 9-48).
(c) Use the *same radius* and draw an arc with center *D* that intersects the ray as shown. Label the intersection of the arc and the ray point *E* (Figure 9-49).
(d) See whether you can complete the construction on your own. If not, go on to parts (e) and (f).
(e) Now measure *BC* with the span of your compass and use the same span as you place the compass point on *E* and draw an arc intersecting the arc that is already there (Figure 9-50).

Figure 9-47

Figure 9-48

Figure 9-49

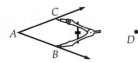 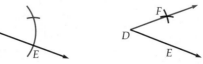

Figure 9-50                 Figure 9-51

(f) Label the intersection of your two arcs *F* and draw $\overrightarrow{DF}$ (Figure 9-51). ∠*FDE* ≅ ∠*CAB!*

Why does the procedure for copying an angle work? You begin with ∠*A* and mark an equal distance on each side (Figure 9-52 on page 508). That distance is copied on each side of ∠*D*.

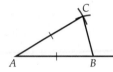
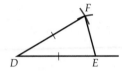

Figure 9-52

You measure $\overline{BC}$ and make $\overline{EF}$ the same length. So you have constructed two congruent triangles, $\triangle ABC$ and $\triangle DEF$ (Figure 9-53).

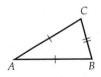
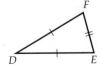

Figure 9-53

**D** Lesson Exercise 9.31

(a) Why is $\triangle ABC \cong \triangle DEF$?
(b) Why does this mean $\angle A \cong \angle D$?

So the construction for copying an angle is based upon the SSS triangle property! Now, try copying a triangle given two sides and the angle between them.

Lesson Exercise 9.32

**Copying a Triangle (SAS method)**

(a) Can you figure out a way to construct a copy of $\triangle ABC$ (Figure 9-54) by copying two of its sides and the angle formed by those sides (such as $\overline{AB}$, $\overline{BC}$, and $\angle B$)? If not, go on to part (b).

If your method did work, compare it to the method outlined in parts (b)–(e).

(b) Copy angle $B$, employing the method of Lesson Exercise 9.30. Label the vertex of the new angle $E$ (Figure 9-55).

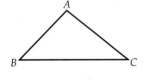

Figure 9-54

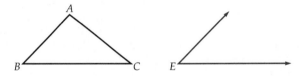

Figure 9-55

(c) See whether you can complete the construction on your own. If not, go on to parts (d) and (e).

(d) Mark the lengths *BC* and *BA* from point *E* on the two rays and label the points *F* and *D*, respectively (Figure 9-56).

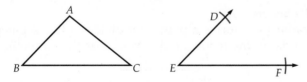

**Figure 9-56**

(e) Draw $\overline{DF}$ to complete △*DEF*, which is congruent to △*ABC*.

---

The construction in Lesson Exercise 9.32 suggests that making $m\angle B = m\angle E$, $BC = EF$, and $AB = DE$ will make △*DEF* ≅ △*ABC*. This is an example of the SAS property of triangle congruence.

---

**SAS Triangle Congruence**

If two sides and the included angle of one triangle are congruent, respectively, to two corresponding sides and the included angle of another triangle, then the two triangles are congruent.

---

## Lesson Exercise 9.33

You want to measure indirectly the distance *AB* across a lake (Figure 9-57). After selecting a point *C*, you measure *AC* and *BC*.

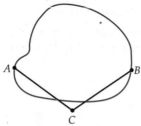

**Figure 9-57**

Next, you lay out ∠*BCD* so that ∠*BCD* ≅ ∠*BCA* and *CD* = *CA* (Figure 9-58). Explain why *BD* must be the same as the length across the lake (*AB*).

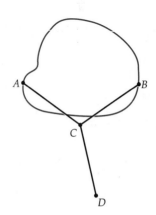

**Figure 9-58**

## Constructing Bisectors

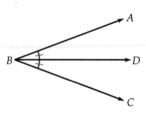

**Figure 9-59**

A compass and a straightedge can also be used to divide an angle or a line segment into two congruent parts. This is called **bisection.** An **angle bisector** is a ray that divides an angle into two congruent parts. In Figure 9-59, $\overrightarrow{BD}$ bisects $\angle ABC$.

A **midpoint** (bisector) is a point that divides a line segment into two congruent parts. In the following diagram, $M$ is the midpoint of $\overline{AY}$.

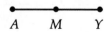

First, try bisecting an angle.

## Lesson Exercise 9.34

**Bisecting an Angle** (Figure 9-60).

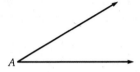

**Figure 9-60**

(a) Place the compass point on $A$ and draw an arc intersecting both sides of the angle. Label the intersection points $B$ and $C$ (Figure 9-61).

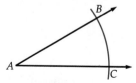

**Figure 9-61**

(b) Now select a radius and place the compass point on $B$. Draw an arc across the interior of the angle (on the opposite side of $\overline{BC}$ from $A$) (Figure 9-62).

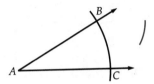

**Figure 9-62**

(c) Place the compass point on $C$ and use the same radius to draw an arc intersecting the arc that has center $B$ (Figure 9-63). Label the intersection point $D$.

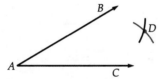

Figure 9-63

(d) Connect the intersection point to $A$. Now $\overrightarrow{AD}$ is the angle bisector of $\angle BAC$ (Figure 9-64).

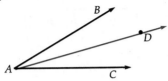

Figure 9-64

This construction also works because of the SSS property. (This SSS property is very handy for explaining constructions!)

In the construction in Figure 9-65, $AB = AC$ and $BD = CD$ because the lengths in each pair were drawn with the same radius.

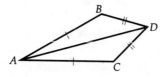

Figure 9-65

**D** Lesson Exercise 9.35

(a) In Figure 9-65, why is $\triangle ABD \cong \triangle ACD$ by SSS?

(b) If $\triangle ABD \cong \triangle ACD$, explain why $\overrightarrow{AD}$ must be an angle bisector of $\angle BAC$.

Now try bisecting a line segment.

## Lesson Exercise 9.36

**Bisecting a Line Segment**

$A$          $B$

(a) Select a compass radius slightly less than $AB$. Place the compass point on $A$ and draw an arc through $\overline{AB}$ as shown in Figure 9-66.

**Figure 9-66**

(b) Use the same radius. Place the compass point on $B$ and draw an arc above and below $\overline{AB}$ that intersects the other arc at two points (Figure 9-67). Label the intersection points $C$ and $D$.

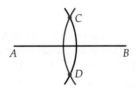

**Figure 9-67**

(c) Connect those two intersection points with a line segment. Label as $M$ the point of intersection with $\overline{AB}$. Not only is $M$ the midpoint of $\overline{AB}$, but $\overleftrightarrow{CD}$ is the perpendicular bisector of $\overline{AB}$ (Figure 9-68). So this procedure can also be used to construct a 90° angle.

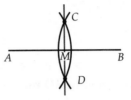

**Figure 9-68**

You can use the SSS and SAS properties to prove why this construction works.

## Lesson Exercise 9.37

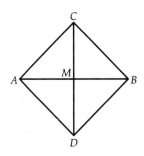

**Figure 9-69**

In the construction in Figure 9-69, $AC = CB = AD = DB$ because the lengths were all drawn with the same radius.
(a) Why is $\triangle ACD \cong \triangle BCD$?
(b) Why is $\angle ACM \cong \angle BCM$?
(c) Why is $\triangle ACM \cong \triangle BCM$?
(d) Why is $M$ the midpoint of $\overline{AB}$?

## The Isosceles Triangle Theorem

All isosceles triangles have at least two congruent sides. Must an isosceles triangle also have two congruent angles? The SSS triangle congruence property can be used to deduce the answer to this question.

Suppose that $\triangle JAN$ (Figure 9-70) is an isosceles triangle with $JA = AN$. Is $\angle J \cong \angle N$?

Draw a line segment from $A$ to the midpoint $M$ of $\overline{JN}$ (Figure 9-71).

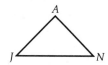

**Figure 9-70**

## D Lesson Exercise 9.38

(a) Explain why $\triangle JAM \cong \triangle NAM$.
(b) Explain why $\angle J \cong \angle N$.

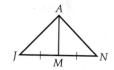

**Figure 9-71**

The angle property you proved in Lesson Exercise 9.38 is called the Isosceles Triangle Theorem.

---

**The Isosceles Triangle Theorem**

If two sides of a triangle are congruent, then the angles opposite them are congruent.

---

The Isosceles Triangle Theorem can sometimes be used to find missing angle measures in polygons.

## Lesson Exercise 9.39

Fill in the missing angle measures in Figure 9-72.

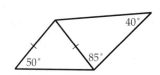

**Figure 9-72**

## Answers to Selected Lesson Exercises

**9.26** (a) yes

**9.27** (a) They are the same length.

**9.29** (a), (c)

**9.31** (a) SSS triangle congruence
(b) The triangles are congruent, so the corresponding parts are congruent.

**9.33** Since $AC = CD$, $BC = BC$, and $\angle ACB \cong \angle DCB$, $\triangle ACB \cong \triangle DCB$ by SAS. If the triangles are congruent, then $BD = BA$.

**9.35** (a) $AB = AC$, $BD = CD$, and $AD = AD$
(b) Since $\triangle ABD \cong \triangle ACD$, $\angle BAD \cong \angle CAD$. This means that $\overrightarrow{AD}$ is the angle bisector of $\angle BAC$.

**9.37** (a) by SSS ($AC = BC$, $AD = BD$, $CD = CD$)
(b) because $\angle ACD \cong \angle BCD$
(c) by SAS ($AC = BC$, $\angle ACM \cong \angle BCM$, $CM = CM$)
(d) Since $\triangle ACM \cong \triangle BCM$, $AM = MB$. So $M$ is the midpoint of $\overline{AB}$.

**9.38** (a) by SSS ($JA = NA$, $JM = NM$, $AM = AM$)
(b) Since $\triangle JAM \cong \triangle NAM$, $\angle J \cong \angle N$.

**9.39**

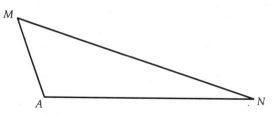

## 9.2  Homework Exercises

### Basic Exercises

1. The lateral surface of a cone can be built from a region like the one shown in Figure 9-73. Try it.

**Figure 9-73**

(a) Draw a circle with a compass and cut it out.
(b) Draw two radii and cut out the smaller closed region.

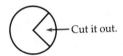

(c) Put the two cut edges together to form the lateral surface of a cone.

2. (a) Construct a copy of $\triangle MAN$ called $\triangle BCD$ so that $\triangle MAN \cong \triangle BCD$.

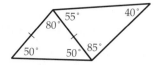

(b) Explain why $\triangle MAN \cong \triangle BCD$.

3. Construct a copy of $\triangle CDE$.

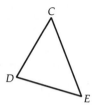

4. Which of the pairs of triangles shown at the top of the first column on page 515 must be congruent by SSS?

(a) 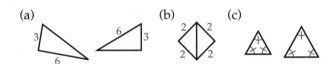 (b) (c)

5. An architect constructs triangular roof supports each with sides of length 0.7 m, 1.8 m, and 2.3 m. Are all the triangular supports congruent? Why or why not?

6.

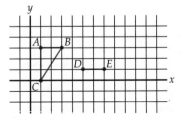

(a) Construct a copy of ∠MAY called ∠BCD.
(b) Explain why ∠MAY ≅ ∠BCD.

7. Construct a copy of ∠TED.

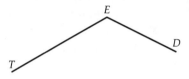

8.

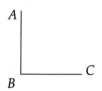

Give all possible coordinates of F that would determine a △DEF that is congruent to the triangle that has vertices A, B, and C.

9. AB = BC and m∠ABC = 90°. Construct the square ABCD.

A

B ———— C

10.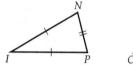

(a) Why is △NIP ≅ △ACR?
(b) Why is ∠I ≅ ∠C?

11. **Copying a Triangle** (ASA method)

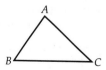

Show how to construct a copy of △ABC by copying two angles and the side between them (such as ∠B, ∠C, and $\overline{BC}$). This suggests the validity of the ASA triangle congruence property.

12. Would an AAS triangle congruence property work? Use the ASA property to show why.

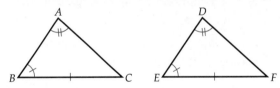

Assume that ∠A ≅ ∠D, ∠B ≅ ∠E, and $\overline{BC}$ ≅ $\overline{EF}$.
(a) Why is ∠C ≅ ∠F?
(b) Why is △ABC ≅ △DEF? (showing that AAS leads to congruent triangles)

13. Decide whether each pair of triangles must be congruent.

(a)          (b)          (c)          (d)

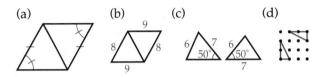

14. Create a counterexample to the SSA congruence property by completing the following. Draw △DEF with DE = AB,

$DF = AC$, and $m\angle B = m\angle E$ so that $\triangle DEF$ is not congruent to $\triangle ABC$.

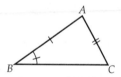

**15.** If possible, sketch two noncongruent triangles with four congruent corresponding parts.

**16.** (a) Construct the angle bisector of $\angle CAT$ and call it $\overrightarrow{AB}$.

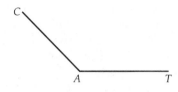

   (b) Explain why your procedure works.
   (c) Use congruent triangles to explain why $\overrightarrow{AB}$ bisects $\angle CAT$.

**17.** Assume that $\overrightarrow{EK}$ bisects $\angle MER$. Fill in all the missing angle measures.

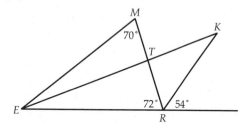

**18.**

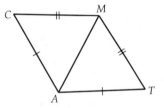

Explain why $\overrightarrow{AM}$ must be the angle bisector of $\angle CAT$.

**19.** Show that a triangle, $\triangle ABC$, with $\angle B \cong \angle C$ has two congruent sides. (*Hint:* Draw the angle bisector of $\angle BAC$.)

**20.** A plane is flying over water from $A$ to $B$ on a clear day with little wind. If there is trouble along the way, construct the point $C$ that can be used to determine whether it would be easier for a plane with engine trouble to go on to $B$ or to return to $A$.

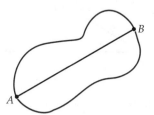

**21.** (a) A **median** of a triangle connects a vertex to the midpoint of the opposite side. Construct a median from $A$ to the midpoint of $\overline{BC}$.

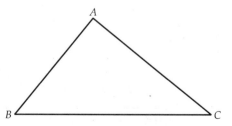

   (b) Cut out a paper triangle and fold the three medians of the triangle. What do you observe?

**22.** Use a straightedge and compass to divide a segment into four equal parts.

**23.** Construct a line segment that is three times the length of $\overline{AB}$.

**24.** (a) Draw a line segment on a piece of paper.
   (b) Locate its midpoint by paper folding.

**25.** (a) Draw an angle on a piece of paper.
   (b) Locate its angle bisector by paper folding.

26. Use the Isosceles Triangle Theorem to explain why an equilateral triangle must have three congruent angles.

27. Which set diagram shows the relationship between equilateral triangles and right triangles?

(a)  (b)  (c)

28. Find all missing angle measures in each diagram.

(a)  (b) (c)

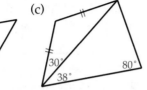

29. Regular hexagon *MARTIN* is inscribed in a circle with center *C*.

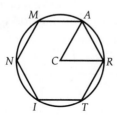

$m\angle ACR =$ _____

30. Find all the angle measures in the diagram.

31. The triangular grid is composed of vertices of equilateral triangles. Consider parallelogram *ABCD*.

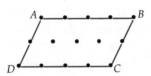

Draw diagonals $\overline{AC}$ and $\overline{BD}$. Check to see if they are congruent or perpendicular, or if they bisect each other.

32. The triangular grid is composed of vertices of equilateral triangles. Consider rhombus *ABCD*.

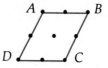

(a) Draw diagonals $\overline{AC}$ and $\overline{BD}$. Check to see if they are congruent or perpendicular, or if they bisect each other.

(b) Since a square is a rhombus, part (a) shows that the diagonals of a square are _____ .

**Extension Exercises**

33. $m\angle PUN = 60°$. Construct an equilateral triangle $\triangle NUT$ with *T* on $\overline{UP}$.

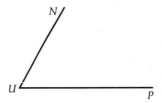

34. Construct a 45° angle.

35. Construct a 135° angle.

36. Construct $\angle GHI$ so that
$m\angle GHI = m\angle ABC - m\angle DEF$.

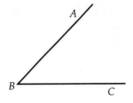 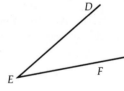

**37.** A jeweler designs a setting with a turquoise in the center surrounded by six pearls as shown. If the turquoise has a radius of 4 mm, what radius should the pearls have?

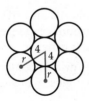

**38.** You are camping out when a friend gets hurt.

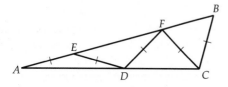

(a) What is the shortest route to the road?
(b) Construct the shortest route.

**39.** $AB = AC$. Find $m\angle A$.

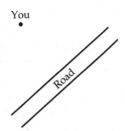

**40.** *ABCDE* is a regular pentagon.
(a) How are *AC, BD, CE, DA,* and *EB* related? (Draw a picture.)
(b) Prove your answer to part (a).

**41.** Suppose that two quadrilaterals have three congruent corresponding sides and two congruent corresponding included angles creating SASAS. Show that the two quadrilaterals must be congruent.

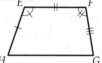

(*Hint:* Show that the remaining three corresponding parts are congruent after drawing diagonals $\overline{AC}$ and $\overline{EG}$.)

**42.** Show that an ASASA quadrilateral property works for *ABCD* and *EFGH*. (*Hint:* Draw $\overline{AC}$ and $\overline{EG}$.)

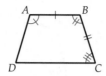

**43.** (a) Draw two noncongruent quadrilaterals showing that an SSSS congruence property would not work.
(b) How does part (a) relate to why quadrilaterals (without diagonals) are not used in structures such as bridges?

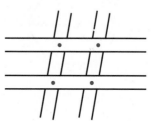

*Computer Exercises*

**44.** Write a Logo program that draws a 50° angle and its bisector.

**45.** Using an automatic drawer, draw $\overline{AB}$ and its perpendicular bisector. Investigate how far a point on the perpendicular bisector is from *A* and *B*. Repeat this for different points on the perpendicular bisector.

46. Using an automatic drawer, draw a parallelogram *ABCD* and its diagonals $\overline{AC}$ and $\overline{BD}$ intersecting at *E*. Compare the measurements of $\triangle AED$, $\triangle AEB$, $\triangle BEC$, and $\triangle CED$ and make a conjecture about parallelograms.

47. Using an automatic drawer, draw a rectangle *ABCD* and its diagonals $\overline{AC}$ and $\overline{BD}$ intersecting at *E*.
    (a) Compare *AC* and *BD*. Make a conjecture about rectangles.
    (b) Compare the measurements of $\triangle AED$, $\triangle AEB$, $\triangle BEC$, and $\triangle CED$ and make a conjecture.

48. Use an automatic drawer to investigate how many side measures or angle measures are needed to determine the shape of a triangle.
    (a) Try to draw two noncongruent triangles with sides *AB* = 7 and *BC* = 12. (SS)
    (b) Try to draw two noncongruent triangles with sides *AB* = 7, *BC* = 12, and *AC* = 10. (SSS)
    (c) Try to draw two noncongruent triangles with $m\angle A = 50°$ and $m\angle B = 70°$. (AA)
    (d) Try to draw two noncongruent triangles with $m\angle A = 50°$, $m\angle B = 70°$, and $m\angle C = 60°$. (AAA)
    (e) Try to draw two noncongruent triangles with $m\angle A = 50°$ and *AB* = 7. (AS)
    (f) Try to draw two noncongruent triangles with *AB* = 7, *BC* = 12, and $m\angle B = 50°$. (SAS)
    (g) Try to draw two noncongruent triangles with *AB* = 7, *BC* = 12, and $m\angle C = 50°$. (SSA)
    (h) Try to draw two noncongruent triangles with *AB* = 7, $m\angle A = 50°$, and $m\angle B = 70°$. (ASA)
    (i) Try to draw two noncongruent triangles with *AB* = 7, $m\angle A = 50°$, and $m\angle C = 60°$. (AAS)
    (j) List the conclusions of your investigation.

*Special Exercise*

49. Using only a compass, straightedge, and pencil or pen, create one of the following designs or make one of your own.

    (a)  (b)  (c)

    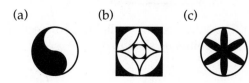

50. A drawing may appear to represent a three-dimensional object, but that object turns out to be impossible to make! The "Penrose triangle" is such a drawing.

    You will need a compass and ruler to make a Penrose triangle.
    (a) Draw an equilateral triangle with sides 12 cm long. Draw the base with a ruler. Locate the top with a compass by measuring 12 cm from each end of the base.

    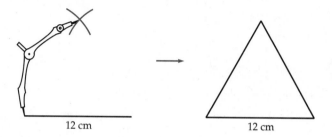

    12 cm                    12 cm

(b) Mark points 1 cm and 2 cm from each corner.

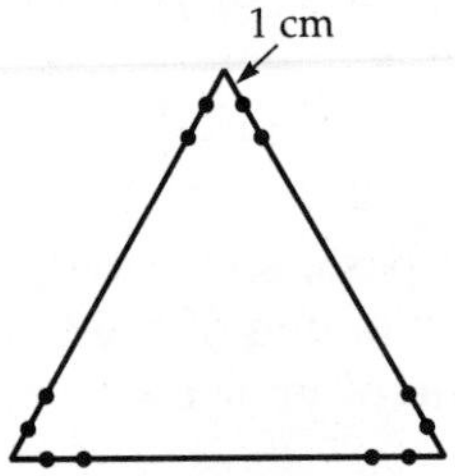


(c) Draw line segments lightly, connecting the points as shown.

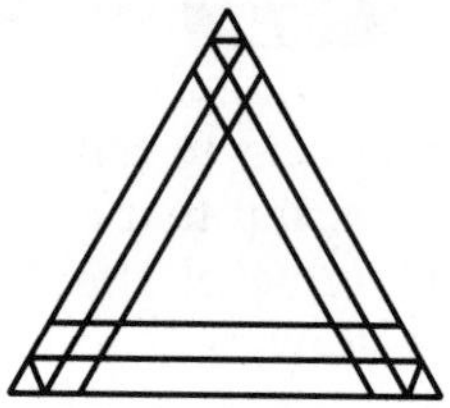

(d) Go over the lines shown. Erase the others.

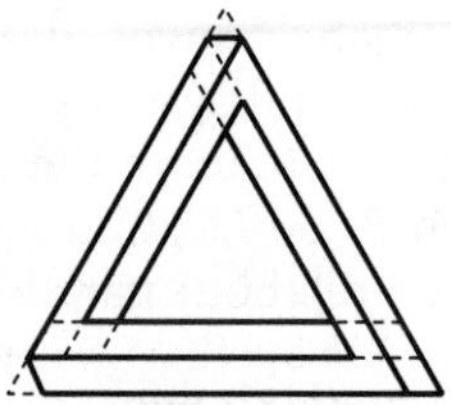

(e) Shade them as shown in the original Penrose triangle.

---

## 9.3 Symmetry

The term "congruence" usually describes a relationship between two figures that are the same size and shape. The term "symmetry" describes a way in which a single figure can be divided into parts that are the same size and shape and possess a particular orientation.

### Symmetry of Plane Figures

Symmetry adds beauty and balance to natural forms and architectural designs (Figure 9-74).

Photo of butterfly (neg. no. 108780) by J. Kirschner. Courtesy Department of Library Services, American Museum of Natural History. Photo of U.S. Capitol courtesy of Library of Congress.

**Figure 9-74**

Can you recognize plane figures that have symmetry?

**D** Lesson Exercise 9.40

Which designs in Figure 9-75 possess some kind of symmetry?

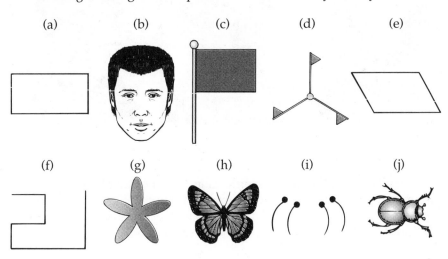

(a)　(b)　(c)　(d)　(e)

(f)　(g)　(h)　(i)　(j)

**Figure 9-75**

In Lesson Exercise 9.40, all but two of the figures are symmetric. You can check your answers with the following test for symmetry.

---

**A Test for Symmetry**

A plane figure is symmetric if you can copy it on tracing paper and find a different position for the tracing paper in which the traced figure coincides with the original figure.

---

## Lesson Exercise 9.41

Use tracing paper to determine which figures in Lesson Exercise 9.40 are symmetric.

---

For each symmetric figure, you moved the tracing paper to a new position, and the traced figure fit on top of the original figure. The motion you used was either a rotation (other than a full turn) or a reflection.

## Reflection Symmetry

(a)                    (b)                    (c)

**Figure 9-76**

A human face is not quite symmetric. Compare the real photograph of my face in Figure 9-76(a) to the two symmetric versions of me. The symmetric versions are each constructed from one half of my face. This example illustrates the most well-known type of symmetry: reflection (line) symmetry.

## Lesson Exercise 9.42

(a) Which shapes in Lesson Exercise 9.40 can be reflected onto themselves? (These figures have reflection symmetry.)

(b) If you have a pocket mirror or a Mira device, confirm your responses to part (a).

(c) Select one of the shapes that has reflection symmetry. Draw a line that divides it into two equal parts such that one part is the reflection image of the other through the given line.

(d) Select one of the shapes that has reflection symmetry. How could you use paper folding to show the symmetry?

A plane figure has **reflection** (line) **symmetry** if and only if it can be reflected through some line so that its image coincides with its original position. Each point in the figure is the same distance as its image point is from the line of symmetry.

Reflection symmetry is also called mirror symmetry since a line of symmetry acts like a double-sided mirror. Points on each side are reflected to the opposite side. Many figures have several reflection (line) symmetries. The equilateral triangle in Figure 9-77 has three lines of symmetry.

**Figure 9-77**

## Lesson Exercise 9.43

Draw all lines of symmetry for the regular pentagon in Figure 9-78.

**Figure 9-78**

**D** ## Lesson Exercise 9.44

Why isn't the line shown in Figure 9-79 a line of symmetry for the shape in the drawing?

## Lesson Exercise 9.45

Complete each figure so that the line acts as a line of symmetry.

(a)    (b)    (c)

**Figure 9-79**

## Rotational Symmetry

Courtesy of National Oceanic and Atmospheric Administration.

**Figure 9-80**

The surfaces of snowflakes (Figure 9-80) suggest a second major type of plane symmetry: rotational symmetry. Natural and manufactured objects that have rotational symmetry possess an order that enhances their beauty and function.

## Lesson Exercise 9.46

Which of the shapes in Lesson Exercise 9.40 can be rotated *less than 360°* (a full turn) onto themselves?

**Figure 9-81**

The figures you selected in Lesson Exercise 9.46 should have rotational symmetry. A plane figure has **rotational symmetry** if and only if it can be rotated less than 360° so that its image coincides with its original position.

Many shapes have several rotational symmetries. The equilateral triangle in Figure 9-81 can be turned 120° or 240° around its center to coincide with its original position. Therefore, it has 120° and 240° rotational symmetry.

## Lesson Exercise 9.47

What rotational symmetries does a regular pentagon have (greater than 0° and less than 360°)?

Can a plane figure have both rotational and reflection symmetry? Can it have one kind of symmetry without the other? Find out in the following exercises.

## Lesson Exercise 9.48

(a) Which shapes in Lesson Exercise 9.40 have rotational *and* reflection symmetry?
(b) Which shapes in Lesson Exercise 9.40 have rotational symmetry but not reflection symmetry?
(c) Which shapes in Lesson Exercise 9.40 have reflection symmetry but not rotational symmetry?

## Lesson Exercise 9.49

Consider the following problem: "Shade in the smallest number of squares in Figure 9-82 so that the pattern has reflection *and* rotational symmetry." Devise a plan and solve the problem.

**Figure 9-82**

## Symmetry of Space Figures

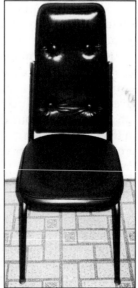

Photo of beetle (neg. no. 122981) by Alex J. Rota. Courtesy Department of Library Services, American Museum of Natural History. Photo of chair by Tom Sonnabend.

**Figure 9-83**

Some three-dimensional figures have the same kinds of symmetry as two-dimensional shapes. The beetle and chair in Figure 9-83 have two halves that are virtually identical. These objects have approximate reflection (plane) symmetry.

**Reflection** (plane) **symmetry** of space figures exists if a plane divides the figure in half so that one half of the figure is a mirror image of the other. To put it more precisely, each point on one side of the plane must have a corresponding point the same perpendicular distance away on the opposite side. This relationship is analogous to the distance relationship for line symmetry.

## Lesson Exercise 9.50

The beetle in Figure 9-83 has approximate reflection symmetry. Where is the plane of symmetry?

Reflection symmetry gives animals greater balance. Most animals and many machines have reflection symmetry.

## Lesson Exercise 9.51

Find an object in your classroom that has approximate reflection symmetry that gives it balance.

Saturn has approximate rotational symmetry. It can be rotated any amount around the line shown in Figure 9-84 and it will coincide with its original position.

**Rotational symmetry** of space figures exists if there is an axis of rotation (a line) around which the figure can be turned (less than a full turn) so that it coincides with itself. The rotational symmetry of an object gives the object "directional flexibility." For example, a square card table can be placed in four different positions that work exactly the same way. In 1888, the Russian mathematician Sonya Kovalevskaya (1850–1891) gained prominence with her research paper *On the Rotation of a Solid About a Fixed Point*.

**Figure 9-84**

## D Lesson Exercise 9.52

(a) Find an object in your classroom that has approximate rotational symmetry that gives it directional flexibility.
(b) Describe the location of the axis of rotation.
(c) What rotational symmetries between 0° and 360° does the object have?

## Answers to Selected Lesson Exercises

9.42 (a) a, b, g, h, i, j

9.43 There are five lines of symmetry.

9.44 A flip through the line does not leave the figure unchanged.

**9.45** (a)  (b) (c)

**9.46** a, d, e, g

**9.47** 72°, 144°, 216°, 288° clockwise (or counterclockwise)

**9.48** (a) a, g    (b) d, e    (c) b, h, i, j

**9.49**

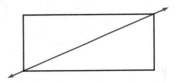

## 9.3   Homework Exercises

### Basic Exercises

**1.** Describe a test for symmetry.

**2.** Does symmetry enhance the beauty of a shape? Cover up the right half of the butterfly. Is it still as pleasing to the eye?

**3.** Which of the following figures have reflection symmetry?

(a)     (b)        (c)            (d)

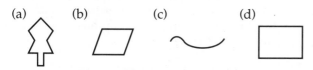

**4.** How many lines of symmetry does each of the following quadrilaterals have?
(a) square         (b) rectangle
(c) rhombus     (d) parallelogram

**5.** Draw all lines of symmetry for each figure. Verify your results using paper folding.

(a)        (b)      (c)                (d)

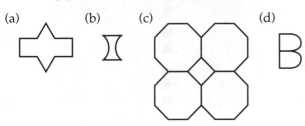

**6.** Draw an octagon that has exactly two lines of symmetry.

**7.** Explain why a diagonal is not a line of symmetry for a rectangle.

**8.** Complete the figure so that it is symmetric to the line.

**9.** (a) Draw two intersecting lines.
(b) Draw the two lines of symmetry for your lines in part (a).
(c) Repeat parts (a) and (b) starting with lines intersecting at a different angle.
(d) Propose a generalization of your results.
(e) Does part (d) involve induction or deduction?

**10.** (a) Fold a sheet of paper in half. Then make a cut so that the unfolded paper shows a heart.
(b) Repeat part (a), but create a pumpkin.
(c) Repeat part (a) and make your own design.

**11.** How many rotational symmetries does each of the following quadrilaterals have?
(a) square         (b) rectangle
(c) rhombus     (d) parallelogram

**12.** You are "O" in tic-tac-toe.

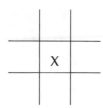

(a) What are four equivalent plays you could make?

(b) How many nonequivalent plays are there?

**13.** What kind of symmetry does each flag have?

(a)     (b)     (c)

    Switzerland      Finland      Great Britain

**14.** What kind of symmetry does each snowflake have?

(a)  (b) 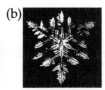 (c)

Courtesy of National Oceanic and Atmospheric Administration.

**15.** (a) Which letters in the word shown have reflection symmetry?

    (b) Which letters have rotational symmetry?

S    Q    U    I    D

**16.** The word HIDE has a horizontal line of symmetry. Write three more words that have a horizontal line of symmetry.

**17.** Examine a deck of playing cards.

(a) Which cards have rotational symmetry?

(b) Which cards have reflection symmetry?

**18.** Draw a plane figure that has reflection symmetry but no rotational symmetry.

**19.** For all plane figures having two or more reflection symmetries, there is a relationship between the number of reflection symmetries and the number of rotational symmetries. Devise a plan and find the relationship.

**20.** What property or properties of a circle help explain why lampshades generally have circular cross sections?

**21.** Shade in the smallest number of squares so that each of the following patterns has rotational symmetry.

(a) 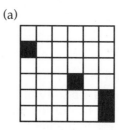      (b)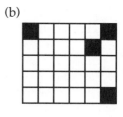

**22.** Mirror cards (developed by Marion Walters) are used to teach symmetry in elementary school. Using the mirror card at the left, where would you place a mirror on the card to obtain the figures shown in parts (a), (b), and (c)?

(a)  (b)  (c)

**23.** A plane figure that looks exactly the same upside down as right side up has what specific symmetry?

**24.**

© 1990 M. C. Escher Heirs/Cordon Art—Baarn —Holland.

Describe all the symmetries of this pattern.

**25.** How many planes of symmetry does a right square pyramid have?

**26.** How many planes of symmetry does a cube have?

**27.** How many planes of symmetry does a right pentagonal prism have?

**28.** How many axes (lines) of rotational symmetry does a cube have?

**29.** How many axes (lines) of rotational symmetry does a cone have?

**30.** A nut  has approximate rotational symmetry. What is the advantage of this?

**31.** If you rotate an isosceles triangle in space about its line of symmetry, what solid would you obtain?

**32.** What kind of symmetry does a lightbulb have, and what is the practical benefit of this symmetry?

**33.** Find a tile floor in your home or school.
(a) What kind of symmetry do the tiles have?
(b) What is the practical benefit of this symmetry?

**34.** (a) What kind of symmetry do birds have?
(b) What is the practical benefit of this symmetry?

**35.** (a) Describe the symmetries of a tennis ball, a tennis racket, and a tennis court.
(b) Explain how the symmetries of each object relate to the function of the object.

**36.** (a) List three objects in your home that have reflection symmetry.
(b) List three objects in your home that have rotational symmetry.

**37.** What kind of symmetry does each of the following figures have?

(a)
(b)
(c)
(d)
(e)

**38.** Pottery and other objects made on a lathe generally have what kind of symmetry?

**39.** In how many ways can a rectangular piece of glass fit into a window frame?

**40.** The driver's door of a two-door car is damaged and has to be refitted. The only available replacement is a passenger door. Will it fit?

**41.** In how many ways can each key be inserted into the corresponding hole from one side?

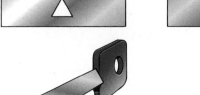

**42.** A kaleidoscope usually has two mirrors placed at a 60° angle as shown. One image is drawn. Fill in all the other images. (*Hint:* Include images of images.)

*Extension Exercises*

**43.**

| + | 0 | 1 | 2 | 3 | 4 | 5 | 6 | 7 | 8 | 9 |
|---|---|---|---|---|---|---|---|---|---|---|
| 0 | 0 | 1 | 2 | 3 | 4 | 5 | 6 | 7 | 8 | 9 |
| 1 | 1 | 2 | 3 | 4 | 5 | 6 | 7 | 8 | 9 | 10 |
| 2 | 2 | 3 | 4 | 5 | 6 | 7 | 8 | 9 | 10 | 11 |
| 3 | 3 | 4 | 5 | 6 | 7 | 8 | 9 | 10 | 11 | 12 |
| 4 | 4 | 5 | 6 | 7 | 8 | 9 | 10 | 11 | 12 | 13 |
| 5 | 5 | 6 | 7 | 8 | 9 | 10 | 11 | 12 | 13 | 14 |
| 6 | 6 | 7 | 8 | 9 | 10 | 11 | 12 | 13 | 14 | 15 |
| 7 | 7 | 8 | 9 | 10 | 11 | 12 | 13 | 14 | 15 | 16 |
| 8 | 8 | 9 | 10 | 11 | 12 | 13 | 14 | 15 | 16 | 17 |
| 9 | 9 | 10 | 11 | 12 | 13 | 14 | 15 | 16 | 17 | 18 |

(a) What kind of symmetry does an addition table have? (Ignore the position of the number within each box.)

(b) What property of addition does this symmetry indicate?

(c) Does a multiplication table for 0 to 9 have the same symmetry?

44. Look at some blank crossword puzzles. Do they have any symmetry?

45. Trace the circle shown here on a sheet of paper. How can you locate its center using paper folding?

46. (a) Which pentominos have reflection symmetry?
    (b) Which pentominos have rotational symmetry?

47. If an isosceles triangle, $\triangle ABC$, has a line of symmetry $\overleftrightarrow{CD}$, what can you say about each of the following?
    (a) $\overline{AD}$ and $\overline{DB}$
    (b) $\angle A$ and $\angle B$

48. Sketch any of the following seven figures that are possible: hexagons with exactly zero, one, two, three, four, five, or six lines of symmetry.

49. Add to the drawing so that it has rotational symmetry and exactly one line of symmetry.

F

*Computer Exercise*

50. The following Logo procedures draw fractal snowflakes.
    (a) Enter the following lines into a computer and experiment with different inputs. Begin with FLAKE 2 100 and try values of N from 1 to 4. (Values of N greater than 4 will take a long time.) Do not clear the screen between inputs.

    TO PATTERN :N :L
    IF :N = 1 [FD :L STOP]
    PATTERN :N=1 :L/3 LT 60
    PATTERN :N=1 :L/3 RT 120
    PATTERN :N=1 :L/3 LT 60
    PATTERN :N=1 :L/3
    END

    TO FLAKE :N :L
    REPEAT 3 [PATTERN :N :L RT 120]
    END

    (b) What kind of symmetry do your drawings have?
    (c) Repeat part (a), but type CS after each run.

*Special Exercise*

51. (a) Copy the following pattern on a nearly transparent piece of paper.

    (b) Trace over the following pattern on each of the six lines.

You have created a snowflake!

# 9.4 Similarity and Size Changes

Scale models of objects are the same shape but not the same size as the object. When you enlarge a photograph, you obtain a new picture in which everything is the same shape but a different size (Figure 9-85).

 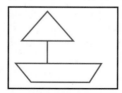

**Figure 9-85**

Beyond a certain age, dolphins grow larger but retain roughly the same shape (Figure 9-86).

Neg. no. 328896. Photo: Rob Mathewson. Courtesy Department of Library Services, American Museum of Natural History.

**Figure 9-86**

## Size Changes

Suppose that you want to enlarge a drawing without changing its shape. How could this be done? This enlargement would correspond to a geometric motion called a size change. A size change is easy to perform on a coordinate plane.

## Lesson Exercise 9.53

(a) Plot $A(0, 0)$; $B(4, 0)$; $C(2, 2)$; and $D(0, 2)$ on a graph.
(b) Connect $A$ to $B$, $B$ to $C$, $C$ to $D$, and $D$ to $A$. What shape do you obtain?
(c) Double the coordinates of $A$, $B$, $C$, and $D$ to obtain $E$, $F$, $G$, and $H$, respectively. Plot $E$, $F$, $G$, and $H$ and connect them.
(d) How are $ABCD$ and $EFGH$ related?
(e) How does $EF$ compare to $AB$? How does $GH$ compare to $CD$?
(f) How do the corresponding angle measures of the two figures compare?
(g) Now triple the coordinates of $A$, $B$, $C$, and $D$ to obtain $I$, $J$, $K$, and $L$. Plot $I$, $J$, $K$, and $L$ and connect them.
(h) How is $IJKL$ related to the other two figures?
(i) How does $IJ$ compare to $AB$? How does $KL$ compare to $CD$?
(j) How do the corresponding angles of $IJKL$ compare to those of $ABCD$?
(k) Propose a generalization about the result of multiplying the coordinates of a shape by a positive number $k$.

Lesson Exercises 9.53 (c) and 9.53(g) are examples of size changes. A size change has a **center** and a positive **scale factor**. A **size change** in a plane multiplies the distance of each point in the plane from the center by the scale factor. In Lesson Exercise 9.53(c), the size change assigns an image to each point of $ABCD$ that is twice as far from the center point $(0, 0)$.

The size change produces an image that has the same shape as the original figure. The size change multiplies the lengths of the original figure by the scale factor but does not change the measures of the angles.

A size change can also be performed on a figure that is not in a coordinate plane.

## Lesson Exercise 9.54

Perform the size change $S_{A, 1.5}$ with center $A$ and scale factor 1.5 by following these instructions.

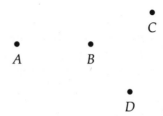

(a) On $\overrightarrow{AB}$, find an image point $B'$ that is 1.5 times as far from $A$ as $B$ is. In the same way, find image points $C'$ on $\overrightarrow{AC}$ and $D'$ on $\overrightarrow{AD}$.

(b) Using a ruler and a protractor, measure the sides and angles of $\triangle BCD$ and $\triangle B'C'D'$.
(c) Describe any relationships that exist between the corresponding sides, angles, and vertices of $\triangle BCD$ and $\triangle B'C'D'$.

## Size Changes and Similar Figures

A size change produces an image that has the same shape and equal corresponding angle measures. The corresponding lengths are multiplied by the scale factor. These properties describe similar figures. **Similar figures** are the same shape but not necessarily the same size.

The results of the size changes suggest criteria for determining whether two polygons are similar.

---

**Definition: Similar Polygons**

**Similar polygons** have
1. congruent corresponding angles and
2. proportional corresponding lengths.

---

The two triangles in Figure 9-87 are similar. They have congruent corresponding angles and proportional corresponding lengths.

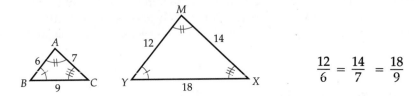

$$\frac{12}{6} = \frac{14}{7} = \frac{18}{9}$$

**Figure 9-87**

The relationship can be written symbolically as $\triangle ABC \sim \triangle MYX$. The symbol $\sim$ means "similar to." The letters in the names of the triangles should match up corresponding vertices.

The scale factor (or ratio of corresponding lengths) is $\frac{2}{1}$, or 2:1, or 2, or $\frac{1}{2}$, or 1:2. Going from the left triangle to the right triangle, the scale factor is 2. Going from the right triangle to the left triangle, the scale factor would be $\frac{1}{2}$.

## Lesson Exercise 9.55

(a) Fill in the blank, putting the vertices for $\triangle DNW$ in the corresponding order (see Figure 9-88). $\triangle FAT \sim$ _____

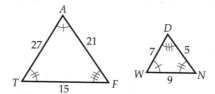

**Figure 9-88**

(b) What is the scale factor going from $\triangle FAT$ to $\triangle DWN$?

## Lesson Exercise 9.56

In each case, use the definition of similar figures to decide if the two figures are similar.

(a)

(b)

When you are given a statement with the names of two similar figures,
such as $ARCX \sim MYTU$, you can tell which angles are congruent and
which lengths are proportional because the vertices are written in corresponding order.

## Lesson Exercise 9.57

$ARCX \sim MYTU$. Fill in the missing lengths.

$$\frac{RC}{\Box} = \frac{RX}{\Box} = \frac{\Box}{MU}$$

If you know the lengths of some sides of two similar polygons, is it
possible to compute the lengths of the remaining sides? In a case like the
following, you could use proportions.

### Example 9.1

You want to enlarge a photograph that is 4 in. by 6 in. so that its longer dimension will be 9 in. How long is the shorter dimension?

**Solution**

An enlarged photograph should retain the same *shape*. Draw two similar rectangles to represent the photograph before and after enlargement (Figure 9-89).

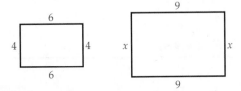

**Figure 9-89**

Since the rectangles are similar, corresponding lengths are proportional. So $\dfrac{6}{9} = \dfrac{4}{x}$.

This is the same as

$$6 \cdot x = 4 \cdot 9$$
$$6x = 36$$
$$x = 6 \text{ in.} \quad \blacksquare$$

## Lesson Exercise  9.58

The two triangles in Figure 9-90 are similar. Find $x$ and $y$.

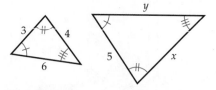

**Figure 9-90**

## Similar Solids

Like similar plane figures, similar solids are the same shape but not necessarily the same size. In similar polyhedra, the lengths of corresponding edges are proportional, and corresponding angles are congruent.

## Lesson Exercise 9.59

The two rectangular prisms in Figure 9-91 are similar. *AB* corresponds to *EF*, *BC* to *FG*, and *CD* to *GH*. Find the lengths x and *y*.

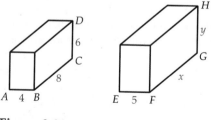

**Figure 9-91**

## Applications of Similarity

On a sunny day, you can use the length of your shadow to compute the height of a building. It's a good way to impress your friends. How does it work?

You and your shadow determine a triangle. This triangle is similar to the same kind of triangle formed by nearby objects and their shadows at the same time of day!

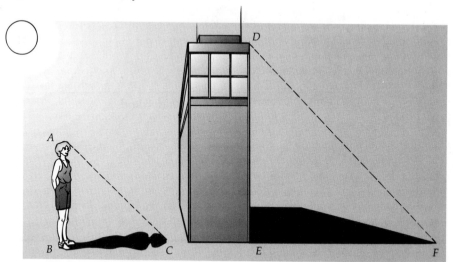

**Figure 9-92**

In Figure 9-92, $\triangle ABC \sim \triangle DEF$. Now suppose that you want to estimate how tall the building is. You can use your height, the length of your shadow, and the length of the building's shadow to compute the height of the building. Example 9.2 illustrates how this is done.

 **Example 9.2**

Jane is 5 ft 3 in. tall. At 4 PM, her shadow is 7 ft 6 in. long. She measures the shadow of a nearby building. It is 500 in. long. About how tall is the building?

**Solution**

**Understanding the Problem** The length of each object and its corresponding shadow have the same ratio.

**Devising a Plan** Draw a picture and set up a proportion with the appropriate units.

**Carrying Out the Plan** Convert the measurements into inches (Figure 9-93).

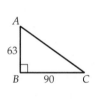 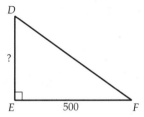

**Figure 9-93**

$$5 \text{ ft } 3 \text{ in. } = 63 \text{ in.} \quad \text{and} \quad 7 \text{ ft } 6 \text{ in. } = 90 \text{ in.}$$

$$\triangle ABC \sim \triangle DEF. \text{ So } \frac{AB}{DE} = \frac{BC}{EF} = \frac{AC}{DF}.$$

Filling in the given information,

$$\frac{63}{?} = \frac{90}{500} = \frac{AC}{DF}$$

Use the first two ratios and solve.

$$\frac{63}{?} = \frac{90}{500} \quad \text{means} \quad 63 \cdot 500 = 90 \cdot (?)$$

Using a calculator, $63 \times 500 \div 90 \approx 350$. So the building is about 350 in. or 29 ft 2 in. tall.

**Looking Back** The building's shadow is about 5 times the length of Jane's shadow. So the height of the building should be about 5 times Jane's height. 29 ft 2 in. is about 5 times 5 ft 3 in. ■

Lesson Exercise 9.60

One sunny morning, Arturo, who is 5 ft tall, cast a shadow 7 ft 10 in. long. A nearby tree cast a shadow 10 ft 10 in. long. About how tall is the tree?

Computing the distance between two cities on a map also involves similar figures. A map shape is approximately similar to the region it represents (although maps are flat and the earth is not). Therefore, map distances are approximately proportional to actual distances.

Lesson Exercise 9.61

A map has a scale ratio of 1 in. $\approx$ 120 miles. New York is $1\frac{5}{8}$ in. from Boston on the map. Approximately how far is New York from Boston?

## Answers to Selected Lesson Exercises

**9.53** (b) trapezoid
(d) They are the same shape.
(e) They are twice as long.
(f) They are equal.
(h) It is the same shape.
(i) They are three times as long.
(j) They are equal.

**9.54** (c) $\triangle BCD$ and $\triangle B'C'D'$ are the same shape. They have congruent corresponding angles. The corresponding sides of $\triangle B'C'D'$ are 1.5 times as long.

**9.55** (a) $\triangle DWN$      (b) 3 to 1

**9.56** (a) no      (b) yes

**9.57** $\dfrac{RC}{YT} = \dfrac{RX}{YU} = \dfrac{AX}{MU}$

**9.58** $x = 6\frac{2}{3}$      $y = 10$

**9.59** $x = 10$      $y = 7\frac{1}{2}$

**9.60** about 6 ft 11 in.

**9.61** about 195 miles

## 9.4  Homework Exercises

*Basic Exercises*

1. Draw a boat like the one shown on a coordinate grid and use a size change to draw a boat that has corresponding length measurements 2.5 times as large. (*Hint:* Place the vertices of the boat at integer coordinates.)

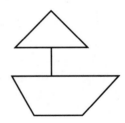

**2.** Perform the size change $S_{P,2}$ on $\overline{AB}$.

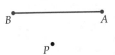

**3.** Perform the size change $S_{P,1/2}$ on $\triangle ABC$.

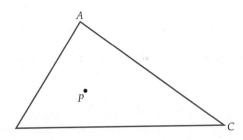

**4.** Look back at the size changes you have done. Under a size change, is the image of a line not containing the center parallel to the original line?

**5.** (a) Fill in the blank, putting the vertices for $\triangle NMR$ in the corresponding order.

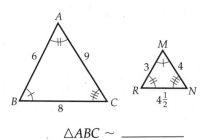

$$\triangle ABC \sim \underline{\hspace{2cm}}$$

(b) What is the scale factor going from $\triangle ABC$ to $\triangle MRN$?

**6.** In each case, decide if the two figures are similar.

(a)                    (b)

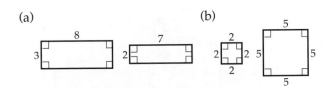

**7.** In each case, decide if the two figures shown at the top of the next column are similar.

(a) 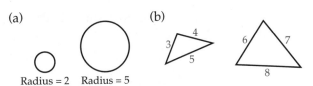 (b)

Radius = 2   Radius = 5

**8.** Are any two squares similar? Why or why not?

**9.** Are any two rhombuses similar? Why or why not?

**10.** Are two congruent figures also similar?

**11.** An overhead projector projects the image of a figure from a transparency to a screen. What is the relationship between the figure and its image?

**12.** $\triangle ANT \sim \triangle REP$. Fill in the blanks.

(a) $\angle T \cong$ _____ (b) $\dfrac{ER}{\square} = \dfrac{\square}{TN}$

**13.** Sketch two similar figures suggested by the equivalent fractions:

$$\frac{8}{10} = \frac{12}{15} = \frac{14.4}{18}$$

**14.** Suppose that you want to enlarge a photograph that is 3 in. by 5 in. so that its longer dimension is 8 in. What will the shorter dimension be?

**15.** The two triangles shown are similar. Find $x$ and $y$.

**16.** Assume that the two triangles in each part are similar and find $x$.

(a) 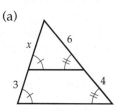 (b)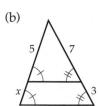

**17.** Assume that all three triangles are similar. Find x.

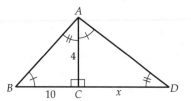

**18.** Find the missing angles in each pair of similar triangles.

(a) $\triangle ACT \cong \triangle RUG$      (b) $\triangle INK \cong \triangle IPS$

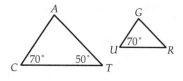

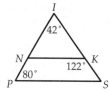

**19.** The two rectangular prisms shown here are similar; $\overline{AB}$ corresponds to $\overline{EF}$, $\overline{BC}$ corresponds to $\overline{FG}$, and $\overline{CD}$ corresponds to $\overline{GH}$. Find the lengths x and y.

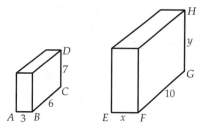

**20.** Would any two cylinders be similar? Why or why not?

**21.** Would any two spheres be similar? Why or why not?

**22.** What is the relationship between a scale model of a bridge and the actual bridge?

 **23.** Bill is 4 ft 4 in. tall. At 3 PM, his shadow is 5 ft 10 in. long. The shadow of a nearby building is 33 ft 4 in. long. How tall is the building?

 **24.** A map has a scale ratio of 1 in. ≈ 60 miles. Sleepytown is $3\frac{1}{4}$ in. from Swingtown on the

map. Based upon this, the actual distance would be _____.

 **25.** A drawing is 10 cm by 15 cm. A copying machine reduces the length and width to 68% of their original size.
(a) What are the dimensions of the reduced drawing?
(b) Is the reduced drawing similar to the original?
(c) The area of the reduced image is _____ % the area of the original drawing.

**26.** A particular magnifying glass enlarges all length measurements to three times their original size. What percent enlargement is this?

**27.** Make a scale drawing of the house shown here with 1 cm representing 4 m.

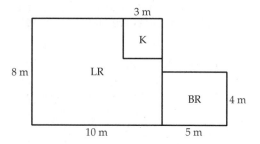

**28.** An engineer wants to build a tunnel from A to B through a mountain as shown. To find the length AB, the engineer sights A and B from C. $AC = 60$ ft, $m\angle A = 90°$, $m\angle B = 32°$, and $m\angle C = 58°$. Make a scale drawing and approximate AB.

*Extension Exercises*

**29.** Materials needed: one ruler, one protractor, one live brain

(a) Draw a triangle and measure its three angles. Now draw a second triangle that has the same three angle measures as the first triangle but with longer or shorter sides.

(b) Now look at your two triangles. What strikes you about their appearance (one compared to the other)?

(c) Measure the sides of each triangle. How do they compare?

(d) Complete the following generalization suggested by this exercise. If three angles of one triangle are congruent to three angles of a second triangle, then the triangles are _____ .

**30.** (a) Draw a triangle with sides of 2 in., 3 in., and 4 in.

(b) Draw a second triangle with sides of 1 in., $1\frac{1}{2}$ in., and 2 in.

(c) Do the triangles appear to be similar?

(d) Repeat parts (a)–(c) for two other triangles with proportional sides.

(e) Based upon your two examples, two triangles with proportional sides appear _____ similar.
(to be, not to be)

**31.** Use a size change to demonstrate a property of triangles.

(a) Draw any $\triangle ABC$ and locate the midpoints of $\overline{AB}$ and $\overline{AC}$. Label them $D$ and $E$ and draw $\overline{DE}$.

(b) Under size change $S_{A,2}$, what are the images of $D$ and $E$?

(c) Based upon part (b), how is $BC$ related to $DE$?

(d) Write a general statement describing the triangle property you found.

**32.** Find the center and scale factor for the size transformation shown. The original figure is black.

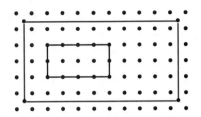

**33.** (a) Plot $A(0, 0)$; $B(4, 0)$; $C(2, 2)$; and $D(0, 2)$ on a graph and connect $A$ to $B$, $B$ to $C$, $C$ to $D$, and $D$ to $A$.

(b) What happens if you multiply all the coordinates by $k < 0$, plot the resulting points, and connect them in the same order?

**34.** Go outdoors on a sunny day and use indirect measure and shadows to find the height of a tree or pole in your neighborhood.

**35.** A quadrilateral has sides of length $a$, $b$, $c$, and $d$. A second quadrilateral has sides of length $2a$, $2b$, $2c$, and $2d$. Must the quadrilaterals be similar?

**36.** A rectangle has dimensions of $b$ and $h$. A second rectangle has dimensions of $b + 6$ and $h + 6$. Are the rectangles similar?

**37.** A rectangle has length $L$ and width $W$. A second rectangle has length $KL$ and width $KW$, with $K > 0$. Are the rectangles similar?

*Computer Exercise*

**38.** Use an automatic drawer to investigate the minimum conditions for lengths of sides or angle measures that would make two triangles similar.

(a) Draw two pairs of triangles with all three corresponding lengths of sides proportional. Are the two triangles similar?

(b) Repeat part (a) with two different triangles.

(c) What conclusion do you draw from parts (a) and (b)?

(d) Draw two pairs of triangles with two

equal corresponding angle measures. Are the two triangles similar?

(e) Repeat part (d) with two different triangles.
(f) What conclusion do you draw from parts (d) and (e)?

**39.** Look at the attractive rectangles below!

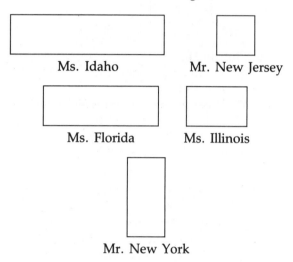

Ms. Idaho      Mr. New Jersey

Ms. Florida      Ms. Illinois

Mr. New York

Which rectangle is the most beautiful? To answer this question, consider which one you would like as the front of a house, the frame of a painting, or the shape of a flag.

**40.** The **golden rectangle** (Ms. Illinois) has been admired since the time of ancient Greece (about 700 B.C.)!

> The **golden rectangle** is any rectangle with a ratio of
> $$\frac{\text{Length}}{\text{Width}} = \frac{1 + \sqrt{5}}{2} \approx 1.1618$$

(a) If the width of a golden rectangle is 4, give its length to three decimal places.
(b) If the length of a golden rectangle is 10, gives its width to three decimal places.

**41.** Take a typical golden rectangle.

Divide it into a square and a rectangle.

(a) Is the new rectangle inside a golden rectangle?
(b) Divide the newly formed rectangle into a square and a smaller rectangle. Is this smaller rectangle golden?
(c) How long could you continue this process of subdividing each new golden rectangle into an even smaller square and smaller golden rectangle?
(d) Note that $\dfrac{1}{0.618} = \dfrac{1.618}{1}$ or $\dfrac{1}{0.618}$
$= \dfrac{1 + 0.618}{1}$. The golden ratio comes from the equation $\dfrac{b}{a} = \dfrac{b + a}{b} = 1 + \dfrac{a}{b}$.
If $r$ is the golden ratio $\dfrac{b}{a}$ then $r = 1 + \dfrac{1}{r}$.
Solve this equation for $r$.

**42.** The Parthenon was built in Athens, Greece, about 2400 years ago. Since the shapes in the sketch shown (see page 543) are approximately similar to those in the building, we can study the sketch and learn about the building! Use a ruler to measure the length and height of the front, including where the roof would be. What is significant about the ratio of the length to the height?

Photo courtesy of Library of Congress.

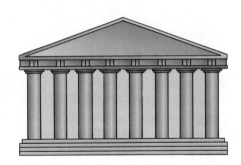

43. Determine how close the following ratios are to the golden ratio.
    (a) your height to the height of your navel
    (b) the length of your index finger to the distance from your index fingertip to the middle of the big knuckle
    (c) the length of your arm to the distance from your middle fingertip to your elbow
    (d) the distance from your left eye to your mouth to the distance from your left eye to the level of your nose

## Summary

Anyone who spends time studying shapes is likely to notice congruence, symmetry, and similarity. Congruence and similarity are two important relationships between pairs of geometric figures. Congruent figures are identical in shape and size, whereas similar figures are the same shape but not necessarily the same size. Symmetry describes a certain kind of balance a figure possesses.

Congruence and symmetry of plane figures are related to rotations, translations, and reflections. Ask a young child whether two shapes are identical, and the child will attempt to fit one shape on top of the other. This is an example of how two plane figures are congruent if and only if one can be mapped onto the other using a rotation, translation, reflection, or some combination of these motions. A plane figure is symmetric if you can find a different position in the plane in which the newly positioned figure coincides with the original figure.

Similarity is related to size changes. A size change uniformly multiplies the lengths of a figure without changing the angle measures or shape. The resulting image is similar to the original figure.

Symmetry enhances the beauty of nature. Reflection symmetry gives balance to birds and kites. Rotational symmetry gives directional flexibility to starfish and bolts. Similarity is useful in measuring heights indirectly and in finding distances represented on maps.

Constructions are a geometric ritual that has been passed on for thousands of years. Using only a compass and straightedge, it is possible to copy or bisect all sorts of plane figures.

## Study Guide

To review Chapter 9, see what you know about each of the following ideas or terms listed that you have studied. You can also use this list to generate your own questions about Chapter 9.

# The NCTM Curriculum Standards
# and Congruence, Symmetry, and Similarity

**Selected NCTM Curriculum Standards**

The following standards come from the NCTM document.

- Explore transformations of geometric figures.
- Develop an appreciation of geometry as a means of describing the physical world.
- Investigate and predict the results of combining, subdividing, and changing shapes.
- Use a mathematical idea to further their understanding of other mathematical ideas.

1. Describe how each standard listed relates to the material you studied in Chapter 9.

2. Select any current elementary-school mathematics textbook series and describe a sample lesson or exercise that illustrates each standard listed.

## Review Exercises

1. What is the relationship between *congruence* and rotations, translations, and reflections?

2. (a) Show the image of $\triangle ABC$ after a reflection through line $m$ followed by a reflection through line $n$.

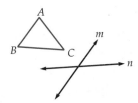

(b) What single motion gives the same image as the two successive reflections?

3. (a) Find the image A′ of point A using the mapping

$$(x, y) \rightarrow (x - 3, y - 4)$$

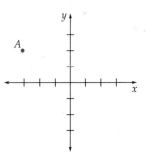

(b) Name the motion that produces the mapping

$$(x, y) \rightarrow (x - 3, y - 4)$$

**4.** *ABCD* is a rectangle.

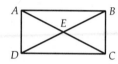

(a) Select a pair of angles that appear to be congruent and name a motion that maps one angle onto the other.

(b) Repeat part (a) for another pair of angles.

**5.** (a) Construct the angle bisector of $\angle AIM$ and call it $\overrightarrow{IT}$. (Assume $AI = MI$.)

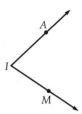

(b) Use congruent triangles to explain why $\overrightarrow{IT}$ bisects $\angle AIM$.

**6.** Shown here is a regular hexagon. Find all the angle measures in the diagram.

**7.** Draw all lines of symmetry for the rectangle shown.

**8.** Are any two regular pentagons similar? Why or why not?

**9.** Draw a figure that has four lines of symmetry and three rotational symmetries less than 360°.

**10.** Shade in the smallest number of squares so that the pattern shown has rotational symmetry.

**11.** Use a ruler to find the image of $\triangle ABC$ after the size change $S_{P, 1.5}$.

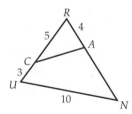

**12.** If $\triangle RUN \sim \triangle RAC$, find $AC$.

**13.** Sandy is 4 ft 10 in. tall. At 1 PM, her shadow is 5 ft 5 in. long. The shadow of a nearby building is 30 ft 2 in. long. How tall is the building?

**14.** A rectangle has length $L$ and width $L + 6$. A similar rectangle has length of 10. What is its width?

**15.** Sketch any of the following six figures that are possible: pentagons with exactly zero, one, two, three, four, or five lines of symmetry.

# Congruence, Symmetry, and Similarity in Elementary School

The following chart shows at what grade level selected geometry topics typically appear in elementary-school mathematics textbooks.

| Topic | Typical Grade Level in Current Textbooks |
| --- | --- |
| Slides, flips, turns | 4, <u>5</u>, <u>6</u> |
| Congruent figures | 2, 3, 4, 5, 6 |
| Line symmetry | 3, 4, 5, 6 |
| Rotational symmetry | 6 (enrichment topic) |
| Similar figures | 4, 5, 6 |
| Constructions | 6 (enrichment topic) |

# Suggested Readings

Hill, J., ed. *Geometry for Grades K–6.* Reston, VA: NCTM, 1987.

National Council of Teachers of Mathematics. 1973 Yearbook. *Geometry in the Mathematics Classroom.* Reston, VA: NCTM, 1973.

National Council of Teachers of Mathematics. 1987 Yearbook. *Learning and Teaching Geometry K–12.* Reston, VA: NCTM, 1987.

O'Daffer, P. and S. Clemens. *Geometry: An Investigative Approach.* 2nd ed. Reading, MA: Addison-Wesley, 1992.

Olson, T. A. *Mathematics Through Paper Folding.* Reston, VA: NCTM, 1975.

Ranucci, E. and J. Teeters. *Creating Escher-Type Drawings.* Palo Alto, CA: Creative Publications, 1977.

Weyl, H. *Symmetry.* Princeton, NJ: Princeton University Press, 1952.

# 10

# Measurement

People created measurement systems to satisfy practical needs such as finding distances between places, heights of horses, and weights of grains. They developed calendars in order to keep track of days, seasons, and years.

All measurements require a unit of measure. People used body measurements as units of length and seeds and stones as units of weight. The first units of time were the cycles of the sun and moon. In recent times, most countries have developed uniform units of measure. Today, most countries in the world use the metric system, while the United States uses the customary (English) system.

People have developed ingenious formulas and methods for computing area and volume of geometric shapes, and they use these formulas to approximate the measures of many everyday objects.

## 10.1 Metric Measure

Any object has a number of attributes that can be measured. When you measure something, you focus on one attribute and ignore all other attributes and qualities. Measurement involves: (1) identifying an attribute, (2) selecting a unit of measure, and (3) comparing the attribute of the object to the unit of measure. The first units of measure were nonstandard units.

### Nonstandard Measuring Units

Historical records indicate that people measured lengths with their hands, feet, and arms (Figure 10-1).

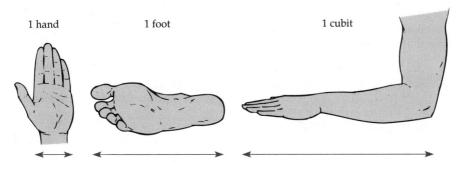

**Figure 10-1**

## Lesson Exercise 10.1

(a) How many hands high is this page of your book?
(b) Why might others in the class obtain different answers?

Hands, feet, and arms are convenient for measuring, but different people have different-sized hands, feet, and arms. This is why we need standard measuring units such as those of the metric system.

## The Metric System

The metric system was developed in France in the late 1700s. A meter was originally defined as $\frac{1}{10,000,000}$ of the distance from the North Pole to the equator. The meter is now defined as the distance light travels in a vacuum in $\frac{1}{299,792,458}$ second.

Nearly every country in the world except the United States and Australia uses the metric system. In what ways is the metric system superior to the customary (U.S.) system?

## Lesson Exercise 10.2

How many people in your class can correctly answer each of the following questions?
(a) How many yards are in a mile?
(b) How many meters are in a kilometer?

Most of you have been using customary measure all your life and metric measure for only a short time. In spite of this fact, more adults in the United States can correctly answer Lesson Exercise 10.2(b) than 10.2(a)!

Two advantages of the metric system are: (1) metric prefixes are the same for length, weight, and liquid volume, and (2) all conversions within the metric system involve powers of 10.

Each pair of students will need a meter stick and a 30-cm ruler to do Lesson Exercises 10.3, 10.7, 10.9, 10.10, and 10.12.

## D  Lesson Exercise 10.3

Look at your meter stick and complete the following.
(a) Find a centimeter on your meter stick.
(b) How many centimeters are in a meter?
(c) The millimeter is the smallest unit of measure on your meter stick. Find a millimeter on your meter stick.
(d) How many millimeters are in a centimeter?
(e) How many millimeters are in a meter?

How does your arm span compare to your height (Figure 10-2)?

## D  Lesson Exercise 10.4

(a) What is your height in centimeters? (Stand against a blackboard and have another student mark your height.)
(b) Give your height using meters and centimeters (such as 1 m 37 cm).
(c) What is your height in meters?
(d) How long is your arm span?
(e) How does your arm span compare to your height?

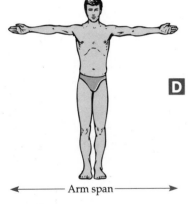
Arm span

**Figure 10-2**

People's heights are most commonly recorded in centimeters as in Lesson Exercise 10.4(a).

## Reference Measures

A good way to learn the approximate size of unfamiliar units of measure is to relate them to measurements of your body or your environment.

## D  Lesson Exercise 10.5

(a) Find an object in your classroom that is about 1 m high.
(b) Find an object in your classroom that is about 1 m long.
(c) Find some part of your hand that is about 1 cm long.
(d) Find an object that is about 1 mm long.

Your answers to Lesson Exercise 10.5 are called reference measures. **Reference measures** are common environmental or body measurements that approximate basic measuring units such as a meter. Reference measures help develop an intuitive understanding (number sense) of metric measure.

You can use reference measures to estimate other measurements. In Lesson Exercise 10.6, use a reference measure from Lesson Exercise 10.5 to select the best estimate.

## Lesson Exercise 10.6

The length of your teacher's shoe is about
(a) 25 mm    (b) 25 cm    (c) 2.5 m    (d) 25 m

## Lesson Exercise 10.7

(a) Use your reference measure for 1 cm to draw a line segment that is about 8 cm long.
(b) Measure your segment to see how close you came.

## D Lesson Exercise 10.8

Use your reference measure for 1 m to obtain an estimate of the area of your classroom floor in square meters. (*Note:* Area will be discussed further in the next section.)

How do metric units compare in size to customary units? Look at your rulers to answer the following questions.

## Lesson Exercise 10.9

(a) What customary unit of length is about the same length as a meter?
(b) Which is longer, an inch or a centimeter?

Why do we need units of different sizes such as centimeters, meters, and kilometers? If we measured traveling distances in centimeters, the numbers would be so large that they would be hard to grasp. For example, the distance from Washington, D.C., to Boston is about 66,000,000 cm. Similarly, measuring the length of your foot in kilometers, you might get a result like 0.00021 km, which would not be very meaningful.

## Conversions Within the Metric System

You have already seen how meters, centimeters, millimeters, and kilometers are related by powers of 10. This same relationship holds for all metric measures, and it makes conversions within the metric system easier than those in the customary system.

The metric prefixes are given in the following chart.

| Prefix | kilo- | hecto-† | deka-† | (none) | deci-† | centi- | milli- |
|--------|-------|---------|--------|--------|--------|--------|--------|
| Symbol | k | h | dk | | d | c | m |
| Meaning | 1000 | 100 | 10 | 1 | $\dfrac{1}{10}$ | $\dfrac{1}{100}$ | $\dfrac{1}{1000}$ |

†not commonly used

Length measurements use these prefixes in front of the basic length unit, the meter. For most everyday measures, kilometers, meters, centimeters, and millimeters are sufficient.

| Kilometer | Hectometer† | Dekameter† | Meter | Decimeter† | Centimeter | Millimeter |
|-----------|-------------|------------|-------|------------|------------|------------|
| km | hm | dkm | m | dm | cm | mm |

†not commonly used in U.S. elementary and secondary schools

Example 10.1 shows how to convert within the metric system.

### Example 10.1

350 cm = _____ m

**Solution**

Compare centimeters to meters. Since 100 centimeters make a meter, divide 350 cm by 100 to convert it to meters: $350 \div 100 = 3.50$ (Move the decimal point two places to the left.)

More formally, one can include the units in the computation and multiply 350 cm by 1 in the form $\dfrac{1 \text{ m}}{100 \text{ cm}}$.

$$350 \text{ cm} \times \frac{1 \text{ m}}{100 \text{ cm}} = \frac{350}{100} \text{ m} = 3.5 \text{ m}$$

This more formal approach with units is part of **dimensional** (unit) **analysis.** ■

As suggested by converting your height from centimeters to meters and the preceding example (350 cm = 3.5 m), metric conversions require nothing more than moving the decimal point since they all involve multiplying or dividing by a power of 10.

Try the following conversions.

D  Lesson Exercise 10.10

(a) 0.5 m = _____ mm     (b) 80 mm = _____ cm

(c) A kilometer is _____ meters (about $\frac{3}{5}$ of a mile).

## Mass and Liquid Volume

### Miracle Diet Program!
### Lose 5/6 of Your Weight:
### Take a Trip to the Moon.

The gram is the basic unit of *mass* in the metric system. People sometimes confuse mass and weight. **Mass** measures the quantity of matter a body contains. **Weight** measures the force exerted by gravity on a body.

If you went to the moon, your mass would remain the same, but your weight would be much less (about $\frac{1}{6}$ of your weight on Earth) because the force of gravity is much weaker on the moon. In everyday usage, kilograms (metric unit of mass) and pounds (customary unit of weight) are used interchangeably. The conversion 1 kg = 2.2 lb works on the surface of Earth, but on the moon, a mass of 1 kg weighs about 0.4 lb.

## Lesson Exercise 10.11

(a) If you flew to Jupiter, the largest planet, would your *mass* be more than, the same as, or less than your mass on Earth?
(b) Would your *weight* be more than, the same as, or less than your weight on Earth?

The most commonly used units of metric mass are milligrams (very small), grams, and kilograms. The prefixes *milli-* $\left(\frac{1}{1000}\right)$ and *kilo-* (1000) have the same meaning with grams as with meters. Do you know any reference measures for grams and kilograms?

## Lesson Exercise 10.12

Name something that has a mass of about 1 g (gram).

## Lesson Exercise 10.13

Name something that has a mass of about 1 kg (kilogram).

A common object that has a mass of 1 g is a solid, well-made paper clip. A textbook you can finish in one semester usually has a mass of about 1 kg.

The liter (L) is the metric unit for liquid volume. Do you know any reference measures for a liter?

## Lesson Exercise 10.14

Name something that holds about 1 L (liter).

## Lesson Exercise 10.15

Grams and liters use the same prefixes as meters.
(a) 80 g = _____ kg
(b) $N$ mL = _____ L          ($N$ is a positive number.)

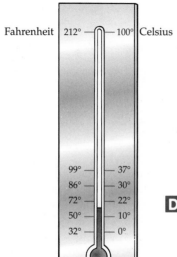

Fahrenheit   212° — 100° Celsius

99° — 37°
86° — 30°
72° — 22°
50° — 10°
32° — 0°

**Figure 10-3**

## Temperature

Do you know what a 35° Celsius day would feel like? Hot! Metric temperatures are often measured in degrees Celsius (C). In this system, 0°C is the freezing point of water and 100°C is the boiling point of water. These are easier to remember than those in the Fahrenheit scale, in which the freezing point of water is 32°F and its boiling point is 212°F. The thermometer shown in Figure 10-3 gives some other common temperatures in Fahrenheit and Celsius.

## D Lesson Exercise 10.16

The temperature inside a working refrigerator is about
(a) 5°C     (b) 15°C     (c) 25°C     (d) 35°C

## Precision and Greatest Possible Error

Whereas exact measurements can be given for perfect geometric shapes, no measurement of an actual object (other than counting a set of objects) is exact. In general, perfect geometric figures have exact measures, and actual objects have approximate measures. In Chapter 3, this textbook distinguished between sets and measures. In order to be consistent, counting a set of objects will not be referred to as a measurement in this chapter.

Geometric shape → Exact measurement
Everyday object → Approximate measurement

A reported numerical measurement should reflect the precision with which it was made. The precision of an approximate measurement is determined by the unit of measure.

## Lesson Exercise 10.17

(a) Measure the height of this page to the nearest centimeter.
(b) Measure the height of this page to the nearest millimeter.
(c) Which measurement is more precise?

Neither measurement of the page height is exact, but using the smaller unit (millimeters) results in a more **precise** measure.

## Lesson Exercise 10.18

People usually give their weight to the nearest pound or kilogram. Suppose that John's correct mass to the nearest kilogram is 53.
(a) What is the smallest decimal number that would be rounded to 53 as the nearest whole number?
(b) What is the largest decimal number that would be rounded to 53 as the nearest whole number?

In the preceding exercise, a measurement given to the nearest 1 kg could be off by as much as 0.5 kg. John's actual mass is somewhere between 52.5 and 53.5 kg (including 52.5). In practice, scientists say "between 52.5 and 53.5 kg" without mentioning whether endpoint measures are included, since no object is likely to weigh *exactly* 52.5 or 53.5 kg. In this example, the greatest possible error is 0.5 kg. The **greatest possible error** (GPE) is half of the smallest unit used.

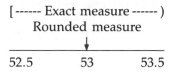

## Lesson Exercise 10.19

Janie's shoe is 27.6 cm long.
(a) What is the smallest unit of measure used?
(b) What is the GPE?
(c) Her actual shoe length is between _____ cm and _____ cm.

Computations involving approximate measurements result in approximate measurements. In adding (or subtracting) measures, the number of decimal places in the resulting sum (or difference) cannot be more than the number that, in the original problem, had the fewest decimal places. In other words, the sum (or difference) can be only as precise as the least precise measurement.

$$
\begin{array}{cc}
36.4 \text{ g} & 36.4 \text{ g} \\
+\ 8.2 \text{ g} & +\ 8.21 \text{ g} \\
\hline
44.6 \text{ g} & 44.61 \text{ g round to } \boxed{44.6} \text{ g}
\end{array}
$$

All precise to          Same precision as
the nearest 0.1 g       least precise 36.4

Usually, all measurements would be given with the same number of decimal places, so a sum or difference would also stop at that decimal place. However, this is not always the case.

## Lesson Exercise 10.20

Kathleen is 146 cm tall. She is wearing shoes that have 2.6-cm heels. How tall is she now?

The next section covers error in multiplying measures, along with the topic of area.

## Answers to Selected Lesson Exercises

10.1 (a)  about 3
    (b)  Their hands are different sizes.

10.3 (b) 100      (d) 10      (e) 1000

10.6 25 cm

10.9 (a) a yard      (b) an inch

10.10 (a) 500      (b) 8      (c) 1000

10.11 (a) the same      (b) more

10.14 a quart milk carton

10.15 (a) 0.08      (b) $\dfrac{N}{1000}$

10.16 (a)

10.17 (c) part (b)

10.19 (a)  one tenth of a centimeter
    (b)  0.05 cm
    (c)  27.55 cm and 27.65 cm

10.20 149 cm

## 10.1    Homework Exercises

### Basic Exercises

1. (a)  How long is your foot in centimeters?
  (b)  Measure the width of your front door using your foot.
  (c)  Convert the width of your door in part (b) into centimeters.

2. (a)  How long is your pace in centimeters?
  (b)  Measure the length of a room in paces.
  (c)  Convert the length of the room in part (b) into centimeters.

3. In what ways is the metric system easier to work with than the customary system?

4. Give a reference measure for
  (a) 1 cm.      (b) 1 m.

5. The width of an adult woman's hand is about _____ cm.

6. Complete the following conversions.
  (a)  0.02 m = _____ mm
  (b)  16 cm = _____ mm

7. Lynn Matthews wants to swim 1 km in a 50-m-long pool. How many pool lengths must she swim?

8. A film is 35 mm wide. How many centimeters wide is it?

9. A town is $T$ km away. How many meters away is it?

10. The length of a new piece of chalk is about
    (a) 1 mm  (b) 1 cm  (c) 10 cm
    (d) 1 m

11. (a) Estimate the length of your arm in centimeters.
    (b) Measure your arm length in centimeters.

12. A pound (on Earth) is about
    (a) 5 g  (b) 5 kg  (c) 50 g  (d) 500 g

13. The average adult man has a mass of about
    (a) 7 kg  (b) 700 kg  (c) 700 g
    (d) 70 kg

14. (a) 65 g = _____ mg
    (b) 47 g = _____ kg
    (c) 346 mL = _____ L

15. A container holds 3.24 liters of milk. How many milliliters is that?

16. A metal strip has a density of 200 g/cm. Express its density in kilograms per meter.

17. A coffee cup holds about
    (a) 25 mL  (b) 250 mL  (c) 2.5 L
    (d) 25 L

18. Your heart pumps about 60 mL of blood per heartbeat. About how much blood will it pump in a day?

19. A box contains 4 kg of paper clips. Each paper clip has a mass of about 0.8 g. About how many paper clips are in the box?

20. (a) Complete the third example, repeating the error pattern in the completed examples and (b) describe the error pattern.
    5 cm = <u>500</u> m
    20 kg = <u>0.02</u> g
    3 mm = _____ m

21. True or false?
    (a) 1 mm is longer than 1 in.
    (b) 1 m is longer than 1 km.
    (c) 1 g is heavier than 1 lb.
    (d) 1 gallon is more than 1 L.

22. For each item, select the most appropriate measuring unit from the following list: mm, cm, m, km, g, and kg.
    (a) the weight of a penny
    (b) your waist size
    (c) the thickness of a page
    (d) your weight
    (e) the distance from Miami to Atlanta

23. Someone who tells you that the temperature is 80° outside is using
    (a) Fahrenheit  (b) Celsius
    (c) could be either Fahrenheit or Celsius

24. A temperature of −10°C is about
    (a) −20°F  (b) 10°F
    (c) 40°F  (d) 70°F

25. The weather outside is sunny and 15°C. Which of the following would you wear?
    (a) a heavy coat  (b) a light sweater
    (c) a swim suit

26. What is the average high temperature in Celsius degrees in May where you are now?

27. Can you walk 1 km in 30 minutes?

28. List the following measurements in increasing order: 37 m, 46 cm, 871 mm, 3 km, 137 cm.

29. Tell whether each number is exact or approximate.
    (a) Joe bought 1 kg of apples.
    (b) Bill bought 2 ears of corn.
    (c) The room is 5 m long.
    (d) Sally has 3 brothers.

30. Which measurement in each pair is more precise?
    (a) 8 cm or 78 mm
    (b) 6 kg or 5820 g

31. I measure the length of my shoe as 28 cm. The actual length of the shoe is between what two measures?

**32.** Give the GPE of each measurement.
(a) 37 m     (b) 5.21 g

**33.** (a) Measure the following line segment to the nearest millimeter.

_____

(b) What is the GPE?
(c) The actual length of the line segment is between _____ and _____ .

**34.** Complete the table.

| Measurement | Precision | GPE | Actual Length Is Between |
|---|---|---|---|
| 32.1 m | nearest tenth of a meter (or nearest dm) | 0.05 m | 32.05 m, 32.15 m |
| (a) 62 g | | | |
| (b) 5.12 cm | | | |
| (c) 4.6 km | | | |

**35.** Compute the answer to the appropriate number of digits.

(a)   4   g          (b)   18.2  cm
    +3.6 g               − 5.01 cm

**36.** The relative error compares the size of the error to the measurement itself. The **relative error** of a measurement is

$\dfrac{\text{greatest possible error}}{\text{reported measurement}}$.

(a) Measure the length and width of a dollar bill to the nearest centimeter.
(b) Give the relative error of each measurement.

*Extension Exercises*

**37.** Draw a rectangle with a length of 5 cm and a diagonal 7 cm long.

**38.** You have a set of black and white centimeter cubes. You could make two different towers that are 1 cm high.

(a) How many different towers could you make that are 2 cm high?
(b) How many different towers could you make that are 3 cm high? (Draw pictures.)
(c) How many different towers could you make that are 4 cm high?
(d) How many different towers could you make that are N cm high? (N is a counting number.)

**39.** A passenger rides in a train going 150 km/hr. The passenger sees a second train pass by in 2 seconds. If the second train is moving at a speed of 150 km/hr in the opposite direction, how long is the second train?

**40.** Make a scale drawing of the solar system in which the distance from the sun to Pluto is somewhere between 30 cm and 1 m. The actual distances of planets from the sun in meters are
Mercury, $5.8 \times 10^{10}$; Venus, $1.1 \times 10^{11}$; Earth, $1.5 \times 10^{11}$; Mars, $2.3 \times 10^{11}$; Jupiter, $7.8 \times 10^{11}$; Saturn, $1.4 \times 10^{12}$; Neptune, $2.9 \times 10^{12}$; Uranus, $4.5 \times 10^{12}$; Pluto, $5.9 \times 10^{12}$.

**41.** The prefix *micro-* represents $10^{-6}$ or $\dfrac{1}{1,000,000}$.

(a) 1 m = _____ micrometers
(b) 60 micrometers = _____ m
(c) 821 micrometers = _____ cm
(d) 4800 mm = _____ micrometers

**42.** The prefix *mega-* means "one million."
(a) 80 megameters = _____ m
(b) 1000 kg = _____ megagrams

**43.** 54 cm/sec = _____ km/hr

**44.** A car that gets 20 km/L of gasoline is getting about _____ miles per gallon.
(a) 10     (b) 20     (c) 30     (d) 45

**45.** $A$ m + $B$ cm = _____ m

## Special Exercises

**46.** When you mix measurement units in a problem, you can get some strange equations. For example, when does 1 + 60 = 25? When it's 1 day + 60 minutes = 25 hours! Provide units for the following equations.

(a) 3 + 120 = 5

(b) 8 + 6 = 2

(c) 3 − 12 = 2

**47.** Make a scale drawing of your classroom on centimeter graph paper.

## 10.2 Perimeter and Area

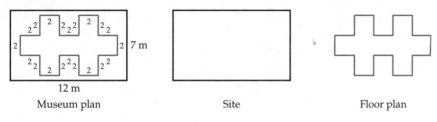

Museum plan          Site          Floor plan

**Figure 10-4**

## D Lesson Exercise 10.21

In Figure 10-4, which is larger, the site or the floor plan?

To answer the question in Lesson Exercise 10.21, one must first decide whether to compare perimeter or area.

## Perimeter

What length of fence will enclose a field? What length of a decorative border would you need for a classroom bulletin board? These situations both call for measuring the perimeter.

In elementary and secondary school, children study the perimeter of polygons and circles. The **perimeter** of a simple, closed plane figure is the distance around the figure. The perimeter is always measured in units of length such as feet or centimeters.

**D** Lesson Exercise 10.22

1 unit

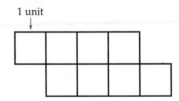

(a) The perimeter is _____ .
(b) Arrange the squares in other configurations in which each square shares at least one side with another square. Compute the perimeter of each configuration.
(c) What is the largest perimeter you can obtain?
(d) What is the smallest perimeter you can obtain?

The perimeter of a polygon is the sum of the lengths of its sides. Some polygons have fairly simple perimeter formulas that are easier to use than adding up the lengths of all the sides. Find the appropriate formula for a rectangle in the following exercise.

**D** Lesson Exercise 10.23

A rectangle has a length $l$ and a width $w$. What is a formula for the perimeter $P$?

The perimeter formula from Lesson Exercise 10.23 will be useful in the following exercise.

Lesson Exercise 10.24

Refer back to the diagram at the beginning of the section. Which has a larger perimeter, the site or the floor plan?

## The Circumference of a Circle

**Figure 10-5**

How far is one lap around a track with semicircular arcs? What is the perimeter of a bicycle tire with a diameter of 26 in. (Figure 10-5)? To answer these questions, one computes the **circumference** (perimeter) of a circle.

In Section 7.6, you saw how $\pi$ originated from studies of the relationship between the circumference and the diameter. The circumference $C$ equals $\pi$ times the diameter $d$, or $C = \pi d$.

The value of $\pi$ is an irrational number, an infinite, nonrepeating decimal that begins as 3.141592654 . . . . In 1987, Hideaki Tomoyori memorized and recited the first 40,000 places of $\pi$. Most of us can get by with 3.14 or $\frac{22}{7}$ as an approximation of $\pi$.

The circumference formula, $C = \pi d$, can be rewritten using $2r$ in place of $d$: $C = 2\pi r$.

---

**The Circumference Formula**

A circle with diameter $d$ and radius $r$ has circumference $C = \pi d$ or $C = 2\pi r$.

---

You can use this formula to find the circumference when you know the length of the radius or diameter. In computations involving $\pi$, use $\pi$ in situations involving perfect geometric figures and approximate $\pi$ as 3.14 (or $\frac{22}{7}$) in situations involving everyday objects.

Perfect Geometric Shapes → Exact Answers → Use $\pi$
Everyday Objects → Approximate Answers → Use 3.14

 ## Lesson Exercise 10.25

A bicycle wheel has a diameter of 26 in. How far would you travel after one full revolution of the tire?

## Area

If you want to know the size of the interior of a field, or which package of gift wrap is a better buy, you measure the area. The **area** of a polygon or circle is the amount of surface inside it.

## Lesson Exercise 10.26

Determine how many of each shape shown are needed to fill in the design in Figure 10-6.

(a) trapezoids

(b) triangles

**Figure 10-6**

Although area can be measured using trapezoids or triangles as units, area is usually measured in square units. An area of "10 square units" would mean that 10 unit squares are needed to cover the interior. An example of a square unit would be a square centimeter (cm²).

What is the area of your hand? To find out, you will need your hand and some centimeter graph paper.

**D** Lesson Exercise 10.27

(a) Trace an outline of your hand on the centimeter graph paper.
(b) Estimate the area of your hand in square centimeters.
(c) Explain how you obtained your answer in part (b).

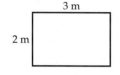

**Figure 10-7**

**D** Lesson Exercise 10.28

(a) Draw to show how many 1-m² squares would cover the interior of the rectangle in Figure 10-7.
(b) What is its area?

Lesson Exercise 10.29

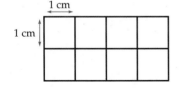

**Figure 10-8**

Each square inside the rectangle in Figure 10-8 is 1 cm by 1 cm.
(a) How many rows and columns of squares are there?
(b) What is the area of the rectangle?
(c) Find the length and width of the rectangle.
(d) How would you compute the area using the length and width?

The rectangle in Lesson Exercise 10.29 has 2 rows and 4 columns of unit squares. The total number of squares is the number of rows times the number of columns (the row-by-column model of multiplication). Since the number of columns is determined by the length of the rectangle and the number of rows is determined by the width, the area can be obtained more quickly by multiplying the length (the number of columns) by the width (number of rows).

---

**Area of a Rectangle**

The area $A$ of a rectangle that has length $l$ and width $w$ is

$$A = lw$$

---

Area formulas are especially useful in problems involving larger numbers when counting squares might take a very long time. Consider the introductory situation.

## Lesson Exercise 10.30

Refer back to the diagram at the beginning of the section. Which has a larger area, the site or the floor plan?

Consumers use the area formula for a rectangle to decide which package of wrapping is a better buy. Consider the following exercise.

## Lesson Exercise 10.31

A store sells two kinds of wrapping paper. Package A costs $4 and has 3 rolls, each $2\frac{1}{2}$ ft by 6 ft. Package B costs $3.25 and has 4 rolls, each 2 ft by 5 ft. Which is a better buy? (*Hint:* Compare the cost per square foot for each package.)

## Area, Perimeter, and Congruence

Do you wonder how area, perimeter, and congruence are related to one another? The following exercises address this question.

## Lesson Exercise 10.32

Would two congruent figures have equal area and equal perimeter?

Next, consider the relationship between area and perimeter.

## D Lesson Exercise 10.33

(a) Draw four different shapes with a perimeter of 8 cm. (Use centimeter graph paper if you have it.)
(b) Do they all have the same area?
(c) What kind of shape tends to have a smaller area?

## D Lesson Exercise 10.34

(a) Draw four different shapes with an area of 16 cm².
(b) Do they all have the same perimeter?
(c) What kind of shape tends to have a smaller perimeter?

**D** Lesson Exercise 10.35

Based upon Lesson Exercises 10.32–10.34, which of the following appears to be true about plane figures $A$ and $B$? If you think a statement is false, give a counterexample.
(a) If the area of $A$ equals the area of $B$, then $A \cong B$.
(b) If $A \cong B$, then the area of $A$ equals the area of $B$.
(c) If $A$ has a larger perimeter than $B$, then $A$ has a larger area than $B$.
(d) If $A$ has a larger area than $B$, then $A$ has a larger perimeter than $B$.

As you may have guessed in Lesson Exercise 10.32, if two figures are congruent, then they have equal areas and perimeters. As you saw in Lesson Exercises 10.33 and 10.34, knowing which of two figures has a larger area does not determine which has a larger perimeter.

### Greatest Possible Error in Area

In computing the possible error in area problems, figure the greatest possible error in each length measurement and then compute the area using the lowest and highest possible lengths.

**Example 10.2**

Suppose that you accurately measure a rectangular room to be 6.2 m by 4.6 m. The actual area is between _____ and _____ .

**Solution**

The actual length is between 6.15 and 6.25 m, and the actual width is between 4.55 and 4.65 m. Compute the smallest and largest possible areas.

$$\begin{array}{lll} \text{Smallest area} & 6.15 \times 4.55 = 27.9825 \text{ m}^2 \\ \text{Largest area} & 6.25 \times 4.65 = 29.0625 \text{ m}^2 \end{array}$$

The actual area is between 27.9825 m² and 29.0625 m². ■

Lesson Exercise 10.36

Suppose that you accurately measure a rectangular carpet to be 6 m by 4 m. The actual area is between _____ and _____ .

## Answers to Selected Lesson Exercises

**10.22** (a) 14     (c) 18     (d) 12                    **10.24** floor plan

**10.23** $P = 2l + 2w$                                   **10.25** $26\pi$ in.

10.26 (a) 4    (b) 12

10.28 (b) 6 m²

10.29 (b) 8 cm²

10.30 site

10.31 B

10.32 yes

10.33 (b) no    (c) longer, thinner shapes

10.34 (b) no    (c) square shape

10.35 only (b) is true

10.36 19.25m² and 29.25 m²

## 10.2 Homework Exercises

### Basic Exercises

**1.** Measure the perimeter of each figure to the nearest tenth of a centimeter.

(a) 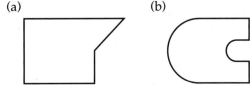 (b)

**2.**

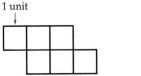

1 unit

(a) The perimeter is _____ .

(b) Arrange the squares in other configurations and compute the perimeter. (Each square must share at least one side with another square.)

(c) What is the largest possible perimeter?

(d) What is the smallest possible perimeter?

**3.** Increase the area of the figure without changing its perimeter.

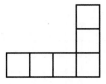

**4.** A square field is enclosed by *T* meters of fence. What are the length and width of the field?

**5.** A lot is 21 ft by 30 ft. A designer wants a post at each corner and a post every 3 feet in between. How many posts are needed?

**6.** A 3 in. by 5 in. photo print costs $.30. I want an enlargement with twice the length and twice the width. I figure that it should cost about twice as much. Am I right?

**7.** Draw a square. Draw a second square whose sides are twice as long.

(a) How do their perimeters compare?

(b) Start with a new square and repeat the exercise.

(c) Make a generalization based upon parts (a) and (b).

**8.** In a circle, how many times longer is the circumference *C* than the diameter *d*?

**9.** Why is $C = 2\pi r$ the same as $C = \pi d$?

 **10.** The dome of the New Orleans Superdome has a diameter of 680 ft. What is the circumference? (Use 3.14 for $\pi$.)

 **11.** The circumference (equator) of the earth is about 25,000 miles. What is the earth's approximate diameter?

**12.** When the radius of a circle increases by 1, the circumference increases by _____ .

 **13.** A car has wheels with radii of 40 cm. How many revolutions per minute must a wheel turn so that the car travels 50 km/hr?

 **14.** On a circular merry-go-round, one horse is 3.0 m from the center, and the other is 5.0 m from the center.

(a) How far does each horse travel in one revolution of the merry-go-round? (Use 3.14 for $\pi$.)

(b) If the merry-go-round revolves 3 times per minute, how fast is each horse traveling?

**15.** (a) Find the perimeter of the inside edge of lane 1. Use 3.142 for $\pi$.

(b) If lane 1 is 1.0 m wide, how much further is a lap around the inside edge of lane 2 than a lap around the inside edge of lane 1?

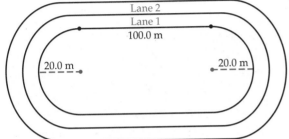

**16.** A satellite is orbiting 1800 km above Earth's surface. The radius of Earth is about 6400 km. About how fast must the satellite travel to orbit Earth in 10 hours?

**17.** What aspect of a polygon or circle does area measure?

**18.**

(a) Estimate the area of the footprint on each grid in the square units.

(b) Which estimate is more precise?

**19.** Use centimeter graph paper to estimate the area of your foot in square centimeters.

**20.** Approximate the area of the circle by counting squares.

**21.** What is the area of the figure at the top of the next column in unit hexagons?

 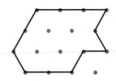

**22.** How many of each shape would it take to cover the hexagon?

(a)     (b)        (c)      (d)

**23.**

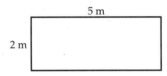

(a) Show how many 1-m squares cover the interior of the rectangle.

(b) What is the area of the rectangle?

**24.** What fraction multiplication is represented by the picture?

**25.** What decimal multiplication is represented by the picture?

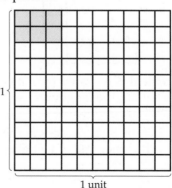

**26.** Use a geoboard or a geoboard drawing and show a shape that has
   **(a)** a perimeter of 8 units and an area of 3 square units.
   **(b)** a perimeter of 10 units and an area of 6 square units.

**27.** The state of Kansas is approximately rectangular. Estimate its area and perimeter.

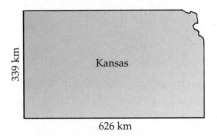

**28.** Use centimeter graph paper and draw seven different shapes composed of centimeter squares that have a perimeter of 16 cm and an area of 12 cm². Each centimeter square should have a common side with at least one other square unit.

**29.** A rectangular garden is 10 ft by 12 ft. A rectangular sidewalk 1 ft wide is built around the outside. What is the area of the sidewalk? (Draw a picture.)

**30.** **(a)** Complete the third example, repeating the error pattern in the completed examples, and **(b)** describe the error pattern.

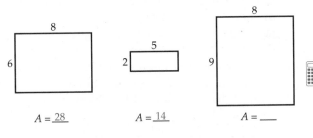

**31.** Which of the following statements about plane figures $A$ and $B$ are true?
   **(a)** If $A \cong B$, then the area of $A$ equals the area of $B$.
   **(b)** If the area of $A$ equals the area of $B$, then $A \cong B$.
   **(c)** If the area of $A$ equals the area of $B$, then

the perimeter of $A$ equals the perimeter of $B$.

**32.** Draw rectangles $A$ and $B$ so that they have the same perimeter, but $A$ has a larger area than $B$.

**33.** A rectangle and a square have equal areas. If the rectangle is 6 ft by 8 ft, how long is a side of the square?

**34.** The Federal Housing Administration (FHA) requires that the window area of a house be at least 10% of the floor space. How many 15-ft² windows are needed to meet FHA requirements for a house with a floor that is 25 ft by 40 ft?

**35.** Find the area, in square units, of the shaded region.

1 unit

**36.** Suppose that the housing authority has valued the house shown here at $220 per ft².

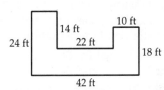

   **(a)** Show two different ways of subdividing the region into rectangles.
   **(b)** Find the assessed value of the house.

**37.** Shown here is a scale drawing $\left(\frac{1}{4} \text{ in.} \approx 12 \text{ ft}\right)$ of the floor plan for the bedroom, hall, and living room of your new apartment.

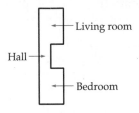

   **(a)** Fill in the missing lengths.

(b) How many square feet of carpet will be needed to cover the floors?

(c) The carpet you want costs $8 per square *yard*. What will the carpet for the apartment cost?

 38. A photo enlargement that is 6 in. by 9 in. costs $1.75, and an enlargement that is 8 in. by 10 in. costs $2.75. Which enlargement costs less per square inch?

 39. A store sells two kinds of wrapping paper. Package A costs $5.25 and has 6 rolls, each 2 ft by 5 ft. Package B costs $7 and has 4 rolls, each 4 ft by 6 ft. Which package is a better buy?

40. (a) How many square feet are in a square yard? (*Hint:* Draw 1-ft² squares in the interior.)

1 yd

1 yd

(b) As you know, 3 ft = 1 yd. So (3 ft)(3 ft) = (1 yd)(1 yd). Simplify both sides and write the resulting equation.

 41. A store sells carpet for $8.99 per square yard. How much does a rug that is 7 ft by 9 ft cost? (*Hint:* See the preceding exercise.)

42. (a) 1 cm² = _____ m²
    (b) 1 cm² = _____ mm²

43. (a) 8 cm² = _____ mm²
    (b) 500 m² = _____ cm²

44. Show that 1 m² = 1,000,000 mm².

45. (a) Complete the third example, repeating the error pattern in the completed examples, and (b) describe the error pattern.

7 cm² = ___70___ mm²
80 m² = __8000__ cm²
26 mm² = _____ cm²

46. A mapmaker wants to represent an area of roughly 20,000 ft² using the scale 1 in. = 20 ft. What area will the map have?

47. How many tiles, each 25 cm by 25 cm, would be needed to cover a floor that is 2 m by 4 m?

48. How many tiles, each 25 cm by 25 cm, would be needed to cover a floor that is 2.2 m by 4.6 m?

49. Suppose that you accurately measure a card to be 6.7 cm by 9.2 cm. The actual area is between _____ and _____ .

### Extension Exercises

50. The earth travels around the sun in an approximately circular path having a radius of 9.3 × 10⁷ miles.
    (a) How far does the earth travel in one trip around the sun? (Use 3.14 for π.)
    (b) If the earth takes 365 days to make one revolution, how far does it travel in 1 hour?
    (c) If the earth is moving so fast, why don't we fall off?

51. Recall the set of pentominos (Section 9.1 Special Exercise).
    (a) What is the area of any pentomino?
    (b) What are all the possible perimeters of pentominos?

52. Suppose that you need a hose at least 20 m long to reach a garden. In your garage, you find a hose that has 20 coils, each having a diameter of about 8 cm.
    (a) Will the hose be long enough?
    (b) Explain how you solved this problem.

53. An engineer is designing a track with semicircular arcs on each end, as shown. One lap around the track should be 400 m.

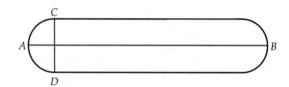

(a) If CD = 40 m, how long would AB be?
(b) If AB = 150 m, how long would CD be?

**54.** (a) A rectangle has a whole-number length and a whole-number width, and its area and perimeter are the same number. What are its dimensions?

(b) Find a second solution to part (a).

 **55.** (a) Consider the following problem. "A rectangle has an area of 4 m². What is the smallest possible perimeter it could have?" Devise a plan and solve the problem.

(b) Repeat part (a) for a rectangle with an area of 9 m².

(c) Generalize your results for a rectangle with an area of $N$ m².

**56.** A rectangle has a length that is 16 m more than its width, and its area is 2961 m². What are the length and width? (Guess and check.)

**57.** A cowhand has 350 yards of fence to enclose equal adjacent rectangular areas for horses and cattle. Find an arrangement that will enclose more area than either one large square or two adjacent squares. (Guess and check.)

**58.** Mrs. Cunningham wants to build a pen for her prize-winning hogs next to her barn with a 3-sided, rectangular, 24-yard fence. What dimensions will enclose the largest area? (Guess and check.)

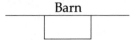

**59.** (a) Make a graph showing the relationship between length and width for all rectangles that have a perimeter of 20.

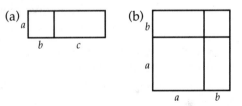

(b) Make a graph showing the relationship

between length and width for all rectangles that have an area of 20.

**60.** Many algebraic formulas can be represented geometrically. Refer to the figure and write an equation related to the area of the entire region.

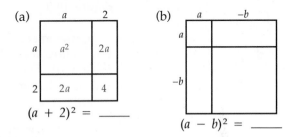

$(a + 2)^2 = $ _____

$(a - b)^2 = $ _____

**61.** What algebraic equation is suggested by each diagram?

**62.** A rectangle is divided into four rectangles. Find $x$.

**63.** Express arc length $s$ in terms of radius $r$ and central angle measure $\theta$.

## 10.3   Areas of Quadrilaterals, Triangles, and Circles

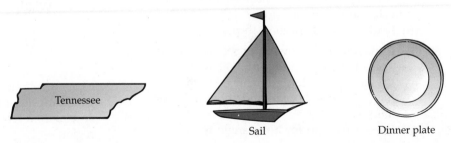

Figure 10-9

To approximate the surface area of each object in Figure 10-9, you could use an area formula. Do you know where such formulas come from? In Section 10.2, you studied the concept of measuring area in square units and how that leads to a more efficient area formula for the rectangle (and square).

We'll pick things up from there. In this section, we will derive in a deductive sequence the area formulas for a triangle, a parallelogram, and a circle.

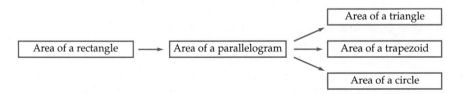

The activities in this section require scissors, a 30-cm ruler, and some paper.

### The Area of a Parallelogram

Before you begin cutting, here is some background information about parallelograms. Any side of a parallelogram can be designated as the **base** (usually it is the bottom side). Then the **height** is the distance from the base to the opposite side. The height is always measured using a segment that is *perpendicular* to the base (or an extension of the base) and the opposite side (Figure 10-10).

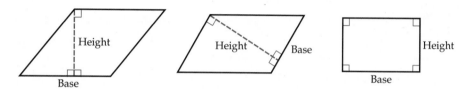

**Figure 10-10**

The terms "base" and "height" are also used for triangles and trapezoids, but more on that later. The following exercise will show you how the area formula for a parallelogram is related to the area formula for a rectangle.

**D** Lesson Exercise 10.37

(a) Cut out a rectangle that is 7 cm by 5 cm.
(b) Draw a parallelogram with the dimensions shown in Figure 10-11 and label its vertices *A*, *B*, *C*, and *D* inside the parallelogram as shown. It's tricky to draw a parallelogram with these measurements. *Draw the top first, then the height,* and see whether you can finish it from there.
(c) Cut out the parallelogram.
(d) What is the perimeter of the rectangle?
(e) What is the perimeter of the parallelogram?
(f) Compare the areas of the two figures by placing one paper over the other. Is one larger in area, or are they equal in area?

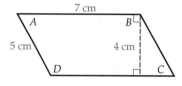

**Figure 10-11**

**D** Lesson Exercise 10.38

To find the exact area of the parallelogram, do the following.
(a) Cut the parallelogram into pieces by cutting along the perpendicular segment from *B* to $\overline{CD}$. Rearrange these two pieces into a rectangle.
(b) What are the dimensions of the rectangle you formed?
(c) What is the area of the rectangle you formed from the parallelogram?
(d) What is the area of the original parallelogram?

**D** Lesson Exercise 10.39

(a) Based upon Lesson Exercises 10.37 and 10.38, describe a general method for finding the area of a parallelogram such as the one in Figure 10-12.
(b) What is the area of any parallelogram in terms of its base *b* and its height *h*?

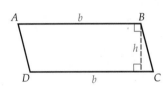

**Figure 10-12**

The answer to Lesson Exercise 10.39(b) is the parallelogram area formula.

---

**Area of a Parallelogram**

The area $A$ of a parallelogram that has a base of length $b$ and height $h$ is

$$A = bh$$

---

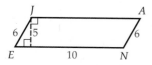

**Figure 10-13**

## Lesson Exercise 10.40

Use the area formula for a parallelogram to find the area of *JANE* in Figure 10-13.

## The Area of a Triangle

How big are the sails on your new sailboat? The formula for the area of a triangle will tell you. This formula can be derived from the area formula for a parallelogram. Do you have scissors ready?

**D** ## Lesson Exercise 10.41

(a) Cut out two congruent triangles. Label one side as the base $b$ and draw the perpendicular height from $b$ to the opposite vertex (Figure 10-14).
(b) Figure out how to put the two triangles together to form a parallelogram.
(c) What is the area of the parallelogram in terms of $b$ and $h$?
(d) What is the area of each triangle in terms of $b$ and $h$?

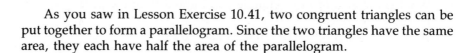

**Figure 10-14**

As you saw in Lesson Exercise 10.41, two congruent triangles can be put together to form a parallelogram. Since the two triangles have the same area, they each have half the area of the parallelogram.

---

**Area of a Triangle**

The area $A$ of a triangle that has a base of length $b$ and height $h$ is

$$A = \frac{1}{2}bh$$

## Lesson Exercise 10.42

Use the area formula for a triangle to find the area of the triangle in Figure 10-15. (*Hint:* The height of a triangle is the perpendicular distance from the base to the opposite vertex.)

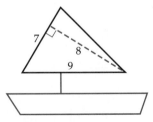

**Figure 10-15**

The area of any polygon can be found by subdividing it into rectangles or triangles or both! After finding the area of each rectangle and triangle, add up the areas to obtain the area of the polygon.

## The Area of a Trapezoid

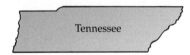

Tennessee

**Figure 10-16**

The state of Tennessee is shaped like a trapezoid (Figure 10-16). You could approximate its land area if you had an area formula for a trapezoid.

The area formula for a parallelogram can be used to deduce the formula for the area of a trapezoid! Two congruent triangles can be put together to form a parallelogram, and so can two congruent trapezoids! You don't believe me? Try Lesson Exercise 10.43.

**D** Lesson Exercise 10.43

(a) Cut out two congruent trapezoids and label them as shown in Figure 10-17. (The parallel sides of the trapezoids are its bases $b_1$ and $b_2$.)

(b) Put them together to form a parallelogram.

(c) What is the area of the parallelogram in terms of $b_1$, $b_2$, and $h$?

(d) What is the area of the trapezoid?

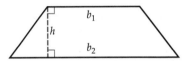

**Figure 10-17**

You have discovered another area formula!

---

**Area of a Trapezoid**

The area $A$ of a trapezoid that has parallel sides of lengths $b_1$ and $b_2$ and height $h$ is

$$A = \frac{1}{2}(b_1 + b_2)h$$

---

**Lesson Exercise 10.44**

Tennessee is approximately a trapezoid (Figure 10-18).

Figure 10-18

(a) What is the approximate surface area of Tennessee?
(b) Land is not perfectly flat. Would this fact make the surface area greater or less than the area of a perfectly flat surface?

---

## The Area of a Circle

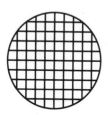

Figure 10-19

What is the surface area of a dinner plate that has a 12-in. diameter? To answer this question, one would compute the area of a circle. It is difficult to count the number of squares inside a circle. Figure 10-19 illustrates why circle areas rarely come out to a whole number of unit squares.

As with the triangle and trapezoid, the formula for the area of a circle is suggested by its relationship to the area formula for a parallelogram! However, in this case, the parallelogram representation is approximate. Calculus is needed for a precise derivation of the area formula for a circle.

Again, the idea is to make the new figure (a circle) look like a parallelogram. Suppose that a circle is cut into six equal parts, as shown in Figure 10-20.

The parts can be arranged as shown in Figure 10-21.

Figure 10-20

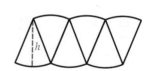

Figure 10-21

**D** Lesson Exercise 10.45

(a) What shape does the rearranged circle in Figure 10-21 approximate?

(b) The "base" of the new figure is about $\frac{1}{2}$ the _____ of the original circle, and the "height" of the figure is about the same as the _____ of the original circle.

(c) Using the parallelogram formula $A = bh$, the area of the circle is about _____ .

---

Lesson Exercise 10.45 suggests that the area of the circle is $\frac{1}{2} \cdot C \cdot r$.

Using $C = 2\pi r$, we can obtain the familiar area formula from $A = \frac{1}{2} \cdot C \cdot r$.

It goes like this (see Figure 10-22).

$$A = \frac{1}{2} \cdot C \cdot r = \frac{1}{2} \cdot 2\pi r \cdot r = \pi r^2 \qquad \text{(look familiar?)}$$

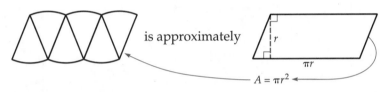

**Figure 10-22**

Figure 10-23 (see page 576) shows a lesson in the sixth-grade textbook of *Mathematics Unlimited*, which derives the area formula of a circle in a similar way.

The more pieces the circle is cut into, the closer the shape would be to a parallelogram with base $\pi r$ and height $r$.

---

**Area of a Circle**

The area $A$ of a circle that has a radius $r$ is

$$A = \pi r^2$$

---

You can use this formula to find the area of a circle when you know the length of the radius or diameter.

Lesson Exercise 10.46

How would a pizza with a 16-in. diameter compare in size to two pizzas with 8-in. diameters?

(a) Guess the answer.

(b) Work out the areas and find out if you're right.

## Area of a Circle

**A.** "Pieces of eight" were Spanish coins minted in Mexico during the 1700's. The coins could be chopped into smaller pieces, called *bits*. You can use the bits to find the area of one side of the coin.

The pieces of the coin can be put together to form a figure that looks like a parallelogram.

So, the area of the circle is approximately equal to the area of the parallelogram.

Area of the circle ≈ Area of the parallelogram

$A \approx \text{base} \times \text{height}$

$A \approx \frac{1}{2} \times C \times r \quad \boxed{C = 2\pi r}$

$A \approx \frac{1}{2} \times (2\pi r) \times r$

$A \approx \pi r^2$

From *Mathematics Unlimited*, Grade 6 (San Diego, CA: Harcourt Brace Jovanovich, 1992), p. 354.

**Figure 10-23**

---

### Lesson Exercise 10.47

A dinner plate has a diameter of 12.0 in. The exact area is between _____ and _____ . (Use π).

---

Some area problems require using more than one area formula.

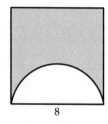

**Figure 10-24**

**Example 10.3**

Figure 10-24 shows a square and a semicircle. Find the shaded area.

**Solution**

***Understanding the Problem***  The shaded area is inside the square but outside the semicircle.

*Devising a Plan* In these types of problems: (1) identify familiar shapes and their area formulas and (2) determine how the shaded area is related to the familiar shapes.

The familiar shapes are a square ($A = s^2$) and half of a circle $\left(A = \frac{1}{2}\pi r^2\right)$. The shaded area is the area of the square minus the area of the half circle.

*Carrying Out the Plan*

$$A_{\text{shaded}} = A_{\square} - \frac{1}{2}A_{\circ} = (8^2) - \frac{1}{2}\pi \cdot 4^2 = (64 - 8\pi) \text{ square units}$$

*Looking Back* The same method would work if the square and circle were replaced by other shapes such as triangles and rectangles. ■

Try one yourself.

## Lesson Exercise 10.48

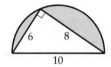

Consider the following problem. "Figure 10-25 shows a semicircle. Find the shaded area."

Devise a plan and solve the problem.

**Figure 10-25**

## Answers to Selected Lesson Exercises

**10.37** (d) 24 cm  (e) 24 cm
(f) The rectangle has a larger area.

**10.38** (d) 28 cm²

**10.39** (a) Translate the right triangle as shown to form a rectangle.

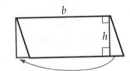

The area of the rectangle is *bh*.

parallelogram area =
rectangle area = *bh*

(b) $A = bh$

**10.40** 50 square units

**10.41** (c) *bh*  (d) $\frac{1}{2}bh$

**10.42** 28 square units

**10.43** (c) $(b_1 + b_2) \cdot h$

**10.44** (a) about 42,000 square miles  (b) more

**10.45** (a) parallelogram

(b) circumference, radius  (c) $\frac{1}{2} \cdot C \cdot r$

**10.46** (b) One 16-in. pizza has twice as much pizza as two 8-in. pizzas!

**10.47** $35.700625\pi$ and $36.300625\pi$ in.²

**10.48** $12.5\pi - 24$ square units

## 10.3   Homework Exercises

### Basic Exercises

**1.** Use the area formula for a rectangle ($A = bh$) to explain why the area of the parallelogram shown is $A = bh$.

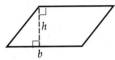

**2.** Which figure shown has a larger area?

(1)

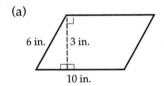

(2)

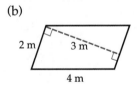

    (a) 1    (b) 2    (c) Their areas are equal.

**3.** Find the area and perimeter of each parallelogram.

(a)

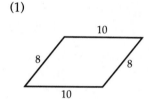

(b)

    2 m    3 m    4 m

**4.** A parallelogram has adjacent sides of length 4 cm and 6 cm.
    (a) Find the largest possible area the parallelogram could have.
    (b) Could the parallelogram have an area of 1 cm²?

**5.** Use the area formula for a parallelogram ($A = bh$) to explain why the area of the triangle shown is $A = \frac{1}{2}bh$.

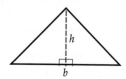

**6.** Find the area of each triangle.

(a)

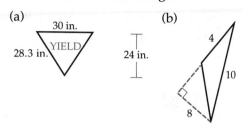

(b)

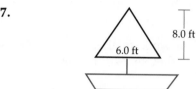

**7.**

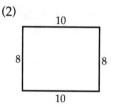

    (a) Mentally compute the area of the sail.
    (b) The exact area of the sail is between _____ and _____ .

**8.** Use a geoboard or a geoboard drawing and show a triangle with each of the following areas. (Make a drawing of your answers if you use a geoboard.)
    (a) 2 square units    (b) 4.5 square units

**9.** Find the area of the kite.

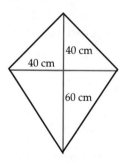

**10.** Find the area of the triangle.

**11.** Use the area formula for a parallelogram

$(A = bh)$ to explain why the area of the trapezoid shown is $A = \frac{1}{2}(b_1 + b_2) \cdot h$.

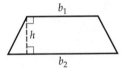

**12.** Since a square is a type of rectangle, the area
formula for a rectangle works for squares.
Which of the following have area formulas
that would work for any rhombus?
   (a) rectangle
   (b) triangle
   (c) parallelogram
   (d) square

**13.** Use a ruler to find the area of the trapezoid
in square millimeters.

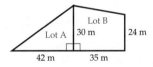

**14.** Two adjacent lots are for sale. Lot A costs
$20,000 and lot B costs $27,000.

   (a) Which lot has a lower cost per square
meter?
   (b) The exact area of lot A is between
_____ and _____ .

**15.** Find the approximate land area of Nevada.

**16.** A Boeing 747 airplane wing is shown. What
is the area of the top surface of the wing?
(Assume that it is flat.)

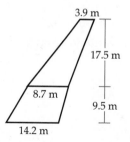

**17.** About 3600 years ago, Egyptians used the
area formula $A = \dfrac{(a + c)(b + d)}{4}$ for
quadrilaterals that have lengths of successive
sides equal to $a$, $b$, $c$, and $d$. For what quadrilaterals does this formula give the correct
area?

**18.** A circle is rearranged as shown.

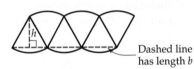

   Show how to derive an approximate area formula for a circle using the area formula for a
parallelogram.

**19.** Explain why $\frac{1}{2}Cr = \pi r^2$ for any circle.

**20.** Suppose that you know how to find the area
of a square but not the area of a circle. How
could you approximate the area of the circle
shown?

**21.** (a) When the radius of a circle is doubled,
the circumference is multiplied by
_____ .

   (b) When the radius of a circle is doubled,
the area is multiplied by _____ .

**22.** (a) How many times larger is the area of a
        pizza that has a 14-in. diameter than a
        pizza that has a 10-in. diameter?
    (b) If a 10-in. pizza costs $6, what is a fair
        price for a 14-in. pizza?

**23.** A woman wants to spray a square plot.

40 yd                    40 yd

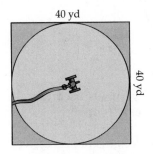   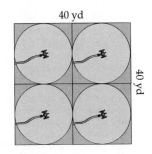

Would using 4 small sprinklers reach more
area than 1 giant sprinkler? (Assume that
they spray the circular areas shown.)

**24.** (a) Complete the third example, repeating
        the error pattern in the completed examples,
        and (b) describe the error pattern.

 $A = 8\pi$    $A = 6\pi$    $A =$ ___

**25.** What is the area of the sector of the circle
      shown? C is the center.

3 ft

C   3 ft

The area = _____ .

**26.** The area of a circle is $25\pi$ m². What is the
      circumference?

**27.** The circumference of a circle is $20\pi$ ft. What
      is the area?

**28.**

(a) Which do you think is larger, the area of
    the inner circle or the shaded region?
(b) Use a ruler and compute each area.

**29.** A circular garden has a diameter of 6.0 m. It
      has a circular path 1.0 m wide around its
      border. What is the area of the path?

**30.** Find the area of the geometric shape (used
      for Norman windows). Assume that the top
      is a circular arc.

3 m                       3 m

1 m

**31.** C is the center of the circle.

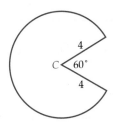

4

C   60°

4

(a) perimeter = _____ .
(b) area = _____ .

**32.** If the radius of a circle increases by 30%,
      then the area of the circle increases by
      (a) 9%      (b) 30%      (c) 69%
      (d) 90%     (e) 130%

*Extension Exercises*

**33.** All of the regions shown have a perimeter of 12π. Which has the largest area?

(a)    (b)    (c)

**34.** You have 40.0 ft of fencing to enclose an area.
   (a) What is the maximum rectangular area you could enclose?
   (b) What area could you enclose with a circle?

 **35.** A lake has a surface area of 800 km². 
   (a) What is the minimum length the shoreline could be?
   (b) What is the maximum length the shoreline could be?

**36.** The figure shows a square and a semicircle.

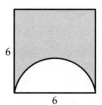

The shaded area = _____ .

**37.** $C$ is the center.

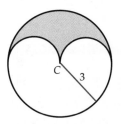

The shaded area = _____ .

**38.** A 3.0-m fence is used to enclose a garden with a circular arc. How long is $L$? (Use 3.14 for π.)

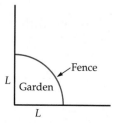

**39.** $C$ is the center. Find the shaded area.

**40.**

Both circles have the same center. The radius of the larger circle is 3 times the radius of the smaller circle. What is the ratio of the shaded area to the area of the smaller circle?

**41.** Make a graph showing the relationship between the radius and circumference of a circle.

Circumference

Radius

**42.** Express the area $A$ of a circle in terms of its circumference $C$.

**43.** True or false? The ratio of the areas of two circles equals the ratio of their radii. If the statement is true, prove it. If it is false, give a counterexample.

**44.** Draw a parallelogram with the measurements shown. (*Hint:* Draw the 8-cm top and the 4-cm height first.)

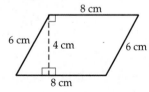

**45.** area *ARNO* = _____

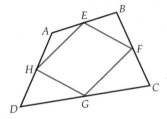

*Special Exercises*

**46.** About 2200 years ago, Eratosthenes measured the circumference of the earth. (It's surprising, considering that many people in more recent civilizations did not even know the earth was spherical.) Eratosthenes measured the angle of a shadow in Alexandria to be 7.5° at the same time the sun was directly overhead in Aswan 500 miles away.

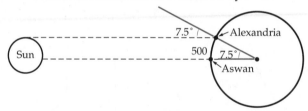

From this, he knew that the central angle shown was 7.5°. Explain how he would compute the circumference of the earth. (Its actual circumference is 24,902 miles.)

**47.** (a) Draw a large quadrilateral *ABCD* on a sheet of paper. Mark the midpoints of each side *E*, *F*, *G*, and *H* and connect *E* to *F* to *G* to *H* to *F*.

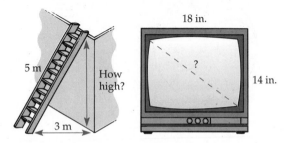

(b) Cut out the four triangles and place them so that they cover *EFGH*.

(c) What relationship does part (b) suggest?

**48.** Write a report on the history of $\pi$.

---

## 10.4  The Pythagorean Theorem

**Figure 10-26**

The lengths in Figure 10-26 can be found using one of the most famous theorems in mathematics: the Pythagorean Theorem.

## Pythagorean Theorem

As you know from Chapter 4, Pythagoras and his followers were interested in numbers and their characteristics. They also studied geometry.

Although the Babylonians knew this property of right triangles, over 3500 years ago, Pythagoras or one of his followers gave the first known proof of the Pythagorean Theorem about 2500 years ago. The theorem describes the relationships between the lengths of the three sides of a **right triangle** (a triangle that has a right angle).

The sides of a right triangle have special names. The side opposite the right angle is called the **hypotenuse,** and the other two sides are called **legs** (Figure 10-27).

The lengths of the sides of any right triangle are related by a single formula.

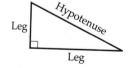

**Figure 10-27**

 **D** Lesson Exercise 10.49

(a) Use a ruler to draw a right triangle. (This could also be done on a computer using an automatic drawer.)
(b) Measure the lengths of the three sides.
(c) Square the lengths of the three sides.
(d) How are the squares of the three lengths related?

In spite of measurement error, your results from Lesson Exercise 10.49 may suggest the Pythagorean Theorem. And now, without further ado, here is one of the most famous and useful theorems in all of mathematics.

---

**The Pythagorean Theorem**

If a right triangle has legs of lengths $a$ and $b$ and a hypotenuse of length $c$, then $a^2 + b^2 = c^2$.

---

How do we know that this theorem is true? Not only has the theorem been proved; it has been proved about 370 different ways! Even James Garfield (later President Garfield) thought up a new proof while he was in Congress.

One proof uses the area formulas for a triangle and a square, and the sum of the angle measures in a triangle. These are all ideas you have studied in this course. Now use them to deduce the Pythagorean Theorem.

**D** Lesson Exercise 10.50

The following proof involves putting together four copies of a right triangle to form a square.

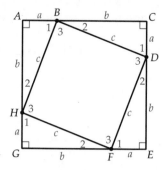

Figure 10-28

First show that *BDFH* (Figure 10-28) is a square.
(a) What is the sum of measures of $\angle 1$ and $\angle 2$?
(b) What is the measure of $\angle 3$?
(c) What kind of figure is *BDFH*?
(d) Find the area of square *ACEG* in terms of *a* and *b* only.
(e) Find the area of square *ACEG* by computing the area of the four right triangles and the square *BDFH*.
Answers to parts (d) and (e) both represent the area of the big square, so they must be equal.
(f) Set your answers to parts (d) and (e) equal to each other and see whether you can derive the Pythagorean Theorem from your equation.

At first, the ancient Greeks used only whole numbers and rational numbers. They may have discovered a geometric representation of a new type of number by solving the following problem.

Figure 10-29

Lesson Exercise 10.51

(a) Find *N* in Figure 10-29.
(b) What new set of numbers is suggested by part (a)?

The Pythagorean Theorem is used in a variety of applications. In any problem in which you know the lengths of two sides of a right triangle, you can use the Pythagorean Theorem to find the length of the remaining side.

 **Example 10.4**

A ladder is 5.0 m long.
(a) If the bottom of the ladder is placed 3.0 m from a wall, how high up the wall will the ladder reach?
(b) The exact length the ladder reaches up the wall is between _____ and _____ .

**Solution**

(a) Draw a picture of the situation (Figure 10-30).

**Figure 10-30**

The ladder, wall, and ground form a right triangle, so the Pythagorean Theorem can be used.

$$N^2 + 3^2 = 5^2$$
$$N^2 + 9 = 25$$
$$N^2 = 16$$
$$N = \pm\sqrt{16} = \pm 4 \ (\pm 4 \text{ means } +4 \text{ or } -4.)$$

Since $N$ represents length, we are interested only in the positive square root (4). This will be true in all Pythagorean Theorem problems. So the length of $N$ is 4 m.

(b) The hypotenuse is actually between 4.95 and 5.05 m. The given leg is actually between 2.95 and 3.05 m.

Largest answer     $N^2 + (2.95)^2 = (5.05)^2$
                            $N^2 = 16.8$
                            $N = \sqrt{16.8} \text{ m}$
Smallest answer     $N^2 + (3.05)^2 = (4.95)^2$
                            $N^2 = 15.2$
                            $N = \sqrt{15.2} \text{ m}$

The exact length is between $\sqrt{15.2}$ and $\sqrt{16.8}$ m.  ∎

**Lesson Exercise 10.52**

A rectangular screen measures 14.0 in. by 18.0 in.
(a) How long is the diagonal, to the nearest tenth of an inch?
(b) The exact diagonal length is between _____ and _____ .

## The Right-Triangle Test

If you know the lengths of the three sides of a triangle, is there a way to tell whether it is a right triangle? Yes. This is the converse of the Pythagorean Theorem. You can complete the proof in the homework exercises. No need to thank me for putting it there.

## Lesson Exercise 10.53

Look at the Pythagorean Theorem and see whether you can write its converse.

According to the converse, any triangle in which the lengths have the relationship $a^2 + b^2 = c^2$ must be a right triangle. The converse, "The Right-Triangle Test," can be used to determine whether a triangle with three given lengths is a right triangle.

> **The Right-Triangle Test (Converse of the Pythagorean Theorem)**
>
> If $a$, $b$, and $c$ are the lengths of the sides of a triangle and $a^2 + b^2 = c^2$, then the triangle is a right triangle.

The Right-Triangle Test is based on the fact that the Pythagorean Theorem works only on right triangles. Use the test in the following exercise.

## Lesson Exercise 10.54

Determine whether each of the following is a right triangle.

(a)                          (b)

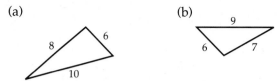

## The Sides of a Triangle

The Right-Triangle Test enables us to recognize three lengths that could form a right triangle. Is it possible to tell whether three lengths could form an **acute triangle** (in which all three angles are acute), an **obtuse triangle** (in which one angle is obtuse), or no triangle at all?

## Lesson Exercise 10.55

Suppose that you are traveling from point $A$ to $B$ (Figure 10-31).
(a)  What is the shortest route?
(b)  What does part (a) imply about the distance from $A$ to $C$ to $B$?
(c)  Parts (a) and (b) suggest that if $C$ is not on $\overline{AB}$, then
      $AC + BC$ _____ $AB$.

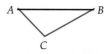

**Figure 10-31**

The result of Lesson Exercise 10.55(c) is called the Triangle Inequality.

---

**The Triangle Inequality**

The sum of the measures of any two sides of a triangle is greater than the measure of the third side.

---

The following exercise uses the Triangle Inequality and the Right-Triangle Test to produce a more general result.

## Lesson Exercise 10.56

Three segments have lengths $a$, $b$, and $c$, with $a < b < c$.
(a)  Under what conditions could segments of lengths $a$, $b$, and $c$ be used to form a triangle?
(b)  What conditions for $a$, $b$, and $c$ would make the triangle a right triangle, an acute triangle, or an obtuse triangle?

## Answers to Selected Lesson Exercises

10.50 (a) $90°$    (b) $90°$    (c) a square
      (d) $(a + b)^2$    (e) $4\left(\frac{1}{2}ab\right) + c^2$

10.51 (a) $\sqrt{2}$    (b) irrational numbers

10.52 (a) 22.8 in.
      (b) $\sqrt{516.805}$ and $\sqrt{523.205}$ in.

10.54 (a) yes, since $6^2 + 8^2 = 10^2$
      (b) no, since $6^2 + 7^2 \neq 9^2$

10.56 (a) $a + b > c$
      (b) $a^2 + b^2 = c^2$; $a^2 + b^2 > c^2$;
          $a^2 + b^2 < c^2$ and $a + b > c$

## 10.4   Homework Exercises

### Basic Exercises

1. Many students know the Pythagorean Theorem as $a^2 + b^2 = c^2$ but do not know anything else about $a$, $b$, and $c$.
   (a) To what geometric shape does the Pythagorean Theorem apply?
   (b) What do $a$, $b$, and $c$ represent?

2. Explain how the shaded area illustrates the Pythagorean Theorem for the white triangle in the center.

3. $ACEG$ is a square. $\triangle ABH \cong \triangle CDB \cong \triangle EFD \cong \triangle GHF$. Explain why $\angle 3$ must be a right angle.

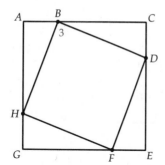

4. Before becoming president, James Garfield proved the Pythagorean Theorem using the trapezoid shown.

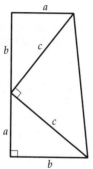

(a) Write formulas for the areas of the three triangles in terms of $a$, $b$, and $c$.
(b) Find the area of the trapezoid.
(c) Set your two areas equal to each other and see whether you can derive the Pythagorean Theorem.

5. Draw a line segment of length $\sqrt{13}$ units on the square lattice.

6. Find the area and perimeter of the right triangle shown on the square lattice.

7. A ladder is 4.0 m long. The bottom of the ladder is placed 0.8 m from the wall. How high up on the wall will the ladder reach?

8.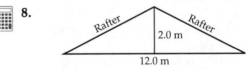

(a) How long are the rafters on the roof?
(b) The exact length of the rafters is between _____ and _____ .

9. In walking from $A$ to $B$ on a square city block, cutting straight across the grass is about _____% the distance of using the sidewalk.

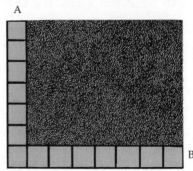

**10.** You want to hang a microphone 3 m above a stage using wires. About how much wire would you need?

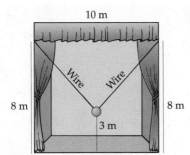

**11.** Two forces act on an object, one pushing east at 4 mph and one pushing north at 4 mph. Where will the object go and at what speed?

**12.** A rectangle has sides of length $b$ and $h$. Compute the length of each diagonal and show that they are equal in length.

**13.** A square television screen measures 20.0 in. along the diagonal. How long is each side of the screen?

**14.** Find the perimeter of the square.

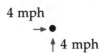

**15.** (a) Complete the third example, repeating the error pattern in the completed examples, and (b) describe the error pattern.

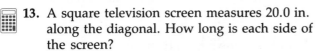

(a)                    (b)                    (c)

Area = $\sqrt{41}$      Area = $\sqrt{13}$      Area = ___

**16.** Find the area of the triangle.

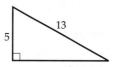

**17.** Find the area of the rhombus if $AC = 8$ and $AB = 12$.

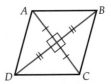

**18.** Find the area of the region on the square lattice. All curves are circular arcs.

**19.** A person in Kansas travels 7 miles north, then 3 miles east, and finally 3 miles south. How far is the person from the starting point?

**20.** Flo and Ken want to carry a tall piece of glass that is 9 ft square through a rectangular doorway that is 3 ft by 8 ft. Will it fit?

**21.** Use the Right-Triangle Test to determine whether each of the following is a right triangle.

(a)                              (b)

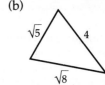

**22.** Use the Right-Triangle Test to determine whether each of the following is a right triangle.

(a)                  (b)

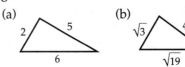

**23.** (a) Select three lengths that make up a right triangle and multiply them all by the same positive number. Do the resulting lengths determine a right triangle?
   (b) Repeat part (a) using three new lengths.
   (c) Propose a generalization of your results.

**24.** Tell whether each set of lengths could form a right triangle, an acute triangle, an obtuse triangle, or no triangle.
   (a) 3, 5, 6      (b) 9, 12, 15
   (c) 3, 5, 10     (d) 2, 3, 4

**25.** Consider the following problem. "A standard stop sign measures 25.0 cm on each side. What is the area of the surface of a stop sign?" Devise a plan and solve the problem.

*Extension Exercises*

**26.** A woman on a pier pulls a rope $d$ meters toward herself. Guess whether the boat will move a distance less than $d$ meters, equal to $d$ meters, or more than $d$ meters.

**27. Pythagorean triples** are three counting numbers that satisfy the relationship $a^2 + b^2 = c^2$. The smallest triple is 3-4-5 ($3^2 + 4^2 = 5^2$). Another triple is 5-12-13 (since $5^2 + 12^2 = 13^2$).
   (a) Double 3, 4, and 5. Does this create a new Pythagorean triple?
   (b) Name three more Pythagorean triples.
   (c) If $a^2 + b^2 = c^2$, show that $ka^2 + kb^2 = kc^2$ for any counting number $k$.

**28.** One of the most amazing Babylonian tablets, dating from around 1700 B.C., is called Plimpton 322 (see photo).

George A. Plimpton Collection, Rare Book and Manuscript Library, Columbia University.

It contains a list of Pythagorean triples! All the triples in the chart are listed in the first three columns ($a$, $b$, $c$). The last two columns list $u$ and $v$ such that $a = 2uv$, $b = u^2 - v^2$, and $c = u^2 + v^2$. Fill in the missing values in the following chart, which shows the first five rows of Plimpton 322.

| $a$ | $b$ | $c$ | $u$ | $v$ |
|---|---|---|---|---|
| 120 | 119 | 169 | 12 | |
| 3456 | 3367 | 4825 | | 27 |
| 4800 | 4601 | | 75 | |
| 13,500 | | 18,541 | | 54 |
| | 65 | 97 | | |

**29.** A famous unsolved problem in mathematics is Fermat's Last Theorem. In 1631, Fermat considered equations of the form $x^2 + y^2 = z^2$, $x^3 + y^3 = z^3$, $x^4 + y^4 = z^4$, and so on. He said that only $x^2 + y^2 = z^2$ has a solution set made up of counting numbers. None of the other equations have any such solutions! After writing this idea down, Fermat wrote in the margin of the paper (in Latin): "I have discovered a truly wonderful proof of this, but the margin is too small to contain it." No one ever found a proof by Fermat, and no one else has ever been able to prove this theorem!

(a) Give three sets of counting-number solutions to $x^2 + y^2 = z^2$.

(b) Consider $x^3 + y^3 = z^3$. Is $x = 5$, $y = 6$, and $z = 7$ a solution set?

**30.** People have found formulas for some Pythagorean triples. One is the following.

For any odd number $N > 1$, $N$, $\dfrac{N^2 - 1}{2}$, and $\dfrac{N^2 + 1}{2}$ will be a Pythagorean triple.

Write four triples using this formula.

**31.** Consider the following problem. "Find the area $A$ in the diagram."

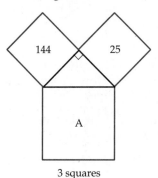

3 squares

$$A = \underline{\hspace{3cm}} .$$

Devise a plan and solve the problem.

**32.**

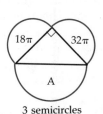

3 semicircles

$$A = \underline{\hspace{3cm}} .$$

**33.**

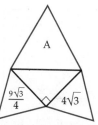

3 equilateral triangles

$$A = \underline{\hspace{3cm}} .$$

**34.** Two congruent 10-by-10 squares overlap so that a vertex of one is the center of the other. One possible drawing is shown. What is the largest possible overlapping area?

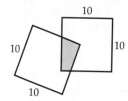

**35.** A regular hexagon has sides of length 10. Find its area. (*Hint:* See the following diagram.)

**36.** The length of each side of the squares, regular hexagons, and equilateral triangles is 1 cm. What is the total area?

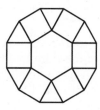

**37.** Consider the following problem. "Home plate in baseball is cut from a square *ABCD*" as shown at the top of page 592.

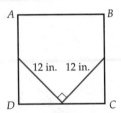

"How long is each side of *ABCD*?" Devise a plan and solve the problem.

**38.** Find the area of the shaded region. *C* is the center of each circle.

(a)
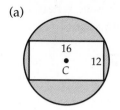

(b)
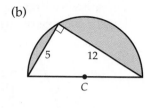

**39.** *C* is the center of both circles. *CB* = 5 and *AB* = 8. Find the shaded area.

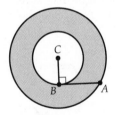

**40.** Find the perimeter and area of the trapezoid.

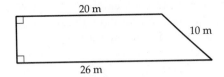

**41.** Compare the following choices for packing one row of canned drinks in a carton. Assume each can has a height and a diameter of 1 unit. Which would be the cheapest *per can* to package?

(a)

(b)

(c)

(d)

**42.** How big a circular pan is needed to fit four slices of bread, each 4.0 in. by 4.0 in. as shown, with 1.0 in. between them?

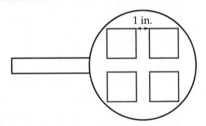

**43.** A cube has edges 2 cm long. How long is a diagonal of the cube? (*Hint:* Draw the diagonal of the base.)

**44.** A closet is 8 ft by 4 ft by 6 ft. Will a 10-ft pole fit inside?

**45.** Read the following proof of the Right-Triangle Test and fill in the missing reasons.

A triangle has lengths *a*, *b*, and *d*, with $a^2 + b^2 = d^2$. How do we show that it must be a right triangle?

Draw another triangle with sides of lengths *a* and *b* and a right angle between them.

(a) Since △*EFG* is a right triangle, the Pythagorean Theorem says:

_____ .

(b) Why must $c^2 = d^2$?

(c) Now, if $c^2 = d^2$, then *c* = *d*. Therefore, △*ABD* ≅ △ _____ because of

_____ .

(d) If the two triangles are congruent, then $m\angle E$ = _____ = 90°. Therefore, △*ABD* is a right triangle!

**46.**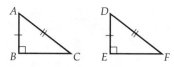

(a) Why is $\overline{BC} \cong \overline{EF}$?
(b) Why is $\triangle ABC \cong \triangle DEF$?
This verifies the *HL* (hypotenuse-leg) congruence property for right triangles.

*Computer Exercises*

 **47.** Write a Logo procedure that draws a 30-by-50 rectangle with one of its diagonals.

**48.** Write a Logo procedure that draws an isosceles right triangle with legs of length 30.

**49.** Write a BASIC program that prints three numbers of the form $T$, $(T^2 - 1)/2$, and $(T^2 + 1)/2$ for $T = 3, 5, 7, 9, \ldots 21$. Then test each set to see if it is a Pythagorean triple.

*Special Exercise*

**50.** Read "Socrates and the Slave" by Plato (from the *Meno*) in *Fantasia Mathematica*, edited by Clifton Fadiman. Write a report that includes a summary of the main ideas and your reaction to them.

## 10.5 Surface Area and Volume

Photo by Tom Sonnabend.

**Figure 10-32**

How much paper is needed for the label of the can in Figure 10-32? How much juice will the container hold? The first question concerns surface area; the second concerns volume. These are two useful measurements of a space figure.

### Surface Area of Rectangular Prisms

How much will a container cost? How much paint is needed to paint your bedroom? In order to answer these questions, you need to compute the surface area (Figure 10-33, page 594).

**Figure 10-33**

The total **surface area** of a closed space figure is the sum of the areas of all its surfaces. A surface area in square units would indicate how many squares it would take to cover the outside of a space figure.

**Figure 10-34**

## Lesson Exercise 10.57

Consider the rectangular prism in Figure 10-34. Compute the total surface area. (In other words, determine how many squares are needed to cover all the faces.)

Computing the surface area of a rectangular prism can help you decide how much paint you would need to paint a room.

 ## Lesson Exercise 10.58

A box-shaped room has two walls that are 8 ft by 12 ft and two walls that are 8 ft by 18 ft. There are two windows that are 3 ft by 5 ft, and a doorway that is 4 ft by 7 ft.
(a) What is the area of the ceiling?
(b) Suppose that you want to paint the walls and ceiling. Excluding the windows and the door, how much area is there to paint?
(c) If 1 gallon of paint covers 400 ft², how many gallons will be needed to paint the four walls and the ceiling?

## Surface Area of Prisms and Cylinders

Computing the total surface area of other prisms and cylinders also requires finding the area of each surface and adding the areas together.

**Example 10.5**

Find the total surface area of the triangular right prism in Figure 10-35.

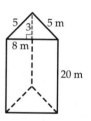

**Figure 10-35**

**Solution**

*Understanding the Problem*   Find the sum of the areas of the five faces of the triangular prism.

*Devising a Plan*   The triangular prism has five faces. There are two isosceles triangles (the bases) and three rectangles (the lateral faces), as shown in Figure 10-36.

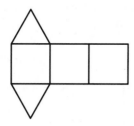

**Figure 10-36**

$$A_{\text{surface}} = A_{\triangle_1} + A_{\triangle_2} + A_{\square_1} + A_{\square_2} + A_{\square_3}$$

*Carrying Out the Plan*   The triangles each have an area of $\frac{1}{2} \cdot 3 \cdot 8 = 12$. The rectangles are 5 by 20, 5 by 20, and 8 by 20. So their areas are 100, 100, and 160.

$$A_{\text{surface}} = 12 + 12 + 100 + 100 + 160 = 384 \text{ m}^2$$

*Looking Back*   The method for finding the total surface area will work if you are able to find the area of each surface.   ■

 Now it's your turn.

**D** Lesson Exercise 10.59

Consider the following problem. "Find the total surface area of the triangular prism in Figure 10-37." Devise a plan and solve the problem.

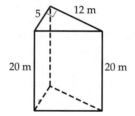

**Figure 10-37**

How do you find the surface area of a cylinder?

**D** Lesson Exercise 10.60

**Figure 10-38**

(a) How many surfaces does the cylinder in Figure 10-38 have?
(b) What shape are its bases?
(c) What shape is the lateral surface? (*Hint:* Roll up a regular sheet of paper.)

A cylinder has two circles for bases. Figure 10-39 shows that the lateral surface of a cylinder is a "rolled-up" rectangle.

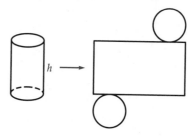

**Figure 10-39**

**D** Lesson Exercise 10.61

(a) If a cylinder has radius $r$ and height $h$, what are the dimensions of the "rolled-up" rectangle (the lateral surface)? It might represent the label of a can.
(b) Compute the area of the two circles and rectangle and find a formula for the total surface area of a cylinder.

The surface area of any prism or cylinder can be computed using a more general formula.

Lesson Exercise 10.62

(a) How can the lateral surface area of a prism or cylinder be computed from the perimeter of the base?
(b) If $B$ is the area of the base, $p$ is the perimeter of the base, and $h$ is the height, what is a formula for the surface area of a prism or cylinder?

The general surface area formula for a prism or cylinder, $A = ph + 2B$, is not commonly used in elementary or middle-school mathematics.

## Volume of Right Rectangular Prisms

Joe Munroe, *Life* Magazine. © 1959 Time, Inc.

**Figure 10-40**

In the late 1950s, college students enjoyed attempting to measure the volume of a phone booth in their own unique way (Figure 10-40). **Volume** tells how much space a three-dimensional figure occupies. Volume is usually measured in cubic units. Whereas surface area measures the area of the faces of a solid, volume measures the capacity of a solid.

## Lesson Exercise 10.63

(a) What is the volume of the solid in Figure 10-41 in cubic units?
(b) What is the total surface area?
(c) If the 3 cubes on the second layer are moved to the first layer so it has 3 rows and 4 columns, how will this change the volume and the surface area?

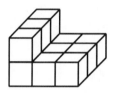

**Figure 10-41**

In Lesson Exercise 10.63, one could compute the volume by counting how many cubes fill up the space figure. With rectangular prisms like the one in the following exercise, there is a shortcut (formula) for counting the cubes.

## Lesson Exercise 10.64

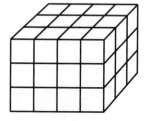

**Figure 10-42**

Imagine building a solid rectangular prism structure out of wooden cubes as shown in Figure 10-42. Each cube is 1 cm³.
(a) How many cubes are there in a layer?
(b) How many layers are there?
(c) What is the volume of the rectangular prism?
(d) What are the length, width, and height of the rectangular prism in centimeters?
(e) How can you compute the volume using the length, width, and height?

The results of Lesson Exercise 10.44 suggest a shorter way to compute the volume of a rectangular prism. The formula $lw$ (length times width) gives the number of cubes in a layer of a rectangular prism, and $h$ (height) is the number of layers. So $lwh$ gives the total number of cubes that fill the interior of the rectangular prism in Figure 10-42.

$4 \times 3$ = number of cubes per layer
3 layers
$4 \times 3 \times 3 = 36$ cubes

---

**Volume of a Right Rectangular Prism**

The volume $V$ of a right rectangular prism that has dimensions $l$, $w$, and $h$ is

$$V = lwh$$

---

Computing the volume of a right rectangular prism can help you decide which freezer is the best buy.

 ## Lesson Exercise 10.65

A store sells two types of freezers. Freezer A costs $310 and measures 1.5 ft by 1.5 ft by 5.0 ft. Freezer B costs $400 and measures 2.0 ft by 2.0 ft by 3.5 ft. Which freezer has a lower unit cost?

## Volume of Prisms and Cylinders

Are you ready for some good news? And no bad news? All right prisms and right circular cylinders have the same general volume formula!

As you have seen, you can compute the volume of a rectangular prism (Figure 10-43) by counting the number of cubes in each layer, which is the *area of the base (lw)*, and multiply by the number of layers, which is the *height (h)*.

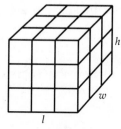

$$V = (l \cdot w) \cdot h$$
$$V = (\text{base area}) \cdot \text{height}$$

**Figure 10-43**

We can apply the same idea to all right prisms and cylinders. Imagine that the shapes in Figure 10-44 are glass containers.

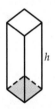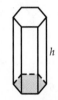

**Figure 10-44**

Visualize filling them up with some water (or orange juice if you prefer). The total amount of liquid can be measured by moving the base area from the bottom to the top of the container. In other words, the volume is the area of the base multiplied by the height.

---

**Volume of Any Right Prism or Right Cylinder**

The volume $V$ of a right prism or a right cylinder that has a base of area $B$ and height $h$ is

$$V = Bh$$

---

Most geometry books use $b$ to denote the *length* of a base (side) of a polygon and $B$ to denote the *area* of a base that is the face of a polyhedron, cone, or cylinder. The general volume formula for prisms and cylinders can be used to derive specific volume formulas.

**D** Lesson Exercise 10.66
_____

Consider a right circular cylinder with radius $r$ and height $h$.
(a) What shape is the base?
(b) What is the area of the base?
(c) What is a formula for the volume obtained by substituting in $V = Bh$?

_____

The following example illustrates how to find the volume of a triangular prism by using the general volume formula.

**Example 10.6**

Find the volume of the right triangular prism shown in Figure 10-45.

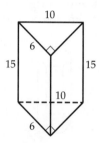

**Figure 10-45**

**Solution**

$V$ (volume) $= B$ (base area) $\times h$ (height of prism)
The bases are right triangles. First, use the Pythagorean Theorem to find the length of the other leg.

$$6^2 + x^2 = 10^2$$
$$36 + x^2 = 100$$
$$x^2 = 64$$
$$x = 8$$

The base has area $B = \frac{1}{2} \cdot 6 \cdot 8 = 24$.

The height of the prism is 15.

$$V_{\text{prism}} = 24 \cdot 15 = 360 \text{ cubic units.} \quad \blacksquare$$

## Lesson Exercise 10.67

Find the volume of the cylinder and prism shown in Figure 10-46.

(a) (could be the design for a
    container)

(b) (could be the shape of a slice
    of cheese)

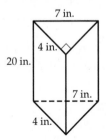

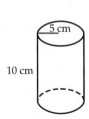

**Figure 10-46**

Think of the right prism in Figure 10-47 as a stack of very, very thin sheets of paper. The related oblique prism would be obtained by shifting the stack. The right cylinder and the oblique cylinder in Figure 10-47 are related in the same way.

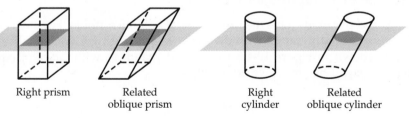

Right prism        Related            Right            Related
                   oblique prism      cylinder         oblique cylinder

**Figure 10-47**

## Lesson Exercise 10.68

(a) How would the volume of the right prism and the oblique prism in Figure 10-47 compare?
(b) How would the volume of the right cylinder and the oblique cylinder in Figure 10-47 compare?

Bonaventura Cavalieri (1598–1647), an Italian mathematician, stated the general relationship between a pair of figures like those in Figure 10-47.

---

**Cavalieri's Principle**

If two solids (1) have bases in the same plane and (2) every plane parallel to the two bases intersects the solids in cross sections of equal area, then the solids have equal volume.

---

Lesson Exercise 10.68 and Cavalieri's Principle suggest why the volume formula for right prisms and right cylinders applies to all prisms and cylinders.

---

**Volume of Any Prism or Cylinder**

The volume $V$ of a prism or cylinder that has a base of area $B$ and height $h$ is

$$V = Bh$$

---

## Volume of Pyramids and Cones

Cones and pyramids have the same general volume formula. For any cone, there is a related pyramid with the same volume (using Cavalieri's Principle) as shown in Figure 10-48. Cones and pyramids with bases of equal area and equal heights have equal volumes.

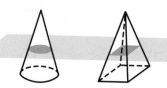

Figure 10-48

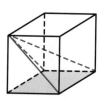

Figure 10-49

By finding the volume formula for a single simple pyramid, one can deduce the volume formula for other pyramids and cones! Consider a square pyramid determined by a face of a cube, a perpendicular edge, and three diagonals drawn from a vertex of an opposite face, as shown in Figure 10-49.

The complete cube can be formed from three congruent square pyramids determined by diagonals drawn from the same vertex, as shown in Figure 10-50.

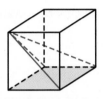 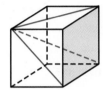 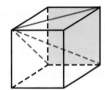

**Figure 10-50**

Since the three pyramids are congruent, the volume of each pyramid is $\frac{1}{3}$ the volume of the cube. So

$$V_{\text{pyramid}} = \frac{1}{3}V_{\text{cube}}$$

This suggests the general relationship between the volume of pyramids and prisms that have the same base and height:

$$V_{\text{pyramid}} = \frac{1}{3}V_{\text{prism}} = \frac{1}{3}Bh$$

Figure 10-51 uses Cavalieri's Principle to show why the same relationship holds between a cylinder and a cone with the same base and height.

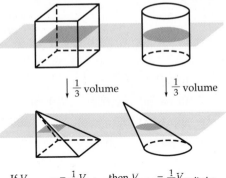

If $V_{\text{pyramid}} = \frac{1}{3}V_{\text{prism}}$ then $V_{\text{cone}} = \frac{1}{3}V_{\text{cyclinder}}$

**Figure 10-51**

## Lesson Exercise 10.69

What is the formula for the volume of a cone that has radius $r$ and height $h$?

If you have models available, you can see that the larger shape in each pair (that is, the prism or cylinder) holds about three times as much water or rice as the smaller shape (the pyramid or cone). The general formula for pyramids and cones is as follows.

---

**Volumes of Any Pyramid or Cone**

The volume $V$ of a pyramid or cone that has a base of area $B$ and height $h$ is

$$V = \frac{1}{3}Bh$$

---

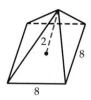

**Figure 10-52**

The general volume formula $V = \frac{1}{3}Bh$ can be used to obtain the volume of cones and pyramids.

### Lesson Exercise 10.70

Find the volume of the square pyramid in Figure 10-52. (It could be a building design.)

---

## Answers to Selected Lesson Exercises

10.57  40 units²

10.58  (a) 216 ft²      (b) 638 ft²      (c) 2

10.59  660 m²

10.60  (a) 3      (b) circles      (c) rectangle

10.61  (a) $2\pi r$ by $h$
       (b) $A = 2\pi rh + 2\pi r^2$ square units

10.62  (a) $ph$
       (b) $A_{surface} = ph + 2B$

10.63  (a) 12      (b) 38
       (c) $V$ and $A$ are the same.

10.64  (a) 12      (b) 3      (c) 36 cm³
       (d) 4 cm, 3 cm, 3 cm
       (e) 4 cm × 3 cm × 3 cm = 36 cm³

10.65  $A$

10.66  (a) a circle      (b) $\pi r^2$      (c) $V = \pi r^2 h$

10.67  (a) $250\pi$ cm³      (b) $40\sqrt{33}$ in.³

10.69  $V = \frac{1}{3}\pi r^2 h$

10.70  $42\frac{2}{3}$ cubic units

---

## 10.5   Homework Exercises

*Basic Exercises*

1. What is the surface area of the rectangular prism?

2. What is the surface area of the rectangular prism?

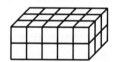

**3.** Show how you would arrange 20 congruent cubes to obtain a rectangular prism with
(a) the largest possible surface area.
(b) the smallest possible surface area.

**4.** Explain in terms of measurement why a potato will bake more quickly if you cut it into smaller pieces and cook them separately.

**5.** How much paper is needed to cover the box shown?

**6.** A rectangular prism has dimensions *l* ft, *w* ft, and *h* ft. What is its total surface area?

**7.** You want to carpet the steps as shown.

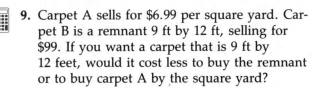

(a) How many square centimeters of carpet will you need?
(b) If the carpet costs $20 per square *meter*, how much will it cost?

**8.** A box-shaped room has two walls that are 8 ft by 10 ft and two that are 8 ft by 16 ft. There is one window that is 3 ft by 6 ft, and a doorway that is 4 ft by 7 ft. If 1 gallon of paint covers 450 ft², how many gallon cans would you buy to paint the four walls and the ceiling?

**9.** Carpet A sells for $6.99 per square yard. Carpet B is a remnant 9 ft by 12 ft, selling for $99. If you want a carpet that is 9 ft by 12 feet, would it cost less to buy the remnant or to buy carpet A by the square yard?

**10.** How much nylon (in square feet) would be needed to make the tent shown, including

the bottom? (You may approximate square roots to one decimal place.)

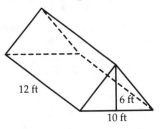

**11.** Find the total surface area of the triangular prism.

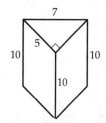

**12.**

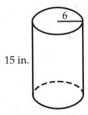

(a) Find the total area of the bases.
(b) The lateral surface can be unwrapped to form a rectangle. What is its area?
(c) What is the surface area of the cylinder?

**13.** Give two possible radii and heights for a cylinder with a surface area of $40\pi$.

**14.** (a) Find the surface area of the sides, front, and back of the house. (Do not include the roof.)

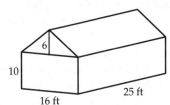

(b) If a gallon of paint covers 400 ft², how much paint would you need to paint the outside of the house?

15. (a) What is the volume of the rectangular prism?

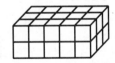

(b) In answering part (a), the most common incorrect answer is 31. How would a child obtain this answer?

16. What is the volume of the swimming pool?

Reprinted by permission: Tribune Media Services.

 17. A store sells two types of freezers. Freezer A costs $350 and measures 2 ft by 2 ft by 4.5 ft. Freezer B costs $480 and measures 3 ft by 3 ft by 3.5 ft. Which freezer is a better buy?

18.

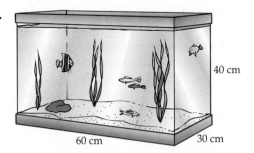

(a) How much water can the fish tank hold?
(b) 1 L = 1000 cm³. How many liters of water does the fish tank hold?
(c) Small tropical fish need about 1500 cm³ of living space. How many fish can live in this tank?

19. Estimate the volume of your refrigerator in cubic meters.

20. Is each quantity related more to volume or to surface area?
(a) the amount of paper needed to make a bag
(b) the amount a bag will hold
(c) your weight

21. (a) Find an open container at home and compute its surface area.
(b) What volume does the container hold?
(c) If you put a top on the container, would this change the answers to part (a) or (b)?

22. (a) Find the volume of a box of tissues.
(b) Compute the ratio of the volume to the surface area.
(c) Would the manufacturer want the ratio in part (b) to be high or low?

23. Suppose that you accurately measure a fish tank and find the length to be 60 cm, the width 30 cm, and the height 40 cm. The actual volume is between _____ and _____ .

24. Suppose that you accurately measure a refrigerator and find the length to be 6.0 ft, the width 3.0 ft, and the height 2.0 ft. The actual volume is between _____ and _____ .

25. The formula $V = Bh$ applies to what kind of figures?

26. A standard 46.00-oz can of juice has a radius of 5.3 cm and a height of 17.5 cm. What is its volume?

**27.** Find the volume of a nickel to the nearest cubic millimeter.

**28.** One can of juice is twice as tall as a second can, but only half as wide. How do their volumes compare?

**29.** (a) Take a sheet of paper $8\frac{1}{2}$ by 11 in. Roll it into a cylindrical tube. What is the length of the diameter?
   (b) Roll the sheet of paper into a cylindrical tube of a different size. What is the length of the diameter?
   (c) Which cylinder has the greater volume?

**30.** Which would appear to hold more, a cube-shaped container, or a tall, thin, box-shaped container with the same volume?

**31.** Find the volume of the oblique prism shown. Its base area is 20 m².

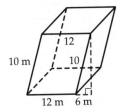

**32.** (a) What is the volume of the piece of cheese shown?

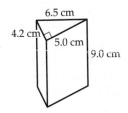

   (b) The exact volume is between _____ and _____ .

**33.** Find the volume of the watering trough.

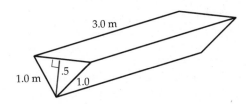

**34.** A cylindrical water tank has a radius of 6.0 m. About how high must it be filled to hold 400.0 m³?

**35.** The formula $V = \frac{1}{3}Bh$ applies to what figures?

**36.** A cylinder-shaped drinking cup holds _____ times more water than a cone-shaped cup that has the same radius and height.

**37.** A 15-step staircase is made out of concrete. Three of the steps are shown. What is the volume of the staircase?

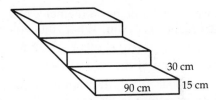

**38.** (a) How much land is needed for the house itself?
   (b) What is the volume of the house?

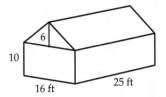

**39.** If 200 in.³ of icing is spread evenly onto a cake to a thickness of 0.5 in., about how much area will it cover?

**40.** A cylindrical hot water heater has a radius of 35 cm and a height of 170 cm. How many liters of water can it hold? (1 cm³ = 1 mL.)

**41.** Find the volume of a 12-oz (355-mL) soda can by
   (a) measuring the radius and height and using a formula.
   (b) using the conversion 1 mL = 1 cm³.

**42.** Find the approximate volume of a standard soup can in cubic centimeters.

**43.** The largest pyramid in the world is in Cho-lula, Mexico. Its base area is 1,960,000 ft² and its height is 177 ft.
(a) What is its volume?
(b) About how many apartments, each 30 ft by 25 ft by 10 ft, would it take to make the same volume?

**44.** The Great Pyramid of Egypt has a square base with sides of 768 ft and a height of 482 ft.
(a) What is its volume?
(b) About how many apartments, each 30 ft by 25 ft by 10 ft, would it take to make the same volume?

**45.** An ice cream cone has a diameter of 2.0 in. and a height of 5.5 in. What is its volume?

**46.** A cone-shaped cup is filled to half its height. What fraction of the cup is filled?

**47.** (a) Complete the third example, repeating the error pattern in the completed examples, and (b) describe the error pattern.

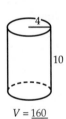  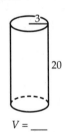

$V = 160$          $V = 96$          $V = \_\_\_$

**48.** A conical tank has an inside diameter of 20 ft and a height of 12 ft. The tank is filled with liquid to a height of 9 ft. How much liquid is in the tank?

*Extension Exercises*

**49.** Consider the following problem. "How heavy is a firefighter's hose? A large hose is 100 ft long and 5 in. in diameter (when full).

Empty, the hose weighs 200 lb. If 1 gallon (231 in.³) of water weighs 8 lb, how much does a full hose weigh?" Devise a plan and solve the problem.

**50.** Given the following floor/wall plan for an apartment, find the cost of redecorating it if you cover the ceiling with 1-ft² tiles costing $.70 each, carpet the floor with carpet costing $8 per square yard, and paint the walls with paint costing $9 per gallon. Each gallon of paint covers 250 ft².

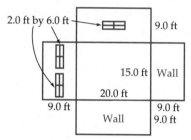

**51.** Suppose that you want to manufacture boxes with a square base as cheaply as possible. The volume must be 2000 cm³. The stronger material on the top and bottom cost $.0002/cm², and the material for the sides costs $.0001/cm². Find the dimensions of the box that minimize the total cost. (Guess and check.)

**52.** A plumber needs to deliver 150 steel pipes to an office building. Her truck can carry 800 kg. Each pipe is 120 cm long, with an outer diameter of 7 cm and an inner diameter of 5 cm. The steel weighs 7.7 g/cm³. How many trips will the plumber need to make?

**53.**

|   |   |   |   |
|---|---|---|---|
| Length of edge | ___ | ___ | ___ |
| Volume | ___ | ___ | ___ |
| Surface area | ___ | ___ | ___ |

(a) Fill in the blanks.
(b) As the cube grows in size, which increases faster, surface area or volume?

**54.** The lengths of the edges of a cube are increased by 20%.
   (a) The surface area will increase by _____ %.
   (b) The volume will increase by _____ %.

**55.** A box with height $h$ contains 6 solid metal cylinders each with radius $r$. What percentage of the box is empty?

**56.** A log has a diameter of 36 cm and a height of 60 cm. Give the dimensions of the largest rectangular solid with a square base that can be cut from it.

**57.** A cylindrical glass jar contains juice. How could you tell without measuring when the jar is half full?

**58.** Consider the following problem. "What size open boxes can you construct from a piece of cardboard 25 cm by 25 cm if you cut off 4 squares from the corners and fold?"

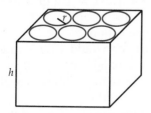

   (a) What size squares can be cut from the corners?
   (b) Devise a plan and solve the problem.

**59.** A cylindrical pipe is hollow inside. What is the volume of the pipe material?

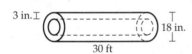

**60.** A cylindrical pipe has length $L$, inner radius

$I$, and overall radius $R$. What is the volume of the pipe material?

**61.** A page in this book is a rectangular prism.
   (a) What are its dimensions? (*Hint:* To find the thickness of a page, measure more than one page.)
   (b) What is the volume of a page?

**62.** A can of tennis balls is 19.3 cm high with a radius of 3.8 cm, and each tennis ball has a radius of 3.2 cm. What percent of the can is occupied by the tennis balls? For a sphere, volume $V = \frac{4}{3}\pi r^3$. Use $\pi = 3.14$.

**63.** A balloon takes 3 seconds to inflate to a radius of 4 in. After 6 seconds, it would have a radius of _____ in. (The answer is not 8 inches.)

**64.** A city water inspector who is 6.0 ft tall is inspecting a spherical water tank. His head touches the tank when he is 18.0 ft away from the lowest point. How did he use this information to find the volume of the tank? (*Hint:* Use the Pythagorean Theorem.)

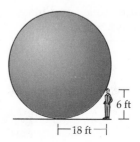

**65.** A garbage can has the dimensions shown. Approximate the volume of the garbage can.

**66.** Find the volume and surface area of the

square pyramid. (Assume that it has rotational symmetry.)

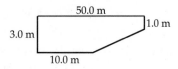

**67.** A swimming pool 20 m wide has the cross section shown. How many liters of water does it hold? (1 L = 1000 cm³.)

**68.** What is the volume of a cube with a surface area of $54N^2$ cm²?

*Special Exercises*

**69.** In the customary system, 1 pint = 1 lb of water, but these measures have no simple relationship to volume measures (such as 1 ft³). The metric system relates volume (cm³), liquid volume (mL), and mass (g) of water in a simple way.

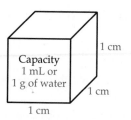

Capacity
1 mL or
1 g of water

(a) What is the volume of the container in cubic centimeters?

So, 1 mL of water = 1 g of water = 1 cm³ of water! Use this information to answer the following questions.

(b) How much would 4 L of water weigh?

(c) A fish tank is 70 cm by 50 cm by 40 cm. About how many liters of water are needed to fill it?

(d) How much would 1 m³ of water weigh?

(e) What is the liquid volume of 1 m³ of water?

**70.** If 1 cm of rain falls uniformly on a field 100 m by 100 m, how much would this rainwater weigh? (1 cm³ weighs 1 g.)

**71.** In order to calibrate a cylindrical beaker with an inside diameter of 2.2 cm to show cubic centimeters, how far apart should the calibration marks be?

---

## 10.6  Length, Area, and Volume of Similar Figures

Do you want to invest in some imaginary real estate? It's safer than investing in real real estate. You are offered two right-triangular pieces of land that are the same shape. One has sides measuring 30 ft, 40 ft, and 50 ft. The other has sides measuring 60 ft, 80 ft, and 100 ft. The second piece of land costs 3 times as much as the first.

**D** Lesson Exercise 10.71

Guess which piece of land is a better buy.

## Similar Plane Figures

The introductory question involves two similar figures. The two triangles are the same shape, but all the sides of the second triangle are twice as long as the corresponding sides of the first. How are their areas related?

First, consider a simpler example.

## Lesson Exercise 10.72

(a) What is the area of the triangle in Figure 10-53?
(b) On a square lattice, draw a similar triangle with the lengths of all its sides tripled.
(c) What is the area of the larger triangle?
(d) The area of the larger triangle is _____ times the area of the smaller triangle.

**Figure 10-53**

Now back to the land problem.

## Lesson Exercise 10.73

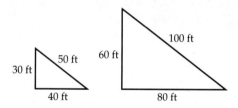

**Figure 10-54**

(a) If you have studied the Right-Triangle Test, show that both triangles in Figure 10-54 are right triangles.
(b) Find the area of each right triangle.
(c) The area of the larger triangle is _____ times the area of the smaller triangle.
(d) Find the perimeter of each triangle.
(e) The perimeter of the larger triangle is _____ times the perimeter of the smaller triangle.
(f) The second triangular piece of land costs 3 times as much as the first. Which is a better buy?

The triangle with twice the lengths had four times the area. What is the general relationship between all corresponding lengths and areas of similar figures? If the suspense is too much for you, do not hesitate to try the next exercise.

Lesson Exercise 10.74

The photographs in Figure 10-55 show the Federal Reserve Bank in Minneapolis, which is designed a lot like a suspension bridge! Enlarging a photo creates two *similar* rectangles.

Photo courtesy of Federal Reserve Bank of Minneapolis.

**Figure 10-55**

(a) The ratio of corresponding sides is _____ : _____ .
(b) The areas of corresponding rectangles are _____ and _____ .
(c) The ratio of their areas is _____ .
(d) The perimeters of the two rectangles are _____ and _____ .
(e) The ratio of their perimeters is _____ .

Try to generalize the results from Lesson Exercises 10.72–10.74 in the following exercise.

Lesson Exercise 10.75

Two similar figures have a ratio of corresponding sides $m:n$.
(a) What is the ratio of their areas?
(b) What is the ratio of their perimeters?

The results of the preceding exercises suggest the following rule.

---

**Length and Area of Similar Plane Figures**

Figures *A* and *B* are similar plane figures with a ratio of corresponding length measurements of *m:n*. The ratio of corresponding area measurements is $m^2:n^2$, and the ratio of their perimeters is *m:n*.

---

Use these properties in the following exercise.

## Lesson Exercise 10.76

Two similar triangles have a ratio of corresponding sides of 4:1. What are the ratios of their areas and their perimeters?

## Similar Space Figures

Relationships between lengths, areas, and volumes in similar figures correspond to relationships among strength, heat loss, and weight in animals. After examining relationships in similar geometric solids, you will use this knowledge to study nature.

**D** ## Lesson Exercise 10.77

Suppose that you have a 1-cm cube and a 3-cm cube. (Use wooden blocks if they are available.)
(a)  What is the ratio of corresponding edge lengths?
(b)  The surface areas of the two figures are _____ and _____ .
(c)  What is the ratio of their surface areas?
(d)  Compute the volume of each figure.
(e)  What is the ratio of their volumes?

Next, consider two similar rectangular prisms and see whether you can generalize the results.

D Lesson Exercise 10.78

Consider the two rectangular prisms in Figure 10-56.

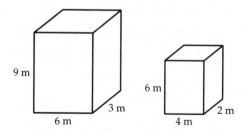

Figure 10-56

(a) What is the ratio of corresponding edge lengths?
(b) What is the ratio of their surface areas?
(c) Guess how the ratio of surface areas is related to the ratio of corresponding edges in similar solids.
(d) What is the ratio of their volumes?
(e) Guess how the ratio of volumes is related to the ratio of their edges in similar solids.

As your results in Lesson Exercises 10.77 and 10.78 suggest, the ratio of volumes is the cube of the ratio of corresponding lengths, and the ratio of corresponding areas is the square of the ratio of corresponding lengths.

> **Length, Area, and Volume of Similar Solids**
>
> $A$ and $B$ are similar solids with a ratio of all corresponding length measurements of $m{:}n$. The ratio of all corresponding area measurements is $m^2{:}n^2$, and the ratio of volumes is $m^3{:}n^3$.

Use these properties to answer the following questions.

Lesson Exercise 10.79

Two similar solids have corresponding heights of 3 m and 12 m.
(a) What is the ratio of their total surface areas?
(b) What is the ratio of their volumes?

## Similarity in Nature

Photo courtesy of Film Stills Archive.

**Figure 10-57**

Do you ever worry that a giant ape might visit your neighborhood (Figure 10-57)? Would this be possible? Similar solids provide the answer! But first we'll consider some friendly dolphins (Figure 10-58).

Neg. no. 328896. Photo: Rob Mathewson. Courtesy of Department of Library Services, American Museum of Natural History.

**Figure 10-58**

The properties of similar solids can be applied to pairs of animals that are approximately the same shape. Young dolphins and adult dolphins are approximately the same shape.

## **D** Lesson Exercise 10.80

What measurements of dolphins are length measurements?

## **D** Lesson Exercise 10.81

In Lesson Exercises 10.81–10.88, suppose that an adult dolphin is 3 times as long as a young dolphin of the same shape. Guess how many times stronger the adult dolphin would be.

According to biologist D'Arcy Thompson, "the strength of a muscle depends upon the size of a cross section (slice)" (Figure 10-59), just as the strength of a steel beam depends upon the cross section of the beam.

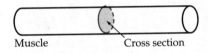

Muscle                 Cross section

**Figure 10-59**

The following exercise concerns the relationship between the strength of a cylindrical muscle and the area of its circular cross section.

## **D** Lesson Exercise 10.82

(a) What is the formula for the area of a circle?
(b) If the cross section of the young dolphin's muscle is circular, with a radius of 1 in., its area is _____ .
(c) The radius of the adult's corresponding muscle would be 3 in. Its area would be _____ .
(d) The adult has a muscle cross section that is _____ times larger in area than that of the young dolphin's, so the adult is _____ times stronger.

## **D** Lesson Exercise 10.83

The ratio of corresponding lengths in the young and adult dolphin is 1:3.
(a) The ratio of strengths is _____ .
(b) The ratio of strengths is the same as the ratio of
    (1) corresponding lengths     (2) surface areas     (3) volumes

Another characteristic of interest would be weight.

**D** Lesson Exercise 10.84

(a) Guess how many times heavier the adult dolphin in the preceding exercises is than the young dolphin.
(b) Would you guess that weight relationships are the same as length relationships, area relationships, or volume relationships?
(c) Would you like to revise your guess in part (a)? (last chance)

In fact, weight corresponds—is proportional—to volume. The following chart shows how a variety of characteristics relate to length, area, or volume.

---

**Classification of Measurements**

*Lengths*—sides, edges, perimeters, heights
*Areas*—surface area, amount of skin, strength
*Volumes*—weight

---

Now it is possible to deduce other facts about the two dolphins. Lesson Exercises 10.85–10.88 refer again to the young and adult dolphins.

**D** Lesson Exercise 10.85

How many times more skin surface does the adult have?

**D** Lesson Exercise 10.86

The adult's waist size is 27 guppy fins (dolphins don't use inches). What is the young dolphin's waist size?

Lesson Exercise 10.87

How many times more material would it take to make a rubber sweater (same thickness) for the adult than for the young dolphin?

Lesson Exercise 10.88

The young dolphin can pull a weight of 8 shells with its dorsal fin. The adult can pull a weight of _____ of the same shells with its dorsal fin.

That's enough of the dolphins. Try the following more general question, and then we'll get back to the giant animals that might visit your neighborhood.

## Lesson Exercise 10.89

In general, when an animal doubles the size of all of its length measurements, its weight becomes about _____ times as much.

## Strength Vs. Weight

Could a giant ape or insect from a horror film exist in real life? The following exercise will help you find out.

**D** ## Lesson Exercise 10.90

In a horror film, a cockroach eats radioactive brussels sprouts and grows 100 times longer in all of its length measurements!
(a)  How many times stronger would the cockroach legs be?
(b)  How many times heavier would the cockroach be?
(c)  Explain why the cockroach could not even stand on its legs, let alone walk around your kitchen.

As animals get larger, supporting their weight with their own legs becomes more difficult. Consequently, heavier animals such as hippos tend to have legs that are relatively thick compared to the rest of their body shape, and giant fictional apes such as King Kong would be unable to stand.

The tallest person on record was Robert Wadlow. He grew to a height of 8 ft 11 in. Unfortunately, his legs could not support his weight. He wore a leg brace to help support his weight, but his joints became diseased, and he died at the age of 22.

## Answers to Selected Lesson Exercises

**10.72** (a) 2 square units    (c) 18 square units
(d) 9

**10.73** (a) $30^2 + 40^2 = 50^2$ and $60^2 + 80^2 = 100^2$
(b) 600 ft² and 2400 ft²    (c) 4
(d) 120 ft and 240 ft    (e) 2
(f)  the second

**10.74** (a) 2:3    (c) 4:9    (e) 2:3

**10.75** (a) $m^2{:}n^2$    (b) $m{:}n$

**10.76**  16:1 and 4:1

**10.77** (a) 1:3    (b) 6 cm² and 54 cm²    (c) 1:9
(d) 1 cm³ and 27 cm³    (e) 1:27

**10.78** (a) 3:2    (b) 9:4    (d) 27:8

**10.79** (a) 1:16    (b) 1:64

**10.82** (b) $\pi$ in.²    (c) $9\pi$ in.²    (d) 9, 9

**10.83** (a) 1:9    (b) 2

**10.85** 9

**10.86** 9 guppy fins

**10.87** 9

**10.88** 72

**10.89** 8

**10.90** (a) 10,000    (b) 1,000,000
(c) Weight has increased 100 times more than strength.

## 10.6  Homework Exercises

### Basic Exercises

**1.** The two rectangles shown are similar.

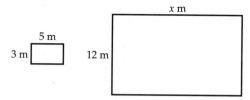

(a) Find $x$.

(b) The ratio of corresponding sides is
_____ : _____ .

(c) The ratio of the areas of the two rectangles is _____ .

(d) The ratio of the perimeters of the two rectangles is _____ .

**2.** The two triangles shown are similar.

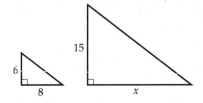

(a) Find $x$.

(b) The ratio of corresponding sides is
_____ .

(c) The ratio of the areas of the two triangles is _____ .

(d) The ratio of the perimeters of the two triangles is _____ .

**3.** A scale drawing of a stop sign and the actual stop sign have a ratio of corresponding sides of $m:n$.

(a) What is the ratio of their perimeters?

(b) What is the ratio of their areas?

**4.** At the Pizza Chalet, a small pizza has an 8-in. diameter, and a medium pizza has a 12-in. diameter.

(a) What is the ratio of their areas?

(b) What is the ratio of their perimeters?

(c) The medium pizza should cost about _____ times more than the small pizza.

**5.** In 1988, I went to Jerry's for pizza. The pizza with a 9-in. diameter was $3.49, the 12-in. pizza was $5.79, and the 16-in. pizza was $7.99.

(a) Which was the best buy?

(b) Which was the worst buy?

**6.** A television screen with a 20-in. diagonal is a rectangle that is about 12 in. by 16 in. A television screen with a 12-in. diagonal is a rectangle that is about 7.2 in. by 9.6 in. Which would be a better buy, a 20-in. color television for $380 or a 12-in. color television for $125?

**7.** Consider the two rectangular prisms shown.

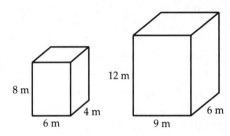

(a) What is the ratio of their corresponding edge lengths?

(b) The surface areas of the two figures are _____ and _____ .

(c) What is the ratio of their surface areas?

(d) How is the ratio of their surface areas related to the ratio of their corresponding edges?

(e) Compute the volume of each figure.

(f) What is the ratio of their volumes?

(g) How is the ratio of volumes related to the ratio of their edges?

8. Two similar solids have a ratio of corresponding heights of $x:y$.
   (a) What is the ratio of their surface areas?
   (b) What is the ratio of their volumes?

9. The earth has about 16 times the surface area of the moon.
   (a) What is the ratio of their circumferences?
   (b) What is the ratio of their volumes?

10. Two similar hexagons have corresponding heights of 3 m and 4 m. If the area of the smaller hexagon is 15 cm², what is the area of the larger hexagon?

11. Two similar cones have heights of 4 m and 7 m.
    (a) If the radius of the smaller cones is 2 m, what is the radius of the larger cone?
    (b) The surface area of the larger cone is _____ times larger than the surface area of the smaller one.
    (c) What is the ratio of the volume of the smaller cone to the volume of the larger cone?

12. Consider the following problem. "Two similar prisms have total surface areas of 100 cm² and 225 cm². If the smaller prism has a height of 10 cm, what is the height of the larger prism?" Devise a plan and solve the problem.

13. The ratio of strengths in similar solids is the same as the ratio of corresponding
    (a) lengths     (b) areas     (c) volumes

14. If a child grows so that all of her length measurements double, her new clothes will

require _____ times as much of the same material as the old ones.

15. A scale model of a car is built in the same shape using the same materials as the actual car, but it is only $\frac{1}{8}$ as long. How many times heavier is the actual car?

16. Suppose a giant existed who was the same shape as you, except that all of the giant's length measurements were triple yours.
    (a) The giant's waist size would be _____ times as big as yours.
    (b) The giant would be _____ times as strong as you are.
    (c) The giant would weigh _____ times as much as you do.

17. Two animals are similar in shape. One is 6 ft long; the other is 4 ft long.
    (a) How many times heavier is the larger animal?
    (b) How many times more skin surface does the larger animal have?

18. Two animals are similar in shape. One weighs 125 lbs; the other weighs 64 lbs.
    (a) How many times longer is the larger animal?
    (b) How many times stronger is the larger animal?
    (c) How many times heavier is the larger animal?
    (d) If the animals walk on their legs, which one will have an easier time walking?

19. In a scale model of a building, 1 ft represents 40 ft. The volume of the scale model is 18 ft³. What will the volume of the building be?

20. Explain why a giant cockroach could not exist.

21. In *Gulliver's Travels*, Gulliver visits the tiny Lilliputians. The Lilliputian emperor finds out that all of Gulliver's length measurements are about 12 times the corresponding measurements of an average Lilliputian. The emperor says that Gulliver will need to eat as

much food as 1728 Lilliputians! Explain the emperor's reasoning.

22. In another scene in *Gulliver's Travels* (see the previous exercise), the emperor wants to make a suit for Gulliver using the same fabric that the tiny Lilliputians wear. How many times more material would Gulliver need for a suit than your average Lilliputian?

23. Lilliputians (see the preceding exercises) are 6 inches tall. About how much would they weigh?

24. A regular can of Blando Ravioli is 12 cm tall and sells for $1.25. A large can is the same shape, 16 cm tall, and it sells for $2.
    (a) How many times more ravioli does the large can hold?
    (b) Which can is a better buy?

25. A child's bicycle might have a 20-in. wheel diameter, while an adult's bicycle might have a 26-in. wheel diameter. If the bicycles are similar and the child's bicycle costs $60, what would be a fair price for the adult's bicycle?

26. Similar triangles can be used to measure objects indirectly. Lyle wants to measure the height of a tree. He stands 20 yards from the tree and sights the top of the tree through a tube at an angle of 35°.

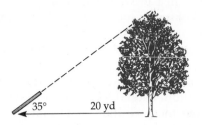

    (a) Using a ruler and protractor, make a scale drawing with 1 in. representing 5 yd.
    (b) Explain why the triangle in your scale drawing is similar to the triangle it represents.
    (c) About how tall is the tree?

*Extension Exercises*

27. Warm-blooded animals such as humans must maintain a reasonably constant body temperature. Animals must balance heat gained from eating (calories) with heat lost through their skin surface.
    (a) Heat gained from eating would be proportional to an animal's
        (1) length    (2) area    (3) volume
    (b) Heat lost through skin surface would be proportional to an animal's
        (1) length    (2) area    (3) volume

28.

Daddy                                    Baby

    (a) Baby and Daddy are similar in shape. Complete the chart.

|       | Length | Surface Area (where heat is lost) | Weight (how heat is gained) |
|-------|--------|-----------------------------------|-----------------------------|
| Baby  | 1 m    | 1 square unit                     | 1 cubic unit                |
| Daddy | 4 m    |                                   |                             |

    (b) Who has an easier time gaining heat relative to heat lost?
    (c) Who has a harder time staying cool?
    (d) As an animal grows larger, will it have more or less difficulty retaining heat?

29. A person eats about $\frac{1}{50}$ of his or her weight each day. Would a smaller animal such as a mouse need to eat a larger or smaller fraction of its body weight each day in order to stay warm enough?

**30.** A larger animal such as a hippopotamus or an elephant has more weight relative to surface area than a person. What problem does this create for these larger animals?

**31.** The following chart gives men's results from the 1989 U.S. Weightlifting Championships.

| Maximum Weight of Weightlifter (kg) | 60.0 | 67.5 | 75.0 | 82.5 | 90.0 |
|---|---|---|---|---|---|
| Snatch Event Weight Lifted (kg) | 102.5 | 120.0 | 132.5 | 145.0 | 150.0 |

Explain how this chart supports the ideas presented in this section about weight and strength.

*Computer Exercise*

**32.** Use an automatic drawer to investigate the relationship between the length of sides, perimeter, and area in similar triangles.

## Summary

Nearly every industrialized nation except the United States uses the metric system. Why? Because it is easier to work with. All metric conversions involve powers of 10, and the same prefixes are used for most metric measurements. In learning a new measurement system such as the metric system, it helps to begin by learning some reference measures for the units of measure.

Some carpentry, building, and consumer problems require finding length, area, or volume. Area is the measure of the surface of a solid or the space inside a polygon or circle. Volume is the measure of the capacity of solids. Area and volume can be measured, respectively, by counting squares or cubes, but formulas exist that simplify these computations for many common figures.

"Students should develop multiplicative procedures and formulas for determining measures. The curriculum should focus on the development of understanding, not on the rote memorization of formulas" (NCTM, *Standards*, p. 116). A number of area formulas are logically related. The parallelogram formula follows from the rectangle formula. The triangle and trapezoid formulas can be deduced from the parallelogram formula.

If you know the lengths of two sides of a right triangle, you can find the length of the third side using the Pythagorean Theorem. The Pythagorean Theorem is frequently applied to right triangles that appear in other figures.

There is one general volume formula and one general surface area formula for all prisms and cylinders. There is also one general volume formula for all pyramids and cones.

All corresponding area measurements of two similar figures are in an equal ratio; all corresponding volume measurements of two similar figures are also in an equal ratio. These ratios are helpful in explaining the relationship between weight and muscle strength and in explaining how well warm-blooded animals of various sizes retain heat.

## Study Guide

To review Chapter 10, see what you know about each of the following ideas or terms listed that you have studied. You can also use this list to generate your own questions about Chapter 10.

# The NCTM Curriculum Standards and Measurement

**Selected NCTM Curriculum Standards**

The following standards come from the NCTM document.

- Extend their understanding of the concepts of perimeter, area, and volume.
- Make and use estimates of measures.
- Make and use measurements in problem and everyday situations.
- Recognize and apply deductive and inductive reasoning.

1. Describe how each standard listed relates to the material you studied in Chapter 10.

2. Select any current elementary-school mathematics textbook series and describe a sample lesson or exercise that illustrates each standard listed.

## Review Exercises

1. On a hot summer day in Washington, D.C., the temperature is about
   (a) 5°C    (b) 35°C    (c) 65°C
   (d) 95°C    (e) 125°C

2. A rectangular prism is 8 m by 6 m by 7 m. How long is the diagonal shown?

3. 8 cm² = _____ m²

4. What is the surface area of the figure?

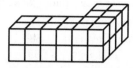

5. The room shown has an area of 58 m². What is the length across the back of the room?

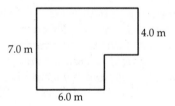

7.0 m    4.0 m    6.0 m

6. A store sells two kinds of wrapping paper. Package A costs \$5 and has 4 rolls, each 2 ft by 7 ft. Package B costs \$4 and has 3 rolls, each $3\frac{1}{2}$ ft by 4 ft. Which is a better buy?

7. A rectangular solid has dimensions of 4 m, 5 m, and $W$ m. Its total surface area is 166 m². What is $W$?

8. If the length, width, and height of a rectangular prism are each multiplied by 4, how does the surface area change?

9. Use the area formula for a parallelogram ($A = bh$) to explain why the area of the triangle shown is $A = \frac{1}{2}bh$.

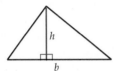

10. A triangular sail is measured as shown.

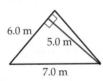

(a) What is the best approximation of its area?
(b) The exact area is between _____ and _____ .

11. Find the surface area of the triangular prism shown.

12. Find the shaded area.

13. The quarter circle has an area of $25\pi$ m². What is its perimeter?

14. Find the shaded area. $\overline{AB}$ is a diameter.

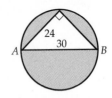

15. The circumference of a circle is 50 cm. What is its area?

16. A 9-in. pizza costs \$5, and a 14-in. pizza costs \$11. Which is a better buy?

17. A cylinder has a radius of 6 ft and a height of 12 ft. What is its surface area?

18. Two similar spheres have radii of 2 ft and 3 ft. What is the ratio of their surface areas?

19. Two similar solids have total surface areas of 400 m² and 900 m². The smaller solid has a volume of 200 m³. What is the volume of the larger solid?

20. Two animals of the same type are the same shape. The larger animal has a waist size of 20 cm; the smaller animal has a waist size of 8 cm.
(a) How many times heavier is the larger animal?
(b) If the larger animal can lift 40 lbs, how many pounds can the smaller animal lift?

## Measurement in Elementary School

The following chart shows at what grade level selected measurement topics typically appear in elementary-school mathematics textbooks.

| Topic | Typical Grade Level in Current Textbooks |
|---|---|
| Metric measure | 1, 2, 3, 4, 5, 6 |
| Perimeter | 2, 3, 4, 5, 6 |
| Rectangle area | 4, 5, 6 |
| Volume | 3, 4, 5, 6 |
| Surface area | 6 |
| Parallelogram area | 6 |
| Triangle area | 5, 6 |
| Circumference | 5, 6 |
| Circle area | 6 |

## Suggested Readings

Beckmann, P. *A History of Pi.* New York: St. Martin's Press, 1971.

Equals. *Get It Together.* Berkeley, CA: Equals, 1989.

Jacobs, H. *Geometry.* 2nd ed. New York: W. H. Freeman, 1987.

Loomis, E. *The Pythagorean Propositions.* Washington, DC: NCTM, 1972.

National Council of Teachers of Mathematics. 1976 Yearbook. *Measurement in School Mathematics.* Reston, VA: NCTM, 1976.

National Council of Teachers of Mathematics. 1987 Yearbook. *Learning and Teaching Geometry K–12.* Reston, VA: NCTM, 1987.

# 11

# Algebra and Coordinate Geometry

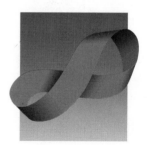

Two-dimensional graphs are widely used in mathematics and everyday life. These graphs show relations between two sets of variables.

Graphing combines ideas from geometry and algebra. Although the ancient Greeks had developed the major ideas of geometry by 300 B.C., algebra developed far more slowly.

Algebra without symbols originated in Babylonia about 4000 years ago. Algebra was done first with words and later with a combination of words and symbols. Around 250, Diophantus was the first to use letters for variables and exponents. It was not until the later 1500s that mathematicians such as Viete were able to solve fairly complicated algebraic equations.

The stage was then set for Descartes and Fermat to connect algebra and geometry using coordinate graphs. In coordinate geometry, algebraic equations are classified according to the shape of their graphs, and geometric shapes can be represented by equations. More recently, Emmy Noether (1882–1935), the greatest woman mathematician of her time, developed more advanced algebra that is now a fundamental part of graduate school mathematics.

In this chapter, you will use formulas, graphs, and tables to represent relations between variables and to solve problems. You will also see how graphs offer another way to study some geometric concepts.

## 11.1 Relations and Functions

How far would a 1993 Honda Civic travel on 10 gallons of gas? How much does it cost to mail a 1.2-oz first-class letter? Both questions involve two related quantities. The distance a car travels can be related to the number of gallons of gas used, and the cost of mailing a letter can be related to its weight. As the word "related" indicates, these are examples of two-set relations and functions, the subjects of this lesson.

### Representing Relations Between Two Sets

Relations between two quantities can be described in words.

627

**D** Lesson Exercise 11.1

Describe the general relationship between
(a) gallons used versus distance traveled in a car.
(b) the supply of apples versus the price of apples.

---

Numerical data can reveal a more precise relation between two sets. Consider a National Motors Garish that gets 36 miles per gallon. We can represent this relation with a table, an equation, or a graph (Figure 11-1). A **relation** pairs the members (for example, numbers) of two sets (or of a set and itself), usually according to some criteria.

| G (gallons of gas) | D (distance traveled–miles) |
|---|---|
| 0 | 0 |
| 1 | 36 |
| 2 | 72 |
| 3 | 108 |
| 4 | 144 |

$D = 36G$

Table          Equation          Graph

**Figure 11-1**

The graph is a ray because 0 is the lowest value for $D$ and $G$, and $G$ can represent any positive decimal number of gallons. When a relation involves countable sets such as the supply of apples, the graph is a **discrete** set of dots, as in Figure 11-2(a). When a relation involves a measurement such as distance or weight, the graph is a **continuous** segment or set of segments, as in Figure 11-2(b).

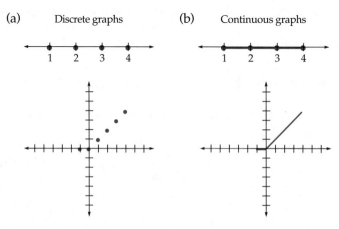

(a)    Discrete graphs          (b)    Continuous graphs

**Figure 11-2**

Three of the most important mathematical relations are "is less than," "is equal to," and "is greater than." The following exercise concerns "is less than."

## Lesson Exercise 11.2

Let the expression "is less than" relate $A = \{1, 2, 3\}$ to $B = \{1, 2, 3, 4\}$.
(a) Complete the table by listing all possible ordered pairs under the relation "is less than."

*A* **"Is Less Than"** *B*

| | |
|---|---|
| 1 | 2 |
| 1 | 3 |
| 1 | 4 |

(b) Graph the set of points from your table in part (a).

A relation can also be represented with an arrow diagram. An **arrow diagram** matches the corresponding elements of two sets with arrows. The arrow diagram for the selected values from the introductory gas mileage problem is shown in Figure 11-3.

The arrow between each pair of elements indicates the order of the two elements in an ordered pair. For example, 1 gallon → 36 miles would correspond to the ordered pair (1, 36).

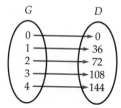

**Figure 11-3**

## Lesson Exercise 11.3

Make an arrow diagram from set $A$ to set $B$ for the relation in Lesson Exercise 11.2.

## Functions

The number of people who buy bananas at your store is a function of the price you charge. The cost of mailing a first-class letter is a function of its weight.

A function is a special kind of relation for which each value of the first variable (called the "input") is related to *exactly one* value of the second variable (called the "output"). Functions result from our observation and analysis of patterns.

Lejeune Dirichlet, a German mathematics professor, defined a function in 1837.

---

**Definition: A Function**

A **function** from set $A$ to set $B$ is a relation in which each member of $A$ is paired with exactly one member of $B$.

---

Whereas a relation may assign any number of outputs to an input, a function gives a single, definite output for each input. The introductory example is a function because each number of gallons $G$ is assigned exactly one distance in $D$. On the other hand, the relation in Lesson Exercise 11.3 is not a function because numbers such as 1 in set A are assigned to more than one number in set $B$. A function is often illustrated with a "function machine" (Figure 11-4).

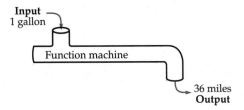

**Figure 11-4**

The set of input values is the **domain,** and the resulting set of output values is the **range.** In the introductory problem, 0, 1, 2, 3, and 4 are in the domain, and 0, 36, 72, 108, and 144 are in the range.

In a standard graph, the domain goes on the horizontal axis, the $x$-axis, and the range goes on the vertical axis, the $y$-axis. Usually, the equation is solved for the variable of the range. For example, it is easier to substitute $G$ and compute $D$ using $D = 36G$ than it would be using $G = \dfrac{D}{36}$.

## Lesson Exercise 11.4

A weight of $W$ (pounds) pulls a spring to a position $H$ (inches) above the ground according to $H = 4 - \dfrac{W}{5}$ (see Figure 11-5).

(a) What is the domain (input set)?     (b) What is the range (output set)?
(c) Explain why the graph exhibits a function from $W$ to $H$.

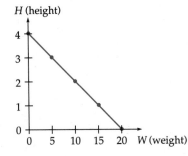

**Figure 11-5**

Not all rules relating two sets are functions.

### Example 11.1

Tell whether each of the diagrams in Figure 11-6 illustrates a function from set $A$ to set $B$.

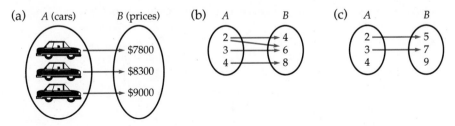

**Figure 11-6**

### Solution

A function must assign a single, definite output to each input. Note that an input or output set can contain objects (or people) as well as numbers.

(a) Is each element in set $A$, or "Cars," assigned exactly one element in set $B$, or "Prices?" Yes. So part (a) represents a function.

(b) No. The value 2 in set $A$ is assigned to two elements, 4 and 6, in set $B$. So part (b) does not represent a function.

(c) No. The value 4 in set $A$ is not assigned to any number in set $B$. So part (c) does not represent a function. ■

Now, it's your turn.

## Lesson Exercise 11.5

Which of the diagrams in Figure 11-7 illustrates a function from set $A$ to set $B$?

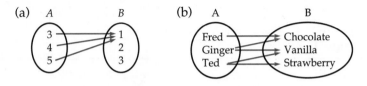

**Figure 11-7**

## Lesson Exercise 11.6

Explain why the relation "is less than" in Lesson Exercise 11.2 is not a function from set $A$ to set $B$.

## Graphs of Relations and Functions

Some graphs represent functions; others do not. In the graph of a function, there is exactly one corresponding value of $y$ for each possible value of $x$.

### Example 11.2

Tell whether each graph in Figure 11.8 represents a function.

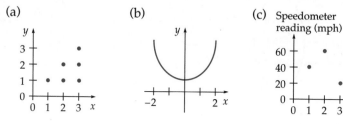

**Figure 11-8**

**Solution**

(a) No, because $x = 2$ is assigned to two $y$-values, and $x = 3$ is assigned to three $y$-values.

(b) Yes. Each $x$-value on $-2 \leq x \leq 2$ is assigned exactly one $y$-value.

(c) Yes. Each time value is assigned exactly one speedometer reading.  ■

## Lesson Exercise 11.7

State whether each graph in Figure 11-9 represents a function.

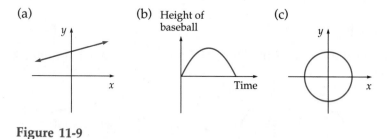

**Figure 11-9**

## Answers to Selected Lesson Exercises

11.1 (a) The distance traveled increases at a fairly uniform rate as the number of gallons used increases.

(b) The retail price of apples decreases as the supply of apples increases.

11.2 (a)

| A "Is Less Than" B | |
|---|---|
| 1 | 2 |
| 1 | 3 |
| 1 | 4 |
| 2 | 3 |
| 2 | 4 |
| 3 | 4 |

11.3

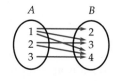

11.4 (a) $0 \leq W \leq 20$      (b) $0 \leq H \leq 4$
(c) Each value for $W$ is assigned exactly one value for $H$.

11.5 (a)

11.6 Some values in set $A$, such as 1, are assigned to more than one value in set $B$.

11.7 (a) yes      (b) yes      (c) no

## 11.1  Homework Exercises

*Basic Exercises*

1. Let "is greater than or equal to" relate $A = \{0, 1, 2, 3, 4\}$ to $B = \{0, 2, 4, 6\}$.
   (a) Complete a table of values or a set of ordered pairs.
   (b) Graph the set of points from part (a).

2. Let "is a factor of" relate $A = \{1, 2, 3, 4\}$ to $B = \{10, 15, 20\}$.
   (a) Complete a table of values or a set of ordered pairs.
   (b) Graph the set of points from part (a).

3. Make an arrow diagram of the data in Exercise 1.

4. (a) What set of ordered pairs corresponds to the following arrow diagram?

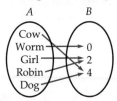

   (b) Describe a rule that relates the two sets.

5. A construction company charges $60,000 plus $65 per square foot to build a house. The total cost $C = 60,000 + 65F$, in which $F$ equals the floor space in square feet.
   (a) If the domain is $500 \leq F \leq 800$, graph the equation.
   (b) What is the range (output set)?
   (c) Explain why your graph exhibits a function from set $F$ to set $C$.

6. Your car gets 36 miles per gallon. You fill up the tank with 15 gallons and drive. The number of gallons, $g$, left after you drive $m$ miles is given by $g = 15 - \dfrac{m}{36}$.
   (a) If the domain is $0 \leq m \leq 540$, graph the equation.

(b) What is the range (output set)?

(c) Explain why your graph exhibits a function from set $m$ to set $g$.

7. (a) Tell which of the following diagrams represents a function from set $A$ to set $B$ and (b) give a possible rule relating the ordered pairs.

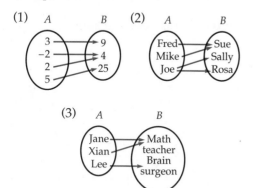

(3)   A           B

Jane ──→ Math
Xian ──→ teacher
Lee ──→ Brain
        surgeon

8. (a) Tell which of the following diagrams represents a function from set $A$ to set $B$ and (b) give a possible rule relating the ordered pairs.

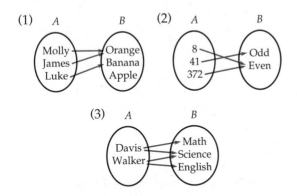

9. Explain why the relation "is greater than" from $A = \{10, 20, 30\}$ to $B = \{10, 20, 30\}$ is *not* a function from set $A$ to set $B$.

10. Is the relation $y$ "is the brother of" $x$ a function from set $x$ to set $y$ if the input set $x$ is all of the students in your mathematics class?

11. Which of the following are functions from $x$ to $y$? (Assume that the entire domain is given.)

(a) {(4,2)  (4,3)  (4,4)  (4,5)}
(b) {(1,7)  (2,8)  (3,9)  (4,10)}
(c) {(2,4)  (3,4)  (4,4)  (5,4)}

12. Tell whether each graph represents a function.

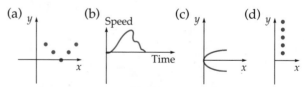

13. The "vertical-line test" is a method for determining whether a graph represents a function. A graph does not represent a function if a vertical line can be drawn through two or more points of the graph.

(a) Draw a vertical line in the graphs of the preceding exercise that are not functions.

(b) Explain why the vertical-line test works.

14. Propose a possible rule for each function shown.

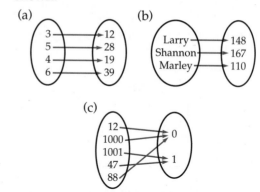

15. Propose a possible rule for each function shown.

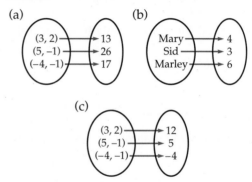

**16.** Give an equation relating $y$ to $x$ in each set of ordered pairs.
(a) {(5,24)  (6,35)  (7,48)}
(b) {(7,18)  (9,22)  (11,26)}

**17.** Consider the following function for the speed and the force of the crash impact of a particular car.

| Speed (in mph) | Force |
|---|---|
| 20 $\longrightarrow$ | 100 |
| 30 $\longrightarrow$ | 225 |
| 40 $\longrightarrow$ | 400 |
| 50 $\longrightarrow$ | 625 |
| 60 $\longrightarrow$ | _____ |

(a) When the speed doubles, the force is multiplied by _____ .
(b) Fill in the force for 60 mph that continues the pattern.
(c) Find a formula relating force to speed.
(d) What factors in addition to speed would affect the impact force of a car?
(e) What is a reasonable domain for this function?

**18.** A function has the rule $P = 8N - 50$. The range (output set) for $P$ is {46, 62, 78}. What is the domain (input set)?

**19.** Measuring creates a relation between two sets. Suppose a 30-cm ruler is used to measure lengths of people's feet. This would create a measuring function.
(a) What could be the domain of the function?
(b) What numbers might be in the range?

**20.** Does the following represent a function for the domain {0, 1, 2, . . . , 90}?

| X = Number of Students Signing Up for Math 130 | Y = Number of Sections of Math 130 |
|---|---|
| 0–7 | 0 |
| 8–32 | 1 |
| 33–62 | 2 |
| 63–90 | 3 |

*Extension Exercises*

(Use these directions for Exercises 21–23.) Often two variables fit one of the following two descriptions.

1. When one variable increases, the other would be expected to increase, as in time elapsed and distance traveled on a car trip.

2. When one variable increases, the other would be expected to decrease, as in price charged and the attendance at a movie theater for a Saturday night show.

**21.** Classify each of the following pairs of variables as type 1 or type 2.
(a) the number of allergy pills taken and the degree of drowsiness you feel
(b) the length of the side of a square and the area of a square
(c) the size of a car's gas tank and the number of stops needed on a long car trip

**22.** Classify each of the following pairs of variables as type 1 or 2.
(a) the winter temperature setting of a home thermostat in Detroit and the amount of heating oil used
(b) the number of people in a car pool and the cost per person of driving to work
(c) the speed of a car and the time it takes to travel 1 mile

**23.** (a) Make up a pair of variables that fits type 1.
(b) Make up a pair of variables that fits type 2.

**24.** Some relations are **transitive.** The relations "is equal to" and "is less than" are transitive, as illustrated by the following.

For real numbers $x$, $y$, and $z$; if $x = y$ and $y = z$, then $x = z$; and if $x < y$ and $y < z$, then $x < z$.

The relation "is a sibling of" is also transitive. If person $x$ is a sibling of person $y$ and person $y$ is a sibling of person $z$, then person $x$ is a sibling of person $z$.

Name two other relations that are transitive.

25. Which of the following represents a function if the domain is the set of all real numbers?
(a) $y = x^2 + 1$    (b) $y^2 = x^2 + 1$

26. $y = x + 2$ and $z = 3y$.
(a) Describe the rule (in words) that relates $x$ to $y$.
(b) Describe the rule (in words) that relates $y$ to $z$.
(c) Find a function that relates $z$ directly to $x$.
(d) Describe the rule (in words) that relates $z$ to $x$.

27. What real numbers *cannot* be used for $x$ in each of the following functions if $y$ must be a real number?

(a) $y = \dfrac{1}{x}$

(b) $y = \sqrt{x}$

(c) $y = \sqrt{25 - x}$

28. Assuming that the domain for $x$ is all real numbers, what is the range for $y$ in each equation?
(a) $y = x^2$    (b) $y = x^3$

29. What is the range for $y$ in each equation?
(a) $y = 8 - x^2$    (domain for $x$: all real numbers)
(b) $y = \dfrac{1}{x}$    (domain for $x$: all real numbers except 0)

30. $A = \{5, 10, 15, 20\}$ and $B = \{9, 18\}$. List the elements $(x, y)$ of $A \times B$ such that $x < y$.

## 11.2  Graphing Functions

The idea of using graphs to represent functions is about 350 years old. In the seventeenth century, René Descartes (1596–1650) and Pierre de Fermat (1601–1665), two Frenchmen (Figure 11-10), had the brilliant idea of using

Photo of Descartes (left) courtesy of Library of Congress. Photo of Fermat (right) from the David Eugene Smith Collection, Rare Book and Manuscript Library, Columbia University.

**Figure 11-10**

coordinates to relate algebraic equations (such as $y = 2x$) to geometric shapes (such as a line).

Descartes was a brilliant but sickly youngster who entered a prestigious private school at age 8. Owing to his ill health, his teachers allowed him to lie in bed in the morning for rest and reflection. Descartes continued this practice throughout his life and came up with many of his philosophical and mathematical ideas during his morning meditation.

Although he was one of the great mathematicians of his time, Fermat was a lawyer who did mathematics as a hobby! Fermat was not well known during his life because he did not try to publish his work. Fermat's achievements include founding the study of number theory, inventing (along with Descartes) coordinate geometry, and helping to lay the groundwork for both probability and calculus.

Today, people use coordinates to locate places and to portray relationships between quantities (Figure 11-11).

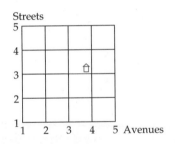

The house is on 4th
Avenue and 3rd Street.

**Figure 11-11**

### $y = mx$

Why are equations of the form $y = mx$ of interest? Many applications have formulas in which one variable equals another variable multiplied by a number ($y = mx$). Try the following exercise.

## Lesson Exercise 11.8

Whole-wheat flakes have 1.5 calories per gram.
(a) Complete the table.

| $g$ (number of grams) | 0 | 20 | 40 | 60 | 80 | |
|---|---|---|---|---|---|---|
| $c$ (number of calories) | | | | | | |

(b) Graph your points with $c$ on the vertical axis and $g$ on the horizontal axis.

(c) Would it be appropriate to connect your points to make a line segment, ray, or line?

(d) An equation relating $c$ and $g$ is $\dfrac{c}{g}$ = _____ or

$c$ = _____ .

___

The preceding exercise illustrates how points that satisfy $c = 1.5g$ all lie on a straight line. The graphs of $c = g$ (tomato catsup), $c = 2g$ (chicken breast), and $c = 3g$ (whole-wheat toast) are similar. Their graphs are shown in Figure 11-12. (You could plot these graphs using a graphing calculator.)

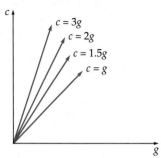

**Figure 11-12**

How are the graphs and equations alike and how do they differ? That's the subject of the following exercise.

## Lesson Exercise 11.9

(a) Are the graphs of $c = g$, $c = 1.5g$, $c = 2g$, and $c = 3g$ all the same shape?

(b) The graphs $c = g$, $c = 1.5g$, $c = 2g$, and $c = 3g$ all pass through the point _____ .

(c) In all four equations, $c = mg$, for a constant $m$. If $c = mg$, then

$\dfrac{c}{g}$ = _____ .

(d) In what way are the four graphs different?

___

For each equation in the calorie example, $\dfrac{c}{g}$ is always the same number.

This means that $c$ is proportional to $g$. For example, $\dfrac{c}{g} = \dfrac{3}{2}$ is a proportion for whole-wheat flakes.

The graphs of all four equations are rays passing through the origin. The calorie examples are rays rather than lines because $g$ and $c$ cannot be negative. If the negative numbers were included in the input set, all of these equations would have graphs that are lines.

The graphs of all equations of the form $y = mx$ (in which $m$ is any real constant) have the same shape! This is an example of the relationship between the shape of a coordinate graph and the form of the corresponding algebraic equation.

---

**Equations of the Form $y = mx$**

The graph of $y = mx$ for all real numbers $x$ and constant $m$ is a line through the origin (0, 0).

---

A line (or ray) through the origin has an equation in two variables in which one variable is proportional to the other. Examples would include total pay and hours worked when you earn $6 per hour, the number of dollars and the equivalent number of British pounds, and the length of a particular type of wire and its weight.

You have seen graphs relating calories and grams of a given food. Consider the example of total pay and hours worked.

## Lesson Exercise 11.10

You earn $6 per hour on a job. If you work a fraction of an hour, you earn that fraction of $6. Make a graph of total pay ($t$) versus hours worked ($h$).

## Slope

The four graphs in the calorie example are the same shape, but they differ in steepness. The graph of $c = 3g$ is the steepest, and the graph of $c = g$ is the flattest. The steepness of a graph is called its **slope**. When the value of $m$ in $y = mx$ changes, the slope of the graph changes.

Mathematicians use the slope to describe lines more precisely. Engineers must compute the slope of a road, a ramp, or a roof when they design it.

Imagine walking along a line from left to right (Figure 11-13). Lines rising from left to right (uphill) have a positive slope. Lines going down from left to right (downhill) have a negative slope. A horizontal line has a slope of 0. Figure 11-14 (page 640) shows some examples.

Figure 11-13

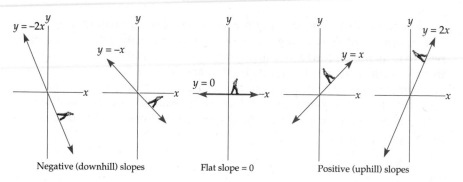

Figure 11-14

## Lesson Exercise 11.11

Classify the slope of each line in Figure 11-15 as one of the following.
(1) slope $< 0$     (2) slope $= 0$     (3) slope $> 0$

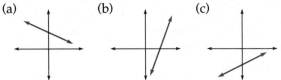

(a)                    (b)                    (c)

Figure 11-15

Since the slope of a line is the same everywhere, you can compute the slope from any two points on the line! For example, (1, 2) and (4, 8) are on the line $y = 2x$, as shown in Figure 11-16.

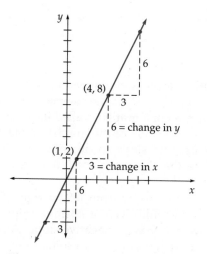

Figure 11-16

Traveling from (1, 2) to (4, 8) involves moving vertically (up 6 in this case) and horizontally (right 3 in this case) a certain distance. For lines with a positive slope, the line is steeper when the vertical change (6) is large relative to the horizontal change (3). For this reason, mathematicians define the slope as

$$\frac{\text{change in } y}{\text{change in } x}$$

or

$$\frac{\text{rise}}{\text{run}}$$

Dividing the vertical change by the horizontal change produces a larger result for steeper lines (with positive slope).

In this example, the slope is $\frac{6}{3} = 2$. Note that 2 is the value of $m$ in the equation in $y = 2x$! In the case of $c = 2g$, the slope 2 corresponds to the $\frac{\text{change in calories}}{\text{change in grams}}$, so it indicates that each change of 1 gram results in a change of 2 calories.

You can compute the slope of a line joining two points using the coordinates of the points.

## Lesson Exercise 11.12

(a) How can the slope of the line joining (1, 2) and (4, 8) be computed using the coordinates 1, 2, 4, and 8 (without making a drawing)?
(b) How can the slope of the line joining $(x_1, y_1)$ and $(x_2, y_2)$ be computed using the coordinates?

Lesson Exercise 11.12 concerns the following two-point slope formula.

---

**The Two-Point Slope Formula**

The slope of the line joining two points $(x_1, y_1)$ and $(x_2, y_2)$, in which $x_1 \neq x_2$, is

$$m = \frac{\text{change in } y}{\text{change in } x} = \frac{y_2 - y_1}{x_2 - x_1}$$

---

Use the slope formula in the following exercise.

## Lesson Exercise 11.13

(a) Points $(-1, -3)$ and $(1, 3)$ lie on the line $y = 3x$. Compute the slope of $y = 3x$ using these two points.
(b) Does the slope equal the value of $m$ in $y = 3x$?
(c) Find two points on $y = 4x$ and see if the slope equals $m$.
(d) Generalize the results of parts (b) and (c).

As you may have guessed from the preceding exercise, the slope of $y = mx$ is $m$. What does the slope tell in an application?

## Lesson Exercise 11.14

(a) In the formula $c = 1.5g$ (for whole-wheat flakes), what is the slope?
(b) What does the slope tell about whole-wheat flakes?

Not all lines have a defined slope. Consider the following exercise.

## Lesson Exercise 11.15

(a) Why can't $x_1 = x_2$ in the two-point slope formula?
(b) Graph $(2, 3)$ and $(2, 4)$. What kind of line passes through these points?

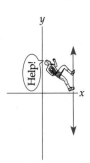

**Figure 11-17**

When $x_1 = x_2$, the line passing through the two points will be vertical. Imagine trying to walk up a vertical line (Figure 11-17)!

Vertical lines have an undefined (infinite) slope, corresponding to the fact that $x_1 = x_2$ makes the two-point slope formula come out undefined.

## $y = mx + b$

A rental car costs $89 per week plus $.26 per mile. The cost $C$ for a week's rental is $C = 0.26D + 89$, in which $D$ is the distance driven in miles. This equation has the form $y = mx + b$.

You have seen that an equation of the form $y = mx$ represents a line (or part of a line) with slope $m$ passing through the origin and that $y$ is proportional to $x$. What happens when you add a constant $b$ to the equation so that it has the form $y = mx + b$?

## Lesson Exercise 11.16

(a) Graph $y = 2x$. (This exercise can be done with a graphing calculator.)

(b) On the same graph, plot four points that are solutions of $y = 2x + 2$ and connect them.

(c) On the same graph, plot four points that are solutions of $y = 2x - 2$ and connect them.

(d) What is the same about all three of the graphs?

(e) What is the relationship between the three equations you graphed?

As the preceding exercise suggests, lines $y = mx + b$ with the same value of $m$ have the same slope and are parallel. The graphs of $y = 3x$, $y = 3x + 2$, and $y = 3x - 2$ are shown in Figure 11-18.

The graph of $y = 3x + 2$ is the same as the graph of $y = 3x$ translated up two units. The graph of $y = 3x - 2$ is the same as the graph of $y = 3x$ translated down 2 units. This pattern suggests the following two properties.

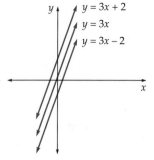

**Figure 11-18**

---

**Slopes of Parallel Lines**

Lines that have the same slope are parallel.

---

**The Relationship Between $y = mx$ and $y = mx + b$**

The graph of $y = mx + b$ is the same as the graph of $y = mx$ translated $b$ units vertically.

---

Use the relationship between $y = mx$ and $y = mx + b$ to answer the following.

## Lesson Exercise 11.17

The graph of $y = 5x - 3$ is the same as the graph of $y = 5x$ translated

_____ .

How can you tell where a line will cross the $y$-axis? The following exercise addresses this question.

## Lesson Exercise 11.18

(a) A point on the $y$-axis has an $x$-coordinate of _____ .
(b) Give the coordinates of the point where $y = mx + b$ crosses the $y$-axis.

The preceding exercise shows that $b$ in $y = mx + b$ tells the $y$-coordinate of the point $(0, b)$ where the line crosses the $y$-axis. This point is called the **$y$-intercept**.

---

**The Slope-Intercept Form of a Line**

The graph of $y = mx + b$ is a line that has slope $m$ and a $y$-intercept $(0, b)$.

---

Some applications have a relationship of the form $y = mx + b$.

## Lesson Exercise 11.19

A car has a ground clearance of 40 cm when it carries no weight. Every 10 kg of weight decreases the ground clearance by 1 cm.
(a) Complete the table.

| $w$ (added weight in kg) | 0 | 10 | 20 | 30 |
|---|---|---|---|---|
| $g$ (ground clearance in cm) | 40 | | | |

(b) A formula relating $w$ and $g$ is $g = 40 -$ _____ .
(c) Find the slope and $g$-intercept of your formula.
(d) What does the slope tell you about the relationship between ground clearance and added weight?
(e) Graph your equation from part (b).

## Is It the Equation for a Line?

The graph of a function $y = mx + b$ is a line. What about other functions such as $y = \sqrt{x}$ and $y = x^2$?

## Lesson Exercise 11.20

(a) Graph $y = x^2$ for $x = -2, -1, 0, 1,$ and 2. Is it a linear equation?
(b) Graph $y = \sqrt{x}$ for $x = 0, 1, 4,$ and 9. Is it a linear equation?

Why must the equation of a line have the form $y = mx + b$?

## Lesson Exercise 11.21

Consider a line through $(x_1, y_1)$ with slope $m$.

(a) Using the slope formula, any other point $(x, y)$ on the line must satisfy $m =$ _____ .

(b) Solve the equation in part (a) for $y$.

In the preceding exercise, $y = mx - mx_1 + y_1$ has the form $y = mx + b$ with $b = -mx_1 + y_1$. Equations such as $y = x^2$ and $y = \sqrt{x}$ that cannot be put into the form $y = mx + b$ do not have straight-line graphs. (*Note: $x = a$ is the equation of a vertical line.*)

---

**A Test for the Equation of a Line**

A function has a straight-line graph if it can be put in the form $y = mx + b$.

---

## Lesson Exercise 11.22

Which of the following have straight-line graphs?

(a) $y = -2x + 7$      (b) $h = -16t^2$      (c) $2R + 4S = 20$

## Parabolas

All equations of the form $y = mx + b$ have a straight-line graph. What happens if $x$ is squared, as in the equation $y = x^2$? Your graph in Lesson Exercise 11.20 suggests the general shape shown in Figure 11-19.

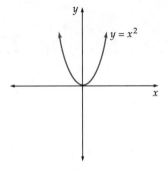

**Figure 11-19**

## Lesson Exercise 11.23

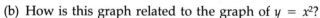

(a) Graph $y = x^2 - 2$ after completing the following table or use a graphing calculator.

| $x$ | $-2$ | $-1$ | $0$ | $1$ | $2$ |
|---|---|---|---|---|---|
| $y$ | | | | | |

(b) How is this graph related to the graph of $y = x^2$?
(c) Figure 11-20 shows a graph of $y = x^2 + 4$. Use the graphs in this problem to write a generalization about the relationship between the graph of $y = x^2$ and the graph of $y = x^2 + c$.

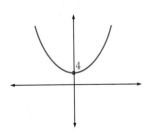

**Figure 11-20**

The preceding exercise illustrates how $y = x^2 + c$ is the same as $y = x^2$ translated $c$ units vertically. The preceding graphs $y = x^2$, $y = x^2 - 2$, and $y = x^2 + 4$ are all the same shape: a parabola.

A **parabola** is a special type of U-shaped curve. The equation of a parabola always has one variable squared and one variable to the first power.

Parabolas describe the path of a ball when it is thrown and the shape of the cable on some suspension bridges (Figure 11-21).

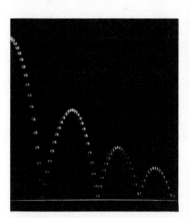 

Photo of bouncing ball from *PSCC Physics*, 2d ed., 1965; © Education Development Center, Inc., and D. C. Heath & Co. Photo of Golden Gate Bridge Courtesy of Library of Congress.

**Figure 11-21**

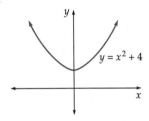

**Figure 11-22**

Parabolas with the form $y = x^2 + c$ (such as $y = x^2$, $y = x^2 - 4$, and $y = x^2 + 2$) all open up and change direction at $x = 0$ (Figure 11-22). What happens with parabolas of the form $y = -x^2 + c$?

## Lesson Exercise 11.24

(a) Graph $y = -x^2$ for $x = -3, -2, -1, 0, 1, 2, 3$. (You may use a graphing calculator.)

(b) How is $y = -x^2$ related to $y = x^2$?

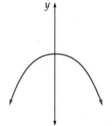

**Figure 11-23**

Parabolas of the form $y = -x^2 + c$ open down and change direction at $x = 0$ (Figure 11-23).

What kind of applications are modeled by parabolas?

## Lesson Exercise 11.25

(a) What is a formula relating the area $A$ of a square to the length $L$ of a side?

(b) Which graph in Figure 11-24 illustrates this relationship with length on the horizontal axis?

(1)    (2)    (3)    (4)

**Figure 11-24**

One of the amazing discoveries of coordinate geometry was that equations of the same form generally have graphs of the same shape. This discovery reveals a fundamental connection between algebra and geometry.

## Answers to Selected Lesson Exercises

**11.8**  (c) ray    (d) $\dfrac{c}{g} = 1.5$ or $c = 1.5g$

**11.9**  (a) yes    (b) (0,0)    (c) $m$

**11.10**

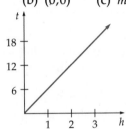

**11.11** (a) (1)      (b) (3)      (c) (3)

**11.13** (a) 3      (b) yes

**11.15** (a) It would make the fraction undefined.
(b) vertical

**11.16** (d) their slope
(e) Their graphs are parallel lines.

**11.17** 3 units down

**11.18** (a) 0      (b) (0, $b$)

**11.19 (b)** $g = 40 - \dfrac{w}{10}$

    **(c)** slope $= \dfrac{-1}{10}$, $g$-intercept is $(0, 40)$

    **(d)** The ground clearance decreases by
        1 cm each time the weight increases by
        10 kg.

**11.20 (a)** no    **(b)** no

**11.21 (a)** $m = \dfrac{y - y_1}{x - x_1}$

    **(b)** $y = mx - mx_1 + y_1$

**11.22 (a)** and **(c)**

**11.23 (b)** the same graph translated down 2
        units

**11.24 (b)** The graph of $y = -x^2$ is the reflection
        of $y = x^2$ through the $x$-axis.

**11.25 (a)** $A = L^2$    **(b)** 3

## 11.2   Homework Exercises

### Basic Exercises

**1.** A marathon runner runs 12 km/hr. So
$d = 12t$, for distance $d$ (in kilometers) and
time $t$ (in hours).
  **(a)** Why must $t \geq 0$?
  **(b)** Why must $d \geq 0$?
  **(c)** Graph $d = 12t$. Put $t$ values on the hori-
      zontal axis and $d$ values on the vertical
      axis.
  **(d)** What shape is the graph?
  **(e)** Is this formula exact or approximate?

**2.** A pump fills up an empty swimming pool at
the rate of 4 m³/min.
  **(a)** Write a formula relating time elapsed $T$
      (in minutes) to the volume of water $V$ (in
      cubic meters) in the swimming pool.
  **(b)** Graph $V$ vs. $T$.

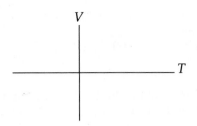

  **(c)** What shape is your graph?

**3.** A store estimates that the daily revenue (in
dollars) $R = 4C$, in which $C$ is the number of
customers that day.
  **(a)** Describe in words what the formula says
      about customers and revenue.
  **(b)** Show why $R$ is proportional to $C$.

**4.** What do the graphs of equations of the form
$y = mx$ have in common?

**5.** Classify the slope of each line as
  **(1)** slope $< 0$    **(2)** slope $= 0$
  **(3)** slope $> 0$

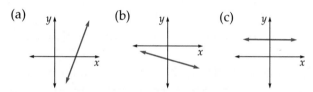

**6.** Which would be steeper, a line in which a
change in $x$ of $-3$ results in a change in $y$ of
6, or a line in which a change in $x$ of $-3$ results in a change in $y$ of 3?

**7.** Give the slope of each line.

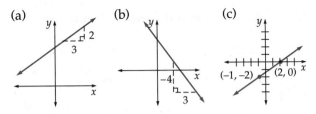

**8.** If a line goes down from left to right, what
do you know about the slope?

**9.** A building entrance is 3 ft above ground
level. A wheelchair ramp with slope $\dfrac{1}{12}$
would have to be how long to go from the
ground to the entrance?

10. A highway grade of 3% means that the highway rises 0.03 miles for every 1 mile of horizontal distance. How much does a highway with a 4% grade rise in 2 miles?

11. (a) Plot $A(2, 3)$, $B(4, 3)$, and $C(5, 6)$.
    (b) Find the coordinates of $D$ so that $ABCD$ is a parallelogram.
    (c) Find the slope of $\overline{BC}$ and $\overline{AD}$.

12. (a) In computing the slope, would $\dfrac{y_2 - y_1}{x_2 - x_1}$
    and $\dfrac{y_1 - y_2}{x_1 - x_2}$ come out the same?
    (b) Explain the significance of your answer to part (a).

13. What one type of line does not represent a function?

14. The graph of $y = 4x + 5$ is the same as the graph of $y = 4x$ translated _____.

15. What is the relationship between the graphs of $y = 5x + 2$ and $y = 5x + 6$?

16. (a) Graph $y = 2x$.
    (b) Draw the image of $y = 2x$ after a translation 3 units to the right.
    (c) What is the equation of the image line?

17. How could you show that the two line segments on the square lattice are parallel?

18. Without graphing, tell whether $y = 3x - 2$ and $y = x - 2$ represent parallel lines.

19. (a) Draw the graph of $y = x + 1$. (You may use a graphing calculator for this exercise.)
    (b) Graph $y = 2x + 1$ on the same graph.
    (c) Graph $y = 3x + 1$ on the same graph.
    (d) What is the same about the three graphs?
    (e) Which graph is the steepest?

20. Find the slope and $y$-intercept of
    (a) $y = 2x - 5$.     (b) $5x + 2y = 10$.

21. What is the equation of the line?

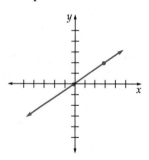

22. What is the equation of the line?

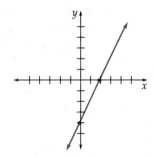

23. A line passes through $(0, 5)$ and $(4, -3)$. What is its equation?

24. (a) Name a point on the graph of $2x - y = 8$.
    (b) Is $(2, -4)$ on the graph of $2x - y = 8$?
    (c) How many different pairs of solutions does the equation $2x - y = 8$ have if $x$ and $y$ can be any real numbers?

25. Without graphing, tell whether each set of points would lie on a straight line.

(a)
| $x$ | 1 | 2 | 3 | 4 |
|---|---|---|---|---|
| $y$ | 5 | 7 | 9 | 11 |

(b)
| $x$ | 1 | 2 | 3 | 4 |
|---|---|---|---|---|
| $y$ | 1 | 2 | 4 | 7 |

(c)
| $x$ | 1 | 2 | 3 | 4 |
|---|---|---|---|---|
| $y$ | 11 | 8 | 5 | 2 |

26. Suppose that you want to cook a hot meal on a camping trip. The higher up you go, the easier it is to boil water. At sea level, the boiling point of water is 212°F. For every

additional 500 ft above sea level, the boiling point decreases by 1°.

(a) Complete the table.

| B (boiling point in degrees F) | 212 | 211 | | |
|---|---|---|---|---|
| A (altitude in feet) | 0 | 500 | 1000 | 1500 |

(b) A formula relating B and A is
$$B = 212 - \underline{\hspace{3cm}}.$$

(c) Graph your equation from part (b).

27. You can time the interval between the lightning flash and the accompanying thunder to estimate how far it is from you. Every 5 seconds in the interval indicates an additional distance of about 1 mile.

(a) A formula relating distance $D$ (in miles) to time $T$ (in seconds) is
$$D = \underline{\hspace{3cm}}.$$

(b) Graph your formula.

(c) What does the slope tell you about the relationship between distance and time?

(d) The formula is based upon the difference between the speed of light (lightning) and the speed of sound (thunder) in reaching us. The speed of light is 186,000 miles per second, and the speed of sound is 0.2 miles per second. Explain how the formula $D = \dfrac{T}{5}$ was obtained.

28. In scuba diving, the water pressure increases as a diver descends. For each additional 20 ft of depth, the pressure increases another 9 pounds per square inch (psi).

(a) Assuming that water pressure $P$ equals 0 at the water surface, a formula relating $P$ to depth, $D$, is $P = \underline{\hspace{2cm}}.$

(b) Graph your formula.

(c) What does the slope tell you about the relationship between water pressure and depth?

(d) Suppose that you do not want to exceed 25 psi added pressure. Use your graph to estimate how deep you could go.

29. (a) Plot $W(1, 4)$, $E(3, 6)$, and $T(6, 9)$.

(b) Find two more points on the same line as $W$, $E$, and $T$.

(c) What pattern do you see in the coordinates of the five points?

(d) What equation relates $y$ to $x$?

30. Which of the following have straight-line graphs?
(a) $x^2 + y^2 = 9$     (b) $y = 4x^2 + 2$
(c) $5x - 2y = 13$

31. (a) Graph $y = x^2 + 1$. Use $x = -3, -2, -1, 0, 1, 2,$ and 3.

(b) Write three ordered pairs that are solutions to $y = x^2 + 1$.

(c) For what values of $x$, $-3 \leq x \leq 3$, is it true that as $x$ increases, $y$ increases?

(d) Use your graph to estimate $x$ when $y = 7$.

32. How is the graph of $y = x^2 + 3$ related to the graph of $y = x^2$?

33. How is the graph of $y = x^2 + 5$ related to the graph of $y = x^2 + 1$?

34. How is the graph of $y = -x^2 - 1$ related to the graph of $y = x^2 + 1$?

35. When you drop a heavy object, its speed increases at every instant until it hits the ground. Which of the following graphs would show the correct relationship between $h$, the height above the ground and $t$, the time elapsed since you dropped the object?

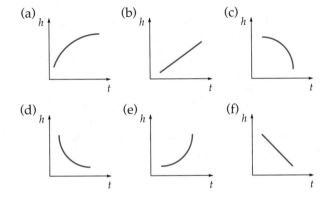

**36.** The graph of the price, *p*, of a television versus the length of its screen diagonal, *d*, is approximately a parabola. Which graph would be correct?

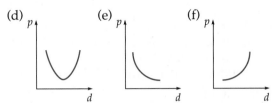

(a) (b) (c)

(d) (e) (f)

**37.** A ball is dropped from a height of 64 ft. Its height *H* (in feet) at time *T* (in seconds) is $H = 64 - 16T^2$.
(a) Graph this equation for *T* = 0, 0.5, 1, 1.5, and 2.
(b) What shape does the graph appear to be?
(c) Why would it be wrong to use *T* = 3 in this equation?

**38.** Revenue, *R*, from ticket sales for a concert depends upon the price, *P*, that you charge, according to $R = -60P^2 + 840P$.
(a) What values of *P* should be excluded?
(b) Graph this equation.

**39.** (a) Plot the points *M*(4, 8), *A*(−2, 8), *R*(4, 2), and *K*(−2, 2). Connect *M* to *A*, *A* to *R*, *R* to *K*, and *K* to *M*.
(b) What shape results?
(c) Plot *MARK* on axes like the one shown here. How is it different?

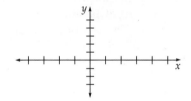

**40.** Use a trapezoid to estimate the shaded area.

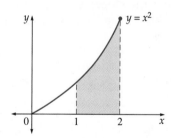

**41.** (a) Graph $y = x^3$. (You may use a graphing calculator for this exercise.)
(b) Guess what the graph of $y = x^3 + 2$ will look like.
(c) Graph $y = x^3 + 2$ and check your guess.

**42.** (a) Plot *M*(0, 0), *A*(3, 0), and *N*(3, 2) and connect *M* to *A*, *A* to *N*, and *N* to *M*.
(b) What shape do you obtain?
(c) Add 3 to the *y*-coordinates of points *M*, *A*, and *N* to obtain coordinates, respectively, for *S*, *K*, and *Y*.
S = (    ,    )   K = (    ,    )
Y = (    ,    )
(d) Plot *S*, *K*, and *Y* and connect *S* to *K*, *K* to *Y*, and *Y* to *S*. What shape do you obtain?
(e) What motion would map △MAN to △SKY?
(f) How does △MAN compare to △SKY?

*Extension Exercises*

**43.**

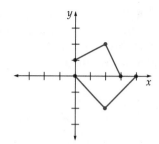

(a) Find the slopes of each pair of perpendicular lines.
(b) Make a conjecture about the relationship between the slopes of perpendicular lines.

**44.** Use the properties of similar triangles to show that the slopes $m_1$ and $m_2$ of perpendicular lines $L_1$ and $L_2$, respectively, satisfy $m_1 m_2 = -1$.

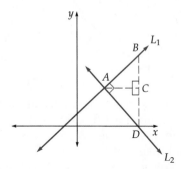

**45.** Motion geometry can also be used to show why two perpendicular lines (which are not horizontal and vertical) have slopes with a product of $-1$. In Figure 11-25, the legs of $\triangle T$ show the slope of $p$. Answer parts (a) and (b) to see why the slope of lines $p$ and $q$ have a product of $-1$.

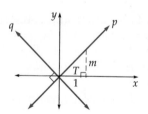

**Figure 11-25**

(a) What is the slope of line $p$?
(b) Rotate line $x$ and $\triangle T$ counterclockwise 90°. Label the image of $\triangle T$ as $\triangle T'$. What is the slope of line $q$?

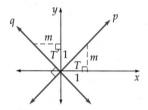

**46.** Use the result of the preceding exercise to explain why the two segments on the square lattice shown form a right angle.

**47.** Use slope properties to determine if $ABCD$ is a rectangle for $A(0, 0)$ $B(3, 6)$, $C(8, 3)$ and $D(5, -3)$.

**48.** (a) Graph $y = 2x$.
(b) Draw the image of $y = 2x$ after a reflection through the $y$-axis.
(c) What is the equation of the image line?

**49.** (a) Graph $y = 3x - 2$.
(b) Draw the image of $y = 3x - 2$ after a reflection through the $y$-axis.
(c) What is the equation of the image line?

**50.** (a) Graph $y = 2x$.
(b) Draw the image of $y = 2x$ after a 90° clockwise rotation around $(0, 0)$.
(c) What is the equation of the image line?

**51.** Use a graphing calculator (or graphing software) to investigate the relationship between the graphs of $y = mx + b$ and $y = -mx - b$ by graphing pairs of equations such as $y = 2x + 3$ and $y = -2x - 3$.

**52.** (a) Use a graphing calculator (or graphing software) to graph $y = \dfrac{1}{x}$.
(b) Investigate the significance of a real number, $a$, in the graph of $y = \dfrac{1}{x - a}$.

*Computer Exercises*

**53.** The Logo command SETX 50 moves the turtle from its current position to horizontal coordinate 50. The $y$-coordinate does not change. There is a similar SETY command.

(a) Start with the turtle at HOME. Enter the following.

SETX 30

SETY 20

SETX 0

SETY 0

What is the result?

(b) Write a procedure using SETX and SETY to draw a rectangle with vertices (−20, 50), (−20, 10), (10, 50), and (10, 10).

54. Investigate the SETXY (IBM Logo) or SETPOS (Apple Logo) command that accepts X- and Y-coordinates as in SETXY 10 20 or SETPOS [10, 20].

## 11.3 Words, Algebra, Tables, and Graphs

Mathematicians communicate using words, equations, tables, and graphs. Each format offers a different way of describing a relation. This lesson makes use of these formats and shows how to change from one to another.

### Translating Words into Algebra

In applying mathematics to everyday situations, one may translate words into algebra. Algebra offers a precise way to communicate information about quantities. Some people enjoy the precision and logic of algebra. But not everyone has this reaction (Figure 11-26).

Reprinted by permission of UFS, Inc.

**Figure 11-26**

Algebra serves as a mathematical language. It is more concise, more abstract, and less ambiguous than English. Algebra is also limited; it can only describe relationships between quantities. I couldn't say $H = M + 5$, in which $H$ = Horace and $M$ = Mitzie. You'd say, "Now hold on, pal! Horace and Mitzie are more than just numbers." And you'd be right.

So how and when do mathematicians translate words into algebra? First, consider English phrases. Some English phrases can be translated into algebraic expressions using two steps.

**Step 1**   Select variables for unknown quantities.

**Step 2**   Write an expression or equation using the variable(s).

### Example 11.3

Translate "five years older than Mitzie" into algebra.

**Solution**

1. Mitzie's age is the unknown quantity. So let $M$ = Mitzie's age in years.

2. Then, "five years older than Mitzie" would be $M + 5$.

So, the answer is: Let $M$ = Mitzie's age

$$M + 5$$

### Example 11.4

Translate "smarter than a literate termite" into algebra.

**Solution**

This phrase does not involve relationships between *quantities*, so it cannot be translated into algebra.   ■

See whether you can translate the following English phrases into algebraic expressions.

## Lesson Exercise 11.26

Translate "25% of the recommended daily allowance of iron" into algebra.

## Lesson Exercise 11.27

Translate "a shower of commanded tears" into algebra.

You have seen how some English *phrases* translate into algebraic **expressions** (an arithmetic operation or operations involving variables and numbers). What does an English sentence look like after being translated into algebra?

### Example 11.5

Translate the following into an algebraic sentence. "The total cost of the repair is $80 for parts plus $30 per hour for labor."

**Solution**

The unknowns are total cost and hours of labor. Let $C$ = total cost and $H$ = hours of labor. Then translate the sentence. The phrase "the total cost of the repair is" translates to "$C =$", and this equals "$80 plus $30 per hour of labor."

If you are not sure how to compute the cost from the number of hours, try it with a number such as 10 hours and see what you would do. To compute the cost of 10 hours, you would multiply 30 by 10 and add 80. To compute the total cost, you would multiply 30 by the number of labor hours ($H$) and add 80.

$$C = 30H + 80$$                            ■

**Example 11.6**

Translate the following into an algebraic sentence. "Sally's income is at least twice as much as Bill's income."

**Solution**

Let $S$ = Sally's income and $B$ = Bill's income. The phrase "at least" would translate to "$\geq$."

$$S \geq 2B$$                               ■

The preceding examples illustrate the ways in which English sentences that describe quantities correspond to equations or inequalities. If possible, translate the English sentences in Lesson Exercises 11.28 and 11.29 into equations or inequalities.

## Lesson Exercise 11.28

Translate the following into an equation or inequality: "Monthly local phone service costs $5 plus $.08 for each call."

## Lesson Exercise 11.29

Translate the following into an equation or inequality: "The sum of the money spent by the U.S. government on transportation and environmental protection in fiscal year 1992 was less than $\frac{1}{6}$ the amount spent on national defense."

One important reason for translating English into algebra is to obtain concise descriptions of rules and properties. For example, instead of saying, "We can add two real numbers in either order and obtain the same sum," we could write "$x + y = y + x$ for real numbers $x$ and $y$."

## Lesson Exercise 11.30

Translate the following into an algebraic equation: "When two rational numbers are multiplied, the result is the product of the numerators divided by the product of the denominators."

A second important reason for translating English into algebra is to obtain a formula. A formula can be obtained by translating an English-language description into an algebraic formula, or by determining how the quantities in a problem are related mathematically, as in the following example.

### Example 11.7

A gas station sells regular unleaded gas for $.96 per gallon and premium unleaded gas for $1.10 per gallon. Write a formula relating total sales to the amount of each type of gas sold.

**Solution**

Let $S$ = total sales in dollars, $R$ = gallons of regular unleaded gas sold, and $P$ = gallons of premium sold. How does one compute $S$ in this problem? By multiplying $R$ by 0.96 and P by 1.10 and then adding the results together. In symbols,

$$S = 0.96R + 1.10P$$

## Lesson Exercise 11.31

A job pays $100 per week plus 5 percent of sales. Write a formula relating total weekly salary to sales.

An algebraic equation or inequality focuses upon some quantifiable aspect of a situation. In Example 11.6, the inequality does not tell us what Bill and Sally do, whether they enjoy their jobs, or whether their work is beneficial to society.

## D Lesson Exercise 11.32

What are some questions that the equation in Lesson Exercise 11.31 does not answer about the quantities involved?

## Translating Algebra into Words

You have practiced translating words into algebra. Now try translating algebra into words (Figure 11-27).

**Figure 11-27**

### Example 11.8

Translate the following expression into English: "$H = 0.2R$, in which $H$ = cost of heat in dollars and $R$ = rent in dollars."

**Solution**

An equal sign can be translated as "is." So, the heat is 0.2 times the rent. Or, in more common English, the heat costs $\frac{2}{10}$ or 20% of the rent.  ■

Try the following yourself.

## Lesson Exercise 11.33

Translate the following equation into an English sentence: $T = 0.15B$, in which $T$ = the tip in dollars and $B$ = the bill in dollars.

## Translating Graphs into Words

Like equations and inequalities, a graph displays a relationship that can also be written in words.

## Lesson Exercise 11.34

Figure 11-28 shows a graph of the progress of a runner.

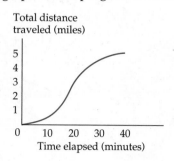

**Figure 11-28**

Which of the following describes the run?
(a) She started slowly and went faster and faster.
(b) She started fast, slowed down, and sped up again.
(c) She started slowly, sped up, and slowed down again.
(d) She started slowly and sped up at the end.

In the next exercise, see whether you can interpret the graph in words.

## Lesson Exercise 11.35

Figure 11-29 shows a graph of a journey by car.

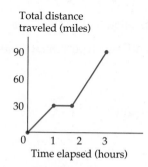

**Figure 11-29**

(a) When might the driver have stopped to rest?
(b) When was the car traveling the fastest?
(c) Describe the progress of the car during the journey.

## Translating Tables and Graphs into Equations

You have probably solved a lot of algebraic equations in your time. Where do such equations come from? Sometimes a formula (equation) can be derived from a table or graph.

Photo courtesy of NASA.

**Figure 11-30**

How much would you weigh on the moon (Figure 11-30)? In order to answer this question, you need a formula. The following data relate people's weights on the earth and the moon.

| Weight on the Earth | 100 lb | 150 | 200 |
|---|---|---|---|
| Weight on the Moon | 16 lb | 24 | 32 |

 Lesson Exercise 11.36

(a) If $E$ = earth weight and $M$ = moon weight, then a formula relating $E$ to $M$ is $M$ = _____ .
(b) Did you use induction or deduction to find the formula?
(c) The author of this book weighs 138 pounds. How much would he weigh on the moon? Would you like to send him there?

You can sometimes translate a graph into an equation. The shape of the graph (for example, a line or parabola) may suggest the appropriate form of the equation. If the graph is a linear function, the equation will have the form $y = mx + b$, and if it is a parabolic function, try the form $y = ax^2 + c$.

## Lesson Exercise 11.37

Write an equation for the graph in Figure 11-31.

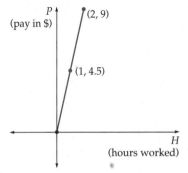

**Figure 11-31**

**D** Lesson Exercise 11.38

Write an equation for the graph in Figure 11-32.

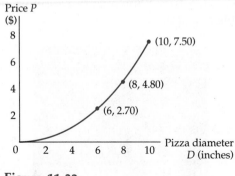

**Figure 11-32**

A graph ("scatter diagram") of statistical data involving two variables will rarely have an exact geometric shape, as shown in Figure 11-33.

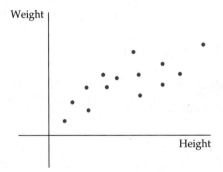

**Figure 11-33**

If the graph approximates a shape such as a line segment or a parabola, the corresponding equation may be tried as a formula relating to two variables.

Lesson Exercise 11.39

A study of the ages of 20 married couples yields the following data in the form (husband's age, wife's age):

| | | | | | | |
|---|---|---|---|---|---|---|
| (35, 30) | (31, 31) | (42, 37) | (29, 26) | (20, 21) | (25, 23) | (36, 34) |
| (40, 39) | (34, 32) | (28, 31) | (47, 47) | (29, 27) | (40, 31) | (37, 36) |
| (37, 36) | (38, 34) | (38, 31) | (24, 20) | (37, 35) | (29, 25) | |

(a) Plot the 20 points on a two-dimensional graph.
(b) Draw a straight line (a "regression line") that seems to fit the data best. Draw it so that about half of the points are below the line and half are above it.
(c) What is the equation of your line?
(d) If it's available, use a calculator or computer software to find the "best fitting" line and compare the results to part (c).

## Answers to Selected Lesson Exercises

**11.26** Let $I$ = recommended daily allowance of iron. $0.25I$ or $\frac{1}{4}I$

**11.27** cannot be translated

**11.28** $M = 5 + 0.08N$, in which $M$ = the monthly charge in dollars and $N$ = the number of local calls made.

**11.29** Let $T$ = transportation budget in dollars. Let $E$ = environmental protection budget in dollars. Let $D$ = defense budget in dollars.

$$T + E < \frac{1}{6}D$$

**11.30** $\frac{a}{b} \times \frac{c}{d} = \frac{a \times c}{b \times d}$ , in which $\frac{a}{b}$ and $\frac{c}{d}$ are rational numbers.

**11.31** $P = 100 + 0.05S$, in which $P$ = weekly pay and $S$ = sales in dollars.

**11.32** what the job is; what others get paid; whether the job is enjoyable or interesting; whether the job is beneficial to society

**11.33** The tip is 0.15 times the bill or, more commonly, the tip is 15% of the bill.

**11.34** (c)

**11.35** (a) after 1 hour
(b) the last part of the trip
(c) The car traveled for an hour at 30 mph. Then it stopped for a little less than an hour. Then the car traveled for a little over an hour at a faster speed.

**11.36** (a) $M = 0.16E$     (b) induction
(c) about 22 lb

**11.37** $P = 4.5H$

**11.38** $P = 0.075D^2$

## 11.3  Homework Exercises

*Basic Exercises*

1. Translate "twelve degrees warmer than the average for this day" into an algebraic expression.

2. Translate "40% off the regular price" into an algebraic expression.

3. (a) Translate "20 dollars is 85% of the list price" into an equation.
   (b) What doesn't this equation tell us about the quantities involved?

4. Which of the following could be represented by an algebraic variable?
   (a) Mary's age
   (b) transportation
   (c) Mike

If possible, translate the English sentences in Exercises 5–7 into algebraic equations or inequalities.

5. The perimeter of a special rectangle is three times its length.

**6.** "The fool thinks he is wise, but a wise man knows he is a fool." (Shakespeare, *As You Like It*)

**7.** Sixty percent of the students at Stellar University are women.

**8.** When an English sentence is translated into algebra, it becomes an _____ or _____ .

**9.** In each case, decide whether the quantity measured is (1) a significant or (2) a trivial feature of the person or object.
   (a) what your score, $S$, on the last mathematics test tells about how much you knew about the material covered
   (b) what your score, $S$, on the last mathematics test tells about you
   (c) what the time, $T$, it takes you to finish a mathematics test tells about your general mathematical ability

**10.** Translate the following into algebra: "The sum of any real number and zero is that real number."

**11.** Translate the following into algebra: "The product of a real number and the sum of two other real numbers is the sum of the products of the real number and each of the other two real numbers."

**12.** Fine Line phone company charges a monthly rate, $R$, of $7 plus $.08 per call.
   (a) What is the total monthly rate, $R$, for 10 calls? $R =$ _____ .
   (b) What is the total monthly rate, $R$, for $N$ calls? $R =$ _____ . (This is a general formula for $R$.)
   (c) For what values of $N$ can you use the formula?
   (d) Is your general formula exact or is it an approximation?
   (e) Graph $R$ (vertical axis) versus $N$ (horizontal axis).

**13.** The annual cost, $C$, of owning some cars can be estimated as $1100 plus $.10 per mile.

   (a) What is the annual cost, $C$, for $M$ miles? $C =$ _____ .
   (b) Graph $C$ (vertical axis) versus $M$ (horizontal axis).

**14.** A rental car from Nightmares costs $11 per day plus $.07 per mile. What is the total cost, $C$, for renting a car $D$ days and driving $M$ miles? (*Hint:* If you're not sure, make up numbers for $D$ and $M$ and see how you compute $C$.)

**15.** After 5 years, a car is worth $3600. After 6 years, the same car is worth $2700. Assume that its decline in value (depreciation) is the same amount each year. What is a formula relating its worth, $W$, to its age in years, $Y$?

**16.** A salesperson earns $120 per week plus a 10% commission on her total sales.
   (a) What is the formula relating total weekly earnings, $E$, to total sales, $S$?
   (b) Graph the formula for $E$ versus $S$ with $E$ on the vertical axis and $S$ on the horizontal axis.

**17.** A man who is 5 ft 8 in. tall weighs 200 pounds.
   (a) If he loses 5 pounds per week, what would he weigh after $W$ weeks?
   (b) Estimate a maximum reasonable value for $W$.

**18.** An airplane at an altitude of 33,000 ft begins descending at a rate of 1200 ft per minute.
   (a) Write a formula relating altitude, $A$, (in ft) to the number of minutes, $M$, after the descent begins.
   (b) What is the domain for $M$?

**19.**

| Sales ($x$) | 0 | 100 | 200 | 300 | 400 |
|---|---|---|---|---|---|
| Salary ($y$) | 100 | 110 | 120 | 130 | 140 |

Write a formula relating sales to salary.

**20.**

| D (km) | 0 | 5000 | 10,000 | 15,000 | 20,000 |
|---|---|---|---|---|---|
| C ($) | 1800 | 2100 | 2400 | 2700 | 3000 |

Write a formula relating the annual cost (C) of driving a National Motors Cheetah SST to the distance driven (D).

In Exercises 21–24, translate each English sentence into an algebraic equation.

**21.** Katie is at least twice as tall as she was last year.

**22.** There are at most 30 more girls than boys.

**23.** The total cost of movie tickets is $5 per adult ticket plus $3 per child's ticket.

**24.** The ratio of students to teachers is 12 to 1.

**25.** In the cartoon, why can't $X$ = Shobert Zangox?

© 1972 Walt Kelly. Reprinted with permission of Los Angeles Times Syndicate.

Translate the algebraic information in Exercises 26–29 into English.

**26.** $0.1P$, in which $P$ = Iowa's population

**27.** $R = 22D + 10$, in which $R$ = rental rate in dollars and $D$ = number of days

**28.** $C > 2P$, in which $C$ = current U.S. population and $P$ = U.S. population in 1940

**29.** $C = 0.025S$, in which $C$ = commission in dollars and $S$ = sales in dollars (Use the word "percent" in your translation.)

**30.**

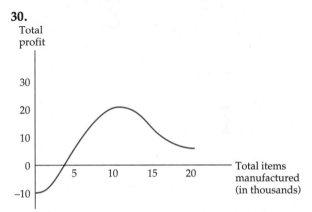

Describe the general relationship between the total number of items sold and the total profit.

**31.** Here is a graph of a journey by car.

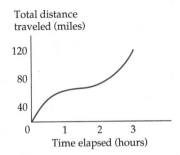

Describe the progress of the car during the journey.

**32.** What does the graph suggest about the relationship between motivation and the difficulty of a lesson?

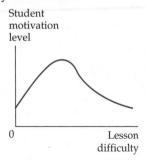

**33.** Match each graph with its description.
(a) 100-yard dash
(b) speed of a pitched baseball
(c) falling object

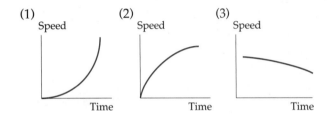

**34.** Make a reasonable sketch of each graph showing a typical relationship between the two variables.

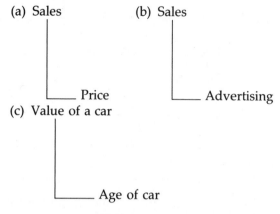

(a) Sales

(b) Sales

Price

Advertising

(c) Value of a car

Age of car

**35.** A roller coaster car moves from left to right over the course shown at the top of the next column. Make a sketch of speed versus time with time on the horizontal axis.

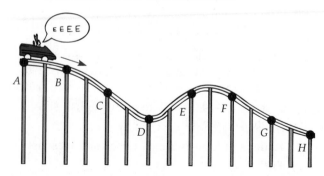

**36.** Julio works in the bakery at the Scrumptious Food Mart. Data on his weekly pay are given in the table.

| H (hours worked) | 20 | 36 | 30 |
| --- | --- | --- | --- |
| P (pay) | $84 | $151.20 | $126 |

(a) Write a formula relating $H$ to $P$.
(b) Did you use induction or deduction to figure out part (a)?

**37.**

| Hours Awake ($x$) | 14 | 15 | 16 | 17 | 18 | 19 |
| --- | --- | --- | --- | --- | --- | --- |
| Hours Asleep ($y$) | 10 | 9 | 8 | 7 | 6 | 5 |

Write a formula relating hours awake to hours asleep.

**38.** An object is dropped from a height of 200 ft. Its height, $H$, in feet after $T$ seconds is given in the table. Write a formula relating $H$ to $T$. (*Hint:* It involves $T^2$.)

| H | 200 | 184 | 136 | 56 |
| --- | --- | --- | --- | --- |
| T | 0 | 1 | 2 | 3 |

**39.** The average weights of 6-year-old boys with selected heights are given in the table.

| H (height, in.) | 42 | 44 | 46 | 48 |
| --- | --- | --- | --- | --- |
| W (weight, lb) | 43 | 49 | 55 | 61 |

Write a formula relating W to H. (*Hint:* Find the slope.)

40. The average weights of 21-year-old women with selected heights are given in the following table.

| H (height, in.) | 60 | 62 | 64 | 66 |
|---|---|---|---|---|
| W (weight, lb) | 112 | 120 | 128 | 136 |

Write a formula relating W to H.

41. Write an equation for the graph.

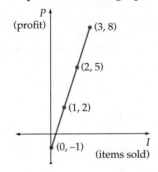

42. Write an equation for the graph.

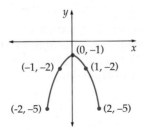

43. The rates for a cab company are shown on the graph. Write an equation relating dollars to miles.

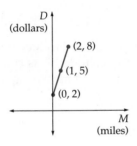

44.

Any polygon can be divided into a *minimum* number of triangular regions by its diagonals. The graph shows the relationship between S (the number of sides of a polygon) and T (the minimum number of triangular regions formed by diagonals).

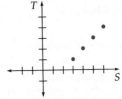

(a) Give the coordinates of each point.
(b) Write a formula relating T to S.

45. Write the equation for the graph. (*Hint:* It involves $x^2$ and $y^2$.)

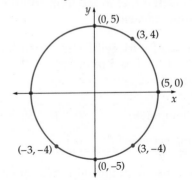

46. The heights (in inches) and weights (in pounds) of ten people in a sample are as follows.

(63, 142)  (69, 152)  (61, 137)  (70, 161)  (68, 148)
(73, 166)  (72, 162)  (64, 140)  (66, 144)  (65, 160)

(a) Plot the ten points on a two-dimensional graph.
(b) Draw a straight line that seems to fit the data best. Draw the line so that about half of the points are below it and half are above it.

(*Exercise continues on next page.*)

(c) What is the equation of your line?
(d) What does the equation suggest about the relationship between height and weight in this sample?

47. The gas tank of a National Motors Titan holds 20 gallons of gas. The following data are collected during a week.

| Fuel in Tank (gallons) | 20 | 18 | 16 | 14 | 12 | 10 |
|---|---|---|---|---|---|---|
| Dist. Traveled (miles) | 0 | 75 | 157 | 229 | 306 | 379 |

(a) Plot the points on a two-dimensional graph.
(b) Draw a straight line that seems to fit the data best. Draw the line so that about half of the points are below it and half are above it.
(c) What is the equation of your line?
(d) What is the slope and what does it tell about the fuel in the tank and the distance traveled?

48. A community tries different speed limits on a stretch of road and records the following number of accidents in a month.

| S (speed limit, mph) | 40 | 45 | 50 | 55 | 60 | 65 |
|---|---|---|---|---|---|---|
| A (accidents per month) | 3 | 7 | 13 | 18 | 21 | 25 |

(a) Plot the six points on a two-dimensional graph.
(b) Draw a straight line that seems to fit the data best. Draw the line so that about half of the points are below it and half are above it.
(c) What is the equation of your line?
(d) What does your equation suggest about the relationship between the speed limit and the number of accidents on this stretch of road?

*Extension Exercises*

49. Suppose that you want to fence in a rectangular area of 30 m². Answer the following to investigate the length and width such a rectangular area could have.
(a) Complete the table.

| L | 3 | 5 | 7 | |
|---|---|---|---|---|
| W | 10 | | | |

(b) Write a formula relating L and W.
(c) Graph your formula.
(d) Describe the shape of the graph. (It is called a **hyperbola**.)
(e) What are the possible values of L and W?

50. You plan to go on a 200-mile car trip. The time it takes is related to the rate at which you drive.
(a) Complete the chart.

| R (rate, mph) | 20 | 30 | 40 | 50 | 60 |
|---|---|---|---|---|---|
| T (time, hr) | 10 | | | | |

(b) Graph R (vertical axis) vs. T.

51. The time needed to cook a piece of chicken in a microwave oven is about 6 minutes at a setting of 500 watts. Additional information is provided in the table.

| W (watts) | 200 | 300 | 400 | 500 | 600 |
|---|---|---|---|---|---|
| T (time, min) | 15 | 10 | 7.5 | 6 | |

(a) Write a formula relating W and T.
(b) How long would it take to cook the chicken at 600 watts?
(c) Graph the formula for W and T.

52. (a) In a vacuum, the product of the pressure, P, and the volume, V, is constant. For example, PV could always equal 4. Graph

$PV = 4$ using positive numbers for $P$ and $V$.

(b) The graph shows that as $P$ increases, $V$ _____ .

**53.** Compare $x^2 - 9$ and $(x + 3)(x - 3)$ by
(a) plotting $y = x^2 - 9$ and $y = (x + 3)(x - 3)$ using a graphing calculator.
(b) comparing the values of $x^2 - 9$ and $(x + 3)(x - 3)$ for $x = -2, -1, 0, 1$, and 2.
(c) multiplying out $(x + 3)(x - 3)$.
(d) Which part or parts—(a), (b), or (c)—*prove* that $x^2 - 9 = (x + 3)(x - 3)$?

**54.** Use the information in the table to write an algebraic equation in three variables.

| Total Cost (*T*) | $11 | 14 | 41 |
|---|---|---|---|
| Pounds of Peanuts (*P*) | 1 | 2 | 3 |
| Pounds of Cashews (*C*) | 1 | 1 | 4 |

**55.** Bill makes 50% more money this year than he did last year. Translate this sentence into algebra. (This cannot be translated word for word.)

**56.** (a) The length of a rectangle is 4 cm more than its width. Express this relationship with an equation.
(b) Write the area of this rectangle in terms of its width.

**57.** The graph shows the speed of a roller coaster throughout the ride. Draw a sketch of the roller coaster track.

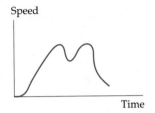

**58.** The graph shows the speed of a car versus time. Sketch a graph of distance versus time for the same trip.

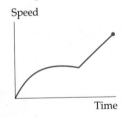

**59.** In its February 1989 issue, *Consumer Reports* rated 26- and 27-inch color television sets. The table gives the price and rating of each set.

| Set | Score | Price | Set | Score | Price |
|---|---|---|---|---|---|
| Hitachi | 90 | $609 | Zenith | 79 | $639 |
| Panasonic | 86 | $680 | GE | 76 | $519 |
| Magnavox | 84 | $729 | Sears | 76 | $740 |
| Sylvania | 84 | $572 | Sony | 74 | $747 |
| JC Penney | 83 | $800 | Toshiba | 73 | $539 |
| Mitsubishi | 83 | $799 | Emerson | 71 | $525 |
| RCA | 83 | $579 | Fisher | 70 | $659 |
| NEC | 81 | $640 | JVC | 70 | $659 |

(a) Plot price (vertical axis) versus score.
(b) How strong is the relationship between the price and the score?
(c) Suppose that it were always true that the higher the price is, the higher the score is. What would the graph look like?

**60.** One of the most famous formulas is $E = mc^2$.
(a) What do $E$, $m$, and $c$ represent?
(b) What is the formula used for?

*Computer Exercise*

**61.** Statistical software such as MINITAB can be used to display data, analyze data, perform simulations, or find a best-fitting line. Further exercises on MINITAB occur in Chapter 13.

In this exercise, use MINITAB to find a best-fitting line for the data in the last exercise from the lesson (husband's and wife's ages). First, type in the data as follows.

MTB > READ HUSBAND IN C1, WIFE IN C2
DATA > 35 30

DATA > 31 31
       .
       .

Then type:

mtb > REGRESS 'WIFE' ON 1, 'HUSBAND'

## 11.4   Solving Problems with Formulas, Tables, and Graphs

Consider the following word problems.

- "Jane's age is 1 less than one-third her grandmother's age. Six years ago, Jane's age was one-fourth her grandmother's age. How old are they both today?"
- "I have 74 coins in all, consisting of dimes and quarters totaling $14.75. How many dimes and quarters do I have?"

Please don't try to solve these problems. Age and coin problems make nice puzzles, but they are not important enough to be done by the pageful, as many algebra classes do.

In this lesson, you will see more realistic applications of algebra that people encounter in everyday life. These applications should be the focus of our algebra classes.

$$\boxed{\text{Word problem}} \longrightarrow \boxed{\text{Translate into formula, table or graph}}$$

$$\boxed{\text{Solve word problem}} \longleftarrow \boxed{\text{Solve mathematical problem}}$$

### Isolating Different Variables in a Formula

Your car gets 26 miles to the gallon. How much gas will you use on a 500-mile trip? The formula

$$D = M \cdot G \quad \text{or} \quad G = \frac{D}{M}$$

$$\text{Distance} = \begin{bmatrix} \text{miles} \\ \text{per} \\ \text{gallon} \end{bmatrix} \cdot \begin{bmatrix} \text{number} \\ \text{of} \\ \text{gallons} \end{bmatrix} \quad \begin{matrix} \text{Number} \\ \text{of} \\ \text{gallons} \end{matrix} = \text{distance/mpg}$$

can be used to solve this problem.

In order to find the unknown quantity $G$, you must have values for *all other variables and constants* in the formula. It's easiest to use a formula when this one unknown $G$ is isolated on one side of the equation.

## Lesson Exercise 11.40

Tickets for the Sonic Boom's rock concert sell for $12. The expenses for setting up the gig are $30,000. So the profit $P = 12 \cdot T - 30{,}000$, in which $T$ is the number of tickets sold.
(a) Solve for $T$.
(b) Select one of the two formulas to solve the following. The profit for the concert was $3000. How many tickets were sold?

## Solving Problems with Formulas

Are you ready to solve some word problems? Wait. Come back here. You've studied everything you need to know: (1) translating words into algebra, (2) writing an equation relating the quantities in a problem, and (3) solving an equation for an unknown.

You can use the following five-step procedure.

### Understanding the Problem

1. Read the problem and assign a variable to the quantity you are looking for.

### Devising a Plan

2. Write an English sentence describing how the quantities in the problem are related.

3. Write an equation (or equations) relating the quantities in the problem.

### Carrying Out the Plan

4. Solve for the unknown variable (or variables) in the equation (or equations) and answer the original question.

### Looking Back

5. Check to see whether your answer makes sense.

The following example illustrates two methods for solving an algebraic word problem: the guess-and-check strategy and the five-step procedure.

### Example 11.9

A saleswoman earns a commission of 6% of her sales. How much must she sell to earn a commission of $1000?
(a) Solve it using the guess-and-check strategy.
(b) Use the five-step procedure.

**Solution**

(a) Guess an answer for sales and compute the commission on it. See how close you are to $1000. Then adjust your answer accordingly.

For example, I might guess $20,000 in sales. The commission would be ($20,000)(0.06) = $1200. Since $1200 > $1000, $20,000 is a little too high. I would guess a little lower than $20,000 and continue in this fashion. I should end up with an answer around $16,700. This method avoids the use of algebra.

(b) Follow the five steps.

*Understanding the Problem*

**1.** We are asked to find total sales. Let $S$ = total sales.

*Devising a Plan*

**2.** To find her earnings, we would multiply 0.06 by her total sales.

**3.** 1000 = 0.06$S$

*Carrying Out the Plan*

**4.** Solve 1000 = $S \cdot 0.06$ for $S$.

$$\frac{1000}{0.06} = S$$

Since $S$ represents money, round it to two decimal places.

$$\$16,666.67 = S$$

She must sell $16,666.67 of goods to earn $1000.

*Looking Back*

**5.** Is the answer reasonable? Yes, her earnings are a small fraction of the amount she sells. 6% is about $\frac{1}{20}$.

$$6\% \text{ of } \$16666.67 \approx \frac{1}{20} \text{ of } \$20,000 = \$1000 \qquad \blacksquare$$

Now try some exercises using the guess-and-check strategy or the five-step procedure.

## D Lesson Exercise 11.41

A college has 300 places in the entering class. In the past, about 46% of the students who are accepted attend the school. How many students should the college accept?

(a) Solve it by the guess-and-check strategy.

(b) Solve it using a formula.

(c) Explain how your formula is similar to the one in Example 11.9.

**D** Lesson Exercise 11.42

Joe sells squirrel-powered vacuum cleaners. He earns $230 a week plus 14% of his sales. How much must he sell in a week in order to earn $400?

Some problems can be solved algebraically with two equations.

 **Example 11.10**

Some state inspection centers check automobile exhaust for carbon monoxide (CO) and carbon dioxide ($CO_2$). CO is 43% carbon and $CO_2$ is 27% carbon.

A sample of 1200 mg of exhaust has 31% carbon. How many milligrams of the sample are CO and how many milligrams are $CO_2$?

**Solution**

*Understanding the Problem*

1. We are asked to find milligrams of CO and $CO_2$ in the sample. Let $m$ = milligrams of CO and $d$ = milligrams of $CO_2$.

*Devising a Plan*

2. A problem with two unknowns generally requires two sentences or equations. The milligrams of CO in the sample plus the milligrams of $CO_2$ add up to 1200 mg; also, 43% of the milligrams of CO plus 27% of the milligrams of $CO_2$ makes 31% of 1200.

3.
$$m + d = 1200$$
$$0.43m + 0.27d = (0.31)(1200)$$

*Carrying Out the Plan*

**4.** Find values of $m$ and $d$ that satisfy both equations using substitution.

$$m + d = 1200 \quad \longrightarrow \quad d = 1200 - m$$

and substitute for $d$ in the other equation.

$$0.43m + 0.27(1200 - m) = (0.31)(1200)$$
$$0.43m + 324 - 0.27m = 372$$
$$0.16m + 324 = 372$$
$$0.16m = 48$$
$$m = 300 \text{ mg}$$
$$d = 1200 - 300 = 900 \text{ mg}$$

The sample contains 300 mg of CO and 900 mg of $CO_2$.

*Looking Back*

**5.** Check by substituting in the second equation.

$$(0.43)(300) + (0.27)(900) \stackrel{?}{=} (0.31)(1200)$$
$$129 \quad + \quad 243 \quad \stackrel{?}{=} \quad 372$$
$$372 \quad = \quad 372 \qquad \blacksquare$$

### Lesson Exercise 11.43

You are planning to buy a dishwasher. Choice A sells for $280 and costs $12 per month to operate. Choice B sells for $220 and costs $20 per month to operate.

(a) Find the number of months for which the total cost of purchasing and operating each machine is the same. (*Hint:* Write a formula for the total cost of purchasing and operating each machine.)

(b) Solve the problem without using the equations.

## Solving Problems with Tables

Suppose that you invest $1000 earning 8% interest compounded annually. How long will it be before your account is worth $1500? You can solve this problem by making a table. (Solving the problem using the equation $1000(1.08)^T = 1500$ would require logarithms.) Example 11.11 illustrates how to solve the problem using a table.

### Example 11.11

You invest $1000 earning 8% interest compounded annually. How long before your account is worth $1500?

*Understanding the Problem*   An account starts with $1000 and earns 8% per year.

*Devising a Plan*   Make a table of values. Experiment until you reach values above and below $1500.

*Carrying Out the Plan*

| Time (years) | 0 | 1 | 2 | 3 | 4 | 5 | 6 |
|---|---|---|---|---|---|---|---|
| Amount | $1000 | 1080 | 1166.40 | 1259.71 | 1360.49 | 1469.33 | 1586.88 |

It will take a little more than 5 years.

*Looking Back*   $1500 represents a 50% increase. At 8% annual interest, it should take about 6 years to gain 50%, so the answer is reasonable.  ■

 Lesson Exercise 11.44

You invest $1000 earning 10% interest compounded annually. How long before your account is worth $1500?

## Solving Problems with Graphs

In Section 11.3, you found the equation of a line that seemed to fit a set of data. You can make predictions using such equations.

**D** Lesson Exercise 11.45

Fifteen people are surveyed. The following data give the average miles driven per month and the average cost per month of maintaining a 3-year-old car.

| | | | | |
|---|---|---|---|---|
| (800, $70) | (1200, $110) | (1000, $120) | (900, $85) | (900, $105) |
| (800, $100) | (900, $95) | (800, $80) | (400, $40) | (1400, $130) |
| (800, $75) | (1100, $105) | (700, $50) | (700, $65) | (600, $60) |

(a) Plot the 15 points on a two-dimensional graph. (Use graph paper.)
(b) Estimate where the graph passes through the *y*-axis.
(c) Draw a straight line that seems to fit the data best.
(d) What is the equation of your line?
(e) What monthly expense does your equation predict for someone who drives a 3-year-old car 1300 miles per month?

You can also use graphs to compare alternatives represented by two equations. Graphing two equations together may clarify the relative merits of the two alternatives.

## **D** Lesson Exercise 11.46

You are currently paying an average of $52 per month for heat. After installing solar panels at a cost of $610, you can reduce your monthly heating costs to about $20 per month (this would depend upon how much sun your town gets).

(a) What is a formula relating the number of months to total heating cost under the current scheme?
(b) Graph your equation from part (a) on graph paper [or you could use a graphing calculator in parts (b), (d), and (e)].
(c) What is a formula relating the number of months to total heating cost using solar panels (including the installation cost)?
(d) Graph your equation from part (c) on the same axes you used in part (b).
(e) Estimate the intersection point of the two graphs.
(f) What is the significance of the intersection point as far as which approach is more economical?

Earlier in the lesson, you studied how to solve problems involving two equations algebraically. These problems can also be solved by graphing the two equations.

## Lesson Exercise 11.47

(a) Solve Lesson Exercise 11.43 from this lesson by graphing the two equations on the same graph. (Use graph paper or a graphing calculator.)
(b) Which method do you think is easier, using algebra or using a graph?

## An Experiment

Scientists and statisticians search for patterns in experimental data in order to answer questions such as: "How is the length of a pendulum related to the time it takes to complete a full swing?"

In order to do this experiment, you will need some string and some weights of uniform size (for example, a set of washers).

## Lesson Exercise 11.48

(a) Attach a weight to the end of a string and hang the string over the edge of a table. Determine how long it takes for the pendulum to complete one full swing. Vary the length of the string and collect data for the following table.

| Length of String | | | | | | |
|---|---|---|---|---|---|---|
| Time for One Full Swing | | | | | | |

(b) Graph the data on a two-dimensional graph.
(c) Describe any pattern you see in the data or the graph.
(d) Make a conjecture in words about the relationship between the length of a pendulum and the time for one full swing.

## Lesson Exercise 11.49

Conduct a similar investigation of the relationship between the weight and the time for ten swings (keeping the length the same).

## Answers to Selected Lesson Exercises

**11.40** (a) $T = \dfrac{P + 30,000}{12}$    (b) 2750

**11.42** $1214.29

**11.43** (a) 7.5 months

**11.44** a little over 4 years

**11.46** (a) $H = 52M$, in which $M$ is the number of months and $H$ is the total heating cost
(c) $H = 610 + 20M$
(e) around $M = 19$
(f) The current scheme is cheaper for a period of less than 19 months. Installing solar panels would be cheaper for time periods beyond 19 months.

## 11.4  Homework Exercises

*Basic Exercises*

1. The cost of printing photos at Blurry's is $.27 per picture plus $1.80 for development. So $C = .27P + 1.80$, in which $C$ is cost and $P$ is the number of pictures.

   (a) Suppose that you got a bill for $3.69. How would you figure out, *without* using a formula, how many pictures were printed?
   (b) Solve for $P$ in the equation.
   (c) Suppose that you bring in 12 negatives featuring your new nephew Baby Drew L. Alot. Your total bill is $3.69 plus tax.

   Using one of the two formulas, compute how many pictures, $P$, of the baby they were able to print.

2. An approximate formula for a man's shoe size is $S = 3F - 24$, in which $F =$ foot length in inches.

   (a) Solve for $F$ in the formula.
   (b) A man has an 11-inch foot. Use one of the formulas to compute his shoe size.
   (c) A man wears a size-8 shoe. Use one of the formulas to approximate his foot length.

**3.**

By permission of Johnny Hart and Creators Syndicate, Inc.

Did you know that you can estimate the Fahrenheit temperature by counting cricket chirps?

(a) Let $N$ equal the number of chirps per minute and $T$ equal the temperature in Fahrenheit. Derive a formula for $T$ from the first frame of the cartoon.

(b) Solve for $N$.

(c) Use one of the formulas to figure out what the temperature is when crickets chirp 100 times per minute.

(d) It's 95°F outside. About how many times per minute will the crickets be chirping?

**4.** Density $D = \dfrac{M}{V}$ (mass ÷ volume).

(a) Solve for $V$.

(b) Use one of the formulas to find the volume if the mass is 8 g and the density is 10 g/cm³.

**5.** A person's I.Q. (intelligence quotient) is 100 times his or her mental age divided by actual age.

(a) Write a formula for I.Q.

(b) How do psychologists attempt to measure people's mental ages?

(c) Find the I.Q. of an 8-year-old child with a mental age of 10.

**6.** Light travels at a speed of 186,000 miles per second.

(a) Write a formula relating time, $T$ (seconds), to distance traveled, $D$ (miles).

(b) The world's fastest human runs 1 mile in about 4 minutes. How long does it take light to travel 1 mile?

(c) The distance from the sun to the Earth is about 93,000,000 miles. How long does light from the sun take to reach the Earth?

**7.** A rental van costs $120 per day plus $.32 per mile. What length trips could you take for less than $280?

**8.** The total bill in a restaurant, including 5% tax, was $16.17. How much was the meal without the tax? (*Hint:* The 5% tax was computed on what amount?)

**9.** An item is marked up 30%. Its selling price is $442. What is the cost?

**10.** A dress is on sale for $26. This is 35% off the regular price. What is the regular price?

**11.** (a) Women make up 36% of a college student body. There are 261 women. How many students are there at the college?

(b) This exercise has the same form as which lesson exercise?

**12.** An ice cream store sells a cone and a scoop for $1.25 and a cone with two scoops for $2.10.

(a) Assume that each scoop costs the same amount. How much is the cone?

(b) Write a formula relating the price, $P$, of a complete ice cream cone to the number of scoops, $S$.

**13.** Tickets for a college basketball game were $10 for adults and $4 for children. The paid attendance was 2460, and total ticket sales were $21,060. How many adult and children's tickets were sold?

**14.** A sample of 1400 mg of automobile exhaust contains 36% carbon (from CO and $CO_2$). If CO is 43% carbon and $CO_2$ is 27% carbon, how many milligrams of exhaust are CO and how many milligrams are $CO_2$?

**15.** In a chicken recipe, you make a coating using 3 oz of bread crumbs for every 2 oz of parmesan cheese. If you want 16 oz of coating, what amount of bread crumbs and parmesan cheese do you need?

16. Consider the following problem. "Suppose that you invest $1000 earning 6% interest compounded annually. About how long will it be before your account is worth $1500?" Devise a plan and solve the problem.

17. Suppose that you invest $1000 earning 12% interest compounded annually. About how long will it be before your account is worth $1500?

18. Suppose that you invest $5000 earning 9% interest compounded annually. About how long will it be before your account is worth $8000?

19. Suppose that a certain new car costs about $11,000 in 1992. If inflation is about 7% per year, in about how many years will a comparable new car cost about $22,000?

20. A store rents an average of 200 videos at $3 per day. For each increase of $.10 in the price (up to $4), the store owners estimate that they will lose an additional 10 rentals per day. Each $.10 decrease in price (down to $2) is expected to result in a gain of 10 rentals per day. What rental price will maximize their daily revenue (total money collected from sales)?

21. A woman is driving home from work. The graph shows her speed throughout the trip.

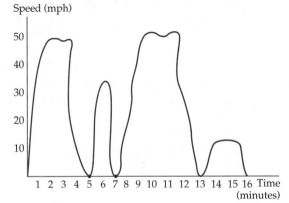

Speed (mph)

(a) Describe her trip.
(b) About how many miles long is the drive?

22. Here is a graph of a journey by car. What was the average speed of the car?

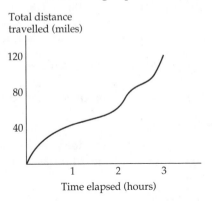

Total distance travelled (miles)

Time elapsed (hours)

23. The graph shows the cost of producing a certain type of sneaker and the revenue from selling them.

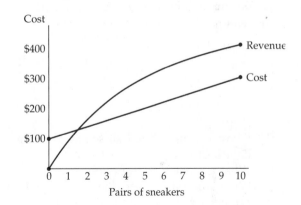

Pairs of sneakers

(a) What is the cost of producing 5 pairs of sneakers?
(b) What is the profit or loss on 5 pairs of sneakers?
(c) What is the profit or loss on 8 pairs of sneakers?
(d) At least how many pairs must be sold in order to make a profit?

24. Suppose that you sample 20 people who began full-time work last year and ask them about their years of education and their starting salary (in thousands of dollars). The results are as follows (years of education, salary in thousands of dollars).

(14, 18)    (16, 22)    (10, 13)    (20, 27)
(12, 10)    (16, 21)    (16, 20)    (11, 12)
(17, 22)    (12, 16)    (12, 18)    (18, 24)
(12, 15)    (16, 21)    (12, 14)    (16, 23)
(19, 23)    (12, 16)    (14, 20)    (20, 25)

(a) Plot the 20 points on a two-dimensional graph.
(b) Draw a straight line that seems to fit the data best.
(c) What is the equation of your line?
(d) What starting salary does your equation predict for someone who has 17 years of school?

25. You sample 15 businesses in an industry and ask them how many thousands of dollars they spent on advertising and how many millions of dollars they made in sales. The results are as follows (advertising dollars in thousands, sales dollars in millions):

(35, 10)    (48, 11)    (26, 8)     (28, 7)     (0, 3)
(8, 5)      (32, 9)     (15, 5)     (40, 12)    (38, 12)
(37, 11)    (30, 10)    (56, 15)    (52, 14)    (50, 13)

(a) Plot the 15 points on a two-dimensional graph.
(b) Draw a straight line that seems to fit the data best.
(c) What is the equation of your line?
(d) What amount of sales does your equation predict for a company that spends $20,000 in advertising?

26. Stopping distance $D = 1.1S + 0.05S^2$, in which $D$ is distance in feet and $S$ is speed in miles per hour (mph). ($1.1S$ is the reaction distance and $0.05 S^2$ is the braking distance.)

(a) Find the stopping distance for a car traveling at 30 mph.
(b) Find the stopping distance for a car traveling at 50 mph.
(c) Graph $D$ vs. $S$, with $D$ on the vertical axis.

(d) Using your graph or a calculator, estimate the speed of a car that took 136 ft to stop.
(e) This formula is only an approximation. What factors in addition to speed should affect stopping distance?

27. An object is tossed up in the air with a velocity of 80 ft/sec. Its height, $h$, in feet after $t$ sec is $h = -16t^2 + 80t$.
(a) Find the height after 3 seconds.
(b) Graph $h$ vs. $t$, with $h$ on the vertical axis.
(c) Using your graph or a calculator, estimate when the object is at height of 50 ft.

28. Scientists can estimate people's heights from the length, $L$, (in centimeters) of their femur (thigh bone). For a female, height in centimeters $H \approx 2.3L + 61.4$.
(a) Why would anyone want to estimate a women's height from the length of her femur?
(b) Estimate the height of a female with a femur of length 42.1 cm.
(c) Graph the equation.
(d) What does the slope tell you about the relationship between the length and the height?

29. A rectangle has a perimeter of 10 ft.
(a) Write a formula relating the length, $L$, and the width, $W$.
(b) Is this formula exact or approximate?
(c) Use the formula to find the width when the length is 3 ft.
(d) What values can the length and width have?
(e) Graph length vs. width.

30. A ball is dropped from a height of 144 ft. Its height, $H$, (in feet) at time $T$ (in seconds) is $H = 144 - 16T^2$.
(a) Graph this equation.
(b) What shape is the graph?
(c) When does the ball hit the ground?
(d) How high does the ball go?

**31.** Revenue, $R$, from ticket sales for a concert depends upon the price you charge according to $R = -50P^2 + 600P$.
  (a) Graph this equation.
  (b) Approximately what price gives the maximum revenue?

**32.** You light a 25-cm candle at a romantic dinner you have prepared. Its height $H$ after $T$ hours is shown.

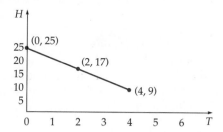

  (a) Extend the graph to estimate when the candle will burn out.
  (b) Write an equation relating $H$ to $T$.

**33.** You are planning to buy a new air conditioner. Choice A costs $400 and costs $30 per month to run. Choice B costs $550 and is more energy-efficient, so it costs $20 per month to run.
  (a) Write a formula for the cost, $C$, of purchasing and operating each air conditioner for $M$ months.
  (b) Graph both equations on the same graph. (You may use a graphing calculator for parts (b) and (c).)
  (c) Find the intersection point on the graph.
  (d) Find the intersection point algebraically.
  (e) What is the significance of the intersection point as far as which air conditioner is the best buy?
  (f) What other factors might you consider besides price in deciding which air conditioner to buy?

**34.** You are choosing between two health insurance plans that cost the same amount. One pays 80% of all expenses *beyond* the first $500

(a $500 deductible). The second pays 60% of all expenses with no deductible.
  (a) Write a formula for the amount, $A$, that each policy pays on a claim of $C$ dollars.
  (b) Graph both equations on the same graph. (You may use a graphing calculator for parts (b) and (c).)
  (c) Find the intersection point.
  (d) What is the significance of the intersection point as far as which plan is the better?
  (e) In choosing a plan, what other factors might you consider in addition to price?

**35.** You are offered two sales jobs. Job A pays $800 per week plus 5% commission. Job B pays $300 per week plus a 15% commission.
  (a) Write a formula for the weekly pay for each job.
  (b) Graph both equations on the same graph. (You may use a graphing calculator in parts (b) and (c).)
  (c) Find the intersection point.
  (d) What is the significance of the intersection point as far as which job pays more?
  (e) In choosing a sales job, what other factors might you consider in addition to pay?

**36.** A marketing research department makes the following forecast:

| Price | $4 | $5 | $6 | $7 | $8 |
|-------|-----|-----|-----|-----|-----|
| Sales | 18  | 15  | 13  | 11  | 9   |

  (a) Estimate the sales at a price of $6.50.
  (b) Plot the data on a graph.
  (c) Extend the graph to estimate the sales at a price of $10.
  (d) Find an approximate formula relating price to sales.

*Extension Exercises*

**37.** Consider the following problem. "A job pays $6.10 an hour. If 23% is deducted for taxes, union dues, and benefits, how many hours must you work at this job in order to take home $100?" Devise a plan and solve the problem.

 **38.** A job pays $7.25 an hour. If 34% is deducted for taxes, union dues, and benefits, how many hours must you work at this job in order to take home $500?

 **39.** Your employer deducts 37% for taxes and benefits. You take home $312 for 40 hours of work. What does your job pay per hour?

**40.** In 1992, first-class mail costs $.29 for the first ounce and $.23 for each additional ounce or fraction thereof. (Fractional amounts are rounded up to the next whole ounce.)
   (a) Find the cost of a 2.6-ounce first-class letter in 1992.
   (b) A postal clerk in 1992 weighs your first-class package and says the charge is $1.67. How much could the package weigh?
   (c) Let $C$ be the cost of a $W$-ounce letter. Graph $C$ (on the vertical axis) versus $W$ (on the horizontal axis).
   (d) What is the input set in part (c)?
   (e) The formula cost $C = 0.23W + 0.06$ works for what values of $W$ (weight in ounces)?
   (f) What shape is the graph?

**41.** In deciding between a National Motors Integer Maxima with a gas engine or a diesel engine, you collect the following information. First, the gas car costs $7200 and the diesel car costs $8500. Second, the gas car gets 38 mpg and the diesel car gets 45 mpg. Third, gas costs $1.10 per gallon and diesel fuel costs $1.18 per gallon. Under what conditions would each car be a better buy?

**42.** A school group already has $600 in an account. They need a total of $900 to pay for a concert. If they sell concert tickets for $D$ dollars, how many tickets must they sell to break even?

**43.** A manufacturer of television sets has weekly expenses $E = 1500 + 100T$ dollars for manufacturing $T$ televisions. The total revenue (money received) from selling $T$ televisions is $180T$.
   (a) What is the *profit or loss* on manufacturing and selling 100 sets in a week?
   (b) What is the *profit or loss* on manufacturing and selling 20 sets in a week?
   (c) What number of sets is the break-even point?

**44.** Do you know what day of the week you were born on? The following formula gives the day of the week for any given date. $D$ is the number of days in the latest year up to and including the date; $Y$ is the year.

$$W = D + Y + \left[\frac{Y-1}{4}\right] - \left[\frac{Y-1}{100}\right] + \left[\frac{Y-1}{400}\right]$$

The notation $[\ \ ]$ means take the quotient without any remainder. For example,

$$\left[\frac{11}{4}\right] = 2.$$

To obtain the day of the week, take the remainder when $W$ is divided by 7 (1 = Sunday, 2 = Monday, . . . , 0 = Saturday)
   What day of the week was the author born on (January 11, 1952)?

$$W = 11 + 1952 + \left[\frac{1951}{4}\right] - \left[\frac{1951}{100}\right] + \left[\frac{1951}{400}\right]$$
$$= 11 + 1952 + 487 - 19 + 4 = 2435$$

$$7 \overline{\smash{\big)}\, 2435} \quad \frac{347 \text{ R } 6}{} \rightarrow \text{sixth day} = \text{Friday.}$$

So the author was born on a Friday.
   (a) Use the formula to find out what day of the week you were born on.
   (b) What day of the week is January 1, 2000?

**45.** The graph (see p. 681) shows $y = x^2 - 9x + 4$. Use the graph or a graphing calculator to estimate the solutions to

(a) $x^2 - 9x + 4 = 2$
(b) $x^2 - 9x + 4 = -3$

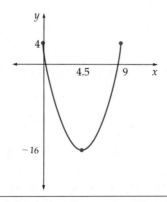

*Special Exercise*

46. Read Chapters 1–7 of *The Education of T. C. Mits* by Lillian Lieber and write a report that includes a summary of the main ideas and your reaction to them.

---

## 11.5  Geometry with Coordinates

Coordinate geometry establishes a connection between algebra and geometry, enabling mathematicians to describe geometry problems algebraically.

### The Distance Formula

How can we find the length of a line segment using coordinates?

Lesson Exercise 11.50
___

(a) Plot $D(2, 1)$, $E(5, 3)$, and $F(5, 1)$ on a graph and draw right triangle $\triangle DEF$.
(b) The legs of $\triangle DEF$ have lengths _____ and _____ .
(c) Find $DE$ using the Pythagorean Theorem.

___

The Pythagorean Theorem is the basis for computing the distance between any two points on a two-dimensional graph. Complete the following exercise to derive the distance formula.

**D**  Lesson Exercise 11.51
___

(a) For two points $A(x_1, y_1)$ and $B(x_2, y_2)$, construct a right triangle with hypotenuse $\overline{AB}$ as shown in Figure 11-34.
(b) What are the coordinates of $C$?
(c) The legs of $\triangle ABC$ have lengths _____ and _____ .
(d) By the Pythagorean Theorem, $(AB)^2 =$ _____ .
(e) Solving for $AB$ in part (c) yields, $AB =$ _____ .

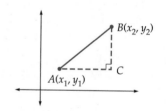

**Figure 11-34**

If the slope of $\overline{AB}$ is negative, the derivation is similar and the resulting formula is the same. The **distance formula** tells us how to find the length of a line segment using the coordinates of its endpoints.

---

**The Distance Formula**

The distance between two points $A(x_1, y_1)$ and $B(x_2, y_2)$ is

$$AB = \sqrt{(x_2 - x_1)^2 + (y_2 - y_1)^2}$$

---

## Lesson Exercise 11.52

A quadrilateral $ABCD$ has coordinates $A(0, 0)$, $B(5, 0)$, $C(8, 4)$, and $D(3, 4)$. Use the distance formula to show that $ABCD$ is a rhombus.

The distance formula can also be used to find the algebraic equation of a circle.

## D Lesson Exercise 11.53

A circle has center $(3, 2)$ and a radius of 4.
(a) This circle is the set of all points that are _____ from

_____ .

(b) Use the distance formula to write an algebraic equation for all points $(x, y)$ that are 4 units from $(3, 2)$. [*Hint:* Represent the distance between the center and a point on the circle $(x, y)$ using the distance formula as shown in Figure 11-35.]

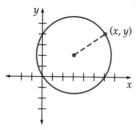

**Figure 11-35**

Use the same procedure to find a more general equation for a circle in the following exercise.

## Lesson Exercise 11.54

A circle has center $(h, k)$ and a radius of $r$ (Figure 11-36).
Find an algebraic equation for the circle.

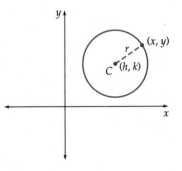

The result of Lesson Exercise 11.54 is the general equation of a circle.

---

**The Equation of a Circle**

The equation of a circle with center $(h, k)$ and radius $r$ is

$$(x - h)^2 + (y - k)^2 = r^2$$

---

**Figure 11-36**

Use this general formula in the following exercise.

## Lesson Exercise 11.55

Find the equation of a circle with center $(2, -3)$ and a radius of 4.

## The Midpoint Formula

How are the coordinates of the midpoint of a line segment related to the coordinates of the endpoints?

## Lesson Exercise 11.56

(a)  Plot the following points: $A(3, 2)$, $B(-1, 4)$, $C(5, 6)$ and draw $\triangle ABC$.
(b)  Find the coordinates of the midpoint of $\overline{AC}$.
(c)  Find the coordinates of the midpoint of $\overline{AB}$.
(d)  Find the coordinates of the midpoint of $\overline{BC}$.
(e)  What is the relationship between the coordinates of the endpoints of a line segment and the coordinates of the midpoint?
(f)  Using parts (b)–(d) to answer part (e) is an example of what kind of reasoning?

The next exercise asks you to generalize your results even further.

## Lesson Exercise 11.57

Given two points $A(x_1, y_1)$ and $B(x_2, y_2)$, what are the coordinates of the midpoint of $\overline{AB}$?

The answer to Lesson Exercise 11.57 is the midpoint formula.

---

**The Midpoint Formula**

Given $A(x_1, y_1)$ and $B(x_2, y_2)$, then the midpoint $M$ of $\overline{AB}$ is

$$M\left[\frac{x_1 + x_2}{2}, \frac{y_1 + y_2}{2}\right]$$

---

The midpoint and distance formulas can be used to find properties of triangles and quadrilaterals.

**D** Lesson Exercise 11.58

$\triangle ABC$ is a right triangle with $A(0, 0)$, $B(8, 0)$, and $C(0, 6)$.
(a) Plot $\triangle ABC$ on a coordinate graph.
(b) Find the coordinates of $M$, the midpoint of the hypotenuse.
(c) Compare the lengths $AM$, $BM$, and $CM$.
(d) Repeat parts (a)–(c) with a new right triangle.
(e) Make a generalization based upon your results.

In Chapter 8, you studied properties of parallelograms. The following exercise shows how to use coordinate geometry to prove one such property: that the diagonals of a parallelogram bisect each other.

Lesson Exercise 11.59

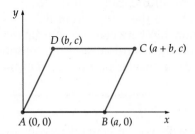

**Figure 11-37**

(a) Prove that $ABCD$ in Figure 11-37 is a parallelogram.
(b) Prove that the midpoint of $\overline{AC}$ is the midpoint of $\overline{BD}$.

## Taxicab Geometry

Suppose that you travel the shortest route along the grid arrangement of streets in Figure 11-38 from point $A$ to point $B$. The distance formula at the beginning of this section would not give the correct **taxicab distance** from $A(2, 1)$ to $B(4, 2)$ along "streets."

The taxicab distance from $A$ to $B$ is 3, denoted by $d_T(AB) = 3$.

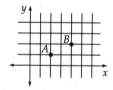

**Figure 11-38**

### Lesson Exercise 11.60

How many different routes of taxicab distance 3 are there from $A$ to $B$?

### Lesson Exercise 11.61

Find the taxicab distance from $(-2, 3)$ to $(4, 1)$.
Which is longer, taxicab distance or standard (Euclidean) distance?

Are taxicab and standard distance ever the same? Try the following exercise.

### Lesson Exercise 11.62

If possible, draw points $A$, $B$, $C$, and $D$ on a graph such that
(a) $d_T(AB) = AB$.      (b) $d_T(AB) < AB$.      (c) $d_T(AB) > AB$.

As you saw in the preceding exercise, $d_T(AB) \geq AB$ for all points $A$ and $B$. The following exercise presents the taxicab equivalent of a geometric shape you studied earlier in this lesson.

### Lesson Exercise 11.63

Point $E$ has coordinates $(2, 4)$.
(a) Plot all points that are a taxicab distance of 2 from point $E$.
(b) What shape do these points form?
(c) If you plotted the corresponding set of points in standard two-dimensional coordinate geometry, what shape would you obtain?

## Answers to Selected Lesson Exercises

11.50 (b) 2, 3     (c) $\sqrt{13}$

11.51 (b) $(x_2, y_1)$     (c) $x_2 - x_1$ and $y_2 - y_1$
      (d) $(x_2 - x_1)^2 + (y_2 - y_1)^2$
      (e) $\sqrt{(x_2 - x_1)^2 + (y_2 - y_1)^2}$

**11.52** $AB = BC = CD = DA = 5$

**11.53** (a) 4 units from (3, 2)

(b) $(x - 3)^2 + (y - 2)^2 = 16$

**11.55** $(x - 2)^2 + (y + 3)^2 = 16$

**11.56** (b) (4, 4)     (c) (1, 3)     (d) (2, 5)

(e) The coordinates of the midpoint are the average of the coordinates of the two endpoints.

(f) inductive

**11.57** $\left(\dfrac{x_1 + x_2}{2}, \dfrac{y_1 + y_2}{2}\right)$

**11.58** (b) $M(4, 3)$     (c) $AM = BM = CM = 5$

(e) The midpoint of the hypotenuse is equidistant from the three vertices.

**11.59** (a) *Hint:* Show that the slopes of the opposite sides are parallel.

(b) The midpoint of both diagonals is $\left(\dfrac{a + b}{2}, \dfrac{c}{2}\right)$.

**11.60** 3

**11.61** 8

**11.62** (b) is impossible

**11.63** (b) a square     (c) a circle

## 11.5   Homework Exercises

*Basic Exercises*

1. What is the distance between (4, 6) and (5, 10)?

2. Explain why the distance between $A(x_1, y_1)$ and $B(x_2, y_2)$ is:

$$AB = \sqrt{(x_2 - x_1)^2 + (y_2 - y_1)^2}$$

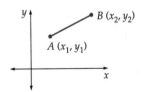

3.

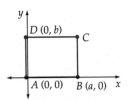

ABCD is a rectangle.
(a) What would the coordinates of C be?
(b) Show that $AC = BD$.

4. Three vertices of a parallelogram are (1, −2), (0, 2), and (2, 0). Find three possible coordinates for the fourth vertex.

5. Find the perimeter of $\triangle ABC$ with coordinates $A(3, 6)$, $B(3, 9)$, and $C(5, 7)$.

6. Determine whether or not (0, 4), (4, 5), and (6, −3) are the vertices of a right triangle.

7. A circle has center (2, −1) and a radius of 3. Find the equation of the circle.

8. A circle has the equation $(x + 4)^2 + (y - 1)^2 = 16$. What are its center and radius?

9. A circle has center (2, 3) and the point (−2, 7) is on the circle. Find the equation of the circle.

10. A modern-day pirate wants to locate a treasure in a park. The water fountain is at (3, −2) and the swings are at (1, −4). The treasure is somewhere 4 units east of the water fountain and 2 units north of the swings. Where is the treasure?

11. Point $A$ has coordinates (4, −1) and point $B$ has coordinates (2, 7). What are the coordinates of the midpoint of $\overline{AB}$?

12. Point $M$ is the midpoint of $\overline{AB}$. Point $A$ has coordinates (3, 7) and $M$ has coordinates (−2, 1). Find the coordinates of $B$.

**13.**

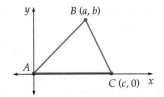

(a) Find the coordinates of the midpoints D of $\overline{AB}$ and E of $\overline{BC}$.
(b) Show that $\overline{DE} \parallel \overline{AC}$.
(c) Show that $DE = \frac{1}{2}AC$.

**14.**

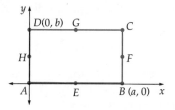

(a) Find the coordinates of the midpoints of the four sides, E, F, G, and H.
(b) Show that EFGH is a rhombus.

**15.** A circle has center (4, −2) and (3, 1) is a point on the circle. Find another point on the circle. (*Hint:* Find a diameter of the circle.)

**16.** Points (3, −1) and (5, 3) are endpoints of the diameter of a circle. Find the equation of the circle.

**17.** Find the taxicab distance from (2, 4) to (1, −2).

**18.** If $d_T(AB) = AB$, then describe the relationship between the coordinates of A and B.

**19.** (a) How would the air distance and the road distance from Dallas to St. Louis compare?
(b) Explain how part (a) relates to the concepts of standard (Euclidean) distance and taxicab distance.

**20.** Find points A, B, C, and D on a graph such that $d_T(AB) = d_T(CD)$ and $AB > CD$.

**21.** Point E has coordinates (1, −1). Plot all points that are a taxicab distance of 4 from E.

**22.** Roy (R) and Paula (P) each live three blocks from school. Where could the school be?

*Extension Exercises*

**23.**

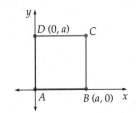

ABCD is a square.
(a) What would the coordinates of C have to be?
(b) Show that AC = BD.
(c) Use slopes to show that $\overline{AC} \perp \overline{BD}$.

**24.** The **center of gravity** of a polygon on a two-dimensional graph is $(\bar{x}, \bar{y})$ where $\bar{x}$ is the average (mean) of the x-coordinates of the vertices and $\bar{y}$ is the average (mean) of the y-coordinates of the vertices.
(a) Find the center of gravity of a quadrilateral with vertices at coordinates A(−1, −3), B(2, 4), C(5, 4), and D(6, −3).
(b) Cut out a piece of cardboard that has the shape of ABCD and balance it on the tip of a pin. Is the center of gravity very close to the location you obtained in part (a)?

**25.** A city has four retirement homes at A, B, C, and D. Where should the city build a medical center M so that the sum of the four distances from $M$ to the four homes is as small as possible?

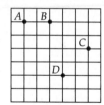

**26.** A **parabola** is the set of points equidistant from a line and a point not on that line. Follow steps (a)–(b) to find the equation of the parabola that is equidistant from $y = -2$ and $(0, 4)$.

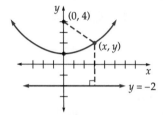

(a) Any point $(x, y)$ on the parabola is equidistant from $(0, 4)$ and $y = -2$. What are the coordinates of the point where $y = -2$ intersects the perpendicular?

(b) Complete the following equation.

$(0, 4)$ to $(x, y)$ dist. = $(x, -2)$ to $(x, y)$ dist.

$$\sqrt{(\ \ )^2 + (\ \ )^2} = \sqrt{(\ \ )^2 + (\ \ )^2}$$

(c) Square both sides and combine like terms to obtain the equation of the parabola.

**27.** Follow the instructions to create a curve by folding waxed paper.

(a) Crease a line segment $\overline{AB}$ and a point $C$ on the waxed paper as shown.

$$.C$$
$$A \text{———} B$$

(b) Fold the point onto the segment and crease. Repeat this about 20 times, folding the point onto different places on the segment.

(c) What shape is suggested by the crease?

(d) How does this work? (*Hint:* See the preceding exercise.)

**28.** If $(3, k)$ is equidistant from $A(5, -3)$ and $B(-1, -5)$, find the value of $k$.

**29.** Find a point that is $\frac{3}{4}$ of the way from $(2, 5)$ to $(4, 1)$.

**30.** Find the area of a triangle with vertices $(-1, 4)$, $(3, 1)$, and $(7, 2)$. (*Hint:* Enclose the triangle in a rectangle.)

**31.**

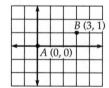

A **taxicab midpoint** $M$ of $A$ and $B$ would be any point such that if $d_T(AB) = c$, then

$$d_T(AM) = d_T(MB) = \frac{1}{2}c.$$ Find all taxicab midpoints of $A$ and $B$.

**32.** Devise a formula for computing the taxicab distance from the coordinates of a point. If $A$ has coordinates $(x_1, y_1)$ and $B$ has coordinates $(x_2, y_2)$, then

$$d_T(AB) = \text{———————}.$$ (*Hint:* Look at the change in $x$ and change in $y$.)

**33.**

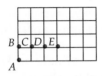

(a) How many different taxicab routes of the shortest distance are there from A to B?

(b) How many different taxicab routes of the shortest distance are there from A to C?

(c) How many different taxicab routes of the shortest distance are there from A to D?

(d) How many different taxicab routes of the shortest distance are there from A to E?

(e) Use the pattern from parts (a)–(d) to determine how many taxicab routes of the shortest distance there would be from (0, 0) to (10, 1).

**34.**

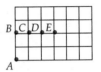

(a) How many different taxicab routes of the shortest distance are there from A to B?

(b) How many different taxicab routes of the shortest distance are there from A to C?

(c) How many different taxicab routes of the shortest distance are there from A to D?

(d) How many different taxicab routes of the shortest distance are there from A to E?

(e) Use the pattern from parts (a)–(d) to determine how many taxicab routes of the shortest distance there would be from (0, 0) to (6, 2).

**35.** Does the point $(-1, 4)$ lie inside or outside the circle with center (0, 1) and radius 3?

## Summary

In many mathematics problems, one examines a relation between two sets of numbers. A relation can be represented with a graph, a table, an equation, an arrow diagram, or words.

Algebra and calculus focus upon a special group of relations called functions, in which each $x$-value has exactly one corresponding $y$-value. The most important functions are linear functions. In linear functions of the form $y = mx$, $y$ is proportional to $x$, and the graph passes through the origin and has a slope of $m$.

Equations can be grouped by their form so that they correspond with graphs of a particular shape. All equations of the form $y = mx + b$ represent lines, and all equations of the form $y = ax^2 + bx + c$ (in which $a \neq 0$) represent parabolas. Some other forms of equations also correspond to specific geometric shapes.

Algebra is a mathematical language used to express relationships between quantities. Algebra cannot be used to analyze nonquantifiable relationships nor the merit of relationships that do exist between quantities.

The most common applications of algebra involve formulas. Formulas can be derived from words, tables, or graphs. After they are derived, such formulas may be used to solve problems in which all but one of the quantities are known. Tables and graphs offer alternate ways to solve problems.

Two thousand years after Euclid died, Fermat and Descartes devised coordinate geometry. Coordinate geometry unifies algebra and geometry. Coordinate geometry gives an algebraic perspective to many basic geometry concepts, including length, slope, and parallelism, and a new way of examining midpoints, circles, right triangles, and quadrilaterals.

## Study Guide

To review Chapter 11, see what you know about each of the following ideas or terms listed that you have studied. You can also use this list to generate your own questions about Chapter 11.

# The NCTM Curriculum Standards and Algebra

**Selected NCTM Curriculum Standards**

The following standards come from the NCTM document.

- Represent situations and number patterns with tables, graphs, verbal rules, and equations and explore the interrelationships of these representations.
- Analyze functional relationships to explain how a change in one quantity results in a change in another.
- Relate their everyday language to mathematical language and symbols.
- Understand the concepts of variable, expression, and equations.
- Use functions to represent and solve problems.

1. Describe how each standard listed relates to the material you studied in Chapter 11.
2. Select any current elementary-school mathematics textbook series and describe a sample lesson or exercise that illustrates each standard listed.

## Review Exercises

1. Where possible, translate the following phrases or sentences into algebraic expressions, equations, or inequalities.
   (a) Joe weighs more than twice as much as his sister.
   (b) Sara Lee is the sweetest woman in Texas.

2. Tell whether each graph represents a function.

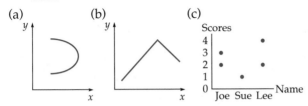

(a)
(b)
(c)

3. What real numbers cannot be used for $x$ if $y = \sqrt{3 - x}$?

4. (a) Graph $y = 2x + 1$.
   (b) What is the equation of the image of $y = 2x + 1$ after a reflection through the $y$-axis?

5. What is the slope of $5x - 2y = 6$?

6. The height of an automobile jack is a function of the number of times you crank it. Before cranking, a jack might be 10 in. high. Each crank raises the jack (and car) 0.5 in.
   (a) Write a formula relating the height of the jack, $h$, to the number of cranks, $n$.
   (b) Graph your formula.
   (c) What shape is your graph?

7. A waiter earns $1 per hour plus tips. Tips average $2 per table.
   (a) Write a formula relating total earnings, $E$,

to number of hours, $H$, and number of tables, $T$.

(b) How many tables must he serve in an 8-hour shift to earn \$40?

**8.** A salesperson earns a commission of 8% of her sales. Her boss then deducts 26% of the commission for taxes. How much must the salesperson sell in order to take home \$500?

**9.** How is the graph of $y = x^2 + 2$ related to the graph of $y = x^2$?

**10.** The typical weight $W$ (in pounds) of a man of height $H$ (in inches) can be estimated by $W = 5.5H - 220$.

(a) Solve for $H$.

(b) Which formula would be easier to use to find the typical weight of a man 5 feet 8 inches tall?

**11.** Suppose that you collect the following data on a group of 50 boys.

| Age | 3 | 4 | 5 | 6 | 7 | 8 |
|---|---|---|---|---|---|---|
| Av. Height (cm) | 100.0 | 106.6 | 112.8 | 119.5 | 126.0 | 133.0 |

(a) Plot the points on a two-dimensional graph.

(b) Draw a straight line that seems to fit the data best.

(c) What is the equation of your line?

(d) What average height does your equation predict at age 15?

**12.** The graph shows distance traveled versus time for a car trip. Draw a graph of speed versus time for the car trip.

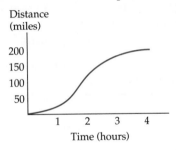

**13.** Explain why the distance between $A(x_1, y_1)$ and $B(x_2, y_2)$ is:

$$AB = \sqrt{(x_2 - x_1)^2 + (y_2 - y_1)^2}$$

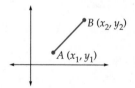

**14.**

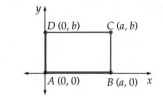

Show that the midpoint of $\overline{AC}$ is the midpoint of $\overline{BD}$.

**15.** How many different taxicab routes of the shortest distance are there from $A$ to $B$?

# Algebra and Coordinate Geometry in the Elementary School

The following chart shows at what grade level selected algebra and graphing topics typically appear in elementary-school mathematics textbooks.

| Topic | Typical Grade Level in Current Textbooks |
|---|:---:|
| Variables | <u>5</u>, <u>6</u> |
| Formulas and equations | 5, <u>6</u> |
| Graphing in the coordinate plane | 6 |

# Suggested Readings

Davis, R. *Discovery in Mathematics*. New Rochelle, NY: Cuisenaire, 1980.

Gardner, M. *Aha!* New York: W. H. Freeman, 1978.

Jacobs, H. *Algebra*. New York: W. H. Freeman, 1979.

National Council of Teachers of Mathematics. *A Sourcebook of Applications of School Mathematics*. Washington, DC: MAA, 1980.

National Council of Teachers of Mathematics. 1988 Yearbook. *The Ideas of Algebra, K–12*. Reston, VA: NCTM, 1988.

National Council of Teachers of Mathematics. 1992 Yearbook. *Calculators in Mathematics Education*. Reston, VA: NCTM, 1992.

# 12

# Computers and BASIC

How can a mathematics teacher utilize computers? Classroom uses include: (1) software that teaches concepts, skills, or problem solving; (2) software such as an automatic drawer that allows students to conduct investigations; (3) programming that gives insight into mathematical concepts or algorithms; and (4) simulations that mimic random events (see Chapter 14).

Logo is well suited to geometry, and BASIC is particularly appropriate for algebra and number theory. In this chapter, you will study BASIC programs for working with equations, algebraic formulas, number theory, and statistics. In the process of studying BASIC programs, you will develop a better understanding of how the computer works.

## 12.1 Introduction to BASIC

Programmers communicate with languages such as BASIC. In this lesson, you will use the BASIC language to write, store, change, or erase computer programs that do arithmetic or print messages. In doing this, you will also see how a computer works: first taking in information, then doing something with it, and finally printing out a result. Later in the chapter, you will study programs that use algebraic formulas and programs that find divisors.

### The BASIC Language

Computers are not very intelligent. They speak limited, inflexible languages. In the most widely used computer language, BASIC, a programmer can get by with about 30 words. Many microcomputers have BASIC built into their memories. So they can speak BASIC as soon as someone turns on the power.

The following investigation of BASIC can be done by pairs of students working at computer terminals or by an instructor using a demonstration computer in front of the class. (Your instructor can show you how to prepare your school computers to do BASIC.)

Which words does a computer speaking BASIC understand? Type the following:

HI THERE

and press the RETURN or ENTER key. (Pressing this key lets the computer know that you are finished typing in information.) What response did you get to your greeting? (Sorry, the computer does not understand the phrase "HI THERE.")

Type the following:

PRINT 842 − 279

and press the RETURN or ENTER key. PRINT is a BASIC word, so the computer understood what you wanted done, and it did it!

Type the following:

PRINT "HELLO GORGEOUS."

and press the RETURN or ENTER key. The computer understood this. See how intelligent the computer is! It recognizes your good looks. Remember what happened when you typed HI as the first word? The *first* word of the line has to be in BASIC.

Type the following:

PRINT "842 − 279"

and press the RETURN or ENTER key.

## Lesson Exercise 12.1

Why didn't the computer type 563 this time?

Figure 12-1 (page 696) shows how the fourth-grade textbook of *Mathematics Unlimited* introduces the PRINT statement.

## Running and Editing Programs

A computer program enables you to give a computer a set of instructions. A BASIC computer program has numbered lines. Line numbers are used in program editing.

# TECHNOLOGY

Your computer speaks a language called BASIC. The PRINT statement is an instruction in BASIC that your computer understands.

You type this.
PRINT "HI THERE"

The computer prints this.
HI THERE

You type this.
PRINT "BLUE CAT"

The computer prints this.
BLUE CAT

When you use the PRINT statement with quotation marks, the computer prints whatever is between the quotation marks.

You can also use the PRINT statement as a caculator.

You type this
PRINT 12 + 3

The computer prints this.
15

You type this.
PRINT 12 – 3

The computer prints this.
9

Use the PRINT statement without quotation marks to compute.

From *Mathematics Unlimited*, Grade 4 (San Diego, CA: Harcourt Brace Jovanovich, 1992), p. 134.

**Figure 12-1**

I resent this program!

Type the following program into the computer. Press RETURN or ENTER after each numbered line. If you make a typing error, you can press RETURN or ENTER and simply type that line over again. Your instructor may show you other ways to correct errors.

10 PRINT "HELLO."

20 PRINT "COMPUTERS ARE LIKE PARROTS."

Notice that when the lines are numbered, the computer does not perform them. It has not printed anything yet, but the computer has recorded the lines in its memory. To see what lines are in memory, type

LIST

and press RETURN or ENTER. The computer should have listed your two-line program. Now enter

RUN

The computer should have performed your program. As you have seen, numbered statements are stored in memory. To ascertain what is in memory, you enter LIST. To perform statements in memory, you enter RUN.

You can correct or rewrite a line by typing in a new version of it. Enter:

20 PRINT "PEOPLE ARE ILLOGICAL."

LIST

See how the program in memory changed? Now enter:

RUN

When you are finished with a program, enter NEW to erase the program from memory. Try it.

NEW

LIST

Nothing is left in memory to LIST. If you don't enter NEW before starting a new program, some old program lines may get mixed into the new program.

Enter the following:

10 PRINT "NOT"

20 PRINT "LUCKY"

RUN

Now, you decide to embellish the phrase.

15 PRINT "VERY"

## Lesson Exercise 12.2

**What will happen?**

LIST

RUN

As you saw, the computer puts numbered statements in order in its memory. Now, suppose that you want to erase line 10 because your luck has changed.

10

LIST

RUN

NEW

To erase any line in a program, type the line number with nothing after it, and press RETURN or ENTER.

## Arithmetic in BASIC

How does a computer do arithmetic? Incredibly fast. The following programs illustrate computer arithmetic. Enter the following program.

10 PRINT 76 * 57
20 PRINT "IS MORE THAN"
30 PRINT 76 + 57
LIST

Check your program for typing errors. Now RUN it.

RUN

In BASIC, spacing around the operation sign does not affect the result of a computation. You can type 76+57 or 76 + 57.

## Lesson Exercise 12.3

What does 76 * 57 mean?

Change line 10 to PRINT SQR(64) and line 30 to PRINT 76 / 57.

10 PRINT SQR(64)
30 PRINT 76 / 57
LIST

RUN it.

RUN

## Lesson Exercise 12.4

(a) What does SQR(64) mean?
(b) What does 76 / 57 mean?

What rules do computers use for doing a sequence of operations? Try the following.

## Lesson Exercise 12.5

(a) Predict what the computer will give as the answer to 7 + 3 * 6 − 1.
(b) Type in a statement that has the computer calculate and write the result.

Because the expression in the preceding exercise is ambiguous, mathematicians have made rules for the order of operations.

---

**Order of Operations**

When there are no parentheses, do multiplication and division
from left to right first, and then do addition and subtraction from
left to right.

---

The order of operations is set up this way to be compatible with
algebraic symbolism. The notation $3 + 4N$ suggests that 4 and $N$ are
multiplied *before* adding 3, since the 4 and $N$ are closer together.

## Lesson Exercise 12.6

Compute $6 - 18 \div 3 - 7 \times 2$ using the correct order of operations and
check your result on a computer or calculator.

---

Computers also work with exponents. The expression $3^8$ is usually
written $3 \wedge 8$ or $3 * * 8$ in computer languages. Try using these symbols in a
new version of line 10 to see which one works in your computer. For
example:

10 PRINT 3 $\wedge$ 8

LIST

RUN

## Lesson Exercise 12.7

(a) What happens in the computer when you type: 10 PRINT 3 $\wedge$ 8 and
    press RETURN or ENTER? (If $\wedge$ is not the appropriate symbol,
    change it.)
(b) What happens in the computer when you type: PRINT 3 $\wedge$ 8 and
    press RETURN or ENTER?

---

The following chart summarizes arithmetic symbols in BASIC.

---

**Arithmetic Symbols in BASIC**

| Mathematical Notation | BASIC Notation |
|---|---|
| 3 + 4 | 3 + 4 |
| 3 − 4 | 3 − 4 |
| 3 × 4 or 3 · 4 | 3 * 4 |
| 3 ÷ 4 | 3 / 4 |
| $3^4$ | _____ |
| | (Fill in for your computer.) |
| $3\frac{1}{2}$ | 3.5 or 7 / 2 |
| $\sqrt{3}$ | SQR(3) |

---

Clear the memory.

NEW

Recall how mathematicians and scientists abbreviate lengthy numerals.

## Lesson Exercise 12.8

Write 30,000,000,000,000,000 in scientific notation.

To see how your computer handles large numbers, type in the following program. The number in line 10 has a 3 followed by 16 zeroes. Do *not* insert commas in the number.

10 PRINT 30000000000000000
RUN

## D Lesson Exercise 12.9

Explain what the computer output means.

If computations involve numbers that are too large for a calculator, one can use a computer. Consider the following famous computation from number theory.

## Lesson Exercise 12.10

In the seventeenth century, Marin Mersenne, a French monk, examined numbers of the form $2^p - 1$, now known as Mersenne numbers. Mersenne substituted different values for $p$ and obtained the following results.

$2^2 - 1 = 3$            $2^3 - 1 = 7$
$2^4 - 1 = 15$ is not prime.    $2^5 - 1 = 31$
$2^6 - 1 = 63$ is not prime.    $2^7 - 1 = 127$, a prime
$2^8 - 1 = 255$ is not prime.   $2^9 - 1 = 511$ is not prime.
$2^{10} - 1 = 1023$ is not prime.   $2^{11} - 1 = 2047$, a prime
$2^{13} - 1$ and $2^{17} - 1$ are prime.

(a) Based upon these results, it appears that if $p$ is _____, then $2^p - 1$ is prime.
(b) Mersenne proposed that $2^p - 1$ is prime when $p$ is prime. In 1903, F. N. Cole said that Mersenne was wrong for $2^{67} - 1$. He said that $2^{67} - 1$ is divisible by 193,707,721. Check this on a computer.

Although not all Mersenne numbers are prime, the formula has been used to find the largest known prime number. In 1992, a supercomputer showed that the 227,832-digit number $2^{756,839} - 1$ is a prime. The computations to check the number took 19 hours.

## What Computers Do

All work with computers tends to involve three steps: first, you give the computer some instructions and some information to work with; second, the computer follows your directions; and third, the computer responds with some result. These three steps are called input, processing, and output.

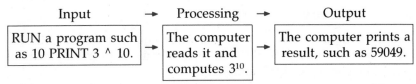

| Input | → | Processing | → | Output |
|---|---|---|---|---|
| RUN a program such as 10 PRINT 3 ^ 10. | → | The computer reads it and computes $3^{10}$. | → | The computer prints a result, such as 59049. |

**Input** is the information the computer receives from you. Then, the computer **processes** the information you type in. Finally, the computer responds with **output** as a result of running your program. For a computer, input is like listening, processing is like thinking, and output is like speaking.

The parts of a computer match up with input, processing, and output (Figure 12-2).

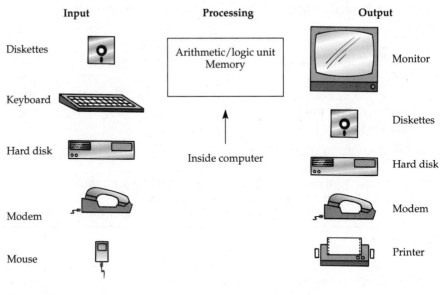

Figure 12-2

## Lesson Exercise 12.11

A supermarket cashier has a computer scanner that reads the bar code on a package and prints the price on a display. What would be the input, the processing, and the output for the computer in this case?

## Computer Memory

How does a computer know what to do when you type LIST or RUN? If your computer has built-in BASIC, the read-only memory (ROM) includes programs (directions) for LIST and RUN.

A computer has two types of memory: permanent read-only memory (ROM) and temporary random-access memory (RAM). **ROM** stores the directions that operate the computer. **RAM** holds the new BASIC programs that you write as well as programs the computer reads from a diskette. ROM is like a page in a book, since it is built in and cannot be erased. RAM is like a chalkboard, since it can be erased and used again to store other information.

## Lesson Exercise 12.12

When you turn off the computer, which is erased, RAM or ROM?

## Lesson Exercise 12.13

You type a BASIC program into your computer. Is it stored in RAM or ROM? (The answer depends upon your specific computer set-up.)

---

**Summary of BASIC Language**

| Commands | Function |
|----------|----------|
| LIST | lists all statements currently in computer memory |
| RUN | performs the program currently in computer memory |
| NEW | erases all statements currently in computer memory |

| Statement | Function | Example |
|-----------|----------|---------|
| PRINT | types out values and messages | 10 PRINT "I LIKE YOU." |

---

## Answers to Selected Lesson Exercises

12.1 because of the quotation marks

12.3 76 times 57

12.4 (a) $\sqrt{64}$    (b) $76 \div 57$ or $\frac{76}{57}$

12.5 (b) PRINT $7 + 3 * 6 - 1$

12.6 $-14$

12.7 (a) It stores the line in memory.
     (b) It computes $3^8$.

12.9 It changed the number to a shorthand that means $3 \times 10^{16}$.

12.11 input: bar code; processing: look up price that goes with the code; and output: prints the price

12.12 RAM

12.13 RAM

## 12.1   Homework Exercises

*Basic Exercises*

1. You type the following into the computer.

   NEW
   10 PRINT "MAD"
   20 PRINT "MAN"
   20 PRINT "DOG"

   (a) What will the computer type as output when you enter LIST?
   (b) What will the computer type when you enter RUN?

2. What would you type into the computer to change line 20 in a program to the following?

   20 PRINT "SUSAN"

3. What would you type into the computer to insert PRINT "NOT" between the two following statements?

   10 PRINT "IT IS"
   20 PRINT "RIGHT."

**4.** What will be in the memory of the computer after you enter the following lines?

10 PRINT "MIKE"

20 PRINT "SALLY"

30 PRINT "ROSA"

20 PRINT "LIKES"

10 PRINT "TONY"

**5.** What would you type into the computer to erase line 20?

10 PRINT "PLEASE"

20 PRINT "STOP"

30 PRINT "HER"

**6.** What is the output of each of the following programs?
(a) 10 PRINT 5 * 3      (b) 10 PRINT "5*3"
(c) 10 PRINT "5*3="; 5 * 3 (*Note:* the semi-colon is used to separate the two expressions, and it will not be printed.)

**7.** Write each of the following in BASIC notation.
(a) $4x^2$    (b) $\frac{2}{3}$    (c) $\frac{1}{2}(x \div 3)$
(d) $D = RT$

**8.** Write a BASIC expression to evaluate the thirtieth power of the sum of 28.9 and 37.6 and 0.8.

**9.** Is PRINT 3 + 4 * 5 the same as PRINT (3 + 4) * 5 or PRINT 3 + (4 * 5)? (If you're not sure, type these statements into a computer.)

**10.** Without using a computer, give the output of each of the following.
(a) PRINT 5 − 6 * 2 / 4
(b) PRINT 4 + 2 * 5 + 8 / (2 + 2)
(c) PRINT 8 + 4 * 2 − 6 / 3
(d) PRINT (8 − 6 / 2) + 8 * 3 − 2

 **11.** Compute the following on a calculator. Each correct answer should spell a word when you turn the calculator display upside down.

(a) 1150.7 + 8 × 8.5 × 102 − 348.7 = _____ (telephone inventor)
(b) 3 − 3 × 2 + 3998 × 2 + 82 = _____ (not neat)
(c) Make up your own.

**12.** Which of the following would be equal to $e + f \cdot g - h$?
(a) $f \cdot g + e - h$      (b) $e - h + f \cdot g$
(c) $(e + f) \cdot g - h$    (d) $h - e + f \cdot g$

**13.** What is the output of the following?

PRINT 3000000 * 4000000

**14.** Tell whether it is most appropriate to do each of the following mentally, with a calculator, or with a computer, assuming that you want an exact answer.
(a) 8.617 ÷ 2.3      (b) 30 × 700      (c) $5^{153}$

**15.** Write each of the following in decimal notation.
(a) 4.31 $E$ −05 (Apple)
    4.31 $D$ −05 (IBM)
(b) 3.2 $E$ 03 (Apple)
    3.2 $D$ 03 (IBM)

**16.** Write each decimal number in computer $E$-notation.
(a) 468,000      (b) 0.0013

**17.** Write a one-step BASIC program that has the computer write the message

"I'M A PRETTY COMPUTER."

**18.** Write a one-line BASIC program that calculates and prints $(4 + 0.1)^{60}$ and RUN it on a computer.

**19.** Fill in the blanks.

| Input | Processing | Output |
|-------|-----------|--------|
| 4, 6 | → Square the larger number. → | _____ |
| _____ | → Divide by 5 and add 2. → | 12 |

**20.** (a) Name two ways to input information into a computer.
(b) Name two computer output devices.

**21.** A building has a computerized thermostat on its air conditioner. Describe what would be input, processing, and output for the thermostat.

22. Which is permanent memory, RAM or ROM?

23. Find all the places computers are used in your home.

24. (a) What are some things computers have made easier for us to do?
    (b) How have computers detracted from the quality of our lives?

25. Give an example of how computers can improve the operations of a library.

*Extension Exercises*

26. Write a single PRINT statement that finds the balance on $5000 earning 8% interest compounded annually for 10 years.

27. Use the order of operations to explain why $2 + 3 \cdot x$ is not $5x$.

28. Use the order of operations to explain why $3 + 2\sqrt{2}$ is not $5\sqrt{2}$.

29. Look at a current mathematics textbook series for Grades 1–6. What do they teach about computers in each grade?

*Special Exercises*

30. In the game Krypto, you are dealt five cards and must combine them using any arithmetic operations to obtain the value on a sixth card. For example, if you are dealt 3, 4, 6, 8, and 10, and the sixth card is 2, you could write: $(10 - 3 - 6) \times 8 \div 4 = 2$. Parentheses are needed so that the subtraction is done before the multiplication and division.

    Try the following Krypto exercises.
    (a) Use 5, 7, 9, 10, and 12 to obtain 3.
    (b) Use 4, 8, 12, 15, and 20 to obtain 15.

31. Using five 3's, parentheses, and any of the four operations, try to write expressions equal to all the numbers from 1 to 10. Here is a solution for 0.

$$0 = [(3 \div 3) - (3 \div 3)] \times 3$$

## 12.2  Algebra on the Computer

To make effective use of computers, it helps to know what computers can do better than people, and what people can do better than computers. One thing computers do better is working with formulas. BASIC is especially well suited for working with formulas.

### What Computers Do Better Than People

The ingenious people who design computers try to develop computer capabilities to perform certain tasks better than people.

Lesson Exercise 12.14

What do computers do better than people? (*Hint:* Look at the cartoons in Figure 12-3, page 706.)

"SURE IT'S DEPRESSING. THIS THING HAS A MEMORY OF 3 TRILLION BITS, AND I CAN'T RECALL WHAT I HAD FOR LUNCH."

"SAY, BROWN — TAKE 14 YEARS AND CHECK THIS ANSWER."

© 1982 by Sydney Harris, *What's So Funny About Computers?* (Los Altos, CA: William Kaufman, Inc.).

**Figure 12-3**

## Lesson Exercise 12.15

(a) Time how long it takes you to add 364,921 + 847,972.
(b) The problem in part (a) takes some computers about 1 microsecond (1 millionth of a second). How many problems like this could such a computer solve in the time it took you to do part (a)?

Computers do arithmetic and make logical decisions faster and more accurately than people do. An example of a logical decision would be determining whether an equation (or inequality) is true or false. Computers do not become bored by repeating a set of instructions over and over and over.

## What People Do Better Than Computers

Computers are quite limited. They have trouble finding patterns. While you could easily find the pattern in 3, 5, 7, 9, . . . , a computer could not find a pattern like this without a relatively complicated program.

People are also much better at interpreting words and symbols that have different meanings in different contexts (such as the words "watch" and "bright").

Computers have difficulty interpreting statements that have even minor errors in spelling or punctuation. For example, when a computer asks you for two numbers, it may understand if you write: 3,4 but not if you write: 3 and 4. Computers understand only particular words and symbols. For example, a computer may understand "LET X = 3" but not "Let X equal 3" or "SET X = 3".

## Lesson Exercise 12.16

What else do people do better than computers? (*Hint:* Look at the cartoons in Figure 12-4.)

"NOT BAD FOR A COMPUTER, BUT THE CHIMPANZEE'S WORK HAD MORE FEELING."

© 1982 by Sydney Harris, *What's So Funny About Computers?* (Los Altos, CA: William Kaufman, Inc.).

**Figure 12-4**

## Using Formulas

In the last chapter, you studied applications of algebraic formulas. With their large memories and extraordinary computational capabilities, computers are well suited to work with formulas. In businesses, computers sometimes deal with hundreds of equations containing hundreds of variables. The following activities will give you an idea about how computers do algebra.

Enter the following program into the computer.

NEW
10 LET A = 3
15 LET C = 4
20 LET P = 7 * A + 4 * C
25 PRINT P

## Lesson Exercise 12.17

What do you think the computer will print when you RUN this program?

LIST it and RUN it.

LIST
RUN

LET is another BASIC word. LET is always followed by an equation. The equal sign in BASIC has a different meaning than it does in algebra. The computer performs two steps with a LET statement:

*Step 1*  It finds the value on the right side of the equal sign.

*Step 2*  It assigns this value to the variable address (actually a location inside the computer) on the left side.

So, for example, 10 LET A = 3 tells the computer to take 3 and put it in a memory mailbox labeled A. You can model this result with a drawing.

A
3

## Lesson Exercise 12.18

Make a mailbox drawing for lines 15 and 20 in the program just presented.

Edit the program as follows:

15 LET C = 2
LIST

## Lesson Exercise 12.19

Now what will the output be?

RUN it and see if you are right.

RUN

Try the following program.

```
NEW
100 LET R = 2
200 LET PI = 3.14159
300 LET A = PI * (R ^ 2)
400 PRINT "AREA = "; A ;" SQUARE UNITS"
```

## Lesson Exercise 12.20

What do you think the output will be?

LIST it and RUN it.

LIST
RUN

Did your program print 12.56636SQUARE UNITS without a space? If so, you did not put a space *between the quotation marks* before SQUARE UNITS.

The preceding program always uses R = 2. There is another BASIC statement that would enable the person running the program to INPUT any value of R he or she wanted! Try the following.

```
90 PRINT "ENTER THE RADIUS."
100 INPUT R
```

LIST the edited program and RUN it.

LIST
RUN

You should see a question mark.

?

This tells you that the computer has read line 100 and is waiting for you to input a value for R.

## Lesson Exercise 12.21

(a) Pick any decimal number for R and enter it. What happens?
(b) Run the program again and use a different value for R.

The INPUT statement allows you to pick the value for variables in a program after the program is running. Usually these variables are part of the right side of a formula.

Enter the following.

```
NEW
10 PRINT "MAY I SERVE YOU?"
20 PRINT "PROGRAM FINDS SLOPE OF LINE JOINING 2 POINTS"
30 PRINT "ENTER FIRST POINT-WRITE TWO COORDINATES
   SEPARATED BY A COMMA"
40 INPUT X1, Y1
50 PRINT "ENTER SECOND POINT"
60 INPUT X2, Y2
70 LET S = (Y2 - Y1) / (X2 - X1)
80 PRINT "THE SLOPE IS "; S
```

This time each input is *two numbers separated by a comma*. RUN the program and select input.

```
RUN
```

## Lesson Exercise 12.22

RUN the program again and select different input values.

Figure 12-5 shows how a sixth-grade textbook of *Mathematics Unlimited* introduces the INPUT statement.

Many programs using formulas have the following parts.

**1.** PRINT statement describing the purpose of the program

**2.** PRINT statement asking for input

**3.** INPUT statement

**4.** LET statement to process input

**5.** PRINT statement to print the result

TECHNOLOGY

Here's a BASIC program that uses an INPUT statement.

```
10  PRINT "TYPE A NUMBER"
20  INPUT N
30  LET T = 2 * N
40  PRINT "TWICE YOUR NUMBER IS"; T
```

When you RUN this program, your screen might look like this.

```
RUN
TYPE A NUMBER
?  16
TWICE YOUR NUMBER IS 32
```

Whatever number you type is stored in the variable N.

If you RUN this program again and type in a different number, that new number will be stored in N.

From *Mathematics Unlimited*, Grade 6 (San Diego, CA: Harcourt Brace Jovanovich, 1992), p. 186.

Figure 12-5

It is often possible to combine parts 4 and 5 into one statement. For example, in the preceding program:

70 LET S = (Y2 − Y1) / (X2 − X1)

80 PRINT "THE SLOPE IS "; S

could be replaced by:

70 PRINT "THE SLOPE IS "; (Y2 − Y1) / (X2 − X1)

Try writing some programs like these yourself.

D Lesson Exercise 12.23

(a) What is the surface area $A$ of a rectangular prism that has length $L$, width $W$, and height $H$?

(b) Write a program that asks a person for the length $L$, width $W$, and height $H$ of a rectangular prism and computes the total surface area $A$.

D Lesson Exercise 12.24

Clear the memory and write a program that will print out the rental charge for a car when someone types in the number of days and the number of miles driven. Assume that the rental charges are $26.50 per day and $.22 per mile driven.

---

**Summary of New BASIC Statements**

| Statement | Function | Example |
|-----------|----------|---------|
| LET | computes and assigns values | 35 LET X = A ∗ B |
| INPUT | allows program user to select numerical values for variables | 12 INPUT C, T |

## Answers to Selected Lesson Exercises

12.18  C        P

| 4 | | 37 |

## 12.2  Homework Exercises

*Basic Exercises*

1. (a) Name two things computers do better than people.
   (b) Name two things computers do not do as well as people.

2. (a) What kind of mathematics topics are most suitable for computer instruction?
   (b) What kind of mathematics topics are more effectively taught by a teacher?

3. Correct the following BASIC programs.
   (a) 10 LET A = 4
       20 LET 3 = B
       30 PRINT A ∗ B
       40 RUN
   (b) 10 SET A = 3
       14 LET T = 3A
       18 PRINT TOTAL PRICE IS T

4. (a) What is the output of the following program?

10 LET A = 5
15 PRINT 4 ∗ A
10 LET A = 8
RUN

   (b) In answering part (a), did you use inductive or deductive reasoning?

5. Which set of pictures correctly illustrates what is contained in the computer's memory after running the following program?

10 LET M = 3
20 LET T = 2 ∗ M + 5
30 PRINT T

(a)  M        T
| 3 | | 2M + 5 |

(b)  M     T
| 3 | | T |

(c)  M     T
| 3 | | 11 |

6. Draw mailboxes that show what is contained in the computer's *memory* after the following program is run.

   10 INPUT C
   20 LET T = 3.10 + 0.05 * C
   30 PRINT "YOUR MONTHLY RATE IS $"; T
   RUN
   ? 10

7. What is the output of the following programs?
   (a) 10 LET A = 3
       20 LET B = 4
       30 LET C = 4 * A − 5 * B
       40 PRINT C
   (b) 100 LET A = 5
       200 LET B = 2 + 3 * A
       300 PRINT B

8. What is the output of the following programs?
   (a) 20 INPUT N
       30 LET T = 4 + N / 40
       40 PRINT T ; " DEGREES"
       RUN
       ? 100
   (b) 5 PRINT "BASE, HEIGHT"
       10 INPUT B, H
       15 LET A = 0.5 * B * H
       20 PRINT "THE AREA IS "; A
       RUN
       BASE, HEIGHT
       ? 3, 6

9. Correct the following program.

   10 INPUT B, H
   20 PRINT A = B * H

10. (a) Type the following into your computer.

    PRINT ABS(− 2)
    PRINT ABS(3)

    (b) What does ABS do?

*Extension Exercises*

11. Can computers think? Look up definitions of the word "think" in a dictionary. List each definition in brief form and write whether or not you believe computers can think in that way.

12. Many banks pay interest "daily" (usually counted 360 days a year or exactly 30 times each month). The following program computes interest compounded daily. (You may have studied this topic in Chapter 7.)
    (a) Enter the following program into a computer.

       10 PRINT "HOW MUCH MONEY WILL YOU DEPOSIT?"

       20 INPUT P

       30 PRINT "HOW MANY YEARS IS IT IN FOR?"

       40 INPUT T

       50 PRINT "TYPE IN THE ANNUAL % INTEREST RATE AS A DECIMAL (LIKE 0.065)."

       60 INPUT I

       70 LET A = P * (1 + I / 360) ^ (360 * T)

       80 PRINT "YOU WILL END UP WITH $"; A

    (b) RUN the program using the input of your choosing.
    (c) Find the output if P = 1000, T = 3, and I = 0.06.
    (d) Have the program compute interest compounded annually instead of daily by changing line 70 to

       70 LET A = P * (1 + I) ^ T

       Use the data from part (c) in your new program. How does daily compounding compare to annual compounding?
    (e) Use the program in part (d) to find out how many years it would take your investment to double if you earn 8% interest compounded annually.
    (f) Use the program in part (d) to find out

how many years it would take your investment to double if you earn 10% interest compounded annually.

13. A phone company charges a basic rate of $4 plus $.06 per local call.
   (a) Write a formula for computing the total cost C for a month.
   (b) Write a program that asks a person how many local calls were made last month and then computes the total monthly charge.

14. The following BASIC program computes phone bills based upon a monthly rate R (in $) plus a charge per call C (in $).

```
10 PRINT "TYPE THE MONTHLY RATE
   AND CHARGE SEPARATED BY A COMMA
   (LIKE 6.50,.09)."
20 INPUT R, C
30 PRINT "HOW MANY CALLS WERE
   MADE?"
40 INPUT N
50 PRINT "THE MONTHLY BILL IS $";
```

   (a) Complete line 50 with an appropriate formula.
   (b) RUN the program and find the cost of making 63 calls when the monthly rate is $8.40 and the cost per call is $.08.

(c) Modify the program so that it also adds 3% tax to the bill.

15. Write a program for a rental car agency that accepts two sets of input. First, you input the charge per day and the charge per mile. Then, you input the number of days driven and the number of miles driven. The program prints out the rental charge for the car.

16. (a) Write a program that accepts input for the radius and height of a cylinder and prints out the volume.
   (b) Modify your program so that it also prints out the surface area.

17. Write a program that asks for the lengths of the two legs of a right triangle and prints out the length of the hypotenuse. (*Hint:* Use SQR.)

18. Write a program that asks for the total number of test questions and the number right and prints out the percent of questions that are right.

19. Write a program that asks for an old price and a new price and prints out the percent increase or decrease.

20. If you have spreadsheet software available, set up a spreadsheet for one of the preceding four exercises. Make up and display five sets of data.

## 12.3　Branches

In all computer languages, programs rely on two basic structures: branches and loops. This lesson deals with branches; the next deals with loops.

Suppose a program asks a person his or her height and then tells the person if he or she is tall enough to be a police officer. This program would need two different output messages: one for people who are tall enough and one for people who are not.

YES
Height over ——→ You're tall enough.
66 in.?

↓ NO
You're not
tall enough.

Such a program would have a branch. A **branch** tests a statement to see if it is true or false. If it is true, the program branches to one group of statements. Otherwise, the program branches to a second group of statements.

To write a branch, you will need three new BASIC statements: GOTO, IF-THEN, and END.

## GOTO Instruction

The GOTO instruction tells the computer to jump to another line number in the program. For example, when the computer reads: GOTO 50, it will go to line 50.

## Lesson Exercise 12.25

What is the output of the following program?

10 GOTO 30
20 PRINT "NO"
30 PRINT "EXIT"

## END and IF-THEN Instructions

The END instruction stops a program. The IF-THEN instruction checks a condition, and if the condition is true, the computer jumps to another part of the program or performs the instructions after THEN.

The following program utilizes these two new BASIC instructions in a branch.

## D Lesson Exercise 12.26

Consider the following program.

10 PRINT "HOW MANY SHIRTS DO YOU WANT?"
20 INPUT N
30 IF N > 4 THEN 60
40 PRINT "THE COST IS $"; N * 10
50 GOTO 70
60 PRINT "THE COST IS $"; N * 8
70 END

Without using a computer, do parts (a) and (b).
(a) What is the output of the program if N = 2?
(b) What is the output of the program if N = 6?
(c) RUN the program on a computer and check your answers to parts (a) and (b).

## Branch Flowcharts and Outlines

The structure of a branch can be illustrated with a flowchart or an outline. Flowcharts have four main types of boxes, as shown in Figure 12-6.

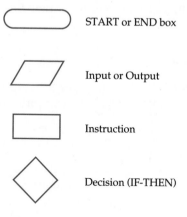

START or END box

Input or Output

Instruction

Decision (IF-THEN)

**Figure 12-6**

The branch for a police officer's height is shown in Figure 12-7.

**Branch flowchart**          **Branch outline**

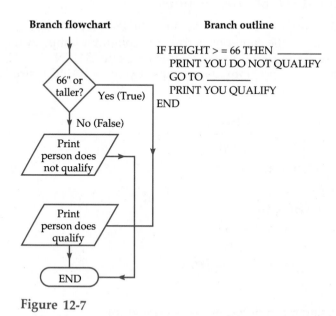

IF HEIGHT > = 66 THEN _____
PRINT YOU DO NOT QUALIFY
GO TO _____
PRINT YOU QUALIFY
END

**Figure 12-7**

Any two-way branch can be written with this structure.

## Lesson Exercise 12.27

Complete the flowchart in Figure 12-8 on retirement age for a particular company.

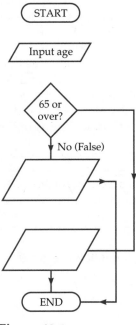

**Figure 12-8**

## Branch Programs

The following BASIC program performs the branch for police officers' heights. It contains the three new BASIC statements: IF-THEN, GOTO, and END. Type the program into a computer and RUN it, trying some different heights.

```
10 PRINT "PLEASE ENTER YOUR HEIGHT IN INCHES AND PRESS
   RETURN."
20 INPUT H
30 IF H >= 66 THEN GOTO 60
40    PRINT "I AM SORRY BUT YOU ARE TOO SHORT."
50    GOTO 70
60    PRINT "YOU QUALIFY."
70 END
```

How does line 30 work? Suppose you enter 70 for H in line 20. When the computer reaches line 30, it checks the IF condition to see if it is true. Is

70 >= 66? Yes! So the computer reads the line number after THEN and goes to line 60. After performing line 60, the computer automatically stops when it reads the word END in line 70.

What if you enter 60 for H in line 20? When the computer reaches line 30, it finds that the IF condition 60 >= 66 is false. Therefore, it does not follow the THEN part. It simply proceeds to the next line, 40, as it would normally do. After performing line 40, line 50 causes the computer to jump to line 70, which then stops the program.

One can indent in a BASIC program (see lines 40–60) to indicate where a branch (or a loop in Section 12.4) begins and ends. Depending upon your computer and software, it may be necessary to type colons between the line number and the first BASIC word in order to retain the indentation when you LIST the program. Indenting is optional, a matter of style.

**D** Lesson Exercise 12.28

Write a program that asks a person for his or her age and tells the person if he or she is old enough to retire. Choose the retirement age, and follow the example of the police officers' height program.

A branch outline has the following general form.

```
Summary of Branch Outline

    IF condition THEN _____⌐   (condition true)
        do something                │
        GOTO _____         │
        do something ◄──────────────┘   (condition false)
    END ◄───────────────────────────
```

The following chart summarizes the new BASIC statements in this lesson.

```
Summary of New BASIC Statements
```

| Statement | Purpose | Example |
|---|---|---|
| END | stops a program | END |
| GOTO | jumps to a particular line number in a program | GOTO 60 |
| IF . . . THEN . . . | checks to see if the statement after IF is true. If it is true, it follows the instruction after THEN. Otherwise, it goes to the next line of the program. | IF X > 5 THEN GOTO 100 |

## Answers to Selected Lesson Exercises

12.25 EXIT

## 12.3 Homework Exercises

### Basic Exercises

1. Consider the following program.

   10 PRINT "WHAT IS YOUR GPA?"

   20 INPUT G

   30 IF G >= 3.5 THEN 60

   40 PRINT "NOT QUITE"

   50 GOTO 70

   60 PRINT "HONORS"

   70 END

   Without using a computer, answer the following.
   (a) What is the output of the program if G = 2?
   (b) What is the output of the program if G = 3.5?
   (c) In answering parts (a) and (b), did you use inductive or deductive reasoning?

2. Without using a computer, give the output of the following program.

   10 INPUT AGE

   20 IF AGE > 17 THEN GOTO 50

   30 PRINT 12 * AGE

   40 GOTO 60

   50 PRINT 220 − AGE

   60 END

   RUN

   ?4

3. The following program has one unnecessary line. Removing this line would not change the program. (It is not line 70.) Which one is it?

   10 INPUT A

   20 IF A > 60 THEN 60

   30 IF A <= 60 THEN 40

   40 PRINT "FAILS"

   50 GOTO 70

   60 PRINT "PASSES"

   70 END

4. Use the following flowchart to diagnose each patient (*AMA Family Medical Guide*, p. 129).

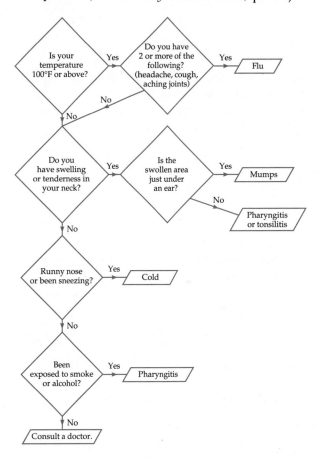

   (a) Clara: Her only symptoms are a runny nose, a 101°F temperature, and a sore throat.
   (b) Malcolm: His only symptoms are a cough, a headache, a runny nose, and a 100°F temperature.

5. Complete the following flowchart for checking if a fraction is in simplest form.

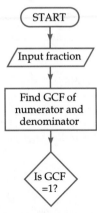

6. Complete the following flowchart that checks if a number is in $A \cap B$.

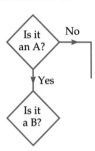

7. Construct a flowchart using the following instructions.

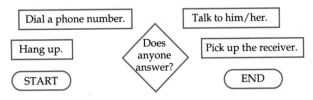

8. Write a BASIC program for the following flowchart.

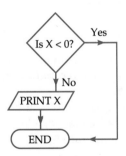

9. Write a BASIC program for the following flowchart.

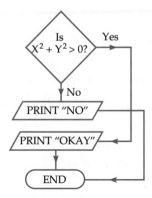

10. Dress shirts are $18 each if fewer than 5 are purchased and $16 each when at least 5 are purchased. Fill in line 40 to complete the program so that it computes the total cost of any number of shirts.

   10 PRINT "TYPE IN THE NUMBER OF SHIRTS YOU WANT."

   20 INPUT N

   30 IF N < 5 THEN 60

   40 _____

   50 GOTO 70

   60 LET C = 18 ∗ N

   70 PRINT "THE TOTAL COST IS $"; C

   80 END

11. Write a library program that asks a person how many books he or she wants to borrow. If the person says 6 or fewer, respond that it is okay. Otherwise, tell the person that he or she is over the limit.

12. Write a program that asks a person's age and tells the price of admission. If the person is under 18, the cost is $3. If the person is 18 or over, the cost is $5.

*Extension Exercises*

13. A job pays $5.76 per hour for the first 40 hours during a week and time and a half for each hour worked over 40.
   (a) Write a formula that relates $H$, the

number of hours worked, to $T$, total pay, for someone who worked over 40 hours.

(b) Write a program that will print out the total weekly pay for any given number of hours worked.

14. In Washington, D.C., one type of monthly phone service costs $10.25 for up to 60 local calls and $.09 for each additional call.

(a) Write a formula for computing the total rate for a person who makes over 60 calls.

(b) Write a program that will print out the monthly rate for any given number of local phone calls.

15. The following program computes the slope using the two-point formula.

10 PRINT "MAY I SERVE YOU?"

20 PRINT "PROGRAM FINDS SLOPE OF LINE JOINING 2 POINTS"

30 PRINT "ENTER FIRST POINT-WRITE TWO COORDINATES SEPARATED BY A COMMA"

40 INPUT X1, Y1

50 PRINT "ENTER SECOND POINT"

60 INPUT X2, Y2

70 LET S = (Y2 − Y1) / (X2 − X1)

80 PRINT "THE SLOPE IS"; S

Modify the program so that it checks for the special case of undefined slope and prints an appropriate message.

16. Write a program that asks a person if he or she wants to change West German marks to U.S. dollars or dollars to marks. (Use the conversion rate 1 mark = $.62.) Then ask how many and print the conversion.

17. Write a program that asks a person for the radius of a circle. Then ask the person to enter a 1 for the circumference or a 2 for the area. The program should then type out the appropriate measurement. (Use 3.14159 as an approximation for $\pi$.)

18. Computer chips can add, multiply, and square voltages. For example, a "× 4 chip" is shown here.

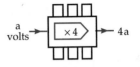

Find the output of the following.

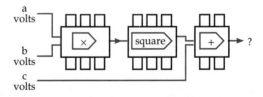

19. Use only the following chips:
Begin with three inputs, $a$, $b$, and $c$, and produce each of the following outputs.

(a) $a(b + c)$      (b) $(a^2 + 2b)c$

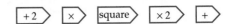

# 12.4  Loops

Suppose that a teacher wishes to enter four test scores for each student in a class and have the computer print each student's average. The teacher could run the following program over again for each student, but that would be inefficient!

10 PRINT "ENTER 4 SCORES SEPARATED BY COMMAS."
20 INPUT A, B, C, D
30 LET AVG = (A + B + C + D) / 4
40 PRINT "THIS STUDENT AVERAGES "; AVG

### Loop Flowcharts and Outlines

When a group of statements needs to be repeated over and over, it can be done efficiently with a **loop.** A loop that repeatedly finds student averages can be shown with a flowchart or an outline, as illustrated in Figure 12-9.

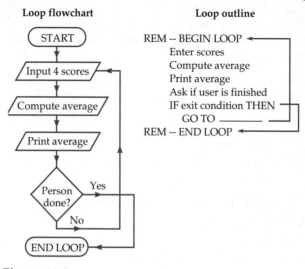

Figure 12-9

All loops can be written using this organization. The following exercise contains a loop program that prints multiples of 5.

## Lesson Exercise 12.29

Complete the flowchart in Figure 12-10 for a program of counting by 5's from 5 up to 100.

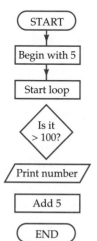

Figure 12-10

The following program computes the average of four test scores for a series of students. The program repeats over and over until the user tells it to stop.

10 PRINT "ENTER 4 SCORES SEPARATED BY COMMAS."
20 INPUT A, B, C, D
30 LET AVG = (A + B + C + D) / 4
40 PRINT "THIS STUDENT AVERAGES "; AVG

50 PRINT "ARE YOU DONE? TYPE 1 FOR YES AND 0 FOR NO. THEN
   PRESS RETURN."

60 INPUT R

70 IF R = 1 THEN 90

80 GOTO 10

90 END

## Lesson Exercise 12.30

(a) Type the preceding program into a computer and RUN it.

(b) Explain what happens when R = 0 in line 60.

## Counters

Many loop programs require a counter. The following rather curious look-ing equation can work as a counter.

30 LET C = C + 1

   Remember that an equal sign in BASIC has a different meaning than it does in algebra. It tells the computer to store the value of the right side of the equation at the memory location on the left side of the equation.

## Lesson Exercise 12.31

(a) What three values of C do you think would be printed by the follow-ing program?

   10 LET C = 0

   20 PRINT C

   30 LET C = C + 1

   40 PRINT C

   50 LET C = C + 10

   60 PRINT C

(b) RUN the program and see.

   How did the program in the preceding exercise work? After line 10, C = 0.

C

| 0 |
|---|

In line 20, the computer prints 0. In line 30, the computer places the value C + 1, which is 1, at memory location C.

C

| 1 |
|---|

In line 40, the computer prints 1. In line 50, the computer places C + 10, which is 11, at memory location C.

C

| 11 |
|----|

In line 60, the computer prints 11.

**D** Lesson Exercise 12.32

Write a program with a loop that prints all multiples of 5 beginning with 5 and ending with 100. Use the flowchart from Lesson Exercise 12.29 to help design it. (*Hint:* You will need a LET statement with an equation that increases the value of a number by 5.)

## FOR-NEXT Loops

There is a shorter way to write a loop if the number of repetitions can be specified before the loop begins. For example, in Lesson Exercise 12.32, if you figured out that you would be printing 20 multiples of 5, you could write the program as a FOR-NEXT loop.

RUN the following program.

```
10 FOR N = 1 TO 20
20    PRINT 5 * N
30 NEXT N
```

How does this program work? The FOR statement tells the computer to start with N = 1 and consider in turn the numbers 1, 2, 3, . . . , 20 for N. For each of these numbers in turn, the computer proceeds line by line until it encounters the NEXT statement. So when N = 1, the computer performs line 20 and prints 5. Then it reads line 30, which picks the next N, 2.

Since 2 is in the range of numbers given in the FOR statement, the computer begins the loop again at line 10 with N = 2. It performs line 20 and prints 10. Then it reads line 30, which assigns 3 to N.

The FOR-NEXT loop is then repeated in this fashion for N = 1, 2, 3, . . . , 20, and line 20 prints out the multiples of 5.

## Lesson Exercise 12.33

An object is tossed in the air from a height of 192 ft. The height H of the object after T seconds is given by $H = -16T^2 + 64T + 192$.
(a) RUN the following program.

```
10 FOR T = 0 TO 10
20  PRINT T; " SECONDS", -16*T*T + 64*T + 192;" FEET"
30 NEXT T
```

(b) Use the program to estimate when the object is at its high point and when it hits the ground.
(c) What do negative heights mean?

## Lesson Exercise 12.34

You are offered two sales jobs. One pays $500 per week plus 10% commission on total sales. The other pays $400 per week plus a 15% commission.
(a) Write a formula for the weekly pay, W, for D dollars in sales for the first job.
(b) Write a formula for the weekly pay, W, for D dollars in sales for the second job.
(c) Write a computer program that prints the total pay of each job for weekly sales of $500, $1000, $1500, . . . , $5000. You could print the results in columns with the following headings.

| Sales | Job 1 Pays | Job 2 Pays |
|---|---|---|

(d) Under what conditions does each job pay better?

### The INT Instruction

BASIC has a special rounding instruction (INT) that is useful in number theory programs. The INT instruction rounds all numbers *down* to the nearest integer. What use is such a statement? After an introduction to INT statements, you'll see how they are used to find divisors and prime numbers.

### Example 12.1

Find the value of each computer expression.
(a) INT(3.6)       (b) INT(7)       (c) INT(−4)
(d) INT(−4.2)     (e) INT(5 / 3)   (f) INT(−5 / 3)

**Solution**

INT rounds the value in the parentheses *down* to the nearest integer.
(a) INT(3.6) = 3     (b) INT(7) = 7     (c) INT(−4) = −4
(d) INT(−4.2) = −5

−5          −4.2   −4

(e) INT(5 / 3) = 1

1               $\frac{5}{3}$          2

(f) INT(−5 / 3) = −2

−2        $\frac{-5}{3}$        −1

## Lesson Exercise 12.35

Find the value of each computer expression.
(a) INT(20 / 3)     (b) INT(3)     (c) INT(−3.2)

## Lesson Exercise 12.36

If A = 27 and B = 5 then INT(A / B) = _____ .

## Lesson Exercise 12.37

If X = INT(X) then X is _____ .

## Lesson Exercise 12.38

If X ≠ INT(X) then X is _____ .

In programs involving factors, multiples, and primes, it is often helpful to compare INT(A / J) to A / J.

## D Lesson Exercise 12.39

(a) Suppose that A = 8. For what counting numbers J in the set
    {1, 2, 3, 4, 5, 6, 7, 8} does A / J = INT(A / J)?
(b) In part (a), what mathematical term describes how the numbers in
    the set you listed are each related to 8?
(c) Based upon part (b), it appears that if A / J = INT(A / J),
    then _____ .

## Lesson Exercise 12.40

(a) RUN the following program on a computer.

```
10 FOR J = 1 TO 8
20    IF 8 / J = INT(8 / J) THEN 40
30       GOTO 50
40       PRINT J
50 NEXT J
```

(b) What is the purpose of this program?
(c) Modify the program to print all factors of 50.
(d) Modify the program so that the user can input any number.

## Answers to Selected Lesson Exercises

12.34 (a) $W = 500 + 0.1D$
     (b) $W = 400 + 0.15D$

12.35 (a) 6    (b) 3    (c) $-4$

12.36 5

12.37 an integer

12.38 not an integer

## 12.4 Homework Exercises

### Basic Exercises

**1.** Complete the following flowchart for a program counting by 8's up to 200.

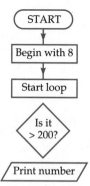

**2.** Complete the following flowchart for a program that counts down from 20 to 0 by 2's.

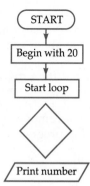

**3.** If A = 20 and B = 12, what is the output of
the following flowchart?

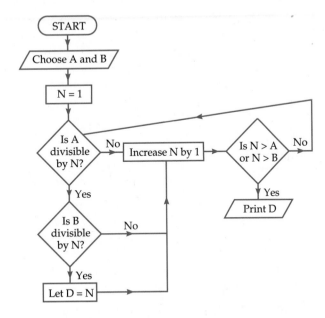

**4. (a)** RUN the following program on a computer.

10 PRINT " L", " W", " P"

20 FOR L = 1 TO 16

30 LET W = 16/L

40 LET P = (2 ∗ L) + (2 ∗ W)

50 PRINT L, W, P

60 NEXT L

**(b)** What shape is this program about?

**(c)** What is true about the area of this shape?

**(d)** Explain what the program is about and what it shows.

**5.** Without using a computer, give the output of the following program.

10 LET N = 4

20 LET M = 5

30 PRINT N

40 LET N = N ^ 2 + M ^ 2

*(Program continues in next column.)*

50 IF N > 300 THEN 70

60 GOTO 30

70 END

**6.** What is the output of the following program?

10 INPUT C

20 LET C = C + 100

30 PRINT C

RUN

? 8

**7.** Write a program that prints all multiples of 9 beginning with 9 and ending with 180.

**8.** RUN the following program on a computer.

10 PRINT " X                Y"

20 FOR X = −3 TO 3

30    LET Y = X ^ 2 + 3 ∗ X − 2

40    PRINT X; "             " ;Y

50 NEXT X

**(a)** What is the output of the program? (If necessary, edit line 10 or 40 to line up the table.)

**(b)** Use the table to graph $y = x^2 + 3x − 2$.

**9.** Write a program that prints a table of values for $y = x^3 − 2x + 7$ for $x = -5, -4, -3,$ . . . , 5. (See the preceding exercise.)

**10.** Rewrite the following program using a FOR-NEXT loop.

10 LET T = 100

20 PRINT T

30 LET T = T + 1

40 IF T > 110 THEN 60

50 GOTO 20

60 END

**11.** Write a program that prints the squares of the first ten odd numbers.

**12.** An object is tossed in the air. The height, $H$, of the object after $T$ seconds is given by $H = -16T^2 + 32T + 1280.$

(a) Write a program that computes the height after 1, 2, 3, . . . , 10 seconds.

(b) When does the object reach its high point?

13. You are choosing between two health insurance plans. One pays 60% of all expenses beyond the first $100. The second pays 80% of all expenses beyond the first $500.

(a) Write a formula for *A*, the amount the first policy pays on a claim of *C* dollars.

(b) Write a formula for *A*, the amount the second policy pays on a claim of *C* dollars.

(c) Write a computer program that prints the total amount paid under each plan for claims of $250, $500, $750, . . . , $2000.

(d) Describe the conditions under which each plan pays more.

14. Find the value of each computer expression.
    (a) INT(10.2)     (b) INT(−8.1)
    (c) INT(21.7)

15. If INT(T) = T then T is _____ .

16. Suppose R = 20. For what counting numbers does INT(R/S) = R/S?

17. What is the output of the following program?

```
10 INPUT A
20 FOR J = 2 TO A
30   IF INT(A / J) = A / J THEN 50
40      GOTO 60
50      PRINT J
60 NEXT J
RUN
? 186
```

*Extension Exercises*

18. The following program will compute the average of 5 numbers.

```
10 SUM = 0
20 FOR I = 1 TO 5
30    PRINT "TYPE IN THE NEXT
         NUMBER."
```

*(Program continues in next column.)*

```
40    INPUT R
50    LET SUM = SUM + R
60 NEXT I
70 PRINT "THE AVERAGE IS "; SUM / 5
```

Modify the program so it asks a person how many numbers will be entered and then computes the average of this set of numbers.

19. A FOR statement does not have to count by ones.

(a) RUN the following BASIC program on a computer and find the output.

```
10 FOR T = 1 TO 15 STEP 2
20    PRINT T
30 NEXT T
```

(b) Write a FOR statement that counts the multiples of 5 from 5 to 100.

(c) Predict the output of the following. Then check it on a computer.

```
10 FOR T = 10 TO 0 STEP −2
20    PRINT T
30 NEXT T
```

20. (a) Enter the following BASIC program into a computer.

```
10 PRINT "TYPE TWO WHOLE
      NUMBERS SEPARATED BY A
      COMMA AND PRESS RETURN. TYPE
      THE SMALLER NUMBER FIRST."
20 INPUT M, N
30 FOR D = M TO 1 STEP −1
40    IF M / D = INT(M / D) AND N / D
         = INT(N / D) THEN 60
50 NEXT D
60 PRINT "THE GREATEST COMMON
      FACTOR OF "; M ;" AND
      ";N;" IS "; D ;"."
```

(b) RUN the program and type in 20, 36. What is the output?

(c) Use the program to find the greatest common factor of 1457 and 1581.

21. The LCM of two numbers can be computed by multiplying the two numbers and dividing by their greatest common factor.
    (a) Revise the program in the previous exercise so that it prints the GCF and the LCM.
    (b) RUN the program for 1581 and 1457.

22. In 1992, the post office charged $.29 for up to 1 ounce for first-class letters and $.23 for each additional ounce or fraction of an ounce. Write a program that asks for a weight and gives the rate. (*Hint:* Use INT, but ingeniously, since INT rounds down and you want to round up.)

23. Write a program that uses INT to round a decimal number to the nearest integer using the rounding rules from Chapter 3. (*Hint:* Add 0.5.)

24. A man has $100,000 in savings when he retires on January 1, 1994. Each year, he withdraws $20,000 at the beginning of the year. The rest of the money earns 9% interest compounded annually. How many years will his money last?

25. (a) RUN the following nested loops program on a computer and find the output.

    10 FOR I = 1 TO 3
    20   FOR J = 2 TO 3
    30     PRINT J
    40   NEXT J
    50 NEXT I

    (b) Explain the resulting output using mailboxes for I and J.

26. Write a program that tells if any input counting number greater than 1 is a prime.

## Summary

Computers can enhance the teaching of mathematics. Logo and BASIC are helpful in teaching selected mathematics topics, and a number of excellent software programs are available that teach and reinforce concepts, skills, or problem solving.

Writing BASIC programs that do mathematics requires that the programmer think more precisely about mathematics; in the process, the programmer also learns more about how a computer works. All computer programs, no matter how complicated, contain no more than three different program structures: straight sequential order, branches, and loops. Both the branch and the loop have standard formats that most programmers use.

In a program, the computer takes input and usually does arithmetic, makes comparisons, stores data, and/or recalls data. The computer then prints the results of the program.

## Study Guide

To review Chapter 12, see what you know about each of the following ideas or terms listed that you have studied. You can also use this list to generate your own questions about Chapter 12.

# The NCTM Curriculum Standards and Computers

**Selected NCTM Curriculum Standards**

The following standards come from the NCTM document.

- Relate everyday language to mathematical language and symbols.
- Apply algebraic methods to solve a variety of real-world problems.
- Recognize and apply deductive reasoning.

1. Describe how each standard listed relates to the material you studied in Chapter 12.
2. Select any current elementary-school mathematics textbook series and describe a sample lesson or exercise that illustrates each standard listed.

## Review Exercises

1. (a) Name two things computers do better than people.
   (b) Name two things people do better than computers.

2. Convert the IBM computer notation 4.987 D −5 to a decimal notation.

3. Compute the answer to
   $4 + 3 * 5 - (10 - 8 / 2)$.

4. (a) What is the output of the following program?

   ```
   10 PRINT "TYPE TWO NUMBERS
      SEPARATED BY A COMMA."
   20 INPUT A, B
   30 LET C = A * (B ^ 2) + B
   40 PRINT C
   RUN
   TYPE TWO NUMBERS SEPARATED BY
   A COMMA.
   ? 3, 7
   ```

   (b) In working out this problem, did you use inductive or deductive reasoning?

5. Write a BASIC program that asks a person how many adult and children's tickets they want to buy and then gives them the price. Assume that adult tickets cost $12 each and children's tickets cost $8 each.

6. Suppose that you have typed the following program into the computer.

   ```
   NEW
   10 PRINT "A FRIED"
   15 PRINT "EGG"
   20 PRINT "IS GOOD"
   15 PRINT "SQUID"
   ```

   (a) What will the computer type when you enter LIST?
   (b) What will the computer type when you enter RUN?

7. A group of salespersons make $400 plus 12% commission on all of their sales beyond the first $200. Write a program that asks a salesperson to input his or her total sales and prints out what the commission is.

8. What is the output of the following program?

   ```
   10 INPUT B, H, C
   20 IF C = 1 THEN 50
   30 LET V = 2 * B * (H ^ 2)
   40 GOTO 60
   50 LET V = B * (H ^ 3)
   60 PRINT V
   RUN
   ? 6, 4, 2
   ```

9. A job pays $8.60 per hour for the first 40 hours each week and double pay for each hour beyond 40. Write a program that will print out the total weekly pay for any given number of hours per week.

10. Find the output of the following program.

    ```
    10 FOR J = 1 TO 12
    20     IF INT(12 / J) = 12 / J THEN 40
    30         GOTO 50
    40         PRINT J
    50 NEXT J
    ```

11. You are choosing between two health insurance plans. One pays 50% of all expenses beyond the first $200. The second pays 75% of all expenses beyond the first $500.
    (a) Write a formula for $A$, the amount the first policy pays on a claim of $C$ dollars.
    (b) Write a formula for $A$, the amount the second policy pays on a claim of $C$ dollars.
    (c) Write a computer program that prints the total amount paid under each plan for claims of $500, $750, . . . , $2000.
    (d) Describe the conditions under which each plan pays more.

## Computers in Elementary-School Mathematics

There is considerable variation in the way in which current elementary-school mathematics textbooks present BASIC and computer literacy topics. Some books teach about computers in supplementary materials, the appendix, or the last chapter. The books that do integrate computer literacy and BASIC into the text tend to present flowcharts and the parts of the computer around Grades 3–6 and principal BASIC topics in Grades 4–6.

## Suggested Readings

Harris, S. *What's So Funny About Computers?* Los Altos, CA: William Kaufmann, Inc., 1982.

Luehrmann, A. and H. Peckham. *Computer Literacy: A Hands-On Approach.* New York: McGraw Hill, 1986.

National Council of Teachers of Mathematics. 1984 Yearbook. *Computers in Mathematics Education.* Reston, VA: NCTM, 1984.

National Council of Teachers of Mathematics. 1990 Yearbook. *Teaching and Learning Mathematics in the 1990's.* Reston, VA: NCTM, 1990.

# 13

# Statistics

$P$ick up a newspaper and you'll read statistics about what the typical citizen eats, earns, and believes. Statistics help us predict election results and tomorrow's weather. People use statistics to evaluate TV shows, schools, and government programs. An educated citizen should be able to tell whether statistics are being used appropriately in all of these situations.

Data collection is as old as written history, but the first comprehensive application of statistics was completed in 1662. Graunt tabulated and published information about births and deaths in England. Insurance companies used these data to set their rates.

The term "statistics" refers to both a set of data and the methods used to analyze the data. Statistical methods enable us to organize and simplify a set of data to reveal essential characteristics and relationships.

First, we select some quantifiable aspect to measure. Then, data are collected. From there, statistical methods enable us to organize and interpret the data.

Throughout this process, certain information is discarded. For example, a graph or table removes the original order of the numbers. An average reduces a whole set of data to just one number. These methods can reveal underlying patterns, or they can obscure reality. That is the difference between good and bad statistics.

## 13.1 Statistical Graphs and Tables

Statisticians often communicate information about data by using a graph or a table (see the top of page 735). Reading and interpreting graphs and tables is the most important part of statistics for most people. Graphs and tables can organize numerical data in a simple, clear way. Because graphs and tables simplify information, they also have the potential of being misleading.

Graphs and tables are part of descriptive statistics. **Descriptive statistics** involves all of the techniques that are used to describe and summarize the characteristics of numerical data.

## "That's the last time I go on vacation."

HERMAN copyright 1981 Universal Press Syndicate. Reprinted with permission. All rights reserved.

## Line Graphs, Bar Graphs, and Circle Graphs

Most elementary-school textbook series discuss four types of graphs: line graphs, bar graphs, pictographs, and circle graphs. Each type of graph is more suitable for presenting certain types of information.

## Lesson Exercise 13.1

Which graph in Figure 13-1, (a) the line graph or (b) the bar graph, is more suitable for displaying the data?

(a)

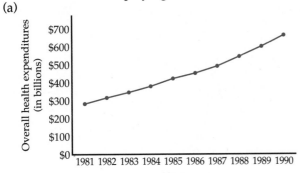

(b)

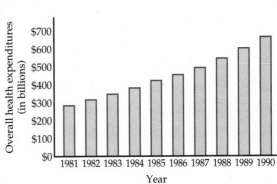

*1992 World Almanac* and *USA Today,* 2-15-89.

**Figure 13-1**

Statisticians most often use a line graph to show a trend in one variable over time.

## Lesson Exercise 13.2

Which graph in Figure 13.2, (a) the line graph or (b) the bar graph, is more effective for displaying the data?

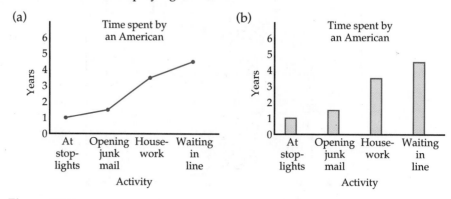

**Figure 13-2**

Statisticians generally use bar graphs to compare the values of several variables. Each bar shows the frequency of one of the variables. In most vertical bar graphs, a simple comparison of the height of each bar shows the relationships among the variables.

If the bars are replaced with pictures, the result is a pictograph. A **pictograph** employs pictures or symbols for quantities (Figure 13-3).

The homework exercises introduce the stem-and-leaf plot, another type of graph that shows individual data values.

Circle graphs are useful for showing the relative size of subgroups of a whole. Governments often use circle graphs to show how they distribute their funds (Figure 13-4).

Number of books read in June

Jay

May

Kay

**Figure 13-3**

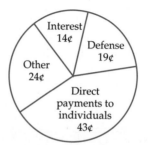

1993 federal budget dollar (estimated)

**Figure 13-4**

If there are more than six or seven parts, a circle graph becomes difficult to subdivide and label. The following chart summarizes the different types of graphs and their common uses.

| Graph | Best for |
| --- | --- |
| Line | Showing trends over time |
| Bar or pictograph | Comparing values of several categories |
| Circle | Comparing sizes of parts of a whole |

## Lesson Exercise 13.3

For each of the following, would the best choice be a line graph, a bar graph, or a circle graph?
(a) showing what percent of a family budget is devoted to each of the following: housing, clothing, food, taxes, and other
(b) showing the change in the consumer price index during the 12 months of 1992

A statistician would probably display the graph in Lesson Exercise 13.3(a) with a circle graph. However, if the budget were subdivided into eight or more categories, the circle graph would be difficult to read, so a bar graph would be better.

## Reading and Interpreting Graphs

Do you feel confident reading and interpreting a graph? In reading and interpreting a graph, you should be able to:

**1.** Read specific data from the graph.
**2.** Summarize the overall pattern of the graph and any significant deviations from that pattern.
**3.** Assess the reliability of the data.
**4.** Note any important information that is not included in the graph.
**5.** Make decisions or predictions using the graph.

Use these steps in the following exercises.

## Lesson Exercise 13.4

Estimate the following from the graphs in Figure 13-5 (page 738).
(a) What percentage of people in North America were under 15 years of age in 1991?
(b) What percent change is expected in the world population 65 years and older between 1991 and 2010?

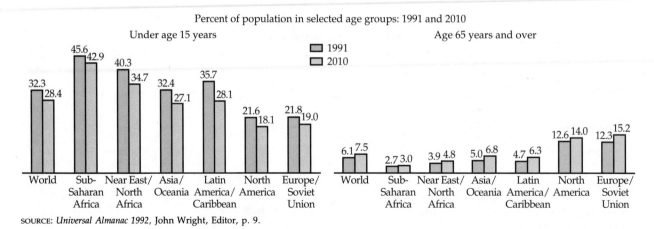

Percent of population in selected age groups: 1991 and 2010

SOURCE: *Universal Almanac 1992*, John Wright, Editor, p. 9.

**Figure 13-5**

In describing the overall pattern in each graph, note the highest points and the trends of increase and decrease.

**D** Lesson Exercise 13.5

(a) Compare the age distribution of younger and older people in each region in 1991.
(b) Speculate about why the age distributions differ as they do.
(c) Compare the predicted change in the age distribution in each region.

**D** Lesson Exercise 13.6

Do you think the data in these graphs are accurate? Why or why not?

**D** Lesson Exercise 13.7

What additional information would be useful in understanding the difference among the age distributions in the various regions?

## Constructing Graphs

A graph should be a simple, visual summary of a set of data. A statistical graph should have the following characteristics: (1) a title and labels on both axes, (2) a complete vertical axis or a break showing that it is not complete, and (3) vertical bars (for bar graphs) unless there is a good reason not to use them.

A statistician selects 20 U.S. families at random and records their annual family incomes (in thousands of dollars). Suppose that the results are as follows.

| 34 | 62 | 18 | 126 | 35 | 24 | 50 | 96 | 11 | 46 |
| 37 | 40 | 83 | 14 | 40 | 21 | 57 | 60 | 6 | 32 |

The statistician wants to construct a graph of these data. The first step is to decide how to group the data. The **range** of the data is found by computing the difference between the highest score and the lowest score: $126 - 6 = 120$. For a small data set, the data would be grouped into about five classes (subintervals). In order to make them equal in width, each one should be about $\frac{120}{5} = 24$.

If the endpoints of the classes are chosen so that no data value falls at an endpoint, it will be clearer which class contains each value. Thus, start the first class at 5.5 instead of 6. Lowering the first value by 0.5 means that we should make the width of the classes slightly larger—say, 25—in order to include all values.

Data are tallied in a **frequency distribution** table showing the frequency of each result. When data are tallied within classes, the result is a **grouped frequency distribution.**

| Annual Income (in thousands of dollars) | Frequency |
| --- | --- |
| 5.5–30.5 | |
| 30.5–55.5 | |
| 55.5–80.5 | |
| 80.5–105.5 | |
| 105.5–130.5 | |

Why is five intervals a reasonable number? Ideally, the data values within each interval represent similar results and also differ from the results in other intervals. A much larger or much smaller number of intervals would not give a meaningful display of the overall distribution. It would have many short bars or a few very big bars.

Statisticians usually select classes of equal width, making it possible to compare frequencies in different intervals by looking at the heights of the bars.

After tabulating the data in a table, statisticians usually display the frequency distribution of a *single* variable using a histogram. A **histogram** has the following properties: (1) the bars are always vertical, (2) the width of each bar is based upon the size of the interval it represents, and (3) there are no gaps between adjacent bars (if bars of height 0 are included).

The histogram in Figure 13-6 (page 740) shows the distribution of frequencies of family income. The histogram shows a pattern in which most families have incomes at the lower or middle level (5.5–55.5) and a few are at the upper end.

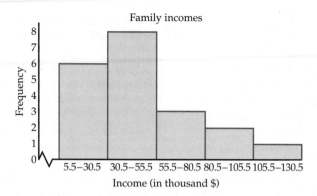

**Figure 13-6**

## Lesson Exercise 13.8

(a) Put the same income data into eight classes of equal width and construct a histogram.

(b) How does your histogram compare to the one with the five intervals?

Histograms have no gaps because their bases cover a continuous range of possible values of a variable such as the days of the year. If all days of the year are included, there are no gaps between them. In a bar graph, the gaps between bars indicate that each bar describes a different item.

## Lesson Exercise 13.9

Which graphs in Figure 13-7 are histograms?

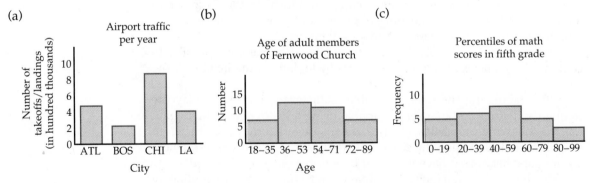

**Figure 13-7**

The *area* of each bar is proportional to the number of items or length of the corresponding interval. Usually intervals are equal in size, so the reader can look at the *height* of the bars to compare the frequencies of different intervals.

The next exercise uses *live* data from your class!

## Lesson Exercise  13.10

(a) Suppose that you find out what month everyone in your class was born. Predict the results you will obtain.

(b) Find out what month everyone in your class has a birthday. Construct a frequency distribution table.

| Month | Jan | Feb | Mar | Apr | May | Jun | Jul | Aug | Sep | Oct | Nov | Dec |
|---|---|---|---|---|---|---|---|---|---|---|---|---|
| **Number of Birthdays** | | | | | | | | | | | | |

(c) Construct a bar graph of the frequency distribution. Assume that each interval is the same size (although they are slightly different).

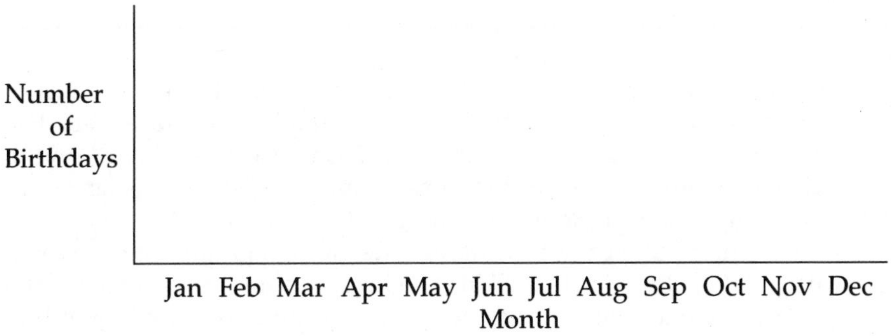

Number
of
Birthdays

Jan Feb Mar Apr May Jun Jul Aug Sep Oct Nov Dec
Month

(d) Do you see any pattern in the results? If so, why do you think the pattern occurs?

## Distorted Graphs

Graphs convey visual information in a simple dramatic way, but sometimes the display is distorted. People most commonly distort graphs by stretching and shrinking scales on the vertical axis without indicating what they have done (Figure 13-8).

Average pay at the Acme Electric Washcloth Company

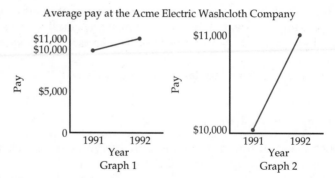

Figure 13-8

## Lesson Exercise 13.11

(a) Suppose that you manage the company and want to show that wages have increased sharply. Which graph in Figure 13-8 would you prefer?
(b) Suppose you want to present the data in an undistorted way. Which graph would you use?
(c) What additional information would be helpful in assessing the wage situation at Acme?

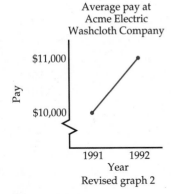

Average pay at
Acme Electric
Washcloth Company

Revised graph 2

**Figure 13-9**

The most common method for distorting graphs is to start from a number other than 0 on the *vertical* axis as in graph 2 in Figure 13-8. The correct way to make a graph such as graph 2 is to use a "squiggle" on the vertical axis to indicate a distortion in the numbering scale between 0 and the next number. This is shown on the graph in Figure 13-9.

In deciding on the overall width and height of a graph, many statisticians use the "3/4 high" rule, making the height about three fourths of the width, as is done in graph 1 and the revised graph 2, but not in graph 2.

## Lesson Exercise 13.12

### Average Teachers' Salaries
### (in thousands of dollars)

| Year   | 1986 | 1988 | 1990 | 1992 |
|--------|------|------|------|------|
| Amount | 25.3 | 28.3 | 30.9 | 33.1 |

(a) Construct an undistorted line graph of this data.
(b) Construct a distorted line graph that makes the salary increase from 1986 to 1992 look larger.

If someone glances quickly at a distorted graph without reading the numbers on the axes, he or she may be deceived by the distorted shape of the graph. If you don't want to be fooled by distorted graphs, read the numbers on the axes.

## Answers to Selected Lesson Exercises

**13.1**   line graph

**13.2**   bar graph

**13.3**   (a) circle graph     (b) line graph

**13.4**   (a) 21.6%     (b) an increase of 1.4%

**13.5**   (a) In 1991, the world had about 32% in the younger group and 6% in the older group. The two African regions had a greater percentage of people in the younger group and a smaller percentage of people in the older group than the world average. The Asia/Oceania and Latin American/Caribbean regions had age distributions similar to the world average. The North American and European/former Soviet Union regions had a smaller percentage of people in the younger group and a greater percentage in the older group than the world average.
   (b) People in the two African regions lived shorter-than-average lives. People in the North American and European/former Soviet Union regions lived longer-than-average lives.
   (c) All age distributions are predicted to change in the same way so that all the populations will become somewhat older.

**13.6**   The data for 1991 should be fairly accurate. The data for 2010 are highly speculative.

**13.7**   the life expectancy in each region; the age distributions for the groups between 15 and 65 years old; the age distributions for countries within each region

**13.9**   (b) and (c)

**13.11**  (a) 2     (b) 1
   (c) the rate of inflation, the benefits, the kind of training required, what other similar companies pay

**13.12**  (b) *Hint:* Do not start the vertical axis at 0.

## 13.1   Homework Exercises

*Basic Exercises*

1. For each of the following, determine whether the best choice would be a line graph, a bar graph, or a circle graph.
   (a) showing the percentage of people who sleep an average of 4, 5, 6, 7, 8, 9, or 10 hours per night
   (b) showing the annual U.S. government budget for environmental protection from 1973 to 1992

2. For each of the following, determine whether the best choice would be a line graph, a bar graph, or a circle graph.
   (a) showing the percentage of people who favor each of three candidates in an election
   (b) showing the frequency of 15-, 30-, 45-, and 60-second commercials on television during a 24-hour period

3. The pictograph at the top of page 744 shows how many books each child read in March.

Number of books read in March

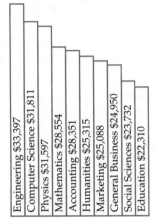

(a) How does a pictograph differ from a bar graph?
(b) What additional information would be useful?

4.

Major and estimated starting salary for bachelor's degree in 1992

(Engineering $33,397; Computer Science $31,811; Physics $31,597; Mathematics $28,554; Accounting $28,351; Humanities $25,315; Marketing $25,088; General Business $24,950; Social Sciences $23,732; Education $22,310)

(a) Which degree earned the lowest average starting salary?
(b) Which degree earned the highest average starting salary?
(c) Summarize the overall trend in starting salaries and various degrees.
(d) Is there any degree whose relative average salary surprises you?
(e) Do you think the data are reliable? Why or why not?
(f) What additional information would be useful?

5. In *State of the World* (1984), Lester Brown lists data on causes of premature deaths in the United States. (Data for 1992 would be similar.)

| Cause of Death | Number of Premature Deaths |
| --- | --- |
| Tobacco use | 375,000 |
| Alcohol use | 100,000 |
| Motor vehicle accident | 50,000 |
| Use of hard drugs | 30,000 |
| Suicide | 27,500 |
| Murder | 19,000 |

(a) Make a bar graph of the data.
(b) What conclusions could be drawn from the data?
(c) What additional information would be useful?

6. A **double bar graph** compares two sets of data that use the same units. Complete the double bar graph of fall semester enrollments for the two years given in the table.

| Student Enrollment | Math | English | Business | Psych. |
| --- | --- | --- | --- | --- |
| Fall 1991 | 2421 | 2260 | 1572 | 874 |
| Fall 1992 | 2580 | 2501 | 1610 | 710 |

Enrollment in four subject areas in fall 1991 and fall 1992

7. The line graph at the top of the next page shows the percent of persons living below the poverty level from 1974 to 1989.
(a) Describe the overall trends.
(b) Can you explain why these trends occurred?
(c) What additional information would be useful?

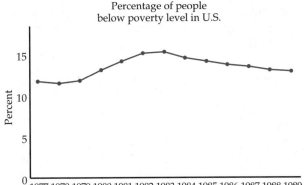

Percentage of people
below poverty level in U.S.

SOURCE: U.S. Bureau of the Census, *1991 Stat Abstract*, p. 462.

| Age | Man's Life Expectancy | Woman's Life Expectancy |
|-----|-----------------------|-------------------------|
| 20  | 71 | 78 |
| 30  | 72 | 79 |
| 40  | 73 | 79 |
| 50  | 74 | 80 |
| 60  | 77 | 82 |
| 70  | 81 | 84 |
| 80  | 87 | 89 |

**8.** The circle graph shows the marital status of U.S. women ages 20–24 in 1990. The data come from the *Universal Almanac 1992*, John Wright, ed.

Marital status of U.S. women
ages 20-24 in 1990

Married
34.3%

Single
62.8%

Divorced or
widowed
2.9%

(a) According to the graph, what percentage of women ages 20–24 have ever been married?

(b) Guess what the data for men ages 20–24 would look like.

**9.** The data in the table at the top of the next column come from *How You Rate* by T. Bicaree.

(a) Why is an older person's life expectancy higher?

(b) A woman's life expectancy is about _____ years longer than that of a man.

(c) Speculate why women tend to live longer than men.

**10.** The Perky Academy annual budget for 1992–1993 is as follows.

**Revenues**

| | |
|---|---|
| Tuition and fees | $4,374,000 |
| Alumni gifts | 194,000 |
| Endowment interest | 109,000 |
| Bookstore and vending machines | 204,000 |
| Summer day camp | 90,000 |
| Other | 93,000 |
| Total | $5,064,000 |

**Expenditures**

| | |
|---|---|
| Teachers' salaries and benefits | $2,269,000 |
| Administration salaries and benefits | 769,000 |
| Maintenance and renovation | 654,000 |
| Scholarships | 504,000 |
| Bookstore and vending machines | 194,000 |
| Summer day camp | 63,000 |
| Student activities | 21,000 |
| Utilities, phone, and postage | 501,000 |
| Insurance | 114,000 |
| Other | 130,000 |
| Total | $5,219,000 |

(a) What percent of the money spent goes for teachers' salaries and benefits?

(b) How much profit does the school make running the summer camp?

(c) What is the school's total deficit (loss) for the year?

**11.**

| Pregnancies per 1000 15- to 19-year-olds (Alan Guttmacher Institute) | |
| --- | --- |
| United States | 96 |
| England/Wales | 45 |
| Canada | 44 |
| France | 43 |
| Sweden | 35 |
| Netherlands | 14 |

| Percent of Teenagers Who Are Sexually Active | | | |
| --- | --- | --- | --- |
| | Age | | |
| | 16 | 17 | 19 |
| United States | 31% | 44% | 72% |
| Canada | 14% | 19% | 41% |
| England/Wales | 22% | 37% | 66% |
| France | 16% | 28% | 74% |
| Netherlands | no data | 35% | 64% |
| Sweden | 34% | 58% | 89% |

(a) Which countries have the most sexually active teenagers?

(b) Which countries have the most teenage pregnancies?

(c) To what extent do teenage pregnancies seem to be related to the degree of sexual activity?

(d) Why might two countries with equal rates of sexual activity among teenagers have different pregnancy rates?

(e) Speculate as to how these data were collected.

**12.** The data in the second column are based on a Gallup poll conducted on November 9–12, 1984.

| Eligible Voters in the 1984 Presidential Election | | | |
| --- | --- | --- | --- |
| Voted | 60% | | |
| Did Not Vote | 40% | Did not like candidates | 7% |
| | | Not interested in politics | 6% |
| | | Working | 5% |
| | | Inconvenient | 5% |
| | | Illness | 5% |
| | | Out of town | 4% |
| | | New resident | 4% |
| | | Other | 4% |

(a) About _____ out of every 10 eligible voters actually votes for president.

(b) If a president is elected by between 50% and 60% of *the voters*, then about _____ out of every 10 eligible voters voted for him.

(c) About _____ out of every 10 eligible voters does not vote for president.

(d) For the 4% who gave other reasons for not voting, name a reason they might have given.

Use your judgment to estimate answers to parts (e) and (f).

(e) _____ % of the people did not vote because they had more important commitments.

(f) _____ % of the people did not vote because of a lack of interest in the election.

**13.**

# USA SNAPSHOTS®

A look at statistics that shape the nation

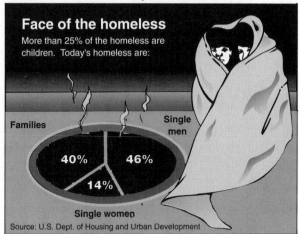

**Face of the homeless**
More than 25% of the homeless are children. Today's homeless are:

Families

Single men

40%

46%

14%

Single women

Source: U.S. Dept. of Housing and Urban Development

Copyright 1992, *USA Today*. Reprinted with permission.

The central angles for each region of the circle graph are obtained by computing the corresponding percentage of 360°. For example, 40% of the homeless are families, so the central angle of the region representing families would be 40% of 360° = 144°. How big is the central angle for the region representing single men?

**14.** In 1990, each dollar in the federal budget was divided up as follows: 32¢ for income/social security, 24¢ for defense, 15¢ for interest, 12¢ for health, and 17¢ for other programs.
(a) What percent of the budget was spent on health?
(b) How big should the central angle for health be?
(c) Use a protractor to draw a circle graph of the 1990 federal budget.

(d) What are some governmental programs included in the part labeled "other"?
(e) What additional information would be useful?

**15.** Juan Gomez's average monthly budget is broken down as follows:

Food $150    Clothing $50    Rent $300
Entertainment $40    Other $60

(a) Find out what percent each category is of the total monthly budget.
(b) Use a protractor to construct a circle graph of Juan's average monthly budget.

**16.**

1990 world energy consumption

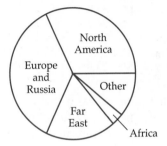

North America

Europe and Russia

Other

Far East

Africa

(a) Estimate the percentage of energy consumption for each place.
(b) Measure each angle in the circle graph and compute what percent of the 360° circle each place has.

**17.** Construct a circle graph showing how you spend time during an average school week. Include the following categories: sleeping, eating, working, going to school, watching television, recreation, and other.

**18.** You want to collect data to rate how livable the 100 largest cities in the United States are.
(a) Name five categories of data you would collect.

(b) If it is available, look at *The Places Rated Almanac* by R. Boyer and D. Savageau. What categories do they use?

**19.** Following are the 1990 average annual salaries (in thousands of dollars) of U.S. elementary-school teachers by state from the *Statistical Abstract*.

| | | | |
|---|---|---|---|
| AL 25.5 | IL 31.3 | MT 24.5 | RI 36.0 |
| AK 42.6 | IN 30.0 | NE 25.5 | SC 26.6 |
| AZ 29.4 | IA 25.7 | NV 29.8 | SD 21.1 |
| AR 21.4 | KS 28.7 | NH 29.0 | TN 27.0 |
| CA 35.6 | KY 25.6 | NJ 35.0 | TX 26.9 |
| CO 30.0 | LA 23.9 | NM 24.8 | UT 23.6 |
| CT 40.0 | ME 26.3 | NY 37.6 | VT 28.1 |
| DE 32.3 | MD 35.0 | NC 27.7 | VA 30.0 |
| DC 38.0 | MA 34.2 | ND 22.9 | WA 29.8 |
| FL 28.8 | MI 35.9 | OH 30.3 | WV 22.5 |
| GA 27.9 | MN 31.4 | OK 22.4 | WI 30.7 |
| HI 32.0 | MS 23.9 | OR 30.2 | WY 28.0 |
| ID 23.4 | MO 26.4 | PA 32.9 | |

(a) Select intervals and make a table showing the frequency distribution.

(b) Make a histogram of the data.

**20.** Following are the ages of every U.S. president from Washington to Bush at inauguration.

| | | | | | | | | |
|---|---|---|---|---|---|---|---|---|
| 57 | 61 | 57 | 57 | 58 | 57 | 61 | 54 | 68 |
| 51 | 49 | 64 | 50 | 48 | 65 | 52 | 56 | 46 |
| 54 | 49 | 50 | 47 | 55 | 55 | 54 | 42 | 51 |
| 56 | 55 | 51 | 54 | 51 | 60 | 62 | 43 | 55 |
| 56 | 61 | 52 | 69 | 64 | | | | |

(a) Make a table of the data showing the frequency distribution.

(b) Make a bar graph of these data.

**21.** (a) Time the next 20 commercials you see on television.

(b) Select intervals for a frequency distribution of the commercial lengths.

(c) Make a graph showing the frequency distribution of commercial lengths.

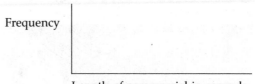

Length of commercial in seconds

**22.** Which of the following graphs are histograms?

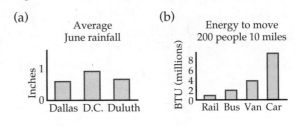

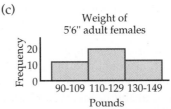

**23.** The following graph of median (average) family income appeared in the March 2, 1992, issue of *Newsweek*. The headline for the

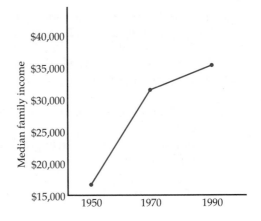

graph read "Income Slowdown." The graph appears to show a major increase from 1950 to 1970, followed by a slight increase from 1970 to 1990.

(a) How did the statistician distort this graph?

(b) How many times higher does the 1970 median family income *appear* to be than the 1960 median family income?

(c) Make an undistorted graph using the same data.

24. The following graph appeared in the May–June 1989 issue of *Learning 89*. It compares the lengths of school years in six countries.

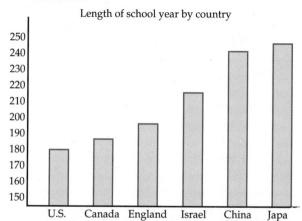

Length of school year by country

(a) Graph the same data on an undistorted graph.

(b) Which country is made to look the worst by the distortion in the original graph?

25. What is misleading about the size of the regions in the following graph?

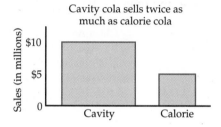

Cavity cola sells twice as much as calorie cola

26. Find a graph in a magazine or newspaper. Write a paragraph telling what the graph is supposed to show and whether it is accurate and useful or misleading.

## Extension Exercises

27. A women's group claims that a graduate school is discriminating against women in admissions. The college admits 40% of the men who apply and only 30% of the women who apply.

|       | Applied | Admitted | Percent Admitted |
|-------|---------|----------|------------------|
| Men   | 150     | 60       | 40%              |
| Women | 150     | 45       | 30%              |

The college has two graduate departments. They claim that departmental breakdowns of admissions data show that there is no discrimination.

|                |       | Applied | Admitted | Percent Admitted |
|----------------|-------|---------|----------|------------------|
| Scuba dept.    | Men   | 50      | 10       | 20%              |
|                | Women | 100     | 20       | 20%              |
| Astrology dept.| Men   | 100     | 50       | 50%              |
|                | Women | 50      | 25       | 50%              |

In this situation, which argument is more valid, that of the women's group or that of the college?

28. A company hires men and women for jobs in three categories: executive, bureaucrat, and laborer.

| Category | Men | | Women | |
|---|---|---|---|---|
| | Number Applied | Number Hired | Number Applied | Number Hired |
| Executive | 600 | 60 | 100 | 5 |
| Bureaucrat | 100 | 50 | 400 | 100 |
| Laborer | 100 | 20 | 300 | 30 |
| Total | 800 | 130 | 800 | 135 |

The company claims that they are not discriminating against female applicants since they hire about the same overall proportion of men and women (130/800 compared to 135/800).

(a) A women's group claims otherwise. Fill in the chart to obtain a different perspective.

| Category | Percentage of Applicants Hired | |
|---|---|---|
| | Men | Women |
| Executive | | |
| Bureaucrat | | |
| Laborer | | |

(b) In this situation, which argument is more valid, that of the women's group or that of the company?

29. A class received the following test scores:
61, 63, 65, 68, 69, 75, 81, 82, 91, 92, 94, 97.
   (a) Construct a table with score intervals that show that most of the scores were either high or low.

(b) Construct a shorter, deceptive table using intervals that make the scores appear to be evenly distributed.

30. A poll is taken to see how people in different age groups feel about candidate Hope. One hundred people in each age group are asked whether they would vote for Hope rather than his opponent. The results are as follows.

| Age | <20 | 21–30 | 31–40 | 41–50 | 51–60 | >60 |
|---|---|---|---|---|---|---|
| Votes for Hope | 6 | 66 | 40 | 36 | 40 | 20 |

Make a table with different groupings that makes it appear that Hope receives similar support from young, middle-aged, and older voters.

31. A **stem-and-leaf plot** uses the actual data numbers to make a sideways bar graph. Individual scores can be read from the plot. For example, 27 with a stem of 2 and a leaf of 7 is shown.

$$2\,|\,7$$

Stem-and-leaf plots work best for small data sets with positive numbers such as the following mathematics test scores.
Class A: 58, 62, 62, 70, 72, 75, 80, 81, 85, 92, 98.

1. First plot the trunk and each stem (in this case, the tens digit).

**Class A**

```
9 |
8 |
7 |
6 |
5 |
```

2. Then plot leaves for all scores.

$$
\begin{array}{r|l}
\multicolumn{2}{c}{\textbf{Class A}} \\
9 & 28 \\
8 & 015 \\
7 & 025 \\
6 & 22 \\
\text{Stem} \rightarrow 5 & 8 \leftarrow \text{Leaf}
\end{array}
$$

Test scores for a second math class were as follows.
Class B: 42, 65, 65, 68, 75, 80, 82, 90, 91, 99
(a) Make a stem-and-leaf plot for class B.
(b) Look at the stem-and-leaf plots from classes A and B and describe the difference in the distribution of scores in the two classes.

32. The following list shows the retirement ages of the last 15 teachers who retired at Brain Power High.

| 64 | 52 | 68 | 72 | 65 | 47 | 59 |
| 43 | 56 | 48 | 49 | 51 | 58 | 66 |
| 58 | | | | | | |

(a) Make a stem-and-leaf plot of the data.
(b) Summarize in words what the stem-and-leaf plot indicates about the retirement ages.
(c) Make a bar graph of the same data.
(d) State one advantage of using the stem-and-leaf plot and one advantage of using the bar graph.

33. Write a paragraph or two that summarizes the information in the graphs and quote from *USA Today* (3-25-92) shown at the top of the next column.

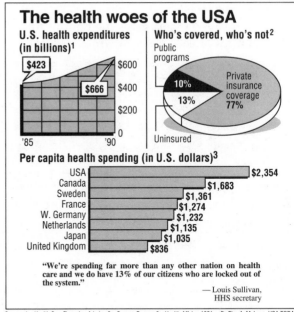

The health woes of the USA

"We're spending far more than any other nation on health care and we do have 13% of our citizens who are locked out of the system."
— Louis Sullivan,
HHS secretary

Source: 1—Health Care Financing Admin.; 2—Census Bureau; 3—Health Affairs, 1991   By Elys A. McLean, USA TODAY
Copyright 1992, *USA Today*. Reprinted with permission.

*Computer Exercises*

34. (a) Write a BASIC program that prints 100 random numbers using PRINT RND(1).
(b) Select class intervals and construct a frequency distribution table of your results.
(c) Construct a histogram of the frequency distribution.
(d) Describe any pattern you see in your results.

35. Use MINITAB to construct a histogram and a stem-and-leaf plot for the family income data from the lesson.

```
MTB> SET THE FOLLOWING DATA INTO C1
DATA> 34 62 18 126 35 24 50 96 11 46
DATA> 37 40 83 14 40 21 57 60 6 32
MTB> HISTOGRAM OF C1
MTB> STEM C1
MTB> STOP
```

*Special Exercises*

**36.** The following table gives the percent frequencies of each letter in written English.

| Letter | A | B | C | D | E | F | G |
|---|---|---|---|---|---|---|---|
| Percent Frequency | 8% | 1% | 3% | 4% | 13% | 3% | 2% |

| Letter | H | I | J | K | L | M | N |
|---|---|---|---|---|---|---|---|
| Percent Frequency | 5% | 7% | 0.2% | 0.5% | 4% | 0.3% | 4% |

| Letter | O | P | Q | R | S | T | U |
|---|---|---|---|---|---|---|---|
| Percent Frequency | 8% | 2% | 0.2% | 6% | 7% | 9% | 3% |

| Letter | V | W | X | Y | Z |
|---|---|---|---|---|---|
| Percent Frequency | 1% | 2% | 0.3% | 2% | 0.1% |

(a) Name the four most frequently occurring letters.

(b) Plot the data for the 11 most frequently occurring letters as a bar graph.

Frequency

Letters

(c) Codes can sometimes be deciphered by looking at the frequency of the letters. Tabulate the frequency of each letter in the following coded message and make a bar graph.

UAC   QCCUWPT   IWNN
XC   GU   UAC   ZWCS

(d) The most frequent letter in the coded message in part (c) represents E. Which letter in the coded message represents E?

(e) Try to decode the whole message. (*Hint:* W stands for I in the coded message.)

**37.** The frequency of letters in Scrabble is as follows.

| | | | | | |
|---|---|---|---|---|---|
| A—9 | B—2 | C—2 | D—4 | E—12 | F—2 |
| G—3 | H—2 | I—9 | J—1 | K—1 | L—4 |
| M—2 | N—6 | O—8 | P—2 | Q—1 | R—6 |
| S—4 | T—6 | U—4 | V—2 | W—2 | X—1 |
| Y—2 | Z—1 | | | | |

(a) Construct a bar graph of the frequencies of each Scrabble letter.

(b) Compare this graph to the one in the preceding exercise. Which letters are significantly more frequent in Scrabble than in written English? Which letters are significantly less frequent in Scrabble?

## 13.2   Statistical Deceptions

### Miracle Yellow Food Diet!
Eat only yellow foods . . . as much as you like.
LEMONS     POTATO CHIPS     SQUASH
GRAPEFRUITS     BANANAS     EGG YOLKS
Lose as much as 8 pounds in a week!

If you don't learn to recognize common statistical deceptions, some people will deceive you. By learning about the deceptions presented in this chapter, you will become a more shrewd individual who can cut through the b.s. (butchered statistics).

In Section 13.1, you learned some common deceptions involving graphs and tables. Some other kinds of deceptions are presented in this section.

## Deceptions Involving Percents

Some statistical deceptions involve percents of numbers of different sizes. In Lesson Exercises 13.13–13.15, try to find the mistake in the italicized conclusion and correct it. If you can't find the deception, go on to the next problem. (*Hint:* All of the deceptions in Lesson Exercises 13.13–13.15 are based on the assumption that taking the same percent of different numbers will give you the same answer.)

**D** Lesson Exercise 13.13

Suppose the United States and an African nation both have GNP (gross national product) growth of 5% in 1993. *Both nations have increased their wealth by the same amount.*

**D** Lesson Exercise 13.14

Suppose food prices went up 10% last year and 10% again this year. Over the 2 years, food prices went up *20%*. (*Hint:* Assume that food prices started at 100 and see where they end up.)

**D** Lesson Exercise 13.15

Last year, profits in a business went down 20%. This year, profits rose 20%. *Now profits are the same amount* as they were 2 years ago.

**D** Lesson Exercise 13.16

Your landlord's heating bill went up 25% this year. Does this justify his raising your rent 25%? Why or why not?

**D** Lesson Exercise 13.17

"SUDS 'N CRUD IS AMERICA'S FASTEST GROWING BEER!"
(a) Fill in the last column of the chart.

|  | **1991 Sales** | **1992 Sales** | **Percent Increase in Sales** |
|---|---|---|---|
| Blubber Beer | $2,000,000 | $2,200,000 |  |
| Lo-Cal Beer | $1,500,000 | $2,100,000 |  |
| Slob's Beer | $ 800,000 | $1,000,000 |  |
| Suds 'n Crud | $      300 | $      600 |  |

(b) What is deceptive about the headline at the beginning of this problem?

Lesson Exercises 13.13–13.17 concern deceptions involving percents. Remember that taking the same percent of a larger number will give you a larger amount, so all 50%'s are not equal. Beware of a percent standing alone. Every percent is a percent of *something*.

---

**Percents of Numbers of Different Sizes**

$A$, $B$, and $C$ are positive numbers. If $A > B$ then $C\%$ of $A$ is greater than $C\%$ of $B$.

---

## Deceptions Involving Mathematical Language

The following ad copy appeared in the March 1989 issue of *Seventeen* magazine.

---

**BEAUTIFUL THICK HAIR**

Your hair will be up to 136% thicker in 10 days. We guarantee it, or your money back.

---

Certain phrases, such as "up to" and "as much as," enable advertisers to include highly unlikely results in their slogans.

### Lesson Exercise 13.18

"LOSE AS MUCH AS 8 POUNDS IN A WEEK!"
(a) If the claim is true, what is the maximum amount of weight you might lose in a week?
(b) If the claim is true, what is the minimum amount of weight you might lose in a week?

---

**"Up To" and "As Much As"**

The phrase "up to a number $A$" can mean any number $\leq A$. The phrase "as much as a number $A$" can mean any number $\leq A$.

---

The phrase "nothing is better" makes it sound as if a product is the best.

Lesson Exercise 13.19

---

"NOTHING CLEANS SHOES BETTER THAN WASHOUT."

(a) Suppose that there are five different shoe-cleaning products on the market, all equally effective. Is the advertising headline true?

(b) Assume that there are five equally effective products. Would it also be true to say that "NO OTHER SHOE-CLEANER IS WORSE AT CLEANING SHOES THAN WASHOUT"?

---

> **"Nothing Is More Than"**
>
> The phrase "nothing is more than a number $A$" can mean all numbers that are $\leq A$.

Lesson Exercises 13.18 and 13.19 concern deceptions involving mathematical language. As you have seen, the phrases "as much as a number" and "up to a number" mean that any amount is possible from 0 "up to" the number mentioned. "Nothing is better" means that other products may be the same as this one.

## Deceptions Involving Comparisons and Time Intervals

In making a comparison based upon statistics, consider unmentioned factors that are also important.

Lesson Exercise 13.20

---

"THE NATIONAL MOTORS PARAKEET GETS THE BEST MILEAGE OF ANY COMPACT CAR!"

Oh, come on, I move faster than that!

What are some other facts a prospective buyer should find out about the Parakeet when comparing it to other compact cars?

---

People presenting historical statistics often select time intervals that are not representative. In examining data from a specific time period, consider whether there is anything special about that time that would affect the data.

### Lesson Exercise 13.21

"SALARIES INCREASE MORE SLOWLY IN THESE HARD TIMES."
A politican notes that U.S. salaries have increased an average of 25% from 1980 to 1984 compared to an increase of 34% from 1976 to 1980. What additional information is needed?

Lesson Exercises 13.20 and 13.21 illustrate deceptions involving comparisons and time intervals. Advertisers often choose a particular factor that makes their products compare favorably by ignoring other important factors. In discussing trends over time, people sometimes select a time period that supports their viewpoint but is not truly representative.

## Answers to Lesson Exercises

**13.13** "Therefore, the United States has increased its wealth by a greater amount."

**13.14** 21%

**13.15** 4% lower than

**13.16** No. The heating bill is only a small part of the total expenses.

**13.17** (a) last column would have 10%, 40%, 25%, 100%
(b) It is the highest percent increase but a

much lower dollar increase in sales than the other three companies show.

**13.18** (a) 8 lb    (b) 0 lb

**13.19** (a) yes    (b) yes

**13.20** price, repair record, safety record, trunk space

**13.21** the rate of inflation during each time period; whether anything unusual happened in 1976, 1980, or 1984

## 13.2   Homework Exercises

*Basic Exercises*

1. Oil prices went up 20% one year and 30% the next. Over the two years, oil prices rose _____ %.

2. My rent went down 10% last year and then rose 20% this year. Over the two years, my rent went up _____ %.

3. New computers enable a company to increase productivity by 20% (assume that profits increase by the same amount). Labor demands a 20% increase in wages. Management claims that if wages increase at the same rate as productivity, no additional profits will be made. Is management right? (*Hint:* Make up a situation with numbers.)

4. The numbers $c$, $x$, and $y$ are positive. If $x < y$, then ($c$% of $x$) _____ ($c$% of $y$).
$$(<, >, =)$$

5. Last year, a company made a 10% profit. If its profit margin decreased by 60%, what percent profit did the company make this year?

6. Sidney's expenses for food, rent, and miscellaneous all increased 20% this year. Sidney figures that his total expenses went up 60%. Explain what is wrong with his reasoning.

7. What important information is missing from the following statement? "After 100,000 miles of test driving, less than 1% of National Motors Cars needed any repairs."

8. Last year, the Social Security budget rose 12%. This year, the rate of increase is down 25%. This year's Social Security budget is _____ % _____ than last
   (higher, lower)
   year's budget.

9. What important information is missing from the following statement? "Eighty percent of all dentists surveyed recommend sugarless gum for their patients who chew gum."

10. "FALL SALE: SAVINGS UP TO 50%!"
    (a) If the claim is true, what is the most you will save on an item?
    (b) If the claim is true, what is the least you will save on an item?

11. In *USA Today*, March 17, 1989, Dodge took out a full-page ad with the following announcement in large type.

# HERE'S TO YOU AMERICA.
UP TO
## $3000
## SAVINGS

Then in very small type at the bottom of the page was the following:

*Total savings = pkg. savings + cash back. $50–$1,200 pkg. savings (depending on pkg.), based on list prices of pkg. items if sold separately, avail. on all model lines, but not on each individual model. $300–$2,000 cash back (depending on model) or 4.9% annual percentage rate financing on all new vehicles in stock except Caravans & diesel pickups.

What does the phrase "up to $3000" really mean in this ad?

12. Find any misleading statements in the following advertisement that once appeared in *Seventeen* magazine.

"LONDON UNIVERSITY CRASH-BURN WONDER DIET Of all medically safe and sound reducing programs

### FASTEST WEIGHT-LOSS METHOD KNOWN TO MEDICAL SCIENCE!
(EXCEPT FOR TOTAL STARVATION)

Compared to the Scarsdale diet, weight-watchers, Duke Univ., even Atkins or Pritikin it burns away as much as:

4 TIMES FASTER THAN HIGH SPEED DIETS
11 TIMES FASTER THAN EXERCISE!"

13. The statement "$A$, $B$, and $C$ are not more than $X$" means
    (a) $A = B = C = X$
    (b) $A$, $B$, and $C$ are less than $X$
    (c) $A$, $B$, and $C$ are greater than or equal to $X$
    (d) $A$, $B$, and $C$ are less than or equal to $X$

14. "NO DETERGENT CLEANS CLOTHES BETTER THAN SLUDGE."

According to the headline, which of the following statements is true?
    (a) Sludge cleans clothes better than other detergents.
    (b) Sludge removes chocolate stains.
    (c) Sludge cleans clothes at least as well as other detergents.

15. "TANDY COMPUTERS ARE CLEARLY SUPERIOR."

According to this slogan, which of the following is (are) true?
    (a) Tandy computers are the best computers.
    (b) Tandy computers are superior to Apple computers.
    (c) Tandy computers work well.

16. "More people drink Jitters Instant Coffee than any other brand."

    If there are ten brands of instant coffee, the percent of all instant coffee drinkers drinking Jitters is between _____ % and _____ %.

17. In each of the following, explain the flaw in the claim or suggestion made about the product.
    (a) A store sells for $8.98 tapes that have a list price of $10.98. You save 27%.
    (b) Alpo's beef-flavored dinner has "as much meat protein in a serving as 7 ounces of the finest steak."

18. The following report describes an actual study involving Aim toothpaste.

**Lever Brothers Company**

Lever Brothers clinically tested Aim with fluoride . . . Thousands of children were enrolled in two studies . . . The dentists reported their findings as the reduction of dental decay of Aim with fluoride compared to Aim without fluoride in all of the teeth and their surfaces. After two years the dentists concluded that a significant reduction of dental decay resulted from the use of Aim with fluoride.

**Summary of Clinical Trials of Aim with Fluoride**

|  | Study I | Study II |
| --- | --- | --- |
| Duration | 2 years | 2 years |
| Number of children | 1107 | 1154 |

**Reduction of Cavities of Aim with Fluoride versus Aim Without Fluoride**

| Whole mouth | 25% | 29% |
| --- | --- | --- |
| Between teeth | 38% | 37% |
| Newly erupted teeth | 21% | 25% |

(a) What two products are being compared in the study?
(b) Does the study show that Aim is better than any other fluoride toothpaste? If not, what does it show?

19. An ad by the Beef Industry Council gives the following information about a 4-oz serving of beef. It contains the following percentages of the recommended daily allowances: 76% of the protein, 35% of the niacin, 51% of the zinc, 19% of the iron, 100% of the vitamin B-12, and 13% of the calories. What important nutritional information about beef is omitted?

20. In graph F in his speech of November 23, 1982, former president Reagan illustrated the declining share of the federal budget spent on defense. Note that the defense budget was especially high from 1962–67.

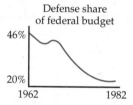

(a) Is there anything special about this time period that accounts for the higher defense spending?
(b) How is the graph distorted?
(c) Does the distortion favor or undermine Reagan's viewpoint?

21. In 1970, roughly 331,000 people died from cancer in the United States. In 1991, roughly 527,000 people died from cancer in the United States. Explain why it is possible that deaths from cancer could be increasing even though medical treatments for cancer are improving.

22. More students are taking mathematics courses than ever before. One could conclude that mathematics has become a well-

liked subject. Why might the conclusion be incorrect?

23. "More people die in hospitals than at home." From this statement you might conclude that you are better off staying at home when you are sick. Explain why this conclusion is unjustified.

*Extension Exercises*

24. In the United States, women's average income is 60% of men's average income. Speculate about what this statistic shows.

25. On the same day, two New York newspapers published conflicting headlines. One said "ELECTRIC POWER USAGE INCREASES." The other said "ELECTRIC POWER USAGE DECLINES." Both were right! How is this possible?

26. Consider the following problem. "A price $P$ rises 20% and then rises 30%. Prove that the overall change is an increase of 56%. (*Hint:* Show that the final price is $1.56P$.)" Devise a plan and solve the problem.

27. A price $P$ rises 10% and then declines 20%. Prove that the overall change is a decline of 12%.

## 13.3 Averages

It is possible to use a single number to describe a whole set of numbers. Sounds amazing, doesn't it? Whereas graphs and tables are useful for presenting statistical data, a set of numbers can be described more simply with an average. However, information is also lost in this simple description of a data set.

### The Mean and Median

I asked my students how long it takes each of them to travel from home to mathematics class. The results in minutes were as follows: 30, 20, 10, 15, 15, 20, 15, 15, 10, 30, 40, 45.

### Lesson Exercise 13.22

Describe two common ways to find the students' average travel time.

The most commonly used average is called the mean.

> **Definition: Mean**
>
> The **mean** of a set of numbers is their sum, divided by how many numbers there are. The mean $\bar{x}$ of the numbers $x_1, x_2, x_3, \ldots x_N$ is
>
> $$\bar{x} = \frac{x_1 + x_2 + x_3 + \cdots + x_N}{N}$$

The mean (short for "arithmetic mean") is the average most people use, since it gives equal weight to all measurements. The word "average" usually refers to the mean. The mean in the example is the sum of the travel times, 265 divided by 12, or $\frac{265}{12} = 22\frac{1}{12}$ minutes.

The mean is a balance point. If you hung equal weights from a rod at positions representing each student's travel time, the rod would balance at the mean (Figure 13-10).

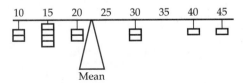

**Figure 13-10**

Another useful kind of average is the median.

---

**Definition: Median**

The **median** is the middle value of a set of numbers when the numbers are arranged in order. If there is an even number of values, the median is the mean of the two middle values.

---

To find the median in the example, arrange the numbers in order.

$$\{10, 10, 15, 15, 15, 15, 20, 20, 30, 30, 40, 45\}$$

↑  ↑

The two middle numbers are 15 and 20, so the median is $\frac{15 + 20}{2} = 17\frac{1}{2}$ minutes. Sometimes, people use the word "average" to refer to the median. This usage leads to confusion between the mean and the median.

## Lesson Exercise 13.23

(a) Find out the travel time from home to mathematics class for each person in your class today.
(b) Compute the mean and median times.
(c) Write a paragraph comparing your class's travel times to those of my class.

**D** Lesson Exercise 13.24

The Nielsen ratings estimate what percent of all U.S. television sets are tuned in to each show. The hourly prime-time Nielsen ratings for two of the major networks for the week of 3/20/89 were as follows.

*NBC:* 17.2, 12.4, 12.4, 12.5, 15.8, 11.8, 16.7, 15.0, 12.9, 21.3, 18.4, 19.5, 16.1, 16.1, 11.7, 13.8, 20.1, 16.4, 9.4, 9.4, 14.9

*ABC:* 14.3, 24.5, 24.5, 21.3, 22.3, 15.6, 17.5, 11.9, 11.1, 8.2, 10.9, 8.1, 14.5, 14.7, 15.6, 8.7, 8.8, 6.4, 14.7, 14.7, 14.7

How would you determine which network did the best for the week?

## Finding the Mean and Median of a Frequency Distribution

Statisticians usually tabulate larger data sets as frequency distributions. The following example shows how to compute the mean and median of a frequency distribution: my students' travel times.

**Example 13.1**

The following chart shows the frequency distribution of travel times for my class. Find the mean and median.

| Time | Frequency | | | | |
|------|-----------|---|---|---|---|
| 10 | 2 | 10 | 10 | | |
| 15 | 4 | 15 | 15 | 15 | 15 |
| 20 | 2 | 20 | 20 | | |
| 30 | 2 | 30 | 30 | | |
| 40 | 1 | 40 | | | |
| 45 | 1 | 45 | | | |

**Solution**

The *mean* is the total number of minutes divided by the total number of students. There are

2(10 minutes) + 4(15 minutes) + 2(20 minutes) +
2(30 minutes) + 1(40 minutes) + 1(45 minutes) = 265 minutes.

There are 2 + 4 + 2 + 2 + 1 + 1 = 12 students.

So the mean is $\frac{265}{12} = 22\frac{1}{12}$ minutes.

The mean of a frequency distribution is computed more quickly by multiplying each data number by its frequency, adding them together, and dividing by the total number of scores. The *median* is the middle number. Since there are 12 numbers, the middle numbers are the sixth and seventh numbers, which are 15 and 20. Writing out the travel time for each student in increasing order confirms this.

$$\{10, 10, 15, 15, 15, \underline{15}, \underline{20}, 20, 30, 30, 40, 45\}$$

So the median is $\dfrac{15 + 20}{2} = 17\frac{1}{2}$ minutes.   ■

The mean in Example 13.1 is the balance point of the histogram for the frequency distribution (Figure 13-11).

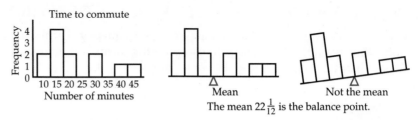

Figure 13-11

The formula for finding the mean of a frequency distribution is as follows.

---

**The Mean of a Frequency Distribution**

The mean $\bar{x}$ of the frequency distribution

| Scores | Frequency |
|--------|-----------|
| $x_1$ | $f_1$ |
| $x_2$ | $f_2$ |
| . | . |
| . | . |
| $x_N$ | $f_N$ |

is $\bar{x} = \dfrac{x_1 f_1 + x_2 f_2 + \cdots + x_N f_N}{f_1 + f_2 + \cdots + f_N}$.

---

## Lesson Exercise 13.25

A class obtained the following scores on a test.

| Score | Frequency |
|-------|-----------|
| 100   | 1         |
| 90    | 3         |
| 80    | 4         |
| 70    | 3         |
| 60    | 0         |
| 50    | 2         |

(a) How many students received a 70?
(b) How many students are in the class?
(c) Find the mean. Be sure to count each score the correct number of times and divide by the total number of students in the class.
(d) Find the median. (*Hint:* Write out all 13 scores from lowest to highest.)

## Mean or Median?

How does a statistician decide whether to represent an average with the mean or the median? In Example 13.1, the median travel time $\left(17\frac{1}{2}\right)$ was slightly lower than the mean $\left(22\frac{1}{12}\right)$. Which is a better indicator of the average travel time? How do you know which one to use with a particular set of data?

Sometimes, a set of data has a small subset of scores that are quite different from the rest of the scores. Would this group of scores be better represented by the mean or by the median? It depends upon whether you want to include the effect of extreme values or whether you want to minimize the effect of extreme values. In the travel time example, the 40- and 45-minute travel times are particularly high. To give these scores equal weight, you would use the mean rather than the median.

## Lesson Exercise 13.26

Pat played in six basketball games. She scored the following number of points in each game: 2, 22, 26, 28, 30, 30. She scored 2 points during a game in which she had the flu and played only for 3 minutes. Which would be a better indicator of her typical scoring game, the mean or the median score?

As Lesson Exercise 13.26 illustrates, the median is a better choice when you want to minimize the effect of an extreme value. Since the median involves only the middle value or values, it is not affected by a change in size of an extreme value. Economists usually compute average family income as a median so that a small number of very wealthy families do not have a large impact on the average.

The mean, on the other hand, gives weight to all scores. The mean is a better choice if you want to include the effect of extreme values. When scores are scattered or there are very few scores, the mean may be a better indicator than the median. For example, the mean (72) of a set of test scores such as {30, 40, 90, 100, 100} is more representative than the median (90). When there are no extreme scores, the mean and median will usually be about the same.

## Lesson Exercise 13.27

For each of the following sets, (1) without computing, tell whether the mean or median would be higher; and (2) tell which would be a better indicator of the average.
(a) {23, 25, 28, 68, 71, 75, 78}
(b) {10, 12, 14, 16, 16, 23, 95} (Assume that you want to minimize the impact of the 95.)

People sometimes choose the average that promotes their viewpoint. They may even neglect to say whether they are using the mean or the median. Lesson Exercise 13.28 illustrates such a situation.

## Lesson Exercise 13.28

The Washington Black and Blueskins have salaries (in thousands of dollars) as follows:

| 100 | 100 | 150 | 200 | 200 | 400 | 400 | 400 | 600 | 900 |

(a) The owner wants to demonstrate how high average salaries are. Would he prefer the mean or the median?
(b) The players' association wants to demonstrate how low average salaries are. Would they prefer the mean or the median?

## Answers to Selected Lesson Exercises

**13.24** Compute the mean or median for each network and compare them.

**13.25**  3     (b) 13     (c) $76\frac{12}{13}$     (d) 80

**13.26** median

**13.27** (a) (1) median; (2) mean
(b) (1) mean; (2) median

**13.28** (a) mean     (b) median

## 13.3 Homework Exercises

*Basic Exercises*

1. Tom bowls 136, 158, and 129. Jean bowls 160, 120, 118, and 137. Find a way to determine who bowled better.

2. A set contains five numbers. Each number is either 1, 2, or 3. What must the five numbers be if the mean is 1?

3. (a) A teacher wants to find the mean of test scores $V$, $W$, $X$, $Y$, and $Z$. What is the mean?
   (b) The mean of a set of five test scores is $M$. What is the *sum* of the five test scores?

4. If $\bar{x}$ is the mean of $x_1, x_2, \cdots, x_n$ and $\bar{y}$ is the mean of $y_1, y_2, \cdots, y_m$, what is the formula for the mean $\bar{z}$ of $x_1, x_2, \cdots, x_n, y_1, y_2, \cdots, y_m$ in terms of $\bar{x}$ and $\bar{y}$?

5. How much lower is the mean cost of the three generic drugs shown than the mean cost of the three brand-name drugs?

| Brand Name | Cost of 100 Units | Generic | Cost of 100 Units |
|---|---|---|---|
| Librium | $13.98 | Chlordiazopoxide | $3.98 |
| Sumycin | $ 7.85 | Tetracycline | $3.75 |
| Polycillin | $25.50 | Ampicillin | $9.98 |

6.

ANY 11 for $1 plus shipping handling

if you join the Columbia Classical Club now and agree to buy 8 more selections (at regular Club prices) in the next 3 years

Courtesy of Columbia Classical Club, CBS Records.

If postage and handling averages 50 cents per tape and the regular club price is $8.98, what is the mean cost per tape for the minimum number of tapes you must buy?

7. Find the mean and median of {4, 7, 10, 7, 5, 2, 7}.

8. Match the expressions in columns A and B.

| A | B |
|---|---|
| Uses order of scores | Mean |
| Equal weight to each score | Median |
| Middle | |

9. You have 5 stacks of books with 3, 5, 7, 2, and 3 books, respectively.
   (a) How would you show the median number of books in a stack?
   (b) How would you show the mean number of books in a stack?

10.

| | | |
|---|---|---|
| World | 27 | |
| U.S. | 112 | |
| France | 91 | |
| Italy | 77 | |
| United Kingdom | 71 | |
| Japan | 41 | |
| China | 24 | |
| India | 2 | |

The world population was about 5 billion in 1990.
   (a) How much meat did all the countries in the world consume in 1990?
   (b) What percent of all the meat was consumed in the United States if the population was about 260 million?

11. Which four numbers in the following group have a mean of 8 and a median of 8.5?

   3    5    5    7    8    9    10    10

12. In "straight-line" depreciation, an accountant will assume that the same amount of depreciation occurs each month. If a new computer costs $3000 and is worth $1000 after 2 years, what is the average (mean) monthly depreciation?

13. Find the mean for each set *without* adding up all the numbers and dividing.
    (a) {7, 7, 7, 7, 7}       (b) {56, 57, 58}
    (c) {5, 7, 9, 11, 13}     (d) {42, 42, 46, 46}

14. (a) Use a shortcut to find the mean of {9, 10, 11}.
    (b) Use a shortcut to find the mean of {20, 21, 22, 23, 24, 25}.
    (c) Use a shortcut to find the mean of {36, 37, 38, . . . , 100}.

15. A newspaper editorial says, "About half of our fifth-graders scored below average on a standardized mathematics test. A major remediation effort must begin." Explain why these test results are not very alarming. (*Hint:* Look at the cartoon.)

© David Pascal, 1978.

16. A class obtained the following test scores.

| Score | Frequency |
|-------|-----------|
| 90    | 2         |
| 80    | 4         |
| 70    | 9         |
| 60    | 5         |
| 50    | 3         |
| 40    | 1         |

    (a) How many students are in the class?
    (b) Find the mean and the median for the class.
    (c) Using the mean average, how many students scored above average?
    (d) Using the median average, how many students scored above average?

17. In 1988, Senate incumbents running for re-election received the campaign contributions shown over a two-year period.

| Total Two-Year Donations for U.S. Senate Campaign (to nearest million dollars) | Frequency |
|-------|-----------|
| 1     | 5         |
| 2     | 8         |
| 3     | 4         |
| 4     | 5         |
| 5     | 2         |
| 6     | 2         |
| 7     | 1         |
| 8     | 1         |
| 9     | 1         |
| 10    | 0         |
| 11    | 1         |

Find the mean and median campaign contributions to an individual senator.

18. The following chart gives the heights of students in a particular class.

| Height (in cm) | Frequency |
|----------------|-----------|
| 177            | 1         |
| 175            | 2         |
| 173            | 2         |
| 171            | 4         |
| 170            | 3         |
| 169            | 2         |
| 168            | 3         |
| 166            | 2         |
| 163            | 1         |
| 160            | 1         |
| 158            | 1         |
| 156            | 1         |

Find the mean and median heights for the class.

19. Following are Karen Svenson's grades for the fall semester. Compute her grade point average (A = 4, B = 3, C = 2, D = 1, F = 0).

| Course | Credits | Grade |
|--------|---------|-------|
| Calculus | 4 | B |
| Biology | 4 | C |
| Literature | 3 | B |
| French II | 3 | A |
| Badminton | 1 | D |

**20.** A class of 23 students has a mean of 78 on a mathematics test. The 10 boys in the class had a mean of 76.2. What was the mean of the girls' test scores?

**21.** Ross wants to prepare a 20-quart orange juice mixture that will sell for \$3/qt. He will use Valencia OJ that sells for \$3.75 per qt and Parson OJ that sells for \$2.50 per qt. How many quarts of each should he use? (Make a table and guess and check.)

**22.** Blair's bowling average after 3 games is 150.
(a) Is a bowling average a mean or a median?
(b) He bowls 170. How much does his average go up?
(c) If he bowls 170 again, how much does his average go up?
(d) Why does the second 170 raise his average less than the first 170?
(e) Blair has an average of $A$ after $N$ games. If he bowls 170, what is his new average?

**23.** Without computing, tell which would be higher, the mean age or the median age in your mathematics class.

**24.** The salaries of the executives of a certain company are shown. Find the mean and the median. Which statistic seems to describe the average salary best?

| Position | Salary |
|----------|--------|
| President | \$90,000 |
| First vice-president | \$35,000 |
| Second vice-president | \$35,000 |
| Supervisor | \$30,000 |
| Accountant | \$24,000 |
| Personnel manager | \$24,000 |

**25.** In 1983 Chicago civil cases, the median award was about \$8000 and the mean award was about \$69,000. Were most awards closer to \$8000 or to \$69,000?

**26.** An article says that the average number of persons in each car on the road is 1.3 persons. Is this figure a mean or a median?

**27.** Each set shows the ages of a group of college students in a seminar. Which would be a better indicator of the average age, the mean or the median?
(a) {19, 20, 20, 20, 42, 47, 48}
(b) {18, 19, 19, 20, 20, 21, 62} (Assume that you want to minimize the effect of the 62.)

**28.** A class has 8 students with heights in inches as follows:

$$\{60, 62, 64, 66, 68, 68, 70, 72\}$$

(a) Find the mean and the median.
(b) Suppose that a basketball recruit 86 inches tall joins the class. Find the new mean and median.
(c) Which average changed the most because of the new student?

**29.** In the accompanying photograph, which would be higher, the mean height or the median height of the three people?

**30.** The teachers' salaries (in thousands of dollars) at a school are

20    22    22    24    26    28    30    35    40

(a) The teachers' union wants to show how low the average salary is. Would they prefer the mean or the median?

(b) The school board wants to show that the average salary is high enough. Would they prefer the mean or the median?

**31.** A business has five employees. The owners say that the average salary is $30,000. The workers say the average salary is $20,000. Make up a set of data that makes both groups right.

**32.** Make up a set of data for which *neither* the mean nor the median is representative.

**33.** A man bought desserts for 10 people, including himself. Five of the desserts cost $1, three desserts cost $2, and two desserts cost $3. He told his friends, "The desserts cost $1, $2, and $3. So, the average cost was $(1 + 2 + 3)/3 = $2. If each of you gives me $2, we'll be even."

(a) What is the actual mean price of the desserts?

(b) How much extra money will the man have after charging everyone, including himself, $2?

**34.** A business pays $100 to Cindy at $20 per hour, $100 to Max at $10 per hour, $100 to Bart at $5 per hour, and $100 to Wanda at $4 per hour. Is the mean salary paid by the business $\frac{20 + 10 + 5 + 4}{4} = \$9.75$ per hr, or is it some other amount?

**35.** In the 1988 campaign, candidate George Bush said, "We've created 17 million new jobs the past five years . . . [that] paid an average of more than $22,000 per year." Bush's claim was based on the fact that at least half the new jobs were in fields in which average pay was $22,000 or more. Why was his claim inaccurate?

**36.** In the math class you teach, the quiz average counts for 10% of the grade, each unit test counts for 20%, and the final exam counts for 30%. Compute the mean for each student. (*Hint:* This is similar to computing the mean of a frequency distribution.)

| Student | Quiz Average | Unit Test | Unit Test | Unit Test | Final Exam |
|---|---|---|---|---|---|
| Terry Orders | 80 | 70 | 60 | 90 | 90 |
| Kathy Heid | 75 | 80 | 92 | 93 | 70 |

**37.** You have test grades of 68, 79, 88, 74, and 82. The final test counts $\frac{1}{4}$ of your grade. What is the minimum score needed on the final for an 80 (B) average?

**38.** A third statistical average, the **mode,** is the score that occurs most frequently in a set. For example, the mode of {2, 2, 4, 5, 6, 6, 6} is 6, which occurs three times. Statisticians use the mode only for larger data sets, since slight changes in smaller data sets can cause significant changes in the mode.

(a) Find the mode of the following set.

{6, 8, 8, 9, 10, 10, 12, 12, 15, 15, 15, 15, 18, 19, 20, 22}

(b) How would you significantly lower the mode by changing just two scores?

(c) Find the mode of the frequency distribution in Example 13.1.

**39.** A class has 10 students with brown hair, 6 with black hair, and 3 with blonde hair. Would you use the mean, median, or mode to find the "average" hair color?

*Extension Exercises*

**40.** (a) During a 20-mile commute, Jill averages 50 mph for the first 10 miles on the expressway and 30 mph for the last 10 miles in town. What is her mean speed for the whole trip? (It's not 40 mph!)

(b) During a 20-mile commute, Jill averages $M$ mph for the first 10 miles and $N$ mph for the next 10 miles. What is her mean speed for the 20 miles?

41. A truck drives the first half of a trip at a speed of 60 km/hr. How fast must it go during the second half of the trip in order to average 80 km/hr for the entire trip?

42. A professor gives five exams. Two students have the same mean score, although one student scored higher on four of the five exams. Make up a set of possible test scores for each student.

43. (a) A newspaper reports that "average family income in the United States in 1992 is $37,480." What important detail has been omitted from this report?
    (b) Which would be higher, the mean family income or the median family income in the United States?

44. The median age of first marriages in the United States is 22 for women and 25 for men. Would the mean ages be higher or lower?

45. Construct a set of numbers for which the mean and median are 5 and the mode is 4.

46.

Salaries at Fatco (nearest $10,000)

(a) Which would be the highest, the mean, median, or mode?
(b) Which would be the lowest, the mean, median, or mode?

47. Two math classes take a test. The mean is 70 in class A and 80 in class B. What circumstance would guarantee that the mean for the total group will be 75?

48. Another way to compute the mean is to use the *assumed-mean* method. Suppose that you want to find the mean of {72, 86, 89, 90}. You might guess (assume) that the mean is 82. Then see how far each score is from the assumed mean.

| Score | Assumed Mean | Difference |
|-------|--------------|------------|
| 72 | 82 | −10 |
| 86 | 82 | 4 |
| 89 | 82 | 7 |
| 90 | 82 | 8 |
| | TOTAL | +9 |

The sum of the four scores is 9 above the assumed mean. If each score contributed equally to the +9, it would be $\frac{9}{4}$ above the mean. The actual mean is $82 + \frac{9}{4} = 84\frac{1}{4}$.

(a) Find the mean of {65, 71, 75, 84} using the assumed-mean method.
(b) Find the mean of {25, 40, 42, 51, 58} using the assumed-mean method.
(c) Show why $\dfrac{72 + 86 + 89 + 90}{4}$ is the same as $82 + \dfrac{-10 + 4 + 7 + 8}{4}$.
    (*Hint:* The 82 results from $\dfrac{82 + 82 + 82 + 82}{4}$.)

49. One day in the *New York Times*, NBC and CBS advertised their success in the Nielsen ratings. Both said they had "The Biggest Average Nighttime Audience!" How is this possible?

## Special Exercises

50. (adapted from Walter Penney's problem in the 12/79 *Scientific American*)

### A New Tax Plan

A society has four economic classes, each containing one quarter of the people. Class 1 is the richest, Class 2 is the second richest, Class 3 is the second poorest, and Class 4 is the poorest.

Senator Trickledown proposes that each pair of consecutive classes beginning with the richest (1 and 2, then 2 and 3, then 3 and 4) will have their wealth averaged and redistributed evenly to everyone in those two classes. Senator Dragdown proposes the same thing, but wants to begin the averaging with the poorest classes (3 and 4, then 2 and 3, then 1 and 2).

Suppose that the money is distributed as follows.

| Class | Money in Trillions of Quaggles |
|-------|-------------------------------|
| 1     | 20                            |
| 2     | 12                            |
| 3     | 6                             |
| 4     | 4                             |

(a) How would the money be distributed after Senator Trickledown's redistribution is completed?
(b) How would the money be distributed after Senator Dragdown's redistribution is completed?
(c) Which classes would prefer which plan?
(d) Which class would lose under both plans?
(e) Which classes would gain under both plans?

**51.** Read "Milo and the Mathemagician" by Norton Juster in *The Mathematical Magpie* edited by Clifton Fadiman or in *The Phantom Tollbooth* by Norton Juster. Write a report that includes both a summary of the story and your reaction to it.

## 13.4   Measuring Spread

If two people have the same test average, can there be any significant differences in their test scores? Milly and Billy have each taken six mathematics quizzes. Their scores are as follows.

| | |
|---|---|
| Milly | 2, 4, 6, 7, 7, 10 |
| Billy | 4, 5, 6, 7, 7, 7 |

### Lesson Exercise 13.29

Find the mean and median for Milly and Billy.

According to the statistics in Lesson Exercise 13.29, Milly and Billy's scores are the same.

### Lesson Exercise 13.30

How do Milly and Billy's scores differ?

As this example suggests, an average does not always sufficiently distinguish between two sets of data.

## Percentiles and Boxplots

Statisticians usually describe a set of data using a measure of the center (mean or median) and a measure of the spread. In the case of Milly and Billy, their average scores are the same, but the spread of their scores is different.

Statisticians sometimes describe the spread with percentiles. A score is in the **pth percentile** if about p% of the scores in the distribution are below that score.

In describing the spread with percentiles, statisticians use a five-number summary that includes the median, the maximum and minimum scores, and the first and third quartiles. The median indicates the 50th percentile. The **first (lower) quartile** indicates the 25th percentile, and the **third (upper) quartile** indicates the 75th percentile.

---

**The Five-Number Summary**

1. Find the minimum, median, and maximum scores.

2. The first quartile is the median of the scores below the location of the median.

3. The third quartile is the median of scores above the location of the median.

---

Statisticians use these five numbers to construct a picture called a **boxplot.**

**Example 13.2**

Graph Milly's distribution in a boxplot.

**Solution**

Milly's minimum, median, and maximum are 2, 6.5, and 10. The first quartile is the median of {2, 4, 6}, which is 4. The third quartile is the median of {7, 7, 10}, which is 7. The five-number summary is 2, 4, 6.5, 7, and 10. The boxplot uses these five numbers (Figure 13-12). The ends

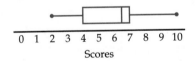

```
0  1  2  3  4  5  6  7  8  9  10
              Scores
```

**Figure 13-12**

of the box are at the quartiles. The median determines the line segment inside the box. Line segments (called "whiskers") extend outside the box to the minimum and maximum data values.   ■

Boxplots provide an excellent way to compare two distributions.

## Lesson Exercise 13.31

(a) Draw boxplots for Milly and Billy's scores (one above the other) on the same graph.
(b) Describe how the boxplots for Milly and Billy differ.

While boxplots are useful for comparing distributions, a bar graph displays a single distribution with greater clarity and detail.

### The Standard Deviation

The standard deviation is the most common measure statisticians use to describe the spread. The standard deviation complements the mean, and, like the mean, it takes all scores into account.

The standard deviation measures how far scores tend to be from the mean. Consider two sets that both have a mean of 24: {22, 23, 24, 24, 24, 25, 25, 25} and {2, 13, 17, 24, 31, 33, 48}. The standard deviation for the first set is 1; for the second set, it is about 14.

Visually, a frequency distribution that has a lower standard deviation has more scores closer to the mean, while a distribution that has a higher standard deviation has more scores further from the mean. In Figure 13-13, compare a set of scores or a graph with a lower standard deviation to one with a higher standard deviation.

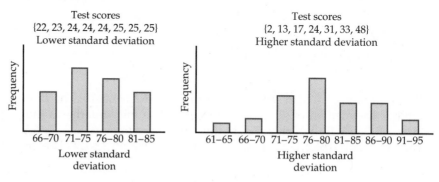

**Figure 13-13**

Determining the standard deviation usually requires some lengthy calculations with a calculator or computer. You can gain some understanding of the standard deviation by computing it for small sets of numbers.

The standard deviation is based upon the **deviation** of each score from the mean.

---

**Definition: Deviation**

The **deviation** of a score $x$ from the mean $\bar{x}$ is $x - \bar{x}$.

---

For example, Milly's mean is 6. Her score of 2 has a deviation of $2 - 6 = -4$.

## Lesson Exercise 13.32

Compute the deviation for each of Milly's scores.

Once you compute the deviations, is it possible simply to add the deviations and take the average (mean) of them?

## Lesson Exercise 13.33

Compute the sum of the deviations for Milly's scores.

The sum of the deviations is always 0. The balance property of the mean suggests why positive and negative deviations cancel each other out.

In order to combine the deviations and not end up with 0, first square the deviations so that none are negative. (Squaring the deviations gives greater weight to scores that have larger deviations.) Next, add the squared deviations and divide the sum by the total number of scores to obtain a mean of the squared deviations.

Computing the mean squared deviation squares the units of data. To obtain a number that has the same units as the original data, compute the **standard deviation**—the positive square root of the mean squared deviation.

---

**Definition: Standard Deviation**

The **standard deviation** $s = \sqrt{\text{mean of squared deviations}}$.

---

A standard deviation of 0 indicates no variation from the mean. All other standard deviations are positive. The larger the standard deviation, the greater the spread of the data. Like the mean, the standard deviation includes all scores and is significantly affected by extreme values.

The following example illustrates how to compute the standard deviation.

 **Example 13.3**

Find the standard deviation of Milly's scores.

**Solution**

**Step 1**   The mean $\bar{x} = 6$.

**Step 2**   Find the deviation of each score from the mean.

| Scores | Deviation from the Mean |
|:------:|:-----------------------:|
| 2 | −4 |
| 4 | −2 |
| 6 | 0 |
| 7 | 1 |
| 7 | 1 |
| 10 | 4 |

**Step 3**   Square each of the deviations.

| Scores | Deviation from the Mean | Squared Deviations |
|:------:|:-----------------------:|:------------------:|
| 2 | −4 | 16 |
| 4 | −2 | 4 |
| 6 | 0 | 0 |
| 7 | 1 | 1 |
| 7 | 1 | 1 |
| 10 | 4 | 16 |

**Step 4**   The sum of the squared deviations is 38. The mean squared deviation $= \dfrac{38}{6} = 6.3$

**Step 5**   The standard deviation $s = \sqrt{6.3} \approx 2.5$.  ■

The five steps needed to compute the standard deviation are:

---

**Computing the Standard Deviation for $N$ Scores**

1. Find the mean.
2. Find the deviation of each score from the mean.
3. Square each of the deviations.
4. Add up the squared deviations and divide by $N$.
5. Take the square root to obtain the *standard deviation*.

The standard deviation measures how far scores tend to be from the mean. It is something like an average deviation. (*Note:* In some situations, statisticians divide by $N - 1$ instead of $N$ in Step 4. We shall not concern ourselves with this distinction in this course.)

 Lesson Exercise 13.34

(a) Would you expect Billy's standard deviation to be higher than, the same as, or lower than Milly's?
(b) Follow the five-step procedure and compute Billy's standard deviation.

Lesson Exercise 13.35

The Teenytown Hamsters (basketball players) have heights of 60, 60, 64, 68, and 68 inches. The starting five for the Leantown Lizards have heights of 62, 62, 64, 65, and 67 inches.
(a) What is the mean height of each team?
(b) Without computing, tell which team's heights would have a larger standard deviation?

Together, the mean and standard deviation tell a lot about a set of measurements that have an approximately normal distribution.

## Normal Distribution

A large random sample of measurements of a homogeneous population often has the same pattern! Consider the following exercise.

## Lesson Exercise 13.36

Suppose that you took a random sample of 500 women at your college and measured their heights.
(a)  Describe the pattern you would expect to find in the results.
(b)  Sketch a histogram of your guess.

In the 1830s, the Belgian statistician Quetelet collected measurements, including heights, weights, and limb lengths, from a large sample of people. For each measurement, Quetelet found that most of the measurements clustered around the mean and that there were fewer scores further away from the mean in either direction.

The data on 50 women's heights in centimeters might be as shown in the table and charted in Figure 13-14.

| Interval (cm) | Frequency | Relative Frequency |
|---------------|-----------|--------------------|
| 140–149       | 4         | 0.8%               |
| 150–159       | 90        | 18%                |
| 160–169       | 285       | 57%                |
| 170–179       | 112       | 22.4%              |
| 180–189       | 9         | 1.8%               |

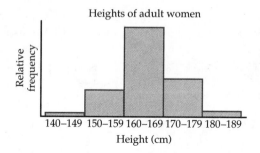

**Figure 13-14**

If progressively larger samples were taken and the interval sizes decreased, the relative frequency histogram of women's heights would approach a certain shape, as shown in Figure 13-15.

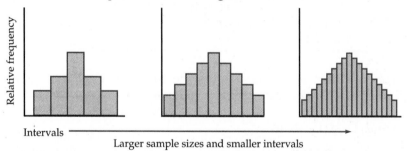

**Figure 13-15**

The histograms approach a theoretical graph called a **normal distribution** or "bell curve," that is continuous and perfectly symmetric on each side of the mean. Three examples of normal distributions are shown in Figure 13-16.

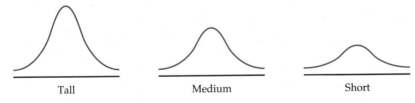

Tall    Medium    Short

**Figure 13-16**

As with a histogram, the area under the curve for an interval is proportional to its frequency. Figure 13-17 shows the distribution of heights (in inches) of 16-year-old-boys. Since 30%, or 0.30, of the heights fall between 62 and 64 inches, the interval from 62 to 64 has a frequency proportional to the area 0.30. The region looks like a bar with a curved top.

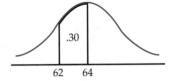

**Figure 13-17**

Statisticians use the standard deviation to describe the normal distribution in greater detail.

## Lesson Exercise 13.37

College women have a mean height of about 5 ft 5 in. and a standard deviation of about 2.5 in.
(a) Estimate what percent of college women are within 2.5 in. (one standard deviation) of 5 ft 5 in. That is, estimate what percent of women have heights between 5 ft 2.5 in. and 5 ft 7.5 in. (You could survey your class.)
(b) Estimate what percent of college women are within 5 in. (two standard deviations) of 5 ft 5 in.

The theoretical normal distribution provides approximate answers to the preceding two questions: 68% and 95%. The normal distribution has the following properties (see Figure 13-18).

---

**Properties of the Normal Distribution**

**1.** It is symmetric around the mean.

**2.** About 68% of all measurements fall within one standard deviation of the mean (34% on each side).

**3.** About 95% of all measurements fall within two standard deviations (47.5% on each side).

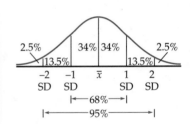

**Figure 13-18**

While the normal distribution was developed for continuous data (for example, all lengths between 0 and 10 cm), it can also be applied to large sets of discrete data (such as quiz scores that are all whole numbers between 0 and 10) (Figure 13-19).

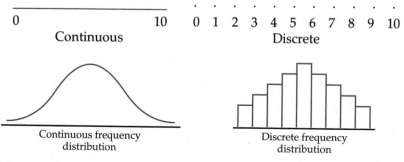

0                                10    0  1  2  3  4  5  6  7  8  9  10
       Continuous                                Discrete

Continuous frequency                   Discrete frequency
    distribution                           distribution

Figure 13-19

Measurements including heights, weights, I.Q.'s, and shoe sizes have an approximately normal distribution for large homogeneous populations. Just knowing the mean and standard deviation of a normal population enables one to estimate what percent of the population data falls between two measurements.

### Example 13.4

The mean height of U.S. adult men is 68.0 in., with a standard deviation of 2.5 in. Assume a normal distribution. What percent of adult men have the following heights?
(a) between 65.5 and 70.5 in.
(b) between 63 and 73 in.
(c) greater than 73 in.

Solution

Sketch a graph of the distribution. It is a normal distribution, so it is bell-shaped, with the mean 68 in the center (Figure 13-20).
Since $s = 2.5$, count off 2.5 units in each direction from the mean (Figure 13-21).

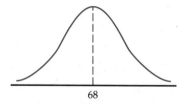

68

Figure 13-20

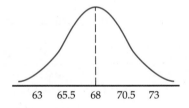

63    65.5   68   70.5   73

Figure 13-21

Fill in the percentages for the normal distribution (Figure 13-22).

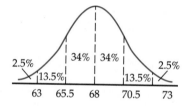

(a) 68% of the heights are between 65.5 and 70.5 in.
(b) 95% of the heights are between 63 and 73 in.
(c) 2.5% of the heights are greater than 73 in.  ■

**Figure 13-22**

## Lesson Exercise 13.38

The heights of U.S. adult women have a mean of 64.5 inches, with a standard deviation of 2.5 in. Assume a normal distribution. What percent of adult women have the following heights?
(a) between 62 and 67 in.
(b) between 59.5 and 64.5 in.
(c) above 64.5 in.

You can also report measurements from normal distributions in percentiles.

## Lesson Exercise 13.39

Using the data from Example 13.4, give the percentile for each man.
(a) N. B. Tween, 68 in. tall
(b) Hy Mann, 73 in. tall
(c) Stan Dup, 63 in. tall

You can estimate the standard deviation for a small set of measurements using the fact that about 68% of the scores are within one standard deviation of the mean.

## D Lesson Exercise 13.40

A group of 10 has the following heights (in inches).

$$\{52, 55, 56, 56, 58, 60, 61, 62, 64, 66\}$$

The mean height is 59 in. Instead of computing the standard deviation, estimate it by finding how many inches you must go from the mean in both directions to include 68% of the scores.

A data distribution can be classified as approximately **symmetric** (for example, the normal distribution) or **skewed** in one direction. When a nonsymmetric curve has a longer left-hand "tail," as shown in Figure 13-23(a), it is **skewed to the left.** A curve with a longer "tail" on the right, as shown in Figure 13-23(b), is **skewed to the right.**

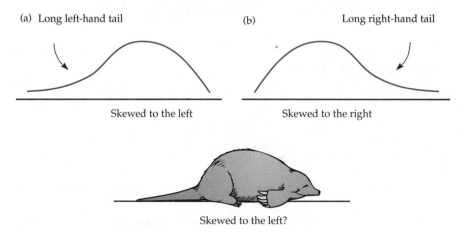

(a)  Long left-hand tail                                    (b)                         Long right-hand tail

Skewed to the left                              Skewed to the right

Skewed to the left?

**Figure 13-23**

## Lesson Exercise 13.41

Decide whether each set of discrete data is most likely to be approximately symmetric, skewed to the left, or skewed to the right.
(a)  second-grade students' test scores on a fourth-grade standardized test
(b)  fourth-grade students' test scores on the same test
(c)  sixth-grade students' test scores on the same test

As with discrete distributions, the mean is the balance point of a continuous distribution (Figure 13-24).

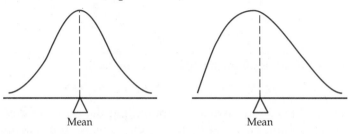

Mean                                    Mean

**Figure 13-24**

The median divides the area under the curve into two regions of equal area since half the measurements are above it and half are below (Figure 13-25).

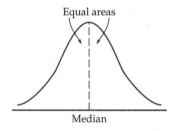

Figure 13-25

## Lesson Exercise 13.42

How do the mean and median compare for each of the following?
(a) a normal distribution
(b) a distribution skewed to the left

## Answers to Selected Lesson Exercises

**13.29** median = 6.5, mean = 6

**13.30** Milly's scores are more spread out than Billy's.

**13.32** −4, −2, 0, 1, 1, 4

**13.33** 0

**13.34** (a) lower    (b) about 1.2

**13.35** (a) T. H. mean = 64, L. L. mean = 64
(b) the Teenytown Hamsters

**13.38** (a) 68%    (b) 47.5%    (c) 50%

**13.39** (a) 50th    (b) 97.5th    (c) 2.5th

**13.40** about 4 in.

**13.41** (a) skewed to the right    (b) normal
(c) skewed to the left

**13.42** (a) They are equal.
(b) The median is higher.

## 13.4 Homework Exercises

*Basic Exercises*

1. A brochure for a new lakefront resort, Muddy Lake, says that the lake has a mean depth of 6 ft. Explain why it may not be possible to swim or canoe in the lake.

2. Mary scores in the 80th percentile on a mathematics test. What does this mean?

3. The hourly prime-time Nielson ratings for NBC and ABC during the week of 3/20/89 were as follows.

   *NBC:* 17.2, 12.4, 12.4, 12.5, 15.8, 11.8, 16.7, 15.0, 12.9, 21.3, 18.4, 19.5, 16.1, 16.1, 11.7, 13.8, 20.1, 16.4, 9.4, 9.4, 14.9

   *ABC:* 14.3, 24.5, 24.5, 21.3, 22.3, 15.6, 17.5, 11.9, 11.1, 8.2, 10.9, 8.1, 14.5, 14.7, 15.6, 8.7, 8.8, 6.4, 14.7, 14.7, 14.7

   (a) Make a boxplot for each network on the same graph.
   (b) Describe how their ratings compare based upon the boxplots.

4. Two mathematics classes have the test scores shown.

   $A = \{56, 67, 73, 78, 81, 84, 90, 92, 97\}$
   $B = \{68, 73, 75, 79, 80, 82, 84, 89, 91\}$

(a) Make a boxplot for each class on the same graph.

(b) Describe how their scores compare based upon the boxplots.

5. Give the five-number summary for the box-plot shown.

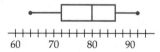

6. Without computing the standard deviation, tell which set of scores has a higher standard deviation.

(a) {4, 5, 6, 7, 8}

(b) {0, 3, 6, 9, 12}

7. Without computing the standard deviation, tell which histogram has a higher standard deviation.

(a)

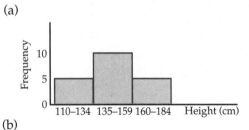

(b)

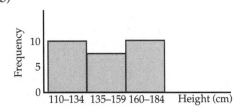

8. My wife has two routes to work. She can drive on back roads that never have much traffic. Or, she can drive on an expressway that is faster when there is not much traffic, but can take a lot longer when there is a traffic jam. Which would tend to have a higher standard deviation, a set of daily travel times on the back roads, or a set of daily travel times on the expressway?

9. (a) Find the mean and standard deviation of {80, 90, 90, 90, 100}.

(b) The range, from Section 13.1 (highest score minus the lowest score), is the simplest measure of spread. What is the range of this set?

10. (a) Find the mean and standard deviation of {3, 7, 8, 10}.

(b) If your calculator has a $\sigma_n$ (standard deviation) key, use it to compute the standard deviation of {3, 7, 8, 10}.

11. Which would have a higher standard deviation, the weights of all 3-year-old boys in the United States or the weights of all 9-year-old boys in the United States?

12. Each number in a set of five numbers is either 0, 1, or 2.

(a) If the mean is 1 and the standard deviation is 0, what numbers are in the set?

(b) List the members of a set with the largest possible standard deviation.

13. The following set of heights has a mean of 60 and a standard deviation of 7.7.

{50, 50, 53, 56, 60, 64, 67, 70, 70}

(a) Which heights are within one standard deviation of the mean?

(b) Which heights are more than two standard deviations from the mean?

14. A population has a mean weight of 140 lb, with a standard deviation of 21 lb. What weights would be more than two standard deviations from the mean?

15. Take six coins.

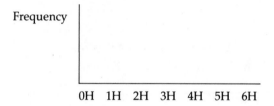

(a) Toss them 50 times and record the number of heads each time.

(b) Graph a frequency distribution of the results.

(c) Do your results suggest a normal curve?

**16.** What are the characteristics of the normal distribution?

**17.** A survey shows that the mean income in Boomtown is $21,000, with $s = $2600$. Assume a normal distribution. What percent of people have the following incomes?
(a) over $21,000
(b) between $18,400 and $26,200
(c) under $18,400

**18.** Surveys indicate that U.S. adults watch television for a mean of 25 hours per week, with a standard deviation of 3 hours. Assume a normal distribution. What percent of adults watch television for the following lengths of time?
(a) between 22 and 28 hours per week
(b) less than 19 hours per week
(c) more than 28 hours per week

**19.** Brand A lightbulbs have a mean life of 1000 hours, with a standard deviation of 20 hours. Brand B lightbulbs have a mean life of 1050 hours, with a standard deviation of 150 hours. Describe the advantages of each lightbulb.

**20.** A standardized test has normally distributed scores with $\bar{x} = 50$ and $s = 5$. Give the percentiles of the following scores.
(a) 55     (b) 40     (c) 54 (Estimate it.)

**21.** Estimate the standard deviation of {2, 4, 6, 8, 10, 12, 14, 16, 18}.

**22.** Estimate the standard deviation of the following set of test scores, with mean 75.

$$\{45, 52, 60, 64, 70, 73, 75, 77,$$
$$79, 80, 84, 86, 89, 92, 99\}$$

**23.** A group of gifted third-grade students take a third-grade standardized test. Would you expect their score distribution to be approximately symmetric, skewed to the right, or skewed to the left?

**24.** Describe the distribution of each of the following as approximately symmetric, skewed to the right, or skewed to the left. (*Hint:* Sketch a graph of each distribution.)
(a) typical scores on a classroom unit test graded 0 to 100%
(b) heights of adult males in the United States
(c) family incomes in the United States

**25.** A distribution is skewed to the right. Which would be higher, the mean or the median?

**26.** Select a page in any book.
(a) Tabulate the length of each word on the page and display the results in a bar graph.
(b) Is your graph approximately symmetric, skewed to the right, or skewed to the left?

*Extension Exercises*

**27.** An ERB standardized test report might include the following information for a sixth-grade class.

| MEAN | S.D. | Q1 | MED | Q3 | SEM |
|------|------|-----|-----|-----|------|
| 426.7 | 6.2 | 422 | 428 | 431 | 18.1 |

"SEM" (standard error of measurement) indicates the typical amount of error in a test score. Tell what all the other numbers represent.

**28.** Suppose that you read an article about a disease you have. The article says that a person with the disease lives an average (mean) of 4 years beyond diagnosis. You have already lived 3 years since being diagnosed.
(a) Explain why this article may be bad news.
(b) Explain why this article may be good news.

**29.** Match each class in column A to all appropriate descriptions in column B.

| A: Class | B: Typical Test Scores |
| --- | --- |
| Class with wide ability range | High mean |
| Honors class | Low standard deviation |
| Students with very similar abilities | High standard deviation |
| Remedial class | Low median |

**30.** (a) If you add two to each number in a set, how does this affect each of the following?
　　(1) the mean
　　(2) the standard deviation
　(b) If you add 10 to each number in a set, how does this affect each of the following?
　　(1) the mean
　　(2) the standard deviation
　(c) Based upon parts (a) and (b), if you increase each score in a data set by a positive number $k$, how do you affect the mean and standard deviation?

**31.** (a) If the salary of each employee in a set is increased by \$2000, how does this change the mean and the standard deviation of the set?
　(b) If the salary of each employee in a set is increased by 10%, how does this change the mean and the standard deviation of the set?

**32.** Find the mean of each distribution.

(a)

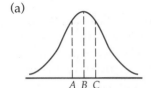

A B C

(b)

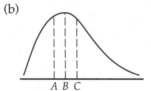

A B C

**33.** Prove that the sum of the deviations for a set of five numbers $A$, $B$, $C$, $D$, and $E$ is 0.

**34.** Suppose that the mean 100-watt Brite light-bulb burns for 2200 hours, with a standard deviation of 200 hours. Assume a normal distribution. What is the chance that a Brite lightbulb will burn for each period of time?
(a) more than 2200 hours
(b) fewer than 1800 hours
(c) more than 2400 hours

**35.**

"Sugar Fix" cereal comes in a 16-oz package. The actual weight of the boxes produced is normally distributed, with a mean of 16.3 oz and $s = 0.3$ oz. What is the chance that a randomly selected box has each of the following weights?
(a) under 16.3 oz　　(b) under 16.0 oz
(c) above 16.9 oz

**36.** Show that the standard deviation of $x_1 + k$, $x_2 + k$, . . . , $x_n + k$ is the same as the standard deviation of $x_1, x_2, . . . , x_n$.

**37.** There is another way to compute the standard deviation of a set. For four numbers $A$, $B$, $C$, and $D$:

$$s = \sqrt{\frac{A^2 + B^2 + C^2 + D^2}{4} - (\bar{x})^2}$$

(a) Write a formula for $\bar{x}$ in terms of $A$, $B$, $C$, and $D$.
(b) Write $s$ as the square root of a mean sum of squared deviations using $A$, $B$, $C$, $D$, and $\bar{x}$.

(c) Square the binomials and combine terms to obtain the formula given at the beginning of the problem.
(*Hint:* $A + B + C + D = 4\bar{x}$.)

**Computer Exercise**

38. The following program uses a shortcut for computing the standard deviation from the preceding exercise. In the program, the computer adds the squares of the scores and divides by $N$, the number of scores. Then it subtracts the square of the mean and takes the square root of the result.

(a) Enter the following program into the computer.

```
10 PRINT "HOW MANY NUMBERS
   DO YOU HAVE?"
20 INPUT N
30 LET T = 0: LET S = 0
40 FOR I = 1 TO N
```

```
50   PRINT "TYPE A DATA NUMBER
     AND PRESS ENTER/RETURN."
60   LET T = T + D
70   LET S = S + D * D
80 NEXT I
90 PRINT "THE MEAN IS "; T / N
100 LET V = S / N − (T / N) * (T / N)
110 PRINT "THE STANDARD
    DEVIATION IS "; SQR(V)
```

(b) RUN the program for $\{65, 74, 80, 82, 86, 95\}$.

39. Use MINITAB to produce data analysis for Milly's scores from the lesson.

```
MTB> SET THE FOLLOWING DATA
     INTO C1
DATA> 2 4 6 7 7 10
MTB> DESCRIBE DATA IN C1
MTB> STOP
```

## 13.5 Sampling

Who do people want as the next president? How do they feel about government spending on education? In order to answer questions like these, would you need to ask every single adult what he or she thinks?

Fortunately, the answer is no. Taking a representative sample of about 1500 will usually give a good estimate of how 190 million U.S. adults stand on an issue! Sampling is a part of inferential statistics.

**Inferential statistics** involves studying how to draw inferences (conclusions) about the larger group (population) based upon information about the subgroup (sample). The preceding lessons in this chapter covered descriptive statistics—techniques used to organize and summarize data. Descriptive statistics and inferential statistics are the two main areas of statistics.

### Surveys

Newspapers frequently report survey results that give us information about our attitudes (Figure 13-26, page 786). A survey is one of the best

## Poll: Fight drugs with more taxes

By M.J. Zuckerman
USA TODAY

WASHINGTON — Most people are willing to pay an average of $50 a year in extra taxes to fight drugs – adding $5.2 billion to the anti-drug battle – a USA TODAY poll shows.

The USA TODAY poll of 612 people found 69 percent "willing to pay more taxes" to "fight illegal drugs"; 28 percent wouldn't pay more; 3 percent are uncertain. Of those willing:

▶ 14 percent would ·pay between $1 and $50.

▶ 40 percent would pay between $51 and $500.

▶ Only 8 percent are willing to pay more than $500.

▶ 38 percent were uncertain how much they'd pay.

If each of the 103.3 million people filing personal tax returns paid $50, it would nearly double the current $5.3 billion in federal anti-drug spending.

The national phone poll, conducted by Gordon S. Black Associates, has a 4 percent margin of error.

**Figure 13-26**

ways to determine the political preferences, moral beliefs, and favorite television programs of a society.

The following experiment will help you understand how surveys work.

### I.  Materials
a paper bag and identical small slips of paper for each class member

## II. Procedure

A. Select a question of interest to the class, one that has two possible responses. Pick a question about which people in the class are likely to disagree. (For example, "Do you prefer plastic or paper bags at the supermarket?" "Would you prefer _____ or _____ in the upcoming election?")

B. Have everyone write a response on a slip of paper and put it in the paper bag.

In a survey, the **population** is the total set of responses you want to study. In this example, the entire collection of responses from your class is the population.

C. Appoint three poll takers. Each in turn will take five slips of paper from the bag, record the results, and return the slips to the bag.

A **sample** is a subset of the population chosen to represent it. In this case, each poll taker collected a sample of five responses. Samples are used because they can provide simple, fairly accurate information about a much larger population. Samples are sometimes the only way to obtain information about a population. For example, would you expect National Motors to crash test every car they make?

D. Ask each poll taker to give his or her sample results and to make a prediction about the population results based upon *his* or *her* sample.

E. Have the class predict the response totals for the class based upon all three samples.

F. Take all the papers out of the bag and tabulate the actual results.

Discuss the following questions about the simulated survey.

## Lesson Exercise 13.43

Was each poll taker's sample random?

## Lesson Exercise 13.44

Was the sample size large enough?

## Lesson Exercise 13.45

(a) How large a sample would have been needed to predict with certainty the class's *preferred* response?
(b) How large a sample would be needed to predict with certainty the *exact results* for the class?

Lesson Exercise 13.46

How could the wording of the survey question or the response choices be modified to obtain different results?

Figure 13-27 shows a sampling activity from the sixth-grade textbook of *Mathematics Unlimited*.

When you cannot find the exact probability of an event, you can approximate through observation or experiments. Act out the following experiment.

**Step 1:**  Have a partner put into an envelope 10 markers, some red and the rest yellow, so that you don't know how many there are of each. Without looking, pick one marker, write down its color, and replace it in the envelope. Shake up the envelope. Repeat this process 4 more times.

  • How many times did you pick a red marker?

  • Based on your picks, what is the probability that the next marker you pick will be red?

**Step 2:**  Now make 5 more picks, making a total of 10 picks. Remember to keep replacing the markers after each pick. Record your results.

  • Based on your 10 picks, what is the probability of picking a red marker?

**Step 3:**  Now make 10 more picks, making a total of 20 picks. Record your results. Based on your 20 picks, what is the probability of picking a red marker?

When do you think the percent of red markers picked would be more likely to be closer to the percent of red markers in the envelope: after 10 picks, after 20 picks, or after 100 picks? Why?

Open the envelope and count the number of red markers. What was the actual probability of picking a red marker?

From *Mathematics Unlimited*, Grade 6 (San Diego, CA: Harcourt Brace Jovanovich, 1992), p. 393.

**Figure 13-27**

## Samples: Randomness, Size, and Error

In a survey, one tries to obtain a sample that is representative of the total population. This requires collecting some type of **random sample** in which everyone in the population has an equal chance of being chosen. A random sample is the ideal, but in practice it is virtually impossible to obtain a perfectly random sample.

## Lesson Exercise 13.47

In a survey of adults in Washington, D.C., telephone numbers are randomly selected from the city phone directory, and these people are called. Why won't the sample obtained be a perfectly random sample of adults in Washington, D.C.?

When you read survey results, check to see whether the sample appears to be nearly random and representative. A reputable pollster uses nearly random samples.

In a national sample, pollsters often use **stratified random sampling**. The pollster groups the population by classifications such as region and community size. Then, the pollster takes appropriately-sized random samples from each of these groups.

## Lesson Exercise 13.48

A pollster wishes to select a total of 200 children from three schools in numbers proportional to the size of each school. If the schools have 641, 410, and 549 students, respectively, how many children should be selected from each school?

Another important consideration in sampling is the size of the sample. As the size of a random sample gets larger, it is more likely to reflect the population more accurately.

While precise computations of statistical error require a more in-depth study of statistics, a bead model can give you some insight into sampling error. Consider the following exercise.

## Lesson Exercise 13.49

Imagine a box containing a large number of identical beads, 30% of which are white.
(a) If you randomly select 100 beads, what kind of results would you expect?
(b) Suppose that you replace 100 beads in the box and mix them up. Then I randomly select 100 beads. How would you expect our results to compare?

I performed such a bead-sampling experiment 50 times and plotted the results as a histogram in Figure 13-28.

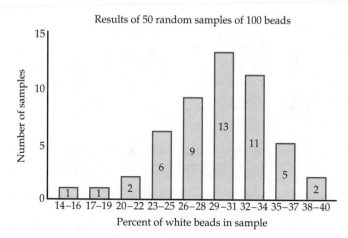

**Figure 13-28**

## Lesson Exercise 13.50

How often did I obtain a sample containing each of the following?
(a) between 26% and 34% white beads
(b) between 20% and 40% white beads

If someone used a random sample of 100 beads to estimate the percent of white beads in the box (the population), he or she would obtain an estimate that was between 26% and 34% about 66% of the time (33 times out of 50) and an estimate that was between 20% and 40% about 96% of the time (48 times out of 50).

Therefore, a pollster could expect that the error in such a sample of 100 would usually be 10% or less. Most of the time, a sample of 100 would show between 20% and 40% white beads, but once in a while, just by chance, someone might pick a sample of 100 beads that has a smaller or larger percent of white beads.

By increasing the sample size, the sampling error can be reduced well below 10%. If you take a course in statistics, you will learn more about the relationship between sample size and sampling error, and how the sampling distribution of percentages of white beads is related to the normal distribution.

Pollsters usually give the range of statistical error expected 95% of the time. The following table gives specific sampling errors for different sample sizes and different percentages of favorable responses.

| Range of Statistical Error Expected 95% of the Time | | | | | | | |
|---|---|---|---|---|---|---|---|
| Favorable Response | Sample Size | | | | | | |
| | 1500 | 1000 | 750 | 600 | 400 | 200 | 100 |
| 10% or 90% | 2% | 2% | 3% | 3% | 4% | 5% | 7% |
| 20% or 80% | 2% | 3% | 4% | 4% | 5% | 7% | 9% |
| 30% or 70% | 3% | 4% | 4% | 4% | 6% | 8% | 10% |
| 40% or 60% | 3% | 4% | 4% | 5% | 6% | 8% | 11% |
| 50% | 3% | 4% | 4% | 5% | 6% | 8% | 11% |

The following example shows how to use the table just given. (You can learn how the table is developed in a probability and statistics course.)

## Example 13.5

A *USA Today* poll (see the beginning of the section) of 612 people found 69 percent "willing to pay more taxes" to fight illegal drugs.
(a) What is the sampling error, and what does it mean?
(b) Write an accurate statement describing what the survey shows.

**Solution**

(a) Find the closest number to 612 in the table under sample size, namely 600. For a 69% favorable response, go down to the row labeled 30% or 70% favorable response. The error is 4%.
(b) We are fairly (95%) sure that the actual percent of adults favoring more taxes to fight illegal drugs is between 65% and 73%. ■

## Lesson Exercise 13.51

In a nationwide Gallup poll on September 26–29, 1991, 35% of 1005 respondents decribed themselves as "overweight." Write an accurate statement describing what the survey tells about U.S. adult opinions.

In analyzing a survey, examine the survey questions, the sample, the error range, and the interpretation of survey results. Sampling is usually reliable in national surveys. Survey reports usually list the error range, but if they don't, you can find the probable error range in the table. Problems are more likely to occur with the questions asked or the interpretation of the results.

## Answers to Selected Lesson Exercises

**13.43** yes

**13.44** yes

**13.45** (b) the entire class

**13.47** All adults do not have telephones, and there is not exactly one adult per telephone number. Also, some people will not be at home to answer the phone.

**13.48** 80, 51, and 69

**13.49** (a) Approximately 30% would be white.
(b) They probably would be similar but not exactly the same.

**13.50** (a) 33 times    (b) 48 times

**13.51** We are 95% sure that between 31% and 39% of all U.S. adults describe themselves as overweight.

## 13.5   Homework Exercises

*Basic Exercises*

1. In a carefully conducted pre-election survey, 58% of those polled said that they preferred Patti Englander. If *P* people vote, what is a good prediction for the number of people who will vote for Patti Englander?

2. The following data were collected from different surveys.

   - About 45% of Americans do not read books at all.
   - The average number of books read by the reading population is 16 per year.
   - About 53% of Americans read fewer than 12 books a year.
   - About 25% of Americans read at least 20 books a year.

   Assume that all of these results are accurate.
   (a) What percent of Americans read at least one book a year?
   (b) What percent of Americans read between 12 and 19 books (inclusive) a year?
   (c) What percent of your class read at least one book in the last year?

 3. An aerial photograph of a forest is divided into 40 sections of equal area. Five sections are randomly selected, and they have 46, 38, 39, 52, and 47 trees, respectively. Estimate the total number of trees in the forest.

4. After President Bush's 1992 State of the Union Address, CBS asked viewers with touch-tone phones to call in and rate the speech. Why didn't the 314,786 responses constitute a perfectly random sample?

5. A telephone survey asking whether people favor or oppose the legalization of marijuana finds that 15% are in favor and 78% are opposed. Why are these results unreliable?

6. A soft drink company says: "In our taste test, the majority of adults preferred our cola to theirs." You find out that they commissioned five different taste tests. Why might their claim be misleading?

7. In a door-to-door daytime survey, an interviewer asks any adult who is at home whether or not he or she uses Bubbly laundry detergent. In a similar survey, an interviewer asks the adult at home to display the box of laundry detergent he or she is using. Would the results tend to be the same? Why or why not?

8. A college has 250 freshmen, 220 sophomores, 200 juniors, and 180 seniors. If a stratified sample of 100 students is chosen, how many should be chosen from each class?

9. A survey question reads as follows: "Would you favor or oppose building a peace shield that might protect us from nuclear attack?" Change the wording of the question so that more people will oppose it.

10. Consider the following survey question with no response choices given. "What should be the three main priorities of the federal government?" How would the results change if the following choices were given?
   (a) gun-control laws
   (b) balancing the budget
   (c) developing solar power
   (d) reducing taxes
   (e) aid to the poor and elderly
   (f) other

11. People are asked to respond to the following survey item. "School teachers are more highly respected than stockbrokers.
   (a) agree     (b) disagree"
   How would the results be affected if we added the following third choice?
   (c) don't know

12. In their 2/90 issue, *Learning 90* reports a survey of 700 substance abuse educators about what drug education approaches are effective, in which 66% of the educators recommended teaching causes and effects, and 66% recommended teaching how to improve self-esteem. Based on sampling error, the actual percent of substance-abuse educators supporting each of these approaches is probably between _____ % and _____ %.

13. In the cartoon, the senator's actual support is probably between _____ % and _____ % of the voters.

Reprinted by permission: Tribune Media Services.

14. A random sample of 2000 U.S. adults shows that 80% like grapes. Which of the following statements is most accurate?
   (a) Eighty percent of all U.S. adults like grapes.
   (b) Close to 80% of all U.S. adults like grapes.
   (c) One can be pretty sure that about 80% of all U.S. adults like grapes.

15. A random sample of 1500 U.S. adults shows that 60% like spinach and 40% do not. Write an accurate statement describing what this survey tells us about all adults in the United States.

16. The following study involved a nationwide random sample of 1500 adults. Based on a poll on July 11–14, 1980, Gallup reported "Public backs drafting women." The poll asked whether women should be required to serve in the armed forces. The results were:

| Should | Should Not | No Opinion |
|--------|-----------|------------|
| 49% | 47% | 4% |

Why is the headline misleading?

17. In a random sample of 50 people who are asked whether they favor stricter gun-control legislation, 58% favor it and 36% oppose it. Why are these results unreliable in showing that most people favor stricter gun control?

18. In December 1975, *Newsweek* reported, "Ford in trouble," based on a Gallup poll showing that Republicans prefer Ronald Reagan over Gerald Ford by 40% to 32%. Why is this headline misleading?

19. A Gallup poll (December 12–15, 1991) reports the following survey results from 1005 telephone interviews with an error of ±3%. The question was, "Do you think abortions should be legal under any circumstances, or certain circumstances, or illegal in all circumstances?" The results showed 31% saying legal under all circumstances, 53% saying only certain circumstances, and 14% saying illegal in all circumstances.

A pro-abortion reporter might say the following about the results. "84% of all Americans favor legal abortions under some or all circumstances." Write a similarly distorted headline that an anti-abortion reporter might write.

20.

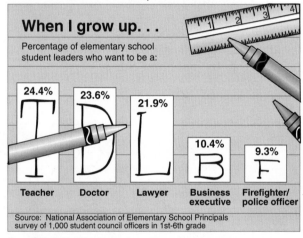

# USA SNAPSHOTS®
A look at statistics that shape our lives

**When I grow up. . .**

Percentage of elementary school student leaders who want to be a:

24.4% Teacher
23.6% Doctor
21.9% Lawyer
10.4% Business executive
9.3% Firefighter/police officer

Source: National Association of Elementary School Principals survey of 1,000 student council officers in 1st-6th grade

   (a) What was the sample size for the survey?
   (b) Approximately what is the statistical error in the 24.4% who said they want to be teachers?
   (c) What additional information would be helpful?

21. On May 5–7 and June 9–11, 1989, Gallup asked 1584 adults the following question. "Students are often given the grades A, B, C, D, and FAIL to denote the quality of their

work. Suppose the public schools themselves in this community were graded the same way. What grade would you give the public schools here?" The results were:

| A | B | C | D | FAIL | Don't Know/ No Answer |
|---|---|---|---|---|---|
| 8% | 35% | 33% | 11% | 4% | 9% |

Why is this survey question a bad one?

22. We all make judgments based upon sampling. For example, if you wanted to decide whether new Squeezie Grapefruit juice is fresh and tasty, you might buy two cartons, try them, and then make your decision.

Give an example of a sample you took and a conclusion you reached about
(a) a restaurant.
(b) a person.

23.                "IS OUR FACE RED!"
So read the headline of the November 14, 1936, issue of *The Literary Digest*. The magazine had conducted a poll just before the 1936 presidential election between Alfred Landon and Franklin Roosevelt. The sample came from a list of 10 million names primarily from telephone directories, automobile registrations, and club membership lists. Each of these people was mailed a questionnaire. Of the 2.4 million people who sent in the questionnaires, 43% preferred Roosevelt, while 57% preferred Landon. This was one of the worst errors ever made in a major survey. Roosevelt won the election 62% to 38%!
(a) Was the sample large enough?
(b) Was the sample representative and random?
(c) Why do you think the prediction was so far off?

*Extension Exercises*
24. The Dow Jones Average is the most widely quoted stock market average. It attempts to represent the trends in the stock market by averaging the prices of the following 30 stocks (as of 1992).

| | | |
|---|---|---|
| Allied Corp. | Alcoa | American Express |
| AT&T | Beth. Steel | Boeing |
| Caterpillar | Chevron | Coca Cola |
| Disney | Dupont | Eastman Kodak |
| Exxon | General Electric | General Motors |
| Goodyear | IBM | Int. Paper |
| McDonald's | Merck | Minn. Mining |
| J.P. Morgan | Phillip Morris | Procter & Gamble |
| Sears | Texaco | Union Carbide |
| United Tech. | Westinghouse | Woolworth's |

Why might the Dow Jones average not be representative of the New York Stock Exchange as a whole?

25. You want to do a survey at your school to determine student preferences in the next presidential election. Describe in detail how you would obtain a representative sample.

26. You own an ice cream store and serve 10 flavors at any one time. How could you decide what flavors to serve?

27. You own a clothing store and want to decide how many of each color pants of a certain style to order. How could you decide?

28. A police department checked the color of clothing worn by pedestrians who were killed in traffic accidents at night. They found that 4/5 were wearing dark-colored clothes and 1/5 were wearing light-colored clothes. The police department concluded that pedestrians wearing white are less likely to be killed in accidents at night. Explain why this conclusion may not be correct.

**29.**

**DOONESBURY**　　　　　　　　　　　　　　　　　**by Garry Trudeau**

(a) In the cartoon, what does Doonesbury mean when he says polls "often become self-fulfilling prophecies"?

(b) Do you agree with Doonesbury?

**30.** In a 6-year study in Seattle, all firearms deaths were investigated. There were 743 firearms deaths, and investigators collected the following information.

**A.** There were 469 suicides, 256 homicides, 11 accidents, and 7 of unknown cause.

**B.** Of the deaths, 473 occurred inside a house (343 involved a handgun).

**C.** Of those 473 deaths, 398 happened in a house involving a firearm that was kept in the house.

**D.** The 398 deaths were divided as follows:

333 suicides (68% from handguns)

50 homicides (42 during a fight in the house)

11 accidents

4 self-inflicted deaths (not known whether they were suicide or accident)

**E.** Of the 65 nonsuicides, 63 involved families or friends and 2 involved strangers (burglars).

What conclusions can be drawn from the study?

**31.** Following are the Nielsen ratings for the top 10 network prime-time television shows during the week 3/15–3/22/92.

|  | Rating | Share |
|---|---|---|
| 1. *60 Minutes* | 23.2 | 38 |
| 2. *Roseanne* | 21.4 | 33 |
| 3. *Murphy Brown* | 21.2 | 32 |
| 4. *Home Improvement* | 19.6 | 31 |
| 5. *Coach* | 18.5 | 29 |
| 6. *Unsolved Mysteries* | 18.4 | 30 |
| 7. *Northern Exposure* | 18.0 | 31 |
| 8. *Designing Women* | 18.0 | 28 |
| 9. *Full House* | 17.8 | 29 |
| 10. *Major Dad* | 17.6 | 27 |

The Nielsen ratings are based on the television-viewing habits of a sample of 1700 U.S. homes (out of 92.1 million). Boxes are attached to all the television sets in each home in order to record each show that is watched for 5 minutes or more. The **rating** is the percentage of the 1700 homes in which a show is watched. The **share** is the percentage of the 1700 homes with a television set on that are tuned to a particular show when it is aired.

(a) Explain why the share is always higher than the rating.

(b) Assuming the Nielsen sampling was done reliably, the error in the ratings is about ___ %.

(c) The Nielsen company attempts to obtain a random sample of 1700, but only about 65% of those they ask are willing to participate. How could they make a good case that the 1700 homes they end up with are representative?

(d) If a show counts after it has been watched for five minutes, how many shows could a person "watch" in a 30-minute period?

32. Suppose the 1700 homes have 3400 television sets. One Tuesday night, 1200 households have a set in use and 400 households are tuned to *Roseanne* for at least 5 minutes.
(a) What share will *Roseanne* receive?
(b) What percent rating will *Roseanne* receive?

33. *Murphy Brown* had a 32 share on 3/16/92. Which of the following must be true?
(a) 32% of all Americans watched *Murphy Brown*.
(b) *Murphy Brown* is the third-best show on television.
(c) Of all televisions in use, 32% were tuned to *Murphy Brown*.
(d) Of all the Nielsen households, 32% had sets tuned to *Murphy Brown*.
(e) Of the people living in Nielsen households, 32% were watching *Murphy Brown*.

34. During the Monday night 8 PM slot, assume that 1700 television sets are counted as being watched. Try answering the following questions.
(a) How many of the 1700 homes have televisions on?
(b) How many people are watching television?
(c) How many people watched the whole program they were watching?
(d) How many television sets were on?

35. Following are the results from a *Newsweek* telephone survey of 756 adults (3-27-89) about pesticides in food. The margin of error is ±4%. Write a few paragraphs interpreting the results.

38% becoming more worried that food is contaminated

  6% becoming less worried

53% feel about the same

52% feel U.S. government makes sure U.S. food is safe

44% feel food from other countries is safe

73% think we should use fewer pesticides/chemicals even if food costs more

45% often or occasionally buy organic foods

47% never or hardly ever buy organic foods

Consumers who are worried have cut down on

| apples | 44% | eggs/poultry | 23% |
|--------|-----|--------------|-----|
| vegetables | 41% | corn | 11% |
| fish | 25% | milk | 9% |

36. How much cheaper are store brands than national brands? Go to a neighborhood food store or drug store that carries store brands. Compare the price of ten national brands to ten store brands, excluding sale items. What is the average (mean) percentage difference?

*Special Exercises*

37. (a) Keep a log of your television watching, including hours spent watching, shows watched, and hours of commercials seen.
(b) Based upon your data from part (a), estimate the number of hours of television you have watched in your lifetime.
(c) How does your answer in part (b) compare to the number of hours you have slept, eaten, or attended school?
(d) Estimate how many hours of commercials you have seen in your lifetime.

**38.** (a) Compile the class data for all three sets of data in the preceding exercise.

  (b) Present these data in appropriate graphs or tables.

**39.** (a) Find an advertisement that makes a claim based upon a survey or research study.

  (b) Write to the company for further details about the study.

  (c) If the company responds, analyze the study and decide whether the company has proved its claim and whether the claim justifies buying the product.

**40.** After the class has composed a list of items that are representative of what the class eats, find the cost of these items at your neighborhood food store. Bring the results to class for a comparison.

**41.** Conduct a college or community survey on a topic of your choice. Consider the following suggestions.

What is your favorite radio station?

Do you prefer paper bags or plastic bags at the grocery store?

What can be done to improve public schools in your county?

## 13.6  Standardized Test Scores

As a teacher, you will receive standardized test reports about your students similar to the one in the following table (which is based on the Stanford Achievement Test). Most standardized test scores are based upon the concepts of the median, percentiles, and the normal distribution.

| Test Score Report | Score Type | Math Comp. | Reading | Vocab-ulary | Math Appl. | Spell. | Lang. |
|---|---|---|---|---|---|---|---|
| Gr 5 Norms Gr 5.2 | RS/NOP OSS | 35/44 | 42/60 | 26/36 | 38/40 | 33/40 | 32/53 |
| Fran Tikley | NAT'L  PR-S | 68-6 | 59-5 | 64-6 | 97-9 | 73-6 | 48-55 |
| Age 10-3 | LOCAL PR-S | 60-6 | 48-5 | 65-6 | 92-8 | 63-6 | 36-4 |
| Test date 10/25/92 | GRADE EQUIV | 5.4 | 5.1 | 5.6 | 8.4 | 6.4 | 4.1 |

**D** Lesson Exercise 13.52

Try to guess the meaning of the various numbers and symbols in the test score report in the table just presented.

Fran Tikley's score report includes raw scores, percentiles, stanines, and grade-level equivalents. The **raw score** is the student's actual score on the exam. Fran received a raw score of 33/40 on spelling, which means he got 33 questions right out of 40.

## Lesson Exercise 13.53

(a)  What is Fran's raw score in math computation?
(b)  What does this score mean?

The test report also gives percentiles. Fran's national percentile for spelling is 73. This means that he scored better in spelling than about 73% of the fifth-grade second-month students in the United States on this exam.

## Lesson Exercise 13.54

(a)  What is Fran's local percentile score in math computation?
(b)  What does this score mean?

## Lesson Exercise 13.55

On the same test as Fran, Hy Skor had a national vocabulary percentile of 66. Does this show that Hy knows more of the vocabulary tested than Fran? Why or why not?

How accurate are these raw scores and percentiles? As you know from personal experience, a student's test score varies somewhat according to how the student feels on a particular day and which questions are chosen for the test. So a percentage or percentile on an exam has some error in it, just as a percentage in a survey does. Repeating a test or a survey on another day will usually result in a slightly different outcome.

Percentile scores can be misleading because they appear more accurate (measuring to the nearest percent) than they really are. This problem led to the development of stanine scores. The term "stanine" is a contraction of "standard nine." **Stanines** divide normally distributed student scores into nine groups based on their percentiles, as shown in Figure 13-29.

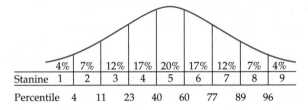

Figure 13-29

For example, a stanine of 6 means that the student is in the 60th to 76th percentile range.

## Lesson Exercise 13.56

A stanine of 2 means that the score is in what percentile range?

In Fran Tikley's score report, the stanines are given to the right of the percentiles.

## Lesson Exercise 13.57

What is Fran's national stanine score in math computation?

Stanine scores do not attempt to make "the fine distinctions which are frequently but improperly made" using percentile scores (NACOME report, 1975).

## Lesson Exercise 13.58

One student has a stanine of 6 and another has a stanine of 7.
(a) What is the smallest possible difference between their percentile scores?
(b) What is the largest possible difference between their percentile scores?

Another type of score reports the student's standing in relation to grade levels. The **grade-level score** indicates the grade level in years and months at which the student's score would be average. Fran has a grade level of 6.4 in spelling. This indicates that he scored the same as the average student in the fourth month of sixth grade.

## Lesson Exercise 13.59

(a) What is Fran's grade-level score in math computation?
(b) What does it mean?

Many educators question the value of grade-level scores because they are commonly misinterpreted in two ways. First, people expect most children to score at or above grade level even though about half the students should score below grade level.

Second, very high or low grade-level scores have little meaning. Fran Tikley scored so well on math applications that his grade-level score was 8.4. Just because he did extremely well on fifth-grade word problems, can we tell whether he can do eighth-grade word problems? A fifth-grade test would have so few eighth-grade-level questions that it could not measure

Fran's ability at that level. These drawbacks in grade-level scoring have led some educators to recommend that it be abandoned.

## Lesson Exercise 13.60

A sixth-grade student receives a grade-level score of 3.2. Why is this score misleading?

## Classroom Use of Standardized Tests

Using standardized test scores in conjunction with other information, you can make a general evaluation of a new student's ability when he or she first comes to your school. The standardized test gives a general score that assesses student progress on topics that are taught in most schools.

## Lesson Exercise 13.61

The following student is transferring to your classroom. His score report (based on the Metropolitan Achievement Test) is given.

| Name | Robert Mark | Grade | 5 |
|------|-------------|-------|---|
| School | Fargo Elementary, N.D. | Date of Test | 10/2/92 |

### Score Summary Box

| Test | Number Possible | Number Right | Grade Equiv. | Percentile | Stanine |
|------|-----------------|--------------|--------------|------------|---------|
| Reading | 60 | 56 | 6.1 | 85 | |
| Mathematics | 50 | 25 | 4.3 | 30 | |
| Language | 60 | 47 | 5.7 | 74 | |
| Science | 45 | 0 | 4.1 | 32 | |
| Social Studies | 45 | 8 | 5.3 | 62 | |

(a) Use the percentile information to fill in the stanine scores for each test.

(b) Give your general assessment of how this student will do at your school.

Some schools routinely use standardized tests to evaluate individual students. Since these tests do not measure student achievement in *specific* areas, and they are not designed to test the particular curriculum the student has been studying, the test results have little value for measuring an individual student's progress with a school's curriculum.

## IQ Scores

Psychologists disagree about what intelligence is and how to measure it. In spite of these disputes, some standardized tests attempt to measure intelligence.

The results of intelligence tests usually are reported as IQ scores. The IQ score compares a child's results with other children the same age. The average (mean) raw score is assigned a standardized IQ score of 100. A raw score one standard deviation above the mean is assigned a standardized IQ score of 115. **Standardized** IQ scores are normally distributed with a mean of 100 and a standard deviation of 15 (Figure 13-30).

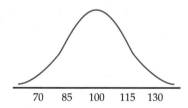

70    85    100    115    130

**Figure 13-30**

### Lesson Exercise 13.62

People who score more than two standard deviations below the mean are classified as mentally retarded. In the distribution in Figure 13-30, what IQ score is two standard deviations below the mean?

### Lesson Exercise 13.63

What percent of children in an age group have IQ's between 85 and 130?

## Answers to Selected Lesson Exercises

13.53 (a) 35/44      (b) 35 right out of 44

13.54 (a) 60
    (b) Fran scored higher in math comp. than 60% of the students in his age group.

13.55 No. Their percentile scores are too close to be considered significantly different. Since the tests are multiple choice, guessing accounts for part of each child's score.

13.56 from the 4th to the 10th percentile

13.57 6

13.58 (a) 1    (b) 28

13.59 (a) 5.4

(b) He scored as well as the average student in the fourth month of fifth grade.

13.60 He is being compared to third-grade students based upon a test with very few third-grade-level questions.

13.61 (a) Stanines are 7, 4, 6, 4, and 6.

(b) If your school is average, this student will be fairly average. He may be a little stronger than average in English and social studies, and a little below average in science and math.

13.62 70

13.63 81.5%

## 13.6  Homework Exercises

*Basic Exercises*

Exercises 1–5 refer to the following test report.

| Test Score Report | Score Type | Math Comp. | Reading | Vocab-ulary | Math Appl. | Spell. | Lang. |
|---|---|---|---|---|---|---|---|
| Gr 6 Norms Gr 6.2 | RS/NOPOSS | 39/44 | 36/60 | 16/36 | 32/40 | 26/40 | 31/53 |
| Susan Porter | NAT'L PR-S | 75-6 | 41-5 | 34-4 | 76-6 | 33-4 | 46-5 |
| Age 11–5 | LOCAL PR-S | 82-7 | 48-5 | 45-5 | 77-7 | 34-4 | 44-5 |
| Test Date 10/22/92 | GRADE EQUIV | 7.4 | 5.2 | 4.9 | 7.1 | 4.8 | 5.5 |

1. (a) What is Susan's raw score in vocabulary?
   (b) What does this score mean?

2. (a) What is Susan's local percentile score in vocabulary?
   (b) What does this score mean?

3. The local percentiles are generally higher than the national percentiles. What does this indicate?

4. (a) What is Susan's national stanine score in spelling?
   (b) What does this score mean?

5. (a) What is Susan's grade-level score in spelling?
   (b) What does it mean?

6. What are two common ways in which grade-level scores are misinterpreted?

7. If Alice scores in the 70th percentile in science, does this mean that she got 70% of the questions right?

8. Why do percentiles tend to be more misleading than stanines?

9. Complete the chart. Refer to the chart in the lesson.

| Stanine | 1 | 2 | 3 | 4 | 5 | 6 | 7 | 8 | 9 |
|---|---|---|---|---|---|---|---|---|---|
| Percentile Range | 0-3 | 4-10 | | | | | | | |

| Name | Izzy Wright | | Grade | | 4 |

### Score Summary Box

| Test | Number Possible | Number Right | Grade Equiv. | Percentile | Stanine |
|------|-----------------|--------------|--------------|------------|---------|
| Reading | 60 | 26 | 3.2 | 42 | |
| Mathematics | 50 | 23 | 3.4 | 43 | |
| Language | 60 | 27 | 2.9 | 31 | |
| Science | 45 | 17 | 2.7 | 24 | |
| Social Studies | 45 | 32 | 5.1 | 70 | |

10. Izzy Wright (see chart above) is transferring to your classroom. His score report (based on the Metropolitan Achievement Test) is given.
    (a) Use the percentile information to fill in the stanine scores for each test.
    (b) Give your general assessment of how this student will do at your school.

11. People who score more than two standard deviations above the mean on intelligence tests are sometimes labeled "gifted". What is the minimum standardized IQ score for a "gifted" student?

12. About what percent of children in an age group score over 115 on an IQ test?

13. What percentile is an IQ score of 85?

14. Joe scored in the 75th percentile in math and Moe scored in the 73rd percentile. Does this show that Joe knows more of the math that was tested than Moe? Why or why not?

### Extension Exercises

15. Is it possible to miss 3 out of 60 questions on a standardized test and still score in the 99th percentile?

16. Why isn't there a 100th percentile?

17. The percentile of an IQ score of 110 is about
    (a) 30th     (b) 50th     (c) 60th     (d) 75th

18. On a standardized test, the first quartile was 35, the median was 42, and the third quartile was 47.
    (a) Sally scored in the 39th percentile. Estimate her score.
    (b) Mike scored in the 9th percentile. Estimate his score.

## Summary

Our society uses statistics to analyze trends and make decisions. Economists analyze financial trends, psychologists measure intelligence, pollsters determine our opinions, and educators assess achievement. Politicians and advertisers try to persuade us with statistics.

These situations make it vital for citizens to understand different ways of collecting, organizing, and interpreting data. People regularly collect data from samples and organize the results into graphs and tables. Data can be further analyzed by computing averages or measures of spread. People who understand these processes will not be fooled by others who collect, organize, or interpret data in a careless or deceptive manner.

"Students need to be actively involved in each of the steps that comprise statistics, from gathering information to communicating results . . . Statistics should focus on the active involvement of students in the entire process: formulating key questions; collecting and organizing data; representing the data using graphs, tables, frequency distributions, and summary statistics; analyzing the data; making conjectures; and communicating information in a convincing way" (NCTM, *Standards*, p. 106).

Even when they are reasonably accurate, statistics only tell part of the story. One also should know what other kinds of important information must be included to give a more complete picture.

Statistical methods are used to design and analyze surveys. After taking a sample that is as representative and random as possible, a well-made survey will still have an error of around $\pm 2\%$. In many large random surveys, the results approximate a special distribution called the normal distribution. In this case, the mean and standard deviation can be used to approximate what percent of scores fall within different intervals.

Teachers regularly receive a collection of statistics about each student: a standardized test report. Since any test score has a certain amount of error, less precise stanine scores tend to be less misleading than percentiles. Grade-level scores that are much above or below the student's grade level are misleading since most test items are related to the student's actual grade level.

Standardized test scores are useful in making general comparisons among schools or students. Standardized tests do not give any specific information about how well a student understands a particular topic in the student's school curriculum.

## Study Guide

To review Chapter 13, see what you know about each of the following ideas or terms listed that you have studied. You can also use this list to generate your own questions about Chapter 13.

# The NCTM Curriculum Standards and Statistics

**Selected NCTM Curriculum Standards**

The following standards come from the NCTM document.

- Construct, read, and interpret displays of data.
- Evaluate arguments that are based on data analysis.
- Collect, organize, and describe data.
- Make convincing arguments that are based on data analysis.
- Apply mathematical thinking and modeling to solve problems that arise in other disciplines.

1. Describe how each standard listed relates to the material you studied in Chapter 13.
2. Select any current elementary-school mathematics textbook series and describe a sample lesson or exercise that illustrates each standard listed.

# Review Exercises

**1.** Use the chart to answer the questions that follow.

| Price per Pound of a Whole Chicken | Chicken Parts Are an Equally Good Buy If the Price per Pound Is | | | |
|---|---|---|---|---|
| | Breast Half with Rib | Thigh | Drumstick | Wing |
| $ .49 | $ .65 | $ .55 | $ .50 | $ .39 |
| $ .59 | $ .78 | $ .66 | $ .61 | $ .48 |
| $ .69 | $ .91 | $ .77 | $ .72 | $ .57 |
| $ .79 | $1.04 | $ .88 | $ .83 | $ .66 |
| $ .89 | $1.17 | $ .99 | $ .94 | $ .75 |

(a) What would the next row in the chart be?

In parts (b)–(d), tell which is a better buy.
(b) a whole chicken for $.59/lb or drumsticks for $.79/lb
(c) a whole chicken for $.72/lb or breasts with ribs for $1.29/lb
(d) drumsticks for $.89/lb or thighs for $.89/lb

**2.** The third-biggest item in the federal budget is interest expense. The graph shows what percent of the U.S. government budget was spent on interest expense from 1970 to 1992. In 1992, the amount was about $200 billion.

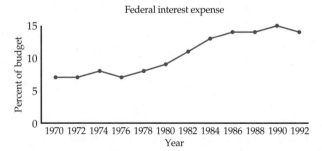

Federal interest expense

(a) Describe the overall trend and any significant exceptions to it.

(b) Why does the government have to pay interest?

**3.** Sugar prices rose 40% one year and declined 20% the next year.
(a) Over the two years, prices rose _____ %.
(b) Prove your answer using $P$ to represent the original price.

**4.** A Listerine ad says "98% of the people reading this ad have plaque. They can reduce it as much as 50% with Listerine." Explain what is deceptive about the ad.

**5.** The following table gives the median salary for employees at a restaurant in 1980, 1985, and 1990.

| Median Salary | 19,800 | 21,500 | 24,000 |
|---|---|---|---|
| Year | 1980 | 1985 | 1990 |

(a) Draw a graph that makes the salary increases look large.
(b) Draw a graph that makes the salary increases look small.

**6.** The following table gives police response times to emergency calls.

| Response Time (in minutes) | 5 | 10 | 15 | 20 | 25 | 30 |
|---|---|---|---|---|---|---|
| Frequency | 3 | 8 | 7 | 2 | 1 | 2 |

Find the mean and the median response times.

**7.** A college has 2000 undergraduates who are ages 18 to 22, 500 undergraduates who are ages 23 to 40, and 100 undergraduates who are ages 41 to 60. Without computing any averages, explain which would be larger, the mean student age or the median student age.

**8.** In a nutrition experiment, two groups want to lower their blood cholesterol level. Group C tries to do it by lowering cholesterol in their diet. Group S tries to do it by lowering the saturated fat in their diet. The change in blood cholesterol level is shown for the ten people in each group.

$$C = \{-10, 8, 0, 2, 5, -2, -5, 4, 1, -2\}$$
$$S = \{-14, -7, 2, -7, -3, 0, -2, 1, -5, -4\}$$

(a) Draw a boxplot for each group on the same graph.
(b) Briefly describe how the two groups compare.

9. The mean of the following set is 120.

$$\{86, 90, 95, 102, 106, 111, 115, 119,$$
$$129, 130, 132, 139, 142, 151, 153\}$$

Estimate the standard deviation and explain how you did it.

10. In a nationwide Gallup poll on August 8–11, 1991, 1013 adults were asked: "Would you like to see the U.S. adopt the metric system?" The results showed that 26% said "yes," 51% said "no," 20% had no knowledge of the metric system and 3% had no opinion. Write an accurate statement describing what the survey tells us about the percentage of all U.S. adults who do not want to adopt the metric system.

11. The diameter of a telephone cable is normally distributed with a mean of 1.20 cm and a standard deviation of 0.02 cm. Determine what percentage of the cables have a diameter
(a) between 1.16 and 1.24 cm.
(b) less than 1.18 cm.

12. The mean weight of an adult woman is normally distributed with a mean of 146 lb and a standard deviation of 22 lb. What percentile is each of the following weights?
(a) 168 lb      (b) 190 lb

13. According to an intelligence test, Mike Goldman has an IQ of 115. What is the percentile rank of his score?
(a) 34th    (b) 65th    (c) 84th    (d) 16th

14. Describe a situation in which grade-level scores are misleading, and explain why they are misleading.

15. Consider the test score report shown below.

(a) What is Kay's raw score in spelling?
(b) What does this score mean?
(c) What is Kay's local percentile score in reading?
(d) What does this score mean?

| Test Score Report | Score Type | Math Comp. | Reading | Vocab- ulary | Math Appl. | Spell. | Lang. |
|---|---|---|---|---|---|---|---|
| Gr 4 Norms Gr 4.2 | RS/NOPOSS | 21/44 | 26/60 | 19/36 | 22/40 | 29/40 | 34/53 |
| Kay O'Brien | NAT'L PR-S | 33-4 | 36-4 | 44-5 | 46-5 | 39-4 | 53-5 |
| Age 11–5 | LOCAL PR-S | 34-4 | 38-4 | 45-5 | 47-5 | 41-5 | 54-5 |
| Test Date 10/22/92 | GRADE EQUIV | 3.1 | 3.2 | 4.1 | 4.3 | 3.7 | 4.5 |

# Statistics in the Elementary School

The following chart shows at what grade levels selected statistics topics typically appear in elementary-school mathematics textbooks.

| Topic | Typical Grade Level in Current Textbooks |
|-------|------------------------------------------|
| Reading graphs | 1, 2, 3, 4, 5, 6 |
| Constructing graphs | 2, 3, 4, 5, 6 |
| Mean | 4, 5, 6 |
| Median and mode | 5, 6 |
| Range | 5, 6 |
| Surveys | 2, 3, 4, 5 |

# Selected Readings

Freedman, D., R. Pisani, R. Purves, and A. Adhikari. *Statistics*. 2nd ed. New York: Norton, 1991.

Gnandeskian, M. et. al. *Quantitative Literacy Series*. Palo Alto, CA: Dale Seymour, 1986.

Horwitz, L. and L. Ferlerger. *Statistics for Social Change*. Boston, MA: South End Press, 1980.

Huff, D. and I. Geis. *How to Lie with Statistics*. New York: Norton, 1954.

*Mathematics Teacher*. February, 1990 Minifocus Issue on Data Analysis. Reston, VA: NCTM, 1990.

Moore, D. and G. McCabe. *Introduction to the Practice of Statistics*. New York: W. H. Freeman, 1989.

Mosteller, F. et. al. *Statistics: A Guide to the Unknown*. 3rd ed. New York: Holden Day, 1989.

Mosteller, F. et. al. *Statistics by Example*. Reading, MA: Addison-Wesley, 1973.

National Council of Teachers of Mathematics. 1981 Yearbook. *Teaching Statistics and Probability*. Reston, VA: NCTM, 1981.

Runyon, R. *How Numbers Lie*. Lexington, MA: Lewis Publ., 1981.

# 14

# Probability

Our futures are uncertain. Will it rain today? Will you enjoy teaching for many years? Will the Cubs win the World Series next season? These questions can be answered only with words such as "unlikely" or "probably" or with numerical probabilities.

People estimate probabilities using intuition and personal experience, but in some cases it is possible to give a more precise numerical probability. If a future event is a repetition of (or very similar to) past events, a numerical estimate of its likelihood can be found. Probability is the study of random phenomena that are individually unpredictable but that have a pattern in the long run.

Although archaeologists have found dice that are 5000 years old, the formal study of probability did not begin until the sixteenth and seventeenth centuries in Italy and France. In 1654, a French gambler asked the mathematician Blaise Pascal (1623–1662) a question about a gambling game. Pascal wrote to another mathematician, Pierre de Fermat (1601?–1665), initiating a correspondence in which they solved gambling problems and developed probability theory. (See Figure 14-1, which shows portraits of Pascal on the left and Fermat on the right.)

You already know Fermat as one of the inventors of coordinate geometry, but who was Blaise Pascal? Pascal's mathematical ability was evident at a young age. Pascal excelled in geometry and wrote a major paper on geometry at the age of 25.

But at 27, Pascal, already in poor health, decided to give up mathematics and devote his life to religion. During the rest of his life, Pascal occasionally returned to mathematics. But, because he lived to be only 39, Pascal is known as the greatest "might-have-been" in the history of mathematics, and his most well known works concern religion.

Pascal and Fermat studied probability in order to understand gambling. People today use probability to estimate the chances of all kinds

Photos courtesy of Library of Congress.

**Figure 14-1**

of repeated events that have patterns in the long run. Insurance companies use probabilities of catastrophes to determine how much to charge for insurance. Testing services design and score standardized tests according to the probabilities of guessing correctly. Meteorologists utilize past frequencies of rain to predict the chance of rain tomorrow. Gambling casinos and some state governments use probabilities to design gambling games and lotteries.

## 14.1  Basic Probability

When someone flips a coin, the result is unpredictable. How likely is it that it will rain tomorrow? We use probability terms such as "unpredictable" and "likely" in an informal way. Numerical probabilities are more precise, but what do they mean?

Lesson Exercise 14.1

Why is the probability of obtaining "heads" on a coin flip $\frac{1}{2}$?

As you probably know, the probability of "heads" being $\frac{1}{2}$ comes from the fact that there are 2 possible results $\{H, T\}$ that are equally likely, and $H$

(heads) is 1 of the 2 possibilities. Each possible result, *H* or *T* in this case, is an **outcome**. The set, {*H, T*}, of all possible outcomes is called the **sample space** of an experiment.

## Lesson Exercise 14.2

Complete the sample space for flipping 2 coins. *HH* means a head on the first coin and a head on the second coin.
{*HH*, ____ , ____ , ____ }

Any subset of the sample space, such as {*HT, TH*}, is called an **event**. Probability questions deal with the probability of an event.

## Equally Likely Outcomes

Probabilities for experiments that have equally likely outcomes (such as a coin flip) are easier to compute. For this reason, it is important to determine whether or not outcomes are equally likely.

## Lesson Exercise 14.3

(a) Are the outcomes 1, 2, and 3 equally likely to occur on the spinner in Figure 14-2?
(b) Explain why the probability of spinning a 3 is not $\frac{1}{3}$.

**Figure 14-2**

Probabilities for a spinner with equally likely outcomes are usually easier to determine, as illustrated in the excerpt from the third-grade textbook of *Mathematics Unlimited* in Figure 14-3.

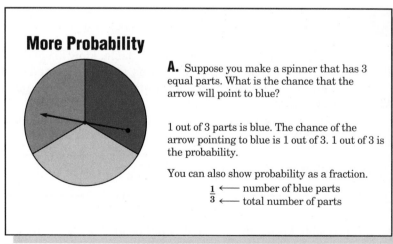

**More Probability**

**A.** Suppose you make a spinner that has 3 equal parts. What is the chance that the arrow will point to blue?

1 out of 3 parts is blue. The chance of the arrow pointing to blue is 1 out of 3. 1 out of 3 is the probability.

You can also show probability as a fraction.
$\frac{1}{3}$ ⟵ number of blue parts
⟵ total number of parts

From *Mathematics Unlimited*, Grade 3 (San Diego, CA: Harcourt Brace Jovanovich, 1992), p. 244.

**Figure 14-3**

Probabilities for an experiment involving equally likely outcomes can be computed as follows.

---

**Definition: Probability with Equally Likely Outcomes**

If all outcomes in a sample space $S$ of an experiment are equally likely, the **probability** of an event $A$ is

$$P(A) = \frac{\text{number of outcomes in } A}{\text{number of outcomes in } S}.$$

---

To use this definition, one must have a sample space that lists equally likely outcomes.

## Lesson Exercise 14.4

You flip 2 coins and want to know the probability of getting 2 heads.
(a) Which explanation, (1) or (2), is correct?
   (1) The possible outcomes are {*HH, HT, TH, TT*}, so the probability of 2 heads is $\frac{1}{4}$.
   (2) The possible outcomes are {0 heads, 1 head, 2 heads} so the probability of 2 heads is $\frac{1}{3}$.
(b) Which of the two preceding spinners in this section is a model for this coin-flipping experiment?
(c) Collect data from coin flips in your class to support the fact that exactly 1 head comes up about half of the time.

---

Probability originated with gambling games. The next exercise concerns probabilities in roulette, a casino gambling game (Figure 14-4).

## Lesson Exercise 14.5

A roulette wheel has 38 numbers. Two numbers, 0 and 00, are green. The other slots are numbered from 1 to 36. Exactly 18 of the numbers are red; 18 are black. Each number is equally likely to occur after a spin of the wheel. What is the probability of each of the following?
(a) a 10
(b) a 10 if a 10 came up on the previous 2 spins
(c) a red or a green number

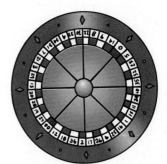

**Figure 14-4**

## Probability Values

What numbers can represent probabilities? Read the cartoon in Figure 14-5 and then try Lesson Exercise 14.6.

**Figure 14-5**

## Lesson Exercise 14.6

(a) Suppose that an event has no chance of happening (for example, spinning a 5 on the spinner in Figure 14-6). What is its probability?
(b) Suppose that an event will definitely occur (for example, spinning a number less than 5). What is its probability?
(c) Parts (a) and (b) suggest that all probabilities are between _____ and _____ (inclusive).

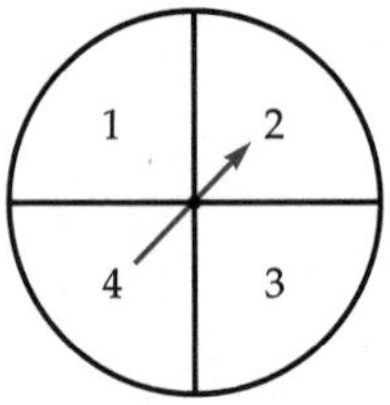

**Figure 14-6**

Lesson Exercise 14.6 illustrates why probabilities can be as low as 0 or as high as 1. In the equally likely outcomes formula,

$$P(A) = \frac{\text{number of outcomes in } A}{\text{number of outcomes in } S}$$

the number of outcomes in $A$ can be as low as 0, making $P(A) = 0$, or as high as the number of outcomes in $S$, making $P(A) = 1$. Put differently, a probability tells what percent of the time an event is likely to happen, so it could be any number between 0% (or 0) and 100% (or 1).

---

**Probability Values of an Event**

If $A$ is any event, then $0 \le P(A) \le 1$.

---

Probabilities are normally expressed as fractions, decimals, or percents. (Odds and ratios are covered in Section 14.4.) For example, if I flip a coin, the probability of heads is given by

$$P(\text{heads}) = \frac{1}{2} = 0.50 = 50\%$$

## Lesson Exercise 14.7

Which of the following could not be the probability of an event?

(a) $\frac{2}{3}$    (b) $-3$    (c) $\frac{7}{5}$    (d) 15%    (e) 0.7

We often discuss probabilities of events using words such as "impossible," "likely," and "certain." How are these words related to numerical probabilities? Figure 14-7 shows possible probabilities of events and some corresponding verbal descriptions.

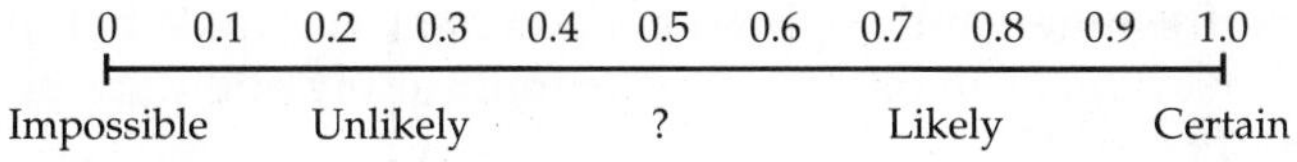

**Figure 14-7**

## Mutually Exclusive Events

How are probabilities involving more than one event computed? One of the simplest cases involves two events that do not intersect.

## Lesson Exercise 14.8

Consider a college with 25% freshman, 25% sophomores, and 25% women.
(a) What is the probability that you pick a freshman *and* a sophomore when you select 1 student?
(b) Name two more nonintersecting groups at the college.
(c) What is the probability of selecting a single student who has both of the characteristics you mentioned in part (b)?

Lesson Exercises 14.8 (a) and (c) suggest the definition of nonoverlapping—that is, mutually exclusive—events. Events $A$ and $B$ are **mutually exclusive** if and only if $P(A \text{ and } B) = 0$ or $A \cap B = \emptyset$. The expression "$P(A \text{ and } B)$" means the probability that both events $A$ and $B$ occur.

For mutually exclusive events, $P(A \text{ or } B)$ is easier to compute than it is for other events.

Lesson Exercise 14.9

A college has 25% freshman, 25% sophomores, and 25% women. A student is picked at random.
(a) Which of the following are mutually exclusive groups?
    (1) freshmen and sophomores      (2) freshmen and women
(b) What is the probability that a randomly chosen student is a freshman or a sophomore?
(c) What is the probability that a randomly chosen student is a freshman or a woman?

In part (b), you could add the probabilities (percentages) because the two groups, freshmen and sophomores, do not overlap. When two events *A* and *B* do overlap, as in part (c), you cannot simply add their probabilities to compute $P(A \text{ or } B)$.

The general rule for $P(A \text{ or } B)$ when *A* and *B* are mutually exclusive is as follows.

---

**The Addition Rule for Mutually Exclusive Events**

If *A* and *B* are mutually exclusive events, $P(A \text{ or } B) = P(A) + P(B)$.

---

The expression "*A* or *B*" combines all the outcomes from event *A* and event *B*. For this reason, $P(A \text{ or } B)$ can also be written as $P(A \cup B)$. However, current middle-school textbooks do not use set symbols in probability.

Probabilities have already been defined for equally likely outcomes. For a sample space with outcomes that are not equally likely, the addition rule can also be used to compute probabilities.

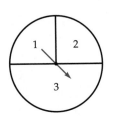

**Figure 14-8**

Lesson Exercise 14.10

How would you compute the probability of spinning a 2 or 3 on the spinner in Figure 14-8?

The preceding exercise illustrates the following.

---

**Definition: The Probability of an Event**

If *A* is any event, $P(A)$ is the sum of the probabilities of all outcomes in set *A*.

---

The addition rule for mutually exclusive events can also be used to derive a formula for events that are complements.

## Complementary Events

The probability of an event and the probability of its opposite have a simple relationship.

## Lesson Exercise 14.11

Suppose that the probability of rain tomorrow is $\frac{1}{4}$. What is the probability that it will *not* rain tomorrow?

The two events, "rain" and "not rain," in the preceding exercise are exact opposites, or **complements**. The complement of any event $A$ can be written "not $A$," or $\overline{A}$. (Some textbooks use the notation $A'$.) Complementary events have no outcomes in common (mutually exclusive), and together they encompass all possible outcomes. In set notation, $A \cap \overline{A} = \emptyset$ and $A \cup \overline{A} = S$.

## Lesson Exercise 14.12

If the probability of an event is $n$, what is the probability of the complement of the event?

Lesson Exercise 14.12 generalizes the rain example. The probability of the complement of an event is 1 (or 100%) minus the probability of the event.

**Probabilities of Complementary Events**

$$P(\overline{A}) = 1 - P(A)$$

The preceding equation follows from the addition rule for mutually exclusive events.

## Lesson Exercise 14.13

(a) $A$ and $\overline{A}$ are mutually exclusive. By the addition rule,

$P(A \text{ or } \overline{A}) =$ _____ .

(b) What is the numerical value of $P(A \text{ or } \overline{A})$?

(c) Combine the equations in parts (a) and (b).

(d) How would you derive the probability rule for complementary events from your equation in part (c)?

## Answers to Selected Lesson Exercises

**14.2** {*HH, HT, TH, TT*}

**14.3** (a) No, 3 is more likely than 1 or 2.

(b) The 3 takes up $\frac{1}{2}$ of the spinner area, so its probability would be $\frac{1}{2}$.

**14.4** (a) (1)

(b) the spinner in Lesson Exercise 14.3

**14.5** (a) $\frac{1}{38}$    (b) $\frac{1}{38}$    (c) $\frac{10}{19}$

**14.6** (a) 0    (b) 1    (c) 0, 1

**14.7** (b) and (c)

**14.8** (a) 0    (b) men and women    (c) 0

**14.9** (a) 1    (b) 50%

(c) cannot be determined

**14.10** $P(2 \text{ or } 3) = P(2) + P(3) = \frac{1}{4} + \frac{1}{2} = \frac{3}{4}$

**14.11** $\frac{3}{4}$

**14.12** $1 - n$

**14.13** (a) $P(A) + P(\overline{A})$    (b) 1

(c) $P(A) + P(\overline{A}) = 1$

(d) Subtract $P(A)$ from both sides of the equation.

## 14.1 Homework Exercises

*Basic Exercises*

1. You roll a fair die and read the result.
   (a) What is the sample space?
   (b) Is each outcome equally likely?

2. In an experiment, people rate 3 brands of orange juice, *A*, *B*, and *C*, from best to worst.
   (a) What is the sample space?
   (b) Is each outcome equally likely?

3. In "in-between," you are dealt 2 cards. Then, you pick a third card from the deck. In order for you to win, its value must be between the values of the other 2 cards. What is the probability of winning if you are dealt each of the following?
   (a) a 6 and a king    (b) a 3 and a 7

4. In a poker game, you have 4 hearts and a spade and you do not know what anyone else has. You discard the spade and pick 1 card. What is the probability of picking a heart (making a "flush")?

5. An experiment consists of spinning a spinner like the one shown.

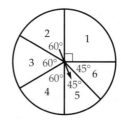

What is the probability of spinning each of the following?
(a) 1    (b) 2    (c) 5
(d) an even number

6. A scientist was asked to explain the "greenhouse effect," which is causing our weather to get warmer. He said that in the 1980s, determining whether you would have a hot, average, or cool summer was like rolling a die with 2 sides labeled "hot," 2 sides labeled "average," and 2 sides labeled "cool." In the 1990s, the die would change to 4 sides labeled "hot," 1 side labeled "average," and 1 side labeled "cool."

(a) Explain what this means in terms of probabilities.

(b) Explain what this means in plain English.

7. What is the probability that a resident of Iowa lives in the United States?

8. Which of the following numbers could not be a probability?
   (a) 0.6    (b) −1    (c) 3    (d) 0%
   (e) $\frac{1}{1000}$

9. An event is very unlikely to happen. Its probability is about
   (a) 0    (b) $\frac{1}{10}$    (c) $\frac{3}{10}$
   (d) $\frac{1}{2}$    (e) $\frac{7}{10}$    (f) $\frac{9}{10}$

10. Estimate the probability that you will eat chicken in the next week.
    (a) 0    (b) 0.3    (c) 0.5
    (d) 0.8    (e) 1

11. In his 1989 bestseller, *Innumeracy*, John Paulos compares the relative danger of being killed by terrorists on a trip abroad to being killed in a car accident at home. Based upon the number of tourists killed abroad by terrorists in a year, Paulos estimated the probability of being killed by terrorists as 1 in 1.6 million. Paulos estimated that the probability of someone being killed in a car crash in a year is 1 in 5300.
    (a) How many times more likely is it for a person to die in a car crash during a year than on a trip abroad?
    (b) How could you make a fairer comparison by considering the time intervals involved?

12. Determine whether or not each pair of events is mutually exclusive.
    (a) getting an A in geometry and a B in English this semester
    (b) getting an A in geometry and a B in geometry this semester

(c) being president of the United States and being 25 years old

(d) being intelligent and being immoral

13. Suppose that you flip a coin once. Name 2 events, A and B, that are mutually exclusive.

14. What is wrong with each of the following statements?
    (a) The probability that a person has black hair is 22%. The probability that a person has brown eyes is 72%. So the probability that a person has either black hair or brown eyes is 94%.
    (b) Since there are 7 continents, the probability of being born in North America is $\frac{1}{7}$.

15. At the Rockville train station, trains run hourly in either direction. If you arrive at the train station at a random time, the next train is 3 times more likely to be northbound rather than southbound. Explain how this could be the case.

16. $P(N) = 0.03$. $P(\text{not } N) = $ _____ .

17. At a college, the probability that a randomly selected student is a freshman is 0.35, and the probability that the student is a sophomore is 0.2. What is the probability that a randomly selected student is neither a freshman nor a sophomore?

*Extension Exercises*

18.

|  | 1980 | 1989 |
|---|---|---|
| Total Traffic Fatalities | 52,600 | 46,900 |
| Number Involving Alcohol | 28,000 | 26,100 |

*Source:* U.S. Department Of Transportation

(a) Estimate the probability that a traffic death may be attributed to a drunken driver.

(b) If about 2% of drivers are legally drunk, about how many times more likely is it for a drunken driver to have an accident than a sober driver?

19. Draw a spinner that has the following characteristics.

(1) The probability of spinning a 2 is $\frac{1}{2}$.

(2) The probability of spinning an odd number is $\frac{1}{4}$.

(3) The probability of spinning a sum of 5 on 2 spins is $\frac{1}{8}$.

20. WIN, designed by Bradley Efron, is a game using unusual cubical dice. The faces are shown here.

A       B       C       D

You pick 1 die and your opponent picks 1 die. Whoever rolls the higher number wins.

(a) Suppose you pick A. Which die would a smart opponent then pick?

(b) Suppose your opponent picks B first. Which die would you then pick?

(c) Suppose your opponent picks C first. Which die would you then pick?

(d) Suppose you pick D first. Which die would a smart opponent then pick?

(e) Is it better to pick first or second?

21. A survey of 1000 elementary-school teachers regarding their preferred subject area yielded the following results.

| | Math/Science | Language/History |
|---|---|---|
| **Male** | 14 | 22 |
| **Female** | 212 | 752 |

Based upon this survey, estimate the probability of each of the following.

(a) that an elementary-school teacher is female

(b) that an elementary-school teacher prefers the math/science area

(c) that a female elementary-school teacher prefers the math/science area

22. Ten people are randomly selected from planet Earth. Use a reference book such as *World Statistics in Brief* from the United Nations to estimate the following.

(a) How many speak English as their native language?

(b) How many of their homes have flush toilets?

(c) How many have sufficient food to eat?

(d) How many out of 10 people over 15 years old can read and write?

(e) How many live under each of the following types of government: free, partly free, and not free?

## 14.2   Experimental and Theoretical Probability

How does someone compute the probability of a sum of 7 on 2 dice or the probability that it will rain tomorrow? You can find the probability of a sum of 7 by listing all possible outcomes, or you can estimate it by rolling some dice a large number of times. Meteorologists estimate the probability of rain using past weather records.

    The probability of some events can be determined two different ways: experimentally or theoretically. Consider for example, the probability of rolling a sum of 7 on 2 dice. This probability can be estimated by rolling 2 dice (that is, hexahedral random digit generators).

**D** Lesson Exercise 14.14

(a) Estimate the probability of rolling a total of 7 on 2 dice.
(b) Roll the dice 30 times and count how many 7's you get.
(c) Based upon your experiment, give a new estimate of the probability of rolling a 7.

Now, collect all the results from the class. Total them up to obtain a class probability of rolling a 7. A probability based upon an experiment such as this one is called . . . are you ready? An **experimental probability!** Such a probability is an estimate of the theoretical probability. The estimate generally improves if you increase the number of experimental trials.

By listing all the possible outcomes on 2 dice, you can compute the **theoretical probability** using the definition of equally likely events. The theoretical probability suggests what number the experimental probability would be expected to approach after a large number of trials.

To find the theoretical probability of rolling a total of 7 on 2 dice, complete Lesson Exercise 14.15.

**D** Lesson Exercise 14.15

(a) Complete the following list of all possible results for rolling 2 dice.

**Sum of 2 Dice**

**First Die**

|            |   | 1 | 2 | 3 | 4 | 5 | 6 |
|------------|---|---|---|---|---|---|---|
|            | 1 | 2 | 3 | 4 | 5 | 6 | 7 |
|            | 2 |   |   |   |   |   |   |
| Second Die | 3 |   |   |   |   |   |   |
|            | 4 |   |   |   |   |   |   |
|            | 5 |   |   |   |   |   |   |
|            | 6 |   |   |   |   |   |   |

(b) How many (different) possible outcomes are there?
(c) Are they equally likely?
(d) The theoretical probability of rolling a sum of 7 is _____ .
(e) How does your answer to part (d) compare to the experimental probability obtained by the class?

## Lesson Exercise 14.16

Use your table of possible dice outcomes to compute the theoretical probability of rolling a sum of 11.

## Lesson Exercise 14.17

Suppose I roll 2 dice and get a sum of 7 three times in a row. How does that affect the probability of rolling a sum of 7 on the next roll?
(a) There is a greater chance of getting a 7 on the next roll.
(b) There is a smaller chance of getting a 7 on the next roll.
(c) It doesn't affect the probability of getting a 7 on the next roll.

How does one describe the connection between the theoretical and experimental probabilities for a particular experiment?

## D Lesson Exercise 14.18

Suppose you select 1 card at random from a regular deck of 52 cards.
The theoretical probability of selecting the ace of spades is $\frac{1}{52}$. Which of the following does this probability tell you?
(a) If I repeat this experiment 52 times, I will pick an ace of spades 1 time.
(b) If I repeat this experiment 520 times, I will pick an ace of spades 10 times.
(c) If I repeat this experiment a large number of times, I will pick an ace of spades $\frac{1}{52}$ of that number of times.
(d) If I repeat the experiment a large number of times. I can expect to pick the ace of spades about $\frac{1}{52}$ of the time.

The following statement describes the relationship between the theoretical probability and experimental probabilities of an event.

---

**Theoretical and Experimental Probability**

If the **theoretical probability** of an event is $\frac{a}{b}$, then $\frac{a}{b}$ approximates the fraction of the time this event is expected to occur when the same experiment is repeated many times under the same conditions.

---

It's amazing that the overall results of a *large number* of coin flips are fairly predictable, but an individual coin toss is completely unpredictable! This is why it is both fair and unpredictable to toss a coin at the beginning of a football game to decide who gets the ball.

In some cases, such as weather forecasting, there is no theoretical probability. A probability of rain tomorrow, such as 80%, is an experimental probability. The meteorologist looks at past records of similar weather conditions and sees that it rained the following day about 80% of the time.

## Lesson Exercise 14.19

The principal of a school is expecting a visitor 2 weeks from today. She wants to estimate the probability that all her teachers will be in school that day. How could she do it?

## Simulations

A couple wants to have children until they have a girl. But they have also decided they will not have more than 3 children. What is the probability they will have a girl? What is the probability they will have 3 children?

When the theoretical probability is difficult or impossible to compute, and it is impractical to find an experimental probability, a simulation can be designed. A **simulation** is a probability experiment that has the same kind of probabilities as the real-life events. Simulations are based upon connections between mathematical models and everyday life.

The result of a coin flip has the same kind of probabilities as the sex of a baby. The probability of heads is $\frac{1}{2}$ , and the probability of tails is $\frac{1}{2}$ , just as the probability of a boy is about $\frac{1}{2}$ , and the probability of a girl is about $\frac{1}{2}$.

Furthermore, each coin flip has no effect on subsequent coin flip probabilities. The same is usually true of the sex of babies.

In this simulation, each coin flip represents the birth of a new child. Furthermore, suppose that each "heads" represents having a girl and each "tails" represents a boy.

**D** Lesson Exercise 14.20

(a) Using $H$ = girl and $T$ = boy, simulate the event of the couple just described having a family. (For example, if you flip "heads" on the first try, they would have 1 girl and would stop having children.) What family do you end up with?

(b) Repeat this experiment 19 more times so that you have created 20 families.

(c) Out of the 20 families, how many have a girl?

(d) Out of the 20 families, how many have 3 children?

The results of a simulation provide an experimental probability that is used to estimate the theoretical probability of the simulated event. A larger number of trials is likely to provide a better estimate. A simulation is sometimes much easier to do than the event it represents.

## Lesson Exercise 14.21

Based upon your results in the preceding problem, estimate the probability of
(a) the family having a girl.     (b) the family having 3 children.

## An Investigation: A Traffic Simulation

A simulation can also be used to analyze a traffic intersection, as in Lesson Exercises 14.22–14.25.

There is an intersection, and you want to decide how long the traffic signal should stay green in each direction. First, consider the cars going from east to west (on a one-way street). A counter can be used to see how many cars pass through the intersection during a given period of time.

Suppose that you find out that during a 10-minute period, 200 cars pass by.

## Lesson Exercise 14.22

One car passes east to west every _____ seconds.

Using a timer, you also compute that cars leave the intersection at a rate of 1 per second when the light is green. What if you make the light alternately red and green every 15 seconds (disregard yellow)? The east-west traffic pattern can be simulated using a die. This will give you an idea of how many cars will get backed up at the traffic light, assuming the traffic and the die both have the same random pattern.

## Lesson Exercise 14.23

One car passes every 3 seconds. If each roll of the die represents 1 second, and the die has _____ possible results, how many of these results should count as a second in which a car passes?

## Lesson Exercise 14.24

Decide which die results represent "car" and which represent "no car" and fill this information in the chart.

**Result on Die**

|        |   |
|--------|---|
| Car    |   |
| No car |   |

## Lesson Exercise 14.25

(a) Now for the simulation. Start with a red light and assume that 1 car can leave the intersection each second. Roll 1 die 120 times (120 seconds) and fill in the results in a chart like the one shown here. Compute how many cars are lined up each second. (*Note:* This simulation could also be done with a computer.)

| Second | 1 | 2 | 3 | 4 | 5 | 6 | 7 | 8 | 9 | 10 | ... |
|---|---|---|---|---|---|---|---|---|---|---|---|
| Result on die | | | | | | | | | | | |
| New car arrives? | | | | | | | | | | | |
| Car leaves? (when light is green) | | | | | | | | | | | |
| Total number of cars lined up | | | | | | | | | | | |

(b) What was the largest number of cars you had backed up? (Get results from other members of the class.) Is this result satisfactory? If not, suggest an alternate timing for the signal.

## An Investigation: A Computer Simulation

A company is buying 10 automobiles from a manufacturer. From past experience, they know that about 1 out of every 6 automobiles needs some kind of adjustment.

## D Lesson Exercise 14.26

Use a die to simulate 20 purchases of 10 automobiles like the one just described.

(a) What roll or rolls on the die will represent an automobile needing adjustment?

(b) If you have a computer available, use the following BASIC program for the simulation. (It could also be done with Logo or MINITAB.) RND(1) randomly selects a decimal number between 0 and 1, including 0 but excluding 1. (In Logo, RANDOM 6 would pick a number at random from {0, 1, 2, 3, 4, 5}.)

```
10 FOR I = 1 TO 10
20    LET ROLL = INT (RND(1) * 6) + 1
30    IF ROLL = 1 THEN PRINT "DEFECTIVE"
40 NEXT I
```

(c) If you have studied INT in BASIC, explain why INT (RND(1) * 6) + 1 simulates the roll of a die.

(*Continued on page 826.*)

(d) Roll the die or use a computer to simulate 20 orders.

(e) Make a frequency graph of the number of automobiles needing adjustment in each of your 20 shipments.

Frequency

Number in shipment needing adjustment

Statisticians often use simulations to approximate probabilities that are difficult to compute using theory or for which there is no theory. Computers offer the possibility of simulating a large number of trials in a short amount of time.

## Answers to Selected Lesson Exercises

**14.15** (b) 36      (c) yes      (d) $\frac{1}{6}$

**14.16** $\frac{1}{18}$

**14.17** (c)

**14.18** (d)

**14.19** Look at attendance records for the past month of school days and see what percent of the days all her teachers were in school.

**14.22** 3

**14.23** 6, 2

**14.26** (c)

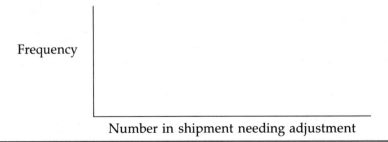

$0 \leq$ RND $(1) < 1$

So $0 \leq 6 *$ RND $(1) < 6$

and $1 \leq 6 *$ RND $(1) + 1 < 7$

Int $(6 *$ RND $(1) + 1)$ produces

$1, 2, 3, 4, 5,$ and $6$ with

equal frequency

## 14.2   Homework Exercises

*Basic Exercises*

1. The following exercise requires flipping 3 coins.

   (a) Flip 3 coins 20 times and record the results.

| | Number of Times |
|---|---|
| 3 heads 0 tails | |
| 2 heads 1 tail | |
| 1 head  2 tails | |
| 0 heads 3 tails | |

(b) Based upon part (a), what is your *experimental* probability for getting exactly 2 heads?

(c) List the different possible equally likely outcomes when flipping 3 coins all at once.

| First Coin | Second Coin | Third Coin |
|---|---|---|
|  |  |  |
|  |  |  |
|  |  |  |

(d) What is the *theoretical* probability of getting exactly 2 heads?

(e) How do your answers to parts (b) and (d) compare?

2. How would you find the experimental probability of your mathematics professor teaching class beyond the end of the period?

3. Two dice are rolled.
   (a) List the theoretical probability of each sum.

| Sum | 2 3 4 5 6 7 8 9 10 11 12 |
|---|---|
| Probability |  |

(b) What is the pattern in your answers to part (a)?

4. When you roll 2 dice, the sum can be 2, 3, 4, 5, 6, 7, 8, 9, 10, 11, or 12. There are 11 possibilities. So $P(\text{sum is 7}) = \frac{1}{11}$. What is wrong with this reasoning?

5. You have vulnerable backgammon men 4 and 6 spaces away from your opponent's pieces. What are your opponent's chances of knocking you off on the next roll of the dice? (Your opponent needs a sum of 4 or 6 on the two dice, or a 4 or a 6 on either of the two dice.)

6. In Chapter 8, you were introduced to regular polyhedra. Usually dice are shaped like cubes, but any of the regular polyhedra could be used.

Tetrahedron        Dodecahedron

(a) Each of two tetrahedral dice has an equal chance of rolling a 1, 2, 3, or 4. What is the probability of rolling a sum of 6 on the 2 tetrahedral dice?

(b) The faces of 2 dodecahedra are numbered from 1 to 12. What is the probability of rolling a sum of 6 on 2 dodecahedra dice?

7. Two dice are numbered 1, 2, 3, 4, 5, and 6, and 1, 1, 2, 2, 3, and 3, respectively. Find the probability of rolling each sum from 2 through 9.

8. (a) Guess how many cards you would have to select from a regular deck of cards (without replacement) to obtain 2 cards of the same denomination (for example, two 7's).

(b) Try it 20 times with a deck of cards and obtain an experimental probability.

9. The IRS audited 2 million out of 82 million taxpayers in 1983. Of those audited, 1.5 million had to make additional payments, and 247 were convicted of fraud.

(a) What is the estimated probability of having to make additional payments if you are audited?

(b) What is the estimated probability of being convicted of fraud if you are audited?

(c) The average IRS auditor collects $10 in extra taxes for every $1 he or she is paid. Based upon this, do you think it would pay to hire more IRS auditors?

10. When we say that the theoretical probability of rolling a 5 on a die is $\frac{1}{6}$ , what does this mean?

11. A meteorologist reports that the chance of rain tomorrow is 60%. What does this mean?

12. You toss a fair coin 1000 times. Which of the following will probably happen?
    (a) You will get 500 heads and 500 tails.
    (b) You will get between 450 and 550 heads.
    (c) You will get 500 to 600 heads.
    (d) none of the above

13. (a) Guess the probability that a thumbtack lands point up.
    (b) Devise an experiment and obtain an experimental probability.

14. A fair coin is tossed 5 times. Two possible results are *HHHHH* and *HTHTH*. Which is more likely to occur?
    (a) *HHHHH*      (b) *HTHTH*
    (c) Both are equally likely.

15. Use a coin flip or a computer program to simulate the birth of a boy or girl. Investigate four-children families by doing the following.
    (a) Create 20 four-children families using $H$ = girl and $T$ = boy.
    (b) Out of the 20 families, how many have exactly 1 girl?
    (c) Use your results to complete the table.

**Four-Children Families**

| Number of Boys | 0 | 1 | 2 | 3 | 4 |
|---|---|---|---|---|---|
| Estimated Probabilities | | | | | |

16. Consider the following problem. "On a game show, a contestant gets to pick box 1, 2, or 3. One box contains $10,000. The other 2 boxes are empty. Use a die to simulate 20 groups of 5 shows (weekly) and estimate the probability that at least 4 people will win during a particular 5-show week." Devise a plan and solve the problem.

17. New Raisin Crumbles come with one of 6 different famous mathematics teacher cards in each box.
    (a) Guess about how many boxes you would have to buy to get all 6 different teacher cards.
    (b) Use a die and simulate collecting all of the cards 30 times to obtain an experimental estimate.

18. Write a sample space for flipping a coin 3 times and find the probability of getting *at least* 2 heads ("at least 2 heads" means 2 or more heads).

19. Assume that the probability of having a baby boy is 50%. If you have 3 children, what are the chances of having 2 boys and 1 girl in any order? (*Hint:* See the preceding exercise.)

20. If you have 4 children, estimate the probability of having 4 girls.

*Extension Exercises*

21. Draw a spinner with sectors labeled 2, 3, 4, . . . , 12 that could be used to simulate rolling 2 dice and computing the sum.

22. Design 2 cubical dice so that the probability of each whole-number sum from 1 to 12 is $\frac{1}{12}$. (*Hint:* Use fractions.)

23. Pascal's triangle relates to a variety of mathematics problems.

$$\begin{array}{ccccccccc} & & & & 1 & & 1 & & \\ & & & 1 & & 2 & & 1 & \\ & & 1 & & 3 & & 3 & & 1 \\ & 1 & & 4 & & 6 & & 4 & & 1 \end{array}$$

    (a) Add a fifth row, continuing the same pattern.
    (b) In flipping 1 coin, there is 1 way to get 0 heads and 1 way to get 1 head. In flipping 2 coins, how many ways are there to get 0 heads? 1 head? 2 heads?
    (c) How does part (b) relate to Pascal's triangle?
    (d) Explain how the third row of the triangle relates to flipping 3 coins.

24. (a) $(x + y)^1 =$ _____
    (b) $(x + y)^2 =$ _____
    (c) How are the results to parts (a) and (b) related to Pascal's triangle?
    (d) Compute $(x + y)^4$ using Pascal's triangle.
25. Consider the following table.

**Probability of Birth Control Being Effective**

|  | Theoretical | Actual |
|---|---|---|
| Abstinence | 100% | ? |
| Vasectomy | 99.8 | 99.8 |
| Pill | 99 | 97 |
| Condom | 97 | 83 |
| IUD | 97 | 94 |
| Diaphragm | 97 | 78 |
| Calendar rhythm | 85 | 65 |
| Chance | 20 | 20 |

Source: *Little Green Book*, by John Lobell, p. 32.

(a) How are the "actual probabilities" obtained?
(b) Why are the actual probabilities usually lower than the theoretical probabilities?

26. Consider the following problem. "One player rolls 2 dice and multiplies the numbers. The other player rolls 1 die and squares the number. The higher number wins. Who will win more often?" Devise a plan and solve the problem.

27. Recall the intersection problem from the lesson. Suppose that cars arrive at the intersection in the north-south direction (one way) at the rate of 1 every 6 seconds. Do a traffic simulation using the light timing of your choice for cars coming in the north-south and east-west directions.

28. The following supermarket checkout simulation is adapted from NCTM's "Student Math Notes" of March 1986.

    You decide to open a supermarket. How many checkout lanes should you have? A die will be used to simulate the arrival of shoppers at the checkout counter. Assume that a new customer arrives at the checkout counter 1 out of every 3 minutes. Assume that it takes the cashier 3 minutes to process each customer.

    (a) What die results would represent a customer arriving during a given minute?
    (b) What die results would represent a customer not arriving during a given minute?
    (c) Roll the die 30 times and simulate 30 minutes at a checkout counter (or use a computer program). See how long the line gets. You could use a chart like the one following to keep a record.

| END OF MINUTE | 1 | 2 | 3 | 4 | 5 | 6 | .... |
|---|---|---|---|---|---|---|---|
| Customer Arrives | A | — | — | B | C | | |
| Checking out | — | A | A | A | B | B | |
| Waiting | — | — | — | — | — | C | |

(d) Complete the following record of your results.

| Customer | A | B | C | D | E | F | ... |
|---|---|---|---|---|---|---|---|
| Minute of Check-out Arrival | | | | | | | |
| Minute Checkout Completed | | | | | | | |
| Minutes-Wait Before Checkout Began | | | | | | | |

(e) Give the following estimates based upon your 30 minutes of data.

Number of customers arriving _____

Total customer waiting time _____

(Continued on page 830.)

Average waiting time    _____

Total clerk idle time    _____

Total time to
process everyone    _____

(f) Repeat parts (c)–(e) using two checkout counters.

(g) Which number of checkout counters works out better? Consider the waiting time and the cost to the store.

## Computer Exercises

29. Recall that the RND(1) statement randomly selects a number between 0 and 1, including 0 but excluding 1.

(a) What are the possible values of INT(2 * RND(1))?

(b) Enter the following program into a computer.

```
10 PRINT "HOW MANY COIN FLIPS?"
20 INPUT N
30 LET H = 0
40 FOR I = 1 TO N
50    LET F = INT(2 * RND(1))
60    IF F = 0 THEN PRINT "HEADS"
70    IF F = 0 THEN H = H + 1
80    IF F = 1 THEN PRINT "TAILS"
90 NEXT I
100 PRINT "YOU GOT "; H ;" HEADS
    AND "; N − H ;" TAILS."
```

(c) RUN the program 20 times for 5 coin flips and use your results to estimate the probability of getting 2 heads and 3 tails.

30. (a) Enter the following program.

```
10 PRINT "HOW MANY ROLLS OF THE DICE?"
20 INPUT N
30 LET S = 0
40 FOR I = 1 TO N
50    LET F = INT(6 * RND(1)) + 1
60    LET G = INT(6 * RND(1)) + 1
70    LET R = F + G
80    IF R = 7 THEN S = S + 1
```

```
90    PRINT "YOU ROLLED A "; R
100 NEXT I
110 PRINT "YOU ROLLED "; S ; " SEVENS."
```

(b) RUN the program for 40 rolls and use it to estimate the probability of rolling a sum of 7.

(c) Edit the program so that you can use it to compute the number of 10's in 100 rolls.

(d) Estimate the probability of rolling a sum of 10.

31. You own two National Motors cars. Suppose that on a given morning, the probability that the Squealer starts is 0.4 and the probability that the Alley Cat starts is 0.2. Use the following computer simulation to estimate the probability that at least one of your cars will start.

(a) Complete the following program.

```
10 PRINT "HOW MANY TIMES DO
   YOU WANT TO RUN THIS
   PROGRAM?"
20 INPUT N
30 FOR I = 1 TO N
40    LET CARS = 0
50    IF RND(1) < 0.4 THEN 80
60       PRINT "OOPS THE SQUEALER
         WON'T START."
70       GOTO 100
80       CARS = 1
90       PRINT "THE SQUEALER IS
         HUMMING TODAY."
100    F RND(1) < 0.2 THEN 130
110
120
130
140
150    IF CARS > 0 THEN PRINT
       "YOU'VE GOT A CAR!"
160 NEXT N
```

(b) In line 50, what is the probability that RND(1) < 0.4?

(c) RUN the program 10 times to obtain an experimental probability that at least one car will start.

(d) Repeat part (c).

(e) Repeat part (c) again.

(f) Estimate the probability that at least one car will start.

32. Some couples have children until they have at least one boy and at least one girl. What is the average number of children such couples would have?

(a) Write a program to simulate this.

(b) RUN the program and estimate the average number of children such a couple would end up having.

33. Twenty people are at a party.

(a) Guess the probability that at least 2 people will have the same birthday.

(b) Use MINITAB (or BASIC or Logo or a calculator) to generate 20 random integers between 1 and 365 (inclusive) and see if at least 2 match. Repeat this 30 times to obtain an experimental probability.

*Special Exercise*

34. Read "Inflexible Logic," by Russell Maloney, in *Fantasia Mathematica*, edited by Clifton Fadiman. Write a report that includes a summary of the story and your reaction to it.

---

## 14.3 Counting

To compute theoretical probabilities, one often counts the number of equally likely results in a sample space. Sometimes the sample space is so large that shortcuts are needed to count all the possibilities.

How do state officials know how many different license plates they can make using three letters followed by three numbers (Figure 14-9)? How does the telephone company know how many people can have the same area code? To answer these questions, they count all possible

**Figure 14-9**

arrangements of a sequence. In order to understand this process, we'll begin by analyzing some simpler counting problems.

## Organized Lists and Tree Diagrams

You have 3 shirts and 2 pairs of pants. How many different choices for an outfit would you have (assuming everything matches)? If the shirts are $s_1$, $s_2$, and $s_3$ and the pants are $p_1$ and $p_2$, you can count the outfits in an organized list or a tree diagram.

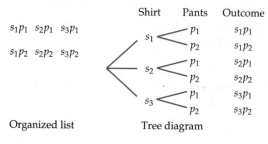

$$s_1p_1 \quad s_2p_1 \quad s_3p_1$$

$$s_1p_2 \quad s_2p_2 \quad s_3p_2$$

| Shirt | Pants | Outcome |

Organized list        Tree diagram

**Figure 14-10**

There are 6 different outfits (Figure 14-10).

**D** Lesson Exercise 14.27

A cafe offers the following menu. Customers choose one appetizer and one main dish.

**LUNCHEON MENU     $4**

Canned fruit du jour
Cream of bamboo shoot

----------------------------------------------------------------

Blowfish thermidor
Woodchuck pilaf
Semi-boneless falcon
Hippo in a blanket

(a) How many different selections can a customer make?
(b) What is a shorter way to compute the answer to part (a) without using a list or diagram?

While the two preceding examples can be solved by making an organized list or a tree diagram, there is a shorter way.

## The Multiplication Principle

Did you recognize the combination model of multiplication from Chapter 3? In both preceding problems, you could multiply the number of ways to make the first choice by the number of ways to make the second choice to obtain the total number of arrangements.

In the outfit problem, there were 3 ways to select a shirt and 2 ways to select a pair of pants. This resulted in $3 \times 2 = 6$ outfits.

$$
\begin{array}{ccc}
(3) & (2) & = & 6 \\
\text{shirt} & \text{pants} & & \text{outfit} \\
\text{choice} & \text{choice} & & \text{choices}
\end{array}
$$

### Lesson Exercise 14.28

Explain how you would use multiplication to count choices in the menu problem.

### Lesson Exercise 14.29

Suppose I want to order a dessert at a restaurant. The menu offers 3 kinds of pie and 2 kinds of cake. How many choices of a dessert do I have?

In Lesson Exercise 14.29, you do not multiply 3 by 2 because you are not picking a cake and then a pie *in sequence*. You are picking only one dessert. The outfit and menu situations are both examples of the Multiplication Principle, whereas the dessert choice is not.

> **The Multiplication Principle**
>
> If an event $E$ can occur in $e$ ways and, after it has occurred, an event $F$ can occur in $f$ ways, then event $E$ followed by event $F$ can occur in $e \cdot f$ ways.

The Multiplication Principle works not only for two events in sequence, but also for any number of events in sequence. The Multiplication Principle can be applied to a complex event if the event can be thought of as a *series of steps* with a specified order.

### Example 14.1

The state of Maryland has automobile license plates consisting of 3 letters followed by 3 digits. How many possible license plates are there?

**Solution**

***Understanding the Problem***   How many ways are there to choose 3 letters followed by 3 digits? A license plate can be created in 6 steps: picking each of the 3 letters and then selecting each of the 3 digits.

***Devising a Plan***   Using the Multiplication Principle, one can compute the total number of choices for each step, and then multiply these numbers together.

***Carrying Out the Plan***   There are 26 choices for each of the 3 letters and 10 choices for each of the 3 digits. The total number of possible license plates is

$$\underset{\text{letter}}{(26)}\quad \underset{\text{letter}}{(26)}\quad \underset{\text{letter}}{(26)}\quad \underset{\text{digit}}{(10)}\quad \underset{\text{digit}}{(10)}\quad \underset{\text{digit}}{(10)} = 17{,}576{,}000$$

***Looking Back***   The same technique would work for many other license plate designs.   ■

 Lesson Exercise 14.30

A state has license plates using 2 letters followed by 4 digits. How many possible license plates can be made?

 Lesson Exercise 14.31

How many possible telephone numbers are there in an area code if you can choose any 7 digits, except that you cannot select 0 or 1 as the first or second digit?

---

One special type of counting problem involves a series of steps in which each step uses up one of the choices.

**Example 14.2**

A club has 10 members. How many ways can they choose a president and vice-president if everyone is eligible?

**Solution**

***Understanding the Problem***   Think of the elections as 2 steps. The first step is to elect a president. Then, the club elects a vice-president from the remaining members.

***Devising a Plan***   Use the Multiplication Principle.

***Carrying Out the Plan***   How many choices are there for president? 10. Once the president is selected, how many choices are there for vice-president? 9. Using the Multiplication Principle, there are $10 \cdot 9 = 90$ ways to select a president followed by a vice-president.

***Looking Back***   This procedure would work on any election in which each position is different.   ■

An ordered arrangement of people or objects (such as a choice of president and vice-president) is called a **permutation.** In the preceding example, the number of permutations is 90, as shown in Figure 14-11.

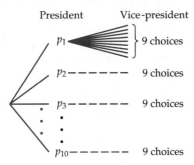

**Figure 14-11**

## Lesson Exercise 14.32

A principal must select a head teacher and an assistant head teacher from her faculty of 30 people. How many ways can she do this?

## Finding Probabilities Using the Multiplication Principle

People who design multiple-choice tests must figure out the probability that someone will guess a correct answer. A test is not very useful if someone who knows nothing about the material does well on it.

Suppose you give a 5-question multiple-choice quiz with 4 choices on each question. What is the probability that someone who randomly selects answers from each set of choices will do well (that is, will get at least 4 out of 5 questions right)?

Example 14.3 shows how to solve part of this problem. You can complete the solution in the exercise that follows Example 14.3. You will need to use the Multiplication Principle on various sets of test responses and then *add* together the number of ways of doing each set of responses.

### Example 14.3

A quiz has 5 multiple-choice questions. Each question has 4 answer choices, of which 1 is the correct answer and the other 3 are incorrect. Suppose that you guess all the answers.

(a) How many ways are there to answer the 5 questions?
(b) What is the probability of getting exactly 4 questions right and 1 wrong?

**Solution**

(a) How many ways can you answer the 5 questions? Consider each question as a step in completing a test. There are 4 ways to do each step. Using the Multiplication Principle:

$$(4)\ (4)\ (4)\ (4)\ (4) = 4^5 = 1024$$

(b) There is more than one way to get 4 right and 1 wrong, depending upon *which question you get wrong*. In the chart, which lists all possible responses involving at least 4 right answers, *R* stands for a right answer and *W* stands for a wrong answer.

    Each type of response (for example, *WRRRR*) can be done 3 ways based upon the Multiplication Principle. Since each of the 5 sets of responses is a complete test result, we add the five 3's together.

| Five Responses | Number of Ways to Fill out the Test |
|---|---|
| *WRRRR* | (3) (1) (1) (1) (1) = 3 |
| *RWRRR* | (1) (3) (1) (1) (1) = 3 |
| *RRWRR* | (1) (1) (3) (1) (1) = 3 |
| *RRRWR* | (1) (1) (1) (3) (1) = 3 |
| *RRRRW* | (1) (1) (1) (1) (3) = 3 |
| | 15 ways |

So there are 15 ways out of the 1024 possible ways that result in 4 right answers and 1 wrong answer.

$$P(4 \text{ right 1 wrong}) = \frac{15}{1024} \approx 1.5\%$$

The chances of getting exactly 4 right by guessing are not very good. It makes more sense to study. ■

## Lesson Exercise 14.33

A quiz has 5 multiple-choice questions. Each question has 4 choices; 1 is the correct answer and the other 3 are incorrect. Suppose you guess all the answers.
(a) How many ways are there to answer the 5 questions?
(b) What is the probability of getting all 5 questions right?
(c) What is the probability of doing well (getting *at least* 4 right)?

    People who construct multiple-choice tests know the probabilities that someone will get different numbers of questions right using random guessing. In order to decrease the probability of someone doing well just by guessing, test constructors use a lot more than 5 questions.

## Lesson Exercise 14.34

A true-false test has 6 questions. What is the probability of getting at least 5 right by guessing the answers at random?

## An Investigation: Seating Arrangements

## Lesson Exercise 14.35

Consider a circular table.
(a) How many ways can 3 people be arranged at a circular table?
(b) How many ways can 4 people be arranged at a circular table?
(c) How many ways can 5 people be arranged at a circular table?
(d) How many ways can $N$ people be arranged at a circular table?

## Answers to Selected Lesson Exercises

**14.27** (a) 8    (b) $2 \cdot 4 = 8$

**14.28** Multiply the number of possible main dishes by the number of desserts.

**14.29** 5

**14.30** 6,760,000

**14.31** 6,400,000

**14.32** 870

**14.33** (a) 1024    (b) $\frac{1}{1024}$    (c) $\frac{1}{64}$

**14.34** $\frac{7}{64}$

## 14.3   Homework Exercises

### Basic Exercises

1. Jane has 4 shirts and 2 skirts that match. How many different outfits can she make?

2. A lottery allows you to select a two-digit number. Each digit may be either 1, 2, 3, 4, or 5. How many different numbers can be selected?

3. The Grain Barn is known for its healthy 3-course dinner with appetizer, entree, and vegetable. How many different dinners are possible if you choose one item for each course?

| Dinner at the Grain Barn |
| :---: |
| Sponge bread |
| Yogurt gumbo |
| Buckwheat balls |
| - - - - - - - - - - - - - - - - - - - |
| Twice-baked kelp |
| Oat bran surprise |
| Flax hash |
| Marinated bulghur |
| - - - - - - - - - - - - - - - - - - - |
| Scalloped kale |
| Lima bean puree |

4. A car dealer offers the National Motors Nag in 5 colors with a choice of 2 doors or 4 doors, and 2 different engines. How many different possible models are there?

5.

## PICK 4 NUMBERS GAME

| DESCRIPTIONS OF POSSIBLE BETS. | EXAMPLE if you bet: | YOU ARE A WINNER if any of these combinations are selected (Example) | |
|---|---|---|---|
| "STRAIGHT" bet is when your number matches the winning number selected in exact order. "BOX" bet is when your number matches the winning number selected in any order. | | | PRI A |
| **STRAIGHT.** To win, the four digit number you select must match in exact order the number drawn on TV. 1 way to win. (ODDS 1 IN 10,000) | 1234 | 1234 ONLY EXACT MATCH WINS. | |
| **4 WAY BOX.** Of the four digits you select, three are the same. To win, all four digits of your number must match the winning number in any order. 4 ways to win. (ODDS 1 IN 2,500) | 1112 | 1112  1121  1211  2111 | |

Explain how the probabilities (incorrectly called "odds") are obtained for the 2 types of payoffs.

6. In theory, a monkey randomly selecting keys on a typewriter would eventually type some English words. If a monkey is at a keyboard with 48 keys, what is the probability that 5 random keystrokes would produce the word "lucky."

7. A club has 15 members. How many different ways can they select a president and vice-president?

8. If 6 horses are entered in a race and there can be no ties, how many different orders of finish are there?

9. My wife's new bicycle lock is a combination lock with 5 dials each numbered 1 to 9. If we forget the combination, how many possible combinations are there to try?

10. In an area code, the first digit cannot be a 0 or a 1, and the second digit must be a 0 or a 1. The third digit can be any number.
    (a) How many possible area codes are there? (In fact, some codes, such as 411 and 911, are used for other purposes.)
    (b) There are currently about 120 different area codes in the United States and Canada. Are the countries close to running out of possible area codes?
    (c) Starting in 1995, the second digit will no longer be restricted. How many possible area codes will there be?

11. A state license plate consists of 1 letter followed by 5 digits.
    (a) How many different license plates can be made?
    (b) If no digit could be repeated, how many possible license plates would there be?

12. A quiz has 4 multiple-choice questions. Each question has 5 choices, 1 being correct and the other 4 being incorrect. Suppose you guess on all 4 questions.
    (a) How many ways are there to answer the 4 questions?
    (b) If someone got "at least 3 right," exactly how many questions could he or she have gotten right?
    (c) What is $P$(at least 3 right)?

13. (a) In the preceding exercise, how many ways are there to get no questions right?
    (b) What is $P$ (none right)?

14. A true-false test has 4 questions. What is the probability of getting at least 3 right by guessing the answers randomly?

*Extension Exercises*

15. Photocopy the 3 characters shown here and

cut each one into 3 separate sections (head, midsection, legs).
(a) Construct some different characters using the pieces.
(b) How many possible characters could you construct?

16. A slot machine has 3 independent dials. Each dial has 20 possible outcomes. How many possible outcomes are there for the 3 dials taken together?

17. A slot machine has the following symbols on its 3 dials. Each dial is spun independently at random and lands on 1 of 20 possibilities.

| Dial 1 | Dial 2 | Dial 3 |
|--------|--------|--------|
| 1 bar | 1 bar | 1 bar |
| 1 bell | 2 bells | 2 bells |
| 2 cherries | 2 cherries | 1 cherry |
| 7 lemons | 1 lemon | 7 lemons |
| 8 oranges | 6 oranges | 4 oranges |
| 1 plum | 8 plums | 5 plums |

The payoffs for each nickel are as follows.

| | | | |
|--------|-------|---------|------|
| 1 cherry | $.10 | 3 bells | $5 |
| 2 cherries | $.50 | 3 bars | $10 |
| 3 cherries | $1 | | |

(a) How many ways are there to get 3 cherries (1 on each dial)?
(b) How many ways are there to get 3 bars?
(c) How many ways are there to get 3 bells?
(d) Give the probabilities of the events in parts (a), (b), and (c) (see the previous exercise).
(e) How many ways are there to spin exactly 1 cherry?
(f) How many ways are there to spin exactly 2 cherries?
(g) Give the probabilities of the events in parts (e) and (f).

18. At Risk High, the football coach also teaches probability. He knows that when the opposition calls the coin flip, they call "heads" 80% of the time. Since "heads" comes up only 50% of the time, he always lets the visiting team call the coin flip. Should he expect to come out ahead this way?

19. On a trip, you plan to visit London, Paris, Avignon, and Nice. You can travel from London to Paris by airplane or by the so-called "boat train." You can travel from Paris to Avignon and Avignon to Nice by car, bus, or train. However, if you rent a car, you would use it for both journeys. Otherwise, you would ride buses or trains between Paris, Avignon, and Nice. How many possible travel arrangements are there for the trip from London to Paris to Avignon to Nice?

20. A quiz has 5 multiple-choice questions. Each question has 4 choices; 1 is the correct answer and the other 3 are incorrect. Suppose that you guess all the answers.
(a) $P(\text{at least 1 right}) = 1 - P(\underline{\hspace{1cm}})$.
(b) Use the equation in part (a) to find the probability of getting at least 1 right.

21. Three couples are sitting together at a show. How many ways can they sit without any of the couples being split up? Find out by answering the following.
(a) How many choices are there for the aisle seat?
(b) Once the aisle seat is filled, how many choices are there for the seat next to it?
(c) Now how many choices are there for the next seat in?
(d) Now, how many choices for the fourth seat?
(e) Now, how many choices for the fifth seat?
(f) Now, how many for the sixth seat?
(g) How many ways then to seat all 6 people?

22. Follow the method of the previous question to find how many ways there are to seat two couples at a concert if a woman sits on the aisle and the remaining people can sit in any possible arrangement.

23. Three couples go to a concert. How many ways can they arrange themselves if all 3 men and all 3 women sit together?

**24.** A survey asks you to list your first 3 choices for the Democratic presidential nomination from a list of 6 contenders and your first 3 choices from a list of 5 Republican contenders. In how many ways can the survey be completed? (Assume that you choose all of your responses from the lists.)

## 14.4   Expected Value and Odds

Have you ever played a lottery or gambled at a casino? Do you know how to compute how much you are going to *lose* in the long run? Do you know what the term "odds" means? This lesson introduces the mathematics of the expected value and odds.

### Fair vs. Unfair Games

Would you play a gambling game in which you roll 2 dice and you win the amount you bet whenever the sum is greater than 10? This is an example of an unfair game.

In a **fair game** involving money, a player would expect to come out even in the long run. In a fair game between two players, neither player has an advantage due to the rules.

### Lesson Exercise 14.36

In an odd-even dice game, you roll 2 dice. If the product is odd, you win. If it is even, your opponent wins. Is this a fair game? If not, whom does it favor?

### Lesson Exercise 14.37

Make up a fair game for 2 players that involves rolling 2 dice.

### Expected Value

Casino games are not fair games. If they were, casino owners would not make any money. Consider the simple model of a casino game in the following example.

#### Example 14.4

Suppose that you pick 1 card at random from the box shown and you win the amount of money printed on the card. The cards are replaced and reshuffled for each new game.

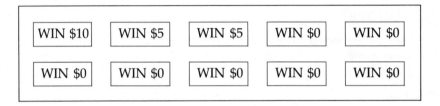

If you play this game often, how much would you expect to be paid on the average?

**Solution**

In the long run, you would expect to pick each of the 10 cards with about the same frequency. You would win about

$$\$10 + \$5 + \$5 + \$0 + \$0 + \$0 + \$0 + \$0 + \$0 + \$0 = \$20$$

every 10 draws. The average per draw would be about $2.  ■

In Example 14.4 the expected average result in the long run was computed. This result is called the **expected value.**

## Lesson Exercise 14.38

Consider a lottery game in which 7 out of 10 people lose, 1 out of 10 wins $25, 1 out of 10 wins $10, and 1 out of 10 wins $5. This can be modeled by selecting 1 card at random from the group shown. What is the expected (average) value of the payoff?

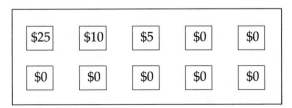

The first state lottery, held in New Hampshire in 1964, created a lot of controversy. Now about 33 states use lotteries to raise money for state programs as an alternative to raising taxes. Is a gambling game a good way to raise money? Many people in the states with no lotteries don't think so.

State officials in lottery states need to know how much money they can expect to raise in the long run—the expected value. People playing the lottery are also interested in the expected value of their lottery tickets.

The next example shows a more widely applicable method for computing expected value in gambling games. In this method, the probability of each possible financial outcome is used.

**Example 14.5**

(a) Find the expected value in Example 14.4 using probabilities.
(b) If the game costs $3 to play, how much should you expect to lose on the average per play?

**Solution**

(a) Because cards are drawn at random, the probability of winning various dollar amounts is as follows.

| Winnings | Probability |
|----------|-------------|
| $10 | $\frac{1}{10}$ |
| $5 | $\frac{2}{10}$ |
| $0 | $\frac{7}{10}$ |

The expected value (denoted by $E$) is a weighted average of the winning amounts. It is computed by multiplying each possible financial outcome by its probability and summing the results.

$$E(\text{winning}) = \$10\left(\frac{1}{10}\right) + \$5\left(\frac{2}{10}\right) + \$0\left(\frac{7}{10}\right) = \$1 + \$1 + \$0 = \$2$$

(b) The average amount won minus the fee gives your expected gain.

$$\$2 - \$3 = -\$1$$

You could expect to lose an average of $1 per play.  ■

The formula used in Example 14.5(a) is as follows.

---

**Definition: Expected Value**

If an experiment has the possible numerical outcomes $n_1, n_2, n_3, \ldots, n_r$ with corresponding probabilities $p_1, p_2, p_3, \ldots, p_r$, then the **expected value,** $E$, of the experiment is

$$E = n_1 p_1 + n_2 p_2 + n_3 p_3 \cdots + n_r p_r$$

---

Use the expected-value formula in the following exercise.

## Lesson Exercise 14.39

Suppose that a lottery game allows you to select a 2-digit number. Each digit may be either 1, 2, 3, 4, or 5. If you pick the winning number, you win $10. Otherwise, you win nothing.

(a) What is the probability that you will pick the winning number?
(b) What is the $E$(winning)?
(c) If the lottery ticket costs $1, how much should you expect to lose on the average (per play)?

Insurance companies also use expected values. In order to determine their rates and payoffs, they estimate the probabilities of different catastrophes.

### Example 14.6

An insurance company will insure your dorm room against theft for a semester. The value of your possessions is $800. Suppose that the probability of your being robbed of $400 worth of goods during a semester is $\frac{1}{100}$, and the probability of your being robbed of $800 worth of goods is $\frac{1}{400}$. Assume that these are the only possible kinds of robberies. How much should the insurance company charge people like you in order to cover the money they pay out and to make an additional $25 profit per person on the average?

**Solution**

*Understanding the Problem*   The insurance company wants $25 per person to be left over after paying out all the claims.

*Devising a Plan*   Compute the expected payout for the insurance. Then, to make $25 profit, charge the expected payout plus an additional $25.

*Carrying Out the Plan*

$$E(\text{payout}) = (\$400) \cdot \frac{1}{100} + (\$800) \cdot \frac{1}{400} = \$4 + \$2 = \$6$$

They should charge $6 + $25 = $31 for the policy in order to make an average gain of $25 per policy.

*Looking Back*   The answer seems reasonable.   ∎

**D** Lesson Exercise 14.40

Consider the following problem. "In a carnival game, you toss a single die. If you roll a 3, you win $3. If you roll a 6, you win $6. Otherwise you win nothing. How much should the carnival operators charge you in order to have an expected gain of $.50 per game?" Devise a plan and solve the problem.

## Odds

In gambling games, probabilities are often stated using odds. Odds compare your chances of losing and winning on each play. For example, on the race card in the following table, the odds against Turf Tortoise winning are 12-1 (12 to 1). This expression means that Turf Tortoise is expected to lose about 12 times for every 1 time he wins. While a probability compares your chances of losing or winning to the total number of possibilities, odds compare your possibilities of losing and winning to each other.

Actually, the real chance of Turf Tortoise winning is slightly worse than 12 to 1. The track pays off bettors based upon the odds *after* taking out about 20% of the money for expenses. For this reason, the track adjusts the odds by a factor of about 20%.

---

**Post Time 1 PM**

Race 1: 6 Furlongs 3YO; CLM $5000

| | |
|---|---|
| Hot Air | 6–5 |
| Dog Lover | 3–1 |
| Wet Blanket | 4–1 |
| Lost Marbles | 5–1 |
| Lead Balloon | 7–1 |
| Turf Tortoise | 12–1 |
| Obstacle | 20–1 |

---

Odds (against) can be defined as follows.

---

Definition: Odds of Experiments with Equally Likely Outcomes

odds against = number of unfavorable outcomes to number of favorable outcomes

---

## Lesson Exercise 14.41

In the table just presented, the odds against Wet Blanket's winning are 4-1 (4 to 1). What does this statement mean?

Probabilities describe the frequency of a (favorable) result in relation to all possible outcomes. "Odds against" compare unfavorable and favorable results like losing to winning. Any probability can be converted to odds, and any odds can be converted to a probability.

### Example 14.7

What is the probability that the director whose door is shown in Figure 14-2 is in his office at 1 PM?

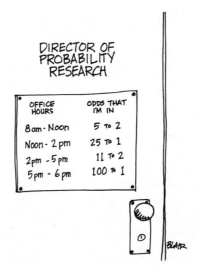

**Figure 14-12**

### Solution

Odds of "25 to 1 against" mean the director will not be there 25 times for each 1 time the director is there. The probability of the director being there is 1 out of 26, or $\frac{1}{26}$. ■

## Lesson Exercise 14.42

The odds against Dead Weight winning the Crabgrass Derby today are 7 to 1. Express this probability using a fraction, a decimal, and a percent.

## Lesson Exercise 14.43

A roulette wheel has 38 numbers. If I bet on 1 number, what are the odds against my winning?

The odds are the basis for payoffs on bets. If the odds were accurate, they would describe a fair bet. For example, if the odds against Dead Weight really are 7 to 1, you gain $7 (an $8 payoff) for every $1 you wager if Dead Weight should happen to lug across in first place. According to these odds, Dead Weight wins about 1 out of 8 races. The expected value can be computed from the following chart.

| Gain | Probability |
|---|---|
| $7 | $\frac{1}{8}$ |
| −$1 | $\frac{7}{8}$ |

$$E(\text{gain}) = \$7\left(\frac{1}{8}\right) + (-\$1)\left(\frac{7}{8}\right) = \$0$$

When the expected value is $0, it is a fair bet, since you would not expect to win or lose money in the long run.

However, the racetrack overestimates the horse's winning chances by about 20%. If the track gives 7 to 1 odds, the true odds are really about 9 to 1. Dead Weight really wins about 1 out of 10 races, so in 10 bets, you could expect to win 1. You would expect to gain $(\$7)\left(\frac{1}{10}\right) + (-\$1)\left(\frac{9}{10}\right) = -\$.20$ for each $1 bet.

## Answers to Selected Lesson Exercises

**14.36** not fair; favors your opponent

**14.38** $4

**14.39** (a) $\frac{1}{25}$   (b) $.40   (c) $.60

**14.40** $2

**14.41** If they are accurate, Wet Blanket would be expected to lose 4 times for every 1 time he wins under these conditions.

**14.42** $\frac{1}{8}$, 0.125, 12.5%

**14.43** 37 to 1

## 14.4   Homework Exercises

*Basic Exercises*

1. In a dice game, you roll 2 dice. If the sum is divisible by 3 or 5, you win. Otherwise, your opponent wins. Who does this game favor?

2. Make up a fair game for 2 players that involves flipping 2 coins.

3. A box contains the cards shown. You randomly select 1 card and win the amount written on that card. What is the expected (average) value of the payoff for a single draw?

| $1000 | $500 | $0 | $0 |
|---|---|---|---|
| $0 | $0 | $0 | $0 |

4. A lottery game allows you to select a 3-digit number using the digits 0, 1, 2, or 3. You may use the same digit more than once. If you pick the winning number, you win $25 on a $1 bet.
   (a) What is the average payoff?
   (b) How much would you expect to lose on the average per $1 bet?

5. Recall that a roulette wheel has 38 slots. Eighteen are red, 18 are black, and 2 are green.
   (a) What is the probability of black?
   (b) If you bet $1, you receive a $2 payoff for black and $0 for red or green. What is the average loss on a $1 bet on black?
   (c) You can also bet on 6 different numbers. If any of them come up, you receive $6 back for each $1 bet. What is the expected gain or loss on a $1 bet?

6. A particular oil well costs $40,000 to drill.

   The probability of striking oil is 1/20.
   (a) If an oil strike is worth $500,000, what is the expected gain from drilling?
   (b) Would you go ahead and drill?

7. (a) The Unshakeable Insurance Company will insure your dorm room against theft. The insurance costs $25 per year. If the probability of getting robbed of an average of $500 worth of possessions is $\frac{1}{100}$, how much profit does the insurance company expect to make from your $25 insurance premium?
   (b) The company sells $100,000 worth of automobile liability insurance that costs $50 per year. In the past, about 1 out of every 1000 people have collected on a claim. The average (mean) claim is $30,000. What is the expected payoff on your $50 investment?
   (c) Why might the insurance in part (b) be worth the investment, while the insurance in part (a) is probably not worth it?

8. Madame Wamma Jamma will predict the sex of a future baby for $5. If she is wrong, she even has a money-back guarantee! If Madame Wamma Jamma has no psychic power (perish the thought!), what is her expected gain per customer? Assume that she cheerfully refunds the $5 whenever she is wrong.

9. An apartment complex has 20 air conditioners. Each summer a certain number of them have to be replaced.

| Number of Air Conditioners Replaced | Probability |
|---|---|
| 0 | 0.21 |
| 1 | 0.32 |
| 2 | 0.18 |
| 3 | 0.11 |
| 4 | 0.11 |
| 5 | 0.07 |

What is the expected number of air conditioners that will be replaced in the summer?

10. The probability that a particular operation is successful is 0.32.
    (a) If the operation is performed 600 times a year at a hospital, about how many successful operations can they expect?
    (b) If you decide to have this operation, give some reasons why the probability of its success for you might be somewhat higher or lower than 0.32.

11. A set of 3 coins is tossed 32 times. How many times would you expect the result to be 3 heads?

12. State Penn Insurance Company will insure your apartment against theft for 1 year. The value of your insured possessions is $4000. In the past, about 1 out of every 100 people has collected on a claim. The average (mean) claim is $1200. How much should the insurance company charge you in order to cover payouts and make an average gain of $20 per policy?

13. You run a check-cashing service. About 1 out of every 500 checks is bad. The average (mean) bad check is for $100. How much of a charge per person would offset the cost of the bad checks?

14. A carnival game costs $2 to play. You roll 2 dice. If the sum is 5, you receive a $5 payoff. If the sum is 10, you receive a $10 payoff. What is the expected payoff $E(\$2 \text{ bet})$?

15. In a gambling game, you pick 1 card from a standard deck. If you pick an ace, you win $10. If you pick a picture card (J, Q, or K), you win $5. Otherwise, you win nothing. How much should a carnival booth charge you to play this game if they want an average profit of $.40 per game?

16. $T$ tickets are sold for $1 each for a lottery drawing with a prize of $100. What is the expected payoff of each ticket in terms of $T$?

17. In a game, whoever spins the higher number wins. Which of the following spinners would be the best one to spin?

(a)                (b)                (c)

18. A roulette wheel has 38 slots, of which 18 are red, 18 black, and 2 green. If I bet on red, what are the odds against my winning?

19. Data indicate that about 3 out of 4 marriages last at least 20 years. The odds against a marriage lasting at least 20 years are _____ .

20. Of the people who purchase handguns, 11 times as many use them on themselves or their family rather than on an intruder. This means that about _____ of every _____ gun owners who uses a handgun will use it on an intruder.

21. Are you ready for a cheery problem? The following table gives the odds against dying in the next year.

| Age | Odds Against Dying in the Next Year | |
|-----|------|--------|
| | Male | Female |
| 15–24 | 576–1 | 1814–1 |
| 25–34 | 560–1 | 1489–1 |
| 35–44 | 384–1 | 743–1 |
| 45–54 | 140–1 | 269–1 |
| 55–64 | 57–1 | 111–1 |
| 65–74 | 25–1 | 49–1 |
| 75–84 | 11–1 | 17–1 |
| 85–up | 6–1 | 7–1 |

What is the probability that you will live another year?

*Extension Exercises*

22. Refer to the slot machine homework exercise from the last section. Use the probabilities you found to compute the expected payoff on a $.05 bet.

**23.** A company wants to test its employees for a drug. The test is 98% accurate. If someone is using the drug, the person will test positive 98% of the time. If someone is not using the drug, the person will test negative 98% of the time.

(a) Suppose the company randomly tests all 10,000 of its employees. Also, assume that 50 people are actually using the drug. How many people will test positive who are not using the drug (false positive)?

(b) In part (a), what is the probability that someone who tests positive is actually using the drug?

(c) Suppose that, instead, the company tests only people who exhibit suspicious behavior. Suppose 100 people act suspiciously, and 30 of them are using the drug. How many people will test positive who are not using the drug (false positive)?

(d) In part (c), what is the probability that someone who tests positive is actually using the drug?

**24.** A company wants to test its employees for a drug. The test is 95% accurate.

(a) Suppose that the company randomly tests all 5000 of its employees. Furthermore, assume that 100 people are actually using the drug. How many people will test positive who are not using the drug (false positive)?

(b) In part (a), what is the probability that someone who tests positive is actually using the drug?

(c) Suppose that, instead, the company tests only people who exhibit suspicious behavior. Suppose 150 people act suspiciously, and 80 of them are using the drug. How many people will test positive who are not using the drug (false positive)?

(d) In part (c), what is the probability that someone who tests positive is actually using the drug?

**25.** A patient has a stroke and must choose between brain surgery and a drug treatment. Of 100 people having surgery, 20 die during surgery, 15 more die after 1 year, and 5 more die after 3 years. Of 100 people having drug therapy, 5 die almost immediately, 20 more die after 1 year, and 30 more die after 3 years. Which treatment would you advise someone to take? Why?

**26.** A lottery game allows you to select any 3-digit number. The first digit cannot be a 0. If you pick just the first 2 digits in the correct order, you win $50 for each $1 bet. If you pick the exact winning number, you win $250 for each $1 bet. What is the expected payoff of a $1 bet?

**27.** Read the Beetle Bailey cartoon and answer the following questions.

(a) If Beetle lives another 50 years, how much money would he win (after taxes)?

(b) Assume that Beetle has a 1-in-5,000,000 chance of winning. What is the expected payoff for his mailing in the entry form?

(c) Is it worth the price of a stamp?

## 14.5   Independent and Dependent Events

If you feel sick in the morning, it affects the probability that you will go to school or work. In computing the probability of two events occurring in succession, it is important to know whether the outcome of one event affects the outcome of the other.

### Lesson Exercise 14.44

Consider the following events.

$R$ = rain tomorrow

$U$ = you carry an umbrella tomorrow

$H$ = coin flipped tomorrow lands on heads

(a) Does the probability of $R$ affect the probability of $U$?
(b) Does the outcome of the coin flip affect whether or not it will rain tomorrow?

In Lesson Exercise 14.44, $R$ and $H$ are independent events, whereas $R$ and $U$ are dependent events.

### Independent Events

When a pair of dice are rolled, each die may show a 1, 2, 3, 4, 5, or 6, and the result on one die does not depend upon the result on the other die. The two die rolls are independent events.

Two events are **independent** if the probability of one event remains the same regardless of how the other event turns out. Events that are not independent are **dependent.**

The following exercise suggests how to compute the probability of a series of independent events.

### Lesson Exercise 14.45

Consider 2 successive draws *with replacement* from the box shown. ("With replacement" means that the number selected first is replaced in the box, and the cards are shuffled before the second draw is made.)

(a) Would the result on one draw affect the result on the other draw?

(b) Suppose that you want to pick two 1's in a row. What fraction of the time would you expect to draw a 1 on your first pick?

(c) Out of those times that you drew a 1 on the first pick, what fraction of the time would you expect to draw another 1 on the second pick?

(d) $\frac{1}{3}$ of $\frac{1}{3}$ = _____ .

---

A geometric model supports the result of Lesson Exercise 14.45.

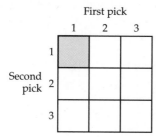

$P(1 \text{ and } 1 \text{ again}) = \frac{1}{9}$

In Lesson Exercise 14.45, $P(1 \text{ and } 1 \text{ again}) = P(1) \cdot P(1 \text{ again})$. This is an example of the independent-events formula.

> **The Independent-Events Formula**
>
> If $A$ and $B$ are independent events, $P(A \text{ and } B) = P(A) \cdot P(B)$.

Lesson Exercise 14.45 can also be modeled with a tree diagram, as in Figure 14.13.

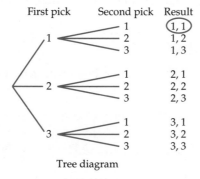

Tree diagram

**Figure 14-13**

One can also use a tree diagram with probabilities (Figure 14-14, page 852). The $P(A \text{ and } B)$ formula justifies multiplying the probabilities in this type of diagram.

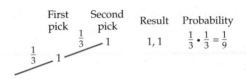

**Figure 14-14**

## Lesson Exercise 14.46

(a) A fair die is tossed twice. What is the probability of getting a 3 on the first toss, followed by an odd number on the second toss?
(b) Illustrate this by shading the geometric model in Figure 14-15.

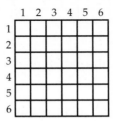

**Figure 14-15**

When there are more than 2 events involved, you can apply probabilities of independent events in the same way. The tree diagram still works in these cases, but geometric models become too complicated.

## Dependent Events

Now consider 2 dependent events *A* and *B* that are steps in a multistage experiment.

## Lesson Exercise 14.47

You make 2 successive draws from a box *without* replacement.

To find $P(2 \text{ and then } 3)$, answer the following.
(a) What is $P(2)$?
(b) What fraction of the time would you expect to pick a 3 after picking a 2?
(c) $P(2 \text{ and then } 3)$ = _____ .

A geometric model supports the result of Lesson Exercise 14.47.

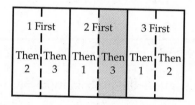

$$P(2 \text{ and then } 3) = \frac{1}{6}$$

In Lesson Exercise 14.47,

$$P(2 \text{ and then } 3) = P(2) \cdot P(3 \text{ second given 2 first})$$

This is usually shortened to

$$P(2 \text{ and } 3) = P(2) \cdot P(3 \text{ given } 2)$$

and it is an example of the following formula.

---

**Multistage Probability**

$P(A \text{ and } B) = P(A) \cdot P(B \text{ given } A)$

---

This formula justifies solving Lesson Exercise 14.47 by multiplying probabilities in a tree diagram (Figure 14-16).

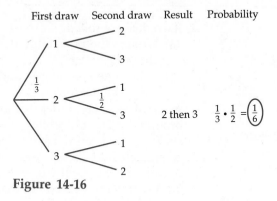

**Figure 14-16**

## Lesson Exercise 14.48

You have a drawer with 10 black socks and 6 white socks. If you select 2 socks at random, what is the probability of picking 2 white socks?
(a) Solve the problem using the formula.
(b) Solve the problem using a tree diagram.

Now, see whether you can find an experimental and a theoretical probability for the following situation.

## Lesson Exercise 14.49

You have 6 black socks and 4 white socks in a drawer. You pick 2 socks at random.
(a) Without computing probabilities, guess the probability of picking a matching pair.
(b) Simulate the experiment 30 times using 2 colors of chips and a bag. What is your experimental probability for matching a pair of socks?
(c) Find the theoretical probability of picking a matching pair.
(d) Model the experiment with a tree diagram.

## Answers to Selected Lesson Exercises

14.44 (a) yes     (b) no

14.45 (a) no     (b) $\frac{1}{3}$     (c) $\frac{1}{3}$     (d) $\frac{1}{9}$

14.46 (a) $\frac{1}{12}$

14.47 (a) $\frac{1}{3}$     (b) $\frac{1}{2}$     (c) $\frac{1}{6}$

14.48 (a) $\frac{1}{8}$

14.49 (c) $\frac{7}{15}$

## 14.5   Homework Exercises

*Basic Exercises*

1. Consider the following events.

   $C$ = you eat cereal tomorrow

   $B$ = you wear blue shoes tomorrow

   $M$ = you drink milk tomorrow

   (a) Are $C$ and $M$ independent or dependent events?
   (b) Are $M$ and $B$ independent or dependent events?

2. Two draws will be made from a standard deck of cards without replacement. Are the draws independent or dependent?

3. (a) When drawing at random with replacement, are the draws independent or dependent?
   (b) Without replacement, are the draws independent or dependent?

4. Two dice are rolled.
   (a) What is the probability that both dice show a 5 or a 6?
   (b) Draw a geometric grid and shade it to show the answer.

5. A man has 2 cars, a Recall and a Sea Bass Brougham. The probability that the Recall starts is 0.1. The probability that the Sea Bass Brougham starts is 0.7. (Assume that the cars operate independently of one another.)
   (a) What is the probability that both cars start?
   (b) What is the probability that neither car starts?
   (c) What is the probability that exactly 1 car starts?

6. The best drug tests are about 98% reliable. This means that there is a probability of 0.98 that the test will correctly identify a drug

user or a nonuser. To be safe, each person is tested twice.
(a) What is the probability that a drug user will pass both tests?
(b) What is the probability that a nonuser will fail at least 1 of the tests?

7. Assume that for a nuclear power plant to have an accident, 4 systems must fail. The probability that each of the 4 systems fails is, respectively, 0.01, 0.006, 0.002, and 0.002. What is the probability that the plant will have an accident?

8. You flip a coin 10 times to test its fairness. What is the probability of getting 10 tails in a row if the coin is fair?

9. A slot machine has 3 independent wheels set up as follows.

| Dial 1 | | Dial 2 | |
|---|---|---|---|
| 1 bar | 2 cherries | 1 bar | 2 bells |
| 1 bell | 7 lemons | 1 lemon | 6 oranges |
| 1 plum | 8 oranges | 2 cherries | 8 plums |

| Dial 3 | |
|---|---|
| 1 bar | 4 oranges |
| 1 cherry | 5 plums |
| 2 bells | 7 lemons |

What is the probability of getting each of the following?
(a) 3 lemons    (b) 3 limes    (c) 0 cherries

10. Suppose that an international phone cable has 300 underwater amplifiers placed at regular intervals. Underwater amplifiers are very difficult to replace. If the probability that an amplifier lasts 20 years is 0.999998, what is the probability that all 300 amplifiers will last 20 years? (Assume that all 300 amplifiers operate independently of one another.)

11. You pick 2 cards from a regular deck *without* replacement. What is the probability of picking 2 aces?

12. In order to repair his knee, a football player must successfully go through 2 operations. The probability that the first operation will be successful is 0.8. If the first operation is successful, the probability that the second operation will be successful is 0.7. What is the probability that both operations will be successful?

13. A drawer contains a mixture of 10 black socks, 8 white socks, and 4 red socks. You select two socks to wear at random. Determine the probability that
(a) both are black.
(b) both are white.
(c) you pick a matching pair.

14. On the average, it rains or snows about 114 days a year in Spokane, Washington.
(a) If you visit for a day, what is the probability that there will be precipitation (rain or snow)?
(b) If there is precipitation one day, the probability of precipitation the next day is 0.5. If you visit for 2 days, what is the probability that it will rain or snow both days?

15. A shipment of radios contains 97 that work and 3 that are defective. An inspector selects 5 at random. What is the probability that they all work?

*Extension Exercises*

16. In a mathematics class that contains 50% boys and 50% girls, 60% of the children are 8 years old and 40% are 9 years old.
(a) What is the largest possible percentage of 9-year-old girls in the class?
(b) What is the smallest possible percentage of 9-year-old girls in the class?
(c) If age and sex are independent, then _____ % of the class is 9-year-old girls.

**17.**

| Pair 1 |
| --- |
| $H$ = a fair coin flip lands on heads today |
| $T$ = your TV works today |

| Pair 2 |
| --- |
| $B$ = you eat a big breakfast today |
| $L$ = you eat a big lunch today |

(a) Tell whether or not each pair of events is independent. Explain your answers.

(b) Tell whether or not each pair of events is mutually exclusive. Explain your answers.

**18.** Consider the following problem. "A football betting service picks 1 game each week. They charge $100 per pick, but only if they pick the game correctly. The service starts with 200 customers. They tell 100 customers to bet on one team and 100 customers to bet on the other team. Assume that this continues for 10 weeks with the following results. Only the customers who win each week continue the next week. Furthermore, the service attracts 40 new customers each week. How much can the service expect to make, if none of the games are ties?" Devise a plan and solve the problem.

**19.** Suppose that tulip bulbs have a probability of 0.6 of flowering. How many bulbs should you buy to have a probability of 0.9 of obtaining at least 1 flower?

**20.**

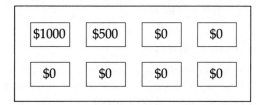

| $1000 | $500 | $0 | $0 |
| --- | --- | --- | --- |
| $0 | $0 | $0 | $0 |

Two cards are drawn at random without re-placement. What is the expected value of the total amount drawn?

**21.** Two basketball teams play a best-2-out-of-3 series, meaning the first team to win two games is the champion. Suppose that team A has a probability of 0.6 of winning each game. Find the probability that team A wins (a) in 2 games.    (b) in 3 games. (*Hint:* Draw a tree diagram.)

**22.** A World Series is a best-4-out-of-7 series. If the American League team has a probability of 0.5 of winning each game, determine the probability that they win the World Series in (a) 4 games.    (b) 5 games.

**23.** A basketball team has a probability of 0.7 of making each free throw. If they shoot 5 free throws at the end of a game, determine the probability that they make
(a) all 5 shots.
(b) at least 4 shots.

*Computer Exercise*

**24.** An airline has booked 50 people for a flight that has 45 seats. If the probability that a passenger shows up is 0.86, RUN the following BASIC program at least 10 times to estimate the probability that the flight will be overbooked.

```
10 LET N = 0
20 FOR P = 1 TO 50
30    IF RND(1) < 0.86 THEN N = N + 1
40 NEXT P
50 IF N < 46 THEN PRINT "OKAY"
60 IF N > 45 THEN PRINT "OVERBOOKED"
```

# Summary

Uncertainty is part of our everyday lives. They say that nothing in life is certain but death and taxes. For this reason, probability theory is helpful in studying the likelihood of everyday events.

Probabilities tell us approximately what we can expect to happen when the same event is repeated a large number of times under the same conditions. If a sample space of equally likely events can be written for an experiment, it may be possible to compute a theoretical probability.

Experimental probabilities are based upon experimental results under identical or similar conditions. If it is impractical or costly to find an experimental probability of a random event, one can sometimes study a simulation of the event using coins, dice, or a computer.

"Students should actively explore situations by experimenting and simulating probability models. Such investigations should embody a variety of realistic situations" (NCTM, *Standards*, p. 109).

In order to decide how many letters and digits to put in license plates, phone numbers, and codes, people use counting techniques. These same techniques indicate how likely one is to guess correctly on a multiple-choice test. In probability, counting techniques are used to determine the size of sample spaces.

How do casinos design gambling games, states design lotteries, and insurance companies set fees? They all use probabilities to estimate the expected average payoffs per person. These payoffs are then used to determine a fee that will cover these payoffs and other expenses.

In computing the probability that events $A$ and $B$ will occur, one multiplies probabilities. If $A$ and $B$ are dependent, one must calculate how much one event affects the probability of the other:

$$P(A \text{ and } B) = P(B \text{ given } A) \cdot P(A)$$

If events $A$ and $B$ are independent, meaning they do not influence each other's probabilities, one can compute $P(A \text{ and } B)$ simply by multiplying $P(A) \cdot P(B)$.

# Study Guide

To review Chapter 14, see what you know about each of the following ideas or terms listed that you have studied. You can also use this list to generate your own questions about Chapter 14.

## The NCTM Curriculum Standards and Probability

**Selected NCTM Curriculum Standards**

The following standards come from the NCTM document.

- Model situations by devising and carrying out experiments or simulations to determine probabilities.
- Model situations by constructing a sample space to determine probabilities.
- Appreciate the power of using a probability model by comparing experimental results with mathematical expectations.
- Apply mathematical thinking and modeling to solve problems that arise in other disciplines.

1. Describe how each standard listed relates to the material you studied in Chapter 14.
2. Select any current elementary-school mathematics textbook series and describe a sample lesson or exercise that illustrates each standard listed.

## Review Exercises

1. (a) What is the probability of rolling a product less than 10 on 2 dice?
   (b) Describe how you could determine the same probability experimentally.

2. What is the probability of getting 3 heads and 1 tail when you flip 4 coins?

3. A true-false quiz has 3 questions. If I guess at random, what is the probability that I will get at least 2 right? (Assume that I answer each question either *true* or *false*.)

4. The theoretical probability of getting 3 heads and 2 tails in 5 coin tosses is 5/16. Explain what this probability tells us about what to expect when we do such a coin-tossing experiment.

5. A judge rates the best and second-best orange juices out of 4 brands *A*, *B*, *C*, and *D*. What is the sample space for his pair of choices?

6. A state has 2 kinds of license plates: plates with 2 letters followed by 2 digits, and plates with 2 letters followed by 3 digits. How many different plates can the state make?

7. You have a spinner like the one shown. You want to simulate each *second* at a one-way traffic intersection. In preliminary work, you found that 150 cars passed in 10 minutes. How would you use the spinner in the simulation?

8.

Photo courtesy of Library of Congress.

| Sure Thing | 1–2 |
| Hopeless | 4–1 |
| Bad Breath | 6–1 |
| Unsettled | 7–1 |
| Lethargic | 10–1 |
| Why Bother | 50–1 |

(a) According to the odds, Unsettled (see photo) wins about 1 out of _____ races.

(b) The probability of Lethargic winning is about _____ .

9. A dice game pays $3 back on a $1 bet if you roll a sum of 7 on two dice and $10 back on a $1 bet if you roll a sum of 11. Otherwise, you lose the $1.
   (a) What is *E*(payoff on $1 bet)?
   (b) What is *E*(gain on $1 bet)?

10. A defective undergarment is inspected by inspector 12 and inspector 14. Each of them has a 0.9 chance of finding the defect. What is the probability that neither one of them will find the defect?

11. An insurance company will insure your home against theft. The value of your possessions that are insurable is $1000. Suppose that the probability of your being burglarized of $500 worth of goods is $\frac{1}{200}$ , and the probability of your being burglarized of $1000 worth of goods is $\frac{1}{1000}$. Assume that these are the only kinds of possible burglaries. How much should the insurance company charge people like you in order to make an average profit of $50 per policy?

12. New Hay Checks come with one of 4 different famous thoroughbreds collectible cards in each box. Using a spinner with regions numbered 1 to 4, I simulated buying boxes until I had collected all 4 cards. The results are shown below.

    1 3 1 2 4
    2 4 1 1 2 2 3
    4 3 1 2
    4 3 4 1 2
    1 3 3 1 4 1 3 2

Based upon these results, how many boxes would you expect to buy to collect all 4 cards?

## Probability in Elementary School

The following chart shows at what grade levels selected probability topics typically appear in elementary-school mathematics textbooks.

| Topic | Typical Grade Level in Current Textbooks |
|---|---|
| Basic probability | 3, 4, 5, 6 |
| Experimental and theoretical probability | 5, 6 |
| Simulations | 5, 6 |
| Predictions (expected value) | 3, 4, 5, 6 |

## Selected Readings

Armstrong, R. and P. Pederson, eds. *Probability and Statistics*. St. Louis, MO: Comprehensive School Mathematics Project, 1982.

Bergamini, D., ed. *Mathematics*. New York: Time, 1963.

Jacobs, H. *Mathematics: A Human Endeavor*. 2nd ed.. New York: W. H. Freeman, 1982.

*Logo Probability*. Portland, ME: Terrapin Software, 1990.

National Council of Teachers of Mathematics. 1981 Yearbook. *The Teaching of Statistics and Probability*. Reston, VA: NCTM, 1981.

Packel, E. *The Mathematics of Games and Gambling*. Washington, DC: MAA, 1981.

Paulos, J. *Innumeracy*. New York: Hill and Wang, 1988.

# Answers to Selected Exercises

## Chapter 1

### 1.1 Homework Exercises

**1.** (b) You end up with 6 more than the original number.

**3.** yes

**5.** with a counterexample

**7.** false; Mike does not drink beer.

**9.** reasonable

**11.** (a) 88,831
   (b) The answer has the same digits in reverse order.
   (c) 68,952, 25,986
   (d) Reversing the order of the digits in two three-digit factors will reverse the order of the digits of their product.
   (e) false

**13.** (a) 16 units    (c) $L = P^2$    (d) 2.2 sec

**15.** (a) For the last 3 weeks, my teacher has given one pop quiz per week. I generalize that my teacher will always do this.
   (b) A mathematician sees three examples in which the sum of two odd numbers is an even number. The mathematician generalizes that this will always occur.

**17.** (a) Generalization (1) is based upon the observation that all through recorded history there have been wars. Generalization (2) could be based upon teaching a few classes in which the boys did better than the girls. Generalization (3) could be based upon seeing a few movie sequels and thinking that they were not as good as the originals.

**19.** (a) true    (b) true    (c) true
   (d) The product of any $N$ consecutive whole numbers is divisible by $N$.

**21.** no

### 1.2 Homework Exercises

**1.** All rectangles are quadrilaterals.

**3.** (a) $\overline{AB}$ is parallel to $\overline{CD}$ and $\overline{AD}$ is parallel to $\overline{BC}$.

(b) *Hypotheses: ABCD* is a rectangle. The opposite sides of a rectangle are parallel. *Conclusion:* $\overline{AB}$ is parallel to $\overline{CD}$ and $\overline{AD}$ is parallel to $\overline{BC}$.

**5.** (e)

**7.** no

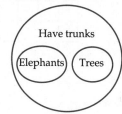

**9.** no

**11.** no

**13.** (a) 0, 1, 2, 6, 7, 9    (b) 8    (c) 3, 5    (e) 358

**15.** If you have your teeth cleaned twice a year, then you will lose fewer teeth.

**17.** Some adults don't have time to read.

**19.** I will have more dates. (false)

**21.** Sandy is a female dachshund that is not white.

**23.** (a) Declaration of Independence (see page 25)
   (b) (1) must be true; (3) must be false.

**25.** 1 honest, 99 crooked

**27.** (a)

(b) (1) and (4)

**29.** If I ask you for the correct route, would you tell me to go right or left?

**31.** Select one ball from "W and Y" and you know if it's really "Y" or "W" and then you can work out the rest.

**33.**

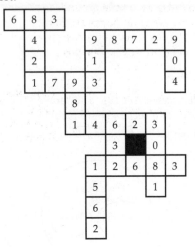

**1.3 Homework Exercises**

1. inductive
3. *Hypotheses*: All boys play baseball. All baseball players chew gum.
   *Conclusion*: All boys chew gum.
5. induction
7. induction
9. inductive
11. (a) It will increase by 4.
    (b) because it may not work for some number that you did not try
    (c) $N \rightarrow 3N \rightarrow 2N \rightarrow 2N + 8 \rightarrow N + 4$
    (d) If you have $2N$ and then you add 8, you can deduce that the result is $2N + 8$.
13. Interchange the hypothesis and the conclusion.
15. (a) yes (in general)
    (b) If you are sick, then you have a fever.
    (c) no
17. (a) If you are smart, then you may be successful.
    (b) If a triangle is equilateral, then it is isosceles.
19. If a triangle has two congruent sides, then it has two congruent angles. If a triangle has two congruent angles, then it has two congruent sides.
21. $2x = 4$ if and only if $x = 2$.
25. (a) an even number
    (b) $2M + 2N$; $(M + N)$; 2 times any whole number is even

**27.** (a) If I do not drive a truck, then I do not need a driver's license.
    (b) If a girl does not use nose powder, then her nose does not look beautiful.
**29.** (a) If you are a real man, then you are a U.S. Marine.
    (b) If you are not a real man, then you are not a U.S. Marine.
    (c) If you are not a U.S. Marine, then you are not a real man.
**31.** (c)
**33.** (a) (2)    (b) (1)
**35.** (a) If $A$, then $B$.    (b) If $B$, then $A$.
    (c) If $A$, then $B$.    (d) If $B$, then $A$.
    (e) If $B$, then $A$.

**1.4 Homework Exercises**

1. (a) 625
   (b) induction to find the general rule of raising to the fourth power and deduction to apply the general rule to 5 and compute $5^4$.
3. 12
5. 132
7. (a) 8 or 7
   (b) multiplying by 2 or adding 1 more each time
9. (a) 1, 1, 2, 3, 5, 8, 13, 21, 34, 55
   (b) The sum is 1 less than the term.    (c) yes
   (d) The sum of three consecutive terms is 1 less than the term that comes two terms later.
11. (a)

| Time (years) | 0 | 5600 | 11,200 | 16,800 | 22,400 |
|---|---|---|---|---|---|
| Fraction of C-14 left | 1 | 1/2 | 1/4 | 1/8 | 1/16 |

   (b) about 15,000 years
13. (a) 2    (b) 4    (c) 8    (d) $2^{12} = 4096$
15. 9, 8, 7, 6, 5
17. (a) 2, 4, 6, 8, . . .    (b) $2n$
    (c) Each term is 2 more than the preceding.
19. (a) 99    (b) 2500
21. (a) 19    (b) $2n + 9$    (c) 89
    (d) deduction
23. (a) 38    (b) $n^2 + 2$    (c) 902
25. (a) $7n - 5$    (b) 695
27. 8
29. (a) $V = L^3$    (b) 125    (c) $n^3$
31. (a) 6, 8, 10, $2N + 2$

(b)

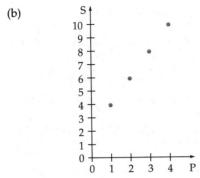

(c) All the points lie on a line.

**33.** 5; 8 − N

**35.** (b)

**37.** (a) 5 and 6

(b) $3^4 + 4^4 + 5^4 + 6^4 = (7)^4$. It is false.

**39.** (a) 3, 7, and 13    (b) $4^2 + 5^2 + 20^2 = (21)^2$, yes

(c) $N^2 + (N + 1)^2 + [N(N + 1)]^2 = [N(N + 1) + 1]^2$

(d)     $N^2 + (N + 1)^2 + [N(N + 1)]^2 \stackrel{?}{=} [N(N + 1) + 1]^2$

$N^2 + N^2 + 2N + 1 + [N^2 + N]^2 \stackrel{?}{=} [N^2 + N + 1]^2$

$2N^2 + 2N + 1 + N^4 + 2N^3 + N^2 \stackrel{?}{=} N^4 + 2N^3 + 3N^2 + 2N + 1$

$N^4 + 2N^3 + 3N^2 + 2N + 1 \stackrel{?}{=} N^4 + 2N^3 + 3N^2 + 2N + 1$

**41.** (a) 12th row       (b) down

(c) 22nd row       (d) down

**43.** (a) 0    (b) 1    (c) 1 − 1 + 1 − 1 + . . .

(d) 1 − 1 + 1 − 1 + . . .    (e) yes

**45.** (161 × 4) + 7 = 651

**47.** $74^2 − 40 = 5436$

**51.** (a) 1    (b) 3    (c) 12

**53.** (a) 128    (b) 2

**55.** no

**57.** The height of each bounce decreases geometrically.

**59.** (a) They add up to 101.    (b) 50    (c) 5050

**61.** (a) 21    (b) N(N + 1)/2

**63.** (15 + 29) · 15/2 = 330

**1.5 Homework Exercises**

**1.** multi-step

**3.** puzzle

**5.** The doctor first tries to understand what is wrong with you. Next, the doctor devises a treatment. Then, the doctor implements the treatment. Finally, the doctor checks to see whether the treatment worked.

**7.** No, it's too high. (2 × $13) + 9 = $35.

**9.** They traveled 40 miles per hour for 2 hours. How much further do they have to go?

**11.** *Understand:* How are the cuts made? Vertically if the log is lying on the ground. *Plan:* Start making cuts and see what happens. *Solve:* 4 cuts. *Look Back:* The first cut creates two pieces, and each additional cut adds another piece.

**13.** (a) 5    (b) 6    (c) N − 1

**15.** $2^{10} = 1024$ including no toppings

**17.** (a) Bea Young is 12 years old. Her father is 2 less than 3 times her age. How old is he?

(b) A room has 3 rows of 12 chairs each. During a film, only 2 of the chairs are empty. How many people are attending the film?

**19.** $3\frac{1}{3}, 3\frac{1}{3}, 3\frac{1}{3}$

**21.** Move the two dots at the ends of the top row to the ends of the third row. Then move the bottom dot to the top.

**23.** Divide the coins into 3 groups: 6, 5, and 5. Put 5 coins on each side of the balance and find which of the three groups has the lighter coin. Take the group of 5 or 6 with the lighter coin and divide it into 3 groups of 2, 2, 2 or 2, 2, 1. Place two coins on each balance and find which of the three remaining groups has the lighter coin. If this group has more than 1 coin, place 1 coin on each balance to find the lighter coin.

**25.** (a) 18    (b) 6

**27.** (a) 1, 2, 1; total = 4

(b) 1, 3, 3, 1; total = 8    (c) $2^{N−1}$

**29.** (a) Switch 2 with 7 and 4 with 9.    (b) 0

(c) 2

(d) For N pairs of checkers in which N is odd, you must move N − 1 checkers.

(e) no    (f) no

(g) For N pairs of checkers in which N is even, you must move N checkers.

(h) 24    (i) 50

**1.6 Homework Exercises**

**1.** devising a plan

**3.** 60

**5.** Wong is off weeks 2, 3, and 6 and Clio is off weeks 2, 5, and 6 (or vice versa).

**7.** 32 and 37

**9.** (a) A worm goes up 4 ft and slides back 1 ft each day.
(b) A worm goes up 6 ft and slides back 3 ft each day.
(c) A worm goes up 9 ft and slides back 6 ft each day.

**11.** (possible answer) The assistant manager is off weeks 1 and 2; one secretary is off weeks 3 and 4; the other is off weeks 5 and 6; One agent is off weeks 1 and 2; the other is off weeks 3 and 4.

**13.** $-2$

**15.** 66 ft

**17.** 17

**19.** (a) 40 yd      (b) $4\sqrt{N}$ yd

**21.** First, he takes the goose across. Then he takes the fox (or corn) across and picks up the goose when he drops off the fox (or corn). He brings the goose back to the starting side and picks up the corn (or fox). Finally, he goes back and brings the goose across again.

**23.** 2, 3, 4, 5, 6, 7, 8, 9, or 10

**25.** minimum of $E - (C - G)$ and a maximum of $G$

**27.** $C = 4T + 2$

**29.** $C = 2T + 4$

**31.** (a) 2      (b) 6      (c) 24
(d) $N \cdot (N - 1) \cdot (N - 2) \cdots 2 \cdot 1$
(e) inductive

**Chapter 1 *Review Exercises***

**1.** the process of reaching a necessary conclusion from given hypotheses

**2.** induction

**3.** deduction

**4.** deduction

**5.** First, the mechanic would find out what was wrong with the car. Next, the mechanic would devise a plan to fix the problem. Then, the mechanic would try out the repair plan. Finally, the mechanic would check to see if the problem no longer occured.

**6.** no

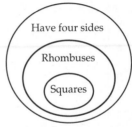

**7.** If a teacher started class by checking attendance 10 days in a row, a student would generalize that the teacher always starts class this way.

**8.** yes

**9.** (a) If the ground gets wet, then it is raining.
(b) no

**10.** $N \rightarrow N + 5 \rightarrow 3N + 15 \rightarrow 3N + 6 \rightarrow 2N + 6 \rightarrow N + 3$

**11.** (a) $21 - n$      (b) $-19$
(c)

| $x$ | 1 | 2 | 3 | 4 |
|---|---|---|---|---|
| $y$ | 20 | 19 | 18 | 17 |

(d) inductive

**12.** (a) 1, 2, 3      (b) $13 + 15 + 17 + 19 = 4^3$; yes

**13.** (a) $7^2 - 4^2 = 3 \cdot 11$
(b) $N^2 - (N - 3)^2 = 3 \cdot (2N - 3)$
(c)      $N^2 - (N - 3)^2 \stackrel{?}{=} 3 \cdot (2N - 3)$
$N^2 - (N^2 - 6N + 9) \stackrel{?}{=} 6N - 9$
$N^2 - N^2 + 6N - 9 \stackrel{?}{=} 6N - 9$
$6N - 9 = 6N - 9$

**14.** I had $10. I spent $3 and then found a $5 bill. How much do I have now?

**15.** 18

**16.** (a) guess and check
(b) 3 tuna and 8 buckwheat

**17.** 6

**18.** (a) 144      (b) bottom row, third from the left

**19.** 9 days

**20.** (a) A snail goes up 7 ft and slides back 5 ft each day.
(b) A snail goes up 5 ft and slides back 3 ft each day.

**21.** (a) Mack owns the sea turtle, Rosie the gorilla, Mona the crocodile, and Ahmad the ant.
(b) deduction

**22.** (a) $142,857 \times 4 = 571,428$
(b) The answer always contains the digits 1, 2, 4, 5, 7, and 8.
(c) The pattern works for 1 to 6 as second factor.

**Chapter 1** *Computer Exercises*
1. (a) 1, 3, 5, 7    (b) 10 FOR N = 2 TO 8 STEP 2
   (c) 10 FOR N = 7 TO 23 STEP 4
   (d) 10 FOR N = 11 TO −1 STEP −3

**Chapter 2**
**2.1** *Homework Exercises*
1. group, batch, bunch, pile, flock
5. (a) and (b)
7. *D* and *F*; *E* and *N*
9. The mathematician removed one rock from the pile as each person returned.
11. Pair off the blocks, taking one from each set. The larger set will have blocks left over that cannot be paired off.
13. (a) $A \subseteq B$    (b) $2 \notin T$
15. (a) $\subseteq$    (b) $\in$
17. (a) at least 4
    (b) All five permanent members joined with sets like the following:
    $\{T_1, T_2, T_3, T_4\}$
    $\{T_1, T_2, T_3, T_5\}$
    $\{T_1, T_2, T_3, T_6\}$
    $\{T_1, T_2, T_3, T_7\}$
    $\{T_1, T_2, T_3, T_8\}$
19. (a) 2    (b) 6    (c) 24
    (d) $N \cdot (N-1) \cdot (N-2) \cdots 2 \cdot 1$
21. (a) 3    (b) 5    (c) 7    (d) $2N - 1$
23. $KN - K + 1$
25. (b) Match each number in *W* with twice itself in *E*.
27. (a) positive multiples of 4
    (b) all whole numbers that end in a 3

**2.2** *Homework Exercises*
1. (a) {3, 9}    (b) {1, 3, 5, 6, 7, 9, 11, 12, 15, 18}
   (c) yes    (d) no
3. (a) yes
   (b)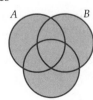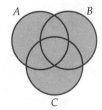

5. (a) 5    (b) 3
7. (a) 14    (b) 4
9. rain or cold or both
11. (a) $\in$    (b) $\cap$    (c) $\subseteq$
13. $A = \{1\}$ and $B = \{1, 2\}$

15. (a)

    (b)

17. (a) II    (b) III    (c) IV
19. (a) red blocks and triangle blocks
    (b) red triangles
21. I is small rectangles that are not blue; II is small blue shapes that are not rectangles; III is small, blue rectangles; and IV is blue rectangles that are not small.
23. (a) The left inner circle is BLUE, the left outer circle is TRIANGLES, and the right-hand circle is RECTANGLES.
    (b) The left circle is RED, the middle circle is TRIANGLES, and the right circle is BLUE.
25. (a) 2    (b) 7    (c) 8    (d) 3
27. (a) false    (b) false    (c) true    (d) false
29. $A = \{1, 2, 3\}$ and $B = \{$red, blue$\}$
31. 90
33. (a) 136%
    (b) Some people put down more than one response.
35. (a) female education majors
    (b) set *U*    (c) { }

37. (a)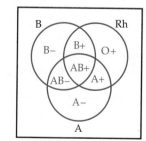

**37.** (b)

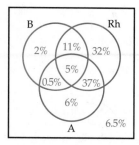

**39.** (b)

**41.** Each line perpendicular to $\overline{AC}$ will match up a point from $\overline{AC}$ with a point from $\overline{AB} \cup \overline{BC}$.

**43.** could be

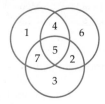

## Chapter 2 *Review Exercises*

**1.**

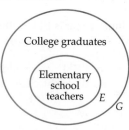

$E \subseteq G$

**2.** thin, red and not triangles
**3.** All are true.
**4.** (a) ∩     (b) ∈
**5.** 8
**6.** (a) 700     (b) 1000
**7.** (a) 8     (b) 6
**8.** 5
**9.** (a) 4     (b) 14

## Chapter 2 *Computer Exercises*

**1.** (b) numbers between 9 and 100 (excluding 9 and 100)
    (c) prints all numbers

## Chapter 3

### 3.1 *Homework Exercises*

**1.** (a) numeral     (b) number

**3.** ꝯꝯꝯ∩∩||||||||

**5.** (a) yes
    (b) Changing the position of different symbols in a Hindu-Arabic numeral changes the value of the numeral.

**7.** (a) 642     (b) 8     (c) 6

**9.** $(A \times 1000) + (B \times 100) + (C \times 10) + D$

**11.** (a) 8062     (b) 23,405

**13.** 3124

**15.** (a) 3 greens, 7 blues, and 2 yellows     (b) green
    (c) Chip trading is more abstract because chips for 1, 10, 100, and 1000 are all the same size, whereas the value of a base-ten block is proportional to its size.

**17.** (a) $600     (b) $36,400

**19.** 2 million

**21.** 499,999

**25.** 6,210,001,000

**27.** (a) 13     (b) $10{,}001_{two}$     (c) $10{,}010_{two}$

**29.** sixty

### 3.2 *Homework Exercises*

**1.** (a)

**3.** (a) combine measures
    (b) the sale price, the current value, the size and condition of the house, the location of the house

**5.** (a) $3 + 5 = 8$     (b) combine measures

**7.** compare measures

**9.** Take 14 blocks. Now remove 3. How many are left? 11. So $14 - 3 = 11$.

**11.** (a) $5 - 3 = 2$     (b) compare measures

**13.** (a) ⊗⊗◯◯◯◯◯◯◯

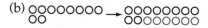

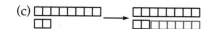

**15.** Problem (a) is about sharing and emphasizes cooperation. Problem (b) has a materialistic and competitive theme.

**17.** Because the enjoyment tends to diminish with each additional dish of ice cream.

**19.** addition, combine sets

**21.** I ran 2 miles yesterday and 3 miles today. How far did I run all together during the 2 days?

**23.** I have 10 oranges. I give 3 to Bill and 5 to Susan. How many do I have left?

**25.**

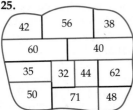

**27.** (a) right
(b) For whole numbers $a$ and $b$, $a < b$ means $a$ is located to the left of $b$ on the number line.
**29.** The 2 should be subtracted from the 27, not added. The women first paid $30 and then got $3 back. So they ended up paying $27, $2 to the bellhop and $25 for the room.
**31.** if $(a - b) \geq c$
**33.** $\{0\}$
**35.** (a)

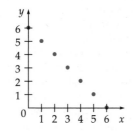

(b) They all lie on a straight line.
(c)

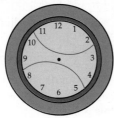

(d) They all lie on a straight line.
(e) If the ordered pairs of any fact family are plotted on a graph, the points will lie on a straight line.
(f) induction
**37.** (a)

(b)

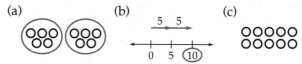

**39.** If 9 were in a corner, then the row, column, and diagonal containing the 9 would all need 6 more to make 15. But there are only 2 ways (not 3) to make 6 more (1 and 5 or 2 and 4).
**41.** $A = 9$, $B = 2$

### 3.3 Homework Exercises
**1.** $3 \cdot 7$
**3.** repeated measures
**5.** repeated sets
**7.** Problem (b) is much more likely to occur in everyday life.
**9.**
(a)      (b)      (c)

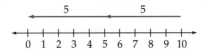

**11.** (a) 74 and $X^2 + 10$    (b) 38 and $4X - 2$
(c) inductive
**13.** (a) $3^2$    (b) $4^3$
**15.** partition measures
**17.** repeated measures
**19.** (a) $8 \div 4 = 2$
(b) Start at 10 on the number line. How many jumps of 5 will it take to get back to 0? 2 jumps. So $10 \div 5 = 2$.

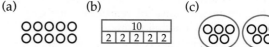

**21.**
(a)      (b)      (c)

**23.** (a) If he puts a maximum of 4 on a page, how many pages will he need?
(b) If he puts 4 on each page, how many extra photographs will be left over?
(c) If 4 photographs fill a page, how many pages can he fill?

**25.** (a) 1     (b) 2     (c) quotient     (d) remainder
**27.** The expression $7 \div 0 = ?$ is the same as $? \times 0 = 7$, which has no answer. So we make $7 \div 0$ undefined.
**29.** some sort of error message; the problem is undefined
**31.** $N/3 - 2$
**33.** 36
**35.** I have 40 pistachio nuts to share equally with you. How many will we each get?
**37.** 608
**39.** $n^2 - (n - 2)^2$ or $4n - 4$
**41.** (a) multiplication, row-by-column sets and subtraction, take away sets
    (b) multiplication, repeated sets and addition, combine sets
**43.** (a) addition, combine sets/measures and subtraction, take away sets/measures, or both subtraction, take away sets/measures
    (b) multiplication, row-by-column sets and subtraction, take away sets
**45.** A school is charging \$3 for lunch and \$6 for a concert. How much will it cost to buy 7 tickets for both events?
**47.** $c/2$
**49.** (a) 5     (b) 1, 5, or 6
**51.** Pour 3 cupfuls into the glass to get 6 oz. Then fill one cup. Pour from one cup into the other until both cups are at the same level. Then each has 1 oz. Pour one of them into the glass.
**53.** They are both odd.
**55.** (a) correct     (b) incorrect
**57.** Take out 1 chip. On successive turns, reduce the pot to 7 chips, 4 chips, and finally 1 chip.
**59.** (a) multiplication, repeated sets
    (b) division, partition sets
**61.** 420
**63.** $1.2(B + C + D + E + F)/A$

### 3.4 *Homework Exercises*

**1.** Multiply any two of the numbers first. Then multiply the answer times the remaining number.
**3.** commutative, multiplication
**5.**

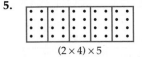     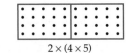

$(2 \times 4) \times 5 \qquad = \qquad 2 \times (4 \times 5)$

**7.** $(8 - 4) - 2 \neq 8 - (4 - 2)$
**9.** Multiply $6 \times 5$ first and then multiply $30 \times 9 = \$270$.

**11.** Each fact that you learn in one order has the same answer when the order of the factors is reversed.
**13.** (b)
**15.** (a) *Hint:* $37 \times 12 = (37 \times 3) \times 4$
**17.** 0, identity, addition
**19.** $(12 \times 34) - 48 = (12 \times 34) - (12 \times 4) = 12 \times (34 - 4) = 12 \times 30 = 360$
**21.** $10 \times (8 + 4)$ or $(10 \times 8) + (10 \times 4) = 120$ ft$^2$
**23.** associative property of addition
**25.** Start with 1 hundred, 8 tens, and 2 ones, and 3 hundreds, 3 tens, and 6 ones. Combine 2 ones and 6 ones to obtain 8 ones. Combine 8 tens and 3 tens to obtain 11 tens. Trade 10 tens for 1 hundred, leaving 1 ten. Combine 1 hundred, 1 hundred, and 3 hundreds to obtain 5 hundreds. The answer is 5 hundreds, 1 ten, 8 ones = 518.
**27.** Addition is associative; addition is commutative; addition is associative; addition is commutative; addition is associative.
**29.** Start with 3 hundreds, 3 tens, and 6 ones. Take away 2 ones, leaving 4 ones. You can't take away 8 tens from 3 tens. Regroup 3 hundreds and 3 tens as 2 hundreds and 13 tens. Take away 8 tens from 13 tens, leaving 5 tens. Take away 1 hundred from 2 hundreds, leaving 1 hundred. The difference is 1 hundred, 5 tens, and 4 ones = 154.
**31.** distributive property of multiplication over addition
**33.**

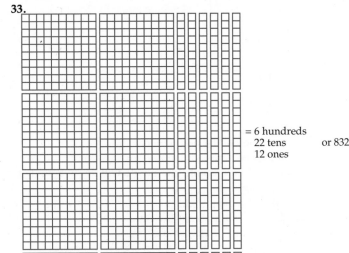

= 6 hundreds
22 tens          or 832
12 ones

**35.** 6 tens $\times$ 3 = 18 tens. 19 tens − 18 tens leaves 1 ten and 7 ones from the next column. The total remaining at this point is 17.

**37.** (a) 175
  (b) adding the number of ones in the second addend to the number of tens in the first addend
**39.** (a) 75
  (b) borrowing 1 ten without subtracting it from the tens column
**41.** (a) 638
  (b) failing to carry the tens from the right-hand multiplication to the tens column
**43.** (a) 46
  (b) placing the digits in the quotient from right to left
**45.** A child might forget to put the 0 in the product, or a child might make an error on a multiplication fact.
**47.** (a) 29    (b) 167
**49.** (a) 1456    (b) 2286
**51.** Take 7 sets of 6 ones to make 42 ones. Trade 40 ones for 4 tens. Then, 7 sets of 2 tens makes 14 tens, plus 4 tens makes 18 tens. Trade 10 tens for 1 hundred. This makes 1 hundred, 8 tens, and 2 ones = 182.
**53.** 372 R 13 (Multiply the decimal remainder by 23.)
**55.** (a) It doubles.    (b) $2a + 2b = 2(a + b)$
  (c) inductive    (d) deductive
**57.** Multiplication over addition is distributive; multiplication over addition is distributive; addition is commutative; addition is commutative.
**59.** (e) The tens digit is 9 and the sum of the ones and hundreds digits is 9.
  (f) inductive
**61.** The dividend could be 1230 or 1236, and the quotient would be 205 or 206, respectively.
**63.** (a) yes    (b) no    (c) no    (d) no

### 3.5 Homework Exercises

**1.** (a) $39 + 90 = 129$ and $129 + 7 = 136$ miles
  (b) commutative property of addition
**3.** $5^3 = 125$ and triple the number of zeroes to obtain 6 zeroes in the answer, 125,000,000.
**5.** $4 \times 3 = 12$ and add the number of zeroes in the two factors to obtain the number of zeroes (5) in the product, 1,200,000 people.
**7.** Round it to $6000 + 8000 + 4000$. Add $6 + 8 + 4 = 18$ and attach three zeroes. 18,000.
**9.** (a) Change $437 \div 55$ to compatible numbers like $400 \div 50 = 8$ hours.
  (b) repeated measures
**11.** If 9000 people attend a game, and each person

paid $8 admission, what is the total amount of sales in dollars?
**13.** too high
**15.** (a) 8    (b) 28    (c) 36    (d) 26    (e) 17
**17.** add $3 + 1 + 21 \approx \$25$ million
**19.** (a) $5 \cdot (800) = 4000$    (b) $4 \cdot (40,000) = 160,000$
**21.** Multiply $18 \times 24$ on the calculator and place two zeroes on the end.
**25.** (a) 225, 625, 1225
  (b) The product ends in 5. Then multiply the tens digit $t$ times $(t + 1)$ to obtain the left-hand digits of the product.
**27.** (a) $631 \times 542$ (guess and check)
  (b) same problem, but use 1, 2, 3, 7, 8, and 9 as the digits
**29.** (a) is the largest; (c) is the smallest
**31.** (a) wrong; the answer should be about $3 \cdot (600) = 1800$
  (b) reasonable, since $30 \times 50 = 1500$
  (c) wrong; the answer should be about $4000 \div 20 = 200$
**33.** (a) calculator; too difficult to do another way
  (b) mental computation (add $750 + 250$ first)
  (c) paper-and-pencil or calculator, depending upon which is more convenient
**35.** (a) $389 + 895 = 384 + 900 = 1284$
  (b) $4990 + 3627 = 5000 + 3617 = 8617$
  (c) $762 - 89 = 763 - 90 = 673$
**37.** (a) $8 \times 1000 - 8 = 7992$    (b) 5994
  (c) $a \times 999 = a \times (1000 - 1) = a \times 1000 - a$
**39.** (a) 24 plus half of 24, and add a 0 on the right.
  $24 + 12 = 36 \rightarrow 360$    (b) 630
**41.** 10 million $\times 70 \times 30$. Now $7 \times 3 = 21$, and there are three zeroes in the factors. The answer is 21,000 million or 21 billion gallons.

### 3.6 Homework Exercises

**1.** (a) 1 eight and 4 ones    (b) 2 fives and 2 ones
**3.** $1_{three}$, $2_{three}$, $10_{three}$, $11_{three}$, $12_{three}$, $20_{three}$, $21_{three}$, $22_{three}$, $100_{three}$, $101_{three}$, $102_{three}$, $110_{three}$
**5.** (a) 61    (b) 113    (c) 139
**7.** (a) 3 quarters, 2 nickels, and 1 penny
  (b) $86 = 321_{five}$
**9.** The last digit is 0.
**11.** $1011_{five}$
**13.** $1314_{five}$
**15.** (a) $13_{five}$    (b) $124_{five}$    (c) $234_{five}$
**17.** Start with 4 longs (1 by 5) and 3 ones. Now take away $24_{five}$ starting with the ones. You cannot

take 4 ones from 3 ones, so trade one of the 4 longs for 5 ones. Now you can take away $24_{five}$ from 3 longs and 8 ones. 8 ones − 4 ones = 4 ones and 3 longs − 2 longs = 1 long. There is 1 long and 4 ones left, so $43_{five} - 24_{five} = 14_{five}$.

**19.** (a) $24_{five}$ R 2      (b) $1204_{five}$ R 1

**21.**

| + | 0 | 1 | 2 | 3 | 4 | 5 | 6 | 7 |
|---|---|---|---|---|---|---|---|---|
| 0 | 0 | 1 | 2 | 3 | 4 | 5 | 6 | 7 |
| 1 | 1 | 2 | 3 | 4 | 5 | 6 | 7 | 10 |
| 2 | 2 | 3 | 4 | 5 | 6 | 7 | 10 | 11 |
| 3 | 3 | 4 | 5 | 6 | 7 | 10 | 11 | 12 |
| 4 | 4 | 5 | 6 | 7 | 10 | 11 | 12 | 13 |
| 5 | 5 | 6 | 7 | 10 | 11 | 12 | 13 | 14 |
| 6 | 6 | 7 | 10 | 11 | 12 | 13 | 14 | 15 |
| 7 | 7 | 10 | 11 | 12 | 13 | 14 | 15 | 16 |

| × | 0 | 1 | 2 | 3 | 4 | 5 | 6 | 7 |
|---|---|---|---|---|---|---|---|---|
| 0 | 0 | 0 | 0 | 0 | 0 | 0 | 0 | 0 |
| 1 | 0 | 1 | 2 | 3 | 4 | 5 | 6 | 7 |
| 2 | 0 | 2 | 4 | 6 | 10 | 12 | 14 | 16 |
| 3 | 0 | 3 | 6 | 11 | 14 | 17 | 22 | 25 |
| 4 | 0 | 4 | 10 | 14 | 20 | 24 | 30 | 34 |
| 5 | 0 | 5 | 12 | 17 | 24 | 31 | 36 | 43 |
| 6 | 0 | 6 | 14 | 22 | 30 | 36 | 44 | 52 |
| 7 | 0 | 7 | 16 | 25 | 34 | 43 | 52 | 61 |

**23.** (a) $25_{eight}$      (b) $244_{eight}$ R 2

**25.** (a) 1, 2, 3, 4, . . . 15 pounds
     (b) 1, 2, 4, and 8 pound weights
     (c) same problem with 1 to 100 pounds

**27.** (a) 182      (b) $10,110,110_{two}$
     (c) The ones digit occupies the first 4 columns in base 2 and 6 → 0110. The sixteens digit occupies the next 4 columns to the left in base 2 and B → 1011. So $B6_{sixteen} = 10,110,110_{two}$.

**29.** (a) 10 is on the second and fourth cards, so you would add 2 + 8 = 10.
     (b) The numbers in the upper left-hand corners of the four cards correspond to the first four place values of base two: ones, twos, fours, eights. The numbers from 1 to 15 are converted to base two and written on the corresponding place-value cards for which they have one as a digit.

**31.** (a) 464      (b) $328_{twelve} = 464$

**33.** (a) $2434_{six}$      (b) $121,110_{four}$

**35.** $1024_{five}$

**37.** $30,424_{six}$

**39.** (a) 4      (b) $26_{five} = 121_b$. What base is $b$?

**41.** $b$ is any whole number greater than 7.

## Chapter 3 *Review Exercises*

**1.** (a)

     (b) commutative property of multiplication

**2.** $362 - 187 = 375 - 200 = 175$

**3.** true for $A = 0$ and $B = C = 1$ and false for $A = B = C = 1$

**4.** (a) $8 \times 40 = 320$
     (b) distributive property of multiplication over addition

**5.** nearest hundred

**6.** In a place-value system, the position of the digit determines its value. In a system that does not have place value, the value of a digit is the same regardless of its position.

**7.** $3 \div 0 = ?$ is the same as $? \times 0 = 3$, which has no solution. So we make $3 \div 0$ undefined.

**8.** (a) 37      (b) 2      (c) 6

**9.**

**10.** (a) Change to compatible $2400 \div 40 = 60$ gallons.
     (b) repeated measures

**11.** (a) no      (b) $8 \div (4 \div 2) \neq (8 \div 4) \div 2$.

**12.** division, repeated sets

**13.** subtraction, compare sets

**14.** multiplication, repeated sets and subtraction, take away sets

**15.** subtraction, take away measures and division, repeated measures

**16.** (a) 1513      (b) 240      (c) 2836

**17.** Represent the numbers with base-ten blocks. The first is 3 flats, 2 longs, and 6 units; the second is 2 flats, 9 longs, and 3 units. Add the ones, then the tens, and then the hundreds. 6 units plus 3 units makes *9 units*. 2 longs plus 9 longs makes 11 longs. Trade in 10 longs for 1 flat and you have *1 long left over*. Finally, combine this 1 flat with 3 flats plus 2 flats for a total of *6 flats*. The answer is 6 flats, 1 long, and 9 units or 619.

**18.** $77 + 666 = 743$

**19.** $HD - S$ dollars

**20.** $46

**21.** $244_{six}$

**22.** $150_{seven}$ R $4_{seven}$

**23.** $b$ is whole number $\geq 3$; $a = 2b + 1$

**Chapter 3** *Computer Exercise*

**1.** (a) 3   6   9   12   15   18 (and so on with each number on a new line)

(b) 10 LET N = 5
      20 LET N = N + 5

(c) 3   9   27   81   243 (and so on with each number on a new line)

**Chapter 4**

**4.1** *Homework Exercises*

**1.** (a) 1, 2, 4, 7, 14, 28

(b) There is no whole number $c$ such that $6 \cdot c = 28$.

**3.** true

**5.** 1210

**7.** true, $A = 4$, $B = 8$, $K = 3$

**9.** true, $A = 2$, $B = 10$, $C = 20$

**11.** true, $A = 2$, $B = 4$, $C = 6$

**13.** 3, $B$, $A$, $B$

**15.** Divisibility-of-a-Product Theorem

**17.** $8 \mid (C + 16)$

**19.** $A \mid 8C$

**21.** false, $B = 5$

**23.** true, by the Divisibility-of-a-Product Theorem, if $A \mid B$ then $A \mid B \cdot B$ or $A \mid B^2$.

**25.** true, by the Divisibility-of-a-Product Theorem, if $2 \mid B$ then $2 \mid BC$. So $BC$ is divisible by 2.

**27.** true

 1. $A \mid B$, $B \mid C$, and $A \neq 0$
 2. $A \cdot K = B$ and $B \cdot L = C$, in which $K$ and $L$ are whole numbers
 3. $A \cdot K \cdot L = C$ and $KL$ is a whole number
 4. $A \mid C$

**29.** true

 1. $C$ and $D$ are odd numbers
 2. $C = 2W + 1$ and $D = 2X + 1$, in which $W$ and $X$ are whole numbers
 3. $CD = (2W + 1)(2X + 1) =$ $4XW + 2X + 2W + 1$
 4. $CD = 2(XW + X + W) + 1$ and $(XW + X + W)$ is a whole number
 5. $CD$ is odd

**31.** $N^3 - N = N(N + 1)(N - 1)$. Either $N - 1$, $N$, or

$N + 1$ must be divisible by 3. By the Divisibility-of-a-Product Theorem, $N^3 - N$ must be divisible by 3. So $3 \mid (N^3 - N)$.

**4.2** *Homework Exercises*

**1.** 0, 7, 14, 21, . . .

**3.** There is no whole number $C$ such that $6 \cdot C = 3$.

**5.** (a) factor      (b) factor      (c) multiple

(d) factor

**7.** no

**9.** (a) 1, 4, or 7      (b) The last digit is 0.

(c) 1, 4, or 7 followed by 0

**11.** (a) no

(b) Any amount made with \$.25 and \$.15 stamps must be divisible by 5.

**13.** (a) false      (b) 15      (c)

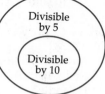

**15.** (a) false      (b) 24      (c)

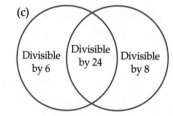

**17.** 1, 3, and 5

**19.** $\underline{A}\ \underline{B}\ \underline{C} = 100 \cdot A + 10 \cdot B + C$, in which $C = 0$, 2, 4, 6, or 8. Now $100 \cdot A$, $10 \cdot B$, and $C$ are each divisible by 2. By the Divisibility-of-a-Sum Theorem, $100 \cdot A + 10 \cdot B + C$, in which $C = 0, 2$, 4, 6, or 8 is divisible by 2.

**21.** (a) last 2 digits are 0      (b) (1), (3), (4)

**23.** The last 2 digits are divisible by 25.

**25.** (a) The last digit must be 0 or 4.

(b) for 2, the last digit must be 0, 2, 4, or 6; for 7, the sum of the digits must be divisible by 7

**27.** 222,456,564

**29.** false, 15 with $A = 2$ and $B = 3$

**31.** true

 1. $A$ is a multiple of $B$
 2. $A = KB$ for some whole number $K$
 3. $2A = 2KB$ where $2K$ is a whole number
 4. $2A$ is a multiple of $B$

**33.** (a) or (b)

**35.** (a) yes     (b) yes     (c) Let the larger number be $\underline{A}\,\underline{B}$. Then $\underline{A}\,\underline{B} - \underline{B}\,\underline{A} = (10A + B) - (10B + A) = 9A - 9B = 9(A - B)$, which must be divisible by 9.

**37.** (a) yes     (b) yes
(c) All 8-digit numbers of the form $\underline{A}\,\underline{B}\,\underline{C}\,\underline{D}\,\underline{A}\,\underline{B}\,\underline{C}\,\underline{D}$ are divisible by 73.
(d) $\underline{A}\,\underline{B}\,\underline{C}\,\underline{D}\,\underline{A}\,\underline{B}\,\underline{C}\,\underline{D} = A \cdot 10,000,000 + B \cdot 1,000,000 + C \cdot 100,000 + D \cdot 10,000 + A \cdot 1000 + B \cdot 100 + C \cdot 10 + D = A \cdot 10,001,000 + B \cdot 1,000,100 + C \cdot 100,010 + D \cdot 10,001$
The numbers 10,001,000; 1,000,100; 100,010; and 10,001 are all divisible by 73, so $A \cdot 10,001,000 + B \cdot 1,000,100 + C \cdot 100,010 + D \cdot 10,001$, which equals $\underline{A}\,\underline{B}\,\underline{C}\,\underline{D}\,\underline{A}\,\underline{B}\,\underline{C}\,\underline{D}$, is divisible by 73.

**39.** (c) yes     (d) yes     (e) yes     (g) 1001
(h) 382,382
(i) Any number of the form $\underline{A}\,\underline{B}\,\underline{C}\,\underline{A}\,\underline{B}\,\underline{C}$ is divisible by 1001, so it must also be divisible by 7, 11, and 13.

### 4.3 *Homework Exercises*

**1.** (a) prime

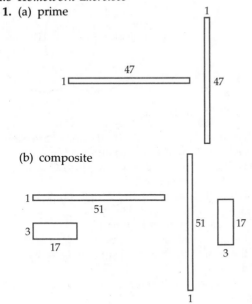

(b) composite

**3.** All the results are prime.
**5.** (a) 257

(b) 4,294,967,297 and 4,294,967,297 ÷ 641 = 6,700,417

**7.** 2, 3, 5, 7, 11, 13, 17, 19
**9.** (a) prime     (b) composite
**11.** exactly one prime factorization
**13.** (a) $76 = 2^2 \cdot 19$     (b) $320 = 2^6 \cdot 5$
**15.** 101 and 103, 107 and 109, 137 and 139, 149 and 151, 179 and 181, 191 and 193, 197 and 199
**17.** (a) 5 + 7     (b) 13 + 17 or 11 + 19 or 23 + 7
(c) 5 + 103 is one answer.
**19.** $17 = 1 + 4^2, 37 = 1 + 6^2, 101 = 1 + 10^2$
**21.** (a) 6     (b) 6
(c) Either at the beginning or second from the end of a row.
(d) $(6n + 1)^2 + 17 = 36n^2 + 12n + 18 = 12(3n^2 + n + 1) + 6$, which will have remainder 6 when divided by 12. $(6n - 1)^2 + 17 = 36n^2 - 12n + 18 = 12(3n^2 - n + 1) + 6$, which will have remainder 6 when divided by 12.
**23.** start at 27,722
**25.** (a) $2 \times 3 \times 5 \times 7 + 1 = 211, 2 \times 3 \times 5 \times 7 \times 11 + 1 = 2311$
(b) yes
(c) $22 \times 3 \times 5 \times 7 \times 11 \times 13 + 1 = 30,031$ and $30,031 \div 59 = 509$
**27.** (a) no     (b) yes
**29.** (a) It is divisible by 3, 5, 7, 11, 13, etc.
(b) It is divisible by 2.     (c) It is divisible by 5.
**31.** (g) 2, 3, 5, 7, 11, 13, 17, 19, 23, 29, 31, 37, 41, 43, 47

### 4.4 *Homework Exercises*

**1.** (a)

| Factors of 10 | | Factors of 24 |
| --- | --- | --- |
| 5 | 1 | 3 |
| 10 | 2 | 4   12 |
| | | 6   24 |
| | | 8 |

(b) 1 and 2     (c) 2
**3.** 18
**5.** (a) 1, 2, 1, 4, 1, 2, 1, 4
(b) The sequence of GCF's will have the repeating pattern 1, 2, 1, 4, 1, 2, 1, 4, . . .

**7.** $2^2 \cdot 3 \cdot 5^6$

**9.** (a) and (c)

**11.** (a) 60, 120, 180    (b) an infinite number

   (c) 60

**13.**

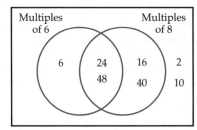

**15.** 4320

**17.** 15

**19.** (a) $2^3 \cdot 3^4 \cdot 5^7 \cdot 7 \cdot 11$    (b) $2 \cdot 3^2 \cdot 5 \cdot 11$

**21.** $2 \cdot 3^2 \cdot 5^4 \cdot 7$

**23.** none

**25.** (b)

**27.** (a) $2^{10}$    (b) $10^6$

**29.** true, $A = 2$ and $B = 8$

**31.** $3y$

**33.** (b) and (c)

**35.** 6 in. by 6 in.

**37.** (b) $ab = \text{GCF}(a, b) \cdot \text{LCM}(a, b)$

**39.** (a) $104 \div 40 = 2 \text{ R } 24 \rightarrow 40 \div 24 = 1 \text{ R } 16 \rightarrow$
   $24 \div 16 = 1 \text{ R } 8 \rightarrow 16 \div 8 = 2$. So
   $\text{GCF}(40, 104) = 8$.

   (b) $\text{GCF}(40, 104) = \text{GCF}(24, 40) = \text{GCF}(16, 24) = \text{GCF}(8, 16) = 8$

**Chapter 4** *Review Exercises*

**1.** 840

**2.** There is a whole number $C$ such that $8 \cdot C = N$.

**3.** $312 = 2^3 \cdot 3 \cdot 13$

**4.** 3 and 7

**5.** 4, GCF

**6.** $x - 2$ is a factor of any whole number multiplied by $x - 2$, including $(x + 3)(x - 2)$.

**7.** true, $A = 2$, $B = 4$, $C = 5$

**8.** true, $\text{GCF}(3, 7) = 1$

**9.** true, $A = 3$ and $B = 6$

**10.** true, $XY \mid Z$ and $XY \mid XY$. So $XY \mid (XY + Z)$.

**11.** false, 2 and 4

**12.** 0, 3, 6, or 9 followed by 0

**13.** (a) $2 \cdot 5^2 \cdot 11^2$    (b) $2^3 \cdot 3 \cdot 5^4 \cdot 11^3$

**14.** 2, 3, 5, 7, 11, 13, 17, 19, 23

**15.** $\underline{A} \ \underline{B} \ \underline{5} = A \cdot 100 + B \cdot 10 + 5$ and $\underline{A} \ \underline{B} \ \underline{0} =$
   $A \cdot 100 + B \cdot 10$. Now $A \cdot 100$, $B \cdot 10$, and 5 are
   all divisible by 5. Therefore, $A \cdot 100 + B \cdot 10 + 5$
   and $A \cdot 100 + B \cdot 10$ are divisible by 5.

**Chapter 4** *Computer Exercise*

**1.** (b) The second number in each pair is not a whole number.

   (c) prime    (d) composite

**Chapter 5**

**5.1** *Homework Exercises*

**−1.** (a) loss of yardage

   (b) more exports than imports

   (c) below sea level

**1.** (a), (b), and (d)

**3.** −1

**5.** (a) none

   (b) integers greater than or equal to 0

   (c) integers less than 0

**7.** (a) 3    (b) 7    (c) $-x$

**9.** $-4 + -2 = -6$

**11.** (a) Go to $-5$. Add the second number 3 by moving 3 to the right from $-5$. You end up at $-2$. So $-5 + 3 = -2$.

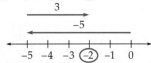

   (b) combine measures

**13.** (a) $86 + -30 + -20 = \$36$

   (b) combine sets/measures

**15.** $2 + -1 = 1$, $2 + -2 = 0$

**17.** (a) $10 + ? = 7$    (b) $-2 + ? = -3$

**19.** (b)

**21.** It is $-6°$ and the temperature drops $4°$. What is the new temperature? $-10°$. So $-6 - 4 = -10$.

**23.** $5 - 1 = 4$, $5 - 0 = 5$, $5 - (-1) = 6$, $5 - (-2) = 7$

**25.** Go to 5. Subtracting $-2$ is the opposite of adding $-2$, so go 2 to the right. You end up at 7. So $5 - (-2) = 7$.

**27.** (a) $-73$    (b) $38$
**29.** (c)
**31.** true
**33.** (a) $-10 - 30 = -40$    (b) $-40$ ft
(c) take away measures
**35.** (a) loss of 7 yards
(b) addition, combine measures or subtraction,
take away measures
**37.** Wang: change $= -3$, Texas Oil and Gas: Tues.
price $= \$83$, K-Mart: Mon. price $= \$55$
**39.**

**41.** (a) all odd integers
(b) all positive and negative multiples of 3
**43.** 7 and $-3$
**45.** (a) true, $x = 3$, $y = 2$    (b) false if $x < y$
**47.**

| $-12$ | $9$ | $-6$ |
|---|---|---|
| $3$ | $-3$ | $-9$ |
| $0$ | $-15$ | $6$ |

**49.** (b) smoking, weight, and family health


**5.2** *Homework Exercises*
**1.** $-5 \cdot -1 = 5$, $-5 \cdot -2 = 10$
**3.** (a) $-24$ pounds    (b) $-6 \times 4 = -24$
(c) repeated measures
**5.** Clem loses 5 pounds a week for 4 weeks in a row.
What is the total change in his weight?
**7.** It is now 0°C. The temperature has been dropping
6°C per hour. What was the temperature 4 hours
ago?
**9.** (a) At least one of $a$ and $b$ is 0.
(b) One of them is negative and the other one is
positive.
**11.** $x \cdot x \cdot x \cdot x$
**13.** (a) $-3 \times \underline{\hspace{1cm}} = 0$, 0
(b) $0 \times \underline{\hspace{1cm}} = -3$, undefined
**15.** (a) $-\$40,000$    (b) $-480,000 \div 12 = -40,000$
(c) partition sets/measures
**17.** You hope to lose 40 pounds at the rate of
5 pounds per week. How long will it take?
**19.** (b)
**21.** (a) 5, 7
(b) The sum of two negatives is a positive.
**23.** mixing up the addition and multiplication rules
**25.** (a) All are positive.    (b) One is 0.
(c) All are negative.
**27.** (a)

**29.** (a) $-8 + -8 + -8 + -8 = -32$
(b) $-5 + -5 = -10$
**31.** for all $x$ and $y$
**33.** positive, negative, positive

**5.3** *Homework Exercises*
**1.** (a) addition and multiplication
(b) addition and multiplication
**3.** Compute $-5 \times -8$ first and then multiply by 7.
**5.** commutative and associative properties of addition
**7.** Compute $-20 \times 6 + -7 \times 6$.
**9.** $(2 - 5)n$
**11.** (a) $(-12 \times 100) - (-12 \times 1) = -1188$
(b) distributive property of multiplication over
subtraction
(c) $-3366$
**13.** Any counterexample showing that whole-number
division is not associative would also show that integer division is not associative.
**15.** 1, identity element, multiplication
**17.** closure property of subtraction
**19.** (b)
**21.** 0.1
**23.** (a) $0 = 2 \cdot 4 + -2 \cdot 4$
(b) $0 = 2 \cdot 4 + -2 \cdot 4 = 8 + -2 \cdot 4$.
So $-2 \cdot 4 = -8$.
**25.** $(2m)(2n) = 4mn = 2(2mn)$, which is even.

**Chapter 5** *Review Exercises*
**1.** $8 - (4 - 2) \neq (8 - 4) - 2$
**2.** addition and multiplication
**3.** The temperature is now $-3$°C. If the temperature
drops 6°C, what will the new temperature be?
$-9$°C. So $-3 - 6 = -9$.
**4.** I now have $\$0$. I lost $\$5$ per hour. How much did I
have 3 hours ago?
**5.** $4 - 1 = 3$, $4 - 0 = 4$, $4 - (-1) = 5$,
$4 - (-2) = 6$
**6.** Go to $-4$. Subtracting $-2$ is the opposite of
adding $-2$, so move 2 to the right. You end up at
$-2$. So $-4 - (-2) = -2$.

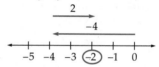

**7.** (a) 500 soldiers better
(b) $-300 - (-800) = 500$    (c) compare sets
**8.** (a) $-18 \div 9 = -2$ lb/month
(b) partition measures

**9.** (a) $-30 + 20 = -10$ ft

(b) addition, combine measures

**10.** when $a = b$ and neither is 0

**11.** (c)

**12.** (b) and (e)

**13.** additive inverses, closure for subtraction

### Chapter 5 *Computer Exercise*

**1.** (b) works for $x > 0$

### Chapter 6

**6.1 *Homework Exercises***

**1.** (c)

**3.** (a), (b), and (d)

**5.** (a)

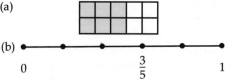

(b)

0        $\frac{3}{5}$     1

**7.** $\frac{1}{3}$ represents:

*Fraction of a whole*     *Fraction of a set/measure*

1 of 3 equal parts     1 out of every 3

*Division*
$1 \div 3$

Numerator ÷
denominator

*Number line location*

0     $\frac{1}{3}$

Divide the interval from 0 to 1 into 3 equal parts and count over 1

**9.** (a) (2)    (b) (4)    (c) (1)    (d) (3)

**11.** (a) $13 \div 3 = 4\frac{1}{3}$

(b) Show with a picture that 13 thirds make 4 wholes and 1 third.

**13.** $\frac{0}{5}$ means $0 \div 5$, which is 0.

**17.** (a) and (c)

**19.** Eating 4 pieces of a 4-slice pizza is 4/4, and eating 8 slices of an 8-slice pizza is 8/8. $4/4 = 8/8$.

**21.** $\frac{x}{y} = \frac{x \cdot 2x}{y \cdot 2x} = \frac{2x^2}{2xy}$

**23.** in writing a check

**25.** (a) 21/58    (b) $1/yz$    (c) 2/11    (d) 2

**27.** Both fractions represent the same amount.

**29.** $4 \cdot 9 = 6 \cdot 6; \frac{12}{18} = \frac{12}{18}; \frac{2}{3} = \frac{2}{3}$

**31.** (a) $2\frac{1}{2}$    (b) 6 or $-6$    (c) $\frac{5}{6}M$ if $M \neq 0$

**33.** 1600 say yes in the second group.

**35.** $\frac{60}{105} > \frac{56}{105}; 4 \cdot 15 > 8 \cdot 7$

**37.** What fraction of each class is girls? Which class has a higher proportion of boys?

**39.** (a) 1/13    (b) 3/13

**41.** 1/2

**43.** (a) yes    (b) reasonable

**45.** $a > b \rightarrow \frac{a}{ab} > \frac{b}{ab} \rightarrow \frac{1}{b} > \frac{1}{a}$

**6.2 *Homework Exercises***

**1.** (a) $3x/n$    (b) $2x/(x + 1)$

**3.** (a) $\frac{1}{3} + \frac{1}{4}$ would equal the shaded region shown, but we cannot name it unless we use a common denominator (twelfths).

$\boxed{\frac{1}{3}}\,\boxed{\frac{1}{4}}\,\square$

(b) $\frac{1}{3} + \frac{1}{4} = \frac{4}{12} + \frac{3}{12} = $ 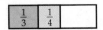 $= \frac{7}{12}$

**5.** (a) Show $\frac{1}{4}$.

$\boxed{\frac{1}{4}}\,\square\,\square\,\square$

Now take away $\frac{1}{6}$.

$\underbrace{\phantom{xxx}}_{\frac{1}{6}\text{ difference}}$

We cannot name the difference unless we use a common denominator (twelfths).

(b) $\frac{1}{4} - \frac{1}{6} = \frac{3}{12} - \frac{2}{12} = $ ▨ $= \frac{1}{12}$

**7.** 31/357

**9.** 67/1800

**11.** $4\frac{1}{5} = 4 + \frac{1}{5} = \frac{20}{5} + \frac{1}{5} = \frac{21}{5}$

**13.** (a) $2\frac{3}{4}$ hours

(b) subtraction, take away measures

**15.** You have a $5\frac{1}{4}$-hour job to do. You have been working for $2\frac{1}{2}$ hours. How much more time is

needed? $2\frac{3}{4}$ hours.

**17.** 5/12 and 1/6

**19.** (a) $\frac{1}{2} + \frac{1}{4}$    (b) $\frac{1}{13} + \frac{1}{26}$    (c) $\frac{1}{2} + \frac{1}{8}$

    (d) $\frac{1}{9} + \frac{1}{2} + \frac{1}{6}$

**21.** (a) 14     (b) 3

**23.** $\frac{a}{b} = \frac{c}{d} \rightarrow \frac{a}{b} + \frac{b}{b} = \frac{c}{d} + \frac{d}{d} \rightarrow \frac{a+b}{b} = \frac{c+d}{d}$

### 6.3 Homework Exercises

**1.** $3/4 \times \$1500 = \$1125$

**3.** $3 \times 3\frac{1}{2}$

**5.** $\frac{1}{5} \times \frac{1}{3}$ means $\frac{1}{5}$ of $\frac{1}{3}$. First show $\frac{1}{3}$.

Now darken $\frac{1}{5}$ of $\frac{1}{3}$.

$\frac{1}{15}$ of the figure is darkened. So $\frac{1}{5} \times \frac{1}{3} = \frac{1}{15}$.

**7.** $\frac{3}{4} \times \frac{4}{5}$ means $\frac{3}{4}$ of $\frac{4}{5}$. First show $\frac{4}{5}$.

Now darken $\frac{3}{4}$ of $\frac{4}{5}$.

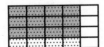

$\frac{12}{20}$ of the figure is darkened. So $\frac{3}{4} \times \frac{4}{5} = \frac{12}{20} = \frac{3}{5}$.

**9.** (a) $\frac{5}{9} \times \frac{7}{10} = \frac{\cancel{5}^1 \times 7}{9 \times \cancel{10}_2} = \frac{7}{18}$

    (b) $2\frac{1}{3} \times 1\frac{1}{5} = \frac{7}{3} \times \frac{6}{5} = \frac{7 \times \cancel{6}^2}{\cancel{3}_1 \times 5} = \frac{14}{5} = 2\frac{4}{5}$

**11.** $2 \div \frac{1}{4}$ means how many $\frac{1}{4}$'s does it take to make 2?

It takes 4 quarters to make 1. So, it takes 8 quarters to make 2. So $2 \div \frac{1}{4} = 8$.

**13.** How many dimes would make \$5?

**15.** 3 and 1/3

**17.** $\frac{1}{2} \div \frac{3}{4} = \dfrac{\frac{1}{2}}{\frac{3}{4}} = \dfrac{\frac{1}{2} \times \frac{4}{3}}{\frac{3}{4} \times \frac{4}{3}} = \dfrac{\frac{1}{2} \times \frac{4}{3}}{1} = \frac{1}{2} \times \frac{4}{3}$

**19.** (a) $1\frac{2}{5}$     (b) $3x/y$

**21.** $\frac{3}{2}$

**23.** $\frac{1}{6}$ cup

**25.** (a) $1\frac{1}{2}$ cups

    (b) multiplication, repeated measures

**27.** (a) 15     (b) division, repeated measures

**29.** \$154

**31.** \$12

**33.** If it takes 3/4 of an hour to write a page, about how long will it take to write 22 pages?

**35.** (a) 8 for Wacky, 6 for Harpo, and 3 for Young Loopy II

    (b) because the fractions $\frac{4}{9} + \frac{1}{3} + \frac{1}{6} = \frac{17}{18}$

    (c) debatable

**37.** (a) 20 ft    (b) 40 ft    (c) 50 ft    (d) 55 ft

    (e) a little less than 60 ft

**39.** $23\frac{1}{13}$ ft

**41.** 24 or 27

**43.** $\frac{1}{9}$

**45.** 6

**47.** (a) $3\frac{3}{4}$    (b) $8\frac{3}{4}$

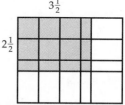

    (c) $15\frac{3}{4}$

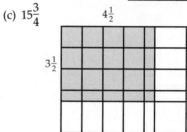

(d) The whole-number part is $b(b + 2)$, and the fraction part is $\frac{3}{4}$.

(e) $(18 \times 20) = 360 \rightarrow 360\frac{3}{4}$

**49.** (a) $x > 0$ and $y < 0$      (b) never

(c) $x$ and $y$ both positive or both negative

**51.** (a) $2^2$    (b) $2^3$    (c) $2^{N-1}$

(d) Write $\frac{1}{3}$ of $3^5$

as a power of 3. Next, do the same for $3^6$. Finally, generalize your results for $3^N$.

**53.** (a) $\frac{1}{3} \div \frac{3}{4} = \frac{1}{3} \times \frac{4}{3} = \frac{4}{9}$ or $\frac{1}{3} \div \frac{3}{4} = \frac{4}{12} \div \frac{9}{12} =$

$\frac{4}{12} \times \frac{12}{9} = \frac{4}{9}$.

**55.** $L/P$ days

**57.** Measure the thickness and divide by the number of pages. It should be about 3/1000 of a centimeter.

**6.4** *Homework Exercises*

**1.** (a) addition and multiplication

(b) addition and multiplication

**3.** $\left(\frac{1}{2} \cdot 4\right) \cdot x$

**5.** Multiply $\frac{1}{3} \times 18$ and $\frac{1}{5} \times 20$ first. Then

$6 \times 4 = 24$.

**7.** $2\frac{1}{2}$

**9.** $2 - 3 \neq 3 - 2$ would be a counterexample for whole numbers, integers, and rational numbers.

**11.** $\left(-\frac{4}{3} + \frac{2}{3}\right)n$

**13.** $-\frac{2}{5}$

**15.** (a) density      (b) multiplicative inverses

**17.** false

**19.** true

**21.** false for $a = -4$ and $b = c = d = -2$

**23.** $\frac{1}{4}$ of 40 is the same as $\frac{1}{4} \times 40 = 40 \times \frac{1}{4} =$

$40 \div 4$ or $\frac{1}{4} \times 40 = \frac{40}{4} = 40 \div 4$

**25.**

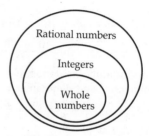

Rational numbers
Integers
Whole numbers

**27.** (a) $S = \dfrac{1 - \frac{1}{3^{40}}}{2}$    (b) $\dfrac{1 - \frac{1}{3^N}}{2}$ or $\dfrac{3^N - 1}{2 \cdot 3^N}$

**29.** $\left(\dfrac{u}{v} \cdot \dfrac{w}{x}\right) \cdot \dfrac{y}{z} = \dfrac{uw}{vx} \cdot \dfrac{y}{z} = \dfrac{uwy}{vxz}$ and

$\dfrac{u}{v} \cdot \left(\dfrac{w}{x} \cdot \dfrac{y}{z}\right) = \dfrac{u}{v} \cdot \dfrac{wy}{xz} = \dfrac{uwy}{vxz}$

**6.5** *Homework Exercises*

**1.** (a) $\frac{5}{6} + \frac{10}{11} \approx 1 + 1 = 2$      (b) too high

**3.** $5\frac{3}{4} \times 8\frac{1}{4} \approx 6 \times 8 = 48$ cups

**5.** too high

**7.** $62\frac{1}{2} \div 14\frac{3}{4} \approx 60 \div 15 = 4$ lessons

**9.** (a) 8      (b) 3

**11.** (b)

**13.** $6 \times 50 + \frac{1}{2} \times 50 = 300 + 25 = \$325$

**15.** (a) 100, 2 halves make 1 yard, so $50 \times 2$ or 100 halves make 50 yards.

(b) division, repeated measures

**17.** (d)

**19.** (a) mental computation      (b) paper-and-pencil

(c) calculator

**21.** (a) $1\frac{9}{3} = 4$, $4\frac{9}{5} = 5\frac{4}{5}$

(b) In regrouping, the child adds 10 to the numerator of the fraction.

**23.** (a) $\frac{5}{12}$, $\frac{11}{20}$

(b) After obtaining the common denominator, the child adds the numerators and denominators.

**25.** The child does not understand what a denominator represents.

**27.** (a) $\frac{1}{48}$, $\frac{1}{96}$      (b) $1/(3 \cdot 2^N)$

**29.** (c)

**31.** (a) $8\frac{1}{3} - 3\frac{2}{3} = 8\frac{2}{3} - 4 = 4\frac{2}{3}$

**31.** (b) $5\frac{1}{4} - 2\frac{3}{4} = 5\frac{1}{2} - 3 = 2\frac{1}{2}$

**33.** (a) $\dfrac{2}{(1+1)} \neq \dfrac{2}{1} + \dfrac{2}{1}$  (b) $\dfrac{(10+10)}{2} \neq \dfrac{10}{2} + 10$

**35.** (a) Add and multiply the denominators to get the new numerator and denominator, respectively.

(b) $\dfrac{1}{3} + \dfrac{1}{5} = \dfrac{8}{15}$ and $\dfrac{1}{2} + \dfrac{1}{6} = \dfrac{8}{12} = \dfrac{2}{3}$

(c) $\dfrac{1}{N} + \dfrac{1}{M} = \dfrac{M+N}{NM}$  (d) inductive

(e) $\dfrac{1}{N} + \dfrac{1}{M} = \dfrac{M}{NM} + \dfrac{N}{NM} = \dfrac{M+N}{NM}$

## Chapter 6 *Review Questions*

**1.** Compute $24 \times 2 = 48$ and $24 \times \dfrac{1}{2} = 12$.

$48 + 12 = 60$.

**2.** $A > 11\frac{3}{7}$

**3.** $\dfrac{5}{6}$ represents:

*Fraction of a whole*　　*Fraction of a set/measure*

5 of 6 equal parts　　5 out of every 6

*Division*　　*Number line location*
$5 \div 6$

Numerator $\div$　　$0 \qquad\qquad \frac{5}{6}\ 1$
denominator

Divide the interval from 0 to 1 into 6 equal parts and count over 5.

**4.**

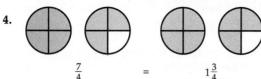

$\dfrac{7}{4} \qquad = \qquad 1\dfrac{3}{4}$

**5.** denseness or multiplicative inverses

**6.** (b)

**7.** $20\frac{3}{4}$

**8.** $\dfrac{5}{0}$ means $5 \div 0$. No number multiplied by 0 equals 5, so $5 \div 0$ and $\dfrac{5}{0}$ are both undefined.

**9.** (a) $6\frac{2}{3}$　　　(b) repeated measures

**10.** (a) $\dfrac{17}{30}$

(b) addition, combine sets/measures and subtraction, take away measures/sets

**11.** (a) $\dfrac{7}{20}$ lb　　(b) division, partition measures

**12.** (a) $\dfrac{4}{9} = \dfrac{20}{45}$ and $\dfrac{2}{5} = \dfrac{18}{45}$ so $\dfrac{4}{9} > \dfrac{2}{5}$

(b) $4 \cdot 5 > 2 \cdot 9$ so $\dfrac{4}{5} > \dfrac{2}{9}$

**13.** $\dfrac{2}{3} + \dfrac{1}{6}$ would equal the shaded region shown, but we cannot name it unless we use a common denominator (sixths).

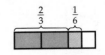

$\dfrac{2}{3} + \dfrac{1}{6} = \dfrac{4}{6} + \dfrac{1}{6} =$ ▭▭▭▭▭ $= \dfrac{5}{6}$

**14.** (a)

**15.** $\dfrac{2}{5} \div \dfrac{7}{9} = \dfrac{\frac{2}{5}}{\frac{7}{9}} = \dfrac{\frac{2}{5} \times \frac{9}{7}}{\frac{7}{9} \times \frac{9}{7}} = \dfrac{\frac{2}{5} \times \frac{9}{7}}{1} = \dfrac{2}{5} \times \dfrac{9}{7}$

**16.** (a) Multiply $\dfrac{1}{5} \times 15$ and $\dfrac{3}{4} \times 8$. Then $3 \times 6 = 18$.

(b) commutative and associative properties of multiplication

**17.** $5 \times (3 + 2) = 5 \times 3 + 5 \times 2$

**18.** $\dfrac{2}{3} \times \dfrac{3}{5}$ means $\dfrac{2}{3}$ of $\dfrac{3}{5}$.

Show $\dfrac{3}{5}$.

Now darken $\dfrac{2}{3}$ of $\dfrac{3}{5}$.

$\dfrac{6}{15}$ or $\dfrac{2}{5}$ is darkened. So $\dfrac{2}{3} \times \dfrac{3}{5} = \dfrac{2}{5}$.

**19.** (a) $1\frac{1}{3}$

(b) The child adds the denominators to obtain the common denominator. Then the child uses addition to obtain the new numerators.

(c) $\dfrac{1}{4} + \dfrac{2}{3} < \dfrac{1}{3} + \dfrac{2}{3}$ so the answer should be less than 1.

**Chapter 6** *Computer Exercise*

**1.** (b) It multiplies fractions.

(c) 30 PRINT A $*$ D "/" B $*$ C

**Chapter 7**

**7.1** *Homework Exercises*

**1.** $100, \dfrac{1}{100}$

**3.** (a) 41.16    (b) 7.005

**5.** Represent 0.40 as 40 small squares. Represent 0.4 as 4 columns.

$$0.40 \quad = \quad 0.4$$

**7.** (a) since 2.3 > 2.1

**9.** Extend $10^3 = 1000$, $10^2 = 100$, $10^1 = 10$. What would $10^0$ be to continue this pattern? $10^0 = 1$.

**11.** (a) $1/10^N$    (b) $1/X^N$

**13.** (a) $2^2$

(b) Subtract the exponent of the denominator from the exponent of the numerator.

(c) $10^3$    (d) $5^{10}$    (e) $x^4$

**15.** $0.321 + 0.127 = \dfrac{321}{1000} + \dfrac{127}{1000} = \dfrac{(321 + 127)}{1000}$

**17.**

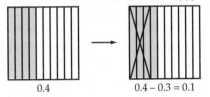

$$0.4 \qquad\qquad 0.4 - 0.3 = 0.1$$

**19.** *Example:* The Russells buy 2 orders of Szechuan chicken and 1 order of Hunan shrimp. What is their total bill before tax?

**21.** $0.6 \times 0.7 = 0.42$

**23.** $(2.64)(0.3) = \dfrac{264}{100} \cdot \dfrac{3}{10} = 264 \cdot 3 \cdot \left(\dfrac{1}{100} \cdot \dfrac{1}{10}\right) =$

$264 \cdot 3 \cdot \dfrac{1}{1000}$

**25.** (a) 72 calories    (b) repeated measures

**27.** 10

**29.** (a) $1000 \div 4 = 250$    (b) $24 \div 2 = 12$

**31.** division, repeated measures

**33.** multiplication, repeated sets/measures and addition, combine sets/measures

**35.** $\dfrac{10}{3}$

**37.** 0.00128

**39.** 300,000

**41.** (a) 1.5, 2.5    (b) $3 \times 4 + 0.25 = (3.5)^2$

(c) yes

**43.** (a) $23    (b) $183

**45.** about $40 to $75 (depends upon gas mileage)

**47.** (a)

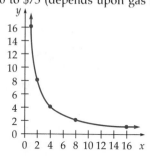

(b)

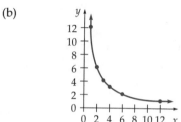

(c) The graph always has the same general shape. It approaches the positive $y$-axis at one end and the positive $x$-axis at the other end.

**49.** (b) $12.00, $13.01, $14.02, $15.03, $16.04, $18.06, or $19.07

**51.** none

**53.** (a) $\dfrac{1}{5}$ and $\dfrac{1}{25}$    (b) $2 \cdot 5 + 4 + 2 \cdot \dfrac{1}{5} + 1 \cdot \dfrac{1}{25}$

**55.** (a) 0.33333 . . .    (b) $0.1_{\text{three}}$    (c) $0.2_{\text{six}}$

(d) nine; $0.3_{\text{nine}}$

**57.** about $90

**7.2** *Homework Exercises*

**1.** (a) $8847.6 - 7132.1 \approx 8800 - 7100 = 1700$ m

(b) subtraction, compare measures

**3.** (b)

**5.** price per item for something sold in a set

**7.** (d)

**9.** $129 \div 46 \approx 120 \div 40 = 3¢$

**11.** too high

**13.** $24 \div 0.5$ means how many halves make 24? 48. So $24 \div 0.5 = 48$.

**15.** (a) and (c)

**17.** (a) Move the decimal two places to the right.
Answer: $329.
(b) repeated sets/measures

**19.** $3,600,000,000,000

**21.** 20,000 hours

**23.** (b) 31.7 years

**25.** (a), (c), and (d)

**27.** 0.0000054

**29.** $3.4 \times 10^{12}$

**31.** (a) 12,000,000     (b) 12 million

**33.** 48 is greater than 10.

**35.** (a) $3 \times 10^{27}$    (b) It's shorter!    (c) | 3     27 |

**37.** (a) Saturn    (b) 40    (c) 0.4

**39.** (a) $4.275 \times 10^{11}$    (b) 427,500,000,000
(c) 427 billion, 500 million

**41.** 0.36 mile

**43.** (a) 5.1, 18.3
(b) The remainder is written as the first place to the right of the decimal point.

**45.** A child might line up the decimal in the answer with the decimals in the factors, or a child might not use a decimal point in the answer.

**47.** $20 \times 4.25$ is $(20 \times 4) + \left( 20 \times \dfrac{1}{4} \right)$, which is
$80 + 5 = 85$.

**49.** $y < z < x < w$

**51.** $5.75 \times 20 = (5 \times 20) + \left( \dfrac{3}{4} \times 20 \right) = 100 + 15 = \$115$

**53.** less than 1 and greater than 0

### 7.3 *Homework Exercises*

**1.** yes

**3.** (a) 0 to 600
(b) The second number would be 0.

**5.** (a) 8 to 30    (b) 4/15    (c) how steep it is

**7.** (a) 17.3:1, 24.0:1, 18.2:1, 18.3:1, 17.5:1, 17.7:1,
17.3:1, 24.7:1    (b) Tampa    (c) San Diego
(d) lower

**9.** (a) $11\dfrac{2}{3}$    (b) $\pm\sqrt{48}$

**11.** (a) 10    (b) 5    (c) 15

**13.** 1195

**15.** (b) $1\dfrac{5}{7}$ quarts of orange juice and $1\dfrac{1}{7}$ quarts of
skim milk

**17.** 400,000 cars

**19.** 660 men, 440 women

**21.** $93\dfrac{1}{3}$ lb

**23.** $x = 8\dfrac{1}{3}$, $y = 21\dfrac{2}{3}$

**25.** $2.27

**27.** 18 oz

**31.** $.94

**33.** The bus is more efficient than the car when it carries more than 4 times as many people. The train is more efficient than the bus when it carries more than 3 times as many people as the bus.

**35.** 250 fish

**37.** $3529.41

**39.** 51

**41.** (c)

**43.** *MH/G*

**45.** *QC/D*

### 7.4 *Homework Exercises*

**1.** per 100

**3.** (a) $\dfrac{34}{100}$, 0.34    (b) $1\dfrac{4}{5}$, 1.8    3. (c) $\dfrac{6}{1000}$, 0.006

**5.** (a) 4%    (b) 18.75%

**7.** $.72

**9.** 74.5%

**11.** 6%

**13.** $33\dfrac{1}{3}$%

**15.** 995, 996, . . . , 1050, 1051

**17.** (a) 1%    (b) 0.033%

**19.** $4716.98

**21.** 91%

**23.** (a) $12.78    (c) $13.29

**25.** about 58%

**27.** (a) $2253.65    (b) 12.68%

**29.** $16,289

**31.** (a) 5.5 billion    (b) 6.1 billion    (c) 13.6 billion

**35.** $16

**37.** 33.6 mpg

**39.** *Example:* Which has a higher percentage markdown, Hippo or Bolt shoes?

**41.** (a) first row: $0, $100, $200, $300, $400; second row: $0, $70, $140, $210, $280
(b)    30% off the price

(c) about $320

**43.** (a) We are with you completely.
(b) half for you and half for me

**45.** (a) Prices will go up in the next year.
(b) No, it is 17.6% higher.

**47.** $125,000

**49.** $3000, $2500, $2000

**51.** about 98.2%

**53.** (c)

**55.** 4%

**57.** about 7 years

**59.** $\frac{28}{64} = \frac{7}{16}$

**61.** $100(M - N)/N$

**63.** (a) at least 12% chicken
(b) no more than 30% breading
(c) no more than 30% fat and 10% added water
(d) at least 35% turkey
(d) at least 4% chicken

**7.5 Homework Exercises**

**1.** (a) 1/2 of 222 = 111   (b) 1/4 of 6 = 1.5
(c) 1/10 of 470 = 47   (d) 1/100 of 37 = 0.37

**3.** $8.80

**5.** $6 \times (10\% \text{ of } 2000) = 6 \times 200 = 1200$

**7.** $.72

**9.** (a) 18   (b) 1800   (c) 7400

**11.** (a) $8N$   (b) $5N^2$   (c) $25N$

**13.** 20%

**15.** (a) $\frac{1}{5}, \frac{1}{10}$   (b) $\frac{1}{3}, \frac{1}{7}$

**17.** 56% of 136 million ≈ 50% of 140 million = 70 million

**19.** 80% of 28, 19% of 400, 37% of 420, 52% of 807

**21.** (a) calculator   (b) mental computation
(c) mental computation

**23.** double tax to $3 and add a little to get $3.25; 10% of bill is $2.10 plus half ($1.05) makes $3.15; 1/6 of $21.00 ≈ $3.50

**25.** 4 times tax (4 × .35) is $1.40; 10% of bill $.90 plus half ($.45) makes $1.35; 1/6 of $9 is $1.50

**27.** (a) 75
(b) The second 50% is of a smaller number (50) than the first 50% (of 100).

**29.** 45% of 689 is close

**31.** 48% of 117, 86% of 90, 11% of 1000, 31% of 642

**33.** 80%

**7.6 Homework Exercises**

**1.** (a) 0.6   (b) 2.22 . . .

**3.** $0.3\overline{4}$

**5.** (a) $52\frac{35}{99}$   (b) $\frac{3917}{9999}$   (c) 1

**7.** A square has an area of 5. How long are its sides?

**9.** 24.2 in.

**11.** (b) $\sqrt{5}$ is an infinite decimal.

**13.** (a) and (c) are irrational.

**15.** (a) 25 mph   (b) 36 mph
(c) irrational and rational

**17.** (a) about 1.3 sec   (b) 400 cm   (c) $\sqrt{L/5}$
(d) $25T^2$

**19.** 1/3 or 3,333,333/10,000,000

**21.** $\sqrt{13}$ is irrational and real; $-6$ is an integer, rational, real; $\sqrt{9}$ is whole, integer, rational, real; $-0.317$ is rational, real.

**23.** true

**25.** (a) 3   (b) 5   (c) an infinite number

**27.** (a) no   (b) yes   (c) no

**29.** 1/3 + 1/6

**31.** 1/7

**33.** 22/7

**35.** $\pi$ is an infinite nonrepeating decimal.

**37.** (a) 550, 490   (b) 66%, 62%   (c) 36, 34

**39.** commutative, addition

**41.** 0.41798

**43.** $3 - 2 \neq 2 - 3$

**45.** $6 \times 8 = 48$ plus $0.5 \times 8 = 4$ and $48 + 4 = 52$

**47.** $8 + (3 \cdot 4) \neq (8 + 3) \cdot (8 + 4)$

**49.** (a) some pairs   (b) all pairs
(c) no real numbers

**51.** Some numbers on the number line (like $\sqrt{2}$) are not rational.

**53.** (a) (1), (2), and (4)   (b) (1), (2), and (4)
(c) 5, $5^2$, $3^2$, $2^3 \cdot 5^2$, 7   (d) 2, 5

**55.** The number of digits is equal to the larger of $a$ and $b$.

**57.** only if $M = 0$ or $N = 0$

**59.** (a) 1.414   (b) 1.412   (c) yes

**61.** irrational

**63.** true, $x + \frac{1}{x} \geq 2 \rightarrow x^2 + 1 \geq 2x \rightarrow$
$x^2 - 2x + 1 \geq 0 \rightarrow (x - 1)^2 \geq 0$, which is true because all real numbers squared are greater than or equal to 0

**65.** Assume $\sqrt[3]{2}$ is rational. Then $\frac{p}{q} = \sqrt[3]{2}$, in which $p$ and $q$ are counting numbers. Then $p = \sqrt[3]{2}q$ or $p^3 = 2q^3$. If $p^3$ is the cube of a counting number, then the number of prime factors it has is a multiple of 3. $2q^3$ has a number of prime factors equal to a multiple of 3 plus 1. So $p^3$ and $2q^3$ are equal numbers that have a different number of prime factors. This is impossible, so $\sqrt[3]{2}$ must be irrational.

**Chapter 7** *Review Exercises*

1. (a) $(3 \times 1/1000) + (7 \times 1/10,000)$
   (b) $3.7 \times 10^{-3}$
2. Represent 0.3 as 3 columns. Represent 0.25 as 25 small squares.

$$0.3 \quad > \quad 0.25$$

3. $GC/3$ gallons
4. 6%
5. Move the decimal point two places to the left. Answer: $0.0076.
6. (a) $\dfrac{2000}{130} = \dfrac{x}{150}$ and $x = 2308$ calories

   (b) $2000 \cdot \dfrac{150}{130} = 2308$ calories

7. $0 < m < 1$
8. about 85 million
9. 44%
10. 0.04
11. Move the decimal two places to the left. Answer: $72.50
12. $42 \div 0.06 = \dfrac{42}{0.06} = \dfrac{42 \times 100}{0.06 \times 100} = \dfrac{4200}{6} = 4200 \div 6$
13. (d)
14. $46 +$ half of $46 = 69.$
15. division, partition measures
16. subtraction, compare measures
17. (d) and (e)
18. additive inverses
19. $3(4 - 2) = 3 \cdot 4 - 3 \cdot 2$
20. $2.37 \times 10^7$
21. $0.2 \times 0.3$ means 0.2 of 0.3. Dot 0.3 of a decimal square.

Now, darken 0.2 of the 0.3.
0.06 of the decimal square is darkened.
So $0.2 \times 0.3 = 0.06$.

**Chapter 7** *Computer Exercise*

1. (a) $A = 1$, $B$ and $C$ are any real numbers
   (b) all real numbers    (c) $A = 0$ or $B = 0$

**Chapter 8**

**8.1** *Homework Exercises*

1. earth measure
3.
5. (a) false     (b)

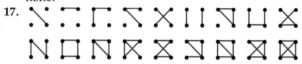

7. It has no length or width.
9 (a) 3    (b) 1    (c) 2
11. cone, cylinder, triangle, square, line segment, angle, rectangle, pyramid, prism, hemisphere
13. different endpoints, opposite directions
15. A line segment has two endpoints; a line has none.
17.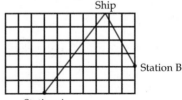

19. Inches measure length.
21.

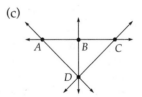

23. $W$, $M$, $Z$, $N$
25. the first
27.     (a)

     (b)

     (c)

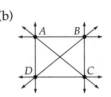

**29.** (a) 2    (b) 3    (c) 4
**31.** (a) 1    (b) 1    (c) 1 and 3
**33.** (a) 5 AM and 7 AM    (b) 2:30 AM and 9:30 AM
**37.**

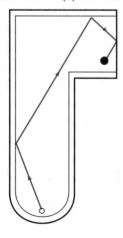

### 8.2 Homework Exercises

**1.**

**3.** (a) octagon    (b) trapezoid
**5.**

**7.** (b) and (c)
**9.**

**11.** stability
**13.** 8
**15.**

**17.** (a) 4 from Group 1 or 2 from Group 1 and 2 from
   Group 2
   (b) 1 from Group 3 with 1 or 2 from Group 1 and
   2 or 1 from Group 2
   (c) 4 from Group 1

**19.** all of them
**21.** (b), (d)
**23.** rectangle, parallelogram, pentagon, hexagon,
   triangle, kite
**25.** (a) three angles    (b) right angles
**27.** all of them
**29.** All squares are rectangles.
**31.** (a) $S$    (b) yes    (c) $Q$
**35.** points, 8 in., $N$
**37.** By cutting a straight line that passes approximately through the center, you divide a pie
   approximately in half.
**39.** 105
**41.** (a)
**43.** (a)                          (b)

   (c)                          (d)

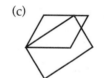
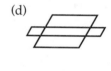

**45.**
   (a)          (b)          (c)          (d)

### 8.3 Homework Exercises

**1.** (c) The sum of the angles should be close to 180°,
   but it may not be exactly 180° because of drawing and measuring error.
**3.** (a) possible    (b) possible
**5.** Their measures add up to 180°.
**7.** The angles of the five triangles do not form the
   angles of the pentagon.
**9.** (a) No; angles may not be congruent.
   (b) No; sides may not be congruent.
**11.** (a) 120°    (b)

**13.** (a) yes    (b) yes
**15.** (a) 6    (b) 10    (c) 15    (e) 36

**17.** (a) $\dfrac{(n-2)180°}{n}$   (b) because $\dfrac{(n-2)}{n}$ is less than 1

**19.** 28

**21.** (b) triangle and parallelogram   (c) 1/8

(d)
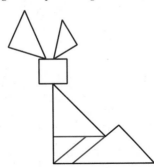

(e)
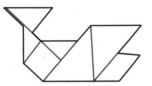

(f)
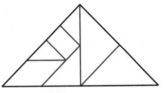

**8.4 Homework Exercises**

**1.** (a) false
(b) the three line segments that meet at the corner of a room

**3.** (a) an infinite number   (b) one   (c) one
(d) an infinite number

**5.** parallel, intersecting in one point, or the line lies in the plane

**7.** (a) true
(b) line on the floor and a line on the ceiling

**9.** yes

**11.**

**13.** true

**15.** (a) parallel   (b) perpendicular

**17.** true

**19.** (a) false
(b) two parallel lines on the floor and a line from the ceiling to the floor that intersects one of them

**21.** true

**23.** (a) and (d)

**25.** (a) 8   (b) 18   (c) 12

**27.** (a) "in space" instead of "in a plane"
(b) point, circle

**29.** (c)

**31.** (a), (c), (d)

**33.** (a)    (b) 7   (c) 7   (d) 12

**35.** (a) $F = 9,\ V = 9,\ E = 16$
(b) $F = 7,\ V = 10,\ E = 15$
(c) $F = 18,\ V = 14,\ E = 30$

**37.**

**39.** (a) right circular cylinder   (b) rectangular prism

**41.** uniform curvature

**43.** (a) plane   (b) plane   (c) line

**45.** true

**47.** false

**49.** (a) $n + 2$   (b) $2n$   (c) $3n$   (d) yes

**51.** (a) octahedron   (b) tetrahedron   (c) cube

**53.** (c) The line on the regular loop is on one side. The line on the Möbius strip goes all around it on both "sides." It has only one side!

**8.5 Homework Exercises**

**1.** (b) $CD$ is longer than $AB$
(c) We tend to look for depth, a third dimension.

**3.** The room is not rectangular. The back of the room on one side is closer to the camera.

**9.**

**11.** hexagonal prism

**13.** (a) triangle   (b) ellipse

**15.** right triangle

**17.** so we don't injure ourselves drinking from them

**19.**

**23.** *A* and *E*, or *I*

**25.**

**27.** (a)

**29.** 4, 5, 7, 6, 2, 3, 1

**31.** The fisherman in the bottom right reaches the water with his pole. The man in the upper right on the hill lights the woman's lantern. The man on one side of the bridge shoots his rifle on the other side. The banner from the building hangs out among the trees.

**33.** (b) It could not exist as the three-dimensional figure it appears to be.

**35.**

**37.** (a) drawing 2     (b) drawing 1

**39.**

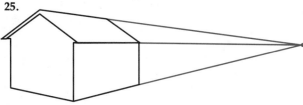

**43.** (a) 64     (b) 24     (c) 24     (d) 8     (e) 0
(f) 8

**45.** (a) 96, 48, 8, 0, 64
(b) $6(N-2)^2$, $12(N-2)$, 8, 0, $(N-2)^3$

**8.6 *Homework Exercises***

**1.** (a)          (b)

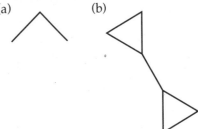

**3.** *T*

**5.** (a) 135°     (b) 45°
(c) REPEAT 8 [FD 30 RT 45]

**7.** REPEAT 360 [FD 1 RT 1]

**9.** FD 50 RT 135 FD 25 LT 90 FD 25 RT 135 FD 50

**11.** REPEAT 4 [FD 30 LT 90 FD 30 RT 90]

**13.** REPEAT 5 [FD 60 RT 144]

**15.** 180° in first 3 blanks; 540°, 180°, 360°

**8.7 *Homework Exercises***

**1.** (a) TO SQUARE
        REPEAT 4 [FD 35 RT 90]
        END
(b) a rotational design with 6 squares

**3.** (a) TO HEXA :S
        REPEAT 6 [FD :S RT 60]
        END

**5.** (a) a pentagram     (b)

**7.** TO ANGBI
    FD 50 RT 100 FD 50 BK 50 RT 40 FD 50
    END

**9.** (a) TO SQUARE :N
        REPEAT 4 [FD :N RT 90]
        END
    TO GROW
        SQUARE 10
        SQUARE 20
        SQUARE 30
        SQUARE 40
        END
(b) TO BOX
        REPEAT 4 [FD 30 RT 90]
        FD 15 RT 45

*(Continued on next page.)*

REPEAT 4 [FD 21 RT 90]
END

**11.** (a) TO TRI
REPEAT 3 [FD 30 RT 120]
END
TO PW
LT 30
TRI
RT 180
TRI
RT 90
TRI
RT 180
TRI
END

(b) TO HUMAN
LT 45
REPEAT 4 [FD 30 RT 90]
LT 45 FD 30 BK 60 FD 30
LT 90 FD 45 RT 45 FD 30
BK 30 LT 90 FD 30 BK 30
END

**13.** (a) TO WHEEL
REPEAT 50 [FD 2 RT 9]
TO CAR
PU LT 90 FD 60 RT 90 PD
WHEEL
LT 180 FD 30 BK 120 RT 90 FD 30
LT 90 FD 40 RT 90 FD 20
LT 90 FD 40 LT 90 FD 20 RT 90 FD 40
LT 90 FD 30 LT 90 FD 90
WHEEL
END

(b) TO CONE
FD 50 RT 135 FD 50
END
TO SCOOP
REPEAT 70 [FD 3 RT 9]
END
TO DESSERT
PU FD 50 PD
SCOOP
LT 180
SCOOP
REPEAT 22 [FD 3 RT 9]
CONE
END

**15.** (a) TO L
RT 180 FD 60 LT 90 FD 35
END

(b) TO O
REPEAT 20 [FD 4 RT 18]
END

(c) TO G
REPEAT 30 [FD 4 RT 18]
FD 30
REPEAT 10 [FD 4 RT 18]
END

(d) TO MASTER
PU FD 30 LT 90 FD 80
RT 90 PD
L
PU FD 25 LT 90 PD
O
PU RT 90 FD 50 LT 90 PD
G
PU RT 90 FD 50
LT 90 FD 30 PD
O
END

**17.** (a) a 15° angle
(c) an infinite loop that draws a "sun"
(d) The last command (in the procedure) calls for the procedure SUN to start again. This results in an infinitely repeating program.

**Chapter 8** *Review Exercises*
**1.** In order to define space figures properly, one must first study the components of these figures.
**2.** It is finite and it has thickness.
**3.** (a) ∠*ABC*     (b) { }
**4.** an infinite number
**5.** false
**6.** (a) false     (b) Two intersecting lines on the ceiling are both parallel to the floor.
**7.**

**8.**

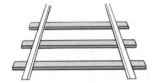

**9.** (b)
**10.** no
**11.** (b), (d)
**12.**

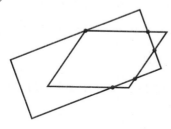

**13.** A pentagon can be divided into three triangles (see p. 428). The angle sum of each triangle is 180°, so the angle sum of the pentagon is $3 \cdot (180°) = 540°$.
**14.** Each angle of a regular hexagon is 120°, so 3 regular hexagons will fit together around a point as shown.

**15.** 7 faces, 7 vertices, and 12 edges
**16.** 9
**17.**

**18.** REPEAT 8 [FD 50 RT 45]
**19.**

**20.**

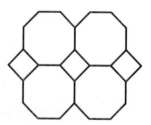

**Chapter 9**
**9.1** *Homework Exercises*
**1.**

**3.** 32°, $P'O$
**5.** Move the flag 4 cm to the left.
**7.** $\overleftrightarrow{AB}$; $\overleftrightarrow{P'B}$
**9.** (a)                     (b) 3

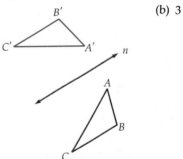

**11.**

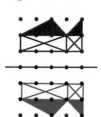

**13.** (a)           (b)

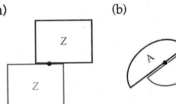

**15.** (a) 90° clockwise around $C$, which is 1 unit to the right of $B$

(b) a line through $C$ that rises up and to the left at a 45° angle

**17.** baseball gloves and desks

**19.**

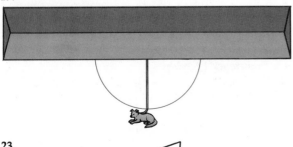

**23.**

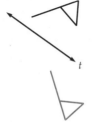

**25.** (a) false

(b) Reflect the vertical line across any line that is not horizontal or vertical.

**27.** (b) Neither pair is congruent.

**29.**

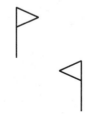

**31.** (a) 180° rotation     (b) reflection

**33.**

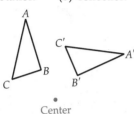

Center

**35.** (a) reflection through $\overleftrightarrow{AM}$ or a counterclockwise rotation around $A$ of $m\angle CAT$

(c) reflection through $\overleftrightarrow{AM}$; $\angle ACT \cong \angle ATC$

**37.** (a) the same thing!     (b) *TIM*

**39.** (a) if they are the same length

(b) if they have one side of equal length

(c) All rays are congruent.

**41.** (a) Rotate 120° clockwise around the point where their "noses" meet.

(b) Reflect through the body line that passes between the eyes.

**43.** (a) yes

**47.** The boy is photographed in one mirror while holding another.

**49.** about half of your height positioned around the middle half of your body

**51.** translation

**53.** (a) $A(2, 4)$     $B(2, 1)$     $C(6, 1)$

(b) $A'(-2, 5)$     $B'(-2, 2)$     $C'(2, 2)$

(d) translation

**55.** (a) $A(1, 2)$     $B(3, -1)$     $C(1, -2)$

(b) $A'(-1, 2)$     $B'(-3, -1)$     $C'(-1, -2)$

(d) reflection through the $y$-axis

**57.**          (a)                    (b)

**59.** (a) 24     (b) 15

**61.** TO ROTATE
       REPEAT 3 [FD 30 RT 120]
       RT 140
       REPEAT 3 [FD 30 RT 120]
       END

**63.** TO SQUARE
       REPEAT 4 [FD 30 RT 90]
       END
       TO PATTERN
       REPEAT 4 [SQUARE RT 90]
       END

**65.** (c) This exercise could lead to a generalization about congruent alternate interior angles or congruent corresponding angles.

**9.2 *Homework Exercises***

**5.** yes, by the SSS property

**9.** You could construct a right angle at $A$. Then, mark off the distance $AB$ on the new side and label the endpoint $D$. Connect $D$ to $C$.

**13.** (a) no     (b) yes     (c) no     (d) yes

**15.** impossible

**17.**

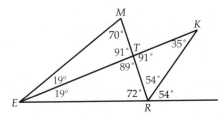

**19.** Draw the angle bisector of ∠A and label the point where it intersects side $\overline{BC}$ as point $D$. Since $AD = AD$, ∠B ≅ ∠C, and ∠BAD ≅ ∠CAD, △ABD ≅ △ACD by AAS. Since the triangles are congruent, corresponding sides $\overline{AB}$ and $\overline{AC}$ are congruent.

**21.** (a) Bisect $\overline{BC}$ to locate the midpoint. Then connect the midpoint to $A$.
   (b) The three medians intersect at one point.

**23.** Use the span of the compass.

**25.** (b) Fold one side of the angle onto the other.

**27.** (c)

**29.** 60°

**31.** They bisect each other but are not congruent or perpendicular.

**33.** Mark the distance $NU$ on $UP$ to locate $T$. Connect $T$ to $N$.

**35.** Take the 45° angle from the last exercise and construct a perpendicular on one side. The sum of the two adjacent angle measures will be 135°.

**37.** 4 mm

**39.** 20°

**41.** △ABC ≅ △EFG by SAS. So $AC = EG$ and ∠BAC ≅ ∠FEG. By subtraction, ∠DAC ≅ ∠GEH. Then △ADC ≅ △EHG by SAS. This means $DC = HG$ and ∠H ≅ ∠D. Since ∠ACD ≅ ∠EGH and ∠ACB ≅ ∠EGF, we can add to obtain ∠BCD ≅ ∠FGH.

**43.** (a)

   (b) It indicates that a quadrilateral is not rigid.

**45.** A given point on the perpendicular bisector is equidistant from $A$ and $B$.

**47.** (a) $AC = BD$. The diagonals of a rectangle are equal in length.
   (b) Each "opposite" pair of triangles is congruent.

### 9.3 Homework Exercises

**1.** See the lesson.

**3.** (a), (d)

**5.** (a)     (b)

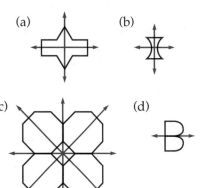

(c)     (d)

**7.** If the rectangle is reflected through the diagonal, the image rectangle will not be in the same position as the original rectangle.

**9.** (c) The two lines of symmetry are perpendicular. The two lines of symmetry bisect the angles formed by the intersecting lines.
   (e) induction

**11.** (a) 3    (b) 1    (c) 1    (d) 1

**13.** (a) and (c) have rotational and reflection; (b) has reflection

**15.** (a) $U, I, D$    (b) $S, I$

**17.** usually: (a) all 2's, 4's, 10's, J's, Q's, K's and the A, 3, 5, 6, 8, and 9 of diamonds
   (b) none

**19.** (number of rotational symmetries) = (number of reflection symmetries) − 1

**21.** (a)     (b)

**23.** rotational

**25.** 4

**27.** 5

**29.** 1

**31.** right circular cone

**33.** (a) usually rotational
   (b) can be laid down in a number of ways

**35.** (a) A tennis ball has rotational and reflection symmetry if one ignores the ridges; a tennis racket has reflection symmetry; a tennis court has rotational symmetry, and the surface has reflection symmetry.

**35.** (b) The tennis ball will bounce well and can be hit at any point without it making a difference; one can strike the ball with either face of the tennis racket; the court on either side of the net is the same, and the court is comparable on the left and right sides on each side of the net.

**37.** (a), (c), (d), and (e) have rotational and reflection; (b) has none.

**39.** 4 if both surfaces are the same

**41.** 3 and 1

**43.** (a) reflection     (b) commutative     (c) yes

**45.** Fold the circle in half from two different positions to create two different diameters. The intersection of the two diameters (folds) is the center.

**47.** (a) They are congruent.
(b) They are congruent.

**49.** impossible

### 9.4 *Homework Exercises*

**3.**

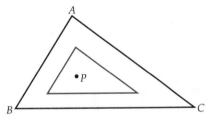

**5.** (a) $\triangle RMN$     (b) 1/2

**7.** (a) yes     (b) no

**9.** No. Corresponding angles may not be congruent.

**11.** They are similar.

**13.**

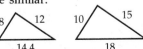

**15.** $x = 17\frac{1}{7}$     $y = 22\frac{6}{7}$

**17.** 1.6

**19.** $x = 5, y = 11\frac{2}{3}$

**21.** Yes, they are all the same shape.

**23.** about 297″ or 24′ 9″

**25.** (a) 6.8 cm by 10.2 cm     (b) yes     (c) 46%

**27.** Hint: 8 m would be represented by 2 cm. 10 m would be represented by 2.5 cm.

**29.** (b) They are similar.
(c) Corresponding sides are proportional.
(d) similar

**31.** (b) $B$ and $C$     (c) $BC = 2 \cdot DE$
(d) The segment joining the midpoints of two sides of a triangle is half the length of the third side.

**33.** (b) You obtain a similar figure. The original figure can be mapped to the image figure using a rotation around the origin followed by a size change.

**35.** no

**37.** yes

**41.** (a) yes     (b) yes     (c) forever
(d) $r = \dfrac{1 \pm \sqrt{5}}{2}$

### Chapter 9 *Review Exercises*

**1.** Two figures are congruent if one can be mapped onto the other using a rotation, reflection, or translation.

**2.** (a)

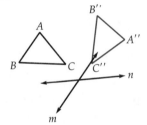

(b) a rotation around the intersection point of the two lines

**3.** (a) $(-6, -2)$     (b) a translation

**4.** (a) could say $\angle DAB \cong \angle BCD$, 180° turn around $E$
(b) $\angle AEB \cong \angle CED$, 180° turn around $E$

**5.** (b) From the construction, $AI = MI$, $TI = TI$, and $AT = MT$. So $\triangle AIT \cong \triangle MIT$ by SSS. Then, $\angle AIT \cong \angle MIT$, so $\overrightarrow{IT}$ is the angle bisector.

**6.** The angles of the hexagon are 120°; smaller angles of the triangle are 30°; the remaining two angles adjacent to the 30° angles are 90°.

**7.** two, each passing through the midpoints of the opposite sides

**8.** Yes, all their angles measure 108°, and corresponding sides are proportional.

**9.** a square

**10.**

**11.**

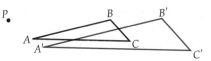

**12.** 5

**13.** 26 ft 11 in.

**14.** $\dfrac{10L + 60}{L}$

**15.**

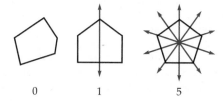

0          1          5

## Chapter 10

### 10.1 *Homework Exercises*

**3.** All conversions within the metric system involve powers of 10. Conversions within the English system are more difficult to do and to remember.

**5.** 8 cm

**7.** 20

**9.** 1000T

**13.** 70 kg

**15.** 3240

**17.** 250 mL

**19.** 5000

**21.** (a) false     (b) false     (c) false     (d) true

**23.** (a)

**25.** (b)

**27.** Most college students can.

**29.** (a) approximate     (b) exact     (c) approximate     (d) exact

**31.** 27.5 and 28.5 cm

**33.** (a) 50 mm     (b) 0.5 mm     (c) 49.5 and 50.5 mm

**35.** (a) 8 g     (b) 13.2 cm

**39.** 0.17 km

**41.** (a) 1,000,000     (b) 0.00006     (c) 0.0821     (d) 4,800,000

**43.** 1.944

**45.** $A + 100B$

### 10.2 *Homework Exercises*

**1.** (a) 8.4 cm     (b) 8.0 cm

**3.** Draw another square adjacent to the second highest square on its left.

**5.** 34

**7.** (a) The second has twice the perimeter.
(b) same as (a)
(c) The ratio of the perimeters of two squares equals the ratio of their corresponding sides.

**9.** because $2r = d$

**11.** 7962 miles

**13.** 332

**15.** (a) 325.7 m     (b) 6.3 m

**17.** the space in its interior

**21.** 3

**23.** (a) Show 2 rows of 5 squares.     (b) 10 m²

**25.** $0.2 \times 0.3 = 0.06$

**27.** $A =$ about 212,214 km², $P = 1930$ km

**29.** 48 ft²

**31.** (a)

**33.** $\sqrt{48}$ ft

**35.** 4 square units

**37.** (b) 504 ft²     (c) $448

**39.** Package $B$

**41.** $62.93

**43.** (a) 800     (b) 5,000,000

**45.** (a) 2.6
(b) converting square units as if they were units

**47.** 128

**49.** 60.8475, 62.4375 cm

**51.** (a) 5 square units     (b) 10, 11, 12

**53.** (a) 177.17 m     (b) 87.60 m

**55.** (a) 8 m     (b) 12 m     (c) $4\sqrt{N}$ m

**57.** Each rectangle could have $L = 42.5$ ft and $W = 60$ ft.

**59.** (a) a line segment connecting (10, 0) to (0, 10) excluding its endpoints
(b)

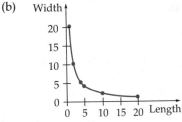

**61.** (a) $ab + ac = a(b + c)$
(b) $(a + b)^2 = a^2 + 2ab + b^2$

**63.** $s = 2\pi r\theta/360°$

### 10.3 *Homework Exercises*

**1.** See Lesson Exercise 10.39.

**3.** (a) 32 in., 30 in.²     (b) 12 m, 6 m²

**5.** Put together two of the triangles as shown to form a parallelogram.

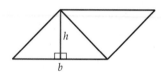

$$A_\triangle = \frac{1}{2} A_{parallelogram} = \frac{1}{2}bh.$$

**7.** (a) 24 ft$^2$     (b) 23.65125 and 24.35125 ft$^2$

**9.** 4000 cm$^2$

**11.** Put together two of the trapezoids as shown to form a parallelogram.

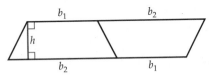

$$A_{trapezoid} = \frac{1}{2} A_{parallelogram} = \frac{1}{2}(b_1 + b_2) \cdot h.$$

**13.** 253 mm$^2$

**15.** 106,950 square miles

**17.** squares and rectangles

**19.** $\frac{1}{2}Cr = \frac{1}{2}(2\pi r)r = \pi r^2$

**21.** (a) 2     (b) 4

**23.** same area either way

**25.** 2.25$\pi$ ft$^2$

**27.** 100$\pi$ ft$^2$

**29.** 7$\pi \approx$ 22m$^2$

**31.** (a) 8 + 20$\pi$/3     (b) 40$\pi$/3 square units

**33.** (c)

**35.** (a) 100.2 km     (b) no theoretical limit

**37.** 2.25$\pi$ square units

**39.** 9$\pi$ − 18 square units

**41.** a ray starting at (0, 0) and passing through (1, 2$\pi$)

**43.** false; circles with radii of 1 and 2 have areas in a ratio of 1:4, not 1:2

**45.** 56 square units

**47.** area $EFGH = \frac{1}{2}$ (area of $ABCD$)

## 10.4 *Homework Exercises*

**1.** (a) right triangles
    (b) $a$ and $b$ are the lengths of the legs; $c$ is the length of the hypotenuse.

**3.** m$\angle ABH$ + m$\angle AHB = 90°$. Since $\angle DBC \cong \angle AHB$, m$\angle ABH$ + m$\angle DBC = 90°$.

m$\angle ABH$ + m$\angle DBC$ + m$\angle 3 = 180°$, so m$\angle 3 = 90°$.

**5.** Draw a line segment that goes up 2 and over 3.

**7.** 3.9 m

**9.** 70%

**11.** 4$\sqrt{2}$ mph NE

**13.** 14.1 in.

**15.** (a) 10     (b) finding the length of the hypotenuse

**17.** 8$\sqrt{128}$ or 64$\sqrt{2}$ square units

**19.** 5 miles

**21.** (a) yes     (b) no

**23.** (a) yes     (b) yes
    (c) If $a$, $b$, and $c$ are the lengths of sides of a right triangle, then $ka$, $kb$, and $kc$ ($k > 0$) also are the lengths of sides of a right triangle.

**25.** 3017.8 cm$^2$

**27.** (a) yes     (b) 6, 8, 10; 5, 12, 13; 9, 12, 15
    (c) If $a^2 + b^2 = c^2$ then $k(a^2 + b^2) = kc^2$ or $ka^2 + kb^2 = kc^2$.

**29.** (a) $x = 3, y = 4, z = 5$; $x = 6, y = 8, z = 10$; $x = 9, y = 12, z = 15$
    (b) no

**31.** 169

**33.** $\frac{25\sqrt{3}}{4}$

**35.** 30$\sqrt{75}$ or 150$\sqrt{3}$ square units

**37.** 12$\sqrt{2} \approx$ 17 in.

**39.** 64$\pi$ square units

**41.** (a), (b), and (c)

**43.** $\sqrt{12}$ cm

**45.** (a) $a^2 + b^2 = c^2$
    (b) They both equal $a^2 + b^2$.
    (c) $\triangle GFE$, SSS property

**47.** TO RECT
    REPEAT 2 [FD 30 RT 90 FD 50 RT 90]
    RT 59 FD 58
    END

**49.** 10 PRINT "TYPE IN A VALUE FOR T"
20 INPUT T
30 PRINT T, (T^2 − 1)/2, (T^2 + 1)/2
40 IF T^2 + [(T^2 − 1)/2]^2 = [(T^2 + 1)/2]^2
    THEN 70
50 PRINT "IS NOT A PYTHAGOREAN TRIPLE."
60 GOTO 80
70 PRINT "IS A PYTHAGOREAN TRIPLE."
80 PRINT "WANT TO DO ANOTHER? TYPE 1
    FOR YES, 0 FOR NO."
90 INPUT A
100 IF A = 1 THEN 10
110 END

## 10.5 *Homework Exercises*

1. 32 square units
3. (a) 1 by 1 by 20    (b) 2 by 2 by 5
5. 2700 cm$^2$
7. (a) 12,150 cm$^2$    (b) $24.30
9. by the square yard
11. $120 + 15\sqrt{24}$ or $120 + 30\sqrt{6}$ square units
13. $r = 2, h = 8$ or $r = 4, h = 1$
15. (a) 30 cubic units
    (b) The child counts the number of squares that are visible.
17. B
21. (c) Surface area would increase; volume would stay the same.
23. 69,332.375 and 74,732.625 cm$^3$
25. prisms and cylinders
27. 693 mm$^3$
29. (a) and (b) 2.7 in. and 3.5 in.
    (c) the cylinder with $d = 3.5$ in.
31. 160 m$^3$
33. $\dfrac{3\sqrt{3}}{4}$ m$^3$
35. cones and pyramids
37. 303,750 cm$^3$
39. 400 in.$^2$
41. (b) 355 cm$^3$
43. (a) 115,640,000 ft$^3$    (b) 15,419
45. 5.8 in.$^3$
47. (a) 180    (b) omitting $\pi$ from the answer
49. 1016 lb
51. $L = W = 10$ cm, $H = 20$ cm
53. (a) 1, 2, 3; 1, 8, 27; 6, 24, 54    (b) volume
55. 21%
57. Lay it on its side.
59. 16,200$\pi$ in.$^3$
63. $4\sqrt[3]{2}$ in.
65. 1145 in.$^3$
67. 2,200,000 L
69. (a) 1 cm$^3$    (b) 4000 g    (c) 140    (d) 1000 kg
71. 0.263 cm

## 10.6 *Homework Exercises*

1. (a) 20    (b) 1:4    (c) 1:16    (d) 1:4
3. (a) $m:n$    (b) $m^2:n^2$
5. (a) 16 in.    (b) 9 in.
7. (a) 2:3    (b) 208 and 468 m$^2$    (c) 4:9
    (d) It is the square of the ratio of the edges.
    (e) 192 and 648 m$^3$    (f) 8:27
    (g) It is the cube of the ratio of the edges.

9. (a) 4:1    (b) 64:1
11. (a) 3.5 m    (b) $3\frac{1}{16}$    (c) 64:343
13. (b)
15. 512
17. (a) $3\frac{3}{8}$    (b) $2\frac{1}{4}$
19. 1,152,000 ft$^3$
21. Food consumption is proportional to volume. Cube the 12 from the ratio of lengths to obtain 1728.
23. 0.1 lb
25. $131.82
27. (a) 3    (b) 2
29. larger
31. *Hint:* Find the cube root of each number in the first row and the square root of each number in the second row.

## Chapter 10 *Review Exercises*

1. (b)
2. $\sqrt{149}$ m
3. 0.0008
4. 72 units$^2$
5. 10.0 m
6. *A*
7. 7
8. multiplied by 16
9. Put together two of the triangles as shown to form a parallelogram.

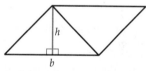

$A_{\triangle} = \dfrac{1}{2} A_{\text{parallelogram}} = \dfrac{1}{2}bh.$

10. (a) 15.0 m$^2$    (b) 14.72625 and 15.27625 m$^2$
11. $80 + 12\sqrt{20}$ or $80 + 24\sqrt{5}$ square units
12. $100 - 25\pi$ m$^2$
13. $20 + 5\pi$ m
14. $225\pi - 216$ square units
15. $625/\pi$ cm$^2$
16. 14 in.
17. 216$\pi$ ft$^2$
18. 4:9
19. 675 m$^3$
20. (a) 15.625    (b) 6.4 lb

## Chapter 11
### 11.1 *Homework Exercises*
1. (a) {(0,0), (1, 0), (2, 0), (2, 2), (3, 0), (3, 2), (4, 0), (4, 2), (4, 4)}

   (b)

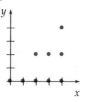

3.

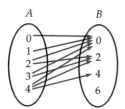

5. (a)

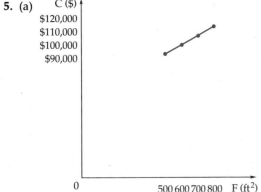

   (b) 92,500 ≤ C ≤ 112,000

   (c) Each $F$-value in the domain has exactly one $C$-value in the range.

7. (a) $a$ and $c$

   (b) (1) squaring     (2) "is a friend of"

      (3) "wants to be a"

9. 30 from set $A$ would be assigned to more than one number in set $B$.

11. (b) and (c)

13. (a)

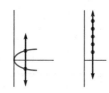

(b) If the line intersects more than one point on the curve, it indicates more than one point with the same $x$-value and a different $y$-value.

15. (a) Add the sums of the squares of the two numbers.

   (b) number of letters in each name

   (c) Multiply the first number in the ordered pair by the square of the second number.

17. (a) 4     (b) 900        (c) $F = S^2/4$

   (d) weight, direction     (e) $0 < S \le 100$ mph

19. (a) the set of feet measured

   (b) the measurements between 4 and 25 cm

21. (a) 1     (b) 1     (c) 2

25. (a)

27. (a) 0     (b) $x < 0$     (c) $x > 25$

29. (a) $y \le 8$     (b) $y \ne 0$

### 11.2 *Homework Exercises*
1. (a) Time cannot be negative.

   (b) Distance cannot be negative.

   (c and d) a ray with endpoint at (0, 0) going through (1, 12)

   (e) approximate

3. (a) The average revenue is $4/customer.

   (b) $R/C = 4$

5. (a) (3)     (b) (1)     (c) (2)

7. (a) 2/3     (b) −4/3     (c) 2/3

9. 36 ft

11. (a)

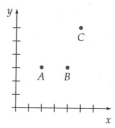

   (b) (3, 6)     (c) both 3

13. vertical

15. parallel

17. Both have a slope of 1/2.

19. (a) a line through (0, 1) and (1, 2)

   (b) a line through (0, 1) and (1, 3)

   (c) a line through (0, 1) and (1, 4)

   (d) the $y$-intercept (0, 1)

   (e) $y = 3x + 1$

21. $y = \dfrac{2}{3}x$

**23.** $y = -2x + 5$

**25.** (a) yes    (b) no    (c) yes

**27.** (a) $T/5$    (b) a line through $(0, 0)$ and $(5, 1)$

(c) Each change of 1 second is an additional 1/5 mile of distance.

(d) The lightning (light) reaches one in virtually no time, so the formula simply estimates the distance the thunder (sound) travels at the rate of 0.2 mi/sec.

**29.** (a) 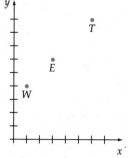    (b) $(2, 5)$ and $(4, 7)$

(c) $y$ is 3 more than $x$.

(d) $y = x + 3$

**31.** (a) 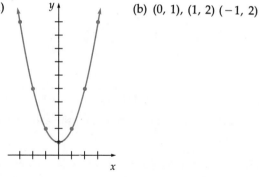    (b) $(0, 1)$, $(1, 2)$ $(-1, 2)$

(c) for $0 \le x \le 3$    (d) about 2.5

**33.** Translate $y = x^2 + 1$ up 4 units.

**35.** (c)

**37.** (a) 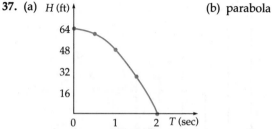    (b) parabola

(c) The object hits the ground at $t = 2$.

**39.** (a) 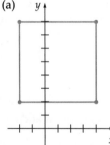    (b) rectangle

(c) It looks longer and skinnier.

**41.** (a) 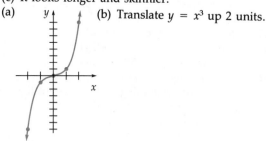    (b) Translate $y = x^3$ up 2 units.

**43.** (a) $-1$ and $1$; $1/2$ and $-2$

(b) The product of the slopes is $-1$.

**45.** (a) $m$    (b) $-1/m$

**47.** no

**49.** (a) a line through $(0, -2)$ and $(1, 1)$

(b) a line through $(0, -2)$ and $(-1, 1)$

(c) $y = -3x - 2$

**51.** One is the image of the other for a reflection through the $x$-axis.

**53.** (a) a rectangle with base 30 and height 20

(b) TO RECT
       PU SETX 10 SETY 10 PD
       SETY 50 SETX $-20$ SETY 10 SETX 10
       END

## 11.3 Homework Exercises

**1.** $a + 12$, in which $a$ is the average temperature for this day in degrees

**3.** (a) $20 = 0.85P$, in which $P$ is the list price in dollars

(b) the wholesale price, the quality of the item, what the item is

**5.** $P = 3L$, in which $L$ is the length and $P$ is the perimeter.

**7.** $0.60S = W$, in which $S$ is the number of students and $W$ is the number of female students

**9.** (a) (1)     (b) (2)     (c) (2)

**11.** $a(b + c) = ab + ac$, in which $a$, $b$, and $c$ are real

**13.** (a) $1100 + 0.1M$
    (b) a ray with endpoint (0, 1100) through
       (100, 1110)

**15.** $W = 8100 - 900Y$

**17.** (a) $200 - 5W$ lb     (b) 6

**19.** $Y = 100 + X/10$

**21.** $y \geq 2x$, in which $x$ is last year's height and $y$ is this year's height

**23.** total cost $C = 5X + 3Y$, in which $X$ is the number of adult tickets and $Y$ is the number of children's tickets

**25.** $X$ must represent a quantity.

**27.** The rental rate is $10 plus $22/day.

**29.** The commission is 2.5% of sales.

**31.** The car went 120 miles in 3 hours, traveling more quickly at the beginning and the end of the trip.

**33.** (a) (2)     (b) (3)     (c) (1)

**35.**

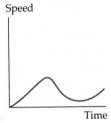

**37.** $y = 24 - x$

**39.** $W = 3H - 83$

**41.** $P = 3I - 1$

**43.** $D = 3M + 2$

**45.** $x^2 + y^2 = 25$

**47.** (a)

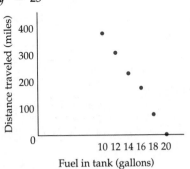

(d) about $-37.5$, which means that the car travels about 37.5 miles per gallon

**49.** (a)

| L | 3 | 5 | 7 | 9 | 11 |
|---|---|---|---|---|---|
| W | 10 | 6 | 30/7 | 10/3 | 30/11 |

(b) $LW = 30$

(c)

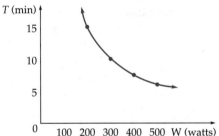

(d) It is all in the first quadrant, and $y$ decreases less and less rapidly (from left to right). The curve gets very close to the $x$-axis.

(e) any positive number

**51.** (a) $WT = 3000$     (b) 5 minutes

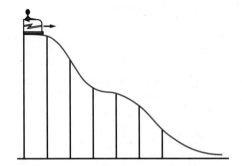

**53.** Parts (a), (b), and (c) come out the same for both expressions.
(d) part (c)

**55.** $S = 1.5x$, in which $S$ is his new salary and $x$ is his old one.

**57.**

**59.** (a)

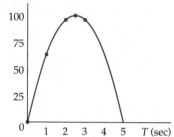

(b) very slight
(c) a line with positive slope
**61.** $y = 0.880x + 1.563$

**11.4 Homework Exercises**

**1.** (a) Subtract $1.80 to get $1.89 and divide that by $.27 to get 7 photos   (b) $P = \dfrac{C - 1.80}{.27}$

(c) formula from part (b), $P = 7$

**3.** (a) $T = \dfrac{N}{4} + 40$   (b) $N = 4(T - 40)$

(c) 65°F   (d) 220

**5.** (a) $I = 100M/A$, in which $M$ = mental age and $A$ = actual age
(b) with tests   (c) 125

**7.** less than 500 miles

**9.** $340

**11.** (a) 725   (b) 2

**13.** 1870 adults and 590 children

**15.** 9.6 oz bread, 6.4 oz cheese

**17.** 4 years

**19.** 10 years

**21.** (a) She drove for 5 minutes, then 2 minutes, then 6 minutes, and finally 3 minutes, accelerating at the beginning and decelerating at the end of each time interval. She averaged about 25 mph.
(b) 6 miles

**23.** (a) $200   (b) $100 profit
(c) about $100 profit
(d) 2

**25.** (a)

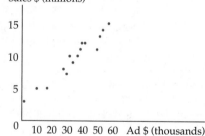

(d) Substitute $20,000 for $x$ and find $y$.

**27.** (a) 96 ft   (b)

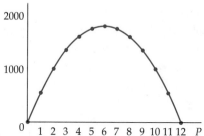

(c) $t = 0.7, 4.3$ sec

**29.** (a) $10 = 2L + 2W$   (b) exact   (c) 2 ft
(d) between 0 and 5 ft
(e) line segment excluding its endpoints (0, 5) and (5, 0)

**31.** (a)

(b) $6

**33.** (a) $A = 400 + 30M$ and $B = 550 + 20M$
(b) $A$ is a ray with endpoint (0, 400) through (10, 700). $B$ is a ray with endpoint (0, 550) through (10, 750).
(c) (15, 850)   (d) (15, 850)
(e) For less than 15 months, $A$ is cheaper. For more than 15 months, $B$ is cheaper.
(f) reliability, design, size

**35.** (a) $A = 800 + 0.05S$ and $B = 300 + 0.15S$, in which $S$ = sales dollars
   (b) $A$ is a ray with endpoint $(0, 800)$ through $(1000, 850)$. $B$ is a ray with endpoint $(0, 300)$ through $(1000, 450)$.
   (c) $(5000, 1050)$
   (d) For less than $5000 in sales, $A$ pays more. For more than $5000 in sales, $B$ pays more.
   (e) location, co-workers, product being sold

**37.** 21.3 hours

**39.** $12.38

**41.** The diesel would be cheaper only after driving about 500,000 miles, so the gas car is a better buy.

**43.** (a) $6500 profit      (b) $100 profit
   (c) $18.75 \approx 19$

**45.** (a) 0.2, 8.8      (b) 0.9, 8.1

**11.5 Homework Exercises**

**1.** $\sqrt{17}$

**3.** (a) $(a, b)$
   (b)
$$AC \stackrel{?}{=} BD$$
$$\sqrt{(a - 0)^2 + (b - 0)^2} \stackrel{?}{=} \sqrt{(a - 0)^2 + (0 - b)^2}$$
$$\sqrt{a^2 + b^2} = \sqrt{a^2 + b^2}$$

**5.** $3 + 2\sqrt{2} + \sqrt{5}$

**7.** $(x - 2)^2 + (y + 1)^2 = 9$

**9.** $(x - 2)^2 + (y - 3)^2 = 32$

**11.** $(3, 3)$

**13.** (a) $D(a/2, b/2)$, $E((a + c)/2, b/2)$
   (b) slope of $\overleftrightarrow{DE}$ = slope of $\overleftrightarrow{AC}$ = 0
   (c) $DE = \sqrt{[(a + c/2) - a/2]^2 + (b/2 - b/2)^2}$
$$= \sqrt{c^2/4} = c/2 \text{ and } AC = c \text{ so } DE = \frac{1}{2}AC.$$

**15.** $(5, -5)$

**17.** 7

**19.** (a) The air distance is shorter, excluding distances traveled going up and down.
   (b) The air distance is more like a straight line joining two points, and the road distance is restricted to certain longer routes like taxicab geometry.

**21.**

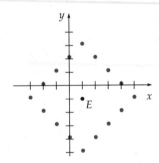

**23.** (a) $(a, a)$
   (b)
$$AC \stackrel{?}{=} BD$$
$$\sqrt{(a - 0)^2 + (a - 0)^2} \stackrel{?}{=} \sqrt{(a - 0)^2 + (0 - a)^2}$$
$$\sqrt{2a^2} = \sqrt{2a^2}$$
   (c) slope of $\overleftrightarrow{AC}$ = 1 and slope of $\overleftrightarrow{BD}$ = $-1$ so $\overleftrightarrow{AC} \perp \overleftrightarrow{BD}$.

**25.** 6 points including: $B$, the two points just below it, and the 3 points each one to the right of these first 3 points

**27.** (c) a parabola
   (d) Each fold creates a point equidistant from the point and the line, which is what defines the points on a parabola.

**29.** $(3.5, 2)$

**31.** $(1, 1)$ and $(2, 0)$

**33.** (a) 1      (b) 2      (c) 3      (d) 4      (e) 11

**35.** outside

**Chapter 11 Review Exercises**

**1.** (a) $J \geq 2S$, in which $J$ = Joe's weight and $S$ = his sister's weight
   (b) untranslatable

**2.** (a) no      (b) yes      (c) no

**3.** $x > 3$

**4.** (a) line through $(0, 1)$ and $(1, 3)$
   (b) $y = -2x + 1$

**5.** 5/2

**6.** (a) $h = 10 + 0.5n$
   (b) a ray with endpoint $(0, 10)$ through $(2, 11)$
   (c) a ray

**7.** (a) $E = H + 2T$      (b) 16

**8.** $8445.95

**9.** It is $y = x^2$ translated up 2 units.

**10.** (a) $H = \dfrac{W + 220}{5.5}$    (b) the original

**11.** (a)

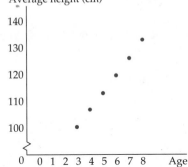

Average height (cm)

(d) about 178 cm

**12.**

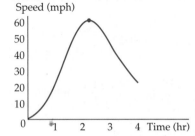

Speed (mph)

**13.** Form a right triangle as shown. The lengths of the legs are $(x_2 - x_1)$ and $(y_2 - y_1)$. By the Pythagorean Theorem,
$$AB = \sqrt{(x_2 - x_1)^2 + (y_2 - y_1)^2}.$$

**14.** The midpoint of $\overline{AC}$ is $((a + 0)/2, (b + 0)/2)$ and the midpoint of $\overline{BD}$ is $((a + 0)/2, (0 + b)/2)$. So they both have the same midpoint $(a/2, b/2)$.

**15.** 3

# Chapter 12

## 12.1 *Homework Exercises*

**1.** (a) 10 PRINT "MAD"    (b) MAD
     20 PRINT "DOG"        DOG

**3.** 15 PRINT "NOT"

**5.** 20

**7.** (a) $4 * X ^ 2$    (b) 2/3
    (c) $.5 * (X / 3)$    (d) $D = R * T$

**9.** PRINT 3 + (4 * 5)

**11.** (a) BELL    (b) SLOB

**15.** (a) 0.0000431    (b) 3200

**17.** 10 PRINT "I'M A PRETTY COMPUTER."

**19.** 36, 50

**21.** Input would be room temperature; processing would be comparing room temperature to the setting; output would be turning the air conditioner on or off or leaving it as is.

**25.** Computer terminals can be available to patrons to check upon the availability of books.

**27.** Multiplication must be done before addition, so you cannot add the 2 + 3.

**31.** $3 - (3 \div 3) - (3 \div 3) = 1, 33 \div 3 - (3 \times 3) = 2,$
    $3 + 3 + 3 - 3 - 3 = 3, 3 \div 3 + 3 + 3 - 3 = 4,$
    $3 \div 3 + 3 \div 3 + 3 = 5, 3 \times (3 - 3) + 3 + 3 = 6,$
    $3 \times 3 - 3 + (3 \div 3) = 7, (3 + 3) \div 3 + 3 + 3 = 8,$
    $3 + 3 + 3 + 3 - 3 = 9, 3 \div 3 + 3 + 3 + 3 = 10$

## 12.2 *Homework Exercises*

**1.** (a) making logical decisions; performing lengthy computations
    (b) finding patterns, interpreting errors

**3.** (a) 20 should say B = 3 and RUN should not be numbered.
    (b) 10 should say LET, 14 should say 3 * A, 18 should have quotes around TOTAL PRICE IS T

**5.** (c)

**7.** (a) $-8$    (b) 17

**9.** take A = out of line 20

**13.** (a) $C = 4 + .06N$, in which $N$ is the number of calls
    (b) 10 PRINT "COMPUTE YOUR PHONE BILL."
       20 PRINT "HOW MANY LOCAL CALLS
          WERE MADE?"
       30 INPUT N
       40 PRINT "THE MONTHLY BILL IS $";
          4 + .06 * N

**15.** 10 PRINT "COMPUTE YOUR RENTAL CAR FEE."
    20 PRINT "TYPE IN THE CHARGE PER DAY
       AND CHARGE PER MILE SEPARATED BY
       A COMMA WITHOUT $."
    30 INPUT X, Y

*(Continued on next page.)*

  40 PRINT "TYPE IN THE NUMBER OF DAYS
       DRIVEN AND THE NUMBER OF
       MILES DRIVEN."
  50 INPUT D, M
  60 PRINT "THE RENTAL CHARGE IS \$";
       X * D + Y * M

**17.** 10 PRINT "FIND THE LENGTH OF THE
       HYPOTENUSE."
  20 PRINT "HOW LONG ARE THE TWO LEGS?"
  30 INPUT A, B
  40 PRINT "THE HYPOTENUSE IS ";
       SQR(A ^ 2 + B ^ 2)

**19.** 10 PRINT "COMPUTE A PERCENT INCREASE."
  20 PRINT "INPUT THE OLD PRICE AND NEW
       PRICE SEPARATED BY A COMMA."
  30 INPUT A, B
  40 PRINT "THE PERCENT INCREASE IS ";
       ((B − A) / A) * 100 ;"%"

## 12.3 Homework Exercises

**1.** (a) NOT QUITE     (b) HONORS
     (c) deductive

**3.** line 30

**5.** for the decision box: YES goes to IN SIMPLEST
FORM as output and NO goes to NOT IN SIM-
PLEST FORM

**7.**

**9.** 10 IF X ^ 2 + Y ^ 2 > 0 THEN 40
  20 PRINT "NO"
  30 GOTO 50
  40 PRINT "OKAY"
  50 END

**11.** 10 PRINT "HOW MANY BOOKS DO YOU WANT
       TO BORROW?"
  20 INPUT N
  30 IF N > 6 THEN 60
  40 PRINT "OKAY"
  50 GOTO 70
  60 PRINT "OVER THE LIMIT"
  70 END

**13.** (a) $T = 230.40 + 8.64(H − 40)$
   (b) 10 PRINT "COMPUTE YOUR WEEKLY PAY."
       20 PRINT "HOW MANY HOURS DID YOU
          WORK?"
       30 INPUT H
       40 IF H > 40 THEN 70
       50 PRINT "YOUR PAY IS \$"; 5.76 * H
       60 GOTO 80
       70 PRINT "YOUR PAY IS
          \$"; 230.40 + 8.64 * (H − 40)
       80 END

**15.** Add the following lines.
  65 IF X2 = X1 THEN 100
  90 GOTO 110
  100 PRINT "SLOPE IS UNDEFINED."
  110 END

**17.** 10 PRINT "AREA OR CIRCUMFERENCE"
  20 PRINT "WHAT IS THE RADIUS?"
  30 INPUT R
  40 PRINT "TYPE 1 FOR CIRCUMFERENCE AND
       2 FOR AREA."
  50 INPUT N
  60 IF N = 1 THEN 90
  70 PRINT "THE AREA IS "; 3.14159 * R ^ 2;"
       SQUARE UNITS."
  80 GOTO 100
  90 PRINT "THE CIRCUMFERENCE IS
       "; 2 * 3.14159 * R
  100 END

**19.**
(a)

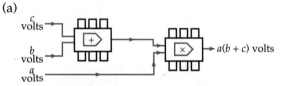

(b)

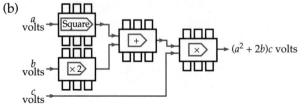

**12.4** *Homework Exercises*
**1.**

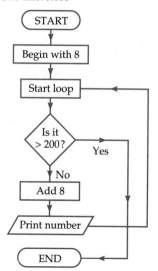

**3.** 4
**5.** prints 4 and 41
**7.** 10 FOR I = 1 TO 20
  20 PRINT 9 * I
  30 NEXT I
**9.** 10 PRINT " X    Y"
  20 FOR X = −5 TO 5
  30   LET Y = X ^ 3 − 2 * X + 7
  40   PRINT X ;"    "; Y
  50 NEXT X

**11.** 10 FOR I = 1 TO 10
  20   LET N = 2 * I − 1
  30   PRINT N ^ 2
  40 NEXT I
**13.** (a) $A = 0.6(C − 100)$    (b) $A = 0.8(C − 500)$
  (c) 10 FOR I = 1 TO 8
    20 LET C = 250 * I
    30 PRINT "PLAN 1 PAYS $"; 0.6 * (C − 100)
    40 PRINT "PLAN 2 PAYS $"; 0.8 * (C − 500)
    50 NEXT I
  (d) The first policy pays more for claims under
    $1700; the second pays more for claims over
    $1700.
**15.** an integer
**17.** 2, 3, 6, 31, 62, 93, 186
**19.** (a) 1, 3, 5, 7, 9, 11, 13, 15
  (b) FOR I = 5 TO 100 STEP 5
  (c) 10, 8, 6, 4, 2, 0
**21.** (a) Add the following lines.
    70 LET L = M * N / D
    80 PRINT " THE LEAST COMMON
      MULTIPLE OF "; M ;" AND
      "; N ;" IS "; L ;"."
  (b) GCF = 31, LCM = 74,307
**23.** 10 PRINT "ROUNDING PROGRAM"
  20 PRINT "TYPE IN A DECIMAL NUMBER."
  30 INPUT N
  40 PRINT INT(N + 0.5)
**25.** (a) prints 2, 3, 2, 3, 2, 3
  (b) First, I = 1 while J = 2 and then J = 3. The
    computer prints the 2 and 3. Then I = 2 while
    J = 2 and then J = 3. The computer prints the
    2 and 3 again. Then I = 3 while J = 2 and
    then J = 3. The computer prints the 2 and 3
    again.

**Chapter 12** *Review Exercises*
**1.** (a) making logical decisions; performing lengthy
    computations
  (b) finding patterns, interpreting errors
**2.** 0.00004987
**3.** 13
**4.** (a) 154    (b) deductive
**5.** 10 PRINT "TOTAL TICKET CHARGE"
  20 PRINT "TYPE THE NUMBER OF ADULT
    TICKETS AND CHILDREN'S TICKETS
    SEPARATED BY A COMMA."

*(Continued on next page.)*

30 INPUT A, C
40 PRINT "THE TOTAL CHARGE IS $"; 12 * A + 8 * C

6. (a)  10 PRINT "A FRIED"          (b) A FRIED
        15 PRINT "SQUID"                SQUID
        20 PRINT "IS GOOD"              IS GOOD

7.  10 PRINT "COMPUTE PAY"
    20 PRINT "TYPE IN THE AMOUNT OF SALES."
    30 INPUT S
    40 IF S > 200 THEN 70
    50 PRINT "YOUR PAY IS $400."
    60 GOTO 80
    70 PRINT "YOUR PAY IS $";
       400 + 0.12 * (S − 200)
    80 END

8. 192

9.  10 PRINT "TOTAL WEEKLY PAY"
    20 PRINT "TYPE IN THE NUMBER OF HOURS WORKED."
    30 INPUT H
    40 IF H > 40 THEN 70
    50 PRINT "YOUR PAY IS $"; 8.6 * H
    60 GOTO 80
    70 PRINT "YOUR PAY IS $"; 344 + (H − 40) * 17.2
    80 END

10. prints 1, 2, 3, 4, 6, 12

11. (a) A = 0.5(C − 200)    (b) A = 0.75(C − 500)
    (c)  10 FOR C = 500 TO 2000 STEP 250
         20    PRINT "PLAN 1 PAYS $"; 0.5 * (C − 200)
         30    PRINT "PLAN 2 PAYS $"; 0.75 * (C − 500)
         40 NEXT C
    (d) The first policy pays more for claims under
        $1100; the second pays more for claims over $1100.

## Chapter 13

### 13.1 Homework Exercises

1. (a) bar    (b) line
3. (a) The bars are constructed from pictures.
   (b) type of books read, age of the readers
5. (a)

No. of premature deaths (thousands) — bar chart with values: Tobacco use ~380, Alcohol use ~100, Motor vehicle accident ~50, Use of hard drugs ~30, Suicide ~30, Murder ~25.

Cause of death

(b) Tobacco use is the major cause of premature deaths. Alcohol contributes to more deaths than does illegal drug use. Suicide accounts for more deaths than murder.

(c) how numbers were derived, breakdown of types of murders

7. (a) lower from 1977 to 1979, then rose from 1979 to 1982, stayed up from 1982 to 1984, and declined slightly from 1984 to 1989
   (c) unemployment data from this time, data on wealthier people

9. (a) because they have already survived for some number of years    (b) 6

11. (a) U.S., Sweden    (b) U.S.    (c) not much
    (d) birth control devices
    (e) by confidential surveys

13. 165.6°

15. (a) food 25%, clothing 8.3%, rent 50%, entertainment, 6.7%, other 10%
    (b) Make the central angles: food 90°, clothing 30°, rent 180°, entertainment 24°, other 36°

23. (a) The vertical axis is distorted between 0 and 15,000.
    (b) 2 or 3
    (c)

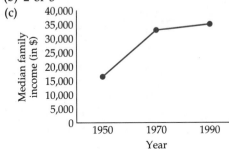

25. The first region is 4 times bigger in area.
27. debatable; probably that of the college
29. (a) Use 60–69, 70–79, 80–89, 90–99.
    (b) Use 60–79 and 80–99.
31. (a) Class B

| 9 | 019 |
|---|-----|
| 8 | 02 |
| 7 | 5 |
| 6 | 558 |
| 5 | |
| 4 | 2 |

(b) Class B has more extreme scores than Class A.

**33.** *Hint:* Comment on overall health costs, amount of insurance coverage, and hospital charges.

**37.** (b) more frequent: I, N    less frequent: H, S, T

**13.2 *Homework Exercises***

**1.** 56%

**3.** No. 20% of wages is less than 20% of overall costs.

**5.** 4%

**7.** how far each car traveled

**9.** how many dentists

**11.** hard to tell; could be as low as $350 savings

**13.** (d)

**15.** none

**17.** (a) No one sells them at list price.
   (b) The meat protein in steak has little to do with the appeal of steak.

**19.** data on saturated fat and cholesterol

**21.** worsening external conditions such as water and air pollution

**23.** People in hospitals are generally much sicker than people who are not.

**25.** They were using different time periods.

**27.** $P \to 1.1P \to 0.88P$. Overall change is a decline of 12%.

**13.3 *Homework Exercises***

**1.** One method would be to compare their means; Tom's is 141 and Jean's is 133.75.

**3.** (a) $(V + W + X + Y + Z)/5$    (b) $5M$

**5.** $9.88

**7.** mean = 6, median = 7

**9.** (a) Place the stacks in order of increasing size; the median is the height of middle stack (3).
   (b) Redistribute the books so that each of the five stacks has the same number of books (4).

**11.** {5, 8, 9, 10}

**13.** (a) 7    (b) 57    (c) 9    (d) 44

**15.** In most large groups, close to 50% of the people score below average.

**17.** mean = $3.7 million, median = $3 million

**19.** 2.8

**21.** 12 Parson and 8 Valencia

**23.** probably the mean

**25.** $8000

**27.** (a) mean    (b) median

**29.** median

**31.** {10,000, 10,000, 20,000, 30,000, 80,000}

**33.** (a) $1.70    (b) $3

**35.** New employees in a profession generally earn lower-than-average salaries.

**37.** 85.4

**39.** mode

**41.** 120 km/hr

**43.** (a) mean or median?    (b) mean

**45.** {4, 4, 4, 5, 5, 6, 7}

**47.** the same number of students in each class

**49.** They computed the average over different time periods.

**13.4 *Homework Exercises***

**1.** It may be 30 ft deep in a limited area and 2 ft deep everywhere else.

**3.** (a)

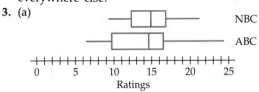

   (b) NBC is doing better overall than ABC, but ABC has two shows with a very high rating.

**5.** minimum = 64, Q1 = 72, median = 80, Q3 = 86, maximum = 92

**7.** (b)

**9.** (a) mean = 90, $s$ = 6.3    (b) 20

**11.** 9-year-olds

**13.** (a) 53, 56, 60, 64, 67    (b) none

**17.** (a) 50%    (b) 81.5%    (c) 16%

**19.** $A$ is more likely to last close to 1000 hours. $B$ lasts longer than 1000 hours on the average.

**21.** 5

**23.** skewed to the left

**25.** mean

**27.** mean, standard deviation, first quartile, median, third quartile

**29.** class with wide ability range → high standard deviation

   honors class → high mean, low standard deviation

   students with very similar abilities → low standard deviation

   remedial class → low standard deviation, low median

**31.** (a) The mean increases by $2000, and the standard deviation stays the same.
   (b) The mean increases by 10% and the standard deviation increases by 10%.

**33.** The mean is $(A + B + C + D + E)/5$. So the sum of the deviations is $A - (A + B + C + D + E)/5 +$

$B - (A + B + C + D + E)/5 + C - (A + B + C + D + E)/5 + D - (A + B + C + D + E)/5 + E - (A + B + C + D + E)/5 = A + B + C + D + E - A - B - C - D - E = 0$

**35.** (a) 50%     (b) 16%     (c) 2.5%

**37.** (a) $(A + B + C + D)/4$

(b) $s = \sqrt{\dfrac{(A - \bar{x})^2 + (B - \bar{x})^2 + (C - \bar{x})^2 + (D - \bar{x})^2}{4}}$

(c) $\sqrt{\dfrac{A^2 - 2\bar{x}A + \bar{x}^2 + B^2 - 2\bar{x}B + \bar{x}^2 + C^2 - 2\bar{x}C + \bar{x}^2 + D^2 - 2\bar{x}D + \bar{x}^2}{4}}$

$= \sqrt{\dfrac{A^2 + B^2 + C^2 + D^2 - 2\bar{x}(A + B + C + D) + 4\bar{x}^2}{4}}$

Use hint.

$= \sqrt{\dfrac{A^2 + B^2 + C^2 + D^2}{4} - (\bar{x})^2}$

### 13.5 Homework Exercises

**1.** 0.58P
**3.** 1776
**5.** Some people will not answer honestly.
**7.** No, the first group is more likely to lie to please the interviewer.
**9.** "Would you favor or oppose building an expensive new missile system?"
**11.** Fewer people would agree or disagree.
**13.** 0% and 4%
**15.** We are 95% sure that between 57% and 63% of all U.S. adults like spinach.
**17.** The sample is too small.
**19.** 67% OF ALL AMERICANS OPPOSE ABORTIONS UNDER SOME OR ALL CIRCUMSTANCES.
**21.** Grades mean different things to different people.
**23.** (a) yes     (b) no
     (c) The respondents were not at all representative of voters.
**27.** Look at past sales records of similar clothing by color.
**29.** (a) The results of a poll can influence what people think, and, consequently, how they respond to subsequent polls.
**31.** (a) The rating is the percent of *all* TV sets; the share is out of a smaller sample, only those sets that are on.
     (b) 2%
     (c) By showing that the 35% who do not respond are similar to the 65% who do.
     (d) 6
**33.** none of these

### 13.6 Homework Exercises

**1.** (a) 16     (b) She got 16 questions right.
**3.** Students in this area score below the national average.
**5.** (a) 4.8
     (b) She scored the same as the average child in the eighth month of fourth grade.
**7.** no
**11.** 130 or above
**13.** 16th
**15.** yes
**17.** (d)

### Chapter 13 Review Exercises

**1.** (a) .99, 1.30, 1.10, 1.05, .84     (b) whole
     (c) whole                   (d) thighs
**2.** (a) The amount was fairly steady from 1970 to 1978; then it rose from 1978 to 1984 and remained at this higher level from 1984 to 1992.
     (b) The U.S. government spends more than it collects in taxes, so it borrows money and pays interest on it.
**3.** (a) 12%
     (b) $P \to 1.4P \to 1.12P$; overall change is 12%
**4.** The phrase "as much as 50%" could mean anywhere from 0 to 50%.
**5.** (a) Start the vertical axis at 19,000.
     (b) Scale the vertical axis accurately.
**6.** mean = 14.1 minutes, median = 15 minutes
**7.** The mean age will be higher because the older students will pull it up, while the median age will be around 20.
**8.** (a)

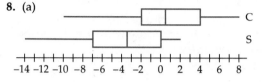

     (b) The saturated fat group has more success lowering cholesterol. The other group shows little change on average.
**9.** About 10 of the scores would fall within 1 standard deviation. This requires going 22 from the mean to include 142. So it's about 22.

10. We are 95% sure that between 47% and 55% of all U.S. adults do not want to adopt the metric system.
11. (a) 95%   (b) 16%
12. (a) 84th   (b) 97.5th
13. (c)
14. When the grade level is a few grades higher or lower than the general level of the test. Such a score would be based upon test items that are mostly written for a significantly higher or lower grade level.
15. (a) 29   (b) She got 29 questions right.   (c) 38
    (d) In her region, she scored better than 38% of those in her age group in reading.

**Chapter 14**
**14.1 Homework Exercises**
1. (a) {1, 2, 3, 4, 5, 6}   (b) yes
3. (a) 12/25   (b) 6/25
5. (a) 1/4   (b) 1/6   (c) 1/8   (d) 11/24
7. 1
9. (b)
11. (a) about 300
    (b) Compare the average amount of time traveling abroad per person to the average time spent in a car per person.
13. $A = \{heads\}$, $B = \{tails\}$
15. The northbound train generally arrives about 15 minutes before the southbound train.
17. 0.45
19. 180° for 2, 90° for 1, 90° for 4
21. (a) 0.964   (b) 0.226   (c) 212/964 = 53/241

**14.2 Homework Exercises**
1. (c) HHH, HHT, HTH, THH, TTH, THT, HTT, TTT
   (d) 3/8
3. (a) 1/36, 1/18, 1/12, 1/9, 5/36, 1/6, 5/36, 1/9, 1/12, 1/18, 1/36
   (b) The denominator is always 36, and the numerator counts from 1 up to 6 and then back down to 1.
5. 13/18
7. $P(2) = 1/18$, $P(3) = 1/9$, $P(4) = 1/6$, $P(5) = 1/6$, $P(6) = 1/6$, $P(7) = 1/6$, $P(8) = 1/9$, $P(9) = 1/18$
9. (a) 0.75   (b) 0.0001235   (c) yes
11. It rained on 60% of the days that were like this in the past.
19. 3/8

21. 2 and 12 are 10°, 3 and 11 are 20°, 4 and 10 are 30°, 5 and 9 are 40°, 6 and 8 are 50°, and 7 is 60°.
23. (a) 1  5  10  10  5  1   (b) 1, 2, 1
    (c) It's the second row.
    (d) If you flip a coin 3 times, add up the numbers in the third row to get the denominator (8), and the numerators of the probabilities are the numbers in the third row: 1 for 0 heads, 3 for 1 head, 3 for 2 heads, and 1 for 3 heads.
25. (a) from statistical studies
    (b) People make mistakes.
29. (a) 0 or 1
31. (a) 110 PRINT "OOPS THE ALLEY CAT WON'T START."
       120 GOTO 150
       130 CARS = CARS + 1
       140 PRINT "THE ALLEY CAT IS PURRING TODAY."
    (b) about 1/3

**14.3 Homework Exercises**
1. 8
3. 24
5. STRAIGHT, 10 choices for each of 4 digits (10)(10)(10)(10) = 10,000 choices, 1/10,000 to pick the correct number
   4 WAY BOX, 4 ways to match out of 10,000 or 1/2500
7. 210
9. 59,049
11. (a) 2,600,000   (b) 786,240
13. (a) 1   (b) 1/625
15. (b) 27
17. (a) 4   (b) 1   (c) 4
    (d) 1/2000, 1/8000, 1/2000   (e) 1692   (f) 148
    (g) 423/2000, 37/2000
19. 10
21. (a) 6   (b) 1   (c) 4   (d) 1   (e) 2
    (f) 1   (g) 48
23. 72

**14.4 Homework Exercises**
1. you
3. $187.50
5. (a) 9/19   (b) $.05 loss   (c) $.05 loss
7. (a) $20   (b) $30
   (c) Part (b) protects you from a possible catastrophic loss, while part (a) does not.

**9.** 1.8
**11.** 4
**13.** $.20
**15.** $2.32
**17.** (a)
**19.** 1:3
**23.** (a) 199     (b) 49/248     (c) about 1 (1.4)
  (d) about 29.4/30.8 ≈ 0.95
**25.** Discussion question; note that people choosing
  surgery have a better chance of surviving more
  than three years.
**27.** (a) $180,000 (assuming a 40% tax)
  (b) about $.04 after taxes     (c) no

### 14.5 *Homework Exercises*
**1.** (a) dependent     (b) independent
**3.** (a) independent     (b) dependent
**5.** (a) 0.07     (b) 0.27     (c) 0.66
**7.** $2.4 \cdot 10^{-10}$
**9.** (a) 0.006125     (b) 0     (c) 0.7695
**11.** 1/221
**13.** (a) 15/77     (b) 4/33     (c) 79/231
**15.** 0.86
**17.** (a) Pair 1 has independent events, since the occurrence of one event does not affect the chance
  that the other event occurs. Pair 2 has dependent events, since the occurrence of one event
  affects the chance that the other event occurs.
  (b) Pair 1 and Pair 2 both have events that are not
  mutually exclusive, since both events in each
  group could occur on a given day.
**19.** 3
**21.** (a) 0.36     (b) 0.288
**23.** (a) 0.17     (b) 0.53

### Chapter 14 *Review Exercises*
**1.** (a) 17/36
  (b) Roll two dice 30 times and see what fraction of
  the time a product less than 10 occurs.
**2.** 1/4
**3.** 1/2
**4.** After a large number of repetitions, we would
  expect 3 heads and 2 tails about $\frac{5}{16}$ of the time.
**5.** {*AB, BA, AC, CA, AD, DA, BD, DB, BC, CB, CD, DC*}
**6.** 743,600
**7.** 1 and 2 represent a car; 3, 4, 5, 6, 7, and 8 represent no car passing.
**8.** (a) 8     (b) 1/11
**9.** (a) $1.06     (b) $.06
**10.** 0.01
**11.** $53.50
**12.** about 6 (expected value is 5.8)

# Index

# CURRICULUM STANDARDS FOR GRADES 5–8

## STANDARD 1: MATHEMATICS AS PROBLEM SOLVING

In grades 5–8, the mathematics curriculum should include numerous and varied experiences with problem solving as a method of inquiry and application so that students can—

- use problem-solving approaches to investigate and understand mathematical content;
- formulate problems from situations within and outside mathematics;
- develop and apply a variety of strategies to solve problems, with emphasis on multistep and nonroutine problems;
- verify and interpret results with respect to the original problem situation;
- generalize solutions and strategies to new problem situations;
- acquire confidence in using mathematics meaningfully.

## STANDARD 2: MATHEMATICS AS COMMUNICATION

In grades 5–8, the study of mathematics should include opportunities to communicate so that students can—

- model situations using oral, written, concrete, pictorial, graphical, and algebraic methods;
- reflect on and clarify their own thinking about mathematical ideas and situations;
- develop common understandings of mathematical ideas, including the role of definitions;
- use the skills of reading, listening, and viewing to interpret and evaluate mathematical ideas;
- discuss mathematical ideas and make conjectures and convincing arguments;
- appreciate the value of mathematical notation and its role in the development of mathematical ideas.

## STANDARD 3: MATHEMATICS AS REASONING

In grades 5–8, reasoning shall permeate the mathematics curriculum so that students can—

- recognize and apply deductive and inductive reasoning;
- understand and apply reasoning processes, with special attention to spatial reasoning and reasoning with proportions and graphs;
- make and evaluate mathematical conjectures and arguments;
- validate their own thinking;
- appreciate the pervasive use and power of reasoning as a part of mathematics.

## STANDARD 4: MATHEMATICAL CONNECTIONS

In grades 5–8, the mathematics curriculum should include the investigation of mathematical connections so that students can—

- see mathematics as an integrated whole;
- explore problems and describe results using graphical, numerical, physical, algebraic, and verbal mathematical models or representations;
- use a mathematical idea to further their understanding of other mathematical ideas;
- apply mathematical thinking and modeling to solve problems that arise in other disciplines, such as art, music, psychology, science, and business;
- value the role of mathematics in our culture and society.

## STANDARD 5: NUMBER AND NUMBER RELATIONSHIPS

In grades 5–8, the mathematics curriculum should include the continued development of number and number relationships so that students can—

- understand, represent, and use numbers in a variety of equivalent forms (integer, fraction, decimal, percent, exponential, and scientific notation) in real-world and mathematical problem situations;
- develop number sense for whole numbers, fractions, decimals, integers, and rational numbers;
- understand and apply ratios, proportions, and percents in a wide variety of situations;
- investigate relationships among fractions, decimals, and percents;
- represent numerical relationships in one- and two-dimensional graphs.

## STANDARD 6: NUMBER SYSTEMS AND NUMBER THEORY

In grades 5–8, the mathematics curriculum should include the study of number systems and number theory so that students can—

- understand and appreciate the need for numbers beyond the whole numbers;
- develop and use order relations for whole numbers, fractions, decimals, integers, and rational numbers;
- extend their understanding of whole number operations to fractions, decimals, integers, and rational numbers;
- understand how the basic arithmetic operations are related to one another;
- develop and apply number theory concepts (e.g., primes, factors, and multiples) in real-world and mathematical problem situations.